MW01114166

McGraw-Hill — offering digital solutions to your paralegal questions.

This valuable CD, available only with the purchase of a new book, provides users with sample forms and documents. Referenced throughout the text, these forms offer practical application of the concepts covered in the text, including:

- Sample legal correspondence
- Sample pleadings, motions, interrogatories
- Federal tax forms
- Sample state-specific corporation and business forms
- Sample UCC forms
- Sample contracts
- Sample proxy statement
- Sample retail contracts
- Sample bankruptcy filings
- Sample will and estate documents
- Sample inventories and checklists
- Sample affidavits
- Sample summons
- Sample real estate documents and agreements

Comprehensive and relevant, the CD is a great place for students and legal professionals alike to connect the concepts they learn in the text to on-the-job applications and procedures.

MCGRAW-HILL PARALEGAL TITLES: WHERE EDUCATIONAL SUPPORT GOES BEYOND EXPECTATIONS.

Building a solid foundation for a successful paralegal career is becoming more challenging as the needs of students and instructors continue to grow. The McGraw-Hill paralegal texts offer the solution to this ever-changing environment. Integrated real-world applications in each chapter teach students the practical skills needed for a thriving career in the field. A common vocabulary among all McGraw-Hill titles ensures consistency in learning. Up-to-date coverage of the available technology used in a legal setting and a purposefully designed set of pedagogical features with shared goals across the list provide the systems needed for students to fully grasp the material and apply it in a paralegal setting. With a thorough set of ancillaries and dedicated publisher support, these texts will facilitate active learning in the classroom and give students the skills sets desired by employers.

Introduction to Law & Paralegal Studies
Connie Farrell Scuderi
ISBN: 0073524638
© *2008*

Introduction to Law for Paralegals
Deborah Benton
ISBN: 007351179X
© 2008

Basic Legal Research, Second Edition
Edward Nolfi
ISBN: 0073520519
© 2008

Basic Legal Writing, Second Edition
Pamela Tepper
ISBN: 0073403032
© 2008

Contract Law for Paralegals
Linda Spagnola
ISBN: 0073511765
© 2008

Civil Law and Litigation for Paralegals
Neal Bevans
ISBN: 0073524611
© 2008

Wills, Trusts, and Estates for Paralegals
George Kent
ISBN: 0073403067
© 2008

Legal Terminology Explained for Paralegals
Edward Nolfi
ISBN: 0073511846
© 2008

The Law Office Reference Manual
Jo Ann Lee and Marilyn Satterwhite
ISBN: 0073511838
© 2008

The Paralegal Resource Manual
Charles Nemeth
ISBN: 0073403075
© 2008

Ethics for Paralegals
Linda Spagnola
ISBN: 0073376981
© 2009

Family Law for Paralegals
George Kent
ISBN: 0073376973
© 2009

Legal Research and Writing for Paralegals
Neal Bevans
ISBN: 007352462X
© 2008

The Professional Paralegal
Allan Tow
ISBN: 0073403091
© 2009

Torts for Paralegals
ISBN: 0073376930
© 2009

Criminal Law for Paralegals
ISBN: 0073376965
© 2009

Real Estate Law for Paralegals
ISBN: 0073376957
© 2009

Law Office Management for Paralegals
ISBN: 0073376949
© 2009

The Paralegal Resource Manual

Charles P. Nemeth

Boston   Burr Ridge, IL   Dubuque, IA   Madison, WI   New York   San Francisco   St. Louis
Bangkok   Bogotá   Caracas   Kuala Lumpur   Lisbon   London   Madrid   Mexico City
Milan   Montreal   New Delhi   Santiago   Seoul   Singapore   Sydney   Taipei   Toronto

The McGraw·Hill Companies

THE PARALEGAL RESOURCE MANUAL

Published by McGraw-Hill/Irwin, a business unit of The McGraw-Hill Companies, Inc., 1221 Avenue of the Americas, New York, NY, 10020. Copyright © 2008 by The McGraw-Hill Companies, Inc. All rights reserved. No part of this publication may be reproduced or distributed in any form or by any means, or stored in a database or retrieval system, without the prior written consent of The McGraw-Hill Companies, Inc., including, but not limited to, in any network or other electronic storage or transmission, or broadcast for distance learning.

Some ancillaries, including electronic and print components, may not be available to customers outside the United States.

This book is printed on acid-free paper.

1   2   3   4   5   6   7   8   9   0   QPD/QPD   0   9   8   7

ISBN 978-0-07-340307-6
MHID 0-07-340307-5

Editorial director: *John E. Biernat*
Publisher: *Linda Schreiber*
Associate sponsoring editor: *Natalie J. Ruffatto*
Developmental editor II: *Tammy Higham*
Marketing manager: *Keari Bedford*
Lead media producer: *Damian Moshak*
Project manager: *Marlena Pechan*
Production supervisor: *Jason Huls*
Lead designer: *Marianna Kinigakas*
Typeface: *10/12 Times New Roman*
Compositor: *Aptara, Inc.*
Printer: *Quebecor World Dubuque Inc.*

Library of Congress Cataloging-in-Publication Data

Nemeth, Charles P., 1951-
    The paralegal resource manual / Charles P. Nemeth.
        p. cm. — (McGraw-Hill business careers paralegal titles)
    Includes index.
    ISBN-13: 978-0-07-340307-6 (alk. paper)
    ISBN-10: 0-07-340307-5 (alk. paper)
    1. Legal assistants—United States. I. Title.
KF320.L4N466 2008
340.023'73—dc22

                                            2007000503

www.mhhe.com

To God and Family, the only meaningful sources of inspiration

To St. Thomas Aquinas

Man will rise again without any defect of human nature, because as God founded human nature without a defect, even so will He restore it without defect. Now human nature has a twofold defect. First, because it has not yet attained to its ultimate perfection. Secondly, because it has already gone back from its ultimate perfection. The first defect is found in children, the second in the aged: and consequently in each of these human nature will be brought by the resurrection to the state of its ultimate perfection which is in the youthful age, at which the movement of growth terminates, and from which the movement of decrease begins. (*Summa Theologica,* III Part, Question 81, Article 1)

Charles P. Nemeth, J.D., Ph.D. LL.M.

Charles P. Nemeth, Professor of Professional Studies and Director of Graduate Criminal Justice/Legal Studies for the University, has spent the vast majority of his professional life in the study and practice of law and justice. A recognized expert on ethics and the legal system, appellate legal practice and private-sector justice, he also is a prolific writer, having published numerous texts and articles on law and justice throughout his impressive career. His most recent works include three titles: *Criminal Law* (Prentice Hall, 2003), *Law & Evidence: A Primer for Criminal Justice, Criminology, Law, and Legal Studies* (Prentice Hall, 2001) and *Aquinas in the Courtroom* (Greenwood and Praeger Publishing, 2001). In addition, recently published were *Private Sector and Public Safety: A Community Based Approach* (Prentice-Hall, 2005), *The Prevention Agency* (California University of PA Press-ILPP, 2005) and *Private Security and the Law, 3rd Edition* (Elsevier, 2005). His most recent venture is a philosophical discussion on *Aquinas and Criminal Law* which was recently accepted for publication by St. Augustine's Press.

An educator for more than 30 years, Nemeth's distinctive career in Law and Justice is founded on an exemplary education, including a Master of Laws from George Washington University, a Juris Doctor from the University of Baltimore, and a Master of Arts and Ph.D. from Duquesne University. In addition, he was awarded a M.S. from Niagara University and received an undergraduate degree from the University of Delaware. He holds memberships in the New York, North Carolina and Pennsylvania Bars.

At California University of Pennsylvania, Dr. Nemeth directs the University's graduate programs in Criminal Justice and Legal Studies, as well as the newly implemented Online B.S. in Legal Studies. Dr. Nemeth also directs the development of new academic programs at CAL-Pittsburgh as Director of Program Development. He has also erected a think tank of legal and justice policy issues–the Institute of Law and Public Policy—which publishes the tri-annual *Homeland Security Review* and *The Monitor,* a quarterly newsletter.

His previous academic appointments include Niagara University (1977–1980), the University of Baltimore (1980–1981), Glassboro State College (1981–1986), Waynesburg College (1988–1998) and the State University of New York at Brockport (1998–2003). He is a much sought-after legal consultant for security companies and a recognized scholar on issues involving law and morality.

Well-known is the fact that paralegalism is a dynamic occupational endeavor. Employment projections and opportunities within this field indicate a very bright future for those choosing to enter. This is a reference text which seeks to lay out the world of paralegal practice. This is a reference manual which exposes both the inquisitive and the established paralegal to the diverse fields encountered in the day to day lives of paralegals. Within its 14 chapters, the reader will discover an unbridled world of opportunity and growth and will surely discover that the world of the paralegal remains both dynamic and professionally meaningful. While this manual cannot accomplish everything, it was crafted with certain fundamental principles in mind.

First, the text is written from both a theoretical and practical slant. It is this author's unreserved judgment that paralegals are much more than mere technicians—functionaries who file documents and pleadings without little understanding of content and purpose. To be truly competent, paralegals need to know those steps and procedures, but they need also some level of conceptual understanding, some appreciation and awareness of the law's theoretical foundations. Hence the text introduces the occupation to legal principles in each field and at every imaginable level.

Second, the text is shaped with the working paralegal in mind. Reference texts should be friendly companions to those who labor in the marketplace. As such, the manual is filled with practice tools such as charts, diagrams, checklists, exhibits and forms. These are practice tools to assist in daily undertakings. We have compiled many of these practical tools into a companion CD. Use these tools to enhance the professional experience and modify to fit the occupational experience.

Third, the textbook addresses pleadings and litigation tactics. So much of what paralegals do involves the administration and documentary processes of litigation. Where appropriate, numerous examples of pleadings, from complaints to motions, are inserted. Again, use these as a starting point and be mindful of local rules and custom.

Fourth, the manual never looses sight of its primary aim—to be a reference source and tool for the paralegal. Being referential requires a high level of scholarship. Take time to review the wealth of information outlined in the footnotes. No work in this field, at least that this author has been able to detect, has as many scholarly references and resources.

Finally, the text features discussion questions and case examples for your resolution. With the publication this text, I welcome your comments and suggestions. The strength of the Paralegal Resource Manual reflects its learned readership.

In more specific terms, the manual covers a lot of territory. At Chapter 1, the reader will find not only the history of paralegalism, but the trends and movements afoot in the field. What makes up the definition of a paralegal or legal assistant? What types of career opportunities exist in the field? What skills and competencies are essential to success for the practicing paralegal?

Chapter 2 outlines how the profession is regulated. Special emphasis is given to professional associations and corresponding standards, and the role and function of judicial and regulatory oversight in the control of paralegal practice. In a nutshell how are paralegals regulated? What ethical obligations are attached to being a paralegal? How are paralegal ethics defined? Do these ethical standards become entangled in the lawyerly craft? Readers will soon discover that both private and public entities play a crucial role in the regulation of paralegals.

Covered as well will be educational standards for licensure and certification as well as relevant academic curricula for career preparation.

Chapter 3 delivers an overview on the nature of law and institutions that administer it. Exactly what is law and how should it be defined? Readers are encouraged to gain some historic insight into how our present system of law and legal administration came about and to discern the roots and foundations of law in our society. This crucial analytical step is often forgotten by busy practitioners.

Once this is accomplished, the chapter turns its attention to the institutions of law, especially courts at the state, local and federal level. Rules regarding the exercise of jurisdiction and venue are comprehensively assessed.

In Chapter 4, the reader will tackle the first of the substantive bases in law, that of the business and corporate forms. Business organizations provide a steady stream of work for the practicing paralegal. In this section, the reader is exposed to the primary forms of business entities, namely the sole proprietorship, partnership, and corporation. In addition, emerging forms of business ownership such as the LLC and joint venture are reviewed. Full analysis of not only form but also operational requirements is provided. The chapter ends will a review of common litigation problems in the business world.

Chapter 5 covers the law of contracts from simple to complex forms. Special emphasis is given to the formal requirements of contract and questions of enforceability. Various schools of interpretation are analyzed with suggestions regarding litigation approaches in the event of breach fully examined. Both common, statutory and the law of Restatements involving are reviewed.

Chapter 6's coverage encompasses Article 3 and 9 of the Uniform Commercial Code—the most relevant provisions regarding commercial practice. In Article 3, the world of commercial paper, from checks to bearer paper, is delved into. How merchants and bankers exchange proceeds for goods represents a major purpose of Article 3. Article 9 deals with secured transactions, those goods secured by financing or other collateral. Article 9 transactions are more typical than most people think since the auto industry relies on the practices for financing. The formal requirements for perfection of the security interest are fully outlined.

Chapter 7 reviews the law of bankruptcy. Extraordinary changes in bankruptcy procedure and practice have taken place in the last few years so the chapter is replete with new rules, forms, and eligibility requirements. The enhanced role of paralegals as to service providers in bankruptcy is highlighted.

Chapter 8 comprehensively covers the world of estates and their administration, wills, trusts, and other predeath planning. The role of the paralegal in estate and probate practice is well documented. From initial interview to the preparation of fiduciary tax returns, the mark of paralegals is everywhere in this area of law. Novel approaches to will and trust instruments are examined as are formal requirements for effective wills and trusts. Tax strategies for the preservation of wealth are reviewed.

Chapter 9 provides an overview of investigative practice for paralegals. There is little doubt that paralegals are often foot soldiers for the employer. As such, they are frequently asked to find out information, to discover the whereabouts of a party and to collect and assimilate facts relevant to the case or question at hand. Chapter 9 lays out the professional steps and practices essential for the investigator.

Chapter 10 scrutinizes the law of crimes and criminal culpability. Aside from an intense examination of the major felonies and misdemeanors, the reader will be exposed to traditional and emerging defenses to criminal culpability and the regular procedural requirements witnessed in criminal litigation.

Chapter 11 analyzes the civil actions and corresponding remedies. From negligence to intentional torts, from strict liability claims to statutory civil actions, the typical paralegal will experience much of the subject matter of this chapter during the professional career. Personal injury practice, malpractice, and workers' compensation practice are fully outlined. The chapter is replete with litigation documents as well as suggestions for appropriate pleadings.

Chapter 12 encompasses the world of family law. The chapter commences with a look at the torrid pace in which family law relations have evolved in the last century and critiques current and proposed statutory models to deal with this level of change. Included too will be a thorough look at divorce, alimony and support, child custody, and visitation as the various formal requirements for the resolution of same.

Chapter 13 comprises the world of real estate where paralegals surely earn their keep. In a world of documentary requirements, searches, and the orchestration of diverse parties and personalities, the paralegal is best described as a ringmaster of sorts. In real estate the tasks are as numerous they get. From initial negotiation to closing, from title search to flood insurance purchase, the typical real estate transaction needs the skill and expertise of the paralegal.

Finally, Chapter 14 reviews the usual steps witnessed in litigation. Commencing with the initial efforts to achieve compromise or settlement, or leading to the filing of a complaint or petition, paralegals are major players in the world of litigation. More specifically, paralegals will be delegated much of the responsibilities relating to the discovery and disclosure process. So too with motion practice where paralegals will track and docket the various processes. Even at trial the paralegal contributes to the preparation of a trial notebook, exhibit and evidence construction, and the evaluation of trial tactics and witnesses.

A work of this magnitude has many players, all of whom deserve recognition and appreciation. It is next to impossible to identify every person who has played some role in the production of this work, but I will attempt to list those individuals and entities that were integral forces in this authorship.

First and foremost, to my family, including my beloved spouse, Jean Marie, and my children—the unrivaled blessing and the certain basis for motivation in the authoring of any text—I extend my heartfelt thanks. My children, Eleanor, Stephen, Anne Marie, John and Joseph, Mary Claire, and Michael Augustine, could not make me a prouder father.

Second, unending plaudits must be granted to Hope Haywood whose editorial control, oversight, opinion and general input vivify this work. Our joint efforts and collaboration in this massive undertaking has been memorable. I am fully aware of my own inadequacy in this enterprise and my true reliance on the skill and acumen of Hope Haywood.

At McGraw Hill, it has been a pleasure working with Tammy Higham. Marlena Pechan, and Linda Schreiber. I am grateful that this project has been brought back to life. At Carlisle, Beth Baugh continues to exert her excellence in the editorial phase.

I acknowledge the following reviewers, who provided thoughtful comments and suggestions:

Laura Alfano
Virginia College at Birmingham

Angela Masciulli
MTI College

James Bartlett
Western Business College

Kathryn L. Myers
Saint Mary-of-the-Woods College

Sally Bisson
College of Saint Mary

Barbara A. Ricker
Andover College

Donna Bookin
Mercy College

Linda Oliver
Chippewa Valley Technical College

Joni Boucher
Sonoma State University

Debbie Vinecour
SUNY-Rockland

Kevin Derr
Pennsylvania College of Technology

Debra Wicks
Pittsburgh Technical Institute

Linda Wilke Heil
Central Community College

Linda Wimberly
Eastern Kentucky University

Terri Lindfors
Minnesota School of Business

On the permission end, I wish to acknowledge various publishers and providers who had the foresight to see the importance of this project and who granted permission to use multiple sources. Those publishers include: Lawyer's Co-operative Publishing Company, Matthew Bender and Company, Inc., McGraw-Hill/Glencoe, New York Times Agency, Callaghan and Company, G .A. Thompson Company, George T. Bisel Company, LexisNexis, West Publishing, The Company Corporation, Kerkering Barberio Financial, Cargo Express, PIAA Corporation USA, The Missing Person Search Bureau, First Advantage, Indox Consulting, SmartDraw.com, ATD AMERICAN CO., Abacus Data Systems, Inc., Legalnurses.com, TASA, Californians Allied for Patient Protection, John Wiley and Sons, Michigan Institute of Continuing Legal Education,

View Plan, Inc., Legal Assistant Today, the National Association of Legal Assistants, the Legal Assistant Management Association, the National Federation of Paralegal Assistants, and the American Legal Institute–American Bar Association.

At California University of Pennsylvania, I am fortunate to work under an administration that sees the value in these types of projects. President Angelo Armenti, Provost Don Thompson, and Dean Len Colelli all display exceptional support in the world of scholarly productions. In my own office, I appreciate the assistance provided by Laurie Manderino whose administrative skill provides that extra time I need to finish these works. Thanks too to Rose Mahouski who works with fervor. Finally, I was thoroughly blessed to have an extraordinary graduate assistant on this project, Adam Young. I shall never forget the many and varied tasks he undertook. All of it was done professionally.

The *Paralegal Resource Manual* is a comprehensive tool for any paralegal student, as well as anyone working in a law office—paralegals, legal assistants, and lawyers. It is filled with practice tools such as charts, diagrams, checklists, exhibits, and forms. It also features discussion questions and case examples to encourage discussion of the content.

Chapter Outlines give readers an easy-to-navigate look into what each chapter covers.

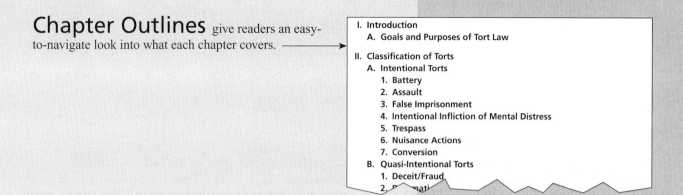

I. Introduction
  A. Goals and Purposes of Tort Law

II. Classification of Torts
  A. Intentional Torts
    1. Battery
    2. Assault
    3. False Imprisonment
    4. Intentional Infliction of Mental Distress
    5. Trespass
    6. Nuisance Actions
    7. Conversion
  B. Quasi-Intentional Torts
    1. Deceit/Fraud
    2. Defamati...

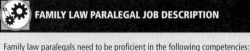

FAMILY LAW PARALEGAL JOB DESCRIPTION

Family law paralegals need to be proficient in the following competencies:

- Attend initial interviews with attorneys and clients.
- Collect background information about clients.
- Complete domestic relations questionnaire forms.
- Perform legal research.
- Draft notices to produce.
- Serve notice on opposing counsel.
- Arrange for service of documents.
- Conduct follow-up filing petitions and check service.
- Conduct timely briefing of clients concerning status of cases.

Paralegal Job Descriptions in chapters 4-13 provide students and users a look into the life of a paralegal as it relates to each substantive area covered.

Chapter Summary
provides a quick review of the key concepts presented in the chapter.

Summary

Much has been said in this chapter about the nature of torts, negligence, strict liability, and the common practice areas of personal injury, malpractice, and product liability. More particularly, the chapter covered the following information:

The Law of Intentional Torts

An examination of the following intentional torts was made:

- Battery.
- Assault.
- False imprisonment.
- Intentional infliction of mental distress.
- Trespass.
- Theories of nuisance.
- Conversion.

Under the quasi-intentional classification, these areas were discussed:

- Deceit.
- Defamation.
- Invasion of privacy:

Discussion Questions in

each chapter present opportunities to delve into the chapter material on a deeper level, providing insight into the material as it relates to on-the-job activities.

Discussion Questions

1. Contact a local realtor in your area. Collect forms for real estate practice and learn about the Multiple Listing Service process in your jurisdiction.
2. Have you ever considered becoming a real estate agent? Do you think the professions of paralegal and real estate agent are complementary or antagonistic?
3. How would you classify the property you currently live in? Is it fee simple? Is it a life estate? Is it a leasehold?
4. What type of lease assures the least protection?
5. Married people own real property by what designation?
6. What would be defined as a fixture within your residence?
7. Why are condominiums slightly different from traditional fee simple estates?
8. What techniques of legal description exist?
9. Why is title insurance important when lawyers have underlying malpractice insurance?
10. What are the most common disagreements that might arise relative to any agreement of sale?
11. What conditions or contingencies can be expected in a typical real estate transaction?

Research Exercises in

each chapter give users hands-on experience with the manual, allowing for continued practice of skills needed on the job.

Research Exercise

1. Abe Lanko left his wife and children and over a period of five years has provided no support at all. He has moved 10 times, each time avoiding a contempt order or other enforcement technique. Every effort to enforce the support order for his three children has been unsuccessful. He simply moves from state to state, thumbing his nose at out-of-state court orders. Eileen Khought, a domestic relations paralegal, has been asked what remedies and options the Uniform Reciprocal Enforcement of Support Act (U.R.E.S.A.) recommends in light of these circumstances:

   A. Asserting jurisdiction under U.R.E.S.A. is a flexible argument when compared to other jurisdictional findings. Eileen Khought writes a draft memorandum to her supervisor indicating that because Abe had sexual relations in a hotel in a foreign state, whereby a child was conceived, personal jurisdiction exists despite present nonresidence. Is this true or false?

   B. Eileen is also asked whether attorneys' fees are awardable in a contested support case. She writes in the memorandum that the answer is yes, but only reasonable fees are awarded. Is this true or false?

Practical Exercises

1. A broker receives a 6 percent commission on the sale of a house for $42,000. What is the amount of the commission? (The commission equals the sale price times the commission rate.)
2. If a broker received a commission of $8,000 on the sale of a property and his commission rate was 7 percent, what was the price of the house? (Selling price equals commission divided by commission rate.)
3. As a rule of calculation the following applies: Interest equals principal times rate times time. Find the interest on $2,000 at 6 percent per annum for three months.
4. Calculate the interest on $1,000 at 7 percent per annum for two months and five days.
5. Points or other origination charges are based on the value of the money borrowed. The term *two points* equals 2 percent. Four and one-half points equals 4½ percent. A loan amount is $110,000. If there is a two and one-half point origination fee, what will be its amount?
6. Most jurisdictions have a transfer tax of 1 or 2 percent. Solve the following problem: The sale price of a house is $300,000. The transfer tax rate is 2 percent. Calculate the transfer tax. If the transfer tax is to be split between seller and buyer, what will each have to pay?
7. Prorations are made on taxes, assessments, water bills, utilities, and possibly insurance. Prorations will be made on an annualized to daily basis. Calculate the following problem: With the fiscal year commencing July 1, 2007, the taxes are $312 and have not been paid. The home is sold, and the transaction closing took place on February 15, 2008. What amount would be credited to the buyer at closing?
8. Sale of a property is to take place on April 5, 2007. The 2006 tax bill was paid in full and equaled $462. The tax for 2007 is not known. Compute the prorated taxes that will be credited to a purchaser.[117]
9. Complete a blank settlement sheet based on the following facts:

Practical Exercises in each

chapter offer users hands-on practice with tools and procedures used by paralegals in the workplace.

Internet Resources

in each chapter list other important references and resources that paralegals and law office employees need. ⟶

Internet Resources

National Association of Realtors—www.realtor.org

NAR Ebooks—ebooks.realtor.org

ABA Real Estate, Probate and Trust Section—www.abanet.org/rppt/home.html

American Land Title Association—www.alta.org/index.cfm

National Association of Insurance Commissioners—www.naic.org/

U.S. Department of Housing and Urban Development—www.hud.gov/

National Association of Mortgage Brokers—www.namb.org

National Association of Mortgage Field Services—www.namfs.org

Mortgage Bankers Association of America—www.mbaa.org

Home Inspectors Nationwide Directory—www.homeinspections-usa.com

National Association of Certified Home Inspectors—www.nachi.org

A series of interrogatory requests are also made in the standard divorce process, again high-lighting economic interests, property rights, wages and salaries, and other pertinent information for the determination. (See Form 12.26 on the accompanying CD.)

Naturally paralegals play an integral role in the discovery process. Written interrogatories and oral and/or written depositions will be a continuous responsibility of the paralegal. A notice of deposition form is shown in Form 12.27 on the accompanying CD. Other documentation about the discovery process is included in Form 12.28.

Defense Strategies

A complaint filed alleging a fault or no-fault ground may be defended like any other cause of action.[51] Singular or plural defenses may be presented by defense counsel in a divorce action and include, but are not limited to, the following strategies.

Connivance The defense may assert that the grounds for divorce are nothing more than a sham. A party who originally consented to the grounds of fault cannot later be permitted to change his or her mind and say that he or she no longer consents. *Connivance* is the setting up of a situation so that the other person commits a wrongdoing, example, a wife who imputes her hus-

An accompanying CD with valuable sample forms is packaged with the text,

providing a number of relevant forms for each chapter. The forms are noted in the text, and an icon appears in the margin whenever a form in mentioned, indicating to the user to access the CD. ⟵

Online Learning Center Users

can access the Web sites for each of the McGraw-Hill paralegal texts from the main page of the Paralegal Super Site. Each OLC has a similar organization. An Information Center features an overview of the text, background on the author, and the Preface and Table of Contents from the book. The OLC can be delivered multiple ways—users can access the site directly through the textbook Web site, through PageOut, or within a course management system (i.e., WebCT, Blackboard, TopClass, or eCollege).

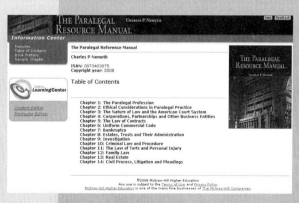

APPENDIXES

The Paralegal Profession

CHAPTER OUTLINE

INTRODUCTION: DEFINING THE PROFESSION

This commentary assumes that readers have a sincere interest in a career as a paralegal. Whether you become a full-time paralegal or practice part-time, you are embarking on an innovative, creative, and dynamic career path. The American workforce has been influenced by the substantial undercurrents of professional assistants in the fields of law, dentistry, medicine, and business. Professional assistants and, in particular, paralegals offer valuable services to the American legal and justice system on both the public and private fronts.

What is a paralegal or legal assistant? The American Bar Association appears to have promulgated an accurate definition:

> *A legal assistant or paralegal is a person qualified by education, training, or work experience who is employed or retained by a lawyer, law office, corporation, governmental agency, or other entity who performs specifically delegated substantive legal work for which a lawyer is responsible.*[1]

1

States may define *paralegal* for the purposes of regulation and discipline. The Indiana Supreme Court has exclusive jurisdiction relative to paralegals and defines the profession in its rules as follows:

> *"Paralegal" means a person who is qualified through education, training, or work experience and is employed by a lawyer, law office, governmental agency, or other entity to work under the direction of an attorney in a capacity that involves the performance of legal work that usually requires a sufficient knowledge of legal concepts and that would be performed by an attorney in the absence of the paralegal.*[2]

Although this definition is customary, it is not uniformly agreed upon.

Not only does the definition of *paralegal* vary by jurisdiction—the occupational title changes as well. Some say *paralegal*, whereas others say *legal assistant*. In a few places the term *legal technician* applies. Legal technicians are witnessed in few American jurisdictions and deliver lawful services in select areas such as Social Security, real estate, ADR, divorce mediation, and administrative processes. Paralegals are sometimes designated either *freelance* or *independent*. In the case of a freelance paralegal, the paralegal always works under an attorney who serves as a supervisor. Independent paralegals provide services that do not impinge upon unauthorized practice rules. The lines frequently blur regarding the practice of law and these occupational designations.[3] At other times, paralegals are labeled *self-help legal service providers*, a reference to nonlawyers who offer self-help legal services to the public for compensation. It is agreed that the profession defines itself in differing ways. Connie Kretchmer, former President of the National Association of Legal Assistants, appreciates this confusion:

> *The terms being used interchangeably to identify these individuals are legal assistant, paralegal, free-lance legal assistant, independent paralegal, and legal technician. Each refers to nonlawyers engaged in a career related to legal services. The important distinction among these terms is how those legal services are delivered.*[4]

This occupational confusion is compounded by a historic resistance to regulation, a wariness of academic and research approaches, and the existence of competing philosophical approaches to the paralegal profession. The *Journal of Paralegal Education and Practice* calls this preliminary occupational analysis a time of *diffusion*. In diffusion, the profession evolves—from legal secretary to administrator, from file clerk to functionary. Exactly when the status of *paralegal* emerges is difficult to pin down.[5] Eventually diffusion gives way to clarity in the occupational definition realized by education, self-regulation, and defined goals. This is a path recently begun for the field. A more widely accepted standard of exactly what a paralegal is will evolve as the profession defines itself.

The paralegal/legal assistant career track has been subject to enormous pressure regarding its occupational roles. The paralegal profession, like any other, goes through periods of occupational growth and stagnation. At present it is developing "independent" dimensions. The independent paralegal works, operates, and acts still in concert with an attorney but runs his or her own paralegal enterprise. Legal only in a few jurisdictions, the independent paralegal's practice borders on the unauthorized practice of law. The independent paralegal is also called *freelance*. For a discussion of what constitutes unauthorized practice of law, see Chapter 2. Another example of the profession's maturation is in the paralegal's direct delivery of legal services. Contracting with clients to provide direct legal services is done by a legal technician. The organized bar sees the legal technician's activities as the unauthorized practice of law. The nonprofit group HALT (Help Abolish Legal Tyranny) has been the legal technician's most outspoken advocate. From HALT's vantage point, the exorbitant costs of legal representation and the locked-up market that lawyers dominate combine to make the occupation of legal technician long overdue. Promoters of the concept say that an administrative proceeding, a bureaucratic filing, and small claims court representation is mundane work that any private citizen can do. If so, why not permit legal technician providers to do the same?[6] See HALT's Web site at www.halt.org.

Even the entry-level paralegal position offers great opportunity. As the paralegal career steadily advances, so do the roles and responsibilities attached to it. It is certainly not static. According to Ann Bailus,

> *Recent graduates, both those with and without legal training, will start in semiclerical positions. As they gain experience, those with good organizational skills will have the advantage and will get additional responsibilities. Different paralegal levels or grades have been emerging over the past few years.*[7]

Even state legislatures throughout the nation have allocated a day out of the legislative calendar for paralegal recognition. New Jersey, Maryland, Ohio, and North Carolina, to name a few, set aside time to recognize this remarkable profession.[8]

The Inevitable Comparison with Attorneys

Like it or not, paralegals are inevitably compared with attorneys. The functions of lawyer and paralegal consistently overlap. In some states either a lawyer or a paralegal can perform a closing at a real estate settlement. A lawyer can research legal questions in the local library; so can the paralegal. The American Bar Association's definition of a paralegal (or legal assistant) refers to this natural alliance or symbiotic relationship between lawyers and paralegals. This inevitable alliance is summed up in the ABA Model Guidelines for the Utilization of Paralegals:

> Under the principles of agency law and the rules of professional conduct, lawyers are responsible for the actions and the work product of the nonlawyers they employ. Rule 5.3 of the Model Rules of Professional Conduct requires that supervising lawyers ensure that the conduct of nonlawyer assistants is compatible with the lawyer's professional obligations.[9]

By way of analogy, if the law is a learned profession (and, of course, most believe, propose, or hope that it is), it follows that paralegalism must have some semblance of *learnedness*. Robert Stevens, president of Haverford College, urges,

> To be a competent lawyer over any extended period of time, one must have learned to learn. Injecting the notions of learning, by learning the job of ordering one's life and work labels, one is able to become a better craftsman, a better technician, as well as a more broadly gauged lawyer. These skills or qualities, in the long run, develop the sense of responsibility to client, to court, and to society as a whole.[10]

Characterizing lawyers as *learned* requires that paralegals strive for educational excellence. Anyone preparing to enter the paralegal profession must take the task of intellectual and educational development seriously. Amanda Flatten, editor of *Legal Assistant Today*, sums it up well:

> Education is the way to stay competitive in the paralegal field. Seeking out the best program for higher education, getting a graduate-level degree, educating others in important issues facing the legal industry . . . and attending classes in continuing legal education on ever-changing issues such as corporate compliance—these are all examples of the important role education plays in the paralegals' lives.[11]

The crossover between the functions of the lawyer and the paralegal does not detract from the unique occupational role that paralegals play. The challenge is in determining how involved paralegals will be in function, practice, and theory.

No paralegal can successfully function in the workplace without having some fundamental understanding of the content and process of lawyering. Because lawyering is heavily geared toward the theoretical and procedural, it follows that a paralegal must possess synonymous capacities. Certain theoretical content areas and technical insights that are applicable in both settings must be mastered.[12] Paralegals need to understand the law, its basis, and its applications.

As lawyers come to more extensively depend on these services, and paralegals lawfully assume a larger range of legal functions, the future of the paralegal profession will be very fruitful. The codependency between lawyers and paralegals may not be as pronounced in the future as it is now. The emergence of legal technicians and independent paralegals may foretell less reliance on one another in the future.

A Professional/Vocational Mix

Paralegalism is a blend of technical action dependent on an understanding of theoretical law. At one end of the spectrum, the paralegal should never be characterized as an errand person, paper pusher, or drone for a firm or agency. At the other extreme, the paralegal cannot be expected to engage in the legal decision making, analysis, and policy making that require specialized law school training. However, these two ends eventually converge, requiring an almost dual persona— the ability to accomplish technical tasks while simultaneously being aware of the reasoning behind the application. Edward Wheat correlates the role of education in paralegal practice and theory because the profession so deeply needs systematic, lifelong learning.[13]

As in any profession, long-range career satisfaction is guided by internal and external growth opportunities. Given the dynamic nature of American law and jurisprudence, there are few reasons why paralegal functions and responsibilities cannot become more challenging in the future. Robert Ulrich, a member of the ABA's Standing Committee and a long-time advocate and scholar of paralegalism, insists that law firms, agencies, and other paralegal employers must take the initiative to ensure substantial personal and professional growth opportunities. He cites the following specific recommendations:

1. Have legal assistants participate in designing law practice systems and procedures.
2. Have attorneys learn to delegate more efficiently.
3. Hire temporary or part-time employees for routine clerical functions.
4. Assign jobs that require legal research and writing.
5. Use paralegals in law office management.
6. Provide opportunities for continuing educational opportunities and new work experience.
7. Use a team approach to meet objectives and make the paralegal a part of the team.
8. Encourage each legal assistant to form his or her own plan for growth and development.[14]

Solid educational programs, a professorate, and accredited institutional operations also help to forge a professional image. Before that image is solidified, however, the academic discipline of paralegal studies has a long way to go. Rod Hughes understands the need for educational evolution:

> If there has been a profession in which educational standards vary, it's the legal assistant field. Depending on your region or locality, the criteria for experience and education—not to mention the title variations for paralegal positions—run the gamut. In a profession lacking solid enforcement of educational standards, those who have taken it upon themselves to pursue graduate-level education are understandably unique.[15]

Few could argue that national standards for educational preparation, let alone licensure and certification, are sorely missing in the field. Education is the key to future professionalism. The role of the AAFPE in standardizing education programs and insisting on measurable academic quality has been undeniable. The American Alliance of Paralegals Inc. has been just as zealous in its advocacy of educational preparedness. Education is fully integrated into the AAPI's Code of Ethics:

> 7. A paralegal shall attain a high degree of competency through education, training, and experience.
> 8. A paralegal shall maintain a high degree of competency by engaging in continuing paralegal education on an annual basis.[16]

In sum, how the profession develops largely depends on its members' sense of self-worth, their drive to evolve both intellectually and occupationally, and their ability to make the profession indispensable to those they serve.

CHARACTERISTICS OF PARALEGALS

Generic Traits

Successful paralegals possess varied personal and professional characteristics. Character traits, education, experience, geographic residency, and area of general knowledge or legal specialization all combine to create the paralegal persona. In small and midsize law firms, the skills that office supervisors have cited as most important for the paralegal to possess are these:

1. Organizational skills.
2. Communications skills.
3. Ability to evaluate and analyze.[17]

Clearly a paralegal must be first a human engineer, an individual who is able to track circumstances, events, conditions, people, and personalities. Also important are the abilities to handle personal interactions and to collect data and information. The National Association of Legal Assistants' (NALA) *Model Standards and Guidelines for the Utilization of Legal Assistants*[18] cites the following functions as essential to paralegalism:

- Conduct client interviews and maintain general contact with the client, so long as the client is aware of the status and function of the legal assistant, and the legal assistant works under the supervision of the attorney.
- Locate and interview witnesses.
- Conduct investigations and statistical and documentary research.
- Conduct legal research.
- Draft legal documents, correspondence, and pleadings.
- Summarize depositions, interrogatories, and testimony.
- Attend executions of wills, real estate closings, depositions, court or administrative hearings, and trials with the attorney.
- Author and sign correspondence provided the legal assistant status is clearly indicated and the correspondence does not contain independent legal opinions or legal advice.

Professionally, a paralegal's time for substantive legal work (as opposed to clerical or administrative work) is billed to clients much like an attorney's time but at a lower hourly rate.[19]

Occupational Requirements

In the 2004 *Legal Assistant Profession: National Utilization and Compensation Survey Report*,[20] NALA surveyed a reliable sample of paralegal practitioners. The results illustrate a paralegal's functions during a typical career experience (see Figure 1.1).

FIGURE 1.1
Functions and Duties/ Frequencies

Source: NATIONAL ASSOCIATION OF LEGAL ASSISTANTS, 2004 NATIONAL UTILIZATION AND COMPENSATION SURVEY REPORT, Table 2.16 (2004). Reprinted with permission of the National Association of Legal Assistants, www.nala.org, 1516 S. Boston, #200, Tulsa, OK 74119.

Functions and Duties/Frequencies Number of Responses and % of Responses Shown					
	Rarely	Monthly	Weekly	Daily	Total Responses
Assist at trial	79%	19%	2%	1%	743
Assist with client contact	15%	17%	25%	44%	1,096
Assist/attend mediations	67%	27%	6%	1%	528
Automation systems/computers	17%	12%	16%	56%	936
Calendar deadlines	10%	6%	21%	63%	1,079
Case management	4%	6%	18%	72%	1,036
Client/witness interviews	36%	24%	26%	14%	871
Court filings	21%	13%	33%	33%	950
Deposition summaries	60%	28%	10%	2%	730
Document analysis/summary	13%	19%	32%	36%	993
Draft correspondence	4%	5%	18%	74%	1,214
Draft pleadings, etc.	13%	11%	30%	46%	994
General factual research	7%	17%	37%	40%	1,134
Investigation	21%	23%	31%	26%	882
Law library maintenance	74%	16%	7%	4%	528
Legal research	33%	31%	25%	12%	996
Office matters	21%	14%	21%	44%	991
Personnel management	53%	13%	13%	22%	606
Prepare/attend depositions	50%	32%	16%	2%	672
Prepare/attend closings	65%	18%	9%	8%	509
Train employees	50%	25%	0%	13%	708
Other	29%	13%	13%	46%	320

FIGURE 1.2   **Characteristics Desired of Prospective Law School Students, According to Law School Admissions Service**

Source: Law School Admissions Council, Law School Admission Service, The Official Guide to ABA-Approved Law Schools Preparing for Law SchoolCore Skills and Values (2005) at http://officialguide.lsac.org/docs/cgi-bin/home.asp.

• Analytic/problem-solving skills	• General research skills
• Critical reading abilities	• Task organization and management skills
• Writing skills	• The values of serving others and promoting justice
• Oral communication and listening abilities	• General knowledge

These results concur with the findings of previous studies. They indicate a pronounced dedication to

- Document analysis and preparation.
- Research.
- Pleadings and litigation.
- Client contact.
- Law office management.
- Office matters.
- Depositions.
- Real estate.
- Personal injury actions.
- Factual and legal investigations.[21]

Not surprisingly, the Law School Admissions Service, in its own independent studies of skills necessary for prospective law students, insists on similar characteristics, traits, and subject matter mastery (see Figure 1.2).

Paralegals are more than technocrats, and they need substantive preparation in critical thinking, critical reasoning, and wording. As noted earlier, educational preparation must mirror the demands of the occupation itself. The U.S. Government's 2006–2007 *Occupational Outlook Handbook* states,

> *One of a paralegal's most important tasks is helping lawyers prepare for closings, hearings, trials, and corporate meetings. Paralegals investigate the facts of cases and ensure that all relevant information is considered. They also identify appropriate laws, judicial decisions, legal articles, and other materials that are relevant to assigned cases. After they analyze and organize the information, paralegals may prepare written reports that attorneys use in determining how cases should be handled. Should attorneys decide to file lawsuits on behalf of clients, paralegals may help prepare the legal arguments, draft pleadings and motions to be filed with the court, obtain affidavits, and assist attorneys during trials. Paralegals also organize and track files of all important case documents and make them available and easily accessible to attorneys.*
>
> *In addition to this preparatory work, paralegals perform a number of other vital functions. For example, they help draft contracts, mortgages, separation agreements, and instruments of trust. They also may assist in preparing tax returns and planning estates. Some paralegals coordinate the activities of other law office employees and maintain financial office records. Various additional tasks may differ, depending on the employer.[22]*

NALA further dissects work product and subject matter according to percentages of time. Paralegal duties, based on time spent on a given category of task, can be categorized as shown in Figure 1.3.

With this occupational responsibility and task range, paralegals have almost unlimited opportunities to grow professionally. An individual's perception of his or her occupational role will be gauged by the performance of certain tasks and duties. Paralegals are fortunate that the selection process affords varied opportunities. Indeed, the professionalization of paralegals is producing intelligent, skillful people who can find value, utility, and functional relevance in their professional experience.[23]

FIGURE 1.3
Duties and Responsibilities in Order of Popularity Average Ranking

Source: NATIONAL ASSOCIATION OF LEGAL ASSISTANTS, 2004 NATIONAL UTILIZATION AND COMPENSATION SURVEY REPORT, Table 2.18 (2004). Reprinted with permission of the National Association of Legal Assistants, www.nala.org, 1516 S. Boston, #200, Tulsa, OK 74119.

Rank 2002 Survey	Duty and 2004 Rank	Average Estimate of Time
1	1. Draft correspondence	3.7
4	2. General factual research	3.1
2	3. Assist with client conference/client contact	3
5	4. Calendar deadlines	3.4
6	5. Case management	3.6
8	6. Legal research	2.2
5	7. Draft pleadings/document responses/discovery	3.1
7	8. Document analysis/summary	2.9
10	9. Office matters	2.9
9	10. Court filings	2.8
13	11. Automation systems/computerized support	3.1
12	12. Investigation	2.6
11	13. Client/witness interviews	2.2
14	14. Assist at trial	1.3
15	15. Deposition summaries	1.6
16	16. Training employees	1.5
17	17. Prepare for/attend depositions	1.7
18	18. Personnel management	2
20	19. Law library maintenance	1.4
21	20. Assist/attend mediations	1.4
19	21. Prepare for/attend closings	1.6
22	22. Other	2.8

Generalization or Specialization: An Ongoing Debate

A paralegal generalist engages in all aspects of paralegal practice—from real estate to labor law, and from mortgage foreclosure to pension law. A specialist refines and hones a single legal area. The issue of whether one method is better than another has caused much debate. Conceptually, the American Bar Association classifies certain practice areas as generalist—namely criminal law, litigation, and real estate.

In Figure 1.4, the following areas achieve the greatest occupational concentration: civil litigation, 45 percent; corporate, 29 percent; personal injury, 26 percent; and real estate, 23 percent. By inference, we can conclude that many generalize. NALA confirms that occupational specialization is uncommon, noting, "The data from this survey show that legal assistants do not specialize as many believe. We found that, as a group, few spend 100 percent of their time on litigation, probate, etc."[24] Its 1990–1991 report confirmed this resistance to specialization on the part of paralegals: "In comparison with the 1988 study, we find consistent results and in many cases, the responses are identical. We are again finding a median value of three specialty areas."[25] Those fields were litigation, personal injury, and real estate, with a secondary but less significant participation in corporate law and probate law. By 2004 the trend to generalized practice appeared entrenched. The most significant level of specialty occurs in litigation. See the NALA survey results in Figure 1.4.

The National Federation of Paralegal Associations (NFPA) has also weighed in on the specialist–generalist debate. According to the responses of more than 7,700 paralegals, the NFPA categorized specialty areas for paralegals (see Figure 1.5). The NFPA also determined that areas of specialization are often connected to levels of experience (see Figure 1.6).

In the International Paralegal Management Association's 2004 *National Compensation Survey and Report of Findings*, fields of specialization for paralegals were identified (see Figure 1.7).

The generalist paralegal can help with real estate closings, prepare criminal defense pleadings, review and assess probate matters, and complete most other tasks delegated by an attorney. It is too early to tell whether the generalist paralegal will go the way of the generalist attorney. The complexities of legal practice will surely cause pressure to do so. The American Bar Association, in its report titled *Legal Assistant Programs: A Guide to Effective*

FIGURE 1.4   Specialty Area of Practice

Source: NATIONAL ASSOCIATION OF LEGAL ASSISTANTS, 2004 NATIONAL UTILIZATION AND COMPENSATION SURVEY REPORT, Table 2.20 (2004). Reprinted with permission of the National Association of Legal Assistants, www.nala.org, 1516 S. Boston, #200, Tulsa, OK 74119.

Specialty Area	Number of Respondents 2004	Percentage of Respondents				
	2004	2004	2002	2000	1997	1995
Civil litigation	648	45%	50%	51%	54%	51%
Corporate	421	29%	35%	33%	33%	22%
Personal injury	372	26%	32%	34%	37%	30%
Real estate	337	23%	29%	30%	32%	25%
Contracts	351	24%	28%	26%	27%	n/a
Probate/estates	263	18%	26%	26%	28%	20%
Trusts and estates	259	18%	24%	23%	n/a	n/a
Administrative/ government/public	273	19%	23%	25%	24%	9%
Family law	183	13%	21%	21%	24%	19%
Medical malpractice	232	16%	21%	21%	22%	13%
Bankruptcy	216	15%	20%	19%	20%	12%
Employment/labor law	239	17%	20%	20%	20%	n/a
Collections	188	13%	20%	n/a	n/a	n/a
Insurance	241	17%	19%	21%	24%	8%
Office management	245	17%	19%	21%	22%	15%
Product liability	185	13%	18%	n/a	n/a	n/a
Workers' compensation	166	12%	17%	17%	18%	11%
Banking/finance	152	11%	17%	14%	16%	6%
Intellectual property	170	12%	16%	15%	14%	n/a
Criminal	137	10%	16%	17%	17%	10%
Mergers and acquisitions	134	9%	14%	n/a	n/a	n/a
Tax	108	8%	13%	13%	14%	4%

FIGURE 1.5   Percentage of Paralegals with at Least 40 Percent of Their Time in a Specialty Area

Source: Lu Hangley, *National Survey Provides Insight into Specialty Areas*, 16 NATIONAL PARALEGAL REPORTER 16 (Summer 1992). Reprinted with permission from the National Federation of Paralegal Associations, Inc., P.O. Box 33108, Kansas City, MO 64114.

Administrative	4.8%
Asbestos	2.2%
Banking	1.6%
Bankruptcy	4.0%
Collections–foreclosure	3.2%
Contracts	1.8%
Corporate	8.3%
Criminal	1.4%
Environmental	2.1%
Employee benefits	1.5%
Insurance	4.2%
Labor	1.6%
Litigation (not elsewhere)	20.1%
Matrimonial	2.9%
Medical malpractice	2.3%
Patent/trademark	1.4%
Personal injury	8.5%
Product liability	2.2%
Real estate	8.2%
Securities	2.1%
Trusts, estate, probate	7.9%
Workers' compensation	2.1%

FIGURE 1.6 Specialty Area Breakdown

Sources: NFPA, A GUIDE TO QUALITY PARALEGAL EDUCATION http://www.paralegals.org/displaycommon.cfm?an=1&subarticlenbr=116. See also Lu Hangley, *National Survey Provides Insight into Specialty Areas,* 16 NATIONAL PARALEGAL REPORTER 16 (Summer 1992). Reprinted with permission from the National Federation of Paralegal Associations, Inc., P.O. Box 33108, Kansas City, MO 64114.

• Alternate dispute resolution (ADR)	• Foreclosure
• Appellate practice	• Immigration
• Asbestos litigation	• Intellectual property
• Bankruptcy and debt collection	• Labor/employment
• Business/corporate	• Litigation
• Collections	• Paralegal management/administration (related career)
• Computer litigation	• Personal injury/medical malpractice/product liability
• Construction	• Probate and estate administration
• Contract administration	• Public benefits
• Criminal law	• Real property
• Domestic relations/family law	• Securities/municipal bonds
• Employment benefits	• Tax
• Environmental law	• Workers' compensation

Program Implementation and Maintenance, urges educational programs to foster a generalized approach:

> The generalist legal assistant is one who is trained in several (usually four or five) areas of the law. The generalist is better equipped to work for the small and medium-size firms whose members practice in many different legal areas.[26]

Other professional organizations have urged a similar philosophy. The American Association for Paralegal Education (AAFPE), the ABA Standing Committee on Legal Assistants, the Association of Legal Administrators (ALA), the International Paralegal Management Association (IPMA), the National Association of Legal Assistants (NALA), and the National Federation of Paralegal Associations Inc. (NFPA) have resolved this in part as follows:

> In recognizing the accomplishments in the education of legal assistants and the utilization of legal assistants' services and acknowledging the commitment necessary to continue the development of

FIGURE 1.7

Fields of Paralegal Specialization

Sources: IPMA 2005 UTILIZATION SURVEY, available at http://www.zoomerang.com/reports/public_report.gi?ID=L229M2HH5D87. See also INTERNATIONAL LEGAL ASSISTANT MANAGEMENT ASSOCIATION, 1993 NATIONAL COMPENSATION SURVEY AND REPORT OF FINDINGS 10 (1993). Copyright 1993. Used with permission of the International Legal Assistant Management Association.

Please Indicate the Practice Areas in Your Organization in Which Paralegals Are Utilized. Check All That Apply.	Number of Responses	Response Ratio
Antitrust	31	46%
Bankruptcy	44	65%
Blue sky/securities	36	53%
Communications	13	19%
Corporate	54	79%
Criminal	12	18%
E-commerce	10	15%
Environmental	38	56%
Family law	6	9%
Immigration	22	32%
Insurance law	25	37%
Intellectual property	48	71%
International	25	37%
Labor/employment	34	50%
Litigation (i.e,. product liability, mass tort, toxic tort, and general personal injury)	55	81%
Medical malpractice	13	19%
Real estate	47	69%
Regulatory practices	27	40%
Tax	25	37%
Trusts and estates	28	41%
Other—please specify	18	26%

FIGURE 1.8   National Average Salaries for Paralegals in the United States

Source: Data are from Salary.com (retrieved January 19, 2007).

Job Description	10th Percentile	25th Percentile	75th Percentile	90th Percentile
Paralegal I Associate's degree or its equivalent and 0–2 years of experience	$30,863	$36,337	$49,343	$55,710
Paralegal II Associate's degree or its equivalent and 2–5 years of experience	$39,013	$45,069	$55,404	$64,488
Paralegal III Bachelor's degree and 5–8 years of experience	$42,742	$48,660	$62,486	$69,157
Paralegal IV Bachelor's degree and at least 8 years of experience	$49,942	$57,454	$76,183	$85,722

the legal assistant profession as well as the well-educated, qualified integral part of the legal assistant's delivery team, we discussed the following:

II A.   We agree the general education requirements in paralegal training serve to eliminate disparity in background that students bring to their training.

III A.   We recognize that in the field of paralegal education, good general education is essential.[27]

Critics of specialization emphasize that a generally educated person will perform more ably over the long haul. Although a specialist may feel comfortable in the short term, a specialist's opportunities to grow professionally are limited.

Compensation Levels

Although information about paralegal compensation varies significantly, paralegal salaries can extend anywhere from $8,000 per year to as high as $75,000 per year. NALA's 2006 survey on salaries can only be labeled positive. The results for 2005–2006 are charted in Figure 1.8. The U.S. Department of Labor paints a fairly positive picture of potential earnings in Figure 1.9.

Earnings of paralegals and legal assistants vary greatly. Salaries depend on education, training, experience, the type and size of employer, and geographic location. In general, paralegals who work for large law firms or in large metropolitan areas earn more than those who work for smaller firms or in less populated regions. In addition to earning a salary, many paralegals receive bonuses. In May 2004, full-time wage and salary paralegals and legal assistants had median annual earnings, including bonuses, of $39,130. The middle 50 percent earned between $31,040 and $49,950. The top 10 percent earned more than $61,390, while the bottom 10 percent earned less than $25,360. Median annual earnings in the industries employing the largest numbers of paralegals in May 2004 were as shown.

It can reasonably be assumed that the predominant starting salary for paralegals ranges from the teens to the low thirties, depending on geographic location, education, and personal skills. Of critical importance in determining salary scale and structure is the size of the law firm. Predictably, larger firms pay higher salaries than smaller ones.

FIGURE 1.9   Potential Earnings of Paralegals

Source: BUREAU OF LABOR STATISTICS, U.S. DEPARTMENT OF LABOR, OCCUPATIONAL OUTLOOK HANDBOOK, 2006–2007 EDITION, *Paralegals and Legal Assistants*, on the Internet at http://www.bls.gov/oco/ocos114.htm (visited April 3, 2006).

Federal government	$59,370
Local government	$38,260
Legal services	$37,870
State government	$34,910

FIGURE 1.10   Paralegal Income Tracking

Sources: 2003 PARALEGAL COMPENSATION AND BENEFITS REPORT, EXECUTIVE SUMMARY, available at http://www.paralegals.org/displaycommon.cfm?an=1&subarticlenbr=111. *See also* Lu Hangley, *National Survey Provides Insight into Specialty Areas*, 16 NATIONAL PARALEGAL REPORTER 16 (Summer 1992). Reprinted by permission from the National Federation of Paralegal Associations, Inc. www.paralegals.org

		Percentage or Average of Population with Characteristic					
Characteristic	**Average Response**	**2003**	**2001**	**1999**	**1997**	**1995**	**1993**
Gender	Female	90.64%	91%	91%	92%	94%	93%
Race	Caucasian	78.57%	88%	88%	91%	95%	94%
Age	Average	40	39	38	38	38	37
Education— college	Bachelor	54.47%	49%	53%	53%	54%	55%
Education— paralegal	Paralegal studies	69.59%	84%	83%	67%	85%	n/a
	ABA-approved			64%	85%	64%	n/a
Employer type	Law firm	69.10%	74%	70%	71%	71%	71%
Time employed	Average	7–10	7–10	7–10	7–10	7–10	3–10
Billing rate	$81–90/hour	46%	41%	53%	66%	74%	75%
Salary	Average	$44,337	$41,742	$38,085	$34,514	$32,875	$31,021
Bonus	Average bonus	$2,165	$2,468	$2,225	$2,094	$1,869	$1,620
	Percent receiving a bonus	60%	65%	64%	64%	63%	68%
Benefits	Vacation	84%	87%	85%	90%		
	Paid sick leave	68%	73%	74%	78%		
	Life insurance	65%	68%	65%	68%		
	Fully paid medical insurance	40%	43%	50%	52%		
	Pension or retirement plan	40%	39%	40%	45%		
	Savings plan (401(k) type)	67%	71%	65%	65%		

The NFPA study weighed paralegal income longitudinally, and the results show a continuing climb for the better (see Figure 1.10).

Once beyond entry-level positions, paralegal salaries tend to rise. The results of a salary survey conducted by the International Paralegal Assistant Management Association (IPAMA) corroborate this finding.[28]

Naturally, paralegals with greater responsibility—in terms of both task expectations and the management of people—command higher salaries. In addition, compensation levels for paralegals frequently are measured by region or locale, firm size, or degree of experience in the field. Identifiable distinctions between salary levels exist in various parts of the country and different metropolitan areas (see the NALA findings in Figure 1.11). Compensation rates will vary based on the size of firm and existing employees. Like other support staff, paralegals have a pecking order—see the NALA data in Figure 1.12.

FIGURE 1.11   Annual Salary and Compensation by Region

Source: NATIONAL ASSOCIATION OF LEGAL ASSISTANTS, 2004 NATIONAL UTILIZATION AND COMPENSATION SURVEY REPORT, Table 4.11 (2004). Reprinted with permission of the National Association of Legal Assistants, www.nala.org, 1516 S. Boston, #200, Tulsa, OK 74119.

Region	2004 Average Salary	2004 Average Compensation	2004 Responses	2002 Average Salary	2002 Average Compensation
Region 1: New England/East	$49,305	$51,479	44	$43,045	$46,268
Region 2: Great Lakes	$42,266	$44,415	89	$39,365	$41,500
Region 3: Plains States	$40,565	$42,694	128	$36,344	$38,333
Region 4: Southeast	$43,168	$45,460	527	$39,644	$42,429
Region 5: Southwest	$45,194	$47,709	274	$40,803	$44,306
Region 6: Rocky Mountains	$40,558	$43,609	72	$34,863	$37,667
Region 7: Far West	$51,993	$55,760	150	$50,379	$55,068

FIGURE 1.12
Annual Salary and Compensation by Number of Attorneys

Source: NATIONAL ASSOCIATION OF LEGAL ASSISTANTS, 2004 NATIONAL UTILIZATION AND COMPENSATION SURVEY REPORT, Table 4.13 (2004). Reprinted with permission of the National Association of Legal Assistants, www.nala.org, 1516 S. Boston, #200, Tulsa, OK 74119.

Number of Attorneys	2004 Average Salary	2004 Average Compensation	2004 Responses	2002 Average Salary	2002 Average Compensation
Sole	$42,452	$45,569	189	$36,401	$38,818
2–5	$43,378	$45,893	396	$38,200	$40,749
6–10	$43,168	$45,092	220	$39,988	$42,858
11–15	$43,631	$45,366	132	$41,441	$44,906
16–20	$45,202	$47,088	56	$42,178	$44,267
21–25	$47,044	$48,713	51	$42,119	$45,398
25–30	$51,724	$54,247	40		
31–35	$42,015	$44,941	30	$43,426	$46,065
36–40	$42,133	$44,013	20	$42,787	$45,901
41–45	$59,250	$61,684	13	$40,936	$43,472
46–50	$43,907	$45,632	15	$44,255	$47,433
51–55	$44,723	$46,071	8	$41,752	$45,149
56–60	$48,743	$52,914	7	$46,071	$49,975
61–65	$48,833	$50,167	3	$42,920	$44,418

Educational Levels

On-the-Job Training

Before proprietary and collegiate programs, paralegals were informally educated or trained through experience by performing various legal functions. The American Bar Association (ABA) definition of a legal assistant supports this by stating, "A legal assistant is a person, qualified through education, training, or *work experience* [emphasis added]."[29] The ABA's 1978 report, *Legal Assistant Education and Utilization*, acknowledged,

> A great deal of the training of legal assistants is conducted in nonformal settings such as inhouse educational programs, clinics, or continuing education programs sponsored by bar associations, legal assistant associations, or CLE units of educational institutions.[30]

NALA's 2004 survey reported on the level of educational opportunity provided by industries, law firms, and corporate entities, revealing the provisions generally made for formal in-house training. The results are illustrated in Figure 1.13. These statistics indicate that law firms and corporations need to become more involved in the education of paralegals.

Continuing education plays an undeniable role in paralegal development and growth. John Reinard's article "Paralegal Career Advancement" advocates the in-house approach by urging

FIGURE 1.13
Participation in Continuing Education

Source: NATIONAL ASSOCIATION OF LEGAL ASSISTANTS, 2004 NATIONAL UTILIZATION AND COMPENSATION SURVEY REPORT, Table 2.27 (2004). Reprinted with permission of the National Association of Legal Assistants, www.nala.org, 1516 S. Boston, #200, Tulsa, OK 74119.

Tools and Techniques for Professional Growth General Findings		
Which Tools and Techniques Have You Utilized for Professional Growth?		
Responses	**Frequency**	**Percentage**
Attend continuing legal education seminars	1,152	89%
Ask/seek more complex work in your practice area	797	62%
Seek the CLA, CLA specialist, or state certification	708	55%
Become involved in your professional association	663	51%
Change practice areas	492	38%
Switch work environments (such as move from large to small firm)	416	32%
Attend work-related courses at community colleges or online	386	30%
Serve as a speaker at continuing legal education seminars	254	20%
Develop freelance opportunities	133	10%
Write educational article for a law-related publication	100	8%

firms and agencies to deliver education and training. Targets should include skills and competencies that benefit the paralegal and the firm, and seminars should be created to use job experiences as learning resources so that relevance of content is enhanced.[31] In-house training is the obligation of the firm and the supervising attorney. According to Thomas J. Calvocoressi and Ronald A. Villanova, a continuing education program for the midsize to large firm or corporate law department "should prepare paralegals to render competent service" and "be an integrated part of the firm's operations."[32]

Certification and Licensure

The question of certification is continuously contested. Having a *certificate* in paralegal studies is not the same thing as being *certified*. Certification implies not only a level of educational preparedness but also successful absorption of content areas relevant in the life of a paralegal. The professional associations, namely NALA, NALS, AAFPE, and the NFPA, administer certification programs. Independently, or with the support of the employer, paralegals should seek all relevant certifications. If the paralegal profession has accomplished anything, it is diversity of certifications and exams. A summary of each follows.

1. PACE: PACE (Paralegal Advanced Competency Exam), offered by the National Federation of Paralegal Associations (NFPA), tests general and specialized practice areas. As noted by NFPA,

    > *The Paralegal Advanced Competency Exam (PACE) is offered by the National Federation of Paralegal Associations Inc. (NFPA) to test the competency level of experienced paralegals.*

    > Exam for experienced paralegals—*PACE is offered to paralegals who have a minimum of two years' experience and meet specific educational requirements. PACE is designed for professional paralegals who want to pioneer the expansion of paralegal roles for the future of the profession, not to restrict entry into the profession.*

    > Two-tier exam—*Each tier addresses different areas. Tier I addresses general legal issues and ethics. As the need arises, a section for state-specific laws may also be developed. Tier II addresses specialty sections.*

    > Fair and independent—*PACE has been developed by a professional testing firm, assisted by an independent task force including paralegals, lawyers, paralegal educators, and content specialists from the general public who are legal advocates. Ongoing administration will be handled by PES.*

    > Voluntary—*Paralegals will have the option to sit for the exam at more than 200 Sylvan Technology Centers. As activities and proposals for regulation of the profession increase, all paralegals will be encouraged to take the exam.*

    > Credential maintenance—*To maintain the PACE RP credential, paralegals are required to obtain 12 hours of continuing legal education, including at least one hour in ethics, every two years.*

2. CLA: NALA offers the Certified Legal Assistant (CLA) examination. Long in the forefront of educational certification, NALA delivers a meaningful measure of paralegal competency.

    > *To be eligible for the CLA examination, a legal assistant must meet one of the following alternate requirements:*
    > a. *Graduation from a legal assistant program that is one of the following:*
    >   - *Approved by the American Bar Association.*
    >   - *An associate degree program.*
    >   - *A postbaccalaureate certificate program in legal assistant studies.*
    >   - *A bachelor's degree program in legal assistant studies.*
    >   - *A legal assistant program that consists of a minimum of 60 semester hours (900 clock hours or 90 quarter hours) of which at least 15 semester hours (225 clock hours or 22.5 quarter hours) are substantive legal courses.*
    > b. *A bachelor's degree in any field plus one year's experience as a legal assistant. Successful completion of at least 15 semester hours (or 22.5 quarter hours or 225 clock hours) of substantive legal assistant courses will be considered equivalent to one year's experience as a legal assistant.*

    c. A high school diploma or equivalent plus seven (7) years' experience as a legal assistant under the supervision of a member of the bar, plus evidence of a minimum of twenty (20) hours of continuing legal education credit to have been completed within a two (2) year period prior to the examination date.

3. ALS, PLS, and PP: Three certifications are offered by the National Association of Legal Specialists (NALS). The certifications differ based on subject matter, education, and experience. NALS highlights the certifications in this way:

> *NALS offers members and nonmembers the opportunity to sit for three unique certifications dedicated to the legal services profession. The exams are of varying levels and are developed by professionals in the industry. ALS . . . the basic certification for legal professionals and PLS . . . the advanced certification for legal professionals are two certifications dedicated to legal professionals of all types. The third certification is dedicated to those professionals performing paralegal duties. The Professional Paralegal (PP) certification was developed by paralegals for paralegals. Each of the three certifications is developed by NALS and takes advantage of the more than 75 years of experience and dedication to the legal services industry only NALS has to offer.*

As for licensure, the regulatory process has been slow to come on board. Some states are silent on the profession, whereas others are increasingly getting involved. Review the chart in Figure 1.14 for a summary.

Proprietary/Vocational/Technical Education

For some time, proprietary institutions of higher education provided the force behind academic development in the paralegal profession. Four-year colleges and universities are now becoming involved in the growth of the profession, although such support has been slow. Institutions like the American Institute for Paralegal Studies (AIPS),[33] founded in 1977, have given nontraditional students throughout the United States an opportunity to pursue this career track. The Institute for Paralegal Training (IPT) also has been an active participant in the development of the profession.

    Currently over 500 institutions of higher learning in the proprietary sector provide paralegal study opportunities. Lists of institutions providing paralegal education are available from the American Association for Paralegal Education (AAFPE), Legal Assistant Today Inc., and the American Bar Association.[34]

    Proprietary institutions may take a generalist or specialist approach; but because their programs are shorter than traditional education programs, less attention tends to be paid to liberal arts curricula and more attention given to a vocational orientation. Preparation for life and its occupational challenges is not an insignificant task.[35] An enormous debt is owed to the proprietary sector for its aggressive involvement in the development of the paralegal profession.

Colleges and Universities

In its 1978 status report on legal assistant education and utilization, the American Bar Association cited 150 colleges and universities that have received their approval.[36] Today most recent estimates hold that there are over 700 paralegal schools.[37] To assure high-quality education programs, the ABA's Approval Commission offers on-site visitation and team analysis and approval of paralegal training programs. The ABA solicits participation of practicing paralegals to be part of on-site team reviews.

    The American Association of Paralegal Education has established four broad classifications of college and university membership:

1. Public community or junior colleges.

2. Public colleges or universities offering baccalaureate degrees or higher.

3. Nonprofit colleges or universities.

4. Proprietary schools.

However, some organizations (such as nonprofit institutes, vocational schools, and comprehensive technical institutes) do not fit neatly into these categories.[38] In general, paralegals are a

FIGURE 1.14 **Summary of State Licensure Requirements**

Source: As seen in the March/April 2006 issue of Legal Assistant Today. Copyright 2007 James Publishing, Inc. Reprinted courtesy of Legal Assistant Today magazine. For subscription information call (800) 394-2626, or visit www.legalassistanttoday.com.

Alabama	Alabama Code Section 6-5-572 includes legal assistants and paralegals in its definition of a *legal service provider*, which is anyone "engaged in the practice of law." (www.legislature. state.al.us/codeofalabama/1975/coatoc.htm)
Alaska	Alaska Rule of Professional Conduct 5.3 doesn't define *paralegals* but considers *paraprofessionals* as nonlawyer assistants. The rule states that lawyers must directly supervise their assistants and are responsible for their assistants' conduct. (www.state.ak.us/courts/prof.htm#5.3)
Arizona	Effective July 1, 2003, anyone preparing legal paperwork without an attorney's supervision must be certified as a legal document preparer pursuant to the Arizona Code of Judicial Administration Section 7-208. Legal document preparers can provide general legal information but can't give legal advice. Paralegals can receive a legal document preparer's certification if they already have earned a paralegal certificate from an ABA-approved program or a non-ABA-approved, accredited institution with a minimum of 24 completed semester units in legal specialization courses. (www.supreme.state.az.us/orders/admcode/pdfcurrentcode/ 7-208%20section2.pdf)
Arkansas	Arkansas Rule of Professional Conduct 5.3 doesn't define *paralegals* but considers *paraprofessionals* as nonlawyer assistants. The rule states that lawyers must directly supervise their assistants and are responsible for their assistants' conduct. (http://courts.state.ar.us/rules/ profcond5.html)
California	Signed into law in 2000 and effective in 2001, the California Business and Professions Code Section 6450–6456 defines a *paralegal* as someone who is qualified by education, training, or work experience and performs substantial legal work under the supervision of an active member of the state bar. The code also defines a paralegal's duties, states minimum educational standards and continuing legal education requirements, and sets fines and jail time for anyone who violates the law. For more information, go to www.leginfo.ca.gov. Also, the voluntary California Advanced Specialty certification program was created in 1994 through an agreement between the National Association of Legal Assistants and the California Alliance of Paralegal Associations. It's suspended until late 2006, when it will return as a Web-based program.
Colorado	Colorado Rule of Professional Conduct 5.3 doesn't define *paralegals* but considers *paraprofessionals* as nonlawyer assistants. The rule states that lawyers must directly supervise their assistants and are responsible for their assistants' conduct. (www.coloradosupremecourt. com/regulation/Rules/appendix20/statdspp0b99.html)
Connecticut	Connecticut Rule of Professional Conduct 5.3 doesn't define *paralegals* but considers *paraprofessionals* as nonlawyer assistants. The rule states that lawyers must directly supervise their assistants and are responsible for their assistants' conduct. (www.jud.ct.gov/ Publications/PracticeBook/PB1.pdf)
Delaware	Although the state doesn't regulate paralegals, the Delaware Paralegal Association in 2005 approved voluntary certification, which establishes minimum educational standards. Certified members must follow the DPA's ethics code and renew certification status every two years. (www.deparalegals.org/dcpp.php)
Florida	At press time, the Florida Bar Board of Governors opposed two bills to license paralegals, saying more study is needed. Rep. Juan Zapata, R-Miami, filed House Bill 395 after his previous legislation died in committee in 2005. The bill aims to establish the Paralegal Professional Act, which would set educational requirements, an ethics code, and other rules. It and a companion senate bill will be discussed during legislative sessions in March. A state bar special committee also will meet in March to discuss regulation options. In 1980, the Paralegal Association of Florida Inc. established the voluntary Certified Florida Legal Assistant program and began administering the CFLA exam in 1983.
Georgia	There are no regulation activities reported.
Hawaii	In 2001 the Hawaii State Bar Association rejected a mandatory paralegal certification proposal by its Task Force on Paralegal Certification. The proposal attempted to impose a degree of regulation on paralegal use and would have required certification of legal assistants in the state. The next year, the state supreme court also declined to approve paralegal certification. There are no new regulation activities reported.
Idaho	Idaho Rule of Professional Conduct 5.3 doesn't define *paralegals* but considers *paraprofessionals* as nonlawyer assistants. The rule states that lawyers must directly supervise their assistants and are responsible for their assistants' conduct. (http://www2.state.id.us/isb/pdf/irpc.pdf)

FIGURE 1.14 (*continued*)

Illinois	In 2005 two state initiatives to monitor nonattorney legal service providers failed. Illinois statutes define a *paralegal* as "a person who is qualified through education, training, or work experience, and is employed by a lawyer, law office, governmental agency, or other entity to work under the direction of an attorney in a capacity that involves the performance of substantive legal work that usually requires a sufficient knowledge of legal concepts and would be performed by the attorney in the absence of the paralegal." (www.ilga.gov/legislation/ilcs/ilcs2.asp?chapterid=2 under "Statute on Statutes")
Indiana	After more than two years, an Indiana supreme court committee will accept comments through April 3 on its planned voluntary paralegal registration before submitting the proposal to the supreme court. The proposal defines *paralegals*, establishes educational requirements, and bans disbarred attorneys, felons, and those convicted of UPL from registering.
Iowa	Iowa Rule of Professional Conduct 32:5.3 doesn't define *paralegals* but considers *paraprofessionals* as nonlawyer assistants. The rule states that lawyers must directly supervise their assistants and are responsible for their assistants' conduct. (www.legis.state.ia.us/rules/current/court/courtrules.pdf)
Kansas	Kansas Supreme Court Rule 5.3 doesn't define *paralegals* but considers *paraprofessionals* as nonlawyer assistants. The rule states that lawyers must directly supervise their assistants and are responsible for their assistants' conduct. (http://www.kscourts.org/ctruls/rule5.htm#5.3)
Kentucky	Reportedly the first to address paralegal utilization, the Kentucky supreme court in 1979 established Rule 3.700, which defines a paralegal, prohibits UPL, and includes other rules such as allowing a paralegal's name on attorney letterhead as long as the "paralegal's status is clearly indicated." Also, the Kentucky Paralegal Association currently is developing a statewide voluntary paralegal certification exam and study guide. (http://kybar.org/documents/scr/scr3/scr_3.700.pdf)
Louisiana	The Louisiana State Paralegal Association established a voluntary certification exam in 1996 to set professional standards and promote recognition of the profession. (www.la-paralegals.org)
Maine	In 1999 the governor signed into law a bill that includes a definition of a *legal assistant* and *paralegal*, based on the ABA definition. Violators of this law are subject to a fine of up to $1,000. (http://janus.state.me.us/legis/statutes/4/title4sec921.html)
Maryland	In 2005 the state's Rules Committee submitted to the Maryland Court of Appeals amendments to Rule 5.3 to allow disbarred, suspended, or inactive attorneys to work as paralegals under certain circumstances, such as working in an office under the supervision of a full-time lawyer who has been in good standing with the state bar for at least five years. (www.courts.state.md.us/rules/ruleschanges.html#rule16760)
Massachusetts	Amended in 2002, Massachusetts Rule of Professional Conduct 5.3 doesn't define *paralegals* but considers *paraprofessionals* as nonlawyer assistants. The rule states that lawyers must directly supervise their assistants and are responsible for their assistants' conduct. (www.mass.gov/obcbbo/rpc5.htm)
Michigan	Michigan Rule of Professional Conduct 5.3 doesn't define *paralegals* but considers *paraprofessionals* as nonlawyer assistants. The rule states that lawyers must directly supervise their assistants and are responsible for their assistants' conduct. (www.michbar.org/generalinfo/pdfs/mrpc.pdf)
Minnesota	In 1994 the Minnesota legislature appointed a special committee to consider paralegal licensure procedures, but the regulation movement never progressed. There are no new regulation activities reported.
Mississippi	Effective in 1987, Mississippi Rule of Professional Conduct 5.3 doesn't define *paralegals* but states that lawyers must directly supervise their assistants and are responsible for their assistants' conduct. (www.mslawyer.com/mssc/profcond.html)
Missouri	Adopted in 1993 and effective in 1995, Missouri Supreme Court Rule 4-5.3 includes *paraprofessionals* in its definition of *nonlawyer assistants*. Attorneys must directly supervise their assistants and are responsible for their assistants' conduct, according to the rule. (www.courts.mo.gov/courts/clerkhandbooksp2rulesonly.nsf/supreme%20court%20rules?openview)
Montana	Amended in 2001, Montana Code Section 37-60-101 defines a *paralegal* or *legal assistant* as a person, qualified through education, training, or work experience, who performs

FIGURE 1.14   (*continued*)

	substantive legal work while employed or retained by a lawyer, firm, or other entities. (http://data.opi.state.mt.us/bills/mca/37/60/37-60-101.htm)
Nebraska	Effective September 2005, the Nebraska Rules of Professional Conduct Rule 5.3 defines *support person* and *paraprofessionals* in its definition of *nonlawyer assistants*. The rule states attorneys must supervise their assistants and are responsible for their assistants' conduct. (http://court.nol.org/rules/RulesProfConduct.34.pdf)
Nevada	Effective in 1986, Nevada Supreme Court Rule 187 doesn't define *paralegals* but states that lawyers must directly supervise their assistants and are responsible for their assistants' conduct. (http://www.leg.state.nv.us/courtrules/scr.html)
New Hampshire	The New Hampshire Supreme Court Administrative Rule 35 defines a *paralegal* as a person not admitted to the practice of law in the state who is under the direct supervision of an active member of the New Hampshire State Bar. (www.courts.state.nh.us/rules/scr/scr-35.htm)
New Jersey	In 1999 the New Jersey supreme court denied a proposal from its special committee calling for the mandatory licensing of paralegals, but encouraged the local associations to look into the development of a credentialing system. The New Jersey State Bar Association Committee on Paralegals currently is working on a registration system for paralegals. Previous attempts to register paralegals have stalled.
New Mexico	The state supreme court in January 2004 amended its rules to include a new definition stating that paralegals are highly trained support staff who engage in substantive legal work. The amendments also establish minimum standards for calling oneself a *paralegal* and discourage using the title *paralegal* by those not qualified and by attorneys disbarred or suspended from practicing law. (www.nmlaws.org)
New York	No regulation activities are reported.
North Carolina	The supreme court of North Carolina approved the voluntary certification of paralegals in October 2004. The North Carolina State Bar Board of Paralegal Certification began accepting applications on July 1, 2005. To qualify, paralegals must fulfill educational and work experience requirements. (www.nccertifiedparalegal.org)
North Dakota	Both the North Dakota Century Code and the North Dakota Rules of Professional Conduct have rules defining a *legal assistant* as someone who works under the direct supervision of a licensed lawyer and whose work product is the complete responsibility of the attorney. (www.ndcourts.com/court/rules/conduct/rule5.3.htm)
Ohio	The state's five paralegal associations are helping the Ohio State Bar Association's Paralegal Committee formulate a proposal for a voluntary certification program, according to the Paralegal Association of Northwest Ohio. No timetable has been set.
Oklahoma	In the 1994 *Taylor v. Chubb* case, the Oklahoma supreme court ruled that charges for legal assistants should be included by courts in attorney fee award decisions. The court's paralegal definition is based on the one established by the ABA and lists paralegal duties such as interviewing clients, drafting pleadings, and performing legal research.
Oregon	No regulation activities are reported.
Pennsylvania	Pennsylvania Consolidated Statutes Section 2524(a) of Title 42 states that paralegals and legal assistants can't deliver legal services without attorney supervision and can't present themselves as people entitled to practice law. The law was passed in 1996 in response to widespread concern that it was misleading to potential clients for people using the terms *paralegal* and *legal assistant* in ads.
Rhode Island	Rhode Island Supreme Court Provisional Order No. 18 was established in 1983 and defines a *legal assistant* as "one who under the supervision of a lawyer, shall apply knowledge of the law and legal procedures in rendering direct assistance to lawyers, clients and courts; design, develop, and modify procedures, techniques, services, and processes; prepare and interpret legal documents; detail procedures for practicing in certain fields of law; research, select, access, and compile information from the law library and other references; and analyze and handle procedural problems that involve independent decisions." For more information, call the supreme court clerk's office at (401) 222-3272.
South Carolina	Rule 5.3 of the Supreme Court of South Carolina Rules of Conduct doesn't define *paralegals* but considers *paraprofessionals* as nonlawyer assistants. The rule states that lawyers must directly supervise their assistants and are responsible for their assistants' conduct. (www.judicial.state.sc.us/courtreg/listapprules.cfm)

FIGURE 1.14   *(concluded)*

South Dakota	The Legal Assistants Committee of the State Bar of South Dakota is lobbying to replace the term *legal assistant* with *paralegal* in state statutes and to tighten the qualifications on who can be called a paralegal. South Dakota Supreme Court Rule 97-25 defines *legal assistants* as a distinguishable group that assists attorneys and has expertise regarding the legal system, substantive and procedural law, the ethical considerations of the legal profession, and state rules, which qualify them to do work of a legal nature under the direct supervision of a licensed attorney. (http://legis.state.sd.us/statutes/displaystatute.aspx?type=statute&statute=16-18-34)
Tennessee	According to Tennessee Supreme Court Rule 5.3, effective in 1981, a lawyer should give *nonlawyer assistants* and *paraprofessionals* appropriate instruction and supervision "concerning the ethical aspects of their employment, particularly regarding the obligation not to disclose information relating to representation of the client, and should be responsible for their work product." (www.tsc.state.tn.us/opinions/tsc/rules/tnrulesofcourt/06supct1_9.htm)
Texas	Established in 1974 by the state supreme court, the Texas Board of Legal Specialization offers voluntary specialty certification for attorneys and legal assistants. Legal assistants can become certified in six different specialty areas of law, each requiring an exam and a minimum amount of experience, education, and CLE. (www.tbls.org)
Utah	Amended in March 2005, the Utah Supreme Court Rule of Professional Conduct 5.3 states that paralegals work under the ultimate supervision of attorneys, who are responsible for their paralegals' work product and must give appropriate instruction concerning the ethical aspects of their employment, particularly regarding the obligation not to disclose information relating to representation of the client. (www.utcourts.gov/resources/rules/ucja/13_proco/5_3.htm)
Vermont	Vermont Rule of Professional Conduct 5.3 doesn't define *paralegals* but states that lawyers must directly supervise their assistants and are responsible for their assistants' conduct. (www.vermontjudiciary.org/committes/prbrules/vtpcframespage.htm)
Virginia	Amended in 2004, Virginia Supreme Court Rule 5.3 doesn't define *paralegals* but states that lawyers must directly supervise their assistants and are responsible for their assistants' conduct. (www.courts.state.va.us/scv/amendments/rule3_5_rule5_3_092603.pdf)
Washington	In December 2005 the Washington State Practice of Law Board drafted a regulation proposal, which the bar's board of governors will consider in early 2006. If the board approves the draft, it will be submitted to the state supreme court for consideration. The proposal includes a definition, certification, and educational requirements. (www.wsba.org/lawyers/groups/practiceoflaw/default.htm)
West Virginia	West Virginia Professional Conduct Rule 5.3 states that lawyers must directly supervise their assistants and are responsible for their assistants' conduct. (www.wvbar.org/barinfo/rulesprofconduct/rules5.htm)
Wisconsin	The Wisconsin State Bar's Paralegal Practice Task Force petitioned the state supreme court in 2004 to regulate paralegals and is awaiting a decision or additional hearing. The proposal includes a definition of a *paralegal*, educational requirements, and an ethics policy. (www.wisbar.org/committees/ptf/definitions.html)
Wyoming	Wyoming Rule of Professional Conduct 5.3 doesn't define *paralegals* but considers *paraprofessionals* as nonlawyer assistants. The rule states that lawyers must directly supervise their assistants and are responsible for their assistants' conduct. (http://courts.state.wy.us/rules/professional conduct for attorneys.html)

well-educated population. Figure 1.15 is a graphic composition of educational backgrounds of practicing paralegals who responded to the 2004 NALA survey.

Given the high achievement level of paralegals, education will be critical during the job search. Nancy Murphy, a Detroit paralegal, views education as the key to success:

> *Because of today's economic climate, employers should be extremely selective. A bachelor's or associate's degree shows a prospective employer that you are both disciplined and dedicated. More often than not a candidate with a degree will be given first consideration in the selection process.*[39]

FIGURE 1.15   General Educational Degree Attained 1988 through 2004 (Percentages of the population)

Source: National Association of Legal Assistants, 2004 National Utilization and Compensation Survey Report, Table 1.6 (2004). Reprinted with permission of the National Association of Legal Assistants, www.nala.org, 1516 S. Boston, #200, Tulsa, OK 74119.

Response	2004	2002	2000	1997	1995	1993	1991	1988
High school diploma	18%	21%	27%	29%	31%	33%	32%	30%
Associate's degree	33%	33%	28%	26%	26%	22%	27%	36%
Bachelor's degree	44%	41%	40%	41%	40%	40%	38%	31%
Master's degree	5%	4%	4%	4%	4%	3%	3%	3%
Doctorate	1%	1%	—	—	—	—	—	—

OCCUPATIONAL OPPORTUNITIES

Opportunities in the paralegal sector are ample. The 2006–2007 data indicate a profession that will grow faster than average. Jobs at the federal level, such as the posting at Figure 1.16, are quite common.

To find a professional position, a paralegal should take some of the following steps:

1. Establish contact with the right people.

2. Scrutinize job advertisements.

3. Locate appropriate professional associations and groups.

4. Consider private employment agencies.

5. Consult reference book listings of law firms and corporations.

6. Review government civil service bulletins.

7. Make telephone inquiries.[40]

Paralegal job opportunities exist on both public and private fronts. Career opportunities are not exclusive to the law firm. Paralegals work in almost every institution, including prisons,

FIGURE 1.16   Paralegal Specialist Job Listing

Source: Please visit www.usajobs.com for current listings of government employment opportunities.

Paralegal Specialist

SALARY RANGE: 40,190.00–99,111.00 USD per year

SERIES & GRADE: CU-0950-09/12

PROMOTION POTENTIAL: 12

WHO MAY BE CONSIDERED: All U.S. Citizens

OPEN PERIOD: Monday, March 27, 2006 to Monday, April 3, 2006

POSITION INFORMATION: Career/Career–Conditional Permanent

DUTY LOCATIONS: 1 vacancy—Alexandria, VA

JOB SUMMARY:

The National Credit Union Administration (NCUA) is the federal agency that charters and supervises federal credit unions and insures savings in federal and most state-chartered credit unions across the country through the National Credit Union Share Insurance Fund (NCUSIF), a federal fund backed by the full faith and credit of the United States government.

The position is located in the Office of the General Counsel (OGC) at the National Credit Union Administration (NCUA). The incumbent provides paralegal and technical support to the general counsel, associate general counsel, and staff of OGC.

KEY REQUIREMENTS:

- You must be a U.S. citizen.
- All federal payments must be directly deposited to a financial institution.
- You must successfully complete a background/security investigation.
- Relocation costs will not be authorized.
- A one-year probationary period is required.

FIGURE 1.17   Qualification Chart for Federal Service Positions

Source: U.S. Office of Personnel Management, "Qualification Standards for General Schedule Provisions." On the Internet at: http://www.opm.gov/qualifications/SEC-IV/A/gs-admin.asp (retrieved January 19, 2007).

Grade	Education or Experience	General	Specialized
GS-5	4-year course of study above high school leading to a bachelor's degree	3 years, 1 year of which was at least equivalent to GS-4	None
GS-7	1 full academic year of graduate-level education or law school or superior academic achievement	None	1 year at least equivalent to GS-5
GS-9	2 full academic years of graduate-level education or a master's or equivalent graduate degree or LL.B. or J.D.	None	1 year at least equivalent to GS-7
GS-11	3 full academic years of graduate-level education or a Ph.D. or equivalent doctoral degree	None	1 year at least equivalent to GS-9
GS-12 and above	None	None	1 year at least equivalent to next lower grade level

Equivalent combinations of education and experience are qualifying for all grade levels for which both education and experience are acceptable.

hospitals, neighborhood centers, nursing homes, real estate development companies, title companies, legal aid and legal service offices, state governments, the federal government, the military, accounting firms, banks, construction companies, entertainment facilities, high-technology companies, publishing companies, professional associations, oil and gas companies, recruiting agencies, and numerous other organizations. Government agencies and paralegal associations can help the job-hunting paralegal.

Government Employment Opportunities

Paralegals are employed at all levels of government. On the local, state, and federal levels there are numerous opportunities for paralegals. Federally, positions are graded by specialty and are classified according to a general schedule, abbreviated as GS-1 through GS-15. Shelley Widoff, a paralegal, has developed a qualification chart for federal service positions (see Figure 1.17).

A greater variety of positions and higher salaries have encouraged more paralegals to work in government service. General information about paralegal careers in federal service can be obtained from the U.S. Office of Personnel Management, Room 5245, 1600 E. Street NW, Washington, DC 20415.

State Civil Service Opportunities

State civil service opportunities are equally extensive. Most states have official definitions of paralegal/legal assistant job descriptions. Government agencies that have positions within their bureaucratic structures include some of those outlined in Figure 1.18.

Civil service opportunities exist within all areas of state and local government. The secretaries of state, divisions of business and corporations, offices of the attorneys general, offices of district attorneys and public defenders, and offices of taxation, estates, and trusts all provide related occupational opportunities. However, because of the newness of the profession, career opportunities may not use the term *paralegal*. Melanie Baker and Thomas Eimermann conducted a study suggesting that the difficulty in breaking into the state civil service network is related to (a) the fact that many positions have not been properly identified, (b) the recent budget crisis, and (c) the bureaucratic process itself, which has prevented the funding of positions for which needs have been recognized.[41]

FIGURE 1.18   State Government Agencies

ALABAMA
Personnel Dept.
Montgomery, AL
36130

ALASKA
Dept. of Administration
Div. of Personnel
Pouch C-0201
Juneau, AK 99811

ARIZONA
Dept. of Administration
Personnel Division
1831 West Jefferson
Phoenix, AZ 85007

ARKANSAS
Dept. of Finance &
Admin.
Office of Personnel
Mgmt.
P.O. Box 3278
Little Rock, AR 72203

CALIFORNIA
State Personnel Bldg.
801 Capital Mall
Sacramento, CA 95814

COLORADO
Dept. of Personnel
State Continental Bldg.
1313 Sherman St.
Denver, CO 80203

CONNECTICUT
Personnel Div.
Dept. of Admin.
Services
P.O. Box 806
Hartford, CT 06115

DELAWARE
State Personnel Office
Townsend Bldg.
P.O. Box 1401
Dover, DE 19901

DISTRICT OF COLUMBIA
D.C. Personnel Office
613 C. St. NW
Washington, DC 20001

FLORIDA
Dept of Administration
Carlton Bldg., Rm 530
Tallahassee, FL 32301

GEORGIA
State Merit System of
Personnel
Administration
200 Piedmont Ave.
Atlanta, GA 30334

GUAM
Office of Attorney
General
Pacific News Bldg. 7th
floor
238 O'Hara St.
Agana, GU 96910

HAWAII
Dept. of Personnel
Services
830 Punchbowl St.
Honolulu, HI 96813

IDAHO
Personnel Commission
700 West State St.
Boise, ID 83720

ILLINOIS
State Civil Service
Comm.
425 ½ S. Fourth St.
Springfield, IL 62701

INDIANA
State Personnel Dept.
State Office Bldg., Fm 513
100 N. Senate Ave.
Indianapolis, IN 40204

IOWA
Merit Employment Dept.
Grimes State Office Bldg.
E. 14th & Grand
Des Moines, IA 50319

KANSAS
Dept. of Administration
Div. of Personnel
Services
State Office Bldg.
Topeka, KS 66612

KENTUCKY
Dept. of Personnel
Capitol Annex
Frankfort, KY 40601

LOUISIANA
Dept. of Civil Service
P.O. Box 44111
Capitol Station
Baton Rouge, LA 70804

MAINE
Dept. of Personnel
State Office Bldg.
State House Station 4
Augusta, ME 04333

MARYLAND
Dept. of Personnel
301 W. Preston St.
Baltimore, MD 21201

MICHIGAN
Dept. of Civil Service
Lewis Cass Bldg.
320 S. Walnut St.
Box 30002
Lansing, MI 48909

MINNESOTA
Dept. of Employee
Relations
Space Center, 3rd Floor
444 LaFayette Rd.
St. Paul, MN 55101

MONTANA
Dept. of Administration
Personnel Division
Mitchell Bldg. Rm 130
Helena, MT 59601

NEBRASKA
Dept. of Personnel
Box 94905
Lincoln, NE 68509

NEW HAMPSHIRE
Dept. of Personnel
State House Annex
Room 1
Concord, NH 03301

NEW JERSEY
Dept. of Civil Service
Div. of Classification
E. State & Montgomery
Sts. CN 310
Trenton, NJ 08625

NEW MEXICO
State Personnel Office
130 So. Capitol
Sante Fe, NM 87501

NEW YORK
Dept. of Civil Service
State Office Bldg.
Campus
Albany, NY 12239

NORTH CAROLINA
Office of State
Personnel
116 West Jones St.
Raleigh, NC 27611

NORTH DAKOTA
Personnel Office
1000 E. Divide Ave.
Box 1537
Bismarck, ND 58502

OHIO
Dept. of Admin. Services
Div. of Personnel
30 E. Broad St.
Columbus, OH 43215

OREGON
Executive Dept.
Personnel Div.
155 Cottage St., NE
Salem, OR 97310

PENNSYLVANIA
Office of
Administration
Bureau of Personnel
517 Finance Bldg.
Harrisburg, PA 17120

SOUTH CAROLINA
Budget & Control Board
Div. of Human Resource
Mgmt.
1205 Pendleton St.
P.O. Box 12547
Columbia, SC 29211

TENNESSEE
Dept of Personnel
J.K. Polk Bldg., 1st Fl.
505 Deaderick St.
Nashville, TN 37219

TEXAS
Atty. Gen. of Texas
Supreme Court Bldg.
Austin, TX 78711

VERMONT
Agency of
Administration
Dept. of Personnel
110 State St.
Montpelier, VT 05602

WASHINGTON
State Dept. of
Personnel
P.O. Box 1789
Olympia, WA 98504

WEST VIRGINIA
Civil Service System
1900 Washington St.
East Room B-456
Charleston, WV 25305

WISCONSIN
Dept. of Employee
Relations
149 E. Wilson St.
P.O. Box 7855
Madison, WI 53707

FIGURE 1.19   Type of Employer: 1993–2004

Source: NATIONAL ASSOCIATION OF LEGAL ASSISTANTS, 2004 NATIONAL UTILIZATION AND COMPENSATION SURVEY REPORT, Table 2.2 (2004). Reprinted with permission of the National Association of Legal Assistants, www.nala.org, 1516 S. Boston, #200, Tulsa, OK 74119.

Employer	2004 Response	2004 Percentage	2002 Percentage	2000 Percentage	1997 Percentage	1995 Percentage	1993 Percentage
Private law firm	928	69%	71%	74%	75%	75%	77%
Insurance company	26	2%	2%	2%	2%	1%	2%
Public sector/ government	101	8%	7%	8%	8%	7%	7%
Self-employed	21	2%	2%	2%	2%	2%	2%
Health/medical	8	1%	1%	1%	1%	1%	n/a
Bank	16	1%	1%	1%	1%	1%	1%
Corporation	182	14%	12%	10%	11%	9%	8%
Court system	15	1%	1%	n/a	n/a	n/a	n/a
Nonprofit corporation, foundation, or association	17	1%	1%	n/a	n/a	n/a	n/a
Other	0	—	1%	n/a	n/a	n/a	n/a
Student	0	—	—	—	0	n/a	n/a
Unemployed	4	0	—	—	0	n/a	n/a

Law Firm Employment

According to the *National Utilization and Compensation Survey Report, 2004*, more than half of all occupational opportunities in the paralegal profession remain in the law office environment (see Figure 1.19). The utilization rate for paralegals depends on firm or agency size. Not surprisingly, larger firms employ more paralegals (see Figure 1.20).

When engaged in a job search, a useful resource is the *Martindale-Hubbell Law Directory*, the premier compendium of practicing lawyers, which gives access to

- An areas of practice index for locating lawyers by specialty.

- A single-volume corporate law department section with information about in-house counsel.

- A services and suppliers consultants section listing companies that serve the legal profession.

- Comprehensive digests of the laws of the United States, Canada, and 60 other countries, prepared by preeminent practitioners in each jurisdiction.

- Three international volumes containing information about lawyers in over 130 countries worldwide.

- Practice profiles of virtually every attorney in the United States and Canada.

The *National Law Journal* performed an extensive analysis of the employment of paralegals in 250 of the largest law firms in the country. The study focused on large, urban law firms but failed to account for the employment influence of small to midsize law firms.[42]

Nontraditional Positions

Paralegals, like lawyers, find their skills welcome in a series of nontraditional paralegal careers. Marsha A. Rattermann characterizes paralegalism as "adaptable to so many different areas of law, business, and society." It is likely that the skills and competencies of paralegals will continue to find new niches.[43] In *Where Do I Go From Here?* Chere Estrin and Andrea Wagner emphasize how experienced paralegals have enormous opportunities in nontraditional fields. They list the following career directions:

Accounting services

Actuarial planners

Advertising companies

Air pollution control

Appraisal services

Arbitration and mediation

Architecture/interior design

Artist or literary agent

Automotive industry

Bank management

FIGURE 1.20
Ratio of Attorneys to Legal Assistants

Source: NATIONAL ASSOCIATION OF LEGAL ASSISTANTS, 2004 NATIONAL UTILIZATION AND COMPENSATION SURVEY REPORT, Table 2.11 (2004). Reprinted with permission of the National Association of Legal Assistants, www.nala.org, 1516 S. Boston, #200, Tulsa, OK 74119.

Ratio of Attorneys to Legal Assistants			
Number of Attorneys	**Number of Attorneys per Legal Assistant**	**Number of Responses**	**Summary**
Sole	.7	172	
2–5 attorneys	1.4	369	
6–10	1.8	197	1.3 attorneys to paralegals (2–10 size)
11–15	2.4	112	
16–20	3	52	
21–25	2.9	48	
26–30	3.4	36	2.7 attorneys to paralegals (11–30 size)
31–35	2.9	28	
36–40	2.8	18	
41–45	1.4	8	
46–50	3	15	
51–55	3.5	9	
56–60	2.8	8	2.8 attorneys to paralegals (31–60 size)
61–65	4.4	3	
66–70	3.3	4	
71–75	4.3	5	
76–80	3.7	13	
81–85	3.5	9	
86–90	4.3	7	
91–95	4.8	1	
96–100	2.1	12	
More than 100	5	45	4.2 attorneys to paralegals (61–100 size)

Better Business Bureaus

Bookkeeping services

Broadcasting

Brokerage houses

Building construction

Business agents

Chambers of Commerce

Circulation and distribution

Communication companies

Computer hardware/software manufacturers

Consumer affairs directors

Conventions and exhibiting services

Counseling and vocational guidance

Data processing

Escrow officers

Examiners (title, banking)

Export–import businesses

Finance and credit companies

Food industry

Foundations (charitable and research)

Fundraising

Gerontology-related services

Graphic arts

Health care industry

Home furnishings manufacturers

Industrial relations

Information processing

Insurance industry

Investments, securities

Journalism

Labor unions

Lecturers

Libraries

Linguistics (translation, interpretation)

Landscaping services

Law enforcement

Mailing and delivery services

Market research

Marketing

Mental health

Merchandising

Motion picture industry

Museums

Music industry

Newspapers and news/wire services

Office equipment and products

Packaging design and manufacture

Paper and paper pulp industry

Personnel agencies

Petroleum industry

Photography

Planning (urban, city, financial)

Politics (government service, elections, polling services)

Printing services (legal and financial)

Public health

Public relations

Publishing

Purchasing

Radio and TV

Real estate (brokers, agents)

Records management

Recreation services (hotel/motel, vacation planning, health resorts)

Research

Retail business

Sales

School and education

Security services

Shipping industry

Social work

Statistics testing services

Textile industry

Trademarks and patents

Transportation

Travel industry

Trucking industry

Utility companies

Warehouse/storage services

Welfare services

Wholesalers

Writer (author/press)[44]

Future Employment Projections

Career opportunities will develop at a rapid pace in the profession. The U.S. Department of Labor continues to paint an extremely positive picture of growth in the profession.

> *Employment for paralegals and legal assistants is projected to grow much faster than average for all occupations through 2014. Employers are trying to reduce costs and increase the availability and efficiency of legal services by hiring paralegals to perform tasks formerly carried out by lawyers. Besides new jobs created by employment growth, additional job openings will arise as people leave the occupation. Despite projections of rapid employment growth, competition for jobs should continue as many people seek to go into this profession; however, experienced, formally trained paralegals should have the best employment opportunities.*
>
> *Private law firms will continue to be the largest employers of paralegals, but a growing array of other organizations, such as corporate legal departments, insurance companies, real estate and title insurance firms, and banks, hire paralegals. Corporations in particular are boosting their in-house legal departments to cut costs. Demand for paralegals also is expected to grow as an expanding population increasingly requires legal services, especially in areas such as intellectual property, health care, international law, elder issues, criminal law, and environmental law. Paralegals who specialize in areas such as real estate, bankruptcy, medical malpractice, and product liability should have ample employment opportunities. The growth of prepaid legal plans also should contribute to the demand for legal services. Paralegal employment is expected to increase as organizations presently employing paralegals assign them a growing range of tasks and as paralegals are increasingly employed in small and medium-size establishments. A growing number of experienced paralegals are expected to establish their own businesses.*
>
> *Job opportunities for paralegals will expand in the public sector as well. Community legal service programs, which provide assistance to the poor, elderly, minorities, and middle-income families, will employ additional paralegals to minimize expenses and serve the most people. Federal, state, and local government agencies, consumer organizations, and the courts also should continue to hire paralegals in increasing numbers.*
>
> *To a limited extent, paralegal jobs are affected by the business cycle. During recessions, demand declines for some discretionary legal services, such as planning estates, drafting wills, and handling real estate transactions. Corporations are less inclined to initiate certain types of litigation when falling sales and profits lead to fiscal belt tightening. As a result, full-time paralegals employed in offices adversely affected by a recession may be laid off or have their work hours*

reduced. However, during recessions, corporations and individuals are more likely to face other problems that require legal assistance, such as bankruptcies, foreclosures, and divorces. Paralegals, who provide many of the same legal services as lawyers at a lower cost, tend to fare relatively better in difficult economic conditions.[45]

For example, paralegals are discovering the enormous opportunities for work as independent contractors. Hal Cornelius, in *Career Guide for Paralegals*, portrays the freelance career option as follows:

> *To be sure, freelance paralegals need control of their wits, need to be skilled in sales and human persuasion, and need to appreciate the incredible ethical dilemmas that might be present in this activity. Mostly, the freelancer is the risk taker, ready and willing to sacrifice initial security for long-term intellectual and personal freedom.*[46]

Even legal representation at select state and federal agencies by paralegal practitioners is now permissible under certain regulatory frameworks. Some examples, as compiled by the National Federation of Paralegal Associations, include these:

Board of Immigration Appeals

Immigration and Naturalization Service

Bureau of Indian Affairs

Civil Aeronautics Board

Consumer Product Safety Commission

Department of Agriculture

Department of Commerce

Patent and Trademark Office[47]—Office of the Secretary

Food and Drug Administration

Department of Justice

Department of Labor

Department of Transportation

Veterans Administration

Federal Deposit Insurance Corporation[48]

Federal Energy Regulatory Commission

Federal Maritime Administration[49]

Federal Mine Safety and Health Review Commission[50]

General Accounting Office[51]

Internal Revenue Service[52]

Interstate Commerce Commission[53]

National Credit Union Administration

National Mediation Board

National Transportation Safety Board[54]

Occupational Safety and Health Review Commission

Small Business Administration

Social Security Administration

U.S. Customs Service

U.S. Environmental Protection Agency

In addition to nonlawyer representation at federal agencies, also compiled was a list of state and local agencies that allow nonlawyer representation. Here is a partial listing:

Alaska—Human Rights Commission

California—Workers Compensation, Labor, Unemployment

Illinois—Department of Unemployment Security, Workers Compensation

Michigan—Unemployment Compensation

Minnesota—Workers Compensation

New York—70 percent of state agencies and 63 percent of New York City agencies allow some form of nonlawyer representation.

Ohio—Workers Compensation

Washington—Seattle (King County) Courts, King County Bar Association Opinion: Nonlawyers are allowed to present ex parte orders that have been agreed on. Tacoma (Pierce County) Courts, Pierce County Bar Association Opinion: Nonlawyers are allowed to present ex parte orders that have been agreed on.

Wisconsin—Workers Compensation[55]

In direct competition with the traditional bar are an emerging lot of paraprofessionals delivering legal services to the general public. Is such a movement justified by soaring legal costs and the need to provide the poor with legal services?[56]

Aside from this altruistic purpose, a new class of paralegal known as the *legal technician* is beginning to deliver direct legal services in permissible fields. "Some legal technicians are computerized form-filing services. Others have *practiced* legally and successfully before federal agencies for years. Some are former legal assistants and paralegals pushing out from under the supervision of lawyers to market their services directly to the public. And some may be rip-off artists."[57] The line between unauthorized practice of law and paralegal delivery becomes more muddled by the day. It is clear that paraprofessional delivery is here to stay, and lawyers have come to depend on it.[58]

Prospects for increased delegation of administrative responsibilities in the law firm and further developed senior legal assistant career tracks are excellent. That paralegals will continue to evolve to higher levels of sophistication is now undeniable. Carol Milano speaks to paralegals about these expansive opportunities:

> *Did you know your colleagues are now making corporate business decisions, representing clients at administrative hearings without an attorney, and conducting arbitration sessions?*
>
> *As a member of America's fastest-growing profession, you're in a very dynamic situation. Today's legal assistants are far more familiar and accepted staff members than they were five or ten years ago. In law firms, corporate departments, governmental agencies, and nonprofit organizations, they are taking on a wide array of new responsibilities.*[59]

The picture is almost rosy. The legal assistant profession is projected to grow by 33 percent during the first 10 years of 2000, according to the Bureau of Labor Statistics, Office of Employment Projections. Compared with other occupations, this is an above-average growth rate. Private law firms are the largest employers of paralegals, but a growing number of other organizations are hiring them too. These organizations include corporate legal departments, insurance companies, real estate and title insurance firms, and banks.[60]

Summary

The paralegal profession is a dynamic and viable occupation. A competent paralegal needs certain traits—such as human relations, organizational, and administrative skills. Paralegals must also have some general understanding of both the theoretical and procedural applications of the law. Eventually a path of legal generalization or specialization must be chosen. Educational opportunities range from in-house training to college coursework, and compensation levels vary significantly.

This chapter has considered occupational opportunities in the private and public sectors. The growth of nontraditional career opportunities and independent paralegalism was also discussed.

In sum, the growing, multifaceted paralegal profession offers its participants wide-ranging opportunities for personal and professional growth. Educational levels are high, compensation rates are climbing, and traditional higher education is becoming more involved.

Discussion Questions

1. What changes can you envision for the paralegal profession in the next 50 years?
2. Why might paralegals take offense when unenlightened parties characterize them as legal secretaries?
3. What schools and educational institutions exist in your area to prepare people for practice as paralegals?
4. What are the addresses and phone numbers of local paralegal associations that you are eligible to join?
5. What do you think the average compensation of paralegals in your jurisdiction is?
6. Do you think it will ever be possible or permissible for paralegals to participate in profit-sharing in a law firm?
7. What type of education do you think is most helpful in preparation for a career as a paralegal?
8. Do you think practical tasks are all that is required by a functional and competent paralegal? Do you think some attention to theory and substantive knowledge is necessary?

9. What do you find most attractive about paralegal practice and procedure? What do you find least attractive about it?

10. Name 10 tasks that could be performed by a paralegal.

11. Identify five major skills a paralegal should have.

Research Exercises

1. Locate statutes in your state relevant to paralegal practice, duties, certification, and regulation.

2. Locate a paralegal journal or law review article that discusses future employment and income projections in your home state.

Practical Exercises

1. Civil service employment opportunities—contact your state's civil service office and answer the following questions:
   - Does the office publish either a print or e-newsletter that lists job opportunities?
   - Does the civil service office have a job definition/description for paralegals or legal assistants? If so, include the description number/job category.
   - Search the office's job listings and find four recent listings that are relevant to a paralegal background.
   - List contact information for your state civil service office, including mailing and e-mail address, phone and fax numbers, and Web site.

2. Locate at least three academic programs in your area that provide paralegal training. Are these programs ABA approved? Are they offered by a proprietary institution, junior college, college/university, or other type of establishment? Do they offer online courses or programs?

3. Using a local newspaper, online job resource center, or paralegal publication, find job advertisements for the following positions: paralegal; legal secretary/law office assistant; law clerk; attorney; litigation support personnel; paralegal manager; law librarian; legal administrator; legal assistant manager.

Internet Resources

National Association of Legal Assistants—www.nala.org

National Federation of Paralegal Associations—www.paralegals.org

American Association for Paralegal Education—www.aafpe.org

National Paralegal Association—www.nationalparalegal.org

California Alliance of Paralegal Association—www.caparalegal.org

Paralegal Jobs—www.paralegaljobs.com

ABA Standing Committee on Paralegals—www.abanet.org/legalservices/paralegals

Endnotes

1. At the August 1997 ABA Annual Meeting, the ABA House of Delegates adopted this current definition of *legal assistant/paralegal* as recommended by the standing Committee on Legal Assistants.

2. Rule 2.2, Section 1 (2) (a), Indiana Rules for Admission to the Bar and the Discipline of Attorneys (2005).

3. Jacqueline M. Nolan-Haley, *Lawyers, Nonlawyers, and Mediation: Rethinking the Professional Monopoly from a Problem-Solving Perspective*, 7 HARV. NEGOTIATION L. REV. 235 (Spring 2002).

4. Connie Kretchmer, National Association of Legal Assistants Inc., *The Issues: What Are They? Who Are They Talking About?* 1 (1991).

5. Donald Green, Joel Snell, Raylene Corgiat, & Tony Paramanith, *The Professionalism of the Legal Assistant: Identity, Maturation States, and Goal Attainment*, 7 J. PARALEGAL ED. & PRACTICE 35, 36 (1990).

6. See the organization's Web site at http://www.halt.org/about_halt/press_room/pdf/Full_Media_Kit.pdf#Quick_Facts.

7. Ann Bailus, *A More Professional Future*, LEGAL ASSISTANT TODAY, Nov.–Dec. 1992, at 87, 90.

8. Patrick Yuong, *Proclaiming Paralegal Celebrations*, LEGAL ASSISTANT TODAY, Jan.–Feb. 2006, at 30.

9. ABA, STANDING COMMITTEE ON PARALEGALS, ABA MODEL GUIDELINES FOR THE UTILIZATION OF PARALEGAL SERVICES, Guideline 1, at 2 (2004).

10. Robert Stevens, *The Nature of a Learned Profession*, 34 J. LEGAL ED. 577, 579 (1984).

11. Amanda Flatten, *The Education Game*, LEGAL ASSISTANT TODAY, Jan.–Feb. 2006, at 10; *see also* Lindsey Bower, "The Increasing Phenomena of Debarred Lawyers Donning the 'Cap' of Paralegal" in *Pseudo-Paralegal "Runners" Stumble*, NAT'L PARALEGAL REP., Oct.–Nov. 2004, at 22.

12. RICHARD BOLLES, WHAT COLOR IS YOUR PARACHUTE? 7 (1985). *See also Note: Your Secretary: Paralegal in Disguise*, CASE & COMM. 12–15 (1983).

13. Edward Wheat, *Paralegal Regulation and the New Professionalism*, 3 J. PARALEGAL EDUC. & PRAC. 3 (1986).

14. Robert Ulrich, *Long-Term Legal Assistant & Job Enrichment*, PARALEGAL, July–Aug. 1987, at 1.

15. Rod Hughes, *Master Plan*, LEGAL ASSISTANT TODAY, Jan.–Feb. 2006 at 60.

16. American Alliance of Paralegals Inc., Code of Ethics, at 7–8.

17. Deborah A. Howard, *Using Paralegals in Small and Mid-Size Law Firms*, 5 J. PARALEGAL EDUC. & PRAC. 67, 68 (1988); *see also* Nancy L. Helmich & Roger A. Larson, *Legal Assistants in Public Law: Their Role in Attorney Generals' Offices*, 5 LEGAL ASSISTANT UPDATE 118 (1986). What is obvious is that marketability depends on skills. *See Dale Smith Thomas: Keynote Speaker, NALS 2006*, @LAW, Winter 2005–2006, at 22.

18. NATIONAL ASSOCIATION OF LEGAL ASSISTANTS INC., MODEL STANDARDS AND GUIDELINES FOR UTILIZATION OF LEGAL ASSISTANTS ANNOTATED (1985, 2004–2005).

19. NATIONAL ASSOCIATION OF LEGAL ASSISTANTS INC., MODEL STANDARDS AND GUIDELINES FOR UTILIZATION OF LEGAL ASSISTANTS ANNOTATED (1985, 2004–2005).

20. H. Archibald Kaiser, *Educating Students about Transition from School to Work*, 3 J. PARALEGAL EDUC. & PRAC. 13, 19 (1986).

21. *Id.* at 53–54 (1987); *see also* Mary L. Guinan, *Paralegals in Administration: A Natural Progression*, 2 NAT'L L. J. 14 (1984).

22. BUREAU OF LABOR STATISTICS, U.S. DEPARTMENT OF LABOR, OCCUPATIONAL OUTLOOK HANDBOOK, 2006–2007 Edition, *Paralegals and Legal Assistants*, on the Internet at http://www.bls.gov/oco/ocos114.htm (visited April 3, 2006).

23. *See* Patrick Yuong, *Are You Happy as a Paralegal?* LEGAL ASSISTANT TODAY, Jan.–Feb. 2005, at 16.

24. NATIONAL ASSOCIATION OF LEGAL ASSISTANTS, 1988 NATIONAL UTILIZATION AND COMPENSATION SURVEY REPORT 38 (1987).

25. NATIONAL ASSOCIATION OF LEGAL ASSISTANTS INC., THE LEGAL ASSISTANT PROFESSION: NATIONAL UTILIZATION AND COMPENSATION SURVEY REPORT 26 (1991).

26. AMERICAN BAR ASSOCIATION, LEGAL ASSISTANT PROGRAMS: A GUIDE TO EFFECTIVE PROGRAM IMPLEMENTATION AND MAINTENANCE 58–59 (1978).

27. Report from the American Association for Paralegal Education, Association of Legal Administrators, Legal Assistant Management Association, National Association of Legal Assistants, and National Federation of Paralegal Associations Inc. (March 11–12, 1988).

28. See set forth in IPMA, ANNUAL COMPENSATION SURVEY FOR PARALEGALS/LEGAL ASSISTANTS AND MANAGERS (2005); *see also* LEGAL ASSISTANT MANAGEMENT ASSOCIATION, 1993 NATIONAL COMPENSATION SURVEY REPORT OF FINDINGS 5 (1993).

29. ABA MEMORANDUM, ABA STANDING COMMITTEE ON LEGAL ASSISTANTS, POSITION PAPER ON LICENSURE, CERTIFICATION, AND DEFINITION OF LEGAL ASSISTANTS (1986).

30. AMERICAN BAR ASSOCIATION, ABA STANDING COMMITTEE ON LEGAL ASSISTANTS, POSITION PAPER ON LICENSURE, CERTIFICATION, AND DEFINITION OF LEGAL ASSISTANTS (1986); *see also* AMERICAN BAR ASSOCIATION, REPORT ON A SURVEY OF NONDEGREE LEGAL ASSISTANT TRAINING IN THE UNITED STATES (1972); *see also* Patricia Lyons, *I Don't Need Paralegal Education . . . or Do I?*, NAT'L PARALEGAL REP., Dec.–Jan. 2006, at 26.

31. John R. Reinard, *Paralegal Career Advancement*, 6 J. PARALEGAL EDUC. & PRAC., Oct. 1989, at 1, 4.

32. Thomas J. Calvocoressi & Ronald A. Villanova, *Approaches for Continuing Legal Education of Paralegals*, 7 J. PARALEGAL EDUC. & PRAC., Oct. 1990, at 43, 45–46.

33. The American Institute for Paralegal Studies administrative offices are located at Honeywell Center, Suite 225, 17515 West Nine Mile Road, Southfield, MI 48075.

34. For more information, contact the American Association for Paralegal Education (AAFPE), P.O. Box 40244, Overland Park, KS 66204; Legal Assistant Today Inc., 3520 Cadillac Avenue, Suite E, Costa Mesa, CA 92626; American Bar Association (ABA), 750 North Lake Shore Drive, Chicago, IL 60611. For an excellent update of case law decision impacting paralegal practice, *see* Georgette Lovelace, *Case Law Update*, NAT'L PARALEGAL REP., Oct.–Nov. 2005, at 20.

35. *See* H. Archibald Kaiser, *Educating Students about Transition from School to Work*, 3 J. PARALEGAL EDUC. & PRAC. 13 (1986).

36. American Bar Association, *supra* note 26; *see also* AMERICAN BAR ASSOCIATION, REPORT ON A SURVEY OF NONDEGREE LEGAL ASSISTANT TRAINING IN THE UNITED STATES (1972); *see also* CHARLES P. NEMETH, DIRECTORY OF CRIMINAL JUSTICE EDUCATION INCLUDING CRIMINOLOGY AND JUSTICE-RELATED PROGRAMS (1991).

37. Carole A. Bruno, *Measuring Progress: How Far Have We Come?* LEGAL ASSISTANT TODAY, Nov.–Dec. 1992, at 38, 42; *see also* CHARLES P. NEMETH, DIRECTORY OF CRIMINAL JUSTICE EDUCATION INCLUDING CRIMINOLOGY AND JUSTICE-RELATED PROGRAMS (1997).

38. George D. Schrader, *The Core Curriculum: An Idea for Today*, 5 J. PARALEGAL EDUC. & PRAC. 48 (1988).

39. Nancy Murphy, *The Road to Legal Assistant Success: Education Is the First Leg of Your Journey*, 70 MICH. B. J. 1172, 1173 (Nov. 1991). *See also* Ann F. Dunkin, *Being a Life Long Learne*r, @LAW, Spring 2005, at 44.

40. CAROLE A. BRUNO, PARALEGAL'S LITIGATION HANDBOOK (1977).

41. Melanie Baker & Thomas Eimermann, *Paralegal Employment Opportunities in State Government*, 6 J. PARALEGAL EDUC. & PRAC. 9, 21 (Oct. 1989).

42. *See* D. Howard, *supra* note 17; *see also* Nancy L. Helmich & Roger A. Larson, *Legal Assistants in Public Law: Their Role in Attorney Generals' Offices*, 5 LEGAL ASSISTANT UPDATE 67 (1986). *See also* Ronald J. Daniels, *Growing Pains: The Why and How of Law Firm Expansion*, 43 UNIV. TORONTO L. J. 147–206 (1993).

43. Marsha A. Ratterman, *Nontraditional Paralegal Careers: Finding Your Niche*, 8 LEGAL ASSISTANT TODAY 75, 80 (Jan.–Feb. 1991).

44. CHERE B. ESTRIN & ANDREA WAGNER, WHERE DO I GO FROM HERE? CAREER CHOICES FOR THE EXPERI-ENCED LEGAL ASSISTANT, 106–108 (1992). Reprinted with permission of the publisher. Copyright 1992 by Estrin Publishing, Los Angeles, CA.

45. BUREAU OF LABOR STATISTICS, U.S. DEPARTMENT OF LABOR, OCCUPATIONAL OUTLOOK HANDBOOK, 2006–2007 Edition, *Paralegals and Legal Assistants*, on the Internet at http://www.bls.gov/oco/ocos114.htm (visited April 3, 2006).

46. HAL CORNELIUS, CAREER GUIDE FOR PARALEGALS 127 (1983).

47. Only registered practitioners are permitted to practice. Nonlawyers become registered by passing a character and fitness review and an examination. Nonlawyers who have served four years in the examining corps of the Patent and Trademark Office may waive the exam. See 57 CFR 1.341.

48. Only qualified nonlawyers are permitted to represent.

49. Only registered nonlawyers are permitted to appear. Certificates of registration are issued on payment of processing fee and completion of application form indicating sufficient educational qualifications and recommendations. There is no testing or formal licensing.

50. Appearances are made at trial hearings before administrative law judges and at appellate reviews before commissioners. A nonlawyer may practice only if the nonlawyer is a party, a representative of minors as described in 30 CFR § 10.1(b), or the owner, partner, full time [sic] officer or employee of the party–business entity; otherwise a nonlawyer is permitted to appear for limited purpose in special proceedings.

51. Permitted in adverse actions, grievance proceedings, and discrimination complaints.

52. Nonlawyers must become enrolled agents by passing a character and fitness review and successfully completing a special enrollment examination testing on federal taxation and related matters. A nonlawyer may also qualify based on former employment with the IRS, provided such duties qualify the individual.

53. Only registered nonlawyers are permitted to practice. To register, an applicant must (1) meet educational and experience requirements, (2) undergo a character and fitness review, (3) pass an exam administered by the agency testing knowledge in the field of transportation, and (4) take an oath. See 49 CFR § 1103.3.

54. Nonlawyer appearances are infrequent except at investigatory levels. Nonlawyer participation is discouraged because technical expertise is required.

55. National Federation of Paralegal Associations Inc. P.O. Box 2016, Edmonds, Washington 98020.

56. *See* HERBERT M. KRITZER, RETHINKING BARRIERS TO LEGAL PRACTICE JUDICATURE 100–103 (1997), where the author states that instead of being prohibited from providing legal services, nonlawyers should be regulated and controlled, just like lawyers.

57. Geoffrey S. Yuda, *A Piece of Your Business: Competition from Nonlawyer "Technicians": Cause for Alarm?* 15 PENN. LAW. 6 (May 1993).

58. *See* RACHEL L. BERKEY, NEW CAREER OPPORTUNITIES IN THE PARALEGAL PROFESSION 113 (1983).

59. Carol Milano, *New Responsibilities Being Given to Paralegals*, 8 LEGAL ASSISTANT TODAY 27 (Nov.–Dec. 1990).

60. See http://www.nala.org/whatis.htm#Occupational. Carole Bruno concurs: "Progress has been monumental. In 1983, the paralegal profession was the fastest-growing occupation. At that time there were 32,000 paralegals. The United States Department of Labor projected that by the year 1990, there would be an employment increase of 109 percent. Today there are over 115,000 paralegals according to the DOL, at a 359 percent increase, far surpassing its 1983 predictions." Carole A. Bruno, *Measuring Progress: How Far Have We Come?* LEGAL ASSISTANT TODAY 38, 45 (Nov.–Dec. 1992).

Ethical Considerations in Paralegal Practice

INTRODUCTORY COMMENT

The measure of any profession is tied to its ethical standards and guidelines. Without a reputation for integrity, any self-praise or proclamation of *profession* is an empty ambition. The word *professional* is used quite liberally these days. Shoe consultants, landscapers, aroma therapists—all have been known to toss about this label. By doing so, these occupations dilute the meaning of *profession* whereby three things are necessary: a body of knowledge and skills for an occupation; a body of literature and scholarly analysis available to the participant; and finally, a series of rules and ethical parameters to guide the occupation. In each of these categories, paralegalism strives to meet the criteria. That paralegals continue to change the face of legal services is now undeniable. "The expansion in the use of paralegals is expected to continue into the next millennium. It is projected that the number of paralegals assisting attorneys in private practice will increase 58 percent between 1994 and 2005, resulting in the addition of 64,000 paralegal positions during that time period."[1]

With growth comes an increasing clamor for personal and professional responsibility. That the profession has yet to achieve a unified ethical framework is obvious. The lack of standardized practices in the occupation has long been an issue of contention. The American Alliance for Paralegals Inc. (AAPI) has emerged in the last decade for this reason. Its charter notes,

> *The American Alliance supports the regulation of paralegals and advocates the following components to be a part of any regulatory scheme: formal paralegal education, experience, continuing legal education, and a code of ethics. Further, its members recognize that any regulatory scheme and its contents (preference for certification, licensure, registration, bar/court rules, etc.) will vary in each jurisdiction. The American Alliance will be proactive in advocating the supporting regulation that enhances the growth of the paralegal profession and will assist any local paralegal organization by responding to regulatory activities within that organization's jurisdiction.*[2]

The AAPI, as well as the American Association for Paralegal Education (AAFPE), regularly advocate the need for higher standards. Despite this call for standardization, tensions and pulls from other groups, as well as a general lack of regulatory and legislative interest at the state level, manifest the difficult road ahead. The profession is making strides but has much to do to truly achieve the status of a pure profession. It is inevitable that this day will come.

From its close association with the legal profession, it is unlikely that paralegals and legal assistants could avoid ethical standards. In a symbiotic way, the paralegal is tied to the lawyer's public image. Unfortunately, when the legal profession suffers public scorn, the paralegal suffers as well. If lawyers are viewed negatively, the paralegal is saddled with the same critique. Without question, lawyer bashing is common and widely accepted.[3] Kenneth Jost states,

> *There was a time, not long ago, when lawyers were proud to work in the Justice Department; law school graduates were happy to be paid $15,000 for their privilege of working in New York's finest firms; partners in law firms expected to stick together for their entire careers; and attorneys tried their cases in courtrooms, not on courtroom steps. When business lawyers provided legal advice to hold big corporations together while managers, executives, and directors conducted the real business of America—that was before the 1980s.*
>
> *Positive images of America's lawyers—never dominant in the public's mind—had faded further with the headlines of the last few years. The result, according to a wide range of observers, is that the image of lawyers today ranges somewhere between "poor" and not much worse than before.*[4]

It has become fashionable to cast aspersions on lawyers; and indeed lawyers, by their ethical lapses, cause a great deal of their own negative image.[5] Public perceptions have been negatively forged for various reasons. First, the nature of the adversarial process itself often promotes natural distrust between plaintiffs' and defendants' attorneys, and the battle of advocacy erodes the gentility and collegiality of the profession. Tim Baker sees a systematic problem—an image even judges conclude in his home state of Indiana:

> *These respected jurists' observations support the conclusion that in Indiana, and throughout the nation, the image of lawyers and the legal profession has spiraled downward—and not necessarily undeservedly.*
>
> *While lawyer bashing is nothing new, it is imperative that those who care about the legal profession obtain a better understanding of the root causes of these problems. Doing so will allow for more effective steps to be taken to address and correct these issues.*[6]

The Honorable R.J. Gerber comments insightfully,

> *Much as one would like to believe our profession is undeserving of its low image, and that our image is correctable simply by doing charitable deeds, ample reason remains for incisive examination of our professional conscience. Though unethical behavior runs well beyond the courthouse, some practices of the average courtroom litigator offer more than enough pangs*

> *of compunction. . . . Somehow our adversary system seems to elicit a kind of ethics at once both commonplace and uncommonly out of place in a profession priding itself on the pursuit of justice.*[7]

Advocacy, instead of a search for factual truth, has become a field of battle with combative strategies becoming the norm. Little help comes from the judiciary, who as neutral parties become passive witnesses to this form of combat. Most judges previously advocated in a similar way and cannot discern the difficulty. This leads to a lack of serious self-examination and constructive criticism of the bar.

Second, in the advocate's quest for a favorable resolution for the client, the line between victory and truth becomes muddled. Naturally, the primary function of the judicial process is to determine truth and mete out corresponding justice. However, the reality is that victory is more important than a finding of inherent and undeniable truth. In place of fact finding and truth, the art of advocacy descends into drama and cunning.[8]

Third, some lawyers have little regard for the truth, and by their carelessness paint the entire profession in a negative light. Trial advocacy is guided by an ethics of situation and circumstances.[9] The client result takes precedence over the right result.

Fourth, the absence of professional courtesy and respect amongst lawyers themselves significantly adds to a low public perception. Historically the bar and the bench have been described as a collegial, respectful body whose word and handshake were golden. Although lawyers and members of the judiciary need not personally care for or even like one another, their interpersonal relationships send a clear message to a doubting public. If lawyers treat each other with such disrespect, what type of profession is it? With a win-at-any-cost mentality, the *hired gun* rationalization, and aggressive litigation posturing, professional courtesies are often ignored.

This form of personal discourtesy is obvious in the day-to-day interactions between attorneys, legal assistants, paralegals, and judicial personnel. Sadly, the image of lawyers suffers. Ellen Mercer Fallon categorizes the essential courtesies for every lawyer and paralegal:

1. *A lawyer should never knowingly deceive another lawyer.*
2. *A lawyer should honor promises or commitments made to another lawyer.*
3. *A lawyer should make all reasonable efforts to schedule matters with opposing counsel by agreement.*
4. *A lawyer should maintain a cordial and respectful relationship with opposing counsel.*
5. *A lawyer should seek sanctions against opposing counsel only where required for the protection of the client and not mere tactical advantage.*
6. *A lawyer should not make unfounded accusations of unethical conduct about opposing counsel.*
7. *A lawyer should never intentionally embarrass another lawyer and should avoid personal criticism of another lawyer.*
8. *A lawyer should always be functional.*
9. *A lawyer should seek informal agreement on procedural and preliminary matters.*[10]

Fifth, the size of verdicts and judgments emerging from today's courtroom goes beyond the notion of bonanza. Damage awards are in some cases obscenely disproportionate to the actual injuries suffered. Excessive awards foster cynicism in the profession and the public. Even if these multimillion-dollar awards are the exception rather than the rule, they have "caused many to conclude that the jury in civil cases has become more of a mechanism for the redistribution of wealth than a dispenser of justice with hordes of hungry attorneys urging them on."[11]

Tied to excessive awards have been the inculcation and unbridled acceptance of the contingent fee system. According to some, contingency fees nurture ethical failure. Others argue the practice affords larger levels of representation. What is undeniable is that contingent fees are awards in expectancy—and that without a case, legitimate or not, there is no payment of the fee. It is easy enough to find unfounded cases granted life within the contingency fee system. The *Model Code of Professional Responsibility*, specifically at Rule 1.5(a), states that "A lawyer shall not make an agreement for, charge, or collect an unreasonable fee or an unreasonable amount for expenses."[12] This guideline is subject to interpretation because gauging what is excessive depends on facts, circumstances, and the economic expectations of the participants. However, multimillion-dollar verdicts that result in sizable legal fees always produce a suspect impression in the public's eye, deserved or not. Excessive fees add to the public's impression of a lawyer being an ambulance chaser. While claiming justice and the honored nature of their profession, a few lawyers take advantage of tragedy, aggressively pursuing a signature on a contingency fee arrangement.

Sixth, various advocacy techniques and the pursuit of unmeritorious cases cause extensive damage to the image of lawyers and paralegals. While certainly the exception, frivolous lawsuits unfortunately are becoming commonplace. Under the *Model Code of Professional Responsibility's* disciplinary rules, a lawyer should not

1. File a suit, assert a position, conduct a defense, delay a trial, or take other action on behalf of a client when he or she knows or when it is obvious that such action would serve merely to harass or maliciously injure another.

2. Knowingly advance a claim or defense that is unwarranted under existing law, except that a lawyer may advance such claim or defense if it can be supported by good faith argument for an extension, a modification, or a reversal of existing law.[13]

A *frivolous lawsuit* is defined as an action without merit or legal justification. In the zealous representation of a client, a lawyer's case will be deemed as frivolous if "the position taken is not supported by the law or is not supportable by any good faith argument for an extension, modification, or reversal of the law."[14] Exactly what *good faith* connotes is the subject of significant debate. Merit in what portion of the case? Is a peripheral matter meritorious while the heart of the case is flawed? How do we judge the good faith of the advocate? Aside from a lack of merit, litigation tactics often lack a caring and precise approach with any and every imaginable defendant named in a cause of action, with boilerplate pleadings that cover the universe of legal actions and not the specific case at hand, and the averment that seeks absurd levels of damages. Additionally, the tactics of delay are well known. "In both civil and criminal litigation, a widespread belief exists that delay benefits the defendant because incriminating witnesses disappear, die, or forget as the case ages. Delay is neither new nor creative. In the hands of the game-playing litigator, it takes many ingenious forms advantageous to the client and detrimental to justice."[15]

Judge Gerber presents the dilemma persuasively:

> Today the road to delay is paved with stipulated extensions of time to answer, stipulated continuances, motions to continue on the inactive calendar, controverting certificates filed to avoid a trial date, strategic changes of judges, and spurious discovery disputes. All these modes of delay line lawyer's pockets while delaying justice and clients' return to normalcy. Few courts have the gumption to describe delay for what it really is: a vexing and expensive sport oriented to victory, not truth.[16]

These litigation tactics foster a poor image of the American lawyer that finds further corroboration in abusive discovery processes, unwillingness to settle and reconcile, and lack of preparation in advocacy.

Seventh, lawyer advertising and marketing programs of recent memory further diminish the profession's reputation.[17] Historically lawyer advertising was relegated to the business card because the *profession* of lawyer was above crass commercialism. Today marketing uses any medium with dramatic characterizations of the lawyer's ability and grand promises of money. In general, the gloves are off when it comes to advertising legal services.[18]

Eighth, the steady increase in the number of American lawyers in the last two decades, escalating from approximately 250,000 lawyers in 1960 to more than a million in 2000, has surely affected the integrity of legal practice. With shrinking opportunity comes careless ethical thinking.[19]

Finally, some credence must be given to the influence of prepaid legal services, the performance of traditional legal activities by laypeople (such as will preparation and real estate settlement), and various opportunities for *pro se* representation. In a way these influences water down a profession that was once sure of itself. As legal practice suffers these stresses and strains, the lines between acceptable practice and entrepreneurship blur. Quality suffers as everyone jumps in the mix of legal practice.

So much of this negative dilemma is triggered by a misunderstanding of what it means to be a legal professional. Lawyers, judges, and paralegals are more than mere functionaries. They are players in a system that seeks justice and truth. It is, as Joseph Allegritti indicates, a calling, a vocation dedicated to a higher end:

> The work of a lawyer is referred to by many names—it is a job, an occupation, a career, and a profession. Each of these words captures something true and important about being a lawyer. But is it possible to approach the practice of law as something else, something more than a job or a career or even a profession? Can law be viewed as a form of service, a kind of ministry? To explore these

questions, I propose to examine the practice of law through the lens of the religious doctrine of calling or vocation (I will use the words interchangeably). This article will consider several related issues: What is a calling? Is law a calling? If so, what are the implications for lawyers? And how does the idea of a calling promote an understanding of legal practice as a form of healing?[20]

As noted, paralegals cannot avoid these ethical and practice dynamics. As a result, it is crucial that the practicing paralegal understand the ethical guidelines authored by courts and local and state bar associations as well as by professional organizations.

REGULATION, LICENSING, AND ETHICAL CONTROL

Governmental Regulations and Paralegals

The once scorned paralegal profession has passed the threshold of acceptability in most quarters. Lawyers cannot construct a professional life without them.[21] "It is by now axiomatic that paralegals—or legal assistants—are playing a salutary and evolving role in the justice system."[22] The legal system itself is aware of the major role paralegals play in the administration of justice. States too see the need for some level of regulation, licensing, and general oversight. By way of example, Indiana has sought to formalize paralegalism through its regulatory process.

Encouraged by the Indiana Paralegals Association (IPA), the state has promulgated some significant legislation relative to paralegals. IPA was the voice behind legislation that defines a paralegal and allows for the recoverability of paralegal fees when attorney's fees are awarded.[23] The association has also adopted education guidelines, a code of ethics and professional responsibility, and rules for enforcement.[24]

Indiana Rules of Professional Conduct, adopted by the state supreme court in 1994, provide guidelines for attorneys in the use of paralegals and legal assistants. Subject to the provisions in Rule 5.3, all lawyers may use legal assistants in accordance with the following guidelines:

Indiana Rules of Professional Conduct, 9.1–9.10, Use of Legal Assistants

Guideline 9.1. Supervision.

A legal assistant shall perform services only under the direct supervision of a lawyer authorized to practice in the state of Indiana and in the employ of the lawyer or the lawyer's employer. Independent legal assistants, to wit, those not employed by a specific firm or by specific lawyers, are prohibited. A lawyer is responsible for all of the professional actions of a legal assistant performing legal assistant services at the lawyer's direction and should take reasonable measures to ensure that the legal assistant's conduct is consistent with the lawyer's obligations under the Rules of Professional Conduct.

Guideline 9.2. Permissible delegation.

Provided the lawyer maintains responsibility for the work product, a lawyer may delegate to a legal assistant any task normally performed by the lawyer; however, any task prohibited by statute, court rule, administrative rule or regulation, controlling authority, or Indiana Rules of Professional Conduct may not be assigned to a nonlawyer.

Guideline 9.3. Prohibited delegation.

A lawyer may not delegate to a legal assistant:
(a) responsibility for establishing an attorney–client relationship;
(b) responsibility for establishing the amount of a fee to be charged for a legal service; or
(c) responsibility for a legal opinion rendered to a client.

Guideline 9.4. Duty to inform.

It is the lawyer's responsibility to take reasonable measures to ensure that clients, courts, and other lawyers are aware that a legal assistant, whose services are utilized by the lawyer in performing legal services, is not licensed to practice law.

Guideline 9.5. Identification on letterhead.

A lawyer may identify legal assistants by name and title on the lawyer's letterhead and on business cards identifying the lawyer's firm.

Guideline 9.6. Client confidences.

It is the responsibility of a lawyer to take reasonable measures to ensure that all client confidences are preserved by a legal assistant.

Guideline 9.7. Charge for services.

A lawyer may charge for the work performed by a legal assistant.

Guideline 9.8. Compensation.

A lawyer may not split legal fees with a legal assistant nor pay a legal assistant for the referral of legal business. A lawyer may compensate a legal assistant based on the quantity and quality of the legal assistant's work and the value of that work to a law practice, but the legal assistant's compensation may not be contingent, by advance agreement, upon the profitability of the lawyer's practice.

Guideline 9.9. Continuing legal education.

A lawyer who employs a legal assistant should facilitate the legal assistant's participation in appropriate continuing education and pro bono publico activities.

Guideline 9.10. Legal assistant ethics.

All lawyers who employ legal assistants in the state of Indiana shall ensure that such legal assistants conform their conduct to be consistent with the following ethical standards:

(a) A legal assistant may perform any task delegated and supervised by a lawyer so long as the lawyer is responsible to the client, maintains a direct relationship with the client, and assumes full professional responsibility for the work product.

(b) A legal assistant shall not engage in the unauthorized practice of law.

(c) A legal assistant shall serve the public interest by contributing to the delivery of quality legal services and the improvement of the legal system.

(d) A legal assistant shall achieve and maintain a high level of competence, as well as a high level of personal and professional integrity and conduct.

(e) A legal assistant's title shall be fully disclosed in all business and professional communications.

(f) A legal assistant shall preserve all confidential information provided by the client or acquired from other sources before, during, and after the course of the professional relationship.

(g) A legal assistant shall avoid conflicts of interest and shall disclose any possible conflict to the employer or client, as well as to prospective employers or clients.

(h) A legal assistant shall act within the bounds of the law, uncompromisingly for the benefit of the client.

(i) A legal assistant shall do all things incidental, necessary, or expedient for the attainment of the ethics and responsibilities imposed by statute or rule of court.

(j) A legal assistant shall be governed by the American Bar Association Model Code of Professional Responsibility and the American Bar Association Model Rules of Professional Conduct.[25]

The push toward state or national regulation has varied between incremental and almost sluggish. Although some states have enacted legislation regarding paralegals, and select supreme courts have promulgated rules, the bulk of the legislative landscape is devoid of involvement.[26] California has made extraordinary contributions to the legislative underpinnings of the paralegal profession. The state legislature sets out both definition and practice parameters in its statutory guidelines. The law states in part,

§ 6450. Paralegal defined; prohibited activities; qualifications; continuing legal education.

(a) "Paralegal" means a person who holds himself or herself out to be a paralegal, who is qualified by education, training, or work experience, who either contracts with or is employed by an attorney, law firm, corporation, governmental agency, or other entity, and who performs substantial legal work under the direction and supervision of an active member of the State Bar of California, as defined in Section 6060, or an attorney practicing law in the federal courts of this state, that has been specifically delegated by the attorney to him or her. Tasks performed by a paralegal include, but are not limited to, case planning, development, and management; legal research; interviewing clients; fact gathering and retrieving information; drafting and analyzing legal documents; collecting, compiling, and utilizing technical information to make an independent decision and recommendation to the supervising attorney; and representing clients before a state or federal administrative agency if that representation is permitted by statute, court rule, or administrative rule or regulation.

(b) Notwithstanding subdivision (a), a paralegal shall not do the following:

(1) Provide legal advice.

(2) Represent a client in court.

(3) Select, explain, draft, or recommend the use of any legal document to or for any person other than the attorney who directs and supervises the paralegal.

(4) Act as a runner or capper, as defined in Sections 6151 and 6152.

(5) Engage in conduct that constitutes the unlawful practice of law.

(6) Contract with, or be employed by, a natural person other than an attorney to perform paralegal services.

(7) In connection with providing paralegal services, induce a person to make an investment, purchase a financial product or service, or enter a transaction from which income or profit, or both, purportedly may be derived.

(8) Establish the fees to charge a client for the services the paralegal performs, which shall be established by the attorney who supervises the paralegal's work. This paragraph does not apply to fees charged by a paralegal in a contract to provide paralegal services to an attorney, law firm, corporation, governmental agency, or other entity as provided in subdivision (a).

(c) A paralegal shall possess at least one of the following:

(1) A certificate of completion of a paralegal program approved by the American Bar Association.

(2) A certificate of completion of a paralegal program at, or a degree from, a postsecondary institution that requires the successful completion of a minimum of 24 semester, or equivalent, units in law-related courses and that has been accredited by a national or regional accrediting organization or approved by the Bureau for Private Postsecondary and Vocational Education.

(3) A baccalaureate degree or an advanced degree in any subject, a minimum of one year of law-related experience under the supervision of an attorney who has been an active member of the State Bar of California for at least the preceding three years or who has practiced in the federal courts of this state for at least the preceding three years, and a written declaration from this attorney stating that the person is qualified to perform paralegal tasks.

(4) A high school diploma or general equivalency diploma, a minimum of three years of law-related experience under the supervision of an attorney who has been an active member of the State Bar of California for at least the preceding three years or who has practiced in the federal courts of this state for at least the preceding three years, and a written declaration from this attorney stating that the person is qualified to perform paralegal tasks. This experience and training shall be completed no later than December 31, 2003.

(d) All paralegals shall be required to certify completion every three years of four hours of mandatory continuing legal education in legal ethics. All continuing legal education courses shall meet the requirements of Section 6070. Every two years, all paralegals shall be required to certify completion of four hours of mandatory continuing education in either general law or in a specialized area of law. Certification of these continuing education requirements shall be made with the paralegal's supervising attorney. The paralegal shall be responsible for keeping a record of the paralegal's certifications.

(e) A paralegal does not include a nonlawyer who provides legal services directly to members of the public, or a legal document assistant or unlawful detainer assistant as defined in Section 6400, unless the person is a person described in subdivision (a).

(f) This section shall become operative on January 1, 2004.[27]

In the state of Washington there is no requirement that a person be licensed, certified, or registered in any way before he or she can work as a paralegal. There is, however, a statute prohibiting the practice of law without a license. This is sometimes applied to those purporting to be paralegals and providing services directly to the general public. Currently paralegals are required to practice under the supervision of an attorney, or pursuant to court rule or federal or state law.[28]

GENERAL RULE 24—DEFINITION OF THE PRACTICE OF LAW

(a) General definition: The practice of law is the application of legal principles and judgment with regard to the circumstances or objectives of another entity or person(s) that require the knowledge and skill of a person trained in the law. This includes but is not limited to:

(1) Giving advice or counsel to others as to their legal rights or the legal rights or responsibilities of others for fees or other consideration.

(2) Selection, drafting, or completion of legal documents or agreements that affect the legal rights of an entity or person(s).

     (3) *Representation of another entity or person(s) in a court, or in a formal administrative adjudicative proceeding or other formal dispute resolution process or in an administrative adjudicative proceeding in which legal pleadings are filed or a record is established as the basis for judicial review.*

     (4) *Negotiation of legal rights or responsibilities on behalf of another entity or person(s).*

  (b) *Exceptions and exclusions: Whether or not they constitute the practice of law, the following are permitted:*

     (1) *Practicing law authorized by a limited license to practice pursuant to Admission to Practice Rules 8 (special admission for a particular purpose or action; indigent representation; educational purposes; emeritus membership; house counsel), 9 (legal interns), 12 (limited practice for closing officers), or 14 (limited practice for foreign law consultants).*

     (2) *Serving as a courthouse facilitator pursuant to court rule.*

     (3) *Acting as a lay representative authorized by administrative agencies or tribunals.*

     (4) *Serving in a neutral capacity as a mediator, arbitrator, conciliator, or facilitator.*

     (5) *Participation in labor negotiations, arbitrations, or conciliations arising under collective bargaining rights or agreements.*

     (6) *Providing assistance to another to complete a form provided by a court for protection under RCW chapters 10.14 (harassment) or 26.50 (domestic violence prevention) when no fee is charged to do so.*

     (7) *Acting as a legislative lobbyist.*

     (8) *Sale of legal forms in any format.*

     (9) *Activities that are preempted by federal law.*

     (10) *Serving in a neutral capacity as a clerk or court employee providing information to the public pursuant to supreme court order.*

     (11) *Such other activities that the supreme court has determined by published opinion do not constitute the unlicensed or unauthorized practice of law or that have been permitted under a regulatory system established by the supreme court.*

  (c) *Nonlawyer assistants: Nothing in this rule shall affect the ability of nonlawyer assistants to act under the supervision of a lawyer in compliance with Rule 5.3 of the Rules of Professional Conduct.*

  (d) *General information: Nothing in this rule shall affect the ability of a person or entity to provide information of a general nature about the law and legal procedures to members of the public.*

  (e) *Governmental agencies: Nothing in this rule shall affect the ability of a governmental agency to carry out responsibilities provided by law.*

  (f) *Professional standards: Nothing in this rule shall be taken to define or affect standards for civil liability or professional responsibility.*

RULE 5.3—RESPONSIBILITIES REGARDING NONLAWYER ASSISTANTS

With respect to a nonlawyer employed or retained by or associated with a lawyer:

  (a) *A partner in a law firm shall make reasonable efforts to ensure that the firm has in effect measures giving reasonable assurance that the person's conduct is compatible with the professional obligations of the lawyer;*

  (b) *A lawyer having direct supervisory authority over the nonlawyer shall make reasonable efforts to ensure that the person's conduct is compatible with the professional obligations of the lawyer; and*

  (c) *A lawyer shall be responsible for conduct of such a person that would be a violation of the Rules of Professional Conduct if engaged in by a lawyer if:*

     (1) *The lawyer orders or, with the knowledge of the specific conduct, ratifies the conduct involved; or*

     (2) *The lawyer is a partner in the law firm in which the person is employed, or has direct supervisory authority over the person, and knows of the conduct at a time when its consequences can be avoided or mitigated but fails to take reasonable remedial action.*[29]

But government regulations are not merely definitional. Qualifications, experience, and education are criteria often overlooked by statutory authority. Some standardization is essential for professional identity. California, Texas, Hawaii, New Jersey, and others are struggling to minimally define these requirements.[30]

The National Federation of Paralegal Associations (NFPA) believes in an expanded, far-reaching regulatory framework, calling for not only specific qualifications but nonlawyer delivery of legal services:[31]

NFPA's Position on Regulation

NFPA members adopted a position to endorse regulation of paralegals, recommending that paralegals be able to do more under the regulatory plan than they were previously doing. Included within NFPA's position on regulation for paralegals working in this expanded role are recommendations for
- *a two-tiered licensing plan, which constitutes mandatory regulation;*
- *another form of regulation, such as certification or registration, that may be appropriate in a given state;*
- *standards for ethics;*
- *standards for discipline;*
- *standards for education;*
- *a method to assess advanced competency of paralegals;*
- *establishing a disciplinary process; and*
- *defining those tasks that may be performed by paralegals in numerous specialty areas of law.*[32]

NFPA agrees that nonlawyer activity is best addressed at the state level and, in accordance with its grassroots structure and position on regulation, deems states' rights issues to be dominant in the forum of nonlawyer practice issues. However, the legal profession must recognize its responsibility to provide the public with the opportunity to choose different levels of expertise and cost, depending on the type of services needed. The continued existence of unmet legal needs is of paramount concern to lawyers, paralegals, and nonlawyers alike. The legal community must strive to provide a greater variety of legal services to allow more freedom of choice, easier access to professional services for the public, and reduced costs.[33] Within this liberal context, NFPA advocates a state-by-state approach in paralegal regulation.[34]

Regulation of independent or freelance paralegals or technicians has been a greater challenge to governmental and legal authorities. The New Jersey supreme court set aside a ban on independent or freelance paralegals. The court felt that the legal system should be more accessible and less costly for the poor and should provide more efficient delivery of legal services in general. A freelance paralegal is still supervised but solicits business from as many lawyers as desired on a contract basis.

The more direct delivery of services by legal technicians has also met growing opposition. A *legal technician* sells legal services without attorney supervision. This entrepreneurial approach in the delivery of legal services is viewed by critics as promoting the unauthorized practice of law. Carl Sellinger argues that these independent paralegals have their place but not an unlimited one:

First, independent paralegals should be able to handle usually uncomplicated matters in personal areas of the law without regard to their lucrativeness. Second, an individual paralegal should only be permitted to practice in a single personal area of the law. Third, independent paralegals should be able to handle uncomplicated matters in non-personal areas of the law only on behalf of clients who could not afford to hire a lawyer for the matter. Fourth, independent paralegals should not be permitted to handle complex matters in any area of the law except on behalf of clients who could not afford to hire a lawyer for the matter, and then only if the legal system had failed within a reasonable time to provide some other legal assistance safety net for such clients. Finally, independent paralegals should be subject to both remedial and preventive regulation.[35]

Naturally, the organized bar has reservations about direct delivery.[36]

Bar Associations and Paralegals

Bar association involvement in the paralegal profession at the state, local, and national levels has been consistent and influential. At the forefront has been the Standing Committee on the Use of Paralegals by the American Bar Association. Since 1993 the ABA has taken a keen interest in the workings of paralegal practice. As a result, in 1993 the ABA instituted a Commission on Non-lawyer Practice to study the expanding role of nonlawyers. Here are the ABA's chief initiatives in the area of paralegal practice:

- The ABA endorsed the use of paralegals in 1967 and established the first committee on paralegals in 1968.
- Since 1975 the ABA has approved paralegal programs that satisfy the rigorous standards of the *ABA Guidelines for the Approval of Paralegal Education Programs.*

- The ABA adopted Model Guidelines for the Utilization of Legal Assistant Services in 1991. The *ABA Model Guidelines for the Utilization of Paralegal Services* were revised in February 2004. Many states, such as Indiana, New Hampshire, North Dakota, Pennsylvania, Rhode Island, South Carolina, South Dakota, Texas, Utah, Virginia, Washington, West Virginia, and state bar associations, such as those in Colorado, Connecticut, Michigan, Missouri, New Mexico, New York, and North Carolina, have adopted these guidelines or their own versions.[37]

The ABA has become the approval mechanism for educational institutions offering paralegal programs. ABA approval is not mandatory, but numerous institutions of higher learning have followed its arduous path of compliance to obtain the prestige that comes from endorsement.[38] Approval guidelines for paralegal instruction and education include specific standards for

- Faculty.
- Libraries.
- Curriculum content—both procedural and substantive.
- The definition of specializations and general studies.
- Physical plant.
- Student and faculty services.
- Other educational criteria.[39]

The ABA has published the Model Code of Professional Responsibility and the more recently revised Model Rules of Professional Conduct[40] as well as the Model Guidelines on the Utilization of Paralegal Services.[41] The pertinent provisions of these codes will be summarized in the third section of this chapter.

At the state and local levels, various bar associations have standing or ad hoc committees on paralegal practice.[42] State and local bar associations usually include regulatory concerns on the following topical issues:

- Paralegal advertising and marketing.
- Services, functions, and duties performed by paralegals.
- The nature of unauthorized practice of law and the paralegal/attorney.

State-by state-legislation is charted by the NFPA (see Figure 2.1).

States such as New Jersey lay out the requirements for paralegal practice as well. New Jersey Rules of Professional Conduct at 5.3 make lawyers ethically responsible for their paralegals' acts under the following conditions:

> *RPC 5.3. Responsibilities Regarding Nonlawyer Assistants*
>
> *With respect to a nonlawyer employed or retained by or associated with a lawyer:*
>
> *(a) every lawyer, law firm, or organization authorized by the Court Rules to practice law in this jurisdiction shall adopt and maintain reasonable efforts to ensure that the conduct of nonlawyers retained or employed by the lawyer, law firm, or organization is compatible with the professional obligations of the lawyer.*
>
> *(b) a lawyer having direct supervisory authority over the nonlawyer shall make reasonable efforts to ensure that the person's conduct is compatible with the professional obligations of the lawyer.*
>
> *(c) a lawyer shall be responsible for conduct of such a person that would be a violation of the Rules of Professional Conduct if engaged in by a lawyer if:*
>
> > *(1) the lawyer orders or ratifies the conduct involved;*
> >
> > *(2) the lawyer has direct supervisory authority over the person and knows of the conduct at a time when its consequences can be avoided or mitigated but fails to take reasonable remedial action; or*
> >
> > *(3) the lawyer has failed to make reasonable investigation of circumstances that would disclose past instances of conduct by the nonlawyer incompatible with the professional obligations of a lawyer, which evidence a propensity for such conduct.[43]*

FIGURE 2.1   State-by-State Paralegal Legislation

- Arizona:
  - Arizona Consumers Benefit from Supreme Court Rules Change—January 16, 2003.
  - Arizona State Bar Rule Change Proposals 10/01.
  - NFPA response to Arizona UPL Committee.
- California:
  - County of Sacramento—Authorization for Nonattorney Court Document Preparer, posted June 11, 2003.
  - California Bill 3027, posted August 8, 2002.
  - Defining a *paralegal*.
  - Defining *unlawful detainer assistant and legal document assistant*.
  - NFPA's Response to California Senate Bill AB 1761.
  - Response of the San Francisco Paralegal Association to Assembly Bill 1761.
  - SAMPLE DECLARATION re: Business & Professions Code §6450.
  - Status of Laws Affecting Paralegals in California, March 2002.
- Florida:
  - UPL cases.
- Hawaii:
  - Second Response to Hawaii's Regulating of Paralegal, Legal Assistants, and Lawyer Assistants.
  - Regulating Paralegal, Legal Assistants, and Lawyer Assistants.
- Illinois:
  - Establishing a Supreme Court Commission on the UPL—January 28, 2002.
- Missouri:
  - Guidelines for Practicing with Paralegals.
- Nebraska:
  - NFPA's response to "proposed Rules Governing the Unauthorized Practice of Law"—June 17, 2003.
- New Hampshire:
  - 2003 Senate Bill Number 83 Bills on Paralegals in Court, Litigation, Judicial Issues Advance.
  - NFPA's Response to 2003 Senate Bill Number 83.
- New Jersey:
  - Response to New Jersey Supreme Court.
- North Carolina:
  - North Carolina plan for certification—effective October 1, 2004.
  - Response to Senate Bill 922/House Bill 957 Paralegal Profession Act—June 19, 2003.
  - Senate Bill 922/House Bill 957 Paralegal Profession Act.
- Oklahoma:
  - Minimum Qualification Standards for Legal Assistants/Paralegals.
- Texas:
  - General Guidelines for the Utilization of the Services of Legal Assistants by Attorneys—May 1993 (19 pages).
- Vermont:
  - Vermont HB 464—Appropriations Bill and Vermont Paralegal Organization appointee June 2003.
- Washington:
  - Washington State Practice of Law Board.
  - Comments to the Supreme Court State of Washington regarding rule changes (GR 22 and 25).
- Wisconsin:
  - Board approves Paralegal Task Force Report.
  - Wisconsin's Paralegal Practice Task Force Final Report—January 2004.

Professional Associations and Groups

Paralegals are lucky to have a vibrant menu of professional organizations. Besides the American Bar Association, other professional associations and groups include these:

- American Alliance for Paralegals.
- American Academy of Legal Assistants.
- American Association for Paralegal Education.

- American Association of Law Libraries.
- ABA Standing Committee on Legal Assistants.
- American Paralegal Association.
- Association of Legal Administrators.
- Legal Assistant Management Association.
- National Association of Enrolled Agents.
- National Association of Law Firm Marketing.
- National Association of Legal Assistants.
- National Association of Legal Specialties.
- National Federation of Paralegal Associations.
- National Indian Paralegal Association.
- National Legal Assistant Conference.
- National Notary Association.
- National Paralegal Association.
- National Shorthand Reporters Association.
- Professional Legal Assistants Inc.

Each of these professional associations lays out a template for paralegal professionalism and ethical best practices. The National Federation of Paralegal Associations has made a significant impact on the need for regulatory oversight. Early in the organization's history it held,

> *NFPA recognizes that as a representative national voice for the paralegal profession it must provide guidance on the issue of regulation which critically impacts the paralegal profession. This refined policy is in direct response to the increasing activity across the United States of proposed paralegal regulations.*
>
> *NFPA recognizes that, since the paralegal profession emerged, the legal profession and practice of law have undergone significant changes. Society has become more conscious of legal rights and better informed about the legal process. One obvious consequence of these changes is that the line between what constitutes practicing law and what is permissible business and professional activity by nonlawyers is indistinct. Many legal services have become so common and standard that nonlawyer practice in these areas is now woven into the socioeconomic fabric of society. Nonlawyers such as title agents, ombudsmen, real estate brokers, accountants, mediators, arbitrators, escrow agents, and estate and trust officers are and have been performing these services successfully, satisfactorily, efficiently, and less expensively to the public's benefit for years. In the wake of these changes, state legislatures, courts, and bar associations are attempting to determine the implications of nonlawyer practice for society, the client, and the legal profession.* [44]

The National Federation of Paralegal Associations sets forth minimal educational standards, including a proficiency examination and standards of character and fitness. "NFPA recommends that future practitioners should have a four-year degree to enter the profession. Individuals receiving a formal paralegal education should have 24 semester hours or the equivalent of legal specialty courses to enhance their ability to practice as paralegals."[45]

The Association of Trial Lawyers of America (ATLA) established a Paralegal Advisory Committee in 1989 and has since granted affiliate membership to paralegals. ATLA doesn't doubt the importance of paralegals:

> *The private practice of law in America is undergoing extraordinary changes that will have a lasting impact on the way lawyers work. Attorneys are now facing the reality that the law is a business as well as a profession. Increased use of paralegals and legal assistants, for example, is carrying law firms in uncharted directions.* [46]

On the state and local levels, even more associations exist. See Appendix A for a comprehensive list.

The Association of Trial Lawyers of America (ATLA) is also a major player in the evolution of the paralegal. The ATLA chart at Figure 2.2 summarizes the regulatory climate involving paralegal practice.

FIGURE 2.2 **Summary of the Regulatory Climate Involving Paralegal Practice**

Sources: See the Association of Trial Lawyers of America (ATLA) Web site at http://www.atla.org/Networking/Tier3/ParalegalAffiliates.aspx; *see also* NALA's Web site (www.nala.org) at issues relating to licensure; Revised Statutes of Nebraska Annotated, Chapter 71, Article 62—Nebraska Regulation of Health Professions Act. Although this statute deals specifically with the regulation of health professionals, its review is instructive; Connie Kretchmer, National Association of Legal Assistants Inc., Facts and Finding "Career Chronicle" (1991). Reprinted with permission of the National Association of Legal Assistants, www.nala.org, 1516 S. Boston, #200, Tulsa OK 74119

California	Title 2, Div. 2, Part 1, Chapter 1.5, Article 8. Legislative oversight of state board formation and licensed professional practice. Secs. 9148.4, 9148.10.	New Mexico	Ch. 12, Article 9A. Sunrise Act. Secs.12-9A-1-12-9A-6.
Colorado	24-34-104.1. General assembly sunrise review of new regulation of occupations and professions	South Dakota	Ch. 36-1A.
Florida	Title III. 11.62. Legislative review of proposed regulation of unregulated functions.	Vermont	Title 26. Ch. 57. Review of licensing statutes, boards, and commissions. Sec. 3105.
Georgia	Title 43. Ch. 1A. Occupational regulation legislation review.	Virginia	Title 54.1, Subtitle 1, Chapter 1. Sec. 54.1-100–54.1-311.
Hawaii	Division 1, Title 4, Ch. 26H. Hawaii Regulatory licensing reform act.	Washington	Title 18. Ch. 18.118. Regulation of business professions.
Maine	Title 32, Ch. 1-A, Subchapter II. Sunrise review procedures. Sec. 60-J-60L.	Wisconsin	Criteria for evaluating need to draft a regulatory legislative proposal of the State of Wisconsin Dept. of Regulation and Licensing.

The AAFPE delivers significant contributions to the ethical debate involving paralegals.[47] At NALS the thrust is similar—with a push for professionalism and integrity in practice. NALS posts timeless advice for the practicing paralegal:

- *A mastery of procedural skills and communication skills.*
- *An advanced knowledge of procedural law, the law library, and the preparation of legal documents.*
- *A working knowledge of substantive law and the ability to perform specifically delegated substantive legal work under an attorney's supervision.*
- *The ability to interact on a professional level with attorneys, clients, and other staff.*
- *The discipline to assume responsibility and exercise initiative and judgment while adhering to legal ethical standards at all times.*

Working under the supervision of a practicing lawyer or a judge, the Certified PP is expected to possess

- *The same high standard of ethical conduct imposed upon members of the bar.*
- *Excellent written and verbal communication skills.*
- *Knowledge and understanding of legal terminology and procedures, as well as procedural and substantive law.*
- *The ability to assume responsibility, exercise initiative and judgment, and prepare substantive legal documents within the scope of assigned authority.*

Attaining this goal demonstrates dedication to professionalism and acceptance of the challenge to be exceptional. Personal motivation is necessary to attain such a goal.[48]

Professional organizations serve many functions, some of which are discussed next.

Education and Certification Policy

Ideally paralegal organizations promote the advancement and professionalism of legal assistants and paralegals. Aside from mandating specific educational levels, there is a continuous push for certification. Certification assures standardized competencies. Professional organizations are taking the lead in this push for certification.

The National Association of Legal Assistants (NALA) has been strongly supportive. Through its Certified Legal Assistant Program (CLA),[49] the association calls for mastery of the following:

- Ability to analyze and categorize facts and evidence.
- Capacity to develop relationships with lawyers, legal secretaries, clients, courts, and other law firms.
- Ability to react to different situations.
- Ability to handle telephone situations.
- Ability to comprehend and interpret data.
- Familiarity with the rules of professional conduct to possess logical reasoning skills.[50]

NALA further distinguishes topical areas by specialty testing. As of 2006, certification specializations are

- Civil litigation.
- Probate and estate planning.
- Corporate and business law.
- Criminal law and procedure.
- Real estate.[51]

NALA's dedication to certification correlates to its push for professionalism. NALA notes,

> *Many of NALA's philosophies and concepts are embedded in its certification program. The program encourages, supports, and exemplifies an attitude of professionalism and professional development through discipline and self-study. It is a voluntary program neither mandated nor required by any state or bar association. Individuals who take the examination are committed to the concepts of professionalism and achievement.*[52]

Kathleen Rasmussen sees major inroads being made by those who advocate certification:

> *Certification or some other form of licensing appears to be the wave of the future for legal assistants. It serves several purposes. It is yet another way that legal assistants can demonstrate their knowledge and expertise in the legal field. It is another way that legal assistants can exhibit their commitment to professional development and gain an edge over their competitors for jobs in the legal field.*[53]

While not a strong advocate of educational and professional certification, the American Bar Association through its approval mechanism for educational programs does call for specific standards and skills attainment. In its guidelines for obtaining ABA approval of legal assistant educational programs,[54] the ABA gives far-reaching proposals on curricula compositions. Its general methodological stance, outlined at Standard G-302, Section B, states,

> *The curriculum should be constructed in a way that provides opportunity for students to achieve upward mobility. A maximum number of credits should be applicable toward continued education for higher degrees or certificates with minimum loss of time and duplication of efforts.*[55]

ABA standards further differentiate courses as *law related* or content that is a *legal specialty*. A law-related course is one that has theoretical law content but does not emphasize the development of a paralegal competency.[56] The ABA's voluntary oversight of the educational process and certification system does provide a means to regulate paralegals and legal assistants.

NALS promotes a series of certification exams that test hierarchical levels of legal skill and knowledge. Summaries of the tests follow.

The ALS examination

- Demonstrates ability to perform business communication tasks.
- Gauges ability to maintain office records and calendars, and prioritize multiple tasks when given real-life scenarios.
- Measures understanding of office equipment and related procedures.
- Denotes aptitude for understanding legal terminology, legal complexities, and supporting documents.

- Assesses recognition of accounting terms in order to solve accounting problems.
- Appraises knowledge of law office protocol as prescribed by ethical codes.[57]

The PLS examination demonstrates possession of

- A mastery of office skills.
- The ability to interact on a professional level with attorneys, clients, and other support staff.
- The discipline to assume responsibility and exercise initiative and judgment.
- A working knowledge of procedural law, the law library, and how to prepare legal documents.[58]

The PP (professional paralegal) examination demonstrates

- A mastery of procedural skills and communication skills.
- An advanced knowledge of procedural law, the law library, and the preparation of legal documents.
- A working knowledge of substantive law and the ability to perform specifically delegated substantive legal work under an attorney's supervision.
- The ability to interact on a professional level with attorneys, clients, and other staff.
- The discipline to assume responsibility and exercise initiative and judgment while adhering to legal ethical standards at all times.[59]

NFPA administers the PACE exam, which measures skill and knowledge in the following areas:

- Administration of client legal matters.
- Development of client legal matters.
- Factual and legal research.
- Factual and legal writing.
- Office administration.

The American Alliance for Paralegal Inc. (AAPI), a new professional organization for paralegals, ties higher levels of education to traditional certification. The AAPI has been quite critical of continued resistance to certification programs that do not call for an undergraduate degree:

> *The American Alliance advocates a bachelor's degree that includes, or is combined with, a paralegal studies program for persons entering the profession. Members are encouraged to continue their education throughout their careers. It is recommended that they participate in no less than 9 hours of continuing education annually, including at least one hour of ethics.*[60]

Certification and educational uniformity on a national level are difficult but honorable objectives. Given the wealth of opportunities for certification, the paralegal profession has accepted increasing responsibilities for its self-regulation and self-competence.

ETHICAL CODES OF CONDUCT FOR PARALEGALS

Ethical guidelines set a tone and pave standards for professional conduct. Paralegals, like other professions, are guided by codes of conduct that are generally promulgated by professional organizations and groups.

National Association of Legal Assistants

Certain minimum standards have been proposed by the National Association of Legal Assistants.[61] See Figure 2.3 for the NALA Model Standards and Guidelines for Utilization of Legal Assistants/Paralegals.

NALA's professional influence is a bold step in outlining minimum requirements of experiential, intellectual, and occupational qualifications. The code seeks to delineate acceptable delegation from attorney to paralegal to avoid the charge of unauthorized practice. *NALA's Code of Ethics and Professional Responsibility* expects paralegals "to adhere strictly to the accepted standards of legal assistants and to live by general principles of proper conduct."[62] Its specific canons of conduct, mirroring the authorized style of the *ABA Model Code of Professional Responsibility*, provide a forum for the measure of professional conduct (see Figure 2.4).

FIGURE 2.3   NALA Model Standards and Guidelines for Utilization of Legal Assistants/Paralegals

Source: Copyright 1984; adopted 1984; revised 1991, 1997, 2005. Reprinted with permission of the National Association of Legal Assistants, **www.nala.org**, 1516 S. Boston, #200, Tulsa, OK 74119.

INTRODUCTION

The purpose of this annotated version of the National Association of Legal Assistants Inc. Model Standards and Guidelines for the Utilization of Legal Assistants (the "Model," "Standards," and/or the "Guidelines") is to provide references to the existing case law and other authorities where the underlying issues have been considered. The authorities cited will serve as a basis upon which conduct of a legal assistant may be analyzed as proper or improper.

The Guidelines represent a statement of how the legal assistant may function. The Guidelines are not intended to be a comprehensive or exhaustive list of the proper duties of a legal assistant. Rather, they are designed as guides to what may or may not be proper conduct for the legal assistant. In formulating the Guidelines, the reasoning and rules of law in many reported decisions of disciplinary cases and unauthorized practice of law cases have been analyzed and considered. In addition, the provisions of the American Bar Association's Model Rules of Professional Conduct, as well as the ethical promulgations of various state courts and bar associations, have been considered in the development of the Guidelines.

These Guidelines form a sound basis for the legal assistant and the supervising attorney to follow. This Model will serve as a comprehensive resource document and as a definitive, well-reasoned guide to those considering voluntary standards and guidelines for legal assistants.

I
PREAMBLE

Proper utilization of the services of legal assistants contributes to the delivery of cost-effective, high-quality legal services. Legal assistants and the legal profession should be assured that measures exist for identifying legal assistants and their role in assisting attorneys in the delivery of legal services. Therefore, the National Association of Legal Assistants Inc. hereby adopts these Standards and Guidelines as an educational document for the benefit of legal assistants and the legal profession.

COMMENT

The three most frequently raised questions concerning legal assistants are (1) How do you define a legal assistant? (2) Who is qualified to be identified as a legal assistant? and (3) What duties may a legal assistant perform? The definition adopted in 1984 by the National Association of Legal Assistants answers the first question. The Model sets forth minimum education, training, and experience through standards assuring that an individual utilizing the title "legal assistant" or "paralegal" has the qualifications to be held out to the legal community and the public in that capacity. The Guidelines identify those acts that the reported cases hold to be proscribed and give examples of services the legal assistant may perform under the supervision of a licensed attorney.

These Guidelines constitute a statement relating to services performed by legal assistants, as defined herein, as approved by court decisions and other sources of authority. The purpose of the Guidelines is not to place limitations or restrictions on the legal assistant profession. Rather, the Guidelines are intended to outline for the legal profession an acceptable course of conduct. Voluntary recognition and utilization of the Standards and Guidelines will benefit the entire legal profession and the public it serves.

II
DEFINITION

The National Association of Legal Assistants adopted the following definition in 1984:

Legal assistants, also known as paralegals, are a distinguishable group of people who assist attorneys in the delivery of legal services. Through formal education, training, and experience, legal assistants have knowledge and expertise regarding the legal system and substantive and procedural law that qualify them to do work of a legal nature under the supervision of an attorney.

In recognition of the similarity of the definitions and the need for one clear definition, in July 2001 the NALA membership approved a resolution to adopt the definition of the American Bar Association as well. The ABA definition reads as follows:

A legal assistant or paralegal is a person qualified by education, training, or work experience who is employed or retained by a lawyer, law office, corporation, governmental agency, or other entity who performs specifically delegated substantive legal work for which a lawyer is responsible. (Adopted by the ABA in 1997)

COMMENT

These definitions emphasize the knowledge and expertise of legal assistants in substantive and procedural law obtained through education and work experience. They further define the legal assistant or paralegal as a professional working under the supervision of an attorney as distinguished from a nonlawyer who delivers

FIGURE 2.3   *(continued)*

services directly to the public without any intervention or review of work product by an attorney. Such unsupervised services, unless authorized by court or agency rules, constitute the unauthorized practice of law.

Statutes, court rules, case law, and bar association documents are additional sources for legal assistant or paralegal definitions. In applying the Standards and Guidelines, it is important to remember that they were developed to apply to the legal assistant as defined herein. Lawyers should refrain from labeling those as paralegals or legal assistants who do not meet the criteria set forth in these definitions and/or the definitions set forth by state rules, guidelines, or bar associations. Labeling secretaries and other administrative staff as legal assistants/paralegals is inaccurate.

For billing purposes, the services of a legal secretary are considered part of overhead costs and are not recoverable in fee awards. However, the courts have held that fees for paralegal services are recoverable as long as they are not clerical functions, such as organizing files, copying documents, checking docket, updating files, checking court dates, and delivering papers. As established in *Missouri v. Jenkins*, 491 U.S.274, 109 S.Ct. 2463, 2471, n.10 (1989), tasks performed by legal assistants must be substantive in nature that, absent the legal assistant, the attorney would perform.

There are also case law and Supreme Court rules addressing the issue of a disbarred attorney serving in the capacity of a legal assistant.

III
STANDARDS

A legal assistant should meet certain minimum qualifications. The following standards may be used to determine an individual's qualifications as a legal assistant:

1. Successful completion of the Certified Legal Assistant (CLA)/Certified Paralegal (CP) certifying examination of the National Association of Legal Assistants, Inc.
2. Graduation from an ABA-approved program of study for legal assistants.
3. Graduation from a course of study for legal assistants that is institutionally accredited but not ABA approved and that requires not less than the equivalent of 60 semester hours of classroom study.
4. Graduation from a course of study for legal assistants, other than those set forth in (2) and (3), plus not less than six months of in-house training as a legal assistant.
5. A baccalaureate degree in any field, plus not less than six months of in-house training as a legal assistant.
6. A minimum of three years of law-related experience under the supervision of an attorney, including at least six months of in-house training as a legal assistant.
7. Two years of in-house training as a legal assistant.

For purposes of these Standards, "in-house training as a legal assistant" means attorney education of the employee concerning legal assistant duties and these Guidelines. In addition to review and analysis of assignments, the legal assistant should receive a reasonable amount of instruction directly related to the duties and obligations of the legal assistant.

COMMENT

The Standards set forth suggest minimum qualifications for a legal assistant. These minimum qualifications, as adopted, recognize legal related work backgrounds and formal education backgrounds, both of which provide the legal assistant with a broad base in exposure to and knowledge of the legal profession. This background is necessary to assure the public and the legal profession that the employee identified as a legal assistant is qualified.

The Certified Legal Assistant (CLA) /Certified Paralegal (CP) examination established by NALA in 1976 is a voluntary nationwide certification program for legal assistants. (*CLA and CP are federally registered certification marks owned by NALA.*) The CLA/CP designation is a statement to the legal profession and the public that the legal assistant has met the high levels of knowledge and professionalism required by NALA's certification program. Continuing education requirements, which all certified legal assistants must meet, assure that high standards are maintained. The CLA/CP designation has been recognized as a means of establishing the qualifications of a legal assistant in supreme court rules, state court and bar association standards, and utilization guidelines.

Certification through NALA is available to all legal assistants meeting the educational and experience requirements. Certified Legal Assistants may also pursue advanced certification in specialty practice areas through the APC, Advanced Paralegal Certification, credentialing program. Legal assistants/paralegals may also pursue certification based on state laws and procedures in California, Florida, Louisiana, and Texas.

IV
GUIDELINES

These Guidelines relating to standards of performance and professional responsibility are intended to aid legal assistants and attorneys. The ultimate responsibility rests with an attorney who employs legal assistants to educate them with respect to the duties they are assigned and to supervise the manner in which such duties are accomplished.

FIGURE 2.3   *(continued)*

COMMENT

In general, a legal assistant is allowed to perform any task that is properly delegated and supervised by an attorney, as long as the attorney is ultimately responsible to the client and assumes complete professional responsibility for the work product.

ABA Model Rules of Professional Conduct, Rule 5.3 provides:

With respect to a nonlawyer employed or retained by or associated with a lawyer:

(a) A partner in a law firm shall make reasonable efforts to ensure that the firm has in effect measures giving reasonable assurance that the person's conduct is compatible with the professional obligations of the lawyer.

(b) A lawyer having direct supervisory authority over the nonlawyer shall make reasonable efforts to ensure that the person's conduct is compatible with the professional obligations of the lawyer.

(c) A lawyer shall be responsible for conduct of such a person that would be a violation of the rules of professional conduct if engaged in by a lawyer if
   (1) The lawyer orders or, with knowledge of the specific conduct, ratifies the conduct involved; or
   (2) The lawyer is a partner in the law firm in which the person is employed, or has direct supervisory authority over the person, and knows of the conduct at a time when its consequences can be avoided or mitigated but fails to take remedial action.

There are many interesting and complex issues involving the use of legal assistants. In any discussion of the proper role of a legal assistant, attention must be directed to what constitutes the practice of law. Proper delegation to legal assistants is further complicated and confused by the lack of an adequate definition of the practice of law.

Kentucky became the first state to adopt a Paralegal Code by Supreme Court rule. This code sets forth certain exclusions to the unauthorized practice of law:

For purposes of this rule, the unauthorized practice of law shall not include any service rendered involving legal knowledge or advice, whether representation, counsel, or advocacy, in or out of court, rendered in respect to the acts, duties, obligations, liabilities, or business relations of the one requiring services where

A. The client understands that the paralegal is not a lawyer.

B. The lawyer supervises the paralegal in the performance of his or her duties.

C. The lawyer remains fully responsible for such representation including all actions taken or not taken in connection therewith by the paralegal to the same extent as if such representation had been furnished entirely by the lawyer and all such actions had been taken or not taken directly by the attorney. Paralegal Code, Ky.S.Ct.R3.700, Sub-Rule 2.

South Dakota Supreme Court Rule 97-25 Utilization Rule a(4) states,

The attorney remains responsible for the services performed by the legal assistant to the same extent as though such services had been furnished entirely by the attorney and such actions were those of the attorney.

Guideline 1

Legal assistants should

1. Disclose their status as legal assistants at the outset of any professional relationship with a client, other attorneys, a court or administrative agency or personnel thereof, or members of the general public.
2. Preserve the confidences and secrets of all clients.
3. Understand the attorney's Rules of Professional Responsibility and these Guidelines in order to avoid any action that would involve the attorney in a violation of the Rules or give the appearance of professional impropriety.

COMMENT

Routine early disclosure of the paralegal's status when dealing with people outside the attorney's office is necessary to ensure that there will be no misunderstanding as to the responsibilities and role of the legal assistant. Disclosure may be made in any way that avoids confusion. If the person dealing with the legal assistant already knows of his/her status, further disclosure is unnecessary. If at any time in written or oral communication the legal assistant becomes aware that the other person may believe the legal assistant is an attorney, immediate disclosure should be made as to the legal assistant's status.

The attorney should exercise care that the legal assistant preserves and refrains from using any confidence or secrets of a client, and should instruct the legal assistant not to disclose or use any such confidences or secrets.

The legal assistant must take any and all steps necessary to prevent conflicts of interest and fully disclose such conflicts to the supervising attorney. Failure to do so may jeopardize both the attorney's representation of the client and the case itself.

Guidelines for the Utilization of Legal Assistant Services adopted December 3, 1994, by the Washington State Bar Association Board of Governors state,

FIGURE 2.3 (*continued*)

"Guideline 7: A lawyer shall take reasonable measures to prevent conflicts of interest resulting from a legal assistant's other employment or interest insofar as such other employment or interests would present a conflict of interest if it were that of the lawyer."

In re Complex Asbestos Litigation, 232 Cal. App. 3d 572 (Cal. 1991), addresses the issue wherein a law firm was disqualified due to possession of attorney–client confidences by a legal assistant employee resulting from previous employment by opposing counsel.

In Oklahoma, in an order issued July 12, 2001, in the matter of *Mark A. Hayes, M.D. v. Central States Orthopedic Specialists, Inc.,* a Tulsa County District Court Judge disqualified a law firm from representation of a client on the basis that an ethical screen was an impermissible device to protect from disclosure confidences gained by a nonlawyer employee while employed by another law firm. In applying the same rules that govern attorneys, the court found that the Rules of Professional Conduct pertaining to confidentiality apply to nonlawyers who leave firms with actual knowledge of material, confidential information, and a screening device is not an appropriate alternative to the imputed disqualification of an incoming legal assistant who has moved from one firm to another during ongoing litigation and has actual knowledge of material, confidential information. The decision was appealed, and the Oklahoma Supreme Court determined that, under certain circumstances, screening is an appropriate management tool for nonlawyer staff.

In 2004 the Nevada Supreme Court also addressed this issue at the urging of the state's paralegals. The Nevada Supreme Court granted a petition to rescind the court's 1997 ruling in *Ciaffone v. District Court*. In this case, the court clarified the original ruling, stating, "mere opportunity to access confidential information does not merit disqualification." The opinion stated instances in which screening may be appropriate and listed minimum screening requirements. The opinion also set forth guidelines that a district court may use to determine if screening has been or may be effective. These considerations are

1. Substantiality of the relationship between the former and current matters.
2. The time elapsed between the matters.
3. Size of the firm.
4. Number of individuals presumed to have confidential information.
5. Nature of their involvement in the former matter.
6. Timing and features of any measures taken to reduce the danger of disclosure.
7. Whether the old firm and the new firm represent adverse parties in the same proceeding rather than in different proceedings.

The ultimate responsibility for compliance with approved standards of professional conduct rests with the supervising attorney. The burden rests upon the attorney who employs a legal assistant to educate the latter with respect to the duties that may be assigned and then to supervise the manner in which the legal assistant carries out such duties. However, this does not relieve the legal assistant from an independent obligation to refrain from illegal conduct. Additionally, and notwithstanding that the Rules are not binding upon nonlawyers, the very nature of a legal assistant's employment imposes an obligation not to engage in conduct that would involve the supervising attorney in a violation of the Rules.

The attorney must make sufficient background investigation of the prior activities and character and integrity of his or her legal assistants.

Further, the attorney must take all measures necessary to avoid and fully disclose conflicts of interest due to other employment or interests. Failure to do so may jeopardize both the attorney's representation of the client and the case itself.

Legal assistant associations strive to maintain the high level of integrity and competence expected of the legal profession and, further, strive to uphold the high standards of ethics.

NALA's Code of Ethics and Professional Responsibility states, "A legal assistant's conduct is guided by bar associations' codes of professional responsibility and rules of professional conduct."

Guideline 2

Legal assistants should not

1. Establish attorney–client relationships; set legal fees; give legal opinions or advice; or represent a client before a court, unless authorized to do so by said court.
2. Engage in, encourage, or contribute to any act that could constitute the unauthorized practice law.

COMMENT

Case law, court rules, codes of ethics and professional responsibilities, and bar ethics opinions now hold which acts can and cannot be performed by a legal assistant. Generally, the determination of what acts constitute the unauthorized practice of law is made by state supreme courts.

FIGURE 2.3   (*continued*)

Numerous cases exist relating to the unauthorized practice of law. Courts have gone so far as to prohibit the legal assistant from preparation of divorce kits and assisting in preparation of bankruptcy forms and, more specifically, from providing basic information about procedures and requirements, deciding where information should be placed on forms, and responding to questions from debtors regarding the interpretation or definition of terms.

Cases have identified certain areas in which an attorney has a duty to act, but it is interesting to note that none of these cases states that it is improper for an attorney to have the initial work performed by the legal assistant. This again points out the importance of adequate supervision by the employing attorney.

An attorney can be found to have aided in the unauthorized practice of law when delegating acts that cannot be performed by a legal assistant.

Guideline 3

Legal assistants may perform services for an attorney in the representation of a client, provided

1. The services performed by the legal assistant do not require the exercise of independent professional legal judgment.
2. The attorney maintains a direct relationship with the client and maintains control of all client matters.
3. The attorney supervises the legal assistant.
4. The attorney remains professionally responsible for all work on behalf of the client, including any actions taken or not taken by the legal assistant in connection therewith.
5. The services performed supplement, merge with, and become the attorney's work product.

COMMENT

Paralegals, whether employees or independent contractors, perform services for the attorney in the representation of a client. Attorneys should delegate work to legal assistants commensurate with their knowledge and experience and provide appropriate instruction and supervision concerning the delegated work, as well as ethical acts of their employment. Ultimate responsibility for the work product of a legal assistant rests with the attorney. However, a legal assistant must use discretion and professional judgment and must not render independent legal judgment in place of an attorney.

The work product of a legal assistant is subject to civil rules governing discovery of materials prepared in anticipation of litigation, whether the legal assistant is viewed as an extension of the attorney or as another representative of the party itself. Fed.R.Civ.P. 26 (b) (3) and (5).

Guideline 4

In the supervision of a legal assistant, consideration should be given to

1. Designating work assignments that correspond to the legal assistant's abilities, knowledge, training, and experience.
2. Educating and training the legal assistant with respect to professional responsibility, local rules and practices, and firm policies.
3. Monitoring the work and professional conduct of the legal assistant to ensure that the work is substantively correct and timely performed.
4. Providing continuing education for the legal assistant in substantive matters through courses, institutes, workshops, seminars, and in-house training.
5. Encouraging and supporting membership and active participation in professional organizations.

COMMENT

Attorneys are responsible for the actions of their employees in both malpractice and disciplinary proceedings. In the vast majority of cases, the courts have not censured attorneys for a particular act delegated to the legal assistant, but rather have been critical of and imposed sanctions against attorneys for failure to adequately supervise the legal assistant. The attorney's responsibility for supervision of his or her legal assistant must be more than a willingness to accept responsibility and liability for the legal assistant's work. Supervision of a legal assistant must be offered in both the procedural and substantive legal areas. The attorney must delegate work based upon the education, knowledge, and abilities of the legal assistant and must monitor the work product and conduct of the legal assistant to ensure that the work performed is substantively correct and competently performed in a professional manner.

The Michigan State Board of Commissioners has adopted Guidelines for the Utilization of Legal Assistants (April 23, 1993). These guidelines, in part, encourage employers to support legal assistant participation in continuing education programs to ensure that the legal assistant remains competent in the fields of practice in which the legal assistant is assigned.

The working relationship between the lawyer and the legal assistant should extend to cooperative efforts on public service activities wherever possible. Participation in pro bono activities is encouraged in ABA Guideline 10.

FIGURE 2.3 (*continued*)

Guideline 5

Except as otherwise provided by statute, court rule or decision, administrative rule or regulation, or the attorney's rules of professional responsibility, and within the preceding parameters and proscriptions, a legal assistant may perform any function delegated by an attorney, including but not limited to the following:

1. Conduct client interviews and maintain general contact with the client after the establishment of the attorney–client relationship, so long as the client is aware of the status and function of the legal assistant, and the client contact is under the supervision of the attorney.
2. Locate and interview witnesses, so long as the witnesses are aware of the status and function of the legal assistant.
3. Conduct investigations and statistical and documentary research for review by the attorney.
4. Conduct legal research for review by the attorney.
5. Draft legal documents for review by the attorney.
6. Draft correspondence and pleadings for review by and signature of the attorney.
7. Summarize depositions, interrogatories, and testimony for review by the attorney.
8. Attend executions of wills, real estate closings, depositions, and court or administrative hearings and trials with the attorney.
9. Author and sign letters providing the legal assistant's status is clearly indicated and the correspondence does not contain independent legal opinions or legal advice.

COMMENT

The United States Supreme Court has recognized the variety of tasks being performed by legal assistants and has noted that use of legal assistants encourages cost-effective delivery of legal services: *Missouri v. Jenkins*, 491 U.S.274, 109 S.Ct. 2463, 2471, n.10 (1989). In *Jenkins* the court further held that legal assistant time should be included in compensation for attorney fee awards at the market rate of the relevant community to bill legal assistant time.

Courts have held that legal assistant fees are not a part of the overall overhead of a law firm. Legal assistant services are billed separately by attorneys and decrease litigation expenses. Tasks performed by legal assistants must contain substantive legal work under the direction or supervision of an attorney, such that if the legal assistant were not present, the work would be performed by the attorney.

In *Taylor v. Chubb*, 874 P.2d 806 (Okla. 1994), the court ruled that attorney fees awarded should include fees for services performed by legal assistants and, further, defined tasks that may be performed by the legal assistant under the supervision of an attorney including, among others: interviewing clients; drafting pleadings and other documents; carrying on legal research, both conventional and computer aided; researching public records; preparing discovery requests and responses; scheduling depositions and preparing notices and subpoenas; summarizing depositions and other discovery responses; coordinating and managing document production; locating and interviewing witnesses; organizing pleadings, trial exhibits, and other documents; preparing witness and exhibit lists; preparing trial notebooks; preparing for the attendance of witnesses at trial; and assisting lawyers at trials.

Except for the specific proscription contained in Guideline 1, the reported cases do not limit the duties that may be performed by a legal assistant under the supervision of the attorney.

An attorney may not split legal fees with a legal assistant, nor pay a legal assistant for the referral of legal business. An attorney may compensate a legal assistant based on the quantity and quality of the legal assistant's work and value of that work to a law practice.

CONCLUSION

These Standards and Guidelines were developed from generally accepted practices. Each supervising attorney must be aware of the specific rules, decisions, and statutes applicable to legal assistants within his/her jurisdiction.

Addendum

For further information, the following cases may be helpful to you:

Duties

Taylor v. Chubb, 874 P.2d 806 (Okla. 1994)
McMackin v. McMackin, 651 A.2d 778 (Del.Fam Ct 1993)

Work Product

Fine v. Facet Aerospace Products Co., 133 F.R.D. 439 (S.D.N.Y. 1990)

Unauthorized Practice of Law

Akron Bar Assn. v. Green, 673 N.E.2d 1307 (Ohio 1997)
In re Hessinger & Associates, 192 B.R. 211 (N.D. Calif. 1996)

FIGURE 2.3   (*concluded*)

In the Matter of Bright, 171 B.R. 799 (Bkrtcy. E.D. Mich)
Louisiana State Bar Assn v. Edwins, 540 So.2d 294 (La. 1989)

Attorney–Client Privilege

In re Complex Asbestos Litigation, 232 Cal. App. 3d 572 (Calif. 1991)
Makita Corp. v. U.S., 819 F.Supp. 1099 (CIT 1993)

Conflicts

In re Complex Asbestos Litigation, 232 Cal. App. 3d 572 (Calif. 1991)
Makita Corp. v. U.S., 819 F.Supp. 1099 (CIT 1993)
Phoenix Founders, Inc., v. Marshall, 887 S.W.2d 831 (Tex. 1994)
Smart Industries v. Superior Court, 876 P.2d 1176 (Ariz. App. Div.1 1994)

Supervision

Matter of Martinez, 754 P.2d 842 (N.M. 1988)
State v. Barrett, 483 P.2d 1106 (Kan. 1971)
Hayes v. Central States Orthopedic Specialists, Inc., 2002 OK 30, 51 P.3d 562
Liebowitz v. Eighth Judicial District Court of Nevada Nev Sup Ct., No 39683,
November 3, 2003 clarified in part and overrules in part *Ciaffone v. District Court*, 113 Nev 1165, 945. P2d 950 (1997)

Fee Awards

In re Bicoastal Corp., 121 B.R. 653 (Bktrcy.M.D.Fla. 1990)
In re Carter, 101 B.R. 170 (Bkrtcy.D.S.D. 1989)
Taylor v. Chubb, 874 P.2d 806 (Okla.1994)
Missouri v. Jenkins, 491 U.S. 274, 109 S.Ct. 2463, 105 L.Ed.2d 229 (1989) 11 U.S.C.A.'330
McMackin v. McMackin, Del.Fam.Ct. 651 A.2d 778 (1993)
Miller v. Alamo, 983 F.2d 856 (8th Cir. 1993)
Stewart v. Sullivan, 810 F.Supp. 1102 (D.Hawaii 1993)
In re Yankton College, 101 B.R. 151 (Bkrtcy. D.S.D. 1989)
Stacey v. Stroud, 845 F.Supp. 1135 (S.D.W.Va. 1993)

Court Appearances

Louisiana State Bar Assn v. Edwins, 540 So.2d 294 (La. 1989)

In addition to these referenced cases, you may contact your state bar association for information regarding guidelines for the utilization of legal assistants that may have been adopted by the bar, or ethical opinions concerning the utilization of legal assistants. The following states have adopted a definition of *legal assistant* or *paralegal* either through bar association guidelines, ethical opinions, legislation, or case law:

Legislation	South Carolina	Kansas
California	Washington	Kentucky
Florida	**Guidelines**	**Bar Associations (Cont.)**
Illinois		Massachusetts
Indiana	Colorado	Michigan
Maine	Connecticut	Minnesota
Pennsylvania	Georgia	Missouri
Supreme Court Cases or Rules	Idaho	Nevada
	New York	New Mexico
Kentucky	Oregon	New Hampshire
New Hampshire	Utah	North Carolina
New Mexico	Wisconsin	North Dakota
North Dakota	**Bar Association Activity**	Ohio
Rhode Island		Oregon
South Dakota	Alaska	Rhode Island
Virginia	Arizona	South Carolina
Cases	Colorado	South Dakota
	Connecticut	Tennessee
Arizona	Florida	Texas
New Jersey	Illinois	Virginia
Oklahoma	Iowa	Wisconsin

FIGURE 2.4 NALA Code of Ethics and Professional Responsibility

Source: Copyright 1975; revised 1979, 1988, 1995. National Association of Legal Assistants Inc. Reprinted with permission of the National Association of Legal Assistants, www.nala.org, 1516 S. Boston, #200, Tulsa, OK 74119.

Canon 1.	A legal assistant must not perform any of the duties that attorneys only may perform nor take any actions that attorneys may not take.
Canon 2.	A legal assistant may perform any task that is properly delegated and supervised by an attorney, as long as the attorney is ultimately responsible to the client, maintains a direct relationship with the client, and assumes professional responsibility for the work product.
Canon 3.	A legal assistant must not (a) engage in, encourage, or contribute to any act that could constitute the unauthorized practice of law; (b) establish attorney–client relationships, set fees, give legal opinions or advice, or represent a client before a court or agency unless so authorized by that court or agency; or (c) engage in conduct or take any action that would assist or involve the attorney in a violation of professional ethics or give the appearance of professional impropriety.
Canon 4.	A legal assistant must use discretion and professional judgment commensurate with knowledge and experience but must not render independent legal judgment in place of an attorney. The services of an attorney are essential in the public interest whenever such legal judgment is required.
Canon 5.	A legal assistant must disclose his or her status as a legal assistant at the outset of any professional relationship with a client, an attorney, a court or administrative agency or personnel thereof, or a member of the general public. A legal assistant must act prudently in determining the extent to which a client may be assisted without the presence of an attorney.
Canon 6.	A legal assistant must strive to maintain integrity and a high degree of competency through education and training with respect to professional responsibility, local rules, and practice, and through continuing education in substantive areas of law to better assist the legal profession in fulfilling its duty to provide legal service.
Canon 7.	A legal assistant must protect the confidences of a client and must not violate any rule or statute now in effect or hereafter enacted controlling the doctrine of privileged communications between a client and an attorney.
Canon 8.	A legal assistant must do all other things incidental, necessary, or expedient for the attainment of the ethics and responsibilities as defined by statute or rule of court.
Canon 9.	A legal assistant's conduct is guided by bar associations' codes of professional responsibility and rules of professional conduct.

National Federation of Paralegal Associations

The National Federation of Paralegal Associations publishes its *Model Code of Ethics and Professional Responsibility*. The federation attempts to define its general principles of professional conduct by discussing and providing general traits and characteristics necessary for paralegal practice. See Figure 2.5 for the NFPA Code of Ethics.

The American Alliance of Paralegals Inc.

The American Alliance of Paralegals Inc. (AAPI) was born out of a driving passion to give substance to the claim of professionalism in the paralegal community. The AAPI has long criticized those who refuse to set standards, refuse to establish minimum educational qualifications, or reject standardization in the industry. Coupled with this has been the organization's enthusiasm about ethics in the profession. Its code holds the following:

1. *A paralegal shall not engage in the unauthorized practice of law.*

2. *A paralegal shall keep confidential any and all information, documents, and other materials entrusted to him or her or acquired in some other way during the course of the legal representation of a client. The confidentiality shall be maintained before, during, and after the legal representation unless the client has given consent or disclosure is required by law or by court order.*

3. *A paralegal shall avoid conflicts of interest and shall immediately disclose any potential conflicts of interest to his or her employer.*

4. *A paralegal shall ensure that his or her status as a paralegal is disclosed at the beginning of any professional relationship with the attorney, client, personnel of a court, or personnel of an administrative agency.*

5. *A paralegal shall follow all provisions of the rules of professional conduct for a paralegal or legal assistant of the state in which he or she is employed. If no such specific code for*

FIGURE 2.5   NFPA Model Code of Ethics and Professional Responsibility and Guidelines for Enforcement

Source: Reprinted by permission from The National Federation of Paralegal Associations Inc., www.paralegals.org.

---

§1. NFPA MODEL DISCIPLINARY RULES AND ETHICAL CONSIDERATIONS

1.1 A PARALEGAL SHALL ACHIEVE AND MAINTAIN A HIGH LEVEL OF COMPETENCE.

Ethical Considerations

EC-1.1(a) A paralegal shall achieve competency through education, training, and work experience.

EC-1.1(b) A paralegal shall aspire to participate in a minimum of twelve (12) hours of continuing legal education, to include at least one (1) hour of ethics education, every two (2) years in order to remain current on developments in the law.

EC-1.1(c) A paralegal shall perform all assignments promptly and efficiently.

1.2 A PARALEGAL SHALL MAINTAIN A HIGH LEVEL OF PERSONAL AND PROFESSIONAL INTEGRITY.

Ethical Considerations

EC-1.2(a) A paralegal shall not engage in any ex parte communications involving the courts or any other adjudicatory body in an attempt to exert undue influence or to obtain advantage or the benefit of only one party.

EC-1.2(b) A paralegal shall not communicate, or cause another to communicate, with a party the paralegal knows to be represented by a lawyer in a pending matter without the prior consent of the lawyer representing such other party.

EC-1.2(c) A paralegal shall ensure that all timekeeping and billing records prepared by the paralegal are thorough, accurate, honest, and complete.

EC-1.2(d) A paralegal shall not knowingly engage in fraudulent billing practices. Such practices may include, but are not limited to, inflation of hours billed to a client or employer; misrepresentation of the nature of tasks performed; and/or submission of fraudulent expense and disbursement documentation.

EC-1.2(e) A paralegal shall be scrupulous, thorough, and honest in the identification and maintenance of all funds, securities, and other assets of a client and shall provide accurate accounting as appropriate.

EC-1.2(f) A paralegal shall advise the proper authority of nonconfidential knowledge of any dishonest or fraudulent acts by any person pertaining to the handling of the funds, securities, or other assets of a client. The authority to whom the report is made shall depend on the nature and circumstances of the possible misconduct (ethics committees of law firms, corporations and/or paralegal associations, local or state bar associations, local prosecutors, administrative agencies, etc.). Failure to report such knowledge is in itself misconduct and shall be treated as such under these rules.

1.3 A PARALEGAL SHALL MAINTAIN A HIGH STANDARD OF PROFESSIONAL CONDUCT.

Ethical Considerations

EC-1.3(a) A paralegal shall refrain from engaging in any conduct that offends the dignity and decorum of proceedings before a court or other adjudicatory body and shall be respectful of all rules and procedures.

EC-1.3(b) A paralegal shall avoid impropriety and the appearance of impropriety and shall not engage in any conduct that would adversely affect his/her fitness to practice. Such conduct may include, but is not limited to, violence, dishonesty, interference with the administration of justice, and/or abuse of a professional position or public office.

EC-1.3(c) Should a paralegal's fitness to practice be compromised by physical or mental illness, causing that paralegal to commit an act that is in direct violation of the Model Code/Model Rules and/or the rules and/or laws governing the jurisdiction in which the paralegal practices, that paralegal may be protected from sanction upon review of the nature and circumstances of that illness.

EC-1.3(d) A paralegal shall advise the proper authority of nonconfidential knowledge of any action of another legal professional that clearly demonstrates fraud, deceit, dishonesty, or misrepresentation. The authority to whom the report is made shall depend on the nature and circumstances of the possible misconduct, (ethics committees of law firms, corporations and/or paralegal associations, local or state bar associations, local prosecutors, administrative agencies, etc.). Failure to report such knowledge is in itself misconduct and shall be treated as such under these rules.

EC-1.3(e) A paralegal shall not knowingly assist any individual with the commission of an act that is in direct violation of the Model Code/Model Rules and/or the rules and/or laws governing the jurisdiction in which the paralegal practices.

EC-1.3(f) If a paralegal possesses knowledge of future criminal activity, that knowledge must be reported to the appropriate authority immediately.

1.4 A PARALEGAL SHALL SERVE THE PUBLIC INTEREST BY CONTRIBUTING TO THE IMPROVEMENT OF THE LEGAL SYSTEM AND DELIVERY OF QUALITY LEGAL SERVICES, INCLUDING PRO BONO PUBLICO SERVICES.

Ethical Considerations

EC-1.4(a) A paralegal shall be sensitive to the legal needs of the public and shall promote the development and implementation of programs that address those needs.

FIGURE 2.5 *(continued)*

EC-1.4(b) A paralegal shall support efforts to improve the legal system and access thereto and shall assist in making changes.

EC-1.4(c) A paralegal shall support and participate in the delivery of Pro Bono Publico services directed toward implementing and improving access to justice, the law, the legal system, or the paralegal and legal professions.

EC-1.4(d) A paralegal should aspire annually to contribute twenty-four (24) hours of Pro Bono Publico services under the supervision of an attorney or as authorized by administrative, statutory, or court authority to persons of limited means; or charitable, religious, civic, community, governmental, and educational organizations in matters that are designed primarily to address the legal needs of persons with limited means; or individuals, groups, or organizations seeking to secure or protect civil rights, civil liberties, or public rights.

The twenty-four (24) hours of Pro Bono Publico services contributed annually by a paralegal may consist of such services as detailed in this EC-1.4(d), and/or administrative matters designed to develop and implement the attainment of this aspiration as detailed above in EC-1.4(a) B (c), or any combination of the two.

1.5 A PARALEGAL SHALL PRESERVE ALL CONFIDENTIAL INFORMATION PROVIDED BY THE CLIENT OR ACQUIRED FROM OTHER SOURCES BEFORE, DURING, AND AFTER THE COURSE OF THE PROFESSIONAL RELATIONSHIP.

Ethical Considerations

EC-1.5(a) A paralegal shall be aware of and abide by all legal authority governing confidential information in the jurisdiction in which the paralegal practices.

EC-1.5(b) A paralegal shall not use confidential information to the disadvantage of the client.

EC-1.5(c) A paralegal shall not use confidential information to the advantage of the paralegal or of a third person.

EC-1.5(d) A paralegal may reveal confidential information only after full disclosure and with the client's written consent; or when required by law or court order; or when necessary to prevent the client from committing an act that could result in death or serious bodily harm.

EC-1.5(e) A paralegal shall keep those individuals responsible for the legal representation of a client fully informed of any confidential information the paralegal may have pertaining to that client.

EC-1.5(f) A paralegal shall not engage in any indiscreet communications concerning clients.

1.6 A PARALEGAL SHALL AVOID CONFLICTS OF INTEREST AND SHALL DISCLOSE ANY POSSIBLE CONFLICT TO THE EMPLOYER OR CLIENT, AS WELL AS TO THE PROSPECTIVE EMPLOYERS OR CLIENTS.

Ethical Considerations

EC-1.6(a) A paralegal shall act within the bounds of the law, solely for the benefit of the client, and shall be free of compromising influences and loyalties. Neither the paralegal's personal or business interest, nor those of other clients or third parties, should compromise the paralegal's professional judgment and loyalty to the client.

EC-1.6(b) A paralegal shall avoid conflicts of interest that may arise from previous assignments, whether for a present or past employer or client.

EC-1.6(c) A paralegal shall avoid conflicts of interest that may arise from family relationships and from personal and business interests.

EC-1.6(d) In order to be able to determine whether an actual or potential conflict of interest exists, a paralegal shall create and maintain an effective recordkeeping system that identifies clients, matters, and parties with which the paralegal has worked.

EC-1.6(e) A paralegal shall reveal sufficient nonconfidential information about a client or former client to reasonably ascertain if an actual or potential conflict of interest exists.

EC-1.6(f) A paralegal shall not participate in or conduct work on any matter where a conflict of interest has been identified.

EC-1.6(g) In matters where a conflict of interest has been identified and the client consents to continued representation, a paralegal shall comply fully with the implementation and maintenance of an Ethical Wall.

1.7 A PARALEGAL'S TITLE SHALL BE FULLY DISCLOSED.

Ethical Considerations

EC-1.7(a) A paralegal's title shall clearly indicate the individual's status and shall be disclosed in all business and professional communications to avoid misunderstandings and misconceptions about the paralegal's role and responsibilities.

EC-1.7(b) A paralegal's title shall be included if the paralegal's name appears on business cards, letterhead, brochures, directories, and advertisements.

FIGURE 2.5   (*continued*)

EC-1.7(c) A paralegal shall not use letterhead, business cards, or other promotional materials to create a fraudulent impression of his/her status or ability to practice in the jurisdiction in which the paralegal practices.

EC-1.7(d) A paralegal shall not practice under color of any record, diploma, or certificate that has been illegally or fraudulently obtained or issued or that is misrepresentative in any way.

EC-1.7(e) A paralegal shall not participate in the creation, issuance, or dissemination of fraudulent records, diplomas, or certificates.

1.8 A PARALEGAL SHALL NOT ENGAGE IN THE UNAUTHORIZED PRACTICE OF LAW.

Ethical Considerations

EC-1.8(a) A paralegal shall comply with the applicable legal authority governing the unauthorized practice of law in the jurisdiction in which the paralegal practices.

§2. NFPA GUIDELINES FOR THE ENFORCEMENT OF THE MODEL CODE OF ETHICS AND PROFESSIONAL RESPONSIBILITY

2.1 BASIS FOR DISCIPLINE

2.1(a) Disciplinary investigations and proceedings brought under authority of the Rules shall be conducted in accord with obligations imposed on the paralegal professional by the Model Code of Ethics and Professional Responsibility.

2.2 STRUCTURE OF DISCIPLINARY COMMITTEE

2.2(a) The Disciplinary Committee ("Committee") shall be made up of nine (9) members including the Chair.

2.2(b) Each member of the Committee, including any temporary replacement members, shall have demonstrated working knowledge of ethics/professional responsibility–related issues and activities.

2.2(c) The Committee shall represent a cross-section of practice areas and work experience. The following recommendations are made regarding the members of the Committee:

1) At least one paralegal with one to three years of law-related work experience.
2) At least one paralegal with five to seven years of law-related work experience.
3) At least one paralegal with over ten years of law-related work experience.
4) One paralegal educator with five to seven years of work experience, preferably in the area of ethics/professional responsibility.
5) One paralegal manager.
6) One lawyer with five to seven years of law-related work experience.
7) One lay member.

2.2(d) The Chair of the Committee shall be appointed within thirty (30) days of its members' induction. The Chair shall have no fewer than ten (10) years of law-related work experience.

2.2(e) The terms of all members of the Committee shall be staggered. Of those members initially appointed, a simple majority plus one shall be appointed to a term of one year, and the remaining members shall be appointed to a term of two years. Thereafter, all members of the Committee shall be appointed to terms of two years.

2.2(f) If for any reason the terms of a majority of the Committee will expire at the same time, members may be appointed to terms of one year to maintain continuity of the Committee.

2.2(g) The Committee shall organize from its members a three-tiered structure to investigate, prosecute, and/or adjudicate charges of misconduct. The members shall be rotated among the tiers.

2.3 OPERATION OF COMMITTEE

2.3(a) The Committee shall meet on an as-needed basis to discuss, investigate, and/or adjudicate alleged violations of the Model Code/Model Rules.

2.3(b) A majority of the members of the Committee present at a meeting shall constitute a quorum.

2.3(c) A Recording Secretary shall be designated to maintain complete and accurate minutes of all Committee meetings. All such minutes shall be kept confidential until a decision has been made that the matter will be set for hearing as set forth in Section 6.1 below.

2.3(d) If any member of the Committee has a conflict of interest with the Charging Party, the Responding Party, or the allegations of misconduct, that member shall not take part in any hearing or deliberations concerning those allegations. If the absence of that member creates a lack of a quorum for the Committee, then a temporary replacement for the member shall be appointed.

2.3(e) Either the Charging Party or the Responding Party may request that, for good cause shown, any member of the Committee not participate in a hearing or deliberation. All such requests shall be honored. If the absence of a Committee member under those circumstances creates a lack of a quorum for the Committee, then a temporary replacement for that member shall be appointed.

FIGURE 2.5 (*continued*)

2.3(f) All discussions and correspondence of the Committee shall be kept confidential until a decision has been made that the matter will be set for hearing as set forth in Section 6.1 below.

2.3(g) All correspondence from the Committee to the Responding Party regarding any charge of misconduct and any decisions made regarding the charge shall be mailed by certified mail, return receipt requested, to the Responding Party's last known address and shall be clearly marked with a "Confidential" designation.

2.4 PROCEDURE FOR THE REPORTING OF ALLEGED VIOLATIONS OF THE MODEL CODE/DISCIPLINARY RULES

2.4(a) An individual or entity in possession of nonconfidential knowledge or information concerning possible instances of misconduct shall make a confidential written report to the Committee within thirty (30) days of obtaining same. This report shall include all details of the alleged misconduct.

2.4(b) The Committee so notified shall inform the Responding Party of the allegation(s) of misconduct no later than ten (10) business days after receiving the confidential written report from the Charging Party.

2.4(c) Notification to the Responding Party shall include the identity of the Charging Party unless, for good cause shown, the Charging Party requests anonymity.

2.4(d) The Responding Party shall reply to the allegations within ten (10) business days of notification.

2.5 PROCEDURE FOR THE INVESTIGATION OF A CHARGE OF MISCONDUCT

2.5(a) Upon receipt of a Charge of Misconduct ("Charge"), or on its own initiative, the Committee shall initiate an investigation.

2.5(b) If, upon initial or preliminary review, the Committee makes a determination that the charges are either without basis in fact or, if proven, would not constitute professional misconduct, the Committee shall dismiss the allegations of misconduct. If such determination of dismissal cannot be made, a formal investigation shall be initiated.

2.5(c) Upon the decision to conduct a formal investigation, the Committee shall

1) mail to the Charging and Responding Parties within three (3) business days of that decision notice of the commencement of a formal investigation. That notification shall be in writing and shall contain a complete explanation of all Charge(s), as well as the reasons for a formal investigation, and shall cite the applicable codes and rules;

2) allow the Responding Party thirty (30) days to prepare and submit a confidential response to the Committee, which response shall address each charge specifically and shall be in writing; and

3) upon receipt of the response to the notification, have thirty (30) days to investigate the Charge(s). If an extension of time is deemed necessary, that extension shall not exceed ninety (90) days.

2.5(d) Upon conclusion of the investigation, the Committee may

1) dismiss the Charge upon the finding that it has no basis in fact;

2) dismiss the Charge upon the finding that, if proven, the Charge would not constitute Misconduct;

3) refer the matter for hearing by the Tribunal; or

4) in the case of criminal activity, refer the Charge(s) and all investigation results to the appropriate authority.

2.6 PROCEDURE FOR A MISCONDUCT HEARING BEFORE A TRIBUNAL

2.6(a) Upon the decision by the Committee that a matter should be heard, all parties shall be notified and a hearing date shall be set. The hearing shall take place no more than thirty (30) days from the conclusion of the formal investigation.

2.6(b) The Responding Party shall have the right to counsel. The parties and the Tribunal shall have the right to call any witnesses and introduce any documentation that they believe will lead to the fair and reasonable resolution of the matter.

2.6(c) Upon completion of the hearing, the Tribunal shall deliberate and present a written decision to the parties in accordance with procedures as set forth by the Tribunal.

2.6(d) Notice of the decision of the Tribunal shall be appropriately published.

2.7 SANCTIONS

2.7(a) Upon a finding of the Tribunal that misconduct has occurred, any of the following sanctions, or others as may be deemed appropriate, may be imposed upon the Responding Party, either singularly or in combination:

1) letter of reprimand to the Responding Party; counseling;

2) attendance at an ethics course approved by the Tribunal; probation;

3) suspension of license/authority to practice; revocation of license/authority to practice;

4) imposition of a fine; assessment of costs; or

5) in the instance of criminal activity, referral to the appropriate authority.

FIGURE 2.5   *(concluded)*

2.7(b) Upon the expiration of any period of probation, suspension, or revocation, the Responding Party may make application for reinstatement. With the application for reinstatement, the Responding Party must show proof of having complied with all aspects of the sanctions imposed by the Tribunal.

2.8 APPELLATE PROCEDURES

2.8(a) The parties shall have the right to appeal the decision of the Tribunal in accordance with the procedure as set forth by the Tribunal.

paralegals exists, then a paralegal shall follow the attorney's code of ethics as it applies to paralegals within that state.

6. *A paralegal shall maintain personal and professional integrity.*
7. *A paralegal shall attain a high degree of competency through education, training, and experience.*
8. *A paralegal shall maintain a high degree of competency by engaging in continuing paralegal education on an annual basis.*[63]

NALS

NALS also holds dear the need for standards and ethical rules. All NALS members are exhorted and urged to

- Encourage respect for the law and the administration of justice.
- Observe rules governing privileged communications and confidential information.
- Promote and exemplify high standards of loyalty, cooperation, and courtesy.
- Perform all duties of the profession with integrity and competence.
- Pursue a high order of professional attainment.

Integrity and high standards of conduct are seen as fundamental to the success of this professional association. This code is promulgated by NALS and accepted by its members to accomplish these ends. Figure 2.6 provides the NALS Code of Ethics.

FIGURE 2.6   **NALS Code of Ethics**

Source: Reprinted with permission.

Canon 1.	Members of this association shall maintain a high degree of competency and integrity through continuing education to better assist the legal profession in fulfilling its duty to provide quality legal services to the public.
Canon 2.	Members of this association shall maintain a high standard of ethical conduct and shall contribute to the integrity of the association and the legal profession.
Canon 3.	Members of this association shall avoid a conflict of interest pertaining to a client matter.
Canon 4.	Members of this association shall preserve and protect the confidences and privileged communications of a client.
Canon 5.	Members of this association shall exercise care in using independent professional judgment and in determining the extent to which a client may be assisted without the presence of a lawyer and shall not act in matters involving professional legal judgment.
Canon 6.	Members of this association shall not solicit legal business on behalf of a lawyer.
Canon 7.	Members of this association, unless permitted by law, shall not perform paralegal functions except under the direct supervision of a lawyer and shall not advertise or contract with members of the general public for the performance of paralegal functions.
Canon 8.	Members of this association, unless permitted by law, shall not perform any of the duties restricted to lawyers or do things that lawyers themselves may not do and shall assist in preventing the unauthorized practice of law.
Canon 9.	Members of this association not licensed to practice law shall not engage in the practice of law as defined by statutes or court decisions.
Canon 10.	Members of this association shall do all other things incidental, necessary, or expedient to enhance professional responsibility and participation in the administration of justice and public service in cooperation with the legal profession.

American Bar Association

The American Bar Association, recognizing the staggering growth of paralegals in both number and occupational responsibilities, has promulgated Model Guidelines for the Utilization of Paralegal Services.[64]

American Association for Paralegal Education

Although the American Association for Paralegal Education (AAfPE) has no explicit ethical guidelines in place, its sole purpose is to advance the profession through higher levels of education. Education is a common way to assure some level of critical inquiry in the employee. Instead of merely performance of function, the educated person has a wider and larger understanding of context and situation. Education serves the profession in not only content-based subject matter but also the means and methods of delivery of service. The AAfPE publishes criteria for college and university programs, and its member base is on the cutting edge of field and practice issues. Its statement on educational quality says much for the organization.[65] See Figure 2.7.

FIGURE 2.7   AAfPE Statement on Academic Quality

Source: Reprinted with the permission of the American Association for Paralegal Education (AAfPE).

Preamble

Paralegal education is a unique academic curriculum, composed of both substantive legal knowledge and professional skills that incorporate legal theory with an understanding of practical applications. This intellectually demanding course of study is derived from the responsibilities of paralegals as legal professionals. It is the philosophy of this organization that a person is qualified as a paralegal with (1) an associate or baccalaureate degree or equivalent coursework; and (2) a credential in paralegal education completed in any of the following types of educational programs: associate degree, baccalaureate degree (major, minor, or concentration), certificate, or master's degree. AAFPE recognizes these essential components of quality paralegal education programs:

Curriculum Development

Quality paralegal education programs monitor the responsibilities and competencies expected by employers on an ongoing basis. They regularly incorporate this information into a well-designed curriculum with a logical sequence of courses that emphasizes interactive learning (student to student and faculty to student) and assignments that teach practical job-related paralegal skills in conjunction with underlying theory.

Facilities

Quality paralegal education programs have a physical learning environment that provides (1) access to legal research library facilities that include computer-based resources; (2) classrooms that provide opportunities for interaction among students and between students and the instructor and include the necessary equipment and technology to facilitate learning; (3) a convenient physical location for administration/support staff and the provision of student services; and (4) accessibility pursuant to the Americans with Disabilities Act (ADA) requirements.

Faculty

The faculty of quality paralegal education programs consists of legal professionals and, where appropriate, other similarly qualified persons in good standing in their profession who (1) possess expertise and experience in their subject area; (2) have background working as or with paralegals; (3) can demonstrate teaching ability; (4) hold a graduate degree or possess exceptional expertise in the legal subject to be taught; and (5) are committed to the role of paralegals in the delivery of legal services. Evaluation is conducted on a frequent and regular basis to ensure that quality instruction is maintained and enhanced. Quality programs strive to achieve diversity in the composition of faculty.

Marketing and Promotion

Quality paralegal education programs advertise in an ethical manner and in full compliance with all applicable laws and regulations. All representations in the following areas are factual as well as current and can be substantiated: (1) the job market, employment opportunity, compensation, and placement; (2) the knowledge and skills necessary to meet entry-level paralegal job qualifications; and (3) the transferability of coursework to other educational institutions. Quality programs strive to achieve diversity in the composition of their student body.

Paralegal Instruction

Quality paralegal education programs maintain standards of excellence and include, either as separate classes or with the overall course of study, the following topics: ethics, substantive and procedural law, the American

FIGURE 2.7 (*concluded*)

legal system, delivery of legal services, law offices and related environments, the paralegal profession, legal research and writing, law-related computer skills, legal interviewing and investigation, and areas of legal practice such as those described in AAFPE's Core Competencies for Paralegal Programs; such programs offer an experiential learning component, such as internship, practicum, or clinical experience. Program director quality paralegal education programs provide adequate release time, funding for professional development opportunities, and administrative support for the program director to develop, monitor, and accomplish the goals and objectives of the program, as well as assess the program's effectiveness in achieving these goals and objectives. The director is primarily responsible for the paralegal program. A program director is a legal professional or other similarly qualified person appropriately credentialed and in good standing in his or her profession, with knowledge, involvement, and understanding of the paralegal profession and paralegal education.

Related Competencies

Quality paralegal education programs assist their students in acquiring these essential related competencies, primarily in general education: (1) critical thinking skills (analysis, judgment, research, and problem solving); (2) communication skills (oral, written, nonverbal, and interpersonal); (3) computer skills; (4) computational skills; (5) understanding of ethics; and (6) organizational skills. Graduates also possess a basic understanding of American history, business, and political systems.

Student Services

Quality paralegal education programs offer student services that include (1) academic counseling, (2) career information and placement assistance, and (3) information and/or opportunities for participation in such activities as honor societies, pro bono activities, professional and paralegal associations, and continuing legal education.

The Paralegal Definition as amended now reads as follows:

Paralegals perform substantive and procedural legal work as authorized by law, which work, in the absence of the paralegal, would be performed by an attorney. Paralegals have knowledge of the law gained through education, or education and work experience, which qualifies them to perform legal work. Paralegals adhere to recognized ethical standards and rules of professional responsibility.

LAWYERS, ETHICS, AND PARALEGAL PRACTICE

How lawyers are regulated directly impacts paralegal practice. States regulate the practice of law by exercising their police power and the enforcement authority of the judiciary and disciplinary boards. From the outset of a legal career, admission to the practice of law is governed by state guidelines. State bar associations work cooperatively with these bodies to create entrance and testing requirements.[66] Disciplinary commissions, bars, and boards are empowered to make decisions about lawyer conduct.

States and localities are not obliged to adopt any specific form of rules but have previously relied heavily on the promulgations of the American Bar Association. Although membership in the ABA is voluntary, its policy making and procedures relative to ethical conduct and standards are quite influential. The ABA has drafted a series of professional guidelines relative to the professional conduct of lawyers and judges:

- The ABA Code of Judicial Conduct.
- The ABA Model Code of Professional Responsibility.
- The ABA Model Rules of Professional Conduct.

Although not legally binding, these codes informally bind the profession due to custom and lack of any serious alternative. In a sense, these rules have garnered the force of law simply by their long-standing adoption. States may or may not adopt all of these codes, but for the most part states emulate the content in their own rules. The *Model Code of Professional Responsibility* was adopted by the American Bar Association in 1969. However, a mixture of internal as well as external pressures from the profession called for a reexamination of those rules. By 1977 the ABA used "a committee of distinguished members of the profession . . . appointed to either revise it [the rules] or start afresh. The committee chose to start afresh, and it ultimately produced the ABA *Model Rules of Professional Conduct,* a document designed to replace the ABA Code and to become a new model for the individual states to follow."[67]

By the early 1980s most states had adopted either a portion or all of the newly revised *Model Rules*. There are some stylistic differences between the *Code of Professional Responsibility* and the *Model Rules*. In the ABA *Code of Professional Responsibility,* a series of canons with illustrative ethical considerations and disciplinary rules are published.

In general, the terms of the canon propose that the lawyer is responsible and must act in accordance with certain ethical considerations (commonly referred to as ECs). In the Disciplinary Rules section, a lawyer is advised that he will be subject to specific discipline for failure to perform a specific act or for a commission or omission of conduct or acts. Footnoting, commentary, and case law analysis are provided at the end of each section.[68]

Under the *Model Rules of Professional Conduct* adopted by the American Bar Association on August 2, 1983, the EC/DR format is eliminated. In its place are enumerated Rules.

Regardless of format, both the *Model Rules* and the *Code of Professional Responsibility* address the essential issues of ethical performance. Although created expressly for lawyers and judges, the rules naturally subsume and sweep up aligned occupations like that of the paralegal. Paralegals, just like lawyers, should be concerned about these issues:

- The definition of competence.
- The design and structure of fees.
- The nature of a meritorious claim.
- The use of delay.
- The requirements of candor.
- The description of what is the unauthorized practice of law.
- The assurance of the expectation of honesty and integrity within the profession.

The more pertinent provisions of the Model Rules relating to paralegals follow.

The Unauthorized Practice of Law

Lawyers may delegate many tasks and duties in a law firm, particularly to paralegals. See Figure 2.8 for Rule 5.5, which discusses the unauthorized and multijurisdictional practice of law. Other nonlawyer personnel who help lawyers in their practice of law include bookkeepers, accountants, secretarial personnel, and expert consultants. The employment of nonlawyers is unreservedly accepted, although the ultimate responsibility rests with the attorney. In a 1967 opinion the ABA noted,

> *A lawyer can employ lay secretaries, lay investigators, lay detectives, lay researchers, accountants, lay scriveners, nonlawyer draftsmen, or nonlawyer researchers. In fact, he may employ nonlawyers to do any task for him except counsel clients about law matters, engage directly in the practice of law, or appear in formal proceedings as part of the judicial process, so long as it is he who takes the work and vouches for it to the client and becomes responsible to the client.[69]*

With the enhanced use of paralegals in the law firm, this well-defined rule of professional conduct becomes even more critical. The ABA specifically enunciates that

> *Paragraph (b) does not prohibit a lawyer from employing the services of paraprofessionals and delegating functions to them, so long as the lawyer supervises the delegated work and retains responsibility for their work.[70]*

The line between performing paralegal tasks and duties and the actual practice of law can sometimes blur.[71]

Both the *Code of Professional Responsibility* and the *Model Rules* envision reasonable delegation. In the *New Jersey Code of Professional Responsibility,* which emulates ABA principles, specific guidelines on the use of legal assistants are delivered:

> *A legal assistant may perform any function delegated by an attorney, including but not limited to the following:*
>
> *1. Conduct client interviews and maintain general contact with the client after the establishment of an attorney–client relationship, so long as the client is aware of the status and function of the legal assistant and the client contact is under supervision by the attorney.*
>
> *2. Locate and interview witnesses, so long as the witnesses are aware of the status and function of the legal assistant.*

FIGURE 2.8   ABA Model Rules of Professional Conduct, Rule 5.5

Source: ABA *Model Rules of Professional Conduct,* 2006 Edition. © 2006 by the American Bar Association. Reprinted with permission. Copies of ABA *Model Rules of Professional Conduct,* 2006 Edition are available from Service Center, American Bar Association, 321 North Clark Street, Chicago, IL 60610, 1-800-285-2221.

Rule 5.5 Unauthorized Practice of Law; Multijurisdictional Practice of Law

(a) A lawyer shall not practice law in a jurisdiction in violation of the regulation of the legal profession in that jurisdiction, or assist another in doing so.

(b) A lawyer who is not admitted to practice in this jurisdiction shall not:

   (1) except as authorized by these Rules or other law, establish an office or other systematic and continuous presence in this jurisdiction for the practice of law; or

   (2) hold out to the public or otherwise represent that the lawyer is admitted to practice law in this jurisdiction.

(c) A lawyer admitted in another United States jurisdiction, and not disbarred or suspended from practice in any jurisdiction, may provide legal services on a temporary basis in this jurisdiction that:

   (1) are undertaken in association with a lawyer who is admitted to practice in this jurisdiction and who actively participates in the matter;

   (2) are in or reasonably related to a pending or potential proceeding before a tribunal in this or another jurisdiction, if the lawyer, or a person the lawyer is assisting, is authorized by law or order to appear in such proceeding or reasonably expects to be so authorized;

   (3) are in or reasonably related to a pending or potential arbitration, mediation, or other alternative dispute resolution proceeding in this or another jurisdiction, if the services arise out of or are reasonably related to the lawyer's practice in a jurisdiction in which the lawyer is admitted to practice and are not services for which the forum requires pro hac vice admission; or

   (4) are not within paragraphs (c)(2) or (c)(3) and arise out of or are reasonably related to the lawyer's practice in a jurisdiction in which the lawyer is admitted to practice.

(d) A lawyer admitted in another United States jurisdiction, and not disbarred or suspended from practice in any jurisdiction, may provide legal services in this jurisdiction that:

   (1) are provided to the lawyer's employer or its organizational affiliates and are not services for which the forum requires pro hac vice admission; or

   (2) are services that the lawyer is authorized to provide by federal law or other law of this jurisdiction.

COMMENT

(1) A lawyer may practice law only in a jurisdiction in which the lawyer is authorized to practice. A lawyer may be admitted to practice law in a jurisdiction on a regular basis or may be authorized by court rule or order or by law to practice for a limited purpose or on a restricted basis. Paragraph (a) applies to unauthorized practice of law by a lawyer, whether through the lawyer's direct action or by the lawyer assisting another person.

(2) The definition of the practice of law is established by law and varies from one jurisdiction to another. Whatever the definition, limiting the practice of law to members of the bar protects the public against rendition of legal services by unqualified persons. This Rule does not prohibit a lawyer from employing the services of paraprofessionals and delegating functions to them, so long as the lawyer supervises the delegated work and retains responsibility for their work. See Rule 5.3.

(3) A lawyer may provide professional advice and instruction to nonlawyers whose employment requires knowledge of the law; for example, claims adjusters, employees of financial or commercial institutions, social workers, accountants and persons employed in government agencies. Lawyers also may assist independent nonlawyers, such as paraprofessionals, who are authorized by the law of a jurisdiction to provide particular law-related services. In addition, a lawyer may counsel nonlawyers who wish to proceed pro se.

(4) Other than as authorized by law or this Rule, a lawyer who is not admitted to practice generally in this jurisdiction violates paragraph (b) if the lawyer establishes an office or other systematic and continuous presence in this jurisdiction for the practice of law. Presence may be systematic and continuous even if the lawyer is not physically present here. Such a lawyer must not hold out to the public or otherwise represent that the lawyer is admitted to practice law in this jurisdiction. See also Rules 7.1(a) and 7.5(b).

(5) There are occasions in which a lawyer admitted to practice in another United States jurisdiction, and not disbarred or suspended from practice in any jurisdiction, may provide legal services on a temporary basis in this jurisdiction under circumstances that do not create an unreasonable risk to the interests of their clients, the public or the courts. Paragraph (c) identifies four such circumstances. The fact that conduct is not so identified does not imply that the conduct is or is not authorized. With the exception of paragraphs (d)(1) and (d)(2), this Rule does not authorize a lawyer to establish an office or other systematic and continuous presence in this jurisdiction without being admitted to practice generally here.

FIGURE 2.8 (*continued*)

(6) There is no single test to determine whether a lawyer's services are provided on a "temporary basis" in this jurisdiction, and may therefore be permissible under paragraph (c). Services may be "temporary" even though the lawyer provides services in this jurisdiction on a recurring basis, or for an extended period of time, as when the lawyer is representing a client in a single lengthy negotiation or litigation.

(7) Paragraphs (c) and (d) apply to lawyers who are admitted to practice law in any United States jurisdiction, which includes the District of Columbia and any state, territory or commonwealth of the United States. The word "admitted" in paragraph (c) contemplates that the lawyer is authorized to practice in the jurisdiction in which the lawyer is admitted and excludes a lawyer who while technically admitted is not authorized to practice, because, for example, the lawyer is on inactive status.

(8) Paragraph (c)(1) recognizes that the interests of clients and the public are protected if a lawyer admitted only in another jurisdiction associates with a lawyer licensed to practice in this jurisdiction. For this paragraph to apply, however, the lawyer admitted to practice in this jurisdiction must actively participate in and share responsibility for the representation of the client.

(9) Lawyers not admitted to practice generally in a jurisdiction may be authorized by law or order of a tribunal or an administrative agency to appear before the tribunal or agency. This authority may be granted pursuant to formal rules governing admission pro hac vice or pursuant to informal practice of the tribunal or agency. Under paragraph (c)(2), a lawyer does not violate this Rule when the lawyer appears before a tribunal or agency pursuant to such authority. To the extent that a court rule or other law of this jurisdiction requires a lawyer who is not admitted to practice in this jurisdiction to obtain admission pro hac vice before appearing before a tribunal or administrative agency, this Rule requires the lawyer to obtain that authority.

(10) Paragraph (c)(2) also provides that a lawyer rendering services in this jurisdiction on a temporary basis does not violate this Rule when the lawyer engages in conduct in anticipation of a proceeding or hearing in a jurisdiction in which the lawyer is authorized to practice law or in which the lawyer reasonably expects to be admitted pro hac vice. Examples of such conduct include meetings with the client, interviews of potential witnesses, and the review of documents. Similarly, a lawyer admitted only in another jurisdiction may engage in conduct temporarily in this jurisdiction in connection with pending litigation in another jurisdiction in which the lawyer is or reasonably expects to be authorized to appear, including taking depositions in this jurisdiction.

(11) When a lawyer has been or reasonably expects to be admitted to appear before a court or administrative agency, paragraph (c)(2) also permits conduct by lawyers who are associated with that lawyer in the matter, but who do not expect to appear before the court or administrative agency. For example, subordinate lawyers may conduct research, review documents, and attend meetings with witnesses in support of the lawyer responsible for the litigation.

(12) Paragraph (c)(3) permits a lawyer admitted to practice law in another jurisdiction to perform services on a temporary basis in this jurisdiction if those services are in or reasonably related to a pending or potential arbitration, mediation, or other alternative dispute resolution proceeding in this or another jurisdiction, if the services arise out of or are reasonably related to the lawyer's practice in a jurisdiction in which the lawyer is admitted to practice. The lawyer, however, must obtain admission pro hac vice in the case of a court-annexed arbitration or mediation or otherwise if court rules or law so require.

(13) Paragraph (c)(4) permits a lawyer admitted in another jurisdiction to provide certain legal services on a temporary basis in this jurisdiction that arise out of or are reasonably related to the lawyer's practice in a jurisdiction in which the lawyer is admitted but are not within paragraphs (c)(2) or (c)(3). These services include both legal services and services that nonlawyers may perform but that are considered the practice of law when performed by lawyers.

(14) Paragraphs (c)(3) and (c)(4) require that the services arise out of or be reasonably related to the lawyer's practice in a jurisdiction in which the lawyer is admitted. A variety of factors evidence such a relationship. The lawyer's client may have been previously represented by the lawyer, or may be resident in or have substantial contacts with the jurisdiction in which the lawyer is admitted. The matter, although involving other jurisdictions, may have a significant connection with that jurisdiction. In other cases, significant aspects of the lawyer's work might be conducted in that jurisdiction or a significant aspect of the matter may involve the law of that jurisdiction. The necessary relationship might arise when the client's activities or the legal issues involve multiple jurisdictions, such as when the officers of a multinational corporation survey potential business sites and seek the services of their lawyer in assessing the relative merits of each. In addition, the services may draw on the lawyer's recognized expertise developed through the regular practice of law on behalf of clients in matters involving a particular body of federal, nationally-uniform, foreign, or international law.

FIGURE 2.8   *(concluded)*

(15) Paragraph (d) identifies two circumstances in which a lawyer who is admitted to practice in another United States jurisdiction, and is not disbarred or suspended from practice in any jurisdiction, may establish an office or other systematic and continuous presence in this jurisdiction for the practice of law as well as provide legal services on a temporary basis. Except as provided in paragraphs (d)(1) and (d)(2), a lawyer who is admitted to practice law in another jurisdiction and who establishes an office or other systematic or continuous presence in this jurisdiction must become admitted to practice law generally in this jurisdiction.

(16) Paragraph (d)(1) applies to a lawyer who is employed by a client to provide legal services to the client or its organizational affiliates, i.e., entities that control, are controlled by, or are under common control with the employer. This paragraph does not authorize the provision of personal legal services to the employer's officers or employees. The paragraph applies to in-house corporate lawyers, government lawyers and others who are employed to render legal services to the employer. The lawyer's ability to represent the employer outside the jurisdiction in which the lawyer is licensed generally serves the interests of the employer and does not create an unreasonable risk to the client and others because the employer is well situated to assess the lawyer's qualifications and the quality of the lawyer's work.

(17) If an employed lawyer establishes an office or other systematic presence in this jurisdiction for the purpose of rendering legal services to the employer, the lawyer may be subject to registration or other requirements, including assessments for client protection funds and mandatory continuing legal education.

(18) Paragraph (d)(2) recognizes that a lawyer may provide legal services in a jurisdiction in which the lawyer is not licensed when authorized to do so by federal or other law, which includes statute, court rule, executive regulation or judicial precedent.

(19) A lawyer who practices law in this jurisdiction pursuant to paragraphs (c) or (d) or otherwise is subject to the disciplinary authority of this jurisdiction. See Rule 8.5(a).

(20) In some circumstances, a lawyer who practices law in this jurisdiction pursuant to paragraphs (c) or (d) may have to inform the client that the lawyer is not licensed to practice law in this jurisdiction. For example, that may be required when the representation occurs primarily in this jurisdiction and requires knowledge of the law of this jurisdiction. See Rule 1.4(b).

(21) Paragraphs (c) and (d) do not authorize communications advertising legal services to prospective clients in this jurisdiction by lawyers who are admitted to practice in other jurisdictions. Whether and how lawyers may communicate the availability of their services to prospective clients in this jurisdiction is governed by Rules 7.1 to 7.5.

3. *Conduct investigations and statistical documentary research for review by the attorney.*

4. *Conduct legal research for review by the attorney.*

5. *Draft legal documents for review by the attorney.*

6. *Draft correspondence and pleadings for review by and signature of the attorney.*

7. *Summarize depositions and interrogatories and testimony for review by the attorney.*

8. *Attend execution of wills, real estate closings, depositions, and court or administrative hearings and trials with the attorney.*

9. *Author and sign letters, provided the legal assistant's status is clearly indicated and correspondence does not contain independent legal opinions or legal advice.*[72]

Unquestionably, each day paralegals perform tasks that a lawyer regularly may undertake. Using skills in legal analysis, and more particular competencies in practice areas, paralegals run close to lawyering daily.[73] As for the tactics of advocacy, the lawyer remains primarily responsible, though paraprofessional representation appears to be on the upswing.[74]

In bankruptcy, paralegals can now represent debtors; in Social Security claims, the paralegal may advise and represent the claimant; and in real estate, some states now permit paralegal oversight of the closing and settlement. There is certainly a remarkable push for relaxation of traditional advocacy rules when it comes to delivery of legal services to the poor and other pro bono work.[75]

As paralegals expand their occupational persona, the issue of what "unauthorized practice of law" actually consists of gets more difficult to resolve. In sum, paralegals deliver services with extraordinary efficiency, and as a result are being looked to in matters involving law and lower-income and poor individuals.[76]

The California Bar has confronted these definitional problems relating to the nature of unauthorized practice. The California Committee on Unauthorized Practice concluded,

> *"[U]nauthorized practice of law" is a concept no longer capable of definition or enforcement. Moreover, specifically with respect to legal technicians, we believe it would be unwise for the State Bar to undertake, under the guide of unauthorized practice, the policing of activities that, if injurious to the public, are essentially consumer fraud.*
>
> *We recommend that the State Bar actively support legislation that (1) makes it unlawful for a person who is not an active member of the State Bar to claim to be a lawyer, (2) requires the registration of legal technicians, (3) requires legal technicians to disclose that they are not lawyers, and (4) renders legal technicians liable, both civilly and criminally, for misfeasance and nonfeasance.*[77]

In 2004 the state of California went even further by listing what a paralegal cannot undertake.

Business & Professions Code

§6450. *Paralegals—Definition; Scope and Limitations of Lawful Activities; Qualifications; Certification*

a. *"Paralegal" means a person who holds himself or herself out to be a paralegal, who is qualified by education, training, or work experience, who either contracts with or is employed by an attorney, law firm, corporation, governmental agency, or other entity, and who performs substantial legal work under the direction and supervision of an active member of the State Bar of California, as defined in Section 6060, or an attorney practicing law in the federal courts of this state, that has been specifically delegated by the attorney to him or her. Tasks performed by a paralegal include, but are not limited to, case planning, development, and management; legal research; interviewing clients; fact gathering and retrieving information; drafting and analyzing legal documents; collecting, compiling, and utilizing technical information to make an independent decision and recommendation to the supervising attorney; and representing clients before a state or federal administrative agency if that representation is permitted by statute, court rule, or administrative rule or regulation.*

b. *Notwithstanding subdivision (a), a paralegal shall not do the following:*
   1. *Provide legal advice.*
   2. *Represent a client in court.*
   3. *Select, explain, draft, or recommend the use of any legal document to or for any person other than the attorney who directs and supervises the paralegal.*
   4. *Act as a runner or capper, as defined in Sections 6151 and 6152.*
   5. *Engage in conduct that constitutes the unlawful practice of law.*
   6. *Contract with, or be employed by, a natural person other than an attorney to perform paralegal services.*
   7. *In connection with providing paralegal services, induce a person to make an investment, purchase a financial product or service, or enter a transaction from which income or profit, or both, purportedly may be derived.*
   8. *Establish the fees to charge a client for the services the paralegal performs, which shall be established by the attorney who supervises the paralegal's work. This paragraph does not apply to fees charged by a paralegal in a contract to provide paralegal services to an attorney, law firm, corporation, governmental agency, or other entity as provided in subdivision (a).*

c. *A paralegal shall possess at least one of the following:*
   1. *A certificate of completion of a paralegal program approved by the American Bar Association.*
   2. *A certificate of completion of a paralegal program at, or a degree from, a postsecondary institution that requires the successful completion of a minimum of 24 semester, or equivalent, units in law-related courses and that has been accredited by a national or regional accrediting organization or approved by the Bureau for Private Postsecondary and Vocational Education.*
   3. *A baccalaureate degree or an advanced degree in any subject, a minimum of one year of law-related experience under the supervision of an attorney who has been an active member of the State Bar of California for at least the preceding three years or who has practiced in the federal courts of this state for at least the preceding three years, and a written declaration from this attorney stating that the person is qualified to perform paralegal tasks.*
   4. *A high school diploma or general equivalency diploma, a minimum of three years of law-related experience under the supervision of an attorney who has been an active member of the State Bar of California for at least the preceding three years or who*

has practiced in the federal courts of this state for at least the preceding three years, and a written declaration from this attorney stating that the person is qualified to perform paralegal tasks. This experience and training shall be completed no later than December 31, 2003.

d.   *All paralegals shall be required to certify completion every three years of four hours of mandatory continuing legal education in legal ethics. All continuing legal education courses shall meet the requirements of Section 6070. Every two years, all paralegals shall be required to certify completion of four hours of mandatory continuing education in either general law or in a specialized area of law. Certification of these continuing education requirements shall be made with the paralegal's supervising attorney. The paralegal shall be responsible for keeping a record of the paralegal's certifications.*

e.   *A paralegal does not include a nonlawyer who provides legal services directly to members of the public, or a legal document assistant or unlawful detainer assistant as defined in Section 6400, unless the person is a person described in subdivision (a).*

f.   *This section shall become operative on January 1, 2004. (Added by Stats. 2000, ch. 439. Amended by Stats. 2001, ch. 311; Stats. 2002, ch. 664.)*[78]

The act also lays out express educational requirements for the paralegal profession—a finding that has received generous praise from many sectors of the paralegal community.

Although the usage of legal assistants in limited advocacy programs is clearly on the upswing, paralegals have no license to practice law.[79] The rules still set a definable standard. Deborah Orlik's *Ethics for the Legal Assistant* cogently remarks,

> *The activities which constitute the arcane "unauthorized practice of law" are subject to the interpretation of each state. Unfortunately, therefore, there does not seem to be a standard by which the paralegal profession can be guided. Most states provide no definition; others, on a case-by-case basis, have laid the foundation for some common themes. The most predominant of these themes are:*
>
> *(1) representation of others in court proceedings;*
>
> *(2) preparation of legal documents; and*
>
> *(3) giving legal advice.*[80]

The NFPA has catalogued the clear trend regarding paralegal representation and the slow erosion of the traditional definition of unauthorized practice. In a word, it is difficult to see how the paralegal role and function will not continue to increase; and the understanding of what constitutes unauthorized practice of law continues to change. NFPA lists agencies that permit paralegal representation at the state and federal level. See Chapter 1 for a partial list, or visit the NFPA's Web site for a complete list.[81]

Resolving unauthorized practice cases is tougher than it seems. Debra Levy Martinelli sums it up well: "Sometimes it's black. Other times, it's white. But most of the time, it's a murky, muddy gray."[82]

Case-by-case determinations are possible only after an evaluation of these factors:

1. The activity is one "traditionally" practiced by lawyers.[83]

2. The activity is one "commonly understood" to involve the practice of law.[84]

3. The activity requires legal skill or knowledge beyond that of a layperson.[85]

4. The activity is characterized by the personal relationship between attorney and client.[86]

5. The activity is such that the public interest is best served by limited performance to those who are attorneys.[87]

6. To the contrary, the activity is "incidental to transactions caused by nonattorneys.[88],[89]

The ABA's *Model Guidelines for the Utilization of Paralegal Services* address the delegation question in Guideline 3 (see Figure 2.9).

The mantle of supervision implies many things. First, the lawyer should understand his or her responsibility to control the behavior of subordinates. And second, the paralegal should understand the nature of the delegation and seeks to honor its scope. Figure 2.10 presents Rule 5.4, which outlines the professional independence of a lawyer. Paralegals and lawyers can get in all sorts of trouble under this rule.

FIGURE 2.9 ABA Model Guidelines for the Utilization of Paralegal Services, Guideline 3

Source: Excerpted from the *ABA Model Guidelines for the Utilization of Paralegal Services,* 2004, published by the American Bar Association Division for Legal Services. © 2004 by the American Bar Association. Reprinted with permission.

Guideline 3: A lawyer may not delegate to a paralegal

(a) Responsibility for establishing an attorney–client relationship.

(b) Responsibility for establishing the amount of a fee to be charged for a legal service.

(c) Responsibility for a legal opinion rendered to a client.

Comment to Guideline 3

Model Rule 1.4 and most state codes require lawyers to communicate directly with their clients and to provide their clients information reasonably necessary to make informed decisions and to effectively participate in the representation. While delegation of legal tasks to nonlawyers may benefit clients by enabling their lawyers to render legal services more economically and efficiently, Model Rule 1.4 and Ethical Consideration 3-6 under the Model Code emphasize that delegation is proper only if the lawyer "maintains a direct relationship with his client, supervises the delegated work, and has complete professional responsibility for the work product." The National Association of Legal Assistants ("NALA"), Code of Ethics and Professional Responsibility, Canon 2, echoes the Model Rule when it states, "A legal assistant may perform any task which is properly delegated and supervised by an attorney as long as the attorney is ultimately responsible to the client, maintains a direct relationship with the client, and assumes professional responsibility for the work product." Most state guidelines also stress the paramount importance of a direct attorney–client relationship. *See* Ohio EC 3-6 and New Mexico Rule 20-106. The direct personal relationship between client and lawyer is critical to the exercise of the lawyer's trained professional judgment.

Fundamental to the lawyer–client relationship is the lawyer's agreement to undertake representation and the related fee arrangement. The Model Rules and most states require lawyers to make fee arrangements with their clients and to clearly communicate with their clients concerning the scope of the representation and the basis for the fees for which the client will be responsible. Model Rule 1.5 and Comments. Many state guidelines prohibit paralegals from "setting fees" or "accepting cases." *See, e.g.,* Pennsylvania Eth. Op. 98-75, 1994 Utah Eth. OP. 139. NALA Canon 3 states that a paralegal must not establish attorney–client relationships or set fees.

EC 3-5 states, "[T]he essence of the professional judgment of the lawyer is his educated ability to relate the general body and philosophy of law to a specific legal problem of a client; and thus, the public interest will be better served if only lawyers are permitted to act in matters involving professional judgment." Clients are entitled to their lawyers' professional judgment and opinion. Paralegals may, however, be authorized to communicate a lawyer's legal advice to a client so long as they do not interpret or expand on that advice. Typically, state guidelines phrase this prohibition in terms of paralegals being forbidden from "giving legal advice" or "counseling clients about legal matters." *See e.g.,* New Hampshire Rule 35, Sub-Rule 1, Kentucky SCR 3.700, Sub-Rule 2. NALA Canon 3 states that a paralegal must not give legal opinions or advice. Some states have more expansive wording that prohibits paralegals from engaging in any activity that would require the exercise of independent legal judgment. *See, e.g.,* New Mexico Rule 20-103. Nevertheless, it is clear that all states and the Model Rules encourage direct communication between clients and a paralegal insofar as the paralegal is performing a task properly delegated by a lawyer. It should be noted that a lawyer who permits a paralegal to assist in establishing the attorney–client relationship, in communicating the lawyer's fee, or in preparing the lawyer's legal opinion is not delegating responsibility for those matters and, therefore, is not in violation of this guideline.

Assume a lawyer continually orders a paralegal to do any of the following functions:

1. Lie to a client about the whereabouts of a child in a visitation or custody problem.
2. Forge checks or documents in the settlement of a personal injury case.
3. Make affirmations to a client regarding the research of a given subject when in fact that research never took place.
4. Pad bills to reflect more time expended than is realistically possible.

Can a paralegal willingly accept these instructions and carry them out? Can the paralegal retort that "I was simply following orders"? Despite their reliance on attorney supervision, paralegals remain free agents making free choices. Although ABA principles may not expressly mention paralegals in this context, paralegals have a moral as well as a legal obligation in the performance of task. Paralegals who hitch their horses to corrupt lawyers will surely garner the same culpability as the lawyer. The sins of the lawyer will be imputed to the paralegal. And while the

FIGURE 2.10   ABA Model Rules of Professional Conduct, Rule 5.4

Source: ABA *Model Rules of Professional Conduct*, 2006 Edition. © 2006 by the American Bar Association. Reprinted with permission. Copies of ABA Model Rules of Professional Conduct, 2006 Edition are available from Service Center, American Bar Association, 321 North Clark Street, Chicago, IL 60610, 1-800-285-2221.

Rule 5.4 Professional Independence of a Lawyer

(a) A lawyer or law firm shall not share legal fees with a nonlawyer, except that:

  (1) an agreement by a lawyer with the lawyer's firm, partner, or associate may provide for the payment of money, over a reasonable period of time after the lawyer's death, to the lawyer's estate or to one or more specified persons;

  (2) a lawyer who purchases the practice of a deceased, disabled, or disappeared lawyer may, pursuant to the provisions of Rule 1.17, pay to the estate or other representative of that lawyer the agreed-upon purchase price;

  (3) a lawyer or law firm may include nonlawyer employees in a compensation or retirement plan, even though the plan is based in whole or in part on a profit-sharing arrangement; and

  (4) a lawyer may share court-awarded legal fees with a nonprofit organization that employed, retained or recommended employment of the lawyer in the matter.

(b) A lawyer shall not form a partnership with a nonlawyer if any of the activities of the partnership consist of the practice of law.

(c) A lawyer shall not permit a person who recommends, employs, or pays the lawyer to render legal services for another to direct or regulate the lawyer's professional judgment in rendering such legal services.

(d) A lawyer shall not practice with or in the form of a professional corporation or association authorized to practice law for a profit, if:

  (1) a nonlawyer owns any interest therein, except that a fiduciary representative of the estate of a lawyer may hold the stock or interest of the lawyer for a reasonable time during administration;

  (2) a nonlawyer is a corporate director or officer thereof or occupies the position of similar responsibility in any form of association other than a corporation ; or

  (3) a nonlawyer has the right to direct or control the professional judgment of a lawyer.

COMMENT

[1] The provisions of this Rule express traditional limitations on sharing fees. These limitations are to protect the lawyer's professional independence of judgment. Where someone other than the client pays the lawyer's fee or salary, or recommends employment of the lawyer, that arrangement does not modify the lawyer's obligation to the client. As stated in paragraph (c), such arrangements should not interfere with the lawyer's professional judgment.

[2] This Rule also expresses traditional limitations on permitting a third party to direct or regulate the lawyer's professional judgment in rendering legal services to another. See also Rule 1.8(f) (lawyer may accept compensation from a third party as long as there is no interference with the lawyer's independent professional judgment and the client gives informed consent).

ABA may not have enforcement power over paralegals, infractions of expected ethical conduct will prompt some reaction from the professional associations discussed earlier. The associations may exert informal and formal means of admonition. The NFPA, NALA, and NALS may revoke a paralegal's certification and expel him or her from membership. Also, the traditional tort remedies are available to wronged clients, and paralegals surely would be potential defendants.

The provisions of Rule 5.4 reflect the common law, traditional limitations on the sharing, splitting, or division of fees between lawyers and nonlawyer individuals or entities. This extends to the division of any interest, proprietary or economic, in the value of a law practice. Given the increased role of paralegals in the daily practice of law, there is a temptation to share and divide the economic rewards of the law practice. Any substantial or even minimal economic exchange between lawyers and nonlawyers is unethical. Some of the highlights of Rule 5.4 can be gleaned from the following fact patterns:

Example 1

Paralegal A wishes to become part of the pension plan of XYZ law firm in New York City. All lawyers within the firm are currently part of the profit-sharing plan. Upon initial inquiry, the senior partner of the firm told the paralegal that including paralegals in the plan would be a violation of the *Model Rules of Professional Conduct.* Is this a correct determination? (See 5.4(a)(3).)

Example 2

John Smith, a solo practitioner for almost 20 years, developed a strong working relationship with a paralegal in his office. Lawyer Smith was always impressed with the substantive and intellectual depth of his paralegal and wanted to form a partnership with him as a reward for his loyalty and expertise. Can John Smith, attorney at law, enter into a partnership with his long-standing paralegal? (See 5.4(b).)

Example 3

Sally Paralegal is a freelance, independent contract provider of paralegal services to various law firms in Cincinnati, Ohio. She has a long-term and profitable relationship with ABC law firm, which has used her services intermittently for the last five years. She has begun to refer personal injury clients that she discovers during her volunteer work at a local hospital. To thank her for her excellent referrals, ABC law firm decides to split the contingent fee upon any eventual settlement or award. Is this a correct practice? (See 5.4(c).)

Each example resulted in ethical violations under the *Model Rules of Professional Conduct.* Paying fee percentages to paralegals is a direct violation of DR 3-102A. In *State Bar of Texas v. Faubion*[90] the practice was declared illegal:

> *The principle purpose of the prohibition against sharing legal fees is to prevent solicitation of clients by laypersons and to avoid encouraging or assisting nonlawyers in the practice of law. The exceptions [payment to the estate of a deceased lawyer or payments to a retirement plan] involve situations where the sharing of fees is unlikely to encourage solicitation or the unauthorized practice of law. The Rule merely forbids sharing of legal fees with nonlawyers; it does not mandate that employees be paid a fixed salary. Thus the payment of an annual or other bonus does not constitute the sharing of legal fees if the bonus is neither based on a percentage of the law firm's profits or on a percentage of particular legal fees nor given as a reward for conduct forbidden to lawyers.*[91]

As the legal profession becomes more attuned to the paralegal's role and acknowledges the skills and professional status of paralegals and legal assistants, the desire to economically integrate will intensify. Rule 5.4 assures the professional independence of lawyers and sends a clear message on the impropriety of such alliances.

The way a paralegal represents her or his status is also judicially scrutinized. When paralegals misrepresent themselves by claiming to be attorneys, placing their names, without qualification, on letterhead, business cards, or advertising, they undermine the professional independence of the lawyer.

"*In the Matter of Martinez*[92] the court found that the legal assistant's failure to identify himself as a nonlawyer, quoting legal fees, and cashing a settlement check payable to the client with no supporting documentation constituted improper conduct. The attorney's failure to identify his assistant as a nonlawyer was the attorney's improper conduct, and all of the improper conduct of the legal assistant was imputed to the attorney by virtue of the lawyer's duty to ensure that the conduct of the assistant comported with the attorney's own professional obligations."[93]

Finally, a lawyer cannot delegate functions that he or she knows go beyond ethical bounds.

As Model Rule 5.2 holds, a lawyer is bound by the Rules of Professional Conduct, even though acting under the direction of another party. Likewise, when the lawyer delegates duties to a subordinate lawyer or paralegal, they must act in accordance to the Rules of Professional Conduct.[94]

Client–Lawyer Relationship

RULE 1.1 Competence

The issue of paralegal competence becomes even more pressing because the actions of a paralegal are vicariously tied to the lawyer. Similarly, traditional tort liability theories, such as master–servant relationships and the doctrine of *respondeat superior,* as well as theories of assignment and delegation, add to the importance of paralegal competence. Although it is not certain that a paralegal will incur any sort of liability for the incompetence of a supervising attorney, it is clear that an incompetent paralegal only adds to the evidence of lawyer incompetence.

RULE 1.3 Diligence

Figure 2.11 presents Rule 1.3: Diligence. As the comments of Rule 1.3: Diligence point out,

> *[3] Perhaps no professional shortcoming is more widely resented than procrastination. A client's interests often can be adversely affected by the passage of time or the change of conditions; in extreme instances, as when a lawyer overlooks a statute of limitations, the client's legal position may be destroyed. Even when the client's interests are not affected in substance, however, unreasonable delay can cause a client needless anxiety and undermine confidence in the lawyer's trustworthiness.*[95]

FIGURE 2.11 **ABA Model Rules of Professional Conduct, Rule 1.3**

Source: ABA *Model Rules of Professional Conduct*, 2006 Edition. © 2006 by the American Bar Association. Reprinted with permission. Copies of ABA Model Rules of Professional Conduct, 2006 Edition are available from Service Center, American Bar Association, 321 North Clark Street, Chicago, IL 60610, 1-800-285-2221.

Rule 1.3 Diligence

A lawyer shall act with reasonable diligence and promptness in representing a client.

COMMENT

[1] A lawyer should pursue a matter on behalf of a client despite opposition, obstruction or personal inconvenience to the lawyer, and take whatever lawful and ethical measures are required to vindicate a client's cause or endeavor. A lawyer must also act with commitment and dedication to the interests of the client and with zeal in advocacy upon the client's behalf. A lawyer is not bound, however, to press for every advantage that might be realized for a client. For example, a lawyer may have authority to exercise professional discretion in determining the means by which a matter should be pursued. See Rule 1.2. The lawyer's duty to act with reasonable diligence does not require the use of offensive tactics or preclude the treating of all persons involved in the legal process with courtesy and respect.

[2] A lawyer's work load must be controlled so that each matter can be handled competently.

[3] Perhaps no professional shortcoming is more widely resented than procrastination. A client's interests often can be adversely affected by the passage of time or the change of conditions; in extreme instances, as when a lawyer overlooks a statute of limitations, the client's legal position may be destroyed. Even when the client's interests are not affected in substance, however, unreasonable delay can cause a client needless anxiety and undermine confidence in the lawyer's trustworthiness. A lawyer's duty to act with reasonable promptness, however, does not preclude the lawyer from agreeing to a reasonable request for a postponement that will not prejudice the lawyer's client.

[4] Unless the relationship is terminated as provided in Rule 1.16, a lawyer should carry through to conclusion all matters undertaken for a client. If a lawyer's employment is limited to a specific matter, the relationship terminates when the matter has been resolved. If a lawyer has served a client over a substantial period in a variety of matters, the client sometimes may assume that the lawyer will continue to serve on a continuing basis unless the lawyer gives notice of withdrawal. Doubt about whether a client-lawyer relationship still exists should be clarified by the lawyer, preferably in writing, so that the client will not mistakenly suppose the lawyer is looking after the client's affairs when the lawyer has ceased to do so. For example, if a lawyer has handled a judicial or administrative proceeding that produced a result adverse to the client and the lawyer and the client have not agreed that the lawyer will handle the matter on appeal, the lawyer must consult with the client about the possibility of appeal before relinquishing responsibility for the matter. See Rule 1.4(a)(2). Whether the lawyer is obligated to prosecute the appeal for the client depends on the scope of the representation the lawyer has agreed to provide to the client. See Rule 1.2.

[5] To prevent neglect of client matters in the event of a sole practitioner's death or disability, the duty of diligence may require that each sole practitioner prepare a plan, in conformity with applicable rules, that designates another competent lawyer to review client files, notify each client of the lawyer's death or disability, and determine whether there is a need for immediate protective action. Cf. Rule 28 of the American Bar Association Model Rules for Lawyer Disciplinary Enforcement (providing for court appointment of a lawyer to inventory files and take other protective action in absence of a plan providing for another lawyer to protect the interests of the clients of a deceased or disabled lawyer).

RULE 1.4 Communication

Lawyers who fail to communicate with clients run the risk of ethical scrutiny. Client dissatis-faction often results from a failure to communicate. Regular phone calls, correspondence, and outlining of current case status go a long way to ensuring client goodwill. "The guiding principle is that the lawyer should fulfill reasonable client expectations for information consistent with the duty to act in the client's best interests, and the client's overall requirements as to the character of representation."[96]

Evaluate these situations:

Example 1

A disgruntled client has written to the law office 15 times and has never received a response. The paralegal is told by the lawyer not to contact this client. There are no justifiable reasons for this instruction. Is the attorney subject to discipline under this rule?

Example 2

A personal injury attorney has received an offer from an insurance company for a sum he feels is plainly too small. He refuses to communicate that dollar sum settlement offer to the client. He orders the paralegal not to divulge the amount either. Is the attorney subject to discipline?

RULE 1.5 Fees

Although paralegals do not have the authority or power to negotiate fees and are expressly forbidden to do so under the *Model Rules and the Code of Professional Responsibility,* the record keeping and documentation necessary to substantiate fees are a regular paralegal activity. See Figure 2.12 for Rule 1.5: Fees. "Only four states, Alaska Supreme Court Civil R. 79, Fla. Stat. § 57.104 (1993), NJ Court R. § 4:42-9(b) (1989) and Ind. Code Ann. § 1-1-4-6 (Burns 1993), have statutes or court rules which permit the recoverability of paralegal time in an attorney's application for fees. Only five federal statutes permit such an award. They are the Civil Rights Attorney's Fee Award Act of 1976, 42 U.S.C.S. § 1988; Sherman Anti-Trust Act and Clayton Act, 15 U.S.C.S. Dec. 1, et seq.; Employee Retirement Income Security Act of 1974, 29 U.S.C.S. § 1001; U.S. Bankruptcy Code as amended 1978, 11 U.S.C.S. 330(a)(1); Annotation, Award of Attorneys' Fees pursuant to §§ 520(d), 520(f), 525(e), or 703(c), The Surface Mining Control and Reclamation Act of 1977, 30 U.S.C.S. §§ 1270(d), 1270(f), 1275(e), 1293(c)."[97]

Nothing is more general than Rule 1.5's assertion that fees must be *reasonable.* The deter-mination and factual analysis of how a fee is determined are governed by various factors listed within the rule. The determination of reasonableness is a departure from the clearly excessive or illegal standard under the *Model Code of Professional Responsibility.*[98] This change in policy has both subtle and major implications in fee setting. V. Adler comments,

> *The abolition of the standard of "clear excess," and the implementation of a standard of mere "reasonableness," widens the court's scope of inquiry because disciplinary authorities need no longer prove that a lawyer charged a clearly excessive fee to warrant discipline.*[99]

To mitigate the increasing amounts of bad faith disputes and litigation over fees, the *Model Rules of Professional Conduct* are much more rigorous in their instruction. As an example, written fee agreements are now required under the rules. "A written statement concerning the fee reduces the possibility of misunderstanding. Furnishing the client with a simple memorandum or a copy of the lawyer's customary fee schedule is sufficient if the basis or the rate of the fee is set forth."[100] Referral fees or fee splitting is still frowned upon in both the *Code of Professional Responsibility* and the *Model Rules of Professional Conduct.*[101] Fee splitting between lawyers who are not in the same firm can be made if

1. The division is in proportion to the services performed by each lawyer, or by written agreement with the client. Each lawyer assumes joint responsibility for the representation;
2. The client is advised of and does not object to the participation of all the lawyers in-volved; and
3. The total fee is reasonable.[102]

FIGURE 2.12   **ABA Model Rules of Professional Conduct, Rule 1.5**

Source: ABA *Model Rules of Professional Conduct*, 2006 Edition. © 2006 by the American Bar Association. Reprinted with permission. Copies of ABA Model Rules of Professional Conduct, 2006 Edition are available from Service Center, American Bar Association, 321 North Clark Street, Chicago, IL 60610, 1-800-285-2221.

Rule 1.5 Fees

(a) A lawyer shall not make an agreement for, charge, or collect an unreasonable fee or an unreasonable amount for expenses. The factors to be considered in determining the reasonableness of a fee include the following:

  (1) the time and labor required, the novelty and difficulty of the questions involved, and the skill requisite to perform the legal service properly;

  (2) the likelihood, if apparent to the client, that the acceptance of the particular employment will preclude other employment by the lawyer;

  (3) the fee customarily charged in the locality for similar legal services;

  (4) the amount involved and the results obtained;

  (5) the time limitations imposed by the client or by the circumstances;

  (6) the nature and length of the professional relationship with the client;

  (7) the experience, reputation, and ability of the lawyer or lawyers performing the services; and

  (8) whether the fee is fixed or contingent.

(b) The scope of the representation and the basis or rate of the fee and expenses for which the client will be responsible shall be communicated to the client, preferably in writing, before or within a reasonable time after commencing the representation, except when the lawyer will charge a regularly represented client on the same basis or rate. Any changes in the basis or rate of the fee or expenses shall also be communicated to the client.

(c) A fee may be contingent on the outcome of the matter for which the service is rendered, except in a matter in which a contingent fee is prohibited by paragraph (d) or other law. A contingent fee agreement shall be in a writing signed by the client and shall state the method by which the fee is to be determined, including the percentage or percentages that shall accrue to the lawyer in the event of settlement, trial or appeal; litigation and other expenses to be deducted from the recovery; and whether such expenses are to be deducted before or after the contingent fee is calculated. The agreement must clearly notify the client of any expenses for which the client will be liable whether or not the client is the prevailing party. Upon conclusion of a contingent fee matter, the lawyer shall provide the client with a written statement stating the outcome of the matter and, if there is a recovery, showing the remittance to the client and the method of its determination.

(d) A lawyer shall not enter into an arrangement for, charge, or collect:

  (1) any fee in a domestic relations matter, the payment or amount of which is contingent upon the securing of a divorce or upon the amount of alimony or support, or property settlement in lieu thereof; or

  (2) a contingent fee for representing a defendant in a criminal case.

(e) A division of a fee between lawyers who are not in the same firm may be made only if:

  (1) the division is in proportion to the services performed by each lawyer or each lawyer assumes joint responsibility for the representation;

  (2) the client agrees to the arrangement, including the share each lawyer will receive, and the agreement is confirmed in writing; and

  (3) the total fee is reasonable.

COMMENT

Reasonableness of Fee and Expenses

[1] Paragraph (a) requires that lawyers charge fees that are reasonable under the circumstances. The factors specified in (1) through (8) are not exclusive. Nor will each factor be relevant in each instance. Paragraph (a) also requires that expenses for which the client will be charged must be reasonable. A lawyer may seek reimbursement for the cost of services performed in-house, such as copying, or for other expenses incurred in-house, such as telephone charges, either by charging a reasonable amount to which the client has agreed in advance or by charging an amount that reasonably reflects the cost incurred by the lawyer.

Basis or Rate of Fee

[2] When the lawyer has regularly represented a client, they ordinarily will have evolved an understanding concerning the basis or rate of the fee and the expenses for which the client will be responsible. In a new client-lawyer relationship, however, an understanding as to fees and expenses must be promptly established. Generally, it is desirable to furnish the client with at least a simple memorandum or copy of the lawyer's

FIGURE 2.12 *(concluded)*

customary fee arrangements that states the general nature of the legal services to be provided, the basis, rate or total amount of the fee and whether and to what extent the client will be responsible for any costs, expenses or disbursements in the course of the representation. A written statement concerning the terms of the engagement reduces the possibility of misunderstanding.

[3] Contingent fees, like any other fees, are subject to the reasonableness standard of paragraph (a) of this Rule. In determining whether a particular contingent fee is reasonable, or whether it is reasonable to charge any form of contingent fee, a lawyer must consider the factors that are relevant under the circumstances. Applicable law may impose limitations on contingent fees, such as a ceiling on the percentage allowable, or may require a lawyer to offer clients an alternative basis for the fee. Applicable law also may apply to situations other than a contingent fee, for example, government regulations regarding fees in certain tax matters.

Terms of Payment

[4] A lawyer may require advance payment of a fee, but is obliged to return any unearned portion. See Rule 1.16(d). A lawyer may accept property in payment for services, such as an ownership interest in an enterprise, providing this does not involve acquisition of a proprietary interest in the cause of action or subject matter of the litigation contrary to Rule 1.8 (i). However, a fee paid in property instead of money may be subject to the requirements of Rule 1.8(a) because such fees often have the essential qualities of a business transaction with the client.

[5] An agreement may not be made whose terms might induce the lawyer improperly to curtail services for the client or perform them in a way contrary to the client's interest. For example, a lawyer should not enter into an agreement whereby services are to be provided only up to a stated amount when it is foreseeable that more extensive services probably will be required, unless the situation is adequately explained to the client. Otherwise, the client might have to bargain for further assistance in the midst of a proceeding or transaction. However, it is proper to define the extent of services in light of the client's ability to pay. A lawyer should not exploit a fee arrangement based primarily on hourly charges by using wasteful procedures.

Prohibited Contingent Fees

[6] Paragraph (d) prohibits a lawyer from charging a contingent fee in a domestic relations matter when payment is contingent upon the securing of a divorce or upon the amount of alimony or support or property settlement to be obtained. This provision does not preclude a contract for a contingent fee for legal representation in connection with the recovery of post-judgment balances due under support, alimony or other financial orders because such contracts do not implicate the same policy concerns.

Division of Fee

[7] A division of fee is a single billing to a client covering the fee of two or more lawyers who are not in the same firm. A division of fee facilitates association of more than one lawyer in a matter in which neither alone could serve the client as well, and most often is used when the fee is contingent and the division is between a referring lawyer and a trial specialist. Paragraph (e) permits the lawyers to divide a fee either on the basis of the proportion of services they render or if each lawyer assumes responsibility for the representation as a whole. In addition, the client must agree to the arrangement, including the share that each lawyer is to receive, and the agreement must be confirmed in writing. Contingent fee agreements must be in a writing signed by the client and must otherwise comply with paragraph (c) of this Rule. Joint responsibility for the representation entails financial and ethical responsibility for the representation as if the lawyers were associated in a partnership. A lawyer should only refer a matter to a lawyer whom the referring lawyer reasonably believes is competent to handle the matter. See Rule 1.1.

[8] Paragraph (e) does not prohibit or regulate division of fees to be received in the future for work done when lawyers were previously associated in a law firm.

Disputes over Fees

[9] If a procedure has been established for resolution of fee disputes, such as an arbitration or mediation procedure established by the bar, the lawyer must comply with the procedure when it is mandatory, and, even when it is voluntary, the lawyer should conscientiously consider submitting to it. Law may prescribe a procedure for determining a lawyer's fee, for example, in representation of an executor or administrator, a class or a person entitled to a reasonable fee as part of the measure of damages. The lawyer entitled to such a fee and a lawyer representing another party concerned with the fee should comply with the prescribed procedure.

The division of fees between nonaligned attorneys is prevalent in the legal marketplace. Referral fees, outside of this specific exception, are unethical. Paralegal fees are properly computed in the lawyer's overall bill. Indeed, various jurisdictions have encouraged the aggressive and widespread use of paralegals as a tool for cost containment.[103]

Rule 1.5 also makes clear that contingency fees are an acceptable form of payment for legal services, though the traditional prohibition against contingency fees for cases in domestic relations and criminal law continues.

Example 1

Can an attorney enter into a contingent fee arrangement, utilizing the proceeds of the sale of property owned by a husband and wife in a protection from abuse case, assuming there is no divorce or separation?

Example 2

Can an attorney receive a car or title to other personal property of a defendant as payment for representation in a criminal case?

Example 3

Assume that Lawyer X took a case on a contingency fee. He happened to be lucky in the representation of this particular matter and resolved the case within two weeks after signing a letter of representation. As a result of the attorney spending 10 hours, he was able to receive a $2 million contingency fee award. Can this type of fee be held reasonable under any set of circumstances?

RULE 1.6 *Confidentiality of Information*

The doctrine of confidentiality and privilege, while primarily a rule for lawyers, has been correctly applied to secondary personnel, including paralegals.[104] Confidentiality in lawyer–client relationships is well documented. "The observance of the ethical obligation of a lawyer to hold inviolate confidential information of the client not only facilitates the full development of facts essential to proper representation of the client but also encourages people to seek early legal assistance."[105] The concept of confidentiality affords some sanctity and certainty to lawyer–client relationships. Those less enamored with the confidentiality doctrine see a system of continuing fraud and protectionism for criminals. The profession undoubtedly will continue to grapple with these competing interests.

Paralegals must expect that the same principles of confidence that apply to the lawyer apply to them. A breach of confidence can easily occur in office conversation or discussions with outside friends, associates, courtroom personnel, and other individuals.

Both the contents and the purpose of the communication during conversation between an attorney and an actual or prospective client determine whether the communication is privileged. "Confidential communications made to an attorney in his professional capacity"[106] are privileged. Those made on a purely personal basis or in other contexts that are not relevant to the attorney–client relationship are not privileged.[107]

Paralegals who have moved from one firm to another may be caught in a confidential situation. In the case of *In re Complex Asbestos Litigation*[108] paralegals were disqualified where a conflict or previous confidences existed. Where the paralegal has access to confidential information, the law firm must obtain informed written consent from the previous employer or face a rebuttable presumption that client confidences have been violated. The opinion stated,

> *The easiest way for law firms to rebut the presumption, said the court, is to impose a "cone of silence" around nonlawyers and screen them off from matters they had worked on previously.*[109]

RULE 1.7 *Conflict of Interest: Current Clients*

As we have seen, the ABA's *Rules* uphold the traditional rule on conflicts. See Figure 2.13 for Rule 1.7: Conflict of Interest: Current Clients. Because a client's interests are the attorney's responsibility, conflicts of interest must be avoided. "A lawyer's duty of loyalty to a client is the linchpin of the historical ethical prohibition against impermissible conflict of interest."[110]

FIGURE 2.13 ABA Model Rules of Professional Conduct, Rule 1.7

Source: ABA *Model Rules of Professional Conduct,* 2006 Edition. © 2006 by the American Bar Association. Reprinted with permission. Copies of ABA Model Rules of Professional Conduct, 2006 Edition are available from Service Center, American Bar Association, 321 North Clark Street, Chicago, IL 60610, 1-800-285-2221.

Rule 1.7 Conflict of Interest: Current Clients

(a) Except as provided in paragraph (b), a lawyer shall not represent a client if the representation involves a concurrent conflict of interest. A concurrent conflict of interest exists if:

   (1) the representation of one client will be directly adverse to another client; or

   (2) there is a significant risk that the representation of one or more clients will be materially limited by the lawyer's responsibilities to another client, a former client or a third person or by a personal interest of the lawyer.

(b) Notwithstanding the existence of a concurrent conflict of interest under paragraph (a), a lawyer may represent a client if:

   (1) the lawyer reasonably believes that the lawyer will be able to provide competent and diligent representation to each affected client;

   (2) the representation is not prohibited by law;

   (3) the representation does not involve the assertion of a claim by one client against another client represented by the lawyer in the same litigation or other proceeding before a tribunal; and

   (4) each affected client gives informed consent, confirmed in writing.

COMMENT

General Principles

[1] Loyalty and independent judgment are essential elements in the lawyer's relationship to a client. Concurrent conflicts of interest can arise from the lawyer's responsibilities to another client, a former client or a third person or from the lawyer's own interests. For specific Rules regarding certain concurrent conflicts of interest, see Rule 1.8. For former client conflicts of interest, see Rule 1.9. For conflicts of interest involving prospective clients, see Rule 1.18. For definitions of "informed consent" and "confirmed in writing," see Rule 1.0(e) and (b).

[2] Resolution of a conflict of interest problem under this Rule requires the lawyer to: 1) clearly identify the client or clients; 2) determine whether a conflict of interest exists; 3) decide whether the representation may be undertaken despite the existence of a conflict, i.e., whether the conflict is consentable; and 4) if so, consult with the clients affected under paragraph (a) and obtain their informed consent, confirmed in writing. The clients affected under paragraph (a) include both of the clients referred to in paragraph (a)(1) and the one or more clients whose representation might be materially limited under paragraph (a)(2).

[3] A conflict of interest may exist before representation is undertaken, in which event the representation must be declined, unless the lawyer obtains the informed consent of each client under the conditions of paragraph (b). To determine whether a conflict of interest exists, a lawyer should adopt reasonable procedures, appropriate for the size and type of firm and practice, to determine in both litigation and non-litigation matters the persons and issues involved. See also Comment to Rule 5.1. Ignorance caused by a failure to institute such procedures will not excuse a lawyer's violation of this Rule. As to whether a client-lawyer relationship exists or, having once been established, is continuing, see Comment to Rule 1.3 and Scope.

[4] If a conflict arises after representation has been undertaken, the lawyer ordinarily must withdraw from the representation, unless the lawyer has obtained the informed consent of the client under the conditions of paragraph (b). See Rule 1.16. Where more than one client is involved, whether the lawyer may continue to represent any of the clients is determined both by the lawyer's ability to comply with duties owed to the former client and by the lawyer's ability to represent adequately the remaining client or clients, given the lawyer's duties to the former client. See Rule 1.9. See also Comments [5] and [29].

[5] Unforeseeable developments, such as changes in corporate and other organizational affiliations or the addition or realignment of parties in litigation, might create conflicts in the midst of a representation, as when a company sued by the lawyer on behalf of one client is bought by another client represented by the lawyer in an unrelated matter. Depending on the circumstances, the lawyer may have the option to withdraw from one of the representations in order to avoid the conflict. The lawyer must seek court approval where necessary and take steps to minimize harm to the clients. See Rule 1.16. The lawyer must continue to protect the confidences of the client from whose representation the lawyer has withdrawn. See Rule 1.9(c).

FIGURE 2.13   (*continued*)

Identifying Conflicts of Interest: Directly Adverse

[6] Loyalty to a current client prohibits undertaking representation directly adverse to that client without that client's informed consent. Thus, absent consent, a lawyer may not act as an advocate in one matter against a person the lawyer represents in some other matter, even when the matters are wholly unrelated. The client as to whom the representation is directly adverse is likely to feel betrayed, and the resulting damage to the client-lawyer relationship is likely to impair the lawyer's ability to represent the client effectively. In addition, the client on whose behalf the adverse representation is undertaken reasonably may fear that the lawyer will pursue that client's case less effectively out of deference to the other client, i.e., that the representation may be materially limited by the lawyer's interest in retaining the current client. Similarly, a directly adverse conflict may arise when a lawyer is required to cross-examine a client who appears as a witness in a lawsuit involving another client, as when the testimony will be damaging to the client who is represented in the lawsuit. On the other hand, simultaneous representation in unrelated matters of clients whose interests are only economically adverse, such as representation of competing economic enterprises in unrelated litigation, does not ordinarily constitute a conflict of interest and thus may not require consent of the respective clients.

[7] Directly adverse conflicts can also arise in transactional matters. For example, if a lawyer is asked to represent the seller of a business in negotiations with a buyer represented by the lawyer, not in the same transaction but in another, unrelated matter, the lawyer could not undertake the representation without the informed consent of each client.

Identifying Conflicts of Interest: Material Limitation

[8] Even where there is no direct adverseness, a conflict of interest exists if there is a significant risk that a lawyer's ability to consider, recommend or carry out an appropriate course of action for the client will be materially limited as a result of the lawyer's other responsibilities or interests. For example, a lawyer asked to represent several individuals seeking to form a joint venture is likely to be materially limited in the lawyer's ability to recommend or advocate all possible positions that each might take because of the lawyer's duty of loyalty to the others. The conflict in effect forecloses alternatives that would otherwise be available to the client. The mere possibility of subsequent harm does not itself require disclosure and consent. The critical questions are the likelihood that a difference in interests will eventuate and, if it does, whether it will materially interfere with the lawyer's independent professional judgment in considering alternatives or foreclose courses of action that reasonably should be pursued on behalf of the client.

Lawyer's Responsibilities to Former Clients and Other Third Persons

[9] In addition to conflicts with other current clients, a lawyer's duties of loyalty and independence may be materially limited by responsibilities to former clients under Rule 1.9 or by the lawyer's responsibilities to other persons, such as fiduciary duties arising from a lawyer's service as a trustee, executor or corporate director.

Personal Interest Conflicts

[10] The lawyer's own interests should not be permitted to have an adverse effect on representation of a client. For example, if the probity of a lawyer's own conduct in a transaction is in serious question, it may be difficult or impossible for the lawyer to give a client detached advice. Similarly, when a lawyer has discussions concerning possible employment with an opponent of the lawyer's client, or with a law firm representing the opponent, such discussions could materially limit the lawyer's representation of the client. In addition, a lawyer may not allow related business interests to affect representation, for example, by referring clients to an enterprise in which the lawyer has an undisclosed financial interest. See Rule 1.8 for specific Rules pertaining to a number of personal interest conflicts, including business transactions with clients. See also Rule 1.10 (personal interest conflicts under Rule 1.7 ordinarily are not imputed to other lawyers in a law firm).

[11] When lawyers representing different clients in the same matter or in substantially related matters are closely related by blood or marriage, there may be a significant risk that client confidences will be revealed and that the lawyer's family relationship will interfere with both loyalty and independent professional judgment. As a result, each client is entitled to know of the existence and implications of the relationship between the lawyers before the lawyer agrees to undertake the representation. Thus, a lawyer related to another lawyer, e.g., as parent, child, sibling or spouse, ordinarily may not represent a client in a matter where that lawyer is representing another party, unless each client gives informed consent. The disqualification arising from a close family relationship is personal and ordinarily is not imputed to members of firms with whom the lawyers are associated. See Rule 1.10.

FIGURE 2.13 *(continued)*

[12] A lawyer is prohibited from engaging in sexual relationships with a client unless the sexual relationship predates the formation of the client-lawyer relationship. See Rule 1.8(j).

Interest of Person Paying for a Lawyer's Service

[13] A lawyer may be paid from a source other than the client, including a co-client, if the client is informed of that fact and consents and the arrangement does not compromise the lawyer's duty of loyalty or independent judgment to the client. See Rule 1.8(f). If acceptance of the payment from any other source presents a significant risk that the lawyer's representation of the client will be materially limited by the lawyer's own interest in accommodating the person paying the lawyer's fee or by the lawyer's responsibilities to a payer who is also a co-client, then the lawyer must comply with the requirements of paragraph (b) before accepting the representation, including determining whether the conflict is consentable and, if so, that the client has adequate information about the material risks of the representation.

Prohibited Representations

[14] Ordinarily, clients may consent to representation notwithstanding a conflict. However, as indicated in paragraph (b), some conflicts are nonconsentable, meaning that the lawyer involved cannot properly ask for such agreement or provide representation on the basis of the client's consent. When the lawyer is representing more than one client, the question of consentability must be resolved as to each client.

[15] Consentability is typically determined by considering whether the interests of the clients will be adequately protected if the clients are permitted to give their informed consent to representation burdened by a conflict of interest. Thus, under paragraph (b)(1), representation is prohibited if in the circumstances the lawyer cannot reasonably conclude that the lawyer will be able to provide competent and diligent representation. See Rule 1.1 (competence) and Rule 1.3 (diligence).

[16] Paragraph (b)(2) describes conflicts that are nonconsentable because the representation is prohibited by applicable law. For example, in some states substantive law provides that the same lawyer may not represent more than one defendant in a capital case, even with the consent of the clients, and under federal criminal statutes certain representations by a former government lawyer are prohibited, despite the informed consent of the former client. In addition, decisional law in some states limits the ability of a governmental client, such as a municipality, to consent to a conflict of interest.

[17] Paragraph (b)(3) describes conflicts that are nonconsentable because of the institutional interest in vigorous development of each client's position when the clients are aligned directly against each other in the same litigation or other proceeding before a tribunal. Whether clients are aligned directly against each other within the meaning of this paragraph requires examination of the context of the proceeding. Although this paragraph does not preclude a lawyer's multiple representation of adverse parties to a mediation (because mediation is not a proceeding before a "tribunal" under Rule 1.0(m)), such representation may be precluded by paragraph (b)(1).

Informed Consent

[18] Informed consent requires that each affected client be aware of the relevant circumstances and of the material and reasonably foreseeable ways that the conflict could have adverse effects on the interests of that client. See Rule 1.0(e) (informed consent). The information required depends on the nature of the conflict and the nature of the risks involved. When representation of multiple clients in a single matter is undertaken, the information must include the implications of the common representation, including possible effects on loyalty, confidentiality and the attorney-client privilege and the advantages and risks involved. See Comments [30] and [31] (effect of common representation on confidentiality).

[19] Under some circumstances it may be impossible to make the disclosure necessary to obtain consent. For example, when the lawyer represents different clients in related matters and one of the clients refuses to consent to the disclosure necessary to permit the other client to make an informed decision, the lawyer cannot properly ask the latter to consent. In some cases the alternative to common representation can be that each party may have to obtain separate representation with the possibility of incurring additional costs. These costs, along with the benefits of securing separate representation, are factors that may be considered by the affected client in determining whether common representation is in the client's interests.

Consent Confirmed in Writing

[20] Paragraph (b) requires the lawyer to obtain the informed consent of the client, confirmed in writing. Such a writing may consist of a document executed by the client or one that the lawyer promptly records and transmits to the client following an oral consent. See Rule 1.0(b). See also Rule 1.0(n) (writing includes

FIGURE 2.13 *(continued)*

electronic transmission). If it is not feasible to obtain or transmit the writing at the time the client gives informed consent, then the lawyer must obtain or transmit it within a reasonable time thereafter. See Rule 1.0(b). The requirement of a writing does not supplant the need in most cases for the lawyer to talk with the client, to explain the risks and advantages, if any, of representation burdened with a conflict of interest, as well as reasonably available alternatives, and to afford the client a reasonable opportunity to consider the risks and alternatives and to raise questions and concerns. Rather, the writing is required in order to impress upon clients the seriousness of the decision the client is being asked to make and to avoid disputes or ambiguities that might later occur in the absence of a writing.

Revoking Consent

[21] A client who has given consent to a conflict may revoke the consent and, like any other client, may terminate the lawyer's representation at any time. Whether revoking consent to the client's own representation precludes the lawyer from continuing to represent other clients depends on the circumstances, including the nature of the conflict, whether the client revoked consent because of a material change in circumstances, the reasonable expectations of the other client and whether material detriment to the other clients or the lawyer would result.

Consent to Future Conflict

[22] Whether a lawyer may properly request a client to waive conflicts that might arise in the future is subject to the test of paragraph (b). The effectiveness of such waivers is generally determined by the extent to which the client reasonably understands the material risks that the waiver entails. The more comprehensive the explanation of the types of future representations that might arise and the actual and reasonably foreseeable adverse consequences of those representations, the greater the likelihood that the client will have the requisite understanding. Thus, if the client agrees to consent to a particular type of conflict with which the client is already familiar, then the consent ordinarily will be effective with regard to that type of conflict. If the consent is general and open-ended, then the consent ordinarily will be ineffective, because it is not reasonably likely that the client will have understood the material risks involved. On the other hand, if the client is an experienced user of the legal services involved and is reasonably informed regarding the risk that a conflict may arise, such consent is more likely to be effective, particularly if, e.g., the client is independently represented by other counsel in giving consent and the consent is limited to future conflicts unrelated to the subject of the representation. In any case, advance consent cannot be effective if the circumstances that materialize in the future are such as would make the conflict nonconsentable under paragraph (b).

Conflicts in Litigation

[23] Paragraph (b)(3) prohibits representation of opposing parties in the same litigation, regardless of the clients' consent. On the other hand, simultaneous representation of parties whose interests in litigation may conflict, such as coplaintiffs or codefendants, is governed by paragraph (a)(2). A conflict may exist by reason of substantial discrepancy in the parties' testimony, incompatibility in positions in relation to an opposing party or the fact that there are substantially different possibilities of settlement of the claims or liabilities in question. Such conflicts can arise in criminal cases as well as civil. The potential for conflict of interest in representing multiple defendants in a criminal case is so grave that ordinarily a lawyer should decline to represent more than one codefendant. On the other hand, common representation of persons having similar interests in civil litigation is proper if the requirements of paragraph (b) are met.

[24] Ordinarily a lawyer may take inconsistent legal positions in different tribunals at different times on behalf of different clients. The mere fact that advocating a legal position on behalf of one client might create precedent adverse to the interests of a client represented by the lawyer in an unrelated matter does not create a conflict of interest. A conflict of interest exists, however, if there is a significant risk that a lawyer's action on behalf of one client will materially limit the lawyer's effectiveness in representing another client in a different case; for example, when a decision favoring one client will create a precedent likely to seriously weaken the position taken on behalf of the other client. Factors relevant in determining whether the clients need to be advised of the risk include: where the cases are pending, whether the issue is substantive or procedural, the temporal relationship between the matters, the significance of the issue to the immediate and long-term interests of the clients involved and the clients' reasonable expectations in retaining the lawyer. If there is significant risk of material limitation, then absent informed consent of the affected clients, the lawyer must refuse one of the representations or withdraw from one or both matters.

[25] When a lawyer represents or seeks to represent a class of plaintiffs or defendants in a class-action lawsuit, unnamed members of the class are ordinarily not considered to be clients of the lawyer for purposes of applying paragraph (a)(1) of this Rule. Thus, the lawyer does not typically need to get the consent of

FIGURE 2.13 (*continued*)

such a person before representing a client suing the person in an unrelated matter. Similarly, a lawyer seeking to represent an opponent in a class action does not typically need the consent of an unnamed member of the class whom the lawyer represents in an unrelated matter.

Nonlitigation Conflicts

[26] Conflicts of interest under paragraphs (a)(1) and (a)(2) arise in contexts other than litigation. For a discussion of directly adverse conflicts in transactional matters, see Comment [7]. Relevant factors in determining whether there is significant potential for material limitation include the duration and intimacy of the lawyer's relationship with the client or clients involved, the functions being performed by the lawyer, the likelihood that disagreements will arise and the likely prejudice to the client from the conflict. The question is often one of proximity and degree. See Comment [8].

[27] For example, conflict questions may arise in estate planning and estate administration. A lawyer may be called upon to prepare wills for several family members, such as husband and wife, and, depending upon the circumstances, a conflict of interest may be present. In estate administration the identity of the client may be unclear under the law of a particular jurisdiction. Under one view, the client is the fiduciary; under another view the client is the estate or trust, including its beneficiaries. In order to comply with conflict of interest rules, the lawyer should make clear the lawyer's relationship to the parties involved.

[28] Whether a conflict is consentable depends on the circumstances. For example, a lawyer may not represent multiple parties to a negotiation whose interests are fundamentally antagonistic to each other, but common representation is permissible where the clients are generally aligned in interest even though there is some difference in interest among them. Thus, a lawyer may seek to establish or adjust a relationship between clients on an amicable and mutually advantageous basis; for example, in helping to organize a business in which two or more clients are entrepreneurs, working out the financial reorganization of an enterprise in which two or more clients have an interest or arranging a property distribution in settlement of an estate. The lawyer seeks to resolve potentially adverse interests by developing the parties' mutual interests. Otherwise, each party might have to obtain separate representation, with the possibility of incurring additional cost, complication or even litigation. Given these and other relevant factors, the clients may prefer that the lawyer act for all of them.

Special Considerations in Common Representation

[29] In considering whether to represent multiple clients in the same matter, a lawyer should be mindful that if the common representation fails because the potentially adverse interests cannot be reconciled, the result can be additional cost, embarrassment and recrimination. Ordinarily, the lawyer will be forced to withdraw from representing all of the clients if the common representation fails. In some situations, the risk of failure is so great that multiple representation is plainly impossible. For example, a lawyer cannot undertake common representation of clients where contentious litigation or negotiations between them are imminent or contemplated. Moreover, because the lawyer is required to be impartial between commonly represented clients, representation of multiple clients is improper when it is unlikely that impartiality can be maintained. Generally, if the relationship between the parties has already assumed antagonism, the possibility that the clients' interests can be adequately served by common representation is not very good. Other relevant factors are whether the lawyer subsequently will represent both parties on a continuing basis and whether the situation involves creating or terminating a relationship between the parties.

[30] A particularly important factor in determining the appropriateness of common representation is the effect on client-lawyer confidentiality and the attorney-client privilege. With regard to the attorney-client privilege, the prevailing rule is that, as between commonly represented clients, the privilege does not attach. Hence, it must be assumed that if litigation eventuates between the clients, the privilege will not protect any such communications, and the clients should be so advised.

[31] As to the duty of confidentiality, continued common representation will almost certainly be inadequate if one client asks the lawyer not to disclose to the other client information relevant to the common representation. This is so because the lawyer has an equal duty of loyalty to each client, and each client has the right to be informed of anything bearing on the representation that might affect that client's interests and the right to expect that the lawyer will use that information to that client's benefit. See Rule 1.4. The lawyer should, at the outset of the common representation and as part of the process of obtaining each client's informed consent, advise each client that information will be shared and that the lawyer will have to withdraw if one client decides that some matter material to the representation should be kept from the other. In limited circumstances, it may be appropriate for the lawyer to proceed with the representation when the clients have agreed, after being properly informed, that the lawyer will keep certain information

FIGURE 2.13 (*concluded*)

confidential. For example, the lawyer may reasonably conclude that failure to disclose one client's trade secrets to another client will not adversely affect representation involving a joint venture between the clients and agree to keep that information confidential with the informed consent of both clients.

[32] When seeking to establish or adjust a relationship between clients, the lawyer should make clear that the lawyer's role is not that of partisanship normally expected in other circumstances and, thus, that the clients may be required to assume greater responsibility for decisions than when each client is separately represented. Any limitations on the scope of the representation made necessary as a result of the common representation should be fully explained to the clients at the outset of the representation. See Rule 1.2(c).

[33] Subject to the above limitations, each client in the common representation has the right to loyal and diligent representation and the protection of Rule 1.9 concerning the obligations to a former client. The client also has the right to discharge the lawyer as stated in Rule 1.16.

Organizational Clients

[34] A lawyer who represents a corporation or other organization does not, by virtue of that representation, necessarily represent any constituent or affiliated organization, such as a parent or subsidiary. See Rule 1.13(a). Thus, the lawyer for an organization is not barred from accepting representation adverse to an affiliate in an unrelated matter, unless the circumstances are such that the affiliate should also be considered a client of the lawyer, there is an understanding between the lawyer and the organizational client that the lawyer will avoid representation adverse to the client's affiliates, or the lawyer's obligations to either the organizational client or the new client are likely to limit materially the lawyer's representation of the other client.

[35] A lawyer for a corporation or other organization who is also a member of its board of directors should determine whether the responsibilities of the two roles may conflict. The lawyer may be called on to advise the corporation in matters involving actions of the directors. Consideration should be given to the frequency with which such situations may arise, the potential intensity of the conflict, the effect of the lawyer's resignation from the board and the possibility of the corporation's obtaining legal advice from another lawyer in such situations. If there is material risk that the dual role will compromise the lawyer's independence of professional judgment, the lawyer should not serve as a director or should cease to act as the corporation's lawyer when conflicts of interest arise. The lawyer should advise the other members of the board that in some circumstances matters discussed at board meetings while the lawyer is present in the capacity of director might not be protected by the attorney-client privilege and that conflict of interest considerations might require the lawyer's recusal as a director or might require the lawyer and the lawyer's firm to decline representation of the corporation in a matter.

Thus opposing parties shall not be represented by the same attorney unless consent and waiver are demonstrated. Sellers and buyers, insured and insurer, husbands and wives, debtors and creditors, and conspiratorial defendants in criminal cases are typical conflict situations. Screening potential conflicts at the initial client interview is an extremely crucial step for the legal professional. "Once the interview begins, describe the job opening and your practice in a fair amount of detail. If the candidate is an experienced paralegal with background in your practice areas, it is imperative to discuss any possible conflicts of interest before the interview proceeds too far—there have been instances of law firms being disqualified from cases due to nonlawyer employee conflicts of interest."[111] Guideline 7 in the ABA's *Model Guidelines for the Utilization of Paralegal Services* confirms the need to root out all conflicts of interest (see Figure 2.14).

Rule 1.7 requires attorneys to remain loyal to the client, providing representation without an actual or implied appearance of impropriety. Conflict situations frequently arise in an age of career mobility. A Kentucky Bar Association Opinion,[112] cited in the *National Reporter on Legal Ethics and Professional Responsibility,* held that paralegals can breach the loyalty standard by their previous employment:

> *The former firm also must request that the new firm not permit the paralegal to work on matters involving the former firm's client; that the new firm withdraw if it does not so advise the paralegal; and that the new firm provided written assurance of this. The former firm must advise the client of the facts and move to disqualify the new firm if the client requests.*[113]

FIGURE 2.14 ABA Model Guidelines for the Utilization of Paralegal Services, Guideline 7

Source: Excerpted from the *ABA Model Guidelines for the Utilization of Paralegal Services,* 2004, published by the American Bar Association Division for Legal Services. © 2004 by the American Bar Association. Reprinted with permission.

Guideline 7: A lawyer should take reasonable measures to prevent conflicts of interest resulting from a paralegal's other employment or interests.

Comment to Guideline 7

Loyalty and independent judgment are essential elements in the lawyer's relationship to a client. Model Rule 1.7, comment 1. The independent judgment of a lawyer should be exercised solely for the benefit of his client and free from all compromising influences and loyalties. EC 5.1. Model Rules 1.7 through 1.13 address a lawyer's responsibility to prevent conflicts of interest and potential conflicts of interest. Model Rule 5.3 requires lawyers with direct supervisory authority over a paralegal and partners/lawyers with managerial authority within a law firm to make reasonable efforts to ensure that the conduct of the paralegals they employ is compatible with their own professional obligations, including the obligation to prevent conflicts of interest. Therefore, paralegals should be instructed to inform the supervising lawyer and the management of the firm of any interest that could result in a conflict of interest or even give the appearance of a conflict. The guideline intentionally speaks to "other employment" rather than only past employment because there are instances where paralegals are employed by more than one law firm at the same time. The guideline's reference to "other interests" is intended to include personal relationships as well as instances where the paralegal may have a financial interest (as a stockholder, trust beneficiary, or trustee, etc.) that would conflict with the clients in the matter in which the lawyer has been employed.

"Imputed Disqualification Arising from Change in Employment by Nonlawyer Employee," ABA informal Opinion 1526 (1988), defines the duties of both the present and former employing lawyers and reasons that the restrictions on paralegals' employment should be kept to "the minimum necessary to protect confidentiality" in order to prevent paralegals from being forced to leave their careers, which "would disserve clients as well as the legal profession." The opinion describes the attorney's obligations (1) to caution the paralegal not to disclose any information and (2) to prevent the paralegal from working on any matter on which the paralegal worked for a prior employer or respecting which the employee has confidential information.

Disqualification is mandatory where the paralegal gained information relating to the representation of an adverse party while employed at another law firm and has revealed it to lawyers in the new law firm, where screening of the paralegal would be ineffective, or where the paralegal would be required to work on the other side of the same or substantially related matter on which the paralegal had worked while employed at another firm. When a paralegal moves to an opposing firm during ongoing litigation, courts have held that a rebuttable presumption exists that the paralegal will share client confidences. *See, e.g., Phoenix v. Founders,* 887 S.W. 2d 831, 835 (Tex. 1994) (the presumption that confidential information has been shared may be rebutted upon showing that sufficient precautions were taken by the new firm to prevent disclosure including that it (1) cautioned the newly hired paralegal not to disclose any information relating to representation of a client of the former employer; (2) instructed the paralegal not to work on any matter on which he or she worked during prior employment or about which he or she has information relating to the former employer's representation; and (3) the new firm has taken reasonable measures to ensure that the paralegal does not work on any matter on which he or she worked during the prior employment, absent the former client's consent). But adequate and effective screening of a paralegal may prevent disqualification of the new firm. Model Rule 1.10, comment 4. Adequate and effective screening gives a lawyer and the lawyer's firm the opportunity to build and enforce an "ethical wall" to preclude the paralegal from any involvement in the client matter that is the subject of the conflict and to prevent the paralegal from receiving or disclosing any information concerning the matter. ABA informal Opinion 1526 (1988). The implication of the ABA's informal opinion is that if the lawyer, and the firm, do not implement a procedure to effectively screen the paralegal from involvement with the litigation, and from communication with attorneys and/or co-employees concerning the litigation, the lawyer and the firm may be disqualified from representing either party in the controversy. *See In re Complex Asbestos Litigation,* 232 Cal. App. 3d 572, 283 Cal. Rptr. 732 (1991) (law firm disqualified from nine pending asbestos cases because it failed to screen paralegal that possessed attorney–client confidences from prior employment by opposing counsel).

Some courts hold that paralegals are subject to the same rules governing imputed disqualification as are lawyers. In jurisdictions that do not recognize screening devices as adequate protection against a lawyer's potential conflict in a new law firm, neither a "cone of silence" nor any other screening device will be recognized as a proper or effective remedy where a paralegal who has switched firms possesses material and confidential information. *Zimmerman v. Mahaska Bottling Company,* 19 P. 3d 784, 791-792 (Kan. 2001) ("[W]here screening devices are not allowed for lawyers, they are not allowed for nonlawyers either."); *Koulisis v. Rivers,* 730 So. 2d 289 (Fla. Dist. Ct. App. 1999) (firm that hired paralegal with actual knowledge of

FIGURE 2.14 *(concluded)*

protected information could not defeat disqualification by showing steps taken to screen the paralegal from the case); Ala. Bar R-02-01, 63 Ala. Law 94 (2002). These cases do not mean that disqualification is mandatory whenever a nonlawyer moves from one private firm to an opposing firm while there is pending litigation. Rather, a firm may still avoid disqualification if (1) the paralegal has not acquired material or confidential information regarding the litigation, or (2) if the client of the former firm waives disqualification and approves the use of a screening device or ethical wall. *Zimmerman,* 19 P. 3d at 822.

Other authorities, consistent with Model Rule 1.10(a), differentiate between lawyers and nonlawyers. In *Stewart v. Bee Dee Neon & Signs. Inc.,* 751 So. 2d 196 (Fla. Dist. Ct. App. 2000) the court disagreed with the Koulisis rule that paralegals should be held to the same conflicts analyses as lawyers when they change law firms. In *Stewart,* a secretary moved from one law firm to the opposing firm in midlitigation. While Florida would not permit lawyer screening to defeat disqualification under these circumstance, the *Stewart* court emphasized that "it is important that nonlawyer employees have as much mobility in employment opportunity as possible" and that "any restrictions on the nonlawyer's employment should be held to the minimum necessary to protect confidentiality of client information." *Stewart,* 751 So. 2d at 203 (citing ABA Informal Opinion 1526 (1988)). The analysis in *Stewart* requires the party moving for disqualification to prove that the nonlawyer actually has confidential information, and that screening has not and cannot be effectively implemented. *Id.* at 208. In *Leibowitz v. The Eighth Judicial District Court of the State of Nevada,* 79 P. 3d 515 (2003), the Supreme Court of Nevada overruled its earlier decision in *Ciaffone v. District Court,* 113 Nev. 1165, 945 P. 2d 950 (1997), which held that screening of nonlawyer employees would not prevent disqualification. In *Leibowitz,* the court held that when a firm identifies a conflict, it has an absolute duty to screen and to inform the adversarial party about the hiring and the screening mechanisms. The *court* emphasized that disqualification is required when confidential information has been disclosed, when screening would be ineffective, or when the affected employee would be required to work on the case in question.

Still other courts that approve screening for paralegals compare paralegals to former government lawyers who have neither a financial interest in the outcome of a particular litigation, nor the choice of which clients they serve. *Smart Industries Corp v. Superior Court County of Yuma,* 876 P. 2d 1176, 1184 (Ariz. App. 1994) ("We believe that this reasoning for treating government attorneys differently in the context of imputed disqualification applies equally to nonlawyer assistants . . ."); *accord, Hayes v. Central States Orthopedic Specialists, Inc.,* 51 P. 3d 562 (Okla. 2002); Model Rule 1.11 (b) and (c).

Comment 4 to Model Rule 1.10(a) states that the rule does not prohibit representation by others in the law firm where the person prohibited from involvement in a matter is a paralegal. But paralegals "ordinarily must be screened from any personal participation in the matter to avoid communication to others in the firm of confidential information that both the nonlawyers and the firm have a legal duty to protect." *Id.*

Because disqualification is such a drastic consequence for lawyers and their firms, lawyers must be especially attuned to controlling authority in the jurisdictions where they practice. *See generally,* Steve Morris and Chirstina C. Stipp, Ethical Conflicts Facing Litigators, ALI SH009ALI-ABA 449, 500-502 (2002).

To assist lawyers and their firms in discharging their professional obligations under the Model Rules, the NALA Guidelines requires paralegals "to take any and all steps necessary to prevent conflicts of interest and fully disclose such conflicts to the supervising attorney" and warns paralegals that any "failure to do so may jeopardize both the attorney's represenation and the case itself." NALA, Comment to Guideline 1. NFPA Model Code of Professional Ethics and Responsibility and Guidelines for Enforcement, EC-1.6, requires paralegals to avoid conflicts of interest and to disclose and to disclose any possible conflicts to the employer or client, as well as to the prospective employers or clients. NFPA. EC-1.6 (a)–(g).

Even if paralegals are not subject to the discipline of Rule 1.7, paralegals must remember that their actions are imputed vicariously to the attorney. Paralegals, even if in doubt, should disclose to their supervising attorney any relationships that may have developed at other places of employment. The Comment to Rule 1.7 states the philosophy of the conflict rules:

> *Loyalty is an essential element in the lawyer's relationship to a client. An impermissible conflict of interest may exist before representation is undertaken, in which event the representation should be declined. If such a conflict arises after the representation has been undertaken, the lawyer should withdraw from the representation.*[114]

RULE 1.15 Safekeeping Property

Lawyers have a grave responsibility to safely hold a client's assets in trust—whether cash, personal property, or other papers and documents. See Figure 2.15 for Rule 1.15: Safekeeping Property. Paralegals can be expected to catalog items. Consider the following examples:

Example 1

Lawyer Jones has possession of 1,000 shares of Chrysler Motor Corporation stock that were entrusted to him by Client Able. Jones places the stocks in an unlocked desk drawer that is completely unsecured. If the shares are stolen, is it reasonable to assume that the lawyer may be disciplined for violation of Rule 1.15?

Example 2

Assume that in a personal injury case, the insurance company has disbursed the settlement check, which the attorney has deposited into her escrow account. As required under federal banking laws, the attorney must wait seven days before the out-of-state check is cleared and credited to her account. Her client says this is a stall tactic and insists that the check be drawn immediately. Can the attorney's client assert that holding a check for a period of seven days in the settlement of a personal injury claim is a violation of Rule 1.15?

Separate escrow or trust accounts that hold client proceeds prevent ethical challenges. Retainers and advanced expense payments are not subject to deposit in trust accounts because these are forms of compensation and reimbursement, unless these sums have yet to be earned. Check with local rules to determine the suitable placement. How a firm accounts for advanced expenses is a relevant tax question.[115]

FIGURE 2.15 **ABA Model Rules of Professional Conduct, Rule 1.15**

Source: ABA *Model Rules of Professional Conduct*, 2006 Edition. © 2006 by the American Bar Association. Reprinted with permission. Copies of ABA Model Rules of Professional Conduct, 2006 Edition are available from Service Center, American Bar Association, 321 North Clark Street, Chicago, IL 60610, 1-800-285-2221.

Rule 1.15 Safekeeping Property

(a) A lawyer shall hold property of clients or third persons that is in a lawyer's possession in connection with a representation separate from the lawyer's own property. Funds shall be kept in a separate account maintained in the state where the lawyer's office is situated, or elsewhere with the consent of the client or third person. Other property shall be identified as such and appropriately safeguarded. Complete records of such account funds and other property shall be kept by the lawyer and shall be preserved for a period of [five years] after termination of the representation.

(b) A lawyer may deposit the lawyer's own funds in a client trust account for the sole purpose of paying bank service charges on that account, but only in an amount necessary for that purpose.

(c) A lawyer shall deposit into a client trust account legal fees and expenses that have been paid in advance, to be withdrawn by the lawyer only as fees are earned or expenses incurred.

(d) Upon receiving funds or other property in which a client or third person has an interest, a lawyer shall promptly notify the client or third person. Except as stated in this rule or otherwise permitted by law or by agreement with the client, a lawyer shall promptly deliver to the client or third person any funds or other property that the client or third person is entitled to receive and, upon request by the client or third person, shall promptly render a full accounting regarding such property.

(e) When in the course of representation a lawyer is in possession of property in which two or more persons (one of whom may be the lawyer) claim interests, the property shall be kept separate by the lawyer until the dispute is resolved. The lawyer shall promptly distribute all portions of the property as to which the interests are not in dispute.

COMMENT

[1] A lawyer should hold property of others with the care required of a professional fiduciary. Securities should be kept in a safe deposit box, except when some other form of safekeeping is warranted by special circumstances. All property that is the property of clients or third persons, including prospective clients, must be kept separate from the lawyer's business and personal property and, if monies, in one or more trust accounts. Separate trust accounts may be warranted when administering estate monies or acting in

FIGURE 2.15   *(concluded)*

similar fiduciary capacities. A lawyer should maintain on a current basis books and records in accordance with generally accepted accounting practice and comply with any recordkeeping rules established by law or court order. See, e.g., ABA Model Financial Recordkeeping Rule.

[2] While normally it is impermissible to commingle the lawyer's own funds with client funds, paragraph (b) provides that it is permissible when necessary to pay bank service charges on that account. Accurate records must be kept regarding which part of the funds are the lawyer's.

[3] Lawyers often receive funds from which the lawyer's fee will be paid. The lawyer is not required to remit to the client funds that the lawyer reasonably believes represent fees owed. However, a lawyer may not hold funds to coerce a client into accepting the lawyer's contention. The disputed portion of the funds must be kept in a trust account and the lawyer should suggest means for prompt resolution of the dispute, such as arbitration. The undisputed portion of the funds shall be promptly distributed.

[4] Paragraph (e) also recognizes that third parties may have lawful claims against specific funds or other property in a lawyer's custody, such as a client's creditor who has a lien on funds recovered in a personal injury action. A lawyer may have a duty under applicable law to protect such third-party claims against wrongful interference by the client. In such cases, when the third-party claim is not frivolous under applicable law, the lawyer must refuse to surrender the property to the client until the claims are resolved. A lawyer should not unilaterally assume to arbitrate a dispute between the client and the third party, but, when there are substantial grounds for dispute as to the person entitled to the funds, the lawyer may file an action to have a court resolve the dispute.

[5] The obligations of a lawyer under this Rule are independent of those arising from activity other than rendering legal services. For example, a lawyer who serves only as an escrow agent is governed by the applicable law relating to fiduciaries even though the lawyer does not render legal services in the transaction and is not governed by this Rule.

[6] A lawyers' fund for client protection provides a means through the collective efforts of the bar to reimburse persons who have lost money or property as a result of dishonest conduct of a lawyer. Where such a fund has been established, a lawyer must participate where it is mandatory, and, even when it is voluntary, the lawyer should participate.

The Lawyer as an Advocate

RULE 3.1 Meritorious Claims and Contentions

As discussed previously, the concept of a meritorious case can be hard to pin down.[116] Some cases stand out as egregious, and paralegals must never involve themselves in litigation driven to harass and abuse the opposing party. Attorneys Rodney Arthur and Ellen Brandt remind practitioners of the consequences of advocating a malpractice case without merit:

> *The four aspects of a malpractice claim are*
>
> *a. Was the primary case meritorious?*
>
> *b. Given the facts of your case, what was the standard of care required of the attorney (i.e., what is "good practice")?*
>
> *c. How did the attorney depart from that standard?*
>
> *d. Finally, was this departure the proximate cause of the loss or damage?*[117]

Any legal action should be brought forth in good faith. Aside from the disciplinary consequences of rules and enforcement authorities, the paralegal, by his or her participation, chips away at the moral foundation. Maintaining one's integrity is a critical component in any professional's life, and the costs of an unmeritorious life are self-evident. Richard Matasar writes most eloquently,

> *Being a zealous advocate is an intellectually rigorous business. Lawyers become masters of manipulation, reconstructing the words or rules and fitting them to a client's goals. They cajole and coax cases into precedential value. They create distinctions, creatively. They revel in ambiguity, a desirable tool utilized to serve the client. Skillful practitioners operate instrumentally, understanding that pliability of legal principles is essential to the craft. The lawyer who represents the plaintiff today defends the defendant tomorrow. To make it work, the law provides wiggle room for both sides.*[118]

Merit or the lack thereof is unquestionably an imprecise science. The rules do a poor job of laying out concrete and uniform principles. Elasticity rather than specificity appears to be the rule.

FIGURE 2.16 ABA Model Rules of Professional Conduct, Rule 3.2

Source: ABA *Model Rules of Professional Conduct*, 2006 Edition. © 2006 by the American Bar Association. Reprinted with permission. Copies of ABA Model Rules of Professional Conduct, 2006 Edition are available from Service Center, American Bar Association, 321 North Clark Street, Chicago, IL 60610, 1-800-285-2221.

Rule 3.2 Expediting Litigation

A lawyer shall make reasonable efforts to expedite litigation consistent with the interests of the client.

COMMENT

[1] Dilatory practices bring the administration of justice into disrepute. Although there will be occasions when a lawyer may properly seek a postponement for personal reasons, it is not proper for a lawyer to routinely fail to expedite litigation solely for the convenience of the advocates. Nor will a failure to expedite be reasonable if done for the purpose of frustrating an opposing party's attempt to obtain rightful redress or repose. It is not a justification that similar conduct is often tolerated by the bench and bar. The question is whether a competent lawyer acting in good faith would regard the course of action as having some substantial purpose other than delay. Realizing financial or other benefit from otherwise improper delay in litigation is not a legitimate interest of the client.

RULE 3.2 *Expediting Litigation*

Delay techniques that sometimes occur in litigation will be often tied to the practices of a paralegal. See Figure 2.16 for Rule 3.2: Expediting Litigation. Paralegals should seek continuances, extensions, and other modifications of the formal calendar of events sparingly. The continuous abuse of these processes reduces a professional's integrity.

RULE 3.3 *Candor toward the Tribunal*

Paralegals who purposely engage in falsehood before the tribunal put the supervising attorney at risk. Paralegals who participate in fraud, misrepresentation, evidence tampering, or perjury will suffer disciplinary consequences. Consider these examples:

Example 1

A paralegal claims that certain evidence he has submitted was acquired at a crime scene. In fact the evidence was found in his closet at home and is completely unrelated to the case at hand. Is the attorney subject to discipline for the acts of this paralegal?

Example 2

In performing a research task for her supervising attorney, a paralegal refuses to research the law properly and instead of reviewing New Jersey law decides she likes Montana law better. In a short list of case law and an accompanying memorandum, the paralegal completely mis-cites a variety of cases and submits this material to the judge's law clerk upon instructions of the attorney. Can the lawyer be subject to discipline for these activities?

Candor was evaluated in *Castillo v. St. Paul Fire & Marine Insurance Co.*[119] The court sanctioned an attorney for ethical failure. After he constantly interfered with opposing counsel's questioning, stonewalled his client's responses to the tribunal, failed to adhere to timetables for discovery and conferences, and threatened physical harm to opposing parties, he was suspended for a year. In the finding, the court stated,

> *The panel also extensively discussed the lawyer's lack of civility in his interactions with the court and opposing counsel, specifically noting the lawyer's conduct when opposing counsel attempted to use the lawyer's phone. The panel found that the lawyer's conduct was "yet another example of the deterioration in civility that is now endemic to the legal profession."*[120]

RULE 3.4 *Fairness to Opposing Party and Counsel*

Paralegal functions are readily evident in this rule. See Figure 2.17 for Rule 3.4: Fairness to Opposing Party and Counsel. A ludicrous, absurd, or unfair discovery request certainly will be unwelcome. The submission of irrelevant, untrue, and unsubstantiated documentation or evidence before a tribunal will be construed as a violation of the rule. Any dishonesty toward opposing counsel should be met with serious reservation and discipline. Unfortunately paralegals often become snared in this sort of situation. Do not become a pawn of an unethical attorney.

FIGURE 2.17 ABA Model Rules of Professional Conduct, Rule 3.4

Source: ABA *Model Rules of Professional Conduct*, 2006 Edition. © 2006 by the American Bar Association. Reprinted with permission. Copies of ABA Model Rules of Professional Conduct, 2006 Edition are available from Service Center, American Bar Association, 321 North Clark Street, Chicago, IL 60610, 1-800-285-2221.

Rule 3.4 Fairness to Opposing Party and Counsel

A lawyer shall not:

(a) unlawfully obstruct another party's access to evidence or unlawfully alter, destroy or conceal a document or other material having potential evidentiary value. A lawyer shall not counsel or assist another person to do any such act;

(b) falsify evidence, counsel or assist a witness to testify falsely, or offer an inducement to a witness that is prohibited by law;

(c) knowingly disobey an obligation under the rules of a tribunal except for an open refusal based on an assertion that no valid obligation exists;

(d) in pretrial procedure, make a frivolous discovery request or fail to make reasonably diligent effort to comply with a legally proper discovery request by an opposing party;

(e) in trial, allude to any matter that the lawyer does not reasonably believe is relevant or that will not be supported by admissible evidence, assert personal knowledge of facts in issue except when testifying as a witness, or state a personal opinion as to the justness of a cause, the credibility of a witness, the culpability of a civil litigant or the guilt or innocence of an accused; or

(f) request a person other than a client to refrain from voluntarily giving relevant information to another party unless:

    (1) the person is a relative or an employee or other agent of a client; and

    (2) the lawyer reasonably believes that the person's interests will not be adversely affected by refraining from giving such information.

COMMENT

[1] The procedure of the adversary system contemplates that the evidence in a case is to be marshalled competitively by the contending parties. Fair competition in the adversary system is secured by prohibitions against destruction or concealment of evidence, improperly influencing witnesses, obstructive tactics in discovery procedure, and the like.

[2] Documents and other items of evidence are often essential to establish a claim or defense. Subject to evidentiary privileges, the right of an opposing party, including the government, to obtain evidence through discovery or subpoena is an important procedural right. The exercise of that right can be frustrated if relevant material is altered, concealed or destroyed. Applicable law in many jurisdictions makes it an offense to destroy material for purpose of impairing its availability in a pending proceeding or one whose commencement can be foreseen. Falsifying evidence is also generally a criminal offense. Paragraph (a) applies to evidentiary material generally, including computerized information. Applicable law may permit a lawyer to take temporary possession of physical evidence of client crimes for the purpose of conducting a limited examination that will not alter or destroy material characteristics of the evidence. In such a case, applicable law may require the lawyer to turn the evidence over to the police or other prosecuting authority, depending on the circumstances.

[3] With regard to paragraph (b), it is not improper to pay a witness's expenses or to compensate an expert witness on terms permitted by law. The common law rule in most jurisdictions is that it is improper to pay an occurrence witness any fee for testifying and that it is improper to pay an expert witness a contingent fee.

[4] Paragraph (f) permits a lawyer to advise employees of a client to refrain from giving information to another party, for the employees may identify their interests with those of the client. See also Rule 4.2.

Former U.S. Attorney Bennett L. Gershman critiques prosecutorial behavior as proof of a lack of candor or fairness. He lists some trouble spots in prosecutorial advocacy:

- Assassinating a defendant's character.
- Introducing improper evidence.
- Inflaming juror prejudice.
- Violating the privilege against self-incrimination.
- Denigrating defense counsel.
- Exploiting prosecutorial prestige.

- Misrepresenting the record.
- Finding remedies.[121]

The rules are, at best, advisory guidelines for the human condition. Any paralegal will see that most standards of conduct are nothing more than exercises of common sense. Courteous, respectful, compassionate conduct generates goodwill, produces competent and professional legal services, and creates a reputation that is respected and trusted.

The practicing paralegal should recognize that displacement of an attorney's own value system often results in subversion of the paralegal's value system. Richard Matasar warns practitioners that the conscience of their clients must not replace their own:

> *In this essay the conflicting demands placed on the good lawyer are highlighted: as advisor, facilitator, and advocate; as zealous representative and manipulator; as self and alter ego of the client. I ask what it means to be a moral lawyer in a system that often sets practice norms at odds with one's own moral vision. I explore lawyers' partial and inadequate coping strategies and conclude they have no simple cure for their conflicts and must learn to live with the pain of moral lawyering.*[122]

In the final analysis, ethics is about treating others with justice and decency. Professionalism calls for not only competency but decency in human action. The steps are not that difficult:

1. Explain the fee agreement in plain and simple English.
2. Contact and communicate with clients on a regular and continuous basis.
3. Return phone calls.
4. Do not split fees or services with nonlawyers (unless permitted by local rules).
5. Let the lawyers do their jobs and the paralegals, legal assistants, and other nonlawyers theirs.
6. Adhere to the rules of court and the statutory and legislative guidelines for conduct and behavior.
7. Protect secrets and confidences of all clients.
8. Live a good, decent, and honorable life.
9. Have no conflicts in either people, knowledge, or economic interests.
10. Improve one's knowledge base and grow intellectually in the law.
11. Be diligent, hardworking, and persevering.
12. Be a person of your word—always forthright, always honest.
13. Treat others as you would expect to be treated.

With these suggestions, the paralegal will remain honest and valuable.

Summary

Paralegals face enormous ethical demands in their occupational activities. Although little direct licensing and regulation exist at the federal, state, or local level, the standards for lawyers are often imputed to the paralegal. Additionally, the regulatory atmosphere at the state and local level is increasingly taking aim at the profession. In a more informal vein, bar associations, professional associations, and accreditation organizations are making their mark on levels of conduct and proficiency expected of paralegals.

The codes adopted by the NFPA, AAPI, NALS, and NALA play an integral role in the formulation of ethical standards.

The prohibition against engaging in the unauthorized practice of law is of primary importance to paralegals. Equally important is the adherence to client–lawyer confidentiality, as well as avoidance of conflicts of interest and other potentially compromising situations. The paralegal must be competent, confident, communicative, accurate, and diligent in the protection of property. Paralegals are expected to exhibit the same candor before the tribunal as other legal professionals.

Discussion Questions

1. Do you have any local associations or groups that publish ethical standards or guidelines on paralegal practice and process?

2. Explain how a paralegal can become an unwilling victim in an ethical dilemma in a law firm.

3. What role do paralegals play in expediting litigation?

4. What disciplinary processes exist at the state or local level regarding your conduct?

5. Are written fee agreements now necessary under the *Model Rules of Professional Conduct*?

6. How could you determine whether a legal fee was fair, reasonable, and just?

7. What are the requirements for safekeeping client properties under the Model Rules?

8. In your association with other paralegals, attorneys, and judicial officers, what standard of conduct is expected under the Model Rules of Professional Conduct?

9. Should paralegals act as hired guns?

10. Can paralegals advertise? If so, how?

11. Find out about your state and local disciplinary boards for lawyers. Does the board or association issue opinions or standards regarding paralegals?

12. Read the DCBA Brief at http://www.dcba.org/brief/mayissue/2002/art40502.htm. Focus on the cases cited. Which case represents the strongest unauthorized practice allegation?

Research Exercise

1. Locate your state Rule of Professional Conduct at the court and bar association level. What provisions are made for paralegals in the rules?

Practical Exercises

1. Discuss the ethical ramifications present in the following scenario.

   Sally Stevens, attorney at law, has hired a paralegal to assist her in her busy practice. She has assigned the following tasks to the paralegal:

   1. Drafting release forms for personal injury cases.

   2. Interviewing eyewitnesses to accidents.

   3. Advising whether a client should take a settlement agreement in an insurance case.

   Review the guidelines for the use of legal assistants adopted by your state bar or court. Determine whether the tasks Attorney Smith has assigned violate this code.

2. Review ABA Model Rule of Professional Conduct 5.5:
   A lawyer shall not:

   (a) practice law in a jurisdiction where doing so violates the regulation of the legal profession in that jurisdiction; or

   (b) assist a person who is not a member of the bar in the performance of activity that constitutes the unauthorized practice of law.

   How do paralegals fit within this unauthorized practice provision? Consider how the delegation of responsibilities for paralegals and legal assistants might sometimes border on unauthorized practice. Think creatively and list five examples of a delegation of responsibility that might violate these provisions.

3. Review ABA Model Rule of Professional Conduct at Rule 1.15. Answer the following question:

In an estate case, jewelry worth a substantial amount of money has been entrusted to the law firm. A paralegal has been asked by an associate in the law firm to guard or preserve the jewelry. The jewelry is placed in an unlocked desk drawer, though the paralegal has indicated that he will take better care of the property the next day. Overnight the jewelry is stolen. Can the attorney be subject to discipline?

Internet Resources

American Alliance of Paralegals Inc., Position on Paralegal Regulation—www.aapipara.org/Positionstatements.htm

Washington Paralegal Associations—www.wspaonline.org/regulation.htm

NFPA—www.paralegals.org

ABA Standing Committee on Paralegals—www.abanet.org/legalservices/paralegals

ABA Paralegal Program Approval Page—www.abanet.org/legalservices/paralegals/process.html

AAFPE—www.aafpe.org

NALS—www.nals.org

Illinois Paralegal Association—www.ipaonline.org

ABA Center for Professional Responsibility Library—www.abanet.org/cpr/ethsrbib.html

Endnotes

1. Jacqueline Meile Rasmussen & Paul M. Sedlacek, *Paralegals: Changing the Practice of Law*, 44 S. D. L. R. 319 (1999).

2. The American Alliance of Paralegals Inc., *Position on Paralegal Regulation,* available at http://www.aapipara.org/Positionstatements.htm.

3. *See* Kenneth Jost, *Public Image of Lawyers: What Image Do We Deserve?* 74 A.B.A. J. (1988); Rupert Warren, *A Profession under Review,* N.Y. St. B. J. 15 (January 1985).

4. Kenneth Jost, *Public Image of Lawyers: What Image Do We Deserve?* 74 A.B.A. J. 47 (1988).

5. *See* Phillip Stern, Lawyers on Trial (1980); Jay Underwood, *Curbing Litigation Abuses,* 56 St. John's L. Rev. 625 (1981); Melvin I. Friedman, Lawyer's Ethics in the Adversary System (1975); Richard K. Burk, *An Essay on Lying and Deceit in the Practice of Law,* 38 Ark. L. Rev. 1 (1984).

6. Tim A. Baker, *Survey: Professionalism and Civility: A Survey of Professionalism and Civility,* 38 Ind. L. Rev. 1305 (2005).

7. Rudolph J. Gerber, *Victory vs. Truth: The Adversary System and Its Ethics,* 19 Ariz. St. L. J. 3–4 (1987).

8. David S. Machlowitz, *Lawyers on TV,* 74 A.B.A. J. 56 (1988).

9. *See* Charles P. Nemeth, Aquinas in the Courtroom (2001).

10. Ellen Mercer Fallon, *Making Idealism a Reality: The Commission on the Vermont Lawyer,* Vt. B. J. & L. Dig. 3 *citing Kansas City Metropolitan Bar Association Guidelines* (June 1988).

11. Rupert Warren, *A Profession under Review,* 57 N.Y. St. B. J. 15, 16 *citing John H. Lehnert, When in Doubt Sue* (1983), (January 1985).

12. Model Rules of Professional Conduct Rule 1.5(A) (2004).

13. Model Code of Professional Responsibility DR 7–102(A)(1) and (2) (1983).

14. *Id.* at EC 7–4.

15. Rudolph J. Gerber, *Victory vs. Truth: The Adversary System and Its Ethics,* 19 Ariz. St. L. J. 3, 9 (1987).

16. Rudolph J. Gerber, *Victory vs. Truth: The Adversary System and Its Ethics,* 19 Ariz. St. L. J. 3, 11 (1987).

17. *See* Ward W. Reynoldson, *The Case against Lawyer Advertising,* 75 A.B.A. J. 60 (1989).

18. Former U.S. Supreme Court Chief Justice Warren Burger was a vociferous critic of the deregulation of advertising and marketing in the legal profession. *See* Bates v. State Bar of Arizona, 433 U.S. 350 (1977); Zauderer v. Office of Disciplinary Counsel, 471 U.S. 626 (1985).

19. Rupert Warren, *A Profession under Review,* N.Y. St. B. J. 15, 17 (January 1985).

20. Joseph Allegretti, *Can the Ordinary Practice of Law Be a Religious Calling?: I. Theological and Philosophical Underpinnings of Law as a Religious Calling: Clients, Courts, and Calling: Rethinking the Practice of Law,* 32 Pepp. L. Rev. 395, 395 (2005).

21. *See* Gloria McPherson, *Legal Assistants: An Evolving Role in the Practice of Law in Alabama,* Ala. Law., May 2002, at 178.

22. Andrew Fede, *Analysis: Wider Use of Paralegals Raises Ethical Issues,* 121 N.J.L.J. 1426 (1988).

23. Ind. Code §1-1-4-6 (2006).

24. *See* the Indiana Paralegals Association's Web site at www.indianaparalegals.org.

25. Ind. R. Prof. Conduct §9.1–9.10 (2006).

26. For some examples of state efforts to regulate the profession, see Cal. Bus. & Prof. Code § 6450 (West 2003); N.H. Sup. Ct. R., Administrative Rules R. 35; Provisional Order No. 18, 454 A.2d 1222 (R.I. 1983); Minn. Stat. Ann. § 481.02(3)(5) (West 2002); Va. Sup. Ct. R. 6:1-6-103; In re Unauthorized Practice Rules, 422 S.E.2d 123, 125 (S.C. 1992); WASH. CT. R., GEN. R. 24(b)(7).

27. Cal. Bus. & Prof.Code § 6450 (West 2006). Paralegal defined; prohibited activities; qualifications; continuing legal education January 1, 2004. *See also Avoiding the Unauthorized Practice of Law: Proposed Regulations for Paralegals in South Carolina,* 53 S.C.L. REV. 487 (2002); *Looking Closely at the Role of Paralegals: The California, New Jersey, and Wisconsin Experiences,* 80 MICH. B.J. 56 (2001); Quintin Johnstone, *Connecticut Unauthorized Practice Laws and Some Options for Their Reform,* 36 CT. L. REV. 303 (Winter, 2004); Washington Paralegal Association's Web page regarding paralegal regulation at www.wspaonline.org/regulation.htm.

28. *See* Wash. Ct. R. GR 24; Wash. R. Prof. Conduct 5.3 (2006).

29. *Id.*

30. For an excellent summary of state attempts to regulate paralegals, *see* http://www.paralegals.org/displaycommon.cfm?an=1&subarticlenbr=38; *see also* Daniel R. Ray, *Regulating Legal Assistant Practice: A Proposal That Offers Something,* 11 WASH. UNIV. J. L. & POLICY 249 (2003).

31. *See* Jacqueline Meile Rasmussen & Paul M. Sedlacek, *Paralegals: Changing the Practice of Law,* 44 S.D. L. REV. 319, 330 (1999).

32. *See* NFPA's position on regulation at its Web site under professional development at www.paralegals.org.

33. NATIONAL FEDERATION OF PARALEGAL ASSOCIATIONS, INC., STATEMENT ON ISSUES AFFECTING THE PARALEGAL PROFESSION (2001), available on NFPA's Web site under professional development—miscellaneous at www.paralegals.org.

34. Mark Dowdy, *NFPA's Wind of Change,* LEGAL ASS'T TODAY, Jan.–Feb. 1993, at 28.

35. Carl Sellinger, *The Retention of Limitations on the Out-of-Court Practice of Law by Independent Paralegals,* 9 GEORGETOWN J. L. ETH. 879 (Spring 1996).

36. *See What Constitutes Unauthorized Practice of Law by Paralegal,* 109 A.L.R.5th 275 (2003).

37. ABA Standing Committee on Paralegals, Information for Lawyers: How Paralegals Can Improve Your Practice*,* available at http://www.abanet.org/legalservices/paralegals/lawyers.html (2005).

38. *See* ABA Guidelines for the Approval of Paralegal Education Programs (2003), available online at http://www.abanet.org/legalservices/paralegals/downloads/2003guidelines.pdf.

39. Guidelines and fee information on the approval process for paralegal education programs are available on the ABA's Web site at http://www.abanet.org/legalservices/paralegals/process.html.

40. Model Code of Professional Responsibility (1983); Model Rules of Professional Conduct (1998).

41. *See* Julie A. Flaming, *Avoiding the Unauthorized Practice of Law: Proposed Regulations for Paralegals in South Carolina,* 53 S. C. L. REV. 487 (Winter 2002).

42. *Id.; see also* Andrew Fede, *Analysis: Wider Use of Paralegals Raises Ethical Issues,* 121 N.J.L.J. 1426 (1988).

43. *See* N. J. R. Prof. Conduct §5.3(c); *see also* In re Shaw, 88 N.J. 433-41 (1982).

44. National Federation of Paralegal Association, *NFPA Updates Its Position on Regulation of Paralegals* (2001).

45. *Id.;* NFPA, *Paralegal Education Position* (1999), available at http://www.paralegals.org/displaycommon.cfm?an=1&subarticlenbr=358; *see also* Mark Dowdy, *NFPA's Wind of Change,* LEGAL ASS'T TODAY Jan.–Feb. 1993, at 28.

46. Association of Trial Lawyers of America, *ATLA's Paralegal Affiliates Grow in Numbers,* ADVOC., March 1993, at 15; ATLA Member Resources, *Paralegal Affiliates,* at http://www.atla.org/Networking/Tier3/ParalegalAffiliates.aspx.

47. AAFPE'S Web site at http://www.aafpe.org/p_about/mission.htm.

48. NALS Web site at http://www.nals.org/certification/ProfessionalParalegal/Index.html.

49. *See* NATIONAL ASSOCIATION OF LEGAL ASSISTANTS, INC., GUIDELINES ON CERTIFIED LEGAL ASSISTANT PROGRAMS (1993).

50. *Id.*

51. *Id.* at 21.

52. NATIONAL ASSOCIATION OF LEGAL ASSISTANTS, CERTIFICATION—A PROFESSIONAL GOAL 2 (1992).

53. Kathleen A. Rasmussen, *Legal Assistants: A Growing Role in the Practice of Law in Alabama,* 52 ALA. LAW. 214, 219 (July 1991).

54. AMERICAN BAR ASSOCIATION, GUIDELINES AND PROCEDURES OF LEGAL ASSISTANT EDUCATION PROGRAMS 8–9 (2003).

55. *Id.*

56. *Id.; see also* RAYMOND MARCIN, BASIC SUBSTANTIVE LAW FOR PARALEGALS: CONTRACTS, TORTS, AND DUE PROCESS (1973).

57. http://www.nals.org/certification/ALS/index.html.

58. http://www.nals.org/certification/PLS/index.html.

59. http://www.nals.org/certification/professionalparalegal/ index.html.

60. http://aapipara.org/Positionstatements.htm.

61. NALA's MODEL STANDARDS AND GUIDELINES FOR UTILIZATION OF LEGAL ASSISTANTS, (2005).

62. *Id.*

63. AAPI Code of Ethics.

64. Note, *ABA Adopts Model Guidelines for Use of Legal Assistants*, LEGAL ASS'T TODAY 12 (Nov.–Dec. 1991).

65. For a recent series of articles about the importance of education in the paralegal community, *see The Education Gam*e, LEGAL ASSISTANT TODAY, Jan.–Feb. 2006.

66. Many states are now involved in the definition of the term *paralega*l. Recently Indiana has jumped in the game. See Rule 2.2: Paralegals, Indiana Rules for Admission to the Bar and the Discipline of Attorneys, Supreme Court of Indiana 2005; State Bar of California, Bar Disciplinary Rule across the Nation, Cal. B. Rev. 1–3 (1980).

67. RICHARD C. WYDICK, PROFESSIONAL RESPONSIBILITY (1988).

68. Model Code of Professional Responsibility at Comment (1983).

69. *See* ABA COMM. ON PROFESSIONAL ETHICS, FORMAL OP. 316 (1967).

70. *See* ABA COMM. ON PROFESSIONAL ETHICS, FORMAL OP. 316 at comment (1967).

71. In the military context, the lines are more than fuzzy. *See* Charles J. Dunlap, Jr., *Speeches and Comments the Revolution in Military Legal Affairs: Air Force Legal Professionals in 21st Century Conflicts*, 21. 51 A.F.L. REV. 293 (2001).

72. Andrew Fede, *Analysis: Wider Use of Paralegals Raises Ethical Issues,* 121 N.J.L.J. 1426, 1426 (1988); *see also* Note, *Representation of Clients before Administrative Agencies: Authorized or Unauthorized Practice of Law?* 15 VALPARISO L. REV. 567 (1981); Comment, *The Unauthorized Practice of Law by Laymen and Lay Associates,* 54 CALIF. L. REV. 1331 (1966); ADVISORY COMMITTEE ON PROFESSIONAL ETHICS, OPINION No. 471, 107 N. J.L.J. *See also* NJ Bar Association Web site at http://www.judiciary.state.nj.us/rules/apprpc.htm.

73. For a case in which the court drew the line of demarcation, *see* Doe v. Condon, 532 S.E.2d 879 (4th Cir. 2000).

74. DEBORAH K. ORLICK, ETHICS FOR THE LEGAL ASSISTANT (1992).

75. Janet M. Price, *Access to Justice Pro Bono and Paralegals: Helping to Make a Difference* COLO. LAW., Sept. 2001, at 55.

76. "Other trends have encouraged nonlawyers to respond to this unmet demand. An increasing specialization in legal work, coupled with a growing reliance on paralegals and routine case-processing systems, undercuts some of the traditional competence-related justifications for banning lay competitors. Law school and bar exam requirements provide no guarantee of expertise in areas where the need for low-cost services is greatest: divorce, landlord/tenant disputes, bankruptcy, immigration, welfare claims, tax preparation, and real estate transactions. In many of these contexts, secretaries or paralegals working for a lawyer already perform a large share of routine services, and this experience has equipped a growing number of employees to branch out on their own." Deborah L. Rhode, *The Delivery of Legal Services by Nonlawyers*, 4 GEO. J. LEGAL ETHICS 209, 215 (Fall 1990).

77. STATE BAR OF CALIFORNIA, REPORT OF THE PUBLIC PROTECTION COMMITTEE, 1 (April 22, 1988).

78. Cal. Bus. & Prof. Code §6450 (West 2006).

79. For an excellent article on the subtleties of unauthorized practice and paralegals, *see* Debra Levy Martinelli, *Are You Riding a Fine Line? Learn to Identify and Avoid Issues Involving the Unauthorized Practice of Law,* 18 UTAH BAR J. (December 2002). People v. Landlords Professional Services, 215 CAL. APP. 3D 1599, 264 CAL. RPTR. 548 (1989) (nonlawyer service provider and UPL); UPL Committee v. State Department of Worker's Compensation, 543 A.2d 662 (R.I 1998) (nonlawyer assistants in administrative agency proceedings); In re Welch, 185 A.2d 458, 459 (Vt. 1962) (definition of practice of law).

80. DEBORAH K. ORLIK, ETHICS FOR THE LEGAL ASSISTANT 38 (1993).

81. NFPA, PROFESSIONAL DEVELOPMENT, AGENCIES THAT ALLOW NONLAWYER PRACTICE http://www.paralegals.org/displaycommon.cfm?an=1&subarticlenbr=334.

82. *Are You Riding a Fine Line? Learn to Identify and Avoid Issues Involving the Unauthorized Practice of Law,* 15 UTAH B.J., Dec. 2002, at 18, 18.

83. State Bar of Arizona v. Arizona Land Title and Trust Co., 366 P.2d 1 (Ariz 1961).

84. *Id.*

85. Baron v. City of Los Angeles, 469 P.2d 353 (Cal. 1970).

86. New York County Lawyers Association v. Davey, 234 N.E2d 459 (N.Y.1967),

87. Le Doux v. Credit Research Corp., 125 Cal. Rptr.166 (1975).

88. State Bar of New Mexico v. Guardian Abstract and Title Co., Inc., 575 P.2d 943 (N.M. 1978).

89. Orlik, *supra* note 80 at 39.

90. State Bar of Texas v. Faubion, 821 S.W.2d 203 (Tex. 1990).

91. Orlik, *supra* note 80, at 54–55.

92. In the Matter of Martinez, 745 P.2d 842 (N.M. 1988).

93. Orlik, *supra* note 80, at 58.

94. MODEL RULES OF PROFESSIONAL CONDUCT RULE 5.2 (1998).

95. Model Rules, *supra* note 95, at Rule 1.3(4) comment.

96. *Id.* at Rule 1.3(4) comment.

97. See the NFPA's Web site at www.paralegals.org. For an interesting discussion of the role of paralegals and billable hours, *see* THERESE A. CANNON, CONCISE GUIDE TO PARALEGAL ETHICS 114 (2002); *see also* In re Hessinger & Assoc., 171 B.R. 366 (Bankr. N.C. Cal. 1994) (bankruptcy court sanctions attorney for fee splitting, excessive fees, and partnership with nonlawyers).

98. MODEL CODE, *supra* note 96, at EC 1-5.

99. Vicki G. Adler, *Lawyer's Fees: A Cornucopia for Client Complaints*, 19 ARIZ. ST. L.J. 71, 73 (1987).

100. MODEL RULES, *supra* note 95, at Rule 5.5 comment.

101. *See* MODEL CODE, *supra* note 96, at EC 1-5(e) and MODEL RULES, *supra* note 95, at Rule 1.5.

102. *See* MODEL RULES, *supra* note 95, at Rule 1.5(e).

103. See Absher Const. Co. v. Kent School Dist., 79 Wash. Ct. App. 841, 917 P.2d 1086 (1995) (appellate court case upholds fee award with paralegal fees and sets forth list of criteria for determining if fees should be awarded); Missouri v. Jenkins, 491 U.S. 274 (1989) (landmark U.S. Supreme Court case upholds award of attorney's fees that included compensation for paralegal time at market rates); Taylor v. Chubb, 874 P.2d 806 (Okla. 1994) (Oklahoma Supreme Court case upholds award of attorney's fees with paralegal fees at market rates). *See also* Great American Leasing Corp. v. Cool Comfort Air, No. 165/03-1581 (Iowa Sup. Jan. 28, 2005), available at www.nala.org/Iowa-SCDecision-Jan05.pdf.

104. *See generally* Cannon, *supra* note 99, at 44; see also Samaritan Found. v. Super. Ct., 844 P.2d 593 (Ariz. App. Divl. 1 1992) (extension of privilege to paralegals).

105. *See* MODEL RULES, *supra* note 95, at Rule 1.6.

106. JAMES MCCARTHY, MAKING TRIAL OBJECTIONS 8.2 (1986).

107. CHARLES P. NEMETH, EVIDENCE HANDBOOK FOR PARALEGALS 245 (1993).

108. In re Complex Asbestos Litigation, 232 Cal. App. 3d 572, 283 CAL. REPTR. 732 (1991).

109. Stephanie B. Goldberg, *Disqualified (Switching Sides by Legal Assistants in Litigation)*, 77 A.B.A. J. 88 (October 1991).

110. THE PENNSYLVANIA BAR INSTITUTE, ETHICAL ISSUES FOR CIVIL LITIGATORS 41 (1993).

111. Ann E. Dunkin, *Finding, Interviewing, Hiring, and Retaining the Best Paralegal for Your Practice*, TEX. B.J., March 2000, at 276, 278.

112. *See* KENTUCKY BAR ASSOCIATION, OP. E-308 (1985).

113. Andrew Fede, *Analysis: Wider Use of Paralegals Raises Ethical Issues*, 121 N.J.L.J. 1426, 11 (1988).

114. *See* MODEL RULES, *supra* note 95, at Rule 1.7 comment; for a related analysis of former clients, *see* MODEL RULES, *supra* note 95, at Rule 1.9 comment.

115. Richard C. Montgomery, *Ethical and Legal Issues in Law Firm Accounting*, 64 PENN. B. ASS'N Q. 39, 40 (Jan. 1993).

116. *See* Samuel J. Levine, *Seeking a Common Language for the Application of Rule 11 Sanctions for What Is "Frivilous,"* 78 NE. L. R. 677 (1999).

117. Rodney M. Arthur & Ellen F. Brandt, *Making the Malpractice Case against the Lawyer*, 16 ALI-ABA COURSE MATERIAL J. 89–90 (1992); *see also* Mary Margaret Penrose & Dace A. Caldwell, *Articles: A Short and Plain Solution to the Medical Malpractice Crisis: Why Charles E. Clark Remains Prophetically Correct about Special Pleading and the Big Case,* 39 GA. L. REV. 971 (2005).

118. Richard Matasar, *The Pain of Moral Lawyering*, 75 IOWA L. REV. 974, 976 (1990).

119. Castillo v. St. Paul Fire and Marine Insurance Co., No. Misc. S-92-4, U.S.D.C., C.D.Ill., 1992, LLR. No. 9211041 C. FTC.

120. Note, *Federal District Court Suspends Lawyers for "Unbecoming Conduct,"* 7 LAW. LIABILITY REV. Q. 19, 20 (Jan. 1993).

121. Bennett L. Gershman, *Tricks Prosecutors Play*, TRIAL, April 1992, at 46, 47–49.

122. Matasar, *supra* note 121, at 974

Chapter 3

The Nature of Law and the American Court System

RATIONALIZATIONS FOR LAW

Anyone embarking upon a legal career, whether it be as a paralegal, law clerk, judge, or attorney, will eventually develop a reverence for the law. It is a funny thing, this concept known as *law*. Civilizations come to depend on its promulgation and enforcement for survival, and these civilizations fall when they forget its true purpose: adherence to justice. In Western tradition, notions of law are bound up in history—where principles of law and equity are passed down though the ages. This concept of the common law, whereby law is not codified but agreed on by consensus, represents this attachment to the historical nature of law. The American experience with law has been both colorful and simultaneously honorable. What is indisputable is this nation's decision to put *law* at its foundation and to depend on it for all sorts of things: from the enforcement of rights and obligations to the assurance of due process in a world filled with inequality. Exactly what law is has been the subject of much debate over the centuries. Most of us are comfortable with the notion that law is a promulgation or an enactment of sorts. State statutes, the Model Penal Code, and the Federal Rules of Criminal Procedure, to name a few, are the chief ways we define laws. Others see the idea of law in a more abstract way. For example, Cicero, the great Roman lawyer and thinker, thought that law and nature were somehow intertwined.[1] And in a way this makes perfect sense—that law sits very obviously in nature. Others like Thomas Aquinas saw law as the rule and measure of reason. It was deposited in our intellect, so to speak, and we already know what is lawful and what is not.[2] In other schools, like Marxism, law was an expression of the ruling class and a reflection of power. While this short exposé cannot do justice to these many definitions, it is obvious that law means more than a codification.

Although our laws have been created in an orderly and logical way, multiple influences have come to bear on their enactment and interpretation. For example, what roles have custom, habit, and social mores played in the evolution of law? Do religion and morality intersect with law and have some integral place in the draftsmanship of codified law?[3] Former Supreme Court Justice Benjamin Cardozo's *The Nature of the Judicial Process* fully appreciates the complexities in the definition of law and urges practitioners to realize that *law* has its own life and history:

> . . . *the judge in shaping the rules of law must heed the mores of his day. Law is indeed a historical growth, for it is an expression of customary morality that develops silently and unconsciously from one age to another...but law is also the conscience or purpose of growth, for the expression of customary morality will be false unless the mind of the judge is directed to the attainment of the moral end and its embodiment in legal forms. Nothing less than conscious effort will be adequate if the end in view is to prevail. The standards or patterns of utility in morals will be found by the judge in the life of the community.*[4]

What role do public opinion and consensus have in the interpretation of laws and their judicial construction? Should the interpretation of laws be political? Or should law be simply the product of humanity and science? Is there a place for disobedience and revolt against existing laws? Is the citizen bound to obey laws that are inherently unjust? Or may that citizen "disobey" such content?[5] How closely should contemporary jurists follow the original intent and language of the American Constitution? In short, law does not emerge in a vacuum, and its full understanding and mastery of definition will come to depend on other forces and factors in its making. Codification or case law opinion is not enough.

Why and how law comes about can be described only as a complex process and with enormous variety of opinion. Some may argue that law comes about by pure necessity; this is the notion that we cannot function without it. Others posit that law reflects something higher—a transcendent notion such as God, nature, or the inner cravings for order that each person seems to possess.[6] Others might opine that law comes about due to economic, cultural, and military influence. It is a safe bet that all of these schools have something to offer.

Law as the Product of Necessity

For some thinkers, law arises by necessity. This view propounds the notion that law must come into existence in order for the culture to survive. Without it, disorder and anarchy reign. Law gives stability and order to a society.

According to some scholars, "The history of law in relation to society reveals that humanity's earliest efforts of lawmaking were prompted by the basic desire of self-preservation. Although engulfed by a society that necessitated such combinations as clans and tribes for protection, as well as for social and economic advancement, the nature of the individual led to the development of certain expressed general rights with regard to person and property."[7]

Thus necessity dictates law for "both reasons of utility and man's lack of perfection."[8] Without it, order is replaced by chaos, and no viable means of social control exists. Law by that becomes a means of formal, social control—a mandatory step to ensure social order.

Law as the Formalization of Customs, Habits, and Mores

Customs, habits, and mores are informal means of control in a society.[9] Consider the workings of your own family. Can certain habits and customs be described as binding though unwritten rules of conduct and behavior? Are there rules or practices regarding social gatherings, driving habits, or forms of holiday observance? Social parameters and expectations shape how people dress, engage sexually, practice religious beliefs, or employ manners of speech. In these situations, methods of formal control are supplanted by informal mechanisms in the form of habit and customs.

Venerable legal scholar Roscoe Pound used common sense in describing how law is initially the product of informal means and social consensus. He characterized law as no more or no less than

1. The product of certain moral judgment on conduct.
2. The product of common sense about common things.
3. Drafted without absolute language or exact content but subject to relative interpretation during differing times, places, and circumstances.[10]

Others paint the idea of custom in a more global context—that nations and countries appear to have some set of interactive principles in their dealings with one another even if these things are not written down anywhere. This is often labeled as *ius gentium*—an international law of nations and tribes that has its own tradition. As Messner propounds,

> *It is upon the same human nature, with the same reason, the same conscience, and the same weaknesses, that people of all ages have established their social systems, having found by experience what was necessary and expedient for securing the common utility.*[11]

Unfortunately the complexity of modern society makes it impossible to retain only an informal means of control—between either individuals or nations. Although there are many things that the bulk of the culture can agree upon, and thereby permit or proscribe, the range and breadth of these commonly shared beliefs shrinks each passing day. Diverse philosophical and theological points of view, toleration of once prohibited behaviors, and a shaky moral consensus on human action cause the shared consensus on norms, habits, and customs to crumble.

Law as the Product of Natural Law

A significant school of legal thought can be characterized as encompassing the *natural law*. By natural law, the proponent poses a series of precepts and predilections that are deposited in the human species and are part of their makeup.[12] In other words, there are rules and laws that guide our operation, and these tenets of the natural law can be discovered in reason and the intellect. In this sense, we already can identify things that are right and good and actions we should avoid. Self-preservation, family, community, procreation, and care of children, as well as a belief in God, are the fundamental tenets of the natural law. Simply put, law, according to the natural law proponent, can be discovered in our very construction, or even discerned in the rules and laws so evident in nature itself. Joseph Boyle sums it up well:

> *The first of these components is the view that there are moral principles which all mature human beings can know, the naturally known principles which are written on the human heart. According to natural law theory, these principles, the foundational prescriptions of the natural law, are accessible to all, . . . (and) that specific moral norms follow from these principles in such a way for people to see their truth, even though it is possible, because of cultural distortion or personal immorality, that people be ignorant of them.*[13]

The depth and breadth of natural law reasoning is well documented. From Cicero's naturalism,[14] which discovers truth in natural processes, to the delineations of natural law principles outlined in the *Summa Theologica* of St. Thomas Aquinas,[15] the yearning for some dependable and reliable underpinnings for law has been continuous. In a nutshell, the natural law advocate seeks legal truth in the truth of higher things, whether in the natural order, the cosmos, or the transcendent imprint of the Creator who gave life to the human player. In Aquinas, the idea of a *law* rooted in higher things would be forever forged. "Law, for St. Thomas, leaps far beyond the text. Its essence is formulated in God Himself, by and through the Eternal Law. The *lex aeterna* is the divine exemplar and that perfection that is the supreme rationality of the Creator. The law that is God eventually finds its imprint in His creatures, especially the rational ones, by and through the imprint of the natural law."[16]

Adhering to the tenets of the natural law leads, according to its proponents, to not only a legal life but a very happy one. Alisdair MacIntyre vividly portrays the impact of a life led in the natural law:

> *It follows that human beings who fail to discover what their true good and happiness consist in will be perpetually balked and frustrated. . . . Obeying the precepts of the natural law is more than simply refraining from doing what those precepts prohibit and doing what they enjoin. These precepts become effectively operative only as we find ourselves with motivating reasons for performing actions inconsistent with those precepts; what the precepts can then provide us with is a reason which can outweigh the motivating reasons for disobeying them—that is, they point us to a more perfect good than do the latter.*[17]

For most of the American legal experience, this search for the higher or transcendent principle when deciding legal cases has been part of the landscape. Indeed, the infant American nation fully proclaimed its dependence on a deity as part of its foundation, and it is not difficult to find natural law influences in the writings of the Founding Fathers.[18] Considering the metaphysical in judicial reasoning has become a lost art in the American courtrooms and legislative halls.[19]

Law as a Product of Positivism

Even classical theorists like St. Thomas accepted and applauded positive (human) law but not without its dependence and interdependence on the eternal natural law. If anything, human law corrals and controls those inclined to do wicked things.[20] Human law is not only desirable but fully necessitous for the maintenance of order.[21] Positive laws are those laws set out and decided upon by humans for their own purposes—a combination of rules and political determinations. Despite this necessity, human law has historically looked to other criteria in its promulgation. Positivism, in and of itself, without guidance from the transcendent, is a relatively modern phenomenon. The picture has changed dramatically in the last 200 years of Western culture.

John Austin, a late 19th century legal philosopher, in his *Lectures on Jurisprudence*,[22] characterized law in a more utilitarian context: that which is useful for the many or the most can be deemed good law.[23] Along with David Hume, John Stuart Mill, and others, he deemed law "good" if it was "good" for humanity. But humans, although not changing essentially, do change their opinions, and they are readily subject to whim, fancy, and the roar of the mob.[24] Hence human enactments, dependent solely on what men and women desire or want, are tricky by design. Positivism radically alters the legal landscape because the basic view of the positivist harkens for a separation from any standard of morality that is set by authorities other than the sovereign. At first glance, this appears to provide certainty about what must be accepted as binding law and ensures stability by rejecting any outside test of validity. The role of judges under positivist theory is to apply the law of the sovereign, not to substitute personal or religious notions of their own about what is wise.[25] However, it was positivism that justified slavery. It was positivism that enabled the fascism of Hitler's state. In a sense, the 20th century mirrors the abandonment of the transcendent in favor of the temporal. Heinrich Rommen lived through the Nazi state and wrote exquisitely about the collapse of modern Germany:

> *We have recorded the victory of positivism. But this must not be taken to mean that positivism won a definitive and total victory on all intellectual, moral, and political fronts. The victory, such as it was, was the outcome of the eventual undermining of metaphysics and the progressive dilution of the Christian heritage . . .*[26]

The acceptance of positivistic legal thinking over other legal philosophies has not been universal. If anything, the American tradition placed significant emphasis on law being related to or influenced by religious and theological tenets. A short look at our history indicates this from Sunday Blue Laws relating to store closings, to proscriptions against public indecency, intoxication, lewdness, and other moral charges. With the rise of evangelical political power in the 21st century, our legislators are increasingly witnessing calls for a return to earlier, even colonial conceptions of law. On the other hand, others are upset by using any law to *legislate morality*. Although modern positivism has many allies, it remains to be seen whether positivism can justify the existence of any law based solely on human experience and utility.

TYPES AND SOURCES OF LAW

Law is further defined and organized by the subject matter of the enactment. In the broadest sense, law falls into two main categories: substantive and procedural. In the former, the content of the law, whether it be agriculture or property, represents the *substance* of the law. In the latter, how one goes about advocating the law—its processes, rules, and regulations—defines *procedural law*. The scope of law can be general in design, with legal principles (such as equity) coursing their way through multiple law coverage, to the specialized topics, like maritime or medical malpractice, that continually emerge in our very lively legal system.

The following list covers the common *categories of law:*

- Criminal law.
- Civil law.
- Domestic relations law.
- Corporate law.
- Contract law.
- Tort law.
- Personal injury law.
- Medical malpractice law.
- Product liability law.
- Environmental law.
- Housing law.
- Oil and gas law.
- Tax law.
- ERISA law.
- Pension law.
- Admiralty law.
- Maritime law.
- International law.
- Immigration law.
- Communications law.
- Municipal law.
- Federal law.
- Litigation law.
- Arbitration law.
- Labor law.
- Zoning law.
- Real estate law.
- Insurance law.
- Hospital law.
- Age discrimination law.
- Legal aid law.
- Appellate law.
- Social Security law.
- Government agencies law.
- Constitutional law.
- Conflicts of law.
- Secured transactions.
- Equity law.
- Commercial paper.
- Sales law.
- Estates, trust, and probate law.
- Agency law.
- Patent and trademark law.
- Intellectual property law.
- Computer and media law.
- Sports and entertainment law.
- Bankruptcy law.
- Debtor/creditor law.
- International law.
- Litigation law.

When considering this list, we can imagine various career tracks and specialties, as well as why it is so difficult to master all areas of legal practice. It is no wonder that law practice tends to be specialized. Law is also classified according to the topics discussed throughout the remainder of this section.

Common Law

Despite its maze of codified statutes and legislative materials, the American legal system relies heavily on principles of common law. Dating from the time of the Greek and Roman empires, and inculcating the decisions and general principles of commonwealth nations such as Canada, England, and Australia, certain principles, ideas, and legal postulates are universally accepted in Western tradition. An example of this proposition would be the right to a jury, a common-law proposition that Western nations agree on. Common-law principles or findings are commonly employed and commonly understood by these common cultures. From the Norman Conquest onward, certain principles of English law became understood and known by the masses. Laws generally were not written until the mid-1500s. Thus legal principles, definitions of crime, and standards of conduct were well understood by the populace and the existing legal system, though limited it might have been.[27]

Upon colonization of the Americas, these principles, common ideas, and common legal maxims were infused into our legal thinking. Brody, describing the common law in colonial America, states articulately,

> *That body of principles described as the common law does not consist of absolute, fixed, or inflexible rules, but rather broad and comprehensive principles based on justice, reaction, and common sense. Its principles have been decided by the social needs of the community, and it reflects changes in such needs. Most important, the common law can adapt to new conditions, interests, relations, and usages as the progress of society may require.*[28]

Currently all American jurisdictions possess vestiges of the common law. The common law is a live and viable force whether incorporated into the statutory or legislative construction or recognized in the body of law applicable to judicial decision making. Judges are often faced with cases that lack a statutory or legislative basis, and in making a decision often call upon common-law principles. This is particularly so in commonwealth jurisdictions such as Pennsylvania, Kentucky, and Virginia.

Case Law

Judicial decisions of the local, state, and federal courts craft case law. Legal decisions, which interpret existing laws, are reported to the public in the form of case law. Cases result from disputes between parties, *plaintiffs* and *defendants*, which cannot be resolved by informal or other means. A typical case caption lays out the parties and the jurisdiction in the following manner:

PLAINTIFF v. DEFENDANT
e.g., LiCause v. Canton
42 Ohio St. 3d 109 (1989)

Reproduced in Figure 3.1 is a sample case. Note the plaintiff and defendant, court of jurisdiction, case number, and the body of the case, which includes

- Caption: Referencing jurisdiction of court.
- Headnotes: short summary of case content.
- Decision: judicial resolution.
- Holding: reasoning of the court.

Within the confines of a case decision rests a judge's ruling. Case law determinations may depend on common-law principles, as well as statutory, legislative, or administrative rules and regulations. However, sometimes there is an insufficient basis in law or an obvious lack of a legal or equitable remedy. When this occurs, depending on judicial philosophy and the facts at hand, a judge will essentially craft a law by a case decision or refuse to resolve the matter between the litigants and advise the legislature to deal with the question. Judges who are labeled *active* do not hesitate to shape new law; judges that are less inclined are known as *strict constructionists*. In the former case, the judge latches onto a particular law, its language, and its content but does not hesitate to imply or jump out of the statutory box to reach a resolution. The abortion decision *Roe v. Wade* is an example of classic activism, whereas its dissent pines for more rigor and urges the advocates to stay within the written words of the statute or amendment in question.

Decisions of the trial courts of record are published within various national and state reporter systems. Case law eventually becomes assembled into a body of cases with similar reasoning justifying the decisions. A decision may or may not become legal precedent. The principle of *stare decicis* informally regulates the courts by urging caution in the overthrow of a precedent. *Let the decision stand* means that judges should be wary of disregarding or overturning precedent. Precedents are given substantial weight by jurists in cases bearing similar circumstances and fact patterns. Decisions are accorded precedential value. *Precedent* is defined as

> *An authority to be followed in courts of justice; a judicial decision on a point of law arising in a given case; a written form of proceedings which have been approved by the courts, or by professional usage, and is thus to be followed.*[29]

FIGURE 3.1   Sample Case

Source: FEDERAL REPORTER, 2nd Series. Reprinted with permission from Thomson/West.

UNITED STATES v. GROSS
Cite as 603 F.2d 757 (1979)

UNITED STATES of America, Appellee,
v.
Jackie Yvonne Gross, Appellant.
No. 78–2379.

United States Court of Appeals,
Ninth Circuit.

Aug. 30, 1979

Defendant was convicted in the United States District Court for the Southern District of California, Howard B. Turrentine, J., of assaulting a federal officer, and she appealed. The Court of Appeals held that (1) evidence was sufficient to sustain defendant's conviction, but (2) it was prejudicial error to admit, over her objection, defendant's two prior narcotics convictions to impeach her.

Reversed.

1. Assault and Battery ⟜91
Evidence that defendant grabbed the hair of a federal agent who was in an argument with her husband involving alleged drug trafficking was sufficient to support her conviction for assaulting a federal officer. 18 U.S.C.A. § 111.

2. Criminal Law ⟜1170 ½ (1)
   Witnesses ⟜337(6)
In prosecution for assaulting a federal officer arising from incident in which defendant grabbed the hair of a federal officer who was in an argument with her husband concerning alleged drug trafficking, it was prejudicial error to admit, over her objection, defendant's two prior narcotics convictions to impeach her. Fed.Rules Evid.rules 609, 609(a), 28 U.S.C.A.

3. Criminal Law ⟜627.6(1)
Evidence favorable to an accused must be disclosed upon request where evidence is material to guilt or punishment; standard of materiality varies depending upon nature of information withheld and type of request made by defendant.

4. Criminal Law ⟜627.6(1), 700
If a general request or no request is made, disclosure of evidence is required only if omitted evidence creates reasonable doubt that did not otherwise exist; however, if a specific request for disclosure of evidence was made, standard of materiality is whether evidence might have affected the outcome of trial.

Robert L. Miller, Miller & Miller, Los Angeles, Cal., David P. Curnow, Amos & Curnow (argued), San Diego, Cal., for appellant.

John J. Robinson, Asst. U.S. Atty. (on the brief), Michael H. Walsh, U.S. Atty., John J. Robinson, Asst. U.S. Atty. (argued), San Diego, Cal., for appellee.

Appeal from the United States District Court for the Southern District of California.

Before HUFSTEDLER and TRASK, Circuit Judges, and McNICHOLS,* District Judge.

PER CURIAM:

Appellant was convicted for assaulting a federal officer in violation of 18 U.S.C. § 111. She complains that (1) the evidence was insufficient to support her conviction; (2) the district court prejudicially erred in admitting, over objection, two prior narcotics convictions to impeach her; (3) *Brady* material was improperly suppressed; and (4) the jury was improperly instructed.

On February 24, 1978, DEA Agent Hu, and a government informant, Bogan, tried to buy cocaine from Warren Gross, appellant's husband. Bogan was given $1,500 Government money with which to purchase the cocaine. Warren Gross and Bogan transacted their business outside Hu's presence. Thereafter, Bogan gave Hu a bag of white powder, which turned out to be either extremely poor cocaine or a substance that was not cocaine. Later on the same day a strip search of Bogan revealed $700 of the Government's money in one of his shoes.

After Bogan's "rip-off," DEA Agents Hu and McKinnon, among other agents, together with Bogan, went to visit Warren Gross, who was staying at the apartment of Norris. Hu, McKinnon, and Bogan reached the apartment about 11:00 p.m. When appellant's husband answered the door, a loud argument ensued. Appellant joined the group. Warren Gross refused the agents' request to go inside the apartment. Thereafter, a shoving match between Warren and McKinnon occurred. Agent Hu turned to help McKinnon, and appellant grabbed Agent Hu by the hair. Waiting agents joined the melee, and eventually appellant, her husband, and the other occupants of the apartment were subdued.

Appellant's defense at trial was that she was justifiably acting in defense of her husband. She claimed that she had heard nothing about any mention of drugs, that she had only heard references to "a package."

I

[1]   The evidence was sufficient to support her conviction. The jury was not obliged to believe her version of the events. Nevertheless, her defense and her credibility with respect to that defense become important on the Rule 609 and *Brady* issues to which we now turn.

At the time this case was tried, neither the court nor counsel had the benefit of a number of cases,

---

*Honorable Ray McNichols, Chief Judge, United States District Court, District of Idaho, sitting by designation.

FIGURE 3.1   (*concluded*)

throughout the country, interpreting Rule 609(a) of the Federal Rules of Evidence. We held this case pending the *en banc* determination of *United States v. Cook,* (9th Cir., *en banc,* 1979) [Slip Op'n 2303].

Appellant's prior convictions for narcotics offenses are not technically within the concept of *crimen falsi,* and, therefore, were inadmissible unless the Government bore its burden of proving that the probative value of the prior convictions for impeachment purposes exceeded the prejudicial effect of their admission. (*E.g., United States v. Cook, supra; United States v. Ortega,* 561 F.2d 803 (9th Cir. 1977) (shoplifting); *United States v. Hayes,* 553 F.2d 824 (2d Cir. 1977) (importing cocaine); *United States v. Hastings,* 577 F.2d 38 (8th Cir. 1978) (narcotics).) The Government offered no theory explaining how the probative value of appellant's prior narcotics convictions could outweigh the prejudice. To the extent that this issue was discussed at the time of trial, the argument was presented by defense counsel, who pointed out "as soon as the jury hears that she has been convicted previously of either smuggling or using narcotics—heroin—they are going to just assume, because of that, that she was involved with whatever Warren was supposed to have done, and it is going to unduly prejudice the jury's mind against her because she is only charged with assault, not anything else." The court did not require that any kind of showing be made by the Government in response. The court's explanation in overruling the objection does not suggest that the court was weighing the prejudicial effect against the probative value, for the only purpose for which it could have been admissible, which was impeachment.[1]

When appellant testified, she did not represent herself as a person who had no knowledge of drugs or drug trafficking. Therefore, nothing developed between the time at which the court issued its preliminary ruling and the conclusion of her testimony, that lent any added strength to the probative value of the evidence for impeachment purposes. Under these circumstances, the Government did not carry its burden of proving that the probative value was greater than the prejudicial effect of the evidence.

UNITED STATES V. BAKER
Cite as 603 F.2d 759 (1979)

[2]   Of course, we cannot know what factors the jury weighed in deciding the credibility issues against appellant. But we would be entirely unrealistic if we failed to perceive that the very prejudice that defense counsel anticipated occurred when the Government impeached her with her prior narcotics convictions. At least a hint that the jury was thus influenced appears from the jury's acquittal of a third defendant, who lived in the apartment and who asserted a defense of property. The acquittal occurred even though that defendant was involved in an extended brawl with several agents that lasted long after appellant had ceased resisting. We conclude that the erroneous admission of the prior convictions was prejudicial.

II

Appellant moved for disclosure of "all internal affairs records, files, and reports relating to complaints filed against and discipline imposed upon Agents Raymond J. McKinnon and Ululaulani M. B. Hu for the use of excessive force or other aggressive behavior." The Government thereupon produced certain documents for an *in camera* inspection. The district court determined that the material was not subject to disclosure.

[3, 4]   Evidence favorable to an accused must be disclosed upon request where the evidence is material to guilt or to punishment. (*Brady v. Maryland,* 373 U.S. 83, 83 S.Ct. 1194, 10 L.Ed.2d 215 (1963).)

The standard of materiality varies depending on the nature of the information withheld and the type of request made by a defendant. (*United States v. Agurs,* 427 U.S. 97, 96 S.Ct. 2392, 49 L.Ed.2d 342 (1976); *Skinner v. Cardwell,* 564 F.2d 1381 (9th Cir. 1977).) If a general request or no request is made, disclosure is required only "if the omitted evidence creates a reasonable doubt that did not otherwise exist." (*United States v. Agurs,* supra, 427 U.S. at 112, 96 S.Ct. at 2402.) If a specific request is made, the standard of materiality is whether the evidence "might have affected the outcome of the trial." (*Id.* at 104, 96 S.Ct. at 2398.) Appellant's request was unquestionably specific; "[i]t gave the prosecutor notice of exactly what the defendant desired." (*Id.* at 106, 96 S.Ct. at 2399; *United States v. Shelton,* 588 F.2d 1242 (9th Cir. 1978).) Implicit in the district court's decision that the information need not be produced is the court's determination that the disclosure could not have affected the outcome of the trial.

We have concluded that it is unnecessary for us to decide whether the district court correctly determined the materiality of the documents produced by the Government for *in camera* inspection. Although we must reverse for Rule 609 error, Gross will not be retried. She has served her sentence while the case was pending on appeal. For the same reason, it is unnecessary specifically to address any of the remaining questions that she raises.

REVERSED.

[1.] The court said, "I will charge the jury that it isn't to be considered in arriving at her guilt or innocence. It only goes to her credibility. It is not evidence of the guilt of the crime. It just goes to the credibility. I will give the usual instruction and I think it will be more advantageous to the jury to understand this than it will be prejudicial to her. If she wishes to take the stand. I am afraid she will have to suffer the consequences.

Constitutional Law

Constitutional law finds its way into the legal arena with extraordinary rapidity. Claims that are constitutional have dramatically increased over the last 50 years and directly reflect what has often been labeled the *Age of Rights*. The data on the rise of litigation have been staggering. The federal courts display no signs of slowdown:

> *The 28,376 case increase in civil filings in FY 2004 stemmed from a 16 percent increase in federal question filings, chiefly because of a doubling of special statutory actions related to financial investment cases. Federal question filings are actions under the Constitution, laws, or treaties of the U.S. in which the U.S. is not a party in the case. Federal question filings relating to personal injury/product liability more than doubled to 2,221 cases. Filings relating to labor law filings, and filed largely under the Fair Labor Standards Act, increased 6 percent. Filings relating to protected property rights actions, mostly copyright and patent cases, increased 7 percent.*
>
> *There also was an 11 percent increase in diversity of citizenship filings, largely as a result of a 62 percent surge in personal injury/product liability filings.[30]*

Figure 3.2 provides a graphic illustration of the number of civil cases filed from 2000 to 2004.

Our "constitution is a system of fundamental laws or principles for the government of a nation or a state. In the United States a constitution is a written charter adopted by the people, creating a government and outlining the forms and powers thereof and defining the basic rights of people. . . ."[31] The *Constitution of the United States*, with the resulting laws and treaties made under the authority of the United States, is the supreme law of the nation.[32] The entire text of the Constitution can be found at any local library; but those provisions having their greatest influence on the lives of paralegals, namely the *Bill of Rights*, are reproduced in Appendix B.

Most constitutional litigation is rooted in the Bill of Rights, with explicit provisions that impart certain express rights in criminal and civil proceedings. A summary is shown in Figure 3.3.

The influence of the Bill of Rights in current constitutional reasoning has been amply documented. Constitutional remedies, either implied or explicit, are adopted with little reservation. For the last century the U.S. Supreme Court has shown little restraint in its legal decision making relative to constitutional foundations, even if the language of the Constitution is silent or suffers from ambiguity.[33] *Rights* have been created by inference in the following matters:

- The right to birth control.[34]
- The right to free speech.[36]
- The decriminalization of sodomy.[38]
- The right to an abortion.[35]
- The right to an attorney in nontrial situations.[37]

FIGURE 3.2
Number of Civil Cases Filed, 2000–2004

Source: Filings Climbed in Federal Courts in Fiscal Year 2004, 37 THE THIRD BRANCH, March 2005. Published by U.S. Courts Office of Public Affairs. Available at http://www.uscourts.gov/ttb/mar05ttb/caseload/index.html (accessed October 6, 2006).

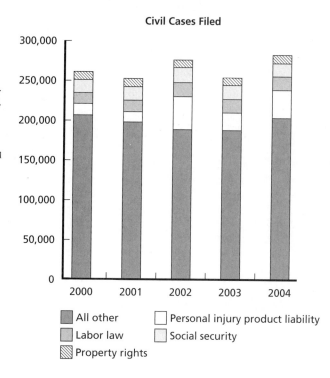

Civil Cases Filed

Legend: All other, Labor law, Property rights, Personal injury product liability, Social security

FIGURE 3.3 Summary of Bill of Rights

AMENDMENT I—Contains clauses covering the establishment of religion, freedom of speech, the right to a free press, the right to assemble, and the right to petition.

AMENDMENT II—Discusses the right to bear arms.

AMENDMENT IV—Contains clauses covering unreasonable search and seizure, warrants, probable cause standard, and oath or affirmation regarding seizures.

AMENDMENT V—Contains clauses covering the federal indictment requirement, the double jeopardy standard, federal due process, the right against self-incrimination, and eminent domain principles.

AMENDMENT VI—Contains clauses covering the right to a speedy and expeditious trial, the right to a public forum, the right to a preliminary hearing or other appearance, the right to confrontation, and the right to an attorney.

AMENDMENT VIII—Contains clauses covering the right not to be excessively fined, a general right to reasonable bail, and a right not to be punished cruelly or unusually.

AMENDMENT XIII—Abolishes slavery.

AMENDMENT XIV—Contains clauses covering state due process, "privacy," privileges and immunities, and equal protection.

However, the Court did demonstrate some hesitancy to grant a constitutional right to die in *Washington v. Glucksberg.*[39]

At the state level, the power and energy of the U.S. Constitution show few or no signs of waning since the Court has taken favor with the language of the Fourteenth Amendment. Federalism, at least for the present, dwarfs any real notion of states' rights. The provisions of the Fourteenth Amendment, which incorporate federal rights into the state arena, are outlined in Figure 3.4.

Whether by voluntary choice or legal necessity, state constitutions emulate these federal principles and, in some cases, liberally provide additional remedies not described or accounted for in the federal document. Consider Article I of the Commonwealth of Pennsylvania's Constitution, shown in Figure 3.5.

FIGURE 3.4 The Fourteenth Amendment

AMENDMENT XIV [1868]

Section 1. All persons born or naturalized in the United States and subject to the jurisdiction thereof are citizens of the United States and of the State wherein they reside. No State shall make or enforce any law which shall abridge the privileges or immunities of citizens of the United States; nor shall any State deprive any person of life, liberty, or property, without due process of law; nor deny to any person within its jurisdiction the equal protection of the laws.

Section 2. Representatives shall be apportioned among the several States according to their respective numbers, counting the whole number of persons in each State, excluding Indians not taxed. But when the right to vote at any election for the choice of electors for President and Vice President of the United States, Representatives in Congress, the Executive and Judicial officers of a State, or the members of the Legislature thereof, is denied to any of the male inhabitants of such State, being twenty-one years of age, and citizens of the United States, or in any way abridged, except for participation in rebellion, or other crime, the basis of representation therein shall be reduced in the proportion which the number of such male citizens shall bear to the whole number of male citizens twenty-one years of age in such State.

Section 3. No person shall be a Senator or Representative in Congress, or elector of President and Vice President, or hold any office, civil or military, under the United States, or under any State, who, having previously taken an oath, as a member of Congress, or as an officer of the United States, or as a member of any State legislature, or as an executive or judicial officer of any State, to support the Constitution of the United States, shall have engaged in insurrection or rebellion against the same, or given aid or comfort to the enemies thereof. But Congress may by a vote of two-thirds of each House, remove such disability.

Section 4. The validity of the public debt of the United States, authorized by law, including debts incurred for payment of pensions and bounties for services in suppressing insurrection or rebellion, shall not be questioned. But neither the United States nor any State shall assume or pay any debt or obligation incurred in aid of insurrection or rebellion against the United States, or any claim for the loss or emancipation of any slave; but all such debts, obligations, and claims shall be held illegal and void.

FIGURE 3.5   Article I of the Commonwealth of Pennsylvania's Constitution

ARTICLE I
DECLARATION OF RIGHTS

That the general, great and essential principles of liberty and free government may be recognized and unalterably established, WE DECLARE THAT—

Inherent rights of mankind

Section 1.   All men are born equally free and independent, and have certain inherent and indefeasible rights, among which are those of enjoying and defending life and liberty, of acquiring, possessing and protecting property and reputation, and of pursuing their own happiness.

Political powers

Section 2.   All power is inherent in the people, and all free governments are founded on their authority and instituted for their peace, safety and happiness. For the advancement of these ends they have at all times an inalienable and indefeasible right to alter, reform or abolish their government in such manner as they may think proper.

Religious freedom

Section 3.   All men have a natural and indefeasible right to worship Almighty God according to the dictates of their own consciences; no man can of right be compelled to attend, erect or support any place of worship, or to maintain any ministry against his consent; no human authority can, in any case whatever, control or interfere with the rights of conscience, and no preference shall ever be given by law to any religious establishments or modes of worship.

Religion

Section 4.   No person who acknowledges the being of a God and a future state of rewards and punishments shall, on account of his religious sentiments, be disqualified to hold any office or place of trust or profit under this Commonwealth.

Elections

Section 5.   Elections shall be free and equal; and no power, civil or military, shall at any time interfere to prevent the free exercise of the right of suffrage.

Trial by jury

Section 6.   Trial by jury shall be as heretofore, and the right thereof remain inviolate. The General Assembly may provide, however, by law, that a verdict may be rendered by not less than five-sixths of the jury in any civil case. Furthermore, in criminal cases the Commonwealth shall have the same right to trial by jury as does the accused.

Freedom of press and speech; libels

Section 7.   The printing press shall be free to every person who may undertake to examine the proceedings of the Legislature or any branch of government, and no law shall ever be made to restrain the right thereof. The free communication of thoughts and opinions is one of the invaluable rights of man, and every citizen may freely speak, write and print on any subject, being responsible for the abuse of that liberty. No conviction shall be had in any prosecution for the publication of papers relating to the official conduct of officers or men in public capacity, or to any other matter proper for public investigation or information, where the fact that such publication was not maliciously or negligently made shall be established to the satisfaction of the jury; and in all indictments for libels the jury shall have the right to determine the law and the facts, under the direction of the court, as in other cases.

Security from searches and seizures

Section 8.   The people shall be secure in their persons, houses, papers and possessions from unreasonable searches and seizures, and no warrant to search any place or to seize any person or thing shall issue without describing them as nearly as may be, nor without probable cause, supported by oath or affirmation subscribed to by the affiant.

Rights of accused in criminal prosecutions

Section 9.   In all criminal prosecutions the accused hath a right to be heard by himself and his counsel, to demand the nature and cause of the accusation against him, to be confronted with the witnesses against him, to have compulsory process for obtaining witnesses in his favor, and, in prosecutions by indictment or information, a speedy public trial by an impartial jury of the vicinage; he cannot be compelled to give evidence against himself, nor can he be deprived of his life, liberty or property, unless by the judgment of his peers or the law of the land. The use of a suppressed voluntary admission or voluntary confession to impeach the credibility of a person may be permitted and shall not be construed as compelling a person to give evidence against himself. Notwithstanding the provisions of this section, the General Assembly may by statute provide

FIGURE 3.5 (*continued*)

for the manner of testimony of child victims or child material witnesses in criminal proceedings, including the use of videotaped depositions or testimony by closed-circuit television.

Criminal information; twice in jeopardy; eminent domain

Section 10. Except as hereinafter provided no person shall, for any indictable offense, be proceeded against criminally by information, except in cases arising in the land or naval forces, or in the militia, when in actual service, in time of war or public danger, or by leave of the court for oppression or misdemeanor in office. Each of the several courts of common pleas may, with the approval of the Supreme Court, provide for the initiation of criminal proceedings therein by information filed in the manner provided by law. No person shall, for the same offense, be twice put in jeopardy of life or limb; nor shall private property be taken or applied to public use, without authority of law and without just compensation being first made or secured.

Courts to be open; suits against the Commonwealth

Section 11. All courts shall be open; and every man for an injury done him in his lands, goods, person or reputation shall have remedy by due course of law, and right and justice administered without sale, denial or delay. Suits may be brought against the Commonwealth in such manner, in such courts and in such cases as the Legislature may by law direct.

Power of suspending laws

Section 12. No power of suspending laws shall be exercised unless by the Legislature or by its authority.

Bail; fines and punishments

Section 13. Excessive bail shall not be required, nor excessive fines imposed, nor cruel punishments inflicted.

Prisoners to be bailable; habeas corpus

Section 14. All prisoners shall be bailable by sufficient sureties, unless for capital offenses or for offenses for which the maximum sentence is life imprisonment or unless no condition or combination of conditions other than imprisonment will reasonably assure the safety of any person and the community when the proof is evident or presumption great; and the privilege of the writ of habeas corpus shall not be suspended, unless when in case of rebellion or invasion the public safety may require it.

Special criminal tribunals

Section 15. No commission shall issue creating special temporary criminal tribunals to try particular individuals or particular classes of cases.

Insolvent debtors

Section 16. The person of a debtor, where there is not strong presumption of fraud, shall not be continued in prison after delivering up his estate for the benefit of his creditors in such manner as shall be prescribed by law.

Ex post facto laws; impairment of contracts

Section 17. No ex post facto law, nor any law impairing the obligation of contracts, or making irrevocable any grant of special privileges or immunities, shall be passed.

Attainder

Section 18. No person shall be attainted of treason or felony by the Legislature.

Attainder limited

Section 19. No attainder shall work corruption of blood, nor, except during the life of the offender, forfeiture of estate to the Commonwealth.

Right of petition

Section 20. The citizens have a right in a peaceable manner to assemble together for their common good, and to apply to those invested with the powers of government for redress of grievances or other proper purposes, by petition, address or remonstrance.

Standing army; military subordinate to civil power

Section 22. No standing army shall, in time of peace, be kept up without the consent of the Legislature, and the military shall in all cases and at all times be in strict subordination to the civil power.

Quartering of troops

Section 23. No soldier shall in time of peace be quartered in any house without the consent of the owner, nor in time of war but in a manner to be prescribed by law.

Titles and offices

Section 24. The Legislature shall not grant any title or nobility or hereditary distinction, nor create any office the appointment to which shall be for a longer term than during good behavior.

FIGURE 3.5 *(concluded)*

Reservation of powers in people

Section 25.   To guard against transgressions of the high powers which we have delegated, we declare that everything in this article is excepted out of the general powers of government and shall forever remain inviolate.

No discrimination by Commonwealth and its political subdivisions

Section 26.   Neither the Commonwealth nor any political subdivision thereof shall deny to any person the enjoyment of any civil right, nor discriminate against any person in the exercise of any civil right.

Natural resources and the public estate

Section 27.   The people have a right to clean air, pure water, and the preservation of the natural, scenic, historic and esthetic values of the environment. Pennsylvania's public natural resources are the common property of all the people, including generations yet to come. As trustee of these resources, the Commonwealth shall conserve and maintain them for the benefit of all the people.

Prohibition against denial or abridgment of equality of rights because of sex

Section 28.   Equality of rights under the law shall not be denied or abridged in the Commonwealth of Pennsylvania because of the sex of the individual.

Statutory or Legislative Materials

Legislative bills are created by legislative action. When legislative bills are passed, they become laws, statutes, or codes. Laws are codified for general dissemination. Codified laws are laws that are systematically organized in the form of code books. Laws are continually enacted by the legislative branches of federal and state governments. A legislative bill arises as a response to various social demands, including environmental issues, crime, Social Security and health benefits, civil rights legislation, immigration law, and others. Figure 3.6 includes some examples of codified laws from the federal realm that address drug distribution.

Examples of state materials are reproduced in Figures 3.7 and 3.8.

Ordinances are regulations that are created at the municipal or local government level. Part of the process involves publishing an intention to pass such an ordinance. (See Figure 3.9 for an example.)

Statutory and codified laws often incorporate all common-law principles. On the other hand, statutory and legislative materials may simply supplement current common-law standards. Because consensus building is a significant part of the legislative process, a deliberating body's resolution usually delays the creation of the resulting law. Statutory and codified law is subject to judicial review by courts with authorized jurisdiction. These checks and balances at the federal and state levels assure legislative integrity. As such, ordinances that are contrary to general constitutional principles (such as acquisition of property without just compensation) are often overturned. If procedural defects in the legislative process occur, unconstitutionality may be judicially declared.

Administrative Regulations

Some people consider administrative law and its authorized agencies a fourth arm of government.[40] At every level of our daily existence, administrative agencies impact us. Governmental agencies touch most aspects of living, including housing and urban development, health and human services, environmental issues, defense strategy, and other agencies controlling property interests. Paralegals will come into regular contact with governmental agencies whose administrative action creates legal implications. Some examples are

- Customs and Immigration.
- Civil Aeronautics Board.
- Consumer Product Safety Commission.
- Department of Commerce.
- Patent and Trademark Office.
- Department of Health and Human Services.
- Department of Justice.
- Department of Labor, Benefits Review Board.
- Department of Labor, Compensation Appeals Board.
- Department of Labor, National Railroad Adjustment Board.
- Department of Labor, Wage and Appeals Board.

FIGURE 3.6
Federal Law Addressing Drug Distribution

Source: 21 U.S.C. §§859, 860(a) & (b) (2003).

Section 859. Distribution to persons under age twenty-one

(a) First offense

Except as provided in section 860 of this title, any person at least eighteen years of age who violates section 841(a)(1) of this title by distributing a controlled substance to a person under twenty-one years of age is (except as provided in subsection (b) of this section) subject to (1) twice the maximum punishment authorized by section 841(b) of this title, and (2) at least twice any term of supervised release authorized by section 841(b) of this title, for a first offense involving the same controlled substance and schedule. Except to the extent a greater minimum sentence is otherwise provided by section 841(b) of this title, a term of imprisonment under this subsection shall be not less than one year. The mandatory minimum sentencing provisions of this subsection shall not apply to offenses involving 5 grams or less of marihuana.

(b) Second offense

Except as provided in section 860 of this title, any person at least eighteen years of age who violates section 841(a)(1) of this title by distributing a controlled substance to a person under twenty-one years of age after a prior conviction under subsection (a) of this section (or under section 333(b) of this title as in effect prior to May 1, 1971) has become final, is subject to (1) three times the maximum punishment authorized by section 841(b) of this title, and (2) at least three times any term of supervised release authorized by section 841(b) of this title, for a second or subsequent offense involving the same controlled substance and schedule. Except to the extent a greater minimum sentence is otherwise provided by section 841(b) of this title, a term of imprisonment under this subsection shall be not less than one year. Penalties for third and subsequent convictions shall be governed by section 841(b)(1)(A) of this title.

Section 860. Distribution or manufacturing in or near schools and colleges

(a) Penalty

Any person who violates section 841(a)(1) of this title or section 856 of this title by distributing, possessing with intent to distribute, or manufacturing a controlled substance in or on, or within one thousand feet of, the real property comprising a public or private elementary, vocational, or secondary school or a public or private college, junior college, or university, or a playground, or housing facility owned by a public housing authority, or within 100 feet of a public or private youth center, public swimming pool, or video arcade facility, is (except as provided in subsection (b) of this section) subject to (1) twice the maximum punishment authorized by section 841(b) of this title; and (2) at least twice any term of supervised release authorized by section 841(b) of this title for a first offense. A fine up to twice that authorized by section 841(b) of this title may be imposed in addition to any term of imprisonment authorized by this subsection. Except to the extent a greater minimum sentence is otherwise provided by section 841(b) of this title, a person shall be sentenced under this subsection to a term of imprisonment of not less than one year. The mandatory minimum sentencing provisions of this paragraph shall not apply to offenses involving 5 grams or less of marihuana.

(b) Second offenders

Any person who violates section 841(a)(1) of this title or section 856 of this title by distributing, possessing with intent to distribute, or manufacturing a controlled substance in or on, or within one thousand feet of, the real property comprising a public or private elementary, vocational, or secondary school or a public or private college, junior college, or university, or a playground, or housing facility owned by a public housing authority, or within 100 feet of a public or private youth center, public swimming pool, or video arcade facility, after a prior conviction under subsection (a) of this section has become final is punishable (1) by the greater of (A) a term of imprisonment of not less than three years and not more than life imprisonment or (B) three times the maximum punishment authorized by section 841(b) of this title for a first offense, and (2) at least three times any term of supervised release authorized by section 841(b) of this title for a first offense. A fine up to three times that authorized by section 841(b) of this title may be imposed in addition to any term of imprisonment authorized by this subsection. Except to the extent a greater minimum sentence is otherwise provided by section 841(b) of this title, a person shall be sentenced under this subsection to a term of imprisonment of not less than three years. Penalties for third and subsequent convictions shall be governed by section 841(b)(1)(A) of this title.

FIGURE 3.7
New Jersey State Laws: Abating Nuisance and Smoking in Public

Source: N.J. Rev. Stat. §2C:33-12.1.& §2C:33-13.

Abating Nuisance

a. In addition to the penalty imposed in case of conviction under N.J.S.2C:33-12 or under section 2 of P.L.1995, c.167 (C.2C:33-12.2), the court may order the immediate abatement of the nuisance, and for that purpose may order the seizure and forfeiture or destruction of any chattels, liquors, obscene material or other personal property which may be found in such building or place, and which the court is satisfied from the evidence were possessed or used with a purpose of maintaining the nuisance. Any such forfeiture shall be in the name and to the use of the State of New Jersey, and the court shall direct the forfeited property to be sold at public sale, the proceeds to be paid to the treasurer of the county wherein conviction was had.

b. If the owner of any building or place is found guilty of maintaining a nuisance, the court may order that the building or place where the nuisance was maintained be closed and not used for a period not exceeding one year from the date of the conviction.

Smoking in Public

a. Any person who smokes or carries lighted tobacco in or upon any bus or other public conveyance, except group charter buses, specially marked railroad smoking cars, limousines or livery services, and, when the driver is the only person in the vehicle, autocabs, is a petty disorderly person. For the purposes of this section, "bus" includes school buses and other vehicles owned or contracted for by the governing body, board or individual of a nonpublic school, a public or private college, university, or professional training school, or a board of education of a school district, that are used to transport students to and from school and school-related activities; and the prohibition on smoking or carrying lighted tobacco shall apply even if students are not present in the vehicle.

b. Any person who smokes or carries lighted tobacco in any public place, including but not limited to places of public accommodation, where such smoking is prohibited by municipal ordinance under authority of R.S.40:48-1 and 40:48-2 or by the owner or person responsible for the operation of the public place, and when adequate notice of such prohibition has been conspicuously posted, is guilty of a petty disorderly persons offense. Notwithstanding the provisions of 2C:43-3, the maximum fine which can be imposed for violation of this section is $200.

- Department of Transportation, Maritime Administration.
- FDIC Corp.
- Federal Energy Regulatory Commission.
- Federal Maritime Commission.
- Federal Mine Safety and Health Review Commission.
- Internal Revenue Service.

- National Transportation Safety Board.
- Occupational Safety and Health Review Commission.
- Small Business Administration.
- Social Security Administration.
- U.S. Environmental Protection Agency.
- U.S. Department of Homeland Security.

FIGURE 3.8
Michigan State Laws Addressing Prize Fights

Source: Mich. Penal Code §§750.442, 750.443 & 750.444.

750.442 Participating in prize fights; felony.

Any person who shall be a party to, or engage in a prize fight in this state, or who shall aid or abet therein, shall be guilty of a felony.

750.443 Training party for prize fight; aiding and abetting, felony.

Any person who shall engage in the training of any party to a prize fight, or shall assist therein, or who shall knowingly carry any person or persons to or from a prize fight shall be deemed aiders and abettors, within the meaning of the preceding section.

750.444 Attending prize fight; misdemeanor.

Any person who shall willfully be present at such prize fight in this state, or shall give or publish notice thereof or invite any person or persons to attend the same, shall be guilty of a misdemeanor.

FIGURE 3.9

Example of Local Ordinance

Source: Borough of Chambersburg, Franklin County, PA Web site. Proposed Ordinances available at http://borough.chambersburg.pa.us/html/proposedordinance.asp, last visited 1/23/2006.

NOTICE OF PUBLIC HEARING AND PROPOSED ADOPTION OF AN ORDINANCE TO AMEND CHAPTER 300, ZONING, OF THE CODE OF THE BOROUGH OF CHAMBERSBURG TO RECLASSIFY VARIOUS TRACTS OF LAND IN THE SECOND WARD AND THE THIRD WARD

NOTICE is hereby given that the Mayor and Town Council of the Borough of Chambersburg will hold a public hearing on MONDAY, NOVEMBER 14, 2005, at 7:00 p.m. in the Council Chambers, 100 South Second Street, Second Floor (enter through Police Entrance), Chambersburg, PA, to hear public comment and then consider the following proposed ordinance amending the Code of the Borough of Chambersburg to reclassify (rezone) various tracts of land in the Second Ward and in the Third Ward.

In accordance with the Americans with Disabilities Act, any person who needs an accommodation in order to gain access to or participate in this public hearing should call 261-3232 (TDD 261-3227) prior to the public hearing date.

The full text of the proposed ordinance along with a plan showing the proposed zoning classification changes is available for public inspection during normal business hours at the Office of the Borough Secretary, 100 South Second Street, Chambersburg, Pennsylvania. Copies of the proposed ordinance have been furnished to the Public Opinion, 77 North Third Street, and the Franklin County Law Library, 100 Lincoln Way East, Chambersburg, and are available for inspection during normal business hours at those offices.

A summary of the proposed ordinance is provided below. Any person desiring more information regarding this proposed ordinance may call Phil Wolgemuth, Planning/Zoning/CDBG Administrator at 261-3232. Copies of the proposed ordinance will be made available upon the payment of reasonable and customary costs of duplication.

SUMMARY:

Section 1. Legislative Findings: The Mayor and Town Council of the Borough of Chambersburg have determined it to be in the public interest to revise the Borough Zoning Ordinance to rezone certain tracts of land in the Second Ward and the Third Ward. The Second Ward rezoning is from Low Density Residential (LDR) to Distributed Commercial Highway (DCH). The Third Ward rezoning is from Medium Manufacturing (MM) to Moderate Density Residential (MDR).

Section 2. The following tracts in the Second Ward will be rezoned from Low Density Residential (LDR) to Distributed Commercial Highway (DCH):

. . .

Section 3. The following tracts in the Third Ward will be rezoned from Medium Manufacturing (MM) to Moderate Density Residential (MDR):

. . .

Administrative agencies are required under both statutory and due process arguments to create a specific administrative procedure that includes a discussion of agency scope, rule making, adjudications, decision making, hearings, and a claimant's rights and powers. Petitions or complaints seeking judicial review of administrative agency decisions are often drafted by paralegals.[41]

Distinguishing Criminal Acts from Civil Wrongs

The largest of the categories of law fall under the designations *criminal* or *civil.* Although these two categories are different, they share much in common. The following case should assist the reader in distinguishing between civil and criminal law:

First, in this scenario is there identifiable criminal conduct? Has the security officer committed assault or battery? Or is the conduct defensible because the method of restraint was reasonable? Do the facts demonstrate a criminal violation based on the Civil Rights Act? Has there been an egregious violation of Mr. X's constitutional rights? Who can be prosecuted for these actions? What penalties are likely upon conviction? How likely is a sentence or fine?

Second, what type of civil action exists in this situation? Does an accosted customer at a large department store have a cause of action that leads to an award of damages, such as assault or false imprisonment? How does one determine the value of an injury and damage award under these facts? What other specific civil actions underlie these facts? On what basis could a court uphold an award of $75,800?

Case Fact Pattern

Mr. X and his fiancée, Ms. Z, were shopping in a large department store in the state of Missouri. The evidence at trial indicated that Mr. X left the department store after picking up a tool. Soon thereafter Mr. X was accosted by a security officer; the interchange was extremely hostile. Mr. X was handcuffed after engaging in a physical altercation with the security guard. Mr. X's face was bleeding, his ribs were bruised, and he suffered other injuries. Mr. X was eventually acquitted at trial on all charges brought forth by the department store.

The contrast between a crime and a civil action can be striking. Intentionality is much less rigorous than in the law of crimes. This is why OJ Simpson was innocent under criminal prosecution yet liable under lawsuit. Crimes are generally considered acts against the commonwealth, whereas civil actions are personal. Crimes are serious and substantial acts that society has an obligation to prosecute. The desires of the damage victims, while relevant, do not compel the same obligation. In this sense, crimes are generally more grievous acts than civil harms.

A civil harm is a cause of action that is uniquely personal. An individual who is victimized by a bad product or by an unsafe design in a consumer good suffers a personal victimization. On the other hand, crimes, though personal, also damage the security and well-being of neighborhoods and community interests. In other words, crimes have impact beyond the person who was harmed.

Civil causes of actions or wrongs are sometimes referred to as torts. A *tort* is a generic term that signifies a personal harm. Torts are fully discussed in Chapter 11. A *crime* broadly describes many violations that individuals and other entities commit against the society. Civil law also encompasses a multitude of other actions aside from torts, including but not limited to contract remedies, equitable actions, family law processes, and other coverage not criminal in design.

The law of torts includes many causes of actions, including *assault, battery, abuse of process, malicious prosecution, conversion, deceit, defamation, false imprisonment, intentional infliction of emotional distress, invasion of privacy, negligence,* and *trespass.* Each cause of action requires a proof of its particular *elements.* Whereas criminal law is primarily concerned with protecting society and restoring the public good, tort law is designed "to compensate the victim for his loss, to deter future conduct of a similar nature, and to express society's disapproval of the conduct in question."[42] In a way, civil remedies are more concerned with making injured parties physically, emotionally, and economically whole. Criminal remedies are more preoccupied with punishment of the perpetrator, either by fines or incarceration as well as restoration of the public good. Tort law is concerned with *damages,* whereas criminal law is concerned with terms of imprisonment, punishment, and other sorts of limitations on personal freedom. Of course, criminal law is also empowered to order restitution or to assess fines.

Even though civil and criminal actions are clearly distinguishable, "the same conduct by a defendant may give rise to both criminal and tort liability."[43] The decision to pursue either remedy does not exclude the other. In sum, the "law of torts and civil remedies is intertwined with the law of crimes, but for the most part stands apart."[44]

Success in the civil arena is generally more likely because the burden of proof is less rigorous. Remember that the evidentiary burden in proof in crime requires *proof beyond a reasonable doubt.* A successful civil action merely mandates *proof by a preponderance of the evidence.* The previous case reveals these specific civil actions:

1. Assault:
   An act: an actual or attempted offensive touching;
   With *intent* to cause harm or apprehension of harm.
   Victim's apprehension is imminent.
   Causation: That act causes the apprehension.

2. *Battery:*
   An act: an offensive touching and resulting harm.
   With *intent* to cause harmful or offensive conduct.
   Harmful or offensive conduct actually results.
   Causation: Offensive contact causes damages.

3. *False imprisonment:*
   An act: confines within fixed boundaries.
   With *intent* to confine plaintiff.
   Plaintiff was conscious of his own confinement or was harmed by it.
   Causation: Confinement causes harm.

4. *Intentional infliction of emotional distress:*
   An act: extreme and outrageous conduct.
   With *intent* to cause severe emotional distress.
   Actual emotional distress is suffered.
   Causation: The extreme act causes distress.

5. *Malicious prosecution:*
   An act: initiation of legal proceedings without probable cause and with malice.
   Defense wins underlying case.
   Causation: Unjustifiable legal action causes harm in another.

Finally, criminal actions usually create the opportunity for multiple charges to be pursued. Clearly a plaintiff in the example might allege assault and battery, and in some jurisdictions a criminal complaint for false imprisonment may be a possibility. Unquestionably there are similarities and differences between the law of torts and the law of crimes. For a concise overview, see the chart in Chapter 11.

THE AMERICAN COURT SYSTEM

The forum for the resolution of litigation is generally a court of particular or general jurisdiction. The American judicial system primarily consists of the federal and state court structure with a series of smaller courts at the local and municipal levels. Choosing the correct forum for litigation is a critical step for any paralegal entrusted with this task. The organization of federal courts will be discussed first.

To ensure the independence of a federal judiciary, the Founding Fathers within Article III of the Constitution called for the establishment of an independent Supreme Court and inferior courts. Article III states in part:

> *The judicial Power of the United States, shall be vested in one supreme Court, and in such inferior Courts as the Congress may from time to time ordain and establish. The Judges, both of the supreme and inferior Courts, shall hold their Offices during good Behaviour, and shall, at stated Times, receive for their Services, a Compensation, which shall not be diminished during their Continuance in Office.*[45]

The United States Supreme Court

Credit: Hisham F. Ibrahim/ Getty Images

FIGURE 3.10
Major
Characteristics of the
U.S. Supreme Court

U.S. Supreme Court Characteristics	
Composition	One chief justice, eight associate justices.
Quorum	A quorum consists of six.
Commencement of term	First Monday in October; permitted to have special terms.
Seniority	Plays a special role in the replacement of Chief Justice and in the ranking associate justices.
Salaries of justices	Determined by Congress.
Occupational requirements for position	Need not be a lawyer.
Jurisdiction	By *certiorari* or by original jurisdiction.

The primary aim of Article III is to promote stability in the American judiciary. The judiciary maintains judicial independence through our checks and balances and tripartite system of government. Ideally, with this separation of powers, the "wisdom, justice, propriety, necessity, utility, and expediency of legislation are matters solely for the determination of the legislature. Further, this prevents the court from substituting their judgment for that of the legislature by declaring a statute invalid on these grounds, unless it violates some specific constitutional provision."[46] The federal system follows a typical hierarchical order with a trial to appellate courts in the sequence.

The United States Supreme Court

The major characteristics of the United States Supreme Court are outlined in Figure 3.10. The Supreme Court's decisions are considered the supreme law of the land unless overturned by constitutional amendment.

The establishment of a lower federal court system is provided in Article I, Section 8, Clause 9, which states that Congress has the power to "constitute tribunals inferior to the Supreme Court."[47] Inferior courts in the federal system include courts of general trial jurisdiction, appeals, and specialized jurisdiction.

Federal Circuit Courts

The 13 federal judicial districts are listed in Figure 3.11.

Circuit courts of appeal are assigned to specific geographic districts. Each court of appeals consists of circuit judges in regular, active service. "The circuit justice and justices or judges designated or assigned shall also be competent to sit as judges of the court."[48] Appointment and tenure of circuit judges are guided by presidential selection and legislative confirmation. The circuits and corresponding number of judges that can be appointed during the tenure of the presidency are noted in Figure 3.12.

A chief judge presides over each circuit of the United States Court of Appeals. This judge must possess the following qualifications:

- Be 64 years of age or younger.
- Have served for one year or more as a circuit judge.
- Have not served previously as chief judge.[49]

A chief judge's term of appointment is seven years.

A majority of the number of judges constituting a court or panel constitutes a quorum for judicial decisions.[50] The Court of Appeals also holds regular sessions at any of the places listed in Figure 3.13 within their respective circuits or as each court may designate by rule.

Federal District Courts

As in the case of the U.S. Court of Appeals, the president has the power, upon the advice and consent of the Senate, to appoint judges for the judicial districts shown in Figure 3.14.

As in the federal courts of appeal, district judges are appointed after congressional advice and consent.[51] Actual or potential appointments by the president of the United States make a significant imprint on the philosophical direction of these courts. Some individuals have argued that former President Ronald Reagan's most powerful legacy was the appointment of 50 percent of the total population of the federal judiciary during his tenure.

FIGURE 3.11

The 13 Federal Judicial Districts

Source: THE FEDERAL PROCEDURAL SYSTEM: A RULE AND STATUTORY SOURCE BOOK 22 (1989).

Circuits	Composition
District of Columbia	District of Columbia
First	Maine, Massachusetts, New Hampshire, Puerto Rico, Rhode Island
Second	Connecticut, New York, Vermont
Third	Delaware, New Jersey, Pennsylvania, Virgin Islands
Fourth	Maryland, North Carolina, South Carolina, West Virginia
Fifth	District of the Canal Zone, Louisiana, Mississippi, Texas
Sixth	Kentucky, Michigan, Ohio, Tennessee
Seventh	Illinois, Indiana, Wisconsin
Eighth	Arkansas, Iowa, Minnesota, Missouri, Nebraska, North Dakota, South Dakota
Ninth	Alaska, Arizona, California, Idaho, Montana, Nevada, Oregon, Washington, Guam, Hawaii
Tenth	Colorado, Kansas, New Mexico, Oklahoma, Utah, Wyoming
Eleventh	Alabama, Florida, Georgia
Federal	All federal judicial districts

The 13 Judicial Districts That Constitute the Federal Circuit Courts

FIGURE 3.12

Circuits and Number of Judges That Can Be Appointed during the Tenure of the Presidency

Source: 28 U.S.C. §44.

Circuits	Number of Judges
District of Columbia	12
First	6
Second	13
Third	14
Fourth	15
Fifth	17
Sixth	16
Seventh	11
Eighth	11
Ninth	28
Tenth	12
Eleventh	12
Federal	12

FIGURE 3.13

Court of Appeals Session Locations

Source: 28 U.S.C. §48.

Circuits	Places
District of Columbia	Washington
First	Boston
Second	New York
Third	Philadelphia
Fourth	Richmond, Asheville
Fifth	New Orleans, Fort Worth, Jackson
Sixth	Cincinnati
Seventh	Chicago
Eighth	St. Louis, Kansas City, Omaha, St. Paul
Ninth	San Francisco, Los Angeles, Portland, Seattle
Tenth	Denver, Wichita, Oklahoma City
Eleventh	Atlanta, Jacksonville, Montgomery
Federal	District of Columbia, and in any other place listed above as the court by rule directs

In the recent U.S. Supreme Court nominations of Chief Justice Roberts and Justice Samuel Alito, the stakes appeared contentious and emotional. What played out directly reflected the depth and breadth of disagreement over the rules and functions of judges and judging. Some desire activism and the continuing extension of rights in the constitutional framework; others wish for judicial restraint and the reining in of what they label as an *imperial judiciary*[52] that knows no bounds.

FIGURE 3.14
District Judge Appointments
Source: 28 U.S.C. §133.

District Judge Appointments

Districts		Judges
Alabama:		
	Northern	7
	Middle	3
	Southern	3
Alaska		3
Arizona		12
Arkansas:		
	Eastern	5
	Western	3
California:		
	Northern	14
	Eastern	6
	Central	27
	Southern	8
Colorado		7
Connecticut		8
Delaware		4
District of Columbia		15
Florida:		
	Northern	4
	Middle	15
	Southern	17
Georgia:		
	Northern	11
	Middle	4
	Southern	3
Hawaii		3
Idaho		2
Illinois:		
	Northern	22
	Central	4
	Southern	4
Indiana:		
	Northern	5
	Southern	5
Iowa:		
	Northern	2
	Southern	3
Kansas		5
Kentucky:		
	Eastern	5
	Western	4
	Eastern and Western	1
Louisiana:		
	Eastern	12
	Middle	3
	Western	7
Maine		3
Maryland		10
Massachusetts		13
Michigan:		
	Eastern	15
	Western	4
Minnesota		7
Mississippi:		
	Northern	3
	Southern	6

FIGURE 3.14
(concluded)

Missouri:		
	Eastern	6
	Western	5
	Eastern and Western	2
Montana		3
Nebraska		3
Nevada		7
New Hampshire		3
New Jersey		17
New Mexico		6
New York:		
	Northern	5
	Southern	28
	Eastern	15
	Western	4
North Carolina:		
	Eastern	4
	Middle	4
	Western	3
North Dakota		2
Ohio:		
	Northern	11
	Southern	8
Oklahoma:		
	Northern	3
	Eastern	1
	Western	6
	Northern, Eastern, and Western	1
Oregon		6
Pennsylvania:		
	Eastern	22
	Middle	6
	Western	10
Puerto Rico		7
Rhode Island		3
South Carolina		10
South Dakota		3
Tennessee:		
	Eastern	5
	Middle	4
	Western	3
Texas:		
	Northern	12
	Southern	19
	Eastern	7
	Western	11
Utah		5
Vermont		2
Virginia:		
	Eastern	11
	Western	4
Washington:		
	Eastern	4
	Western	7
West Virginia:		
	Northern	3
	Southern	5
Wisconsin:		
	Eastern	5
	Western	2
Wyoming		3

Specialized Federal Courts

Bankruptcy Courts

In every judicial district, a bankruptcy court is a unit of the district court. Bankruptcy judges are judicial officers of the district court and exercise authority conferred on them by the provisions of Article III. Bankruptcy judges are appointed under the United States District Court under Article III of the U.S. Constitution, somewhat differently than the Article I analysis discussed previously.[53] Such appointments are made after considering the recommendations of a judicial conference. There has been considerable constitutional litigation regarding the tenures of bankruptcy judges because they have been deemed non–Article I in design.

United States Court of Claims

By presidential appointment and the advice and consent of the Senate, 16 judges constitute a court of record known as the United States Court of Claims. The jurisdictional basis for the court is disputes in which the United States is named a plaintiff or defendant.[54]

Court of International Trade

Another specialized court is the Court of International Trade. The president appoints, with the advice and consent of the Senate, nine judges to the United States Court of International Trade. Its subject matter jurisdiction involves trade disputes. Judicial decisions are made either by a single jurist or by three-judge panels. The location of this court is in the offices of the Court of International Trade in New York City.[55]

United States Tax Court

Jurisdiction of the United States Tax Court is conferred by Title 26 of the United States Code and is dependent on the issuance by the commissioner of the Internal Revenue Service of any notice of deficiency in income, gift, or estate taxes.[56]

Other Significant Courts

Criminal and civil jurisdiction involving military personnel are granted to the U.S. Court of Military Appeals.[57] Matters involving customs law rest with the United States Court of International Trade.[58]

STATE COURT SYSTEMS

In a dual system of federal and state judicial power, state court systems rest side by side with their federal partners. Although this has not always been true, federal courts appear preeminent in most territory, even in areas once unthinkable. In a culture once convinced of states' rights, it is easy to see how a federal system that entangles itself in most aspects of a citizen's life would restrain itself in matters of judicial reasoning. When federal decisions involve federal rights, state courts cannot abridge these rights. The federal system preempts the state courts from legal decision making on subject matter federal in design. In other words, states can't regulate Indian Affairs or Department of Defense actions because the federal system preempts them from doing so. U.S. Supreme Court decisions on uniquely federal issues are binding and are given full faith and credit by state judicial authorities. Hence the federal courts are the preeminent players on the judicial horizon.

Organizationally, court systems throughout the nation are far from uniform. A prototype of the "typical" state court structure is charted by the National Center of State Courts in Figure 3.15.[59]

All state systems, however, contain a jurisdictional and hierarchical system of superior and inferior courts. State courts, like their federal counterparts, are described by these designations and terms:

1. *Court of record:* A court that keeps a transcript of the proceedings, usually at the upper levels of a judicial hierarchy.

2. *Court of last resort:* A court to which an appeal can finally be taken.

3. *Trial court:* A court in which adjudication litigation takes place.

4. *Appellate court:* A court in which an appeal is taken, usually from a trial, magistrate, or district court.

5. *Superior court:* Any court above an inferior court.

6. *Inferior court:* Any court below any court superior to it.

FIGURE 3.15

**State Court Structure
Prototype**

Source: NATIONAL
CENTER FOR STATE COURTS,
STATE COURT CASELOAD
STATISTICS, 2004 at State
Court Structure Charts 7
(2004).

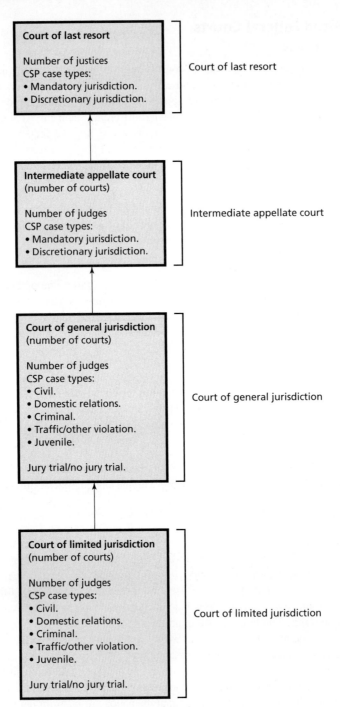

Courts can be further differentiated by specific jurisdictional limits based on subject matter, monetary dollar figures, and geographical limitations. As a specific example of state court hierarchies, the Arkansas court system is delineated in Figure 3.16.

Arkansas displays the usual structure of a court system with higher to lower jurisdictions. The supreme court rests atop and hears appeals from the lower divisions. The circuit courts are the courts of general jurisdiction, whereas the court of appeals hears select appellate cases. The district courts handle smaller cases and do not permit jury trials.

The Florida court system is a multitiered judicial process that consists of the appellate division, the highest court, an intermediate appellate division called a district court of appeals, as well as courts of general jurisdiction, the district circuit courts. The county courts handle smaller caseloads. (See Figure 3.17.)

In Michigan the supreme court is the court of last resort; the court of claims handles actions against state government and other specialized matters; and the circuit courts take on the tasks of general jurisdiction. (See Figure 3.18.)

FIGURE 3.16 Arkansas Court Structure

Source: National Center for State Courts, State Court Caseload Statistics, 2004 at State Court Structure Charts; http://www.ncsconline.org/D_Research/Ct_Struct/AR.htm.

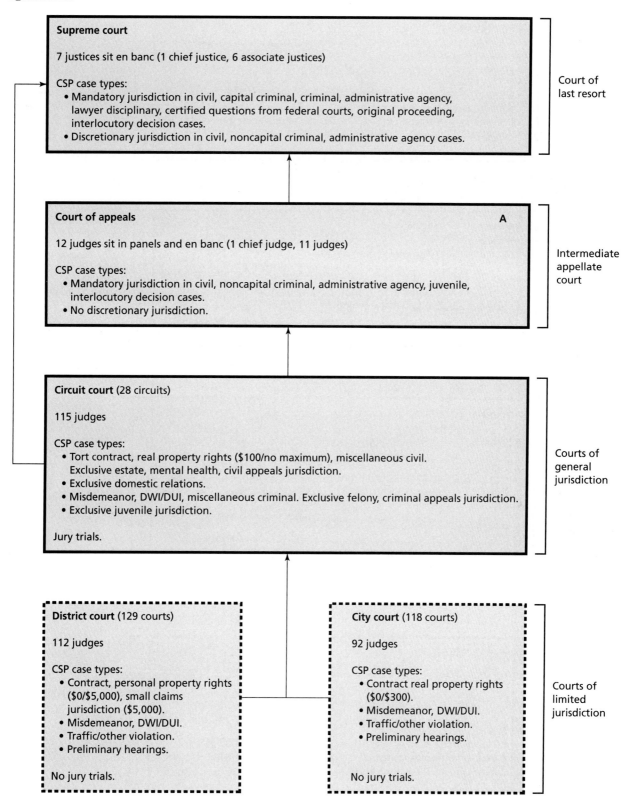

Note: In 2001 Arkansas combined the chancery and probate court with the circuit court and reduced the number of limited jurisdiction courts from six to two by combining the county police common pleas and justice of the peace courts into the municipal court, which was renamed and is now the district court.

FIGURE 3.17 Florida Court System

Source: NATIONAL CENTER FOR STATE COURTS, STATE COURT CASELOAD STATISTICS, 2004 at State Court Structure Charts http://www.ncsconline.org/D_Research/Ct_Struct/FL.htm.

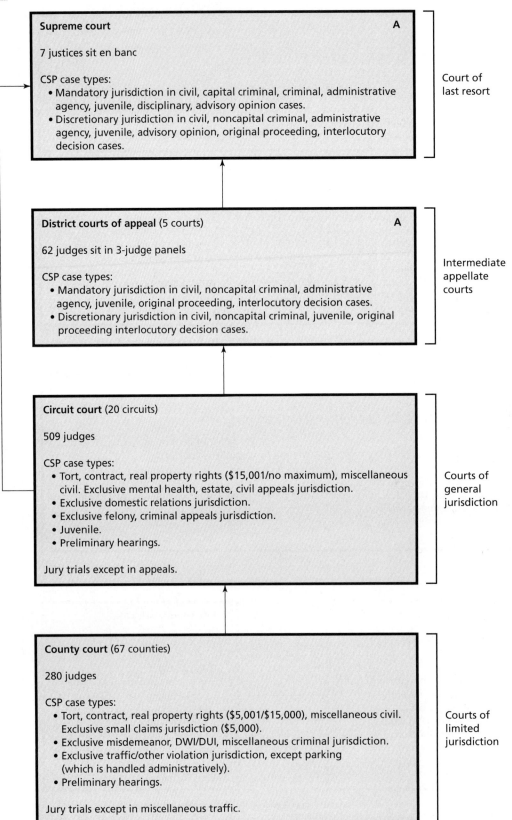

Supreme court   A

7 justices sit en banc

CSP case types:
- Mandatory jurisdiction in civil, capital criminal, criminal, administrative agency, juvenile, disciplinary, advisory opinion cases.
- Discretionary jurisdiction in civil, noncapital criminal, administrative agency, juvenile, advisory opinion, original proceeding, interlocutory decision cases.

Court of last resort

District courts of appeal (5 courts)   A

62 judges sit in 3-judge panels

CSP case types:
- Mandatory jurisdiction in civil, noncapital criminal, administrative agency, juvenile, original proceeding, interlocutory decision cases.
- Discretionary jurisdiction in civil, noncapital criminal, juvenile, original proceeding interlocutory decision cases.

Intermediate appellate courts

Circuit court (20 circuits)

509 judges

CSP case types:
- Tort, contract, real property rights ($15,001/no maximum), miscellaneous civil. Exclusive mental health, estate, civil appeals jurisdiction.
- Exclusive domestic relations jurisdiction.
- Exclusive felony, criminal appeals jurisdiction.
- Juvenile.
- Preliminary hearings.

Jury trials except in appeals.

Courts of general jurisdiction

County court (67 counties)

280 judges

CSP case types:
- Tort, contract, real property rights ($5,001/$15,000), miscellaneous civil. Exclusive small claims jurisdiction ($5,000).
- Exclusive misdemeanor, DWI/DUI, miscellaneous criminal jurisdiction.
- Exclusive traffic/other violation jurisdiction, except parking (which is handled administratively).
- Preliminary hearings.

Jury trials except in miscellaneous traffic.

Courts of limited jurisdiction

FIGURE 3.18   Michigan Court Structure

Source: National Center for State Courts, State Court Caseload Statistics, 2004 at State Court Structure Charts; http://www.ncsconline.org/D_Research/Ct_Struct/MI.htm.

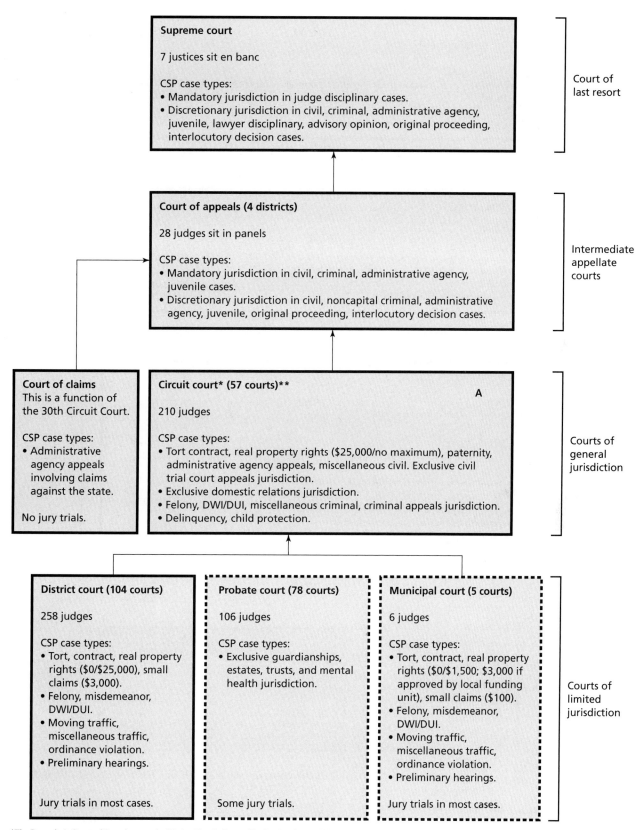

*The Recorder's Court of Detroit merged with the Circuit Court effective October 1, 1997.

**A Family Division of Circuit Court became operational on January 1, 1998.

FIGURE 3.19   **Missouri Court Structure**

Source: National Center for State Courts, State Court Caseload Statistics, 2004 at State Court Structure Charts; http://www.ncsconline.org/D_Research/Ct_Struct/MO.htm.

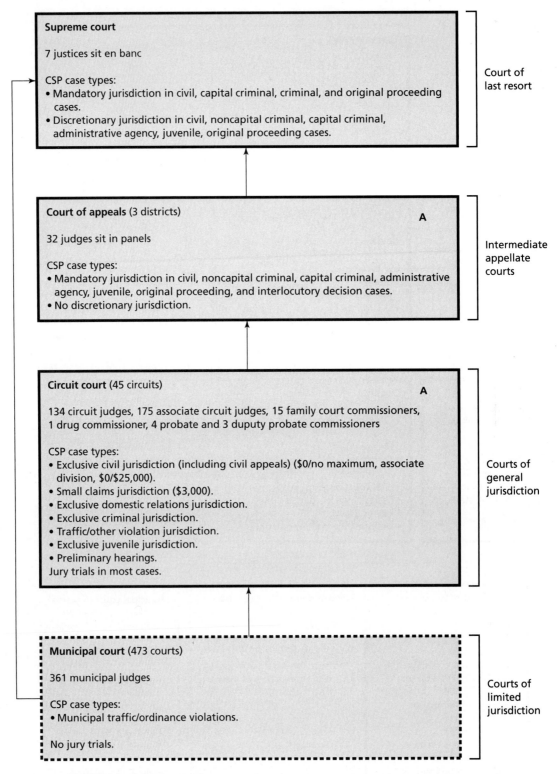

The supreme court of Missouri is the court of last resort in that state; the court of appeals is the intermediate appellate division, and the circuit court is the trial court. Figure 3.19 illustrates the Missouri court system.

The New York system is a more complex state court system. (See Figure 3.20.)

The court of appeals is the court of last resort, with a designated appellate division that hears cases from the New York court of general jurisdiction—the Supreme Court. Given New York's

FIGURE 3.20   New York Court Structure

Source: NATIONAL CENTER FOR STATE COURTS, STATE COURT CASELOAD STATISTICS, 2004 at State Court Structure Charts; http://www.ncsconline.org/D_Research/Ct_Struct/NY.htm.

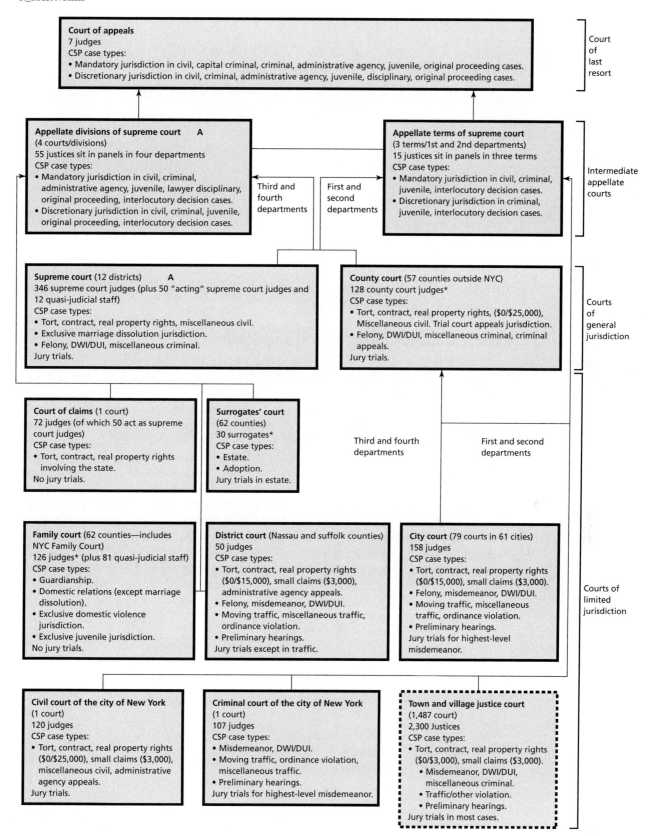

*Unless otherwise noted, numbers reflect statutory authorization. Many judges sit in more than one court, so the number of judgeships indicated in this chart does not reflect the actual number of judges in the system. Fifty county court judges also serve surrogates' court, and six county court judges also serve family court.

massive size, it has erected specialized courts that deal with special subjects such as estates and trusts, family court, and surrogates' practice.

Understanding the structure of courts is a major challenge for a practicing paralegal. Another is to determine the proper jurisdiction and venue for filing claims.

THE NATURE OF JURISDICTION AND VENUE

Jurisdiction can rest on many theories:

1. Geographic area.
2. Subject matter of controversy.
3. Statutory or legislative grant of jurisdiction.
4. Dollar amount in controversy.
5. Level of appeal or resolution.
6. Exhaustion of specific remedies.

Subject Matter Jurisdiction

Specific courts have been developed to handle specific subject matters or claims. Keep some of the examples in Figure 3.21 in mind.

Exclusive Jurisdiction: Federal and State

Certain rights, obligations, and legal questions are exclusively confined to the federal realm. Federal tax matters belong in federal tax courts; but controversies arising over federal issues, such as the interpretation of a federal law or statute, also belong in a federal court. Exclusive jurisdiction is also exercised over any subject matter court if the court is granted an exclusive right to determine a particular dispute. For example, constitutional questions at the federal level are plainly the subject matter of the federal court. Section 2 of Article III of the Constitution states, "The judicial power shall extend to all cases in law and equity arising under this constitution, the laws of the United States and treaties made or which shall be made under authority."[60]

Conversely, all state matters are generally within the purview of state court decision making. "At the time this nation was formed, the colonist considered each state to be a nation in itself; the central government was given only those limited powers thought necessary for the common survival, protection, and economic well-being of all the states. All powers that were not exclusively granted to the central government were reserved by the individual states."[61] Thus a case involving a state law on licensure or regulation is exclusively a state problem and under state jurisdiction. Federal oversight of such an issue would be a constitutional infringement, though exceptions to this principle exist.

FIGURE 3.21
Examples of Subject Matter Jurisdiction

Subject Matter	Court of Jurisdiction
Federal taxes	U.S. Tax Court
Federal international trade disputes	U.S. Court of International Trade
Military criminal prosecutions	U.S. Military Court of Appeals
Actions against the U.S. as defendant	U.S. Court of Claims
Bankruptcy	U.S. Bankruptcy Courts
Estate disputes	State Probate or Surrogates' Court
State family law problems	State Family Law Court
Traffic ticket	State Magistrate, Aldermans', or District Court
Crime against a state	State, Commonwealth, or Court of Claims
Court appeals	Appellate Division beyond Court of Record

Original Jurisdiction

Certain courts have original jurisdiction over specific matters. Original jurisdiction has been granted to the U.S. Supreme Court under the Constitution and Title 28 of the United States Code.[62] The statute states in part,

(a) *The Supreme Court shall have original and exclusive jurisdiction of all controversies between two or more States.*

(b) *The Supreme Court shall have original but not exclusive jurisdiction of*

(1) *All actions or proceedings to which ambassadors, other public ministers, consuls, or vice consuls of foreign states are parties;*

(2) *All controversies between the United States and a State;*

(3) *All actions or proceedings by a State against the citizens of another State or against aliens.*[63]

At the state level, the concept of original jurisdiction is also applicable.

Jurisdiction Based on *Certiorari*

Jurisdiction is grounded in *certiorari,* a policy of discretionary review in both the federal and state systems. Congress provided this authority to the Supreme Court of the United States under the Judiciary Act of 1789. Under Rule 17 of the Rules of the U.S. Supreme Court, review by *certiorari* is not an inherent right but a discretionary one:

A review on writ of certiorari *is not a matter of right but of judicial discretion, and will be granted only when there are special and important reasons therefore. The following, while neither controlling nor fully measuring the court's discretion, indicate the character of reasons that will be considered.*

A. When a federal court of appeals has rendered a decision in conflict with the decision of another federal court of appeals on the same matter; or has decided a federal question in a way in conflict with a state court of last resort; or has so far departed from the accepted and usual course of judicial proceedings, or so far sanctioned such a departure by a lower court, as to call for an exercise of this court's power of supervision.

B. When a state court of last resort has decided a federal question in a way in conflict with the decision of another state court of last resort or of a federal court of appeals.

C. When a state court or a federal court of appeals has decided an important question of federal law which has not been, but should be, settled by this court, or has decided a federal question in a way in conflict with applicable decisions of this court.[64]

The grant of *certiorari* is often the result of political undercurrents or pressure from an irregular and inconsistent pattern of decision making in the lower courts. In response to a *certiorari* request, courts will determine the issues without comment or request that oral arguments be presented at a later date to assess the evidence.[65]

Concurrent Jurisdiction

Concurrent jurisdiction exists when two or more courts have control over specific subject matter or can exercise jurisdiction based on other claim or right. Often when there is concurrent jurisdiction forum shopping, looking for the best judge or the most favorable pattern of decision making, occurs. In the federal courts such forum shopping, while severely frowned on, is rampant. Courts should be selected based on convenience to the parties, on economic considerations, and in the interest of reaching a quick and just resolution to the matter. Concurrent jurisdiction is most likely seen in these circumstances:

1. A state case alleging civil rights violation based on state and federal constitutions.

2. A case of collective bargaining infringement based on state and federal labor laws.

3. A case of personal injury against a municipal police department in which civil rights violations are alleged.

4. A case of dispute over territorial boundary lines or riparian water rights that would be subject to the control of federal and state authorities concurrently.

Choosing the most favorable forum available is an important tactical consideration when litigating any case. Some states have a more liberal case law background when compared to federal decision making.

Appellate Jurisdiction

Appellate jurisdiction rests in those courts that have the jurisdiction to hear inferior court decisions. As a rule, the following principles apply:

1. Any court above a trial court is an appellate court.
2. Any court above the district or magistrate levels is an appellate court.
3. Any court above an intermediate court of appeals can be construed as an appeals court.
4. Federal courts can be characterized as appeals courts for state decisions if a federal matter or question is involved.

If a court has the control, power, and authority to review the decision of a lower court, the label *appellate* is appropriate. The next step necessary for a review of a decision of either a court or an administrative agency determines appellate jurisdiction. Failure to follow procedural requirements in the appellate framework can result in an irreversible dismissal. The federal system publishes an entire set of Federal Rules of Appellate Procedure.[66]

Appeals can be available as a matter of right or a discretionary grant. Acceptability of an appeal has procedural implications like specific time periods for filing and argument.

Ancillary Jurisdiction

"Ancillary jurisdiction is jurisdiction assumed by federal courts that extends beyond the judicial power expressly conferred upon them by the Constitution or by federal statutes. Under the concept of ancillary jurisdiction, a federal district court acquires jurisdiction over issues that otherwise would be determinable only in a state court as an incident of disposition on a closely related federal matter that is properly before such federal court."[67] This type of jurisdiction is granted as an accommodation to the litigating parties.[68]

Pendent Jurisdiction

Pendent jurisdiction exists in a case in which a plaintiff has both a federal and a state law claim. The court must construe whether a series of events or a singular transaction may be said to constitute a single cause of action in deciding whether to exercise pendent jurisdiction. In the federal system, the term *pendent* has been replaced with *supplemental*.[69] In *United Mine Workers of America v. Gibbs*, 383 U.S. 715 (1966), the Court had held that district courts, when adjudicating federal law claims within their subject matter jurisdiction under 28 U.S.C. 1331, also may adjudicate state law claims over which they would not otherwise have jurisdiction if the federal law and state law claims "derive from a common nucleus of operative fact" and thus comprise "but one constitutional *case*" under Article III.[70]

Federal Jurisdiction Based on Diversity

To ensure the just resolution of cases between plaintiffs and defendants from differing states, the federal courts exercise diversity jurisdiction. Diversity is defined as follows:

> (a) *The district courts shall have original jurisdiction of all civil actions where the matter in controversy exceeds the sum or value of $75,000, exclusive of interest and costs, and is between—*
>> (1) *Citizens of different States;*
>> (2) *Citizens of a State and citizens or subjects of a foreign state;*
>> (3) *Citizens of different States and in which citizens or subjects of a foreign state are additional parties; and*
>> (4) *A foreign state, defined in section 1603(a) of this title [28 USCS § 1603(a)], as plaintiff and citizens of a State or of different States.*[71]

Diversity jurisdiction has opened a litigation floodgate in the federal system. The mere residences of the parties determine the forum rather than federal subject matter. Consider the following fact pattern to discern the ease of stumbling into diversity jurisdiction:

A citizen driving a car from the state of Delaware gets into a serious accident with a citizen from the commonwealth of Pennsylvania. Damages exceed $100,000.

Diversity jurisdiction exists. Be aware, however, that state jurisdiction also exists concurrently.

Federal Jurisdiction Based on a Federal Question

Federal jurisdiction can also exist when a plaintiff or defendant advocates a purely federal question. As discussed, district courts have original jurisdiction over civil actions arising under the Constitution, laws, and treaties of the United States. Common federal questions that emerge may include

- Civil rights violations.
- National labor relations problems.
- OSHA appeals.
- Immigration problems.
- International treaties and trade problems.
- Federal crimes such as kidnapping and terrorist threats to the president.
- Constitutional questions about tax law.
- A state disregarding a federal law.
- Preemption of federal law by states' rights advocates.
- Refusal of a state authority to honor a federal court order.
- Voting rights questions.
- Freedom of speech questions.
- Privacy questions.
- Fourth, Fifth, and Sixth Amendment questions.

Venue

Venue is based on the geographic implications of the parties and the events surrounding them rather than the subject matter of the lawsuit. Venue determines in what geographic location that civil or criminal action must take place. Under Chapter 87 of the Judiciary Judicial Procedure Act of Title 28, venue is described in the following context:

> *(a) A civil action wherein jurisdiction is founded only on diversity of citizenship may, except as otherwise provided by law, be brought only in (1) a judicial district where any defendant resides, if all defendants reside in the same State, (2) a judicial district in which a substantial part of the events or omissions giving rise to the claim occurred, or a substantial part of property that is the subject of the action is situated, or (3) a judicial district in which any defendant is subject to personal jurisdiction at the time the action is commenced, if there is no district in which the action may otherwise be brought.*

> *(b) A civil action wherein jurisdiction is not founded solely on diversity of citizenship may, except as otherwise provided by law, be brought only in (1) a judicial district where any defendant resides, if all defendants reside in the same State, (2) a judicial district in which a substantial part of the events or omissions giving rise to the claim occurred, or a substantial part of property that is the subject of the action is situated, or (3) a judicial district in which any defendant may be found, if there is no district in which the action may otherwise be brought.*

> *(c) For purposes of venue under this chapter [28 USCS §§ 1391 et seq.], a defendant that is a corporation shall be deemed to reside in any judicial district in which it is subject to personal jurisdiction at the time the action is commenced. In a State which has more than one judicial district and in which a defendant that is a corporation is subject to personal jurisdiction at the time an action is commenced, such corporation shall be deemed to reside in any district in that State within which its contacts would be sufficient to subject it to personal jurisdiction if that district were a separate State, and, if there is no such district, the corporation shall be deemed to reside in the district within which it has the most significant contacts.*

> *(d) An alien may be sued in any district.*

(e) A civil action in which a defendant is an officer or employee of the United States or any agency thereof acting in his official capacity or under color of legal authority, or an agency of the United States, or the United States, may, except as otherwise provided by law, be brought in any judicial district in which (1) a defendant in the action resides, (2) a substantial part of the events or omissions giving rise to the claim occurred, or a substantial part of property that is the subject of the action is situated, or (3) the plaintiff resides if no real property is involved in the action. Additional persons may be joined as parties to any such action in accordance with the Federal Rules of Civil Procedure and with such other venue requirements as would be applicable if the United States or one of its officers, employees, or agencies were not a party.

The summons and complaint in such an action shall be served as provided by the Federal Rules of Civil Procedure except that the delivery of the summons and complaint to the officer or agency as required by the rules may be made by certified mail beyond the territorial limits of the district in which the action is brought.

(f) A civil action against a foreign state as defined in section 1603(a) of this title [28 USCS § 1603(a)] may be brought—

(1) in any judicial district in which a substantial part of the events or omissions giving rise to the claim occurred, or a substantial part of property that is the subject of the action is situated;

(2) in any judicial district in which the vessel or cargo of a foreign state is situated, if the claim is asserted under section 1605(b) of this title [28 USCS § 1605(b)];

(3) in any judicial district in which the agency or instrumentality is licensed to do business or is doing business, if the action is brought against an agency or instrumentality of a foreign state as defined in section 1603(b) of this title [28 USCS § 1603(b)]; or

(4) in the United States District Court for the District of Columbia if the action is brought against a foreign state or political subdivision thereof.

(g) A civil action in which jurisdiction of the district court is based upon section 1369 of this title [28 USCS § 1369] may be brought in any district in which any defendant resides or in which a substantial part of the accident giving rise to the action took place.[72]

At the state level, venue is determined by county or district. The determination of appropriate venue is based on where the event occurred, the plaintiffs and defendants reside, and the interest in question takes place, whether real property or other matter in dispute. Defendants in criminal cases often want a change of venue if the nature of their crime has generated prejudicial and inflammatory publicity. Venue can be and is changed across county lines, and in certain rare circumstances it can be moved to another state jurisdiction.

Two essential questions are necessary in analyzing venue:

1. Given the particular facts and parties, what court has jurisdiction?
2. Given the jurisdiction of the court, what geographic location is the appropriate venue for this dispute to be resolved?

Summary

This introductory chapter's content has given an overview of the nature and definition of law. Many types of law were discussed and differentiated, from common law to administrative regulation. The second part of this chapter covered the hierarchical structure of American courts, both federal and state. The powers and duties of the U.S. Supreme Court, the circuit courts, the district courts, and the specialized federal courts were assessed. Various state model court systems, including those of New York and Michigan, were profiled.

Methods of determining jurisdiction, from subject matter jurisdiction to federal jurisdiction based on diversity, were outlined. Practical problems and suggestions were made for choosing the proper forum for litigation.

Discussion Questions

1. Can it be said that law exists out of expedience or necessity alone?
2. What are proponents who claim that the law has a higher authority called?
3. A holding in a case decision is considered law. Why?
4. Administrative agencies publish rules and regulations. Are these forms of law?

5. Make a chart or diagram outlining the courts that exist within your jurisdiction. What is the highest court?

6. How does one distinguish between a civil and a criminal wrong?

7. How would you describe a judicial activist versus a strict constructionist?

8. Name several federal courts based solely on subject matter jurisdiction.

9. If jurisdiction is exclusive, can it be concurrent with another forum?

10. "The grant of jurisdiction by *certiorari* is not a matter of right." True or false?

11. "Any case with citizens from diverse states can qualify for federal jurisdiction. A showing of two statehoods is all that is necessary." True or false?

Research Exercises

1. Locate two subject-specific secondary legal resources for each of the following topics:
   - Criminal law.
   - Civil law.
   - Domestic relations law.
   - Corporate law.
   - Contract law.
   - Tort law.
   - Personal injury law.
   - Medical malpractice law.
   - Product liability law.
   - Environmental law.

2. Using online or library resources, locate your state court and the federal court rules for the following. Include proper citation of applicable rules. How are these processes similar or different?
   - Appearance by out-of-state lawyers.
   - Stipulations regarding discovery.
   - Depositions by medical experts.
   - Admissibility of duplicates.

Practical Exercises

1. Using Internet and print resources, chart your state and local/municipal court systems. How are they similar to and different from the federal court organization?

2. Complete the following questionnaire after visiting a courtroom and observing a current case proceeding:
   - Identify the court personnel who were present during your visit to the courtroom. Name their positions and give your perception of their duties.
     - If possible, name the exact case that you observed.
     - If possible, name the attorneys who represented plaintiffs and defendants.
     - Was a jury present? If so, what was your impression of the jury and its conduct during our observation?
     - What impressions did you form regarding the conduct of the judge during this adjudication?
     - Do you think that the attorneys presented clear, concise arguments regarding the issue?
     - What was your impression of the attorneys as they advocated their positions?
     - If the judge gave instructions to a jury or ruled on a matter of law or other motion, do you think the judge presented a clear position?
     - How do all of these impressions differ from your previous expectations and perceptions?
     - It is often said that advocacy is more drama than a pure application of law. Is there any truth to this comment?

3. Locate your state's directory of courts either online or in print. Which district are you in? Report addresses, phone numbers, e-mail addresses, and Web sites for all of the state courts

that have jurisdiction over your area of residence. Do any of these courts allow electronic or online filing of documents? If so, what are the fees in relation to paper filing?

Internet Resources

U.S. Courts Web site—www.uscourts.gov

Federal Courts Finder—www.law.emory.edu/FEDCTS

U.S. Court Forms—www.uscourtforms.com

PACER Service Center—pacer.psc.uscourts.gov

Cornell Legal Information Institute State Court opinion page—www.law.cornell.edu/opinions.html

Internet Legal Research Group U.S. State & Federal Courts—www.ilrg.com/caselaw

Federal Judicial Branch on First.gov—www.firstgov.gov/Agencies/Federal/Judicial.shtml

Law Library of Congress—www.loc.gov/law/guide/usjudic.html

Endnotes

1. Cicero, *On the Laws*, in Selected Works of Cicero (Harry M. Hubbet trans., Walter J. Black, 1948).

2. St. Thomas Aquinas, Summa Theologica, pt. I-II, Q 90, et seq.

3. *See generally* Roslyn & Matthew Muraskin, Morality and the Law (2001).

4. Benjamin Cardozo, The Nature of the Judicial Process 104 (1970).

5. Charles P. Nemeth, Aquinas in the Courtroom 48 (2001).

6. Nemeth, *supra* note 5, at 179–194 for a full exposition on this school of thought.

7. Robert Waldron, The Criminal Justice System: An Introduction 5 (1976); *see also* Robert P. George, Making Men Moral (1995).

8. Nemeth, *supra* note 5, at 47. *See also* Vincent McNabb, St. Thomas Aquinas and The Law (1955); Barry F. Smith, *Of Truth and Certainty in the Law: Reflections on the Legal Method*, 30 Am. J. Juris. 119 (1985).

9. *See* Harry Barnes & Negley Teeters, New Horizons in Criminology (1951); Gerold Geis, Man, Crime, and Society (1962); Walter C. Reckless, The Crime Problem 1967).

10. Roscoe Pound, An Introduction to the Philosophy of Law 58 (1968).

11. J. Messner, Social Ethics: Natural Law in the Modern World, 202 (trans. J.J. Doherty, 1952).

12. *See* Nemeth, *supra* note 5, at 32–40.

13. Joseph Boyle, *Natural Law and the Ethics of Tradition*, in Natural Law Theory: Contemporary Essays 11 (Robert P. George ed., 1994).

14. Cicero, *supra* note 1.

15. Aquinas, *supra* note 2.

16. Nemeth, *supra* note 5, at 25.

17. Alisdair MacIntyre, Whose Justice? Whose Rationality? 193–194 (1988).

18. *See* Brian Tierney, the Idea of Natural Rights: Studies on Natural Rights, Natural Law, and Church Law 1150–1625, 346 (1997).

19. *See* Charles P. Nemeth, *Some Brave Ideas on an Old Rule of Law: Jacques Maritain and the Application of Natural Law*, 25 Cath. Law. 8 (1979); Roscoe Pound, *The Revival of Natural Law*, 17 Notre Dame L. Rev. 287 (1942).

20. Aquinas, *supra* note 2, at Q. 95, a. 4, c.

21. M. Gilson, Law on The Human Level, Moral Values, and Moral Life: The System of St. Thomas, 204 (L. Ward trans., 1931); Aquinas, *supra* note 2, at Q 93, a. 3, ad. 2.

22. John Austin, Lectures on Jurisprudence (1885).

23. *See* Daniel Lyons, Forms and Limits of Utilitarianism (1965); Roscoe Pound, Jurisprudence (1959).

24. *See* Peter Radcliff, Limits of Liberty: Studies on Mill's on Liberty (1966).

25. David Brody, The American Legal System: Concepts and Principles 9 (1978).

26. Heinrich Rommen, The Natural Law 133 (Thomas R. Hanley trans., 1948).

27. The classic work and treatise is Sir William Blackstone, Commentaries.

28. Brody, *supra* note 25, at 9.

29. J. Kendrick Kinney, A Law Dictionary and Glossary 540 (1987).

30. *Filings Climbed in Federal Courts in Fiscal Year 2004*, March 2005, Third Branch—The Newsletter of the Federal Courts, available at http://www.uscourts.gov/ttb/mar05ttb/caseload/index.html.

31. Richard Kimbrough, Summary of American Law §4.1 at 38 (1985).

32. *Id.*

33. *See generally* Roe v. Wade, 410 U.S. 113 (1973); Planned Parenthood v. Casey, 505 U.S. 833 (1992); Romer v. Evans, 517 U.S. 620 (1996); Bowers v. Hardwick, 478 U.S. 186 (1986).

34. Griswold v. Connecticut, 381 U.S. 479 (1965); *see also* R. H. Clark, *Constitutional Sources of the Penumbrae Right to Privacy*, 119 Vill. L. Rev. 833 (1974).

35. Roe v. Wade, 410 U.S. 133 (1973).

36. U.S. Const. Amend. I; *Note, From Private Places to Personal Privacy*, 43 N.Y.U.L. Rev. 96 (1968).

37. Powell v. Alabama, 287 U.S. 45 (1932).

38. Lawrence v. Texas, 539 U.S. 558 (2003); Bowers v. Hardwick, 478 U.S. 186 (1986).

39. 521 U.S. 702 (1997).

40. *See* Walter Gellhorn, Administrative Law (1980).

41. *See* for example 5 U.S.C. §7123.

42. Arthur J. Bilek, John C. Klotter, & R. Keegan Federal Jr., Legal Aspects of Private Security 158 (1980); *see also* Charles P. Nemeth, Private Security and the Law (Elsevier: London 2005).

43. Arthur J. Bilek, John C. Klotter, & R. Keegan Federal Jr., Legal Aspects of Private Security 158 (1980); *see also* Charles P. Nemeth, Private Security and the Law 110 (1989, 2005).

44. Charles P. Nemeth, Criminal Law 32 (2004).

45. U.S. Const. art. III, sec. 1.

46. Kimbrough, *supra* note 31, at §4.1 at 42.

47. U.S. Const. art. I, §8 Cl. 9.

48. 28 U.S.C. §43.

49. 28 U.S.C. §45.

50. 28 U.S.C. §46.

51. 28 U.S.C. §§133 (2003).

52. Justice Antonin Scalia remarked in Planned Parenthood v. Casey, "The Imperial Judiciary lives. It is instructive to compare this Nietzschean vision of us unelected, life tenured judges—leading a Volk who will be "tested by following," and whose very "belief in themselves" is mystically bound up in their "understanding" of a Court that "speak[s] before all others for their constitutional ideals"—with the somewhat more modest role envisioned for these lawyers by the Founders." 505 U.S. 833; 112 S. Ct. 2791; 120 L. Ed. 2d 674 (1992).

53. 28 U.S.C. §152; *see also* Charles P. Nemeth, *The Retired Judges Service Act in the District of Columbia: Can It Withstand Constitutional Challenge?* Feb.-Mar. 1990, Judicature, at 253.

54. 28 U.S.C. §171.

55. 28 U.S.C. §§251, 254, 255.

56. 26 U.S.C. §7441.

57. 28 U.S.C. §1259.

58. 28 U.S.C. §1581.

59. National Center for State Courts, *State Court Caseload Statistics*, 2004 at State Court Structure Charts 7 (2004).

60. U.S. Const. art. III, §2.

61. *See* Brody, *supra* note 25, at 70; *see also* The Federalist Papers Nos. 45 and 46.

62. 28 U.S.C. §1251.

63. 28 U.S.C. §1251.

64. Rule 17 of the U.S. Supreme Court, *Jurisdiction on a Writ of Certiorari.*

65. For an excellent example of the certiorari grant, *see* Scheidler v. N.O.W., 126 S. Ct. 1264; 164 L. Ed. 2d 10.

66. *See* The Federal Procedural System: A Rule and Statutory Source Book, 710 *et seq.*

67. Brody, *supra* note 25, at 74.

68. For an excellent analysis of ancillary jurisdiction, *see* Exxon Mobil v. Allapattah Services, Nos. 04-70 & 04-79, 545. U.S. (2005).

69. Congress enacted the supplemental jurisdiction statute as part of the Judicial Improvements Act of 1990, Pub. L. No. 101-650, 104 Stat. 5089, to codify the common-law doctrines of pendent and ancillary jurisdiction. See H.R. Rep. No. 734 (House Report), 101st Cong., 2d Sess. 27-29 (1990); City of Chicago v. International Coll. of Surgeons, 522 U.S. 156, 165 (1997).

70. 28 U.S.C. §725.

71. 28 U.S.C. §1332.

72. 28 U.S.C. §1391.

Chapter 4

Corporations, Partnerships, and Other Business Entities

 BUSINESS LAW PARALEGAL JOB DESCRIPTION

Business law paralegals need to be proficient in the following competencies:

- Draft a preincorporation share subscription.
- Draft an outline or checklist of preincorporation activities.
- Select a jurisdiction for corporate formation that is most favorable for corporate liability and taxation.
- Select, check availability of, and reserve a corporate name.
- Draft articles of incorporation.
- Draft a series of bylaw provisions.
- File all necessary documents at the state and local level that permit the formation of a corporation, including the following:
  - Statement of intent to incorporate.
  - Advertisement of intent to incorporate.
  - Fictitious name affidavit.
  - Articles of incorporation.
  - Powers of the corporation.
  - Any corresponding amendments.
- Draft a notice of initial shareholder or promoter meetings.
- Draft notices of directors' organizational meetings.
- Set up agendas or itineraries for meetings.
- Draft all necessary documentation for shareholder activity and business.
- Draft a proxy.
- Draft resolutions to be considered by the board of directors.
- Draft all other documents necessary for corporate activity.
- File amendments to the articles of incorporation.
- Draft a merger document.
- Draft a consolidation document or agreement.
- Draft an acquisition agreement.
- Draft a contract for the sale of corporate assets.
- Draft a mortgage on corporate assets.
- File necessary documents for a voluntary or involuntary dissolution.
- Contact the secretary of state or other governmental authority about the intent to dissolve.
- File necessary documents at the state or local level regarding liquidation of corporate assets.
- File necessary documents for notice granted to governmental authorities, creditors, shareholders, and other interested parties in a liquidation action.
- Correspond and document derivative actions with dissenting shareholders.[1]
- Complete and file qualification of foreign corporations.

- Complete and file election by small business corporations and subsequent shareholders' consents to such elections.
- Complete and file applications for employer identification number.
- Complete and file applications for workers' compensation.
- Complete and file applications for unemployment insurance.
- Complete and file applications for employer withholding tax registration.
- Complete and file for appropriate licenses to operate specific business.
- Complete and file trade name applications, copyright applications, and financing statements.
- Draft notices, minutes, and consents of organization meetings.
- Draft banking resolutions and shareholder agreements.
- Draft and proofread employment agreements.
- Draft and file applications for proper licensing when forming professional or special-purpose corporations.
- Draft responses to auditors' requests for information.
- Draft notices, proxy materials, ballots, affidavits of mailing, and agendas for annual meeting and special meetings.
- Draft oaths and reports of judges of election for annual meetings, as well as shareholders' and directors' minutes.
- Draft written consents in lieu of meetings.
- Draft stock option plans; maintain stock option registers and related charts.
- Draft and organize closing documents for corporate acquisitions.
- Draft lease agreements.
- Draft articles of merger or consolidation and plans of merger or consolidation.
- Draft closing checklists and memoranda.
- Draft partnership agreements and amendments.
- Draft statements of partnership and certificates of limited partnership
- Draft certificates of amendment to certificates of limited partnership.
- Draft minutes of partnership meetings.
- Draft noncompetition agreements for selling partners.
- Draft agreements for dissolution of partnership.
- Draft and publish terminations of partnership (or continuation of successor businesses).
- Draft certificates or cancellations of certificates of limited partnership.
- Draft analysis for tax planning.
- Draft state and federal tax returns and prepare for accountants' audits.
- Draft and file certificates of trade names and certificates of assumed names with the appropriate county and state offices.
- Prepare necessary documents for opening corporate bank accounts.
- Prepare and file S corporation elections.
- Prepare and file annual reports and registrations.
- Prepare closing files and assist in closing transactions.
- Prepare and issue public notices of substance of certificates of general and limited partnership.
- Prepare documents for qualification to do business in foreign jurisdictions.
- Prepare necessary documents to amend and restate articles of incorporation and amend corresponding bylaws.
- Prepare and file governmental applications and reports.
- Obtain good-standing certificates from the secretary of state.
- Issue and transfer stock; prepare stock and shareholder registers; prepare and maintain analyses and charts of outstanding securities.
- Order (or prepare) the minute book, stock book, and corporate seal.
- Maintain a tickler system for annual stockholders' meetings and board of directors' meetings.
- Collect information and draft documents and correspondence necessary to adopt qualified profit-sharing and pension plans, as well as related trust agreements and other documents.
- Submit such materials to IRS for determination letters.
- Conduct due diligence investigation.
- Compile and index documents in corporate transactions.
- Collect information from, and verify filings with, the secretary of state and other state and local agencies.
- Change the registered office and agent.

INTRODUCTION

The formation of a business, whether a sole proprietorship, joint venture, partnership, or corporation, is a recurring paralegal responsibility. Even after formation, the tracking and administration of business forms remains a continuing obligation of the paralegal. The challenges and demands of corporate practice in the life of a paralegal are many. Paralegal and author Julie Bassett calls the corporate setting a unique "culture" to which the paralegal must adapt:

> *The typical corporate paralegal, whether working within a corporation or a law firm, is not typical at all. The education and experience each brings to the job is as diverse as the "corporate culture" in which the job exists.*[2]

Paralegals are a natural fit in the legal office specializing in corporate law.[3] By any measure, choosing a corporate specialization will result in both rewards and challenges. It is a dynamic area filled with evolving and complex legal standards. The field calls for sharp minds. Bassett suggests five ways to enhance a corporate career choice:

1. Become a specialist.
2. Seek new challenges.
3. Become active in a national professional organization.
4. Build a good reputation.
5. Sharpen writing skills.[4]

The opportunities for personal and professional growth in business paralegal practice are unlimited.

CHOICE OF BUSINESS ENTITY

From the outset, it is crucial that the client business plan match the choice of business entity. The question of which form is best for the client is never easy to answer. Before you make any recommendation, consider these questions:

- What kind of business is the individual interested in?
- Does the individual have the mental and physical capacity to enter the business?
- Is it a business that has specific equipment or specialized equipment needs?
- Is the business likely to be of a long-range nature?
- Where is the business going to be located?
- Does the business fulfill a need?
- Does the business have an exact market?
- What is the competition?
- What are its capital requirements?
- How much money does the business have?
- Is any private sector financing available?
- Are any government programs available to help?
- Is any venture capital available?
- Are there any laws or restrictions on the nature of the business?
- Are any licenses or permits required?
- What other filings must take place before a business can be effected?
- Might any investors be of assistance?
- Might any government agencies provide assistance?
- What are the tax requirements under the business scheme selected?
- Is the client capable of handling this form of business?

Figure 4.1 categorizes the chief choices of business forms or entities.

FIGURE 4.1 Types of Business Entities

Source: Law offices of David J. Reed Web site, *Services, Business Law*, available at http://www.davidjreed.com/Corporate/business_types.htm (last modified April 8, 2003; accessed October 23, 2006).

Business Type	Advantages	Disadvantages	Limited Liability	Pass-Through Taxation
Sole proprietorship	Simple	Limited growth No limited liability	No	Yes
C corporation	Unlimited growth Deductible health insurance	Double taxation	Yes	No
S Corporation	Well-established law	Shareholder limitations	Yes	Yes
LLC	Simple creation and administration	Law not well established	Yes	Yes
General partnership	Simple creation and administration	No limited liability	No	Yes
Limited partnership	Well-established law	Must have general partner Limited partners cannot manage	Yes (for limited partners)	Yes
LLP	Very simple creation and administration	Must not have three or more corporate attributes	Yes	Yes

Each of the business forms in Figure 4.1 has a particular advantage depending on the client's circumstance.[5] Some provide favorable tax treatment; others limit liability, whether personal or vicarious in nature; others allow faster and more expeditious generation of profit. Generally business forms fall into three major categories: the sole proprietorship, the partnership, and the corporation.[6] In each of these instances, as well as other forms of business structure, the client needs to be educated and the paralegal must conduct sufficient background analysis.

The following resources will help the paralegal make a recommendation:

- Publications of the Internal Revenue Code on "Small Business."
- Publications of the Internal Revenue Code on "Partnership Income."
- Passive loss descriptions as to taxability under the Internal Revenue Code's standards of the Tax Reform Act of 1986.
- Community Development Corporation (CDC) programs, policies, and procedures (check locally).
- The local Small Business Administration office.
- Local small business investment companies (SBICs).[7]
- A copy of the state or local Business Corporations Act.
- A copy of the Uniform Securities Act, if applicable in your jurisdiction.
- A copy of state tax guides for business and industry.
- Office of Economic Development literature that outlines small business requirements.
- Rules and regulations regarding licenses and permits.
- Rules and regulations regarding federal identification numbers.
- Rules and regulations regarding state occupational licenses.
- Rules and regulations regarding sales tax and other occupational and business taxes.
- Wage tax and withholding information.
- Workers' compensation insurance information.
- Fire insurance information.
- Rules and requirements for establishing a corporation.
- Paperwork and documents necessary to choose or register a specific corporate name.
- Chamber of Commerce information.

- State business and commerce information.
- Corporate kits and other minute books.

Choice of business form largely depends on liability considerations, extent of documentary requirements, and tax structure and accounting demands. Andrew Beckerman-Rodau classifies the variables of choice as follows:

1. Type of business.
2. Number of participants in the business.
3. Desired length of existence of the business.
4. Business location.
5. Use of the customary form.
6. Potential liability.
7. Financing and capital requirements.
8. Cost and complexity of formation.
9. Ongoing requirements.
10. Management and control.
11. Transferability of ownership interests.[8]

The precise intent and purpose for the business formation must also be evaluated.

Choosing a business entity should reflect the client's overall needs. The strengths, weaknesses, and significant characteristics of the various choices are charted in Figure 4.2.

Sole Proprietorship

The individual or sole proprietorship is the oldest, least complicated, and most frequently established business enterprise in the United States. With minimal regulation and simplicity of management and control, the sole proprietor essentially "sinks or swims" alone. More specifically, when compared to the corporation, the business lacks a perpetual nature, lapses upon the death or retirement of the proprietor, and is taxed at rates that may or may not be preferable. The advantages of an individual proprietorship are

1. Few formalities.
2. Few filing fees at the state, local, or federal levels.
3. No stockholder or shareholder input.
4. Unilateral decision making.
5. No board of directors or other formal body to answer to.
6. Capacity to trade in other localities without registration or other filings.
7. Deemed a citizen as a person would be because an individual owns the business.
8. Less regulation and fewer reporting requirements.
9. No double tax as in some corporate distributions.
10. Ability to create merging or cohesive tax shelters.
11. Right to operate under a fictitious name.
12. Liberal, easy to set up, and simplified employee pension plans, profit-sharing plans, and Keogh plans are available.[9]

Not all is rosy with the sole proprietorship form. The choice does have some disadvantages:

1. The owner of a sole proprietorship has unlimited personal liability for all the obligations of the business. That liability can result from tort claims, creditors' actions, and any other causes of action related to the business operation.
2. Personal creditors can also access or attack sole proprietorship assets because they are viewed as personal assets.
3. Capital cannot be raised through stock offerings.
4. Investors, venture capitalists, and other equity owners cannot be attracted.

FIGURE 4.2 **Six Preferred Legal Forms of Business**

Source: Adapted from Hawaii State Government. Available at: http://hbe.ehawaii.gov/BizEx/faq.eb;jsessionid=4470D91C910A4396D0C3CFD695884A79 (accessed February 2, 2007).

	Sole Proprietorship	Partnership	Corporation	Sub-S Corporation	Limited Liability Partnership	Limited Liability Company
Ownership	By a single individual	By two or more persons	By unlimited number of shareholders	By shareholders: number of shareholders limited to 75	2 or more persons or entities (except law firms)	1 or more persons or entities (except certain providers of professional services and law firms)
Advantages	Uncomplicated—ease of formation Greater flexibility of action Singleness of control Economy of operation Tax advantage by avoiding corporate income tax Maximum centralized authority	Division of responsibilities Ease of formation Greater flexibility of action Increased sources of capital Incentive to key employees Tax advantage by avoiding corporate income tax	Legal entity separate from individuals Limited personal liability Continuity of existence Continuity of management Easier to raise capital Incentive to key employees Readily transferable interests Possible separation of ownership and management	Legal entity separate from individuals Limited personal liability Continuity of existence Continuity of management Readily transferable interests Possible separation of ownership and management Net operating loss deductible by shareholders	Division of responsibilities Ease of formation Limited personal liability Greater flexibility of action Increased sources of capital Incentive to key employees Tax advantage by avoiding corporate income tax	Legal entity separate from individuals Limited personal liability Continuity of existence Continuity of management Easier to raise capital Incentive to key employees Readily transferable interests Possible separation of ownership and management
Disadvantages	Unlimited personal liability Legal life ends with owner's death Difficulty in raising capital Possible personnel difficulties Owner's salary cannot be treated as expense, hence, not tax deductible	Unlimited personal liability Impermanence of existence Division of control/authority Difficult to find compatible partners Difficult to raise additional capital Owners' salary/wage cannot be treated as expense, hence, not tax deductible	Difficult, costly formation Subject to close government regulation Scope limited by corporate charter Inflexibility of operations Double taxation by paying both corporate and personal income taxes	Only one class of stock outstanding Difficult, costly formation Subject to close government regulation Inflexibility of operations	Impermanence of existence Division of control/authority Difficult to find compatible partners Difficult to raise additional capital Owners' salary/wage cannot be treated as expense, hence, not tax deductible	Difficult, costly formation Subject to close government regulation Scope limited by company charter Inflexibility of operations

5. After the owner dies or becomes incapacitated, the business can disintegrate.

6. The profits of a sole proprietorship are taxed personally to the owner.

7. The owner is personally responsible for decision making and cannot as easily delegate other responsibilities and agency relationships.[10]

The owner of a sole proprietorship is the owner of the business. If the client wishes to maintain centralized control with little outside input, a sole proprietorship provides the mechanism. "If maintaining control of the business is an important consideration to an individual, a sole proprietorship is an appropriate choice."[11]

The requirements for sole proprietorship creation are few. First an application for an employer identification number (EIN), which may or may not differ from a personal Social Security number, needs to be completed. See Federal SS-4 at Form 4.1 on the accompanying CD. In some cases, licenses and permits must be acquired to operate the business of the sole proprietorship; this is a frequent requirement for the trades or crafts. Information regarding necessary licenses is available from individual state governments. In Pennsylvania the Bureau of Professional and Occupational Affairs, a branch of the Department of State, issues and renews licenses. Depending on the jurisdiction, if the name of the proprietorship differs from the proprietor, a fictitious name registration must be completed. See Form 4.2 for an example from Pennsylvania and Form 4.3 for an example from Texas. This document advises regulatory authorities of the nature and identity of ownership.

Reporting income and computing tax liability varies a bit from simple wage and tax calculations. The sole proprietor usually calculates income and corresponding expenses on Schedule C of the IRS Form 1040. See Form 4.4 on the accompanying CD. Sole proprietors with employees need to prepare W-4s for withholding purposes. Social Security, Medicare and Medicaid, federal, state, and local withholding are all reported on the employee W-4 (see Form 4.5). Payments may now be made by coupon or electronic wire. See Form 4.6 for a sample payment coupon. Finally, IRS Form 941 recapitulates taxes collected and deposited (see Form 4.7).

Aside from these requirements, the sole proprietor is free to carry out the aim and goal of the proprietorship. Sole proprietorship delivers a flexible and adaptable business form for the American entrepreneur.

Partnerships

Partnerships are generally defined by the parties and the corresponding agreement to enter the business relationship. The State of Delaware defines the partnership as so:

> *"Partner" means a person who has been admitted to a partnership as a partner of the partnership.*
>
> *(11) "Partnership" means an association of two or more persons formed under § 15-202 of this title, predecessor law or comparable law of another jurisdiction to carry on any business, purpose or activity.*
>
> *(12) "Partnership agreement" means the agreement, whether written, oral or implied, among the partners concerning the partnership, including amendments to the partnership agreement. A partnership is not required to execute its partnership agreement. A partnership is bound by its partnership agreement whether or not the partnership executes the partnership agreement. A partnership agreement may provide rights to any person, including a person who is not a party to the partnership agreement, to the extent set forth therein. A partner of a partnership or a transferee of an economic interest is bound by the partnership agreement whether or not the partner or transferee executes the partnership agreement.*

Most partnerships are guided by statute. Model acts, such as the Uniform Partnership Act and the Uniform Limited Partnership Act, serve as guides for legislative process and are well regarded.[12]

General Partnership

In contrast to a sole proprietorship, a partnership requires more than one person. In addition, the partnership must evidence co-ownership or a division of assets or other allocation explicitly in a partnership agreement. Partners jointly own identifiable and tangible assets, divisibly share in the profit, and share authority in decision making. All "partners have equal rights in the management of the business. The day to day decisions of the firm are decided by the majority vote of the partners."[13] General partners also bind one another as agents for the partnership. As each carries out his or her tasks in good faith and in accordance with law and the scope of the partnership agreement, the other partners are bound to that action. The State of Delaware sets out the general policy:

> ***SECTION 15-301. PARTNER AGENT OF PARTNERSHIP.*** *Subject to the effect of a statement of partnership existence under Section 15-303:*
>
> *(1) Each partner is an agent of the partnership for the purpose of its business, purposes or activities. An act of a partner, including the execution of an instrument in the partnership name, for apparently carrying on in the ordinary course the partnership's business, purposes or activities or business, purposes or activities of the kind carried on by the partnership binds the partnership, unless the partner had no authority to act for the partnership in the particular matter and the person with whom the partner was dealing had notice that the partner lacked authority.*
>
> *(2) An act of a partner which is not apparently for carrying on in the ordinary course the partnership's business, purposes or activities or business, purposes or activities of the kind carried on by the partnership binds the partnership only if the act was authorized by the other partners.*[14]

Without express direction from the partnership agreement, a partner's share in the business will be deemed equally or proportionately divisible as outlined in the Uniform Partnership Act. Each partner shall be repaid his or her contributions (whether by capital or by advances of the partnership property) and share equally in the profits and surplus remaining after all liabilities, including those to partners, are satisfied. Each partner must also contribute toward the losses, whether of capital or otherwise, sustained by the partnership according to his or her share in the profits.[15]

Just as in the sole proprietorship, foundational documentation is required when a partnership is established. First, as outlined previously in Form 4.1 on the accompanying CD, a Form SS-4 must be completed. Second, partnerships may need business licenses, certificates, or other permits. Third, fictitious name registrations and in some cases name reservations may be required. Fourth, notice may need to be given to the appropriate state agency regarding the partnership formation. See Form 4.8 for Florida's Partnership Registration Statement. Fifth, as in all other business forms, income and corresponding tax liability must be reported on designated forms. In the case of a partnership, IRS Form 1120 serves this purpose. States and localities may also have reporting documents (see Form 4.9). Partnership income is taxed directly to the individual partners because the partnership has no specific income and specified rates of taxation.

Sixth, and most critically, the nature, scope, and purpose of the partnership are memorialized in a partnership agreement. (See Form 4.10 on the accompanying CD.) A partnership agreement fully outlines the rights and obligations of the partners and usually covers the following topics:

1. The term, parties, and purpose of the agreement.

2. The organizational structure of the firm and the method of firm governance and management, including how partners (and possibly associates) are elected or appointed to managerial positions.

3. The decisions reserved to the partnership (duties and responsibilities of all partners) and voting requirements for decisions.

4. The duties and responsibilities of the executive or management group of the firm.

5. The method of determining partners' voting rights (such as cumulative or one person, one vote).

6. The method of voting, including voting rights, quorum, and limitation of voting.

7. The method of determining initial capital contributions, ongoing capital contributions, and return of capital under various conditions and whether interest is to be paid on capital accounts.

8. The approach to setting partner compensation—that is, the sharing of profits and losses, including who makes such determinations and when.

9. The voluntary or involuntary withdrawal of partners, including expulsion, retirement, death, or disability, and payments to the withdrawing partner under these circumstances.

10. The activities of a withdrawing partner—that is, noncompetition clauses and penalties for violating them, ethical considerations when partners leave to become judges, and so on.

11. The limitation on payments (as a percentage of net profits) to be paid to retiring, disabled, withdrawing, expelled, or deceased partners.

12. The dissolution of the firm, including how to liquidate assets and distribute the proceeds.

13. The ownership of accounts receivable and work in process—the method and principles of accounting.

14. The indemnification of partners under a variety of conditions and events.

15. The handling of professional ethics issues (advertising, conflicts of interests, and the like).

16. Any special provisions required by state law to protect the firm in the event of a partner's divorce.[16]

The partnership agreement will especially focus on the nature of the partnership's property, including provisions relating to transferability or liquidation upon death or disability of any general partner. Partnership property must be clearly and distinctly defined. Nevada Revised Statute 87.080 defines partnership property as follows:

1. *All property originally brought into the partnership stock or subsequently acquired by purchase or otherwise, on account of the partnership, is partnership property.*

2. *Unless the contrary intention appears, property acquired with partnership funds is partnership property.*

3. *Any estate in real property may be acquired in the partnership name. Title so acquired can be conveyed only in the partnership name.*

4. *A conveyance to a partnership in the partnership name, though without words of inheritance, passes the entire estate of the grantor unless a contrary intent appears.*[17]

The partners' respective contributions to the partnership, in specific dollar sums, should be outlined in the content of the agreement. This calculation focuses on each partner's individual interest, comprising all intangible interests including a partner's proportionate share of assets and liabilities and corresponding rights in subsequent profits.

As for management and governance policy, the partnership agreement should delineate the partners' respective rights and restrictions. The Uniform Partnership Act holds that management decision making is an equal right unless otherwise stated. In reality, management rights are often delegated to one or two individuals because of their expertise or in exchange for the skills and services of other individuals handling designated business affairs. Partnership agreements may include language that limits or restricts certain action on the part of the partners. Nevada Revised Statute 87.090 lays out the following language:

1. *Every partner is an agent of the partnership for the purpose of its business, and the act of every partner, including the execution in the partnership name of any instrument, for apparently carrying on in the usual way the business of the partnership of which he is a member binds the partnership, unless the partner so acting has in fact no authority to act for the partnership in the particular matter, and the person with whom he is dealing has knowledge of the fact that he has no such authority.*

2. *An act of a partner which is not apparently for the carrying on of the business of the partnership in the usual way does not bind the partnership unless authorized by the other partners.*

3. *Except as otherwise provided in subsection 5, unless authorized by the other partners or unless they have abandoned the business, one or more but less than all the partners have no authority to:*
   (a) *Assign the partnership property in trust for creditors or on the assignee's promise to pay the debts of the partnership;*
   (b) *Dispose of the goodwill of the business;*
   (c) *Do any other act which would make it impossible to carry on the ordinary business of a partnership;*
   (d) *Confess a judgment; or*
   (e) *Submit a partnership claim or liability to arbitration or reference.*

4. *No act of a partner in contravention of a restriction on authority shall bind the partnership to persons having knowledge of the restriction.*

5. *One or more of the partners designated in an agreement among all of the partners may sell all or substantially all of the property of the partnership without the unanimous approval or consent of the partners if:*
   (a) *The sale is approved by a vote; or*
   (b) *The prior consent of the partners for a sale of all or substantially all of the property has been given in an agreement among the partners,*

and written notice of the sale is sent by registered or certified mail to all partners at least 15 days before the date of the sale.[18]

In the case of a general partnership, the delegation of power, decision making, and management control tends to be spread evenly because the partners share equally in the governance process.

Partnership agreements should explain compensation, expense allowances, and other permissible means of economic reward and incentive for management. A general partner, who manages and operates the partnership, rightfully seeks a higher form of compensation compared to a limited partner, who seeks a return on investment and principal.

The profits and losses of the partnership, and their respective allocation and distribution, should be adequately described in the partnership agreement. The agreement may establish a specific formula for this distribution. Other relevant provisions in the partnership agreement might be

- An indemnification clause in the event that personal assets are attached for creditors or other rights.
- The dissolution and termination processes to be followed if the partnership desires to close down.
- A winding-up process in which claims of creditors, claims of partners, and other interested parties are resolved.
- Arbitration and accounting clauses.
- Signatures, witnesses, and other executory provisions as locally required.

The drafter of the partnership agreement must attend to a host of factors involving not only the partners themselves, but also the operation of the partnership as legal entity. A coherent, enforceable partnership agreement will cover these issues:

- What are the purpose and philosophical direction of the partnership?
- What is the exact amount of each partner's contribution to the partnership?
- What are the distribution rights for partners?
- How will profits and losses be allocated between the partners?
- Who has specific management rights, and what are these rights?
- Are the partners general or limited?
- What is the procedure for calculating profits and losses in the partnership for purposes of distribution?
- What is the procedure for paying profits within the partnership?
- What happens if one of the general partners dies? To whom does his or her interest inure?
- How is liability avoided or imposed on the partners?

Technically a partnership agreement need not be in writing, and it is not uncommon to witness informal promises binding the partnership together.[19] However, given the diverse demands of the partnership, a formal document outlining enumeration of specific contributions, management authority, voting powers, duties, and rights and responsibilities of each partner will prevent and minimize disputes and provide stability to the partners.

Limited Partnership

Limited partnerships are special partnerships created by statute. A limited partnership must have one or more general partners who are typically subject to the same rules as the partners in a general partnership. Additionally, a limited partnership must have one or more limited partners who have a restricted role in the operation of the enterprise. Limited partners can invest cash, property, or services in the entity with the expectation that their investment will pay a meaningful return. The limited partner's risk is directly tied to the amount of the investment itself:[20]

(a) *Except as otherwise provided in subsections (b) and (c), all partners are liable jointly and severally for all obligations of the partnership unless otherwise agreed by the claimant or provided by law.*

(b) *A person admitted as a partner into an existing partnership is not personally liable for any obligation of the partnership incurred before the person's admission as a partner.*

(c) *An obligation of a partnership incurred while the partnership is a limited liability partnership, whether arising in contract, tort or otherwise, is solely the obligation of the partnership. A partner is not personally liable, directly or indirectly, by way of indemnification, contribution, assessment or otherwise, for such an obligation solely by reason of being or so acting as a partner.*[21]

As a result, the limited partner has less at risk than the general partner, whose responsibility extends to the full allocation of profit as well as loss. Due to their limited investment in the business, however, limited partners cannot engage in the management or control of the business.

General partners assume losses and liabilities of the partnership business, whereas limited partners bear limited liability based on their proportionate interest in the overall partnership. The avoidance should not be construed in any negative light; rather, it is a vehicle for investment in the American economy and its engines for economic growth. Limited partners are significant contributors to the American economy—consider capital contributors to low-income housing projects, historical rehabilitation funds, movie and television projects, and diverse other business ventures.

Limited partners can be further defined as follows:

1. The limited partner makes an agreed-upon economic contribution.

2. The limited partner's name does not appear in the partnership name.

3. The limited partner has no participatory management rights in the business.

4. The limited partner is not in any sense a principal in the business.

5. The limited partner's liability extends only to his or her contribution.

6. The limited partner is given a preferred priority upon liquidation against general partners and other creditors.

7. The limited partner's proceeds and distributions will be taxed at an individual rate.

Whether or not there are formal requirements for the creation of a limited partnership depends on the jurisdiction.[22] Some issue no requirements, whereas others may insist on a centralized filing. A Certificate of Limited Partnership is the most common filing for this purpose. See Form 4.11 on the accompanying CD. The state Corporations Bureau or Secretary of State usually publishes the form.

Any subsequent amendments to the certificate must be filed with the Secretary of State. The requirements for filings are typically outlined in a state's statutory authority. See the example from Mississippi below:

> *(a) One (1) original of a certificate of limited partnership and of any certificates of amendment, dissolution or cancellation, or of any judicial decree of amendment, dissolution or cancellation must be delivered to the Secretary of State. A person who executes a certificate as an agent or fiduciary need not exhibit evidence of his authority as a prerequisite to filing. If the Secretary of State finds that the certificate meets the requirements of this article and all filing fees required by Section 79-14-1104 have been paid, he shall:*
> *(1) Endorse on the original the word "Filed" and the day, month and year of the filing thereof;*
> *(2) File the original in his office; and*
> *(3) Return a copy to the person who filed it or his representative.*
>
> *(b) Upon the filing of a certificate of amendment or judicial decree of amendment in the office of the Secretary of State or upon the future effective date of a certificate of amendment or judicial decree thereof, as provided for therein, the certificate of limited partnership shall be amended as set forth therein. Upon the filing of a certificate of dissolution or cancellation or a judicial decree thereof in the office of the Secretary of State or upon the future effective date of a certificate of dissolution or cancellation or a judicial decree thereof, the certificate of limited partnership is dissolved or cancelled, as the case may be.[23]*

Form 4.12 on the accompanying CD contains a sample limited partnership agreement delineating terms and conditions relative to voting rights; liability to third parties; forms of contributions and respective interests in profits, losses, and distributions; withdrawal rights; management rights; assignment rights dissolution; and derivative actions.

In summary, the most compelling characteristic of the limited partnership is the opportunity for investors to make a limited capital contribution and incur minimal personal and business liability.

Joint Venture

A *joint venture* (also known as a joint adventure, co-adventure, business consortium, syndicate, group, pool, joint enterprise, joint undertaking, or joint speculation) is an unincorporated association created by the co-owners of a business venture, usually to carry out a particular venture, as contrasted with a partnership's operation of a business. (An example of a joint venture agreement is Form 4.13 on the accompanying CD.) Joint ventures frequently display an inordinate amount of risk. Because profit is the primary motive, the conduct of the members of the joint venture may be less attentive to law and ethics than in the corporate setting. A frequently seen venture involves exploration for oil and gas reserves. Be sure to advise clients of the many pitfalls.[24]

In some circles, the joint venture is labeled a *joint stock association*. The association displays all the qualities of a corporation but is not incorporated. It issues shares and carries out the business of the association with annual meetings and typical protocols, though it remains unincorporated. Georgia defines a joint stock association as follows:

> *"Joint-stock association" includes any association of the kind commonly known as a joint-stock association or joint-stock company and any unincorporated association, trust, or enterprise having members or having outstanding shares of stock or other evidences of financial and beneficial interest therein, whether formed by agreement or under statutory authority or otherwise, but does not include a corporation, partnership, or nonprofit organization. A joint-stock association as defined in this paragraph may be one formed under the laws of this state, including a trust created pursuant to Article 3 of Chapter 12 of Title 53, or one formed under or pursuant to the laws of any other state or jurisdiction.[25]*

Corporations

The corporate form constitutes a legal entity in its own right. It is operated by a board of directors and operating or managing officers and in most cases, a body of shareholders, each of whom fractionally owns some portion of the entity. "Corporations are owned by shareholders, who purchase shares of stock in the corporation. In order to sell these shares to the general public, it is often necessary that documentation be filed by the corporation with the Securities and Exchange Commission (SEC)."[26] All corporations are regulated by state authorities such as the Secretary of State or a Corporations Bureau. Most states have adopted provisions similar to the Model Business Corporation Act. Idaho is one such state. Below is a list of the areas covered by the Idaho Business Corporation Act:

Part 1. General Provisions	Part 10. Amendment Of Articles Of Incorporation And Bylaws
Part 2. Incorporation	Part 11. Merger And Share Exchange
Part 3. Purposes And Powers	Part 12. Disposition Of Assets
Part 4. Name	Part 13. Appraisal Rights
Part 5. Office And Agent	Part 14. Dissolution
Part 6. Shares And Distributions	Part 15. Foreign Corporations
Part 7. Shareholders	Part 16. Records And Reports
Part 8. Directors And Officers	Part 17. Transition Provisions
Part 9. Domestication	

Advantages of the Corporate Form

The corporation has many attractive advantages in the business sector, especially regarding the limitations on personal liability, business continuity of life, the centralization of management, the ability to transfer and alienate interests, and increased potential for capital and tax preferences.

A Nonhuman Entity A corporation is a legal enterprise geared and driven by the profit motive. It lacks a personal quality and is instead a legal entity in its own right serving the shareholders. In this context, the corporation shields its owners, shareholders, and other interested parties from personal liability.

A Separate Legal Entity Corporations are entities different and apart from the parties who manage or control them.[27] For purposes of legal liability, the corporate entity itself remains the responsible party rather than its officers and directors. To hold responsible those individuals who run the corporation, one must "pierce the corporate veil."[28] Piercing the corporate veil is an extraordinary legal occurrence that takes place in cases of fraud or injustice. Even as a debtor, the corporation has limited liability. In larger corporations, which consist of multiple layers of management and bureaucratic structure, the capacity to pierce is a lot less than the close corporation. In the smaller corporation the shareholders are often running the show and will be accountable in a more intimate way.[29] "Personal liability means that a creditor of an organization may seek personal satisfaction from a member of the organization to the extent that the assets of such organization are insufficient to satisfy the creditor's claims."[30] However, the protection provided by the corporate form makes this approach unlikely. Debtors in corporate bankruptcy, for example, are usually left hanging. Corporations shield the personal officers and directors not only in claims for debt but also in other forms of liability. Fines, sanctions, and penalties against the corporate entity are the prime means of exacting punishment on the corporation. Some hold that this is simply not enough to reign in errant directors and officers. Others, such as Steven Walt and William S. Laufer, argue that the imposition of penalties on the corporate entity is meaningful enough. Although immunization from liability is attractive, it is hardly foolproof:

> *In addition, a good counselor should disabuse prospective shareholders of the commonly held notion that shareholder-officers are insulated from liability for all actions that they take on behalf of the corporation. To the contrary, as individuals, they may be legally responsible for the individual acts though performed within the scope of their employment. By way of example, if a shareholder-officer (or shareholder-employee) commits an act of fraud, he or she may be individually liable for such act. However, he or she would not be liable for a fraudulent act committed by another corporate employee in which he or she did not participate or for which he or she had no supervisory responsibilities. In short, the corporate form primarily provides protection against vicarious liability.*[31]

Making corporations liable for action in both the civil and criminal context is becoming more common. "The imposition of criminal culpability upon corporations through the application of the traditional civil law concept of *respondeat superior*, or vicarious liability, is a relatively recent idea but one that has become solidly entrenched. Despite the description of various forms of *mens rea* (criminal intent) that might arguably demonstrate what some believe would be genuine corporate fault, most prosecutions are successful upon the mere showing that an agent acted criminally while within the scope of his employment and to benefit the corporation."[32] Yet the imposition of potential criminal liability on corporate officers and agents appears to have barely dented the avalanche of corporate criminality. For some, this obsession with criminality distracts regulators and prosecutors from the thing that really hurts the corporate pocketbook—corporate damages, fines, and other assessments.[33]

Continuity of Life In the event of death, disability, mental incapacity, bankruptcy, retirement, or resignation of shareholders or corporate directors, or any other extraordinary event, the life of the corporation goes on. Without express durational limitation, a corporation is dubbed "perpetual." A corporation has a continuing identity that is detached from its relationship to its stockholders.

Centralization of Management In both hierarchical and bureaucratic terms, corporations are the most complicated of the alternative business forms. Statutory controls and regulations of the corporation call for the naming of officers, boards of directors, registered agents, and specific locations for conducting business. Rules regarding voting, proxy rights, the issuance of stocks, and general fiscal and financial accountability are enumerated by governmental and other authority. The Model Business Corporation Act, an act that most American states emulate, provides generic recommendations on the compilation of bylaws; the holding of mandatory shareholder meetings; the establishment of quorums; the making of rules and restrictions on voting trusts and agreements; the establishment of a board of directors; and the promulgation of rules regarding the number and election of directors, classification of directors, removal of directors, establishment of committees, appropriate distributions to shareholders, appointment of officers, removal of officers, and other pertinent requirements.[34]

Ability to Transfer and Alienate Interests Corporations bear few restrictions as to the sale, transfer, or alienation of assets. In a corporation, property rights are evidenced by the number of shares, and real assets are freely alienable by subsequent transfer. The downside of full alienability of property interests is manifest in cases of leveraged buyouts, corporate raiding, and hostile takeovers—activities that cause a burden to company stability and management security.

Increased Potential for Capital Through the issuance of stock, a corporate entity can raise capital for expansion, growth, reduction of debt, or other legal purposes. A share of stock is a fractional share of ownership in a corporation or company. The corporation is legally empowered to issue a certain number of shares, depending on its type and the applicable regulatory framework. Outstanding shares are those that are currently on the market and held by differing parties.

Tax Preferences The choice of a corporate format leads to certain preferential tax treatments. Under the passive tax loss rules and limitations promulgated by the Tax Reform Act of 1986, individuals, sole proprietorships, partnerships, and other noncorporate entities are severely restricted in their use of passive losses as a deflection of active or passive income.

Traditional corporations (called C corporations because they are taxed according to Subchapter C of the Internal Revenue Code) are exempt from the restrictive implications of these rules. The tax aspects are generally beyond normal paralegal responsibility. However, the passive loss exemption should be a factor in the client's selection analysis. Furthermore, within a C corporation, disability, health, and medical premiums are still permissible deductions that are not subject to any ceilings. C corporations with low profit margins (less than $50,000) are taxed at the lowest rate available under the current Internal Revenue Code standard, though current legislation may modify this.

Besides these advantages, the corporation permits liberal pension and profit-sharing plans. This is true as long as the aggregate amount, under what is known as a defined contribution plan, a defined benefit plan, or a profit-sharing plan, does not exceed published shareholder limits.

Disadvantages of the Corporate Form

At times the corporate form will generate negative results for the client and may be less advantageous. Corporations are more costly entities than many other business forms.[35] The widely agreed negative side of the corporation includes

1. Increased filing costs for initial operation.
2. Increased accounting costs.
3. Multiple tax returns.
4. More taxes for employee wages.
5. Less authority and management given shareholder rights.
6. Registered agent fees.
7. Extension of credit limited to corporate assets.
8. Indemnification expenses.
9. Recordkeeping regarding shares transfer.
10. Taxation of income and dividends.
11. Costs of notices, proxy mailings, annual reports.
12. Costs of annual meetings, minutes, and record keeping.
13. Filings with the Securities and Exchange Commission (SEC).
14. Costs of formation, dissolution, and termination.
15. Accumulated earnings tax.
16. Insurance costs.
17. Potential or actual litigation about trade secrets, patents, shareholder rights and derivative actions, employment and labor relations, product liability, and other related matters.

Although these drawbacks are significant, selection of the corporate status depends on comparative and critical inquiry. The well-known traditional advantages, such as limited liability, perpetual existence, transferability of interest, and centralized management, usually outweigh the burdens imposed by the additional formalities of establishing, operating, and dissolving a corporation.[36]

Special Corporate Entities

S Corporations

A legal hybrid, the S corporation gets its name directly from Subchapter S of the Internal Revenue Code.[37] Often selected by small business interests, the S corporation is a mix of a partnership and a C corporation. It is designed to permit smaller, less capitalized businesses to be taxed at regular rates rather than corporate rates.[38] The S corporation embraces these traits:

1. An S corporation cannot have more than 75 shareholders.
2. Shareholders must be individuals, estates, or qualifying trusts.
3. An S corporation must not have more than one class of outstanding stock.
4. Election of S form must be no later than the fifteenth day of the third month after original incorporation.

The choice of S corporation status is driven by economic factors. Of special concern is the question of tax liability. Usually the beginning years of corporate operation generate large losses. As a result, if the company were taxed as a traditional C corporation, those losses could be carried forward or held for other shelter purposes at a later or even former tax year. Under Subchapter S, these losses are directly passed to the individuals who own that company. The S corporation is a "pass-through" corporation as far as federal taxation is concerned. The corporation pays no federal corporation tax; instead the profits are passed through to the shareholders and then taxed at individual rates.

 Finally, an S corporation is not subject to the double taxation that C corporations must pay on the distribution of dividends. S corporations must file consent forms as required under Internal Revenue Code Section 1362(a). In addition, federal income tax Form 2553, at Form 4.14 on the accompanying CD, should be submitted to the appropriate Internal Revenue Service office. Check various state jurisdictions for a declaration regarding the election when a C corporation converts to S status.

Close (Closely Held) Corporations

The close or closely held corporation is a legislative phenomenon. A close corporation is an entity owned by two or more shareholders who exercise extraordinary control over governance and share transfer. Shareholders are restricted by agreement in the transference of their interests to outside parties. And due to the smallness of the operation they owe one another an imputed higher fiduciary loyalty. Courts appear empathetic with the disgruntled shareholder in the close corporation.[39]

In Ohio, as an illustration, close corporations can effect agreements that modify, eliminate, or restrict the following activities:

- Elimination of a board of directors.
- Terms and conditions of employment.
- Designation of officers.
- Distribution of profits.
- Voting requirements and arrangements.
- Deadlock resolution by arbitration.[40]
- Dissolution.

A close corporation is a desirable format when governance or dissolution struggles are a probability, or when the owners wish to restrict outside influence by new or unfriendly shareholders. Thus, the most compelling provisions in any close corporation bylaws will be the restrictive language relative to stock. William Jacobs recommends the following:

- The triggering event should be clearly defined. Usually this will be the shareholder receiving a bona fide written offer from another person who is sent to the corporation and shareholders. The stock must be transferred on the same terms as in the written offer.

- The planner must determine whether the right of first refusal is to be held by the corporation, the shareholders, or both in succession. If the shareholders are to have this option, provision should be made for the situation in which some shareholders exercise their options, so that those who so desire should have the right to purchase prorated portions of the stock of the transferring shareholder to avoid upsetting the remaining balance of power.

- Probably the options should be exercised with respect to the entire block of stock in question. This is in fairness to the transferer; otherwise he or she may be left with a small, unmarketable block of securities.

- If the corporation is an option holder, neither the transferring shareholder nor his or her board nominee should be able to veto the corporation's decision. One way of dealing with this is to delegate this decision to the shareholders and provide that the decision shall be made without regard to the votes of the shares held by the transferring shareholder.

- The clients must decide whether the restrictions or transfers are intended to apply to transfers between existing shareholders or only transfers to nonshareholders.

- The shareholders must also decide whether the restrictions should apply to transfers to family members. If so, a different process mechanism must be worked out because such transfers are usually gifts. This problem is better resolved in the context of buy–sell agreements.

- The agreement should provide clearly for written notice and time periods within which the corporation or shareholders may exercise their respective options. These periods should not be unreasonably lengthy.[41]

Professional Service Corporations

Lawyers, accountants, doctors, dentists, and other professionals are now empowered, in some jurisdictions, to create what is known as a professional service association or corporation. In Illinois, for example, a "certificate of registration is required for any medical corporation or professional corporation to 'open, operate, or maintain an establishment.' These corporations must submit an application to the Department of Financial and Professional Regulation (Department) stating the name and address of the corporation and identifying information for all directors, officers, shareholders, and incorporators. For professional service corporations, all directors, officers, shareholders, and incorporators must be licensed by the proper agency or authority. The secretary, however, does not have to be licensed."[42]

To create this form, the paralegal needs to consult statutory guidelines. Here is an example:

(a) *A professional corporation may lawfully render professional services only through officers, employees, or agents who are licensed persons. The corporation may employ persons not so licensed, but such persons shall not render any professional services . . .*

(b) *This section shall not be interpreted to preclude the use of clerks, secretaries, nurses, administrators, bookkeepers, technicians, and other assistants who are not usually and ordinarily considered by law, custom, and practice to be rendering the professional service or services for which the professional corporation was incorporated, nor to preclude the use of any other person who performs all his employment under the direct supervision and control of a licensed person; but no person shall, under the guise of employment, render professional services unless duly licensed or admitted to practice as required by law.*

(c) *Despite any other provision of law, a professional corporation may charge for the professional services of its officers, employees, and agents, may collect such charges, and may compensate those who render such professional services.*[43]

The notable advantages of the professional corporation are

- The creation of profit-sharing and pension plans.
- The ability to receive up to $50,000 in group life insurance, accident, and health plans.

The Limited Liability Corporation (LLC)

The limited liability corporation is a relatively recent organizational invention. At its heart, the LLC is a nontaxable entity because its owners, known as *members*, are taxed at individual rates. "The managerial control of an LLC is vested in the members. . . . A majority of these decision makers decide the direction of the organization."[44] This compares quite identically to the partnership format, where money flows to the members. The difference lies with the liability issue. The LLC provides a shield of personal liability for its members in the same way the corporation protects its officers and directors.[45]

All 50 states now permit the formation of LLCs. Two steps are required in the formation process:

1. Articles of organization.

2. Operating agreement: Similar to corporate bylaws, the agreement highlights profit sharing, ownership, responsibilities, and ownership changes.

For an example of LLC articles of organization, see Form 4.15 on the accompanying CD.

BUSINESS PRACTICE AND PROCEDURE: A PARALEGAL'S ROLE

The paralegal's role in business practice may include the preparation, upkeep, and filing of the business's documentation. Once a decision on form of business has been made, the paralegal function is administrative in scope. The corporate form, which requires the most paperwork and documentation, will be the paralegal's major task.

FIGURE 4.3

An Example of a For-Profit Incorporation Service Provider

Source: The Company Corporation home page: www.corporate.com (accessed October 23, 2006).

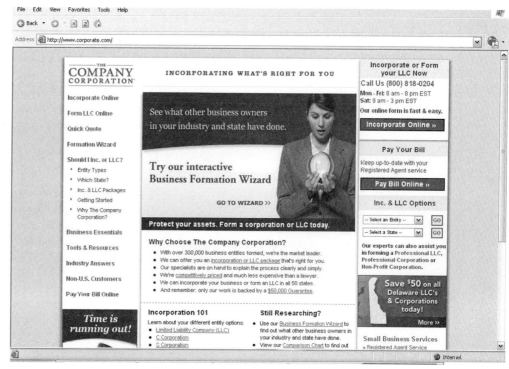

Incorporation services can be performed either by the law firm directly or in consort with for-profit providers. Delaware ranks first in corporate service providers (see Figure 4.3).[46]

Preliminary Conference

During the initial conference or consultation, an incorporation information worksheet will help the paralegal gather necessary information (see Form 4.16 on the accompanying CD). The essential information for incorporation includes the following:

- Who are the incorporators?
- What types of shares will be issued?
- Who is the registered or authorized agent?
- Who will be the officers and directors?
- When does the corporation plan on holding its initial meeting?

Selection, Clearance, and Reservation of a Corporate Name

Corporations need legal names for formal records and must register their chosen names at the designated office. Because names of business entities are subject to trademark, copyright, or intellectual property rights, choosing a name is a serious undertaking. One of the paralegal's tasks in the preincorporation phase is to search the database of corporate records to be assured of no infringement and to guarantee a reserved, protected name. As an example, if the name "Nembar Enterprises, Inc." is selected by the originators of the corporation, an application to reserve that name is required. See Form 4.17 on the accompanying CD. If the corporation elects to use a name other than its true legal name, the paralegal will need to complete a form similar to that shown in Form 4.18. The required fee is usually between $25 and $50. If the chosen name does not conflict with other corporate names already on record and is not deceptively similar, the name can be formally adopted.

Trademark registration is required in most American jurisdictions (see Form 4.19 on the accompanying CD). As an alternative route, if the supervising attorney requests, paralegals can retain private, for-profit bodies to perform this service for a charge.

Subscription Agreements

A subscription agreement is a contract by a party who wishes to purchase common stock or shares of a company using money or other assets. Subscription agreements can be produced either during the preincorporation phase or during the life of a corporation. Financing and venture capital play a crucial role in establishing corporate viability. Making subscription agreements available (by public or private memoranda) to specific individuals, as guided by Securities and Exchange Commission (SEC) rules, is one of the chief techniques of raising capital. Subscription agreements are often the work of promoters and financiers involved in the preincorporation phase of corporate formation. (A subscription agreement is provided in Form 4.20 on the accompanying CD.) A promoter is "Any person who, acting alone or in conjunction with one or more other persons, directly or indirectly takes initiative in founding and organizing the business or enterprise of an issuer."[47]

Preincorporation Agreements

Certain preincorporation activities may also need to be addressed by the paralegal and supervising attorney. Preincorporation activity encompasses the promoter's activity and the shareholder's interests in purchasing shares by either option or direct exchange. Acting as agents for the corporation, promoters often draft the preliminary articles of association, articles of agreement, or other preliminary documentation.

Registered Agent and Registered Office

A corporation must maintain a registered office and a designated registered agent within the state selected as its jurisdictional base. The registered office is not required to be in the principal place of business. The overwhelming majority of American businesses are located in a few states—namely Delaware, New York, Pennsylvania, and New Jersey.[48]

Increasingly, other states are attempting to follow Delaware's lead in promoting easy incorporation and other benefits. Such benefits include low minimum capital requirements; limitation of stockholder liability; creation of voting trusts and other voting pools; no taxation on the shares of stock held by nonresidents; no "blue sky" law (state regulations on securities offerings and sales); no corporate income tax for businesses not doing business in Delaware; the ability to hold stockholders' and directors' meetings outside the state; and other rights regarding classes of stock, dividends, and officers' and directors' rights and liabilities.

Normally the registered agent is designated in the articles of incorporation. To change a registered agent, a state form has to be filled out and a corresponding fee included (see Form 4.21 on the accompanying CD). A registered agent has limited responsibilities on a day-to-day basis but is the recipient of all formal notices, service of process, and in some jurisdictions (such as Delaware) annual tax returns. Any subsequent changes in registered agent status must be reported (see Form 4.22).

Articles of Incorporation

Once the preincorporation activities have been completed, a name has been reserved, and an agent has been named, the corporation is prepared to file its articles or certificate of incorporation. A standardized form must include the corporate name, registered agent address, number of shares, general corporate purpose, and amount of capital invested initially in the company's operation. Examples of articles and certificates of incorporation are provided (see Forms 4.23 and 4.24 on the accompanying CD).

When articles of incorporation are drafted, a powers or purpose clause must be drafted. Under the Idaho Business Corporation Act (based on the ABA Model Business Corporation Act), general powers of corporations are outlined at Section 3. Corporations have the authority, control, and right to do any of the following:

30-1-302   GENERAL POWERS.

Unless its articles of incorporation provide otherwise, every corporation has perpetual duration and succession in its corporate name and has the same powers as an individual to do all things necessary or convenient to carry out its business and affairs, including without limitation power:

(1) To sue and be sued, complain and defend in its corporate name;

(2) To have a corporate seal, which may be altered at will, and to use it, or a facsimile of it, by impressing or affixing it or in any other manner reproducing it;

(3) To make and amend bylaws, not inconsistent with its articles of incorporation or with the laws of this state, for managing the business and regulating the affairs of the corporation;

(4) *To purchase, receive, lease, or otherwise acquire, and own, hold, improve, use, and otherwise deal with real or personal property, or any legal or equitable interest in property wherever located;*

(5) *To sell, convey, mortgage, pledge, lease, exchange, and otherwise dispose of all or any part of its property;*

(6) *To purchase, receive, subscribe for, or otherwise acquire; own, hold, vote, use, sell, mortgage, lend, pledge, or otherwise dispose of; and deal in and with shares or other interests in, or obligations of, any other entity;*

(7) *To make contracts and guarantees, incur liabilities, borrow money, issue its notes, bonds, and other obligations, which may be convertible into or include the option to purchase other securities of the corporation, and secure any of its obligations by mortgage or pledge of any of its property, franchises or income;*

(8) *To lend money, invest and reinvest its funds, and receive and hold real and personal property as security for repayment;*

(9) *To be a promoter, partner, member, associate or manager of any partnership, joint venture, trust or other entity;*

(10) *To conduct its business, locate offices, and exercise the powers granted by this chapter within or without this state;*

(11) *To elect directors and appoint officers, employees, and agents of the corporation, define their duties, fix their compensation, and lend them money and credit;*

(12) *To pay pensions and establish pension plans, pension trusts, profit sharing plans, share bonus plans, share option plans, and benefit or incentive plans for any or all of its current or former directors, officers, employees and agents;*

(13) *To make donations for the public welfare or for charitable, scientific, or educational purposes;*

(14) *To transact any lawful business that will aid governmental policy;*

(15) *To make payments or donations, or do any other act, not inconsistent with law, that furthers the business and affairs of the corporation.*[49]

These powers allow corporations to buy, sell, convey, make contracts, and conduct the affairs of the business enterprise. Proponents of more particularized purposes insist that more explicit descriptions and express language be used when filing initial articles of incorporation. The paralegal can refer to many form books that offer examples of language authorizing direct and precise powers.[50]

Critics of such specificity say that a general powers grant is politically and economically open-ended, promoting product and service diversity. Literally any activity that is legal and not wasteful of the corporation's assets is permissible.

When completing business documentation, the paralegal should create a form file. All jurisdictional incorporators are required to sign the articles of incorporation before the document is submitted to state authorities. Some filing and licensing fees are required.

Under the Idaho Business Corporation Act, the articles or certificate of incorporation must set forth the following:

30-1-202. ARTICLES OF INCORPORATION.

(1) *The articles of incorporation must set forth:*
   (a) *A corporate name for the corporation that satisfies the requirements of section 30-1-401, Idaho Code;*
   (b) *The number of shares the corporation is authorized to issue;*
   (c) *The street address of the corporation's initial registered office and the name of its initial registered agent at that office; and*
   (d) *The name and address of each incorporator.*

(2) *The articles of incorporation may set forth:*
   (a) *The names and addresses of the individuals who are to serve as the initial directors;*
   (b) *Provisions not inconsistent with law regarding:*
      (i) *The purpose or purposes for which the corporation is organized,*
      (ii) *Managing the business and regulating the affairs of the corporation,*
      (iii) *Defining, limiting and regulating the powers of the corporation, its board of directors, and shareholders,*
      (iv) *A par value for authorized shares or classes of shares,*
      (v) *The imposition of personal liability on shareholders for the debts of the corporation to a specified extent and upon specified conditions;*

    (c) Any provision that under this chapter is required or permitted to be set forth in the bylaws;

    (d) A provision eliminating or limiting the liability of a director to the corporation or its shareholders for money damages for any action taken, or any failure to take any action, as a director, except liability for:

        (i)   The amount of a financial benefit received by a director to which he is not entitled,

        (ii) An intentional infliction of harm on the corporation or the shareholders,

        (iii) A violation of section 30-1-833, Idaho Code, or

        (iv) An intentional violation of criminal law; and

    (e) A provision permitting or making obligatory indemnification of a director for liability, as defined in section 30-1-850(5), Idaho Code, to any person for any action taken, or any failure to take any action, as a director, except liability for:

        (i)   Receipt of a financial benefit to which he is not entitled,

        (ii) An intentional infliction of harm on the corporation or its shareholders,

        (iii) A violation of section 30-1-833, Idaho Code, or

        (iv) An intentional violation of criminal law.

(3) The articles of incorporation need not set forth any of the corporate powers enumerated in this chapter.

(4) Provisions of the articles of incorporation may be made dependent upon facts objectively ascertainable outside the articles of incorporation in accordance with section 31-1-120(11) [30-1-120(11)], Idaho Code.[51]

The state acknowledges the acceptance of the articles or certificate by the return of an endorsed certificate of incorporation, accepted and filed with the Office of the Secretary of State. In some jurisdictions, notice of incorporation through publication in a public forum such as a newspaper or legal review is an additional required step.

In this case, paralegals should ensure that a Statement of Intention to Incorporate, or the articles or certificate itself, is publicly disseminated for review. A newspaper advertisement for this purpose is shown in Figure 4.4. This is a rule of local control and custom.

Once a certificate of incorporation has been endorsed or issued, it is conclusively presumed that a corporation has met all conditions and statutory requirements. Over the life of a corporate enterprise, amendment of the original articles or certificate of incorporation will take place. For example, if the corporation wants the right to authorize the creation and sale of more shares of stock, to change its existing powers, or to allow for voting trusts or voting pools, the proper technique for changing the original articles is through filing of amended articles or a certificate of amendment with the Secretary of State. Form 4.25 on the accompanying CD contains the amendment language. Requisite filing fees, cover sheets, and other documents for amendment are a local concern.

Issuance of Shares

Stock falls into two categories: common and preferred. A common stock is "the capital of a corporation, usually divided into equal shares of a fixed nominal value, the ownership of which is evidenced by a certificate."[52] Preferred stock is "the shares of capital stock of a corporation,

FIGURE 4.4
Example of a Newspaper Advertisement for Intention to Incorporate

---

NOTICE OF INCORPORATION OF

_____.

Notice is hereby given that the undersigned have formed a corporation under the laws of the {*insert state or commonwealth*}:

1. The name of the corporation is {*insert name as registered with state or commonwealth*}.
2. The address of the initial registered office and registered agent is {*insert name and address of registered agent/office*}.
3. The general nature of the business to be transacted is {*insert purpose of incorporation and purpose of business as well as what states/commonwealths business will be transacted in*}.
4. {*Insert statement regarding issuance of stock, detailing number of certificates, total amount of stock, etc.*}.
5. {*Insert statement regarding method of incorporation and duration of company*}.
6. {*Insert statement regarding the governance/hierarchy of the corporation*}.

which under its bylaws have priority as to payment of dividends, up to a fixed amount, over the common stock; preferred does not have priority over debts due creditors, however."[53]

Preincorporation and postincorporation activities often concern the issuance of shares. The articles or certificate of incorporation explicitly state the number of shares the corporation can issue. The articles also describe in detail the classes of stock and whether they are common or preferred.

Under the Idaho Business Corporation Act, corporations have the authority to do the following:

30-1-621. ISSUANCE OF SHARES

(1) The powers granted in this section to the board of directors may be reserved to the shareholders by the articles of incorporation.

(2) The board of directors may authorize shares to be issued for consideration consisting of any tangible or intangible property, including cash, promissory notes, services performed, or other securities of the corporation.

(3) Before the corporation issues shares, the board of directors must determine that the consideration received or to be received for shares to be issued is adequate. That determination by the board of directors is conclusive insofar as the adequacy of consideration for the issuance of shares relates to whether the shares are validly issued, fully paid and nonassessable.

(4) When the corporation receives the consideration for which the board of directors authorized the issuance of shares, the shares issued therefor are fully paid and nonassessable.

(5) The corporation may place in escrow shares issued for a promissory note, or make other arrangements to restrict the transfer of the shares, and may credit distributions in respect of the shares against their purchase price, until the note is paid. If the note is not paid, the shares escrowed or restricted and the distributions credited may be cancelled in whole or part.

(6) (a)   An issuance of shares or other securities convertible into or rights exercisable for shares, in a transaction or a series of integrated transactions, requires approval of the shareholders, at a meeting at which a quorum consisting of at least a majority of the votes entitled to be cast on the matter exists, if:

(i) The shares, other securities, or rights are issued for consideration other than cash or cash equivalents; and

(ii) The voting power of shares that are issued and issuable as a result of the transaction or series of integrated transactions will comprise more than twenty (20) percent of the voting power of the shares of the corporation that were outstanding immediately before the transaction.

(b) In this subsection:

(i) For purposes of determining the voting power of shares issued and issuable as a result of a transaction or series of integrated transactions, the voting power of shares shall be the greater of:

(A) The voting power of the shares to be issued; or

(B) The voting power of the shares that would be outstanding after giving effect to the conversion of convertible shares and other securities and the exercise of rights to be issued.

(ii) A series of transactions is integrated if consummation of one (1) transaction is made contingent on consummation of one (1) or more of the other transactions.[54]

 In some cases shareholder agreements may be appropriate because the agreement lays out parameters for the sale and transfer of stock. Shareholder agreements provide both certainty and flexibility in the operation of a closely held corporation. By placing restrictions on the transfer of stock, organizers have some control over who their "partners" will be in the future. Rules for the operation of the corporation can be set down, and mechanisms for future decision making can be established. Plans regarding what to do in the event of death, disability, and retirement can be formulated to limit the uncertainties that often surround these events.[55] Comprehensive language is supplied on the accompanying CD at Form 4.26, which outlines preferences, privileges, and restrictions on the various classes of stock.

Tabulation of Voting Interests

Another paralegal responsibility relates to the tabulation of voting shares. Each share of stock carries either a single or a cumulative vote. Cumulative voting allows the shareholder to multiply the number of votes he or she has (determined by the number of shares held) by the number of directors to be elected and to cast all of his or her votes for any one candidate or to distribute the votes among the candidates.[56] Cumulative voting rights have a substantial impact on both the tenure of the board and on the power of the corporation to act on extraordinary matters. Form 4.27 on the accompanying CD contains an agreement delineating cumulative rights of shareholders. Proxy voting allows a block of votes to be cast by one shareholder. "Proxy solicitation is the process by which one shareholder asks another for his or her voting right."[57]

Additionally, voting trusts or pools may be suitable for the corporate form. A voting pool or trust represents a body or group of people that accords one individual the right to vote their shares en masse. Voting pools concentrate voting power by contractual agreement.[58] (See the voting trust agreement at Form 4.28 on the accompanying CD. [59])

Drafting of Bylaws

Bylaws are a set of rules and standards for governing and managing the daily affairs of the corporation. "It is binding upon all shareholders but not third parties unless the third parties have knowledge of it."[60] Paralegals may help draft bylaws.

The ABA Committee on Corporate Laws of the Section on Corporations has proposed model bylaws that would be acceptable in all jurisdictions. Standard bylaw clauses and provisions generally cover the following issues:

1. Where is the office located? Where is the office of the registered agent?
2. What are the rules and guidelines for the annual meeting?
3. Structural and mechanical aspects of corporate operations comprising

- Quorum standards.
- Proxy procedures.
- Directors: number, tenure, and general qualifications.
- Types of directors.
- Rights to special meetings.
- Replacement of directors or officers.
- Removal of directors or officers.
- Compensation schemes.

- Appointment of executive committees.
- Terms of office.
- Number of officers.
- Officers' tasks and duties.
- Certificates and transfer of shares.
- Transfer agents.
- Dividends.
- Seals.
- Rights to amend.

A full set of bylaws for a Delaware corporation is reproduced in Form 4.29 on the accompanying CD.

Administrative Activities

Corporations are required to keep extensive, accurate records. Corporate kits assist the paralegal in this important task. The traditional corporate kit contains

- Corporate seal.
- Record book for shareholders.
- Minutes forms and books.

- Share certificates.
- Transfer ledgers.
- Additional bond paper for resolutions.

Organizational Meetings

Once the previously discussed steps have been completed, organizational meetings need to be scheduled. Organizational meetings call directors, shareholders, and the original incorporators to discuss and resolve corporate business. Notice of the upcoming meetings must be communicated to all interested parties, though the requirement may be consensually waived. See Form 4.30 on the accompanying CD for a waiver document. The minutes of a board of directors' first meeting are illustrated in Form 4.31.

Any business conducted by the board of directors should be memorialized by either resolution or documented consent. See Form 4.32 on the accompanying CD.

Other Matters of Corporate Concern

In corporations operating under SEC guidelines and blue sky laws, the issuance of securities is governed by complex federal legislation. Extensive consideration of issuance or payment of share subscriptions is an area of extreme specialization. Be alert for governmental complexities.

Document and preserve minutes of serious corporate intentions and actions. Paralegals may be asked to compile minutes proving and corroborating decisions on the issuance of stock, the election and termination of officers and other key employees, and any other extraordinary action a corporation may decide to engage in.

Paralegals must be extremely attentive to the following administrative questions:

1. Are organizational meetings required?

2. Can organizational meetings be waived or held through means other than personal visitation?

3. May action be taken by the directors without the written consent of the shareholders?

4. Who has the right to call a specific meeting?

5. What notice of such meeting is required? Can notice be waived under statutory guidelines?

6. What voting rights are outlined in the corporate bylaws and articles of incorporation?

7. May a person vote by proxy?

In general, the paralegal must display the skills of a seasoned administrator and track and catalog the many activities of corporate governance.

ALTERATION OR TERMINATION OF THE CORPORATE FORM

Despite the perpetuity of the corporate form, a corporation's form can be changed or modified during its lifetime. This can take place via termination, conversion, merger, or dissolution.

Termination

Corporations can simply terminate their operations. In this event most states require a termination statement (see Form 4.33 on the accompanying CD).

Conversion

A business entity may convert to another form. For example, a for-profit corporation may choose to convert to a nonprofit form. In this case it is necessary to file articles or a certificate of conversion (see Form 4.34 on the accompanying CD).

Merger

Merging with other business entities is another viable modification for the corporate form. Besides filing articles or a certificate of merger, governmental authorities require a merger plan that lays out the mechanics of the merger. (See Form 4.35 on the accompanying CD for an example of articles of merger.)

It is also sound practice to conduct due diligence, or background, investigations on companies, their directors, and their officers before effecting a merger. Consulting companies make these services available. See Figure 4.5 for a description of the due diligence background investigation services offered by one such company.

Dissolution

Dissolving the corporate entity can be either a voluntary or an involuntary act. In a voluntary case, the corporation simply winds down its affairs and distributes its remaining assets. By

FIGURE 4.5
Example of
Information Provided
in Due Diligence
Investigation

Source: Record Time Retrieval & Investigations. Available at http://www.rtr-i.com/ (retrieved February 1, 2007).

Example of the type of information that can be obtained in due diligence investigations:

- Detailed information on the prospective M&A's corporate structure/size.
- Detailed background information on the prospective M&A's key executives/managers.
- General publicly available information on the prospective M&A's cost/liquidity base.
- Detailed history of the prospective M&A's legal liabilities, claims, or criminal activity.
- Detailed background information on the prospective M&A's product/service quality.
- Information on their receptivity/viability for a M&A proposal.
- Detailed background information on all potential investors to confirm their legitimacy.

filing articles of dissolution, the corporation sets out a plan of distribution and gives assurance that no liabilities are unaccounted for or legal actions unresolved (see Form 4.36 on the accompanying CD).

By contrast, an involuntary dissolution results by judicial decree, actions by shareholders or deadlocked management, or governmental authority. The filing of articles of involuntary dissolution is required (see Form 4.37 on the accompanying CD).

SOME RECURRING PROBLEMS IN BUSINESS LITIGATION

Paralegals must realize that litigation activity occurs regularly in business and corporate practice. Disgruntled shareholders, disaffected owners and directors, and other parties with any stake make litigation a natural consequence of the corporate environment.

Partnerships in Turmoil

Our previous analysis showed that partnerships, whether general or limited, are basically ventures entered for profit. Often the decision making of the managing general partner(s) causes dissension among the remaining general partners. Partners owe one another a duty of due care, and just as critically they owe the partnership the duty to obey its purpose and its provisions.[61] Limited partners can challenge the actions of general or managing partners.

If partners no longer trust each other or are suspicious of internal accounting or profit or loss, they can petition for dissolution. To accomplish this, a form or petition (depending on the jurisdiction) requesting the dissolution of a partnership must be drafted. (For Louisiana's format, see Form 4.38 on the accompanying CD.)

Rights of Creditors

Corporations are sometimes badly managed. Creditors who are not paid may challenge management. Creditors legitimately concerned about corporate directors and officers "looting" the company's assets can file a motion for the appointment of a receiver—an individual who will take over the operation of the company to ensure its business stability (see Form 4.39 on the accompanying CD).

In Form 4.40 on the accompanying CD, a plaintiff advances a complaint in the federal court that seeks enforcement of a loan obligation. Because the defendant corporation is insolvent or nearing insolvency, creditors can ask the court to appoint a receiver to ensure some chance of collection in this matter.

Litigation and the Board of Directors

Corporate boards of directors have become favorite targets of disgruntled shareholders. Decision making by the board, although it must adhere to intelligent business judgment, is sometimes plainly inexplicable. Directors have been granted broad authority in the operation of a business enterprise, a reality long protected under the business judgment rule, a principle of considerable judicial favoritism.[62] When a corporate board is sensibly exercising discretion, the judiciary has been hesitant to intervene in its activities. "When reviewing a board's ordinary business decisions to determine whether the directors have breached their fiduciary duties, courts have traditionally applied the business judgment rule. The rule affords a presumption that they acted on an informed basis, in good faith, and in the honest belief that they took the action in the best interests of the corporation and its stockholders."[63]

The fiduciary nature of a director's obligation to a corporation obligates the director to good-faith efforts and to exhibit unyielding loyalty to the corporate interest. This good-faith fiduciary requirement does not require business genius, nor does it require infallible decision making. Not all market economies view this duty in an identical way; indeed, there are vast disagreements about what the duty really is. Is it merely avoidance of illegality or something far more metaphysical? In Eastern Europe and Russia, for example, the complexities of the system make entrepreneurial thinking and inventive leadership difficult. In the American experience, governance theory and the fiduciary duty are imbued with the legal sensibilities unique to their time and place, but in other nations there simply is little understanding of what fiduciary concepts are.[64] Solid corporate governance and adherence to fiduciary requirements call for good intentions and reasonable conduct. If a shareholder or other party shows that the board is careless, grossly negligent, corporately wasteful, or bereft of elementary business practice and procedure, then some action against that board is plausible. In an article about regulating U.S. corporations Robert Deutsch argues,

> *The board must give undue deference to the fact either that there is an ongoing corporate culture in place, or that appeal can be taken to the forces of the marketplace. When waste is condoned because it has become an accepted part of operations, or when a level of executive compensation is justified as necessary to meet the market rather than fill the corporate goal, the board has revealed that it is not meeting its responsibility. The new dimension added to the activities of the board is acceptance of the proposition that prudence is a matter of activity rather than passive acceptance of what is.[65]*

How we should measure gross negligence or most other governance standards is unclear.[66]

To support an action against a director, the evidence must show that the director acted "on an uninformed basis, in bad faith, or primarily or solely for the purpose of preventing a change in control to keep themselves in office."[67] The pleading shown in Form 4.41 on the accompanying CD is used to challenge the actions of a director or other individual who has taken advantage of a position by wrongful conduct.

Shareholders' Derivative Suits

Whether management likes it or not, shareholders own the company. Challenging the actions of officers or directors can be best accomplished by a derivative action—an action of one shareholder on behalf of all. "In order to bring a derivative suit, a shareholder must also own stock at the time of the injury and the time of suit. This is known as the rule of contemporary ownership."[68]

The suit, analogous to a class action, represents a last-resort remedy to alter the conduct of the corporation. If the business judgment rule can be bypassed and will not afford a defense, a derivative action representing other shareholders is a permissible strategy if all other potential remedies have been exhausted within the corporation.[69]

Litigation committees, a recent legislative phenomenon, have been established to respond to stockholder challenges. These are committees that address legal problems with the hope that shareholder dissatisfaction can be resolved. In some jurisdictions, committee process and review are mandatory before a derivative suit can proceed. Because a derivative lawsuit is a suit by one shareholder representing the entire stockholder group or class, it must consist of these elements:

1. The complainant shareholder must have the capacity to maintain the suit.

2. The shareholder must have actual or contemporaneous ownership at the commencement of suit.

3. All other remedies available under the bylaws or other statutory or legislative authority must be exhausted.

4. There must be a demand for a resolution of a specific problem.

5. There must be no defenses that may be imposed against the shareholders' actions.

6. If required, security for expenses for the suit must be posted to cover costs.

7. The shareholder's action must be representative of the entire shareholder group's dilemma.[70]

Similar to a class action, the derivative suit is a hybrid form of litigation—not personal to a specific stockholder but representative of the corporation per se because shareholder rights are being adversely affected. In more general terms, a derivative suit is a stockholders' suit on behalf of the corporation's own welfare and benefit.

Under the Federal Rules of Civil Procedure, Rule 23.1,

> *. . . a derivative action brought by one or more shareholders or members to enforce a right of a corporation or of an unincorporated association, the corporation or association having failed to enforce a right which may properly be asserted by it, the complaint shall be verified and shall allege (1) that the plaintiff was a shareholder or member at the time of the transaction of which the plaintiff complains or that the plaintiff's share or membership thereafter devolved on the plaintiff by operation of law, and (2) that the action is not a collusive one to confer jurisdiction on a court of the United States which it would not otherwise have. The complaint shall also allege with particularity the efforts, if any, made by the plaintiff to obtain the action the plaintiff desires from the directors or comparable authority and, if necessary, from the shareholders or members, and the reasons for the plaintiff's failure to obtain the action or for not making the effort. The derivative action may not be maintained if it appears that the plaintiff does not fairly and adequately represent the interests of the shareholders or members similarly situated in enforcing the*

right of the corporation or association. The action shall not be dismissed or compromised without the approval of the court, and notice of the proposed dismissal or compromise shall be given to shareholders or members in such manner as the court directs.[71]

Examples of times when derivative actions are appropriate include

- Wrongful merger.
- Wrongful reorganization.
- Wrongful dissolution.
- Wrongful termination of stock rights.
- Wrongful renunciation of preemptive or cumulative voting rights.
- Improper or wrongful redemption of a class of shares.

New York's Business Corporation Law at Section 720 permits the following mandatory actions against directors and officers for specific misconduct:

> *An action may be brought against one or more directors or officers of a corporation to procure a judgment for the following relief:*
>
> *(1) To compel the defendant to account for his official conduct in the following cases:*
> *(a) the neglect of or failure to perform or violation of his duties in the management and disposition of corporate assets committed to his charge;*
> *(b) the acquisition by himself, transfer to others, loss, or a waste of corporate assets due to the neglect of or failure to perform or violation of other duties.*
>
> *(2) To set aside an unlawful conveyance, assignment, or transfer of corporate assets.*
>
> *(3) To enjoin a proposed unlawful conveyance, assignment, or transfer of corporate assets where there is sufficient evidence that it will be made . . .*[72]

Paralegals need to consult with business valuation experts to objectively assess the conduct of management. Mere allegations do not suffice.

Paralegals must sometimes prepare shareholder actions making directors, officers, and other responsible parties accountable for misconduct or gross mismanagement. A derivative action format is outlined in Form 4.42 on the accompanying CD.

Deadlocked Directors: Deadlocked Corporation

In close corporations, deadlock is a common occurrence. Dissension, disagreement, and disputes between the parties are quite regular even in larger enterprises.[73] Deadlock for definitional purposes can include

> *Any implacable disagreement between two or more persons or groups of persons. . . . Conceivably, every person in a corporation may have one or more implacable disagreements with every other person in a corporation, yet corporate affairs may run smoothly either because parties find some method of resolving their disputes or because any party who may desire to impose his view on the other lacks the power to do so.*[74]

Ordinarily deadlock results from evenly divided voting rights between parties proclaiming opposite positions. "Among shareholders a deadlock is a clear-cut division in voting interests. When the impasse occurs among directors, another factor enters. The shareholders have the power to elect and remove directors; hence, unless they are also equally divided, they can break the deadlock on the board simply by electing one or more new directors."[75] Before taking formal steps to resolve the deadlock, the directors may wish to consider the appointment of a provisional director to handle corporate affairs until the deadlock is resolved. The provisional director would have a series of powers, some of which are enumerated in the following proposed statute:

> **Model Provisional Director Statute**
>
> *§ 000—Appointment of Provisional Director for Deadlock*
>
> *(A) Grounds, Standing, and Exhaustion of Nonjudicial Remedies. If the directors or those in control of the corporation are deadlocked in the management of the corporation's affairs, the shareholders are unable to break the deadlock, and the business and affairs of the corporation can no longer be conducted to the advantage of the shareholders generally or there is danger that the corporation's property and business will be impaired or lost because of the deadlock, the court may appoint a provisional director upon the petition of any complaining shareholder or director.*

If the petitioner has agreed in writing to pursue a nonjudicial remedy to resolve disputed matters, the petitioner may not commence a proceeding under this section with respect to the matter unless (i) the nonjudicial remedy has been exhausted or (ii) the petitioner establishes that the terms of the agreement are patently unfair or inadequate in light of current circumstances.

(B) *Impartiality and Qualifications. The provisional director shall be an impartial person who is neither a shareholder, creditor, nor debtor of the corporation or of any subsidiary or affiliate of the corporation and who has no close personal, business, or financial relationship with the members of any contending faction within the corporation. Persons who have a proven business background or who are conversant with corporate affairs shall be strongly preferred.*

(C) *Rights, Powers, and Duties. The provisional director shall have the right to notice of meetings of directors and the power to vote at such meetings on all matters upon which the parties are deadlocked, unless the parties request and the court prescribes a limited set of matters upon which the provisional director may vote. The duty of the provisional director is to cast votes in the best interest of the corporation with the purpose of breaking the deadlock upon such disputed matters. Upon the request of the court, the provisional director shall report to the court, periodically and in the presence of the parties, concerning the status of the deadlock and the corporation's business and shall submit recommendations to the court as to the appropriate disposition of the matter.*

(D) *Removal and Compensation. The provisional director shall serve until such time as the deadlock is broken or the provisional director is removed by order of the court or by a vote of the holders of a majority of the shares having voting power. The provisional director shall be entitled to reasonable compensation for services rendered, such compensation to be determined by agreement between the provisional director and the corporation with the approval of the court. The court may fix the compensation of the provisional director in the absence of agreement or in the event of disagreement between the corporation and the provisional director. All amounts shall be paid by the corporation. The corporation shall also reimburse or make direct payments to the provisional director for reasonable costs and expenses incurred during the term of the provisional director's appointment.*

(E) *Immunity. The provisional director shall be immune from civil liability for any acts or omissions within the scope of the performance of the provisional director's powers and duties, so long as the provisional director acted in good faith, without malice, and not for improper personal enrichment.*

(F) *Attorneys' Fees. If the court finds that the petitioner acted arbitrarily, vexatiously, or in bad faith in initiating a proceeding under this provision, the court may award one or more other parties their reasonable expenses, including attorneys' fees, incurred in the proceeding.*[76]

Judicial resolution also is an acceptable technique of ending deadlock. A motion or petition can be made for a court to adjudge a corporation in a deadlock status with a corresponding request for the appointment of a receiver or trustee. For an example of such petition or motion, see Form 4.43 on the accompanying CD.

Other strategies indicating good sense include the following:

- Buyout arrangements of a disgruntled director.
- Exercise of a specific contract related to deadlock arbitration.
- Equitable remedies.
- Voluntary or involuntary dissolution.
- Appointment of a custodian/trustee or provisional director or receiver.
- Purchase of a disgruntled party's shares.
- Compromise or plan of reorganization.[77]

Small businesses frequently have managerial disputes and disagreements. The checklist in Form 4.44 on the accompanying CD (provided by Richard Tinney in *Dissension or Deadlock of Corporate Directors and Shareholders*) is a guide to determining whether a deadlock has taken place.

Antitrust

To ensure a competitive marketplace, Congress has enacted a series of laws governing monopolization of industry and commerce. Commonly known as *antitrust laws*, they apply to virtually all industries and to every level of business, including manufacturing, transportation, distribution, and marketing. These laws prohibit a variety of practices that restrain trade, such as price-fixing conspiracies, corporate mergers likely to reduce the competitive vigor of particular markets, and predatory acts designed to achieve or maintain monopoly power.[78]

The historic goal of the antitrust laws is to protect economic freedom and opportunity by promoting competition in the marketplace. Competition in a free market benefits American consumers through lower prices, better quality, and greater choice. Competition lets businesses compete on price and quality in an open market, unhampered by anticompetitive restraints. Competition also tests and hardens American companies at home, the better to succeed abroad. Enforcement under antitrust provisions generally resides in the Department of Justice by and through its Antitrust Division, which is portrayed in the chart in Figure 4.6.[79]

FIGURE 4.6
U.S. Department of Justice, Antitrust Division Organization Chart

Source: U.S. Department of Justice, Antitrust Division, Organization Chart; updated January 24, 2002, available at http://www.usdoj.gov/atr/org.htm.

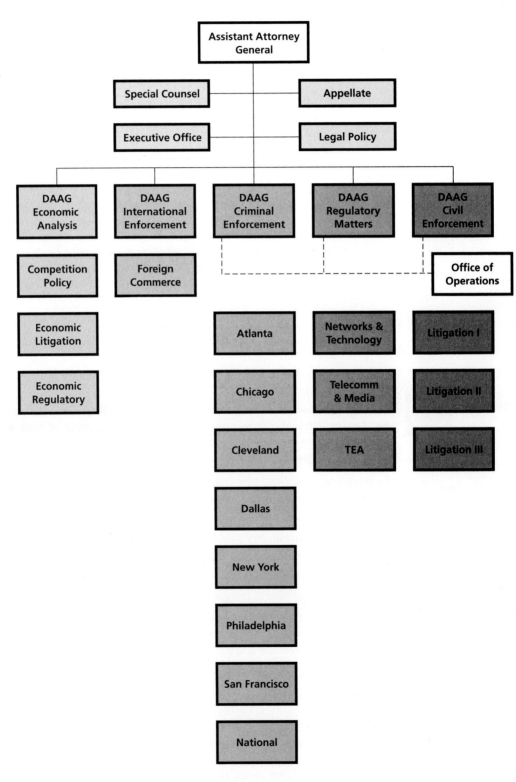

Various field offices have been erected for the investigation and resolution of antitrust claims. These offices provide the paralegal with a wealth of information on how to file and process an antitrust complaint:

Division Headquarters

Office of Deputy Assistant Attorney General for Criminal Enforcement
Antitrust Division, U.S. Dept. of Justice
950 Pennsylvania Ave. NW., Suite 3218
Washington, DC 20530
202-514-3543

Citizen Complaint Center
Antitrust Division, U.S. Dept. of Justice
950 Pennsylvania Ave. NW., Suite 3322
Washington, DC 20530
1-888-647-3258 (toll-free in U.S. and Canada)
202-307-2040

Field Offices

Atlanta Field Office
Antitrust Division, U.S. Dept. of Justice
Richard B. Russell Building
75 Spring Street SW, Suite 1176
Atlanta, GA 30303-3308
404-331-7100

Chicago Field Office
Antitrust Division, U.S. Dept. of Justice
Rookery Building
209 South LaSalle Street, Suite 600
Chicago, IL 60604-1204
312-353-7530

Cleveland Field Office
Antitrust Division, U.S. Dept. of Justice
Plaza Nine Building
55 Erieview Plaza, Suite 700
Cleveland, OH 44114-1816
216-522-4070

Dallas Field Office
Antitrust Division, U.S. Dept. of Justice
Thanksgiving Tower
1601 Elm Street, Suite 3900
Dallas, TX 75201-4717
214-880-9401

National Criminal Enforcement Section
Antitrust Division, U.S. Dept. of Justice
1401 H Street NW, Suite 3700
Washington, DC 20530
202-307-6694

New York Field Office
Antitrust Division, U.S. Dept. of Justice
26 Federal Plaza, Room 3630
New York, NY 10278-0140
212-264-0390

Philadelphia Field Office
Antitrust Division, U.S. Dept. of Justice
Curtis Center
One Independence Square West
7th and Walnut Streets, Suite 650
Philadelphia, PA 19106-2424
215-597-7405

San Francisco Field Office
Antitrust Division, U.S. Dept. of Justice
450 Golden Gate Avenue, Room 10-0101
Box 36046
San Francisco, CA 94102-3478
415-436-6660

In sum, litigation is now expected in the American business enterprise. In addition, corporate counsel and paralegals must be aware that criminal investigations and prosecutions are becoming more common under both SEC and criminal statutes. Legal insulation of officers and directors is no longer guaranteed under doctrines of privilege or immunity. Joel M. Androphy argues,

Officers, directors, and employees, as well as the corporation, may be indicted for a broad range of criminal activity. "He did it, not me" is no defense. Criminal liability may be imposed for acquiescence or tacit approval of another's criminal conduct or conspiring with others who actually commit the illegal act. Even if your criminal exposure originally is tenuous at most, you enhance your chances of indictment if you help others in destroying documents or otherwise obstructing an investigation.[80]

Officers and directors can also be responsible for tortious conduct outside the scope of their employment. A director who participates in fraudulent conduct by the corporation may be personally liable to the third party.[81]

Even if negligence or criminal conduct has not occurred, poor company management or poor profit margins may give rise to shareholder challenges. To some, these actions indicate a decline in director and officer loyalty to the company. Bevies Longstretch poses the basis for shareholders' turmoil:

There are two issues here and they are often confused with each other: (1) Is management (the agent) serving itself rather than the corporation and its shareholders (the principal)?—this is a matter of loyalty; and (2) Is management, in seeking to serve the corporation and its shareholders, acting in a stupid or otherwise incompetent way?—this is a matter of care.[82]

Summary

This chapter has blended the theoretical and practical aspects of business operation. There are various choices of business entities, including sole proprietorship, partnership, and the corporation; the paralegal must be aware of the advantages and disadvantages of these various forms of business. Substantial attention was given to the advantages of the corporate form, including continuity of life, centralization of management, preferential tax treatment in the area of passive income, and the capacity to raise financing for growth and expansion.

The paralegal's role in corporate operations received significant attention. Topics such as clearance and reservation of a corporate name; the drafting of subscription and preincorporation agreements; tracking registered agents and offices; preparing articles of incorporation; shares; drafting of bylaws; and other administrative tasks were covered. Discussion also included modification of the corporation—from termination to dissolution to conversion.

Some specialized forms of business litigation were discussed, highlighting the rights of creditors, deadlocked corporations and partnerships, and shareholders' derivative suits.

A corporate paralegal has a diverse range of duties. After studying this chapter, a paralegal should have the information required to take all steps necessary to form a business entity and to maintain its status.

Discussion Questions

1. What paperwork and documentation must be completed before the formation of a business entity?

2. What does it mean to pierce the corporate veil?

3. "Under the interpretation of the business judgment rule, directors and officers are not permitted to make mistakes." True or false?

4. Which business entity requires the least paperwork?

5. Where is personal exposure and liability most limited—in general partnerships or in limited partnerships?

6. In what types of corporate record-keeping functions will paralegals regularly participate?

7. Are there any tax advantages to particular business entities? Explain in detail.

8. To file a derivative action, what argument does the proponent have to demonstrate?

9. Can a lawyer, doctor, or accountant form a corporation? If so, what would it be called?

10. Write to the Secretary of State for Delaware and request a packet of information about incorporating in the state of Delaware. Address: Secretary of State, State of Delaware Division of Corporations, P.O. Box 898, Dover, DE 19903. Phone: 302-739-3073.

11. Write to your own state office that regulates corporations and other business entities. Create a form file for registration and reporting.

12. Create a fee data sheet for the various business entities in your jurisdiction. How much do corporate or partnership filings cost? Be specific.

Research Exercise

The law firm of Steele and Gray has a longtime corporate client, AJAX Repossession, Inc., wishing for a change in its tax status. Because there are fewer than 10 shareholders, the board, after consultation with its accounting firm, wishes to change from its C status to an S (close corporation) status. You have been asked to research the following issues:

1. Can a Delaware C corporation convert to a close corporation?
2. If shareholders' approval is required, what percentage must vote in favor?
3. What is the preferred and statutorily suggested way to accomplish this conversion?

Practical Exercises

1. Obtain the following forms from your state's corporations department or bureau. Use hypothetical information of your own choosing:

    Name reservation form

    Application for registration of fictitious name

    Trade or service mark registration

2. Use the following information to complete an article or certificate of incorporation endorsed by your home jurisdiction:

Type of corporation:	Business stock
Number/classes of shares:	10,000 par
Total authorized capital:	$100,000.00
Par value of shares:	$10
Term of existence:	Perpetual
Name/address of incorporator:	John Stephens, 472 Marx Street, Wilmington, DE 19116
Number and class of shares owned by incorporators:	10,000
Effective date:	November 3, 2006
Registered agent:	CSS
Registered agent address:	31 Tally Road, Wilmington, DE 19809
Period of liability:	November 3, 2006, to November 3, 2007
Limited liability purpose:	To invest and develop a movie production company
Company assets:	$2,000,900
Company liabilities:	$1,476,000

3. Using the following information complete a waiver of notice for a first meeting of a board of directors.

Date of notice:	July 18, 2006
Place of meeting:	Luau Hotel, Honolulu, Hawaii 99888
Date of meeting:	December 23, 2006
Time:	4:00 p.m.

Due to the holiday, the scheduled meeting is canceled. In its place a resolution in lieu of first meeting of board of directors needs to be drafted. Using the following facts, draft the necessary document:

Officers appointed:	President, John Regina; vice president, Joseph Aloysius; secretary, Anne Marie Huguenot; treasurer, Stephen Charles
Directors:	Same
Date:	August 23, 2006
Bank:	Mellon/Honolulu Branch
Fiscal year:	July 1–June 30
Corporate name:	Nembar Enterprises, Inc.
Shares issued:	1,000 common—$30.00 per share
Capital:	$60,000
Subscription date and place:	September 30, 2006 Honolulu, Hawaii

Internet Resources

Findlaw Practice Areas, Corporation & Enterprise Law—www.findlaw.com/01topics/08corp/index.html

Findlaw for Small Business, Incorporation, Legal Structures, and Business Formation—smallbusiness.findlaw.com/business-structures

Findlaw State Resources—www.findlaw.com/11stategov/index.html

ABA Business Law Section—www.abanet.org/buslaw/home.shtml

Law.Com, Business Law Practice Center—www.law.com/jsp/pc/buslaw.jsp

Internal Revenue Service business page—www.irs.gov/businesses/index.html

Endnotes

1. *See* ILLINOIS PARALEGAL ASSOCIATION, THE FINDINGS OF THE COMPETENCY COMMITTEE RELATING TO THE QUALITY OF PARALEGAL SERVICES 10–13 (1989).

2. Julie Bassett, *The Corporate Paralegal,* LEGAL ASSISTANT TODAY, Nov.–Dec. 1990, at 21; *see also* Alan Freeman, *A Critical Look at Corporate Legal Practice,* 37 J. LEGAL EDUC. 315, 320–321 (1987).

3. *See* Dianne Molvig, *Defining the Role of Paralegals,* WIS. LAW., Dec. 1998, at 10.

4. J. Bassett, *supra* note 2, at 24.

5. *See* Michael C. Riddle, T. Christine Butts, & Karen K. Akiens, *Choice of Business Entity in Texas,* 4 HOUS. BUS. & TAX L.J. 292 (2004).

6. Some have argued for a unified system of business codification. *See* Harry J. Haynsworth, *The Unified Business Organizations Code: The Next Generation,* 29 DEL. J. CORP. L. 83 (2004).

7. You may purchase a directory from the National Association of Small Business Investment Companies at 1156 15th St. NW, Washington, DC 20005; *see also The National Directory of SBICs* by writing to SBA, Washington, DC.

8. Andrew Beckerman-Rodau, *Selecting Entity for a Small Business: Non-Tax Considerations,* 93 DICK. L. REV. 519, 526–527 (Spring 1993).

9. *See* CHESTER ROHRUCH, ORGANIZING AND OTHER CORPORATE AND OTHER BUSINESS ENTERPRISES (1967).

10. *See* HAROLD S. BLOOMENTHAL, GOING PUBLIC AND THE PUBLIC CORPORATION (1987).

11. A. Beckerman-Rodau, *supra* note 8, at 519, 550.

12. Both acts are available at the University of Pennsylvania Law School's Web site and the National Conference of Commissioners on Uniform State Laws Web site at http://www.law.upenn.edu/bll/ulc/upa/upa1200.htm and http://www.law.upenn.edu/bll/ulc/ulpa/final2001.htm.

13. GORDON W. BROWN & PAUL A. SUKYS, BUSINESS LAW WITH UCC APPLICATIONS 688 (11th Ed. 2006).

14. Delaware Code §15-301. 72 Del. Laws, c. 151, §1.

15. *See Id.* §18.

16. Chuck Santangelo & Gerry Malone, *Partnership Agreements: Don't Dance around the Issues,* TRIAL, April 1988, at 58.

17. Nevada Revised Statute 87.080 Property of partnership. [8:74:1931; 1931 NCL § 5028.07]

18. Nevada Revised Statute 87.090 Partner agent of partnership; restrictions on authority. [9:74:1931; 1931 NCL § 5028.08]—(NRS A 1987, 375)

19. For a fascinating look at how a court will find partnership without a writing, *see* Patrick Mastrogiacomo, *A Partnership Is Formed by Parties Merely Intending to Carry On Business for Profit as Co-Owners, Byker v. Mannes, 641 N.W.2d 210 (Mich. 2002),* 82 U. DET. MERCY L. REV. 157 (Fall 2004).

20. See Unif. Act, *supra* note 14, §306.

21. Delaware Code §15-306: Partner's liability.

22. *See* Daniel S. Kleinberger, *A User's Guide to the New Uniform Limited Partnership Act*, 37 Suffolk U. L. Rev. 583 (2004).

23. Mississippi Code, Sec. 79-14-206. Filing in office of Secretary of State. Sources: Laws, 1987, ch. 488, Sec. 206; 1990, ch. 385, Sec. 2; 1995, ch. 362, Sec. 4, eff from and after July 1, 1995.

24. Elizabeth Cosenza, *Co-Invest at Your Own Risk: An Exploration of Potential Remedial Theories for Breaches of Rights of First Refusal in the Venture Capital Context* 55 Am. U.L. Rev. 87 (2005); *see also* Robert W. Hillman, *Law, Culture, and the Lore of Partnership: Of Entrepreneurs, Accountability, and the Evolving Status of Partners*, 40 Wake Forest L. Rev. 793 (2005).

25. Ga. Code §14-3-1101.

26. Anthony L. Liuzzo & Joseph G. Bonnice, Essentials of Business Law 268 (6th ed. 2007).

27. Note, *Real Persons, Corporate Persons, and Vicarious Liability*, 38 Case W. Res. L. Rev. 453 (1987–1988).

28. W.A. Harrington, *Annotation, Personal Civil Liability of an Officer or Director of a Corporation for Negligence of Subordinate Corporate Employee Causing Personal Injury or Death of a Person*, 90 A.L.R. 3d 916 (1976).

29. Brown & Sukys, *supra* note 13, at 708.

30. William R. Jacobs, The Ohio Close Corporation 6 (1991); *see also Note, Corporate Officials Beware: Calder v. Jones May Pierce Your Fiduciary Shield*, 24 Loy. L.A.L. Rev. 809 (April 1991); *See also Note, To Pierce or Not to Pierce? When Is the Question. Developing a Federal Rule or Decision for Piercing the Corporate Veil under CERCLA*, 68 Wash. U.L.Q. 733 (1990); *see also* John A. Swain & Edwin E. Aguilar, *Piercing the Veil to Assert Personal Jurisdiction over Corporate Affiliates: An Empirical Study of the Cannon Doctrine*, 84 B.U.L. Rev. 445 (2004).

31. Steven Walt & William S. Laufer, *Why Personhood Doesn't Matter: Corporate Criminal Liability and Sanctions*, 18 Am. J. Crim. L. 262, 264 (1991).

32. Keith Welks, *Corporate Criminal Capability: An Idea Whose Time Keeps Coming*, 16 Colum. J. Envtl. L. 293, 309 (1991).

33. A recent commentator notes, "This seems puzzling because we would expect that well-organized and well-funded groups (such as corporations) should obtain a large measure of what they want through legislation. Yet in the context of corporate crime legislation the corporations seem to be losing the battle. What might explain this outcome? Overall, my analysis suggests that most of the important players, including many corporations and management, have reasons to support some corporate crime legislation. This is because it helps to avoid or mitigate legislative and judicial alternatives—such as new forms of corporate civil liability and managerial criminal liability—that would be even more costly to corporate interests. Most corporate crime legislation arises at times when there is a large public outcry over a series of corporate scandals during or around a downturn in the economy." Vikramaditya S. Khanna, *Corporate Crime Legislation: A Political Economy Analysis*, 82 Wash. U. L. Q. 95, 97–98 (2004).

34. *See* Model Act, *supra* note 26.

35. *See* O. Lee Reed, Peter J. Shedd, Jere W. Morehead, & Robert N. Corley, The Legal and Regulatory Environment of Business 322 (13th ed. 2005).

36. Institute of Continuing Legal Education, 1 Michigan Basic Practice Handbook 310 (1992).

37. I.R.C. §1361(c)(1).

38. Reed et al., *supra* note 35, at 336.

39. *See* Matthew J. Rossman, *The Descendants of Fassihi: A Comparative Analysis of Recent Cases Addressing the Fiduciary Claims of Disgruntled Stakeholders against Attorneys Representing Closely Held Entities*, 38 Ind. L. Rev. 177 (2005).

40. W. Jacobs, *supra* note 30, at 33–34.

41. *Id*. at 45–46.

42. Robert John Kane, *Survey of Illinois Law: Professional Corporation Licensure*, 29 S. Ill. U. L. J. 687, 688 (2005).

43. 15 Pa. Stat. Ann. §§2902, 2912 (2005).

44. Reed et al., *supra* note 35, at 339.

45. *See* Douglas K. Moll, *Minority Oppression & The Limited Liability Company: Learning (or Not) from Close Corporation History*, 40 Wake Forest L. Rev. 883 (2005).

46. Some corporate service providers include Corporation Service Company, 1013 Centre Road, Wilmington, DE 19805; Corporation Information Services, Inc., P.O. Box 5828, Tallahassee, FL 32314; other states have jumped into the mix with an aggressive spirit. *See* Philip S. Garon, Michael A. Stanchfield, & John H. Matheson, *Developments in Minnesota Law: Challenging Delaware's Desirability as a Haven for Incorporation*, 32 Wm. Mitchell L. Rev. 769 (2006).

47. *See* 17 C.F.R. §230.405 (2003).

48. Earnest L. Falk, The Redbook Digest of Delaware Corporation Procedures (1970); Earnest L. Falk & Peter L. Moye, *Sequestration in Delaware, A Constitutional Analysis*, 73 Colum. L. Rev. 749 (1973).

49. Idaho Business Corporation Act at 30-1-302. General powers.

50. *See* 7 Jacob Rabkin & Mark H. Johnson, Current Legal Forms, 17–1521 (1989).

51. Idaho Business Corporation Act at 30-1-202. Articles of incorporation.

52. Wesley Gilmer Jr., The Law Dictionary 310 (6th ed. 1986).

53. *Id*. at 260.

54. Idaho Business Corporation Act at 30-1-621. Issuance of shares.

55. Kevin B. Scott, *How to Draft a Shareholder Agreement (with Form)*, Prac. Law., Jan. 1990, at 63, 64.

56. June A. Streigel, *Cumulative Voting, Yesterday and Today: The July 1986 Amendments to Ohio's General Corporation Law*, 5S U. Cin. L. Rev. 1265 (1987); *see also* Abrams Glaser, Brenda J. Glaser, & Bernard N. Groffman, *Cumulative Voting in Corporate Elections: Introducing Strategy into the Equation*, 35 S.C. L. Rev. 295 (1984).

57. Brown & Sukys, *supra* note 13, at 721.

58. For some advice to paralegals about corporate document preparation, *see* REED K. BILZ, LEGAL DOCUMENT PREPARATION (1988); ROBERT N. CORLEY, ERIC M. HOLMES, & WILLIAM J. ROBERT, PRINCIPLES OF BUSINESS LAW 740 (1983).

59. For an analysis of increasing shareholder voting power, *see* Lucian Arye Bebchuk, *The Case for Increasing Shareholder Power*, 118 HARV. L. REV. 833 (2000).

60. *See* James R. Burkhard, *Proposed Model Bylaws to Be Used with the Revised Model Business Corporation Act (1984)*, BUS. LAW., Nov. 1990, at 189.

61. Brown & Sukys, *supra* note 13, at 689–690.

62. Dennis J. Block & Adam Prussin, *Termination of Derivative Suits against Directors on Business Judgment Grounds, from Zapata to Aronson*, 39 BUS. L. 1503 (1984); Davis S. Ruder, *Duty of Loyalty—A Law Professor's Status*, 40 BUS. L. 1383 (1985); *see also* Zapata Court v. Maldonado, 430 A. 2d 779 (Delaware 1981).

63. James Farinaro, *Target Directors Fiduciary Duties: Initial Reasonableness Burden*, 61 NOTRE DAME L. REV. 724 (1986).

64. Cally Jordan, *The Conundrum of Corporate Governance*, 30 BROOKLYN J. INT'L L. 983, 992 (2005).

65. Robert Deutsch, *Regulation and the United States Corporation: An Alternative to Law and Economics*, 9 CARDOZO L. REV. 1465, 1486–1487 (1988).

66. Norwood Beveridge says courts are frustrated over the ambiguity of what due care in the corporate setting is. "The confusion in terminology for director duty of care standards in the cases can largely be explained by the tendency in the early cases to put directors in the category of mandatories and by the tendency of courts to use the term 'gross negligence' when they actually mean 'gross error of judgment.' Since directors currently are compensated for their services, 'they should, in any event, be held to the ordinary care standard of paid agents. However, the historical standard for unpaid agents was that of a reasonable person under the circumstances, and unpaid agents were also required to have some reasonable qualifications for the job undertaken unless a lesser standard of care was agreed upon. The argument that there are not enough successful director liability cases is not supported by the facts and, in any event, is irrelevant. Directors do not represent themselves to be infallible, and they should not be held to a higher standard than other business or professional persons." Norwood P. Beveridge Jr.,

The Corporate Director's Duty of Care: Riddles Wisely Expounded, 24 SUFFOLK U. L. REV. 923, 948–949 (1990).

67. J. Farinaro, *supra* note 63, at 724, 726.

68. Brown & Sukys, *supra* note 13, at 726.

69. *Note, Derivative Actions—Presumed Good Faith Deliberations by Special Litigation Committees: A Major Hurdle from Minority Shareholders*, 24 WAKE FOREST L. REV. 127 (1987).

70. Alfred v. Shaw, 318 N.C. 289, 349 S.E. 2d 41 (1986).

71. FED. R. CIV. P. 23.1.

72. N.Y. BUS. CORP. LAW §720 (McKinney 2005).

73. W.J. Dunn, *Annotations, Judicial Relief Other Than by Dissolution or a Receivership in Cases of Intra-Corporate Deadlock*, 47 A.L.R. 2d 365 (1956); Richard C. Tinney, *Dissension or Deadlock of Corporate Directors and Shareholders*, 6 AM. JUR. PROOF OF FACTS 2d 387 (1987).

74. Dunn, *id.* at 397.

75. *Id.*

76. Susanna M. Kim, *The Provisional Director Remedy for Corporate Deadlock: A Proposed Model Statute*, 60 WASH & LEE L. REV. 111 (2003).

77. Model Act, *supra* note 26, §97.

78. Sherman Antitrust Act, 15 U.S.§§; Wilson Tariff Act, 15 U.S.§§; Clayton Act, 15 U.S.§§ 12–27, 29 U.S.§§; Appeals [U.S. is civil complainant, equitable relief sought], 15 U.S.§; Depositions for Use in Suits in Equity Proceedings Open to the Public 15 U.S.§; Antitrust Civil Process Act, 15 U.S.§§ 1311–1314, as Amended; Counsel's Liability for Excessive Costs, 28 U.S.§ 1927; International Antitrust Enforcement Assistant Act of 1994, 15 U.S.§§ 6201–6212.

79. U.S. Department of Justice, Antitrust Division, Organization Chart; updated January 24, 2002; available at http://www.usdoj.gov/atr/org.htm. For a time line on antitrust practice and policy in the American experience, *see Time Line of Antitrust Enforcement Highlights*, available at www.usdoj.gov/atr/timeline.pdf.

80. Joel M. Androphy, *What Corporate Counsel Needs to Know about Criminal Investigations and Prosecutions*, TEX. B. J. 999 (Oct. 1987).

81. R. Corley et al., *supra* note 58, at 765.

82. Bevies Longstretch, *Reflections of the State of Corporate Governance*, 57 BROOK. L. REV. 113, 117 (1991).

The Law of Contracts

III. **Contract Enforceability**
   A. **Statute of Frauds**
   B. **Parol Evidence Rule**
   C. **Incapacity**
   D. **Illegality**
   E. **Mistake**
   F. **Misrepresentation**
   G. **Duress or Undue Influence**
   H. **Breach of Warranty**
      1. **Express Warranties**
      2. **Implied Warranty of Merchantability**
      3. **Implied Warranty of Fitness for a Particular Purpose**
      4. **Lemon Law Litigation**
   I. **Commercial Impracticability**

IV. **Paralegal Practice and Process in the Law of Contracts**
   A. **Preliminary Considerations**
   B. **Initial Conference**
   C. **Choice of Form and Format**
   D. **Standardized Forms**
   E. **Suggestions on Draftsmanship**
   F. **Structure of a Contract**

V. **Contract Litigation**
   A. **Pleadings and Practice**
      1. **Complaint for Breach**
      2. **Damages**
      3. **Restitution**
      4. **Rescission**
      5. **Reformation**
      6. **Specific Performance**
   B. **Uniform Commercial Code Remedies**
      1. **Anticipatory Breach**
      2. **Seller's Remedies**
      3. **Buyer's Remedies**

VI. **Summary**

Discussion Questions

 CONTRACT LAW PARALEGAL JOB DESCRIPTION

Contract law paralegals need to be proficient in the following competencies:

- Identify a legally enforceable contract.
- Draft contracts, under the supervision of an attorney, that contain the requisite elements for enforceability.
- Recognize and explain conditions that terminate an offer or that constitute a counteroffer.
- Recognize the means and methods by which an offer may be revoked.
- Draft correspondence and other documents highlighting the precise nature of an offer and acceptance and outlining the specificity of consideration.
- Distinguish bilateral and unilateral contracts.
- Transmit a proper notice of acceptance.
- Determine whether consideration is legally adequate.
- Chart, list, or graph outlining contracts that require a writing under the Statute of Frauds.

- Pinpoint contracts that do not require a writing.
- Make judgments concerning the legal competency of individuals to enter into contracts, particularly in the consumer finance environment.
- Identify contractual activities that will be void for public policy and are inherently illegal.
- Distinguish normal sales ability from techniques of fraud, misrepresentation, and duress.
- Make recommendations regarding the overall enforceability of a contract defense.
- Draft affirmative defense clauses, under the supervision of an attorney, in a contract between parties.
- List and specify rights in third party beneficiaries including creditors, donees, and subcontractors.
- Draft and design, under the supervision of an attorney, an assignment of rights agreement.
- Enumerate services, tasks, or duties that are delegable.
- Draft and design, under the supervision of an attorney, a delegation of duties contract.
- Draft, under the supervision of an attorney, conditional clauses and contingencies.[1]
- Recognize conduct that can be viewed as a present, actual, and/or anticipatory breach of performance.
- Assess facts regarding the major or minor nature of a breach.
- Make recommendations on a legal rationale or excuse from contract performance including a failure of conditions and waiver and estoppel.
- Identify, recognize, and explain the conditions that result in a discharge of obligations due to factual and legal impossibility.
- Define standardized, consequential, and liquidated damages and explain the circumstances under which each applies.
- Define and explain compensatory, punitive, and nominal damages.
- Calculate damage claims.
- Calculate a liquidated damage claim.
- Draft notices, correspondence, and other documentation putting a defendant on notice of a breach of contract.
- Draft documents and other memoranda, under the supervision of an attorney, highlighting the inability to meet or perform an existing condition for contractual contingency.

INTRODUCTION

As practicing paralegals quickly learn, the law of contracts plays an integral role in their professional lives. Contracts are essentially the stuff of daily living—the interaction among and between individuals and other entities with legal existence and the formalization of economic beliefs, aspirations, and expectations. Contract work primarily resides in the office of the attorney, but working collaboratively with the paralegal promotes high rates of practice efficiency.

Contracts can be formal, informal, written, or oral; or they can simply result from a promise, the performance of an act, silence, or by material reliance on a series of offers.[2] Contracts, for lack of a better definition, are nothing more or less than a *group of promises*.[3]

In the analysis of contracts, certain foundational questions must be posed:

1. What are the legal requisites for a contract?
2. When does a series of exchanges, discussions, or actions become a legally enforceable, binding contract?
3. How does one distinguish preliminary discussion from formal negotiations?
4. How does one define a legal offer and a legal acceptance?
5. What is satisfactory consideration?
6. What are the defenses to the formation of contracts?
7. What issues of public policy and other matters bear on the enforceability of a contract?
8. What remedies exist in the event of breach?

The law of contracts exists to provide civility to transactions undertaken and to provide a framework of predictability in commerce and an assurance that parties involved can engage in commerce. The law of contracts fully recognizes that promises between people, in order to be enforceable, must be judged, evaluated, and enforced by sensible rules of construction and interpretation. When a person offers to purchase 500 shares of General Motors stock, any interpretation would lead to a specific objective numerical purchase of 500. There is no way around this fact. But whether the 500 shares will make their purchaser a millionaire, merely by a promise to purchase and deliver, is not a sensible expectation. The question whether the stock has value is a reasonable expectation, but its appreciation is another issue altogether.

Within this general framework, contract law thrives—to ensure that promises are kept and that legal obligations are adhered to. In essence, the law of contracts is the law of obligation—that is, a description or a delineation of the rights and duties between individuals who make promises to each other. The law of contracts gives meaning to the parties' "expressions of mutual assent."[4] Consider these economic interchanges:

- An employer promises to hire an employee under a specific contract.
- An auto dealer promises to deliver a specific model vehicle to a consumer.
- A painter promises to paint a house for a specific price.
- Litigants agree to release each other in the settlement of a dispute under certain conditions and terms.
- A borrower agrees to make specific monthly payments of principal and interest on a promissory note.
- A purchaser and a vendor of real estate agree to close and settle on a specific real property.

From the commercial marketplace to the corporate boardroom, the real estate broker's office to the auto showroom, most of the major transactions of life are guided by specific contractual terms and conditions.

Contractual activity can be aptly termed a "promissory environment." Vincent A. Wellman, in his work *Conceptions of the Common Law: Reflections on a Theory of Contract*,[5] notes that "the law of contracts is guided by a promise principle—that principle by which persons may impose on themselves obligations where none existed before."[6] Wellman further hypothesizes,

> In promising, Fried argues, we intentionally invoke a social convention whose function it is to give moral grounds to others to rely on our promises. It is wrong to invoke the convention in order to make the promise, and then to break it. We therefore incur a moral obligation to do as we have promised. It is this moral obligation to keep our promises that Fried asserts to be the moral basis of contract law.[7]

Although this formulation lacks legal enforceability, Professor Fried's work is important because it gives heightened emphasis to the moral aspects of individual promises. People have a right to rely on the promises of another. A party who fails to adhere to such promises, to meet his or her obligations, causes a breakdown of relationships. If a society tolerates a haphazard approach to a promise or an action, it can expect little sincerity or dependability in the economic marketplace.

There has been an obvious, unbridled stray from the strict interpretation of contracts toward an activist mentality that interprets beyond the four corners of the instrument. Even when contracts are clear and unambiguous, and even when the parties fully understand the ramifications of the conduct engaged, judicial activists display little hesitancy in bypassing contract language or even inventing clauses and phrases that do not presently exist in the contract language. Formal contract analysis is the path of the strict constructionist. What the document says and contains is sometimes viewed as contrary to equitable theory. This adherence to a contract's wording is known as the *formal* approach.

The mechanical or formal theory of contract suggests that if a certain standard method is followed, and certain prescribed elements are found to be present, a contract exists. Thus if there has been such identifiable conduct as an offer and an acceptance, legally sufficient consideration, mutuality of obligation, and possibly, depending on the theory's complexity, other indications of an intent to contract, a contract exists. We follow the steps and find that a contract either exists completely or fails completely.[8]

Another school of thought is labeled *textualism*. Here the interpreter is bound almost slavishly to the language and the text of a contract and should avoid ever leaping beyond the text to discover the intentions of the parties. Others in opposition see the process of text analysis as too narrow in scope, asserting that it is a mistake to "confine their inquiry in that fashion."[9] Interpretation can no longer, according to these critics, reside in the terms and text alone, and must be evaluated in light of both common law and statutes.

Definitional Issues in Contract Law

Contract

Under the Uniform Commercial Code at §1-201(12), contracts are viewed as agreements and defined as follows:

> *"Contracts" means the total legal obligation that results from the parties' agreement as determined by [the Uniform Commercial Code] as supplemented by any other applicable laws.*[10]

A *contract* can be defined in a various ways. As previously noted, contracts can be formal or informal but essentially reflect the promises between individuals and institutions. The American Law Institute's *Restatement of Contracts*, §1, defines a contract as

> *. . . a promise or a set of promises for the breach of which the law gives a remedy or the performance of which the law in some way recognizes a duty.*[11]

The Uniform Commercial Code exerts significant influence over the contractual behavior between merchants. The Uniform Commercial Code delineates an all-encompassing statutory framework for contracts in the sale of goods, specifically at Article 2. Reference to the Uniform Commercial Code will be seen throughout this chapter with its relevance and scope directed toward the sale and exchange of goods:

> *"Goods" means all things (including specially manufactured goods) which are movable at the time of identification to the contract for sale other than the money in which the price is to be paid, investment securities (Article 8) and things in action. "Goods" also includes the unborn young of animals and growing crops and other identified things attached to realty as described in the section on goods to be severed from realty (Section 2-107).*[12]

Goods must both exist and be identified before any interest in them can pass. Goods that are not both existing and identified are *future* goods. A purported present sale of future goods or of any interest therein operates as a contract to sell.[13]

Given these definitions, it is clear that a contract sets out the rights and obligations of the parties. It is a roadmap for behavior in a particular transaction. It is a document that binds parties. On the other hand, a *gift* lacks the punch of enforceability because its donor need not make the gift, nor is the donor bound in any sense to give for any formal reason. "Realistically, a contract is a legal device to control the future through promises. By definition, a promise is a present commitment, however expressed, that something will or will not be done. Parties are allowed to create rights and duties between themselves and the state will enforce them through legal machinery."[14] As such, contracts need certain prerequisites before being enforceable.

Parties to Contract

With rare exception, any individual or legal entity can be a party to a contract. The following names take on different meanings and implications depending on the type of contract entered into, whether a real estate contract, a consumer contract, or other interchange:

Assignee: A person to whom a right or property is transferred.[15]

Assignor: A person who makes an assignment.[16]

Promisor: A person who makes a promise.

Promisee: A person to whom the promise is made.

Obligor: A person under a duty or obligation to perform.

Obligee: A person who will receive the benefit of a duty or obligation.

Vendor: A seller of real property.

Vendee: A purchaser of real property.

Seller: A party selling any good or service.

Purchaser: A party purchasing any good or service.

Lessor: A party providing real property for lease.

Lessee: A party leasing real property.

Insurer: An entity providing an insurance policy.

Insured: A party paying a premium for an insurance policy.

Subrogor: A person put in the place or substituted for another in upholding a right or claim.[17]

Subrogee: A person who allows another to be substituted for herself or himself as creditor; with a transfer of right and duties.[18]

Donor: A person who makes a gift or confers or a power of appointment.[19]

Beneficiary: A person who is entitled to the benefits of a trust that is administered by a trustee.[20]

As can easily be deduced, there are always two or more parties to a contract because we cannot truly contract with ourselves.

Subject Matter of a Contract

Fundamentally, an enforceable contract requires the meeting of the minds of two or more parties who desire a mutual end—with the end being the contract's purpose and corresponding subject matter. The subject matter of any contract can and does include literally anything that can be bargained for and exchanged, such as the following:

- Personal services.
- Employment.
- Construction.
- Real property.
- Personal property.

- Option rights.
- Specific acts of conduct.
- Settlement.
- Forbearance.
- Legal detriment.

Any legal activity allowed by public policy can be the subject matter of a contract.

Classification and Types of Contracts

Formal Contract

A formal contract expressly employs a writing in documentary form. Informal contracts may be based on everything but a writing. In contract law, whether governed by rule or regulation, formal contracts must be in writing to be enforceable. Common examples of formal contracts include (1) contracts under seal; (2) recognizance; (3) negotiable instruments; and (4) letters of credit.

Contracts under seal include promissory notes, mortgages, or other documentation that is left with a permanent impression, such as a legal ring seal imprinted with wax, a signature or a corporate seal, or an impression made on paper.

Another form of formal contract is a *contract of record* that may include any of the following: a lien, release, satisfaction, accord, documentation relating to judgments, and documentation relating to bail and bond.[21]

Informal Contract

By inference, any contract that is not under seal and not governed by a specific statutory rule or standard can be described as informal. The nature of its enforceability depends not on its form but instead on the representations between the parties themselves. *Informal* does not mean *unenforceable*. Oral promises, consumer purchases under $500, and contracts performable in a short duration of time are often termed *informal*. Informal contracts are sometimes called *simple* contracts as well.[22]

Express Contract

A contract is considered express when (1) the parties to the contract are fully aware of its terms, conditions, and overall requirements; and (2) there is little dispute about the rights and obligations of either of the parties. Mutual assent between the parties is evidenced by outward verbal or physical expressions that reflect the agreement of both parties.

Both expressed and implied contracts have the same legal effect, though their methods of expressing assent or agreement are distinguishable. Contracts in writing are always described as express. Examples include a lease, an employment contract, or a real estate agreement.

Implied Contract

Contracts can also be founded on implication or reasonable inference. The fine line drawn between express and implied contracts is addressed in *Skelly v. Bristol Savings Bank*:

> *Contracts may be express or implied. These terms, however, do not denote different kinds of contracts, but have reference to the evidence by which the agreement between the parties is shown. If the agreement is shown by the direct words of the parties, spoken or written, the contract is said to be an express one. But if such agreement can only be shown by the acts and conduct of the parties, interpreted in the light of the subject matter and of the circumstances, then the contract is an implied one.*[23]

In finding a contract by implication, courts frequently wrestle with a promisor who performs a specific act to the benefit of another. Assume that a homeowner had entered discussions with a landscaping contractor to redo his entire front yard. Without specific agreement about terms and conditions, the landscaping contractor went forward, performed the activities, and then submitted a bill. No writings existed, and no protests came forth from the homeowner. Within these types of factual situations a party can urge the finding of an implied contract. "Such a contract arises . . . when one person renders services under circumstances indicating that payment for them is expected, and the other person knowing such circumstances accepts the benefit of those services."[24]

Void Contract

A *void* contract is a contract that possesses no legal effect or influence. Commonly confused with the term *voidable*, a void contract fails by operation of law. Void contracts are the bargained-for exchanges that are plainly illegal—such as a "hit man" organized crime contract or contracts with minors—both of which are contrary to a serious public policy determination or statutory interpretation or guideline. The term *void* expresses a "total absence of legal effect."[25]

Voidable Contract

In contrast, a voidable contract is one that has the potential to remain in effect or alternatively to be declared null and void. The American Law Institute defines *voidable* as ". . . one where one or more parties thereto have the power, by a manifestation of election to do so, to avoid the legal relations created by the contract; or by ratification of the contract to make it valid and enforceable."[26] A voidable contract is in all respects a proper contract in which one of the parties involved may have a power to avoid doing what he has promised to do, or by some positive act (ratification) require both parties to perform the contract. A party declared insane or mentally incompetent is incapable of contract formation.[27]

On the other hand, if a party chooses to avoid a contract, both parties are released from the contract. If the party with the power to avoid ratifies, both must perform. Contrasted with void, a contracting party lacking the requisite mental capacity before the formation of a contract would not be in a voidable dilemma because the contract is inherently void.

Certain contracts are fraudulently induced. In this instance, the party defrauded has entered the contract relying on actions or representations by the other party that at the time of their commission or making are known to be false. The guilty party cannot claim the contract to be valid; however, the innocent party may, at its option, accept any benefit of the contract or declare the contract void. Contracts entered into by infants, incompetents, and other parties not mature enough to make such determinations may be totally unenforceable. Voidable contracts are sometimes referred to as *unenforceable contracts*.[28]

Valid or Enforceable Contract

A valid contract is a contract that is proper in its formation—that is, it contains the elements of offer, acceptance, consideration, legality, and capacity. On the other hand, an unenforceable contract is a *valid* contract that is not enforced because a *legal defense exists* to prevent enforcement such as statutes of limitation or the Statute of Frauds. Hence a contract can be valid and unenforceable. A contract may lack statutory language or be a violation of law or other public policy. In these cases, the contract is neither valid nor enforceable. The *Restatement of Contracts* describes an unenforceable contract as "one which the law does not enforce by legal proceedings but recognizes in some indirect or collateral way as creating a duty of performance, though there has been no ratification."[29]

Executed Contract

This contractual classification encompasses contracts in which the parties have fully adhered to the rights, obligations, and formalities of the agreement. Leaving no matters undone or incomplete, the contract is fully performed or executed. An executed contract has necessary signatures and attestations and is appropriately filed.

Executory Contract

An executory contract is one that has yet to be fully performed or has been only partially completed. Formalities of the contract, including signatures and other documentation, have been filed and completed; however, the duties and obligations of the promisor have yet to be fulfilled. Contracts that have conditions and contingencies are frequently considered executory, such as a real estate sales agreement contingent on the acquisition of sufficient financing.[30]

Be aware that a contract that calls for the payment of consideration in full can be totally executed by one party with the reciprocal services, goods, or other obligations yet to be submitted or transferred. These contracts are yet to be executed.[31]

Bilateral Contract

Contracts can be further typified by the offers made by the parties who form a contract. Contracts may be *unilateral* or *bilateral*. Bilateral contracts are two-sided affairs. For example, X promises to sell his house for $10,000, and Y promises to pay $10,000 for the house. As soon as the parties exchange promises, corresponding rights and duties create a bilateral contract. Because the seller is obliged to transfer the property, and the buyer is obliged to pay the appropriate consideration, a bilateral contract exists. *Bilateral* means a *promise for a promise*.

Complex and intricate rules apply in bilateral and unilateral contract theories. Evaluate this example:

Bobby Jones, by written memorandum, writes to Sally Jones, "I promise to sell you my boat on June 1 if you promise to pay me $2,000 at that time."

Because Bobby promises to sell his boat, and Sally, if she so wishes, can promise to pay the consideration of $2,000 on June 1, a bilateral contract has been formed. If Sally does not wish to buy, the contract remains a simple ambition without formality.

When an offeror asks, "Will you buy my contract for $5.00?" that contract has only potentiality rather than actuality. For a contract to exist, the offeree must accept. In this sense the contract is bilateral—a promise for a promise.

Unilateral Contract

Comparatively, a unilateral contract is a promise that has legal effect only if a specific act, duty, or obligation is performed by the offeree, the person to whom the offer is made. Review the following examples:

Example 1

John posts a reward of $100 for anyone who will return his lost dog. The SPCA shows up with his dog seeking collection and asks for the reward of $100.

This is a unilateral contract—one party making a promise that has legal effect when the act is performed.[32]

Example 2

Harry Kowalsky writes to his supplier, Johnny LaRue, and states, "Send me 800,000 pounds of wheat at once at a price of $10 per barrel. Payment will be made upon delivery." Johnny ships, and Harry receives.

This is another classic example of a unilateral contract in which a promise is given legal effect once the offeree has performed.

Until the obligation or duty created by the offeror has been fulfilled, there is merely an offer for a unilateral contract, which has no enforceability.[33]

Quasi-Contract

A quasi-contract is essentially a legal invention—or better stated, a legal fiction—that courts employ to prevent unjust enrichment in a noncontractual situation. Described as an equitable remedy, the doctrine of quasi-contract is employed in situations where "there is no contract between the parties, those in which there was a contract between the parties but it has been avoided, and those in which there was an attempted contract but for some reason the agreement is held illegal and therefore void."[34] Review the following examples in which the doctrine of quasi-contract may be utilized:

Example 1

A construction company enters a work site, performs all work, then finds out that it is at the wrong location. No objection to construction activity was made, and a substantial benefit or improvement was made on the property.

Example 2

A landowner mistakenly believes that she owns an extension on her present land site. As a result, she pays the adjoining landowner's taxes for 10 years. Upon discovery, the landowner seeks restitution.

Example 3

A neighbor discovers that an adjoining house had an exploding pipe during a cold weather spell. To get a plumber to fix the property, he personally had to pay that expense in cash. The owner refuses to pay.[35]

In each example here, the lack of formal, informal, or express terms leads to the conclusion that one party receives benefit without comparable detriment, and as a result is unjustly enriched. A finding of a quasi-contract permits some level of compensation for the party incurring the expense.

REQUISITES OF THE CONTRACT

Whether any contract is valid depends on whether it meets the general standards for contract construction. In other words, what elements are required to make a contract both legal and binding? A valid contract must contain these elements:

1. *Agreement*: There must be a mutual assent, a mutual meeting of the minds, governed by the terms of an offer and a corresponding acceptance.
2. *Consideration*: There must be valid bargained-for consideration or other legal detriment that gives the agreement legal effect and authority.
3. *Competency*: The parties who execute and sign the contract must be competent to do so.
4. *Legal subject matter*: Contracts that promote criminality or are against significant public policy may be void or voidable.

FIGURE 5.1
The Contract Process Element by Element

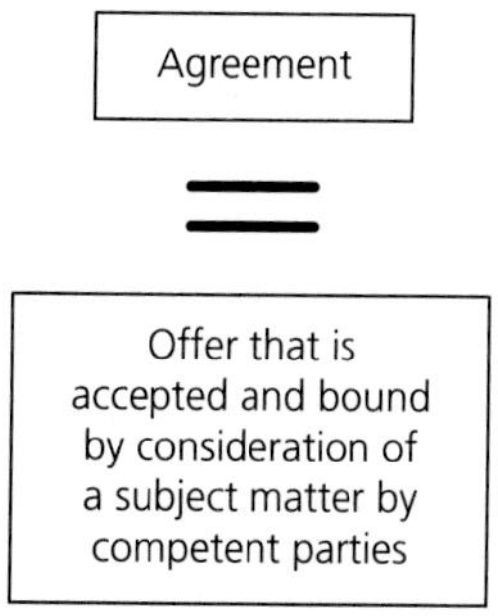

Agreement

=

Offer that is accepted and bound by consideration of a subject matter by competent parties

Practicing paralegals will be amply assisted in their analysis of contracts by reviewing this checklist:

- Is there a document, either standardized or prepared, that governs the conduct of the parties in question?
- Can an offer be determined or discovered?
- Has there been an expression of acceptance by any party empowered to make an offer?
- Has a mutual consensus been arrived at between offeror and offeree that corroborates a meeting of the minds?
- What has been the bargained-for exchange, the consideration, the legal detriment? Has it been money, personal or real property, or forbearance, settlement, or other matter?
- Are there any defenses to the contract in question, such as illegal subject matter, incompetence of the parties, statute of frauds, statute of limitations, mistake of law, or fact? If not, there is a valid, enforceable contract.
- Are the parties competent to contract?[36]

Finding an agreement—a series of acts, words, or expressions that evidences mutual assent and a meeting of the minds—commences contractual inquiry. The *contractual state of mind*, frequently referred to as an accord, a mutual manifestation, a mutual exchange, or a singular promise asking for performance under a unilateral framework, must be initially founded. Whether bilateral or unilateral in design, contracts are "consensual relationships."[37] Determining exactly when, how, if, and under what terms and conditions this mutual assent exists can be a knotty exercise. "Classical common law rules required that the assent of both parties exactly match at the same point in time—that is, that there be a subjective meeting of the minds."[38] In the electronic age, particularly the emerging marketplace of electronic commerce, the rules of contract law still bind. Even though the purchase may be Internet based, the parties must come to terms, although they may do so by different signals. Juliet Moringiello of Widener Law School portrays the new age of contracting as confusing because the "contractual nature of Web site terms of use might be even less obvious than the contractual nature of ski lift tickets. And while the presence of a human in the contracting process is often overrated, when contract terms are delivered by machine, no humans are available to explain the terms."[39]

Discovering the intent of contracting parties, in a perfect sense, whether face to face or in the virtual world, is simply not possible. We must look to the words, the language of the contract, and the actions of the parties to discern intent. Determining the exact time of the formulation of agreement can best be done by evaluating and judging the contractual instrument while simultaneously assessing the parties' conduct.

Contractual Elements

The Offer

An offer is a serious representation to negotiate—a decision to enter a contract, to forge, formulate, or create legal obligations, rights, and duties between an offeror and an offeree. A legal offer encompasses more than mere puffery and preliminary discussions that might anticipate a future contract. Discerning whether a legal offer exists "turns upon the question of fact as to whether they arouse an expectation in the mind of the average, reasonable man in the position of the offeree that, if he purports to do what is requested, nothing further need be done by the one making the proposal in order to form a contract."[40] Expressions of interest or preliminary discussions about the product or service that may be subject to a future contract do not suffice for a formal offer.[41] On the other hand, an offer that delineates express expectations, which is subsequently accepted, creates binding obligations in the parties. Recent U.S. Supreme Court appointee Justice Samuel Alito has historically construed offers in a strict fashion. In denying that the promise of a performance bonus is unenforceable, Justice Alito, joining the majority court, held the following:

> *Further, we reject Advanta's suggestion that the bonuses were unenforceable promises. With regard to the 1998 Retention Bonus and the 1997 Change of Control Bonus, there was sufficient evidence presented at trial for the jury to have concluded (which it did) that the traditional indices of a binding contract offer, acceptance and consideration were present.*[42]

Paralegals must distinguish, contrast, and discriminate ordinary commercial practice, retail activity, and mercantile practice from the formalities of contract formation. Expressions of interest, a willingness to discuss, and other hopeful intentions do not constitute legal offers.

Offers are made by *offerors*. Offerors can be supermarkets, retail establishments, car dealers, employers, boat sales agents, stockholders, stockbrokers, corporations, or any other individual or entity who may legally enter a contract. The party to whom the offer has been communicated is known as the *offeree*.

Technically, an offer is an act by a person giving another the legal power to create an obligation called a contract. Standardized contract forms contain predrafted offers. (See Form 5.1 on the accompanying CD.) A contract may be in proposal form, as is often witnessed in construction or labor contracts. (See Form 5.2.)

The party making the offer will also affect its interpretation. *Merchants*—those who deal daily with commerce—are held to a less tolerant and flexible standard compared to the general citizen. When merchants offer, the offer is deemed *firm* and less easily revoked. The merchant sells to a wider world. The U.C.C. recognizes this distinction:

> *An offer by a merchant to buy or sell goods in a signed writing which by its terms gives assurance that it will be held open is not revocable, for lack of consideration, during the time stated or if no time is stated for a reasonable time, but in no event may such period of irrevocability exceed three months; but any such term of assurance on a form supplied by the offeree must be separately signed by the offeror.*[43]

A labor contract outlines an offer to provide a certain service or product at a specific price. The party who decides to accept the offer, the offeree, by his or her signature, evidences an assent to these terms and conditions. Study in the same contract form the existence of actual consideration and the other terms and conditions that comprise the rights, duties, and obligations of the parties. Once it is determined that an offer has legal effect, acceptance of the offer's terms and conditions formalizes the contract.

For paralegals engaged in contract activity, it is crucial that facts, parties, and circumstances be evaluated with precision and objectivity. Never assume a contract clause or the intent of any contracting party. Never presume that a contract has been formalized or gone beyond the preparatory phase. Analyze closely the lines of communications between offeror and offeree. Consider these suggestions:

1. Communications are to be construed as a whole in light of all correspondence and prior transactions; if inconsistencies exist, later words control over former words.

2. A communication that is sent in response to a buyer's request for a firm offer or a seller's request for an order is more likely to be found to manifest an intention to be presently bound and thus constitute an offer.

3. The more individuals to whom the proposition is addressed, the less likely it is to be an offer because such conduct negates an intention to be presently bound.

4. The more definite a proposal, the more likely it is to be an offer.

5. Language is to be interpreted in light of custom and usage in the trade or community.[44]

In evaluating offer contract language, interpret with these factors in mind:

- Is the offer merely an advertisement without singularly attempting to enter a binding or operative contract?

- How definite were the terms, conditions, or pricing? Certainty of terms and language must be sufficiently definite and precise to be declared a legally binding offer.

- Was the offer made in a circular advertisement distributed to millions of homes?

- Was the offer directed by name and by specific contract to a specific individual?

- Were specific prices quoted?

- Was the offer made through catalog or other bulk mail mechanism?

- Did the offer contain language that represented a serious interest in bargaining rather than general language of puffery?

- Does the offer contain language commonly understood as being a sincere and serious effort to create a contract? Does it use language such as "I hereby offer . . .; I hereby make available . . .; I hereby put up for sale . . .;" or does it sound like "I might consider selling . . .; I will sell . . .; Let's talk prices . . .; Depending on my cash flow, I may accept a reasonable price. . . ."

- What is the custom and trade usage in the business when it comes to determining whether or not an exact offer to buy or sell has been made? Think of the commodities industry or stock sales.

- Are there pieces of correspondence that evidence a series of offers, counteroffers, and other exchanges?

- Has there been a series of written memoranda that supports a regular and consistent pattern of negotiation leading to an eventual formal offer and acceptance?

- Are the terms, requirements, and place of delivery specifications sufficiently definite to lead one to the conclusion that a serious and formal offer is being made?

- Is the offer being made on formal stationery or preprinted or standardized contracts?

- Has the offeror stated a specific time duration for acceptance of the offer?

- Has the offeror provided a means of revocation or exercise on the offer?

To find an offer, quantify and qualify the conduct of the offeror. A car dealer does not really make an offer when, in a less-than-credulous car commercial, he or she proclaims,

> *I'll beat any deal, any time, any place and give you a thousand dollars for any trade-in regardless of condition. Just come on down, and we'll put you in heaven!*

The salesman's exercise is one of commercial jaw-boning, which has little legal effect or impact.[45]

Offers can also be deemed legally defective if they are communicated to the wrong party, suffer from ambiguity and confusion in terms and conditions, or contain a mistake of terms or conditions.

Duration of Offer Absent express language and statutory control or guidelines, courts generally give an offer a reasonable period for viability. In the commercial marketplace, offers need reasonable time frames of negotiation. Thus an offer made to a specific individual without express durational terms would be accorded a reasonable time as generally found by habit, custom, or industrial usage. Under no set of facts will an offer last forever. It can be terminated by death, incapacity, insanity, or destruction of the subject matter or supervening illegality of a proposed contract.[46]

If there is an express term or durational limitation, some courts religiously uphold it, whereas others curiously create a new standard. For example, assume a furniture sales agent sends a written offer to a preferred former customer of the furniture store that states,

> *Due to your past loyalty to our company and the regular business you have provided us, we hereby offer you a $100 gift certificate to be applied toward the purchase of any furniture if you arrive at the store before closing on January 31.*

Because the offeree was out of town and could not exercise this option, he was infuriated. The offeror has the power to create the offer, so he or she may dictate the durational terms in which acceptance can take place.[47]

Termination or Revocation of Offer An offer may also be revoked by the party making it. The right to revoke naturally resides within the offeror. Any time before the offer is accepted, a revocation is possible. Outside of a binding option contract, revocation of an offer can take place at any time before acceptance.

In contract law, a specific offer may be withdrawn even though a specific time was expressly stated in the original offer; in this sense, the power of acceptance influences the duration of any offer. The offer "may be specific in the time within which acceptance may occur. . . ."[48] The guiding principle that governs the revocability of an offer is that an acceptance must not have taken place. However, many jurisdictions require that specific notice of that revocation must be given because the offeree may detrimentally rely on the fact that the offer remains open.[49]

The duration of an offer is also governed by other tests and factual scenarios. A partial listing of those legal issues is provided here:

1. *Lapse of time*: Offers not accepted within the specified time frame are said to have lapsed and are therefore terminated. Offers that do not have an expressly stated period are governed

by the reasonable time standard and eventually will expire due to lapse of time. No offer remains open indefinitely. Review the following example:

Business X receives an offer from Supplier G to sell 4 million tons of corn feed for livestock at a price of $4.50 per bushel as long as Business X accepts this offer on or before July 1, 2008. With no lapse of time and no revocation by notice or other communication indicating that the offer has expired, Business X accepts the offer on July 1, 2007. A contract has been formed.

2. *Rejection*: An offer that is rejected outright or responded to with a counteroffer is terminated. Assume the following facts:

Bob says he will sell his bike to Jim for $1,750. Jim counters with a price of $1,400.

The original offer is terminated because it was originally rejected by the offeree.

3. *Termination by illegal subject matter*: If the original offer under the contract subsequently were to become illegal, such as in cases of usury laws, toxic or narcotic substances, or other matters deemed illegal, an offer would terminate by operation of law.

   While not fully on point, our earlier review of void and voidable contractual undertakings should be reviewed for its applicability to this subject.

4. *Termination by offeror*: An offer made to an explicit party or individual (a specific offeree) is terminated when done so by the offeror. The offeror naturally must consider other offerees to whom she or he can make an offer.

5. *Death or disability of offeror or offeree*: In most American jurisdictions, contractual parties who become totally disabled or die are relieved from any legal contractual responsibility. Their offers terminate upon death. The offers of corporate and business entities with legal perpetuity do not terminate.

Irrevocable Offers   Offers may be irrevocable in either a legal or an equitable sense. Paralegals may see cases in which a party detrimentally relied on an offer, expended money, and incurred economic losses. The offeror, by the nature of the promise, may have waived the right to withdraw or be declared "estopped" from withdrawing. These offers are then irrevocable. Offers granted under an option right (a separately enforceable contract) are irrevocable. Finally, an offeree who has partially performed may argue irrevocability of an offer.

Acceptance

Offers in and of themselves do not create binding contracts. They are unilateral actions that do not fulfill the mutual assent manifestation necessary for an enforceable contract. "Offer followed by acceptance is the substantially universal method."[50] Acceptance accomplishes that goal of the transaction. The power of acceptance rests specifically in the offeree because the terms and conditions of the offer have been communicated directly to him or her. Acceptance implies a conscious, knowledgeable decision-making process on the part of the offeree demonstrating a desire to enter a formal, legally binding contract under the terms and conditions of the offer. The role of acceptance in the creation of a contract cannot be overstated. Russell Wald's well-drafted work, *Offeree's Acceptance of a Contract Offer*, states this precisely:

> *Only when accepted is the offer converted into a binding contract, since prior to acceptance, mutual assent is lacking, and as a rule, to become a binding contract, the offer must be accepted while it is still open and existing, without qualification, by one having the right to do so. The acceptance must be communicated to the offeror, and although the offeror may specify how the offer shall be accepted, failing such a specification, anything that amounts to a manifestation with a determination to accept is sufficient.[51]*

Under Section 2-206 of the Uniform Commercial Code, acceptance in the formation of contract is defined as follows:

> *(1) Unless otherwise unambiguously indicated by the language or circumstances*
> > *(a) an offer to make a contract shall be construed as inviting acceptance in any manner and by any medium reasonable in the circumstances;*
> > *(b) an order or other offer to buy goods for prompt or current shipment shall be construed as inviting acceptance either by a prompt promise to ship or by the prompt or current*

shipment of conforming or nonconforming goods, but such a shipment of nonconforming goods does not constitute an acceptance if the seller seasonably notifies the buyer that the shipment is offered only as an accommodation to the buyer.

(2) *Where the beginning of a requested performance is a reasonable mode of acceptance an offeror who is not notified of acceptance within a reasonable time may treat the offer as having lapsed before acceptance.*[52]

The paralegal must be keenly aware of these legal issues involving acceptance:

1. Has the acceptance been made within the durational time as stated in the offer?
2. Has the acceptance been made while the offer was still in existence?
3. Has the acceptance been communicated without conditions?
4. Has the acceptance been made according to custom, habit, and industrial usage in this particular trade or business?
5. Is the acceptance unequivocal, without change or reservation?
6. Is the right to accept or reject the offer supported by an underlying option contract?[53]
7. Has the acceptance been carried out according to the terms of the offer, such as in a specific place, time, manner, writing, word, sign, or other deed?[54]

Acceptance of an offer must have no variation from the terms of that offer. "To be effective the acceptance must be unequivocal and unconditional, and it may not introduce any additional terms or conditions."[55] As already noted, counteroffers are considered rejections of offers. Additional terms are construed as outright rejections of original offers. However, requests for clarification of terms or explanation of price, conditions, or other matters are not construed as counteroffers. Evidence of acceptance can also be proven in various ways. The following illustrations highlight the methods of performance.

Methods of Acceptance

1. *Acceptance by overt acts*: Any offer that is responded to by mail, by sign, by conduct, by express declaration, by telegram, or by any other terms or conditions that are outlined in the offer are binding methods of acceptance.[56] "Ordinarily, the making of a promise is by overt action."[57]
2. *Acceptance by performance*: Under a unilateral contract whereby a promise will be honored upon the performance of an act, acceptance is evidenced by commencement of performance.[58] When the recipient of this partial performance balks at the enforceability of said contract, the basic principles of contract acceptance by performance will be applied because "honorable men do not repudiate their promises after part performance has been given or tendered."[59]
3. *Acceptance of prizes or rewards*: If an offeror promises that a prize or reward will be granted for specific conduct, such as the return of lost or stolen goods or animals or the apprehension of a specific criminal, the agreed conduct ensures the acceptance.
4. *Express acceptance by words*: Any express affirmation that can reasonably be interpreted as acceptance is viewed as binding on the offeree.
5. *Acceptance by forbearance from action*: A promise that the offeree will not sue, take legal action, or collect a debt or other forbearance constitutes an acceptance.
6. *Silence as a mode of acceptance*: An offeree who does not respond to an offer could hardly be construed as accepting its terms and conditions.[60] However, this situation can occur, particularly between merchants and other individuals who regularly conduct business with each other. Silence can also be inferred as a form of acceptance of or modification of existing contracts between parties who regularly contract.
7. *Acceptance by post—the "mailbox rule"*: The means and methods by which an offer is responded to can include telegraph, telephone, letter, fax, electronic imagery, or any other technique of transmission.[61] Certain governmental entities restrict acceptance to U.S. mail facilities, whose postmark controls the timing and legitimacy of acceptance.

   Acceptance by mail is generally found once the letter has been stamped and posted. In common parlance, this technique is known as the *mailbox rule*. "It is immaterial whether the letter or wire actually reaches the offeror, and the offer cannot be revoked or withdrawn unless the revocation reaches the offeree before the mailing or wiring of the acceptance."[62]

Based on the following facts, determine whether an acceptance has taken place:

> *John and Joe's Fuel Depot makes a formal offer to its preferred customers stating,*
> *"50,000 gallons of heating oil have just arrived at our terminal. In order to clear out old stock, we hereby offer you the right to purchase our heating oil at 40 cents per gallon. Acceptance to this offer may be by mail, telegraph, or telephone. April 15 is the last date to exercise your rights under this offer."*
> *On April 14, Allison's Oil Company writes in a note,*
> *"We hereby accept the offer to purchase your oil at 40 cents per gallon and desire delivery of 33,000 gallons."*
> *The offeror, John and Joe's Fuel Depot, advises Allison's Oil that they received the acceptance on April 17—after what they claimed was the duration of the offer.*

Because the letter was stamped, posted, and delivered, acceptance took place upon posting rather than upon actual delivery to John and Joe's Fuel Depot.

The *Restatement of Contracts* clarifies this stance:

> *An acceptance sent by mail or otherwise from a distance is not operative when dispatched, unless it is properly addressed and such other precautions taken as are ordinarily observed to insure safe transmission of similar messages.*[63]

The Uniform Commercial Code conforms to this general standard. Under §1-201(36), to send or to communicate an acceptance means the following:

> *"Send" in connection with a writing, record, or notice means (A) to deposit in the mail or deliver for transmission by any other usual means of communication with postage or cost of transmission provided for and properly addressed and, in the case of an instrument, to an address specified thereon or otherwise agreed, or if there be none to any address reasonable under the circumstances; or (B) in any other way to cause to be received any record or notice within the time it would have arrived if properly sent.*[64]

8. *Acceptance by written contract*: Common commercial practice is that buyers and sellers, merchants and vendors, and other parties in the regular course of business will submit written offers that are accepted by retention or no counteroffer. "Bills of sale, promissory notes, deeds, and many other writings are customarily signed by one of the contracting parties and delivered to another, who on receipt of the writing orally or by conduct acquiesces therein, and accepting it, holding, and acting on a contract may constitute an assent to its terms . . ."[65]

Revocation of Acceptance   Just as the offeror controls the terms, conditions, and nature of an offer, the offeree has a right to revoke acceptance in a timely fashion. Naturally, for an acceptance to be revoked, it must be halted before the original acceptance has been communicated to the offeror. Significant emphasis is placed on the requirement of notice—that the offeror has received word that any acceptances communicated subsequent to revocation notice are of no legal effect. Essentially this becomes a race between a valid acceptance and a withdrawal of that acceptance. To be effective, a revocation must be received by the offeror.[66]

Consideration

Bargained agreements without an incursion of debt, detriment consequence, or consideration are challengeable as valid contracts. "In the typical bargain, the consideration and the promise bear a reciprocal relation of motive or inducement: the consideration induces the making of the promise and the promise induces the furnishing of the consideration."[67]

In contract litigation, the advocates cannot simply banter about empty and superfluous verbiage between the parties. For the negotiations between parties to be taken seriously, consideration must exist, a serious exchange must occur, and a real-effort bargain must take place. Definitions of *consideration* are varied. The *Restatement of Contracts*[68] states this succinctly:

> *(1) To constitute consideration, a performance or a return promise must be bargained for.*
> *(2) A performance or return promise is bargained for if it is sought by the promisor in exchange for his promise and is given by the promisee in exchange for that promise.*
> *(3) The performance may consist of:*
> *(a) an act other than a promise, or*
> *(b) a forbearance, or*
> *(c) the creation, modification or destruction of a legal right.*[69]

In fundamental terms, consideration can be better described as detriment—a cost or a risk that the parties are taking assuring that their promises have some substance or meaning. Consider these illustrations:

Example 1

Sally offers to buy John's car for $4,000. John agrees.

This is a classic bargained-for exchange—cash for a car; both parties have a detriment.

Example 2

John refuses to accept the $4,000 for the car and says, "Since you are a good friend, you can have it." When he changes his mind, Sally sues on the theory of breach of contract.

This is not an enforceable contract because there is no solid consideration. (Can Sally sue on another theory?)

Illusory promises are generally not binding. However, "courts do not inquire into the adequacy of consideration, particularly where one or both of the values exchanged are difficult to measure."[70]

Example 3

A father tells his son that he knows the debt of $2,000 the son currently has on his real estate is too much of a burden for him. Father promises he will pay for it but tells the son to consider it as just a loan. Son agrees.

This is not a binding contract because the son has incurred no detriment.

Example 4

John tells his brother Steve that if he stops smoking and learns to take care of his health, he will give him $1,000 per year for each year he does not smoke. Steve ceases his smoking and at the end of one year asks for $1,000.

Most courts would hold that even though no economic detriment has been suffered by Steve, his forbearance (his denial of a previous habit) is considered proper and true consideration. Consideration can be noneconomic.

Legal duty, whether preexisting or subsequent, has been a questionable basis for finding consideration. Review this example:

A deputy sheriff in the state of North Carolina promises to apprehend a burglar in the county in which he has jurisdiction if the citizens suffering from this criminality will pay him an extra $2,000. Upon apprehension of the criminal, he seeks to collect and claims that legal consideration existed.

Because a legal duty already exists, no real obligation or risk is being taken by this law enforcement official.[71]

As long as the party asserting an enforceable contract can demonstrate that some legal obligation or detriment has occurred, a claim of consideration is justified and a contract will be deemed truly bargained for. Here are examples of the forms and types of consideration regularly seen in contract relations:

- Assignment of accounts receivable.
- Assignment of the right to litigate.
- Wages, compensation, dividends, bonuses, or money for specific services or activities.
- Execution of a promissory note.
- Refinancing of debt in exchange for increased services.
- A prenuptial agreement in contemplation of marriage that outlines property interests.
- Exchange of a third party's debt for services.
- Forbearance of a specific claim or defense.[72]

- Promise to pay indebtedness discharged in bankruptcy.[73]
- Promise to perform a duty despite nonoccurrence of a condition.[74]
- Promise to be a surety or guarantor.[75]
- Modification of an existing executory contract.[76]
- Any forbearance of an economic or other right.[77]

In summary, consideration may consist of performance or of a return promise. Consideration, by way of performance, may be a specified act of forbearance or any one of several specified acts or forbearances of which the offeree is given the choice or such conduct as will produce a specified result. The issue in any contractual analysis is whether or not offeror and offeree both have an obligation of corresponding benefit or detriment.

The exchange does not have to be equalized, nor must the valuation follow strict economic principles. "Valuation is left to private action in part because the parties are thought to be better able than others to evaluate the circumstances of particular transactions."[78] Hence the issue of adequacy of consideration is rarely a point of argument.

Promises that are illusory, conditional, impossible, or provisional generally will not support the consideration requirement. Consideration is faulty if it is based on any of the following premises:

- The promise is illusory—that is, impossible to fulfill and absurd in scope and design.
- Promises made relate to a preexisting duty—a legal duty either of the parties are already under an obligation to perform.
- The contract is supported by the payment of past consideration—funds the exchange of which is already negotiated under a previous legal obligation.
- Forbearance from bringing forth a lawsuit when one or the other party knows there is a completely invalid and illegal claim.
- Promises that are supported by criminal conduct or illegality that are logically voidable or unenforceable.

CONTRACT ENFORCEABILITY

Offers, acceptances, and their underlying consideration often pass legal muster, yet the contract will still be deemed unenforceable. Needless to say, many technical and substantive challenges in the law of contracts relate primarily to these areas. Some challenges relate to form:

- Does the contract contain all required provisions?
- Is the contract in writing?
- Are the appropriate signatures and executions on the document's face?
- Have there been any alterations or other suspect conduct in the drafting and finalization of the contract?
- Have there been appropriate filings as required by law?
- Does the agreement contain all terms and conditions between the parties and not violate technical rules of interpretation?

Other challenges relate to purpose:

- Does the agreement violate any law, ordinance, statute, or legal principle?
- Does the agreement have the potentiality for being declared void or voidable?
- Is the agreement a fair and rational expression of the parties' intent?
- Is the agreement unconscionable?
- Is the agreement usurious?
- Does the agreement violate a previous contract between the parties?
- Is the agreement an unreasonable restraint of trade under federal guidelines?

Still other challenges address the parties' participation, perception, and capacity:

- Are the parties to the contract competent?
- Are the parties to the contract of age?
- Are the parties to the contract mentally ill, emotionally disturbed, or suffering from other evidence of mental defect?
- Has there been a mistake of law or fact in the construction of the contract?
- Has there been a mistake in price, value, quality, or other terms and conditions under the Uniform Commercial Code?
- Have there been any fraudulent activities related to the construction and negotiation of the contract?
- Have any false statements or other misrepresentations been made?
- Has there been an exercise in the negotiation process of any undue influence or conduct best described as duress?

Certain issues regarding the formation of contracts and their related defenses always seem to crop up. An examination of these recurring problems follows.

Statute of Frauds

Although contractual negotiation and eventual formation may take various forms, many contracts are required to be formally written in order to be enforceable. The significance of this rule cannot be overstated. Even when a party has detrimentally relied on a fraudulent inducement, a claim based on a contract that was not in writing, and as a result was unenforceable, was not upheld. In *Propulsion Technologies v. PowerTech*, a Fifth Circuit Court of Appeals held,

> *Without a binding agreement, there is no detrimental reliance, and thus no fraudulent inducement claim. Because the foundational contract claim has not survived, there remains no legally sufficient basis to support a jury verdict.*[79]

A *writing* means just that—a series of written or otherwise recorded words or other documentation that evidences the intentions of the parties. An enforceable contract cannot be inferred from writings; rather, said writing must contain express terms and provisions to provide a basis for interpretation.[80]

All American jurisdictions employ a Statute of Frauds, which indicates that certain types of contracts need be memorialized in writing to be enforceable.[81] Furthermore, the documents constituting the contract must be signed; or, in the alternative, one document must be signed, so long as the others are significantly related to it.[82]

Under the *Restatement of Contracts*, certain classes of contracts are explicitly covered, including these:

> *(a) A contract of an executor or administrator to answer for a duty of his decedent;*
>
> *(b) A contract to answer for the duty of another (the suretyship provision);*
>
> *(c) A contract made upon consideration of marriage;*
>
> *(d) A contract for the sale of interest in land;*
>
> *(e) A contract that is not to be performed within one year from the making thereof.*[83]

Guidelines on the requirement of a writing for enforceability are fully covered in the U.C.C.

The U.C.C. also provides varied definitions of writing requirements for merchants. The standard under §2-201 is whether a person is in business and understands regular and customary business practices.

In Statute of Frauds analysis, a three-part inquiry is essential:

1. What is the subject matter of the contract? For example, is it realty? Is it for consumer goods over $500?
2. Has there been a sufficient writing, memorandum, or other documentation that meets the standards of common law or the statutory guidelines of the U.C.C.?
3. If the contract does fall within the statute and there is no writing, is there a doctrine or principle that would create an exception for it, such as promissory estoppel, waiver, or other equitable principle or rule?[84]

Paralegals in the typical law firm frequently come into contact with contracts that fall under the statute's governance—namely real estate contracts, contracts for the sale of goods, contracts for qualified executors and administrators under estate administration activities, suretyships and guarantor contracts, contracts for employment extending beyond one year, and contracts for construction or other activities of similar duration. But many contracts do not fall under the scope of the Statute of Frauds. Oral contracts, depending on the subject matter, are just as enforceable as those in written form. The U.C.C. promulgates formal requirements but fully recognizes a variety of transactions neither covered nor unenforceable if lacking a writing:

> (1) *Except as otherwise provided in this section, a contract for the sale of goods for the price of $500 or more is not enforceable by way of action or defense unless there is some writing sufficient to indicate that a contract for sale has been made between the parties and signed by the party against whom enforcement is sought or by his authorized agent or broker. A writing is not insufficient because it omits or incorrectly states a term agreed upon, but the contract is not enforceable under this paragraph beyond the quantity of goods shown in such writing.*
>
> (3) *A contract that does not satisfy the requirements of subsection (1) but which is valid in other respects is enforceable*
>> (a) *if the goods are to be specially manufactured for the buyer and are not suitable for sale to others in the ordinary course of the seller's business and the seller, before notice of repudiation is received and under circumstances which reasonably indicate that the goods are for the buyer, has made either a substantial beginning of their manufacture or commitments for their procurement; or*
>> (b) *if the party against whom enforcement is sought admits in his pleading, testimony, or otherwise in court that a contract for sale was made, but the contract is not enforceable under this provision beyond the quantity of goods admitted; or*
>> (c) *with respect to goods for which payment has been made and accepted or which have been received and accepted (Sec. 2-606).*

Remember that any contract less than one year in duration need not be in writing. Assignments and delegations of rights and duties need not necessarily be in writing. Any consumer transaction involving less than $500 also need not be in writing.[85]

Even if a writing is required, the contract's editorial sufficiency is of significant legal importance. *Restatement of Contracts* makes plain, under Section 131, that a writing will be sufficient if it accomplishes the following:

> (a) *Reasonably identifies the subject matter of the contract.*
> (b) *Is sufficient to indicate that a contract with respect thereto has been made between the parties as offered.*
> (c) *States with reasonable certainty the essential terms of the unperformed promises of the contract.*[86]

Signatories and attestations are technical criteria in the sufficiency of a writing. When clarification of intent is necessary, writings may be supplemented and interpreted using extrinsic documents, such as letters, telegrams, pleadings, depositions, and other evidence showing the usage and custom between the parties.

With the rise of e-commerce, the traditional understanding of the statute has been liberalized. What constitutes a writing and a required signature for said writing can now be electronically memorialized. Various national and international efforts to give predictable practices are evident in worldwide commerce.[87] A suggested legislative provision, the *e-Commerce Act of 2000*, lays out the integration of the "writing" requirement in the virtual world of commerce:

- Information (such as data, writing, or other text) cannot be denied legal effect, validity, or enforceability simply because it is in electronic form (section 9).

- Where a person is required by law or contract to give information in writing, then, in general, this may be given in electronic form by e-mail or otherwise. This would include making an application or request, lodging a claim or return, and recording and disseminating a court order (section 12).

- Where law or contract requires a person to sign a document, this may be given in electronic form (section 13).

- Contracts may not be denied legal effect simply because they are in electronic form (section 19).
- The courts may not deny the admissibility into evidence of documents, information, communications, and contracts simply because they are in electronic form (section 22).

Parol Evidence Rule

Parol evidence is a rule of document interpretation offered to contradict or modify a writing. Generally, extrinsic evidence is not admissible when the writing is ambiguous or was intended to be a final expression of the author's wishes. Contracts should be fully integrated, meaning all terms, conditions, words, and intentions of the parties are within the confines of the contract document. Some see a contract as representing an uncoordinated series of documentations needing extrinsic evidence to interpret contract content—evidence like outside memos or oral conversations. Courts prefer fully integrated documents and call upon a traditional rule to ensure the integrity of such documents: the *parol evidence rule.* By no means is the rule readily mastered. Professor Ralph James Mooney of the Oregon Law School remarks that the "parol evidence rule is so dark and difficult" that there is no "definitive statement of the rule."[88]

Although the rule can sometimes undermine the express provisions of an integrated document, the parol evidence rule seeks to give greatest weight to the final formalized contract between the parties. The contract document is viewed as the final embodiment of negotiations between parties, thereby excluding evidence that alters, varies, contradicts, subtracts, or adds conditions and terms or other information beyond the stated language.

Long considered a rule of "prior" evidence, parol evidence consists of oral or written material that is preliminary to the final formalization of the contract. "Everything that transpires prior to the execution of the written contract is assumed to be integrated into it. The written contract is deemed the only permissible evidence of the agreement."[89] In this sense, the parol evidence rule "determines whether a party may add a term to a written contract."[90]

As a fundamental proposition, evidence of prior discussions outside the document itself is not admissible. If ambiguity exists within the contract document, parol evidence permits a look at extrinsic material or other documentation referenced in the underlying contract—such as a letter or memo. In this sense, the four corners of the contract are not fully integrated but rather are dependent on outside sources. Corbin sets out three queries when determining the suitability of parol evidence:

1. Have the parties made a contract?
2. Is that contract void or voidable because of illegality, fraud, mistake, or any other reason?
3. Did the parties assent to a particular writing as the complete and accurate "integration" of that contract?[91]

The use of parol evidence to clarify any of these issues is a legitimate exercise. Although we must respect the four corners approach, in these instances something extrinsic is essential to understanding and interpretation. Corbin further notes,

> On these issues, no relevant evident, whether parol or otherwise, is excluded. No written document is sufficient, standing alone, to determine any one of them, however long and detailed it may be, however formal, and however many may be the seals and signatures and assertions. No one of these issues can be determined by mere inspection of the written document.[92]

The Uniform Commercial Code provides an exception to the integration doctrine at §2-202:

> Terms with respect to which the confirmatory memoranda of the parties agree or which are otherwise set forth in a writing intended by the parties as a final expression of their agreement with respect to such terms as are included therein may not be contradicted by evidence of any prior agreement or of a contemporaneous oral agreement but may be explained or supplemented
>
> (a) by course of performance, course of dealing, or usage of trade (Section 1-303); and
> (b) by evidence of consistent additional terms unless the court finds the writing to have been intended also as a complete and exclusive statement of the terms of the agreement.[93]

The rule will not exclude evidence that explains, clarifies, or supplements the agreement by the parties. Although the rule functions with exceptions, critics charge that it has little utility. The rule also does not preclude the use of evidence that demonstrates fraud, misrepresentation, duress, mistake, custom, prior course of dealing, or similar matters. "The rule also does not exclude evidence of a prior agreement that the writing was not intended to be a contract at all or that the entire agreement was subject to a condition precedent. If the writing or any portion of it is ambiguous, extrinsic evidence may be used to show the intended meaning of the ambiguous portions."[94]

Paralegals should be wary of documentation that is contemporaneous to a signed, formalized contract. Documents that seek to explain what is already executed and signed by the parties should be strictly scrutinized.

Incapacity

An individual's ability to contract depends on various factors, including mental state, state of intoxication, and age. "A party without mental capacity to contract can avoid the contract or defend on lack of mental capacity."[95] Thus capacity becomes a question of understanding or conceptual awareness, and the individual asserting a lack of capacity to a contract must demonstrate that he or she failed to understand the nature, purpose, and effect of that contract.

A party who successfully asserts a lack of competency or capacity to contract will have a once valid contract declared voidable. A paralegal may come in contact with minors entering contracts with retailers, auto dealerships, or other individuals by their own volition. By their minority, they are considered infants who lack contractual capacity. As a matter of public policy, the law does not close the door on a joint effort between the minor and the retailer, if the minor secures the approval of a party in a position to supervise and ratify the eventual contract. However, most courts hold that minors have the right to disaffirm contracts and to avoid general liability. "A minor's contract which is voidable can be disaffirmed either by the minor himself or by his guardian before he attains his majority or by the minor himself within a reasonable time after reaching majority."[96]

More than one jurisdiction also has rules regarding the capacity to contract for what are deemed as *necessaries*—things that the individual needs regardless of his capacity to contract, such as expenses for education, food, or other goods or services regularly viewed as necessities in life.[97]

On another front, a lack of capacity can be argued as a defense to a contract if the person has been adjudged mentally ill or legally insane. A contract formed by one declared incompetent prior to its formation is void. A contract formed before declaration is voidable. In the case of an insane party, a contract entered into is not a willing or volitional act, and the party who defends on lack of capacity may seek a rescission of that contract. Courts have declared these exchanges as either void or voidable depending on the circumstances.

Illegality

Discussed previously was the influence of illegality on the continuing viability of a contract. A contract that directly violates the law is contrary to public policy and ordinarily will be construed as void or voidable. "When an agreement is illegal, the parties are usually not entitled to the aid of the courts. If the illegal agreement has not been performed, neither party can sue the other to obtain performance. If the agreement has been performed, either party can sue the other for damages to set it aside."[98]

Contracts formulated in violation of licensing laws, statutes or ordinances or those criminal in design automatically fall within this classification. Some federal circuit courts have dealt with allegations relative to usury violations.[99] Contracts promoting civil wrongs or contracts made in restraint of trade or in violation of federal statutes such as the Sherman Antitrust Act, the Clayton Act, or the Federal Trade Commission Act will be declared void for illegality. Fraudulent sales, usurious agreements charging interest rates that exceed statutory standards, and agreements not to compete that are onerous and unfair in the stream of commerce can be declared void for their underlying illegality. Of recent interest has been the inadequate resolution of agreements that involve frozen embryos and sperm. How enforceable are these contracts? Are these contracts in violation of some particular law or public policy? Have state legislatures even dealt with this novel subject matter? Kim Pittman argues that the legislatures have dropped the ball because advocates have been "pleading for legislative guidance."[100]

Closely tied to the defense of illegality is the doctrine of unconscionability, a modern statutory and case law legal remedy that goes to the equity ("fairness") of a contract despite its stated language and provisions. Courts are not in the business of becoming social service agencies and should not serve as arbiters of what is a generally fair or intelligent contract. However, there are instances when provisions of a contract, its clauses and conditions, are so utterly oppressive in construction that judicial intervention is deemed just.

Under the Uniform Commercial Code at §1-201(20), the principles of unconscionability have been implied by the following definition of good faith:

> *"Good faith," except as otherwise provided in Article 5, means honesty in fact and the observance of reasonable commercial standards of fair dealing.*[101]

The U.C.C., in its warranty provisions, either express or implied in nature,[102] tends to impose on merchants in the commercial framework some level of reasonable conduct in the drafting and construction of contracts. U.C.C. §2-302, under its general obligation and construction of contract provisions on unconscionability, states,

> (1) *If the court as a matter of law finds the contract or any clause of the contract to have been unconscionable at the time it was made, the court may refuse to enforce the contract, or it may enforce the remainder of the contract without the unconscionable clause, or it may so limit the application of any unconscionable clause as to avoid any unconscionable result.*
>
> (2) *When it is claimed or appears to the court that the contract or any clause thereof may be unconscionable, the parties shall be afforded a reasonable opportunity to present evidence as to its commercial setting, purpose, and effect to aid the court in making the determination.*[103]

This style of judicial intervention has critics. Unconscionability—the determination that something is unfair in the business and consumer sector—is a finding based on subjective and objective standards, though some have argued that said judgment is essentially subjective on its face.[104] "The fact that a contract is a bad bargain does not make it unconscionable. Moreover, unconscionability is to be determined in light of the circumstances existing at the time when the contract was made."[105]

Under U.C.C. §2-302 the parameters of unconscionability are less than certain and heavily reliant on subjective reasoning; terms like "unfairness, inequalities in bargaining power, overreaching, oppression"[106] appear to be the legal measure. Is this good law? Does it not supplant the intentionality of the parties? "How far can and should a court go in policing a bargain which is one-sided yet where the party seeking relief was fully informed? What factors other than oppression and surprise justify nonenforcement? Economic necessity where the seller has a monopoly and exacts an unreasonable price? A 'one-sided' bargain where the seller has a superior bargaining position?"[107]

Some of the factors listed here may bear on this issue of unconscionability:

- Price versus product.
- Intelligence level of purchaser or buyer.
- Language barriers between the buyer and seller.
- Credit terms.
- Extraordinary remedies provided upon default.
- Custom and usage in the industry and business.

Would it be reasonable for a refrigerator that costs $3,000 to the world market to be sold for $20,000 to an unsophisticated buyer?

Mistake

Mistake as to the facts, conditions, and intentions of the parties is often asserted in the defense of a contract. Mistake can be either unilateral or mutual. Generally unilateral mistakes are not accorded a remedy in law, whereas bilateral mistakes will be afforded a legal remedy. Under *Restatement of Contracts* §152 a mutual mistake is outlined:

> (1) *Where a mistake of both parties at the time a contract was made as to a basic assumption on which the contract was made has a material effect on the agreed exchange of performances, the contract is voidable by the adversely affected party unless he bears the risk of the mistake under the rule stated in Section 154.*
>
> (2) *In determining whether a mistake has a material effect on the agreed exchange of performances, account is taken of any relief by way of reformation, restitution, or otherwise.*[108]

A mistake cannot be peripheral or incidental to the nature of the contract. The mistake must be "material"—going to the essence of the enforcement of the legal obligations and significant to the contract in total. Mere disagreements over terms or language that do not hit the heart of the contract will not provide a basis for this defense.

Mistake as enunciated in the American Law Institute's *Restatement of Contracts* must relate to the "basic assumption" of the contract. "Relief is only appropriate in situations where a mistake of both parties has such a material effect on the agreed exchange of performances as to upset the very basis of the contract."[109] To be aware of the mistake is the initial hurdle for the proponent of this defense.

Consider parties to a real estate contract during negotiations. The price communicated to the seller is higher than the buyer wished to pay. The contract price was incorrectly transcribed. However, the seller is happy with the result and accepts. The buyer would have to bear the cost of the specific mistake unless she can demonstrate that the seller was well aware that there was a mistake in the transmission of the offer.

Mistakes are common in pricing, quality, descriptions of goods or services, and expectations. There are general principles of contract regarding reformation, rescission, or defense based on mistake. The courts eventually must make decisions based on whether the risk ought to be borne by the mistaken party or whether the mistake was truly mutual. "Courts are influenced by the negligence, conscious ignorance, and unequal knowledge of the mistake by any party."[110]

To be permitted a defense of mistake, the proponent of such a defense must demonstrate that it strikes at the heart of the bargained-for exchange; that it is material in nature and scope; that it is an error that both parties are aware of; that to enforce the contract would result in a serious hardship, risk, or even unconscionable result; that either party was grossly negligent; and that prompt notice and a request for reformation took place immediately upon discovery. A pleading asserting the mistake defense is shown in Form 5.3 on the accompanying CD.

Misrepresentation

Contracts that are born of a lie should receive little or no legal protection, except for the innocent party. Contracts should be the result of a volitional exchange, unencumbered by trickery or other subterfuge. Asserting misrepresentation as a defense to a contract calls for proof that material allegations made were patently false, and that in reliance upon these misrepresentations the offeree entered into the agreement. Misrepresentation may take many forms, including written or oral assertions or even pure silence. A misrepresentation is an assertion that is not in accord with the facts. It is basically a nontruth.[111]

Misrepresentation must go to the crux of the contract's intention, the relevant subject matter, the deal itself. For example, any lie or misrepresentation regarding a product's capacity and functionality; an employee's skills, education, and proficiencies for a selected position; or the value of precious stones may give rise to the defense of misrepresentation. Even a failure to disclose essential facts, as often occurs in real property with termite damage, latent defects, or radon problems, can lead a court to determine that a misrepresentation has taken place.

Just as the mistake must relate to the basic assumption of the contract, so too must the misrepresentation. As the *Restatement of Contracts* clarifies,

> *(1) A misrepresentation is fraudulent if the maker intends his assertion to induce a party to manifest his assent and the maker*
> *(a) knows or believes that the assertion is not in accord with the facts, or*
> *(b) does not have the confidence that he states or implies in the truth of the assertion, or*
> *(c) knows that he does not have the basis that he states or implies for the assertion.*[112]

Some of the examples listed here are blatant misrepresentations:

- Changing the odometer on a used motor vehicle.
- Switching engines on a late model motor vehicle.
- Claiming that computer equipment is compatible with certain software when it is not.
- Claiming that a company has skill and expertise in bricklaying when it has no employee who can lay bricks.

For a case of misrepresentation to be upheld, the victim of a misrepresentation must be able to demonstrate some type of detriment based on justifiable reliance. In other words, the party who entered a contract based on a misrepresentation was innocent and unaware, and the decision to contract was guided by false affirmations. A party who knows and is aware of specific latent defects and still enters a contract will have a difficult time asserting reliance. A party who knows or is aware of a specific zoning or ordinance problem that may be coming up in a municipality regarding the transfer of land cannot be held to have justifiably relied on that misrepresentation.

QUILL v. NEWBERRY
238 GA. APP. 184 (GA. CT. APP. 1999)
ELDRIDGE, JUDGE

Plaintiff/appellant Robert Quill appeals from an order of the Superior Court of DeKalb County granting defendant/appellee Scott Newberry's motion for summary judgment on Quill's complaint in equity seeking to rescind a contract of sale for Newberry's former residence based on fraud. Quill contends that said contract was induced by Newberry's allegedly fraudulent misrepresentations about and concealment of an active termite infestation. Because the evidence in this case is in conflict and raises factual issues to be decided by a jury, we conclude that the trial court's grant of summary judgment was error.

Viewed in a light most favorable to the nonmoving party, i.e., Quill, the evidence shows that appellee Scott Newberry purchased a townhouse located at 892 Argonne Avenue in midtown Atlanta, DeKalb County. At that time, a wooden addition had already been added to the ground floor of the back of the house. The addition served as a sunroom/eating area annexed to the kitchen. The floor of the addition was of the same aged hexagonal tile that covered the kitchen floor.

Newberry lived in the house for five years, from February 1992 through July 1997. After moving into the house, Newberry had installed sheetrock walls in the kitchen and addition. By 1997, the sheetrock showed places where the drywall had been repaired since Newberry installed it. Also in January 1997, Newberry replaced a small area rug that for the prior five years had partially covered the center of the addition's tile floor. In its stead, Newberry installed a wall-to-wall carpet that covered the addition's tile floor from baseboard to baseboard. Newberry laid the carpet using carpet tacking strips around the entire perimeter of the floor to ensure that the carpet stayed down. "In the course of installing [the] carpet, [Newberry] saw every inch of the border of that room." Shortly after installing the wall-to-wall carpet, Newberry placed the house for sale-by-owner.

Appellant Robert Quill saw the for-sale-by-owner sign and called about the house. Quill arranged to walk through the house with Newberry. At that time, Newberry told Quill that the residence was a "turnkey" house, meaning to both men that the house was in perfect condition and the purchaser could move in immediately. Newberry also told Quill that he had a continuous contract with an exterminator and that someone came and sprayed once a year.

Quill put a contract on the house. As required by law, Newberry provided to Quill a Seller's Disclosure Form. In that form, Newberry specifically stated that he had no "knowledge of termites, dry rot, or pests on or affecting the property"; that he had no "knowledge of any damage to the property caused by termites, dry rot, or pests"; that his property is "currently under warranty or other coverage by a licensed pest control company"; and that he did not "know of any termite/pest control reports or treatments for the property in the last five years[.]" In addition, Newberry wrote by hand, "Have regular House treatments."

Prior to closing on the house, Quill had a licensed inspector, Ed Gibson, walk through the house. Although Gibson's contract to inspect the house specifically excluded any inspection for termites or termite damage, he would have noted such damage in his report if it had been visible. Gibson noted no damage.

In addition, five minutes before the July 17, 1997, closing on the property was completed, Norman Terrell of Northwest Exterminating arrived with the requisite termite inspection letter, which letter stated that there was no evidence of active termite infestation in the residence. Terrell did not inspect the inside of the house prior to preparing the letter.

The closing was on Wednesday, July 16, 1997. On Saturday, July 19, 1997, Quill arrived at his new house with tools, painting equipment, and two friends to help him. Quill intended to repaint the walls and to refinish the floors. He started in the addition where he pulled up the new carpet. "In . . . the far corner, it was immediately obvious that the floor was sunken. The floor along that one wall . . . was all soft and squishy. And in that corner there was foam coming up around the hexagonal or whatever the shapes of the tile was. The tiles were loose and could be easily picked up, which I did pick up. And it was obvious to me that there was an insect infestation there which I believed to be termites." At that time, Quill enlisted the aid of his friends, and they followed the infestation from the floor itself into the floorboards and up behind the sheetrock walls of the addition. "All three walls the floor and the ceiling [of the addition were] all affected with termite infestation and substantial damage." As Quill pulled open the sheetrock, he followed the infestation into the kitchen and behind the kitchen cabinets. "It was an obvious trail of where the damage was and where the termite damage was, and I continued to explore. And in fact in the exploration in taking sheetrock out and everything, the termites were falling out all over my arms and biting my arms. . . . There were thousands of them."

Further investigation showed that holes had been drilled into the ground outside of the house behind the addition. The holes extended into the back of the house below the ground level. Structural insulating foam had been injected through the holes and up under the collapsed corner of the addition's floor, thereby propping up the floor. The hardened foam had bits of wood in it, demonstrating that the floor was eaten through at the time the foam was injected. Thereafter, the holes on the outside of the house had been covered with concrete. Residual traces of the foam could be seen on the concrete. White landscape gravel had been placed over the concrete, thereby masking it. In the addition, besides the wall-to-wall carpet which concealed the condition of the wood floor, mesh tape had been placed over damaged areas of drywall and then patched and painted over. Estimates placed the amount of termite damage as high as $45,000. Upon order from the Department of Agriculture, Northwest Exterminators informed Quill that they would treat the back addition upon demolition or removal of the entire floor.

Quill immediately filed a complaint seeking to rescind the contract, obtain the money he put down on the house, and return to the status quo. . . .

Newberry also filed the instant motion for summary judgment based upon the record. Inter alia, the record includes:

(a) Newberry's testimony that he did not know about the termite infestation and that, when he installed the wall-to-wall carpet in the addition just before he put the house on the market, he saw no loose tiles, no cracked tiles, no foam coming through the tiles, no damage to the floor around the baseboards, and the floor was solid.

   However, the record also contains multiple pictures taken only six months after the carpet was installed and showing the extent of the termite infestation and damage to the floor of the addition, including the damaged appearance of the tiles, cracked tiles, the appearance of the insulating foam coming between loose tiles, and the extensively damaged flooring around the perimeter of the floor near the baseboards. Quill also testified regarding the fact that the damage to the floor of the addition was immediately apparent once the wall-to-wall carpet was removed. Further, Quill testified that the damage was estimated at $45,000.

(b) Evidence that prior to the sale of the house, Newberry represented to Quill, both orally and on the Seller's Disclosure Form, that Newberry had a continuous pest control contract and that the house was "treated regularly."

   However, the record also contains Newberry's testimony, subsequent to the sale, that he did not have the house treated regularly and that he never had a continuous pest control contract. Norman Terrell, the representative of Northwest Exterminating who Newberry previously alleged treated the house regularly, testified that he had treated the house only once several years earlier for black ants.

(c) Newberry's testimony that a handyman he hired, Roger Amburgy, never "restructured" the back of the house at Newberry's request: "No, [Amburgy] did not restructure the back of the house, no"; Amburgy would not "have done something [Newberry] had not asked him to do"; and if Newberry paid Amburgy for work, "it was not only completed but it was also completed at [Newberry's] request."

   However, the record also includes a paid invoice from Amburgy to Newberry for 18.5 hours over two days spent "restructuring the back of the house."

(d) Newberry's testimony that Amburgy did not "patch and paint drywall" in the kitchen and addition, the only rooms in the house that had sheetrock, not plaster.

   However, the record also contains Amburgy's paid invoice for "paint and patch drywall, ten hours."

(e) Newberry's testimony that during the inspection for the termite letter, Norman Terrell "went in and out of every room."

   However, the record also contains Terrell's testimony that during the inspection for the termite letter, "I [Terrell] did not inspect the interior of the home."

Although the trial court had found that "the evidence is in conflict" when previously denying Quill's motion for interlocutory injunction, the trial court granted Newberry's motion for summary judgment. In so doing, the trial court noted that Newberry had unequivocally stated that he did not know of the termite infestation. Citing our recent case of Supchak v. Pruitt, 232 Ga. App. 680 (503 S.E.2d 581) (1998), the trial court held that,

Plaintiff's inferences disappear in the face of defendant's uncontradicted and unimpeached evidence. The court finds that the evidence is undisputed that defendant Newberry did not know of the termite infestation and that there is no evidence sufficient to create a jury issue on the element of scienter.

Held:

1. In his first enumeration of error, Quill contends that the trial court erred in finding that Newberry's sworn denial of knowledge of the termite infestation negated any circumstantial evidence to the contrary and thereby created no issue of fact for the jury to determine. Quill argues that, if, as is almost always the case, the defendant simply denies his fraudulent conduct under oath, under [the trial court's] approach, absent an eyewitness to the fraudulent conduct, there is no recovery for fraud, as any contrary circumstantial evidence simply "disappears" in the face of a sworn denial. We agree.

(a) The standards applicable to motions for summary judgment generally are announced in Lau's Corp. v. Haskins, 261 Ga. 491 (405 S.E.2d 474) [(1991)]. When ruling on a motion for summary judgment, the opposing party should be given the benefit of all reasonable doubt, and the court should construe the evidence and all inferences and conclusions therefrom most favorably toward the party opposing the motion. Further, when reviewing the grant or denial of a motion for summary judgment, this court conducts a de novo review of the law and the evidence.

(b) Since fraud is inherently subtle, slight circumstances of fraud may be sufficient to establish a proper case. Proof of fraud is seldom ever susceptible of direct proof, thus recourse to circumstantial evidence usually is required. Moreover, it is peculiarly the province of the jury to pass on these circumstances showing fraud. Except in plain and indisputable cases, scienter in actions based on fraud is an issue of fact for jury determination.

(c) Generally, if a defendant did not deny scienter as to what otherwise would be a fraudulent act, neither litigation nor subsequent appeal would even be necessary. Thus, if scienter in a fraud case is normally proved through circumstantial evidence raising inferences to contradict a defendant's denial of scienter, then such inferences cannot be negated simply through the defendant's denial, itself. This is why scienter is "peculiarly" a jury issue; it deals with the choice of what to believe regarding a subjective state of mind seldom capable of direct proof. Clearly, making a choice as to what to believe has no place in summary judgment, which is granted "only where the evidence is plain, palpable, and undisputable." Robinson v. Kroger Co., 268 Ga. 735, 739 (1) (493 S.E.2d 403) (1997).

. . .

(e) Here, the evidence includes the timing of the laying of the wall-to-wall carpet covering the termite-damaged floor in relation to the sale of the home; the extent of the termite damage that was readily apparent when the carpet was removed; the taping, painting, and patching of the addition's sheetrock walls which were otherwise ravaged with termite damage; Newberry's false representation that the house was treated regularly for termites and that he had a contract therefor; Newberry's "restructuring the back of the house" where the termite infestation and damage was at its worst; evidence of the extent of the infestation, including that there were "thousands" of termites in the floor, ceiling, and falling out of the walls; and evidence that $45,000 worth of termite damage had been done to the house, making necessary the removal of the entire floor. This evidence raises the inferences that Newberry was aware of the termite infestation, sought to mask it, and falsely represented to Quill that the house was without a termite problem in order to induce Quill to purchase the property. Contrary to the trial court's finding, Newberry's sworn statement that he did not know of the infestation does not make the above-referenced inferences "disappear," but instead creates a jury issue as to scienter. The trial court's grant of summary judgment was error.

. . .

Judgment reversed. Pope, P. J., and Smith, J., concur.

Finally, if reliance is demonstrated, some measure of damages must be proven. Damages are usually economic in form—the value of a lost bargain or any out-of-pocket expenses incurred in the defense of a contract, such as legal expenses and loss of business due to the contract's defense. Punitive damages are also awardable, depending on the willful or intentional conduct of the person who made such misrepresentation.[113]

Duress or Undue Influence

As elaborated thus far, free will and the volitional capacities of the parties are extremely important in contract formation. Contracts that result from threats, force, coercion, duress, and undue influence do not evidence mutual assent or a meeting of the minds.

Undue influence can take many forms, including physical threats against an individual; threats to leak certain embarrassing information; threats against the professional standing of an individual; threats of criminal prosecution; threats with civil process; and threats that border on extortion, unfair persuasion, or domination of a party in a contractual relationship. Under the *Restatement of Contracts*, conduct constituting duress will make a contract voidable and ineffectual:

> *If a party's manifestation of assent is induced by an improper threat by the other party that leaves the victim no reasonable alternative, the contract is voidable by the victim.*
> *If a party's manifestation of assent is induced by one who is not a party to the transaction, the contract is voidable by the victim unless the other party to the transaction in good faith and without reason to know of the duress either gives value or relies materially on the transaction.*[114]

In any situation in which an unequal bargaining position exists (not limited to economic inequality) or an aura of mental domination or control is apparent, the defense of duress or undue influence may be pertinent. Certain types of individuals often fall prey to unfair bargaining arrangements, including the elderly, the feeble-minded, the incompetent, and certain minors.[115]

Breach of Warranty

A contract may have express clauses or conditions regarding warranty. A warranty is a promise that certain goods, services, or activities will be delivered or performed in a certain way. Under common law, contractual analysis, and the statutory authority[116] of the Uniform Commercial Code, these warranty arguments can be categorized:

- Breach of warranty of title in the sale or transfer of goods (see U.C.C. §2-312).
- Breach of express warranties under U.C.C. §2-313.
- Breach of implied warranties of merchantability (see U.C.C. §2-314).
- Breach of implied warranty for fitness for a particular purpose (see U.C.C. §2-315).
- Breach of implied warranty arising out of the course of dealing or trade usage (see U.C.C. §2-314 (3)).

Any party to a contract who desires to defend based on nonperformance or nonpayment due to defective design may have the right to argue a warranty defense.

Express Warranties

Express warranties are readily accepted and used in the commercial marketplace. The traditional consumer comes in contact with this form of assurance in the purchase of an automobile, television set, refrigerator, or other consumer durable. U.C.C. §2-313 (1) states that express warranties are created as follows:

> (a) *Any affirmation of fact or promise made by the seller to the buyer which relates to the goods and becomes part of the basis of the bargain creates an express warranty that the goods shall conform to the affirmation or promise.*
>
> (b) *Any description of the goods which is made part of the basis of the bargain creates an express warranty that the goods shall conform to the description.*
>
> (c) *Any sample or model which is made part of the basis of the bargain creates an express warranty that the whole of the goods shall conform to the sample or model.*[117]

Express warranties are generally written or are affirmations within the salesperson's presentation or referenced in the sales agreement. Such a warranty should be a direct, clear statement of how the product or services will perform or be performed. No specific words or descriptive terms are necessary to create a warranty—just any affirmation of fact or promise made by a seller to a buyer. In finding a warranty, paralegals must again distinguish pure puffery and opinion from legal obligation. As a rule, a buyer who relies on opinions of a seller, whether through oral or written promise, description, or affirmation, can argue the express warranty theory.

Accordingly, a car dealer who says that an auto power train will last either seven years or 70,000 miles has made an undeniable affirmation of warranty. Express warranties are not strictly guided by the Uniform Commercial Code because any contractual drafter may make specific express warranties or affirmations in a contract regarding the suitability of a product or a service. See Figure 5.2 for an example of an express warranty.

An express warranty is created by "[a]ny affirmation of fact or promise made by the seller to the buyer which relates to the goods and becomes part of the basis of the bargain."[118] "It is not necessary to the creation of an express warranty that the seller use formal words such as 'warrant' or 'guarantee' or that the seller have a specific intention to make a warranty . . ."[119] Nor is it necessary for the promise or affirmation of fact to be incorporated into a written document; oral representations may create an express warranty, even between sophisticated commercial parties.[120]

In product defect cases, the breadth and extent of the warranty remedy may pull in a bevy of parties. "An express warranty may also be available against the seller or intermediate distributor as well as the manufacturer and designer of said product."[121] In express warranty cases, the

FIGURE 5.2
Example of an Express Warranty

Source: Cargo Express 708 S. Division St., Bristol, IN 46507. Phone: 574-848-7441; fax: 574-848-9372; http://www.cargoexpress.com/php/register.trailer/index.php.

J & L's Cargo Express, Inc., Bristol, Indiana 46507 (Cargo Express) hereby warrants the Cargo Express product line for a period of three (3) years to the original purchaser. This warranty covers defects in material and workmanship performed by Cargo Express, but does not include warranties on specific components used within this product line. Certain individual components are warranted by the supplier for their own products and such products are covered by a separate warranty. This includes tires, wheels, axles, couplers, jacks, light fixtures, fiberglass parts, windows, and so forth. Cargo Express does not warrant components warranted by the supplier. Excluded from this three (3) warranty are seals and sealants, doors and windows, fiberglass parts, electrical and paint and undercoating, which are warranted for a period of one (1) year from the date of purchase for the original purchaser. On component parts, the warranty must be filed with the respective component manufacturer for their warranty claims. The Cargo Express warranty will be honored only if the product is returned to Cargo Express or a repair facility authorized by Cargo Express. Reasonable notification and time must be allowed for performance of all warranty repairs. Any service charges, towing charges, or transportation charges are the responsibility of the purchaser and will not be paid by Cargo Express. Loss of time inconvenience, loss of use of trailer, rental of substitute equipment, loss of revenues, or other commercial loss is not covered by this warranty. This warranty is void if the product has been abused, overloaded, neglected, misused, or made to perform beyond the normal use for which the product was intended. Cargo Express reserves the right for final determination whether or not the product has been misused or abused by the initial purchaser.

proponent need not show fault because the "warranty represents a promise by the seller to the buyer, about some aspect of the good's performance or quality, which the buyer relied upon in purchasing the good."[122]

Implied Warranty of Merchantability

The U.C.C. expands traditional warranty analysis under its doctrine of implied warranty of merchantability. The merchantability standard is that certain goods, regardless of the existence of an affirmation, do possess functional, provable characteristics like a shelf life, an engineering capacity, or durability in performance. For a product to be merchantable in an implied sense, performance is governed by these standards:

> (a) pass without objection in the trade under the contract description; and
>
> (b) in the case of fungible goods, are of fair average quality within the description; and
>
> (c) are fit for the ordinary purposes for which such goods are used; and
>
> (d) run, within the variations permitted by the agreement, of even kind, quality, and quantity within each unit and among all units involved; and
>
> (e) are adequately contained, packaged, and labeled as the agreement may require; and
>
> (f) conform to the promise or affirmations of fact made on the container or label if any.[123]

This less than striking description of what a merchantable good is indicates the minimal standard of what is a commercially acceptable product. All products must operate for ordinary purposes, not a Herculean endeavor. Fungible goods must be fair, average, and generally acceptable rather than inferior or superior. At a minimum, the world expects an average product. Figure 5.3 shows a limited warranty.

Implied Warranty of Fitness for a Particular Purpose

An implied warranty lacks the express language of the express warranty. The warranty is "essentially an implied promise by the seller of a product that the product will meet the particular

FIGURE 5.3
Example of a Limited Warranty

Source: PIAA Corporation USA, 15370 SW Millikan Way, Beaverton, OR 97006. Telephone: 503-643-7422; fax: 503-643-9144; http://www.piaa.com/Lamps/PIAAWarranty.html.

With the exception of bulbs, PIAA Corporation, USA ("PIAA") warrants its products to be free from defects in workmanship and materials under normal use for as long as the original purchaser owns them.

EXCLUSIONS   This Limited Warranty specifically excludes defects resulting from misuse, abuse, neglect, alteration, modification, improper installation, unauthorized repairs, submersion, theft, vehicle crash, or by any other type of impact. Except for the Limited Warranty stated above, there are no warranties of PIAA products or any part thereof, whether express or implied. Any implied warranty of merchantability or any warranty of fitness for a particular purpose is expressly disclaimed. Some states do not permit the disclaimer of implied warranties.

EXCLUSION OF DAMAGES   In no event shall PIAA be liable for any damages whatsoever (including, without limitation, consequential damages, incidental damages, or damages for loss of use, loss of business profits, business interruption, loss of business information, loss of time, inconvenience, or other losses) arising out of the use, misuse, or inability to use a PIAA product. PIAA reserves the right to change the design its products without any obligation to modify any previous product. This warranty gives you specific legal rights. You may also have other rights that vary from state to state.

REPAIR OR REPLACEMENT   If a PIAA product is suspected of being defective, it must be submitted freight prepaid, to either an authorized dealer or distributor for warranty inspection. The receipt or other proof of purchase and a description of the problem must be included. The returned product will be inspected. If the product is found to be defective and covered by this Limited Warranty, the sole remedy is repair or replacement, at PIAA's option. A repaired or replacement product will be shipped back at no charge, and will be warranted to be free from defects in workmanship and materials under normal use for as long as the original purchaser owns it. Removal, installation, or reinstallation costs are not covered by this Limited Warranty.

or special needs of the buyer."[124] U.C.C. §2-315 covers products or goods for a specific or particular purpose. Its provisions include the following language:

> *Where the seller at the time of contracting has reason to know any particular purpose for which the goods are required and that the buyer is relying on the seller's skill or judgment to select or furnish suitable goods, there is unless excluded or modified under the next section an implied warranty that the goods shall be fit for such purpose.*[125]

Under this protective language, buyers who explain their needs and requirements accurately expect a specific product or design to meet this expectation. An individual who seeks a tractor that can cut rough-hewn land should not be expected to tolerate the referral of a lawn mower that cannot cut more than one-inch-high grass. So it goes with literally any product that is designed for a specific purpose—such as storage containers for nuclear fuel, truck engines to haul gross poundage of goods, or a precision instrument capable of cutting through stainless steel. "On the other hand, goods do not have to be flawless or perfectly safe to be merchantable."[126] Under Arkansas law the claim or cause under Arkansas Code Annotated § 4-2-314 states the following:

> *Where the seller at the time of contracting has reason to know any particular purpose for which the goods are required and that the buyer is relying on the seller's skill or judgment to select or furnish suitable goods, there is unless excluded or modified under the next section an implied warranty that the goods shall be fit for such purpose.*[127]

Before this doctrine applies, the buyer must be able to demonstrate a specific reliance on the seller's skill, judgment, and knowledge regarding the selection and furnishing of specific goods and services.[128]

Although all manufacturers and providers of products and services attempt to disclaim, modify, or exclude specific express or implied warranties, numerous courts have mitigated these efforts. Terms such as *limited warranty* or *express disclaimer* are often seen in contracts. Read the language on limitations of warranty before asserting the defense or the prosecution of a case based on a breach of warranty. Obviously a product or service that has not performed as expected and violates this fitness definition prompts either an action for damages or a defense for nonpayment. See Form 5.4 on the accompanying CD for a pertinent pleading.

Lemon Law Litigation

Anyone who has ever had repeated difficulties with an automobile will have sympathy with a person who owns a "lemon."[129] A *lemon* automobile is hopelessly flawed or in a state of eternal breakdown. In response to the truckload of consumer complaints about new vehicles that perform miserably, nearly all American jurisdictions have passed *lemon laws*—bills that provide a unique form of protection in new car disputes.[130] At the foundation, lemon laws recognize the "disparity of bargaining power" in the parties in vehicle purchase.[131] In common parlance, there is a view that auto dealers always have the upper hand in the vehicular transaction. Legislators appear to agree, as David Warren points out:

> *Many American consumers do not have the general level of literacy that is required to be able to both read and understand the mass of financial and legal paperwork that is presented to them at the car dealership. . . . This amount of sophistication is much greater than the general ability to read and write. Because of these difficulties, it is unclear to what extent consumers are able to assent to the terms of a contract by agreeing to sign it.*[132]

The acts are generally in addition to common-law contract rights, U.C.C. remedies under §2-601 in which a buyer may refuse to accept, or U.C.C. §2-608 whereby a buyer may revoke acceptance. The acts also supplement federal legislation that protects consumers—more pointedly, the Magnuson–Moss Warranty Act of 1975,[133] whose coverage includes "proscriptions or manufacturers' disclaimers of implied warranties, provisions for low-cost, quick alternative dispute resolution mechanisms, and award of attorneys' fee and litigation costs to successful consumers."[134]

Section 2304 of the Magnuson–Moss Warranty Act, 15 U.S.C.A. §§ 2301-2312, provides, in pertinent part,

(a) *In order for a warrantor warranting a consumer product by means of a written warranty to meet the Federal minimum standards for warranty—*

(1) *such warrantor must as a minimum remedy such consumer product within a reasonable time and without charge, in the case of a defect, malfunction, or failure to conform with such written warranty; [and] . . .*

(4) *if the product (or a component thereof) contains a defect or malfunction after a reasonable number of attempts by the warrantor to remedy defects or malfunctions in such product, such warrantor must permit the consumer to elect either a refund for, or replacement without charge of, such product or parts (as the case may be) . . .* [135]

State-level protections are just as vigorous. Florida, for example, emphasizes its legislative intent in the adoption of its lemon law:

The Legislature recognizes that a motor vehicle is a major consumer purchase and that a defective motor vehicle undoubtedly creates a hardship for the consumer. The Legislature further recognizes that a duly franchised motor vehicle dealer is an authorized service agent of the manufacturer. It is the intent of the Legislature that a good-faith motor vehicle warranty complaint by a consumer be resolved by the manufacturer within a specified period of time; however, it is not the intent of the Legislature that a consumer establish the presumption of a reasonable number of attempts as to each manufacturer that provides a warranty directly to the consumer. It is further the intent of the Legislature to provide the statutory procedures whereby a consumer may receive a replacement motor vehicle, or a full refund, for a motor vehicle which cannot be brought into conformity with the warranty provided for in this chapter. However, nothing in this chapter shall in any way limit or expand the rights or remedies which are otherwise available to a consumer under any other law. [136]

Nonconformity, meaning a defect, is defined in Ohio as follows:

(E) *Nonconformity: means any defect or condition which substantially impairs the use, value, or safety of a motor vehicle and does not conform to the express warranty of the manufacturer or distributor.* [137]

Alabama looks to "significant" defect and impairment as follows:

(6) *Nonconforming Condition. Any condition of a motor vehicle which shall not be in conformity with the terms of any express warranty issued by the manufacturer to a consumer and which (i) significantly impairs the use, value, or safety of the motor vehicle and (ii) occurs or arises solely within the ordinary use of the motor vehicle, and which does not arise or occur as a result of abuse, neglect, modification, or alteration of the motor vehicle not authorized by the manufacturer, nor from any accident or other damage to the motor vehicle which occurs or arises after such motor vehicle was delivered by an authorized dealer to the consumer.* [138]

Rhode Island sets the time frame for corrective action:

Time allowed for correction of nonconformity. A reasonable number of attempts shall be presumed to have been undertaken to conform a motor vehicle to any applicable express or implied warranties if (a) the same nonconformity has been subject to repair four (4) or more times by the manufacturer or its agents or authorized dealers within the terms of protection, but such nonconformity continues to exist or such nonconformity has recurred within the term of protection, or (b) the vehicle is out of service by reason of repair of any nonconformity for a cumulative total of thirty (30) or more calendar days during the term of protection provided, however, that the manufacturer shall be afforded one (1) additional opportunity, not to exceed seven (7) calendar days, to cure any nonconformity arising during the term of protection, notwithstanding the fact that such additional opportunity to cure commences after the term of protection.

Such additional opportunity to cure shall commence on the day the manufacturer first knows or should have known that the limits specified in clause (a) or (b) have been met or exceeded. The term of protection and thirty (30) calendar day period and said additional opportunity to cure shall be extended by any period during which repairs services are not available to the consumer as a direct result of a war, invasion, fire, flood, or other natural disaster. The term of protection, said thirty (30) calendar day period, and said additional opportunity to cure shall also be extended by the period of time during which repair services are not available as a direct result of a strike; provided, however, that the manufacturer, its agent, or authorized dealer makes provision for the free use of a vehicle of comparable year and size by any consumer whose vehicle is out of service by reason of repair during strike. The burden shall be on the manufacturer to show that any event claimed as a reason for an extension under the provisions of this section was the direct cause for the failure of the manufacturer, its agent, or authorized dealer to cure any nonconformity during the time of said event. Extensions for concurrent events shall not be cumulative.[139]

From a statutory perspective, lemon laws generally contain these elements:

1. A warranty breach exists.
2. The breach is substantial and material.
3. Repair efforts were permitted, say three to five times.
4. The auto has been out of service more than so many days or months.
5. The manufacturer or dealer has been put on notice.
6. Attempts have been made to arbitrate.

Given these factors, lemon laws are not an appropriate remedy when the mechanical difficulty is the stuff of wear and tear or minor flaws such as a broken doorknob. A lemon problem is severe, substantial, and resistant to repair. Proving the case calls for substantial record collection. During an initial client interview, the requisite documents and other pertinent material involving the history of the vehicle should be collected. Consider using Form 5.5 found on the accompanying CD.

In most cases, manufacturers wish an amicable resolution under a lemon law claim. If unsuccessful, a complaint instituting a proceeding may be prepared by the paralegal. Review the complaint in Form 5.6 on the accompanying CD, and witness how multiple and alternative remedies to the lemon law action are pled.

Commercial Impracticability

A contract can be defended, discharged, or excused if certain events or conditions make its performance utterly impracticable. Of course, a contract that contains numerous conditions and contingencies will be considered impossible to perform if any of those conditions or contingencies has not been met. This doctrine is predicated on the theory that the parties to a contract made their bargain with specific circumstances in mind—that their basic assumptions about the world in which the contract was negotiated were thereafter upset by a failed contingency or condition. Performance under the contract becomes commercially impracticable and legally excused.[140]

Often these contractual situations in which a condition or a contingency cannot be met, such as the acquisition of financing or zoning permit certifications, result in what is crudely known as contractual frustration. As events, circumstances, and conditions either interfere or cannot be fulfilled, the contract loses its viability. In the commercial realm, especially since the adoption of the Uniform Commercial Code, there has been ample discussion regarding a doctrine of commercial impracticability or commercial impossibility.[141]

These defenses are broadly defined to cover those "sets of circumstances where performance is literally possible but is so radically different from that contemplated by the parties as to become impracticable."[142] In a commercial setting where freedom to contract is essential, what conditions or circumstances should give rise to a discharge or a defense to a contract based on impracticability? Ponder these scenarios:

- Is an extraordinary rise in cost or price that makes a contract counterproductive a basis for commercial impracticability?
- Does an outbreak of hostilities between nations in which commercial trade was once acceptable and now is no longer a basis for asserting commercial impracticability?
- Does the death of a party permit a court to rewrite the contract?
- Do supply problems, demand problems, or problems with labor, royalties, equipment, transportation, or power have anything to do with the right to assert commercial impracticability?[143]

Without doubt, circumstances upon which the original contract was framed dramatically change. Remember the oil crisis of the early 1970s and the recent run-up of fuel in 2005 with their skyrocketing prices? In time of war, nations who were once allies may become hostile enemies, making honored negotiations in commerce and trade and continued contractual enforcement an unlikely event. What about goods, services, and products destroyed when catastrophe hits, such as a typhoon or hurricane? The *Restatement of Contracts* zeroes in on these performance problems:

> *Performance may be impracticable because extreme and unreasonable difficulty, expense, injury, or loss to one of the parties will be involved. A severe shortage of raw materials or of supplies due to war, embargo, local crop failure, unforeseen shutdown of major sources of supply, or the like, which either causes a marked increase in cost or prevents performance altogether, may bring the case within the rule.*[144]

Undoubtedly, any business enterprise has various risks. Is it appropriate for the courts to impose remedies of reformation or contract novation to solve unforeseen problems and difficulties?[145]

Paralegals should view contracts, whether oral or written, as the guiding force in the interpretation of the intentions of the parties. Judicial intervention, though often well-intentioned, generally creates more havoc than reasoned result. Judicial intervention fosters a disregard for the terms and conditions of the contract itself, replacing the contract with a singular judicial impression. This is often far removed from the reality and history of a particular contract.

PARALEGAL PRACTICE AND PROCESS IN THE LAW OF CONTRACTS

As noted thus far, paralegals are critical players in the world of contracts. Now two essential areas must be considered. First, how will paralegals regularly interact with contract clients and their specific contractual desires? And second, what legal remedies and actions are common in contract litigation?

Preliminary Considerations

At the heart of contract practice are five fundamental objectives:

1. Consummate the transaction on schedule.
2. Be certain that the client fully understands the contract.
3. Draft a contract that clearly reflects that understanding.
4. Identify all risks.
5. Achieve the best arrangement for the client.[146]

Initial Conference

To assure that the paralegal achieves these objectives, an initial conference serves as a staging point for the proper assessment of client desires and the simultaneous collection of information and facts regarding a specific case. Success in the initial conference will depend on these steps:

1. Complete a checklist or other documentation necessary to validate the facts.
2. Set up a fee agreement or arrangement that is satisfactory to both parties.
3. Collect all necessary information for the preparation of a first draft if the client requests a formalized contract.

Employ the guide in Figure 5.4 when interviewing clients.

Choice of Form and Format

Busy practitioners have a wide selection of products to assist in the drafting and compilation of contracts. Increasingly law firms are relying on packaged software programs. Form books or software should serve only as general guides because each contract and client has its own personality and circumstance. Some sample contracts can be seen at Forms 5.7 and 5.8 on the accompanying CD.

Bar associations and professional organizations also deliver some exceptional materials in the area of contracts. As an example, Michigan's Institute of Continuing Legal Education advises that the construction and drafting of forms is a lifelong process. Set up a form file and

- Continue to improve your form file.
- Redraft your forms using more persuasive language.
- Do not copy blindly.

FIGURE 5.4
Guide for Contract
Preparation

- Outline the promises, duties, or tasks of the parties.
  - Is the contract workable?
  - Does it provide for all possibilities?
  - Is it arranged logically?
  - Can it be performed according to its terms?
  - Does it answer all conceivable legal questions that are or may become involved?
- Prepare a draft of the contract.
  - Use ordinary, plain English.
  - Choose words that precisely fit the intended meaning.
  - Be consistent in use of terminology.
  - Use abbreviated terms for recurring parties, items, and the like.
  - Avoid legalese where possible.
  - Avoid long sentences.
  - Emphasize important material, terms, or statements by using bold, underlined, capitalized, or italic type.
  - Avoid repetition of a promise or statement.
  - In longer documents, use numbered paragraphs.
  - Be extremely careful in the use of punctuation: Errors can cause confusion and misinterpretation.
  - Make sure every term is included and understandable.
- Review the draft.
  - Be sure to clearly mark on the document that it is a draft copy.
  - If the contract will be reviewed by another attorney, be sure to triple-space the text and include space for notations by the other attorney.
  - Always clearly indicate changes by highlighting, using different inks to mark text, and so on.
- Review the final draft.
  - Proofread.
  - Make sure all blanks are completed.
  - Verify all names, dates, figures, and cross-references to ensure accuracy.
  - Attach and identify all exhibits mentioned in the contract.

- Make sure your forms are up to date and unambiguous.
- Determine whether or not you can improve a specific form.
- Create or use checklists in the organization of thoughts regarding your forms.[147]

Standardized Forms

Transactions involving houses, cars, retail goods, products, services, and employment contracts regularly use standardized preprinted forms. For example, building contracts generally rely on standard documentation. (See Form 5.9 on the accompanying CD.)

Professors Holmes and Thurman of the University of Georgia and the University of Hamburg, respectively, urge caution in the use of standardized contracts because these documents may be subject to modification and judicial reformation. Holmes and Thurman call for a new progressive theory of contract interpretation:

1. *Courts must recognize that control of standard terms is part of the unconscionability doctrine.*

2. *Courts must determine whether the terms were actually read and comprehended.*

3. *Courts must determine whether there were adequate means or notice given to the consumers that they should read the standard terms. The court must be assured that the consumers accepted those terms by signature or manifestation of assent.*

4. *Terms and conditions in a standardized contract must pass a test of substantive fairness.*

5. *Courts must strike any objectionable terms or conditions in a standardized contract.*[148]

These standardized documents create an unintentional injustice by binding the parties to rigid terms and conditions that may or may not apply to the given circumstances. Holmes and Thurman argue that conservative adherence to the terms and conditions of a stated and written contract is unrealistic and unacceptable given today's consumer and commercial complexity. On the other hand, standardization promotes predictability in the marketplace.

Suggestions on Draftsmanship

Despite the proliferation of legalese, a good contract is one that can be read and understood. States like New York now mandate plain-language documents in the bulk of consumer transactions. A seasoned practitioner holds,

> *Speak the client's language. If he is relatively unsophisticated, do not try to impress him with big words, long sentences, and legalese. As much as possible, speak and write in plain English.*[149]

An example from New York State is reproduced here:

> *Requirements for use of plain language in consumer transactions*
>
> a. *Every written agreement entered into after November first, nineteen hundred seventy-eight, for the lease of space to be occupied for residential purposes, for the lease of personal property to be used primarily for personal, family, or household purposes, or to which a consumer is a party and the money, property, or service which is the subject of the transaction is primarily for personal, family, or household purposes must be:*
>   1. *Written in a clear and coherent manner using words with common and everyday meanings;*
>   2. *Appropriately divided and captioned by its various sections.*
>
> *Any creditor, seller, or lessor who fails to comply with this subdivision shall be liable to a consumer who is a party to a written agreement governed by this subdivision in an amount equal to any actual damages sustained plus a penalty of fifty dollars. The total class action penalty against any such creditor, seller, or lessor shall not exceed ten thousand dollars in any class action or series of class actions arising out of the use by a creditor, seller, or lessor of an agreement which fails to comply with this subdivision. No action under this subdivision may be brought after both parties to the agreement have fully performed their obligation under such agreement, nor shall any creditor, seller, or lessor who attempts in good faith to comply with this subdivision be liable for such penalties. This subdivision shall not apply to a good-faith attempt to describe the constant yield or other method of determining the lease charge and depreciation portions of each base rental payment under a lease of personal property. It also shall not apply to agreements involving amounts in excess of fifty thousand dollars nor prohibit the use of words or phrases or forms of agreement required by state or federal law, rule, or regulation or by a governmental instrumentality.*
>
> b. *A violation of the provisions of subdivision a of this section shall not render any such agreement void or voidable nor shall it constitute:*
>   1. *A defense to any action or proceeding to enforce such agreement; or*
>   2. *A defense to any action or proceeding for breach of such agreement.*
>
> c. *In addition to the above, whenever the attorney general finds that there has been a violation of this section, he may proceed as provided in subdivision twelve of section sixty-three of the executive law.*[150]

In general, solid draftsmanship in contracts call for these characteristics:

- Accurate, complete recitation of facts, parties, and individuals.
- Complete, coherent sentences, structurally designed by headings, appropriate numbers, or corresponding keynotes.
- Clear, lucid, understandable English that covers the subject matter precisely and by appropriate legal description.
- Full integration clauses, evidencing the complete intentions of the parties without referral to peripheral or secondary documentation.
- All necessary components and parts present to create a formal and binding contract.
- Depending on jurisdiction, required witnesses to signatories, notary public proof, or other seal or evidence of execution.

- Adherence to statutory guidelines and legal doctrine.
- No vague and illusory language.
- Necessary consideration included as support.
- Understandable by the parties who are signatories.
- Read by all the parties.
- Written with the average person in mind rather than the esoteric needs of a select few.
- Authored with common terms with common meanings for ordinary people.

The Conference of the Legal Writing Institute[151] encourages the legal profession to use English with the following resolution:

> *Resolution*
>
> *At the 1992 Conference of the Legal Writing Institute, which has 900 members worldwide, the participants adopted the following resolution:*
>
> 1. *The way lawyers write has been a source of complaint about lawyers for more than four centuries.*
> 2. *The language used by lawyers should agree with the common speech unless there are reasons for a difference.*
> 3. *Legalese is unnecessary and no more precise than plain language.*
> 4. *Plain language is an important part of good legal writing.*
> 5. *Plain language means language that is clear and readily understandable to the intended readers.*
> 6. *To encourage the use of plain language, the Legal Writing Institute should try to identify members who would be willing to work with their bar associations to establish plain language committees like those in Michigan and Texas.*[152]

In addition, read the contract, no matter what its source. How will the contract withstand the test of time and the barbs and arrows of an antagonist? Never hesitate to "test the effectiveness of your proposed contract by playing out future scenarios against it. Ask your client 'what if?' This exercise will not only point out potential weaknesses in a contract but will also reduce the chances of future unpleasant surprises for your contract."[153]

Structure of a Contract

Contracts, like other legal documents, have various components. Clauses, provisions, and signature lines are general to all contracts, whereas others may have highly specialized language not witnessed in traditional circles. In the broadest terms, all contracts have these components:

1. Statement of the parties.
2. Background or purpose of the contract.
3. Subject matter of the contract.
4. Consideration of the contract.
5. Warranty representations.
6. Risk allocation.
7. Conditions, covenants, or other qualifying clauses.
8. Performance expected under the contract.
9. Term or duration of the contract.
10. Miscellaneous provisions regarding jurisdiction, conflict of laws, damages, assignment, and assumption rights.
11. Signatures.
12. Witnesses.

13. Date.

14. Notary or other required seal.

Review the sample contract at Form 5.10 on the accompanying CD. Identify the structural components of the contract using the topical numbers in the preceding list.

CONTRACT LITIGATION

Unfortunately, contract law is not just about making and shaping terms and provisions. Too often in our highly litigious culture, lawsuits and other challenges emerge to the language of contracts. Contract litigation is a big business with paralegals in the thick of it.

Pleadings and Practice

Some of the more commonly witnessed litigation tactics in contract law will be covered in the pages to come. Contract law consists of a strange mix of actions in law and in equity, and this area is often the subject of judicial activism.

Complaint for Breach

Individuals who do not adhere to the terms of a contract are subject to an action for breach. The breach can be either material or nonmaterial in nature; but if it is of sufficient gravity, it will require the payment of specific compensatory, punitive, consequential, or nominal damages.

To establish a prima facie case for breach of contract, a plaintiff must plead and prove (1) the existence of a contract; (2) a breach of that contract; and (3) damages resulting from the breach.[154] "One who violates his contract with another is liable for all the direct and proximate damages which result from the violation."[155] Causation is an essential element of damages in a breach of contract action. As in tort, a plaintiff must prove that a defendant's breach directly and proximately caused his or her damages.[156]

In the event of a real, actual, or anticipatory repudiation or breach of a contract, under common law the aggrieved party to the contract has a right to file a complaint either seeking specific performance under the contract or pursuing payment of damages. A sample complaint about a standard contract is shown in Form 5.11 on the accompanying CD.

The stated breach needs to be material, significant, or of integral importance to the contract's fulfillment. The *Restatement of Contracts* at §241 elucidates circumstances when a breach is material:

> In determining whether a failure to render or to offer performance is material, the following circumstances are significant:
>
> (a) the extent to which the injured party will be deprived of the benefit which he reasonably expected;
>
> (b) the extent to which the injured party can be adequately compensated for the part of that benefit of which he will be deprived;
>
> (c) the extent to which the party failing to perform or to offer to perform will suffer forfeiture;
>
> (d) the likelihood that the party failing to perform or to offer to perform will cure his failure, taking account of all the circumstances including any reasonable assurances;
>
> (e) the extent to which the behavior of the party failing to perform or to offer to perform comports with standards of good faith and fair dealing.[157]

Thus if "A" promises "B" to paint his house, and "A" fails to do so, a material breach occurs. Even statements that anticipate or preliminarily repudiate a duty under contract can be a breach. The *Restatement* defines an anticipatory breach as

> (a) a statement by the obligor to the obligee indicating that the obligor will commit a breach that would have itself given the obligee a claim for damages for total breach under 243, or
>
> (b) a voluntary affirmative act which renders the obligor unable or apparently unable to perform without such a breach.[158]

The *Restatement* permits an action for either *total* or *partial* breach of contract:

> *(1) A claim for damages for total breach is one for damages based on all of the injured party's remaining rights to performance.*
>
> *(2) A claim for damages for partial breach is one for damages based on only part of the injured party's remaining rights to performance.*[159]

Damages

If a breach is established, a party may aver a claim for damages. Damages are those sums the party would have received if the contract had been fulfilled. To illustrate, here is an example:

> "A" contracts to sell and "B" to buy, on 30 days' credit, 3,000 tons of iron rails at a stated price. "B" purchases iron rails heavily from various sources for use in his business, and in consequence "A" has difficulty in securing 3,000 tons and the market price is subsequently increased. "A" fails to deliver the rails. "B" has a claim against "A" for breach of contract. "B's" purchase of iron rails from other sources for use in his business is not a failure of performance because "B" is under no duty to refrain from purchasing for that purpose. "A's" failure to deliver the rails is therefore a breach.[160]

Restitution

A breach can also be remedied by an action for restitution. When compared to damages, restitution is merely the return of the injured or aggrieved party to his former position. Thus if John paid $8,000 for a car, the seller taking it and never delivering the car, John may be made whole of the $8,000 by restitution. The *Restatement* at §373 discusses the remedy:

> *(1) Subject to the rule stated in Subsection (2) on a breach by nonperformance that gives rise to a claim for damages for total breach or on a repudiation, the injured party is entitled to restitution for any benefit that he has conferred on the other party by way of part performance or reliance.*
>
> *(2) The injured party has no right to restitution if he has performed all of his duties under the contract and no performance by the other party remains due other than payment of a definite sum of money for that performance.*[161]

 A notice of motion for restitution is shown in Form 5.12 on the accompanying CD.

Rescission

 An aggrieved party may rescind a contract for personal or economic motivations. By recission, the aggrieved party extinguishes certain interests in the contract but not necessarily the damages. Troublesome cases of rescission involve partial payments or installment and/or partial performance. Rescission may be the product of mutual assent.

An answer to a complaint for breach may allege the rescission of an existing contract. (See Form 5.13 on the accompanying CD.)

Reformation

The parties are free to reform an existing contract rather than continue performance of the original language of the contract. Reformation is of an existing contract, not a novation producing an entirely new contract.

Specific Performance

 Specific performance is an equitable remedy made available to an injured contractual party. It is applicable in two major areas: real estate and personal service contract litigation. A paralegal can help in these areas. A personal service contract is when an individual with specific talents and skills is hired to perform a specialized service. This service is usually an artistic or otherwise unique skill and quality that cannot be delegated or assigned. Construction contracts illustrate this principle. (See Form 5.14 on the accompanying CD.)

The *Restatement of Contracts* highlights the remedy at §357:

> *(1) Subject to the rules stated in 359-69, specific performance of a contract duty will be granted in the discretion of the court against a party who has committed or is threatening to commit a breach of the duty.*

> *(2) Subject to the rules stated in 359-69, an injunction against breach of a contract duty will be granted in the discretion of the court against a party who has committed or is threatening to commit a breach of the duty if*
> *(a) the duty is one of forbearance, or*
> *(b) the duty is one to act and specific performance would be denied only for reasons that are inapplicable to an injunction.[162]*

A case where the services are unique and utterly personal will qualify.[163]

In addition to any equitable relief granted under theories of specific performance or injunction, the court may award damages in conjunction. Courts also have liberal discretion in authoring specific performance remedies as §358 indicates:

> *(1) An order of specific performance or an injunction will be so drawn as best to effectuate the purposes for which the contract was made and on such terms as justice requires. It need not be absolute in form and the performance that is required need not be identical with that due under the contract.*
> *(2) If specific performance or an injunction is denied as to part of the performance that is due, it may nevertheless be granted as to the remainder.*
> *(3) In addition to specific performance or an injunction, damages and other relief may be awarded in the same proceedings and an indemnity against future harm may be required.[164]*

Uniform Commercial Code Remedies

Additional remedies regarding conduct between merchants are covered under the Uniform Commercial Code at Article 2. Both buyers and sellers of goods are given options on how to resolve a claim or dispute. The remedies provided by the Code are to be liberally administered so that the aggrieved party may be put in as good a position as if the other party had fully performed. The Code rejects the doctrine of election of remedies and provides that the remedies of an aggrieved party are essentially cumulative. Both the buyer and the seller may invoke, in addition to Code remedies, other available legal and equitable remedies.

Anticipatory Breach

Contracting parties, either buyer or seller, can sometimes sense or anticipate a breach to come. Under the U.C.C. remedies are available when an anticipated repudiation occurs. §2-610 defines this state:

> *When either party repudiates the contract with respect to a performance not yet due the loss of which will substantially impair the value of the contract to the other, the aggrieved party may*
> *(a) for a commercially reasonable time await performance by the repudiating party; or*
> *(b) resort to any remedy for breach (Section 2-703 or Section 2-711), even though he has notified the repudiating party that he would await the latter's performance and has urged retraction; and*
> *(c) in either case suspend his own performance or proceed in accordance with the provisions of this Article on the seller's right to identify goods to the contract notwithstanding breach or to salvage unfinished goods (Section 2-704).[165]*

If parties in a commercial setting are concerned about the conduct of contracting parties, they may seek reasonable assurances that performance will take place under an underlying contract. The demand must be based on reasonable belief that a breach may occur. The U.C.C. at §2-609(1) states in part,

> *When reasonable grounds for insecurity arise with respect to the performance of either party the other may in writing demand adequate assurance of due performance and until he receives such assurance may if commercially reasonable suspend any performance for which he has not already received the agreed return.[166]*

Available remedies are categorized according to seller and buyer interests. A brief examination of these rights follows.

Seller's Remedies

Under U.C.C. standards, a seller has various remedies when a buyer defaults in the purchase of specific goods. The seller may exercise any of the following:

1. Withhold delivery (see U.C.C. §2-702 (a)).
2. Resell (see U.C.C. §2-706).

3. Sue for breach (see U.C.C. §2-708).

4. Cancel or rescind (see U.C.C. §2-704).

5. Identify the goods to the contract (see U.C.C. §2-704).

The use of remedies depends on the condition of the goods and their location. If a seller discovers that a buyer is insolvent, the seller may refuse to proceed with delivery of contracted goods. The seller is also entitled to reclaim delivered goods under §2-702 (2)-(3):

> *(2) Where the seller discovers that the buyer has received goods on credit while insolvent he may reclaim the goods upon demand made within ten days after the receipt; but if misrepresentation of solvency has been made to the particular seller in writing within three months before delivery the ten-day limitation does not apply. Except as provided in this subsection the seller may not base a right to reclaim goods on the buyer's fraudulent or innocent misrepresentation of solvency or of intent to pay.*

> *(3) The seller's right to reclaim under subsection (2) is subject to the rights of a buyer in ordinary course or other good-faith purchaser under this Article (Section 2-403). Successful reclamation of goods excludes all other remedies with respect to them.[167]*

An alternative remedy, when goods have not arrived but are in transit, is provided by the Code at §2-705:

> *(1) The seller may stop delivery of goods in the possession of a carrier or other bailee when he discovers the buyer to be insolvent (Section 2-702) and may stop delivery of carload, truckload, planeload, or larger shipments of express or freight when the buyer repudiates or fails to make a payment due before delivery or if for any other reason the seller has a right to withhold or reclaim the goods.*

> *(2) As against such buyer the seller may stop delivery until*
> *(a) receipt of the goods by the buyer; or*
> *(b) acknowledgment to the buyer by any bailee of the goods except a carrier that the bailee holds the goods for the buyer; or*
> *(c) such acknowledgment to the buyer by a carrier by reshipment or as a warehouse; or*
> *(d) negotiation to the buyer of any negotiable document of title covering the goods.*

> *(3) (a) To stop delivery the seller must so notify as to enable the bailee by reasonable diligence to prevent delivery of the goods.*
> *(b) After such notification the bailee must hold and deliver the goods according to the directions of the seller; but the seller is liable to the bailee for any ensuing charges or damages.*
> *(c) If a negotiable document of title has been issued for goods the bailee is not obliged to obey a notification to stop until surrender of possession or control of the document.*
> *(d) A carrier who has issued a nonnegotiable bill of lading is not obliged to obey a notification to stop received from a person other than the consignor.[168]*

Resale is another remedial action available to a seller. As long as the resale effort is in good faith and commercially reasonable, the seller may resell and collect any outstanding differences or incidental damages.[169] The method of sale is outlined in the Code:

> *(2) Except as otherwise provided in subsection (3) or unless otherwise agreed resale may be at public or private sale including sale by way of one or more contracts to sell or of identification to an existing contract of the seller. Sale may be as a unit or in parcels and at any time and place and on any terms; but every aspect of the sale including the method, manner, time, place, and terms must be commercially reasonable. The resale must be reasonably identified as referring to the broken contract, but it is not necessary that the goods be in existence or that any or all of them have been identified to the contract before the breach.*

> *(3) Where the resale is at private sale the seller must give the buyer reasonable notification of his intention to resell.[170]*

The Code upholds traditional actions for the price for the contracted goods and the damages that result therefrom. U.C.C. §2-709 states,

> *(1) When the buyer fails to pay the price as it becomes due the seller may recover, together with any incidental damages under the next section, the price*
> *(a) of goods accepted or of conforming goods lost or damaged within a commercially reasonable time after risk of their loss has passed to the buyer; and*
> *(b) of goods identified to the contract if the seller is unable after reasonable effort to resell them at a reasonable price or the circumstances reasonably indicate that such effort will be unavailing.[171]*

Finally, if the seller is able, he or she can identify those goods, either in a finished or unfinished state, cease manufacture, or resell for scrap or salvage value. Under §2-704,

(1) An aggrieved seller under the preceding section may

    (a) identify to the contract conforming goods not already identified if at the time he learned of the breach they are in his possession or control;

    (b) treat as the subject of resale goods which have demonstrably been intended for the particular contract even though those goods are unfinished.

(2) Where the goods are unfinished an aggrieved seller may in the exercise of reasonable commercial judgment for the purposes of avoiding loss and of effective realization either complete the manufacture and wholly identify the goods to the contract or cease manufacture and resell for scrap or salvage value or proceed in any other reasonable manner.[172]

Under U.C.C. §2-703, the seller's remedies are more specifically delineated:

Where the buyer wrongfully rejects or revokes acceptance of goods or fails to make a payment due on or before delivery or repudiates with respect to a part or the whole, then with respect to any goods directly affected and, if the breach is of the whole contract (Section 2-612), then also with respect to the whole undelivered balance, the aggrieved seller may

(a) withhold delivery of such goods;

(b) stop delivery by any bailee as hereafter provided (Section 2-705);

(c) proceed under the next section respecting goods still unidentified to the contract;

(d) resell and recover damages as hereafter provided (Section 2-706);

(e) recover damages for nonacceptance (Section 2-708) or in a proper case the price (Section 2-709);

(f) cancel.[173]

Pleading documents that comprise seller's remedies are shown in Forms 5.15 and 5.16 on the accompanying CD. Finally, a seller is entitled to file a damage action for repudiation under §2-708. In seeking damages for nonacceptance or repudiation, "the measure of damages for nonacceptance or repudiation by the buyer is the difference between the market price at the time and place for tender and the unpaid contract price together with any incidental damages provided in this Article (Section 2-710), but less expenses saved in consequence of the buyer's breach."[174]

Buyer's Remedies

A buyer has alternative, yet similar, rights under common-law contract principles. The remedies due to the buyer are determined by the manner in which the seller has breached. The likely scenarios are these:

1. The seller refuses to deliver or tenders nonconforming goods, and the buyer rejects them.

2. The seller tenders nonconforming goods and buyer accepts them.

3. The seller refuses delivery and the buyer still wants the goods.

In the first instance, buyer may cancel the obligation:

(1) Where the seller fails to make delivery or repudiates or the buyer rightfully rejects or justifiably revokes acceptance then with respect to any goods involved, and with respect to the whole if the breach goes to the whole contract (Section 2-612), the buyer may cancel and whether or not he has done so may in addition to recovering so much of the price as has been paid

    (a) "cover" and have damages under the next section as to all the goods affected whether or not they have been identified to the contract; or

    (b) recover damages for nondelivery as provided in this Article (Section 2-713).

(2) Where the seller fails to deliver or repudiates the buyer may also

    (a) if the goods have been identified recover them as provided in this Article (Section 2-502); or

    (b) in a proper case obtain specific performance or replevy the goods as provided in this Article (Section 2-716).

(3) On rightful rejection or justifiable revocation of acceptance a buyer has a security interest in goods in his possession or control for any payments made on their price and any expenses reasonably incurred in their inspection, receipt, transportation, care, and custody and may hold such goods and resell them in like manner as an aggrieved seller (Section 2-706).[175]

In the alternative, the buyer may cover or substitute the goods purchased. U.C.C. §2-712 sets out cover practice requesting that the substitute goods be purchased in good faith as to price and timing. Damages can be computed according to the difference between the "cost of cover and the contract price."

A traditional lawsuit for breach of contract is an acceptable remedy. §U.C.C. 2-713 poses this remedy:

> (1) *Subject to the provisions of this Article with respect to proof of market price (Section 2-723), the measure of damages for nondelivery or repudiation by the seller is the difference between the market price at the time when the buyer learned of the breach and the contract price together with any incidental and consequential damages provided in this Article (Section 2-715), but less expenses saved in consequence of the seller's breach.*
>
> (2) *Market price is to be determined as of the place for tender or, in cases of rejection after arrival or revocation of acceptance, as of the place of arrival.*[176]

In the second circumstance listed previously, the seller tendered nonconforming goods and the buyer accepts them. The buyer still has a damage claim set by contract and warranty right. The Code establishes damages in this light:

> (1) *Where the buyer has accepted goods and given notification (subsection (3) of Section 2-607) he may recover as damages for any nonconformity or tender the loss resulting in the ordinary course of events from the seller's breach as determined in any manner which is reasonable.*
>
> (2) *The measure of damages for breach of warranty is the difference at the time and place of acceptance between the value of the goods accepted and the value they would have had if they had been as warranted, unless special circumstances show proximate damages of a different amount.*
>
> (3) *In a proper case any incidental and consequential damages under the next section may also be recovered.*[177]

The buyer is also given the right in U.C.C. §2-717 to deduct damages from the contract price and to file an action for any incidental or consequential damages.[178]

In the last scenario listed previously, the seller refuses to deliver and buyer still wants the goods. The buyer can sue for specific performance or replevin. U.C.C. at §2-716 lays out the action:

> (1) *Specific performance may be decreed where the goods are unique or in other proper circumstances.*
>
> (2) *The decree for specific performance may include such terms and conditions as to payment of the price, damages, or other relief as the court may deem just.*
>
> (3) *The buyer has a right of replevin for goods identified to the contract if after reasonable effort he is unable to effect cover for such goods or the circumstances reasonably indicate that such effort will be unavailing or if the goods have been shipped under reservation and satisfaction of the security interest in them has been made or tendered. In the case of goods bought for personal, family, or household purposes, the buyer's right of replevin vests upon acquisition of a special property, even if the seller had not then repudiated or failed to deliver.*[179]

Summary

The formation, classification, and analysis of contracts and their terms and provisions have been this chapter's primary concerns. The requisites of a contract, including a comprehensive analysis of an offer, acceptance, and consideration and relevant issues regarding enforceability, were covered. Issues regarding requirements of a writing, capacity to contract, illegality, mistake, warranty issues, impracticability, and unconscionability were thoroughly examined. Standardized forms, checklists, and other documents useful to paralegals in contractual practice were provided. Suggestions for draftsmanship and the structural components of contracts were also discussed.

Various examples of pleadings and practice materials involved in contract litigation with both common-law and the Uniform Commercial Code principles were given major emphasis. U.C.C. remedies for both buyers and sellers in a breach of contract were addressed.

Various features of contract litigation were discussed, including preparation of complaints for breach and employment of Uniform Commercial Code remedies for buyers and sellers in a breach of contract situation. Theories regarding anticipatory breach and specific performance were also covered.

Discussion Questions

1. What types of contracts have you entered into? How many of them have been written? How many of them have been oral?

2. Name the elements of a valid contract. Explain the novelty yet legal enforceability of an e-signature.

3. Has anyone else signed a contract on your behalf or taken the responsibility for eventual liability on your contract?

4. What types of contracts could be considered potentially voidable?

5. Measuring the objective and subjective intentions of the parties to a contract is easier said than done. Why is it so difficult to determine these states of mind in contractual negotiations?

6. What types of problems or disagreements usually come about in a personal service contract?

7. An offer can be accepted in many ways. Discuss four or five techniques.

8. If a client came to you asking to be defended in a contract case, what types of legal defenses would you consider first?

9. Warranties are rarely ironclad guarantees. Instead they are full of limitations and conditional language. Discuss some of the conditional aspects of warranty rights.

10. Under what theories can the exact language of a contract be simply disregarded?

11. Some would argue that a contract with a condition is really not an enforceable contract at all. What do they mean?

12. How does the U.C.C. depart or differ from traditional common-law contracts?

Research Assignment

1. Locate and cite your state's statute governing noncompete clauses in employment agreements. What is the name of the legislation that created the statute? What is the benchmark measure of any restriction to compete? Report any findings regarding at-will employment in your state.

Practical Exercises

1. Emply the following fact pattern to complete a standard sales contract. Feel free to create additional facts as needed:

    Principal place of business of seller: *38 James Street, Pinkney, Louisiana*
    Buyer's address: *14 John Street, Pinkney, Louisiana*
    Date of agreement: *September 1, 2007*
    Name of seller: *Maria & Jessica's Rubber Band Company; Maria Gonzales, sales manager: Ted Rinker, secretary*
    Name of buyer: *Pinkney Consolidated School District; Helen Wu, president; Latoya Chambers, secretary*
    Description of product: *4 million cartons of three-inch rubber bands; 2 million cartons of one-inch rubber bands; 10 million cartons of six-inch rubber bands*
    Delivery date: *December 1, 2007*
    Place of shipment: *Buyer's principal place of business*

2. Use the following facts to complete a complaint for breach of contract. Create additional facts as needed:

    Jurisdiction: *Venice County*
    Civil action number: *06-569*
    Attorney's phone number: *555-123-4567*

> Debtor's address: 956 Euclid Street, Murrysville, Ohio, Venice County
> Court of jurisdiction: General Court of Justice, District Court Division
> Amount due plaintiff: $25,547

3. Using the following facts complete a complaint for breach of warranty:

> Date of contract: February 8, 2006
> Defendant: McDonald Construction Company, 9 Appian Boulevard, Knoxville, Tennessee, 41114, Knoxville County
> Jurisdictional authority: General Court of Justice, Marlboro County, Tennessee
> Plaintiff: Melissa Evans, 13 Arlington Avenue, Arlington, Tennessee, 41114, Marlboro County
> Civil action number: 06-289
> Type of pleading: Complaint for breach of warranty and punitive damages
> First claim of relief: Breach of both oral and written express warranties
> Second claim of relief: Punitive damages totaling $11,500
> Contracting status: Not licensed

Internet Resources

Jurist Contract Law Guide—jurist.law.pitt.edu/sg_k.htm

Hieros Gamos, Commercial Law Section—www.hg.org/commerc.html

Findlaw Legal Subjects, Contract Law—www.findlaw.com/01topics/07contracts/index.html

ABA, Public Contract Law Section—www.abanet.org/contract

Legal Information Institute, Contracts—www.law.cornell.edu/wex/index.php/Contracts

U.S. Department of Commerce—www.commerce.gov

Endnotes

1. *See generally* Margie Alsbrook, *Contracting Away an Honest Day's Pay: An Examination of Conditional Payment Clauses in Construction Contracts,* 58 ARK L. REV. 353 (2005).

2. *See* E. Allen Farnsworth, *"Meaning" in the Law of Contracts,* 76 YALE L. J. 939 (1967); RESTATEMENT (SECOND) OF CONTRACTS, §1 (1981); Karl N. Llewellyn, *A Case Law of Contracts: Offer and Acceptance,* 48 YALE L. J. 1 (1938).

3. ARTHUR L. CORBIN, CORBIN ON CONTRACTS §3 (1963).

4. *Id.* §2.

5. Vincent A. Wellman, *Conceptions of the Common Law: Reflections on a Theory of Contract, citing* CHARLES FRIED, CONTRACT AS PROMISE: A THEORY OF CONTRACTUAL OBLIGATION (1981), 41 U. MIAMI L. REV. 925, 932–933 (1987).

6. CHARLES FRIED, CONTRACT AS PROMISE: A THEORY OF CONTRACTUAL OBLIGATION 1 (1981).

7. Wellman, *supra* note 5, at 932–933.

8. Joel Levin & Banks McDowell, *Striking the Balance in Contract Theory,* 40 CLEV. ST. L. REV. 19, 21 (Winter 1992).

9. Edward L. Barrett, *A More Modest Proposal Than a Common Law for the Age of Statutes: Greater Reliance in Statutory Interpretation on the Concept of Interpretative Intention,* 68 ALB. L. REV. 949, 951 (2005).

10. U.C.C. §1–201 (12) (2005).

11. Restatement, *supra* note 2, §1.

12. *See* U.C.C. §2–105(1) (2005).

13. *See* U.C.C. §2–105(2) (2005).

14. ROBERT N. CORLEY, ERIC M. HOLMES, & WILLIAM J. ROBERT, PRINCIPLES OF BUSINESS LAW 185 (1983).

15. J. KENDRICK KINNEY, A LAW DICTIONARY AND GLOSSARY 74 (1987).

16. *Id.* at 75.

17. BRYAN A. GARNER, A DICTIONARY OF MODERN LEGAL USAGE 525 (1987).

18. *Id.* at 525.

19. WESLEY GILMER, THE LAW DICTIONARY 115 (1986).

20. *Id.* at 44.

21. RONALD A. ANDERSON, IVAN FOX, & DAVID P. TWOMEY, BUSINESS LAW 104 (1984).

22. Corbin, *supra* note 3, §5.

23. Skelly v. Bristol Savings Bank, 63 Conn. 83, 26 A. 474 (1893).

24. Anderson et al., *supra* note 21, at 104–105; *see also* European American Bank v. Cane, 79 A.D. 2d 158, 436 N.Y.S. 2d 318 (1981); Marvin v. Marvin, 13 CAL. 3d 660, 134 CAL. RPTR. 815, 557 P. 2d 106 (1976).

25. Corbin, *supra* note 3, §7.

26. Restatement, *supra* note 2, §13 (1981).

27. Earl R. Boonstra, *Contracts: Mutual Assent: Effect of Insanity* 47 Mich. L. Rev., 269, 270 (1948).

28. Corbin, *supra* note 3, §8.

29. Restatement, *supra* note 2, §14; *see also* Republic Steel Corp. v. United Mine Workers, 570 F. 2d 467 (3d Cir. 1978).

30. Charles P. Nemeth, Plain Language And a Finding of Ambiguity—The Delaware Supreme Court Interprets a Real Estate Sales Agreement (1986) (unpublished manuscript, on file with author).

31. Corley et al., *supra* note 14, at 197.

32. Restatement, *supra* note 2, §62.

33. *See* Packard Englewood Motors v. Packard Motor Car Company, 215 F. 2d 503 (3d Cir. 1954).

34. Anderson et al., *supra* note 21, at 107.

35. *See* Deskovick v. Porzio, 78 N.J. Super. 82, 187 A. 2d 610, (1963); Nationwide Mutual Insurance Company v. Chantos, 293 N.C. 431, 238 S.E. 2d 597 (1977); U.S. Controls Corp. v. Wendell, 509 F. 2d 909 (7th Cir. 1975).

36. Corley et al., *supra* note 14, at 186.

37. Juliet M. Moringiello, *Signals, Assent, and Internet Contracting*, 57 Rutgers L. Rev. 1307 (2005).

38. Corley et al., *supra* note 14, at 205.

39. Moringiello, *supra* note 37, at 1315.

40. Gary V. Schaber & Claude D. Rohwer, Contracts 7 (1975).

41. *See generally* Peerless Publications v. County Of Montgomery, 656 A. 2d 9 (Pa. Commw. 1994).

42. Riseman v. Advanta, Nos. 01-3707/01-3844, slip opinion at 10 (3rd Cir. July 8, 2002).

43. U.C.C. §2-205 (2005).

44. Schaber & Rohwer, *supra* note 40, at 11.

45. Pacific Cascade Corp. v. Nema, 25 Wash. App. 552, 608 P. 2d 266 (1980); Natrona Service, Inc. v. Continental Oil Co., 435 F. Supp. 99 (D. Wyo. 1977).

46. Schaber & Rohwer, *supra* note 40, at 21; *see also* Starkwether v. Gleason, 221 Mass. 52, 109 N.E. 635 (1915).

47. There is often a fine line between a fair and equitable offer and a bait-and-switch scheme.

48. Corbin, *supra* note 3, §35.

49. Anderson et al., *supra* note 21, at 117.

50. Corbin, *supra* note 3, §12.

51. Russell Wald, *Offeree's Acceptance of a Contract Offer*, 27 Am. Jur. Proof of Facts 2d 559, 569 (1987); *see also* Corbin, *supra* note 3, §11; 17 Am. Jur. 2d *Contracts* §41 (1987).

52. U.C.C. §2-206 (2005).

53. 1 Samuel Williston, A Treatise on the Law of Contracts 55 (1957).

54. Wald, *supra* note 51, at 572.

55. *Id.* at 574.

56. Goodwin v. Tyson, 167 Ark. 396, 268 S.W. 15 (1925).

57. Corbin, *supra* note 3, §62.

58. Restatement, *supra* note 2, §45.

59. Corbin, *supra* note 3, §63.

60. Trainer v. Fort, 310 Pa. 570, 165 A. 232 (1933).

61. Corbin, *supra* note 3, §78–79; *also* note the arcane mailbox rule, which has been the subject of some substantial debate and scholarship.

62. Wald, *supra* note 51, at 580; Williston, *supra* note 53, §§81, 88.

63. Restatement, *supra* note 2, §66; Williston, *supra* note 53, §84; *Limitations of Liability in Connection with the Transmission of Telegraph Messages*, 61 ICC 541 (1921).

64. U.C.C. §1-201(36) (2005).

65. Wald, *supra* note 51, at 577; 17 Am. Jur. 2d Contracts §§46 & 70 (1987).

66. Williston, *supra* note 53, §89.

67. Restatement, *supra* note 2, §71(1)(b).

68. Restatement, *supra* note 2, §71.

69. Restatement, *supra* note 2, §71; Williston, *supra* note 53, §§99–103; Lon Fuller, *Consideration in Form*, 41 Colum. L. Rev. 799 (1941).

70. Restatement, *supra* note 2, §71(c).

71. Restatement, *supra* note 2, §73.

72. Restatement, *supra* note 2, §74.

73. Restatement, *supra* note 2, §83.

74. Restatement, *supra* note 2, §84.

75. Restatement, *supra* note 2, §88.

76. Restatement, *supra* note 2, §89.

77. Restatement, *supra* note 2, §90.

78. Restatement, *supra* note 2, §79.

79. Propulsion Technologies, Inc. v. Attwood Corporation, No. 03-4065, at 15 (5th Cir. May 26, 2004). *See also* Tex. Bus. & Com. Code Ann. §2.201 (requiring written quantity term); Eastern Dental Corp. v. Isaac Masel Co., Inc., 502 F. Supp. 1354, 1363 (E.D. Pa. 1980) (statute of frauds' requirement of a writing applies to requirements contracts), cited with approval in Merritt-Campbell, 164 F.3d at 963; Willard, Sutherland & Co. v. United States, 262 U.S. 489; 493, 43 S. Ct. 592, 594 (1923); Mid-South Packers, Inc. v. Shoney's, Inc., 761 F.2d 1117, 1120-21 (5th Cir. 1985) (without buyer's commitment to purchase exclusively from the seller either buyer's entire requirements or up to a specified amount, a requirements contract fails for want of consideration); Tex. Bus. & Com. Code Ann. §2.201(c)(3); *see also* Comment 2 following §2.201: "*Partial performance* as a substitute for the required memorandum can validate the contract only for the

goods which have been accepted or for which payment has been made and accepted."

80. *See* Kansas City Power & Light Co. v. Burlington N. R.R. Co., 707 F.2d 1002, 1004 (8th Cir. 1993).

81. *See* Pa. Stat. Ann. tit. 33 §§1, 3, 4 (1987) as an example. For a fuller discussion of statutory jurisdictions see Restatement, *supra* note 2, at the Statute of Frauds, Chapter 5, §§281–286.

82. *See* Vess Beverages, 941 F.2d at 654.

83. Restatement, *supra* note 2, §§281–286.

84. John Sommers, *The Doctrine of Estoppel Applied to the Statute of Frauds*, 79 U. Pa. L. Rev. 440 (1931).

85. U.C.C. §2-201(1)&(3) (2005).

86. Restatement, *supra* note 2, §131; *see also* Peacock Realty v. E. Thomas Crandall, 108 R.I. 593, 278 A. 2d 405 (1971).

87. For example, Canada, Ireland, the EU, and the Philippines have adopted the Electronic Commerce Act of 2000.

88. Ralph James Mooney, *A Friendly Letter to the Oregon Supreme Court: Let's Try Again on the Parol Evidence Rule*, 84 Or. L. Rev 369, 370 (2005).

89. Corley et al., *supra* note 14, at 247; Corbin, *supra* note 3, §532, *et seq.*

90. Mooney, *supra* note 89, at 370.

91. Corbin, *supra* note 3, at 573.

92. Corbin, *supra* note 3, at 573.

93. U.C.C. §2-202 (2005).

94. Schaber & Rohwer, *supra* note 40, at 158.

95. Corley et al., *supra* note 14, at §275.

96. Schaber & Rohwer, *supra* note 40, at 110.

97. For an interesting but very common case involving aspiring child actors and actresses, *see* Pacitti v. Macy's, No. 98–1803 (3rd Cir. October 5, 1999).

98. Anderson et al., *supra* note 21, at 166.

99. *See, e.g.*, Snowden v. Checkpoint Check Cashing, 290 F.3d 631, 637 (4th Cir. 2002); Burden v. Check Into Cash of Kentucky, LLC, 267 F.3d 483, 489–91 (6th Cir. 2001)

100. Kim Pittman, *Resolving Disputes over the Disposition of Frozen Preembryos: Playing Catch-Up with IVF Technologies*, 20 Maine bar. J. 228 (2005); *see also* Jennifer M. Stoller, *Disputing Frozen Embryos: Using International Perspective to Formulate U.S. Policy*, 9 Tul. Int'l & Comp. L. 459 (2002).

101. U.C.C. §1-201(20) (2005).

102. U.C.C. §§2-313 through 2-316 (2005).

103. U.C.C. §2-302 (2005).

104. Paul Bennet Marrow, *Squeezing Subjectivity from the Doctrine of Unconscionability*, 53 Clev. St. L. Rev. 187 (2006).

105. Anderson et al., *supra* note 21, at 169.

106. Marrow, *supra* note 105, at 188.

107. *See* Charles Bunn, Harry Snead, & Richard Speidel, An Introduction to the Uniform Commercial Code 55 (1964).

108. Restatement, *supra* note 2, §152; *see also* Plains Cotton Corp. v. Wolf, 553 S.W. 2d 800, 805 (Tex. Civ. App. 1977).

109. Restatement, *supra* note 2, §152.

110. Corley et al., *supra* note 14, at 279.

111. Williston, *supra* note 53, at Chapter 45; *see also* Michael R. Darby & Edi Karni, *Free Competition and the Optimal Amount of Fraud*, 16 J. L. & Econ. 67 (1973).

112. Restatement, *supra* note 2, §162.

113. Quill v. Newberry, 238 Ga. App. 184 (Ga. Ct. App. 1999).

114. Restatement, *supra* note 2, §175.

115. Williston, *supra* note 53, §1604; *see also* Robert Hale, *Bargaining, Duress, and Economic Liberty*, 43 Colum. L. Rev. 603 (1943).

116. *See generally* J. David Prince, *Other Recent Developments in Minnesota Law: Defective Products and Product Warranty Claims in Minnesota*, 31 Wm Mitchell L. Rev 1677 (2005).

117. U.C.C. §2-313 (1) (2005).

118. Minn. Stat. §336.2-313(1)(a).

119. *Id.* §336.2-313(2).

120. *See, e.g.*, Wilson v. Marquette Elecs., Inc., 630 F.2d 575, 579-80 (8th Cir. 1980).

121. Prince, *supra* note 117, at 1680.

122. Prince, *supra* note 117, at 1683.

123. U.C.C. §2-314 (2) (2005).

124. Prince, *supra* note 117, at 1699.

125. U.C.C. §2-315 (2005).

126. Prince, *supra* note 123, at 1996.

127. Ark. Code Ann. § 4-2-314

128. *See* Great Dane Trailer Sales, Inc. v. Malvern Pulpwood, Inc., 785 S.W.2d 13, 17 (Ark. 1990).

129. For a typical example *see* Md. Com. Law Code Ann. §§ 14-1501–14-1504 (1990 Repl. 1 Vol.; 1996 Supp.).

130. Only Alabama, Arkansas, Idaho, South Carolina, and South Dakota do not have statutory lemon laws.

131. *See* David A. Warren, *Car Trouble: Some Help for the Uninformed Buyer*, 66 Ohio St. L. J. 441 (2005).

132. *Id.* at 448.

133. 15 U.S.C.A. §§2301–2312 (1982; 1997 Supp.)

134. Lawrence A. Tower, *Automobile Warranty Litigation*, 39 Am. Jur. Trials 20 (1989).

135. 15 U.S.C.A. §§2301–2312

136. FLORIDA §681.101.

137. PAGE'S OHIO REVISED CODE ANNOTATED, §1345.71(E) (1992 Supp.).

138. Code of Alabama §8-20A-2 (6) (1992 Supp.).

139. General Laws of Rhode Island, 31-5.2-5 (1992 Supp.).

140. Paula Walter, *Commercial Impracticability in Contracts*, 61 ST. JOHN'S L. REV. 266 (1987); *see also* William T. Birmingham, *A Second Look at the Suez Canal Cases: Excuse for Non-Performance of Contractual Obligation in Light of Economic Theory*, 20 HASTINGS L. J. 1393 (1969).

141. Benjamin N. Henszey, *U.C.C. §2-615—Does "Impracticability" Mean Impossibility?* 10 U.C.C. L. J. 107 (1977); *see also* Stephan J. Sirriana, *The Developing Law of Contractual Impracticability/Impossibility, Part I*, 14 U.C.C. L. J. 30 (1980); John Sommers, *Commercial Impracticability: An Overview*, 13 DUQUESNE L. REV. 521 (1975).

142. Paula Walter, *Commercial Impracticability in Contracts,* 61 ST. JOHN'S L. REV. 225–226 (1987).

143. *Id.* at 228-229; *see also* Marcia J. Speziale, *The Turn of the Twentieth Century Is the Dawn of the Contract "Interpretation," Reflections, and Theories of Impossibility*, 17 DUQUESNE L. REV. 555 (1978–1979).

144. Restatement, *supra* note 2, §261(d).

145. See Vincent A. Wellman, *Conceptions of the Common Law: Reflections on a Theory of Contract*, 41 U. MIAMI L. REV. 925, 965 (1987).

146. Pasco Gasbarro Jr., *A Guide to Contract Negotiations*, 29 PRAC. LAW. 83, 84 (April 15, 1983).

147. INSTITUTE OF CONTINUING LEGAL EDUCATION, MICHIGAN BASIC PRACTICE HANDBOOK 8 (1986).

148. Eric M. Holmes & Dagmar Thurmann, *A New and Old Theory for Adjudicating Standardized Contracts*, 17 G. J. INT'L & COMP. L. 325, 427-429 (1987).

149. Gasbarro, *supra* note 147, at 88.

150. New York Plain English Law N.Y. Gen. Oblig. § 5-702 (as amended L.1994, c. 1, 36.)

151. Visit its Web site at http://www.lwionline.org/activities/conferences.asp.

152. Joseph Kimble, *Plain English: A Charter for Clear Writing (Part Three)*, 71 MICH. B. J. 1302 (Dec 1992).

153. Continuing Legal Education, *supra* note 148, at 16 (1986).

154. RIJ Pharm. Corp. v. Ivax Pharms., Inc., 322 F. SUPP. 2d 406, 412 (S.D.N.Y. 2004); *see also* First Investors Corp. v. Liberty Mut. Ins. Corp., 152 F.3d 162, 168 (2d Cir. 1998).

155. Wakeman v. Wheeler & Wilson Mfg. Co., 101 N.Y. 205, 209 (1886); *accord* Losei Realty Corp. v. City of New York, 254 N.Y. 41, 46 (1930) (quoting Wakeman).

156. Wakeman, 101 N.Y. at 209; *see also* Exxon Co. v. Sofec, Inc., 517 U.S. 830, 839–840 (1996).

157. 2 Restatement, *supra* note 2, §241.

158. 2 Restatement, *supra* note 2, §250.

159. 2 Restatement, *supra* note 2, §236.

160. 2 Restatement, *supra* note 2, at Comments, §218.

161. 2 Restatement, *supra* note 2, §373.

162. 2 Restatement, *supra* note 2, §357.

163. U.C.C. §2-716(2005).

164. 2 Restatement, *supra* note 2, §358.

165. U.C.C. §2-610 (2005).

166. U.C.C. §2-609(1) (2005).

167. U.C.C. §2-702(2)(3) (2005).

168. U.C.C. §2-705 (2005).

169. U.C.C. §2-706 (2005).

170. U.C.C. §2-706(2)(3) (2005).

171. U.C.C. §2-709 (1972).

172. U.C.C. §2-704 Official Comment (2005).

173. U.C.C. §2-703 (2005).

174. U.C.C. §2-708 (2005); *see also* U.C.C. §§2-709-10 (2005).

175. U.C.C. §2-711 (2005).

176. U.C.C. §2-713 (2005).

177. U.C.C. §2-714 (2005).

178. U.C.C. §2-715 (2005).

179. U.C.C. §2-716 (2005).

Chapter 6

Uniform Commercial Code

6. **Retention**
7. **Resale**
8. **Debtor's Rights in Collateral: Redemption and Preservation**

IV. **Summary**

Discussion Questions

 UNIFORM COMMERCIAL CODE PARALEGAL JOB DESCRIPTION

Uniform Commercial Code paralegals need to be proficient in the following competencies:

- Recognize an Article 2 sale of goods.
- Cite when a sale of goods under Article 2 must be perfected under Article 9.
- Make recommendations on unconscionability in a contract's provisions.
- Under the supervision of an attorney, draft and design provisions that provide for implied warranty and merchantability and warranty of fitness for a particular purpose.
- Recommend specific remedies buyers and sellers can take for a contract or sale of goods under the U.C.C.'s Article 2.
- Evaluate fact patterns to give alternative remedies to both buyers and sellers in a typical commercial transaction.
- Recognize all forms of commercial paper.
- Present commercial paper for acceptance in payment.
- Acquire surety documents.
- Prepare and draft a bill of lading.
- Properly endorse negotiable instruments.
- Endorse and transfer a stock certificate and draft an assignment separate from the certificate.
- Register bonds and stocks.
- Negotiate bearer bonds.
- Read and utilize the U.C.C. or applicable state statutes.
- Define an Article 9 secured interest.
- Discern whether attachment of a secured interest has taken place.
- Perfect a security interest.
- Determine who has priority in a secured interest.
- Prepare correspondence necessary under federal and state regulations for consumer finance, including notices and Regulation Z and other financing documents.
- File financing documents with the Secretary of State or county or other local officials as required under local rules and law.
- Finance a transaction using documents as collateral.
- Finance a transaction using inventory as collateral.
- Finance a motor vehicle.
- Finance equipment as a source of collateral.
- Determine which parties must file to perfect their interests.
- Determine where the parties must file to perfect their interests.
- Make recommendations on an outline of ownership priority in a secured interest.
- Perfect a security interest in the following ways:
  - Taking possession of the collateral.
  - Filing a financing statement in a designated public office.
  - Automatic perfection upon the attachment of the security interest.
  - Temporary perfection for a limited period.

INTRODUCTION

At the turn of the 20th century, commercial practices between merchants, businesses, and other entities were far from uniform. Statutory and legislative differences were based on local custom and tradition. The lack of a uniform set of principles and practices often led to chaotic results in the economy. Well-intentioned efforts to nationalize business practices were guided more by tradition than by modern business techniques. As society became more complex, transportation systems became more efficient, and communication and record keeping became revolutionized, the importance of nationalizing business practices acquired added meaning.

With the help of the American Law Institute, a commission drafted the Uniform Commercial Code (commonly abbreviated "U.C.C."). For almost 20 years the commission solicited comments from state and local bar associations, merchants' groups, governmental entities, academicians, and practitioners so that they could compose a code to serve the American commercial marketplace. By 1962 an official text with comments was presented for potential adoption by all American jurisdictions. Although the U.C.C. was originally not a legislative mandate, it has been so well received that all American jurisdictions have adopted at least portions of it. According to U.C.C. §1-103 (a), its purposes are to promote the following goals:

> *(1) to simplify, clarify, and modernize the law governing commercial transactions; (2) to permit the continued expansion of commercial practices through custom, usage, and agreement of the parties; and (3) to make uniform the law among the various jurisdictions.*[1]

Minimally, the Uniform Commercial Code is the product of business necessity and the desire to facilitate standard practices between merchants and other business entities. The U.C.C. covers various topical considerations that are treated according to specific articles. A summary of the articles of the Uniform Commercial Code include these subjects:

> Article 1: *General provisions; definitions and principles of interpretation; territorial applicability; and general rules.*
>
> Article 2: *Sale of goods; contract form, formation, and adjustment; general obligations of parties and construction of contract; title; creditors and good-faith purchasers; performance; breach; repudiation and excuse; remedies.*
>
> Article 2A: *Formation and construction of lease contract; effect of lease contract; performance of lease contract: repudiated, substituted and excused, default by lessee and lessor.*
>
> Article 3: *Negotiable instruments—commercial paper; checks; certified checks; notes; promissory notes; certificates of deposit; forms of endorsement; investment securities.*
>
> Article 4: *Bank deposits and collections—depository banks; methods of payment; payor banks; relationships between banks and customers; collection of documentary drafts.*
>
> Article 4A: *Fund transfers; issue and acceptance of payment order; execution of sender's payment order by receiving bank; payment.*
>
> Article 5: *Letters of credit; requirements of consideration; indemnification.*
>
> Article 6: *Transfer and assignment—bulk transfers.*
>
> Article 7: *Warehouse receipts; bills of lading and other documents of title; liens; negotiation and transfer issues.*
>
> Article 8: *Investment securities; transfer issues; brokers; warranty claims; endorsement issues; creditors' rights; registration requirements.*
>
> Article 9: *Secured transactions—definition of security interest; attachment; perfection of security interest; priority rights; financing statements; filing requirements; default remedies.*

Paralegals will spend little time examining the provisions of the U.C.C. but will engage in many of its practices. In fact, most articles are not germane to paralegal practice, though Articles 2, 3, 4, 5, and 9 will interest the paralegal involved in large retail settings and financial institutions. It is, however, important to understand the scope of the U.C.C. In the introduction to the 1972 version, the Uniform Commercial Code clarifies that its adoption is for numerous purposes:

> *To be known as the Uniform Commercial Code, relating to certain commercial transactions in or regarding personal property and contracts and other documents concerning them, including sales, commercial paper, bank deposits and collection, letters of credit, bulk transfers, warehouse receipts, bills of lading, other documents of title, investment securities and secured transactions,*

including certain sales of accounts, chattel paper, and contract rights; providing for public notice to third party in certain circumstances; regulating procedure, evidence, and damages in certain court actions involving such transactions, contracts, or documents to make uniform the law with respect thereto; and repealing inconsistent legislation.[2]

With this legislative design, it is clear that the U.C.C. standardizes commercial practice. Note that each provision of the U.C.C., as enacted, is accompanied by an "official comment"—that is, the draft discussion committee's review and assessment.

Case law can also be analyzed in annotated versions of the Uniform Commercial Code. It is important to realize that the Code does not displace all forms of law and analysis. Case law, traditional common law, and equitable principles still have a role in the interpretation of commercial practice between merchants. Section 1-103 (b) of the Code directs itself to this issue:

> *(b) Unless displaced by the particular provisions of [the Uniform Commercial Code], the principles of law and equity, including the law merchant and the law relative to capacity to contract, principal and agent, estoppel, fraud, misrepresentation, duress, coercion, mistake, bankruptcy, and other validating or invalidating cause supplement its provisions.*[3]

The drafters of the Uniform Commercial Code had one underlying desire in the promulgation of these principles—that of promoting the freedom to contract. As a result, business traditions of custom and usage, means of performance, and tactics of negotiation are not disregarded. The U.C.C. has been a subject of much scholarly, academic, and practical discussion.

Some commercial activities are not governed by the Uniform Commercial Code.[4] For example, the Code does not cover real estate practices and standards, leases, or certain crops and farm products. Each article will have definitional differences, and the paralegal must fit the applicable Code section to the proper transaction. Three specific articles within the Uniform Commercial Code have the greatest applicability and relevance to paralegal practice and procedure:

Article 2: Sales of Goods

Article 3: Commercial Paper

Article 9: Secured Transactions

Article 2 of the U.C.C., regarding the sale of goods, and geared toward the conduct of merchants, is covered in Chapter 5—Contracts. Again, Chapter 5 examines seller and buyer rights, warranty rights, and remedies of buyers and sellers in case of breach. The provisions of Article 3, covering commercial paper, and Article 9, encompassing secured transactions, are discussed in this chapter. Paralegals often complete commercial documentation, help prepare necessary forms, and make the necessary filings.

ARTICLE 3: COMMERCIAL PAPER

Paralegals working with commercial paper are involved in the law of negotiable instruments.[5] Some negotiable instruments (like checks and promissory notes) have been used in the commercial marketplace by individuals and business entities for generations. Commercial paper is simply a substitute for cash or the delivery of actual money. A *negotiable instrument* represents an underlying obligation between parties. These definitions describe the obligations that arise in the use of commercial paper:

Drawer: A person who writes, executes, or signs a piece of commercial paper, such as an individual who signs a check.

Drawee: A financial institution or other individual where funds are deposited to meet the underlying obligation.

Payee: The person to whom the commercial paper negotiable instrument has been drawn or made out.

Holder: The person who has the right to possess the commercial paper and is defined under the U.C.C. as

> *(A) the person in possession of a negotiable instrument that is payable either to bearer or to an identified person that is the person in possession; or (B) the person in possession of a document of title if the goods are deliverable either to bearer or to the order of the person in possession.*[6]

Endorsement: Whether through general or special means, an endorsement makes the negotiable instrument or commercial paper negotiable or usable.

> *(5) "Bearer" means a person in possession of a negotiable instrument, document of title, or certificated security that is payable to bearer or endorsed in blank.*[7]

What documents are commonly used in this commercial paper market? What documents qualify as a negotiable instrument? Under the U.C.C. a negotiable instrument must, at a minimum, meet the following standards:

> *(a) Except as provided in subsections (c) and (d), "negotiable instrument" means an unconditional promise or order to pay a fixed amount of money, with or without interest or other charges described in the promise or order, if it:*
> *(1) is payable to bearer or to order at the time it is issued or first comes into possession of a holder;*
> *(2) is payable on demand or at a definite time; and*
> *(3) does not state any other undertaking or instruction by the person promising or ordering payment to do any act in addition to the payment of money, but the promise or order may contain (i) an undertaking or power to give, maintain, or protect collateral to secure payment, (ii) an authorization or power to the holder to confess judgment or realize on or dispose of collateral, or (iii) a waiver of the benefit of any law intended for the advantage or protection of an obligor.*[8]

Common sense dictates that commercial paper must have documentary integrity to bind, assure, and make the underlying value of a transaction reasonably predictable. Many businesspeople and some consumers appreciate the unique legal liabilities associated with legal, negotiable instruments. The provisions of Article 3 make sure that negotiable instruments meet specific standards.

Negotiable Instruments: Requirements and Form

A negotiable instrument must

- Be generally in written form.
- Be signed by maker or drawer.
- Be an unconditional promise or order to pay.
- Have a sum certain in the monetary value of the commercial paper.
- Be definite in time.
- Have words of negotiability expressed in the document.

Types of negotiable instruments vary. The following are some examples.

Checks

Article 3 defines a check as a negotiable instrument. First, its negotiability is based on spacing for a drawer's signature in the lower right corner. Second, it has a space for a payee—that is, the person to whom the check is made. The check's language says, "Pay to the order of." Third, there are no conditions or other contingencies that would make the negotiability of this check questionable. Fourth, it is payable at a definite time as dictated by the date provision at the top of the check. All that remains to make the commercial paper negotiable is an endorsement on the back.

Primarily, a check is a payment instrument. "Its primary use is not to evidence or to create an obligation but to pay it. The check is not expected to circulate long or to be negotiated often."[9] A variation on this form of negotiable instrument is a certified or cashier's check in which the bank or other drawee certifies that the requisite funds exist to meet this obligation. In certifying the check, the bank assumes responsibility for its payment.

Promissory Notes

A promissory note is a written promise to pay a specific obligation. The person who makes the promise is called the *maker*.[10] Promissory notes are frequently written on standardized, preprinted forms but also can be prepared by a paralegal using the individual facts of the parties concerned. An example of a promissory note is outlined in Form 6.1 on the accompanying CD.

Often referred to as a *note*, this form of commercial paper is a statement by express provision regarding terms of payment and the promise to repay a debt. "Notes are used in the United States in almost every case where anybody borrows money, whether that anybody is a government, a business, or an individual. They can be written for any period of time from 'on demand' on up, as long as the period is definite."[11] To be enforceable, a note must have the following traits.

Payment at a Definite Time   The U.C.C. outlines what a definite time is by stating,

> *A promise or order is "payable at a definite time" if it is payable on elapse of a definite period of time after sight or acceptance or at a fixed date or dates or at a time or times readily ascertainable at the time the promise or order is issued, subject to rights of (i) prepayment, (ii) acceleration, (iii) extension at the option of the holder, or (iv) extension to a further definite time at the option of the maker or acceptor or automatically upon or after a specified act or event.*[12]

Maker   For a note to have any contractual capacity or protection under the U.C.C., the maker (that is, the person responsible for payment of the note) should be stated.

Payee or Holder   A person who is entitled to receive the benefit of the note (that is, the balance to be paid) is referred to as the *payee*. This party completes the contractual obligation.

Other Provisions   Notes may also contain specific provisions regarding interest rates, installment rates, renewal or extension provisions, acceleration clauses, addresses, and other personal information.

Signature   Under the provisions of §3-401(1), the Code requires an authorized signature. No person is liable on an instrument unless her or his signature appears thereon.[13]

The U.C.C. further provides that a signature may be made by an agent or other representative that is authorized to sign for the represented individual.[14]

The Code mandates these standards for a negotiable instrument:

- The promise must be unconditional.
- There must be a certain sum stated on the document outlining a specific level of payment.
- That payment must be made within a definite time.
- That payment must be made to order or to a specific bearer.

Drafts and Bills of Exchange

A *draft* is any order to pay money. A person who is issuing a draft is known as a *drawer*, and the person to whom the order is addressed is the *drawee*. A draft is a technique to ensure payment upon shipment of goods and is sometimes attached to a bill of lading or other delivery documentation. Draft examples usually require that payment be "at sight or on demand." Do not conclude that a draft is the same as a promissory note. The drawee is obligated to pay on the note rather than the drawer.

Here is how a draft works. In the commercial workplace, goods are shipped, transported, and delivered on oral agreement. The buyer awaits, let's say, shipment of 4,000 pencil sharpeners, while the seller desires payment upon receipt. A bill of lading sets out the contractual details and shipping or transport instructions. Once the buyer sees and inspects the goods, she issues a draft to seller, which in effect gives instructions to her bank to pay the seller a certain amount from a specific account. The draft may appear as shown in Figure 6.1.

Once the seller endorses the draft, the proceeds are remitted. A draft is payable on demand. As U.C.C. §3-108 indicates,

> *Instruments payable on demand include those payable at sight or on presentation and those in which no time for payment is stated.*[15]

A draft is usually an excellent means of ensuring collectible accounts, especially when merchants are not familiar with each other. It is also an effective technique of financing to ensure movement of goods between parties. When commercial merchants' reputations are strong enough, the use of a banker's acceptance of a draft assures that it will be paid.

Certificates of Deposit

A *certificate of deposit* as defined under the Uniform Commercial Code as "an acknowledgment by a bank that a sum of money has been received by the bank and a promise by the bank to repay

FIGURE 6.1   **Example of a Draft**

SPACE BELOW FOR ACCEPTANCE STAMP	DRAWER'S OR FORWARDING BANK'S NUMBER

Drawn under Anytown Commercial Bank

Bank Number XXXXXXX   Due

My City United Bank

Bank Number XXXXXX   *January 31, 2006*

XXXX/XXXX

At sight for value received pay to the order of the

My City United Bank the sum of   **Dollars** *$20,000.00* **U.S.**

Twenty Thousand   **U.S.**

TO *My City United Bank*   All Products Distributor

My City Financial District

RECEIVING BANK'S NUMBER
XXXXX-XXXXX

My Town, State

the sum of money. A certificate deposit is a note of the bank"[16] A sample certificate of deposit form is outlined in Figure 6.2.

The maker of a certificate of deposit is usually a financial institution. The payee is the individual or institution to whom the proceeds of the deposit plus corresponding interest must be paid upon its expiration or termination.

Endorsement Requirements

Endorsement of checks, promissory notes, and other commercial paper is necessary before the underlying funds can be transferred. Under Article 3 of U.C.C. §3-203, the act of endorsement creates a transference of interest:

> (b) *Transfer of an instrument, whether or not the transfer is a negotiation, vests in the transferee any right of the transferor to enforce the instrument, including any right as a holder in due course, but the transferee cannot acquire rights of a holder in due course by a transfer, directly or indirectly, from a holder in due course if the transferee engaged in fraud or illegality affecting the instrument.*
>
> (c) *Unless otherwise agreed, if an instrument is transferred for value and the transferee does not become a holder because of lack of indorsement by the transferor, the transferee has a specifically enforceable right to the unqualified indorsement of the transferor, but negotiation of the instrument does not occur until the indorsement is made.*[17]

The effect of binding negotiation is summarized under U.C.C. §3-201:

> (a) *"Negotiation" means a transfer of possession, whether voluntary or involuntary, of an instrument by a person other than the issuer to a person who thereby becomes its holder.*
>
> (b) *Except for negotiation by a remitter, if an instrument is payable to an identified person, negotiation requires transfer of possession of the instrument and its indorsement by the holder. If an instrument is payable to bearer, it may be negotiated by transfer of possession alone.*[18]

FIGURE 6.2 Sample Certificate of Deposit Form

Certificate of Deposit Receipt

Certificate No.

Primary Owner

Secondary Owner

☐ Certificate of Deposit

    ☐ Retail   ☐ Retirement

    ☐ Fixed Rate   ☐ Variable Rate

☐ Initial Deposit   ☐ Additional Deposit

Date _____   Amount _____

Maturity Date _____   Interest Rate _____ %

Term_____   Annual Percentage Yield _____ %

Interest Payment Method _____

_____
Official Signature

Subject to terms and conditions set forth in bank's Rules and Disclosures for Time Deposits, as amended. A penalty will be imposed for early withdrawal.

NONNEGOTIABLE AND NONTRANSFERABLE TIME DEPOSIT

FIGURE 6.3
Example of a Check Made Out to an Individual

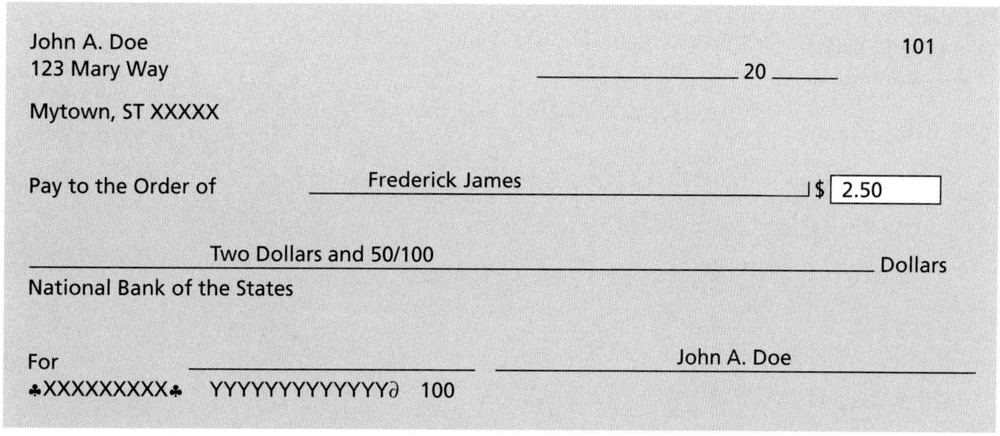

John A. Doe
123 Mary Way
                                                                            101
Mytown, ST XXXXX   _____ 20 _____

Pay to the Order of   Frederick James $ 2.50

                    Two Dollars and 50/100   Dollars
National Bank of the States

For _____   John A. Doe
♣XXXXXXXXX♣   YYYYYYYYYYYYYYϑ 100

The U.C.C. makes no attempt to mandate rights under the partial assignment just cited at subsection (3). Endorsing a check or commercial note, with a stated value, for a qualified, partial assignment gives only those rights to the bearer dictated by local jurisdictions. The Code's official comment relays,

> The partial endorsement does, however, operate as a partial assignment of the cause of action. The provision makes no attempt to state the legal effect of such an assignment, which is left to the local law. In a jurisdiction in which a partial assignee has any rights, either at law or in equity, the partial endorsee has such rights; and in any jurisdiction where a partial assignee has no rights the partial endorsee has none.[19]

Endorsements are either special, general, or in blank. Examples of these endorsements are outlined in the following sections.

Depending on the type of commercial paper, the location of the endorsement varies. On a check, for instance, the endorsement needs to be at the top of the instrument. Examine the instrument closely to determine the appropriate endorsement location. Endorsed commercial paper can be honored in banks, retail establishments, and brokerage houses.

Blank (General) Endorsements

The example of the check shown in Figure 6.3 states, "Pay to the Order of Frederick James." To make this commercial paper negotiable, the payee merely has to turn the check over and sign his name accordingly. It is thereafter treated as bearer paper and is negotiable by mere delivery.[20]

Bearer Paper

The check shown in Figure 6.4 made out to "Cash" is considered bearer paper. "The basic characteristic of bearer paper as distinguished from other commercial paper is that it can be negotiated by delivery without endorsement."[21] Naturally, bearer paper has limitations and dangers. The fact that bearer paper can be negotiated without a normal endorsement means that it can fall into the hands of individuals who may use it illegally or fraudulently.

FIGURE 6.4
Example of a Check Made Out to "Cash"

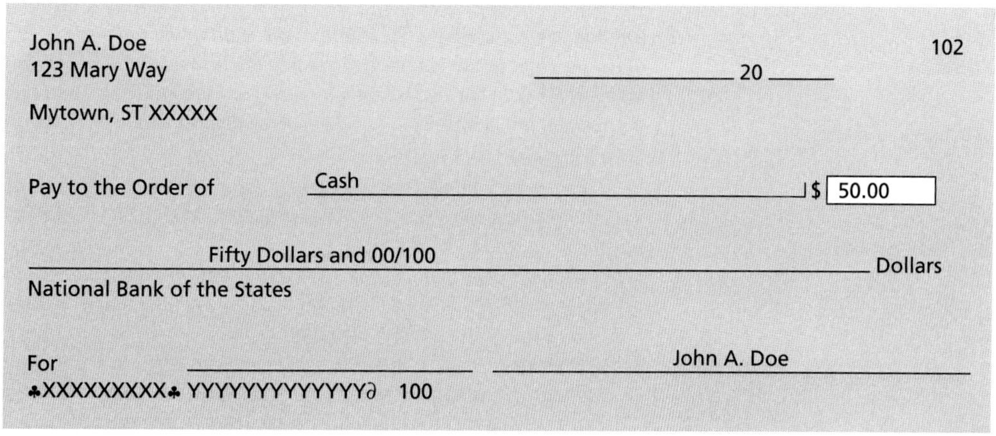

John A. Doe
123 Mary Way
                                                                            102
Mytown, ST XXXXX   _____ 20 _____

Pay to the Order of   Cash $ 50.00

                    Fifty Dollars and 00/100   Dollars
National Bank of the States

For _____   John A. Doe
♣XXXXXXXXX♣ YYYYYYYYYYYYYYϑ 100

FIGURE 6.5
Example of Special Endorsement

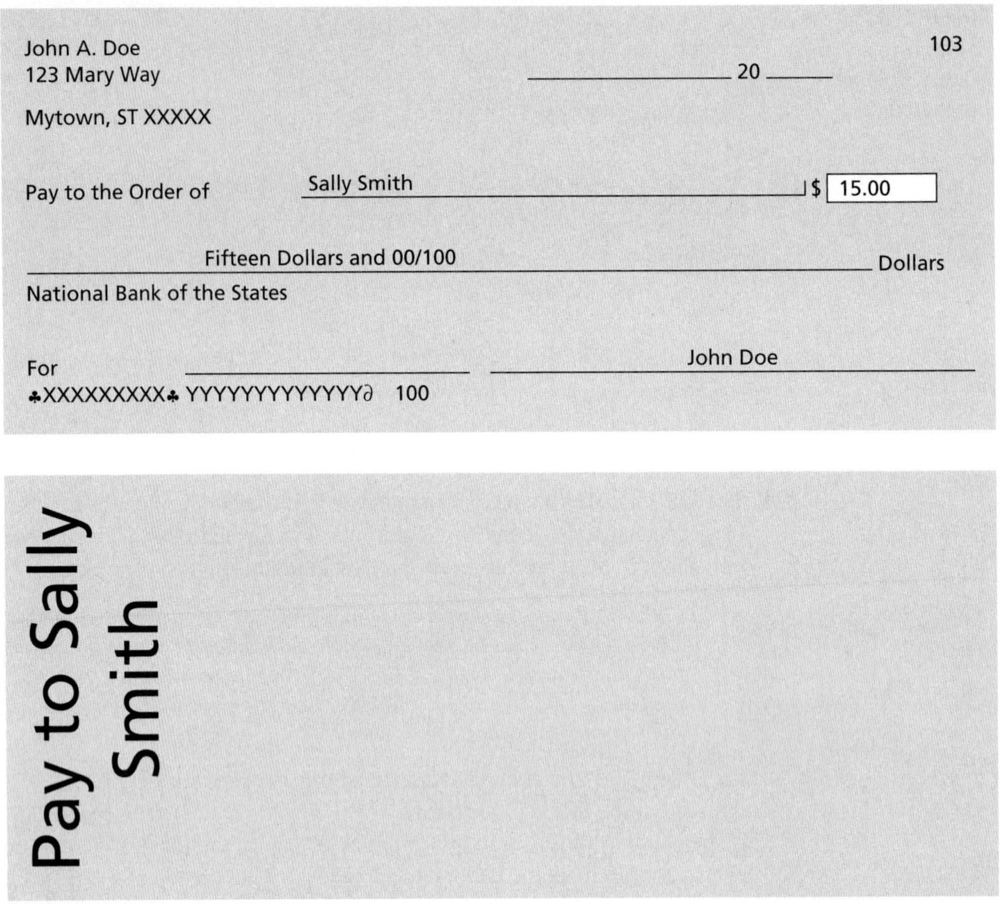

John A. Doe
123 Mary Way

Mytown, ST XXXXX

_____ 20 _____   103

Pay to the Order of   Sally Smith $ [15.00]

Fifteen Dollars and 00/100 _____ Dollars

National Bank of the States

For _____   _____ John Doe _____

♣XXXXXXXXX♣ YYYYYYYYYYYYY∂ 100

Pay to Sally Smith

Special Endorsement

The back of a check can also be the location for a special endorsement. Figure 6.5 uses the language "Pay to Sally Smith" and thereafter requires an endorsement from the individual on the back of the check. "A special endorsement specifies the person to whom or to whose order it makes the instrument payable. When an instrument is specially endorsed, it becomes payable to the order of the special endorsee and requires his endorsement for further negotiation."[22]

Restrictive Endorsements

Uniform Commercial Code §3-205 defines a _restrictive endorsement_ as follows:

(a) _An indorsement limiting payment to a particular person or otherwise prohibiting further transfer or negotiation of the instrument is not effective to prevent further transfer or negotiation of the instrument._

(b) _An indorsement stating a condition to the right of the indorsee to receive payment does not affect the right of the indorsee to enforce the instrument. A person paying the instrument or taking it for value or collection may disregard the condition, and the rights and liabilities of that person are not affected by whether the condition has been fulfilled._

(c) _If an instrument bears an indorsement (i) described in Section 4-201(b), or (ii) in blank or to a particular bank using the words "for deposit," "for collection," or other words indicating a purpose of having the instrument collected by a bank for the indorser or for a particular account, the following rules apply:_

(1) _A person, other than a bank, who purchases the instrument when so indorsed converts the instrument unless the amount paid for the instrument is received by the indorser or applied consistently with the indorsement._

(2) _A depositary bank that purchases the instrument or takes it for collection when so indorsed converts the instrument unless the amount paid by the bank with respect to the instrument is received by the indorser or applied consistently with the indorsement._

> (3) *A payor bank that is also the depositary bank or that takes the instrument for immediate payment over the counter from a person other than a collecting bank converts the instrument unless the proceeds of the instrument are received by the indorser or applied consistently with the indorsement.*
>
> (4) *Except as otherwise provided in paragraph (3), a payor bank or intermediary bank may disregard the indorsement and is not liable if the proceeds of the instrument are not received by the indorser or applied consistently with the indorsement.*
>
> (d) *Except for an indorsement covered by subsection (c), if an instrument bears an indorsement using words to the effect that payment is to be made to the indorsee as agent, trustee, or other fiduciary for the benefit of the indorser or another person, the following rules apply:*
>
> (1) *Unless there is notice of breach of fiduciary duty as provided in Section 3-307, a person who purchases the instrument from the indorsee or takes the instrument from the indorsee for collection or payment may pay the proceeds of payment or the value given for the instrument to the indorsee without regard to whether the indorsee violates a fiduciary duty to the indorser.*
>
> (2) *A subsequent transferee of the instrument or person who pays the instrument is neither given notice nor otherwise affected by the restriction in the indorsement unless the transferee or payor knows that the fiduciary dealt with the instrument or its proceeds in breach of fiduciary duty.*
>
> (e) *The presence on an instrument of an indorsement to which this section applies does not prevent a purchaser of the instrument from becoming a holder in due course of the instrument unless the purchaser is a converter under subsection (c) or has notice or knowledge of breach of fiduciary duty as stated in subsection (d).*
>
> (f) *In an action to enforce the obligation of a party to pay the instrument, the obligor has a defense if payment would violate an indorsement to which this section applies and the payment is not permitted by this section.*[23]

The best example of the restrictive endorsement is a payee's express instructions to a bank that a check is to be deposited to a specific account. The only other individuals who will have some impact on the transferability or negotiability of the document once the payee has deposited it are the banks in the collection process itself. This type of restrictive endorsement ensures a proper credit to an account and minimizes fraud or theft. The check's restrictive language may state,

- Pay only upon completion of a task.
- For collection only.[24]
- For deposit only.

Right of Holders in Due Course

A person who takes, purchases, or acquires a piece of commercial paper is known as a *holder in due course.* In a free market system, commercial paper should be freely alienable and easily transferable to keep the wheels of economic enterprise moving. Paper is transferred to holders for any imaginable reason.

Holders in due course are individuals who take, for some period, control, possession, or actual ownership of a piece of commercial paper. A holder in due course must meet five fundamental conditions as outlined at U.C.C. §3-302:

> 1. *Be a holder;*
> 2. *Of a negotiable instrument;*
> 3. *For value;*
> 4. *Have taken in good faith; and*
> 5. *Without notice that it was overdue or dishonored or subject to defenses.*

Predictably, an individual who purchases commercial paper that is defective, faulty, fraudulent, or subject to other rights or interests is economically injured. The purchaser of commercial paper, a promissory note, a certificate of deposit, or a draft may be immune to specific defenses that the initial makers, acceptors, endorsers, and drawers had upon the original instrument. The paralegal's task is to help the attorney gauge the rights of the parties with competing interests in commercial paper. A holder in due course is within the secondary tier of individual owners. The holder in due course is, of course, a highly refined species of bona fide purchaser who is free of most defenses of prior parties to the instrument and is free of conflicting title claims to the instrument.[25]

Consider a finance company that buys a consumer note, such as a finance agreement on an automobile, at a stated rate of interest. The finance company is not an original party to the contract but by purchase is a holder in due course of the original agreement between the auto company (or the dealer) and the vehicle buyer. Does the finance company take free and clear if the original automobile purchased is subject to an unpublished, unregistered lien? If the finance company can show the purchase was for real value, in good faith, and without notice of any pending or actual litigation on the car's liens, it takes free and clear.[26] Whether or not one has been put on notice of claims or defenses is a common dispute:

> (2) the holder took the instrument (i) for value, (ii) in good faith, (iii) without notice that the instrument is overdue or has been dishonored or that there is an uncured default with respect to payment of another instrument issued as part of the same series, (iv) without notice that the instrument contains an unauthorized signature or has been altered, (v) without notice of any claim to the instrument described in Section 3-306, and (vi) without notice that any party has a defense or claim in recoupment described in Section 3-305(a).[27]

Notice is dependent on actual or constructive knowledge. For a pleading that exhibits the holder in due course status, see Form 6.2 on the accompanying CD.

The specific rights of a holder are delineated at U.C.C. § 3-305:

> To the extent that a holder is a holder in due course he takes the instrument free from
>
> (1) all claims to it on the part of any person; and
> (2) all defenses of any party to the instrument with whom the holder has not dealt, except
>   (a) infancy, to the extent that it is a defense to a simple contract; and
>   (b) such other incapacity, or duress, or illegality of the transaction, as renders the obligation of the party a nullity; and
>   (c) such misrepresentation as has induced the party to sign the instrument with neither knowledge nor reasonable opportunity to obtain knowledge of its character or its essential terms; and
>   (d) discharge in insolvency proceedings; and
>   (e) any other discharge of which the holder has notice when he takes the instrument.[28]

A party that cannot declare itself a holder in due course is nothing more than a holder without due course. U.C.C. §3-306 outlines these reduced interests and rights:

> Unless he has the rights of a holder in due course, any person takes the instrument subject to:
>
> (a) all valid claims to it on the part of any person; and
> (b) all defenses to any party which would be available in an action on a simple contract; and
> (c) the defenses of want or failure of consideration, nonperformance of any condition precedent, nondelivery or delivery for a special purpose; and
> (d) the defense that he or a person through whom he holds the instrument acquired it by theft, or that payment or satisfaction to such holder would be inconsistent with the terms of a restrictive endorsement. The claim of any third person to the instrument is not otherwise available as a defense to any party liable thereon unless the third person himself defends the action for such party.[29]

Obviously a subsequent purchaser who is declared a holder without due course may possess a worthless piece of paper or be liable for the actions of the original parties.

Presentment and Dishonor

Once a piece of commercial paper has been endorsed and made negotiable, its presentment is the next step. "Presentment may be made by personally contacting the primary party and making a demand for acceptance of payment. Presentment may be made by mail or through a clearinghouse."[30] The Code also sets out timetables for presentment, from specific time lines to timetables set by customary habits of particular financial entities at §3-501:

> (a) "Presentment" means a demand made by or on behalf of a person entitled to enforce an instrument (i) to pay the instrument made to the drawee or a party obliged to pay the instrument or, in the case of a note or accepted draft payable at a bank, to the bank, or (ii) to accept a draft made to the drawee.

    (b) The following rules are subject to Article 4, agreement of the parties, and clearinghouse rules and the like:

        (1) Presentment may be made at the place of payment of the instrument and must be made at the place of payment if the instrument is payable at a bank in the United States; may be made by any commercially reasonable means, including an oral, written, or electronic communication; is effective when the demand for payment or acceptance is received by the person to whom presentment is made; and is effective if made to any one of two or more makers, acceptors, drawees, or other payors.

        (2) Upon demand of the person to whom presentment is made, the person making presentment must (i) exhibit the instrument, (ii) give reasonable identification and, if presentment is made on behalf of another person, reasonable evidence of authority to do so, and (iii) sign a receipt on the instrument for any payment made or surrender the instrument if full payment is made.

        (3) Without dishonoring the instrument, the party to whom presentment is made may (i) return the instrument for lack of a necessary indorsement, or (ii) refuse payment or acceptance for failure of the presentment to comply with the terms of the instrument, an agreement of the parties, or other applicable law or rule.

        (4) The party to whom presentment is made may treat presentment as occurring on the next business day after the day of presentment if the party to whom presentment is made has established a cutoff hour not earlier than 2 p.m. for the receipt and processing of instruments presented for payment or acceptance and presentment is made after the cutoff hour.[31]

Presentment may also be at a place of acceptance or payment specified in the instrument or, if there is none, at the place of business or residence of the party to accept or pay. If neither the party to accept or pay nor anyone authorized to act for him or her is present or accessible at such place, presentment is excused.[32] Parties who bring checks, drafts, or other negotiable instruments to a financial institution, or other authority, can be rightfully expected to produce proper identification. Under U.C.C. §3-501 (2) the party to whom presentment is made may without dishonor require the following:

- Display the instrument
- Present identification
- If presentment is being made on behalf of another person give evidence of authority to do so
- Sign a receipt or surrender the instrument. When drafts, checks, promissory notes, and other commercial papers are presented and the underlying obligation cannot be met or satisfied, it sometimes results in a statement by a bank, (payor bank or collection bank) that there are not enough funds; in this case a legal dishonor occurs. Accounts with insufficient funds, forged or altered checks, or suspect collateral all may result in dishonor. The U.C.C. lays out explicit instructions for the banking industry:

    (a) If a payor bank settles for a demand item other than a documentary draft presented otherwise than for immediate payment over the counter before midnight of the banking day of receipt, the payor bank may revoke the settlement and recover the settlement if, before it has made final payment and before its midnight deadline, it

        (1) returns the item;

        (2) returns an image of the item, if the party to which the return is made has entered into an agreement to accept an image as a return of the item; and the image is returned in accordance with that agreement;

        (3) sends a record providing notice of dishonor or nonpayment if the item is unavailable for return.

    (b) If a demand item is received by a payor bank for credit on its books, it may return the item or send notice of dishonor and may revoke any credit given or recover the amount thereof withdrawn by its customer, if it acts within the time limit and in the manner specified in subsection(a).

    (c) Unless previous notice of dishonor has been sent, an item is dishonored at the time when for purposes of dishonor it is returned or notice sent in accordance with this section.

    (d) An item is returned:

        (1) as to an item presented through a clearinghouse, when it is delivered to the presenting or last collecting bank or to the clearinghouse or is sent or delivered in accordance with clearinghouse rules; or

        (2) in all other cases, when it is sent or delivered to the bank's customer or transferor or pursuant to instructions.[33]

For provisions relating to notice of dishonor, see U.C.C. §3-503.

Presentment may be excused or waived if a party is without notice of its due date, or mitigating circumstances beyond the control of the party cause a delay, or presentment is waived or excused. Section §3-504 sets the requirements:

> *(b) Notice of dishonor is excused if (i) by the terms of the instrument notice of dishonor is not necessary to enforce the obligation of a party to pay the instrument, or (ii) the party whose obligation is being enforced waived notice of dishonor. A waiver of presentment is also a waiver of notice of dishonor.*
>
> *(c) Delay in giving notice of dishonor is excused if the delay was caused by circumstances beyond the control of the person giving the notice and the person giving the notice exercised reasonable diligence after the cause of the delay ceased to operate.*[34]

Discharge

Commercial paper, like a contract, outlines an underlying obligation on the part of the maker or drawer. The maker or drawer who meets his or her obligations can be said to have been discharged from that underlying obligation. The reasons or rationales for discharge are governed by various sections within the Uniform Commercial Code.

In the case of discharge, the drawer or maker of a piece of commercial paper has no further obligations under the matter. If fraudulent or material alteration has taken place, other civil or criminal remedies may be available to the drawer or the maker. A party will be discharged from liability on a secured instrument if any of the following takes place:

- Payment or satisfaction (Section 3-602).
- Tender of payment (Section 3-603).
- Cancellation or renunciation (Section 3-604).
- Impairment of right of recourse or of collateral (Section 3-605).
- Reacquisition of the instrument by a prior party (Section 3-207).
- Fraudulent and material alteration (Section 3-407).
- Certification of a check (Section 3-409).
- Acceptance varying a draft (Section 3-410).
- Unexcused delay in presentment or notice of dishonor or protest (Section 3-504).

Section 3-601(a) also discharges a party "by an act or agreement with the party which would discharge an obligation to pay money under a simple contract."[35] A subsequent holder of the instrument need not honor the discharge unless on notice of the discharge.[36]

Paralegals will probably see payment and satisfaction as the most common method of discharge:

> *(1) The liability of any party is discharged to the extent of his payment or satisfaction to the holder even though it is made with knowledge of a claim of another person to the instrument unless prior to such payment or satisfaction the person making the claim either supplies indemnity deemed adequate by the party seeking the discharge or enjoins payment or satisfaction by order of a court of competent jurisdiction in an action in which the adverse claimant and the holder are parties. This subsection does not, however, result in the discharge of the liability if*
>
> > *(1) a claim to the instrument under Section 3-306 is enforceable against the party receiving payment and (i) payment is made with knowledge by the payor that payment is prohibited by injunction or similar process of a court of competent jurisdiction, or (ii) in the case of an instrument other than a cashier's check, teller's check, or certified check, the party making payment accepted, from the person having a claim to the instrument, indemnity against loss resulting from refusal to pay the person entitled to enforce the instrument; or*
> >
> > *(2) the person making payment knows that the instrument is a stolen instrument and pays a person it knows is in wrongful possession of the instrument.*[37]

The Code also provides liberal discretion in any holder merely canceling or renouncing the objection. Section 3-605 states,

> *(a) A person entitled to enforce an instrument, with or without consideration, may discharge the obligation of a party to pay the instrument (i) by an intentional voluntary act, such as surrender of the instrument to the party, destruction, mutilation, or cancellation of the instrument, cancellation or striking out of the party's signature, or the addition of words to the instrument indicating discharge, or (ii) by agreeing not to sue or otherwise renouncing rights against the party by a signed record.*

(b) *Cancellation or striking out of an indorsement pursuant to subsection (a) does not affect the status and rights of a party derived from the indorsement.*

(c) *As used in this section, "signed," with respect to a record that is not a writing, includes the attachment to or logical association with the record of an electronic symbol, sound, or process to or with the record with the present intent to adopt or accept the record.*[38]

A standard discharge document is shown in Form 6.3 on the accompanying CD.

Defense Strategies in Commercial Paper Cases

Paralegals assisting parties sued over commercial paper should recognize the defense strategies available. As summarized previously, a true holder in due course take free and clear and is generally granted immunity to subsequent litigation. However, even holders in due course are not totally impregnable. A holder in due course may still become subject to specific defenses that arise at the time of the transfer of the commercial paper. Also, defenses and other obligations arising before transfer negotiations may attach to any holder. (See §3-305(2) of the Code.)

Other defenses involve the influence of fraud and forgery, material alteration to a document, a lack of signature, and other technical assertions. The burden of proving defenses or claims rests on the individual who asserts that he or she is the owner. Before attempting a defense, get all the information about the commercial paper transaction during a client interview. (See Form 6.4 on the accompanying CD.)

ARTICLE 9: SECURED TRANSACTIONS

Paralegal practice with regard to the U.C.C. also involves the law of secured transactions. For both individuals and businesses, the term *security* means assurance—some level of guarantee, some proof that an obligation of a creditor, a financial institution, or another party will have collateral backing. A transaction that is secured is a "protected" one. Article 9 is basically an extension of the traditional definition of a pledge, a chattel mortgage, or a lien. The purpose of Article 9 is an attempt, to some extent, to provide a uniform approach to the collateralizing of obligations. A security interest is broadly defined to mean any interest in personal property or fixtures that secures the payment of an obligation.[39] Section 9-109 of the Code enunciates its scope:

> *Except as otherwise provided in subsections (c) and (d), this article applies to:*
>
> *(1) a transaction, regardless of its form, that creates a security interest in personal property or fixtures by contract;*
>
> *(2) an agricultural lien;*
>
> *(3) a sale of accounts, chattel paper, payment intangibles, or promissory notes;*
>
> *(4) a consignment;*
>
> *(5) a security interest arising under Section 2-401, 2-505, 2-711(3), or 2A-508(5), as provided in Section 9-110; and*
>
> *(6) a security interest arising under Section 4-210 or 5-118.*[40]

In elementary terms, the law of secured transactions concerns itself with protection for the creditor to ensure repayment of the underlying obligation; and if the debtor fails to repay, the creditors have certain remedies. Here are some examples that demonstrate these principles:

Example 1

A company wishing to borrow funds from a commercial lender enters a secured transaction using inventory.

Example 2

A judgment creditor wishing to ensure his or her eventual payment in a settlement enters a financing and security agreement using the assets of the judgment debtor.

Example 3

Company X wanting to buy a $4 million incinerator enters a financing and security arrangement with the dealer of incinerator granting a secured interest upon payment of all installments.

Article 9 provides a means to secure a transaction, like Article 3, while fostering economic stability. Every credit seller and every credit lender is interested in being paid. Accordingly, every credit seller and every credit lender is interested in any legal advice that will increase the possibility of repayment. Security increases the possibility of repayment. Every credit seller and every credit lender is interested in minimizing collection costs. Security minimizes such costs.[41]

The Vocabulary of Article 9

Paralegals must pay close attention to the terminology and vocabulary of Article 9 to understand its purposes. Here are the essential classifications and definitions frequently used:

Debtor: The party who wishes to acquire goods, inventory, machinery, equipment, or any other property interest outlined under Article 9; the party who remains obliged; the party who owes the debt (§9-105 (1)(d)).

Secured party: The seller, lender, or dealer using the sale item as collateral; the party hoping to protect his or her risk in a noncash transaction (§9-105 (1)(m)).

Security interest: The seller's, lender's, or dealer's interest in specific property, collateral, or inventory; his or her lien or right against the property under the secured transaction. U.C.C. §1-201 at Paragraph 37 defines a *security interest* to mean any interest in personal property or fixtures that secures the payment or performance of an obligation (§1-201 (35)).

Collateral or property: The inventory, goods, machinery, equipment, or assets utilized to secure a transaction (§9-105 (1)(c)).

Security agreement: The contract or document outlining the debtor and secured party's duties and obligations under the agreement. Agreement can be complex or simplistic, and it need not be written. An example of a security agreement with pertinent provisions is shown in Form 6.5 on the accompanying CD (§9-105 (1)(l)).

Financing statement: A financing statement evidences the secured transaction by outlining the obligation. A financing statement filed with appropriate governmental bodies and authorities creates notice of a secured transaction to any parties. A copy of a financing statement usually referred to as U.C.C.-1 is reproduced in Form 6.6 (§9-402).

Purchase money: A security interest taken or retained by the seller of the collateral to secure all or part of its price; or taken by a person who by making or incurring an obligation gives value to enable the debtor to acquire rights in or the use of collateral if such value is so used (§9-107).

The *debtor* is the one who owns but owes the secured interest. The *secured party* is the person with a real interest in the debtor's property. The *financing statement* should reference the property secured and adequately describe the real estate, agricultural crops, goods, and livestock. Other information is self-explanatory.

Classification of Secured Interest: The Nature of Property under Article 9

Under Article 9 property relies on collateral—that is, property is subject to security interest *and* includes accounts and chattel paper. The problem is that *security interest* is not defined in the Code. However, *goods* falls into these common categories:

1. Consumer goods.
2. Equipment.
3. Farm products.
4. Inventory.

These classifications are further subdivided under Article 9 as follows:

Chattel paper: A record or records that evidence both a monetary obligation and a security interest in specific goods, a security interest in specific goods and software used in the goods, or a lease of specific goods. The term does not include charters or other contracts involving the use or hire of a vessel. If a transaction is evidenced both by a security agreement or lease and by an instrument or series of instruments, the group of records taken together constitutes chattel paper.[42]

Collateral: The property subject to a security interest or agricultural lien. The term includes

(A) proceeds to which a security interest attaches;

(B) accounts, chattel paper, payment intangibles, and promissory notes that have been sold; and

(C) goods that are the subject of a consignment.[43]

Goods: All things that are movable when a security interest attaches. The term includes

(i) fixtures, (ii) standing timber that is to be cut and removed under a conveyance or contract for sale, (iii) the unborn young of animals, (iv) crops grown, growing, or to be grown, even if the crops are produced on trees, vines, or bushes, and (v) manufactured homes. The term also includes a computer program embedded in goods and any supporting information provided in connection with a transaction relating to the program if (i) the program is associated with the goods in such a manner that it customarily is considered part of the goods, or (ii) by becoming the owner of the goods, a person acquires a right to use the program in connection with the goods. The term does not include a computer program embedded in goods that consist solely of the medium in which the program is embedded. The term also does not include accounts, chattel paper, commercial tort claims, deposit accounts, documents, general intangibles, instruments, investment property, letter-of-credit rights, letters of credit, money, or oil, gas, or other minerals before extraction.[44]

Not all property forms can be made subject to a security agreement. At U.C.C. §9-109 (d) the Article states explicit exemptions and exclusions from its coverage as follows:

The Article does not apply to

(1) a landlord's lien, other than an agricultural lien;

(2) a lien, other than an agricultural lien, given by statute or other rule of law for services or materials, but Section 9-333 applies with respect to priority of the lien;

(3) an assignment of a claim for wages, salary, or other compensation of an employee;

(4) a sale of accounts, chattel paper, payment intangibles, or promissory notes as part of a sale of the business out of which they arose;

(5) an assignment of accounts, chattel paper, payment intangibles, or promissory notes which is for the purpose of collection only;

(6) an assignment of a right to payment under a contract to an assignee that is also obligated to perform under the contract;

(7) an assignment of a single account, payment intangible, or promissory note to an assignee in full or partial satisfaction of a preexisting indebtedness;

(8) a transfer of an interest in or an assignment of a claim under a policy of insurance, other than an assignment by or to a health care provider of a health care insurance receivable and any subsequent assignment of the right to payment, but Sections 9-315 and 9-322 apply with respect to proceeds and priorities in proceeds;

(9) an assignment of a right represented by a judgment, other than a judgment taken on a right to payment that was collateral;

(10) a right of recoupment or set-off, but:

(A) Section 9-340 applies with respect to the effectiveness of rights of recoupment or set-off against deposit accounts; and

(B) Section 9-404 applies with respect to defenses or claims of an account debtor;

(11) the creation or transfer of an interest in or lien on real property, including a lease or rents thereunder, except to the extent that provision is made for:

(A) liens on real property in Sections 9-203 and 9-308;

(B) fixtures in Section 9-334;

(C) fixture filings in Sections 9-501, 9-502, 9-512, 9-516, and 9-519; and

(D) security agreements covering personal and real property in Section 9-604;

(12) an assignment of a claim arising in tort, other than a commercial tort claim, but Sections 9-315 and 9-322 apply with respect to proceeds and priorities in proceeds; or

(13) an assignment of a deposit account in a consumer transaction, but Sections 9-315 and 9-322 apply with respect to proceeds and priorities in proceeds.[45]

Unless exempted under §9-109 security interests can be created by contract, assignment, chattel mortgage, chattel trust, trust deed, factor's lien, equipment trust, conditional sale, trust receipt, other lien, or title retention contract and lease or consignment intended as security.[46]

The Uniform Commercial Code gives special treatment to various other property or transactional interests. In the broadest context, Article 9 applies to "goods" that are movable when a security interest attaches.[47]

A person who is not a purchaser of a consumer good is labeled a "buyer in the ordinary course of business." Special rules also exist, especially at the state level, regarding filings and paperwork for the financing and registration of motor vehicles. Although the U.C.C. generally has authority and control over such a transaction, departments of motor vehicles and other administrative agencies have preempted and downplayed the influence of the U.C.C. in auto financing practice. In fact, the entire area of consumer finance is guided by a diversity of federal and state legislation. Alternative and ancillary federal legislation guides these financial security practices:

Equal Credit Opportunity Act: 15 U.S.C. §1691.

Fair Credit Reporting Act: 15 U.S.C. §1681.

Installment Sales Agreement Act: See state statutes particularly.

Magnuson Moss Warranty Act: 15 U.S.C. §2301.

Electronic Fund Transfer Act: 15 U.S.C. §1693.

Fair Credit Billing Act: 15 U.S.C. §1666.

Truth in Lending Act: 15 U.S.C. §1601.

Fair Debt Collection Practices Act: 15 U.S.C. §1692.

Formal Requirements in the Creation of a Security Interest

Attachment

In order for a security interest to have any validity and enforceability, it must attach. *Attachment* is defined as those acts necessary to create an enforceable security interest. By attachment, the law assumes that the necessary formal requirements for the security agreement have been fulfilled. U.C.C. §9-203 makes this plain:

(a) *[Attachment.]*
A security interest attaches to collateral when it becomes enforceable against the debtor with respect to the collateral, unless an agreement expressly postpones the time of attachment.

(b) *[Enforceability.]*
Except as otherwise provided in subsections (c) through (i), a security interest is enforceable against the debtor and third parties with respect to the collateral only if:
(1) *value has been given;*
(2) *the debtor has rights in the collateral or the power to transfer rights in the collateral to a secured party; and*
(3) *one of the following conditions is met:*
(A) *the debtor has authenticated a security agreement that provides a description of the collateral and, if the security interest covers timber to be cut, a description of the land concerned;*
(B) *the collateral is not a certificated security and is in the possession of the secured party under Section 9-313 pursuant to the debtor's security agreement;*
(C) *the collateral is a certificated security in registered form and the security certificate has been delivered to the secured party under Section 8-301 pursuant to the debtor's security agreement; or*
(D) *the collateral is deposit accounts, electronic chattel paper, investment property, or letter-of-credit rights or electronic documents, and the secured party has control under Section 7-106, 9-104, 9-105, 9-106, or 9-107 pursuant to the debtor's security agreement.*[48]

The Security Agreement

As a result of formal requirements, debtor and secured creditor will draft and enter a written security agreement as previously outlined in Form 6.5 on the accompanying CD. Some discussion regarding the possessory rights to the collateral security underlying the obligation is found within the security agreement. The debtor has specific rights in the collateral, but the secured party is giving value for an interest in that property. The steps to perfect a security interest may not occur simultaneously; but once all have occurred, a valid Article 9 security interest, enforceable at least against the debtor, comes into existence.

Requirements of a Writing As a rule of practice, a secured interest must be evidenced by a writing. Written security agreements avoid potential fraud and minimize any disputes about terms and conditions. There is a split of authority over whether or not the financing agreement itself is a satisfactory writing.[49] Despite this judicial division, a security agreement should be drafted with explicit terms and conditions. The financing statement is mandatory under the Code.[50] The financing statement usually does not contain a description of the collateral.

Signature Requirements Wisely, the Code requires an authenticated, verifiable, and credible signature on a document, whether it be from the actual debtor, agent, or other legally empowered representative.[51]

Description of the Collateral U.C.C. provisions require that the security agreement sufficiently outline and describe the collateral in question. "There have been substantial numbers of reported cases considering the sufficiency of a description of collateral in a security agreement. In some cases the debtor is challenging the sufficiency of the description; in others the challenger is another creditor of the debtor or a representative of such creditors. . . ."[52] U.C.C. §9-108(a) simply calls for a description that "reasonably identifies what it describes."[53] Attorneys and paralegal practitioners should make sure that the descriptions of the collateral in question adhere to customary standards of specificity and particularity. Imprecise terms, such as "all the equipment in the plant," "all the farm equipment available," or "all the goods and stuff that can be found," should be eliminated. The purpose of a description of collateral in any security agreement is to ensure the identification of the item described to enforce any rights or remedies of the parties upon default.

Existence of Value As in traditional contract analysis, the term *value* is synonymous with *consideration*. The Uniform Commercial Code at §1-204 defines *value* in the following way:

> *Except as otherwise provided in Articles 3, 4, [and] 5, [and 6], a person gives value for rights if the person acquires them:*
>
> *(1) in return for a binding commitment to extend credit or for the extension of immediately available credit, whether or not drawn upon and whether or not a chargeback is provided for in the event of difficulties in collection; (2) as security for, or in total or partial satisfaction of, a preexisting claim; (3) by accepting delivery under a preexisting contract for purchase; or (4) in return for any consideration sufficient to support a simple contract.*[54]

Any security agreement should, to be enforceable, have value. Existence of value may be discerned similarly to how one analyzes consideration in a contract:

- Is the subject matter of the security agreement a preexisting claim?
- Is the subject matter of the security agreement a conditional offer that has no legal effect?
- Is the subject matter of the security agreement crops yet to be planted or harvested?
- Is the subject matter of the security agreement forms of property specifically exempted or excepted from Article 9 coverage?

Process of Perfection

Although not defined by the U.C.C., *perfection* presents rules for formalization and prioritization of the rights, secured or not, of the parties who claim an interest in the collateral. Creating priorities or conflicting claims through statute minimizes litigation. As a result, most states have shaped laws guiding this process. The basic question is this: When will a secured party's security interest in the collateral be subordinate to a third party's interest? Phrased another way, upon the default of the debtor, what are the risks to the third parties? Although perfection appears to be a complex topic, this sorting out of rights is essential to the free market. Consider these situations:

Example 1

A debtor seeking extra capital gives more than one security interest in the same collateral. A bankruptcy trustee attempting to resolve claims of creditors and other interested parties takes a dominant interest in all of the collateral of the debtor in order to ensure an equitable payment of claims.

Example 2

A good-faith purchaser acquires specific collateral and has no idea and no actual or constructive notice that other parties have an interest in the collateral. Governmental entities claim collateral under a federal or state tax lien.

Example 3

Collateral that once was real property has been recharacterized as a fixture, creating other secured interests.

Commonly there are circumstances and situations where claims to property are in competition.[55] Review the following list for examples of this phenomenon:

- Consumer purchases of goods from another consumer.
- The existence of mechanic's or materialman's liens.
- The effect of commingled, repossessed, or returned goods.
- The existence of a floating lien.
- The determination of who has a right to future advances.

These competitive interests prompt a perfection process. The more perfect party naturally deserves the greater protection, while the imperfect party is placed into a lower priority with fewer rights than the perfect party. Article 9 lays out the general standard.

Except as otherwise provided in Sections 9-303 through 9-306, the following rules determine the law governing perfection, the effect of perfection or nonperfection, and the priority of a security interest in collateral:

> *(1) Except as otherwise provided in this section, while a debtor is located in a jurisdiction, the local law of that jurisdiction governs perfection, the effect of perfection or nonperfection, and the priority of a security interest in collateral.*
>
> *(2) While collateral is located in a jurisdiction, the local law of that jurisdiction governs perfection, the effect of perfection or nonperfection, and the priority of a possessory security interest in that collateral.*
>
> *(3) Except as otherwise provided in paragraph (4), while tangible negotiable documents, goods, instruments, money, or tangible chattel paper is located in a jurisdiction, the local law of that jurisdiction governs:*
> *(A) perfection of a security interest in the goods by filing a fixture filing;*
> *(B) perfection of a security interest in timber to be cut; and*
> *(C) the effect of perfection or nonperfection and the priority of a nonpossessory security interest in the collateral.*
>
> *(4) The local law of the jurisdiction in which the wellhead or minehead is located governs perfection, the effect of perfection or nonperfection, and the priority of a security interest in as-extracted collateral.[56]*

Further elucidation of how to resolve conflict is evident in Section 9-322:

> *Except as otherwise provided in this section, priority among conflicting security interests and agricultural liens in the same collateral is determined according to the following rules:*
>
> *(1) Conflicting perfected security interests and agricultural liens rank according to priority in time of filing or perfection. Priority dates from the earlier of the time a filing covering the collateral is first made or the security interest or agricultural lien is first perfected, if there is no period thereafter when there is neither filing nor perfection.*
>
> *(2) A perfected security interest or agricultural lien has priority over a conflicting unperfected security interest or agricultural lien.*
>
> *(3) The first security interest or agricultural lien to attach or become effective has priority if conflicting security interests and agricultural liens are unperfected.[57]*

Hence prioritization of interests mirrors the order of filing and perfection. The Code at §9-324 delineates the prioritization of perfection in purchase money security interests:

> *Except as otherwise provided in subsection (g), a perfected purchase-money security interest in goods other than inventory or livestock has priority over a conflicting security interest in the same goods, and, except as otherwise provided in Section 9-327, a perfected security interest in its identifiable proceeds also has priority, if the purchase-money security interest is perfected when the debtor receives possession of the collateral or within 20 days thereafter.[58]*

Article 9 is not a consumer-oriented statute.[59] It has been designed to protect American business and banking interests in retail consumer transactions that are termed purchase money security interests. Vendors of consumer goods, such as a television set, a bed, or other consumer durable, are not required to perfect any interest in the product because the transaction is complete. If this were done, it would be impossible to monitor. Article 9 at §309 exempts consumer goods from the filing for perfection requirements. If Joe Smithson walks into Sears Roebuck, he should be able to buy with complete assurance. Article 9 recognizes this practical policy.[60] The Code also covers special rules regarding fixtures, agricultural crops, investment property, and other matters.[61]

The issue of attachment dwells upon the rights of the parties in the event of dispute. The U.C.C attempts to promulgate a logical sequence of prioritization of ownership and corresponding rights to property. In short, attachment zeroes in on the following:

Who was first to file? This statute prioritizes and categorizes rights according to the timeliness of the filing, similar to a claim or right asserted in a title dispute.

If no filings have taken place, whose security interest is first attached? Outside of consumer transactions and those activities automatically perfected, priority of rights is determined by which security agreements were entered into first and which attached in order of sequence. Because of these requirements, a paralegal must follow local requirements to ensure perfection.

The following security interests are perfected when they attach:

(1) a purchase-money security interest in consumer goods, except as otherwise provided in Section 9-311(b) with respect to consumer goods that are subject to a statute or treaty described in Section 9-311(a).[62]

Remember that perfection can be automatic only in purchase money security interest cases in which consumers engage. To have automatic perfection, a security agreement that is signed and meets its legal requirements has simply attached. There are cases in which security interests have not been filed. Priority then is determined by which security agreements were entered into first. Because of these requirements, a paralegal must follow local requirements to assure perfection.

Methods of Perfection Aside from the techniques of automatic perfection and those goods or collateral covered by non-Code regulations, such as automobiles, off-track vehicles, and certain real estate fixtures, there are three chief ways to perfect property interests:

1. Transfer of collateral—the so-called collateral pledge.
2. Automatic perfection related to "purchase money security interest."
3. Filing a financing statement.

Of these three, perfection by filing is the most common method of perfection. Filing can take many forms, such as recorded deeds, mortgages, notes, trust agreements, and other documents. Under the provisions of Article 9, filing processes generally require two major forms: the financing statement (Form 6.6 on the accompanying CD) and the general security agreement (Form 6.5). Be sure to have financing statements conformed and impressed with seals by an appropriate governmental officer.

To perfect a security interest, U.C.C. §9-502 requires that a financing statement include the following items:

- Name and address of debtor.
- Name and address of secured party.
- Transmitting utility, if applicable.
- Filing office.
- Description of the collateral.
- Name and address of assignee of secured party, if any.
- Description of crops, timber, minerals, or fixtures, if involved.
- Description of real estate if involved with fixtures.
- Name of record owner.
- Signatures of the debtor and the secured party, if required.[63]

Note that any changes, reformation, or modification of the security agreement must be made with additional filings of U.C.C. Form 3. (See Form 6.7 on the accompanying CD.)

Filing Requirements Security interests have a time limit of three to five years. To halt the termination of that interest, a refiling is necessary. The impact of filing can be summarized as follows:

- If first in time, the secured interest has been perfected and holds a dominant position over all other parties, except those clearly given preferential status by the Code, such as purchase money security interests or consumers.

- If not in a dominant or first position, a record of prioritization or chronological filing will help in the eventual distribution of rights in a disputed claim.

Professors Charles Bunn, Harry Snead, and Richard Speidel of the Harvard Law School comment:

> *Filing perfects the security interest. Perfection insures the validity against lien creditors without knowledge in the trustee and bankruptcy and it can, but does not necessarily, improve the priority of the security interest.*[64]

U.C.C. litigation frequently involves proving priority of time, priority of filing, quality of attachment, and adherence to perfection standards.

Filing Location Deciding where to file documents is primarily dictated by local rules. For example, in New York State, the offices of the Secretary of State, the county clerk, or city register are acceptable depositories for filing. New York, as well as other states, now permits e-filing of U.C.C documents.[65] New York has recently promulgated revised rules regarding physical filings (see Figure 6.6).

It should be stressed that under Revised Article 9 a filing office may refuse to accept a record for filing only for certain specified reasons. The fact that a record is accepted for filing does not necessarily mean that the filing is effective for the purpose intended by the filer. The filer is solely responsible for determining the proper office in which to file and for determining that the record to be filed contains the information necessary to make the record effective to accomplish the filer's purpose.[66]

The U.C.C. promulgates a standard definition for filing practice at §9-501. The provisions of the U.C.C. display extraordinary deference to state schemes for filing. The general underpinning is evident:

> *9-501. FILING OFFICE.*
>
> *(a) [Filing offices.]*
> *Except as otherwise provided in subsection (b), if the local law of this State governs perfection of a security interest or agricultural lien, the office in which to file a financing statement to perfect the security interest or agricultural lien is:*
> *(1) the office designated for the filing or recording of a record of a mortgage on the related real property, if:*
> *(A) the collateral is as-extracted collateral or timber to be cut; or*
> *(B) the financing statement is filed as a fixture filing and the collateral is goods that are or are to become fixtures; or*
> *(2) the office of [(2) the office of [ ] [or any office duly authorized by [ ]], in all other cases, including a case in which the collateral is goods that are or are to become fixtures and the financing statement is not filed as a fixture filing.*[67]

In New York, as in other jurisdictions, the first alternative is known as *central filing.* "If the goods are or are to become fixtures, then file in the office where a mortgage under real estate concern would be filed or recorded; in all other cases in the Office of the Secretary of State or another central office to be selected by the adopting state. The ideal system is called central filing; it was the dream of the drafters of the U.C.C."[68]

Practitioners have long argued the need for uniformity in filing locations. As a rule, states provide both local and centralized filing options. Article 9 "simplifies the choice of law rules governing perfection by providing a general rule that the law of perfection and priority will be the law of the debtor's location. The debtor's location for a debtor created by registration in a state is the state of registration. However, for security interests in fixtures perfected by filing, timber to be cut, and perfection attained by the secured party taking possession of the collateral, the

FIGURE 6.6   Original Financing Statements (UCC1s)

Section 9-501 governs place of filing. Subsection (a) (1) provides that the office in which to file a financing statement to perfect the security interest or agricultural lien is the office designated for the filing or recording of a record of a mortgage on the related real property (this is the office of the county clerk or *New York City Register*) if (1) the collateral is as-extracted collateral or timber to be cut or (2) the financing statement is filed as a fixture filing and the collateral is goods that are or are to become fixtures or (3) the collateral is a cooperative interest. Subsection (a) (2) provides that the office in which to file a financing statement to perfect a security interest is the office of the Secretary of State in all other cases. Pursuant to subsection (b) a fixture filing for a transmitting utility would also be filed with the Secretary of State.

Amendments, Assignments, Continuations, & Terminations (UCC3s)

It is the responsibility of the filer to determine which of the following may best meet the needs of his or her individual situation. (1) In the case of an original financing statement that was filed in the office of a county clerk (or the office of the *New York City Register*) that only provided for collateral that would properly be filed in that office under Revised Article 9, that office is the proper place for filing an amendment, assignment, continuation, or termination statement. (2) In the case of an original financing statement filed with the Department of State that only provided for collateral that would properly be filed with the Department of State under Revised Article 9, the proper place for filing an amendment, assignment, continuation, or termination statement is the Department of State. (3) In the case of an original financing statement filed in the office of a county clerk (or the office of the *New York City Register*) that provided for collateral that would properly be filed with the Department of State under Revised Article 9, the secured party should not file anything with the office of the county clerk (or the office of the *New York City Register*) but, rather, should file an "in lieu of filing" with the Department of State. ("In lieu of" filings are discussed below.) (4) In the case of an original financing statement that was properly filed in both the office of a county clerk (or the office of the *New York City Register*) and with the Department of State that provided for collateral that would be filed with both offices under Revised Article 9 (for example, a fixture filing with other general collateral), the secured party should file an amendment, assignment, continuation, or termination statement with both offices.

"In Lieu of" Filings

Section 9-706 of Revised Article 9 provides for "in lieu of" filings. An "in lieu of" filing is a new UCC1 filed in an office other than the one in which the original financing statement to which it relates was filed. It is intended to provide for the continuity and continued effectiveness of a filing made in an office under former Article 9 but which would not be the office for filing the original financing statement under Revised Article 9. The secured party must file a new UCC1 that complies with the requirements for filing under Revised Article 9. In addition, an "in lieu of" filing must identify the original financing statement by indicating the office in which the financing statement was filed and providing the dates of filing and file numbers of the financing statement and most recent continuation statement, if any, and indicating that the financing statement remains effective. An appropriate place to set forth the information mentioned in the preceding sentence is Item 10 in the National UCC Financing Statement Addendum Form UCC1Ad. An "in lieu of" filing may contain amended information. The Official Comments to Revised Article 9 suggest that an "in lieu of" filing may include language terminating the filing.

perfection is governed by the law of the jurisdiction in which the collateral is located."[69] In fact, Professor Bunn highlights this tendency toward local record keeping:

> You'll notice that each of the above three alternative methods offers progressively more local filing. The third alternative grew out of the experience Massachusetts had when it adopted the U.C.C.: There was a very vocal protest that the record should be readily available to local people. It may be. It is significant though that this argument is often most pressed by the local county clerks whose compensation, at least in some states, turns on the volume of local filings.[70]

If you are in doubt where to file, file everywhere. The notion of proper place of perfection clearly rests upon the locality of the interests in question. Consider these examples:

- Place of inventory.
- Place of business.
- Place of fixtures.
- Place of collateral.
- Place of residence.

- Place of secured party.
- Place of agricultural commodities or crops.
- Place of goods transfer.
- Place of intangible interests.

Commercial practice usually involves diverse locations. Consequently, attorneys and paralegals must be sensitive to competing claims on both intrastate and interstate levels. Multiple-state claims bring further confusion into this ongoing dilemma. However, regardless of its shortcomings, the perfection system has created uniformity in American commerce.

Default

Beside filing secured interest documents and preparing forms, security agreements, and other necessary documentation, the paralegal may be involved in protecting the interests of either debtors or secured parties. On either end, certain remedies for breach or default can take place. This section highlights some of the more common forms of litigation and provides pleadings examples.

Under any security agreement that is evidenced by a financing statement, a secured party is interested in collecting or maintaining an economic interest in the agreement. A debtor who is failing to meet the terms and conditions of the agreement can be considered in default.

Default is generally a failure to adhere to material terms as laid out in the security agreement. Although not explicitly defined by the Code, default or breach can be construed in any of the following fact situations:

1. A debtor fails to pay indebtedness.
2. A debtor fails to punctually perform obligations.
3. A debtor induces a secured party to make a loan under fraudulent conditions or misrepresentations.
4. Collateral has been lost, stolen, damaged, or destroyed.
5. Collateral has been sold or encumbered.
6. A debtor has died.
7. A debtor's business interest has been terminated.
8. A debtor is now insolvent or bankrupt.
9. A debtor's financial condition has deteriorated or is at best described as a misrepresentation.
10. Collateral has become unsatisfactory or insufficient in character or value.
11. Any other event results in the acceleration or maturity of any indebtedness.[71]

Secured Party Remedies

Assuming a default occurs, a secured party has the right to dispose of collateral after a finding of default. Section 9-601 of the Uniform Commercial Code outlines a generic approach to remedies:

> After default, a secured party has the rights provided in this part and, except as otherwise provided in Section 9-602, those provided by agreement of the parties. A secured party:
>
> (1) may reduce a claim to judgment, foreclose, or otherwise enforce the claim, security interest, or agricultural lien by any available judicial procedure; and
>
> (2) if the collateral is documents, may proceed either as to the documents or as to the goods they cover.[72]

Under Section 9-609, a secured party has the right to repossession under a theory of self-help, with or without prior judicial process. The rule states this clearly:

> After default, a secured party:
>
> (1) may take possession of the collateral; and
>
> (2) without removal, may render equipment unusable and dispose of collateral on a debtor's premises under Section 9-610.[73]

If repossession is not possible, judicial actions like these may be necessary:

- File a lawsuit.
- Obtain a judgment.
- Obtain a writ of execution from the court that issues that judgment.
- Cause the sheriff to levy on the property.
- Cause such property to be sold in execution.

Retention

> *In lieu of a resale or other disposition, the secured party is entitled to retain the property, dispose of it, and retain the proceeds from the sale. The retention may fulfill, in whole or part, the underlying obligation (see U.C.C. §9-609). The Code permits a possessory retention of the collateral in lieu of other remedies*[74]

 See Form 6.8 on the accompanying CD for an example of a secured party's notification.

Resale

Secured parties are also entitled to sell the collateral in repossession for a commercially reasonable price.[75] In fact, it is clear that the provisions of the U.C.C. seek to stimulate and motivate the seller to engage in a system of self-help and cure. This tendency toward self-help is a very positive development in commercial law, says Celia R. Taylor:

> *The seller could either supply substitute goods in fulfillment of the contract terms or remit the difference in contract price and market price, plus perhaps some amount to compensate for delay. Because of the low risk involved with resale it is appealing to a seller facing breach. U.C.C authorization of resale, without need for official intervention, is further evidence of the U.C.C.'s support for self-help.*
>
> *While resale is the most important self-help remedy permitting a seller to terminate and protect its interests upon a buyer's breach, the U.C.C authorizes several other actions. The availability of each of these remedies is premised on a wrongful rejection or revocation of acceptance by the buyer, or a failure to make timely payment.*[76]

The U.C.C. sets out a flexible approach to valuation at resale:

> (a) *[Disposition after default.]*
> *After default, a secured party may sell, lease, license, or otherwise dispose of any or all of the collateral in its present condition or following any commercially reasonable preparation or processing.*
>
> (b) *[Commercially reasonable disposition.]*
> *Every aspect of a disposition of collateral, including the method, manner, time, place, and other terms, must be commercially reasonable. If commercially reasonable, a secured party may dispose of collateral by public or private proceedings, by one or more contracts, as a unit or in parcels, and at any time and place and on any terms.*[77]

Sales or other disposition may be as a unit or in parcels and at any time and place and on any terms; but every aspect of the disposition, including the method, manner, time, place, and terms, must be commercially reasonable. Unless collateral is perishable or threatens to decline speedily in value or is of a type customarily sold in a recognized market, reasonable notification of the time and place of any public sale or reasonable notification of the time after which any private sale or other intended disposition is to be made shall be sent by the secured party to the debtor, if he or she has not signed after default a statement renouncing or modifying the right to notification of sale.[78]

The Code is silent as to whether the standard for measuring the resale price is wholesale or retail. Secured parties also have a right to purchase the goods outright under this theory of operation.[79]

Debtor's Rights in Collateral: Redemption and Preservation

Under the same provisions that seek to protect the rights of secured parties, debtors also have specific protection. When a security agreement has been fulfilled, secured parties are required to send a termination statement to the debtors when (1) a debtor makes a written demand for such statement; and (2) there is no secured obligation outstanding and no commitment to make one.[80] Sanctions and fines are available for failure to do so. Debtors who default also have a right to redemption as outlined in U.C.C. §9-623. Though the debtor does not argue from a position of strength, if circumstances change for the better and full tender can be made for past as well as future obligations, a redemption right exists.[81] The Code publishes the process:

(a) *[Persons that may redeem.]*
    A debtor, any secondary obligor, or any other secured party or lien holder may redeem collateral.

(b) *[Requirements for redemption.]*
    To redeem collateral, a person shall tender:
    (1) fulfillment of all obligations secured by the collateral; and
    (2) the reasonable expenses and attorney's fees described in Section 9-615(a)(1).

(c) *[When redemption may occur.]*
    A redemption may occur at any time before a secured party:
    (1) has collected collateral under Section 9-607;
    (2) has disposed of collateral or entered into a contract for its disposition under Section 9-610; or
    (3) has accepted collateral in full or partial satisfaction of the obligation it secures under Section 9-622.[82]

If a debtor cannot or will not exercise the right of redemption or other steps, the secured party may dispose of the property. Although the debtor may possess and utilize collateral, the secured party has a legal and equitable interest in its preservation and ownership. When a secured party has possession of the collateral, the party is obligated to use reasonable care in the custody and preservation of that collateral. U.C.C. §9-207 outlines the terms and conditions regarding the rights and obligations of a secured party in possession of collateral. A debtor may question whether the collateral is being maintained, preserved, or reasonably kept. See Form 6.9 on the accompanying CD for a complaint by a debtor against a secured party for failure to maintain and preserve such property.

Summary

In the law of commercial paper and secured transactions, the paralegal must keep track of filing requirements, paperwork, documentation of financing and security forms, endorsements, checks, drafts, and promissory notes. Evaluating the rights, duties, and obligations of all parties to a financing transaction is a technical undertaking. Proficiency in the Uniform Commercial Code calls for mastery of a complex area of substantive law. Although states are not under any obligation to adopt the U.C.C., the majority of American jurisdictions have adopted its content. The provisions of the U.C.C. attempt to provide a balance between debtors, creditors, payers, drawers, drafters, banks, and various other individuals and institutions. Good record keeping, an open mind, and attention to detail are necessary skills for the paralegal. In the final analysis, the U.C.C hopes to be a major player in the economic development of a nation and seeks

(1) to simplify, clarify, and modernize the law governing commercial transactions; (2) to permit the continued expansion of commercial practices through custom, usage, and agreement of the parties; and (3) to make uniform the law among the various jurisdictions.[83]

Discussion Questions

1. Why isn't it better to have local rules and customs controlling all commercial activities in the American marketplace?

2. If a creditor wants to be certain that a bill is going to be paid, what type of check should she or he ask for?

3. For a document to be negotiable, the promise must meet certain standards. Describe these.

4. What types of endorsement will minimize fraud and ensure that money is used for a specific purpose?

5. If commercial paper is presented and dishonored, what remedies are available?

6. Security agreements are favored by inventory lenders. Why?

7. "Perfection involves a priority of rights." True or false?

8. "An agreement can attach yet not be perfected." True or false?

9. Where would you file a security agreement on livestock and other agricultural commodities in your jurisdiction?

10. Prepare a form file for your jurisdiction's requirements for U.C.C filings.

Practical Exercises

1. Prepare a UCC-1 Financing Statement using the following information:

Debtor:	*Rufus T. Robertson, 1006 Longo Lane, Jamestown, Virginia 23333*
Secured party:	*Billboard Finance Company, 1111 Blacktop Way, Richmond, Virginia 23219*
Size of UCC-1:	*1 sheet*
Date:	*July 1, 2007*
Assignees:	*None*
Statement number:	*5446*
Time of filing:	*When collateral transferred into a new state jurisdiction*
Real estate covered:	*None*
Types of property:	*11 Mack cross-country trucks, serial numbers 1101, 1102, 1103, 1104, 1105, 1106, 1107, 1108, 1109, 1110, and 1111; registered in Sacramento County, Sacramento, California*
To be filed with:	*Virginia Secretary of State*

2. Prepare a UCC-3 Financing Statement Change using the information from the previous question, noting the secured party's July 1, 2007, release of the secured property.

3. Complete a UCC-11 Request for Information or Copies under the assumption that on January 15, 2008, the secured party in the previous questions sought information from the Secretary of State about its current activity with this particular debtor. The secured party also would like copies of all financing statements and statements of assignment. However, at the time of completing the request, the secured party is not aware of how many copies will be received. Complete the form from both the secured party's and filing officer's perspective.

Internet Resources

U.C.C Articles 1–9 from the Legal Information Institute—www.law.cornell.edu/ucc/ucc.table.html

State of Wisconsin, Department of Financial Institutions—http://www.wdfi.org/ucc/

Legal Information Institute, U.C.C locator—http://www.law.cornell.edu/uniform/ucc.html

Boston College, U.C.C Reporter Digest—www.bc.edu/schools/law/lawreviews/uccrd

Federal Trade Commission—http://www.ftc.gov/

Board of Governors of the Federal Reserve System—http://www.federalreserve.gov/

Findlaw, contracts page—http://www.findlaw.com/01topics/07contracts/gov_laws.html

Endnotes

1. U.C.C. §1-103(a) (2003).

2. U.C.C. Introduction to Article I (1972).

3. U.C.C. §1-103(B) (2003).

4. Recent revisions to the Code have not been universally well received. *See* Gregory E. Maggs, *Patterns of Drafting Errors in the Uniform Commercial Code and How Courts Should Respond to Them*, U. Ill. L. Rev. 81 (2002); *see also* Gerald T. McLaughlin, *Symposium: Is the UCC Dead, or Alive and Well? The Evolving Uniform Commercial Code: From Infancy to Maturity to Old Age*, 26 Loy. L.A. L. Rev. 691 (April 1993).

5. For a view on good faith in commercial paper, *see* Patricia L. Heatherman, *Good Faith in Revised Article 3 of the Uniform Commercial Code: Any Change? Should There Be?* 29 Willamette L. Rev. 567 (1993).

6. *See* U.C.C. §1-201(21) (2003).

7. *Id.* §1-201(5).

8. *Id.* §3-104(1).

9. Charles Bunn, Harry Snead, & Richard Speidel, Introduction to the Uniform Commercial Code 212 (1964).

10. U.C.C at §3-103(7).

11. Bunn et al., *supra* note 9, at 218.

12. U.C.C. at §3-108.

13. *Id.* §3-401(1).

14. *Id.* §3-402.

15. *Id.* §3-108.

16. *Id.* §3-104(J).

17. *Id.* §3-203(b) & (c).

18. *Id.* §3-201.

19. *Id.* §3-202, Commentary.

20. *Id.* §3-205.

21. Robert N. Corley, Eric M. Holmes, & William J. Robert, Principles of Business Law 388 (1983).

22. *Id.* at 392.

23. U.C.C. at §3-206.

24. *Id.* §3-206.

25. *See* U.C.C. at §3-305.

26. *Id.* §3-302.

27. *Id.* §3-302 (2).

28. U.C.C. §3-305 (1972).

29. U.C.C. §3-306 (1972); *see also* RESTATEMENT ON CONTRACTS §167 (1932).

30. Corley et al., *supra* note 21, at 419; *see also* U.C.C. at §3-504.

31. U.C.C. at §3-501.

32. *See* U.C.C. at §3-504.

33. *Id.* §4-301.

34. *Id.* §3-504.

35. *Id.* §3-601 (a).

36. *Id.* §3-601 (b).

37. *Id.* §3-602 (e).

38. *Id.* §3-604.

39. *Id.* §9-102 & 103.

40. *Id.* §9-109.

41. *See* DAVID EPSTEIN, SECURED TRANSACTIONS (1976).

42. U.C.C. at §9-102(a)(11).

43. *Id.* §9-102(a)(12).

44. *Id.* §9-102(a)(44).

45. *Id.* §9-109(d).

46. *Id.* §9-109.

47. *Id.* §9-102 (44).

48. *Id.* §9-203.

49. *See* GRANT GILMORE, SECURITY INTERESTS IN PERSONAL PROPERTY, §11.4 at 348 (1965); In re Mann, 8 U.C.C. REP. SERV. 132 (1970).

50. U.C.C. at § 9-502.

51. *Id.* §9-203.

52. Epstein, *supra* note 42, at 6.

53. U.C.C. at §9-108(a).

54. *Id.* §1-204.

55. *See Financing Statement: When Is Filing of Financing Statement Necessary to Perfect an Assignment of Accounts under UCC §9-302(1)(e)?* 85 ALR 3d 1050.

56. U.C.C. at §9-301.

57. U.C.C. at §9-322.

58. U.C.C. at §9-324.

59. For an interesting discussion of the recent revisions to Article 9, *see* David R. Beran, *Financing Statements, Descriptions, Collateral, and Confusion: Arkansas Courts Tackle the New Article 9*, 57 ARK. L. REV. 951 (2005).

60. U.C.C. at § 9-309 (1).

61. *Id.* §9-301-312.

62. *Id.* §9-307 (2).

63. *See* SECRETARY OF STATE OF NEW YORK, THE UNIFORM COMMERCIAL CODE: A GUIDE TO FILINGS (1979).

64. Bunn et al., *supra* note 9, at 436.

65. For one example *see* NEW YORK STATE DEPARTMENT OF STATE, UCC E-FILING SYSTEM INSTRUCTIONS at https://appsext4.dos.state.ny.us/pls/efiling_public/eucc.euccfilingguide.

66. NEW YORK DEPARTMENT OF STATE, FILING UNDER REVISED ARTICLE 9 OF THE UNIFORM COMMERCIAL CODE, available at http://www.dos.state.ny.us/corp/uccfilinguide.html.

67. U.C.C. at §9-501.

68. Bunn et al., *supra* note 9, at 436.

69. Donald W. Garland, *Revised Article 9: Understanding the Changes to Secured Transactions*, TEX. B.J., Nov. 2001, at 974, 975.

70. Bunn et al., *supra* note 9, at 438.

71. Epstein, *supra* note 42, at 12; *see also* U.C.C. at §9-501.

72. U.C.C. at §9-601.

73. *Id.* §9-609.

74. *See What Is "Commercially Reasonable" Disposition of Collateral Required by UCC Sec. 9-504(3)?* 7 A.L.R. 4th 308.

75. U.C.C. at §9-507.

76. Celia R. Taylor, *Self-Help in Contract Law: An Exploration and Proposal*, 33 W. F. L. REV. 839, 876-877 (1998).

77. U.C.C. at §9–610.

78. *Id.*

79. *Id.* §9-610 (c).

80. *Id.* §9-513.

81. *See* Alvin C. Harrell, *Introduction to the Symposium: Revised UCC Article 9*, 54 CONSUMER FIN. L.Q. REP. 140 (2000).

82. U.C.C. at §9-623.

83. *Id.* §9-103.

Chapter 7

Bankruptcy

BANKRUPTCY PARALEGAL JOB DESCRIPTION

Bankruptcy paralegals need to be proficient in the following competencies:

- Provide lists of documents required for filing preparation, such as tax returns, life insurance policies, lists of liabilities, and financial statements.
- Collect personal financial information and prepare lists of assets.
- Maintain tickler and calendar systems, including status sheets.
- Survey court records of lawsuits and judgments against a debtor.
- Obtain U.C.C. and real property searches, as well as appraisals.
- File wage-earner plan schedules and fees with bankruptcy courts.
- Check creditor documentation to ensure proper perfection.
- Attend court hearings with attorney and client.
- Conduct initial interviews to obtain information for filing petitions, schedules, and so on.
- Familiarize clients with general procedures at hearings, meetings, and motions.
- Analyze and summarize factual information.
- Meet with clients to review and sign schedules.
- Draft and file bankruptcy petitions and schedules.
- Draft and file proof of claims for bankruptcy.
- Process letters to creditors with copies of orders for relief.
- Prepare preliminary drafts of questions for first creditor meetings.

- Attend first meetings of creditors.
- Collect data for creditors' proof of claims in bankruptcy.
- Prepare plans of reorganization and disclosure statements.
- Draft, serve, and file Chapter 11 debtors' monthly financial statements.
- Help prepare pleadings for adversary proceedings.
- Compile initial schedules for bankrupt wage-earner plans.
- Write proof of claims of wage-earner plans.
- Prepare preliminary drafts of questions for various hearings.
- Prepare legal, financial, and statistical research.
- Draft reaffirmation agreements.
- Contact creditors and complete related forms.
- Draft various motions, including those for avoidance of liens.
- Handle routine telephone calls and correspondence.
- Draft and file attorney's fee applications with bankruptcy courts.[1]
- Attend court hearings to ease flow of documents and information.
- Draft, serve, and file complaints in adversary proceedings.
- Attend Section 341 (a) meetings.
- Attend Chapter 13 plan confirmation hearing.
- Obtain lists of creditors.

INTRODUCTORY COMMENT

Debt can unexpectedly overwhelm both individuals and institutions. Debt difficulties are caused by multiple factors, including careless management, crisis, or trauma in the business market or poor financial planning. At other times bankruptcy results from catastrophic events, hard luck, and a general turn of economic conditions and events that are unforeseeable. Critics of bankruptcy have long argued that the government should erect a legal process that allows bankrupt parties to avoid or eliminate debt. The number of legal actions borders on the hyperbolic as bankruptcy rates "have soared during the past twenty-five years. From 225,000 filings in 1979, consumer bankruptcies topped 1.5 million."[2] In a sense, the system encourages financial irresponsibility by providing "economic incentives" for going bankrupt.[3] Others argue that bankruptcy provides a free market means for business and individuals to restore their financial health. Some argue that the bankruptcy system is a form of rehabilitation for both individuals and businesses.[4] In the American experience, there has been a supportive and historical tradition for bankruptcy, both in common law and statutorily. The federal Bankruptcy Act of 1898 has an obvious lineage. Bankruptcy laws have a constitutional basis as well.[5]

Bankruptcy legislation resides exclusively in the federal legislative process. Congress has the power to establish uniform laws on bankruptcy throughout the United States. In doing so, the federal government preempts state legislation on the practices and policies of bankruptcy.[6] Subsequent acts culminated in the Bankruptcy Reform Act of 1978, effective on October 1, 1979.[7] The 1978 Act is always referred to as the "code" because the Bankruptcy Act of 1898 was repealed and subsequently codified in 1979. In 2004 the Bankruptcy Act was substantially revised and by most accounts makes the process a bit more difficult for individuals.

Ironically, creditors have in some ways benefited from the adoption of a bankruptcy code. Instead of a cataclysmic, nonproductive collapse of the debtor, whether an individual or an institution, debtors usually emerge from what could have been a total loss to a partial restoration of a debt. Although this is not always true in business bankruptcies, the bankruptcy process distributes by order of priority—in hopes that most interested parties receive some portion of what is owed.[8] Creditors also benefit from the orderly processes the bankruptcy procedure affords a distressed debtor. Creditors have fair opportunity to have their claims prioritized according to their interests and can negotiate their interests with competing creditors in an open, deliberate forum. "It is the task of bankruptcy judges to balance competing interests and arrive at fair solutions."[9] Under recent reforms to the Bankruptcy Act, the debtor appears to have lost some footing when compared to the status of creditors. Debtors now have a higher burden of proof, so to speak. Using a six-month income rule, debtors now must compute earnings for the previous six months, even if laid off or out of work for part of that period. The act also sets "strict limits" as to "housing, transportation and food."[10] In general, the bankruptcy reforms of the last few years are reforms of limitation. Accurate or not, there was a growing sense that the historical bankruptcy laws were being used for a host of reasons, some licit and some illicit. Debtors are feeling the crunch.[11]

On the other hand, there is little dispute that bankruptcy has gotten out of control. Instead of the historic connection between the filing rate and economic conditions, it is apparent that rates rise despite the health or distress of the economy. Todd Zywicki sees the sham of a system that rewards the irresponsible who appear in a bankrupt class of repetitors—"the increased frequency of Americans choosing bankruptcy as the preferred response to those underlying problems."[12]

The statutory framework of the bankruptcy code contains these titles and chapters:

Chapter 1: Definitions and general provisions.

Chapter 3: The administration and procedure to be followed in bankruptcy cases.

Chapter 7: Liquidation processes and techniques in bankruptcy cases.

Chapter 9: Adjustment of debts for municipalities.

Chapter 11: Plans of reorganization for business entities and nonbusiness individuals.

Chapter 12: Adjustment of debts of a family farmer with regular income.

Chapter 13: Debt extension plans or other adjustments for individuals with regular income.

Chapter 15: Discussion of the United States Trustee system.

Bankruptcy practice allows paralegals to perform many valuable tasks. Recent reforms to the Bankruptcy Act appear to substantially benefit the paralegal profession.[13] Under the Debt Relief Agency component of the act, paralegals are essentially permitted to represent debtors and creditors. The act states in part,

> *"Debt Relief Agency" means any person who provides bankruptcy assistance to an assisted person in return for the payment of money or other valuable consideration, or who is a bankruptcy petition preparer under Section 110.*[14]

Bankruptcy paralegals will find a plethora of pleadings, forms, documents, and other necessary filings, as dictated by increasingly favorable legislation. Geoff Giles comments,

> *Paralegal firms are likely to flourish as they get to advertise that they are "debt relief agencies," just like lawyers.*[15]

The bankruptcy process is also guided by specific bankruptcy rules adopted by a congressional advisory committee. Jurisdiction and venue are based on subject matter and the residence of the claimant or debtor. By a grant to the federal courts of original and exclusive jurisdiction, the task of handling bankruptcy has been delegated to a specialized court: the bankruptcy court.[16] Bankruptcy judges are federal judges with limited tenure, unlike other federal colleagues on the bench. Much constitutional litigation has occurred about these courts—more specifically, as to whether such congressional right or authority can be delegated. An equally complicated and intellectual controversy has centered on the designation, title, and duties of bankruptcy judges. Mired in a confused legal status, bankruptcy judges are continually searching for their place as either Article I or Article III judges under the U.S. Constitution. Bankruptcy judges are not granted life tenure and do not have the same protections and emoluments as other federal judges.[17]

Venue in bankruptcy cases can be determined by the domicile of the debtor, the debtor's principal place of business, or the location of principal assets.

In reality, paralegals will be mostly concerned with the liquidation processes of a Chapter 7 bankruptcy—and on occasion have some exposure to Chapter 12, which deals with family farmers. For reorganization of business entities, or simply starting all over, paralegals will work extensively under Chapters 11 and 13. The paralegal specialist should also have a solid library of support material. Here are a few useful works:

- Douglas G. Baird, *Elements of Bankruptcy* (2005).
- Richard E. Boyeer, *Practical Bankruptcy Law for Paralegals* (3rd ed. 2005).

- Brian Blum, *Bankruptcy and Debtor/Creditor (Examples and Explanations)* (2004).
- David G. G. Epstein, *Bankruptcy and Related Law in a Nutshell* (2005).
- *The New Bankruptcy Code: U.S. Bankruptcy Code & Rules Booklet*, Dahlstrom Legal Pub. Ed. (2005).

Make certain your form file is up to date and consistent with your district. Bankruptcy courts now publish all forms online. For the full set of forms, visit http://www.uscourts.gov/bkforms/bankruptcy_forms.html. Local jurisdictions may post additional requirements.

Some excellent Web locations for information about courts, codes, and paralegals engaged in bankruptcy, as well as updates on this ever-changing area of law, are listed here:

- U.S. Bankruptcy Trustee: http://www.usdoj.gov/ust/7_12n13.htm. Names, addresses, and contact information of all trustees in all 50 states.
- Local rules of court for all districts: http://www.uscourts.gov/rules/bk-localrules.html. Local rules for all bankruptcy courts in all 50 states.
- Bankruptcy code online: http://www4.law.cornell.edu/uscode/11. Easy lookup for federal case law and codes.
- Chapter 7 help center: http://law.chapter7.com. Chapter 7 information for consumers and attorneys.
- State bankruptcy exemptions: http://www.debtworkout.com/statex.html.

LIQUIDATION PROCEEDINGS UNDER CHAPTER 7 BANKRUPTCY

Chapter 7 of the bankruptcy code permits individuals, partnerships, corporations, and other entities (with some exceptions) to liquidate all existing assets and distribute the remainder to creditors. The debtor is then discharged from most debts except those that were fraudulently incurred or are priority claims under 11 U.S.C. §507. Discharge will be granted only to specific individuals rather than business entities. "A discharge covers all debts that arose before the date of the order for relief . . . A discharge also operates as an injunction against all attempts to collect the debt—by judicial proceedings, telephone calls, letters, personal contacts, or other efforts."[18] Once Chapter 7 procedures commence, creditors are precluded from any attempt to collect a debt. Despite the liberality of discharge, the debtor can no longer be relieved of every type of obligation. Under the reforms of 2005, the debtor needs to compute and calculate income on a *means test.*[19] This reform targets those who take advantage of the system.[20] Here is the language of the statute:

> *(10A) The term "current monthly income"—*
>> *(A) means the average monthly income from all sources that the debtor receives (or in a joint case the debtor and the debtor's spouse receive) without regard to whether such income is taxable income, derived during the 6-month period ending on—*
>>> *(i) the last day of the calendar month immediately preceding the date of the commencement of the case if the debtor files the schedule of current income required by section 521(a)(1)(B)(ii); or*
>>> *(ii) the date on which current income is determined by the court for purposes of this title if the debtor does not file the schedule of current income required by section 521(a)(1)(B)(ii); and*
>> *(B) includes any amount paid by any entity other than the debtor (or in a joint case the debtor and the debtor's spouse), on a regular basis for the household expenses of the debtor or the debtor's dependents (and in a joint case the debtor's spouse if not otherwise a dependent), but excludes benefits received under the Social Security Act, payments to victims of war crimes or crimes against humanity on account of their status as victims of such crimes, and payments to victims of international terrorism (as defined in section 2331 of title 18) or domestic terrorism (as defined in section 2331 of title 18) on account of their status as victims of such terrorism.*[21]

See Form 7.1 on the accompanying CD for a Statement of Monthly Income and Means Test Calculation.

In addition, debtors are required to complete an instructional course that highlights financial management. See Form 7.2 on the accompanying CD for the subsequent affirmation. Once a debtor is determined to be eligible for bankruptcy protection, the paralegal assists in the next task—the petition.

Voluntary Petition

Bankruptcy cases commence in two ways. First, a voluntary petition can be filed. (See Form 7.3 on the accompanying CD.) The debtor entitled to relief under Chapter 7, Title 11, of the U.S. Code files the petition. The petition has a series of schedules that compute both assets and liabilities:

Schedule A   Real Property

Schedule B   Personal Property

Schedule C   Property Claimed as Exempt

Schedule D   Creditors Holding Secured Claims

Schedule E   Creditors Holding Unsecured Priority Claims

Schedule F   Creditors Holding Unsecured Nonpriority Claims

Schedule G   Executory Contracts and Unexpired Leases

Schedule H   Codebtors

Schedule I   Current Income of Individual Debtor(s)

Schedule J   Current Expenditures of Individual Debtor(s)

Once all schedules are calculated, the debtor prepares a summary of these schedules and declares under penalty of perjury that the calculation is correct. (See Form 7.4 on the accompanying CD.)

Involuntary Petition

An involuntary case can be filed by creditors or other interested parties. An involuntary petition under Chapter 7 is shown in Form 7.5 on the accompanying CD. Notice within its content that creditors whose unsecured claims total more than $5,000 must sign the involuntary petition.

Title 11 at §501 publishes guidelines for a proof of claim:

> (a) *A creditor or an indenture trustee may file a proof of claim. An equity security holder may file a proof of interest.*
>
> (b) *If a creditor does not timely file a proof of such creditor's claim, an entity that is liable to such creditor with the debtor, or that has secured such creditor, may file a proof of such claim.*
>
> (c) *If a creditor does not timely file a proof of such creditor's claim, the debtor or the trustee may file a proof of such claim.*
>
> (d) *A claim of a kind specified in section 502(e)(2), 502(f), 502(g), 502(h), or 502(i) of this title may be filed under subsection (a), (b), or (c) of this section the same as if such claim were a claim against the debtor and had arisen before the date of the filing of the petition.*[22]

Of course, a debtor in a Chapter 7 case has every right to challenge the actions within the petition. The court is not permitted or entitled to grant relief if there exists any of the following:

> *. . . a genuine issue of material fact that bears upon the debtor's liability, or a meritorious contention as to the application of law to undisputed facts, then the involuntary petition must be dismissed.*[23]

Appointment of a Trustee

In both Chapter 7 and Chapter 13 cases a judicial appointment of a trustee takes place. A trustee is the representative of the bankruptcy estate who exercises statutory powers, principally for the benefit of the unsecured creditors, under the general supervision of the court and the direct supervision of the U.S. trustee or bankruptcy administrator. The trustee is a private individual or corporation appointed in all Chapter 7, Chapter 12, and Chapter 13 cases and some Chapter 11 cases. The trustee's responsibilities include reviewing the debtor's petition and schedules and bringing actions against creditors or the debtor to recover property of the bankruptcy estate. In

Chapter 7, the trustee liquidates property of the estate and makes distributions to creditors. Trustees in Chapters 12 and 13 have similar duties to a Chapter 7 trustee and the additional responsibilities of overseeing the debtor's plan, receiving payments from the debtor, and disbursing plan payments to creditors. Bankruptcy trustees are granted wide discretion and authority and have been criticized for their liberal exercise of their power. Title 11 §704 states,

The trustee shall—

(1) collect and reduce to money the property of the estate for which such trustee serves, and close such estate as expeditiously as is compatible with the best interests of parties in interest;

(2) be accountable for all property received;

(3) ensure that the debtor shall perform his intention as specified in section 521 (2)(B) of this title [U.S.C.S. §521 (2)(B)];

(4) investigate the financial affairs of the debtor;

(5) if a purpose would be served, examine proofs of claims and object to the allowance of any claim that is improper;

(6) if advisable, oppose the discharge of the debtor;

(7) unless the court orders otherwise, furnish such information concerning the estate and the estate's administration as is required by a party in interest;

(8) if the business of the debtor is authorized to be operated, file with the court and with the governmental unit charged with responsibility for collection or determination of any tax arising out of such operation, periodic reports and summaries of the operation of such business, including a statement of receipts and disbursements, and such other information as the court requires; and

(9) make a final report and file a final account of the administration of the estate with the court.[24]

In a Chapter 7 case, trustees are required to calculate and reduce all property that is nonexempt or subject to a valid security interest to cash and to distribute the money to creditors expeditiously. The trustee must also ensure that the debtor performs his or her obligations and that the debtor makes no unauthorized transfers. Trustees have the authority and power to set aside what are deemed *preferential transfers*:

(1) The trustee transfer was to pay a debt incurred at some earlier time;

(2) The transfer was made when the debtor was insolvent and within 90 days before filing the bankruptcy petition;[25] *and*

(3) By the transfer, the creditor received more than such creditor would have received in a liquidation of a debtor's estate.

A trustee can, depending on the nature of the transaction, avoid the improper transfer of an interest of the debtor. Fraudulent transfers may also be avoided (see Title 11 §548):

(a) (1) The trustee may avoid any transfer of an interest of the debtor in property, or any obligation incurred by the debtor, that was made or incurred on or within one year before the date of the filing of the petition, if the debtor voluntarily or involuntarily—

(A) made such transfer or incurred such obligation with actual intent to hinder, delay, or defraud any entity to which the debtor was or became, on or after the date that such transfer was made or such obligation was incurred, indebted; or

(B) (i) received less than a reasonably equivalent value in exchange for such transfer or obligation; and

(ii) (I) was insolvent on the date that such transfer was made or such obligation was incurred, or became insolvent as a result of such transfer or obligation;

(II) was engaged in business or a transaction, or was about to engage in business or a transaction, for which any property remaining with the debtor was an unreasonably small capital; or

(III) intended to incur, or believed that the debtor would incur, debts that would be beyond the debtor's ability to pay as such debts matured.

(2) A transfer of a charitable contribution to a qualified religious or charitable entity or organization shall not be considered to be a transfer covered under paragraph (1)(B) in any case in which—

(A) the amount of that contribution does not exceed 15 percent of the gross annual income of the debtor for the year in which the transfer of the contribution is made; or

> (B) the contribution made by a debtor exceeded the percentage amount of gross annual income specified in subparagraph (A), if the transfer was consistent with the practices of the debtor in making charitable contributions.
>
> (b) The trustee of a partnership debtor may avoid any transfer of an interest of the debtor in property, or any obligation incurred by the debtor, that was made or incurred on or within one year before the date of the filing of the petition, to a general partner in the debtor, if the debtor was insolvent on the date such transfer was made or such obligation was incurred, or became insolvent as a result of such transfer or obligation.
>
> (c) Except to the extent that a transfer or obligation voidable under this section is voidable under Section 544, 545, or 547 of this title, a transferee or obligee of such a transfer or obligation that takes for value and in good faith has a lien on or may retain any interest transferred or may enforce any obligation incurred, as the case may be, to the extent that such transferee or obligee gave value to the debtor in exchange for such transfer or obligation.
>
> (d) (1) For the purposes of this section, a transfer is made when such transfer is so perfected that a bona fide purchaser from the debtor against whom applicable law permits such transfer to be perfected cannot acquire an interest in the property transferred that is superior to the interest in such property of the transferee, but if such transfer is not so perfected before the commencement of the case, such transfer is made immediately before the date of the filing of the petition.
>
>   (2) In this section—
>   "value" means property, or satisfaction or securing of a present or antecedent debt of the debtor, but does not include an unperformed promise to furnish support to the debtor or to a relative of the debtor;
>   a commodity broker, forward contract merchant, stockbroker, financial institution, or securities clearing agency that receives a margin payment, as defined in Section 101, 741, or 761 of this title, or settlement payment, as defined in Section 101 or 741 of this title, takes for value to the extent of such payment;
>   (C) a repo participant that receives a margin payment, as defined in Section 741 or 761 of this title, or settlement payment, as defined in Section 741 of this title, in connection with a repurchase agreement, takes for value to the extent of such payment; and
>   (D) a swap participant that receives a transfer in connection with a swap agreement takes for value to the extent of such transfer.
>
>   (3) In this section, the term "charitable contribution" means a charitable contribution, as that term is defined in Section 170(c) of the Internal Revenue Code of 1986, if that contribution—
>   (A) is made by a natural person; and
>   (B) consists of—
>   (i) a financial instrument (as that term is defined in Section 731(c)(2)(C) of the Internal Revenue Code of 1986); or
>   (ii) cash.
>
>   (4) In this section, the term "qualified religious or charitable entity or organization" means—
>   (A) an entity described in Section 170(c)(1) of the Internal Revenue Code of 1986; or
>   (B) an entity or organization described in Section 170(c)(2) of the Internal Revenue Code of 1986.[26]

Generally trustees in a liquidation case have a fiduciary trust obligation in the liquidation process to ensure that assets are maintained and preserved. In a Chapter 13 case, trustees are primarily responsible for making certain that the filed plan of restructuring and debt adjustment is followed. Trustees are also entitled to reasonable compensation for their services.

> (b) The trustee shall—
>   (1) perform the duties specified in Sections 704(2), 704(3), 704(4), 704(5), 704(6), 704(7), and 704(9) of this title;
>   (2) appear and be heard at any hearing that concerns
>   (A) the value of property subject to a lien;
>   (B) confirmation of a plan; or
>   (C) modification of the plan after confirmation;
>   (3) dispose of, under regulations issued by the Director of the Administrative Office of the United States Courts, moneys received or to be received in a case under Chapter XIII of the Bankruptcy Act;

    (4) advise, other than on legal matters, and assist the debtor in performance under the plan; and

    (5) ensure that the debtor commences making timely payments under Section 1326 of this title. [11 U.S.C.S. §1326].[27]

Paralegals often are named trustees in bankruptcy cases—a trend likely to continue.

Duty of a Debtor

In Chapter 7, a debtor must comply with various obligations regarding documentation, cooperation with the trustee, and attendance at legal hearings and meetings with creditors. A statement of financial affairs needs preparation and filing under the original petition. (See Form 7.6 on the accompanying CD.)

    The provisions of the bankruptcy code permit payment of legal fees and compensation that is reasonable in light of services rendered. A statement for attorneys' fees, a standardized form, is regularly used in the bankruptcy division. An official form, *Disclosure of Compensation of Attorney for Debtor*, is filed either with a voluntary petition or no more than 15 days after the order of relief is issued.[28] (See Form 7.7 on the accompanying CD for a compensation statement.)

Distribution of the Bankruptcy Estate

Upon the filing of the bankruptcy petition and the commencement of the case, a new entity titled the *bankruptcy estate* comes into being. "The estate consists of all the debtors' interests in real and personal property as of the date the petition is filed."[29] This total sum of property also must be finally calculated when specific federal and state exemptions as to forms of property are subtracted. Some debtors' exemptions are listed in Figure 7.1.

    The bankruptcy code permits individual states to opt out of this exemption scheme, and 37 American jurisdictions have done so.[30] For a comparison of amounts under an alternative exemption plan, review the Washington State's rules in Figure 7.2.

    Discharge of individuals under Chapter 7 will not cover or exercise certain activities, including taxes, alimony and child support, liability for willful and malicious torts, certain student loans, and tax penalties.[31]

    Under the provisions of 11 U.S.C. §507, once an estate has been thoroughly collected and liquidated by the trustee, the remaining proceeds are distributed to claim holders. Claims are prioritized thus:

    (1) First:

        (A) Allowed unsecured claims for domestic support obligations that, as of the date of the filing of the petition in a case under this title, are owed to or recoverable by a spouse, former spouse, or child of the debtor, or such child's parent, legal guardian, or responsible relative, without regard to whether the claim is filed by such person or is filed by a governmental unit on behalf of such person, on the condition that funds received under this paragraph by a governmental unit under this title after the date of the filing of the petition shall be applied and distributed in accordance with applicable nonbankruptcy law.

        (B) Subject to claims under subparagraph (A), allowed unsecured claims for domestic support obligations that, as of the date of the filing of the petition, are assigned by a spouse, former spouse, child of the debtor, or such child's parent, legal guardian, or responsible relative to a governmental unit (unless such obligation is assigned voluntarily by the spouse, former spouse, child, parent, legal guardian, or responsible relative of the child for the purpose of collecting the debt) or are owed directly to or recoverable by a governmental unit under applicable nonbankruptcy law, on the condition that funds received under this paragraph by a governmental unit under this title after the date of the filing of the petition be applied and distributed in accordance with applicable nonbankruptcy law.

    (2) Second, administrative expenses allowed under Section 503(b) of this title, and any fees and charges assessed against the estate under Chapter 123 of Title 28.

    (3) Third, unsecured claims allowed under Section 502(f) of this title.

    (4) Fourth, allowed unsecured claims, but only to the extent of $10,000 for each individual or corporation, as the case may be, earned within 180 days before the date of the filing of the petition or the date of the cessation of the debtor's business, whichever occurs first, for—

        (A) wages, salaries, or commissions, including vacation, severance, and sick leave pay earned by an individual; or

        (B) sales commissions earned by an individual or by a corporation with only 1 employee, acting as an independent contractor in the sale of goods or services for the debtor in

FIGURE 7.1   Federal Exemptions

Source: 11 U.S.C. §522 (2005).

Type of Property	Amount of Exemption	Statute Creating Exemption
Debtor's interest in real or personal property that the debtor uses as a residence.	$17,425	11 U.S.C 522(d)(1)
One motor vehicle.	$2,775	11 U.S.C 522(d)(2)
Household furnishings.	$9,300 aggregate value limitations with $450 limitation on value of each item.	11 U.S.C 522(d)(3)
Jewelry.	$1,150	11 U.S.C 522(d)(4)
Any property selected by the debtor.	$925 plus up to $8,725 of unused portion of 11 U.S.C 522(d)(1) exemption.	11 U.S.C 522(d)(5)
Implements, professional books, or tools of the trade of the debtor or a dependent of the debtor.	$1,750	11 U.S.C 522(d)(6)
Unmatured life insurance contracts owned by the debtor except credit life insurance contracts.	100%	11 U.S.C 522(d)(7)
Accrued dividends or interest under, or loan value of, any unmatured life insurance contract owned by the debtor in which the insured is the debtor or a person of whom the debtor is a dependent.	$9,300 less any amounts transferred by insurer for payment of premiums.	11 U.S.C 522(d)(8)
Professionally prescribed health aids.	100%	11 U.S.C 522(d)(9)
Social Security, unemployment compensation, or public assistance benefits.	100%	11 U.S.C 522(d)(10)(A)
Veterans' benefits.	100%	11 U.S.C 522(d)(10)(B)
Disability, illness, or unemployment benefits.	100%	11 U.S.C 522(d)(10)(C)
Alimony, support, or separate maintenance.	100% of amount reasonably necessary for support of debtor and dependents.	11 U.S.C 522(d)(10)(D)
Payments under stock bonus, pension, profit sharing, annuity, or similar plan or contract on account of illness, disability, death, age, or length of service.	100% of amount reasonably necessary for support of debtor and dependents.	11 U.S.C 522(d)(10)(E)
Crime victims' reparation law benefits or awards.	100%	11 U.S.C 522(d)(11)(A)
Payments on account of the wrongful death of an individual of whom the debtor was a dependent.	100% of amount reasonably necessary for support of debtor and dependents.	11 U.S.C 622(d)(11)(B)
Payment under a life insurance contract insuring the life of an individual of whom the debtor was a dependent.	100% of amount reasonably necessary for support of debtor and dependents.	11 U.S.C 522(d)(11)(C)
Payments on account of personal bodily injury (does not include compensation for pain and suffering or actual pecuniary loss).	$17,425	11 U.S.C 522(d)(11)(D)
Payments in compensation for loss of future earnings.	100% of amount reasonably necessary for support of debtor and dependents.	11 U.S.C 522(d)(11)(E)

the ordinary course of the debtor's business if, and only if, during the 12 months preceding that date, at least 75 percent of the amount that the individual or corporation earned by acting as an independent contractor in the sale of goods or services was earned from the debtor.

(5) Fifth, allowed unsecured claims for contributions to an employee benefit plan—

(A) arising from services rendered within 180 days before the date of the filing of the petition or the date of the cessation of the debtor's business, whichever occurs first; but only

(B) for each such plan, to the extent of—

(i) the number of employees covered by each such plan multiplied by $10,000; less

(ii) the aggregate amount paid to such employees under paragraph (4) of this subsection, plus the aggregate amount paid by the estate on behalf of such employees to any other employee benefit plan.

FIGURE 7.2 **Washington State Exemptions**

Type of Property	Amount of Exemption	Statute Creating Exemption
Homestead consisting of house or mobile home in which owner resides, plus appurtenances and land, if any, on which situate. *Note:* Homestead declaration must be recorded in county recording office if property is not yet occupied as homestead.	$40,000	R.C.W 6.13.030
All wearing apparel.	No limit, except furs, jewelry, and personal ornaments cannot exceed $1,000.	R.C.W 6.15.010(1)
Private library of debtor.	$1,500	R.C.W 6.15.010(2)
Family pictures and keepsakes.	100%	R.C.W 6.15.010(2)
Household goods, appliances, furniture, and home and yard equipment, including provisions and fuel.	$2,700	R.C.W 6.15.010(3)(a)
Other personal property of debtor and family, except personal earnings.	$1,000 with $100 limit on cash and $100 limit on bank accounts and securities.	R.C.W 6.15.010(3)(b)
Two motor vehicles.	$2,500 aggregate value.	R.C.W 6.15.010(3)(c)
Farm trucks, stock, tools, equipment, supplies.	$5,000	R.C.W 6.15.010(4)(a)
Library and office furniture, equipment, supplies.	$5,000	R.C.W 6.15.010(4)(b)
Tools, instruments, and materials used to carry on trade.	$5,000	R.C.W 6.15.010(4)(c)
Disposable earnings (earnings less deductions required by law).	75% or 30 times the federal minimum hourly wage per week, whichever is greater.	R.C.W 6.27.150
Federal pension benefits.	100%	R.C.W 6.15.020(2)
Debtor's right to retirement, disability, or death benefits from employee benefit plans qualified under Internal Revenue Code.	100% of qualified amounts (support claims and QDRO benefits excepted).	R.C.W 6.15.020(3)
Fire insurance proceeds of policies covering exempt property.	100% of exemption for covered property.	R.C.W 6.15.030(E)
Industrial insurance benefits.	100%	R.C.W 51.32.040
Unemployment compensation benefits.	100% (support claims excepted).	R.C.W 50.40.020
Disability insurance benefits.	100%	R.C.W 48.18.400
Proceeds and avails of life insurance policies wherein beneficiary is person other than insured.	100%	R.C.W 48.18.410
Group life insurance proceeds.	100%	R.C.W 48.18.420
Annuity contract benefits.	$250 per month.	R.C.W 48.18.430
Public assistance grants and payments.	100%	R.C.W 74.08.210, 74.13.070
Income or proceeds from trust for benefit of debtor created and funded by another person.	100%	R.C.W 6.32.250
Personal or family burying grounds.	100%	R.C.W 68.24.220, 68.20.120
City employees' retirement benefits.	100%	R.C.W 41.44.240, 41.28.200, 41.20.180
Police and firefighter's retirement benefits.	100%	R.C.W 41.20.180, 41.24.240, 43.43.310
State employees' retirement benefits.	100%	R.C.W 41.40.052
Teachers' retirement benefits.	100%	R.C.W 41.32.052
Judges' retirement benefits.	100%	R.C.W 2.10.180, 2.12.090
Specific partnership property.	100% of partner's interest.	R.C.W 25.04.250
Crime victim's compensation.	100%	R.C.W 7.68.070, 51.32.040
Earnings from work release.	100%	R.C.W 72.65.060
Property of incompetent.	100%	R.C.W 11.92.060(3)

(6) Sixth, allowed unsecured claims of persons—
   (A) engaged in the production or raising of grain, as defined in Section 557(b) of this title, against a debtor who owns or operates a grain storage facility, as defined in Section 557(b) of this title, for grain or the proceeds of grain, or
   (B) engaged as a United States fisherman against a debtor who has acquired fish or fish produce from a fisherman through a sale or conversion, and who is engaged in operating a fish produce storage or processing facility—but only to the extent of $4,925 for each such individual.

(7) Seventh, allowed unsecured claims of individuals, to the extent of $2,225 [FN1] for each such individual, arising from the deposit, before the commencement of the case, of money in connection with the purchase, lease, or rental of property, or the purchase of services, for the personal, family, or household use of such individuals, that were not delivered or provided.

(8) Eighth, allowed unsecured claims of governmental units, only to the extent that such claims are for—
   (A) a tax on or measured by income or gross receipts for a taxable year ending on or before the date of the filing of the petition—
      (i) for which a return, if required, is last due, including extensions, after three years before the date of the filing of the petition;
      (ii) assessed within 240 days before the date of the filing of the petition, exclusive of—
         (I) any time during which an offer in compromise with respect to that tax was pending or in effect during that 240-day period, plus 30 days; and
         (II) any time during which a stay of proceedings against collections was in effect in a prior case under this title during that 240-day period, plus 90 days.
      (iii) other than a tax of a kind specified in Section 523(a)(1)(B) or 523(a)(1)(C) of this title, not assessed before, but assessable, under applicable law or by agreement, after the commencement of the case;
   (B) a property tax incurred before the commencement of the case and last payable without penalty after one year before the date of the filing of the petition;
   (C) a tax required to be collected or withheld and for which the debtor is liable in whatever capacity;
   (D) an employment tax on a wage, salary, or commission of a kind specified in paragraph (4) of this subsection earned from the debtor before the date of the filing of the petition, whether or not actually paid before such date, for which a return is last due, under applicable law or under any extension, after three years before the date of the filing of the petition;
   (E) an excise tax on—
      (i) a transaction occurring before the date of the filing of the petition for which a return, if required, is last due, under applicable law or under any extension, after three years before the date of the filing of the petition; or
      (ii) if a return is not required, a transaction occurring during the three years immediately preceding the date of the filing of the petition;
   (F) a customs duty arising out of the importation of merchandise—
      (i) entered for consumption within one year before the date of the filing of the petition;
      (ii) covered by an entry liquidated or reliquidated within one year before the date of the filing of the petition; or
      (iii) entered for consumption within four years before the date of the filing of the petition but unliquidated on such date, if the Secretary of the Treasury certifies that failure to liquidate such entry was due to an investigation pending on such date into assessment of antidumping or countervailing duties or fraud, or if information needed for the proper appraisement or classification of such merchandise was not available to the appropriate customs officer before such date; or
   (G) a penalty related to a claim of a kind specified in this paragraph and in compensation for actual pecuniary loss.
      An otherwise applicable time period specified in this paragraph shall be suspended for any period during which a governmental unit is prohibited under applicable nonbankruptcy law from collecting a tax as a result of a request by the debtor for a hearing and an appeal of any collection action taken or proposed against the debtor, plus 90 days; plus any time during which the stay of proceedings was in effect in a prior case under this title or during which collection was precluded by the existence of 1 or more confirmed plans under this title, plus 90 days.

(9) *Ninth, allowed unsecured claims based upon any commitment by the debtor to a federal depository institutions regulatory agency (or predecessor to such agency) to maintain the capital of an insured depository institution.*

(10) *Tenth, allowed claims for death or personal injury resulting from the operation of a motor vehicle or vessel if such operation was unlawful because the debtor was intoxicated from using alcohol, a drug, or another substance.*[32]

Under the new act, the emphasis on child support and its relationship with the bankrupt party responsible for paying it took on heightened importance. In recent reforms, lawmakers are attempting to steer funds to children over detached creditors. As a result, some portion of unpaid child support and alimony takes priority over certain creditors. The bankruptcy court has promulgated a new form for announcing this intention by the support or alimony creditor.[33] Certain priority claims are payable before unsecured claims.

 The bankruptcy petitioner sets out claims of creditors holding either secured or unsecured claims in the original filings. (See Schedules D and E in Forms 7.8 and 7.9 on the accompanying CD.) Claims that are unprioritized are also listed. (See Schedule F in Form 7.10.) After all documents and schedules are filed, a Debtor's Statement of Intention is drafted and recorded (see Form 7.11).

CHAPTER 13 PROCEEDINGS

Chapter 13 proceedings are designed to handle the debts of individuals whose earnings are basically wages and whose debts are small enough and income significant enough that a substantial repayment is a possibility. As a rule, Chapter 13 proceedings cannot have unsecured individual debts of more than $100,000, and secured debts cannot exceed a total of $350,000. Note the petitioner's eligibility determination under 11 U.S.C. §109 as outlined here:

(a) *The plan shall—*

(1) *provide for the submission of all or such portion of future earnings or other future income of the debtor to the supervision and control of the trustee as is necessary for the execution of the plan;*

(2) *provide for the full payment, in deferred cash payments, of all claims entitled to priority under Section 507 of this title, unless the holder of a particular claim agrees to a different treatment of such claim; and*

(3) *if the plan classifies claims, provide the same treatment for each claim within a particular class.*[34]

 In adjustment of individual debts, a plan must be submitted to the bankruptcy judge for review and confirmation. The plan "must provide for the full payment of all claims entitled to priority unless the creditors with priority agree to a different treatment."[35] One of a paralegal's tasks may be to critically evaluate the economic capacity of a potentially bankrupt client. As in Chapter 7, a voluntary petition filed with appropriate schedules commences the process. (See Form 7.3 on the accompanying CD.) A statement of current monthly income is required as well (see Form 7.12) and is attached to Chapter 13's voluntary statement. Fundamentally, a Chapter 13 participant must be prepared to demonstrate three critical factors:

1. That he or she is earning enough money regularly that will result in a stable source of income to pay into the plan.

2. That he or she has debts that are dischargeable rather than not because Chapter 13 does not protect a debtor's bad acts.

3. That he or she is willing to be under a judicial microscope for three years under a Chapter 13 plan.

 A plan is required under Chapter 13 rules. (See Form 7.13 on the accompanying CD.)

Once a plan has been filed and creditors have been put on appropriate notice, a hearing will take place. Creditors have the right to object to the nature and structure of the plan. The trustee and any disgruntled creditors try to resolve any disputes under the proposed plan. For any plan to be eventually confirmed, it must be economically feasible, and the court must be satisfied that there is a likely chance that all payments under the plan will be made according to the plan's general intent.[36] Once the plan is approved, it is binding on the debtor, as well as on interested parties.[37]

CHAPTER 11 PROCEEDINGS: REORGANIZATION OF AN EXISTING BUSINESS

Paralegals may occasionally come into contact with the content and subject matter of Chapter 11 reorganization, a process mainly geared to complex corporate situations. Chapter 11 reorganizations were "designed to provide an efficient, expeditious, and economical vehicle for small, generally privately owned business enterprise."[38]

Chapter 11 is comparable to Chapter 13 in that a business partnership or other entity must reorganize itself with a specific plan. Congress enacted the Chapter 11 procedures to provide a safe haven for struggling yet still potentially viable businesses. Essentially Chapter 11 provides protection to "ongoing businesses worthy of protection and rehabilitation."[39]

During the steel, air, and industrial recession of the last five decades, many companies, such as LTV Corporation, US Airways, United, and others, sought Chapter 11 protection. Larger, more complex companies have numerous dilemmas in need of resolution:

- How will pensions be funded, and how will pension benefits be paid, if the business continues to operate?
- How will the claims of creditors be handled?
- What value of creditors' claims will be paid?
- What health and medical benefits will be available to existing workers and retirees?
- What disadvantage will competing industries have versus a company in Chapter 11?
- How will creditors be protected? Will the creditors' committee approve? (Creditors' committees are significant decision makers in the Chapter 11 reorganization plan.)[40]

The statistics tell a story of a bankruptcy process that imitates the economic life of a nation. Although Chapter 11 reorganizations have recently witnessed less participation in the corporate sector, there is little doubt that this option "provide{s} a level of certainty with respect to the treatment of debtors and creditors when dealing with the inevitable failures and defaults of business."[41]

As in a Chapter 13 case, a Chapter 11 plan must be filed and approved by the bankruptcy court. Among the issues to consider in a Chapter 11 reorganization are these:

- Preparation of a disclosure statement regarding the plan.
- Vote or tally of creditors as to their finding of acceptability of the plan.
- Confirmation hearing on the plan.
- Entry of a confirmation order binding the debtor and its creditors to the plan's provisions.
- Dismissal of the Chapter 11 case.

As in Chapter 7 and 13, a Chapter 11 bankruptcy action is commenced upon the filing of a petition. (See Form 7.3 on the accompanying CD.) Schedules and a financial statement are necessary components in the bankruptcy action. In addition to these items, a list of the 20 largest unsecured creditors needs preparation in a Chapter 11 case (see Form 7.14).

After all payments shown in the plan have been met, debtors will be given a discharge releasing them from any future liability, except on those debts that are exempted by statutory preference.[42] For useful checklists when preparing Chapter 7, 11, and 13 cases, see Forms 7.15–7.17 on the accompanying CD.

CHAPTER 12: THE FAMILY FARM

The passage of the Bankruptcy Abuse Prevention and Consumer Protection Act of 2005 (BAPCPA) made Chapter 12 (as in effect on June 30, 2005) a permanent part of the bankruptcy code effective July 1, 2005. Chapter 12 is the bankruptcy proceeding used for the adjustment of debts of a family farmer or family fisher with regular annual income. Chapter 12 is closely modeled after Chapter 13 procedures but incorporates some Chapter 11 concepts. Relief under this chapter is "voluntary," meaning only the debtor may file a petition for Chapter 12 bankruptcy relief.[43] Chapter 12 allows the family farmer or fisher to reorganize debts by reducing secured debts to

FIGURE 7.3 Chapter 12 Qualifications

Source: Internal Revenue Service Regulations at 5.9.9.2 (1-1-2006).

Characteristics	Family Farmer	Family Fisher
Entity	Individual, partnership, or corporation.	Individual, partnership, or corporation.
Debt limit	$3,237,000.00, subject to periodic adjustment for inflation pursuant to 11 U.S.C §104(b).	$1,500,000.00, subject to periodic adjustment for inflation pursuant to 11 U.S.C §104(b).
Percentage of debt from operation of business	50% of liabilities must be attributable to farming operations (excluding debt for personal residence of the farmer or residence of the farmer partner/shareholder).	80% of liabilities must be attributable to fishing operations (excluding debt for personal residence of the fisher or residence of the fisher partner/shareholder).
Gross income	More than 50% of the debtor's income is received from a farming operation in the tax year prior to the petition, or more than 50% of the debtor's income is received from a farming operation in each of the second and third years before the petition.	More than 50% of the debtor's gross income is received from commercial fishing operations for the tax year preceding the commencement of the case.

the present value of the assets securing the debt and by extending the repayment periods. The bankruptcy code provides that only a family farmer or fisher whose annual income is sufficiently stable and regular to enable the debtor to make payments under a Chapter 12 plan is eligible to file this type of bankruptcy.[44] A debtor may continue to operate the farming or commercial fishing operation as a debtor-in-possession with the duties and rights of a trustee unless the court, for cause, appoints a trustee.[45]

Chapter 12 promulgates specialized rules on debt limits as well as gross income. Review the qualifications in Figure 7.3.

Chapter 12 bankruptcy filing is similar to a Chapter 11 corporate reorganization bankruptcy or a Chapter 13 personal reorganization bankruptcy. After a farmer files for Chapter 12, a stay is imposed, and all actions of creditors to collect from the debtor must cease. After filing for bankruptcy, the farmer has 90 days to file a plan of reorganization with the bankruptcy court. The reorganization plan must reveal all of the farmer's debt and detail how he or she plans to repay the debt over three to five years. If the plan meets all the requirements of Chapter 12, the bankruptcy court must approve it at a hearing held within 45 days of filing. Creditors are given an opportunity to file objections to the plan, but they cannot veto it. After filing for Chapter 12, the farmer almost always is allowed to continue operating the farm. The reorganization plan is supervised by a court-appointed trustee. During the plan, the farmer makes periodic payments to the trustee, who then pays creditors according to the terms of the plan.

Chapter 12 encourages creditors to work at resolving a debt crisis with the debtor so that the farm will remain intact and productive. The provisions of a confirmed plan bind the debtor and each creditor.[46] Once the court confirms the plan, the debtor must make the plan succeed. The debtor must make regular payments to the trustee, which will require adjustment to living on a fixed budget for a prolonged period. Furthermore, although confirmation of the plan entitles the debtor to retain property as long as payments are made, the debtor may not incur any significant new debt without consulting the trustee because additional debt may compromise the debtor's ability to complete the plan.[47] In any event, failure to make the plan payments may result in dismissal of the case.[48] In addition, the court may dismiss the case or convert the case to a liquidation case under Chapter 7 of the bankruptcy code upon a showing that the debtor has committed fraud in connection with the case.[49]

As in all other forms of bankruptcy, creditors need to be put on notice. (See Form 7.18 on the accompanying CD.) Once the debtor has paid down the debt in accordance with the plan, the court will discharge the debtor (see Form 7.19).

Summary

This chapter has briefly addressed the three fundamental techniques of declaring bankruptcy from both a personal and a business point of view. Chapter 7 liquidations, both voluntary and involuntary aspects, and the powers and duties of trustees, the obligations of debtors and creditors, and the processes of distribution in a bankruptcy case, were covered. Chapter 13 proceedings, in which a plan of action is required, were also discussed. Chapter 11's methods of reorganization of existing businesses and its requirements were highlighted. Finally, a short visit to the world of Chapter 12 processes involving family farms ended the analysis.

Discussion Questions

1. Critics of bankruptcy have charged that it is a means of avoiding personal financial responsibility for debt. Does bankruptcy cause or promote a lack of responsibility in financial affairs?
2. What is the difference between voluntary and involuntary processes in bankruptcy?
3. A trustee serves many functions in a bankruptcy action. Discuss them.
4. Distribution of a bankrupt estate can take place. What types of parties should be advised and consulted?
5. How does one ensure that a claim or economic interest will be considered during a bankruptcy proceeding?
6. Which of the bankruptcy proceedings is more a reorganization of debt than a forgiveness or elimination?
7. What types of debts have priority over others in the handling of a bankruptcy estate?
8. Can you think of any other means or methods of providing assistance to individuals in financial trouble outside the bankruptcy procedure?
9. In a Chapter 11 reorganization, what parties must give consent?
10. Who can challenge the distribution of an estate?
11. How would a paralegal get and verify information received from a debtor?
12. What could a paralegal do if a debtor represented false or inaccurate information?

Practical Exercises

1. Any creditor, secured or otherwise, to have any chance to collect the sum or sums owed from a debtor or bankruptcy estate, must file a timely proof of claim. Notice of claim should be sent to all interested parties listed on the original petition. Obtain the necessary federal form and complete it using the following fact pattern:

Secured claim (car):	*$11,610.00*
Unsecured claim (wages):	*$41,000.00*
Date of case:	*November 19, 2007*
Name of creditor:	*Angeli Merics, 1111 Wayne Way, Saratoga, FL 33254*
Date of debt:	*January 11, 2001*
Date of judgment:	*February 10, 2003*
Court:	*Circuit Court of Saratoga, FL*
Account number of claim:	*#353194*
Case number:	*2007-3194*
Name of debtor:	*Larry Loso, 345 Springdale Road, Saratoga, FL*
Only claim filed in the debt.	

2. In publicly held companies, the company's ownership interests are fractionalized by share measures. To own stock is to own some portion of the company. When a company reorganizes, its shares usually metamorphose by valuation and number.
   Prepare a list of equity security holders using the following facts:

   Creditor #1: Wilson Sports, Treasurer Charlie Smith, 1216 Venor Way, Sacramento, CA 91601
   (707)777-7777
   $6,000,000.00 line of credit,
   50% of which is denied as liability.
   $1,000,000.00 pledges by baseball future sales.
   Account—disputed.

Creditor #2: Eggshore Enterprises, President Mike Stern, 1111 Rondo Boulevard, Egg Harbor, NJ 08802 (609)414-4141
$67,000.00 in a personal loan.
Debtor claims it is owed $20,000.00 in past due billings from creditor. None of the loan proceeds were secured.
Account—disputed.

Creditor #3: Dupont Book Company, 1200 King Street, Wilmington, DE 19855 (302) 555-5555
No secured portion.
$11,000,000.00 owed by competition royalty infringement.
Debtor denies all liability.
Account—contingent/unliquidated.
District: Pennsylvania (Eastern)
Debtor: Sargeant Enterprises
Case number: 94-X302
Executive/Signature: President William Ames
No other creditors.

3. Prepare a statement of financial affairs using these facts:

- *Debtor Shirley Remonso is a single, 69-year-old, unemployed woman. She receives $980.00 per month in Social Security benefits.*

- *Vacation home: $300,000.00 in Ocean City, New Jersey, owned by debtor, Shirley Remonso, 18 Guiding Beacon Street, Philadelphia, PA. Sold at foreclosure: August 1, 2007, for $179,100.00. The foreclosure suit was brought by the first mortgage holder, National Bank of Philadelphia.*

- *Subject to a civil action for collection of past due credit in the Court of Common Pleas of Venango County, PA, Case No. 07-616. Plaintiff's Rocket Rubber Bands suit in discovery stage, and the case was initiated prior to bankruptcy filing.*

- *August 1, 2007, 60 days before commencement of bankruptcy, Debtor Shirley Remonso paid Exxon Gas Company of 11 Laurel Way, Sea Isle, New Jersey $6,000.00. Still owes $8,000.00.*

- *Debtor gave her sister Annie Remonso $9,600.00 as a birthday gift on July 30, 2007, not reported.*

- *Debtor gave $600.30 cash to her favorite charity, People of the Light, 11 Webster Street, Baltimore, MD 21222, on September 20, 2007. (NB: As you can see, the debtor likes to give her money away but not pay her debts.)*

- *Debtor spent $1,410.00 for credit counseling payable to Easy Credit Company, 210 Forrester Building, Tolcony Street, Philadelphia, PA 19301. Date: June 11, 2007.*

- *Debtor closed her checking account #327-77777 six years ago at the First Fidelity Bank in Aramingo, PA 19000. Balance was $4,500.00.*

- *Debtor, under her name, has moved two times in the past two years. Addresses are:*
  - *2011 Gondo Avenue, Wildwood, NJ 08070*
  - *411 Wilson Court, Secane, NJ 07430*

- *Debtor was married to William Balkin in 1960 for 39 years until his death in 1999. Debtor then married Lucus Remonso in 2000 until his death in 2002.*

- *Debtor's present accountant is J. Graff, CPA, 59 Washington Place, Wayne, NJ 07777. Duration of representation: 1981 to present.*

- *Debtor's records were destroyed in a flood in 1988. Her accountant, J. Graff, has all records since that date.*

- *Debtor's attorney is Sam Hazo, 944 Plognet Field, Princeton, NJ 07640.*

- *This Chapter 13 case (No. 07-11R6W) was filed in the Southern District of New Jersey.*

Internet Resources

U.S. courts bankruptcy forms page—http://www.uscourts.gov/bkforms/index.html

U.S. courts publications page—http://www.uscourts.gov/library/publications.html

SEC corporate bankruptcy information page—http://www.sec.gov/investor/pubs/bankrupt.htm

Legal Information Institute U.S. bankruptcy code—http://www.law.cornell.edu/uscode/html/uscode11/usc_sup_01_11.html

U.S. Government Printing Office—http://www.access.gpo.gov/

FindLaw bankruptcy code—http://caselaw.lp.findlaw.com/casecode/uscodes/11/toc.html

FindLaw bankruptcy practice area page—http://www.findlaw.com/01topics/03bankruptcy/index.html

U.S. House of Representatives, downloadable U.S. code, Chapter 11—http://uscode.house.gov/download/title_11.shtml

DOJ, U.S. Trustee Program home page—http://www.usdoj.gov/ust/

ABA bankruptcy, pro bono—http://www.abanet.org/legalservices/probono/bankruptcy.html

---

Endnotes

1. ILLINOIS PARALEGAL ASSOCIATION, THE FINDINGS OF THE COMPETENCY COMMITTEE RELATING TO THE QUALITY OF PARALEGAL SERVICES 4–6 (1989).

2. *See* Todd J. Zywicki, *Institutions, Incentives, and Consumer Bankruptcy Reform*, 62 WASH. & LEE L. REV. 1071 (2005).

3. *Id.* at 1072.

4. *See* Harvey R. Miller & Shai Y. Waisman, *The Future of Chapter 11: A Symposium Cosponsored by the American College of Bankrupt: Is Chapter 11 Bankrupt?* 47 B.C. L. REV. 129 (2005).

5. U.S. CONST., Art. I, §8, Cl. 4.

6. International Shoe v. Pinkus, 278 U.S. 261 (1929).

7. 11 U.S.C. §101 et seq.

8. "Two events have helped to raise the prestige and profitability of the field. One is the Bankruptcy Reform Act of 1978, which created a Bankruptcy Code that made it easier for people to file, and that also raised attorneys' fees, making the field more lucrative. The other factor behind the boom is the recession. With so many people declaring bankruptcy, it's become an acceptable way of cleaning up one's debts. And when well-known corporations like R.H. Macy's and TWA file for reorganization, it even becomes respectable." Verna Safran, *The Boom in Going Bust, Opportunities for Paralegals in Bankruptcy Law*, 9 LEGAL ASS'T TODAY, May–June 1992, at 99.

9. INSTITUTE FOR CONTINUING LEGAL EDUCATION, 2 MICHIGAN BASIC PRACTICE HANDBOOK 990 (1988).

10. Geoff Giles, *Bankruptcy: The New Bankruptcy Law: Bad News for Debtors, Worse News for Lawyers*, 13 NEV. LAW., Sept. 2005, at 8.

11. See Henry J. Sommer, *Trying to Make Sense out of Nonsense: Representing Consumers under the Bankruptcy Abuse Prevention and Consumer Protection Act of 2005*, 191, 79 AM. BANKR. L. J. 191 (2005).

12. Zywicki, *supra* note 2, at 1076.

13. *See* The Bankruptcy Abuse Prevention and Consumer Protection Act of 2005, Public Law No. 109-8, 119 STAT. 23 (2005).

14. 11 U.S.C §101(12A) (2005).

15. Giles, *supra* note 10, at 17.

16. 28 U.S.C. §1334(a) (2005).

17. *See* Charles P. Nemeth, *The District of Columbia Retired Judges' Services Act: Can It Pass Constitutional Muster?* JUDICATURE , Feb.–Mar. 1990, at 253.

18. ROBERT N. CORLEY, ERIC M. HOLMES, & WILLIAM J. ROBERT, PRINCIPLES OF BUSINESS LAW 537 (1987); *see also* 11 U.S.C. §362.

19. *See* 11 U.S.C §101(10A) (2005).

20. *See* Sommer, *supra* note 11, at 195; *see also* Official Form B22a, Statement of Current Monthly Income and Means Test Calculation.

21. 11 U.S.C.S. §101(10A) (2005).

22. 11 U.S.C.S. §501 (2005).

23. In re Lough, 57 Bankr. 993 (Bankr. E.D. Mich. 1986).

24. 11 U.S.C.S. §704(9) (2005).

25. 11 U.S.C. §547(B)(4)(a) (2005).

26. 11 U.S.C.S. §548 (2005).

27. 11 U.S.C.S. §1302(b) (2005).

28. 11 U.S.C.S. §329.

29. INSTITUTE FOR CONTINUING LEGAL EDUCATION, 2 MICHIGAN BASIC PRACTICE HANDBOOK 1009 (1988); 11 U.C.C. §541 (2005).

30. *Id.*

31. *Id.*

32. 11 U.S.C. §507(a) (2005).

33. *See* http://www.uscourts.gov/bkforms/official/b281.pdf.

34. 11 U.S.C.C §1322(a)(1-3) (2005).

35. Corley et al., *supra* note 18, at 539.

36. 11 U.S.C. §1325(a) (2005).

37. *See* 11 U.S.C. §1327(a) (2005).

38. Miller & Waisman, *supra* note 4, at 141.

39. In re Winshall, Settler's Trust, 758 F. 2d. 1136 (6th Cir. 1985).

40. 11 U.S.C. §1102 (2005).

41. Miller & Waisman, *supra* note 4, at 132

42. 11 U.S.C. §1328 (2005).

43. *See* 11 U.S.C §303.

44. *See* 11 U.S.C §101(19) & (19B).

45. *See* 11 U.S.C §§1203 & 1204.

46. 11 U.S.C. §1227.

47. 11 U.S.C. §§1222(a)(1), 1227.

48. 11 U.S.C. §1208(c).

49. 11 U.S.C. §1208(d).

Chapter 8

Estates, Trusts, and Their Administration

      7. Trustee's Compensation and Other Rights

      8. Attestation Clauses and Other Executory Requirements

   C. Types of Trusts

      1. Testamentary Trust

      2. Charitable Trust

      3. Inter Vivos Trust

      4. Express Trust

      5. Totten Trust

      6. Honorary Trust

      7. Section 2503(c) Trust

      8. Implied Trust

      9. QTIP Trust

    10. Generation-Skipping Tax Trust

    11. Life Insurance Trust

IV. Decedent's Administration: Preliminary Matters

   A. Accumulation of Assets for Estate Administration

   B. Determination of Heirs and Other Interested Parties

   C. Determining Competency and the Guardianship of Incapacitated Parties

V. Estate Administration Processes

   A. Small Estates

   B. Formal versus Informal Administration

   C. Paralegal Responsibilities in the Estate Administration Process

      1. Confirmation of a Personal Representative

      2. Appointment of a Personal Administrator: Intestate Estate

      3. Grant of Letters Testamentary/Administration

      4. Probate and the Will

      5. The Elective Share of a Surviving Spouse

      6. Compilation of an Inventory

      7. Dealing with Creditors or Other Interested Parties

      8. First and Final Account

      9. Distribution and Discharge

VI. Estate Taxation

   A. Estate Tax Return: Form 706

   B. Schedule Preparation

      1. Schedule A

      2. Schedule B

      3. Schedule C

      4. Schedule D

      5. Schedule E

      6. Schedule F

      7. Schedule G

      8. Schedule H

      9. Schedule I

    10. Schedule J

    11. Schedule K

    12. Schedule L

    13. Schedule M

    14. Schedule O

    15. Schedule P

    16. Schedule Q

    17. Schedule R/R-1

    18. Schedule U

   C. Gift Tax Calculation

   D. Fiduciary Returns

ESTATES AND TRUSTS PARALEGAL JOB DESCRIPTION

Estates and trusts paralegals need to be proficient in the following competencies:

- List all tasks, duties, and obligations of a paralegal in an estate planning practice.
- Chart and diagram the intestate succession laws of the paralegal's jurisdiction.
- Calculate property distribution under an intestate succession statute.
- Draft and design an estate planning interview form and checklist.
- Make a list, diagram, or chart of the formal requirements for drafting wills that covers capacity, execution, and attestation requirements and essential clauses.
- Draft and design, under the supervision of an attorney, specific will clauses and provisions.
- Draft and design, under the supervision of an attorney, residuary estate clauses.
- Draft and design, under the supervision of an attorney, a testamentary trust within a will.
- Draft and design checklists, interview documents, and other materials to help in the collection of information for will construction.
- Designate parties as a donor, donee, settlor, or beneficiary.
- Draft and design, under the supervision of an attorney, a trust for asset or financial management purposes.
- Draft or design a trust, under the supervision of an attorney, for charitable purposes.
- Draft or design a trust, under the supervision of an attorney, for minimization of tax liability.
- Draft or design a general trust that includes provisions for the marital deduction, alternative distribution techniques, and powers of appointment.
- Draft and design forms, checklists, and other exhibits necessary for information gathering in the trust process.
- Understand the functions of trustees and executors.
- Be familiar with the various services offered by the trust departments of local financial institutions in the paralegal's jurisdiction.
- Draft, under the supervision of an attorney, clauses on revocability in a trust document.
- Understand the legal effect of a Totten trust.
- Provide information to clients regarding the implications of the Tax Reform Act of 1986.
- Draft, under the supervision of an attorney, a provision of a trust that outlines the powers, duties, and obligations of a trustee.
- Draft documents, under the supervision of an attorney, signifying the resignation of a trustee.
- Devise checklists, forms, and other materials that chart, track, and provide a history of estate planning assets and important individuals.
- Design personal and family information sheets.
- Locate all necessary legal documents to begin the administration of an estate, including trusts, gift documents, wills, certificates, and titles.
- Search records at governmental offices such as the Registrar of Wills, the Surrogate or Orphan Court, the Office of Vital Statistics, the Veteran's Administration, and the Social Security Administration.
- Create a chart, graph, or diagram listing all government agencies, along with their phone numbers and addresses, that deal with the administration of estates.
- Collect information about the business interests of an estate, including assets owned by corporations, partnerships, or sole proprietorships.
- Collect all forms and documents necessary for initial estate filing.

- Acquire statutory or legislative codes on estate administration.
- Make a list, chart, or diagram of all responsible local court personnel who handle the administration of estates.
- Draft, under the supervision of an attorney, a petition to identify heirs.
- Acquire all forms and documents necessary for either formal or informal, supervised or independent probate proceedings.
- Create preliminary drafts of and file documents, such as a petition for a grant of letters testamentary or probate, or other pleadings necessary to effect a probate proceeding.
- Prepare a notice and/or order of hearing of appointment and admission of will to probate.
- Prepare an inventory of estate assets.
- Prepare an information sheet mailed to beneficiaries under the probate process.
- Prepare a notice to creditors.
- Calculate and determine a spouse's elective right under the statutory code of the paralegal's jurisdiction.
- Calculate and assess multiple problems under a spouse's right of election.
- Pay taxes from an estate administration fund.
- Care for specific claims for which the estate is liable.
- Perform a final accounting of an estate.
- Calculate attorney and/or executor's fees based on agreed formulas.
- Perform a closing procedure on an estate.
- Collect tax forms and documents for estate and gift calculation.
- Calculate unified credits on an estate tax return.
- Identify assets that would be construed as transfers made in contemplation of death.
- Employ and use specific transitional rules in the determination of a gross estate.
- Perform multiple methods of valuation of an estate.
- Complete an estate and gift tax return.
- Compute unified credits, annual exclusions, deductions, and exemptions under the estate and gift tax rules and principles.
- Identify all types of wills recognized by the laws of the paralegal's jurisdiction.
- Identify all parties named in a will by designation, such as testator, testatrix, executor, executrix, guardian, or trustee.
- Develop effective docket procedures to ensure timely filing of all probate and tax documents.
- Develop effective procedures for making a final distribution of assets.

THE NATURE OF ESTATE AND TRUST WORK

Practitioners in the field of estates and trusts have long been characterized as dull and humorless individuals whose chief task in life is to read the dispositive provisions in a will. To the contrary, the services that estate practitioners provide are not only essential but dynamic.[1] The perception of probate and trust works belies its many demands. This is not a field for the uncreative or dull-minded. If anything, the field contains a plethora of complicated subject matter from tax to statutory construction, from legal drafting to planning for the care of others. Estate planners handle legal matters of the living and the dead. For the living, the estate lawyer assists and counsels in the areas of financial planning and living trust administration, in addition to trusts and gifts. Aside from possessing the necessary intellect, estate paralegals and attorneys hone exceptional skills in human relations.[2]

Paralegals assume an integral role in all aspects of estate and trust work. Shari Faulkner argues convincingly about the positive role paralegals play in the world of estate administration:

> *A paralegal can be extremely effective, both in administration of the estate and in cost-effectiveness, in assisting an attorney with the probate process. Because of all of the tax issues, this area of legal practice can be most challenging. Many times the estate is simple. Perhaps the probate client is someone who has just lost his or her spouse and part of the paralegal's duties is to help the client adapt to his or her new situation. On the other hand, it may be a sophisticated estate worth millions of dollars with a variety of assets and tax issues.[3]*

How the paralegal contributes to this esoteric field is the subject of the pages to come.

Financial Planning

Paralegals often deal with estate finance, from tracking assets and investments to assisting with the creation of a family financial plan. Good estate and trust paralegals help the living prepare for the eventualities that arise upon death. Money usually is a major issue in estate administration. During a client's life, the paralegal and attorney will give advice and insight about how to provide for remaining family members. Take this task seriously. Michael C. Hodes, in his work *A Roadmap to Financial Planning*, urges legal professionals to take a more active role in financial planning by becoming competent in areas of taxation and business and retirement planning.[4]

How estate, tax, and fiduciary laws affect the client's assets is a primary focus of the estate plan. The paralegal, under the supervision of the attorney, needs to identify both assets and liabilities in the early stage of the estate plan. Employ Form 8.1 on the accompanying CD to target these issues.

Taxation

As the maxim states, there are two certainties in life: death and taxes. Incredibly, even well-educated individuals overlook the tax bite that will occur at their death. Estate planners and practitioners must have a substantial "familiarity with current tax rules, tax statutes, and judicial decisions, and an appreciation of the movement in the field in taxation through administration, judicial, and legislative actions."[5] Wills, trusts, and the inter vivos transfer of property generate significant tax implications. Professor Gary Randall of the University of Idaho states that death may be the last available tax shelter.[6] His commentary is not facetious when he claims, "it is still advantageous (from a tax standpoint) to die."[7] However, the comment assumes that the client has been given the right advice about tax implications. Tax planning is essential to inter vivos transfers in the form of charitable giving, the establishment of charitable trusts, and gifts to minors or for other tax purposes.

Retirement planning, which highlights tax advantages to the estate, plays a critical role in the estate plan for the living and the deceased. The diversity of products available that shelter income, from the IRA to the Simplified Employee Pension, from the Archer Medical Savings Account to 529 College Plans, provides prolific practice opportunities for the firm and the paralegal.

Human Counseling

A successful estate planning practice requires positive human relations attributes. It is a field in which people do "good work for real people with truly human needs, responses, and emotions."[8] Of course, the emotionalism of death, mortality, and the human experience affects every person, including the estate practitioner. Tragedy—unanticipated or expected—causes the practitioner and his or her clients a sadness that can only be consoled with the care of those that remain. The paralegal must stress this obligation repeatedly—to prepare for the inevitable and leave behind sufficient resources for the living. Naturally, clients avoid the issue of death; because of this, they procrastinate about wills and resist these types of terminal questions. Here the paralegal provides a valuable service by emphasizing this critical need and encouraging clients to think about the unthinkable.

Similarly, the dispositive aspects of wills and trusts must address the psychosocial desires of the client. Parents in less than ideal family settings often are concerned about how assets will be disposed and to whom those dispositions should be made. Clients look to the estate practitioner for guidance on these thorny questions of transfer and testacy. What about a son or daughter the client knows is undeserving and is likely to squander the fruits of the estate plan? Who are the best candidates for executor or executrix? What impact will remarriage have on the provisions of a will? What is the most sensible plan for distribution to multiple categories of beneficiaries? Other legal issues in need of resolution are these:

- Who will be guardian or custodian of the children should both spouses die?
- At what age or in what period should distributions of assets be made for the care, support, and education of children?
- Assuming the client, his or her spouse, and all children die, what dispositive provisions control the distribution of the estate?
- Is there a charitable interest so important to the testator that he or she wishes to address it through an inter vivos or testamentary trust?[9]

The estate practitioner, in a sense, is a mortality ombudsman, a person who has the objective and factual capacity to keep the lines between life and death well drawn. With the advance of aging in the baby boom generation, the opportunities for legal work are lucrative.[10] In this context, the estate paralegal must hone and refine the skills of human interaction.

Preparation of Estate Documentation

Paralegals and lawyers involved in estates and trusts should possess a high level of proficiency in legal draftsmanship. In documents, wills, trusts and living trusts, and papers of every other sort, the paralegal will aid the client.[11] In documents intentions are memorialized.

Estate Questionnaires

Estate planning documents solicit sizable amounts of information about the client's state of affairs. In estate practice, checklists, forms, and other background documents play a critical role in developing an accurate picture of the client served. Standard form books about estate planning, wills, and trusts and probate administration are plentiful, and come in hard or electronic formats:

- 3 *Current Legal Forms,* 7-510–7-518, §1-b
- 4 A. Nichols, *Cyclopedia of Legal Forms,* §4.3567
- 1 Prentice-Hall, *Estate and Gift Taxes,* §101–10
- Sachs, *Modern Tax Planning Checklists,* Chapter 15
- Casey, *Estate Planner's Practice and Procedural Guide,* 101–22
- Practicing Law Institute, *Essential Estate Planning,* 15–20

Software programs and packages are equally plentiful. Here are two prominent firms in this area:

- Easy Soft, Inc.—Estate Planning
  http://www.easysoft-usa.com/
  475 Watchung Avenue
  Watchung, NJ 07069
  800-905-SOFT

- The Lackner Group—The Lackner 6-in-1 for Windows
  http://www.lacknergroup.com/
  Carnegie Office Park, Suite 290
  700 North Bell Avenue
  Pittsburgh, PA 15106
  800-709-1041

Keeping profit margins in sensible view and realizing that efficiency advances the bottom line in estates and trust practice are ideas always on the front burner. Charles McCarter, an estate planner for more than 25 years, says in his work *Cost-Efficient Estate Planning* that efficiency begins at the beginning by being "adequately prepared to ask the right questions at the first meeting with the client."[12] The initial client questionnaire must be shaped and crafted with efficiency in mind.

A "client information package" can be used for multiple estate purposes, including the preparations of wills and trusts, as well as valuation and calculation of asset values. (See Form 8.2 on the accompanying CD.) Send the information package to the client well before the first meeting so the client has time to gather the necessary information. (Another example by Lackner 6-in-1 is provided at Form 8.3.)

Administration of Estates

The administration of any estate, whether formal or informal, small or sizable, will require the completion of a series of documents that tracks the decedent's estate. The process of actual estate administration is labeled *probate* and will be guided by rules and statutory principles unique to each jurisdiction. In general terms, an estate administration will call for these types of legal documents:

- Petitions for probate.
- Petitions for a grant of letters testamentary.

- Petitions for a grant of letters of administration.
- Preparation of an inventory and appraisal schedule for assets of the estate.
- Preparation of a distribution scheme or plan for court approval.
- Will contest pleadings.
- Preparation of a first accounting.
- Preparation of a final account.
- Preparation of a petition for settlement and final distribution.
- Preparation of an estate tax opinion.

Although some of this writing is less than glamorous, these steps are analytically challenging and require dedication to detail. Precision in language of wills and trusts is always required. The consequences of poor draftsmanship are frequently severe.[13]

Litigation and Advocacy

Estate planning and its administration consist of hearings and related challenges, advanced litigation, and the advocacy of claims from many quarters in the estate arena. In the area of wills, the estate practitioner engages in advocacy over construction, interpretation, and verification. Other legal challenges include these:

- Petition to determine the validity of a will.
- Challenge of a probate order on a will regarding undue influence in its execution.
- Challenge of a probate order on a will regarding incompetency of the testator.
- Will contests.
- Petitions to determine heirs.
- Settlement disputes regarding intestate estates and corresponding claims.
- Abatement, abolition, or change in the dispositive provisions of a will.
- Petitions to remove trustees.
- Petitions to remove executors/administrators/guardians.
- Petitions to change the nature and purpose of trusts.
- Petitions to overturn trusts as a violation of public policy.
- Tax litigation regarding a trust's revocability.

Paralegals play a prominent role in the preparation of pleading documentation, as well as in research on specific procedural and substantive estate questions. In addition, they are involved in the ongoing coordination between clients, attorneys, and other parties who have a substantial or incidental interest in estates.

The Indispensability of the Estate Paralegal

> *By any reasonable measure, paralegals are indispensable in the world of estates and trusts. In affairs involving information gathering, client contact and tracking, and assistance with documentation and pleadings, paralegals deliver an impressive array of services.*[14]

What capacities, proficiencies, and responsibilities are eventually delegated to the paralegal will largely depend on the individual's skill, intellectual depth, technical ability, and general experience.[15] What is undeniable is the necessity of the paralegal profession in legal life. From estate filings to probate pleadings, from probate notices to assistance at actual hearings, paralegals earn their keep in the litigation arena. Ralph Blount labels paralegals as "indispensable" and says that their usage permits the firm "to deliver high quality service at less expense to the client."[16]

WILLS

From a legal perspective, a person may die in two ways: with a will (testate) and without a will (intestate). When a will is absent, how assets and property are distributed will no longer be the will of the deceased but rather will be controlled by a statutory substitute known as the *laws of intestacy.* Intestacy is a topic that will be given further consideration in the section about the administration of estates. Dying testate is more desirable because the decedent's express wishes and purposes are fulfilled by a legal document: a *will.* In effect, the decedent who writes a will, thereafter known as a *testator,* is ruling from the grave. He or she is determining how assets will be distributed, deciding which individuals should get specific items of personal property or other bequests or which land should be devised to whom and how. "Rare is the case that a living person cannot materially benefit his estate by leaving a will. Besides the tax savings that often accrue, it is always preferable for an individual to select the manner in which his or her property will be distributed."[17]

Aside from giving full credence to the wishes and desires of the testator, the will instrument can accomplish a bevy of other things, including a reduction of taxes[18] and other benefits such as these:

- Provides care for minors as a guardian or custodian.
- Allows testator to select a fiduciary who will administer his or her estate and trust.
- Permits the orderly transfer of business interests, whether corporate or other legal entity.
- Permits a plan of disinheritance or other exclusion if the testator so desires in children and remarried partners.

From every angle, a will makes perfect sense.

Preliminary Considerations in the Will Process

Collection of Information

Estate practitioners and paralegals assimilate factual data and information into a plan for will preparation. A "will information worksheet" should be presented and completed at the initial client interview. (See Form 8.4 on the accompanying CD.) Before the attorney drafts a will, he or she will rely on the information gathered by the paralegal regarding guardianship, trustee or other fiduciary appointment, and listing of beneficiaries and property subject to bequest, devise, or other distribution scheme. Emphasize full disclosure and accurate reporting of the assets and testator desires.

As the plan for the will unfolds, discuss the alternative options available to the client that are sometimes described as "will substitutes." Inform clients of the nonwill options.

There are three major alternatives to testacy; property covered by these alternatives passes to successors by contract or operation of law, and therefore is not part of any decedent's probate estate. These three alternatives are (1) life insurance proceeds that pass by contract to a designated beneficiary; (2) assets held by joint tenancy with right of survivorship that pass by operation of law to the surviving joint tenant; and (3) property held in trust that is a distinct legal entity from the testator's estate and is controlled by the terms of the trust document. Each of these alternatives may make better sense than the use of a will. In the case of life insurance, the proceeds payable upon death may effectively remain outside the probate process. Alternative strategy requires the assistance of expert financial planners, whom paralegals should befriend.

Guidelines for Will Drafting

Most will contests are rooted in technical issues—most of which are related to a will's structural difficulties. In addition, will drafts often suffer from flaws relating to signatures, witnesses, and the necessary clauses to give the will effect. Faulty seals or impressions, forgeries, and tampering also open the challenge door. Paralegals should be zealously attentive to will requirements as they serve the drafting attorney. Here are some reliable guidelines for proper will drafting:

1. Never use preprinted forms.
2. Be consistent in the method of transcription. Type it all or write it all.
3. Use the same tool or machine for the transcription, such as the same printer and same typeface.
4. So desirous are clarity and precision in language that the will drafter soon finds that certain terms like *devise, bequeath,* and a *legacy* are inventions for this purpose. These terms have little meaning outside the will context.
5. Although will documents have an incredible variety, the dispositive intention of the testator must be apparent, and formal requirements, as statutorily delineated, should be attentively followed.

6. Make no additions, corrections, erasures, or other modifications to the document.

7. In most statutory schemes, the witness must be a credible and competent party.

8. Use consistent spelling for the names of all beneficiaries.

9. The primary aim of any will drafter or estate practitioner is to give pure, unadulterated effect to testator's intentions.

Will interpretation depends on the clarity and precision of the draft, as well as attentiveness to the legal language that gives effect to the dispositions. Even so, the will document should not be overly obtuse and legalistic. Plain English accomplishes the same end as legalese. Attorney Thomas Word Jr. writes,

> *A will should be written for the client's eyes. Of course, it must be sound technically, but it need not be written in legalese. By applying plain English principles in our wills (indeed in all our drafting) we can respond to our clients in language they will understand. We will also improve our instruments technically.*[19]

Legal Formalities of a Valid, Enforceable Will

Certain formal requirements must exist for will validity. What are the requirements and components for a valid will? To discern these requirements, give thought to these legal issues:

1. Who has the capacity to make a will?

2. Has the will been made freely and voluntarily?

3. Who has the right to prepare a will?

4. What clauses, provisions, and components are necessary to make a will valid?

5. What is the effect of competing or contradictory documents?

6. Are signatures required?

7. Is a notary public required?

8. Are witnesses required?

9. Are any filings or certifications or other formal authentications necessary?

10. What language meets minimally the statutory requirements for an effective and constructive will?

11. Do wills have to be written?[20]

The types and formats of wills are as varied as client circumstances. A simple will for an individual without children and limited assets is shown in Form 8.5 on the accompanying CD. In Form 8.6 a more complicated version is provided with significant assets and a series of testamentary trusts.

Attempts to regularize will practice on a statutory basis have been partially successful. "The statutory will is a legislative attempt to ease the increasing cost and complexity of testamentary planning by permitting and encouraging briefer forms for wills. This effort may involve the creation of simple alternatives to intestacy, shorthand methods for writing wills, or both. A well-drafted statute not only should streamline the writing of wills, but also should strike an intelligent balance between several potentially conflicting concerns."[21] The Uniform Probate Code (U.P.C), adopted in about a dozen American states, lays out the general requirements for will construction. These requirements are described in Article 5 of the Arizona Revised Statutes, which is based on the U.P.C. Chapter 5:

> *ARTICLE 5 WILLS*
> *14-2501 Who may make a will*
> *14-2502 Execution; witnessed wills; holographic wills*
> *14-2503 Holographic will*
> *14-2504 Self-proved wills; sample form; signature requirements*
> *14-2505 Witnesses; requirements*
> *14-2506 Execution; choice of law*
> *14-2507 Revocation of will; requirements*
> *14-2508 Change of circumstances; effect on will*

14-2509   Revoking a subsequent will; effect; reviving a revoked will; requirements
14-2510   Incorporating outside document into a will; requirements
14-2511   Testamentary additions to trusts; requirements; effect of revocation
14-2512   Disposition of property by reference to acts of independent significance
14-2513   References to separate lists; requirements
14-2514   Contracts regarding wills; requirements; effect
14-2516   Custodian of will; duties; liability
14-2517   Penalty clause for contest; restriction

That a basic will design can be statutorily mandated is agreed, though the unique profile of each client likely negates the general design. Statutes can insist on technical requirements, but they come up short on standardizing will practice. Even with statutory instructions and guidance, will practice has long relied on common-law principles and the rules issued under local jurisdictions.

When reviewing a will draft, check to see whether the document is compatible with these requirements:

1. Does the preamble (the introduction) identify the testator—the person disposing of property at death?
2. Is the spelling of the client's name correct?
3. Is the client also known ("AKA") as someone else?
4. Does the will address the matters of debt, expenses, and the like?
5. Does the testator have any powers of appointment?
6. Are there funeral and burial arrangements?
7. Is there a disposition for personal, tangible property?
8. Is there a disposition for real property?
9. Is there a satisfactory residuary clause for property that is not disposed?
10. Have provisions been made for guardians, trustees, and executors?
11. Have powers been granted to fiduciaries?
12. Is there a signature or testimonium clause?
13. Is there an attestation clause?
14. Is there a simultaneous death clause?
15. Is there a self-proof clause?[22]

Clauses and Provisions in a Standard Will

Will practice should not be overly difficult but must adhere to fundamental requirements. To be valid, a will needs select clauses.

Preamble, Introduction, Exordium, or Publication   Terms like *preamble* and *exordium* pertain to the introductory clauses in a standard will. Within this clause the testator supplies identification with the general clause, "I (name) do make, publish, and declare this to be my last will." Additionally, the clause can revoke previous wills.

 Provision for Payment of Debts and Funeral Expenses   This clause customarily instructs that all debts are to be paid and that funeral expenses taken care of. (An example is Form 8.7 on the accompanying CD.)

Specific Testamentary Dispositions   In the construction of any will, gifts, transfers, or specific devises are accounted for by clear disposition. Often an individual has certain personal property, extra cash, or financial instruments that he or she wishes to disburse to selected individuals or charitable institutions. Of course, under a residuary clause or other provision, the bulk of personal and real property may inure to the benefit of a surviving spouse, whose own will may delineate an estate plan.

However, paralegals would be wise to ask the testator whether there is some property of high sentimental value or genealogical importance that the testator wishes to transfer with unique instructions. Heirlooms, artwork, books, family bibles, and other items can be listed under the testamentary gift clause. Language regarding specific gifts or testamentary transfers might be as follows:

> *I give $300 to St. Eleanor's Church in Collegeville, Illinois.*
> *or*
> *I bequeath my diamond ring to my daughter Anne Marie with the wish that she keep and maintain it.*
> *or*
> *I give 1,000 shares of stock of General Motors Corporation to my son David.*

Bequests, Legacies, and Devises   *Bequests* are gifts of cash or commercial property. *Devises* are real property passed through the will. *Legacies* are the generic term applicable to all distributions of all other remaining property given under the will's provisions. The order and scope of legacies and devises are important for the estate practitioner unless, of course, the will mandates an ordering to distribution. This is how interests are prioritized:

1. Specific legacies and devises.
2. Demonstrative legacies and devises.
3. General legacies and devises.
4. Residuary legacies and devises.

Legacies and devises are further broken down into either a general or specific category. A specific category is a direct and unequivocal instruction to the executor to take a certain piece of clearly identifiable property and distribute it before any other interests. A general legacy is a general instruction to allow some property to go to an individual but not necessarily at the expense of the specific legatee. Another differentiation of these interests is based on the term *demonstrative,* an example being this:

> *I give and bequeath a hundred thousand dollars from my savings account at the Mellon Bank to my daughter Eleanor.*

Personal property that is not specifically outlined or described in a will testament can be left to the surviving spouse in what is known as a *pour-over trust.* It also can be part of the residue or residuary estate—though the beneficiary of the residuary need not be a spouse. (See Form 8.8 on the accompanying CD.) Note that powers accorded the personal representative under residuary distribution scheme can widely vary.

In most cases the surviving spouse will be appointed as executor or executrix. Therefore, the distribution of tangible property among the children is usually not contested. When the spouse does not survive, problems often occur in the remaining parties eligible for appointment. Will language goes a long way in eliminating misunderstanding and disputes. Weigh the following will provision:

> *In the interest of family harmony, I state that I have not promised any particular item of tangible personal property to any person. Therefore, if there is a dispute between the beneficiaries over which items each should receive, I recommend but do not require that all such items be appraised and that each beneficiary then select in rotation (my personal representative selecting for any person unable to act for himself) items at the appraised value, the order of choice to be determined by lot. I may leave a list dated, and either in my handwriting or signed by me, that sets forth my wishes regarding distribution of my tangible personal property. If I do, I intend it to qualify as an amendment to my will.*

Aside from the resolution of appointment, the clause employs an outside letter or memorandum to delineate the distribution of personal property. This technique is known as the *doctrine of incorporation by reference.* By incorporation, we infer that an outside reference—one that is outside the pages of the will—is tied to the underlying will document. Minnesota Statute 524.2-510 directly mentions this practice.

> *524.2-510 INCORPORATION BY REFERENCE.*

> *Any writing in existence when a will is executed may be incorporated by reference if the language of the will manifests this intent and describes the writing sufficiently to permit its identification.*[23]

Here is another example of incorporation by reference clause:

> *It is my wish and desire that my children (and the issue of any deceased child of mine) will be guided in the division of my tangible personal property by a letter to them that will be found with my personal papers.*

Tangible personal properties are merely one form of testamentary gift. Devises of real property are also known as *general* or *specific demonstrative bequests*. See the examples in Forms 8.9 and 8.10 on the accompanying CD outlining representative language.

Residuary Estates   After all testamentary gifts have been analyzed and provided for, after payment of debts and all expenses have been accounted for, and after taxes have been calculated and remitted, whatever property remains in the estate is referred to as the *residuary*. If a will is visualized as a funnel, whatever remains at the end of the funneling process is what can be characterized as *residue*. A residuary clause typically reads,

> *All the rest, residue, and the remainder of my property, of whatsoever kind and wherever so situated, but excluding any property over which I have a power of appointment, it being my intention not to exercise any power of appointment, I give and bequeath and devise to my wife if she survives me.*

In this standardized residuary clause, the wife is clearly identified as the beneficiary of the residuary.

If funds are insufficient for payment of debts, taxes, and other estate expenses, invasion of the residuary remainder may cause specific gifts, bequests, and devise to be abated. *Abatement* is defined when there are "not enough funds to pay them in full, they are paid in part."[24] Pay close attention to gifts that are subject to exemption due to their destruction or alienation during the lifetime of the testator. Also, gifts may lapse because the initial beneficiary is no longer living. In this form of lapse, the testamentary gift or bequest will often be pooled into the residuary fund. Examine the residuary clause with a trust mechanism in Form 8.11 on the accompanying CD.

Residuary clauses are too often written with confusing and obtuse distribution schemes. In the case of a surviving spouse, the question of distribution is not all that difficult; but when the spouse predeceases, children and more remote beneficiaries become involved. If a residuary trust benefits a spouse and upon her eventual demise benefits the children, how is the remaining residuary to be distributed? There are two formulas of distribution:

> *Per stirpes:* A division of a gift into as many shares as there are beneficiaries, whether living or deceased, in the generation closest to the testator's with members still living.

> *Per capita:* A division of the gift into as many shares as there are beneficiaries then living in the generation closest to the testator.

In the per capita formulation, children and grandchildren would often receive an equal share under a distribution scheme. Because this is frequently not the desired end or the usual distribution desire, if a testator's intentions are challenged, courts tend to favor the per stirpes distribution allocation, emphasizing larger distributions to direct issue (children) rather than grandchildren. The chart in Figure 8.1 portrays the dynamic.

Under a per capita formulation a bequest to A's issue, B through I would receive a 1/7 distribution apiece. Under a per stirpes distribution, B and C would each receive a 1/3 distribution; G, H, and I would divide the difference, each receiving a 1/9 interest.

How *children* are defined affects any distribution plan. Under the Uniform Probate Code, a child is defined as "an individual entitled to take as a child under this Code by intestate succession from the parent whose relationship is involved and excludes a person who is only a stepchild, a foster child, a grandchild, or any more remote descendant."[25] As a result, adopted children and illegitimate children fit within a classification scheme of distribution. Within this definitional framework does *child* also refer to the children of different marriages? Are children inclusive of stepchildren, adoptive children, grandchildren, or illegitimate children?[26]

Is the term *children* synonymous with the terms *issue, offspring, descendants,* and *heirs of the body?* Even more basically, does *a child* mean *children?* As *Page on Wills* concisely states, "The primary meaning of children is the immediate, legitimate offspring of the person indicated as the parent."[27] Will language for per stirpes distribution and per capita is shown in Forms 8.12 and 8.13 on the accompanying CD.

FIGURE 8.1
Illustration of Per Stirpes and Per Capita Distributions

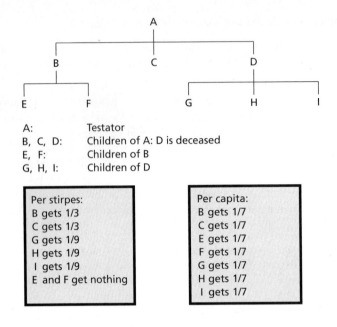

A: Testator
B, C, D: Children of A: D is deceased
E, F: Children of B
G, H, I: Children of D

Per stirpes:
B gets 1/3
C gets 1/3
G gets 1/9
H gets 1/9
I gets 1/9
E and F get nothing

Per capita:
B gets 1/7
C gets 1/7
E gets 1/7
F gets 1/7
G gets 1/7
H gets 1/7
I gets 1/7

Appointment of an Executor/Personal Representative/Guardian Much occurs after the demise of one or both parents. A testator must plan for all possibilities and appoint individuals he or she knows to be capable of carrying out certain responsibilities. Parents must prepare for the risk of their simultaneous deaths. A guardianship provision takes on added meaning for parents concerned with their children's supervision. Appointment of an executor or personal representative—an individual in charge of the administration of the will and estate plan—is also a matter of concern. Executors and personal representatives can be trusted family members, long-time friends of the family, attorneys, bankers, trust departments, financial institutions, and any legal entity empowered to engage in such activities. Whoever is appointed should have the necessary business acumen, skill in negotiation, and capacity to handle complex details. The party chosen should be beyond reproach and of the highest integrity. The estate paralegal should be clear about the types of parties to pick.

The testator should be advised that an executor's role is not honorary but one with duties, responsibilities, and potential liabilities. Although many individuals consider only family members as executors, corporate fiduciaries may be desirable in many circumstances.[28] An executor appointment clause is shown in Form 8.14 on the accompanying CD. An appointment of guardian clause is shown in Form 8.15.

A will should also contain a clause covering simultaneous death. This clause provides that in situations where it is impossible to determine which of the spouses died first, the husband is deemed to have predeceased the wife; then devisees, legatees, and other beneficiaries named in the respective wills of the spouses take the estate when both spouses die in a common accident. The Uniform Simultaneous Death Act creates this presumption to ensure the transfer of probate assets and to resolve other matters regarding property held in joint tenancy, insurance policies, and similar issues.[29] (See Form 8.16 on the accompanying CD.)

Testamentary Trusts A testamentary trust—that is, the creation of a trust within a will document—is an important device to care for a spouse or children. Additionally, the trust has been correctly employed as a tool of tax reduction or deferral of taxable estate income. A testamentary trust also provides a mechanism by which specific goals can be accomplished by the more deliberate distribution of income to minors. Examples include these:

- Trusts for the benefit of children for their education.
- Trusts for the benefit of children once they reach a certain age.
- Trusts for the benefit of children who embark on or pursue a particular business or professional venture.
- Trusts that provide financial planning and upkeep for minors who do not possess monetary skills.
- Trusts that provide for the payment of expenses relating to a long-term illness.

The will should contain provisions on trust advisers. (See Form 8.17 on the accompanying CD.)[30] Two-tiered trusts, first for spouse, then to children, preserve capital and minimize tax liability. (See Form 8.18 for this will clause.)

Testimonium or Execution Clauses   The clause showing that the document has been freely executed and signed by the testator is known as the *testimonium clause*. Its provisions are self-explanatory. See Form 8.19 on the accompanying CD. The North Carolina Bar suggests standard instructions on execution requirements (see Form 8.20). To corroborate the fact that the will is the actual expression of the testator's intention, witness attestation is mandatory. A witness execution clause is drafted in Form 8.21.

Self-Proof Clause   Many jurisdictions permit the use of self-proof clauses as an alternative to formal probate. This clause is simultaneously executed after the attestation and acknowledgement sections of the will. By completing this will provision, the representative or administrator is relieved from formal attestation and verification processes during probate. An example of a self-proof clause that requires a notarial seal or other verification is shown in Form 8.22 on the accompanying CD.

Will Codicils

Amending a will or adding novel dispositive provisions requires either a new will or the drafting of a legal addendum called a *codicil*.[31] "A will or codicil, or any part of either, is revoked (1) by a subsequent inconsistent will or codicil, even though the subsequent inconsistent will or codicil does not expressly revoke all previous wills or codicils, but the revocation extends only so far as the inconsistency exists; (2) by a subsequent written will, codicil, or other writing declaring the revocation, if the same formalities required for the execution of wills are observed in the execution of the will, codicil, or other writing."[32]

Generally a codicil must be executed with the same formalities as an original will. A codicil should refer precisely to the clause, line, provision, or other item subject to change or modification. For added subject matter, a codicil serves the same purpose. (Form 8.23 on the accompanying CD contains a codicil.)

Remember that wills are ambulatory instruments whose language, depending on circumstances and the law, may need modification.

> *Every attorney—even those who do not specialize in estate planning—should know how to review a will. Few attorneys go to others to have a will drawn or reviewed. It is an area that invites a "do it yourself" effort by the general practitioner. Yet a will may be the single most important document the general practitioner ever drafts, and it is certainly an instrument that must be revisited not only at the conclusion of its original scrivening but also regularly.*[33]

Will Contests

A *will contest* is an assertion by an interested party that a defect, inconsistency, or illegality in the will document is the subject of contest. To *contest* a will is to claim that it is not an accurate reflection, in whole or in part, of the testator's intentions. "In most jurisdictions, the statutes prescribing the proceedings for the probate and contest of wills allow a person in interest to file a caveat, petition for contest, or statement of objections to a will offered for probate; this procedure permits such a person to wage a contest before the will has been probated."[34] In a will contest, the challenger may initially argue whether the testator had the capacity to make the will. Questions of testamentary intent and capacity are easier to allege than prove. Testamentary intent generally consists of (1) knowing the material recipients of the testator's bounty and (2) knowing the nature of the testator's property. Advocates of the will contest may maintain that the testator was

- Senile at the time of drafting the will.
- Under the influence of drugs, alcohol, or other substances at the time of drafting the will.
- Completely incoherent and unable to transact ordinary business.
- Completely lacking in memory and mental faculties.
- Unable to formulate the required testamentary capacity.
- Given to extreme passions and prejudices leading to a less than crystalline view of intentions.[35]

A will may also be the result of fraud, duress, and undue influence.[36] "Fraud as sufficient to invalidate a will occurs when, because of misrepresentations and deceptions, a testator is tricked into making dispositions in his will that he would not have otherwise made."[37] In a practical sense, if money or other property is bequeathed to a non–family member, a new marriage partner upon a preceding divorce, or singularly channeled to one heir, devisees, legatees, and other interested parties may erroneously deduce undue influence, duress, and coercion in the making of a will. An alternative explanation could be the testator's displeasure with them or a conscious, volitional decision to leave them out of an estate plan.[38] Paralegals and estate planning practitioners should reserve judgment on claims of undue influence until a complete investigation is conducted.

Furthermore, a will contest petition or complaint goes to the heart of the document's authenticity. Authenticity, the credibility of the document, usually involves questions of legal signature, witness qualification, and other technical requirements relating to the execution of a will document. Forged and feigned signatures are not beyond the scope of this type of examination. The expertise of forensic specialists in documentary analysis is helpful because the analysis of handwriting in a comparative context ensures authentic signatures. Typefaces, pen types, and other forms of micrographic comparisons are also important in the determination of whether a will is authentic.[39] Even a self-proved will may be challenged on grounds of forgery, incapacity, improper execution, or the like, but no witness need be heard or testimony taken if the will is not so challenged. Examples of pleadings challenging the authenticity of a will are provided in Forms 8.24 through 8.27 on the accompanying CD.

Exceptions to Will Formality

The paralegal should be aware of both statutory and common-law exceptions to historic will formalities. Exceptions fall into two main categories: holographic wills and nuncupative wills.

A *holographic will* is one entirely handwritten, dated, and signed by the testator with no adherence to technical requirements, such as witnesses or other execution requirements. In limited circumstances such a will has validity. Check local statutes for rules regarding legitimacy.[40]

A *nuncupative will* lacks the traditional writing and is orally corroborated. This situation occurs in time of war and is a very limited exception. Most jurisdictions place extreme limitations on usage by mandating specific estate valuation thresholds and insisting on strict witness requirements and corroborative proof of the authorship during wartime. A typical nuncupative statute might read as follows:

1. *The estate bequest must not exceed in value the sum of one thousand dollars ($1,000.00).*
2. *It must be proved by two witnesses who were present at the making thereof, one of whom was asked by the testator at the time to bear witness that such was his will, or to that effect.*
3. *The decedent must at the time have been in actual military service in the field, or doing duty on shipboard at sea, and in either case in actual contemplation, fear, or peril of death, or the decedent must have been at the time in expectation of immediate death from an injury received that same day.*[41]

TRUSTS

Purposes and Parties

Trusts can be either inter vivos, taking effect while the testator is living, or testamentary, taking effect upon a testator's demise. Seen thus far in the discussion and analysis of wills is the testamentary trust: a testator's instructions regarding the transfer of estate assets to a surviving spouse, and upon his or her demise, and the establishment of secondary, remainder trusts for children. Trusts serve many purposes:

- Charitable.
- Tax shelters, deferral, and other saving mechanisms.
- Care of surviving spouse.
- Preservation of capital and principal.
- Promotion of specific profit activities.
- Pension plans and annuities.

- Financial management.
- Promotion of educational and professional opportunities for individuals or entities.
- Financial contingencies and conditions for beneficiaries who are inept with money or need to follow certain conduct.
- Preserving capital and business assets for shareholders.
- Certificates of deposit and other bank trusts: Totten trusts.
- Probate and any other lawful purposes.[42]

All trusts contain the following elements and components:

Settlor: Also known as a creator or grantor. A settlor is simply a person who creates a trust.

Trust corpus: The body of the trust; the income, funds, or money of the trust, which is necessary to give the trust substance and effect; also known as the trust res, the fund, the estate, or any property interest that the trustee holds subject to the right of someone else.

Trustee: The person or institution named by the settlor or creator of a trust to administer, manage, or be responsible for the trust corpus.

Beneficiary: The party to whom the benefits of the trust should inure; the person or institution to whom the trustee distributes income earned from the trust corpus and/or the trust corpus itself.

For a formal and valid trust, each component must be present. However, the variety of trust structures can be somewhat confusing. For example, the settlor could be simultaneously designated beneficiary. In this case, though the trust corpus or property is in the legal ownership of the trustee, by express or implied trust appointment, equitable title vests in the beneficiary. A trust agreement created for purposes of financial management is shown in Form 8.28 on the accompanying CD.

The settlor's selection of a trustee should result from conscious and thorough deliberation. The individual can be an institution, whether financial or banking in nature; a government agency; a charitable or nonprofit corporation; or any natural or legal person. Because of financial expertise, banks are often selected to serve as trustees. In most jurisdictions, cotrustees are also an acceptable avenue of appointment. Trustees can be appointed under clauses that are either revocable or irrevocable, giving the beneficiary and/or the settlor authority to terminate the trust instrument.

Trustees are guided by general fiduciary duties and obligations. According to the Uniform Probate Code, a trustee "shall observe the standards in dealing with the trust assets that would be observed by a prudent man dealing with the property of another, and if the trustee has special skills or is named trustee on the basis of representations of special skills or expertise, he is under a duty to use those skills."[43] Trustees are under a fiduciary duty to beneficiaries and are accountable to them and expected to perform faithfully their administrative duties and to exercise good faith in all dealings. Trustees have the legal duty to handle the trusts' assets in an intelligent, beneficial, and productive way.

The Trust Document

The Preamble

Primarily drafted for the purpose of identification of the parties, the preamble describes the settlor, trustee, and beneficiary. Here is an example of introductory language:

> I, _____, Settlor, of Anytown, USA, hereby transfer the properties listed in the annexed schedule to John Stephens, hereinafter known as Trustee, in trust to keep invested and to distribute the net income in principal. . .
> or
> Settlor hereby establishes a trust that will act as a receptacle for his property, which may be transferred to trustee during his lifetime, or at death, be transferred by will or otherwise. Settlor appoints. . .
> Trustee agrees to hold the same in trust for the purposes and the conditions set forth in the trust. . .

Frequently the trust corpus is identified within the initial preamble; or if its appraised value and financial content tend to be variable, reference to a schedule attached to the main document is made. Subsequent withdrawals or additions to the trust corpus can be noted on the attached schedule.

Appointment of Trustee

A legally enforceable trust must also designate a trustee—the person empowered to handle the trust corpus and principal for the benefit of the beneficiary. The trustee is mentioned in most preambles or introductory paragraphs of trust documents. Trustee clauses should also provide for the contingency of original trustee resignation or the elimination of the original trustee by settlor's desire.

Trust Purpose Clause

As previously discussed, a trust may have many purposes, including financial management, the fostering of educational opportunity, or the advancement of any charitable end. A purpose clause should be drafted in a trust document. Make certain the trust is not illegal or void for public policy reasons. Courts have intervened, declaring invalid trust documents that promote racial segregation or a violation of state, federal, or local law.

Revocability Clause

For tax and other legal reasons, revocability is a key issue in the compilation of a trust document. By permitting some reservation or control over the trustee's functions and duties, the Internal Revenue Code has held that for all intents and purposes, taxes on trust income cannot be deferred, transferred, or spun off to other parties. As a result, the corpus of a trust is included in a decedent's estate for estate tax purposes, although it is not included in the decedent's probate estate. The issue of revocability still has tax and governance implications, especially in charitable gifts by trust. A clause, an example following, permits a settlor's continuing control over the trust corpus:

> *Settlor reserves the right to alter, amend, revoke, or terminate this agreement in whole or in part without the consent of trustee, but only upon written notice to trustee; provided, however, that if altered or amended, the duties, powers, and responsibilities of trustee shall not be changed substantially without his consent. Trustee agrees to reassign or reconvey to settlor any property affected by exercising such right.*

If a trust is thoroughly revocable by the settlor, the income derived under the trust is taxable to the settlor who is considered the owner of the trust property. Additionally, the entire trust property is included in the settlor's estate for federal tax purposes because the settlor has not irrevocably disposed of the trust property. The opposite result is reached, sometimes, in an irrevocable trust instrument because the settlor has waived, relinquished, or transferred complete and total right over the property and corresponding benefits in question. Therefore, depending on the provisions of the trust, the income earned on the trust property will be taxed to the settlor, the trust, the trust beneficiaries, or both the trust and the trust beneficiaries at the same time.[44]

A beneficiary and settler, when uncertain of an appointed trustee's capacity to manage money, may opt for a revocable trust to determine the suitability of the appointment. In this temporary situation, the power of revocation makes sense. Few other reasons justify revocable trusts.

Trustee's Powers and Duties

Some clear delineation of a trustee's powers and duties should be outlined in the trust document. Those powers and duties not delineated in the trust document are usually governed by state statute. In most cases, the language contained in Form 8.29 on the accompanying CD will satisfactorily cover all of the trustee's power and authority.

A settlor may feel more comfortable limiting the range and extent of the trustee's authority. A settlor may determine that a trustee should not be handling real estate matters, the exchange of stocks and bonds, debentures, or the purchase of corporate bonds or other matters. Gauge and evaluate powers and responsibilities in light of the client's particular needs and interests.

Trustees may be called on to make regular, though discretionary, distributions of income and principal. Some notation of a distribution plan should be made, whether on a monthly, quarterly, or annual basis, or whether the parties desire a policy of regular reinvestment. The investment powers of a trustee usually are broad.

Durational Requirements

Under a trust's duration clause, the term of the trust is specified, listing for what period the trust will have effect, and also for how long the current trustee may serve.

Trustee's Compensation and Other Rights

A clause should be included in the trust agreement that outlines a trustee's right to notice of removal with or without cause. A trustee's compensation should also be included, whether payment is based on an annual fee, a percentage of the trust principal and profit, or another formula. An example of a trustee's compensation formula based on gross profits is shown in Form 8.30 on the accompanying CD.

Attestation Clauses and Other Executory Requirements

Most jurisdictions have attestation and execution requirements. Although a trustee must accept the terms of the trust, only the settlor is required to execute the trust. Although notarization of the trust may be required to put it into recordable form, attestation is not usually required. A sample clause is included within the whole trust previously shown in Form 8.28 on the accompanying CD. Paralegals should pay close attention to notarial requirements.

Types of Trusts

Trusts come in many shapes and sizes and reflect the specific needs of the settlor and beneficiary. Examples with corresponding forms are discussed in the pages that follow.

Testamentary Trust

Form 8.31 on the accompanying CD[45] lays out a comprehensive example of a testamentary trust. The testamentary trust seeks to preserve accumulated assets, allows expert financial management, and offers greater economic flexibility to both surviving spouse and issue. The most often used testamentary trust is a grant from a testator to a surviving spouse and then, upon that spouse's demise, to remaining children or issue. All of the elements of a trust are required and include the following:

- *Settlor:* testator.
- *Beneficiary:* surviving spouse, then children.
- *Trust corpus:* residuary estate.
- *Legal purpose:* For the economic benefit of the surviving spouse and children.

Charitable Trust

A fund that is created for the benefit of a named charity, whether a religious institution, nonprofit agency, or other worthy cause, can be in the form of a charitable trust. Increasingly these trust formats are being scrutinized for profit making and inordinate benefit to the settlor, trustee, or beneficiaries. Excessive and irregular expenses in the administration of a trust and the payment of unreasonable compensation of the trustee's activities can be construed as inconsistent with federal and state tax law. Charitable trusts that advance public welfare, foster religion and religious education, support missionary work, relieve poverty and human suffering, or fund research into the causes of disease qualify as legitimate charitable trusts.

Of recent interest to estate planners is the *charitable lead trust*. "A charitable lead trust is established by the donor transferring property, such as securities, to the trust. During the trust term, the trust provides for an annual income to be paid to the designated charity (or charities) for a certain period of time. That trust term can be based either on a person's life expectancy or on a set number of years. At the end of the charitable term, the trust terminates and distributes to the children or other family member beneficiaries."[46] Again, do not ignore the structural elements of a formal and legally binding trust:

- *Settlor:* The party making or creating the charitable trust.
- *Trustee:* The party who is managing or administering the trust corpus.
- *Beneficiary:* The charitable institution that will benefit by the donation of funds to the trust principal.
- *Legal purpose:* Charitable in design.

- *Trust corpus:* That property the trust is subject to: cash, stocks, real and personal property.

(See Form 8.32 on the accompanying CD for a charitable trust.)

Inter Vivos Trust

Trusts between living individuals, such as a trust corpus used for an investment vehicle, management or fiscal control of individuals who are incompetent in handling their money, or the creation of a fund for the benefit of a settlor's children, are all examples of inter vivos trusts. A sample inter vivos trust is shown in Form 8.33 on the accompanying CD.

Express Trust

A trust that is either inter vivos or testamentary can be express in nature. Express trusts are generally evidenced by some written documentation, but oral trusts that can be verified or corroborated by other evidence are acceptable for personal property.

Totten Trust

A Totten trust is the standard trust relationship entered into when a depositor makes a deposit of cash into a bank or financial institution. Standard passbook language consists of the following:

> With notation X as Trustee for Y. During X's lifetime, X may deal with a deposit as his own. However, upon X's death, the bank is entitled to treat Y as the owner of the funds then upon deposit.

Review a standard passbook or other certificate of banking deposit literature referencing as a trustee under a Totten trust.

Honorary Trust

An honorary trust is created for a specific noncharitable purpose such as for the care of a grave. No beneficiary exists to enforce the trust, so whether these arrangements are technically a pure trust is an academic argument. Examples of this include trusts for animals and for the care of burial grounds.

Section 2503(c) Trust

By making a specific gift to a minor and simultaneously taking advantage of $12,000 in annual gift tax exclusion, a 2503(c) trust is an attractive option for high-income tax candidates.[47] The requirements for a 2503(c) trust are as follows:

    (1) A gift to a minor through Section 2503(c) will qualify for an annual exclusion—that is, will not be considered a gift of a future interest—if income and principal may be expended by or on behalf of the beneficiary at any time before the beneficiary's becoming 21 years of age.

    (2) Unexpended income and principal must be payable to the beneficiary upon reaching 21.

    (3) If the beneficiary dies before age 21, the trust corpus must go to the minor's estate or to an appointee.

    (4) The trust may continue beyond the donee's 21st birthday while the donee has the ability after reaching 21 years of age to obtain the property held in the trust by exercising a right of withdrawal.[48]

The revocability of this form of trust is also an important tactical consideration because tax benefits will be substantially affected in the event of revocation.[49]

Implied Trust

Certain trusts come about because of an equitable finding. No precise form can be demonstrated because it is implied from specific facts and conditions. Implied trusts are passive in nature and are usually rooted in judicial urgency, such as the prevention of a serious wrong or unjust enrichment. The two main categories of an implied trust are the resulting trust and the constructive trust. "A resulting trust arises by implication of law to carry out the presumed intention of the parties, while a constructive trust arises purely by construction of equity, without regard to the intent of the parties, so as to bring an end to unfairness, bad faith, or fraud; a resulting trust is a passive trust with no duties imposed upon the trustee except to convey the trust property to the beneficiary, while in a constructive trust situation, a trustee is required to exercise reasonable care and skill to preserve the trust property."[50]

Examples of resulting trusts can be discovered in these short fact patterns:

Example 1

A technical failure in the draftsmanship of the trust document: Under that set of facts, courts would not forbid the reacquisition of a trust corpus of a settlor because of a technical or procedural failure in the trust instrument.

Example 2

Failure of a specific trust's purpose—a trust that is illegal in purpose and that cannot be given legal effect or authority: To prevent unjust harm to the settlor and beneficiary, the trust can be declared binding under a theory of resulting trust.

A constructive trust is also imposed by equitable principles. A "court may impose a constructive trust against a trustee who refuses to recognize his status as such, or against the person to whom trust property has been wrongfully transferred, on the ground that he has intermeddled with the management and control of the beneficiary's property by acquiring and holding the legal right to property which, in equity and good conscience, he ought not hold and enjoy."[51] Property acquired through unjust means or unconscionable activities can be reacquired under an argument of constructive trust.

QTIP Trust

A *qualified terminable interest property* or *QTIP trust* affords surviving spouses some declaration options on whether they wish to take full advantage of the marital deduction under most estate distribution strategies. QTIP trusts provide for the welfare of a spouse and keep the assets out of the estate of another (such as a future marriage partner) if the grantor dies first. Such trusts allow assets to be transferred between spouses. The grantor of a QTIP trust directs the income generated from the assets to his or her spouse for life but has the power to distribute the assets upon the death of the spouse. The trust qualifies the grantor for unlimited marital deductions if the spouse dies first.

Some requirements for a QTIP marital trust include the following:

1. The property must pass to the surviving spouse from the decedent.
2. Income must be distributed at least annually.
3. No power of appointment in the surviving spouse or others can benefit anyone except the surviving spouse during the surviving spouse's lifetime.
4. The donor must direct and/or the executor must irrevocably elect on return.
5. The property will be included in the surviving spouse's estate for federal tax purposes.[52]

Generation-Skipping Tax Trust

To shield a future beneficiary from tax liability, draft a generation-skipping tax trust. For the most part, the motivations of a testator/settlor relate to tax minimization—though this conclusion may only be partial. How does one create a trust for a beneficiary that is also shielded from onerous tax liability? The key is to draft multiple or dual trusts that avoid the liability. These dual trusts must be coupled with the will, thereby causing a generational skip.[53] Beneficiaries are subject to normal estate taxes as well as a generation skipping transfer tax. Transfers to grandchildren or more remote descendants may be subject to a "generation-skipping transfer tax," or GST tax. This tax permits the IRS to tax every generation. Fortunately, there is an exemption from the GST tax which is equal to the applicable exclusion amount which is currently $2,000,000.00.

Life Insurance Trust

Life insurance may be distributed by lump sums or in increments. The trust instrument adds the oversight of a specialist concerned with the beneficiary who spends the proceeds. In cases where over a million dollars are about to be distributed to a remaining spouse and children, the client may obviously see the need for a trust. An example of a life insurance trust is shown in Form 8.34 on the accompanying CD.

DECEDENT'S ADMINISTRATION: PRELIMINARY MATTERS

Clearly the paralegal's most compelling role in estate law involves the administrative and mechanical steps in estate administration. Guided by both statutory and common-law principles, the diversity of estate administration processes—from informal to formal, from independent to supervised, from contested to automatic probate—creates challenges for even the most seasoned paralegal. Estate administration processes encompass these steps:

1. Did the decedent leave a will?
2. If the decedent left a will, what is the value of the estate?
3. When evaluating assets, what property is exempt, and what property is included in estate analysis?
4. Can a will be located and probated?
5. Are the provisions of a will contested or disputed?
6. Does the local jurisdiction prevent a family settlement agreement?
7. Does the local jurisdiction provide for an informal administrative process?
8. Does the local jurisdiction permit only formal administration of estates?
9. What processes and requirements are involved in probate?
10. Is there a small estate procedure? If so, what qualifies to be classified as such?[54]

Checklists, forms, and documents that track the administrative process are helpful to the paralegal. An estate administrative file checklist is shown in Form 8.35 on the accompanying CD. Observe that this model form assumes no litigiousness regarding the testator's wishes and that the application for probate, grant of letters, and other formalities have been taken care of.

Many documents and forms have to be accounted for in estate work. A probate cover sheet is shown in Form 8.36 on the accompanying CD. Before we discuss the procedural aspects of probate and related matters, we examine the initial analysis of assets and their accumulation.

Accumulation of Assets for Estate Administration

Once a testator dies, administrative steps must be taken to ensure collection of entitled benefits. Immediately the categorization, collection, and assimilation of information regarding assets within the estate should be conducted. Families, especially those short on economic resources, need counseling on how to pierce the bureaucracies responsible for payments. Here is a partial listing of benefits that may be germane to your client's case:

- Veteran's benefits: burial, life insurance or disability payments.
- Railroad retirement benefits.
- Black lung benefits.
- Life insurance benefits: term or whole life policies.
- Social Security: widow's benefits, pension benefits, burial benefits.
- Insurance policies for accidents.
- Annuities.
- Union death benefits.
- Charitable and professional associations or social organization benefits.
- 401K plans and other pension benefits.

Estate planners will also need to familiarize themselves with the various entitlement programs, such as Social Security, Medicare, Medicaid, prescription coverage and catastrophic illness provisions recently introduced, and other community services available to the elderly.[55]

In any event, an initial visit with a family member who can answer such questions is often a paralegal's responsibility. Although the questions are difficult to pose and the responses sometimes hard to acquire, families soon appreciate the detailed attention the paralegal provides regarding entitlement payments.

Besides these preliminary steps, the paralegal helps the client in multiple areas of concern:

- Be sure the decedent's assets, both real and personal, are physically secure and protected.
- Terminate all mail delivery.
- Be certain the decedent's business interests are being cared for and adequately protected.
- Collect accurate information for preparation of the death certificate.
- Acquire copies of medical reports regarding the cause of death.
- Contact the decedent's clergyperson.
- Make sure specialized funeral arrangements outlined in the will's provision are being adhered to.
- Meet with responsible family representatives about any special matters or concerns they might have.
- Honor anatomical gift provisions if a living will or a special provision within the testator's will has been made.
- Find out who the family spokesperson is and assist with any requests.
- Advise the funeral director that all bills and other obligations for funeral and burial should be forwarded to the law office.
- Collect necessary documentation about the cemetery plot.
- Help family members in the preparation of an obituary.
- Discuss with family members the legal requirements of autopsy if necessary.
- Be certain that minor children who are incapacitated or incompetent adults once dependent on the decedent are cared for.
- Ascertain whether any cash funds can be disbursed for immediate living expenses.
- Advise family members that receipts and other documentation are necessary as the administration of the estate takes place.
- Arrange for the immediate care of the decedent's livestock, agricultural commodities, and other perishable property.
- Put on notice all interested parties that safe deposit boxes and other private domains are off-limits to relatives.
- If a bank is named an executor, request the name of the administration officer.
- Meet with family members to review the estate planning questionnaire filled out previously by the testator, if in the file, to see if it is still accurate.
- Ensure that all property of the decedent is still insured and that all insurance policies are in full force and effect.
- Advise family members, executors, or other administrators not to take any substantial actions.
- Notify all parties who possess the decedent's power of attorney.
- Authorize the decedent's bank that it should continue to honor all checks issued before death.
- Preserve all the decedent's important documents.
- Consider the current will of the surviving spouse.
- Determine whether the decedent's family wishes you to represent them in the estate administration.
- Draft a fee agreement regarding estate administration with family, if chosen.[56]

Employ the checklist shown in Figure 8.2 to categorize assets.

Determination of Heirs and Other Interested Parties

Under both testate and intestate schemes, determining heirs is a critical task in estate administration. Remember that a person who dies with a will is considered testate, having taken the time to designate where and to whom specific bequests, grants, and devises will pass. Under a residuary clause or a testamentary trust, the remainder of the estate customarily remains with the extended family. What the traditional family is has been the subject of some discussion in recent years—particularly how traditional estate tax laws and intestacy schemes fail to reflect the changing American household.

FIGURE 8.2 **Checklist of Decedent's Assets and Liabilities**

Source: David Cleaver, Pennsylvania Probate and Estate Administration 190 (1992). Used with permission of Thomson West. To access the most current version of this form, please visit www.westlaw.com.

ASSETS

A. CASH AND NOTES

1. Checking accounts.
2. Savings accounts.
3. Certificates of deposit.
4. Credit union share accounts.
5. Uncashed checks/travelers checks.
6. Notes held by decedent.
7. Mortgages held by decedent.
8. Debts due decedent.
9. Cash and valuables on decedent at death.
10. Vacation or Christmas clubs.

B. STOCKS AND BONDS

1. Stocks.
2. Bonds.
3. Mutual funds.
4. U.S. savings bonds.
5. U.S. Treasury bills.

C. TANGIBLE PERSONAL PROPERTY

1. Cars, trucks, boats, motorcycles.
2. Household furnishings and contents.
3. Personal property held by others.
4. Gold and silver.
5. Jewelry.
6. Hobby assets (coins, gems, stamps).
7. Contents of safe deposit box.
8. Furs.

D. EMPLOYMENT BENEFITS

1. Wages.
2. Bonuses.
3. Vacation pay.
4. Group insurance.
5. Profit-sharing and pension plan benefits.
6. Savings or thrift plans.
7. Benefits from previous employers.
8. Contract rights.

E. MISCELLANEOUS

1. Business assets.
2. Life insurance.
3. Pets and livestock.
4. Tax refunds.
5. Past-due alimony or child support.
6. Social Security, railroad retirement, and veterans' benefits.
7. Contract rights.
8. Claims in litigation.
9. Accounts receivable.
10. Powers of appointment.
11. Assets held as a fiduciary.
12. Fire or casualty insurance claims.
13. Jointly held property.

F. REAL ESTATE

1. Primary residence.
2. Other residence.
3. Condominium.
4. Apartments.
5. Other real estate—business real estate.
6. Cemetery plots.
7. Remainderman interests.
8. Contracts to buy or sell real estate.
9. Leases.
10. Mortgages held by decedent.
11. Limited partnership interest in real estate.

DEBTS

1. Charge accounts.
2. VISA, Mastercard, American Express.
3. Home mortgage.
4. Installment loans.
5. Demand notes.
6. Lines of credit.
7. Other mortgages.
8. Utilities.
9. Funeral bills.
10. Taxes.
11. Past-due (at death) alimony or child support.
12. Debts due as fiduciary.
13. Hospital.
14. Doctors.
15. Cemetery plot and grave marker.
16. Pledges to charity.
17. Leases or rent.
18. Judgments.
19. Sales contracts.
20. Wages due employees.

Even the plain meaning of will language is affected by an ongoing family disintegration. Questions such as the following are becoming more common:

- What influence does an invalid marriage—that is, a procedurally defective marriage—have on an intestacy or inheritance tax scheme?
- Can a bigamist inherit as a surviving spouse?
- Can a bigamist inherit as the surviving spouse of the bigamist's first spouse?
- What does the law of intestacy and inheritance say about common-law marriages?

- How are homosexual relationships treated by the law?
- What if the parties are legally separated when one of the spouses dies?
- Does the law account for informal adoption techniques?
- How do stepchildren fit into the picture?
- Can children be disinherited by will?

Even the unintentional omission of a later-born child can cause testamentary frustration. States are increasingly substituting a legislative remedy for these omitted children, allowing them an equal share. Illegitimacy no longer has the harsh historical results in the determination of heirs. Statutory designs place the illegitimate heir in the same camp as the legitimate if certain conditions are met, such as these:

(a) *The father, in writing signed in the presence of a competent witness, acknowledges himself to be the father of the child.*

(b) *The father and mother intermarried subsequent to the child's birth, and the father, after such marriage, acknowledged the child as his own or adopted him into his family.*

(c) *The father publicly acknowledged such child as his own, receiving it as such, with the consent of his wife, if he is married, into his family and otherwise treating it as if it were a child born in wedlock.*

(d) *The father was judicially determined to be such in a paternity proceeding before a court of competent jurisdiction.*[57]

Traditional estate legislation fails to account for these kinds of human and familial interests. Whatever statutory inroads have been made are at best controversial and without national support.

The determination of heirship is an important fact that arises in the administration of any decedent's estate.[58] The reasons are obvious. "The right of an heir to succeed in a decedent's property arises on the death of the decedent. Succession plans fully delineated by will, can only be restricted for legitimate legal cause and challenge. In the absence of a will, intestacy, distribution is usually made according to laws of descent and distribution as they existed as of the date of the decedent's death."[59] See Figure 8.3.

FIGURE 8.3 State of Maryland, The Register of Wills

If the Decedent is Survived by:

1. **A spouse and minor children** (does not include stepchildren)—spouse receives one-half; minor children share remaining one-half.
2. **A spouse and all adult children** (not including stepchildren)—spouse receives $15,000 plus one-half of remaining estate; adult children divide the remaining share of the estate (the interest of a predeceased child passes to issue of that child).
3. **Children only**—children (does not include stepchildren) divide estate equally.
4. **A spouse and parents**—spouse receives $15,000 plus one-half of remaining estate; both parents divide the balance or surviving parent receives the balance.
5. **A spouse without other heirs listed above**—entire estate passes to spouse.
6. **Parents without heirs listed above**—both parents divide entire estate or surviving parent takes all.
7. **Brothers and/or sisters without other heirs listed above**—brothers and/or sisters divide estate equally (share of a deceased sibling goes to his or her issue—nieces and nephews of the decedent).
8. **Grandparents without other heirs listed above**—grandparent(s) divide entire estate or, if grandparents are deceased, to issue of the grandparents.
9. **Great-grandparents without other heirs listed above**—great-grandparent(s) divide entire estate or, if great-grandparents are deceased, to issue of the great-grandparents.
10. **Stepchildren will share the estate if there are no other heirs as listed above.**
11. **No living heirs or stepchildren**—the estate will pass to the Board of Education, or to the Department of Health and Mental Hygiene if the decedent was a recipient of long-term care benefits under the Maryland Medical Assistance Program.

As a result, statutes of descent or distribution attempt to formulate a plan or a scheme for intestate situations, marking most heirs as either lineal descendants—that of a direct line of the intestate, such as from a father to a son—or as collateral descendents—that of an indirect line, such as from sister to sister or cousin to cousin. Employing reasoning based on bloodlines, consanguinity, and common ancestry, these statutes of descent and distribution fill the void created by the intestate.[60]

Compare and contrast the Montana version of intestacy laws at http://www.montana.edu/wwwpb/pubs/mt8908.pdf.

Predictably, without a will, the spouse maintains the dominant right and role with his or her issue under both per capita and per stirpes schemes. Intestacy law recognizes the basic lines of descent by giving credence to closer proximity in the relationship. At the bottom of the distribution plan, property will escheat to the governing jurisdiction in which the estate is jurisdictionally based if no sufficient relationships exist based on consanguinity or other legal interrelationship.

The following facts and circumstances tend to establish that a claimant is a rightful heir of the decedent:

Family history.	Photographs.
Relationship to decedent.	Advancements.
Death of decedent in intestacy.	Declarations of decedent.
Nonexistence of other heirs.	Declarations of deceased relative of decedent.
Legitimacy.	Acquaintance with decedent.
Identity of names.	Acquaintance with claimant.
Physical resemblance.	Corroboration of claimant's testimony.[61]

Determining Competency and the Guardianship of Incapacitated Parties

Estate planning, particularly trust activities, often involves the incapacitated or incompetent. Guardianship proceedings are generally guided by statute. As discussed in a previous section, a guardian may be appointed and designated to oversee the affairs of children during their age of minority. Trustees, of course, can be appointed to manage income on behalf of children even up to age of majority. Frequently, however, testators are concerned about the continuing care of individuals within their family who are mentally incapacitated, incompetent, or teetering on the edge of normalcy.

Nominations of guardians can be done by a testamentary instrument or by judicial proceedings in an appropriate court such as Surrogate's or Orphan's. Proceedings can be initiated by testators, trustees, and even potential beneficiaries under a will or trust document. A formal petition for the appointment of a guardian is shown in Form 8.37 on the accompanying CD.

After proper service and notice has occurred, a hearing, usually involving the evaluation of a psychiatrist, medical examiner, or other expert witness, addresses the question of competency. Some factors that should be determined in a case of competency include the following issues:

- Psychiatric reports.
- Specific mental illnesses.
- Abnormal depressions.
- Moodiness.
- Inability to function.
- Total vocational disability.
- Types of irrational conduct.
- Previous mental disorder.
- Reports and records outlining past and present condition.
- Failure to pay bills.
- Failure to fill out tax returns or perform other functions indicating a competent being.
- Breach of the peace.
- Police records.
- Psychological tests and evaluations.
- Expert reports.
- Specific physical conditions.

Courts review these factors before issuing a judgment about a party's suitability and competency. New York lays out express directions regarding the guardianship process:

Guardianship of mentally retarded person.

> *When it shall appear to the satisfaction of the court that a person is a mentally retarded person, defined for purposes of this act as a person certified as incapable to manage himself and/or his affairs because of mental retardation, and that such condition is permanent in nature by at least two licensed physicians or one such physician and one certified psychologist, having qualifications to make such certification, who requires in his best interest the appointment of a guardian of the person or of the property or of both, the court is authorized and empowered to appoint such guardian in the following manner:*

1. *In the court's discretion without a hearing, upon the application of:*
   (a) *Both parents or the survivor, or*
   (b) *One parent and the consent of the other parent, or*
   (c) *Any interested person and the consent of each parent; and*

2. *After hearing, upon the application of:*
   (a) *One parent after citation of the other parent, or*
   (b) *Any interested person after citation of each parent.*

> *When it shall appear to the satisfaction of the court that a parent or guardian not joining in or consenting to the application has abandoned the mentally retarded person, the court may dispense with his consent or citation or hearing upon the application.*
>
> *As used in this section the term parent means only a living, natural or adoptive parent.*[62]

Paralegals should note that "the courts are very liberal in admitting evidence of conduct, and since the vital issue is the mental condition of the alleged incompetent or mentally ill person. . . counsel should try to show the relevant conduct of the subject individual in the recent past. In some cases, he may attempt to establish a pattern of behavior over a period of years to show recent changes in the mental condition of the subject; in such cases, evidence of conduct in the temporarily remote but related past is particularly relevant."[63]

State probate codes promulgate an order of priorities as to candidates for guardians:

(a) *Any competent person or a suitable institution may be appointed guardian of an incapacitated person, except as provided in subsection (c).*

(b) *Subject to a determination by the court of the best interests of the incapacitated person, persons who are not disqualified have priority for appointment as guardian in the following order:*
   (1) *The person or institution nominated in writing by the incapacitated person;*
   (2) *The spouse of the incapacitated person;*
   (2-A) *The domestic partner of the incapacitated person;*
   (3) *An adult child of the incapacitated person;*
   (4) *A parent of the incapacitated person, including a person nominated by will or other writing signed by a deceased parent;*
   (5) *Any relative of the incapacitated person with whom he resided for more than 6 months prior to the filing of the petition;*
   (6) *A person nominated by the person who is caring for him or paying benefits to him.*

(c) *No owner, proprietor, administrator, employee or other person with a substantial financial interest in a facility or institution licensed under Title 22, sections 1817 and 7801, may act as guardian of an incapacitated person who is a resident, as defined in Title 22, section 7852, subsection 13, unless the person requesting to be appointed guardian is one of the following:*
   (1) *The spouse of the incapacitated person;*
   (1-A) *The domestic partner of the incapacitated person;*
   (2) *An adult child of the incapacitated person;*
   (3) *A parent of the incapacitated person or a person nominated by the will of a deceased parent; or*
   (4) *A relative of the incapacitated person with whom the incapacitated person has resided for more than 6 months prior to the filing of the petition for appointment.*[64]

In the representation of an incapacitated person, a guardian has the same powers, rights, and duties that a parent has regarding an unemancipated minor child. Guardians may also resign, be removed, or be terminated.[65]

The relevance of guardianship and incompetency determinations becomes more obvious when the testator has named a personal representative or executor who is himself or herself incompetent. Other situations may arise, especially when individuals have drafted a now-antiquated will that fails to accurately reflect the physical and mental health status of the appointed party. If a surviving spouse's physical and mental health has deteriorated, is a replacement guardian necessary? What about testamentary trusts that nominate guardians who become mentally unbalanced?

ESTATE ADMINISTRATION PROCESSES

In some jurisdictions the entire estate administration process is labeled *probate*. In others, the term *probate* applies merely to proof of will validity. Presently, our analysis will dwell on the particular steps and procedures evident in probate. Probate processes are many and varied. Before taking the first formal step in the probate process, create an environment that fosters information gathering. The checklist in Figure 8.4 provides a good summarization of the probate process. Be mindful that this checklist is generic and may not be applicable to your jurisdiction.

FIGURE 8.4 **Checklist of Personal Representative's Duties during Probate**

- Assist with burial arrangements of decedent. Instructions may appear in will.
- Locate will. If it cannot be found or if it is in decedent's safe deposit box in bank, obtain court order to enter box and remove will.
- Determine state and county where decedent was legally domiciled.
- Deposit will with court.
- Locate and take possession of decedent's records.
- Determine whether a family allowance is necessary.
- If there is a will, read it and discuss its provisions with the family.
- Take measures to protect jewelry, automobiles, and other tangible personal property and arrange for protection of real estate.
- Examine existing insurance coverage and determine whether there is sufficient coverage on real estate and personal property. Increase insurance when necessary.
- Determine whether administration of the estate is necessary and, if so, to what extent.
- If administration is necessary, petition for an order of appointment of personal representative.
- If there is a will, petition court for an order admitting will to probate and for appointment of the personal representative.
- File designation of resident agent, if required; oath of the personal representative; and, if required, the agent's bond.
- Obtain letters of administration.
- File, publish, and serve notice of administration/notice to creditors.
- Determine extent of checking and savings accounts and open account in name of personal representative in his or her representative capacity.
- After obtaining court order (if before issuance of letters), inventory contents of safe deposit box and see that inventory is filed in the court. Take possession of the box or remove contents entirely, as the situation demands. If the box is released, obtain refund for the keys.
- Examine and study all records of decedent in order to locate and collect all other assets of estate.
- If any assets, real or personal, are outside of the state, determine what must be done with respect to that property.
- Arrange for redirecting of mail.
- Determine whether there are any unpaid salaries or benefits due from the employer of decedent.
- Determine whether there any rights of decedent under stock purchase agreements or stock options that could benefit estate, or deferred compensation.
- Determine if there is insurance of the life of decedent. Collect whatever proceeds are payable to the estate. Often it is desirable to assist the beneficiaries in collecting insurance payable to them.
- Obtain treasury form (life insurance statement for a decedent) for each insurance policy, to be filed with the federal estate tax return if one is required.
- Determine whether estate is entitled to any death benefits under the Social Security Act, veterans' acts, or any pension or profit-sharing plan.
- Obtain information on all other nonprobate assets such as inter vivos trusts, joint tenancies, annuities, inter vivos gifts, Totten trusts, and property subject to power of appointment.

- Determine whether expenses of last illness are to be paid in part by accident and health policies or hospitalization insurance. If so, make collection.
- Determine all sums due to estate on any promissory notes, loans, or accounts receivable.
- If decedent was in a partnership, study terms of the partnership agreement governing the death of a partner. Determine how best to handle decedent's interest.
- If decedent left a going business, determine whether it should be liquidated and, if so, how.
- If business is to continued, make plans for continuation and obtain a court order if needed.
- Prepare inventory of estate and file with court within 60 days of death of decedent. An additional copy must be sent to the Department of Revenue.
- Obtain services of appraiser when needed.
- File notice of fiduciary relationship (Form 56) with the Internal Revenue Service. Request employer identification number (Form SS-4) for estate.
- Assign the elective share, if necessary.
- Investigate all claims against estate and file timely objections when necessary, and if a lawsuit is commenced by a claimant, defend the estate.
- Analyze assets of estate and estimate needs for liquidity to meet all debts, funeral and administration expenses and taxes, the family allowance, and monetary legacies; petition the court if required for sale of sufficient assets to meet the requirement of liquidity and for temporary reinvestment in liquid assets.
- Examine all contracts and leases of decedent. Complete, terminate, or negotiate those contracts and leases.
- If real property is to be sold or leased and if there is no power of sale granted by the will, obtain a court order; then proceed to sell or lease without delay.
- Take steps to collect debts due the estate, including court action where necessary, or effect settlement or abandonment of claims when appropriate and obtain a court order authorizing the action if required.
- Prepare and file decedent's final income tax return or returns, Form 1040.
- Prepare and file U.S. Fiduciary Income Tax Return, Form 1041.
- Prepare and file state intangible tax returns and any other tax returns required.
- Prepare and file interim accountings if appropriate.
- Make partial distribution of personal property if not needed for payment of debts of estate, funeral expenses, administration expenses, taxes, and monetary legacies. (Be careful that the distribution does *not* carry out distributable net income.)
- Obtain transfer of title of automobile to the beneficiary.
- Pay promptly all claims against the estate property filed to which no objection was made. Claims bear interest after five months from the first publication of notice of administration.
- Prepare and file federal estate tax return (Form 706) within nine months after date of death. For a U.S. citizen or resident, this is necessary if the value of the gross estate (less adjustments for certain gifts) is over $1,500,000.
- Consider whether apportionment of estate taxes is required. If so, collect contributions due from beneficiaries.
- Pay administration expenses.
- File notice of termination of fiduciary relationship and obtain closing letter (Form L-154) from IRS in connection with estate tax return.
- Obtain release of personal representative from personal liability for estate tax deficiencies.
- File accounting and petition for discharge within one year from issuance of letters, for estates not required to file a federal estate tax return, or 12 months from the date the federal estate tax return is due. Petition should include a statement in the body or in an attached schedule of the amount of compensation paid or to be paid to the personal representative, attorneys, accountants, appraisers, or other agents employed by the personal representative.
- If the estate cannot be closed within the time required by law, petition for an extension of time.
- Send copy of final accounting and petition for discharge to all beneficiaries, with a copy of the notice of filing it.
- If no objections to petition for discharge are filed, make final distribution, obtain receipts from all distributees, and file receipts with court.
- If objections are filed, obtain order approving final accounting and directing distributions.
- File report of distribution if made pursuant to court order.
- Obtain order of final discharge.
- Send certified copy of order of final discharge to surety and a copy to each residuary beneficiary.
- Advise all debtors that the obligations have been transferred to new obligees.
- Deliver to the beneficiaries all data not necessary to be retained.

Small Estates

Estates of small appraised value, usually between $2,000 and $20,000 in sum, are exempted from normal probate or intestate administration. In rare cases the threshold sum is higher, as in Oklahoma where $60,000 qualifies, and in Illinois where the threshold has been elevated to $100,000.[66]

A variety of American jurisdictions also provide a streamlined or abridged probate process for estates solely involving surviving spouses.[67] In other words, the estate receives preferential treatment because of its narrow legacies. With the filing of a simple form (an example is shown in Form 8.38 on the accompanying CD), these small estates are discharged soon after a brief and uncomplicated listing of cash or assets has been posted.

Upon submission of the small estate documentation, an order dismissing and discharging the responsible party is signed by the appropriate court. "This procedure does not require the appointment of a fiduciary or any other formal court proceedings such as hearings, inventories, accountings, or other matters."[68] Most states have some provision for these types of estates. The language usually looks as follows:

> *If it appears from the inventory and appraisal that the value of the entire estate, less liens and encumbrances, does not exceed homestead allowance, exempt property, family allowance, costs and expenses of administration, reasonable funeral expenses, and reasonable and necessary medical and hospital expenses of the last illness of the decedent, the personal representative, without giving notice to creditors, may immediately disburse and distribute the estate to the persons entitled thereto and file a closing statement as provided in Section 3-1204.*[69]

Whether an estate qualifies for this preferential treatment depends on not only the amount of assets but also the amount of property deemed exempt. Some jurisdictions grant an automatic "homestead" or family allowance between $2,000 and $50,000 that avoids computation in the estate process. Exactly who can make claim to the homestead right has been liberally construed to include beneficiaries such as a son or daughter.[70]

In addition, certain types of property designations, such as joint property or bequests to children, are subtracted in a calculation of estate size. Under the Uniform Probate Code, which most states have adopted, a sworn statement regarding the validity and suitability of small estates administration is required.[71]

Formal versus Informal Administration

Whether an estate can be declared formal or informal will depend on its valuation. Naturally, the informal calls for fewer procedural requirements and summarily processes the smaller estates. Larger estates are subject to more steps and requirements. The Uniform Probate Code permits both approaches: first a formal, also known as supervised, probate action, and second an informal, or unsupervised, probate proceeding. Informal processes are designed "to simplify the administration of the decedent's assets without unnecessary intervention or supervision of the court."[72] Formal processes require greater levels of legal representation and skill among the practitioners entrusted with these tasks.[73]

In some cases, even though the informal path appears appropriate, conflicts in family relations, suspicion among the beneficiaries, and potential conflicts will cause the advocate to choose the formal path. In the formal path, judicial oversight and supervision apply, whereas the informal process exercises less diligence. Review the Uniform Probate Code at §§3-301 through 311 for the distinctions.

In informal appointment proceedings, the registrar must determine whether

1. The application for informal appointment of a personal representative is complete.
2. The applicant has made oath or affirmation that the statements contained in the application are true to the best of his or her knowledge and belief.
3. The applicant appears from the application to be an interested person as defined in Section 1-201(23).
4. On the basis of the statements in the application, venue is proper.
5. Any will to which the requested appointment relates has been formally or informally probated; but this requirement does not apply to the appointment of a special administrator.

6. Any notice required by Section 3-204 has been given.

7. From the statements in the application, the person whose appointment is sought has priority entitling him or her to the appointment.[74]

The choice of either forum, whether supervisory or not, is a question of legal and human judgment.

Paralegal Responsibilities in the Estate Administration Process

Confirmation of a Personal Representative

A decedent leaving a will names a personal representative referred to as an *executor* or *executrix*. Under the Uniform Probate Code §3-601, a personal representative qualifies by providing bond or a statement of acceptance of this responsibility. The personal representative is given wide-ranging authority in the administration of the decedent's estate. As a result, the estate team must give meaningful advice on who would make a good choice for these responsibilities. Being a family member alone will not suffice. Even after appointment, it may become obvious that the representative is incapable of carrying out the required duties. In this event, removal is proper. "In determining whether to remove a fiduciary the Court must find that she is either unfit or unwilling or that there has been a persistent failure on her part to administer this Estate effectively. If one of the above requirements is found, the Court must then determine if it is in the best interest of the beneficiaries to force a regime change. The fiduciary may be removed should we find a substantial change of circumstances and determine if removal best serves the needs of the beneficiaries."[75]

 Appointment or designation of executors, personal representatives, or administrators is not an assurance of willing acceptance. These parties may reject the obligation, usually evidenced by a renunciation form. (See Form 8.39 on the accompanying CD.)

 Tracking the processes and responsibilities of personal representatives demands exceptional organizational skills. In some jurisdictions, an oath may be required. (See Form 8.40 on the accompanying CD.) Additionally, some parties, obliged by statute to serve, such as a surviving spouse or next of kin, are sometimes derelict or even obstinate in carrying out their duties. A motion to compel administration will motivate the representative. See Form 8.41.

Appointment of a Personal Administrator: Intestate Estate

 Without benefit of an appointment of an executor or personal representative by will, the decedent's intestate estate will petition the court for the appointment of an administrator. (See Form 8.42 on the accompanying CD.) Intestate appointments occur under an order of preference dictated by statute:

1. Surviving spouses.

2. Those entitled under intestate distribution schemes.

3. Principal creditors.

4. Other fit people.[76]

Grant of Letters Testamentary/Administration

 In cases of both testate and intestate estates, once representatives or administrators are appointed, a grant of letters, giving the representative the right or authority to act in an official capacity, is the next logical step in the administrative process. A governmental authority like a register of wills assesses whether or not letters of administration or letters testamentary should be granted, and if so, to whom.[77] In some jurisdictions the letters are domiciliary. (See Form 8.43 on the accompanying CD.)

 An example of a petition or application for letters testamentary can be reviewed in Form 8.44 on the accompanying CD. Notice that the petition requests initially that the court take notice of certain heirs, legatees, and devisees in the decedent's estate, and the sum of its property is generally described.

If the court is satisfied that the petition for the letters testamentary or letters of administration is procedurally and substantively correct, it will grant an order, triggering the probate and estate administration process.

The grant of letters is a mandatory step before commencement of the estate administration process. Upon the grant of letters, the estate representative is given, at his or her request, a series of "short certificates" that assist him or her in the administration of the estate because the short certificates act as evidence of his or her right to effect the administration of the decedent's estate.[78] A power of attorney may be needed for estate administration purposes.

Probate and the Will

If a decedent dies testate, the probate of his or her will may not be necessary if all of the estate assets are nonprobate assets—that is, exempt assets, property held in joint tenancy with right of survivorship, life insurance proceeds not payable to the estate, and/or property in trust. Hence the process of probate may never occur in select estates because the estate assets and accumulation are outside the probate process. On the other hand, the term *probate* connotes a narrower issue—that of will validity and verification.

When a will is subject to probate and approved, the court is satisfied with its authenticity and regularity, though the interested parties may think otherwise and proceed to formal litigation. Accepting probate means that the decedent's will has been duly executed, published, and attested according to local standards, and is in compliance with statutory and drafting requirements. In addition, a positive probate finding evidences a will free from defects and authored without undue influence or coercion. Of course, probate practice at this initial phase is relevant only to testacy rather than intestacy. A shortcut for probate is announced in the self-proof clause, as shown in Minnesota Statute 524.2-504.

> *524.2-504 SELF-PROVED WILL.*
>
> *(a) A will may be contemporaneously executed, attested, and made self-proved, by acknowledgment thereof by the testator and affidavits of the witnesses, each made before an officer authorized to administer oaths under the laws of the state in which execution occurs and evidenced by the officer's certificate, under official seal, in substantially the following form: I, ..., the testator, sign my name to this instrument this .... day of ...., and being first duly sworn, do hereby declare to the undersigned authority that I sign and execute this instrument as my will and that I sign it willingly (or willingly direct another to sign for me), that I execute it as my free and voluntary act for the purposes therein expressed, and that I am 18 years of age or older, of sound mind, and under no constraint or undue influence.[79]*

Paralegals should become familiar with various pleadings and documentary requirements in the probate process.[80]

First, in Form 8.45 on the accompanying CD is the petition or application to probate a will. Here the court is instructed that the testator left a will; named an executor; listed heirs, legatees, and devisees; and was clear about the nature of the property to be bequeathed or devised. Local rules may require that interested parties be notified of the upcoming probate hearing. (See Form 8.46.)

After examination, if assured of the document's authenticity and legal validity and comfortable that no serious disputes exist, the court will grant an order admitting the will to probate. See Form 8.47 on the accompanying CD.

As a practical matter, probate conflict arises over distribution of estate assets. Part of that challenge relates to allegations involving the form and executory nature of the will as well as various arguments about how the distribution is unfair and unjust.

Once the will is successfully probated, or the intestacy process commences, the important role of the personal representative comes into full view. Figure 8.5 sets out the procedural requirements of the executor or administrator.

Here the personal representative or administrator must attend to these tasks:

- Obtain letters.
- Assemble assets.
- Conserve assets.
- Pay charges.
- Distribute other services.

Loudon County, Virginia, has crafted excellent instructions for executors. Visit the Clerk of Courts Web site at http://www.loudoun.gov/clerk/index.html. Click on the "Forms" link and follow to the 2005 Probate forms, then "Decedent's Estate FYIs." Locate "Instructions and Duties of an Executor or Administrator."

From the outset, the paralegal earns his or her keep. Cataloging government benefits, collecting and valuing assets, and keeping track of any relevant business interests are all part of the paralegal regimen. Additionally, personal effects and papers, accounting records, files, bank accounts, life insurance benefits, and the care of real property in the decedent's estate are central responsibilities of the paralegal guiding the representative or administrator. The services may also include maintenance and tracking of convertible securities, stocks, bonds, and other investment and commercial paper. These initial steps will lead to future documentary and reporting requirements such as the inventory and plan of distribution—neither of these two legal documents being possible without the initial collection of information by the executor and paralegal.

FIGURE 8.5   **Procedural Requirements of the Executor/Administrator**

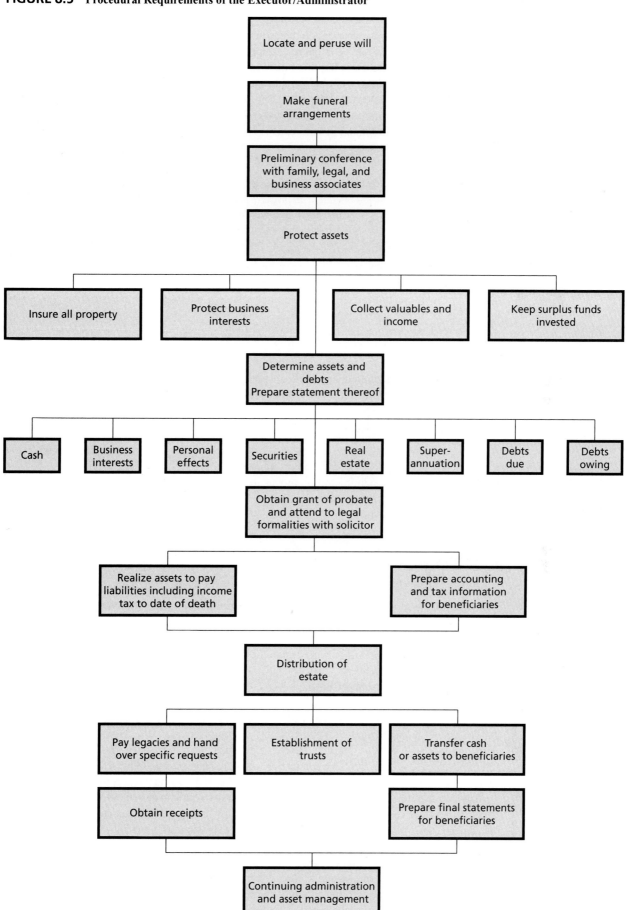

The Elective Share of a Surviving Spouse

Although the provisions of a will may expressly devise assets to a surviving spouse, the level of generosity exhibited by the testator could be stingier or more punishing than the surviving spouse ever imagined. In fact, some testators may adopt language of exclusion whereby the surviving spouse takes nothing. Recognizing this injustice, most jurisdictions permit a spousal option: to choose the provisions of the will or elect a designated share under current law. In this latter case, the surviving spouse decides that the allocation formula chosen by the decedent is not satisfactory. If no will exists, intestacy formulas make obligatory a share to the surviving spouse. The elective share right is grounded in statute, as in the following example:

> The right of election of the surviving spouse may be exercised in whole or in part during his or her lifetime.
>
> The gross size of the elective share is one-third of the value of all property subject to elective rights plus the decedent's interest in all property acquired from the decedent by gift to the surviving spouse which must be conveyed, released or disclaimed, or charged against the elective share. The surviving spouse's quantitative share is a fraction of all property in the denominator. Funeral and administration expenses, charges, debts, and claims are allowed as reduction of the denominator.[81]

 These legal machinations are further complicated by asset exclusionary principles that are not calculated in the elective share. In sum, rejection of the will's provisions regarding a surviving spouse is usually memorialized in a motion or affidavit with corresponding notice (see Forms 8.48 and 8.49 on the accompanying CD).

Elective share practice can be quite turbulent because the pursuit of the elective share evidences an estrangement or favoritism to the disadvantage of the spouse. Presently most American jurisdictions recognize the injustice of economic abandonment of a surviving spouse.[82] In the absence of divorce, annulment, or other legal action, the legislative remedy supersedes any intention of the testator. Provisions to the contrary are void and violate public policy.

Compilation of an Inventory

After the collection of all necessary assets, a calculation of all benefits, a rough finding of what is included in the decedent's estate, and an ascertainment of rights of a surviving spouse, the formal processes of estate administration moves to the inventory stage. Inventory documents have certain general characteristics and categories:

- Real estate.
- Stocks and bonds.
- Mortgage notes and cash.
- Miscellaneous property.

The inventory not only lists these forms of property but declares a valuation and posts the net value of designated assets.

 If market values cannot be easily computed, appraisals should be ordered. Guided by a particular jurisdiction, an inventory must become part of the court's record. In some jurisdictions, such as New York, the inventory constitutes a "date of death valuation."[83] An example of a blank inventory form is shown in Form 8.50 on the accompanying CD. Once the inventory is completed, beneficiaries and other interested parties, after review and analysis, may accept or object to its content.

 In some jurisdictions, the inventory process may be waived by court or, in select cases, by the parties who stipulate to valuation and amount. Upon presentation of application and order, consented to by all the heirs and legatees, a court may waive the requirement. This procedure can save time and expense for the client. An application, consent, and corresponding order that afford waiver of the inventory process are shown in Forms 8.51, 8.52, and 8.53 on the accompanying CD.

 Time frames for the filing of an inventory generally run between 90 and 180 days. If a personal representative or administrator fails to file an inventory despite repeated requests of interested parties and does not have a bona fide excuse, extension, or court approval for a late filing, a petition or application to compel the filing of an inventory is an available legal remedy. (See Form 8.54 on the accompanying CD.)

In the calculation of an inventory, the personal representative or administrator who relies on the advice of estate counsel and the assistance of paralegals should not include property that is outside the decedent's probate estate. Property may be in a decedent's estate for estate tax purposes but not in the decedent's probate estate. Remember that for inventory and appraisal purposes, as well as estate tax purposes, only "qualified" properties that are designated in the gross estate are to be reported. Jointly held property with corresponding rights of survivorship is specifically exempted property—an illustration being the car or home. Exemption rights under family allowance or other elective rights or shares, living expenses, certain forms of trusts, and specifically exempted property do not flow into the decedent's gross estate and should not be calculated or listed on the inventory or, for that matter, any subsequent accounting processes.

Dealing with Creditors or Other Interested Parties

Under informal, supervised, or unsupervised estate administration processes, creditors will be concerned about the viability of their claims. Creditors stand ready to collect at any station, including the estate distribution. Creditors, by statute, are entitled to notice regarding the valuation of assets and the proposed plan of distribution. As noted previously, the inventory valuation may not meet the creditors' desire. Before any distribution can take place under an estate plan, creditors' claims and the payment of such claims must be accounted for. See Form 8.55 on the accompanying CD for the notice pleading.

Alternative methods of notice may be acceptable. Publication in a newspaper of general readership is a common alternative to firsthand delivery. Creditors can submit a proof of claim as to amount indebted. A failure to adhere to time limitations will bar the claim.[84] By statute, the payment of creditor claims will be subservient to these estate liabilities:

1. *Funeral expenses.*
2. *The expenses of the last sickness.*
3. *Funds necessary for the support of the family and allowed by the court pursuant to the provisions of this chapter.*
4. *Taxes to the United States or the state, county, or city.*
5. *Debts having preference under the laws of the United States and of this state.*
6. *Judgments rendered against the decedent in his lifetime, which are liens upon his property and mortgages in the order of their dates.*
7. *Demands or claims that are presented to the executor or administrator for an allowance or proved within two (2) months after the first publication of notice to creditors.*
8. *All other demands against the estate except those set forth in paragraph 9 of this section.*
9. *Interest resulting from the extension of time for payment of federal estate or transfer taxes.*[85]

Each jurisdiction adopts a priority of payment system. Section 3-805 of the Maine Code relays this prioritization:

§3-805. CLASSIFICATION OF CLAIMS

(a) *If the applicable assets of the estate are insufficient to pay all claims in full, the personal representative shall make payment in the following order:*
   (1) *Costs and expenses of administration;*
   (2) *Reasonable funeral expenses;*
   (3) *Debts and taxes with preference under federal law;*
   (4) *Medicaid benefits recoverable under Title 22, section 14, subsection 2-I and reasonable and necessary medical and hospital expenses of the last illness of the decedent, including compensation of persons attending the decedent;*
   (5) *Debts and taxes with preference under other laws of this State;*
   (6) *All other claims.*

(b) *No preference shall be given in the payment of any claim over any other claim of the same class, and a claim due and payable shall not be entitled to a preference over claims not due.* [1979, c. 540, § 1 (new).]

Hence creditors may have a difficult time collecting just debts.

On other occasions, the sale of realty or significant personal property may be a way of generating funds to pay creditors. The personal representative or administrator will file a petition or application regarding the sale. See Form 8.56 on the accompanying CD. Some jurisdictions require a report on the disposition of said property by executor or administrator. (See Form 8.57.)

A creditor who is dissatisfied that a claim has not been paid when it is bona fide and due may file a petition or application to compel. Form 8.58 on the accompanying CD provides the necessary language to file that pleading.

At this stage of the administration process, the personal representative or administrator is busy trying to determine whether sufficient resources exist for the payment of all claims and expenses. This is a serious task because the costs of dying are anything but insignificant with legal, funeral, and burial expenses, debt payment, and taxes swallowing large portions of the estate's value.

First and Final Account

The first and final accounting process summarizes value and assets, claims and obligations, expenses, and legal damage claims asserted against the estate. Charged against that figure are the total assets available to pay costs and debts with an eye toward payment to legatees, devisees, and other interested parties.

The final accounting comes in a wide array of standard formats. Form 8.59 on the accompanying CD is an example of a final account with a corresponding petition by the administrator to permit distribution shown in Form 8.60. A party who objects to such an accounting may do so by petition or motion. Form 8.61 outlines the necessary language.

In the case of a negligent personal representative or administrator, a petition or application forcing the filing of a final accounting, as seen in Form 8.62 on the accompanying CD, can be utilized to prod the tardy.

Many jurisdictions have adopted the Uniform Fiduciary Accounting Principles and Model Accounts Format as the suggested design for a first and final account. Reproduced in Appendix C is an example.[87] This first and final account, like all others, includes these components:

- *A summary of account:* List all expenses, debts, taxes, and other fees and commissions under the estate as well as principal amounts and receipts within the total value of the estate.
- *Receipts of principal:* Any assets listed in inventory and collected throughout the process of estate administration are listed.
- *Gains and losses on sales or other dispositions:* A sale of stock or Treasury bonds is also accounted for on the basis of capital losses or capital gains.
- *Disbursements of principal:* All disbursements of principal for the purposes of payment of debts and other obligations are fully outlined.
- *Debts of the decedent:* Funeral expenses, administration expenses, federal taxes, fees, and commission are highlighted.
- *Distribution of principal to beneficiaries:* Specific bequests and payments of cash, stock, and dividends are computed, as well as receipts of corresponding disbursements of income.
- *Proposed distributions to beneficiaries:* Proposed distributions are listed on the final page of the first and final accounting with a signature line for the executor.

Depending on the intricacy of the estate, a hearing on valuation may be required. As in the inventory process, waivers and consents can bypass confirmatory hearings. Creditors and other individuals who object to the distribution proposal may challenge the first and final accounting.

Distribution and Discharge

Once the final accounting has been approved, the next step involves the means and method of distribution. How are these recognized estate assets divided? In most jurisdictions, the plan will be outlined in a petition for distribution. An example is shown in Form 8.63 on the accompanying CD.

Local legal rules and procedures may require an order from a court approving the account and authorizing distribution. (See Form 8.64 on the accompanying CD.) In other jurisdictions, an additional closing statement is required with a formal order of discharge issued by the court. See Form 8.65 for an example.

ESTATE TAXATION

Estate taxation is a specialized area guided almost exclusively by federal tax law. Although some states have their own estate tax structure, most mimic the federal design. Estate tax is computed by

- Calculating a gross estate value.
- Subtracting expenses and exempt properties.

- Tabulating credits and exempt amounts.
- Computing net taxable estate value.

Estate taxation has come to depend on technology in the calculation. Software programs proliferate in the legal landscape and can accomplish the following:

- Probate court accounting schedules.
- Receipts.
- Disbursements.
- Gains.
- Losses.
- Distributions.
- Investments.
- Capital changes.
- Complete lists of assets for principal and income.
- History of investment assets.
- Cash reconciliation statement.
- Cash position statement.
- Checkbook register.
- Form 706.
- Schedules A through O of the federal estate tax return.
- State estate, inheritance, and fiduciary income tax returns.

Some companies appear to outshine the competition. For example, the 6-in-1 Estate Administration Program by The Lackner Computer Group Inc.[88] continues to deliver quality software packages for the busy practitioner. Others of significant reputation are these:

- BNA Software
  1231 25th Street N.W.
  Washington, D.C. 20037
  www.bnasoftware.com

- Fast-Tax
  2395 Midway Road, Bldg. 1
  Carrollton, TX 75006
  www.fasttax.thomson.com

- Abacus Tax Software
  www.abacustaxsoftware.com

It makes perfect sense to use these excellent software packages for tax preparation. Estate tax rates and corresponding credits are charted in Figure 8.6.

To determine the taxability of any estate, various issues must be resolved:

- What was the gross value of the estate?
- What property was owned by the decedent?
- What types of lifetime transfers should be calculated in the total gross estate?
- Have there been any gifts within three years of death?
- Have there been any transfers of property or other interests with strings attached?
- Is there any retained life interest?
- Is there retention of voting rights in stock?
- Do any transfers take effect only at the time of death?
- Does the decedent retain powers of appointment over the property?
- What influence does jointly held property have?
- What influence does community property have?
- Is the property insured?
- Is the property subject to a QTIP trust?
- Is the property an annuity?
- What other forms of insurance are within the estate?
- What charitable deductions are permissible?
- What marital deduction is permissible?

Calculating a decedent's taxable estate is a matter of valuing the gross estate and then deducting the following items:

- Funeral expenses.
- Administration expenses.

FIGURE 8.6
Estate Tax Rate and
Credits

ESTATE TAX RATE			
Bottom Bracket	Top Bracket	Bracket Tax	Marginal Rate
$0	$10,000	$0	18%
$10,001	$20,000	$1,800	20%
$20,001	$40,000	$3,800	22%
$40,001	$60,000	$8,200	24%
$60,001	$80,000	$13,000	26%
$80,001	$100,000	$18,200	28%
$100,001	$150,000	$23,800	30%
$150,001	$250,000	$38,800	32%
$250,001	$500,000	$70,800	34%
$500,001	$750,000	$155,800	37%
$750,001	$1,000,000	$248,300	39%
$1,000,001	$1,250,000	$345,800	41%
$1,250,001	$1,500,000	$448,300	43%
$1,500,001	$2,000,000	$555,800	45%
$2,000,001	$2,500,000	$780,800	49%
$2,500,000	No limit	$1,025,800	49%*

*This rate will be reduced by 1% for each year between 2004 and 2007 and will return to 50% as of 2011.

APPLICABLE CREDIT AMOUNT		
Year	Applicable Exclusion	Applicable Credit Amount
2003	$1,000,000	$345,800
2004 and 2005	$1,500,000	$555,800
2006, 2007, 2008	$2,000,000	$780,800
2009	$3,500,000	$1,455,800
2010	No estate tax	No estate tax
2011 and beyond	$1,000,000	$345,800

- Commissions.
- Attorney's fees.
- Accountant's fees.
- Appraiser's fees.
- Court costs.
- Claims against the estate.
- Property taxes.
- Unpaid income taxes.
- Unpaid gift taxes.
- Transfers and satisfaction of claims by decedent's former spouse.
- Unpaid mortgages or other indebtedness on property included in the gross estate.
- Casualty and theft losses.
- Transfers to charitable and similar organizations.
- Transfers to surviving spouse.
- Fifty percent of the proceeds from sales of employee securities to an ESOP.

Additional Estate Tax on Excess Retirement Accumulations (Form 706) is the granddaddy document for estate tax, and it is crucial that the preparer be thorough in its preparation. Clients must be the source of information to compute the 706. Be persistent and fully recognize that the quality of the return directly depends on the quality of the information provided. Estate paralegal Diane St. John urges paralegals to be the "fly in the ointment of the client's life."[89]

Estate Tax Return: Form 706

Form 706 and its corresponding instructions pose the historic way of calculating estate tax liability. See Form 8.66 on the accompanying CD. Notice the formula employed at line 1:

$$Total\ gross\ estate - Deductions = Taxable\ estate$$

Although this equation seems simple enough, the preparer must deal with the schedules of 706 first. Schedules A–R provide specialized data for estate tax liability. Form 706 follows a logical path:

Line 4: Add back in taxable gifts and come up with a tentative tax on the sum.

Line 6: A tentative gross estate tax is calculated using Table A.

Line 7: Gift tax payable.

Line 8: Total tentative tax.

Line 9: Computation of the unified credit.

Line 10: Adjustments to unified credit.

Lines 11–15: Allowance for unified credit, state death taxes, federal gift taxes, foreign death taxes, and tax on prior transfers.

Line 16: Net estate tax.

Lines 17–19: Allowance for payments made, redemptions, or miscellaneous credits.

Lines 20: Balance of tax owed.

The concepts can be obtuse and foreign, but the Internal Revenue Service has done a good job of walking us through the complexities of estate valuation.

Schedule Preparation

From this point on, the return digresses into a series of schedules that are summarized in the recapitulation section on page 3 of Form 706. The schedules zero in on specific estate property interests:

Schedule A: Real estate.

Schedule A-1: Section 2032A valuation.

Schedule B: Stocks and bonds.

Schedule C: Mortgages, notes, and cash.

Schedule D: Insurance on a decedent's life.

Schedule E: Jointly owned property.

Schedule F: Miscellaneous property.

Schedule G: Transfers during a decedent's life.

Schedule H: Powers of appointment.

Schedule I: Annuities.

Schedule J: Funeral expenses and expenses in the administration of the estate.

Schedule K: Debts of the decedent and mortgages and liens.

Schedule L: Net losses during administration and expenses incurred in administering the property not subject to claims.

Schedule M: Bequests.

Schedule N: Qualified ESOP sale.

Schedule O: Charitable, public, and similar gifts.

Schedule P: Credit for foreign death taxes.

Schedule Q: Credit on prior transfers.

Schedule R: Generation-skipping transfer tax.

In completing these schedules, the paralegal will describe, value, and appraise numerous forms of property. Schedules A through U are listed on the pages that follow, though the depth and breadth of commentary will vary.[90]

Schedule A

On Schedule A, list real estate the decedent owned or had contracted to purchase. Number each parcel in the left column. Describe the real estate in enough detail so that the IRS can easily locate it for inspection and valuation. For each parcel of real estate, report the area and, if the parcel is improved, describe the improvements. For city or town property, report the street and number, ward, subdivision, block and lot, and so on. For rural property, report the township, range, landmarks, and the like.

> *If any item of real estate is subject to a mortgage for which the decedent's estate is liable; that is, if the indebtedness may be charged against other property of the estate that is not subject to that mortgage, or if the decedent was personally liable for that mortgage, you must report the full value of the property in the value column. Enter the amount of the mortgage under "Description" on this schedule. The unpaid amount of the mortgage may be deducted on Schedule K.[91]*

See Form 8.67 on the accompanying CD.

Schedule B

On Schedule B list the stocks and bonds included in the decedent's gross estate. Number each item in the left column. Bonds are exempt from federal income taxes unless specifically exempted by an estate tax provision of the code. Therefore, list these bonds on Schedule B.

For stocks indicate

- Number of shares.
- Whether common or preferred.
- Issue.
- Par value where needed for identification.
- Price per share.
- Exact name of corporation.
- Principal exchange upon which sold, if listed on an exchange.
- CUSIP number, if available.

For bonds indicate

- Quantity and denomination.
- Name of obligor.
- Date of maturity.
- Interest rate.
- Interest due date.
- Principal exchange, if listed on an exchange.
- CUSIP number, if available.

An identification number for a stock or bond is known as a CUSIP number. (See Form 8.68 on the accompanying CD.)

Schedule C

On Schedule C list mortgages and notes payable to the decedent at the time of death. (Mortgages and notes payable by the decedent should be listed, if deductible, on Schedule K.) Also list on Schedule C any cash the decedent had at the date of death. (See Form 8.69 on the accompanying CD.)

Group the items in the following categories and list the categories in the following order:

1. Mortgages.
2. Promissory notes.
3. Contracts by the decedent to sell land.
4. Cash in possession.
5. Cash in banks, savings and loan associations, and other types of financial organizations.

Schedule D

File Schedule D to figure the life insurance deductible in the gross estate. However, attach a Form 712 for every policy. (See Forms 8.70 and 8.71 on the accompanying CD.)

You must list every policy of insurance on the life of the decedent, whether or not it is included in the gross estate.

Under "Description" list:

- *Name of the insurance company and*
- *Number of the policy.*

For every policy of life insurance listed on the schedule, you must request a statement on Form 712, Life Insurance Statement, from the company that issued the policy. Attach the Form 712 to the back of Schedule D.

If the policy proceeds are paid in one sum, enter the net proceeds received (from Form 712, line 24) in the value (and alternate value) columns of Schedule D. If the policy proceeds are not paid in one sum, enter the value of the proceeds as of the date of the decedent's death (from Form 712, line 25).

If part or all of the policy proceeds are not included in the gross estate, you must explain why they were not included.[92]

Schedule E

Enter on this schedule all property of whatever kind or character, whether real estate, personal property, or bank accounts, in which the decedent held at the time of death an interest either as a joint tenant with right to survivorship or as a tenant by the entirety.

Do not list on this schedule property that the decedent held as a tenant in common, but report the value of the interest on Schedule A if real estate, or on the appropriate schedule if personal property. Similarly, community property held by the decedent and spouse should be reported on the appropriate Schedules A through I. The decedent's interest in a partnership should not be entered on this schedule unless the partnership interest itself is jointly owned. Solely owned partnership interests should be reported on Schedule F, "Other Miscellaneous Property."

. . .Generally, you must include the full value of the jointly owned property in the gross estate. However, the full value should not be included if you can show that a part of the property originally belonged to the other tenant or tenants and was never received or acquired by the other tenant or tenants from the decedent for less than adequate and full consideration in money or money's worth, or unless you can show that any part of the property was acquired with consideration originally belonging to the surviving joint tenant or tenants. In this case, you may exclude from the value of the property an amount proportionate to the consideration furnished by the other tenant or tenants. Relinquishing or promising to relinquish dower, curtesy, or statutory estate created instead of dower or curtesy, or other marital rights in the decedent's property or estate is not consideration in money or money's worth. See the Schedule A instructions for the value to show for real property that is subject to a mortgage.[93]

See Form 8.72 on the accompanying CD.

Schedule F

On Schedule F list all items that must be included in the gross estate and are not reported on any other schedule, including these:

- Debts due the decedent (other than notes and mortgages included on Schedule C).
- Interests in business.
- Insurance on the life of another (obtain and attach Form 712 for each policy).
- Section 2044 property.
- Claims including the value of the decedent's interest in a claim for refund of income taxes (or the amount of the refund actually received).
- Rights.
- Royalties.
- Leaseholds.
- Judgments.

- Reversionary or remainder interests.
- Shares in trust funds (attach a copy of the trust instrument).
- Household goods and personal effects, including wearing apparel.
- Farm products and growing crops.
- Livestock.
- Farm machinery.
- Automobiles.

See Form 8.73 on the accompanying CD.

Schedule G

Five types of transfers should be reported on this schedule:

1. Certain gift taxes—Section 2035(c): Enter at item A of the schedule the total value of the gift taxes that were paid by the decedent, or the estate, on gifts made by the decedent, or the decedent's spouse, within three years before death.

2. Other transfers within three years before death—Section 2035(a). These transfers include only the following:
   a. Any transfer by the decedent of a life insurance policy within three years before death.
   b. Any transfer within three years before death of a retained Section 2036 life estate, Section 2037 reversionary interest, or Section 2038 power to revoke, etc., if the property subject to the life estate, interest, or power would have been included in the gross estate had the decedent continued to possess the life estate, interest, or power until death.

3. Transfers with retained life estate (Section 2306)—These are transfers in which the decedent retained the income from the transferred property or the right to designate the person or person who will possess or enjoy the transferred property, or the income from the transferred property if the transfer was made.

4. Transfers taking effect at death (Section 2037)—These are transfers made on or after September 8, 1916, that took effect at the decedent's death. A transfer that takes effect at the decedent's death is one under which possession or enjoyment can be obtained only by surviving the decedent.

5. Revocable transfers (Section 2038)—These are transfers in which the enjoyment of the transferred property was subject at decedent's death to any change through the exercise of a power to alter, amend, revoke, or terminate.

All transfers (other than outright transfers not in trust and bona fide sales) made by the decedent at any time during life must be reported with the schedule regardless of whether you believe the transfers are subject to tax. If the decedent made any transfers not described in the instructions above, the transfers should not be shown on Schedule G. Instead, attach a statement describing these transfers: List the date of the transfer, the amount or value, and the type of transfer.

The IRS, to increase collections at the estate level, has tried to halt abuses in the transfer of property out of estates in contemplation of death. By setting specific time periods, generally three years, property will be includable in the gross estate if the deceased's chief motive in the transfer was escaping estate tax liability. However, Internal Revenue Code §2035 and §2036 contain even more protective provisions. "A gift made by a decedent within three years of his death is included in his estate whether or not a gift tax return was required if the gift consists of interest in property otherwise included in the gross estate under appropriate Internal Revenue sections."[94] Transfers of interest whereby the decedent maintains control whether through revocability, powers of appointment, or other retention of the right to possess and enjoy the transferred property or income will not be able to escape the gross estate calculations because of those "strings" still being attached.[95] (See Form 8.74 on the accompanying CD.)

Schedule H

On Schedule H include in the gross estate

1. The value of property for which the decedent possessed a general power of appointment on the date of his or her death.

2. The value of property for which the decedent possessed a general power of appointment which he or she exercised or released before death by disposing of it in such a way that if it were a transfer of property owned by the decedent, the property would be includable in the decedent's gross estate.

See Section 2041 and Publication 448 for more details. (See Form 8.74 on the accompanying CD.)

Schedule I

Enter on Schedule I every annuity that meets all of the conditions under General Information and every annuity described in paragraphs (a)–(h) of Annuities under Approved Plans, even if the annuities are wholly or partially excluded from the gross estate. (See Form 8.75 on the accompanying CD.)

Schedule J

On Schedule J itemize funeral expenses and expenses incurred in administering property subject to claims. List the names and addresses of persons to whom the expenses are payable and describe the nature of the expense. Do not list expenses incurred in administering property not subject to claims on this schedule; list them on Schedule L instead. (See Form 8.76 on the accompanying CD.)

Schedule K

List under "Debts of the Decedent" only valid debts the decedent owed at the time of death. List any indebtedness secured by a mortgage or other lien on property of the gross estate under the heading "Mortgages and Liens." If the amount of the debt is disputed or the subject of litigation, deduct only the amount the estate concedes to be a valid claim. If the claim is contested, indicate that fact. (See Form 8.77 on the accompanying CD.)

Schedule L

> *Deduct only those losses from thefts, fires, storms, shipwrecks, or other casualties that occurred during the settlement of the estate. You may deduct only the amount not reimbursed by insurance or otherwise.*
>
> *Describe in detail the loss sustained and the cause. If you received insurance or other compensation for the loss, state the amount collected. Identify the property for which you are claiming the loss by indicating the particular schedule and item number where the property is included in the gross estate.*
>
> *If you elect alternate valuation, do not deduct the amount by which you reduced the value of an item to include it in the gross estate.*
>
> *Do not deduct losses claimed as a deduction on a federal income tax return or depreciation in the value of securities or other property.*
>
> *You may deduct expenses incurred in administering property that is included in the gross estate but that is not subject to claims. You may only deduct these expenses if they were paid before the Section 6501 period of limitations for assessment expired.*
>
> *The expenses deductible on this schedule are usually expenses incurred in the administration of a trust established by the decedent before death. They may also be incurred in the collection of other assets or the transfer or clearance of title to other property included in the decedent's gross estate for estate tax purposes, but not included in the decedent's probate estate.*[96]

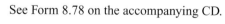

See Form 8.78 on the accompanying CD.

Schedule M

Generally, you may list on Schedule M all property interests that pass from the decedent to the surviving spouse and are included in the gross estate. However, you should not list any "nondeductible terminable interests" (described below) on Schedule M unless you are making a QTIP election. The property for which you make this election must be included on Schedule M. See "qualified terminable interest property" on the following page.

> *For the rules on common disaster and survival for a limited period, see Section 2056(b)(3). You may list on Schedule M only those interests that the surviving spouse takes:*
>
> 1. *As the decedent's legatee, devisee, heir, or donee;*
>
> 2. *As the decedent's surviving tenant by the entirety or joint tenant;*

3. *As an appointee under the decedent's exercise of a power or as a taker in default at the decedent's nonexercise of a power;*

4. *As a beneficiary of insurance on the decedent's life;*

5. *As the surviving spouse taking under dower or curtesy (or similar statutory interest); and*

6. *As a transferee of a transfer made by the decedent at any time.*

You should not list on Schedule M:

1. *The value of any property that does not pass from the decedent to the surviving spouse;*

2. *Property interests that are not included in the decedent's gross estate;*

3. *The full value of a property interest for which a deduction was claimed on Schedules J through L. The value of the property interest should be reduced by the deductions claimed with respect to it;*

4. *The full value of a property interest that passes to the surviving spouse subject to a mortgage or other encumbrance or an obligation of the surviving spouse. Include on Schedule M only the net value of the interest after reducing it by the amount of the mortgage or other debt;*

5. *Nondeductible terminable interests (described below); or*

6. *Any property interest disclaimed by the surviving spouse.*[97]

See Form 8.79 on the accompanying CD.

Schedule O

Estate valuation and resulting tax liability will also be affected by the level and size of charitable bequests. In general, these bequests are deductible to the estate. Schedule O asks for an *ad seriatim* listing of donees and corresponding amounts. See Form 8.80 on the accompanying CD.

Schedule P

The estate may also compute credits for taxes paid to foreign jurisdictions.

> *The credit for foreign death taxes is allowable only if the decedent was a citizen or resident of the United States. However, see Section 2053(d) and the related regulations for exceptions and limitations if the executor has elected, in certain cases, to deduct these taxes from the value of the gross estate.*
>
> *. . . The credit is authorized either by statute or by treaty. If a credit is authorized by a treaty, whichever of the following is the most beneficial to the estate is allowed:*
>
> *The credit computed under the treaty;*
> *The credit computed under the statute;*
>
> *. . . The total credit allowable in respect to any property, whether subjected to tax by one or more than one foreign country, is limited to the amount of the federal estate tax attributable to the property.*[98]

See Form 8.81 on the accompanying CD.

Schedule Q

The estate may also seek a credit for tax paid on prior transfers within designated calendar periods. The term *transferee* means the decedent for whose estate this return is filed. If the transferee received property from a transferor who died within 10 years before, or 2 years after, the transferee, a credit is allowable on this return for all or part of the federal estate tax paid by the transferor's estate with respect to the transfer. There is no requirement that the property be identified in the estate of the transferee or that it existed on the date of the tranferee's death.

Where the transferee predeceased the transferor, if not more than two years elapsed between the dates of death, the credit allowed is 100 percent of the maximum amount. If more than two years elapsed between the dates of death, no credit is allowed.

Where the transferor predeceased the transferee, the percentage of the maximum amount that is allowed as a credit depends on the number of years that elapsed between dates of death. It is determined using the table in Figure 8.7. (See Form 8.81 on the accompanying CD.)

Schedules R and R-1

The Internal Revenue Service will impose a tax on parties/transferees who, by use of trusts and others instruments, have avoided taxation on certain assets. Known as the GST—the

FIGURE 8.7
Table for
Determining
Maximum Amount
Allowed as a Credit

Period of Time Exceeding	Not Exceeding	Percentage Allowable
—	2 years	100
2 years	4 years	80
4 years	6 years	60
6 years	8 years	40
8 years	10 years	20
10 years	—	None

generation-skipping transfer tax—the policy searches for *skip persons*—those who have not incurred tax liability due to estate planning of their predecessors. It is a complex area of tax law.

Schedule R is used to compute the generation-skipping transfer (GST) tax that is payable by the estate. Schedule R-1 (Form 706) is used to compute the GST tax that is payable by certain trusts that are includible in the gross estate.

The GST tax that is to be reported on Form 706 is imposed only on "direct skips occurring at death." Unlike the estate tax, which is imposed on the value of the entire taxable estate regardless of who receives it, the GST tax is imposed only on the value of interest in property, wherever located, that actually pass to certain transferees, who are referred to as "skip persons."

For purposes of Form 706, the property interests transferred must be includible in the gross estate before they are subject to the GST tax. Therefore, the first step in computing the GST tax liability is to determine the property interests includible in the gross estate by completing Schedules A through I of Form 706.

The second step is to determine who the skip persons are. To do this, assign each transferee to a generation and determine whether each transferee is a "natural person" or a "trust" for GST purposes.

The third step is to determine which skip persons are transferees of "interests in property." If the skip person is a natural person, anything transferred is an interest in property. . . .

The fourth step is to determine whether to enter the transfer on Schedule R or on Schedule R-1. . . .

The fifth step is to complete Schedules R and R-1.[99]

See Form 8.82 on the accompanying CD.

Schedule U

To encourage the preservation of land for multiple purposes, Congress enacted the Qualified Conservation Easement program. The program excludes from the estate valuation the appraised value of land.

The exclusion is the lesser of:

The applicable percentage of the value of land (after certain reductions) subject to a qualified conservation easement, or

$500,000.

Once made the election is irrevocable.

Land may qualify for the exclusion if all of the following requirements are met.

The decedent or a member of the decedent's family must have owned the land for a three-year period ending on the date of the decedent's death.

No later than the date the election is made, a qualified conservation easement on the land has been made by the decedent, a member of the decedent's family, the executor of the decedent's estate, or the trustee of a trust that holds the land.

The land is located in the United States or one of its possessions. . .

A qualified conservation easement is one that would qualify as a qualified conservation contribution under Section 170(h). . .

The term conservation purpose *means:*

The preservation of land areas for outdoor recreation by or the education of the public;

The protection of a relatively natural habitat of fish, wildlife, or plants, or a similar ecosystem; or

The preservation of open space (including farmland and forest land) where such preservation is for the scenic enjoyment of the general public, or under a clearly delineated federal, state, or local conservation policy and will yield a significant public benefit.[100]

See Form 8.83 on the accompanying CD.

FIGURE 8.8
Table for Computing Gift Tax

Source: Internal Revenue Service, Form 709 Instructions at 12.

Column A Taxable Amount Over	Column B Taxable Amount Not Over	Column C Tax on Amount in Column A	Column D Rate of Tax on Excess Over Amount in Column A
—	$10,000	—	18%
$10,000	20,000	$1,800	20%
20,000	40,000	3,800	22%
40,000	60,000	8,200	24%
60,000	80,000	13,000	26%
80,000	100,000	18,200	28%
100,000	150,000	23,800	30%
150,000	250,000	38,800	32%
250,000	500,000	70,800	34%
500,000	750,000	155,800	37%
750,000	1,000,000	248,300	39%
1,000,000	1,250,000	345,800	41%
1,250,000	1,500,000	448,300	43%
1,500,000	2,000,000	555,800	45%
2,000,000	—	780,800	47%

Gift Tax Calculation

For estates of significant size, some attention must be given to gift tax calculation. The Internal Revenue Code looks askance at gifts or transfers made in contemplation of death or those that are inordinate relative to the donor's overall income. Gift taxes, as already noted, also play a role in the calculation of the overall gross estate tax and can serve as a credit in that calculation. (See Form 8.84 on the accompanying CD.)

Also be aware that certain types of transfers are not subject to gift tax. These are transfers to

- Political organizations.
- Educational institutions.
- Medical providers.

There is an annual exclusion of $11,000 of gifts per donor to each recipient (donee) during the calendar year. Many complicated issues of tax policy and strategy crop up in gifts by both husbands and wives to third parties and attempts to "skip a generation" in the donor's line of descendants. The paralegal should fully recognize that complex tax questions need the oversight of a specialist in tax law or accounting.

A table outlining the unified credit and calculation formulas is shown in Figure 8.8. Form 709, the official gift tax return, is in Form 8.84 on the accompanying CD.

Fiduciary Returns

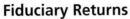

The estate paralegal will soon discern that the federal and state governments are looking at multiple means of raising revenue. Aside from the federal gift and estate taxes and state inheritance taxes, taxes are paid on the income generated by the estate. This return is usually called a *fiduciary tax return.* "The income of a deceased person's estate is taxable at the same rate as the income of an individual. The tax generally is determined in a similar manner as for individuals, with certain exceptions in the computation of deductions and credits. The estate is a separate taxable entity and will have its own taxpayer identification number, which must be applied for. The estate comes into existence as a separate entity upon the death of the taxpayer, and it ceases when the personal representative closes the estate."[101] The tax is collectible at the federal level after preparation of Form 1041. (See Form 8.85 on the accompanying CD.)

The Internal Revenue Code provides for deductions relative to the operation of the estate and the estate alone, which includes distributions to heirs and legatees. The paralegal should also advise the executor or representative that the option exists to include administrative and funeral expenses on Form 1041 or Form 706. A majority of American states also have fiduciary return requirements.

LIVING WILLS

Some examination of the living will is appropriate in estate law analysis. "In an age where life spans are extraordinary, when medical and mechanical intervention prolongs a life beyond normal age barriers, more and more individuals have qualms about the extent of medical interventions in the latter stages of their life when it is clearly terminal. Of course, this analysis prompts numerous ethical questions, both medical and philosophical in nature. But what is factually true is that more and more clients will come into the law office and will freely discuss the matter of extraordinary care, and then request information on whether or not the particular jurisdiction allows some instructions, some voice on the level of medical intervention."[102] Obviously the ethical questions are troubling. Medical and scientific intervention have become so intrusive that there is general sympathy for patients' rights in terminal cases, though whether this moves toward physician-assisted suicide is another story. The U.S. Supreme Court's recent decision on the Oregon Death with Dignity Act by a 6–3 margin has again stirred this debate.[103] Some suggestions for forms and format follow.

Power of Attorney

A durable power of attorney is essential in matters of medical care. "A client may want to deliver a power of attorney to a third party who will take responsibility when the client's health is terminal and his judgment capacity is limited or even nonexistent. A grant of a durable power of attorney to another is an acknowledgment by the client that he leaves personal medical decisions in the hands of a trusted person."[104] An example by the State Bar of Michigan referred to the power as durable. (See Form 8.86 on the accompanying CD.)[105] The Uniform Durable Power of Attorney Act, adopted in a majority of American jurisdictions, sets out the attributes of this authority. (See Form 8.87.)

Living Wills

Living will format is largely influenced by statute. To be sure, "[a] living will is a document with serious implications. It applies only in situations where care is being provided to one in a permanently unconscious state, a terminal condition from which the patient is unlikely to recover. The language popularized in living wills is that 'to a reasonable degree of medical certainty and in accordance with reasonable medical standards, there is no reasonable possibility' that the patient will recover."[106] An example reflecting these fundamental requirements is shown in Form 8.88 on the accompanying CD. The Arkansas Bar Association makes freely available a living will (see Form 8.89).[107]

Closely aligned to the living will is the advance directive on medical care. Also called a durable power of attorney, here the client publishes advance directions relative to medical care and course of treatment and appoints a party to carry out the directive. See the advanced directive and accompanying addenda in Form 8.90 on the accompanying CD.[108]

Summary

This chapter's coverage included an introductory discussion of the nature of estate and trust practice, from the initial client contact to the filing of the first and final account. Special emphasis was given to financial planning, taxation, human counseling skills, preparation of estate documentation, administration of estates, and the litigation and advocacy aspects of the field.

The most common documentation in estate practice is, of course, the will document. The legal formalities of a valid and enforceable will, as well as the structural content of a typical will, were thoroughly assessed. Will contests, will codicils, and alternatives to traditional wills were also part of this chapter's focus.

Of similar importance is trust practice. Reviewing first the nature of a trust document and its appropriate provisions, clauses, and legal requirements, the chapter then analyzed the various forms and purposes for trust documents.

The chapter also considered the administrative aspects of estate and trust practice, also known as probate, including accumulation of assets and other record keeping, determination of heirs, guardianship, determinations of competency, and potential incapacitation. Within the pages the reader contrasted and compared small estates and large estates, formal versus informal estate administrative processes, pleadings and petitions, steps in probate, and the predictable challenges of probate practice. Compilation of an inventory, first and final accounting, and a plan of distribution were other facets of the chapter's direction.

Estate taxation, as guided by Federal Form 706 and its corresponding schedules, is another major component of paralegal estate practice. In addition, a short survey of gift tax and fiduciary returns was provided. The chapter ended with an analysis of living wills.

Discussion Questions

1. Describe your jurisdiction's procedural and substantive requirements in the preparation of a will.

2. Name or identify three or four trust entities in your geographic area. Think of charitable institutions.

3. If a party wishes to challenge the validity of a will, what types of arguments could be made?

4. Describe the many purposes of a residuary clause in a will.

5. Why does the law favor per stirpes distribution over per capita distribution?

6. In what areas of estate planning and practice do questions of guardianship and competency most frequently come up?

7. What types of estates will receive preferential and expeditious processing?

8. Name five or six techniques of minimizing estate taxation.

9. Where do remote cousins generally fit in an intestacy scheme?

10. For what reason would a spouse exercise her elective share rather than accept the disposition of the will?

11. What types of transfers, prior to death, will be includable in the gross estate?

12. What type of situation would create an implied or resulting trust? Outline a fact pattern.

13. Locate your intestate succession statute for your jurisdiction. Explain how property will be distributed under the statute.

14. Contact your local register of wills or other authority that deals with probate. What instructions does the office have about heirs?

Practical Exercises

1. Wills—special bequests of personal and household goods

   Which is the appropriate way of drafting a specific bequest of personal and household goods?

   a. I hereby devise my coin and stamp collection.

   b. I hereby transfer and sell my furniture, clothing, and jewelry.

   c. I hereby give and bequeath my heirlooms, works of art, and silverplate.

2. Estate tax problem—Form 706

   Using the facts presented here, complete a federal estate tax return, Form 706, and accompanying schedules:

Name of decedent:	*Betty B. Dead*
Date of birth:	*May 1, 1924*
Date of death:	*April 12, 1989*
Address:	*666 Cemetery Lane, Pittsburgh, PA 15219*
Death certificate number:	*1452467*
Cause of death:	*Heart failure*
Attending physician:	*Kim Fu Young, M.D.*
Will probated:	*April 17, 1989*
Executor named:	*Frank N. Stein*
Estate federal I.D. number:	*25-2497619*
Probate court number:	*1246 of 1989*

   Items included in gross estate:

   • *300 shares of Duquesne Light Company stock at 27.34 per share.*

   • *19,250 shares of Walt Disney stock at 76.875 per share.*

   • *200 shares of Kodak Company stock at 31.38 per share.*

- *$70,000 Allegheny County Industrial Development Authority Environmental Improvement Revenue Bond, Series A, 7.25%, due May 1, 2000, CUSIP No. 017292BR3 at 93.411.*
- *1½ story dwelling with detached garage located at 666 Cemetery Lane, Pittsburgh, PA 15219, recorded in Deed Book Volume 999, page 333. (Mr. Stein got an appraisal on the property that listed the real estate at fair market value of $250,000.)*

Bank accounts:

- *Mellon Bank checking account number 2479446: $29,406.54 (with IRD interest of $94.23).*
- *Mellon Bank money market account number 9462742: $35,946.76 (was held jointly with Adam Dead, her son).*
- *Certificate of deposit number 1567823: $31,246.00 (with IRD interest of $1,246.00).*
- *Dean Witter cash management account: $94,146.7220.*

Household goods and furnishings totaling $10,500.00.
1989 Mercury Sable valued at $15,200.00.

Stock transactions:

- *250 shares of Duquesne Light sold at $45.00 per share.*
- *2 for 1 split of Kodak stock.*
- *2,000 shares of Walt Disney sold at $75.175 per share.*
- *150 shares of Kodak sold at $30.00 per share.*

Estate administrative expenses:

- *Funeral expenses, J.B. Bloody Funeral Home: $6,456.23.*
- *Yohe Floral Shop: $257.00.*
- *Luncheon after funeral: $125.00.*
- *Executor's commissions: $80,000.00.*
- *Attorney's fees: $75,000.00.*

Betty's husband, Charles, of the same address, will be taking the family exemption of $2,000.00.
Miscellaneous administrative expenses:

- *Appraisal of property: $125.00.*
- *Probate fees: $925.00.*
- *Miscellaneous administrative expenses: $250.00.*
- *Prepayment of inheritance tax:$ 9,450.00.*

Decedent's debts incurred:

- *Duquesne Light: $75.00.*
- *Equitable Gas: $100.00.*
- *Bell of PA: $40.00.*

Bequests as stated in will:

- *Charles B. Dead, husband, same address: 50% of the estate.*
- *Adam Dead, son, same address: 50% of the estate.*
- *Charitable bequest to Salvation Army of $5,000.00.*
- *Any information required to complete the forms, such as Social Security numbers, not provided here may be created by the student as necessary.*

Internet Resources

FindLaw: wills, trusts, estates, and probate—findlaw.com/01topics/31probate

WashLaw WEB: probate/trusts/estates/wills—www.washlaw.edu/subject/estate.html

Estates and trusts: Wex—www.law.cornell.edu/topics/estates_trusts.html

Michigan courts probate forms—courts.michigan.gov/scao/courtforms/probate/gpindex.htm

Estates and Trusts Resource Guide—www.law.csuohio.edu/lawlibrary/EstatesTrustsResource-Guide.htm

U.S. estate and gift tax law—www.law.cornell.edu/topics/estate_gift_tax.html

Internal Revenue Service—www.irs.gov

Endnotes

1. Jeffrey N. Pennell, *Introduction: Whither Estate Planning,* 24 IDAHO L. REV. 339, 341 (1988).

2. CHARLES P. NEMETH, ESTATE PLANNING AND ADMINISTRATION FOR PARALEGALS 2 (1993).

3. Shari Snell Faulkner, *How to Effectively Use a Paralegal in a Probate Matter,* UT. B. J., Jan.–Feb. 2004, at 42. See also Gail E. Cohen, *Using Legal Assistants in Estate Planning,* 30 PRAC. LAW. 73–74 (Oct. 1984).

4. Michael C. Hodes, *A Roadmap to Financial Planning: The Professional's Role,* 20 MD. B. J. 14, 18 (1987).

5. PENNSYLVANIA BAR INSTITUTE, ESTATE PLANNING 1 (1982).

6. Gary C. Randall, *Death as a Tax Shelter—An Overview of Planning for Income Tax Basis Changes,* 24 IDAHO L. REV. 397 (1988).

7. *Id.*

8. Jeffrey N. Pennell, *Introduction: Whither Estate Planning,* 24 IDAHO L. REV. 339, 341 (1988).

9. Robert S. Mucklestone, *Estate Planning Practice, A Team Approach for Lawyers and Legal Assistants,* LEGAL ECON., Dec. 1981, at 35.

10. Jeffrey N. Pennell, *Introduction: Whither Estate Planning,* 24 IDAHO L. REV. 339, 345 (1988). *See* the American Bar Association's Real Property, Probate, and Trust Law section at www.abanet.org/rppt/publications/magazine/home.html.

11. *See* J.M. Zitter, who assesses the fine line between estate assistance and unauthorized practice of law in *What Constitutes Unauthorized Practice of Law by Paralegal,* 109 A.L.R.5th 275 (2005).

12. Charles C. McCarter, *Cost-Efficient Estate Planning,* 53 J. KAN. B. ASSOC. 51 (1984); *see also* Matter of Easler, 275 S.C. 400, 272 S.E.2d 32 (1980), where the court had reservations about estate planning seminars that seemed to imply that paralegals conducting the seminars were able to resolve questions concerning the legal content.

13. Gerold P. Johnston, *Avoiding Malpractice Claims That Arise out of Common Estate Planning Situations,* TAXES, Nov. 1985, at 780, 799; *see also* Ralph G. Miller, *Creating an Estate Plan Database,* TR. & EST., June 1985, at 45.

14. Be cautious about unlawful practice. See Gerold P. Johnston, *Avoiding Malpractice Claims That Arise out of Common Estate Planning Situations,* TAXES, Nov. 1985, at 780, 799. *See also* Gail E. Cohen, *Using Legal Assistants in Estate Planning,* 30 PRAC. LAW. 73, 78 (1984).

15. Robert S. Mucklestone, *Estate Planning Practice, A Team Approach for Lawyers and Legal Assistants,* LEGAL ECON., Dec. 1981, at 35.

16. Ralph Blount, *Could Your Office Use a Paralegal?* 44 ADVOC 23, 25 (2001).

17. INSTITUTE FOR PARALEGAL TRAINING, INTRODUCTION TO ESTATES AND TRUSTS 416 (1978).

18. LOUIS D. LAVRINO, AVOIDING WILL CONSTRUCTION PROBLEMS, 11 ALI-ABA COURSE MATERIALS 83 (1987).

19. Thomas S. Word Jr., *A Brief for Plain English Wills and Trusts,* 14 U. RICH. L. REV. 471, 471–472 (1980).

20. CHARLES P. NEMETH, ESTATE PLANNING AND ADMINISTRATION FOR PARALEGALS 66 (1993).

21. Gregory V. Mersol, *The Statutory Will: A Simple Alternative to Intestacy,* 35 CASE W. RES. L. REV. 307 (1984).

22. CHARLES P. NEMETH, ESTATE PLANNING AND ADMINISTRATION FOR PARALEGALS 177 (1993, Supp. 1995).

23. Minnesota State Statute 524.2-510. Incorporation by reference. *See also* Uniform Probate Code §2-513 (2006). The Uniform Probate Code is available in its entirety at the National Conference of Commissioners on Uniform State Laws Web site at www.law.upenn.edu/bll/ulc/ulc_frame.htm. The incorporated document must describe the property with particularity. The instructions provided by a testator in the secondary document legally guide the distribution of tangible property. *See* L.S. Tellier, *Incorporation of Extrinsic Writings in Will by Reference,* 173 A.L.R. 568.

24. J. Kendrick Kinney, A Law Dictionary and Glossary 4 (1987).

25. Uniform Probate Code §1-201(3) (2006).

26. For a fascinating look at how the Chinese legal system differentiates heirs based on behavior over blood, see Frances H. Foster, *Toward a Behavior-Based Model of Inheritance? The Chinese Experiment*, 32 U.C. Davis L. Rev. 77 (1998).

27. William J. Bowe & Douglas H. Parker, 4 Page on the Law of Wills 430 (1992).

28. Pennsylvania Bar Institute, Estate Planning 15 (1982).

29. D. Hower, Wills, Trusts, and Estate Administration for the Paralegal 196 (1985).

30. See Institute of Continuing Legal Education, 1 Michigan Basic Practice Handbook, 430 (1986), for some salient suggestions regarding trusts and their formation.

31. For general suggestions about wills, see Charles P. Nemeth, the Paralegal Handbook 371 (1987).

32. Stacy L. Ossin, The *"Void" in Florida's Will Revocation Statutes*, Fla. B.J., June 1997, at 79.

33. Stephan R. Leimberg & Charles Plotnick, *How to Review a Will*, Prac. Law., Sept. 1988, at 13–14.

34. Leon Jaworski, *Will Contests,* 9 Am. Jur. Trials 605, 606 (1987).

35. See Annotation, J.E. Macy, *Insane Delusion as Invalidating Will,* 175 A.L.R. 882 (1948); Annotation, *E.H.H. Admissibility and Probative Force, on Issue as to Mental Condition, of Evidence That One Had Been Adjudged Incompetent or Insane, or Has Been Confined in Insane Asylum,* 68 A.L.R. 1318 (1930).

36. See Annotation, G.S.O., *Fraud or Mistake as to Relationship or Status of Legatee or Devisee as Affecting Will,* 17 A.L.R. 247 (1922); Annotation, M.DeL., *Fraud as Distinguished from Undue Influence as a Ground for Contesting Will,* 92 A.L.R. 790 (1934).

37. Leon Jaworski, *Will Contests,* 9 Am. Jur. Trials 605, 623 (1987).

38. See generally J. Kraut, *Effect of Will Provision Cutting Off Heir or Next of Kin, or Restricting Him to Provision Made, to Exclude Him from Distribution of Intestate Property,* 100 A.L.R.2d 325.

39. Leon Jaworski, *Will Contests,* 9 Am. Jur. Trials 605, 618–622 (1987).

40. See Herbert E. Tucker, David M. Swank, & Thomas G. Hill, *Holographic and Nonconforming Wills: Dispensing with Formalities-Part I,* Colo. Law., Dec. 2002, at 57.

41. Okla. Stat. Tit. 84, §46.

42. Charles P. Nemeth, Estate Planning and Administration for Paralegals 212 (1993).

43. Uniform Probate Code §7-302 (2006).

44. Pennsylvania Bar Institute, Estate Planning 32 (1982).

45. See Medlawplus.com.

46. Michael L.M. Jordan, *Charitable Lead Trusts,* S.C. Law., May 2004, at 32.

47. See generally Bradley E.S. Fogel, *Back to the Future Interest: The Origin and Questionable Legal Basis of the Use of Crummey Withdrawal Powers to Obtain the Federal Gift Tax Annual Exclusion,* 6 Fl. Tax Rev. 189 (2003).

48. Pennsylvania Bar Institute, Estate Planning 37 (1982).

49. North Carolina Bar Foundation, VII Practical Skills Course, Wills and Estates 46 (1988).

50. 34 Standard Pa Practice 2d §160:122 at 457 (1987).

51. George A. Locke, *Grantor's Intent That Grantee Hold Realty in Trust,* 4 Am. Jur. Proof of Facts 2d 54 (1975).

52. Pennsylvania Bar Institute, Estate Planning 40 (1982). For a thorough examination of the implications of a Qtip trust in testamentary estate practice, see Covey, Moore, & Cornfield, Question and Answer Session of the Twentieth Annual Institute of Estate Planning, Institute on Estate Planning §200 (1986).

53. Carolyn McCaffrey & Allen Hirschfield, *Restructuring Wills and Trusts to*

Reduce Generation Skipping Taxes, TR. & EST., Mar. 1992, at 9.

54. CHARLES P. NEMETH, ESTATE PLANNING AND ADMINISTRATION FOR PARALEGALS 272–275 (1993).

55. Clare H. Springs, *Probate Lawyer's Role Changing,* TR. & EST., Jan. 1988, at 23.

56. Edward S. Schlesinger, *A Post-Mortem Estate Planning Checklist, Part I,* 30 PRAC. LAW. 11, 13–14 (1984).

57. Okla. Stat. Tit. 84, §215.

58. *See* Donald J. Liddle, *Intentional Omission of a Child from a Will,* 6 AM. JUR. PROOF OF FACTS 2d 95 (1987); Russell L. Ward, *Relinquishment of Parental Claim to Child-Adoption Proceedings,* 10 AM. JUR. PROOF OF FACTS 2d (1987); Annotation, L.S. Tellier, *Descent and Distribution from Step-Parent to Step-Children or Vice Versa,* 63 A.L.R. 2d 303 (1959); Annotation, C.C. Marvel, *Admissibility on Issue of Child's Legitimacy of Parentage, of Declarations of Parent, Relative, or Child Where Declarant Is Unavailable,* 31 A.L.R. 2d 989 (1953).

59. *See* J. Michael Rosso, *Determination of Heirship,* 12 AM. JUR. PROOF OF FACTS 2d 463 (1987).

60. Francis M. Dougherty, J.D, *Descent and Distribution: Rights of Inheritance as between Kindred of Whole and Half Blood,* 47 A.L.R.4th 561.

61. *See* J. Michael Rosso, *Determination of Heirship,* 12 AM. JUR. PROOF OF FACTS 2d 463, 472 (1987).

62. New York State Surrogate Court Act §1750.

63. J. Howard Ziemann, *Incompetency and Commitment Problems,* 8 AM. JUR. TRIALS 483, 501 (1988); *see also* Daniel F. Sullivan, *Discount Rate for Future Damages,* 8 AM. JUR. PROOF OF FACTS 1 (1986).

64. Maine Code §5-311. Who may be guardian; priorities. *See also* Uniform Probate Code §5-311 (2006).

65. *See* Uniform Probate Code §§5-306 to 307, 5-312 (2006).

66. Okla. Stat. Tit. 58 §241; *see also* Helen W. Gunnarsson, *The Ceiling for Small Estate Affidavits Has Doubled from $50,000 to $100,000,* 92 IL. B. J. 508 (2004).

67. Okla. Stat. Tit. 58, §1101 et seq.

68. Ohio Standard Probate §8.09 at 489.

69. Maine Code §3-1203. Small estates; summary administrative procedure. *See also* Uniform Probate Code §3-1203 (2006).

70. Ian S. Oppenheim & Alex L. Moschella, *National Perspective on Expanded Estate Recovery: Case Law Analysis, Emerging Legislative Trends, and Responsive Strategies for the Elder Law Attorney,* NAELAJ 7, 15 (Spring 2005).

71. *See* Uniform Probate Code §3-1204 (2006).

72. INSTITUTE OF CONTINUING LEGAL EDUCATION, MICHIGAN BASIC PRACTICE HANDBOOK 491 (1986).

73. *See* Brenda Mientka, *Colorado Paralegals—Proposed Guidelines to the Next Century and Beyond: Part I,* COLO. LAW., Oct. 1996, at 63.

74. *See* Uniform Probate Code §3-308 (1974).

75. Daniel F. Caruso, *In the Matter of Albert A. Garofalo (Executor Removal),* 18 QUINNIPIAC PROB. L. J. 12 (2004).

76. M. PAUL SMITH, RICHARD L. GROSSMAN, & JOHN L. HOLLINGER, PENNSYLVANIA FIDUCIARY GUIDE 413 (1983).

77. *See* CHARLES P. NEMETH, ESTATE PLANNING AND ADMINISTRATION FOR PARALEGALS 333 (1993).

78. M. PAUL SMITH, RICHARD L. GROSSMAN, & JOHN L. HOLLINGER, PENNSYLVANIA FIDUCIARY GUIDE 63 (1983).

79. Minnesota State Statute 524.2-504. Self-proved will. *See also* Uniform Probate Code §2-504 (2006).

80. For an interesting look at the role and function of a probate judge, *see* Hawaii State Bar Association, *Interview with Judge Colleen K. Hirai,* 22 HI. B. J. (2004).

81. M. PAUL SMITH, RICHARD L. GROSSMAN, & JOHN L. HOLLINGER, PENNSYLVANIA FIDUCIARY GUIDE 153–163 (discussing general calculations and formulas) (1983).

82. John H. Derrick, J.D., *Construction, Application, and Effect of Statutes Which*

Deny or Qualify Surviving Spouse's Right to Elect against Deceased Spouse's Will, 48 A.L.R.4th 972.

83. Uniform Rules for Surrogate's Court §207.20 (c); *see also* Eugene E. Peckham, *New Era for Estate Administration in New York Has Reduced Estate Tax but Many Requirements Still Apply,* N.Y. St. B.J., Sept. 2000, at 30.

84. Daniel F. Carmack, *Action by or against a Decedent's Estate,* 19 Am. Jur. Trials 35 (1972).

85. Okla. Stat. Tit. 58, §591.

86. Maine Code §3-805. Classification of claims. *See also* Uniform Probate Code §3-805 (2006).

87. M. Paul Smith, Richard L. Grossman, & John L. Hollinger, Pennsylvania Fiduciary Guide 26–37 (1983).

88. Lackner Computer Group Inc., Carnegie Office Park, Suite 290, 700 North Bell Avenue, Pittsburgh, Pennsylvania 15106.

89. Diane St. John, *Federal Estate Tax Return,* 9 Legal Ass't Today, May–June 1992, at 116, 118.

90. Instructions for Schedules A–P are fully outlined in the Internal Revenue Service's Instructions for Form 706.

91. Internal Revenue Service, 2005 Form 706 at 5.

92. Internal Revenue Service, 2005 Form 706 at 16.

93. Internal Revenue Service, 2005 Form 706 at 18.

94. RIA, Estate Planning and Taxation Coordinator 5014 at 562–563 (1989).

95. I.R.C. §2036(A)(2); *see also* Treas. Reg. §20.2036-1.

96. Internal Revenue Service, Form 706 Instructions at 18.

97. Internal Revenue Service, 2005 Form 706 at 28.

98. Internal Revenue Service, Form 706 Instructions at 19.

99. Internal Revenue Service, Form 706 Instructions at 21.

100. Internal Revenue Service, Form 706 Instructions at 24–25.

101. David Cleaver, Pennsylvania Probate and Estate Administration 183 (1992).

102. Charles P. Nemeth, Estate Planning and Administration for Paralegals 529 (1993).

103. Slip Opinion, Gonzales, Attorney General, et al. v. Oregon et al. Certiorari to the United States Court of Appeals for the Ninth Circuit No. 0423. Argued October 5, 2005; decided January 17, 2006.

104. Charles P. Nemeth, Estate Planning and Administration for Paralegals 529 (1993).

105. State Bar of Michigan, Elder Law and Advocacy Section, Michael Franck Building, 306 Townsend Street, Lansing, Michigan 48933-2083. Durable power of attorney for health care sample form available at http://www.michbar.org/elderlaw/pdfs/dpoa_hc.pdf.

106. Charles P. Nemeth, Estate Planning and Administration for Paralegals 532 (1993).

107. Arkansas Bar Association Web site at http://www.arkbar.com, What's New Section–April 2005; follow links to "Living Wills & Other Information on End of Life Decisions."

108. Advance Directives: A Guide To Maryland Law on Health Care Decisions, State of Maryland Office of the Attorney General 8–14; available at http://www.oag.state.md.us/Healthpol/adirective.pdf.

Investigation

INVESTIGATIVE PARALEGAL JOB DESCRIPTION

Investigative paralegals need to be proficient in the following competencies:

- Participate in the initial phases of case evaluation to determine whether further investigation is necessary.
- Develop the requisite skills of objectivity, logic, and perseverance in the investigative process.
- Develop good human relations skills in dealing with clients, witnesses, sources, and the like.
- Differentiate the many types of witnesses in an investigative process.
- Locate missing or unknown witnesses.
- Draft and maintain a listing of expert organizations.
- Contact medical and specialty expert organizations for assistance in evaluating evidence.
- Draft correspondence and questionnaires to be sent to witnesses for the attorney's approval.
- Draft interrogatories and direct or cross-examination inquiries for expert witness testimony for the attorney's review.
- Interview, depose, and coach witnesses.
- Develop a solid and ongoing relationship with contacts, both public and private.
- Develop a relationship with private companies that can assist in locating missing witnesses.
- Be aware of and know how to use the many sources of information available in the investigative process.
- Be familiar with and be able to gain access to the investigative documentation and methods employed by police departments.
- Draft checklists and logs for use in collecting physical evidence.
- Develop and maintain a comprehensive investigative kit for the collection and preservation of evidence.
- Be familiar with and practice the various methods of preserving and transmitting evidence.
- Reconstruct events based on the facts at hand.
- Photograph or graphically recreate an accident scene.
- Draft correspondence to medical facilities or personnel necessary to acquire medical records.
- Draft correspondence to state and federal governmental entities to acquire accident details.
- Draft a comprehensive accident scene investigation report.
- Sort, categorize, and maintain the physical evidence, correspondence, statements, and other information collected in the investigative process.

THE PARALEGAL'S ROLE IN THE INVESTIGATIVE PROCESS

Paralegals play an important and active role in the investigative process in the American legal system. The functions of investigation are multifaceted. Its Latin derivative, *vestigare*, implies a tracking, a search, an assimilation or collection of information or facts. Attorneys, law firms, agencies, and many other employers quickly learn the sensibility of delegating investigation to paralegals. This frees attorneys from these time-consuming obligations and provides an efficient and productive mechanism for processing cases. Some of the more common exercises performed by paralegals in the investigative process include

- Claims investigation.
- Divorce investigation.
- Location of missing persons.
- Location of heirs and assigns.
- Civil investigation.
- Criminal investigation.
- Credit investigation.
- Background investigation.
- Undercover investigation.

- Insurance investigation.
- Personal injury investigation.
- Traffic accident investigation.
- Property loss investigation.
- Medical malpractice investigation.
- Government agency investigation.
- Fire, safety, and OSHA investigations.
- Domestic relations investigation.
- Patent and trademark investigations.

- Organized crime investigation.
- Fraud and white-collar crime investigations.
- Employee investigation.
- Polygraph investigation.
- Housing code investigation.
- Building trades investigation.
- Surveillance activities.
- Witness location.
- Workers' compensation cases.
- Corporate investigation.

- Judgment investigation.
- Product liability and consumer claims.
- Public record searches.
- Title searches.
- Marine investigation.
- Construction accident investigation.
- Toxic tort investigation.
- Psychological and psychiatric investigation.
- Questioned document investigation.

This list is a partial attempt to cover investigative techniques; the nature and extent of investigative work and practice in the paralegal community are difficult to categorize fully. Art Buckwalter, former managing director of the Academy of Professional Investigators, indicates that "no list can possibly cover all potentialities";[1] but change is a sure bet in the world of investigative practice. For paralegals, the picture reaffirms this drama, especially due to the diversity of legal practice areas, and the "nature of the investigation varies considerably with the area of law involved, as well as with the particular facts of the case at hand."[2] Whether in workers' compensation or negligence analysis, investigative skills are crucial. To attain a high level of professional standing, paralegals must be competent investigators. Attorneys, agencies, and other employers look to the paralegal to collect information and gather data that resolve factual disputes and inconsistencies. Often paralegal investigative steps lay a foundation, a conceptual framework, upon which a case can be evaluated for settlement, trial, or eventual dismissal.

Investigation is the process of factual assimilation and the systematic collection of evidence. It is a process of observation, inspection, and analysis, involving continuous and regular inquiry into a specific subject. It requires balancing the theories of investigative practice and the information in policy manuals and textbooks with experience and "street smarts." Legal practice depends on facts and hard information. Without these, a case or claim rests on an uneasy and tenuous foundation. A successful paralegal investigator must provide the information necessary to support or refute a claim, cause of action, or criminal prosecution. Solid investigative practice usually relies on the following traits:

- Energy and alertness.
- Knowledge of the law.
- Ability to set realistic objectives.
- Methodical approach.

- Knowledge of human nature.
- Observation and deduction abilities.
- Ability to maintain meaningful notes.[3]

Solid investigative practice operates under an investigative plan, creates a theoretical framework that underlines the investigative process, and proposes a cause or case in law that relates to the investigative regimen.

The investigative process must reconstruct events, conditions, or (as is often stated) the "truth" itself. Finding the truth can be a challenge for even the most seasoned investigators. Objective and fully reliable information is hard to come by. To reconstruct events and circumstances, the paralegal will engage many parties and practices including witnesses, physical and real evidence, documents, forensic science, demonstrative evidence, and the sophistication of expert opinion. In a sense, the investigator reconstructs history for the present. James Davidson and Mark Lytle's *After the Fact* suggests that the investigative process is really a journey into the historical past:

> *"History is what happened in the past." That statement is the everyday view of the matter. . . . The everyday view recognizes that this task is often difficult. But historians are said to succeed if they bring back the facts without distorting them or forcing a new perspective on them. In effect, historians are seen as couriers between the past and present. Like all good messengers, they are expected simply to deliver their information without adding to it.*[4]

In sum, the process of investigation requires the conversion of alleged acts into real and useful evidence.[5]

GENERAL CHARACTERISTICS OF A COMPETENT INVESTIGATOR

As in all occupations, personalities, styles of operation, and professional competencies vary among individuals. Even so, there are universal characteristics germane to the professional investigator. These traits are foundational to success in the investigative process and include objectivity, logic, perseverance, diligence, and skill in human interaction.

Objectivity

Good investigators are driven by facts rather than emotions, preconceptions, biases, or opinions. The search for rock-hard evidence signifies the passion for objectivity. Investigators who operate with preconceived notions of what the facts might be usually are led down a road lacking in objectivity. An initial bias drives the choice of many divergent paths in case analysis. This mindset undermines objectivity. Therefore, the investigator's strongest suit is an open-minded, hypothesis-driven, almost scientific approach. Only when an investigator purges personal feelings, inclinations, and preconceptions will the investigative process have integrity.

If such attention to detail becomes the hallmark of the paralegal's process, then his or her actions inspire others to believe that he or she has integrity, that his or her judgments are reliable, and that he or she is credible in the evaluation of facts and issues in the case at hand. "Their confident, businesslike, and friendly approach creates the atmosphere of professional skill."[6] An important factor to remember is that paralegals are often placed in situations that are extremely emotional. Working in domestic relations, environmental hazards, criminal defense and prosecution, or constitutional and civil rights litigation may affect a person's view of what is right and wrong. Remaining emotionally detached and objective is a continuous struggle.

Objectivity assures that judgments are rooted in fact rather than emotion and that investigative conclusions are the result of an intellectual process rather than a passionate judgment. Objectivity is "the key to things as they are."[7]

Logic

Purging one's emotions and preconceptions is necessary to maintain an objective view. The collection of facts, data, and all forms of knowledge requires rigorous logic. Logic can best be described as the orderly and sensible review of facts, conditions, and events. Once information is gathered, the assessment must continue sequentially. "By querying this way, the investigator looks for correlations."[8] Because logic is an exercise of pure reason, facts can be evaluated by direct, deductive, inferential, or reverse forms of reasoning. Queries in a general sense will include these:

- What does the information mean?
- When was this information collected?
- How was this information acquired?
- Who was responsible for this information?
- Why was this information found in this location?
- What other parties or individuals might be responsible for this information?

Deductive reasoning rightfully dwells on the most fundamental questions—the "who, what, where, when, why, and how" questioning sequence. The competent investigator stays true to the basics.

"Who" Questions

- Who discovered the cause of action or crime?
- Who reported the cause of action or crime?
- Who saw or heard anything of importance?
- Who had a motive or other reason for participation?
- Who was responsible for the cause of action or crime?
- Who can be considered an aider, abettor, coconspirator, or codefendant or coplaintiff?
- With whom did the defendant associate?
- Who are the witnesses?

"What" Questions

- What occurred during this cause of action or crime?
- What are the causes of action or crimes in question?
- What are the elements of these causes of action or crimes?
- What are the facts and actions committed by the defendant or suspect?
- What do the witnesses know?
- What evidence has been obtained?
- What was done with the evidence?
- What tools and other instruments were employed?
- What weapons or other real evidence exists?
- What means of transportation existed in the cause of action or commission of the crime?
- What was the modus operandi?

"Where" Questions

- Where was the cause of action or crime discovered?
- Where was the cause of action or crime committed?
- Where were the suspects or defendants seen?
- Where were the witnesses during the event?
- Where was the victim found?
- Where were the tools and other instruments obtained?
- Where does the suspect or defendant live?
- Where does or did the victim live?
- Where is the suspect or defendant now?
- Where are the places the suspect or defendant is likely to frequent?
- Where was the suspect or defendant tracked down?

"When" Questions

- When did the cause of action or crime take place?
- When was the cause of action or crime discovered?
- When were appropriate parties notified of the crime or cause of action?
- When did the police arrive at the scene?
- When was the victim last seen?
- When was the suspect apprehended?

"Why" Questions

- Why did the cause of action or crime take place?
- Why were particular tools or instruments utilized?
- Why was a particular method employed?
- Why did the witnesses talk?
- Why did the witnesses show reluctance in talking?

"How" Questions

- How did the cause of action or crime take place?
- How did the suspect or defendant get to the scene?
- How did the suspect or defendant depart from the scene?
- How did the suspect or defendant get the necessary information to commit the wrong?
- How much damage was done?
- How much property was stolen?
- How much skill, knowledge, and personal expertise was necessary for this cause of action or crime to take place?

The television character Lieutenant Columbo is a well-known example of an investigator using logical, deductive, and inferential reasoning. Carrying a notepad, he repeatedly states, "I have a few more questions. I hope I don't bother you." By doing so, he is sorting and reviewing the facts, the witnesses, and the evidence. The facts must be drawn out to produce the necessary results. Put another way, investigative logic is an exercise of the imagination. Imagination is not fabrication or delusion; it is the capacity and ability to draw natural inferences, based in logic and reality, from well-grounded facts. The investigator must be able to distinguish, compare, and contrast the reliable from the conjectural.[9]

Perseverance and Diligence

A competent investigator displays persistence and is thorough when obtaining necessary facts. Cases are resolved not by chance but by careful collection and assimilation of information. Most leads result from diligent investigation. When an investigator is able to produce an unknown or unsuspected witness, the discovery of the witness cannot usually be credited to chance; instead the witness is usually discovered because the investigator has followed a lead with tenacity and persistence.[10] In fact, the bulk of investigative work can be tedious. The practices of surveillance, government searches, auditing, record analysis, and title abstraction are often humdrum and repetitive. To succeed one must persist. The investigator needs to exhibit "deliberateness without excuse or mitigating factors."[11]

Contrary to the media's often dramatic portrayal, the investigative process is slow and deliberate. For example, in building a case for divorce based on infidelity, cruelty, or abuse, the investigator corroborates allegations with facts. The investigator objectively weighs the opposing party's position and withholds judgment on allegations of any client until demonstrated. In short, the investigative perspective requires a review of the whole picture—that is, all the parties and all the evidence that support a prima facie case.

Human Relations Skills

Because so much of an investigator's success depends on collecting information, the ability to interact positively with others is a valuable attribute. Investigators who relate poorly to others will struggle in the endeavor. Investigators must interact with clients, witnesses, agency heads, government employees, police and social service personnel, insurance and claims adjusters, and many occupational and social roles. If an investigator alienates individuals or cannot communicate in clear and understandable terms, the quality of response will be questionable. The investigator understands cultural differences, is sensitive to issues of gender and race, is a skilled listener, and understands all levels of human communications from the verbal to the nonverbal. Ideally investigators must have personal characteristics that attract, motivate, and encourage people to cooperate. Investigators must make their subjects comfortable.[12] Human relations include many aspects of interpersonal conduct:

- Express positive attitudes toward others.
- Manifest and show interest in others.
- Build good, solid human relations.
- Express empathy and concern for others.
- Establish personal rapport with others.
- Adapt to different personalities and circumstances.
- Communicate effectively with others.
- Be a believable, credible personality.
- Be clear and accurate in communications with others.
- Persuade and motivate other people.
- Manage conversations effectively in order to elicit information.
- Understand the emotional strengths and shortcomings of others.
- Exercise control of one's emotions.
- Make friends rather than enemies.[13]

From another vantage point, human relations skills encompass the art of communication. Communication can be verbal, nonverbal, or written. It is important that investigators also be attuned to body language and sensory perceptions, including sight, smell, taste, hearing, touch, and other environmental and human conditions.

The professional paralegal will understand these complex dynamics and conduct an investigation with a full appreciation of both the client and the underlying claim. To be effective, the paralegal must adopt effective tactics and strategies that encourage the sharing of information. At a minimum, the investigator must

1. Review the merit, eligibility, and worthiness of the cause or claim.
2. Ensure that the office provides the specific service.
3. Ask hard questions.
4. Don't make waves.
5. Make a record.[14]

Clearly, information gathering and the assimilation and collection of facts will be easier for those who can skillfully interact with others. Certain other personality traits benefit the investigator. Buckwalter outlines various qualities or characteristics necessary for a good investigator:

- *Affable: easy to speak to; amiable; good-natured.*
- *Agreeable: pleasing to the mind or senses; pleasant.*
- *Alert: ready and quick to understand or act; aware.*
- *Believable: one whom other people can believe and trust.*
- *Broad-minded: tolerant and considerate of others' views.*
- *Calm: able to control emotions; free from agitation and excitement.*
- *Courageous: dauntlessly able to meet difficulties and danger.*
- *Commonsense: possessing down-to-earth good judgment.*
- *Courteous: shows courtesy and respect to everyone.*
- *Curious: habitually inquisitive; anxious to learn; prying.*
- *Dependable: worthy of being depended on; reliable and trustworthy.*
- *Determined: resolute; decisive; able to see an investigation through to its finish.*
- *Empathic: able to put oneself in another's place and feel with that person.*
- *Energetic: possesses an active drive; performs with energy and reserve strength.*
- *Enthusiastic: inspired with living; ardent and alive; comes alive with interest.*
- *Faithful: firm in adherence to promises, contracts, and keeping one's word; worthy of confidence.*
- *Gentle: refined in manners; of a gentle rather than harsh nature; has a soothing, respectful influence on others.*
- *Honest: has integrity; truthful, frank, and straightforward in conduct or speech; free from fraud; honorable.*
- *Humble: unassuming but efficient; not aggressively and assertively proud.*
- *Impartial: unbiased; equitable; free from favoritism; fair.*
- *Ingenious: possessed of inventive ingenuity; shrewd; capable of creating a clever and effective solution to an investigative problem.*
- *Just: equitable and impartial in action and judgment.*
- *Kind: deals kindly with others; has a considerate nature.*
- *Law-abiding: conforms to or lives in accordance with law.*
- *Levelheaded: has sound judgment, balanced reasoning.*
- *Likable: is liked for attractive nature and qualities.*
- *Motivated: has inner qualities that impel to action.*
- *Natural: free from artificiality or pretense.*
- *Objective: able to concentrate on facts and external aspects of investigation without focusing on subjective feelings.*
- *Observant: takes careful notice; blessed with keen powers of observation.*
- *Patient: capable of calm waiting and forbearance under provocation; undaunted by obstacles and delays.*
- *Perceptive: discerning; aware; has alert senses.*

- *Persistent: tenacious; dogged; able to see the problem through.*
- *Persevering: steadfast in a pursuit or undertaking; persistent in spite of counterinfluences.*
- *Prudent: capable of directing and conducting self wisely and judiciously; discreet, sensible, reasonable, and skillful in the application of capabilities.*
- *Remembers well: capable of recollection and recall.*
- *Resourceful: able to fall back on other sources or strategies when the usual means are not effective; has reserve abilities and alternative resources.*
- *Responsible: accountable; reliable; able to answer for own conduct and obligations and to assume trust.*
- *Sagacious: has keen sense perceptions; discerning in judging people, motives, and means; shrewdly penetrating and farsighted.*
- *Self-confident: self-reliant and self-determined; able to rely on and have confidence in own efforts and skills.*
- *Self-controlled: in command of self, acts, and emotions; self-disciplined; self-possessed; has self-mastery.*
- *Sincere: is what he or she appears to be; genuine; real; unfeigned; wholehearted; free from hypocrisy or simulation.*
- *Sociable: of a nature to be companionable with others; friendly; able to have pleasant social relations.*
- *Thinker: capable of deliberate and deductive reasoning; able to reflect on and analyze information received and evidence examined.*
- *Thorough: able to carry things through to completion; painstaking, exact, and careful about details.*
- *Tolerant: tolerates practices, habits, and beliefs that differ from his or her own; treats those who differ with consideration.*
- *Understanding: capable of comprehending and discerning true interpretations; has reasoned judgment and rational discernment.*

Paralegal interviewing a witness
Credit: Ryan McVay/Getty Images.

- *Versatile: has many aptitudes; can adapt to circumstances and situations that require changes in tactics or positions.*
- *Vigilant: alertly watchful.*
- *Vigorous: strong; robust; full of physical strength; has the vitality to endure.*
- *Warmhearted: cordial and sympathetic; has feelings for the welfare of fellow beings.*
- *Well-spoken: can speak with propriety under all circumstances.*[15]

INTERVIEW AND QUESTIONING TECHNIQUES

The commencement of any investigation generally begins with an interview of a client, suspect, victim, witness, plaintiff, or defendant. The original interview conducted is usually the first human relations test of a paralegal's investigative skill. The importance of this initial interview cannot be overemphasized because it is here that the paralegal sets the tone of the investigative process. In the *Paralegal's Litigation Handbook*, Carole A. Bruno provides advice by noting that the successful interview and handling of any client depends on the following principles:

1. *A client's confidences are respected.*
2. *A client's cooperation is secured.*
3. *The investigator is friendly, courteous, and polite at all times.*
4. *The paralegal investigator practices the art of conversation.*
5. *The paralegal investigator exudes confidence and reassures the client.*
6. *The paralegal investigator promotes a good, positive attitude on behalf of the law firm he or she represents.*
7. *All information collected is an accurate presentation of the client's representations.*
8. *Regular and constant communication ensures subsequent releases of information called for in the initial interview.*[16]

Letting the client, witness, or other interested party subject to the interview know that he or she is a welcome, critical player promotes a positive interview environment. "An attitude of superiority by the investigator should be avoided. Many people may not have had the educational opportunities that may have been offered to the investigator, and nothing antagonizes . . . people more quickly than a patronizing attitude. Therefore, the investigator should try to meet everyone on as close to an equal level as possible and should show friendship toward those whom he intends to interview."[17] The paralegal investigator should be able to create an environment conducive to discussion. Many documents, litigation needs, forms, and checklists are available in the initial interview process. Various examples are outlined in the forms accompanying this chapter.

 First, a personal injury information worksheet should be filled out during an initial client interview (see Form 9.1 on the accompanying CD). The worksheet seeks background information necessary for permanent records, as well as pertinent data about opposing counsel, economic and personal injury losses, and insurance policy information. Form 9.2 is a wrongful death information worksheet. It includes information regarding the appropriate police agency, emergency medical service unit, and other medical personnel.

Using positive human relations skills is essential during the interview. Skill and expertise in eliciting information from witnesses or clients depends on many factors. The paralegal investigator is conducting and controlling the interview and setting the tone, tenor, and pace at which the information will be given. As a result, the burden rests on the investigator to get the necessary information successfully. Do not forget that the process of collecting information often involves the art of compromise.[18] Using the following guidelines ensures productive solicitation of desired information:

- *Do not prejudge anyone.*
- *Subdue all personal prejudices.*
- *Keep an open mind, receptive to all information, regardless of its nature.*
- *Try to evaluate each development on its own merit.*
- *Do not try to impress the witness.*
- *There is no justification for deliberate lies. At times, a bluff may be acceptable, but use great caution.*

- *Never underestimate the mentality or physical endurance of a witness.*
- *Do not show contempt.*
- *Do not make promises you cannot keep.*
- *Be fair.*
- *Avoid signs of personal nervousness.*
- *Avoid the impression that your only interest is information or confession. The witness must believe your only motivation is a search for the truth.*
- *Never raise your voice. The moment you do, you have endangered the interview.*
- *Avoid antagonizing the witness.*
- *Be a good listener.*
- *Be patient.*
- *Be gentle—you can always get tough after being gentle, but you can never be gentle after being tough.*
- *Be persistent.*
- *Be empathetic.*[19]

The interview process is the gateway to the law firm, agency, or other legal employer—and first impressions really do matter. It is just as crucially the place where counsel formalizes the representation, or at least discusses the issues, such as fees and scope of representation, that lead to formal representation. The initial interview, as Susan Martyn indicates, makes plain the nature of relationship whether formal or "accidental" in design.[20] The "accidental client" is one who thinks you have been hired when your understanding is not even remotely similar. Initial interviews can clear up any ambiguity. Correspondence and other documentation can help explain, outline, and teach the client about the case in question. A letter to the client fully outlining the nature of investigatory practice, settlement procedure, litigation steps and processes, and corresponding fees constitutes good investigative practice. (See Form 9.3 on the accompanying CD). Because most clients are new to the legal game and are unfamiliar with its processes, details about the particulars of the case should be included in the letter. It is helpful to reassure the client in the conclusion:

> *I am always available to discuss any aspect of your claim. I will not call you constantly and advise you of everything we are learning. I am sure you appreciate your peace and privacy at home and do not want constant phone calls advising you of every detail concerning your case. However, I will send requests for updates to you.*

When the paralegal investigator adopts a mentality of service to case and client, the collection of information and corresponding investigative steps are bound to be easier. Advise the client at every stage of the case history.

Each cause of action, whether civil or criminal, should have its own introductory forms, documents, and interview checklists. Regardless of the type of case, a paralegal investigator should delve into general issues that prove or disprove a contention. Bruno offers some interview planning suggestions applicable in every sort of representation:

1. *Determine the scope of the investigation.*
2. *Formulate your investigative plan.*
3. *Conduct your preliminary investigation in the office.*
4. *Be prompt and conduct your investigation in a timely manner.*
5. *Gather and review relevant facts and basic documents carefully.*
6. *Identify basic principles of law.*
7. *Obtain further guidance when necessary.*
8. *Visit the scene of the accident immediately.*
9. *Make contacts and establish credibility in the community.*
10. *Follow leads and develop your sources.*
11. *Interview all witnesses and obtain statements.*
12. *Develop an inquisitive attitude.*
13. *Obtain and preserve evidence properly.*
14. *Document all information.*
15. *Revise your investigative plan when necessary.*

16. *Know when to obtain the assistance of a professional investigator.*

17. *Seek help from professional experts when necessary.*

18. *Report your progress.*

19. *Recognize the necessity for further discovery.*[21]

Some other examples of initial interview information-gathering forms include a client file form for the collection of information regarding addresses, insurance companies, and employers (see Form 9.4 on the accompanying CD). Using a form whereby the client can indicate the location, size, and scope of specific physical injuries is helpful.

Two other useful forms include one that contains information about the motor vehicles of either plaintiff or defendant (see Form 9.5 on the accompanying CD) and one, called a "witness information sheet" (see Form 9.6), that enables information to be collected about witnesses. Both will help the paralegal gather sufficient information.

It is important that the paralegal investigator be aware of the ethical dilemmas that may occur during the initial interview process. Giving legal advice or opinions, or making any representation regarding the merits or value of a case, directly violates the Model Code of Professional Responsibility, as well as the various disciplinary findings of state and local bars.[22] A recent Utah decision publicly admonished and formally disciplined an attorney that "permitted his paralegal to interview clients, provide legal advice, and accept retainers. He shared legal fees with the paralegal."[23] Because the initial interview stage in screening cases is amply documented, the substantive integrity, credibility, and merit of a legal or factual contention should be scrutinized closely. Experienced attorneys frequently can spot questionable cases in the interview process. Be wary of the following characters:

1. *Clients who wish to make a point.*

2. *Clients who are crusaders.*

3. *Clients who simply want revenge.*

4. *Clients who have a "pot of gold at the end of the rainbow" mentality.*

5. *Clients who are mentally or emotionally disturbed.*

6. *Clients who proclaim too much the merits of their case.*

7. *Clients who are mere attorney shoppers.*

8. *Clients who have other underlying and unknown motivations.*[24]

Paralegal investigators are often asked by attorneys whether a case has legal merit and/or whether the party to be represented is worth the price of representation. Experience teaches paralegal investigators that certain cases are not worth the trouble. Paralegal investigators should observe how the client tells the story. "Proving the case may require that this person be a witness; [one] must judge the client's effectiveness in this role and include that judgment in the evaluation of whether the case should be accepted. Clients may be abrasive, dull, neurotic, alcoholic, nervous, argumentative, or entirely inarticulate, yet still be able to testify effectively about potentially winning claims that the attorney can accept."[25]

Allen R. Earl's "Conducting the Initial Interview: Rules and Red Flags" zeroes in on the red flags of suspect potential clients. Keep in mind these characteristics:

- *People who clearly indicate they just want to make money from the "legal system."*
- *People who announce they have a set damages figure in mind.*
- *People who purport to "know the law."*
- *Injury victims who let others do the talking.*
- *Spouses who are not injured but insist that counsel include loss of consortium in the claim.*
- *Cases turned down by other attorneys.*
- *People wanting to engage in a personal vendetta.*
- *People who have major personality conflicts with the lawyer.*[26]

The paralegal investigator can help the attorney filter out potentially troublesome cases during the initial interview stage.[27]

The initial interview process accomplishes various ends. Charfoos and Christensen characterize the interview process as consisting of two phases. Phase I determines the eligibility, merit, and credibility of a case. Phase II is geared to the information-gathering process. A flowchart illustrating these phases is shown in Figure 9.1.

FIGURE 9.1
Flowchart of the Client Interview Process

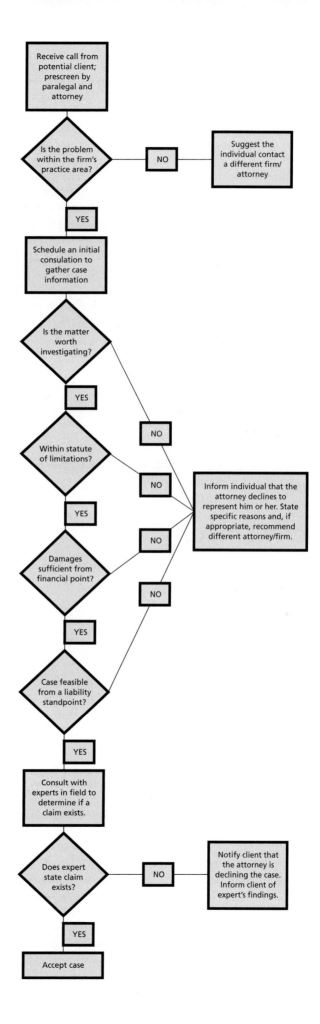

Receive call from potential client; prescreen by paralegal and attorney

Is the problem within the firm's practice area? — NO → Suggest the individual contact a different firm/attorney

YES

Schedule an initial consulation to gather case information

Is the matter worth investigating?

YES

NO

Within statute of limitations?

NO

YES

Inform individual that the attorney declines to represent him or her. State specific reasons and, if appropriate, recommend different attorney/firm.

NO

Damages sufficient from financial point?

NO

YES

Case feasible from a liability standpoint?

YES

Consult with experts in field to determine if a claim exists.

Does expert state claim exists? — NO → Notify client that the attorney is declining the case. Inform client of expert's findings.

YES

Accept case

During Phase II of the interview process, analysis of the legal issues occurs. This is when calculations of damages, determinations of rights, obligations, and liabilities, and findings of affirmative defenses or counterclaims are made. Questions regarding strategy and settlement consultation are presented. It is possible to determine that the legal argument is meritorious yet find that damage collection is at best nominal or remote. By the end of this secondary analysis, a clear-cut decision is made regarding both representation and strategy. What is equally apparent is that the interview process need not end at the initial phase. The paralegal investigator should revisit the client or witness at various stages throughout the case history. "Interviews can be conducted at various stages of the case, including the initial meeting during pretrial preparation, and during trial activity."[28]

Finally, the paralegal investigator needs to accept interviewees as found. Clients may be cooperative, friendly, or resistant to questioning or even hostile to the underlying case. Witnesses, clients, defendants, suspects, or other parties may exhibit personal traits and characteristics that are difficult to accept or gauge.

Considerable time could be spent analyzing all forms of witnesses and their evidentiary qualities. Creating a database including the essential information provided by a witness is a good practice. Such a database should include

- *Name.*
- *Address.*
- *Telephone number.*
- *Issue that witness provides evidence of, along with liability or damages or both.*
- *Elements of cause of action of which the witness provides evidence.*
- *Whether statement was taken.*
- *Abstract of witness statement recounting facts actually witnessed.*
- *An evaluation of the witness's expected performance in court (some rating scale—from 1 to 10, for example—may be used).*[29]

THE INVESTIGATIVE PROCESS

The investigative process serves many purposes in the criminal and civil justice systems:

- *Determine liability or guilt/innocence.*
- *Determine damages, costs, fines, or punishment.*
- *Locate evidence.*
- *Acquire sufficient evidence to meet the burden of proof.*[30]

Investigation depends on the quality and content of evidence collection. Whether a statement of a witness or the report of a forensic scientist on a ballistics issue, the paralegal garners an evidentiary deposit for case and cause. "Without evidence, there is no proof. Without proof, burdens are not met, and convictions, verdicts, or judgments are an impossibility. Evidence directs the tribunal, the jury, and the practitioners advocating its content toward actions to be taken."[31] A survey of the common investigative sources follows.

Witnesses

Testimonial evidence is generally one of the more useful tools in the proof of a civil or criminal case. While always useful, testimonial evidence should never be accepted at face value, but instead scrutinized closely for veracity and reliability. Testimony of any witness is subject to impeachment during cross-examination. A witness may be the plaintiff or defendant in a civil or criminal case. A witness may be an individual party suffering from an act of negligence or medical malpractice or intentional tort. A witness may be an eyewitness who can testify about the facts and conditions of an event. A witness could be qualified as a character witness—a person capable of attesting to the community reputation of an individual's character. A witness may also be expert, qualified to testify in certain fields of expertise that are beyond the scope of the lay witness's knowledge. Witnesses can be further labeled as friendly to one's case or as adverse, unfriendly, or hostile.

The techniques of interviewing a witness call for refined interactive skills. Preparation of background information about a witness is advisable where there is some reason to believe that the witness will be reluctant or hostile. An investigation of the witness (occupation, family friends, –and so forth) will often suggest some method of approach that would otherwise have gone unnoticed.[32] Correspondence with any prospective witness is essential (see Forms 9.7 and 9.8 on the accompanying CD).

Attorneys and investigators should evaluate the quality of the witness as the witness statement (Form 9.9 on the accompanying CD) is completed. Such letters should not be antagonistic or excessively legal in presentation. They amicably request cooperation from an adverse party. Using a witness questionnaire is helpful (see Form 9.10).[33]

Types of Witnesses

Missing or Unknown Witnesses   Paralegals need to realize that witnesses can be difficult to locate. A missing witness is a common phenomenon in civil and criminal litigation.[34] Finding an unknown or missing witness can be cumbersome, particularly in criminal matters. "Missing witnesses sometimes submerge into an underground hiding system, particularly in major metropolitan areas. In domestic relations cases, especially in the prosecution of individuals who neglect support or alimony obligations, investigators have to track down individuals who move from jurisdiction to jurisdiction and create new, illegal identities."[35] Here are some practical suggestions for locating missing witnesses:

- *Telephone books:* Scan all available telephone books for names or aliases that might match the individual in question. Also look in earlier phone books because it is common for names that were once listed to become unlisted pending or during certain legal difficulties. Also, if a number is secured, you might try to call it and use feigned, though not illegal, circumstances to introduce yourself to determine the location of a specific person.

- *Mail and telegrams:* The use of certified mail, telegrams, or other electronic means can be a practical and useful way of tracking a witness if a last known address is found. You may use a subpoena or summons to serve on a witness that will satisfy most jurisdictional requirements.

- *Interview of client:* The client will often have knowledge of secondary addresses, hiding places, or insights into customs and habits regarding travel and location of a given individual.

- *Police reports or other documents:* The client, attorney, or paralegal investigator should check whether other parties who were in attendance at a crime scene or accident setting obtained the names of other witnesses in some type of report or documentation.

- *Canvass of community:* With a picture or other identification aid in hand, paralegal investigators can canvass businesses, shops, restaurants, and people of the community. This is a typical and long-standing investigative technique.

- *Newspaper and other media sources:* Frequently, at scenes of crimes or in personal injury litigation, a reporter will have taken pictures or made some record of the case in question.

- *Public transportation carriers:* Checking with bus drivers, taxi drivers, and other individuals who provide regular service to the public may lead to identification of a specific witness.

- *City address directories:* If a name is not available, a street address can sometimes be cross-referenced with a specific name if a telephone company provides such information. City directories (available at most public libraries) also provide information. Much of this information is now available online through area telephone service providers.

- *Postal service:* Registered mail, certified mail, and other means of address authentication commonly employed in service-of-process techniques are useful ways of verifying the location of a specific witness. Although postal regulations do not provide for the direct disclosure of forwarding addresses, there are indirect methods of finding the location of a specific witness. In criminal actions, under the authority of the postal inspector, this traditionally confidential information is made available to public law enforcement representatives.

- *Internet:* Much information is accessible online. Searching various e-mail providers such as Yahoo!, MSN, and AOL can turn up e-mail addresses. Many online fee-based search services exist as well. Interest-specific newsgroups, chat rooms, and organizational and school-based Web sites can also provide leads.

- *Other leads:* Check social clubs, union halls, professional organizations, schools and educational institutions, utility companies, veterans' offices, government agencies, welfare offices, recreational organizations, public record depositories, departments of motor vehicles, voter registration records, marriage records, birth and death records, police records, and National Crime Information Center (NCIC) records.

In "How to Locate Elusive Witnesses," Elaine Thorp suggests a check of the following records and leads:

1. *Real estate records*
   a. *Deeds*
   b. *Contracts*
   c. *Witness name*
   d. *Spouse name*
   e. *Other relatives' names*

2. *Tax records*
   a. *Real property*
   b. *Personal property*
   c. *Witness name*
   d. *Spouse name*

3. *Divorce records*
   a. *Witness name*
   b. *Ex-spouse name*
   c. *Ex-spouse's address*
   d. *Attorney who handled the divorce*
   e. *Children's names*

4. *Criminal records*
   a. *Witness name*
   b. *Spouse name*
   c. *Attorney name*
   d. *Probation officer*

5. *Probate records*
   a. *Death of witness*
   b. *Death of spouse*
   c. *Death of relative—is witness a personal representative of the estate?*

6. *Marriage license records*
   a. *Witness name*
   b. *Spouse name*
   c. *Name of relatives/parents*
   d. *Name of hometown*

7. *U.S. Postal Service*
   a. *Forwarding address/address search*
   b. *Is mail actually delivered to the address you were given?*
   c. *Does letter carrier know witness?*

8. *City directory*
   a. *Witness name*
   b. *Spouse name*
   c. *Witness occupation*
   d. *Spouse occupation*
   e. *Current or former address*
   f. *Current or former telephone number*
   g. *Names of current or former neighbors*
   h. *Neighbors' addresses, telephone numbers, and occupations*

9. *Bureau of motor vehicles*
   a. *Witness name*
   b. *Witness driver's license number*
   c. *Current address*
   d. *Current city of resident*
   e. *Insurance company and agent name*

10. *Public utilities*
    a. *Current address*
    b. *Confirm service at an address*

FIGURE 9.2
Advertisement for a Tracking Firm

Source: The Missing Person Search Bureau (a division of Worldwide Tracers), P.O. Box 511, Mansfield, TX 76063-0511, (817) 473-0449, fax (817) 473-0113, mail@ missingpersonsearchbureau. com, http://www.missingper-sonsearchbureau.com/ intlsearch.html.

11. *Libraries*
    a. *Telephone directories for various cities*
    b. *City directories*
    c. *List of local businesses*
    d. *Member rosters for local professional organizations, service organizations, clubs, and hobby groups.*[36]

Paralegal investigators also must develop relationships with firms that locate missing heirs, witnesses, and judgment debtors. Firms that specialize in locating missing individuals regularly advertise in legal periodicals and journals. Tracking firms are particularly helpful in the areas of estates and trusts, criminal law and litigation, and debtor/creditor collection practices (see Figure 9.2).

Internet providers are crucial players in the process of finding missing witnesses. Hundreds of private companies now deliver such services on the Web. See the list in Appendix D for some examples.

Character Witnesses   Any legal dispute involving the credibility of a victim or defendant may rely on the use of a character witness. Character witnesses are also used to bolster the credibility of a damage claim or to mitigate potential punishments.[37] Consider a convicted defendant who wishes to minimize the severity of a sentence. He or she will parade before the sentencing judge a selection of individuals who can attest to his or her good and reputable character. Often used are people with prominent reputations in the community, such as teachers, ministers, priests, rabbis, or individuals who have a long-standing relationship with the convicted defendant.[38]

Character evidence is commonly witnessed in these types of cases:

- Proving or defending the credibility of a rape complaint based on some disputed theory of promiscuity.

- Supporting or impeaching the credibility of a white-collar criminal who claims his or her actions were merely accidental or negligent rather than intentional.

- Proving or disproving a person's right to maintain custody of a child.

- Proving or disproving a case of child or spouse abuse.

- Proving or disproving the credibility of a defendant based on previous convictions.

In sexual offense litigation, the role of character evidence can cause additional victimization for the victim. In short, the victim's history of sexual conduct may be scrutinized as relevant not only to the character of the victim and possibly the witness, but also as to questions of credibility. In the federal system, FRE Rule 412 attempts to structure the propriety of evidence dealing with sexual propensities or proclivities in crime victims:

> *Evidence generally inadmissible. The following evidence is not admissible in any civil or criminal proceeding involving alleged sexual misconduct except as provided in subdivisions (b) and (c):*
> *Evidence offered to prove that any alleged victim engaged in other sexual behavior.*
> *Evidence offered to prove any alleged victim's sexual predisposition.*[39]

At subpart (b) of the same rule, an exception has been carved out:

> *In a criminal case, the following evidence is admissible, if otherwise admissible under these rules:*
> *Evidence of specific instances of sexual behavior by the alleged victim offered to prove that a person other than the accused was the source of semen, injury, or other physical evidence.*
> *Evidence of specific instances of sexual behavior by the alleged victim with respect to the person accused of the sexual misconduct offered by the accused to prove consent or by the prosecution, and*
> *Evidence the exclusion of which would violate the constitutional rights of the defendant.*

In a civil case, evidence offered to prove the sexual behavior or sexual predisposition of any alleged victim is admissible if it is otherwise admissible under these rules and its probative value substantially outweighs the danger of harm to any victim and of unfair prejudice to any party. Evidence of an alleged victim's reputation is admissible only if it has been placed in controversy by the alleged victim.[40]

Lay Witnesses A lay witness, simply defined, is any witness who is not an expert. A lay witness must be able to testify, record, recollect, narrate, attest to, and affirm certain conditions and facts. In essence, the ability to relate information corresponds in the most basic sense of the word to the *competency* of the witness. Additionally, the witness must have the mental and emotional competency to outline in some logical sequence the facts, conditions, and events before the trier. Under the Federal Rules of Evidence, a lay witness's testimony "is limited to those opinions or inferences that are (a) rationally based on the perception of the witness and (b) helpful to a clear understanding of the witness's testimony or the determination of a fact in issue."[41]

Generally the law does not favor lay opinion; however, certain opinions that are the result of personal observation and perception are readily accepted, such as those related to alcohol intoxication, speed at which a vehicle was moving, height, distance or other natural perceptions. In any investigative process, the paralegal must be confident that the facts being attested to are objective.

A traditional example of lay witness activity includes a witness's description of a suspect. Figure 9.3 shows a descriptive terms and characterizations sheet used by police officers in attempting to formulate a basic description of a suspect.

Another example of lay witness testimony can be prepared by the compilation of a witness questionnaire involving a negligent auto or DUI case. With Form 9.11 on the accompanying CD, the witness is advised that he or she has been a witness to the accident in question. The witness is asked to share his or her perceptions and understanding of the events that took place. Paralegal investigators should use witness documents and reports as the foundation for any lay witness testimony preparation.

Developing ongoing relationships with lay witnesses in a criminal case is an important function for paralegals who work in the office of a district attorney or public defender. Form 9.12 on the accompanying CD is a sample letter sent to a witness who is deemed important in a criminal matter.

Paralegals play a special role in the preparation of the lay witness for subsequent litigation. Urge the witness to be honest and forthcoming. Encourage the witness to be genuine and natural in response. The National Institute of Trial Advocacy posts unrivaled recommendations on the preparation of lay witnesses:

- *Cross-examination can be as forthright as direct examination.*
- *Obvious weaknesses should be openly acknowledged.*
- *No information should be volunteered.*
- *Answers should be formulated only after questions have been completed.*

FIGURE 9.3 Suspect Description Form

Suspect Description Form

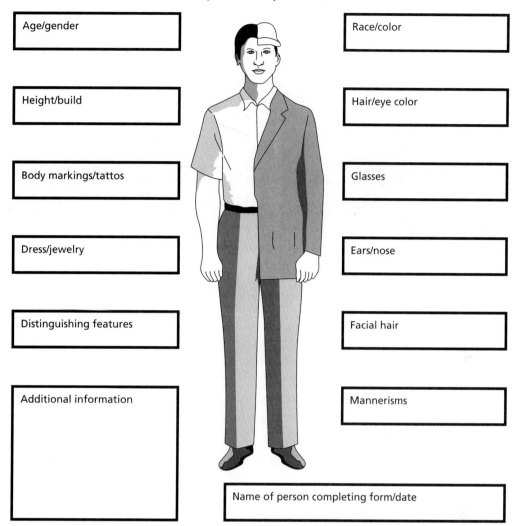

Age/gender

Height/build

Body markings/tattos

Dress/jewelry

Distinguishing features

Additional information

Race/color

Hair/eye color

Glasses

Ears/nose

Facial hair

Mannerisms

Name of person completing form/date

- *Explanation can be requested if a question is unclear.*
- *Answers should not include any speculation.*
- *Answers can be explained.*
- *Never argue with an opposing lawyer.*
- *Witnesses should not look over toward their own lawyers before answering questions.*
- *Prior discussions of testimony should be acknowledged.*
- *Witnesses should listen for objections.*[42]

Expert Witnesses   The role of expert witnesses in litigation is a topic of considerable range and importance.[43] In our complex society, judicial reliance on expert testimony as a form of explanation and understanding has steadily increased over the last five decades. "If scientific, technical, or other specialized knowledge will assist the trier of fact to understand the evidence or to determine a fact in issue, a witness qualified as an expert may testify thereto in the form of an opinion or otherwise."[44] Why and how experts have generated such enthusiasm in the legal system is open to question.[45] It is accepted that an expert has a certain level of knowledge, understanding, and experience that exceeds that of the ordinary layperson. Standards of education, personal qualification, experiential activities, scholarly publication, and production indicate whether a witness can be properly qualified as an expert. The areas of expertise are limited only by judicial decision making (that is, a finding as to whether the field of testimony is scientifically acceptable).

FIGURE 9.4
Commonly Used Expert Witnesses

Actuaries	Geologists
Agricultural experts	Meteorologists
Anthropologists	Metallurgists
Appraisers	Microscopic specialists
Archaeologists	Nuclear scientists
Aviation safety experts	Physicists
Biologists	Psychologists
Botanists	Psychiatrists
Chemists	Radiologists
Criminalists	Security analysts
Electrical contractors	Surveyors
Engineers	Water pollution experts
Foresters	

Courts have historically construed certain disciplines as having "crossed the barrier of the judicial acceptability"[46] while barring the admissibility of those fields suspiciously viewed as untried. Under the *Frye* doctrine (applicable for most of the 20th century), the expert and his or her expertise had to undergo the following tests:

1. The validity of the underlying scientific principle.
2. The validity of the technique or process that applies the principle.
3. The condition of any instrumentation used in the process.
4. Adherence to proper procedures.
5. The qualifications of the person who performs the test.
6. The qualifications of a person who interprets the results.[47]

Not all fields can withstand the scrutiny. For example, the fields of astrology or parasensory perception have not as yet attracted sufficient scientific support to be viewed as legitimate scientific endeavors. On the other hand, psychiatry and psychology (which in longitudinal terms have only recently come into vogue) are judicially noticed. In recent years, at least in the federal courts, evidence tends to be accepted if it is "helpful," regardless of its general reliability. "The federal courts, by and through the pivotal ruling *Daubert v. Merrill Dow Pharmaceuticals, Inc.*,[48] have effectively made the *Frye* rule moot in their jurisdictions."[49] Hard science has been replaced with a theory of helpfulness—and has delegated the primary task of making judgments about the reliability of a science to the judge over the scientists themselves. *Daubert* essentially permitted the admission of things beyond traditional science including "technical and specialized knowledge."[50]

Experts come in many shapes and sizes. The list in Figure 9.4 represents commonly employed scientific, medical, and technical experts.

Experts can be discovered in many sources and directories. The *Lawyer's Desk Reference Manual* contains pertinent information about expert groups and associations. In addition, *American Jurisprudence (Am. Jur.) Trials* contains a directory of experts with appropriate addresses.[51] Experts and their respective expertise are further broken down into specialties and subspecialties. Some examples are shown in Figure 9.5.

Private consulting firms are evident everywhere in the American legal landscape. For a fee, these firms provide a tailor-made witness for the cause behind the litigation. See Figure 9.6 for an example of a consulting firm.

No matter who the witness may be, each will be adjudged by the court for admissibility purposes. Expert witnesses must be grounded in both personal expertise and evidentiary reliability.[52] A foundation for the testimony must be laid to assure relevant testimony. The court must be convinced that "the subject matter of the expert's proposed testimony must be relevant.... Second, the expert's field must be one requiring scientific, technical, or specialized knowledge. Third, the witness must be shown to have the background necessary to qualify an expert in the field."[53] To

FIGURE 9.5
Experts Categorized by Specialties and Subspecialties

Source: David Rubsamen, Locating Medical Experts, 2 Am. Jur. Trials 357–407 (1964) (Supplement 2005). To access the most current version of this form, please visit www.westlaw.com.

Allergies	Nursing
Anesthesiology	Obstetrics
Cardiology	Occupational therapy
Chiropractics	Ophthalmology and optometry
Dentistry	Orthopedics
Dermatology	Osteopathy
Endocrinology	Otolaryngology
Gastroenterology	Pathology
Geriatrics	Pediatrics
Gerontology	Pharmacy
Gynecology	Physical medicine and therapy
Hematology	Plastic surgery
Hospital administration	Preventive medicine
Immunology	Proctology
Industrial medicine	Psychiatry and psychoanalysis
Internal medicine	Psychology
Medical laboratory technology	Surgery
Medical photography	Urology
Neurology and neurosurgery	Veterinary science
Nuclear medicine	X-ray technology

assure these fundamental requirements, use the expert witness questionnaire shown in Form 9.13 on the accompanying CD.

In pretrial practice, experts are prepared; they are informed of all issues and afforded the opportunity to thoroughly scrutinize the case. In a way, paralegals act as coaches. Because experts sometimes appear patronizing or condescending to a jury, advice on mannerisms and personal

FIGURE 9.6
Advertisement for a Legal Consulting Firm

Source: First Advantage, 14030 Thunderbolt Place, Suite 700, Chantilly, VA 20151, 703-375-4340, http://www.fadv.com/Litigation-Consulting/index.html.

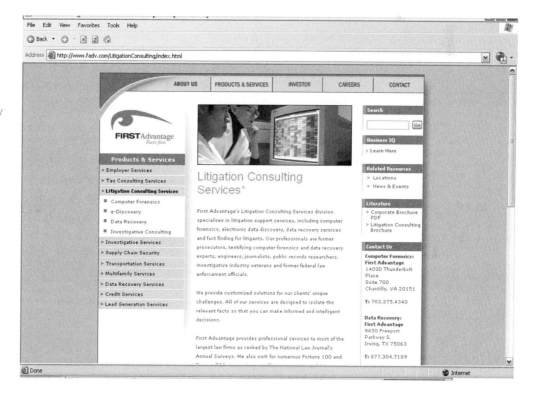

FIGURE 9.7
Advertisement for Medical Expert Service

Source: Indox Consulting, 479 Church Street Suite 2, San Francisco, CA 94114, 415-568-7116, info@indox-consulting.com, http://www.indoxconsulting.com.

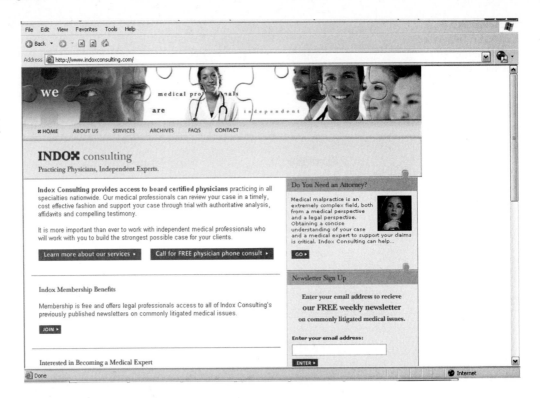

approach can be needed. The bearing, stature, and demeanor of an expert are often important. Check backgrounds to see whether there are any skeletons to unearth, such as false degrees or contradictory reports and results of the same author. Also, research contrary studies or data that refute the expert opinion. An expert who is well qualified, makes a good presentation before a jury and a judge, and can explain the issues in a layperson's terms is the desirable candidate.[54]

The Expert's Role in Screening Cases

Besides their testimonial capacity, experts play a major role in case screening for lawyers, government agencies, and other interested parties. Over the last three decades, myriad private companies, foundations, and entities have assisted the busy practitioner with case evaluation and assessment. These providers review medical records and scientific reports, as well as weigh and evaluate the merits of a given case. See Figure 9.7 for an example of this type of screening tool.

Expert services are not only delivered by the private sector. Experts can be located in a multiplicity of settings, such as these:

- Professional associations.
- Colleges and universities.
- Trade schools.

- Scholarly literature and reviews.
- Who's Who books and series.
- Telephone books.

Expert referral services are well entrenched in the legal system. Such firms catalog and list a cadre of experts in various subject matters. One national firm, Technical Advisory Service for Attorneys (TASA), claims to have more than 18,500 experts under contract, representing more than 1,500 categories of expertise. Figure 9.8 illustrates the breadth of specialty areas covered by such firms.

Paralegals should consult the following directories for location of experts:

The Directory of Medical Specialists
A. N. Marquis Co.
200 East Ohio Street
Chicago, IL 60611

Consultants and Consulting Organization
Directory

Consultant's Project
Box 428
College Park, MD 20740

The Lawyer's Guide to Legal Consultants
Expert Witnesses, Services, Books, and
Products

FIGURE 9.8
Partial Listing of TASA Expert Areas

Source: Technical Advisory Service for Attorneys, Inc., http://www.tasanet.com. Go to "Expertise Directory— Major Category Search." The TASA Group Headquarters, 1166 DeKalb Pike, Blue Bell, PA 19422-1853, 800-523-2319, experts@tasanet.com.

Aerospace	Earth science and oceanography
Agriculture and animal husbandry	Electronic communications
Appraisal and real estate	Electronics and electricity
Athletics, recreation, physical education, and leisure	Environmental
Atmospheric sciences	Fire
Automotive	Industrial engineering
Behavioral and social sciences	Laboratory and testing
Biological and medical sciences	Maritime
Business, finance, management, and economics	Materials
Chemistry	Mechanical engineering
Communicating arts	Nuclear science and technology
Communications (electronic)	Ordnance and explosives
Computer and mathematical sciences	Physics
Construction	Safety and industrial hygiene
	Transportation

Attorney's Profiles International
30700 Bainbridge Road, Suite H
Solon, OH 44139-2291

Locating Scientific and Technical Experts
2 AM. JUR. TRIALS, 302–356 (1987)

Locating Medical Experts
2 AM. JUR. TRIALS, 112–133 (1987)

Professional Safety, Inc. (PSI)
100 Euston Royal
Palm Beach, FL 33411 1-800-562-7233

The Internet also delivers options for finding expert witnesses. The Washburn School of Law has amassed a comprehensive Web directory of expert service providers. (See Appendix E.) Though the field of experts seems quite unlimited, paralegal investigators and attorneys should remember that many experts are close to home, such as the claimant's personal physician. (See Form 9.14 on the accompanying CD). At its base, the choice of an expert must make sense both topically and economically. The expert chosen must corroborate and confirm the basis of the case and must possess the necessary expertise to offer an opinion. "Among the matters to investigate are education, licensure, or board certification, if applicable, and practical experience. Experience should be evaluated for quality as well as quantity. Factors affecting quality include exposure to authorities in the field or recognition by peers through awards or honors or membership in professional societies."[55]

Be cautious in the evaluation and selection of experts. In some ways the process is corrupted, especially when one considers the economic motivation for testimony. Experts, at least in the private sector, hope to deliver a favorable product for client and cause. This payment for services prompts a natural bias.[56] Recognize that this bias alone may taint the integrity of the opinion. Add to this the general unreliability of certain opinions, and one wonders why experts are given the homage they are. Psychiatry exemplifies this irony because there is little doubt that this discipline has room for contrary viewpoints. "Another challenge sometimes made to the admissibility of expert evidence is that the failure of experts in the field to agree—either in the specific case or in general—warrants the exclusion of the evidence. The Court has rejected this challenge in a variety of contexts."[57] Whatever can be said about the field, it is an imprecise undertaking.

Be cautious and skeptical of expert theory. Degrees and experience do not necessary equate with truth. Expert evidence must meet minimal standards of corroboration and confirmation, and the scope of testimony must "have a logical nexus to the case at bar, the content of which is based upon a substantive foundation of data, studies, reports, experiments, and firsthand observation and which can result in meaningful testimony."[58] Paralegals should gauge with caution the testimonial and evidentiary results of experts.[59]

If expert services are needed, prepare a contract that sufficiently sets out the duties of the expert and the corresponding compensation (see Form 9.15 on the accompanying CD).

FIGURE 9.9
Typical Investigative Contacts

Source: Paul Fuqua & James Wilson, Security Investigator's Handbook 21–22 (1979).

Bank officers and personnel	Neighborhood "busybodies" and "snitches"
Body shop and auto repair specialists	Newspaper reporters and editors
Code enforcement officers	Police officers
Corporation registration and licensing employees	Private security employees
County clerks	Recorders of deeds
Credit office employees	Registrars of wills
Department and retail store employees	School and educational personnel
Emergency medical services personnel	Social club heads and board members
Government employees	Tag, title, and inspection employees
Hospital and medical personnel	Tax agents
Insurance company personnel	Telephone employees
	Tow truck operators

The Collection of General Information

Public and private sources of information aid the paralegal investigator. A good investigator develops contacts and sources for gathering information. Police officers, detectives, private security officers, revenue agents, defense investigators, General Accounting Office (GAO) investigators, and any other party engaged in this type of activity develop contacts that can provide information. The practice of law (especially cases of domestic relations, corporate and business litigation, criminal and civil matters, and personal injury litigation) also requires numerous contacts. Typical contacts are shown in Figure 9.9.

Contacts represent individuals willing to provide information that otherwise might be difficult to find. Using various information resources, the paralegal investigator is capable of maneuvering through the maze of government and private entities and institutions that contain information. The talented paralegal investigator knows how to get this information quickly and saves time and energy in the process.

Even if information is available for public review and inspection, knowing the steps and requirements for access can be vexing. According to Paul Fuqua and James Wilson, "the well-prepared investigator knows where information generally is kept, and what kinds of information are kept where. If he knows this, he will have a head start on finding something in particular. If he does not, he will be like a man looking for a needle and not even knowing which haystack to search."[60]

Information and contacts are not exclusively governmental or institutional in nature. Ordinary citizens also know a great deal. Cultivate individuals with access to information; those who have access to the rich, famous, or powerful; and those who have unique opportunities to overhear or observe conduct (because of their positions or duties). Some of those individuals might be

Airline clerks and attendants.	Elevator operators.
Barbers.	Gas station attendants.
Bartenders.	Hairdressers.
Bellhops.	Hat check personnel.
Building managers.	Hosts and hostesses.
Bus drivers.	Hotel clerks.
Cab drivers (trip sheets).	Janitors.
Carhops (drive-ins and the like).	Maids (bars, hotels, motels).
Custodians.	Mail carriers.
Dance hall operators.	Mechanics.
Delivery service personnel.	Neighborhood children.
Dentists.	News vendors.
Door attendants.	Night watch personnel.

Operators of street businesses and entertainment houses.

Paper deliverers.

Parking lot attendants.

Parolees and probationers.

Physicians.

Pool hall operators.

Public utility service personnel.

Railroad ticket agents and conductors.

Restaurant servers.

Shoeshine operators.

Street vendors (especially all-night stands).

Switchboard operators.

Public Sources

Public access to governmental information is guaranteed under statute and common-law principles. Although that access is not absolute and is subject to certain administrative oversights, significant information of public record may be useful to law firms, agencies, and other employers of paralegal investigators. This information includes judgments, birth records, marriage records, filings for incorporation and other business entities, tax records, voter registrations, and motor vehicle and auto licensing documentation. Informed investigators know that federal, state, and local agencies can provide such data and information.

Federal Agencies   A wide variety of federal agencies can provide valuable information. The U.S. Blue Pages Web site at www.usbluepages.gov provides an easy and fast way to search federal agency listings by state, city, area code, agency or service, and keyword (see Figure 9.10).

State and Local Agencies   State and local governments gather and retain extensive information. With information ranging from birth, death, and marriage records to other vital statistics, state and local governments are key places to conduct investigations. Most states publish guides or manuals that outline their operations and other pertinent information. All states have some type of administrative bureaucracy that handles records and other formal documentation. A trained paralegal investigator will be able to get information from these agencies. Some of these agencies include the following:

- Departments of motor vehicles.
- Departments of transportation/streets and highways.
- Departments of labor and industry.
- Departments of corrections.
- Departments of corporations and business.
- Secretaries of state.
- Departments of vocational rehabilitation.
- Medical examiner's offices.
- County recorders of deeds.
- Registers of wills.
- County clerks.

- Tax assessors.
- Voter registration offices.
- Bureaus of vital statistics.
- State revenue commissions.
- Departments of insurance.
- Departments of business, professions, and licensing.
- District attorney's offices.
- Offices of county coroners.
- Traffic departments.
- Departments of public works.
- County and local courthouses.
- Department of Homeland Security offices.

Under most circumstances, the information within these agencies is of public record. Usually found in city halls, courthouses, and county offices, this information includes property deeds and titles; records of lawsuits, marriages, births, deaths, probated wills, financial statements, transfers of property, tax liens, mechanic's liens, property taxes, military discharges, divorces, criminal convictions; records of lunacy hearings; and other matters.[61] Whether a record is open for public inspection has been the subject of considerable litigation, particularly at the federal level. With the passage of the *Freedom of Information Act,* more government publications, reports, and documents are now available to the public than in the past. It is important to note, however, that "[n]ot all records, documents, and writings possessed by the government are made available to the public. In some cases, particularly where communications are made in confidence to officials, public interests may require secrecy."[62]

FIGURE 9.10
U.S. Blue Pages
Web Site

Source: U.S. Blue Pages:
http://www.usbluepages.gov/.

Private Sources

Significant information is also available through private sources. Besides using the services of independent private investigators, detectives, and security companies, paralegal investigators can take advantage of numerous sources that are often bypassed in the investigative process, including directories, databases, atlases, libraries, newspapers, professional associations, and law enforcement agencies.

Directories, Databases, and Atlases   Historically, certain information has been collected in directories, atlases, or other databases. Specific topics include information about trademarks, congressional record announcements, corporate operation and value, affirmative action programs, labor and employment statistics, and other business record keeping. With the arrival of electronic data transmission, considerable information is stored within these directories:

- *Standard & Poor's News.*
- *Standard & Poor's Register of Corporations.*
- *Moody's Corporate News.*
- *Moody's Corporate Profiles.*
- *Mergers and Acquisitions.*
- *Corporate Affiliations.*
- *Insider Trading Monitor.*
- *Business Wire.*
- *Trinet Company Database.*
- *Dun's Electronic Yellow Pages.*
- *Dun's Market Identifiers.*
- *Dun's Million Dollar Directory.*

- *Dun's Financial Records.*
- *Disclosure Database.*
- *Trade & Industry ASAP.*
- *Dow Jones News/Retrieval Database.*
- *Thomas Register Online.*
- *Investext.*
- *PTS Annual Reports Abstracts.*
- *Trade and Industry Index.*
- *Business Dateline.*
- *The Wall Street Journal.*
- *Thomas Register Online.*
- *Publishers, Distributors, and Wholesalers43.*

Libraries   State, county, and municipal libraries are often-forgotten sources of investigative information. Most local and state libraries have significant law collections, as well as various directories, telephone books, and other informational materials. Research librarians can help with historical and contemporary questions that may influence law and legislation.

University and college libraries are usually stocked with a formidable array of scholarly journals, periodicals, and other information necessary to research any technical question. Moreover, state college and university libraries usually participate in interlibrary loan programs that afford access to almost every major library in the continental United States.

In addition, libraries provide access to the multitude of Internet-based search engines and databases. Here are some of the most useful:

U.S. Department of Justice—www.usdoj.gov.

Bureau of Justice Statistics—www.ojp.usdoj.gov/bjs.

Bureau of Justice Assistance—www.ojp.usdoj.gov/bja.

Office for Victims of Crime—www.ojp.usdoj.gov/ovc.

Thomas Legislative Information—www.thomas.loc.gov.

LexisNexis—www.lexisnexis.com.

WestLaw—www.westlaw.com.

Cornell Law School, Legal Information Institute—www.law.cornell.edu.

Newspapers Most major city newspapers have a library or holding acquisition center, usually referred to as a "morgue," for all previous papers. Although not all original editions can be kept, old newspapers are filed under standardized classification systems on microfilm or microfiche or electronically. Stories of topical concern are arranged either chronologically or in some other order for appropriate indexing and cataloging.

Professional Associations and Groups Many private foundations and groups can provide access to relevant information. Consider these:

- U.S. Chamber of Commerce.
- State chambers of commerce.
- Better Business Bureau.
- Nonprofit product and safety commissions.
- Nonprofit groups (such as the Red Cross).
- Private associations and groups such as Rotary International, Lions, and Optimist International Clubs.
- Public utility company records.
- Title insurance companies (which have real estate directories).
- Religious bodies and groups.
- Credit records.
- Insurance records.
- Trade and industrial groups.
- Political parties.

Directories of associations can be explored for further ideas.

Police and Law Enforcement Agencies Paralegal investigators who work in district attorneys' offices, public defenders' offices, large police departments, or law firms that specialize in criminal defense cases will spend substantial time interacting with federal, state, and local law enforcement agents. Testimonial documentation (that is, real and physical evidence collected and assimilated by police agencies) is essential to prove or disprove a case. Gaining access to that information is imperative—but often difficult. The physical evidence alone may include the items listed in Figure 9.11.

The paralegal investigator has the task of collecting and assimilating enough information and data to support or refute a claim, charge, or cause of action. The evidentiary sources are limited only by the scope of the facts and the imagination, creativity, perseverance, logic, and deductive reasoning of the investigator.

FIGURE 9.11
Examples of Physical Evidence

Source: Alexander Joseph & Harrison C. Allison, Handbook of Crime Scene Investigation 29–31 (1980); see also Andre Moenssens & Fred E. Inbau, Scientific Evidence in Criminal Cases (1987).

Blood: wet and dry stains	Hair
Breathalyzer results	Letters and writing
Cartridge casings	Locks and keys
Comparative microanalysis	Metal wire
Contraband illicit goods	Paint
Cords	Poisons
Drugs	Questioned documents
Explosives	Semen stains
Fibers	Shot and shotgun wadding
Firearm and ballistics material	Soil
Flammable liquids	String
Footprint and heel print impressions	Tire imprints and tracks
Forensic studies	Tools
Glass fragments	Twine
Gun powder residue	

Investigation of Criminal Cases

Because of the constitutional and procedural implications of criminal adjudication and the usual forensic demands, the paralegal investigator must achieve a high level of professional sophistication to succeed. The techniques of criminal investigation may be grouped into four general categories relative to collection, preservation, processing, and presentation of evidence:

1. The technical methods by which the investigation has advanced (such as fingerprint systems; photography; plaster casting; the field of criminalistics or forensic science—microscopy, spectrography, serology, chemical analysis, biology, and pathology).

2. Interviews and interrogations of suspects, witnesses, and complainants (the techniques and strategies of interviews, interrogations, and the recording of statements and admissions; the place of lie detector tests and truth serums).

3. The use of records (using records and sources of information motor vehicle bureau records, utility records, mail covers, modus operandi files, and the like as a means of discovery and identification of suspects and witnesses as well as a source of evidence).

4. Surveillance and plant (physical surveillance; stakeouts; the use of undercover operatives and confidential informants; and technical surveillance such as wiretapping and electronic eavesdropping).[63]

Evidence in Criminal Cases

Because the burden of proof in a criminal case is "beyond a reasonable doubt," it is important to make sure that a secure crime scene existed to prevent distortions (see the checklist in Form 9.16 on the accompanying CD).

Crime scene survey sketches are considered a mandatory exercise in all major felonies. Figure 9.12 is an advertisement for one of the many drawing programs now in use by legal professionals.[64]

Computerized graphics, demonstrative models, and animation materials are also helpful in reconstructing events and conditions. Products and services are offered by a variety of suppliers, including Wolf Technical Service Inc. of Indianapolis, IN (simulated railroad accidents; product liability cases; aviation accidents), and A.D.A.M. Software Incorporated of Marietta, GA (software portraying functions of the human body).

Litigation teams have come to heavily depend on demonstrative means. Demonstrative evidence elucidates, clarifies, and is "evidence employed solely for illustrative purposes as

FIGURE 9.12
**Advertisement for
Smart Draw**

Source: Visit www.
smartdrawlegal.com for a
free trial of SmartDraw Legal
Edition.

distinguishing from substantive evidence."[65] Paralegal investigators may be assigned to ensure that real and physical evidence has been collected, whether from a defense or prosecution angle. The paralegal's evaluation of such evidence ensures its evidentiary integrity and admissibility. Criminal litigation generally witnesses the following evidence types.

Fingerprints Fingerprint evidence has exceptionally high probative value due to its unique quality. Because alteration or destruction of a fingerprint pattern is not considered scientifically plausible, a correlation between a fingerprint and criminal opportunity of a crime is highly probative, though some recent commentary raises the questionability of this "given" in forensic science.[66]

Due to environmental and physiological conditions, latent fingerprints can be left behind on various surfaces. A chart outlining fingerprint patterns, including arches, loops, and whorls, is shown in Figure 9.13.

DNA DNA evidence is being aggressively utilized throughout the criminal and civil justice systems. In capital cases, its use has been lifesaving and equally condemnatory. In paternity cases, DNA provides unassailable matches. Sexual offenses, particularly proof of the rapist's

FIGURE 9.13
Fingerprint Patterns

Source: FBI, U.S. Department of Justice, *Fingerprint Identification: An Overview,* www.fbi.gov/hq/cjisd/ident. pdf.

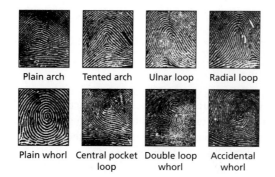

identity, find DNA an unrivaled tool. The National Institute of Justice advises on where DNA samples will work best in victim assistance:

DNA Evidence in Unsolved and Postconviction Cases

Advanced DNA technology, such as PCR, makes it possible to obtain conclusive results in cases in which previous testing might have been inconclusive. This can result in the identification of suspects in previously unsolvable cases or the exoneration of those wrongfully convicted. It is important to realize that while testing or retesting may exonerate an individual, exclusionary results may not necessarily prove actual innocence.

Prosecutors, defense counsel, the court, and law enforcement should confer on the need for testing on a case-by-case basis.

Using CODIS to Solve Crime

CODIS uses two indexes to generate investigative leads in crimes that contain biological evidence. The forensic index contains DNA profiles from biological evidence left at crime scenes, and the offender index contains DNA profiles of individuals convicted of violent crime. Each state in the nation has a DNA database law that defines which convicted offenders must have their profiles entered into CODIS; some states even require that DNA profiles from all felons be entered into the database. CODIS enables federal, state, and local forensic crime laboratories to work together—between jurisdictions and across state lines—to solve crimes.

Identifying DNA Evidence

Since only a few cells are needed for a useful DNA sample, the list below identifies some areas at the crime scene or on the victim that may contain valuable DNA evidence. Remember, even though a stain cannot be seen, there may be enough cells for DNA typing. Furthermore, DNA does more than just identify the source of the sample; it can place a known individual at a crime scene, in a home, or in a room where the suspect claimed not to have been. The more victim service providers know about properly identifying, collecting, and preserving DNA evidence, the more powerful a tool it becomes.

Possible Location of DNA Evidence Source of DNA

Bite mark or area licked—saliva.

Fingernail scrapings—blood or skin cells.

Inside or outside surface of used condom—semen or skin cells.

Blankets, sheets, pillows, or other bed linens—semen, sweat, hair, or saliva.

Clothing, including under garments worn during and after the assault—hair, semen, blood, or sweat.

Hat, bandanna, or mask—sweat, skin cells, hair, or saliva.

Tissue, washcloth, or similar item—saliva, semen, hair, skin cells, or blood.

Cigarette butt; toothpick; or rim of bottle, can, or glass—saliva.

Dental floss—semen, skin cells, or saliva.

Tape or ligature—skin cells, saliva, or hair.[67]

Both public and private companies deliver DNA analysis services.

 Confessions A defendant who gives a voluntary confession provides the prosecution with substantial evidence in the absence of any constitutional challenge. A voluntary confession is considered sufficient in and of itself to sustain a conviction.[68] Form 9.17 on the accompanying CD is a voluntary statement that is frequently used by police departments. In some jurisdictions, there is a move to electronically record all confessions to maintain a permanent record.[69]

Artist's Rendition, Composite, or Photo-Fit Imagery Identification of a suspect can be the result of an artist's rendition, a composite overlay, or a computerized technique, such as comPhotoFit shown at Figure 9.14.

Comparative Microscopy Comparative analyses of tool marks, fragments, ballistics, or the reconstruction of parts to a whole are readily admitted in criminal litigation. Paralegal investigators should evaluate the quality of the comparison to ensure that the comparison of a test plate and the seized evidence matches with significant similarities. This type of sophisticated microanalysis can be performed by the FBI laboratory in Washington, DC, or by criminalistics laboratories located in most major American cities.

FIGURE 9.14
Advertisement for comPhotoFit Composite Description

Source: Sirchie Finger Print Laboratories, 5825 Triangle Drive, Umstead Industrial Park, Raleigh, NC 27613, www.sirchie.com.

Surveillance Photography   Surveillance photography is used in regular investigative practice. Banks, individuals, retail establishments, and the private security industry all rely heavily on surveillance results. Surveillance photography or motion pictures yield convincing results.

Photographic Evidence   Photography must precisely depict the scene, people, or objects to be effective. Thus the investigator performing photographic functions is concerned about two fundamental queries:

1. What is the time relationship between the event or condition in question and the photographic action?

2. What photographic perspective, angle, or plan was employed during the photographic action? (See Form 9.18 on the accompanying CD.)

To be admitted into evidence, a photograph must be authenticated—whereby either the photographer or a third party can personally attest to its content.[70] The process of authentication includes these steps:

1. Is there a witness who is familiar with the event or subject matter of the photo that is depicted?
2. Can that same witness explain in a meaningful way how he or she is familiar with it?
3. Can the witness intelligently identify the content of the photo?
4. Is the photo, in the witness's view, a fair and accurate depiction?[71]

Challenges to photographic evidence are common—though mostly based on theories of tampering or gruesomeness in the presentation.[72] Just as readily seen are challenges based on the chain of custody. Asserting a break in the chain implies alteration and tampering.[73]

Police Documentation   Police regularly complain that, in terms of time, their job relates first to paperwork and secondarily to social work. Paralegal investigators will realize quickly the magnitude of this documentation—from discovery of police reports to field notes. Police agencies use many standardized forms and documents and are increasingly employing software programs to complete these many requirements.[74] An exampleis a uniform traffic ticket. These forms are invaluable to an attorney in a DUI, DWI, or traffic infraction case. An offense report that outlines a criminal complaint by describing the particulars of an offense is shown in Form 9.19 on the accompanying CD. Any information received subsequent to the original offense report filing is added with a supplementary report.

Because there has been such increased emphasis on the defense and prosecution of cases involving driving while intoxicated or driving under the influence of controlled substances, any documents the defense can obtain relative to states of intoxication are helpful. An alcohol influence report form in which test results from a breathalyzer operation become part of the formal record is reproduced in Form 9.20 on the accompanying CD. Contrarily, the defense strategy regarding breathalyzers and alcohol intoxication machines is tactically oriented toward proving improper method and maintenance. In the area of domestic relations, police departments expend considerable time protecting spouses from abuse and seeing that neglect or abuse of children is ameliorated. Increasingly police departments are being expected to file and keep paperwork regarding these matters. The public outcry when such cases are unaccounted for (or are unknown) reflects negatively on social service and law enforcement agencies. A domestic violence offense report, typically completed by a police agency, is effective in corroborating any claim for abuse (as grounds for divorce or as a factor in custody or visitation contests). (See Form 9.21.) Another example of police documentation is the radio log (see Form 9.22). Various 911 dispatch controversies recently have arisen, alleging that police departments, cities, and municipalities have been negligent in their method and speed of response. Discovery of a radio log form may assist in determining whether the dispatcher has been careless or willfully incompetent in handling a 911 call.

Another form regularly used is an arrest report for a narcotics division (see Form 9.23 on the accompanying CD). Police departments frequently set up narcotics units that are solely dedicated to the investigation and prosecution of drug-related matters.

A missing persons report (see Form 9.24 on the accompanying CD) can be useful to investigators working on cases of insurance fraud, escape from prison, violation of probation and parole, change of identity, or other forms of subterfuge.

In cases involving infringed civil rights, an officer's daily activity report (see Form 9.25 on the accompanying CD) demonstrates whether public officials have antagonized or harassed select citizens or whether quota systems have governed police or state action. Although many police departments have argued effectively that such a form is a police work product, a civil rights allegation will sometimes free up this type of document for ordinary discovery. In final record keeping, a police department will frequently maintain a disposition sheet that records the details of arrest, trial, and sentencing (see Form 9.26).

Preservation of Evidence

Collection, preservation, and the assurance of evidentiary integrity in a criminal case are mandatory functions. Investigators who work for public defenders' offices should discern whether the chain of custody has been broken or whether evidence has been contaminated, tampered with, reformulated, recast, or changed in any significant way. Evidence such as tools, guns, glass fragments, hairs, fibers, body parts—any real or physical evidence—is entitled to an environment that maintains its original integrity. According to Leland V. Jones,

> *The investigator himself should bear in mind the possibility that he himself may destroy or contaminate evidence before it is noticed or recognized. Minute spurts of blood, particles of dust, dirt, and debris are not always obvious to the naked eye and can be destroyed or rendered worthless as evidence if the investigator is not sufficiently observant during his investigation. Defense counsel should recognize the possibility or probability of contamination having occurred and conduct his cross-examination accordingly.[75]*

The integrity of evidence can be ensured by using tags, tapes, and various labels. Blood is a common evidentiary problem in chain of custody analysis.[76] Tamper-resistant tapes and seals warn prospective individuals to keep out unless authorized, and are designed to show evidence of tampering or unauthorized entry. Attempts to remove them will result in tape destruction or surface damage to the item being sealed. Figure 9.15 shows an evidence security seal.

FIGURE 9.15
Evidence Security Seal

Source: G. A. Thompson Co., P.O. Box 64681, Dallas, Tx 75206.

```
┌─────────────────────────────────────────────┐
│                 EVIDENCE                      │
│  WARNING!!          DO NOT                    │
│  POLICE SEAL        REMOVE                    │
│      Form #Es-1 G.A. Thompson Co.             │
│      P.O. Box 64681, Dallas, Texas 75206      │
└─────────────────────────────────────────────┘
```

Property/evidence tags are also routinely employed to verify chain of custody. They are usually tied to a bag, box, or other packaging, and they account for the exact chain of possession—from whom, to where, and what date and time are recorded. A property or evidence card may also be kept on file within the police department or forensic unit.

The prosecution's job is to assure the jury that the evidence submitted at trial has not substantially changed in its form or inherent properties. To maintain the integrity of evidence collected, a criminal investigator should have the necessary investigative equipment to perform tasks in a professional, competent manner. A basic investigative kit should include the following items:

- Cameras and film.
- Chalk and chalk line.
- Compass.
- Containers.
- Crayon or felt marker.
- Depressors.
- Envelopes.
- Fingerprint kit.
- First aid kit.
- Flashlight and batteries.
- Knife.
- Labels.
- Magnifier.
- Mirror.
- Money.
- Notebook.
- Paper.
- Picks.
- Plaster of paris.
- Pliers.
- Rope.
- Scissors.
- Screwdriver.
- Scriber.
- Sketching supplies.
- Spatula.
- Steel measuring tape.
- String.
- Tags.
- Tubes.
- Tweezers.
- Wrecking bar.

Numerous commercial companies provide kits for the investigation of blood and other matter, collection of evidence in rape cases, ballistics analysis, and gunshot residue tests. Figure 9.16 describes a narcotics identification kit that contains the equipment necessary for on-site identification of 25 controlled substances.

FIGURE 9.16
Narcotics Identification Kit

Source: Data are from Armorholdings.com (http://www.armorholdings.com/productsdiv/fieldtests.asp) and Copquest.com (www.copquest.com/43-2000.htm#NIK_Narcotic_Field_Test_Kit_Master_-_Pac) (both retrieved January 22, 2007).

Narcotics identification kits contain tests that help investigators identify the most commonly encountered narcotics and street drugs:

- Opiates and Amphetamine Screening Test
- Heroin and Opium Alkaloids Screening Tests
- Barbiturates
- LSD
- Cannibis—Marijuana, Hashish, Hash Oil
- Acid Neutralizer
- Cocaine, Rock Cocaine, Crack, HCL and FreeBase
- Methadone
- PCP Special Opiates Test
- Opiates
- Heroin
- Methaqualone
- Pentazocine
- Propoxyphehe
- Ephedrine
- Methcathinone, Valium® and Rohypnol®
- Methamphetamine/Exstacy (MDMA)

Investigation of Personal Injury and Other Civil Actions

Many of the skills and techniques of investigating criminal actions are equally applicable to civil harms. Paralegals may be extensively involved in the investigative aspects of personal injury, medical malpractice, and negligence litigation. Proof of medical facts is essential before any settlement or adjudication of a civil claim can take place.[77] "Medical facts are crucial to the proper evaluation of whether a case should even be accepted in the first place."[78]

Lawyers engaged in personal injury actions must rely on the investigative acumen of paralegals. It is the paralegal's task to discern, collect, and assimilate the data necessary to support these cases related to medical, economic, emotional, consortium, and related damages. Damages fall into the following major categories:

Actual damages: Real, substantial, and just damages; the amount awarded to a complainant in compensation for his or her actual loss or injury.

Compensatory damages: Damages that compensate the injured party for the injuries sustained and nothing more, such as will simply "make good on" or replace the loss caused by the wrong or the injury.

Consequential damages: Damage, loss, or injury that does not follow directly and immediately from the act of the party, but occurs only from some of the consequences or results of the act.

Direct damages: Damages that follow immediately upon the act done.

Double damages: A grant of actual damages that is multiplied by two (this is only sometimes statutorily permissible).

Excessive damages: Damages awarded by a jury that are grossly more than the amount warranted by law on the facts and circumstances of the case; unreasonable or outrageous damages.

Punitive damages: Damages on an increased scale awarded to the plaintiff over and above what will reimburse his or her property loss; used where the wrong committed was aggravated by circumstances of violence, oppression, malice, fraud, or wanton and wicked conduct on the part of the defendant. These damages are intended to compensate the plaintiff for mental anguish, shame, degradation, or other aggravations of the original wrong.[79]

General damages: Damages accruing from a wrong, complained of for the reason that they are its immediate, direct, and proximate result or necessarily result from the injury.

Inadequate damages: Damages that would not compensate the parties or place them in a position in which they formerly stood.

Irreparable damages: Damages not easily ascertainable at law, applicable in settings of public nuisance in which a private party may enjoin. The term includes wrongs of repeated and continuing character that lead to damage that is estimable only by conjecture and not by any accurate standard.

Liquidated damages: Damages ascertained by the judgment in an action, or when a specific sum of money has been expressly stipulated by the parties to a bond or other contract as to the amount of damages to be recovered by either party for breach of the agreement.

Nominal damages: A trifling sum awarded to a plaintiff in an action where there is no substantial loss or injury to be compensated, yet still the law recognizes a technical invasion of rights or a breach of the defendant's duty. Also used in cases where, although there has been real injury, the plaintiff's evidence entirely fails to show its amount.

Pecuniary damages: Damages that can be estimated and compensated by money.

Permanent damages: Damages awarded on a theory that the cause of injury is fixed and the property will always remain subject to it.

Remote damages: Damages arising from an unusual and unexpected result that is reasonably unanticipated from an accidental or an unusual combination of circumstances—a result beyond which the negligent party had no control.

Special damages: Damages that are the actual, but not the necessary, result of the injury complained of, and which in fact followed as a natural and proximate consequence in the particular case (by reason of special circumstances or conditions).

Substantial damages: Damages that are considerable in amount and intended as real compensation for a real injury (as opposed to nominal damages).[80]

Tracking damages according to category can be accomplished with a damages expense record (see Form 9.27 on the accompanying CD).

Many steps can be taken to ensure proper investigation of a medical, personal injury, or medical malpractice claim. One example is the Personal Injury Case Management System, which provides a computerized method by which law firms can calculate and keep track of information related to these types of claims. In its client/case information form, the investigator is put on the right track in collecting information regarding the case.

Abacus Personal Injury Special Edition is specifically designed to capitalize on the best practices for handling personal injury cases that maximize firm resources, improve case handling efficiency, and decrease time to settlement by providing immediate access to the exact party, accident, insurance, injury, and treatment information you need. (See Figure 9.17.) The software allows you to enter that information into practice-specific matter and name screens, manage a calendar using custom rules, generate documents, and print reports through all phases of a personal injury case. With Abacus Personal Injury Special Edition you can

- Complete a client intake form.

- Collect important information about the case, including details regarding the client, the defendant(s), the parties' insurance coverage, the property damage, the injuries suffered, and medical treatment received.

- Enter party contact information and link it to the accident.

- Calendar client meetings, document drafting, discovery deadlines, trial dates, and case settlement negotiations.

- Use preconfigured mail merge documents to save time by automating the drafting of correspondence common in a personal injury case.

FIGURE 9.17
Advertisement for Abacus Personal Injury Special Edition

Source: Abacus Data Systems Inc. 5230 Carroll Canyon Rd, Suite 306, San Diego, CA 92121; 858-452-4245, fax 858-452-2073; http://www.abacuslaw.com/products/specialeditions/personalinjury.html.

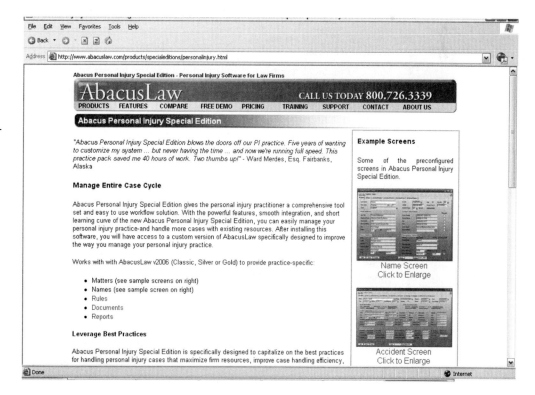

- Manage your caseload by scheduling reminders for record gathering, document drafting, client meetings, statute of limitations deadlines, and trial preparation.
- Generate attorney and/or firm calendars, prioritize your caseload, and access firm productivity and client data.

Personal Injury Special Edition comes with a number of preconfigured documents and reports to simplify the process of managing a personal injury case.[81] Other personal injury software includes Perfect Practice by ADC Legal Systems Inc;[82] Needles Case Management Software by Chesapeake Interlink Ltd.[83] and Stedman's Legal Med Ware by LeMed Inc.[84] These computer applications minimally collect information, evaluate cases, and provide a starting point in the investigator's activity.

Paralegals critically advise legal counsel about the procedural aspects of the case while reviewing the substantive history of the case of claim. Much of what the paralegal does during the investigative process will impact whether or even how a personal injury case will unravel. Personal injury expert Stephen Sullivan knows this better than anyone. He warns of these pitfalls in personal injury practice:

1. Failure to issue proceedings in time.
2. Failure to serve proceedings in time.
3. Delay in relation to reports.
4. Delay in relation to obtaining witness statements.
5. Delay in making routine applications to court.
6. Failure to keep up-to-date with procedural changes.
7. Failure to identify unusual time limits when your claim overlaps with an area in which you do not regularly practice.
8. Failure to warn clients of the weaknesses in their case so that if they are not as successful as they hoped, they don't blame their legal advisers.
9. Failure to give clients comprehensive advice about costs.
10. Failure to follow guidelines set up by steering or other groups dealing with particular kinds of injuries.[85]

Here is where the paralegal earns his or her keep: keeping the case on track and communicating with counsel and client.

Medical Records

Standard medical records are indispensable in the investigation of any medical or personal injury claim. To obtain records, medical releases authorizing the transferal of information from a hospital, physician, consultant, emergency room, or employer should be signed, attested, and submitted.[86] A general medical release is granted to an attorney by a client (see Form 9.28 on the accompanying CD). To obtain copies of an employee's work history, a release is submitted to the employer (see Form 9.29). Wage information that is germane to economic loss considerations requires that a wage release be submitted to the personnel or payroll division of a company or other employer (see Form 9.30). An accompanying letter for the release of medical office records (see Form 9.31) explains to medical personnel that you have a right to obtain them. For copies of X-rays, you can use a letter like that outlined in Form 9.32. A request for a medical admission chart is shown in Form 9.33.

The investigator may seek to access numerous other records. These include admission records (see Form 9.34 on the accompanying CD), discharge records (see Form 9.35), emergency room records (see Form 9.36), medical expense records (see Form 9.37), itemized billing statements (see Form 9.38), patient account billings (see Form 9.39), personnel records (see Form 9.40), life squad reports (see Form 9.41), accident reports (see Form 9.42), and medical forms (see Form 9.43). In the case of medical records, the paralegal must be sensitive to statutory protections regarding their content and to whom these records apply. For example, the Health Insurance Portability and Accountability Act of 1996 (HIPAA) established national standards to guard the privacy of a patient's protected health information. Protected health information includes

- Information created or received by a health care provider or health plan that includes health information or health care payment information plus information that personally identifies the individual patient or plan member.

- Personal identifiers such as a patient's name and e-mail, Web site, and home addresses; identifying numbers (including Social Security, medical records, insurance numbers, biomedical devices, vehicle identifiers, and license numbers); full facial photos and other biometric identifiers; and dates (such as birthdate and dates of admission and discharge or death).

The HIPAA Security Rule, effective April 20, 2005, requires that workforce members adhere to controls and safeguards to (1) ensure the confidentiality, integrity, and availability of confidential information; and (2) detect and prevent reasonably anticipated errors and threats due to malicious or criminal actions, system failure, natural disasters, and employee or user error.

Paralegal investigators will quickly discover that the amount of information in a personal injury or medical records case is substantial. The reports from experts, hospitals, and doctors can be quite voluminous. A document inventory form can be of great assistance in more complex cases (see Form 9.44 on the accompanying CD). Paralegal investigators must also understand that certain hostility may exist between medical professionals and attorneys. The reasons most commonly given for these poor relations include the following:

1. Defensiveness of each group believing that the other is attacking them.

2. Competing economic interests.

3. Difficulty in communicating because attorneys and physicians use words differently.[87]

Paralegals must try to move beyond this antagonism and develop solid, professional, honest relationships with medical professionals.[88] With communication and professional interchange, such animosity can be minimized.

Traffic and Vehicular Investigations

Closely aligned to medical, personal injury, and malpractice investigative practices is the investigation of traffic accidents. A paralegal may work for an insurance company as a claims adjuster, accident investigator, claims analyst, or person responsible for determining damages.

From the outset, make every effort to record and permanently memorialize the accident scene. Typically an investigator will record or tape, photograph, and sketch the scene. Photography still is heavily relied on. Photographic coverage of a scene should include the following:

1. Approach to the scene—from the viewpoint of the driver or drivers involved. It may be necessary to make several photographs of the scene at different distances. Make these from the driver's eye level as he or she would be seated in the vehicle. Remember that the high cab of a tractor–trailer rig may place the driver as much as eight feet from the ground. Climb on a truck or SUV to get the needed height.

2. Eyewitnesses' viewpoints—To corroborate eyewitness statements, take pictures of the scene from the eyewitnesses' position and eye level.

3. Positions of vehicles—Try to get pictures of the final positions of vehicles before they are moved. If they must be moved before they can be photographed, mark their positions with chalk or tape.

4. Positions of victims—If victims were thrown clear of the vehicles, get photographs of the positions of their bodies, or mark the position of an injured victim who is being removed for treatment.

5. Point of impact—If possible, determine and photograph the point of impact of the vehicle or vehicles involved in the accident. This may correspond to the final position of the vehicles, or it may be some distance from that point. Relate the two in a photograph if possible.

6. Overall view of scene—One or several pictures that relate the overall scene elements can be useful to the accident investigator. One viewpoint for such photographs is a high position

overlooking the scene: a rooftop, an embankment, a bridge, or even a truck can provide a commanding position. Other overall shots can be made with the camera at eye level in the direction of vehicle travel and then by looking back through the scene from the opposite direction to show the area of approach.

7. Close-ups of accident details—Details of vehicle damage; skid marks; tire marks; worn or damaged tires; registration plates; oil, water, or gasoline spills; and broken parts provide key information to aid the accident investigator. Photograph questionable items within the car such as wine, beer, and liquor bottles; narcotics; or firearms.[89]

Automobile accidents may involve any number of automobiles, other movable objects, pedestrians, animals, or fixed objects such as telephone poles, buildings, or signs.[90] Photographic examples of vehicular accidents are essential. The investigator's obligation is to photograph the accident scene and to support it with some graphic portrayal or reproduction of the accident case. Usually this is accomplished by a police report written by an official. Richard Congo, a paralegal, emphasizes the photographic tactic in the accident case:

> Photograph the damaged portion of the vehicle from every possible angle. Include close-up pictures of a small portion of the vehicle and short-distance pictures to include a larger portion of the vehicle. Determine the exact point of impact and take extra pictures of that point (this makes it easier to explain your theory of how the accident happened).
>
> The last thing to photograph as soon after the accident as possible is the accident scene itself. This is particularly important in the winter months and early spring if the weather and road conditions change as rapidly as they do in the Northeast.[91]

Auto accident investigators should follow these general suggestions:

1. Locate, identify, and interview all surviving witnesses, drivers, and participants in the accident.
2. Determine climate and road conditions at the time of the accident.
3. Collect police reports outlining the event.
4. Collect weather and meteorological reports.
5. Determine the nature or state of visibility.
6. Determine whether any environmental factors influenced the capacity to see or to engage the roadways.
7. Determine road surface conditions.
8. Determine traffic control at the vicinity of the accident.
9. Determine whether any defects of operation or design are evident in the road design and construction.
10. Verify and corroborate the statements of witnesses, drivers, and other individuals.
11. Determine whether multiple parties were negligent.
12. Determine whether your jurisdiction allows the defense of comparative or contributory negligence.
13. Assess the conditions of the automobiles at the time of and before the accident.
14. Assess whether any of the vehicles violated any statutory guidelines of motor vehicle operation.
15. Assess whether any citations were issued at the time of the accident.
16. Determine whether drivers or pedestrians contributed to the accident.
17. Review and assess the drivers' histories and records.
18. Look for marks on the road or signs of speed, sudden stops, or other visible inertia changes.
19. Determine damage to any objects.
20. Examine tire marks, skid marks, and tire imprints.
21. Determine the nature and extent of vehicle damages and conditions.
22. Collect all accident reports.

FIGURE 9.18
National Safety Council Web Site

Source: Reprinted with permission of National Safety Council Library. Web site: www.nsc.org.

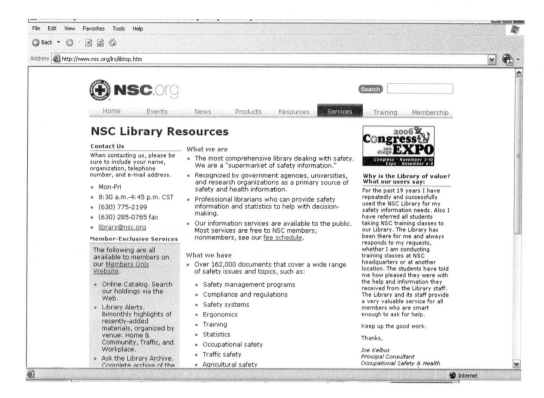

23. Take appropriate photographs.

24. Take witnesses' statements.

25. Use experts in the field of accident analysis and accident reconstruction.

Private, nonprofit entities exist that offer assistance in auto accident investigations. See the National Safety Council Library's Web page in Figure 9.18.

Walter Stroebel, in *The Investigator's Handbook*, provides sound advice. The chain of events leading to the accident consists of

> 1. *Principal event—the time, place, and type of accident (for example, running off the road; collision on the road with a pedestrian).*
>
> 2. *Perception of a hazard—seeing, sensing, or hearing the unusual or unexpected movement or condition that could be taken as a sign of an accident about to happen.*
>
> 3. *The point of perception—the time and place at which the unusual or unexpected movement or condition could have been perceived by a normal person.*
>
> 4. *The point of no escape—the time and place beyond which the accident can no longer be prevented by the person who is watching.*
>
> 5. *Maximum engagement—the time and position in which the objects in a collision are pushed together as far as they will be.*
>
> 6. *The final position—the time and place when objects involved finally come to rest; this is the position before anything is moved.*[92]

Adept auto accident investigators do everything in their power to maintain the integrity of Stroebel's "Stage 6." With the exception of lifesaving issues and the minimization of property destruction, Stage 6 is where things should remain to provide the most untainted picture of this actual or potential collision between two moving objects.[93] Insurance company profits are based on their capacity to analyze and reconstruct accident cases. Paralegal investigators working for plaintiffs in personal injury traffic accidents must possess the same level of dedication and proficiency. Where contributory negligence operates as a pure defense, reconstruction of the accident scene becomes an even more critical step in the investigative process. Finally, a good paralegal investigator will keep in touch with clients. Paralegals investigating a traffic accident case need a fact collection form to supplement any official police reports or insurance company records (see Form 9.45 on the accompanying CD).

Summary

To be an effective paralegal investigator, an individual must be able to evaluate substantial amounts of data and information. Having the ability to refine complex material; possessing strong interpersonal skills; and being persistent, diligent, and objective, as well as creative, are all attributes of an effective investigator. In both civil and criminal settings, the importance of forms and documentation in the corroboration and proof of facts (direct, inferential, or circumstantial) must be continually stressed. Collecting witnesses' statements and analyzing the results of consultants' reports, medical records, and forensic documentation can ensure that the case is guided in the right direction. Playing the mediator and conciliator to fearful and often hostile, adverse, and arrogant witnesses is yet another obligation of the paralegal investigator.

Of all the proficiencies in the investigative process, none is more apparent than the application of common sense to a fact pattern. Novice paralegals can be overwhelmed by the sheer magnitude of information, individuals, and circumstances. Even more likely is the tendency to make simple things unnecessarily complex—to become consumed with the tangential and disregard the obvious. Paralegals must strive to keep it simple.

Discussion Questions

1. Review some newspaper employment ads. What types of positions require investigative capacity?
2. Information collection plays a crucial role in the investigative process—so much so that many experienced trial advocates claim that victory depends on comprehensive pretrial investigative work. Do you think there is truth to this statement?
3. How could you track down a witness with no known address or location?
4. A case involving a bridge collapse would involve what types of expert witnesses?
5. Call or Web research a local college or university to determine whether the institution has a directory of experts on its faculty.
6. Intoxication can be proven by scientific means. Often forgotten are other techniques of proving intoxication. What types of evidence reach a similar conclusion?
7. Why is it so important to develop dependable relationships with police personnel?
8. In a case involving personal injury or medical malpractice, what types of records and documents must be discovered?
9. Discuss generally the techniques of proving liability or fault in a case of auto negligence.
10. Identify state, local, and federal agencies in your area that provide investigative services, personnel, testing, and analysis.

Practical Exercises

1. Police Report Questionnaire – Contact your local police agency and ask what is the procedure and cost involved in acquiring an accident report and accompanying photographs.
   a. Name of police department
   b. Procedure for acquiring a copy of a police report
   c. Cost of acquiring a police report
   d. Ask for a sample police report
   e. Ask about supplemental or follow-up reports, if applicable.
2. Medical Records Questionnaire – Call, visit or correspond with a local hospital, physician, or other medical facility and ask how medical records on a specific patient can be acquired.
   a. Name of physician, hospital or medical care provider
   b. What is the procedure for acquiring copies of medical records?
   c. Are there any specific forms or authorizations published by this agency for this purpose?
   d. Under what rules, statutes or codes does the hospital comply in providing these records?

Internet Resources

American Prosecutors Research Institute
99 Canal Center Plaza, Suite 510
Alexandria, VA 22314
703-549-4253
www.ndaa-apri.org/apri/Index.html

Federal Bureau of Investigation
J. Edgar Hoover Building
935 Pennsylvania Avenue NW
Washington, DC 20535
202-324-3000
www.fbi.gov

National Center for Victims of Crime
2111 Wilson Boulevard, Suite 300
Arlington, VA 22201
703-276-2880
www.ncvc.org

National Commission on the Future of DNA Evidence
Office of Justice Programs
National Institute of Justice
810 Seventh Street NW
Seventh Floor
Washington, DC 20531
202-307-0645
www.ojp.usdoj.gov/nij/dna

National Criminal Justice Reference Service (NCJRS)
PO Box 6000
Rockville, MD 20849-6000
800-851-3420
www.ncjrs.org

Office for Victims of Crime
U.S. Department of Justice
810 Seventh Street NW
Washington, DC 20531
202-307-5983
www.ojp.usdoj.gov/ovc

Office for Victims of Crime Resource Center
PO Box 6000
Rockville, MD 20849-6000
800-627-6872
www.ojp.usdoj.gov/ovc/ovcres

Rape, Abuse, and Incest National Network
635B Pennsylvania Avenue SE
Washington, DC 20003
800-656-HOPE
www.rainn.org

Sexual Assault Nurse Examiner (S.A.N.E.)—Sexual Assault Response Team (S.A.R.T.)
www.sane-sart.com

Speaking Out About Rape Inc. (S.O.A.R.)
69 East Pine Street
Orlando, FL 32801
407-836-9692
www.soar99.org

DNA Genotek Inc.
29 Camelot Dr. Unit 200
Ottawa, Ontario, Canada
K2G 5W6
www.dnagenotek.com/press_five.htm

Psylon Head Office
PO Box 101
Vermont 3133
Victoria, Australia
www.psylon.com

DNA Consulting
1274 Calle de Comercio
Santa Fe, NM 87507
dnaconsultants.com/dna_tests/index.html

Endnotes

1. Art Buckwalter, Investigative Methods 22 (2nd ed. 1987).

2. Thomas Eimermann, Fundamentals of Paralegalism 102–103 (1980).

3. Charles P. Nemeth, Private Security and the Investigative Process 19 (2nd ed. 2000).

4. James Davidson and Mark Lytle, After the Fact: The Art of Historical Detection xv (5th ed,, McGraw Hill: Boston 2005).

5. Patricia W. Kittredge, *Guideposts for the Investigation of a Negligence Case*, 90 Prac. Law. 55 (1973); J. Stannar Baker, *Reconstruction of Accidents*, 17 Traffic Dig. & Rev. 9 (1969); P. Magarick, *Investigating the Civil Case: General Principals*, 1 Am. Jur. Trials 361 (1987).

6. Buckwalter, *supra* note 1, at 36.

7. Charles P. Nemeth, Law and Evidence 1 (Prentice Hall 2001).

8. Nemeth, Security, *supra* note 3, at 21.

9. Edward Smith, Practical Guide for Private Investigators 34 (1982).

10. Magarick, *supra* note 5, at 365.

11. Nemeth, Security, *supra* note 3, at 25.

12. Buckwalter, *supra* note 1, at 34–37.

13. *Id.* at 36.

14. Mark E. Sullivan, *The Legal Assistance Chief's Handbook*, Army Law., Sept. 2004, at 1.

15. Buckwalter, *supra* note 1, at 47–49.

16. Carole A. Bruno, Paralegal's Litigation Handbook 68–83 (1980).

17. Magarick, *supra* note 5, at 374.

18. Bruno, *supra* note 17, at 70.

19. Kathryn L. Andrews, *Legal Investigation & Information Discovery*, Legal Assist. Today, July–Aug. 1990, at 36, 40.

20. Susan R. Martyn, *Accidental Clients*, 33 Hofstra L. Rev. 913 (2005).

21. Bruno, *supra* note 17, at 90.

22. Deborah Larbalestrier, Paralegal Training Manual 22 (1981).

23. *State Bar News: Discipline Corner*, Utah Bar J., May 2002, at 29.

24. Lawrence S. Charfoos & David W. Christensen, Personal Injury Practice: Technique and Technology 42 (1988).

25. *Id.* at 433; *see also* Julius Glickman, *Persuasion in Litigation*, 8 Litig. 30 (1982); Neil Horowitz, *How to Handle a New Client*, 21 Prac. Law. 11–12 (1975).

26. Allen R. Earl, *Conducting the Initial Interview: Rules and Red Flags*, Trial, April 1993, at 59, 61–62.

27. Charfoos & Christensen, *supra* note 24, at 436.

28. Nemeth, Evidence, *supra* note 7, at 158.

29. Charfoos & Christensen, *supra* note 24, at 517–518.

30. Al Cone & Verne Lawyer, The Complete Personal Injury Practice Manual 29 (1988).

31. Nemeth, Evidence, *supra* note 7, at 1.

32. Irv Gross, *Locating and Interviewing Witnesses*, 2 Am. Jur. Trials 264–265 (1964).

33. Nemeth, Evidence, *supra* note 7, at 157.

34. Gross, *supra* note 32, at 5.

35. Nemeth, Security, *supra* note 3, at 71.

36. Elaine Thorp, *How to Locate Elusive Witnesses*, Legal Assist. Today, Nov.–Dec. 1990, at 60, 64.

37. *See* Jason Elliot Nard, *Pennsylvania's Capital Statute: Does the Introduction of Victim Impact Evidence—Into the Evaluation of Mitigating and Aggravating Circumstances—At the Sentencing Hearing of a Murder Trial Introduce Unjust Prejudice into the Imposition of the Death Penalty?* 42 Duq. L. Rev. 825 (2004).

38. The Federal Rules of Evidence Sections 607 through 610 lay out standards regarding the utilization of character witnesses. Fed. R. Evid. §607–610.

39. Fed R. Evid. §412(a).

40. Fed. R. Evid. §412(b). *See also* Charles P. Nemeth, *Character Evidence in Rape Trials in 19th Century New York: Chastity and the Admissibility of Specific Acts*, 6 WOMEN'S RIGHTS L. REP. 3 (1980); Charles P. Nemeth, *An Evaluation of New Jersey's Sexual Offense Statute: Judicial and Prosecutorial Perceptions in Rape Reform*, N.J.L.J. (1983); Michigan v. Lucas, 500 U.S. 145 (1991); Toni Lester, *The Reasonable Woman Test in Sexual Harassment Law—Will It Really Make a Difference?* 26 IND. L. REV. 227 (1993).

41. Fed. R. Evid. §701. *See also Recent Development in Utah Law: III. Evidence Law: Distinguishing between Expert and Lay Testimony*, 2005 UTAH L. REV. 230 (2005).

42. D. Lake Rumsey, *Selecting, Preparing, and Presenting the Direct Testimony of Lay Witnesses, in* MASTER ADVOCATE HANDBOOK 84 (D. Lake Rumsey ed., 1986).

43. Peter B. Oh, *Assessing Admissibility of Nonscientific Expert Evidence under Federal Evidence Rule* 702, DEF. COUNS. J., Oct. 1997, at 556; Michael H. Gottesman, *Should State Courts Impose a "Reliability" Threshold?* TRIAL, Sept. 1997, at 20; Paul S. Miller & Bert W. Rein, *Whither Daubert? Reliable Resolution of Scientifically Based Causality Issues in Toxic Tort Cases*, 50 RUTGERS L. REV. 563 (1998).

44. Fed. R. Evid. §702.

45. Andre Moenssens, *The Impartial Medical Expert: A New Look at an Old Issue*, 25 MED. TRIAL TECHNIQUE Q. 63 (1978); Lancaster Smith, *Impeaching a "National Expert" in a Catastrophic Collision Case*, 23 FOR DEF. 8 (1981).

46. Frye v. U.S., 293 Fed. 1013 (1923); *see also* William Daubert et ux., etc., et al. v. Merrell Dow Pharmaceuticals, Inc., 113 S. Ct. 2786. The *Frye* standard has been relaxed at the federal level in this case.

47. MICHAEL GRAHAM, EVIDENCE, TEXT, RULES, ILLUSTRATIONS, AND PROBLEMS 305–306 (1983).

48. 509 U.S. 579 (1993).

49. NEMETH, EVIDENCE, *supra* note 7, at 178.

50. NORMAN M. GARLAND, CRIMINAL EVIDENCE 131 (5th ed. 2006). Kumho Tire Co. v. Carmichael, 119 S. Ct. 1167 (1999); Robert W. Littleton, *Supreme Court Dramatically Changes the Rules on Experts*, N.Y.ST. B.J., July–Aug. 1999, at 8; Gottesman, *supra* note 43; Miller & Rein, *supra* note 43.

51. *See* David Rubsamen, *Locating Medical Experts*, 2 AM. JUR. TRIALS 112–133 (1987).

52. This was the ambition of *Daubert*, though it miserably failed. Daubert v. Merrell Dow Pharmaceuticals, Inc., 509 U.S. 579, 113 S. CT. 2786, 125 L. ED. 2D 469, 27 U.S.P.Q.2D (BNA) 1200, PROD LIAB. REP. (CCH) ¶13494, 37 FED. R. EVID. SERV. 1, 23 ENVTL. L. REP. 20979 (1993).

53. GARLAND, *supra* note 50, at 131.

54. Beverly Hutson's *Paralegal Trial Handbook* emphasizes the preparation phase in the use of experts. "As part of the trial team, you should be present at the trial preparation conferences. You may be asked to schedule and coordinate the trial preparation conferences for one or more clients. You can assist the attorney a great deal in this portion of the trial preparation." BEVERLY HUTSON, PARALEGAL TRIAL HANDBOOK 3–9 (1991).

55. CHARFOOS & CHRISTENSEN, *supra* note 24, at 493.

56. See Russell G. Donaldson, *Propriety of Cross-Examining Expert Witness Regarding His Status as "Professional Witness,"* 39 A.L.R.4th 742.

57. Brian Sheppard, *Admissibility of Expert or Opinion Evidence—Supreme Court Cases*, 177 A.L.R. FED. 77 at 10 b.

58. CHARLES P. NEMETH, EVIDENCE HANDBOOK FOR PARALEGALS 158 (1993).

59. CHARFOOS & CHRISTENSEN, *supra* note 24, at 502.

60. PAUL FUQUA & JAMES WILSON, SECURITY INVESTIGATOR'S HANDBOOK 17 (1979).

61. *Id.* at 18.

62. Irv Gross, *Locating Public Records*, 2 AM. JUR. TRIALS 414 (1987).

63. Magarick, *supra* note 5, at 365.

64. *See also* NATIONAL INSTITUTE OF JUSTICE, NATIONAL GUIDELINES: A GUIDE FOR THE SCENE INVESTIGATOR, NCJ 167568 (1999).

65. NEMETH, EVIDENCE, *supra* note 7, at 72; *see also* Fed. R. Evid. §403.

66. Tamara F. Lawson, *Can Fingerprints Lie? Reweighing Fingerprint Evidence in Criminal Jury Trials*, 31 AM. J. CRIM. L. 1, 9–10 (2003).

67. US DOJ, UNDERSTANDING DNA EVIDENCE: A GUIDE FOR VICTIM SERVICE PROVIDERS, available at http://www.ncjrs.gov/pdffiles1/nij/bc000657.pdf.

68. Miranda v. Arizona, 384 U.S. 436, 86 S. Ct. 1602 (1966).

69. *See* Roberto Iraola, *The Electronic Recording of Criminal Interrogations,* 40 U. RICH. L. REV. 463 (2006).

70. *See* Brian Barakat & Bronwyn Miller, *Authentication of Digital Photographs under the "Pictorial Testimony" Theory: A Response to Critics,* FLA. B.J., July–Aug. 2004, at 38.

71. NEMETH, PARALEGAL HANDBOOK, *supra* note 58, at 68–69.

72. Mark Dombroff, *Utilizing Photographs as Demonstrative Evidence*, TRIAL, Dec. 1982, at 71; Benjamin Mattison, *Seeing Can Be Deceiving: Photographic Evidence in a Visual Age—How Much Weight Does It Deserve?* 25 WM. & MARY L. REV. 705 (1984).

73. NEMETH, EVIDENCE, *supra* note 7, at 84.

74. George L. Blum, *Admissibility in State Court Proceedings of Police Reports as Business Records*, 111 A.L.R.5th 1 (originally published in 2003).

75. Leland V. Jones, *Locating and Preserving Evidence*, 1 AM. JUR. TRIALS 577 (1988).

76. *See Chain of Custody Requirement for Organic Nonblood Specimens Taken from Human Body for Purposes of Analysis*, 78 A.L.R.5th 1.

77. M. HOUTS, LAWYER'S GUIDE TO MEDICAL PROOF (1984).

78. CHARFOOS & CHRISTENSEN, *supra* note 24, at 530.

79. The issue of punitive damages has been fiercely debated. *See* Brian C. McManus, *Analyzing Excessive Punitive Damages under Massachusetts Law,* 36 SUFFOLK UNIV. L. REV. 559 (2003).

80. CHARLES P. NEMETH, LITIGATION, PLEADINGS, AND ARBITRATION, 117–118 (1992); BLACK'S LAW DICTIONARY (6th ed. 1990).

81. Abacus Personal Injury Special Edition, Abacus Law, Abacus Data Systems Inc., 5230 Carroll Canyon Rd., Suite 306, San Diego, CA 92121, 858-452-4245, http://www.abacuslaw.com/products/specialeditions/personalinjury.htm.

82. PO Box 540086, Orlando, FL 32854, 407-843-8992, http://www.adclegal.com/html_version/personal.html.

83. 8E Music Fair Road, Owings Mills, MD 21117, 410-363-1976, www.needleslaw.com.

84. A Medical Legal Solutions Holding Company, Hoover, Alabama 35216, 205-370-2391, http://www.legalmedware.com.

85. Stephen Sullivan, *Top 10 Pitfalls to Avoid*, 4 J.P.I. Law 250–252 (2004).

86. For an excellent article about how paralegals help in the world of medical records, see Mary Alice McLarty, *Secrets of a Successful Small Office Practice*, TRIAL, Apr. 1998, at 82.

87. Joan M. Gibson & Robert L. Schwartz, *Physicians and Lawyers: Science, Art, and Conflict*, 6 AM. J. L. & MED., 173, 174–175 (1981).

88. *See* Jeffrey W. Stempel, *The Law and Politics of Tort Reform: Not-So-Peaceful Coexistence: Inherent Tensions in Addressing Tort Reform*, 4 NEV. L. J. 337 (2004).

89. Eastman Kodak Co., Photography in Traffic Accident Investigation 4 (1979).

90. SMITH, *supra* note 9, at 108.

91. Richard D. Longo, *Effective Discovery in Small Personal Injury Cases*, Legal Assist. Today, Nov.–Dec. 1990, at 68, 69.

92. WALTER STROEBEL, THE INVESTIGATOR'S HANDBOOK 90 (1984).

93. See NEMETH, SECURITY, *supra* note 3, at 283–290.

Chapter 10

Criminal Law and Procedure

 CRIMINAL LAW PARALEGAL JOB DESCRIPTION

Criminal law paralegals need to be proficient in the following competencies:

- Interpret and analyze criminal statutes.
- Read and brief criminal law cases.
- Establish docket procedures for criminal clients.
- Summarize and annotate lower court transcripts for appeal.
- Analyze bank records and preparation of check spreads.
- Review corporate records, including minutes and financial data.
- Review and analyze tax records and supporting documentation.
- Log exhibits offered and admitted.
- Log objections sustained and overruled.
- Monitor a jury's reactions during trial.
- Help with preparation of opening and closing arguments.
- Prepare outlines of prosecution and defense cases.
- Coordinate specific documents with witnesses during testimony.
- Verify that all depositions have been filed.
- Help in planning and strategy.
- Take notes and monitor related hearings and trials.
- Help prepare witnesses for testimony in trial or deposition.
- Investigate background information on potential jurors.
- Draft jury instructions.
- Help with analysis of voir dire.
- Prepare complete notes of witness testimony.
- Help with interviewing the jury following the verdict.
- Attend and help at trials.
- Attend client and attorney meetings regarding presentence reports.
- Prepare sentencing information and work with probation officers.
- Research law regarding appealable issues.
- Draft assignments of error and arguments.

INTRODUCTION: THE PARALEGAL'S ROLE IN CRIMINAL PRACTICE

Today paralegals are being more widely used by criminal litigation practitioners. With the consistent rise in the crime rate and the growing number of repeat offenders, opportunities in criminal practice will continue to flourish. The practice of criminal law is labor-intensive, particularly its investigative pretrial and appellate responsibilities. In the most general sense, criminal law paralegals must be able to

- Work cooperatively with various public and private agencies, including district attorneys' offices, public defenders' offices, the judiciary, court personnel, police agencies, forensic teams, medical examiners' offices, coroners' offices, and the private security industry.
- Make checklists, exhibits, and other demonstrative tools that illustrate the factual and legal issues.
- Make a chart outlining the elements of a criminal charge.
- Understand, enunciate, and apply specific Bill of Rights provisions regarding governmental conduct and criminal defense, including the Fourth, Fifth, Sixth, and Fourteenth Amendments.
- Develop forms and checklists to ensure that evidence will be admissible and withstand exclusion based on constitutional challenge.
- Read and interpret statutory and legislative materials outlining specific criminal offenses.
- Evaluate criminal fact patterns for possible defenses.
- Create charts, lists, or diagrams outlining the elements of crimes against a person, crimes against property, crimes against habitation, and crimes against the public order and decency.
- Make a checklist or other demonstrative aid that outlines jurisdictional requirements.
- Read and interpret initial police reports and other documentation.
- Draft and prepare pretrial motions, criminal complaints, pretrial conference materials, and pretrial notices.
- Prepare charts, diagrams, and other materials for use at trial.
- Prepare documents for appearances, arraignments, bail, and preliminary hearings.
- Help the attorney prepare pleadings used in motion practice and before and after a trial.
- Help the attorney at trial.
- Research and help complete appellate documents.

As in other areas of legal practice, the paralegal orchestrates and calendars the procedural aspects of criminal law and procedure. The Illinois Bar Association accurately portrays paralegals' responsibilities in criminal work:

- Index documents.
- Draft pleadings.
- Digest and abstract depositions.
- Review personnel and medical records.
- Prepare and have served subpoenas for document production.
- Initiate and respond to correspondence.
- Document telephone conferences and personal meetings.
- Help write reports to state and federal prosecutors to halt an indictment.
- Summarize and annotate lower court transcripts for appeal.
- Coordinate appeal procedures with court reporters in securing transcripts for appeal.
- Participate in document productions to and from government agencies.
- Supervise witness and evidence files.
- Analyze bank records and preparation of check spreads.
- Coordinate documents with testimony at hearings, trials, and depositions.
- Review corporate records, including minutes and financial data.
- Review and analyze tax records along with supporting documentation.
- Research and organize appellate briefs, and help analyze responses.

In the investigative role of criminal law the paralegal may

- Review fingerprints, handwriting, and polygraph results.
- Obtain information regarding blood, hair samples. and other physical evidence.
- Acquire and analyze coroner and autopsy reports.
- Obtain and analyze driving records.
- Prepare memoranda or summaries of investigative interviews.
- Locate and work with accident reconstruction and other appropriate experts.
- Measure and photograph alleged crime scenes.
- Prepare factual chronologies.
- Have knowledge of criminal charges.
- Help in surrendering defendants to authorities for processing.
- Review arresting information and indictments, search warrants, and consents to search.
- Help at search locations and prepare inventories of items seized.
- Interview clients while in custody under special circumstances.
- Obtain and review police reports, photographs, and statements to prosecutors from witnesses.
- Locate and analyze statements, interviews, and depositions of witnesses conducted by third parties.
- Trace property ownerships.
- Conduct or participate in investigative interviews of client, witnesses, character, and expert witnesses.
- Prepare questions for attending depositions.
- Prepare character sketches of client, witnesses, and victims.
- Interview and analyze communities to help decide the need for a change of venue.
- Conduct a survey of community standards and the availability of sexually explicit material relating to First Amendment cases.

At criminal court hearings and trials a paralegal may

- Prepare exhibits.
- Help with preparation of trial briefs.
- Help with jury selection.
- Log exhibits offered and admitted.
- Log objections sustained and overruled.
- Monitor the jury's reactions during trial.
- Help prepare opening and closing arguments.
- Prepare an outline of prosecution and defense cases.
- Coordinate specific documents with witnesses during testimony.
- Verify that all depositions have been filed.
- Prepare charts, diagrams, and other visual aids for use at trial.
- Coordinate telephone contact with offices and witnesses.
- Help in planning and strategy.
- Take notes and monitor related hearing and trials.
- Help prepare witnesses for testimony in trial or deposition.
- Investigate background information about potential jurors, including areas of residence, political affiliations, and other pertinent information.
- Draft jury instructions.
- Help with analysis of voir dire.

- Prepare complete notes of witness testimony.
- Help interview the jury following the verdict.

The paralegal can also be valuable in the sentencing process by

- Helping the client in meetings with probation officer.
- Arranging for bail.
- Obtaining discovery (police reports, search warrant, affidavit, and related documents).
- Drafting motions compelling discovery.
- Doing legal research.
- Subpoenaing and interviewing witnesses.
- Examining physical evidence and tangible objects.
- Examining and photographing the scene of the alleged crime.
- Coordinating and arranging for outside investigators and experts.
- Preparing trial notebooks.
- Drafting supplemental memoranda of law.
- Drafting motions in arrest of judgment, for new trial, for release pending new trial or appeal, and related motions.
- Drafting petitions for leniency or probation.
- Drafting notices of appeal.
- Preparing reports and investigating alternative sentencing methods.
- Helping client effectuate restitutions.
- Helping with change of plea matters, including drafting the petition to enter a plea of guilty.
- Investigating facts for decision to prosecute or prepare defense.
- Interviewing the client to gather information.
- Gathering information for plea bargaining and preparing charges or plea for arraignment.
- Preparing for preliminary hearings or grand jury presentations.
- Drafting testimony of defendants.
- Analyzing cases based on discovery.
- Drafting motions for change of venue.
- Drafting demurrers.
- Drafting motions to set indictment, to suppress, to covert, for civil compromise, for diversion, in limine, for return of property, to postpone trial, to disqualify judges, and to withdraw as attorney of record.
- Drafting and responding to interrogatories.
- Drafting deposition questions and deposition summaries.
- Arranging civil compromises.
- Arranging for rehabilitation or other programs.
- Arranging work release.
- Drafting trial memoranda.
- Attending conferences with prosecutors.
- Attending pretrial conferences with judges and attorneys.
- Drafting jury instructions.
- Attending and helping at trials.
- Attending conferences with clients and attorneys regarding presentence reports.
- Preparing sentencing information and working with probation officers.
- Researching law regarding appealable issues.
- Drafting assignments of error and arguments.[1]

FIGURE 10.1   Procedural Steps in Criminal Litigation

Source: U.S. District Court for the Southern District of Texas, Federal Attorney Practice home page, *Typical Progression of Criminal Litigation,* available at http://www.txs. uscourts.gov/atyadm/fedpractice/progcrimlit.pdf.

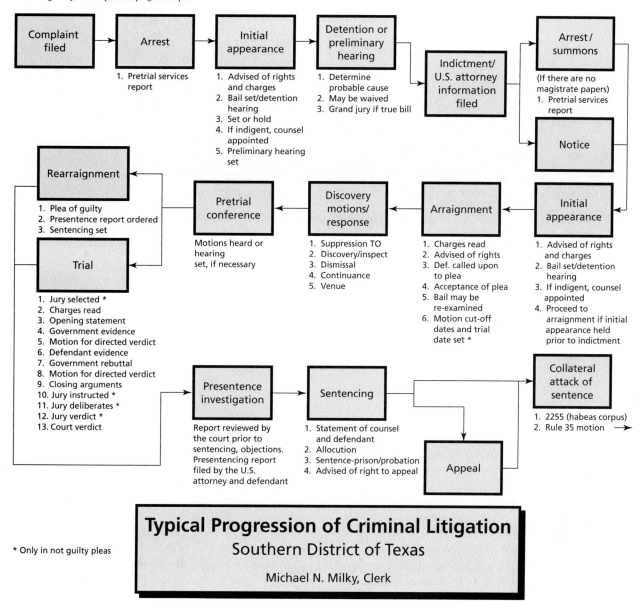

Figure 10.1 charts the diverse procedural steps in criminal litigation, at any of which the paralegal can deliver meaningful services.

Even though procedural steps make up the bulk of the paralegal's responsibilities, it is critical that the paralegal understand the content and concepts of criminal law and the general requirements of culpability. Other topics of importance include the classification of offenses and corresponding definitions.

DEFINING CRIMINAL LIABILITY

The criminal act, in the most general terms, consists of two elements:

Actus reus: the act or deed.

Mens rea: the criminal mind or intent.

Criminal conduct generally assumes some specific, executed activity. Punishing ideas does not sit well in a democracy, and the criminal system focuses on deeds—not thoughts. This is the essence of actus reus. The term *actus reus* means the thing done or carried out, and in the case of a criminal charge, it is elemental that the prosecutor be able to point to an act that constitutes the essence of the offense.

The Model Penal Code mandates the element of actus reus, as well as other components, before any imposition of criminal liability. Section 2.01 states in part:

> *(1) A person is not guilty of an offense unless his liability is based on conduct which includes a voluntary act or the omission to perform an act which it was physically possible to perform.*[2]

Stated simply, to be a criminal, one must do rather than think about doing it.

Criminal culpability also looks to mind and the mental faculty of the perpetrator. Acts alone do not suffice. The sum and substance of criminal culpability assumes not only the act but also the corresponding mindset that manifests intentionality. In Western jurisprudence, more than movement is required. Acts plus the mind trigger culpability:

$$\text{Actus reus} + \text{Mens rea} = \text{Culpability}$$

In short, acts are prompted and nourished by intention.

Elements of a Crime

The Criminal Act (Actus Reus)

Criminal liability attaches only if there is a deed, an act, an offense, a commission, or certain omission or dereliction of some legal responsibility. For example, to be a thief implies the taking of something without right or privilege. Although a person may obsessively want another's property, until some overt act or course of conduct is chosen, there is no actus reus.[3]

A criminal act must be a voluntary act. The mind must desire or intend the specific act in question. Those coerced or forced into action, or those suffering from some sort of mental deficit or incapacitation or other serious mitigation, may not be responsible for the acts in question. Acts must be coupled with a voluntary player to assign criminal liability.

Acts, for criminal purposes, are volitional rather than the product of convulsion, reflex, or somnambulism. To be criminal, the act images free choice and will in the person. Accountability and responsibility can be directed only to those aware of circumstances and those moving unfettered in the choice between one act or another. The sleepwalker and the hypnotically induced do not decide freely.

To act implies a motion of sorts, the doing of some deed. *Commission* describes actus reus. Commission signifies that the criminal agent has carried through the mentally conceived plan of action. Commission represents the culmination of thought and the transformation of mind to deed. To hold otherwise would be contrary to our most fundamental notions of criminal responsibility, whereby a conviction would be improper unless the actor "committed some act in furtherance of the intent."[4]

Plainly commission represents the primary meaning of *actus reus*. Another avenue for criminal conduct can be witnessed in the failure to act—an omission as contrasted with commission. Instead of commission, the criminal act finds its substance in inactivity or failure to do what is required. So acts are either committed or omitted. The Model Penal Code clearly lays out the distinction:

> *(3) Liability for the commission of an offense may not be based on an omission unaccompanied by action unless*
> *(a) the omission is expressly made sufficient by the law defining the offense; or*
> *(b) a duty to perform the omitted act is otherwise imposed by law.*[5]

The concept of omission is particularly complicated because it blends the subtleties of moral and legal obligation. In other words, there are many things we should do in the moral sphere but are not legally obligated to perform. Omission looks for a certain linkage between parties who have specified obligations. For example, a parent has various obligations and responsibilities that involve the care and maintenance of offspring: education, food, shelter, and supervision. This same expectation, however, would not be assigned to strangers and detached citizens, even though there is some moral and spiritual sense of communal obligation to others. Even though troubling, nonobliged parties who see and hear of abuse heaped on others may have little or no obligation to intervene. To omit aiding an injured motorist would be criminal for an emergency medical technician or police personnel, though hardly criminal for someone who drives by. It may be bothersome in a moral sense, but it is not illegal.

The Criminal Mind (Mens Rea)

Determining the state of someone's mind, the mens rea, is a far more complicated exercise than the determination of a criminal act. Discerning someone's mind is a subjective undertaking. For the most part, legal analysis looks to facts and conditions caused by the defendant to impute or infer a mental state. The law also presumes that criminal agents understand and know the consequences of chosen conduct.

Mens rea is about the intentionality of the perpetrator, and the definitions of particular criminal offenses employ the language of the mind. Some common examples are these:

- Felonious intent.
- Criminal intent.
- Malice aforethought.
- Premeditated.
- Guilty knowledge.
- Fraudulent intent.
- Willful.
- With scienter.
- With guilty knowledge.
- Maliciously.
- Viciously.
- Intentionally.
- With gross disregard.
- With depraved heart.
- With an evil purpose.
- Wantonly.
- Unlawfully.
- Without justification.
- With a corrupted mind.
- Criminally negligent.
- With disregard for human life.
- With depraved indifference.
- With moral turpitude.
- Without justification.
- Overtly.
- With mischievous intent.[6]

There are, as the Model Penal Code states, diverse degrees of mental culpability:

Section 2.02. General requirements of culpability.

(1) Minimum requirements of culpability. Except as provided in Section 2.05, a person is not guilty of an offense unless he acted purposely, knowingly, recklessly, or negligently as the law may require with respect to each material element of the offense.

(2) Kinds of culpability defined.
(a) Purposely. A person acts purposely with respect to a material element of an offense when
(i) if the element involves the nature of his conduct or a result thereof, it is his conscious object to engage in conduct; and
(ii) if the element involves the attendant circumstances, he knows the existence of such circumstances.
(b) Knowingly. A person acts knowingly with respect to a material element of offense when
(i) if the element involves the nature of his conduct or the attendant circumstances, he is aware that his conduct is of that nature. . . .; and
(ii) if the element involves a result of his conduct, he is aware that it is practically certain that his conduct will cause such result.
(c) Recklessly. A person acts recklessly with respect to a material element of an offense when he consciously disregards a substantial and unjustifiable risk that the material exists or will result from his conduct . . .
(d) Negligently. A person acts negligently with respect to a material element of an offense when he should be aware of a substantial and unjustifiable risk that the material element exists or will result from his conduct . . .[7]

The task of the criminal practitioner and investigator is to match facts to a particular sort of intentionality. In light of this, the legal player ties the act to the intellect—where the criminal agent knows and wills a certain result. In other words, the act results from the free, willing person with the mind to make decisions. Not every case may have this equation because some defendants may be insane or emotionally disturbed or suffer from such severe mitigation that free choice is substantially affected. In this dual analysis of act and mind, the law insists on a correlation between the two—a view that one causes the other. The courts refer to this as *causation*. In all jurisdictions, the law fully requires a concurrence of act and intent because "criminal liability is predicated upon a union of act and intent or criminal negligence."[8]

In historic terms, the term *mens rea* signified what and how the perpetrator thought as he or she carried out the offense. From its Latin translation, "things thought" or "mind things," this essential component of every criminal offense delves into a region unseen. How can a mind and its content be measured? How are thoughts cataloged and computed? Mens rea is the intellectualization of criminality; it is the mental formulation of malevolent design and plan, the overall thought process by which offenders offend. It means, at a minimum, that a "person intends the natural and probable consequences of his act."[9] Much more than motive, mens rea depicts the criminal's mindset during the commission of the felonious conduct. The carefully chosen words used in statutes connote the mental faculty of the perpetrator and represent what the law demands as proof of mental choice.

At the state level, definitions of act and mental states are part and parcel of criminal codes. Examples from Delaware and Missouri are selectively reproduced to highlight the mental element central to criminal codification:

§231. Definitions relating to state of mind.

(a) *"Intentionally." A person acts intentionally with respect to an element of an offense when*
  (1) *If the element involves the nature of the person's conduct or a result thereof, it is the person's conscious object to engage in conduct of that nature or to cause that result; and*
  (2) *If the element involves the attendant circumstances, the person is aware of the existence of such circumstances or believes or hopes that they exist.*

(b) *"Knowingly." A person acts knowingly with respect to an element of an offense when*
  (1) *If the element involves the nature of the person's conduct or the attendant circumstances, the person is aware that the conduct is of that nature or that such circumstances exist; and*
  (2) *If the element involves a result of the person's conduct, the person is aware that it is practically certain that the conduct will cause that result.*

(c) *"Recklessly." A person acts recklessly with respect to an element of an offense when the person is aware of and consciously disregards a substantial and unjustifiable risk that the element exists or will result from the conduct. The risk must be of such a nature and degree that disregard thereof constitutes a gross deviation from the standard of conduct that a reasonable person would observe in the situation. A person who creates such a risk but is unaware thereof solely by reason of voluntary intoxication also acts recklessly with respect thereto.*

(d) *"Criminal negligence." A person acts with criminal negligence with respect to an element of an offense when the person fails to perceive a risk that the element exists or will result from the conduct. The risk must be of such a nature and degree that failure to perceive it constitutes a gross deviation from the standard of conduct that a reasonable person would observe in the situation.*

(e) *"Negligence." A person acts with negligence with respect to an element of an offense when the person fails to exercise the standard of care which a reasonable person would observe in the situation.*[10]

562.016. Culpable mental state.

1. *Except as provided in Section 562.026, a person is not guilty of an offense unless he acts with a culpable mental state—that is, unless he acts purposely or knowingly or recklessly or with criminal negligence, as the statute defining the offense may require with respect to the conduct, the result thereof, or the attendant circumstances which constitute the material elements of the crime.*

2. *A person "acts purposely," or with purpose, with respect to his conduct or to a result thereof when it is his conscious object to engage in that conduct or to cause that result.*

3. *A person "acts knowingly," or with knowledge,*
  (1) *With respect to his conduct or to attendant circumstances when he is aware of the nature of his conduct or that those circumstances exist; or*
  (2) *With respect to a result of his conduct when he is aware that his conduct is practically certain to cause that result.*

4. A person "acts recklessly" or is reckless when he consciously disregards a substantial and
    unjustifiable risk that circumstances exist or that a result will follow, and such disregard
    constitutes a gross deviation from the standard of care which a reasonable person would
    exercise in the situation.

5. A person "acts with criminal negligence" or is criminally negligent when he fails to be
    aware of a substantial and unjustifiable risk that circumstances exist or a result will follow,
    and such failure constitutes a gross deviation from the standard of care which a reasonable
    person would exercise in the situation.[11]

This is the primary task of the prosecution team: to show mental states coupled with completed
or attempted action. To prove the overwhelming bulk of criminal charges, proof will be proffered
that manifests the intentionality of the accused. Mental motivations, mental plans and designs,
desires, choices, and wills are fundamental to any successful prosecution. From the defense
perspective, disproof of these very same requirements frees the accused. The defense approach
focuses on how an accused may mistakenly have acted, or did so without the requisite malice
or reckless disregard, or operated without grave indifference to human life. From either vantage
point, mens rea acts as lynchpin as the criminal case unfolds. The most efficacious prosecution
or defense depends on its proof or disproof. In the final analysis, mens rea drives juror or judicial thinking as the ultimate issue of guilt or innocence is evaluated. Jurors can readily discern
whether acts have been done (such as murder, arson, or rape), for as witnesses to reality we
decipher motion and activity during our daily existence.

Classification of Offenses and Related Penalties

Statutory guidelines structure crime into these basic categories:

- Felony.
- Misdemeanor.
- Summary offense.
- Treason.[12]

In common law, criminal offenses were defined in a threefold way: treason, felony, and misdemeanor. The distinctions were largely a reflection of the offense's subject matter and its inherent
gravity.

For the typical criminal law practitioner, felonies and misdemeanors will be the common
practice area. Treason and other infamous crimes may result from political espionage, sedition,
or other heinous actions against the government, and are sometimes the practice specialty of civil
liberties specialists. Summary offenses generally consist of public order violations, including
failure to pay parking tickets, creating a temporary obstruction in a public place, public intoxication, or other offenses of a less serious nature rarely punishable by a term of imprisonment.[13]

Paralegals need to be able to differentiate a felony from a misdemeanor. In common law, a
felony constituted an extremely serious offense. Historically felony convictions met with harsh
results from the death penalty to forfeiture of all lands, goods, and other personal property. Customarily a felony was synonymous with specific capital offenses, including murder, manslaughter, rape, sodomy, robbery, larceny, arson, burglary, mayhem, and other violent conduct.[14] *Felony*
was defined "to mean offenses for which the offender, on conviction, may be punished by death
or imprisonment in the state prison or penitentiary; but in the absence of such statute the word is
used to designate such serious offenses as are formally punishable by death, or by forfeiture of
the lands or goods of the offender."[15]

Modern criminal practice sees a bit more confusion because the question of severity and grade
will not always correlate to the felony/misdemeanor distinction. Although generally felonies are
construed as more serious acts than misdemeanors, the reality can be quite different. A President's Commission on Law Enforcement and Administration of Justice, in its *Task Force Report
on the Courts*,[16] relates,

> A study of the Oregon penal code revealed that 1,413 criminal statutes contained a total of 466
> different types and lengths of sentences.
>
> The absence of legislative attention to the whole range of penalties may also be demonstrated
> by comparisons between certain offenses. A recent study of the Colorado statutes disclosed that
> a person convicted of a first degree murder must serve ten (10) years before becoming eligible
> for parole, while a person convicted of a lesser degree of the same offense must serve at least
> fifteen (15) years; destruction of a house with fire is punishable by a maximum twenty (20) years'

> *imprisonment, but destruction of a house with explosives carries a ten (10) year maximum. In California, an offender who breaks into an automobile to steal the contents of the glove compartment is subject to a fifteen (15) year maximum sentence; but if he stole the car itself, he would face a maximum ten (10) year term.*
>
> *Although each offense must be defined in a separate statutory provision, the number and variety of sentencing distinctions that result when legislatures prescribe a separate penalty for each offense are among the main causes of the anarchy in sentencing that is so widely deplored.[17]*

Finally, in defining the term *misdemeanor,* a legislative design that fails to designate a criminal act as either a felony or misdemeanor will automatically label it as a misdemeanor. The practitioner will not always find logic in the application of these principles, and classification systems are often the product of political and social influences. Most sexual offense statutes manifest this extraordinary displacement.[18]

Treason

Treason is a very specialized offense dealing with the betrayal of country. Acts of treason were certainly highlighted by the case of FBI agent Robert Hanssen, whose clandestine activities in union with Russian spies created one of this nation's most notorious cases.

Selling secrets to the enemy—exchanging information for money to the detriment of one's own homeland—represents a daring untrustworthiness that must be dealt with harshly. In Hanssen's case, the offenses committed over a three-decade period led to death and leaks in national security. So serious are these types of infractions that the Founding Fathers of this nation spelled out the crime in explicit detail within the Constitution:

> *Treason against the United States shall consist only in levying war against them, or in adhering to their enemies, giving them aid and comfort. No person shall be convicted of treason unless on the testimony of two witnesses to the same overt act, or on confession in open court. The congress shall have power to declare the punishment of treason; but no attainder of treason shall work corruption of blood or forfeiture except during the life of the person attainted.[19]*

Since medieval times, the offense has further been defined as either *high* or *petit* (lower), though this distinction has largely been lost in contemporary settings. Federal criminal codifications still employ the language of treason, though it is no longer separate from the felony/misdemeanor classification:

> *Sec. 2381. Treason.*
>
> *Whoever, owing allegiance to the United States, levies war against them or adheres to their enemies, giving them aid and comfort within the United States or elsewhere, is guilty of treason and shall suffer death, or shall be imprisoned not less than five years and fined under this title but not less than $10,000; and shall be incapable of holding any office under the United States.[20]*

Treason has also been typed an "infamous crime" since the emergence of the common-law tradition. The term *infamous* described a corrupt disqualification from giving testimony in any legal forum, a deceit and fraudulent character, and a general untrustworthiness that the law could not tolerate. To be infamous is to be famous for all the wrong reasons—just as FBI agent Robert Hanssen has now become. Betrayal of country may also fall under other statutory constructs such as sedition and espionage.[21]

Felonies

The more serious of the major crime classifications, felonies constitute the bulk of first and second degree crimes, or the common-law capital or forfeiture offenses. A capital offense in common law could result in the imposition of death, and it was nearly impossible for the death penalty to be inflicted in misdemeanor cases. A forfeiture offense signified a loss of property right or interest in personalty or realty. Common-law felonies were cataloged as follows:

- Murder
- Manslaughter
- Rape
- Sodomy
- Robbery
- Larceny
- Arson
- Burglary
- Mayhem

Recent statutory constructions have been quite liberal in extending this basic list of felonies. For example, drug possession offenses, habitual offender statutes, and other enhancement provisions involving hate crimes and ethnic intimidation may not be, on close inspection, as morally grave as other conduct that still retains a misdemeanor title. Even so, these politically influenced offenses have achieved felony status. New York's nonparole drug offense has been attacked for more than 20 years for its extraordinary harshness by launching smaller crimes into a larger, graver sphere.[22] DUI and other intoxication offenses, once the province of the petty misdemeanor category, have been recast in felonious mode due to the harm inflicted and public outcry. In other words, things once minor can become major if pressure is substantial enough. Criminal offenses, whether discerned or not, are subject to the push and pull of political factions and public clamor. For this reason alone, one should not become too comfortable holding that all felonies are fundamentally more serious than misdemeanor counterparts.[23]

Aside from the gravity of the offense, the felony definition rests upon how long an accused can be incarcerated or whether the penalty of death is possible. As general rule, felonies allow a minimum of 365 days of incarceration or death, whereas misdemeanor penalties are less than 365 days and afford no chance of death penalty imposition. This is a crude but telling qualification because the felony actor incurs harsher penalty results than the misdemeanant.

Blackstone, an influential legal thinker in Western tradition, laid this out in his *Commentaries* more than three centuries ago:

> *A crime, or misdemeanor, is an act committed, or omitted, in violation of a public law, either forbidding or commanding it. This general definition comprehends both crimes and misdemeanors; which properly speaking are mere synonymous terms: though, in common usage, the word "crimes" is made to denote such offences as are of a deeper and more atrocious dye; while smaller faults, and omissions of less consequence, are comprised under the gentler name of "misdemeanors" only.*[24]

In this way, one looks to the penalty possibilities outlined in the statute governing the offense. In either determinate or indeterminate sentencing schemes, an express time period, say 10 years, or between 2 and 5 years, of potential incarceration will be listed. The more onerous the punishment, anything beyond 365 days will mean the offense is a felony—less, and the opposite conclusion is drawn. "Under such a statute, it is the potential punishment that may be imposed which determines whether an offense is a felony, and not the punishment that is actually imposed in a particular case."[25]

Misdemeanors

In addition to the term of incarceration, the misdemeanor qualification rests on grounds of gravity, seriousness, and diversion to alternative disposition. For the most part, misdemeanors are lower grade or degree offenses in criminal codifications and of lesser gravity and seriousness. Just as in the evolution of felonies, misdemeanors go through varying degrees of growth and ebb, whereby the offense offends our sensibilities depending on the state of our knowledge and moral outrage. Certain sodomy offenses were once designated felony offenses punishable by death—even the consensual variety. Today many of these statutes have been decriminalized or reduced to lower misdemeanor forms. The story of drug law tells a similar story. As the push to decriminalize continues, we regularly see formerly bedrock criminality turned into less strenuous offenses, or as public pressure increases to the level of contagion, once tolerable behavior recast in satanic terms. In general, however, misdemeanors do not undercut the greater good as intensely as the felony counterpart.

Misdemeanor punishments are more commonly diverted to alternative disposition. Instead of filling our prison facilities with less despicable offenders than the felony audience, the penalty infrastructure recognizes the worthiness of other penalty approaches such as community service, probation, work release, or simply far less time spent in correctional facilities. DUI/DWI litigation has shown the systematic willingness to divert a large population of offenders into alternative disposition and to allow the justice model to penalize the infractions with diverse approaches not usually witnessed in the world of felonies.

A sample statute that represents the misdemeanor format is given here:

(E) PENALTY.—

(1) Any person violating any of the provisions of this section is guilty of a misdemeanor of the second degree, except that a person convicted of a third or subsequent offense is guilty of a misdemeanor of the first degree, and the sentencing court shall order the person to pay a fine of not less than $300 and serve a minimum term of imprisonment of

    (i) Not less than 48 consecutive hours.

    (ii) Not less than 30 days if the person has previously accepted Accelerated Rehabilitative Disposition or any other form of preliminary disposition, or been convicted of, adjudicated delinquent, or granted a consent decree under the Juvenile Act (42 Pa.C.S. §6301 et seq.) based on an offense under this section or of an equivalent offense in this or other jurisdictions within the previous seven years.

    (iii) Not less than 90 days if the person has twice previously been convicted of, adjudicated delinquent, or granted a consent decree under the Juvenile Act based on an offense under this section or of an equivalent offense in this or other jurisdictions within the previous seven years.

    (iv) Not less than one year if the person has three times previously been convicted of, adjudicated delinquent, or granted a consent decree under the Juvenile Act based on an offense under this section or of an equivalent offense in this or other jurisdictions within the previous seven years.[26]

Summary/Petty Offenses

Further down the hierarchical schema of crime classifications are the designations *summary* and *petty*. The word *summary* indicates the fluid, almost automatically dispositional nature of the offense, meaning the system deals with the offense summarily. *Petty*, from the French adjective *petit*, means small or insignificant. As a rule, summary offenses are minor in nature and are defined as such to allow the justice system to dispense with them readily. Disorderly conduct or vagrancy, as illustrations, are repetitive offenses witnessed with regularity in the justice system. It would be insensible to dedicate the full machinery of the judicial system to offenses of this nature and far more rational to dispose of them expeditiously. Public intoxication, loitering, first-time shoplifting, and other similar offenses neatly fit this category and allow the justice model to process these recurring cases quickly and efficiently. Common-law tradition provides no precedential authority for enactment of these types of offenses, and legislative tinkering to basic felony and misdemeanors erects this lower infrastructure of criminality.

§168-13. Specific acts and penalties.

The following shall be considered violations and penalties for improper parking and, as such, are prohibited acts:

B. Specific acts and penalty.

    (1) The following are prohibited acts:

        (a) Parking in a no-parking zone.

        (b) Parking in an intersection or in a marked bus stop.

        (c) Parking so as to impede traffic.

        (d) Parking double.

        (e) Parking in a no-standing area.

    (2) The penalty for any violation of this subsection is $17.[27]

Finally, the term *infraction* is sometimes employed in the criminal realm and by most accounts refers to traffic or other municipal offenses, such as failure to shovel a sidewalk or obtain licensure for a pet. Infractions are so innocuous that imprisonment remains impossible, with fines and other collections being the sole means of enforceability and correction.

Specific Types of Crimes and Offenses

Offenses against the Person

This subsection discusses felonious acts of homicide and other crimes that cause injurious actions against the person.

Homicide   Homicide is the killing of another person, though the action may or may not be criminal. Nonculpable homicide occurs when the reaction is excusable, such as the case of self-defense, necessity in time of war, or by legal right, authority, or privilege.[28] Criminal homicide is defined by the Model Penal Code as follows:

> *Section 2.10.1. Criminal Homicide*
>
> *(1) A person is guilty of criminal homicide if he purposely, knowingly, recklessly, or negligently causes the death of another human being.*
> *(2) Criminal homicide is murder, manslaughter, or negligent homicide.*[29]

The Model Penal Code, after this general legislative introduction, precisely defines each type of homicide.

Most murder statutes define the seriousness of the offense with clear-cut terms such as *premeditation, willfulness, knowing,* and *intentional*. Tennessee's template for Murder 1 reflects standard practice in the United States:

> *(a) First degree murder is*
> *(1) A premeditated and intentional killing of another;*
> *(2) A killing of another committed in the perpetration of or attempt to perpetrate first degree murder, arson, rape, burglary, theft, kidnapping, aggravated child abuse, aggravated child neglect, or aircraft piracy; or*
> *(3) A killing of another committed as the result of the unlawful throwing, placing, or discharging of a destructive device or bomb.*[30]

Within this design rests the archetypal elements of the murder charge—namely premeditation, intentional killings, plots and plans that utilize bombs and other destructive devices, and deaths caused during the commission of a major felony. Classic conspiracy plans have been repeatedly held as sufficient evidence for conviction under Murder 1 rules. Telling others of the intent to kill, making public threats to kill, and drawing up plans to carry out the kill signify the type of mental preparation necessary for the most heinous crime.[31]

In common law, murder convictions depended on a finding of premeditation—preparation and planning of the crime before the event and exercise of will and choice unfettered. To premeditate was to plan in advance, to meditate through the sequence to unfold. This intellectual process has also been labeled *deliberation* and *malice aforethought*. Murder was a more unified crime with fewer degrees and grades, as the learned scholar Wharton notes:

> *Although at common law there were no degrees of murder, most jurisdictions have subdivided murder into two or more degrees.*[32]

In contemporary settings the distinction has dissolved somewhat, being redeployed in the sentencing phase more than the charge component. By this, the legal system spends less of its energy trying to prove the purity of the defendant's mental processes and more of its time arguing on behalf of harsher punishments for those who premeditate. Undoubtedly the death penalty appears reserved for those who revel and choose with wild abandon and less for those who act in spontaneity and passion. Murder 1 people know exactly what to do and when to do it. Today the murder construct erects many more degrees and gradations in the definition of murder by adding provisions that account for passion, provocation, gross negligence, and depraved indifference to others.

Murder

> *A charge of murder will be upheld when*
>
> *(a) it is committed purposely or knowingly; or*
> *(b) it is committed recklessly under circumstances manifesting extreme indifference to the value of human life. Such recklessness and indifference are presumed if the actor is engaged or is an accomplice in the commission of or an attempt to commit, or flight after committing or attempting to commit robbery, rape, deviate sexual intercourse by force or threat of force, arson, burglary, kidnapping, or felonious escape.*[33]

Murder calls for the highest level of criminal intentionality. In this sense, the killer wants the end result and is thereby considered to have specific intent. *Specific intent* has been described as premeditation or a mind with malice aforethought. The criminal actor wants, desires, wishes, knows, and realizes the ramifications and repercussions of his or her activity. Although the law does not require an intelligent or an esoteric thinker, it does insist on mental clarity in the decision making. In *People v. Moran,* the level of mind required was keenly described as follows:[34]

> *Malice aforethought is the intention to kill, actual or implied, under circumstances that do not constitute excuse or justification or mitigate the degree of the offense of manslaughter. The intent to kill may be implied where the actor intends to inflict great bodily harm or the natural tendency of his behavior is to cause death or great bodily harm.*[35]

Although the manner of death will lead to deductions about the level of intentionality, paralegals need to evaluate conduct both directly and circumstantially.

When the facts lack the necessary clarity to meet the murder in the first degree burden, a lower grade of murder may be more suitable. Murder in the second degree applies to less crystalline cases of mental intentionality. M2 focuses on the knowledge factor more than the plot. To know and accept the death to be inflicted is to have rationalized and thought about it. To know is to understand the full implications yet still proceed with the criminal agency:

> *§14-17. Murder in the first and second degree defined; punishment.*
>
> *A murder which shall be perpetrated by means of poison, lying in wait, imprisonment, starving, torture, or by any other kind of willful, deliberate, and premeditated killing, or which shall be committed in the perpetration or attempted perpetration of any arson, rape or a sex offense, robbery, kidnapping, burglary, or other felony committed or attempted with the use of a deadly weapon shall be deemed to be murder in the first degree . . . All other kinds of murder, including that which shall be proximately caused by the unlawful distribution of opium or any synthetic or natural salt, compound, derivative, or preparation of opium, or cocaine or other substance described in G.S. 90-90(1)d., when the ingestion of such substance causes the death of the user, shall be deemed murder in the second degree.*[36]

Some jurisdictions have designated certain actions as so depraved and indifferent that the inference of knowledge is permissible. In other words, how else can conduct be rationally explained except that the actor desired the particular end? Nebraska's statute could not be plainer about this:

> *Murder in the second degree; penalty. (1) A person commits murder in the second degree if he causes the death of a person intentionally, but without premeditation.*[37]

In common law, the trier searched for a level of "malice" that subjectively explained objective actions. Why else would the defendant kill except for maliciousness and evil heart? Malice imputes wrongfulness in the actor and partially explains the criminality. However, murderers come in many shapes and sizes and may or may not operate with depravity, malice, or evil at the base of the conduct. The contract "hit man" kills even people he may know or like and rationalizes the conduct as "business" and an occupational risk. Malice may explain some forms of intentionality but not all of them. Hence the contemporary perspective is to weigh the conduct as either expressly or impliedly instructive of the actor's intentions. It is fair to impute and infer from conduct the corresponding depravity and bad motive. It is acceptable to judge another's intentions from the results of his or her decision making. "American law followed the general pattern of the English common law. To the present, American casebooks and treatises consistently define malice as"[38]

> *(1) An intent to kill someone, not necessarily the victim . . . (2) An intent to commit "serious" or "grievous" bodily injury upon someone. (3) A wanton and reckless disregard of a very great risk of causing death or serious bodily injury . . . The older statutes use language such as "depraved heart" or an "abandoned and malignant heart" to refer to this type of culpability. (4) Malice is also implied when the defendant or his accomplice commits a killing in the perpetration of certain felonies.*[39]

Whether an accused "knowingly" attempted to kill his or her victim is a question of fact for the jury.[40] "Intent, which can seldom be proven by direct evidence, may be deduced or inferred by the trier of fact from the character of the assault, the nature of the act, and from all the circumstances of the case in evidence."[41]

Felony Murder.   In felony murder defendants find little solace in mitigation, lack of intentionality, and other traditional defense mechanisms. The theory of felony murder holds the convicted accountable with little or no proof of mens rea and looks first to a series of actions willingly engaged in and last, if at all, at how a defendant thought those actions might unravel. The felony murder rule has two fundamental aims: "(1) to impose liability on a felon for an unintended homicide committed by the felon or someone working in concert with the felon during a felony and (2) to deter a person from committing a felony because of the liability that is attached if a homicide occurs during the felony."[42] A felony murderer not only kills but does so while committing a distinct and underlying felony delineated in the statutory design. Felony murderers kill during the commission of a specified felony, such as robbery, arson, rape, or battery. Felony murderers comprise a unique and distinctive class of accused because guilt may be imposed without achieving the requisite elements of criminal law culpability. Actus reus is what drives this horse, not mens rea. In this way, the penalties of felony murder are extraordinarily harsh in select cases and proportionate in others.

Central to any real understanding of the felony murder doctrine is the requirement that the death of another occur during the commission of particular category of felony. Not all felonies qualify for this treatment, and legislatures list ad seriatim those felonies that trigger the rule. Here is an example:

> *All murder which shall be committed in the perpetration of, or attempt to perpetrate, any rape in any degree, sexual offense in the first or second degree, sodomy, mayhem, robbery, carjacking or armed carjacking, burglary in the first, second, or third degree, a violation . . . of this article concerning destructive devices, kidnapping as defined . . . this article, or in the escape or attempt to escape from . . . any institution or facility under the jurisdiction of the Division of Correction of the Division of Pretrial Detention and Services, or from any jail or penal institution in any of the counties of this State, shall be murder in the first degree.*[43]

The Illinois Code provides useful language as well:

> *Treason, first degree murder, second degree murder, predatory criminal sexual assault of a child, aggravated criminal sexual assault, criminal sexual assault, robbery, burglary, residential burglary, aggravated arson, arson, aggravated kidnapping, kidnapping, aggravated battery resulting in great bodily harm or permanent disability or disfigurement, and any other felony which involves the use or threat of physical force or violence against any individual.*[44]

The reach of the rule's liberal net of potential victims as the underlying felony appears endless. In short, any party who dies prompts the rule's application and includes intended and unintended parties.[45] Thus the concept of victimhood spreads wide under the principle and includes

- The intended victim.
- Any inadvertent victim.
- A bypasser.
- An onlooker.
- A public safety officer responding to the scene.
- EMT/fire personnel.
- A rescuer or good Samaritan.
- Other defendants and perpetrators.
- An accomplice, conspirator, or other participant.

Another facet of the felony murder rule that intrigues legal commentators and jurists relates to how the principal's act will bind all the principal's cohorts whether accessories, conspirators, accomplices, or possibly solicitors, aiders, and abettors. In other words, the felony murder rule grabs each defendant involved in the deed and declares each equally accountable. Hence the escape driver may not pull the trigger while passing time waiting for the getaway, though he or she might as well have.[46] Any perpetrator subsumes each and every colleague into the web of culpability. Naive, dumbfounded, and surprised defendants cannot withstand the tug of the felony murder rule.[47]

A few legal locales simply transfer the intent of the felony to not only the subsequent killing but to all the actors involved. The doctrine of *transferred intent* differs from strict liability in that in the latter case no finding of mens rea is required, whereas in the former a mental state is imputed. Criminals choosing the path of felonious activity have much to answer for under these stringent principles.

One final curiosity of the felony murder rule relates to its competing intentionalities. Although mens rea becomes somewhat irrelevant under the unusual felony murder rule fact pattern because the legislative pattern imposes strict liability, the exemption on proof becomes available only in cases where a demonstration of the underlying felony's mens rea has been achieved. In other words, proof of the rape, robbery, or other qualifying felony mandates satisfactory evidence of the defendant's mental state. Strict liability in the felony murder rule must extend to the felony that affords the rule's existence. A prosecutor unable to convict based on the root felony stands in legal quicksand on felony murder grounds. Hence, to avail oneself of the felony murder rule, proof of the qualifying felony is mandatory. Otherwise the defendant will be prosecuted as any other murderer is—under the fundamental elements of both act and mind. In the last instance, the prosecutor works much harder than the smooth sailing strict liability affords. From this perspective, the felony murder rule really contains two forms of intentionality:

Qualifying felony + Homicide = Felony murder rule

Any failure in the equation negates the felony murder rule case. If a killing does not occur, the issue of murder in any degree, outside of the attempted category, will not meet the threshold. If an underlying felony is not satisfactorily proven, the felony murder rule remains illusory also, and only the murder case survives.

Manslaughter Descending downward on the scale of homicidal responsibility, we next encounter the crime of manslaughter. *Manslaughter* is murder with passion, provocation, and mitigation—circumstances that take the perpetrator out of the realm of the cold and calculating. It comes in two varieties: voluntary and involuntary. In the *involuntary* form, it is an act of extreme or gross negligence. The *voluntary* form closely resembles murder except for the presence of mitigation and provocation. The manslaughter offender kills because of mitigation, which is roughly defined as any explanation prompting the criminal agent to act. The homicide occurs because or on account of

- The defendant's emotional rage and jealousy.
- The defendant's mental, familial, and economic pathology.
- The defendant's addictions and history of substance abuse.
- The defendant's psychological profile.
- The defendant's syndromes, from battered spouse to junk food deprivation.
- The defendant's reaction to provocation.
- The defendant's gross indifference to others but lack of direct intention.
- The defendant's psychiatric profile.

Specific intent is always required for a charge of murder. In the case of manslaughter the mental demands lessen. A murder under passionate circumstances, or caused by an offender suffering from any sort of mitigating factor, may lack the clear thinking necessary for the murder charge. Manslaughter appears to call for a mental state less lucid and more battered by external forces and conditions. These conditions are often referred to as *mitigating*. Essentially, a charge of manslaughter, whether voluntary or involuntary, mandates less of an evidentiary burden as to the defendant's mens rea. A voluntary manslaughter includes facts of substantial mitigation, as well as significant understanding and knowledge. In the involuntary case, gross carelessness and negligence manifest a paucity of thinking. A sample statute is reproduced here:

2503. *Voluntary manslaughter.*

(a) *GENERAL RULE.—A person who kills an individual without lawful justification commits voluntary manslaughter if at the time of the killing he is acting under a sudden and intense passion resulting from serious provocation by*
   (1) the individual killed; or
   (2) another whom the actor endeavors to kill, but he negligently or accidentally causes the death of the individual killed.

(b) UNREASONABLE BELIEF KILLING JUSTIFIABLE.—A person who intentionally or knowingly kills an individual commits voluntary manslaughter if at the time of the killing he believes the circumstances to be such that, if they existed, would justify the killing under Chapter 5 of this title, but his belief is unreasonable.

(c) GRADING.—Voluntary manslaughter is a felony of the first degree.[48]

2504. Involuntary manslaughter.

(a) GENERAL RULE.—A person is guilty of involuntary manslaughter when as a direct result of the doing of an unlawful act in a reckless or grossly negligent manner, or the doing of a lawful act in a reckless or grossly negligent manner, he causes the death of another person.

(b) GRADING.—Involuntary manslaughter is a misdemeanor of the first degree. Where the victim is under 12 years of age and is in the care, custody, or control of the person who caused the death, involuntary manslaughter is a felony of the second degree.[49]

Manslaughter evaluates mitigating circumstances, including provocation, intense passion, and sudden and impetuous events. In involuntary cases the issue of gross negligence is appropriately weighed. *Monroe v. Smith*[50] is one of those cases where it is evident that manslaughter and murder are often closely aligned. Evaluate these facts:

On March 25, 1999, defendant went to the marital home where his estranged wife, the victim, and his children were living. Defendant was admitted to the home by his stepdaughter, Jennifer. Although the screen door of the home was never locked, it was locked after defendant entered the home. Defendant entered the bedroom and spoke with the victim. The victim took her cellular telephone to Jennifer in case something happened. One week prior to this visit by defendant, victim had told neighbors that she feared that defendant would kill her. The couple spoke for an extensive period of time. Defendant told the victim that he thought about killing her, but it was not "worth it." At approximately 9:30 p.m., defendant telephoned his employer to advise that he would be late for work. Defendant indicated that he wanted to reconcile, but the victim was concerned about prior drug and physical abuse by defendant. At approximately midnight, the victim advised defendant that she needed to sleep. Defendant told the victim that she did not need to sleep and began to choke her. Defendant tried to get the victim to enter the basement, but she refused. The couple struggled, and the victim screamed for help. Jennifer tried to call 911, but found that the two telephones in the home had been disabled. Jennifer was unable to contact 911 with the cellular telephone. Jennifer observed defendant strike the victim in the face.

The victim tried to exit the home, but found that the screen door was locked. The victim was able to unlock the door and jump off the porch. Defendant chased after the victim with a knife. The victim was stabbed in the back. The victim struggled to get the knife from defendant. She was stabbed in the neck on two occasions. The victim managed to get the knife from defendant on two occasions and toss it aside. Each time, defendant retrieved the knife and attacked the victim. Neighbors observed the stabbing on the front lawn, called 911, and screamed at defendant to leave the victim alone. Neighbor James Waters jumped off his porch and said, "What in the hell are you doing, Bradford?" Defendant looked and began walking down the street.

The Waters family assisted the victim into their home. There was so much blood that it was difficult to discern where the stabbings wounds were located. The victim told the family to apply pressure to her neck. In addition to the neck and back wounds, the victim suffered numerous cuts to her hands. The victim was taken to the hospital where she was treated by Dr. Kenneth Gibb. Dr. Gibb testified that the neck injuries were life threatening because of the major blood vessels in the neck. However, the back injury was not life threatening because the stabbing had not pierced the victim's lungs. Near the scene, police observed defendant walking. When defendant saw the police, he fled and hid in a field, where he was arrested.

In his opening statement, defense counsel argued that the prosecutor could not establish the element of intent to kill because of defendant's alcohol and drug induced condition. At trial, the victim testified that defendant was "high." When asked to provide a factual support for that conclusion, the victim stated that she "knew" defendant, he had never acted so violently before, and his eyes were red. However, the victim also testified that defendant did not slur his words, did not ramble, and did not stagger. Jennifer testified that she did not smell alcohol on defendant when he arrived at the home. There was no evidence admitted at trial that defendant consumed any alcohol or drugs between the time of his arrival at the home and at the time of the attack. A police officer responsible for defendant's intake, who was trained in signs of alcohol and drug intoxication, did not perceive the conditions that evidence such consumption. Evidence at trial also revealed that defendant normally parked in the driveway or on the street, but during this visit, parked across the street in a plaza parking lot. The prosecution argued that this evidence, coupled with the screen door being locked and the disconnection of the telephones, evidenced the requisite intent and negated the intoxication defense.[51]

In these cases the court instructs the jury on the negligent nature of the act that causes harm. The defendant need not specifically intend the commission of any crime but could have or should have known the consequences. These are acts, mistaken and accidental in nature, that are unresponsive to others. Cases of automobile manslaughter, or the mishandling of weapons while in a drunken stupor, are good examples. Public defenders and defense counsel usually promote mitigating issues, hoping at a minimum for a reduction in charge. The inverse is true of prosecutors who are trying to avoid mitigation because it mucks up the clarity of the case.

A lack of time to deliberate and think things through rationally provides the backdrop for manslaughter when compared to the intellectual choice so evident in murder. Hence, in a rare reversal, a New York appellate court overturned the finding of the trial court when a security guard, reacting to the death of his partner, shot an assailant. Here three youths pummeled a colleague with a steel pipe. Enraged, the security guard fired upon the youths, killing one of them. Reversing the conviction of murder, the opinion relates,

> *The entire incident, including the shooting, unfolded within a matter of seconds leaving defendant with no opportunity for deliberation other than to react emotionally to the extreme circumstances confronting him.*[52]

In this case we identify a man under charged circumstances whose emotions are intense and reactionary. This emotional aura correctly mitigates the claim of the deliberation and premeditation. So too is the result witnessed in passionate and emotionally laden settings like these:

- Battered spouses.
- Sexual abuse.
- Terroristic threats and harassment.
- Love, sex, and betrayal.
- Envy, jealousy, and rage.

Like it or not, homicide occurs in less than deliberate venues. The complexity of human relationships, the unreliability of emotional reaction and overreaction, and the existence of human frailty guarantees some homicidal activity that falls short of the planned and premeditated. To be sure, every person has threatened another with the undignified affront "I could kill you!" Parents, children, and estranged lovers have heard it, as have teachers and police.[53] When the threat becomes more than idle chatter, criminality occurs. Manslaughter takes in these complicated confrontations and affords not exoneration for the acts but only another classification for the finding of culpability. Simply, manslaughter allows the defendant to explain why the homicide occurred in the first place, not necessarily in the sense of excuse or acquittal but as to influence and determinism. The criminal actor moves with forces above and beyond the usual freedom of the human agent. The human agent saddled with mitigation makes intentionality less apparent. Mitigation and mitigating factors are what the defense uses to explain, to elucidate the conduct in question. It is mitigation that catapults the thinking, intentional mind into another dimension filled with obtuse and ill-defined terms like these: *passion, provocation, mental illness, abuse as a child, spousal abuse syndrome, addictions, obsessions, jealousy, paramours, intoxication, neglect, Satanism, the occult, television, music, junk food, chemical imbalance, breastfeeding, bottle feeding, astrological signs, witchcraft, XYY chromosomes, genetic imbalance, religion, messages from God, animal instructions, mental disease and defect, ethnic rage, love, estrangement,* and *betrayal.*

Assault and Battery Assault and battery are threats or actual physical touching that causes harm to another. In a case of assault, the harm is imminent though not actualized. In battery, the harm, the offensive act, has been carried out. Most jurisdictions have merged assault and battery and assigned corresponding grades based on the level of harm.

The Model Penal Code proposed draft states the following:

Section 211.1. Assault.

(1) Simple Assault. A person is guilty of assault if he
 (a) attempts to cause or purposely, knowingly, or recklessly causes bodily injury to another; or
 (b) negligently causes bodily injury to another with a deadly weapon; or
 (c) attempts by physical menace to put another in fear of imminent serious bodily harm.

> *(2) Aggravated Assault. A person is guilty of aggravated assault if he*
>> *(a) attempts to cause serious bodily injury to another or causes such injury purposely, knowingly, or recklessly under circumstances manifesting extreme indifference to the value of human life; or*
>> *(b) attempts to cause or purposely or knowingly causes bodily injury to another with a deadly weapon.*[54]

Assault is a common criminal charge. Personal disturbances, domestic violence, and barroom brawls are likely settings for assault, though the severity can range to the major felony, "aggravated assault," when weaponry is used. Jurisdictions have gone even further by adopting *reckless endangerment*[55] statutes. For example, "a person commits a misdemeanor of the second degree if he recklessly engages in conduct that places or may place another person in danger of death or serious bodily injury."[56] Other criminal statutes possibly applicable in assault situations are

- Terroristic threats.
- Use of tear gas or other noxious substances.
- Harassment.
- Ethnic intimidation.[57]

Assault cases, from simple to aggravated, all contain core elements. First, the harm threatened or done must be of a serious nature, not the petty trifles and insults that civil damages cover. By serious, we mean substantive. One cannot assault another with a feather or spaghetti noodle, nor can a two-day-old baby inflict injury on another. The type of injury in assault has pathological and medical substance—the smash to the face, the broken bone, the tear or laceration, the bruise or contusion. The substantiality of the injury directly correlates to its severity, and the law of assault requires something measurable.

Second, the reaction of the injured party must be one of reasonableness. Threats of imminent harm and injury should be kept in some rational perspective, according to how the average and most reasonable person might react. Thus if a Mafia enforcer says, "I am going to break your face if your payment is not here tomorrow!" the average person appreciates the sincerity of the threat. On the other hand, if a seven-year-old screams at an adult, "I am going to break every bone in your body," the threat is illusory and without reasonable potential. To be a threat in any sense, the harm offered must have a bona fide possibility of being inflicted, and the party communicating the threat needs the capacity to carry it out. Reasonable people know what these words mean and just as intelligently can differentiate the idle or silly insult from the purposeful words of an impending assaulter. In short, the criminal actor must have the present and actual ability to carry out the threatened bodily injury.

Third, the person accused must possess the requisite intent set out in the statute. In the graver versions of assault, the actor wills and intends specifically; in the lower varieties, the actor knows or should know that injury is an inevitable outcome of the confrontation. Accidental touching does not qualify for criminal responsibility, though these mistaken actions can be remedied by damages in the civil courts.

Fourth, for a high grade of assault, such as aggravated, the prosecution team may have to produce a weapon or other instrument capable of inflicting harm. Weapons such as firearms and knives always qualify—but so do blunt instruments like tire irons, tools, wooden planks, baseball bats, chains, and steel bars. Aggravated cases may also involve the commission of a concurrent felony like rape or kidnapping, which generates a greater degree of culpability because of the forcible actions.

In general, the law of assault should not pose many problems for the justice professional as long as the facts fit nicely into the statutory definition.

Kidnapping Kidnapping is the unlawful confinement or restraint of a victim coupled with movement or transportation for ransom, political benefit, or other motivation. Kidnapping can also be a corollary offense in sexual assault and other crimes that witness some level of geographic movement during the commission of the offense. Statutorily, the Model Penal Code requires proof of these elements:

> *Section 212.1. Kidnapping.*
>
> *A person is guilty of kidnapping if he unlawfully removes another from his place of residence or business, or a substantial distance from the vicinity where he is found, or if he unlawfully*

confines another for a substantial period in a place of isolation, with any of the following purposes:

(a) to hold for ransom or reward or as a shield or hostage; or

(b) to facilitate commission of any felony or flight thereafter; or

(c) to inflict bodily injury on or to terrorize the victim or another; or

(d) to interfere with the performance of any government or political function.[58]

The asportation or movement requirement has been the subject of significant litigation. Contemporary case law tends to be liberal when measuring movement and would be satisfied with movement of any sort. Geographic transfer from one locale to another works, but this seems too demanding in light of modern practice. It is "movement" of any sort that qualifies.[59] Statutory constructions tend to dwell on the factors witnessed in North Carolina law here:

§14-39. Kidnapping.

(a) Any person who shall unlawfully confine, restrain, or remove from one place to another, any other person 16 years of age or over without the consent of such person, or any other person under the age of 16 years without the consent of a parent or legal custodian of such person, shall be guilty of kidnapping if such confinement, restraint, or removal is for the purpose of:

(1) Holding such other person for a ransom or as a hostage or using such other person as a shield; or

(2) Facilitating the commission of any felony or facilitating flight of any person following the commission of a felony; or

(3) Doing serious bodily harm to or terrorizing the person so confined, restrained, or removed or any other person; or

(4) Holding such other person in involuntary servitude in violation of G.S. 14-43.2.[60]

Kidnapping also calls, at least by imputation or inference, for proof of the motive behind the act. Motive indicates an improper purpose in the captive act—such as for money, political gain, terroristic threat, or extortion. Although motive is instructive, it may not edify a bevy of other circumstances that connote the kidnap. Kidnapping has evolutionary and piggyback qualities that most felonies do not possess. By *piggyback* we mean the offense rests on other offenses, such as the original rapist, who specifically intends to rape another, but to effectuate the offense, restrains and moves the victim to another location. What was originally rape now assumes the weight of kidnapping. In this sense the offense is evolutionary, as changing and as transient as the offender's itinerary. As the offender moves through time and space while forcibly dragging along the target of the original intent, kidnapping charges evolve out of other offenses. For this reason, kidnapping facilitates the commission of underlying offenses; for example, burglary changes to rape, and rape may be elevated to murder. As long as the movement accompanies the evolving offenses, kidnapping applies.

False Imprisonment Contrasted with kidnapping, the crime of false imprisonment, while often factually similar, tends to refer to the less violent constraint of another. False imprisonment deals more with infringements on freedom of movement rather than concerns about physical safety. False imprisonment restrains freedom of movement without just cause, right, or privilege. The comparison with kidnapping is sometimes fuzzy. Nebraska offers befuddling language that sounds much like kidnapping:

A person commits false imprisonment in the first degree if he or she knowingly restrains or abducts another person (a) under terrorizing circumstances or under circumstances which expose the person to the risk of serious bodily injury; or (b) with intent to hold him or her in a condition of involuntary servitude.[61]

The Model Penal Code emphasizes the restraint of liberty over the violent means to effect the result:

A person commits a misdemeanor if he knowingly restrains another unlawfully so as to interfere substantially with his liberty.[62]

False imprisonment may also leave open the door to a civil remedy. Causes of action involving consumers, shoppers, or other individuals unprotected by merchants' privilege or other statutory immunity are commonly witnessed in American courtrooms. In sum, a person commits a misdemeanor if he knowingly restrains another unlawfully to interfere substantially with his liberty.[63]

Sexual Offenses   Sexual offenses are primarily acts of violence against the sanctity of the human person. All sexual offenses display the invasiveness of person, the disregard of personal dignity, and an assault on personal integrity.

Rape.   The use of force by a male upon a female to submit to sexual intercourse—the act of penetration by a male penis into a female vagina, without consent and with the victim's resistance, summarizes the common-law definition of rape. Rape constituted the forcible imposition of a male person upon an unwilling female partner. Force remains the critical question in all rape case law and adjudication. Consensual sexual activity signifies a willingness to cooperate and participate, whereas force implies a lack of will. Sex by force confronts our fundamental sensibilities of personal and bodily integrity. Without force, rape lacks the seriousness and substantiality to be deemed a high-level felony. Without force, a willing agent engages in sexual activity freely and without objection. This is why questions involving date rape, intoxication, and underage sexual conduct are cumbersome in rape litigation. Although force may exist in these contexts, its clarity is muddled by choice, will, and levels of participation.

In date rape, part of the series of events that lead to the eventual criminality are consensual, and others are not. In statutory rape cases involving young partners, the parties may choose freely and without resistance to engage in sexual intercourse. A female who becomes inebriated, then has little if any recollection of certain sexual conduct, presents a less convincing evidentiary situation for the prosecutor who wants to achieve a rape conviction but is trumped by the persistent reasonable doubts that may emerge in jurors.

The relationship with force and consent is firmly grounded in rape law. A lack of consent implies and imputes the force necessary for a rape conviction. Definitionally, rape statutes are attentive to these standards:

> *§11-37-1 Definitions.—For the purposes of this chapter*
>
> *(2) "Force or coercion" entails any of the following actions by the accused:*
>   *(i) Uses or threatens to use a weapon, or any article used or fashioned in a manner to lead the victim to reasonably believe it to be a weapon;*
>   *(ii) Overcomes the victim through the application of physical force or physical violence;*
>   *(iii) Coerces the victim to submit by threatening to use force or violence on the victim and the victim reasonably believes that the accused has the present ability to execute these threats; or*
>   *(iv) Coerces the victim to submit by threatening to at some time in the future, murder, inflict serious bodily injury upon, or kidnap the victim or any other person and the victim reasonably believes that the accused has the ability to execute this threat.*[64]

Consent, on the other hand, implies willingness and lack of objection. Consent represents intellectual assent and emotional willingness to engage in the activity. Consent explicitly relays permission for the sexual conduct engaged in; a lack of consent declares resistance to the same conduct. Of course, consent can be freely given only by those capable of its issuance. Free, willing, and consenting beings possess the physical and mental capacity to consent to specific conduct. Thus people who are physically incapacitated, in comas, or under the influence of drugs that affect consciousness, or those mentally deficient in reasoning and intellectual skills needed for decision making, lack the power of consent in any sense. Rape statutes have long recognized these incapacities in the analysis of consent:

> *(c) A person is deemed incapable of consent if he is:*
>   *(1) Less than 16 years old; or*
>   *(2) Mentally defective; or*
>   *(3) Mentally incapacitated; or*
>   *(4) Physically helpless.*[65]

Consent negates the issue of force because it makes sexual intercourse a volitional act rather than one of terror and power. Consent signifies acceptance of the agent's movement and a willing toleration of what develops in human sexual activity. Consent is the purest and most effective defense to the crime of rape because its proof strikes at the heart of victimization on the one hand and the mental state of the alleged offender on the other.

Common-law tradition emphasized that sexual intercourse was the exclusive actus reus for any rape charge. Under traditional scrutiny, sexual intercourse consisted of the insertion or penetration of penis into vagina. Penetration, however slight, was part of the order of proof. Ejaculation was not required, but proof of penetration could be easily inferred from the presence of this biological material. Sexual intercourse constituted the act central to rape; these same statutes excluded a wide series of other sexual acts, including anal sex, oral sex, use of foreign object for insertion, and the full range of conduct between same-sex adults.

> *§18.2-61. Rape.*
>
> A. *If any person has sexual intercourse with a complaining witness who is not his or her spouse or causes a complaining witness, whether or not his or her spouse, to engage in sexual intercourse with any other person and such act is accomplished (i) against the complaining witness's will, by force, threat, or intimidation of or against the complaining witness or another person, or (ii) through the use of the complaining witness's mental incapacity or physical helplessness, or (iii) with a child under age thirteen as the victim, he or she shall be guilty of rape.*[66]

The qualification is not as senseless as so many of its critics charge. Pregnancy cannot result from these other practices, whereas it is certainly a frequent consequence of the intercourse. Early drafters, living in an age lacking contraception and legalized abortion, perceived these consequences with gravity exclusive to sexual intercourse.[67]

Deviate Sexual Intercourse. Every American jurisdiction lumps nonrape offenses into other statutory definitions. *Deviate sexual intercourse* is a common descriptor and implies a difference in the act. Under traditional rape statutes, vaginal–penile contact and penetration are required. *Sodomy* was another word commonly employed. Here the act was usually anal or oral in design, and possibly irrelevant to the consent question. A typical statute might be this:

> *§5-14-122. Sodomy.*
>
> (a) *A person commits sodomy if such person performs any act of sexual gratification involving:*
>   (1) *The penetration, however slight, of the anus or mouth of an animal or a person by the penis of a person of the same sex or an animal; or*
>   (2) *The penetration, however slight, of the vagina or anus of an animal or a person by any body member of a person of the same sex or animal.*[68]

Or the language of the statute might employ words of force such as these:

> *§ 18.2-67.1. Forcible sodomy.*
>
> A. *An accused shall be guilty of forcible sodomy if he or she engages in cunnilingus, fellatio, analingus, or anal intercourse with a complaining witness who is not his or her spouse, or causes a complaining witness, whether or not his or her spouse, to engage in such acts with another person.*[69]

Of course, consensual sexual practice, particularly in the homosexual community, where these historic proscriptions have now been declared constitutionally acceptable, has largely minimized the importance of sodomy statutes.[70]

Sexual Abuse of Children. The increases in the sexual abuse of children are staggering. Techniques such as doll portrayal of the sexual abuse are helpful to investigators, though these techniques can be used improperly. In general, the younger the child, the more serious the offense. Missouri's code is one of the laws with clear, succinct recitations of the nature of child molestation:

> *A person commits the crime of child molestation in the first degree if he subjects another person who is less than twelve years of age to sexual conduct.*
> *Child molestation in the first degree is a class C felony unless the actor has previously been convicted of an offense under this chapter or in the course thereof the actor inflicts serious physical injury, displays a deadly weapon or deadly instrument in a threatening manner, or the offense is committed as part of a ritual or ceremony, in which case the crime is a class B felony.*[71]

When compared to sexual intercourse, sexual contact liberally construes any form of sexual behavior between adults and minors. To contact implies penetration and a wide array of other physical touching. To contact could mean no more than an adult male placing his hand on top of genitalia, without insertion or intrusion. Under rape litigation, contact is insufficient to meet the penetration standard. Molestation statutes reflect a type of sexual affront that illegally gratifies the pedophile and fondler, the indecent assaulter and exposer. In terms of sheer gravity, the offense of molestation may or may not be less serious than rape in the first degree. On the other hand, the outrage generated by these types of offenses directly connects to the innocence and age of the victims. Pedophiles are held in enormous contempt not only for what they do but also to whom they do it. "Additionally, pedophilic molestation of children falls into a class of crimes against which society categorically wishes to guard. It is a crime we seek to prevent at all costs. It is true that societies seek to prevent all types of crime."[72]

New statutory constructions attempt to precisely define the range of sexual crimes inflicted on the young, especially under the broad term *exploitation*. Here is an example:

> *§13-3553. Sexual exploitation of a minor; evidence; exemption; classification.*
>
> A. *A person commits sexual exploitation of a minor by knowingly:*
>   1. *Recording, filming, photographing, developing, or duplicating any visual depiction in which minors are engaged in exploitive exhibition or other sexual conduct.*
>   2. *Distributing, transporting, exhibiting, receiving, selling, purchasing, electronically transmitting, possessing, or exchanging any visual depiction in which minors are engaged in exploitive exhibition or other sexual conduct.*[73]

Incest. Incest constitutes an attack on blood (consanguinity) and relations and status (affinity). The ramifications of these acts, from unwanted pregnancy to physical trauma, are exacerbated by the natural and abiding trust that children have for those who oversee their development. From whatever angle the offense is scrutinized, the act and its consequence inexorably alter victims for the remainder of their lives. Research on sexual abusers, prostitution, and deviant sexual lifestyles usually demonstrates the interplay between incestuous experiences and the lifestyle chosen.

Utah lays out a comprehensive statute that includes not only biological offspring but stepchildren as well:

> (1) *A person is guilty of incest when, under circumstances not amounting to rape, rape of a child or aggravated sexual assault, he has sexual intercourse with a person whom he knows to be an ancestor, descendant, brother, sister, uncle, aunt, nephew, niece, or first cousin. The relationships referred to herein include blood relationships of the whole or half blood without regard to legitimacy, relationship of parent and child by adoption, and relationship of stepparent and stepchild while the marriage creating the relationship of a stepparent and stepchild exists.*[74]

As family structures continue to change, it will be difficult to see how this and other forms of criminality will decrease.

Offenses against Property

Property offenses, in sheer numbers alone, exploit the justice system resources more than all other crime forms. Whether theft or arson, robbery or embezzlement, the volume of litigation relating to these offenses continues its meteoric rise. The analysis commences with the most serious of property offenses—arson.

Arson Insurance companies and industrial and business concerns have a grave interest in protecting property assets from arson destruction. Around-the-clock security systems, surveillance systems, and electronic technology aid private enterprise in the protection of commercial property.

Arson is a serious felony. Arson as defined in the Model Penal Code includes the following provisions:

> (1) *A person is guilty of arson, a felony of the second degree, if he starts a fire or causes an explosion with the purpose of:*
>   (a) *destroying a building or occupied structure of another; or*
>   (b) *destroying or damaging any property whether his own or another's, to collect insurance for such loss . . .*[75]

Judicial interpretation of arson statutes has been clear, but the definition of a structure and what constitutes an actual burning or fire have presented some problems. *Structure,* broadly defined, includes any physical plant, warehouse, or accommodation that permits the carrying on of business, or the temporary residence of people, a domicile, and even ships, trailers, sleeping cars, airplanes, and other movable vehicles or structures.[76]

Fire has been broadly described as any burning, substantial smoke discoloration and damage, charring, the existence of an alligator pattern on the burned object, or destruction and damage resulting from explosives, detonation devices, and substantial heat. Total destruction or annihilation of the facilities is not required.[77] Most jurisdictions have also adopted related offenses handling other incendiary circumstances:

- Reckless burning or exploding.
- Failure to prevent a catastrophe.
- Criminal mischief.
- Injuring or tampering with fire apparatus.
- Unauthorized use of or opening a fire hydrant.
- Institutional vandalism.[78]

Although arson is a specific intent crime, proof of motive helps understand the mens rea component. Some common motives are these:

- Economic gain from insurance proceeds.
- Economic gain by halting losses on a distressed property.
- Homicide and personal injury infliction.
- Fire as a means of intimidation.
- Fire as a sign of vengeance and jealousy.
- Fire as senseless destruction.
- Fire as sexual stimulation.

Burglary Burglary is the illegal entry into a home or other structure. Clark and Marshall, in their renowned *Treatise on Crimes,*[79] provide the common-law definition of the crime of burglary:

 1. *The premises must be the dwelling house of another . . .*
 2. *There must be a breaking of some part of the house itself. The breaking must be constructive, as well as actual.*
 3. *There must be an entry. The slightest entry of a hand or even an instrument suffices.*
 4. *The breaking and entering must both be at night; but need not be on the same night.*
 5. *There must be an intent to commit a felony in the house and such intent must accompany both the breaking and entry. The intended felony need not be committed.*[80]

Many statutes have modified this definition. A definition of a *dwelling house* has been liberally construed and includes a chicken coop, cow stable, hog house, barn, smokehouse, mill house, or any other area or any other building or occupied structure.[81]

The term *breaking* does not require an actual destruction of property—merely the breaking of a plane or point of entrance in the occupied structure. Additionally, most jurisdictions have reassessed the nighttime element and made this requirement nonmandatory. Many jurisdictions, however, make the time of the intrusion applicable to the degree of the offense.[82]

A common misconception is that burglary is only a property offense. Appellate decisions have continually held that burglary's requirement that the entry be spurred by the intent to commit a felony within the house is the crux of the matter.[83] The benchmark question then becomes what the accused's intent was at the precise time of the actual breaking and entry.[84] As long as the defendant breaks in to commit any felony, a burglary charge can stick.

Another aspect that prompts confusion involves the dual intent that accompanies the typical burglary prosecution. Initially the perpetrator intends to break and enter a domicile or other structure. At the same time this perpetrator must intend some other felony as part of the master plan of invasion. Which intent controls? Or does each have the same weight? What if the prosecution fails to prove one type of intent?

Entry of some sort is mandated by all burglary statutes. One must enter to burglarize. State codifications fully show the importance of the element of entry. Tennessee, as an illustration, employs the term repeatedly in its construction:

> *39-14-402 Burglary.*
>
> (a) *A person commits burglary who, without the effective consent of the property owner:*
>   (1) *Enters a building other than a habitation (or any portion thereof) not open to the public, with intent to commit a felony, theft, or assault;*
>   (2) *Remains concealed, with the intent to commit a felony, theft, or assault, in a building;*
>   (3) *Enters a building and commits or attempts to commit a felony, theft, or assault; or*
>   (4) *Enters any freight or passenger car, automobile, truck, trailer, boat, airplane, or other motor vehicle with intent to commit a felony, theft, or assault or commits or attempts to commit a felony, theft, or assault.*[85]

New Hampshire follows similar suit:

> *635:1 Burglary.—I. A person is guilty of burglary if he enters a building or occupied structure, or separately secured or occupied section thereof, with purpose to commit a crime therein, unless the premises are at the time open to the public or the actor is licensed or privileged to enter. It is an affirmative defense to prosecution for burglary that the building or structure was abandoned.*[86]

Entry takes the offender toward the aim of the burglary effort and gives life to the unseemly plan about to unfold. In some jurisdictions the entry need not be very significant and the "element of entry is satisfied if any part of the intruder's body enters the structure."[87]

Trespass A related act that has applicability to a secure domicile, land, or other environment is criminal trespass. Trespass is an intrusion without privilege or right. The act confronts the possessory right of ownership. A typical statute might read as follows:

> (1) *Buildings and occupied structures. A person commits an offense if knowing he is not licensed or privileged to do so, he enters or surreptitiously remains in any building or occupied structure or separately secured or occupied portion thereof. An offense under this subsection is a misdemeanor if it is committed in a dwelling at night. Otherwise it is a petty misdemeanor.*[88]

The line between burglary and trespass is relatively thin. Here is an example from Pennsylvania:

> *§3503. Criminal trespass.*
>
> (A) *BUILDINGS AND OCCUPIED STRUCTURES.—*
>   (1) *A person commits an offense if, knowing that he is not licensed or privileged to do so, he*
>   (i) *enters, gains entry by subterfuge, or surreptitiously remains in any building or occupied structure or separately secured or occupied portion thereof; or*
>   (ii) *breaks into any building or occupied structure or separately secured or occupied portion thereof.*[89]

Language like *break into*, *without license or privilege*, or *surreptitiously* identically appears in burglary and trespass laws. What this demonstrates is the central focus of both offenses: *intrusion*. In either offense the perpetrator enters unlicensed space without permission or consent. The law recognizes a wide variety of grades and degrees of trespass activity—from felonious to summary violations.[90]

The Model Penal Code lays out lucid meaning for what it means to enter or intrude by trespass:

> *Section 206.53 Criminal trespass.*
>
> (2) *Definitions. To intrude means to enter or remain without consent express or implied of the person entitled to exclude or of another lawful occupant. Warning means notice that the person entitled to exclude does not consent to intrusion; it may be given by written or oral communication to the actor or by posting notices in a manner prescribed by law or reasonably likely to come to the attention of intruders.*[91]

Although the entry addresses the actus reus of trespass, the mental motivation of trespass involves a little more than mere motion of the actor. There is a motivation in the movement.

Robbery The unlawful acquisition or taking of property by forceful means constitutes robbery. In retail and commercial establishments and banks, people assaulted for property are endangered by the activities of robbery felons. Robbery, though essentially a property crime, is fundamentally a crime of violence. Robbery is often described as a "larceny with force." A typical robbery statute mimics this Model Penal Code provision:

> (1) *Robbery Defined. A person is guilty of robbery if, in the course of committing a theft, he*
> > (a) *inflicts serious bodily injury upon another; or*
> > (b) *threatens another with or purposely puts him in fear of immediate serious bodily injury; or*
> > (c) *commits or threatens immediately to commit any felony of the first or second degree. An act shall be deemed "in the course of committing a theft" if it occurs in an attempt to commit theft or in flight after the attempt or commission.*[92]

Distinguishing robbery from a larceny or theft offense rests on proof of force, violence, or a threat. Threats in robbery must be immediate and capable of being carried out.[93] The harm threatened is usually death or great bodily injury to the victim, a member of the victim's family, or a close relative of the victim.[94] Threats to damage property will not suffice, with the statutory exception in select jurisdictions of a threat to destroy a dwelling house.[95]

The federal criminal code dwells more intently on the nature of robbery in federally insured and regulated banking institutions:

> (a) *Whoever, by force and violence, or by intimidation, takes, or attempts to take, from the person or presence of another, or obtains or attempts to obtain by extortion any property or money or any other thing of value belonging to, or in the care, custody, control, management, or possession of, any bank, credit union, or any savings and loan association; or*
> > *Whoever enters or attempts to enter any bank, credit union, or any savings and loan association, or any building used in whole or in part as a bank, credit union, or as a savings and loan association, with intent to commit in such bank, credit union, or in such savings and loan association, or building, or part thereof, so used, any felony affecting such bank, credit union, or such savings and loan association and in violation of any statute of the United States, or any larceny—*
> > *Shall be fined under this title or imprisoned not more than twenty years, or both.*
> (b) *Whoever takes and carries away, with intent to steal or purloin, any property or money or any other thing of value exceeding $1,000 belonging to, or in the care, custody, control, management, or possession of any bank, credit union, or any savings and loan association, shall be fined under this title or imprisoned not more than ten years, or both; or*
> > *Whoever takes and carries away, with intent to steal or purloin, any property or money or any other thing of value not exceeding $1,000 belonging to, or in the care, custody, control, management, or possession of any bank, credit union, or any savings and loan association, shall be fined not more than $1,000 or imprisoned not more than one year, or both.*
> (c) *Whoever receives, possesses, conceals, stores, barters, sells, or disposes of any property or money or other thing of value which has been taken or stolen from a bank, credit union, or savings and loan association in violation of subsection (b), knowing the same to be property which has been stolen, shall be subject to the punishment provided in subsection (b) for the taker.*[96]

For some, the level of violence and force make robbery less of a property offense and more of a crime against the person. Force is the crux of the matter. Hence robbery statutes display uniform and consistent qualities like this example: "Robbery is the felonious taking of personal property in the possession of another, from his person or immediate presence, and against his will, accomplished by means of force or fear."[97] Taking another's property, without a legitimate claim or right, is felonious conduct in its own right. If the offender meets the requirements of carrying away the stolen property (asportation), and it is determined that the property has value, the prosecutorial staff can rest easy on meeting the evidentiary demands of a larceny case. The same would be true of robbery except that the issue of force must be proven.

In *Zanders v. U.S.*[98] the defendant successfully appealed a robbery conviction under a statute which read,

> *Whoever by force or violence, whether against resistance or by sudden or stealthy seizure or snatching, or by putting in fear, shall take from the person or immediate actual possession of another anything of value, is guilty of robbery, and any person convicted thereof shall suffer imprisonment for not less than two years nor more than 15 years.*[99]

The majority opinion dismissed both robbery counts against the defendant in facts that amounted to nothing more than a subway pickpocketing. The victim was completely unaware until later that he had lost his wallet. With the lack of victim comprehension, it is conclusive that the accused carried out their design without the infliction or threat of imminent harm. The *Zanders* court found neither direct nor indirect evidence of any taking committed by the appellants.[100]

Determining the nature of force in a robbery case subjects both the investigative and prosecutorial teams to intense fact finding and assuring evidentiary sufficiency. To achieve this standard, the evidence will have to demonstrate some, but not necessarily all, of these criteria:

- Infliction of physical injury.
- Real and serious threats to inflict it.
- Threats to perform another felony on the person subject to the robbery.
- Causing the crime victim to be in fear of real and immediate bodily injury.
- Taking the property by force.

Theft   Also known as larceny, theft continuously undermines the business and social fabric in any society. From shoplifting[101] to stock pilferage, from fraudulent accounting and record keeping systems to the embezzling of corporate funds, from theft of benefits and services to theft of cable television signals, larceny and theft undeniably influence the quality of life. Outlined in Figure 10.2 are the requisite elements needed in any successful charge of larceny.

Upon closer inspection, the term *property* applies when any commercial interest is at stake. Essentially anything of value can be stolen. From the roots of the common law, questions of what qualifies as property border on the legendary. Commentary has been presented ranging from whether rabbits and fish are larcenable to whether vegetables, land, or the skins of deer could be the subject of theft.[102] Both common law and current statutory constructions define what goods, services, or commodities are considered to be larcenable commodities. Maryland clarifies the definition of *property* comprehensively as shown here:

> *(H) "Property" means anything of value, including but not limited to*
> *(1) real estate;*
> *(2) money;*
> *(3) commercial instruments;*
> *(4) admission or transportation ticket;*
> *(5) written instruments representing or embodying rights concerning anything of value, or services, or anything otherwise of value to the owner;*
> *(6) things growing on or affixed to, or found on land, or part of or affixed to any building;*
> *(7) electricity, gas, and water;*
> *(8) birds, animals, and fish that ordinarily are kept in a state of confinement;*
> *(9) food and drink;*
> *(10) sample cultures, microorganisms, and specimens;*
> *(11) records, recordings, documents, blueprints, drawings, maps, photographs . . .;*
> *(12) financial instruments, information, electronically produced data, computer software, . . .*[103]

FIGURE 10.2
Requisite Elements for Larceny

To prove a larceny, these elemental principles are required:
- A taking that is unlawful.
- A carrying away or movement thereafter of personal property.
- Property of which the taker is not in rightful ownership or possession.
- A mens rea that is felonious.

Did Maryland's legislators forget something? No matter how comprehensive the list may be, concepts of property evolve in accordance with the commercial marketplace. Cable television signals, electronic funds, and sophisticated versions of intellectual property were never envisioned by our ancestors.

The following Model Penal Code provision on theft is fairly clear:

> *Section 223.2. Theft by unlawful taking or disposition.*
>
> *(1) Movable Property. A person is guilty of theft if he unlawfully takes or otherwise exercises unlawful control over movable property of another with purpose to deprive him thereof.*
>
> *(2) Immovable Property. A person is guilty of theft if he unlawfully transfers immovable property of another or any interest therein with the purpose to benefit himself or another not entitled thereto.*[104]

Commentators from the American Law Institute find it legally necessary to consolidate theft acts or practices. Hence "the general definition of theft consolidates into a single offense a number of heretofore distinct property crimes, including larceny, embezzlement, obtaining by false pretense, cheating, extortion, and all other involuntary transfers of wealth except those explicitly excluded by provisions of this article."[105]

Larceny and theft also break down into various grades and levels that usually reflect the value of what has been taken and the methods employed to unlawfully seize. Definitions that use dollar or other valuations to distinguish one offense from the other are usual players:

> *(A.1) FELONY OF THE THIRD DEGREE.—Except as provided in subsection (a), theft constitutes a felony of the third degree if the amount involved exceeds $2,000, or if the property stolen is an automobile, airplane, motorcycle, motorboat, or other motor-propelled vehicle, or in the case of theft by receiving stolen property, if the receiver is in the business of buying or selling stolen property.*
>
> *(B) OTHER GRADES.—Theft not within subsection (a) or (a.1) of this section constitutes a misdemeanor of the first degree, except that if the property was not taken from the person or by threat, or in breach of fiduciary obligation, and:*
> *(1) the amount involved was $50 or more but less than $200 the offense constitutes a misdemeanor of the second degree; or*
> *(2) the amount involved was less than $50 the offense constitutes a misdemeanor of the third degree.*[106]

A cursory glance at most theft statutes indicates the simplicity of form and content. By way of example, Michigan's statute clearly defines the proscribed conduct:

> *(1) A person who commits larceny by stealing any of the following property of another person is guilty of a crime as provided in this section:*
> *(a) Money, goods, or chattels.*
> *(b) A bank note, bank bill, bond, promissory note, due bill, bill of exchange or other bill, draft, order, or certificate.*
> *(c) A book of accounts for or concerning money or goods due, to become due, or to be delivered.*
> *(d) A deed or writing containing a conveyance of land or other valuable contract in force.*
> *(e) A receipt, release, or defeasance.*[107]

Theft under the Model Penal Code is first and foremost the "unauthorized taking or disposition of movable or immovable property." The essential issues in larceny analysis are these:

- Was the taking temporary or permanent?
- What type of property was subject to taking?
- What type of value did the property have?
- How far was the property carried away?

Paralegals must study the closely related theft provisions and correctly evaluate the facts to discern the applicability of certain offenses. Related theft acts are discussed in the following paragraphs.

Theft by Deception.[108]　Be aware of individuals best described as "flim-flam artists" who create false impressions and deceive others into giving up their possessions. The agent misrepresents in such a way as to cause another party to sign over, assign, release, or bequeath some property, the ownership of which is usually signified by a legal document. At its heart, the offender's false pretenses trick the victim into the taking by appearing utterly legitimate in the context in which the fraud takes place.

Other manifestations of fraud involve acquisition of government benefits by false application for welfare, Food Stamp collusion, and false Medicaid and Social Security filings. Any false statement that secures the payment of government benefits constitutes fraudulent practice.[109] The range of fraudulent theft is further evidenced in the mail and shipping services where corrupt and unconscionable practices of sale, bait and switch, and false and glaring misrepresentation are regular phenomena. The U.S. Postal Service Inspector Division spends the bulk of its time tracking down criminals who use the mail to enable their fraudulent designs.

The Model Penal Code declares the following:

> *Section 206.2 Theft by deception.*
>
> *(1) General. A person commits theft if he obtains property of another by means of deception. A person deceives if he purposely*
> > *(a) creates or reinforces an impression which is false and which he does not believe to be true; or*
> > *(b) prevents another from acquiring information which the actor knows would influence the other party in the transaction; or*
> > *(c) fails to disclose a lien, adverse claim, or other legal impediment to the enjoyment of property being sold or otherwise transferred or encumbered, regardless of the legal validity of the impediment and regardless of any official record disclosing its existence; or*
> > *(d) fails to correct a false impression previously created or reinforced by him; or*
> > *(e) fails to correct a false impression which he knows to be influencing another to whom he stands in a relationship of special trust and confidence.*[110]

The centerpiece of every fraud investigation lies in the falsehood and material misrepresentation that manipulates the transference. The District of Columbia has crafted an enviable statute at 22-3821:

> *§22-3821. Fraud.*
>
> *(a) Fraud in the first degree.—A person commits the offense of fraud in the first degree if that person engages in a scheme or systematic course of conduct with intent to defraud or to obtain property of another by means of a false or fraudulent pretense, representation, or promise and thereby obtains property of another or causes another to lose property.*
> *(b) Fraud in the second degree.—A person commits the offense of fraud in the second degree if that person engages in a scheme or systematic course of conduct with intent to defraud or to obtain property of another by means of a false or fraudulent pretense, representation, or promise.*
> *(c) False promise as to future performance.—Fraud may be committed by means of false promise as to future performance which the accused does not intend to perform or knows will not be performed. An intent or knowledge shall not be established by the fact alone that one such promise was not performed.*[111]

Theft by Extortion.[112] Certainly property can be illegally acquired by making future threats of bodily injury or by threat of disclosing private matters or secrets that will cause serious damage to a party. Similarly, public officials refusing to cooperate officially, or causing unjustifiable harm or injury by their offices, can also be found guilty of theft by extortion.

Extortion conjures images of loan sharks and other tough characters who lend at exorbitant rates and nearly make impossible any reasonable payback. Part of this picture is on the mark, but extortion covers a great deal of generally unknown territory.[113] Extortion contains additional qualities that relate to force, intimidation, or threat to inflict harm. Also known as *blackmail* in some jurisdictions, the end results of this threat are identical to every other class of larceny and theft because a victim relinquishes involuntarily rightful property or some other benefit. In the federal code, drafters have authored a broad and comprehensive set of principles that covers every imaginable form of threat for benefit:

> *18 USC §1951. Interference with commerce by threats or violence.*
>
> *(a) Whoever in any way or degree obstructs, delays, or affects commerce or the movement of any article or commodity in commerce, by robbery or extortion or attempts or conspires so*

to do, or commits or threatens physical violence to any person or property in furtherance of a plan or purpose to do anything in violation of this section shall be fined under this title or imprisoned not more than twenty years, or both.

(b) As used in this section—

(1) The term "robbery" means the unlawful taking or obtaining of personal property from the person or in the presence of another, against his will, by means of actual or threatened force, or violence, or fear of injury, immediate or future, to his person or property, or property in his custody or possession, or the person or property of a relative or member of his family or of anyone in his company at the time of the taking or obtaining.

(2) The term "extortion" means the obtaining of property from another, with his consent, induced by wrongful use of actual or threatened force, violence, or fear, or under color of official right.

(3) The term "commerce" means commerce within the District of Columbia, or any Territory or Possession of the United States; all commerce between any point in a State, Territory, Possession, or the District of Columbia and any point outside thereof; all commerce between points within the same State through any place outside such State; and all other commerce over which the United States has jurisdiction.[114]

Practitioners quickly notice that things or property are subject to the claim, but so are items with a nontangible benefit. Ohio, for example labels this secondary classification the "valuable benefit."[115] What further separates this type of theft from its counterparts is the intimidation to the party victimized. The criminal agent succeeds because he or she frightens and threatens a party with real and actual harm. One major qualification for this method of taking is that the threat never evolves into actual assault or physical injury. Here is a statutory example:

Section 206.3 Theft by intimidation.

A person commits theft if he obtains property of another by means of a threat to

(1) inflict physical harm on the person threatened or any other person or on property; or

(2) subject any person to physical confinement or restraint; or

(3) commit any criminal offense; or

(4) accuse any person of a criminal offense; or

(5) expose any person to hatred, contempt, or ridicule; or

(6) harm the credit or business repute of any person; or

(7) reveal any secret; or

(8) take action as an official against anyone or anything, or withhold official action, or cause such action or withholding; or

(9) bring about or continue a strike, boycott, or other collective unofficial action, if the property is not demanded or received for the benefit of the group which he purports to represent; or

(10) testify or provide information or withhold testimony or information with respect to another's legal claim or defense; or

(11) inflict any other harm which would not benefit the actor.

Retail Theft.   With the increasing number of shoplifting cases, and the commercial lobbying for protective laws, many jurisdictions have adopted specialized retail theft statutes. An example follows:

(a) OFFENSE DEFINED.—A person is guilty of a retail theft if he

(1) takes possession of, carries away, transfers, or causes to be carried away or transferred, any merchandise displayed, held, stored, or offered for sale by any store or other retail mercantile establishment with the intention of depriving the merchant of the possession, use, or benefit of such merchandise without paying the full retail value thereof;

(2) alters, transfers, or removes any label, price tag marking, indicia of value, or any other markings which aid in determining value affixed to any merchandise displayed, held, stored, or offered for sale in a store or other retail mercantile establishment and attempts to purchase such merchandise personally or in consort with another at less than the full retail value with the intention of depriving the merchant of the full retail value of such merchandise;

> *(3) transfers any merchandise displayed, held, stored, or offered for sale by any store or other retail mercantile establishment from the container in or on which the same shall be displayed to any other container with intent to deprive the merchant of all or some part of the full retail value thereof; or*
>
> *(4) under-rings with the intention of depriving the merchant of the full retail value of the merchandise.*
>
> *(5) destroys, removes, renders inoperative, or deactivates any inventory control tag, security strip, or any other mechanism designed or employed to prevent an offense under this section with the intention of depriving the merchant of the possession, use, or benefit of such merchandise without paying the full retail value thereof.[116]*

Can you see any other technique that accurately depicts shoplifting? Is it possible, in an age of television shopping networks, computerized networking, and credit card usage, that this statutory guideline is remiss? For a thorough analysis of retail theft and its legal and commercial applications, review James Cleary's text *Prosecuting the Shoplifter, A Loss Prevention Strategy.*[117]

Forgery.   Individuals who create false documentation, false writings, or forged stamps, seals, trademarks, or other symbols of value, right, privilege, or identification can be charged with forgery.

> *A person is guilty of forgery if, with the intent to defraud or deceive another person or government, he*
>
> *A. Falsely makes, completes, endorses, or alters a written instrument, or knowingly utters or possesses such an instrument; or*
>
> *B. Causes another, by deception, to sign or execute a written instrument, or utters such an instrument.[118]*

Maine also has adopted what it terms "aggravated forgery"[119] to target offenders who are not only con artists but intend without any reservation to effect fraud. The line here seems a little fuzzy, although the language of the statute is definitely one of specific intent:

> *§702. Aggravated forgery.*
>
> *1. A person is guilty of aggravated forgery if, with intent to defraud or deceive another person or government, he falsely makes, completes, endorses, or alters a written instrument, or knowingly utters or possesses such an instrument, and the instrument is*
>
> > *A. Part of an issue of money, stamps, securities, or other valuable instruments issued by a government or governmental instrumentality;*
> >
> > *B. Part of an issue of stocks, bonds, or other instruments representing interests in or claims against an organization or its property;*
> >
> > *C. A will, codicil, or other instrument providing for the disposition of property after death;*
> >
> > *D. A public record or an instrument filed or required or authorized by law to be filed in or with a public office or public employee.[120]*

Oregon's codification speaks well of its drafters:

> *165.013. Forgery in the first degree.*
>
> *(1) A person commits the crime of forgery in the first degree if the person violates ORS 165.007 and the written instrument is or purports to be any of the following:*
>
> > *(a) Part of an issue of money, securities, postage or revenue stamps, or other valuable instruments issued by a government or governmental agency; or*
> >
> > *(b) Part of an issue of stock, bonds, or other instruments representing interests in or claims against any property or person; or*
> >
> > *(c) A deed, will, codicil, contract, or assignment; or*
> >
> > *(d) A check for $750 or more, a credit card purchase slip for $750 or more, or a combination of checks and credit card purchase slips that, in the aggregate, total $750 or more, or any other commercial instrument or other document that does or may evidence, create, transfer, alter, terminate, or otherwise affect a legal right, interest, obligation, or status; or*
> >
> > *(e) A public record.[121]*

Familiar examples of documentation in criminal forgery are wills, deeds, contracts, commercial instruments, negotiable bonds, securities, or any other writing that influences, executes, authenticates, or issues something of monetary value. To constitute forgery, a fraudulent intent is always essential. There must not only be a false making of an instrument; it must be done with intent to defraud.[122]

Simulating Objects of Antiquity or Rarity.   Museums, art centers, or other nonprofit institutions housing articles of antiquity or rarity should always be aware of possible reproduction or simulation of their collections.[123]

Fraudulent Destruction, Removal, or Concealment of Recordable Instruments or Their Tampering.[124]   Another problem of security in business, industrial, and governmental settings is the fraudulent destruction of documentation. The potential for this act is obvious when government employees have access to highly sensitive information.

Bad Check and Credit Card Violations.[125]   The alteration of checks for fraudulent purposes depicts one more nuance in theft by deception.[126] Check offenses in general are statutorily lumped into all types of disconnected categories, although fraud remains a strong choice if the facts warrant. Changing payees and sums due and owed on a series of checks was upheld as fraud in *U.S. v. Laljie*.[127] After altering the checks the defendant used the mail to deposit the proceeds. Evidence was sufficient for conviction of mail fraud because the defendant "engaged in a scheme to defraud… and that scheme was furthered by the use of the mails."[128] A representative statute is shown here:

> Obtaining property or services by bad check. *The person is guilty of obtaining property or services by a bad check when*
>
> *(A) (1) as a drawer or representative drawer, he obtains property or services by uttering a check knowing that he or his principal, as the case may be, has insufficient funds with the drawee to cover it and other outstanding checks; and*
>
> *(2) he intends or believes at the time of utterance that payment will be refused by the drawee upon presentation; and*
>
> *(3) payment is refused by the drawee upon presentation.*[129]

Theft of Services.   For many generations, the common-law idea of what *property* means did not include the value of services rendered. In a service economy, it is natural not only to witness growth in the types of services available to the masses but also to accept that services can be valuated. Criminal codes now have either defined their *property* term to be inclusive or have determined that an additional offense is necessary. The Model Penal Code crafts a new offense titled "Theft of Labor or Services":

> *Section 206.7 Theft of labor or services.*
>
> *(1) A person commits theft if he obtains the labor or service of another by deception or intimidation, knowing that the provision of such labor or service is part of the calling or business of the person providing it.*
>
> *(2) A person commits theft if, having control over the disposition of labor or service of others, to which he is not entitled, he diverts their labor or service to his own benefit or to the benefit of another not entitled thereto.*
>
> *(3) A person commits theft if he obtains transportation, telephone service, or any service available for hire, without the consent of the person authorized to give consent or by means of deception or intimidation.*[130]

In its commentary, the Model Penal Code describes this code addition as somewhat revolutionary, especially when one considers the traditional rules.

Since the time of recommendation, the states continue to experiment with a host of statutory designs that zero in on all the possibilities for this type of theft. New York has an elaborate template that attempts to cover every imaginable tract. Its coverage makes theft of specific services criminal in these scenarios:

- Lodgings.
- Restaurant services.
- Credit cards.
- Public transportation.
- Telecommunications services.
- Telephone access.
- Utilities and tampering with utility devices.
- Entertainment admission.
- Computers and computer services.
- Labor for improper cause.[131]

Auto Theft.   Another staggering rise in criminal conduct has been apparent in vehicular theft. Why lawmakers have determined the necessity for this distinguished offense in the larceny/theft family is open to interpretation. Others hold that the offense is often done with less than permanent motivations—and rather than criminalize the "joy ride" believe we should deal less severely with the unauthorized use of the auto compared to other property forms. Stereotypically, wild and reckless youths are the main players in this offense; but this picture is only a partial caricature. Every second or so, someone is victimized by the national crisis of auto theft.[132] The sheer numbers of auto thefts, just as in shoplifting, have caused the invention of new law. Rather than the harsh reality of felony theft, the justice system affords the less oppressive misdemeanor under various nomenclatures. Pennsylvania's construction is fairly common:

§*3928. Unauthorized use of automobiles and other vehicles.*

(A) *OFFENSE DEFINED.—A person is guilty of a misdemeanor of the second degree if he operates the automobile, airplane, motorcycle, motorboat, or other motor-propelled vehicle of another without consent of the owner.*

(B) *DEFENSE.—It is a defense to prosecution under this section that the actor reasonably believed that the owner would have consented to the operation had he known of it.*[133]

Theft by Receiving Stolen Property.   The array of theft possibilities continues with those offenders who may not directly steal but rely on others who do the taking. When a criminal agent receives or takes into possession property he or she knows is suspect, the law construes the receipt to be a criminal theft no different than the initial larceny. To not declare this conduct illegal would open up a world of endless possibilities for the criminal population, whose innocence could be shielded by second and third parties. Theft statutes are now wise enough to ferret out those who gain and profit from the larceny done by others. The usual statute mimics the recommendations of the Model Penal Code, which contains this language:

Section 206.8 Theft by receiving.

(1) *In General. A person who receives stolen movable property otherwise than for the purpose of restoring it to the owner commits theft if he knows that it is stolen property or, in the case of a dealer, if he believes that it is probably stolen property.*

(2) *Receiving Defined. Receiving means*
  (a) *acquiring possession, control, or title;*
  (b) *selling or lending on the security of the property;*
  (c) *retaining or transferring possession, control, or title after the actor has information leading him to knowledge or belief, as the case may be, that the property is stolen, without notifying the police.*[134]

The statute is unique for many reasons. First the essence of the offense rests in the receipt rather than the real taking. In fact, the novelty of this infraction arises from the receiver who does "not commit the trespassory taking, but instead acquires the property by the voluntary delivery of the original thief."[135]

Theft by Unauthorized Disposition (Embezzlement).   An actor who embezzles takes without right or justification, though in a significantly different fashion. Each offense scrutinized thus far requires a taking, a carrying away, the specific intent to strip away the possessory interest of another without license or privilege to do so. Embezzlement differs in one particular sense—that of right to possess. Embezzlers are entitled to possess the cash, funds, or other property taken. Their positions are ones of trust where the owner grants a license or privilege to the third party to have and to hold. Bank tellers have a possessory right to handle cash because occupational responsibilities demand it. Lawyers hold large sums of money in escrow on behalf of clients, as do money managers and financial consultants, trustees, and guardians. These are custodial positions with fiduciary responsibility. The Model Penal Code promulgates a model statute most states emulate at 206.4:

Section 206.4 Theft by failure to make required disposition of funds received.

(1) *In General. A person who obtains property upon agreement, or subject to a known legal obligation, to make specified payment or other disposition, whether from such property or its*

proceeds or from his own property in equivalent amount, commits theft if he deals with the property obtained as his own and fails to make the required payment or disposition, unless the actor proves that his obligation in the transaction was limited to a promise or other duty to be performed in the future without any present duty to reserve property for such performance. The foregoing applies notwithstanding that it may be impossible to identity particular property as belonging to the victim at the time of the actor's failure to make the required payment or disposition.[136]

Offenses against Public Order and Decency

Riots, loitering, vagrancy, disorderly conduct, harassment, public drunkenness, and other obstructive activities are typical concerns of the criminal law practitioner. Legislative language and executive orders provide substantial charging capacity in this area. A discussion of those most often adopted follows.

Riot   A person is guilty of a riot, felony of the third degree, if he participates with two or more others in disorderly conduct

(1) with intent to commit or facilitate the commission of a felony or misdemeanor;

(2) with intent to prevent or coerce official action; or

(3) when the actor or any other participant to the knowledge of the actor uses or plans to use a firearm or other deadly weapon.[137]

Added to the riot provisions are other offenses that seek to restore the public order. Offenses such as resisting arrest,[138] obstructing highways,[139] loitering and prowling at night time,[140] and failure to disperse upon official order[141] are often seen in criminal codes.

Disorderly Conduct

(a) OFFENSE DEFINED.—A person is guilty of disorderly conduct if, with intent to cause public inconvenience, annoyance, or alarm, or recklessly creating a risk thereof, he
(1) engages in fighting or threatening, or in violent or tumultuous behavior;
(2) makes unreasonable noise;
(3) uses obscene language, or makes an obscene gesture; or
(4) creates a hazardous or physically offensive condition by any act which serves no legitimate purpose of the actor.

(b) GRADING.—An offense under this section is a misdemeanor of the third degree if the intent of the actor is to cause substantial harm or serious inconvenience, or if he persists in disorderly conduct after reasonable warning or request to desist. Otherwise disorderly conduct is a summary offense.

(c) DEFINITION.—As used in this section the word "public" means affecting or likely to affect persons in a place to which the public or a substantial group has access; among the places included are highways, transport facilities, schools, prisons, apartment houses, places of business or amusement, any neighborhood, or any premises which are open to the public.[142]

Legal challenges to disorderly statutes are usually based on vagueness in legislative wording. Critics charge that such statutes afford police too much discretionary power. In the statute just shown, is it possible to be arrested for using obscene language?

Public Drunkenness   Here is the language of a sample statute:

A person is guilty of a summary offense if he appears in any public place manifestly under the influence of alcohol or a controlled substance, as defined in the act of April 14, 1972 (P.L. 233, No. 64), known as The Controlled Substance, Drug, Device and Cosmetic Act, except those taken pursuant to the lawful order of a practitioner, as defined in the Controlled Substance, Drug, Device and Cosmetic Act, to the degree that he may endanger himself or other persons or property, or annoy persons in his vicinity.[143]

Does a restaurant or tavern qualify as a public place under this statute? If so, public or private police would be able to arrest many patrons. Intoxication is engaging in conduct likely to be offensive or cause inconvenience, alarm, or annoyance to persons of ordinary sensibilities.[144]

Prostitution   Every American jurisdiction forbids the commerce of sex for money, except for a few legalized counties in Nevada, and expends considerable funds to eradicate the practice in neighborhoods and communities. Analyze the following statute:

> *§5902. Prostitution and related offenses.*
>
> *(A) PROSTITUTION.—A person is guilty of prostitution if he or she*
> *(1) is an inmate of a house of prostitution or otherwise engages in sexual activity as a business; or*
> *(2) loiters in or within view of any public place for the purpose of being hired to engage in sexual activity.[145]*

The movement for decriminalization of prostitution has been continuous. What are the arguments pro and con?

Drugs and Controlled Substances   As with prostitution, advocacy for the legalization of drugs is rooted in the impossibility of control and the need for proper use of law enforcement resources. Despite these tensions, both the federal and state governments expend considerable energy in the so-called war on drugs. The Controlled Substances Act, published by the federal government in consultation with federal and state law enforcement agencies, lists substances that cannot be used, manufactured, sold, or distributed. A sample page from the Controlled Substances Act[146] is reproduced here:

> *§801. Congressional findings and declarations: controlled substances.*
>
> *The Congress makes the following findings and declarations:*
>
> *(1) Many of the drugs included within this title have a useful and legitimate medical purpose and are necessary to maintain the health and general welfare of the American people.*
>
> *(2) The illegal importation, manufacture, distribution, and possession and improper use of controlled substances have a substantial and detrimental effect on the health and general welfare of the American people.*
>
> *(3) A major portion of the traffic in controlled substances flows through interstate and foreign commerce. Incidents of the traffic which are not an integral part of the interstate or foreign flow, such as manufacture, local distribution, and possession, nonetheless have a substantial and direct effect upon interstate commerce because*
> *(A) after manufacture, many controlled substances are transported in interstate commerce,*
> *(B) controlled substances distributed locally usually have been transported in interstate commerce immediately before their distribution, and*
> *(C) controlled substances possessed commonly flow through interstate commerce immediately prior to such possession.[147]*

Drug provisions further differentiate according to amounts possessed or sold by weight and value of transaction, or whether one is a dealer or distributor. A typical drug offense statute looks like this:

> *§780-113. Prohibited acts; penalties.*
>
> *(a) The following acts and the causing thereof within the Commonwealth are hereby prohibited:*
> *(1) The manufacture, sale or delivery, holding, offering for sale, or possession of any controlled substance, other drug, device, or cosmetic that is adulterated or misbranded.*
> *(2) The adulteration or misbranding of any controlled substance, other drug, device, or cosmetic. . . .*
> *(8) Selling, dispensing, disposing of, or causing to be sold, dispensed, or disposed of, or keeping in possession, control, or custody, or concealing any controlled substance, other drug, device, or cosmetic or any container of any drug, device, or cosmetic with knowledge that the trademark, trade name, or other identifying mark, imprint, or symbol of another, or any likeness of any of the foregoing, has been placed thereon in a manner prohibited by clause (7) hereof.*
> *(9) Making, selling, disposing of, or causing to be made, sold, or disposed of, or keeping in possession, control, or custody, or concealing with intent to defraud, any punch, die, plate, stone, or other thing designed to print, imprint, or reproduce the trademark, trade name, or other identifying mark, imprint, or symbol of another or any likeness of any of the foregoing upon any controlled substance, other drug, device, or cosmetic or container thereof.*

(10) *The sale at retail of a nonproprietary drug except by a registered pharmacist in a licensed pharmacy or by a practitioner.*

(11) *The operation of a drug manufacturing, distributing, or retailing establishment, except by registered pharmacists in a licensed pharmacy, without conforming with such standards respecting sanitation, materials, equipment, and supplies as the secretary, after consultation with the board, may establish by regulation for the protection of the public health and safety.*[148]

The list of controlled substances grows by the moment as users experiment and discern other ways to be taken into another dimension.

Bigamy and Polygamy   Bigamy, the often hidden and nondisclosed practice of being married simultaneously to more than one spouse, raises its ugly head in most communities. By contrast, polygamy constitutes an open and notorious multiple partnering in marriage where the parties consent to the practice. Here is a sample criminal codification:

§4301. Bigamy.

(a) *Bigamy—A married person is guilty of bigamy, a misdemeanor of the second degree, if he contracts or purports to contract another marriage, unless at the time of the subsequent marriage*
  1. *the actor believes that the prior spouse is dead;*
  2. *the actor and the prior spouse have been living apart for two consecutive years throughout which the prior spouse was not known by the actor to be alive; or*
  3. *a court has entered a judgment purporting to terminate or annul any prior disqualifying marriage, and the actor does not know that judgment to be invalid.*

(b) *Other party to bigamous marriage.—A person is guilty of bigamy if he contracts or purports to contract marriage with another knowing that the other is thereby committing bigamy.*[149]

Obscenity   Efforts to codify this crime are evident in the aggressive promulgation of state and federal systems with special controls relative to Internet and cyberspace providers.[150] Criminal sanctions involving obscenity, while tougher than they used to be, have fortunately not been abrogated. Much of the reason these statutes are ineffective relates to their ambiguity and essential relativity. Even the U.S. Supreme Court has been unable to shape a meaningful obscenity standard. Hence the statutes are only as good as existing definitions. For an example see the following statute:

§5903. Obscene and other sexual materials and performances.

(a) *Offenses defined.—No person, knowing the obscene character of the materials or performances involved, shall*
  1. *display or cause or permit the display of any explicit sexual materials as defined in subsection (c) in or on any window, showcase, newsstand, display rack, billboard, display board, viewing screen, motion picture screen, marquee, or similar place in such manner that the display is visible from any public street, highway, sidewalk, transportation facility, or other public thoroughfare, or in any business or commercial establishment where minors, as a part of the general public or otherwise, are or will probably be exposed to view all or any part of such materials;*
  2. *sell, lend, distribute, exhibit, give away, or show any obscene materials to any person 18 years of age or older or offer to sell, lend, distribute, transmit, exhibit, or give away or show, or have in his possession with intent to sell, lend, distribute, transmit, exhibit, or give away or show any obscene materials to any person 18 years of age or older, or knowingly advertise any obscene materials in any manner;*
  3. *design, copy, draw, photograph, print, utter, publish, or in any manner manufacture or prepare any obscene materials;*
  4. *write, print, publish, utter, or cause to be written, printed, published, or uttered any advertisement or notice of any kind giving information, directly or indirectly, stating or purporting to state where, how, from whom, or by what means any obscene materials can be purchased, obtained, or had;*
  5. *produce, present, or direct any obscene performance or participate in a portion thereof that is obscene or that contributes to its obscenity;*
  6. *hire, employ, use, or permit any minor child to do or assist in doing any act or thing mentioned in this subsection;*

7. *knowingly take or deliver in any manner any obscene material into a state correctional institution, county prison, regional prison facility, or any other type of correctional facility;*

8. *possess any obscene material while such person is an inmate of any state correctional institution, county prison, regional prison facility, or any other type of correctional facility; or*

9. *knowingly permit any obscene material to enter any state correctional institution, county prison, regional prison facility, or any other type of correctional facility if such person is a prison guard or other employee of any correctional facility described in this paragraph.*

(a.1) *Dissemination of explicit sexual material via an electronic communication.—No person, knowing the content of the advertisement to be explicit sexual materials as defined in subsection (c)(1) and (2), shall transmit or cause to be transmitted an unsolicited advertisement in an electronic communication as defined in Section 5702 (relating to definitions) to one or more persons within this Commonwealth that contains explicit sexual materials as defined in subsection (c)(1) and (2) without including in the advertisement the term "ADV-ADULT" at the beginning of the subject line of the advertisement. . . .*

(c) *Dissemination to minors.—No person shall knowingly disseminate by sale, loan, or otherwise explicit sexual materials to a minor. "Explicit sexual materials," as used in this subsection, means materials which are obscene or*

1. *any picture, photograph, drawing, sculpture, motion picture film, videotape, or similar visual representation or image of a person or portion of the human body which depicts nudity, sexual conduct, or sadomasochistic abuse and which is harmful to minors; or*

2. *any book, pamphlet, magazine, printed matter however reproduced, or sound recording which contains any matter enumerated in paragraph (1), or explicit and detailed verbal descriptions or narrative accounts of sexual excitement, sexual conduct, or sadomasochistic abuse and which, taken as a whole, is harmful to minors.*

(d) *Admitting minor to show.—It shall be unlawful for any person knowingly to exhibit for monetary consideration to a minor or knowingly to sell to a minor an admission ticket or pass or knowingly to admit a minor for a monetary consideration to premises whereon there is exhibited, a motion picture show or other presentation or performance which, in whole or in part, depicts nudity, sexual conduct, or sadomasochistic abuse and which is harmful to minors, except that the foregoing shall not apply to any minor accompanied by his parent.*[151]

Driving under the Influence/Driving While Intoxicated A typical example of a DUI/DWI provision might be this:

55-10-401. Driving under the influence of intoxicant, drug, or drug-producing stimulant prohibited—alcohol concentration in blood or breath.

(a) *It is unlawful for any person to drive or to be in physical control of any automobile or other motor-driven vehicle on any of the public roads and highways of the state, or on any streets or alleys, or while on the premises of any shopping center, trailer park, or any apartment house complex, or any other premises which is generally frequented by the public at large, while*

(1) *Under the influence of any intoxicant, marijuana, narcotic drug, or drug producing stimulating effects on the central nervous system; or*

(2) *The alcohol concentration in such person's blood or breath is ten-hundredths of one percent (.10%) or more.*[152]

Within this framework, the legislature pinpoints the key elements in each DUI/DWI charge. First, a driver exerts "physical control" over a motor vehicle. Second, that driver operates the vehicle under the influence of some substance, namely a drug or alcohol intoxicant. Third, the level of chemical influence on the operator, as measured in blood, meets or exceeds the sum of ten hundreds of 1% (.10).

Other Selected Provisions Loitering,[153] obstruction of highways and other public places,[154] disrupting lawful meetings or processions,[155] desecration of venerated objects,[156] vagrancy, and tramps[157] are related public offenses of interest to the criminal law practitioner. Doesn't the crime of vagrancy strike you as being imprecise? Maryland, as well as many other states, has had statutes involving people it wished to declare as vagrants. Evaluate the following language:

Every person, not insane, who wanders about in this state and lodges in markethouses, marketplaces, or in other public buildings, barns, outhouses, barracks, or in the open air, without having any lawful occupation in the city, town, or county in which he may so wander, without having any visible means of support, shall be deemed to be a tramp. Penalty, imprisonment, at the discretion of the Court or Justice of the Peace, hearing of the charge, for a period of not less than thirty days nor more than one year.[158]

DEFENSES OF CRIMINAL ACTS

Introduction

Any defense alleged in a criminal case is an effort to free oneself from the allegations. Defenses can either be technical or substantive in nature. Technical defenses often concern timeliness on procedural matters, such as whether a preliminary hearing took place within 48 hours. Substantive defenses go to the heart of the charge. A defendant who pleads alibi has created a substantive defense that he or she is innocent.

The real or feigned claim by defendants is denial. Most defendants will deny responsibility. Paralegals must discern the believable from the unbelievable.

The term *defense* means just what it says: a tactic that makes a party nonresponsible, defensible, not necessarily from the factual reality of the crimes charged but defensible, exonerative of the offense in either a factual or legal sense. A defense differs from a mitigating factor in one prime sense: the fact that successful defenses set perpetrators free while mitigators have the potential to reduce the level of impending culpability. (Revisit the murder/manslaughter discussion for more information about mitigating factors.) Defenses work when directed to the structural components of any crime, pinpointing a lack of act, of causation, or of mental state sufficient to assign responsibility. A legally insane person will be incapable of formulating the type of intent necessary for conviction, as will a comatose party who could not carry out any criminal design due to nonexistent will and an incapable body. These examples edify the power and strength of defenses that exonerate and liberate the defendant.

Self-Help—Protection of Person and Property

Self-Defense

A claim of self-defense must be reasonable; otherwise, the defense may be aggression.[159] Because the preservation instinct is inherent conduct, limits constituting reasonable and justifiable force and defense are desirable.[160] As an example, an article by Chris McGoey describes a "use of force continuum" that helps private security employees determine how much force they should use in self-defense or in apprehending a suspect (see Figure 10.3).[161] The concept of a force continuum has been around for years and is used to help private security personnel as well as police officers prepare for tense and potentially dangerous situations.[162]

FIGURE 10.3   Use of Force Continuum

Source: Adapted from "Security Guards & Officers: Use of Force Continuum" by Chris E. McGoey. Available at http://www.crimedoctor.com/security_guards_2.htm (retrieved January 25, 2007).

Six Levels on the Use of Force Continuum

Level 1: Officer Presence
Merely having a uniformed officer present—either standing, walking, or using vehicle lights—can deter criminal action. At this level, physical gestures should be nonthreatening and professional.

Level 2: Verbal Communication
Both the message and the way the message are delivered can defuse a tense situation. The tone should be firm but nonthreatening. Word choice and intensity level should be increased as necessary to keep control of the situation.

Level 3: Control Holds and Restraints
If words alone do not defuse the aggression, minimal force can be used. Minimal force involves the use of bare hands to guide, hold, and restrain. A baton should be used only for self-defense. Handcuffs may be used only if the security officer has had the correct training.

Level 4: Chemical Agents
Pepper spray and tear gas can be used only when the suspect is violent or threatening. They should not be used to protect property or enforce business rules; they are only used in defense. These chemical sprays provide an element of surprise and distraction, allowing the security officer to get away, call for help, or subdue the suspect, but they do not incapacitate the suspect. Even though these sprays are nondeadly, they can cause severe reactions.

Level 5: Temporary Incapacitation
Temporary incapacitation is used to stop a suspect from injuring the security officer or others long enough to handcuff and restrain them. Both defensive and offensive moves are appropriate at this level. Baton blows to soft tissue are consistent with professional security personnel training. Extreme caution and specialized training need to be taken into account before using restraining neck holds and stun guns.

Level 6: Deadly Force
Deadly force is used only when the officer is in immediate fear of death or great bodily injury. State laws vary on whether or when deadly force is allowed; check your state laws to be certain. After deadly force is used, the use of force continuum is considered to determine whether the other alternatives were used first or were more appropriate. Handguns should never be pulled and used as a deterrent under Level 3.

Excessive force during self-protection is not compatible with reasonable action. The Model Penal Code, as proposed in its official draft in 1962 by the American Law Institute, sets out a well-respected statutory design:[163]

1. *Use of force justifiable in the protection of the person. Subject to the provision of this section and of Section 3.09 the use of force upon or toward another person is justifiable when the actor believes that such force is immediately necessary for the purpose of protecting himself against the use of unlawful force by such other person on present occasion.*

2. *Limitations on justifying necessity for use of force.*
    a. *The use of force is not justifiable under this section:*
       (i) *to resist an arrest which the actor knows is being made by a peace officer although the arrest is unlawful. . . .*
    b. *The use of deadly force is not justifiable under this section unless the actor believes that such force is necessary to protect himself against death, serious bodily harm, kidnapping, or sexual intercourse compelled by force or threat, nor is it justifiable if*
       (i) *the actor, with the purpose of causing death or serious bodily harm, provoked the use of force against himself in the same encounter; or*
       (ii) *the actor knows that he can avoid the necessity of using force with complete safety by retreating or surrendering possession of a thing to a person asserting a claim of right thereto, or by complying with the demand that he abstain from any action which he has no duty to take, except that*
          (a) *the actor is not obliged to retreat from his dwelling or his place of work unless he was the initial aggressor . . .; and*
          (b) *a public officer justified in using force in the performance of his duties, or a person justified in using force in his assistance or a person justified in using force in making an arrest, or preventing an escape is not obliged to desist from efforts to perform such duty, effect such arrest, or prevent such escape . . .*[164]

This statutory guideline places an affirmative duty on the individual who seeks to use force. One who employs force must think of its consequences. Force exerted against the lawful action of law enforcement officers is generally not permissible. To employ force in self-defense, its usage must be immediately necessary. Force is to be employed only in situations where a reasonably prudent person might believe that he or she could suffer serious bodily harm, death, kidnapping, or a sexual assault.

In law enforcement arrest, violent aggression caused by suspects can be met by a proportionate response. Indeed, a defendant's slingshot should not be met with a police officer's rapid-fire weapon. Thus self-defense analysis always looks to proportionality first. By *proportionality* we mean that the means employed to withstand an attack match the force of the attacker. Proportionality does not imply identicality of means, only of effect. Therefore, a knife-wielding assailant can be met with a gun because the knife and gun harken equal potential for injury. One looks to the potential harm for determining the suitability of the defense chosen. A fist cannot justify a machine gun, nor would a pen knife a rocket launcher.

Consider the following fact patterns:

A security official catches a thief in the act. The thief reaches into his side pocket. Before he can withdraw his hand, the security official fires a weapon, inflicting a fatal injury.

Defend the actions selected by the security official. Would this be a case of the use of excessive force for self-protection?

A police officer comes upon a crime scene and sees a juvenile, with stolen goods in hand, riding his bike from the scene of a crime. As the juvenile accelerates his bicycle, he directs the path of the bike toward the police officer. The officer, to protect his life, even though he has an easy retreat and an opportunity to move in another direction, inflicts a fatal injury on the juvenile.

Is this a case of excessive force?

Plainly, the latter case demonstrates the Model Penal Code's demand that the force exerted by a defender be proportionate to that being exhibited by the aggressor. In the last fact pattern here, no weaponry is employed.

More troubling is that the first fact pattern is a modern legal dilemma for police officers every day of their professional lives. In these cases, judgment calls are common and are gauged by an officer's reasonable belief about the circumstances confronted.

The Model Penal Code refers to this equation as what is "immediately necessary" to counter the onslaught. In most statutory designs, deadly force is frowned upon except in necessitous cases. The Model Penal Code confirms this view:

> *Section 3.04. Use of force in self-protection.*
>
> *(2) Limitations on justifying the necessity for use of force.*
> >   *(b) The use of deadly force is not justifiable under this section unless the actor believes that such force is necessary to protect himself against death, serious bodily harm, kidnapping, or sexual intercourse compelled by force or threat; nor is it justifiable if*
> > >   *(i) the actor, with the purpose of causing death or serious bodily harm, provoked the use of force . . .*
> > >   *(ii) the actor knows that he can avoid the necessity of using such force with complete safety by retreating or by surrendering possession of a thing . . .*[165]

The reasonable person reaction will vary according to facts and conditions under which the parties labor and cannot be packaged into a compact formula. Conduct constituting a defense is justified if

> *(1) an aggressor unjustifiably threatens harms to the actor; and*
> *(2) the actor engages in conduct harmful to the aggressor;*
> >   *(a) when and to the extent necessary for self-protection*
> >   *(b) that is reasonable in relation to the harm threatened.*[166]

Protection of Other People

Another slant in the use of self-defense involves the protection of other people. People of social importance, such as entertainers, politicians, business executives, religious leaders, and other public personalities rely heavily on public and private law enforcement for protection. What level of response is permissible in the protection of other people? The Model Penal Code provides, again, some general statutory guidance:

> *(1) Subject to the provisions of this section and of Section 3.09, the use of force upon or toward the person of another is justifiable to protect a third person when*
> >   *(a) the actor would be justified under 3.04 in using such force to protect himself against the injury he believes to be threatened to the person whom he seeks to protect; and*
> >   *(b) under the circumstances, as the actor believes them to be, the person whom he seeks to protect would be justified in using such protective force; and*
> >   *(c) the actor believes that his intervention is necessary for the protection of the other person.*[167]

This statutory scheme allows for a transfer of authority for self-protection. A person who is entrusted with the obligation, particularly professionals in the public or private justice system, may exert such force as is proportionate, reasonable, and necessary given the set of facts within which he or she is operating. When measuring a defender's predicament, the self-defender can take whatever steps or actions a victim would be entitled to take. The defender is placed in the shoes of an actual or potential victim. What the defender believes becomes the key and prominent standard for taking action. However, belief should not be governed by hypersensitivity and delusion. It must be reasonable and justified. There should be "a threat, actual or apparent, to the use of deadly force against the defender; the threat must have been unlawful and immediate, and the defender must have believed that he was in imminent peril of death or serious bodily harm and that his response was necessary to save himself therefrom; such beliefs must not only have been honestly entertained, but also objectively reasonable considering the surrounding circumstances."[168]

The issue of self-defense for both the public and private justice systems has never been more pertinent. The Case Western Reserve University School of Law, in its long-standing publication *Private Police Training Manual,*[169] admonishes the public and private sector to prepare for a further influx of this type of activity. Training in the area of self-defense takes on added significance because

1. Confrontations between the police and the public are far more frequent.

2. Violence against officers has increased greatly.

3. Public clamor has been directed toward police using nonlethal weapons.

4. Police study groups are researching alternatives to violence.[170]

With increasing community pressure, the influence of civil and criminal litigation on police planning and the limits, obligations, and standards of self-defense will become more relevant. The role of self-defense is further affected by the proliferation of defense technology and occupational hardware. Defensive equipment available to public and private police systems, such as the following, makes proportionate self-defense or defense of others harder to measure:

- Revolvers
- Shotguns
- Rifles
- Machine guns
- Flare guns
- Armored vehicles
- Helmets

- Bulletproof vests
- Combat shields
- Tear gas
- Grenade launchers
- Batons
- Water cannons
- Military vehicles

Defense of Property

The value placed on personal property is markedly less than that placed on human life. Most American jurisdictions, with traditional common-law themes, have always placed a heavy burden on those seeking to employ force in the protection of personal property.[171] The Model Penal Code confirms that tradition:

> 1. *Use of force justifiable for the protection of property. Subject to the provisions of this section and of Section 3.09, the use of force upon or toward the person of another is justifiable when the actor believes that such force is immediately necessary:*
>   a. *to prevent or terminate an unlawful entry or other trespass upon land or a trespass against or the unlawful carrying away of tangible, movable property, provided that such land or movable property is or is believed by the actor to be in his possession or in the possession of another person for whose protection he acts; or*
>   b. *to effect an entry or reentry upon land or to retake tangible movable property provided that the actor believes that he or the person by whose authority he acts or a person from whom he or such other person derives title was unlawfully dispossessed . . . provided further, that*
>   (i) *the force is used immediately . . . .*
>   d. *Use of deadly force is not justifiable under this section unless the actor believes that*
>   (i) *the person against whom the force is used is attempting to dispossess him of his dwelling. . .*
>   (ii) *the person against whom the force is used is attempting to commit or consummate arson, burglary, robbery, or other felonious theft or property destruction.*[172]

Common sense dictates that the degree of force permissible is dependent on the totality of circumstances. Factual situations that include entry into one's domicile or residence support the right to exert force. Simple thefts or disputes over tangible property, such as a television, a garden tool, or some other item, do not justify the use of life-threatening force. On its face, the statute insists that if a party wants to resolve a property dispute without the assistance of public law enforcement, it must be done immediately.

The most confused cases occur when a dwelling place is involved. Numerous jurisdictions have grappled with the crosscurrents that occur in this area. Recent history indicates a movement toward favoring the owner to protect his own property.[173] In *State v. Miller*, a 1966 North Carolina case, the court held,

> *When a trespasser enters upon a man's premises, makes an assault upon his dwelling, an attempt to force an entrance into a house in a manner such as would lead a reasonably prudent man to believe that the intruder intends to commit a felony or inflict some serious personal injury upon the inmates, a lawful occupant of the dwelling may legally prevent the entry, even by the taking of the life of the intruder.*[174]

Applying these general standards, which of the following fact patterns would be considered an excessive use of force?

Fact Pattern 1
An employee responsible for the protection of a warehouse is responding to an alarm. As he approaches the point of detection, he is confronted with a man, middle-aged, who is attempting to pilfer some gold ingots from a storage container. The security official professionally requests that the thief halt and return the stolen object. The thief disregards the request, and the security officer inflicts two fatal bullet wounds.

Fact Pattern 2
An owner in a retail establishment confronts a shoplifter. The shoplifter flees from the store; a security officer gives pursuit. After a scuffle in the parking lot, the suspect pulls a switchblade and threatens to seriously harm the officer. The officer pulls his weapon and fires twice into the suspect's leg, causing a serious but not critical injury.

The initial fact pattern outlined is the best case for an excessive force charge. The reason is twofold: First, the utilization of excessive force did not have a basis or was not based on a belief that would lead a reasonable person to conclude that he or she was in imminent danger or harm; second, the force exerted was to protect assets or personal property, something the law does not favor. Alternatively, protection of the gold ingots was a real responsibility. The fault is not in intention but methodology.

The factual scenario outlined in the shoplifting case is a frequent occurrence. The force exerted was reasonable considering the weaponry initially employed by the shoplifter. The weapons chosen were not strictly identical, but their similar capacity to kill supports reasonable judgment.

Defenses Related to the Elements of a Crime

Entrapment

Encouraging, inducing, and influencing a person to engage in criminal activity may signal the defense of entrapment. Entrapment occurs when any law enforcement agent or individual, acting under local, state, or federal authority, or a private individual working for a public agency, induces another to commit an offense by unfair means of persuasion. From another angle, entrapment can be claimed when the criminal design, the plan, or the idea originated with a law enforcement agent rather than the defendant. Subsequent to the design, the officer implants this idea into the mind of an innocent person who lacks a predisposition to commit that offense.

Law enforcement agents or other public officials who induce an individual to commit a criminal act, who directly solicit the offense knowing that the individual would not have been so inclined, can arguably said to have entrapped the defendant. However, conduct that merely enables an individual to commit a criminal offense does not constitute entrapment. The defense of entrapment is extremely difficult to win[175] given a typical defendant's criminal history.

The Model Penal Code's official draft includes the following language:

> Section 2.13 Entrapment—A public law enforcement official or person acting in cooperation with such an official perpetrates an entrapment if, for the attaining of evidence of the commission of an offense, he induces or encourages another person to engage in conduct constituting such offense by either
>
> (a) Making knowingly false representations designed to induce a belief that such conduct is prohibited; or
> (b) Using methods of persuasion or inducement that create a substantial risk that such an offense will be committed by persons other than those who are ready to commit it.[176]

Mental Illness/Insanity

Fewer than 1 percent of American criminals file pleas and notice of insanity, and even fewer succeed in the argument.[177] Questions of legal insanity vastly contrast with any of the medical–psychiatric perspective. Being mentally ill provides no assurance that the legal defense will work. Only by the declaration of legal insanity can a defendant escape culpability. The distinction is not artificial because the law already understands that some portion of the criminal population will suffer from some type of psychiatric disorder. Most clinical studies of criminal lifestyles verify that criminal pathology is the product of many forces, including addictions, obsessions, alienations, antisocial behaviors, and troubled family life. Almost any criminal can find a psychiatrist to diagnose some disorder. To allow these general conditions as an absolute defense in criminal cases would generate not only enormous controversy but also injustice. Legal insanity, therefore, much more narrowly defines the role and influence of mental disease or defect in the exact circumstances leading up to the offense and takes center stage at the actual commission. Insanity is an affirmative defense available to criminal defendants. Although insanity is a debatable condition exacerbated by its weak psychiatric and psychological foundations, its defense is primarily behavioral in design. The defense views mental illness as an escape hatch from a criminal act, freely admitted as to deed, but excused due to lack of intent. A jury was instructed once as follows:

> *If the defendant had not sufficient reason to be able to judge the consequences of his act, or was so far deprived of volition or self-control by the overwhelming violence and mental disease that he was not capable of voluntary action and therefore was not able to choose the right and avoid the wrong, he was not responsible for any act committed while in this condition.*[178]

Professor Herbert Wechsler, in his work "The Criteria of Criminal Responsibility," holds as well,

> *If one conceives the major purpose of the insanity defense to be the exclusion of the non-deterrables from criminal responsibility, a control test seems designed to meet that objective. Furthermore, notions of retributive punishment seem particularly inappropriate with respect to one powerless to do otherwise than he did. Treatment and incapacitation can be accomplished in a mental hospital as well as in a prison.*[179]

In both these comments, a popular proposition crystallizes—that certain conduct is uncontrollable, irresistible, and without clear-cut mens rea. Under the Model Penal Code's Article 4 published in 1955, a mental disease or defect is characterized as a defense or exclusion to pure criminal responsibility. Cited at Section 4.01,

> *(1) A person is not responsible for criminal conduct if at the time of such conduct as a result of "mental disease or defect" he lacks substantial capacity either to appreciate the criminality [wrongfulness] of his conduct or to conform his conduct to the requirements of the law.*
>
> *(2) As used in this article, the terms mental disease or defect do not include an abnormality manifested only by repeated criminal or otherwise antisocial conduct.*[180]

Both historical and contemporary measurements of judging insanity are at best inexact. From the rule of Daniel McNaghten,[181] criminal law practitioners have struggled with recurring themes:

1. Should an individual who has no conception of right or wrong be criminally accountable?
2. If an individual does not understand the nature of right and wrong, is it a defense to his or her criminal conduct?
3. How is mental insanity gauged? By the scientific tests authorized by psychology and psychiatry?
4. What is irresistible conduct?
5. What is diminished capacity?
6. Are there individuals who are mentally ill yet still understand the nature of their conduct?
7. Using the Model Penal Code's test, what condition represents the lacking of substantial capacity?
8. How does an individual not "appreciate" the criminality of an act?
9. Should there be a more rigorous correlation between a mental illness and a finding of non-culpability for the resulting criminality?

The simple fact that a person has a mental disease or defect is not enough to relieve him or her of responsibility for a crime. Required proof is the relationship between the disease and the criminal act; the relationship must be such as to justify a reasonable inference that the act would not have been committed if the person had not been suffering from the disease.[182] In any event, various tests are employed in differing jurisdictions:

The McNaghten Rule: The Right and Wrong/Good and Evil Test

The Durham Rule: Product Analysis

The American Law Institute Rule: The Substantial Capacity Test[183]

Public criticism regarding the insanity plea reached cynical heights during the cases of Mark Chapman, who murdered John Lennon, and David Hinckley, who attempted to assassinate President Reagan. Outraged by the results of these two cases, critics of the insanity defense have called for either its complete abolition or material modification. The success of the defense has led some jurisdictions, while recognizing mental illness as a factor in mens rea, to adopt a new plea nonetheless called guilty but mentally ill.[184] An example of a recently enacted Michigan statute is outlined here:

Section 768.36.

(1) If the defendant asserts a defense of insanity in compliance with Section 20a of this chapter, the defendant may be found "guilty but mentally ill" if, after trial, the trier of fact finds all of the following:

(a) The defendant is guilty beyond a reasonable doubt of an offense.

(b) The defendant has proven by a preponderance of the evidence that he or she was mentally ill at the time of the commission of that offense.

(c) The defendant has not established by a preponderance of the evidence that he or she lacked the substantial capacity either to appreciate the nature and quality or the wrongfulness of his or her conduct or to conform his or her conduct to the requirements of the law.

(2) If the defendant asserts a defense of insanity in compliance with Section 20a of this chapter and the defendant waives his or her right to trial, by jury or by judge, the trial judge, with the approval of the prosecuting attorney, may accept a plea of guilty but mentally ill in lieu of a plea of guilty or a plea of nolo contendere. The judge shall not accept a plea of guilty but mentally ill until, with the defendant's consent, the judge has examined the report or reports prepared in compliance with Section 20a of this chapter, the judge has held a hearing on the issue of the defendant's mental illness at which either party may present evidence, and the judge is satisfied that the defendant has proven by a preponderance of the evidence that the defendant was mentally ill at the time of the offense to which the plea is entered. The reports shall be made a part of the record of the case.

(3) If a defendant is found guilty but mentally ill or enters a plea to that effect which is accepted by the court, the court shall impose any sentence that could be imposed by law upon a defendant who is convicted of the same offense. If the defendant is committed to the custody of the department of corrections, the defendant shall undergo further evaluation and be given such treatment as is psychiatrically indicated for his or her mental illness or retardation. Treatment may be provided by the department of corrections or by the department of community health as provided by law. Sections 1004 and 1006 of the mental health code, 1974 PA 258, MCL 330.2004 and 330.2006, apply to the discharge of the defendant from a facility of the department of community health to which the defendant has been admitted and to the return of the defendant to the department of corrections for the balance of the defendant's sentence. When a treating facility designated by either the department of corrections or the department of community health discharges the defendant before the expiration of the defendant's sentence, that treating facility shall transmit to the parole board a report on the condition of the defendant that contains the clinical facts, the diagnosis, the course of treatment, the prognosis for the remission of symptoms, the potential for recidivism, the danger of the defendant to himself or herself or to the public, and recommendations for future treatment. If the parole board considers the defendant for parole, the board shall consult with the treating facility at which the defendant is being treated or from which the defendant has been discharged and a comparable report on the condition of the defendant shall be filed with the board. If the defendant is placed on parole, the defendant's treatment shall, upon recommendation of the treating facility, be made a condition of parole. Failure to continue treatment except by agreement with the designated facility and parole board is grounds for revocation of parole.

(4) If a defendant who is found guilty but mentally ill is placed on probation under the jurisdiction of the sentencing court as provided by law, the trial judge, upon recommendation of the center for forensic psychiatry, shall make treatment a condition of probation. Reports as specified by the trial judge shall be filed with the probation officer and the sentencing court. Failure to continue treatment, except by agreement with the treating agency and the sentencing court, is grounds for revocation of probation. The period of probation shall not be for less than 5 years and shall not be shortened without receipt and consideration of a forensic psychiatric report by the sentencing court. Treatment shall be provided by an agency of the department of community health or, with the

approval of the sentencing court and at individual expense, by private agencies, private physicians, or other mental health personnel. A psychiatric report shall be filed with the probation officer and the sentencing court every 3 months during the period of probation. If a motion on a petition to discontinue probation is made by the defendant, the probation officer shall request a report as specified from the center for forensic psychiatry or any other facility certified by department of community health for the performance of forensic psychiatric evaluation.[185]

This brief analysis simply gives an overview of the dilemmas and difficulties in an insanity case. However, paralegals must evaluate their clients as they find them, especially those with long and turbulent emotional histories, or those victimized by serious sexual and emotional abuse. Clients who have indulged in years of drug and alcohol abuse, or who have sweeping track records of civil and criminal commitment for mental illness and disturbance, must be realistically evaluated. Form 10.1 on the accompanying CD contains the necessary language to support a motion for the psychiatric examination of an incarcerated defendant.

To be legally insane, the burden is not only narrow—it is extremely heavy. The insane individual acts without the necessary intellectual faculties needed to meet the mens rea standard. In sum, the insane defendant "had not sufficient reason to be able to judge the consequences of this act, or was so far deprived of volition or self-control by the overwhelming violence and mental disease that he was not capable of voluntary action and therefore was not able to choose the right and avoid the wrong, he was not responsible for any act committed while in this condition."[186] The sequence of offer might go like this:

- Give notice of intent to plea insanity well ahead of trial.
- Demonstrate a clear and clinically undeniable mental disease or disorder.
- Employ expert opinion to connect the diagnosis with the criminal conduct.
- Demonstrate that the mental disease or defect interfered with intellectual assent and understanding of the quality of the offense.

Legal insanity should not be confused with questions of legal competency, though the principles sometimes intersect. A finding of incompetency says that a defendant or other civil party lacks the capacity to understand the nature of the proceedings. Mental state may make incongruous any formal trial or hearings.

The criteria that should be used to determine competency include the defendant's capacity to

- Appreciate the charges against him.
- Appreciate the range and nature of possible penalties that may be imposed in the proceedings against him.
- Understand the adversary nature of the legal process.
- Disclose to counsel facts pertinent to the legal process.
- Manifest appropriate courtroom behavior.
- Testify relevantly.
- Perform any other factors deemed relevant.

See Figure 10.4 for a sample motion for determination of competency.

FIGURE 10.4
Motion to Determine Competency

Pursuant to _____, counsel for the Defendant, _____, asks this Court to order a competency examination to determine if he currently has the ability to consult with counsel with a reasonable degree of rational understanding and if he has a rational and factual understanding of the pending proceeding against him. He makes this request for the following reasons:

[List reasons supporting request for examination.]

Based on the above listed reasons, counsel for the defendant in good faith respectfully asks this Court to appoint appropriate mental health experts to examine the defendant to determine his competency to stand trial.

Duress

Defendants who have been charged with criminal conduct that has been allegedly triggered by extreme duress, force, emotional, or physical coercion can sensibly present the affirmative defense of duress. The Model Penal Code defines duress as follows:

> It is an affirmative defense that the actor engaged in conduct charged to constitute an offense because he was coerced to do so by the use of or threat to use, unlawful force against the person or the person of another, that the person of reasonable firmness in his situation would have been unable to resist.[187]

Duress is being witnessed with greater regularity in spousal and child abuse cases as well as cases involving psychological torment. To argue effectively, its proponent will have to demonstrate a lack of alternatives in the choice of conduct. The question depends too on the factual circumstances that compel the individual to act and the reasonableness of the reaction to the coerced circumstances. Some statutes refer to this as a "reasonable firmness"[188] that comports with how average people react to compulsive circumstances. Thus when a Mafia hit man instructs that a delivery of drugs should occur or self or other relatives will suffer consequences, duress exists. It could be argued that a juvenile facility where harm occurred with regularity might be a coercive environment. Although not synonymous with brainwashing, the element of mind control flows through duress analysis because the defense admits the wrongdoing but justifies the action by the impossibility of any other course of conduct. "The courts have generally been unwilling to recognize duress as a defense to escape except in the most egregious of situations. As a general rule, one who escapes from a penal institution is not excused even though faced with an immediate threat of death or serious bodily harm if there is a reasonable and viable alternative to the act of escaping."[189]

Necessity

Certain actions may appear criminal but are justified or excusable by the doctrine and defense of necessity. Clark and Marshall advance the following argument:

> An act that would otherwise be a crime may by excused if the person accused can show that it was done only in order to avoid consequences that could not otherwise be avoided, and which, if they had followed, would have inflicted upon him, or upon others whom he was bound to protect, inevitable and irrespirable evil; that no more was done than was reasonably necessary for that purpose; and that the evil inflicted by it was not disproportionate to the evil avoided.[190]

Essentially facing a choice of evils, the actor chooses not with a criminal purpose but without other reasonable moral choice. Self-defense is a case where deadly force may be exerted by pure necessity. Under Section 3.02 of the Model Penal Code, *justification* is used interchangeably with *necessity*:

> 1. Conduct that the actor believes to be necessary to avoid a harm or evil to himself or to another is justifiable, provided that
>   a. The harm or evil sought to be avoided by such impotency is greater than that sought to be prevented by the law defining the offense charged.
>   b. Neither the code nor other law defining the offense provides exceptions or defenses.
>   c. The legislative purpose used to exclude the justification claim does not otherwise plainly appear.[191]

Review the cannabis case at *United States v. Oakland Cannabis Buyer's Coop.,* 190 F.3d 1109 (9th Cir. 1999). How would the necessity defense play out in these facts?

Consent

Consent negates criminal liability. For example, a conviction for a larceny will not be upheld if the property possessed was given freely to defendant by its former owner. One who gives consent can later revoke consent. Consent defenses habitually arise in cases of assault, battery, and sexual offenses.[192]

Consent statutes emphasize the commonsense features of the defense—namely that consent be given by those capable, that consent be mutual to be consent at all, and that certain types of activities, due to their inherent legality, cannot be consented to. Here is Pennsylvania's version:

> §311. Consent.
>
> (A) GENERAL RULE.—The consent of the victim to conduct charged to constitute an offense or to the result thereof is a defense if such consent negates an element of the offense or precludes the infliction of the harm or evil sought to be prevented by the law defining the offense.

(B) *CONSENT TO BODILY INJURY.—When conduct is charged to constitute an offense because it causes or threatens bodily injury, consent to such conduct or to the infliction of such injury is a defense if*

    (1) the conduct and the injury are reasonably foreseeable hazards of joint participation in a lawful athletic contest or competitive sport; or

    (2) the consent establishes a justification for the conduct under Chapter 5 of this title (relating to general principles of justification).

(C) *INEFFECTIVE CONSENT.—Unless otherwise provided by this title or by the law defining the offense, assent does not constitute consent if*

    (1) it is given by a person who is legally incapacitated to authorize the conduct charged to constitute the offense;

    (2) it is given by a person who by reason of youth, mental disease or defect, or intoxication is manifestly unable or known by the actor to be unable to make a reasonable judgment as to the nature or harmfulness of the conduct charged to constitute the offense;

    (3) it is given by a person whose improvident consent is sought to be prevented by the law defining the offense; or

    (4) it is induced by force, duress, or deception of a kind sought to be prevented by the law defining the offense.[193]

Statute of Limitations

The technical defense of the statute of limitations is available in all jurisdictions and requires that a criminal action be prosecuted within a specific time frame. For example, a rape complaint must be brought to prosecution within 20 years. Statute of limitation defenses may pertain to these criminal processes:

- Durational quality of an arrest or search warrant.
- Speedy trial determinations.
- Period of detention without legal representation.
- Times imposed for posttrial motions and appellate activities.
- Governmental privilege or domestic authority.

Murder, for example, has no statute of limitations.

Legal or Domestic Authority

Undercover activities of police officers, federal agents, and other individuals are immune from prosecution for criminal offenses. Ordinarily the domestic authority or privilege rule arises in cases pertaining to parents and their children, guardians and their responsible parties, police officers and suspects, and teachers and students. The defense can also be posed by any individual given authority under state or federal law who is vicariously liable for another.

Infancy

Most jurisdictions define a minor adult or an infant for both civil and criminal purposes. In criminal law, the defense of infancy should not be overlooked because juvenile courts are generally more liberal in their deliberations. Infancy analysis bears directly on the issue of mens rea, asserting that the mental element necessary for a conviction could not possibly be formulated in a child or juvenile of such youth or tender years.[194]

In common law, infancy was a true defense to criminal liability. In common law, before reaching the age of seven years, a child was not responsible for any criminal act. The child was conclusively presumed to be unable to know right from wrong. Before reaching the age of 14, a child was presumed to be incapable of knowing. This condition was rebuttable when evidence was produced that clearly proved that the child knew right from wrong when the offense was committed. If the child fled the scene or attempted to conceal the offense, those facts were considered to rebut the presumption. After reaching the age of 14, a child was presumed to know right from wrong and was treated as an adult.

Today the picture appears quite bleak. Courts are increasingly imputing criminal culpability to once sacrosanct minors.

EX PARTE STATE OF ALABAMA (IN RE *D.B.Y. V. STATE OF ALABAMA*)
CR-04-0443
COURT OF CRIMINAL APPEALS OF ALABAMA
910 SO. 2D 820; 2005 ALA. CRIM. APP. LEXIS 71
MARCH 18, 2005, RELEASED

SUBSEQUENT HISTORY: Released for Publication July 28, 2005.

PRIOR HISTORY: Montgomery Circuit Court. (CC-01-331 and CC-01-894). *D.Y. v. State,* 841 So. 2d 304, 2002 Ala. Crim. App. LEXIS 89 (Ala. Crim. App., 2002).

DISPOSITION: PETITION FOR WRIT OF MANDAMUS IS GRANTED; WRIT ISSUED.

COUNSEL: For Petitioner: Eleanor Idelle Brooks, district atty., and Trisha L. Mellberg, asst. district atty.

For Respondent: Richard K. Keith, Montgomery.

JUDGES: McMillan, P.J., and Cobb, Baschab, Shaw, and Wise, J.J., concur.

OPINION: PETITION FOR WRIT OF MANDAMUS

PER CURIAM.

The district attorney for the Fifteenth Judicial Circuit filed this petition for a writ of mandamus directing Judge Johnny Hardwick to reinstate D.B.Y.'s[195] probation and to direct that he undergo a sexual offender risk assessment as required by law before he be released from probation.[196] In 2001, D.B.Y. was indicted for six counts of enticing a child in violation of §13A-6-69, Ala. Code 1975. In November 2001, he was granted youthful offender ("YO") status and pleaded guilty to all counts as charged in the indictments. Judge Hardwick sentenced him to three years' imprisonment on each count; the sentences were to run consecutively. D.B.Y. appealed to this Court. In April 2002, we held that the sentence imposed was illegal because Alabama law clearly prohibits consecutive sentences for youthful offenders that exceed the statutory maximum of three years; we remanded the case to the Montgomery Circuit Court to correct its illegal sentence. *D.Y. v. State,* 841 So. 2d 304 (Ala. Crim. App. 2002). In August 2002, Judge Hardwick resentenced D.B.Y. to 12 months in the Montgomery County Detention Facility and two years of supervised probation. Approximately two years later, in November 2004, before D.B.Y.'s probation was scheduled to terminate, the State filed a motion to have D.B.Y. undergo a sexual offender risk assessment as required by §15-20-28, Ala. Code 1975. Judge Hardwick set the motion for a hearing. On December 6, 2004, before the hearing was held, D.B.Y.'s probation officer released D.B.Y. from probation. Judge Hardwick then denied the State's motion for a risk assessment. The district attorney filed this mandamus petition.[197]

The district attorney asserts that Judge Hardwick was without jurisdiction to terminate D.B.Y.'s probation without first complying with §15-20-28, Ala. Code 1975. Section 15-20-28, states, in part,

> (a) Sixty days prior to the projected release of a juvenile criminal sex offender, the treatment provider shall provide a risk assessment of the juvenile to the sentencing court and the juvenile probation officer.

> (b) Upon receiving the risk assessment, the juvenile probation officer shall immediately notify the state, and either the parent, guardian, or custodian of the juvenile criminal sex offender, or attorney for the juvenile criminal sex offender, of the pending release and provide them with the risk assessment.

> (c) Unless otherwise ordered by the sentencing court, the juvenile criminal sexual offender shall not be subject to notification upon release.

> (d) Within thirty days of receiving the risk assessment, the state may petition the court to apply notification.

> (e) No juvenile criminal sex offender shall be removed from the supervision of the court until such time as the juvenile criminal sex offender has completed treatment, the treatment provider has filed a risk assessment with the court, and the state has had an opportunity to file a petition to apply notification.

> (f) Upon receiving a petition to apply notification, the sentencing court shall conduct a hearing on the risk of the juvenile criminal sex offender to the community. The sentencing court may deny the petition or grant the petition based upon, but not limited to, the following factors relevant to the risk of reoffense:

> > (1) Conditions of release that minimize risk of reoffense, including, but not limited to, whether the offender is under supervision of probation or parole; receiving counseling, therapy, or treatment; or residing in a home situation that provides guidance and supervision.

> > (2) Physical conditions that minimize risk of reoffense, including, but not limited to, advanced age or debilitating illness.

> > (3) Criminal history factors indicative of high risk of reoffense, including whether the offender's conduct was found to be characterized by repetitive and compulsive behavior.

> > (4) Other criminal history factors to be considered in determining risk, including

> > > a. The relationship between the offender and the victim.

> > > b. Whether the offense involved the use of a weapon, violence, or infliction of serious bodily injury.

> > > c. The number, date, and nature of prior offenses.

> > (5) Whether psychological or psychiatric profiles indicate a risk of recidivism.

(6) The offender's response to treatment.

(7) Recent behavior, including behavior while confined or while under supervision in the community as well as behavior in the community following service of sentence.

(8) Recent threats against persons or expressions of intent to commit additional crimes.

D.B.Y. does not contest the application of this section to him. He pleaded guilty to six counts of enticing a child. He was granted YO status. According to §15-20-31, Ala. Code 1975, the juvenile registration procedures apply to D.B.Y.

D.B.Y. first argues that this mandamus should not issue because, he argues, the State, has another remedy—it can appeal the circuit court's ruling. However, the State has only a limited right to appeal. As this Court stated in *State v. A.R.C.,* 873 So. 2d 261, 266 (Ala. Crim. App. 2003),

> In Alabama, the State has a limited right to appeal and that right is conditioned on compliance with certain requirements. The State can appeal a pretrial ruling holding a statute unconstitutional, suppressing evidence, dismissing the charges, quashing an arrest or search warrant, or granting a habeas corpus petition and ordering an individual released from custody. See §§12-12-70, 12-22-90, and 12-22-91, Ala. Code 1975, and Rule 15.7, Ala. R. Crim. P.

The State has no right to appeal the ruling made in this case—mandamus is the State's only remedy. See *Smith v. State,* 447 So. 2d 1334 (Ala. 1984); *State v. Monette,* 887 So. 2d 314, 315 (Ala. Crim. App. 2004). See also *State v. Drewry,* 519 S. 2d 591 (Ala. Crim. App. 1987). This case is correctly before this Court by way of mandamus petition.

The district attorney argues that the terms of §15-20-28, Ala. Code 1975, are mandatory and that Judge Hardwick had no authority to deny its request to have D.B.Y. undergo a sexual offender risk assessment. D.B.Y. argues that the State's motion was untimely. He further argues that to place D.B.Y. back on supervised probation so that he may undergo a sexual offender risk assessment would violate his constitutional rights.

In 1999, when the Alabama Legislature rewrote the community notification laws, it enacted §15-20-20.1, Ala. Code 1975. This section specifically addresses the legislative intent in adopting community notification laws for both juvenile and adult sexual offenders. Section 15-20-20.1, as that section relates to juvenile sexual offenders, states, in pertinent part

> Juvenile sex offenders, like their adult counterparts, pose a danger to the public. Research has shown, however, that there are significant differences between adult and juvenile criminal sexual offenders. Juveniles are much more likely to respond favorably to sexual offender treatment. Juvenile offenders have a shorter history of committing sexual offenses. They are less likely to have deviant sexual arousal patterns and are not as practiced in avoiding responsibility for their abusive behavior. Juveniles are dependent upon adults for food and shelter, as well as the emotional and practical support vital to treatment efforts. Earlier intervention increases the opportunity for success in teaching juveniles how to reduce their risk of sexually reoffending. The Legislature finds that juvenile criminal sex offenders should be subject to the Community Notification Act, but that certain precautions should be taken to target the juveniles that pose the more serious threats to the public.

> Therefore, the state policy is to assist local law enforcement agencies' efforts to protect their communities by requiring criminal sex offenders to register, record their address of residence, to be photographed, fingerprinted, to authorize the release of necessary and relevant information about criminal sex offenders to the public, to mandate residency and employment restrictions upon criminal sex offenders, and to provide certain discretion to judges for application of these requirements as provided in this article.

Section 15-20-28(e), Ala. Code 1975, specifically states, "No juvenile criminal sex offender shall be removed from the supervision of the court until such time as . . . the treatment provider has filed a risk assessment with the court."

The Legislature chose to use the term "shall" throughout §15-20-28, Ala. Code 1975. The Alabama Supreme Court in *Ex parte Prudential Insurance Co. of America,* 721 So. 2d 1135 (Ala. 1998), stated the following concerning the Legislature's use of the words "shall" and "must" in §6-5-430, Ala. Code 1975:

> Words used in [a] statute must be given their natural, plain, ordinary, and commonly understood meaning, and where plain language is used a court is bound to interpret that language to mean exactly what it says. Then there is no room for judicial construction and the clearly expressed intent of the Legislature must be given effect.

> *Tuscaloosa County Comm'n v. Deputy Sheriffs' Ass'n of Tuscaloosa County,* 589 So. 2d 687, 689 (Ala. 1991) (citations omitted); see also *Ex parte New England Mutual Life Ins. Co.,* 663 So. 2d 952 (Ala. 1995), and *State Dep't of Transportation v. McLelland,* 639 So. 2d 1370 (Ala. 1994). The word "shall" is clear and unambiguous and is imperative and mandatory. *Tuscaloosa County Comm'n v. Deputy Sheriffs' Ass'n of Tuscaloosa,* supra; *Taylor v. Cox,* 710 So. 2d 406 (Ala. 1998); *Ex parte First Family Financial Services, Inc.,* 718 So. 2d 658 (Ala. 1998) (on application for rehearing) (interpreting the word "shall" as used in §6-3-21.1). The word "shall" has been defined as follows:

> "As used in statutes, contracts, or the like, this word is generally imperative or mandatory. In common or ordinary parlance, and in its ordinary signification, the term "shall" is a word of command, and one which has always or which must be given a compulsory meaning, as denoting obligation. The word in ordinary usage means "must" and is inconsistent with a concept of discretion."

> Black's Law Dictionary 1375 (6th ed. 1991).

721 So. 2d at 1138. Accordingly, we find that compliance with §15-20-28, Ala. Code 1975, is mandatory.[198]

The community notification laws as they apply to juvenile sexual offenders were enacted long after the Legislature enacted the Youthful Offender Act in 1971.

The first rule of statutory construction is that the intent of the legislature should be given effect. *Ex parte McCall,* 596 So. 2d 4 (Ala. 1992); *Volkswagen of America, Inc. v. Dillard,* 579 So. 2d 1301 (Ala. 1991). However, when possible, the intent of the legislature should be gathered from the language of the statute itself. *Dillard,* supra. Thus, where the language of the statute is plain, the court must give effect to the clear meaning of that language. *Ex parte United Service Stations, Inc.*, 628 So. 2d 501 (Ala. 1993); *IMED Corp. v. Systems Eng'g Associates Corp.*, 602 So. 2d 344 (Ala. 1992).

Beavers v. County of Walker, 645 So. 2d 1365, 1376-77 (Ala. 1994) See also *Tuscaloosa County Comm'n v. Deputy Sheriffs' Ass'n of Tuscaloosa County,* 589 So. 2d 687, 689 (Ala. 1991) ("Words used in [a] statute must be given their natural, plain, ordinary, and commonly understood meaning, and where plain language is used a court is bound to interpret that language to mean exactly what it says. If the language of the statute is clear and unambiguous, then there is no room for judicial construction and the clearly expressed intent of the legislature must be given effect.") Moreover, this Court has stated,

"In determining legislative intent, statutes are, where possible, construed in harmony with statutes existing at the time of enactment, so that each is afforded a field of operation." *Sullivan v. State ex rel. Attorney General of Alabama,* 472 So. 2d 970, 973 (Ala. 1985). "It is a fundamental principle of statutory construction that in enacting the statute the legislature had full knowledge and information as to prior and existing law and legislation on the subject of the statute." *Miller v. State,* 349 So. 2d 129, 131 (Ala. Cr. App. 1977). "In cases of conflicting statutes on the same subject, the latest expression of the legislature is the law. Where a conflict exists between statutes, the last enactment must take precedence." [*Baldwin County v.] Jenkins,* 494 So. 2d [584,] 588 [(Ala. 1986)].

"*Hatcher v. State,* 547 So. 2d 905, 906-07 (Ala. Crim. App. 1989)."

Soles v. State, 820 So. 2d 163, 164-65 (Ala.Crim.App. 2001).

Section 15-20-28(e), Ala. Code 1975, provides, "No juvenile criminal sex offender shall be removed from the supervision of the court until such time as . . . the treatment provider has filed a risk assessment with the court. . . ." The mandatory wording of this statute is evidence that the Legislature intended that no juvenile sex offender be released from custody until that offender undergoes a sexual offender risk assessment. With this legislative intent in mind, we conclude that the State's filing of its motion for a sexual offender risk assessment before the expiration of D.B.Y.'s probation operated to toll D.B.Y.'s probation. To reach any other conclusion would foreclose the State from seeking enforcement of §15-20-28, Ala. Code 1975, given that a motion for sexual offender risk assessment is filed near the end of an offender's term of probation.[199]

Based on the mandatory wording of §15-20-28 and on the clearly stated legislative intent, we can reach no other reasonable conclusion—Judge Hardwick had no authority to release D.B.Y. from probation until he underwent a sexual offender risk assessment. Compliance with this section is not discretionary on the part of the sentencing judge but is mandatory and is a prerequisite to implementing the special community notification procedures for juvenile sexual offenders. To hold otherwise would be contrary to the stated legislative intent. Judge Hardwick was obligated to ensure that the mandatory provisions of §15-20-28, Ala. Code 1975, were complied with before D.B.Y. was released from probation.

D.B.Y. also argues that we should not grant this petition because the district attorney failed to file the motion for a sexual offender risk assessment 60 days before D.B.Y.'s projected release date. However, §15-20-28(a), Ala. Code 1975, specifically provides that the "treatment provider" shall provide a risk assessment of the juvenile 60 days before his projected release date. Section 15-20-21(10), Ala. Code 1975, specifically defines the responsible agencies. This section defines "responsible agency" as:

> The person or government entity whose duty it is to obtain information from a criminal sex offender before release and to transmit that information to police departments or sheriffs responsible for providing community notification. For a criminal sex offender being released from state prison, the responsible agency is the Department of Corrections. For a criminal sex offender being released from a county jail, the responsible agency is the sheriff of that county. For a criminal sex offender being released from a municipal jail, the responsible agency is the police department of that municipality. For a criminal sex offender being placed on probation, including conditional discharge or unconditional discharge, without any sentence of incarceration, the responsible agency is the sentencing court. For a criminal sex offender being released from the Department of Youth Services, the responsible agency is the Department of Youth Services.

We see no indication in the documents filed with this Court that the district attorney had any responsibility to comply with or failed to comply with §15-20-28, Ala. Code 1975.

Accordingly, this petition is due to be granted. Judge Hardwick is directed to order that D.B.Y. undergo a sexual offender risk assessment as required by §15-20-28, Ala. Code 1975.

PETITION GRANTED; WRIT ISSUED.

Alibi

Numerous American jurisdictions require that notice of alibi be provided in the defense pleadings. The defendant should produce evidence, such as witnesses who will state that the defendant was in a different place when the crime was committed. An alibi defense must be averred in the initial stages of a criminal prosecution.

Intoxication

Often misunderstood and mischaracterized, intoxication is rarely a pure and absolute defense to criminal conduct. Involuntary force-fed intoxication without consent to alcohol is a defense. Voluntary intoxication is a limited defense technique. Intoxication bears directly on the issue of mental state—the ability to formulate a mental scheme, plan, or a logical series of steps forging the mens rea. The Model Penal Code defines intoxication as follows:

1. *Except at provided in subsection 4 of this Section, intoxication of the actor is not a defense unless it negates an element of the offense.*

2. *When recklessness establishes an element of the offense if the actor, due to self-induced intoxication, is unaware of a risk of which he would have been aware had he been sober. Such unawareness is immaterial.*

3. *Intoxication does not in itself constitute mental disease with the meaning of Section 4.01.*[200]

Other Defenses

The list of defenses that exist in criminal practice is lengthy. Remember that defense arguments may present these issues:

- Mistake or ignorance of law.
- Mistake of fact.
- Mistaken identification.
- Failure of proof.
- Double jeopardy.

- Provocation.
- Collateral estoppel.
- Scientific defenses such as the XYY theory.[201]

New criminal defenses based on psychological, psychiatric, and scientific explanations for behavior will surely be created as time passes. Predictably, some defenses based on genetics, DNA structure and molecules, and other avant garde social and psychiatric explanations will surface from the defense bar. In a way, this type of legal innovation and challenge is inevitable because defense practitioners are obliged to argue legitimate, and even provocative, defenses in their advocacy. Use Form 10.2 on the accompanying CD in your assessment of defense issues.

PROCEDURAL ASPECTS OF CRIMINAL PRACTICE

Preliminary Considerations

Whether working for prosecution or defense interests, a paralegal must be a competent fact evaluator and investigator. Successful criminal practice requires accurate factual collection, assimilation, and analysis. Although many sources provide this information, Chapter 9, which focuses on investigations, discusses this subject briefly. A brief assessment of some investigative reports and documents unique to criminal practice is provided here.

Form 10.3 on the accompanying CD is a police offense report that classifies the conduct into initial criminal categorizations. Look particularly at Section 8, about the object of attack, and Section 15, in which bodily injuries are narrated. In Section 24 the offense is outlined in rough factual terms. This is the starting point for the investigative paralegal.

Critical information is obtained at the client's initial consultation and interview. A confidential client information form contains the pertinent information for proper representation (See Form 10.4 on the accompanying CD.) This document is used to compile key information, including the person's name and address, prior criminal record and bail information, factual recitation, and an analysis of the arrest process.

Client consultation forms can be more specific. Use the informational form for defense of driving while under the influence. (See Form 10.5 on the accompanying CD.)

The paralegal's initial case analysis helps shape tactical and litigation strategy. See Form 10.6, case analysis, on the accompanying CD; this form prompts the paralegal to handle questions of mental state, evidentiary support and litigation theories, identity of the defendant, and the elemental analysis of specific crimes and their related defenses.

Police Documentation

Police documentation and reports are extensive and useful in litigation planning and strategy. Gaining access to this information is not always easy, but with solid professional relationships much information can be acquired. In addition, many documents are subject to disclosure due to constitutional mandates.

Form 10.7, a record of arrest, on the accompanying CD offers substantial insight into the defendant's arrest circumstances. For a full discussion of investigative practice in a criminal case, see Chapter 9.

Initiation of the Criminal Case

Jurisdictional approaches to criminal case initiation are strikingly simple and fairly uniform. At both federal and state levels, a preliminary investigation leads to a specific summons being issued in advance of a full-fledged criminal complaint. In some circumstances, an arrest takes place immediately, with initial appearances and preliminary hearings occurring soon thereafter. In any event, the sequence generally overlaps and evolves in the following steps.

Filing the Criminal Complaint

Criminal complaints may be filed by both public officials and private citizens. A sample criminal complaint for the U.S. District Court appears in Form 10.8 on the accompanying CD. The complaint cites the factual background and charging statutes.

Summons

In response to the criminal complaint that has been filed, a summons is issued to a criminal defendant. Some jurisdictions permit the filing of summons to advise a defendant that a complaint is forthcoming. See Form 10.9 on the accompanying CD. Process service is required under the applicable federal or state rules, though the method of service will depend on the jurisdiction.

Warrant for Arrest

A warrant for arrest can be prepared and carried out in advance of a complaint if the circumstances and conditions warrant. The warrant for arrest for the U.S. District Court in Form 10.10 on the accompanying CD has the required federal information.

Warrants for arrest are not always needed if suspects or defendants are cooperative or if a summons has been successfully employed. The form is irrelevant in warrantless circumstances.

Search Warrants

As part of the investigative process, either pre-arrest or post-arrest in nature, the assigned investigators may wish to perform a full-fledged search of the person or his domicile. In accordance with due process, the officer or affiant must present, by affidavit or other application, to a neutral magistrate, the basis and the grounds for said request. See the application and affidavit for search warrant at Form 10.11 on the accompanying CD.

After an objective and critical examination of the evidence presented by the affiant, the judicial officer or magistrate determines whether a search warrant is supported by probable cause. If so, a search warrant for a specific purpose and time period with other limitations will be granted. (See Form 10.12, which shows a search warrant, on the accompanying CD.)

Initial Appearance

After the arrest, an initial appearance usually takes place unless the defendant chooses to waive this right. Initial appearances are generally held to advise defendants about

- Right to counsel.
- Specific offenses for which they are charged.
- A preliminary hearing or other probable cause determination within a specific period of time.
- The nature of bail or release on personal recognizance.
- The procedural issues related to bail.

Bail

Although bail is not constitutionally guaranteed, most criminal systems provide the bail process if facts and conditions warrant. Rarely do individuals desire to remain in custody, and bail provides a mechanism for early release pending other hearings or eventual trial. Paralegals will spend significant time handling questions of bail. The personal recognizance bond is used when a defendant promises to abide by any judgment entered by the court for eventual surrender or to serve any sentence imposed for failure to honor the personal promise or guarantee. (See Form 10.13 on the accompanying CD.)

Personal recognizance bonds are regularly granted to individuals who have positions of importance or families to support or to defendants who pose little risk of flight. The basis of the grant or denial of bail will depend on many factors:

1. The nature and circumstances of the offense charged.

2. The weight of the evidence against the person.

3. The history and characteristics of the person including
   a. Character.
   b. Physical and mental condition.
   c. Financial resources.
   d. Employment.
   e. Length of residence in the community.

4. The danger that would be posed by a person's release.[202]

To ensure the credibility of a bail determination and the likelihood that a defendant will meet his or her financial obligation, an affidavit of financial status is usually prepared. (See Form 10.14 on the accompanying CD.)

The amendment of bail form (see Form 10.15 on the accompanying CD) is based on the Eighth Amendment argument that bail is excessive; it provides a quantitative basis to challenge the reasonableness of bail in light of the offense charged. As a condition of release, often it is required that a defendant designate a specific person or organization to accept custody and supervision of his or her person. (See Form 10.16 on the accompanying CD.)

Preliminary Hearing or Examination

The preliminary hearing, or the probable cause hearing, is the state's determination of whether sufficient evidence exists to continue with a full-scale prosecution of the offenses contained in a complaint. It also serves as an alternative for bail-setting purposes, as a mock minitrial, and as a quality control test of a prosecutor's charge. Others have described it as an initial discovery opportunity for both the prosecution and the defense. "The primary function of the preliminary hearing is to permit a judicial determination that a crime has been committed and that there is probable cause to believe that the accused committed it, thereby justifying any restraint on his liberty prior to trial. This inquiry should be made as soon after the arrest as possible to prevent any unnecessary detention of the accused."[203]

Paralegals who are involved in any criminal case should attend its preliminary hearing. Discussions of the state's case-in-chief will be presented at this hearing. However, sometimes it is strategically advisable to waive the preliminary hearing and prepare for the trial itself. If this is the case, a waiver of preliminary examination must be drafted to ensure that due process standards under the Fifth and Fourteenth Amendments are adhered to. (See Form 10.17 on the accompanying CD.)

Waiver is an intelligent choice in highly charged cases involving public sexual offenses, political crimes, and other litigation likely to produce extensive press coverage.

Indictment or Bill of Information

Probable cause determinations, to proceed with a full-scale criminal litigation, may also result from a grand jury indictment or a bill of information. State and federal court systems are empowered to summon grand juries to review the record in specific cases and to determine whether a person should be charged with a crime. A federal grand jury consists of between 16 and 23 members. The proceedings have been criticized for being a prosecutorial rubber stamp because of the general aura of secrecy, sealed records, and closed hearing process. Fundamentally, this is a prosecutor's show with no permissible defense counter. Indirectly, the process is an alternative method for determining the credibility of the prosecution's case. Grand jury investigations may also precede arrest. Usually they may be an avenue for testing the credibility and worth of a prosecutor's decision whether to follow through on a particular set of charges. As might be expected, grand juries are viewed with great favor by prosecutors but with disdain by defense counsel.[204] The defense bar claims that grand juries are clandestine operations that are inconsistent with due process principles. Challenges to dismiss an indictment or bill of information may be made by motion. (See Form 10.18 on the accompanying CD.)

Plea Bargaining

Most criminal cases are resolved by eventual plea bargaining. The paralegal again acts as information gatherer and recorder of statements and other documentation that verifies and corroborates prosecutorial and defense promises. A petition to enter a plea of guilty that ensures the voluntary nature of the plea bargain agreement is shown in Form 10.19 on the accompanying CD.

As a practical matter, prosecutors should corroborate the voluntariness of the defendant's plea. To ensure that a defendant understands the nature of a plea, the prosecution team will execute signed Miranda documents and formal plea statements witnessed by others. It is crucial that issues involving coercion, duress, trickery, fraud, and false promises be affirmatively dealt with. See Form 10.20 on the accompanying CD for a voluntary statement and Figure 10.5 for a statement regarding Miranda Rights.

Litigation regarding the voluntariness of confessions and its relationship to incrimination is far too prevalent, with defendants even claiming a change of heart.[205] "The courts have identified many factors that are important in determining whether, in the totality of the circumstances, a statement has been made voluntarily. These factors can be broken down into two broad categories: the police conduct involved and the characteristics of the accused."[206] The validity of a confession or other agreement between prosecution and defendant is also influenced by whether the eventual plea bargaining is satisfactory to the defendant or whether any allegations of broken promises occur.

Pretrial Conference

If plea bargaining fails, the defendant refuses to confess, and there is no likelihood of settlement, the legal teams must prepare for full-fledged adjudication. Pretrial conferences set the stage for the litigation to come. Under both state and federal rules, the litigants are required to meet in conference in order for the trial calendar and its conduct to be memorialized. After the indictment or information is filed, upon motion of any party or upon its own motion, the court may order one or more conferences to consider such matters that will promote a fair and expeditious trial.[207]

The calendar schedule for a pretrial conference and for trial may be prepared by the paralegal. (See Form 10.21 on the accompanying CD.)

Motion Practice

Motion practice occurs at every phase of criminal litigation. A motion is simply a request, a petition, presented to a court calling for an order or a rule on a specific subject matter.

FIGURE 10.5
Statement of Miranda Rights

1. You have the right to remain silent.
2. Anything you say can and will be used against you in a court of law.
3. You have the right to talk to a lawyer and have him present with you while you are being questioned.
4. If you cannot afford to hire a lawyer, one will be appointed to represent you before any questioning, if you wish.
5. You can decide at any time to exercise these rights and not answer any question or make any statements.

WAIVER OF RIGHTS

I have read the above statement of my rights, and I understand each of those rights, and having these rights in mind I waive them and willingly make a statement.

Witnessed by _____
Officer's Name _____
Officer's Department _____
Date: _____, 20__   Time: _____ m.

Motions generally involve issues like jurisdiction, payment of expenses, suppression of evidence, mental and medical state, venue, excessive publicity, and postconviction remedies. Figure 10.6 catalogs the diversity of motions relevant to criminal practice. Motions are shaped by the parties, the evidence, and the circumstances of the client. The range of motion types is limitless.

Discovery and Disclosure Motions

In criminal defense litigation, quality information fosters quality advocacy. In the discovery and disclosure phase, the defendant gains access to a wide diversity of information from the prosecution team. The due process standards of the Fifth and Fourteenth Amendments give the defendant a natural advantage in the discovery of information over the prosecution's case-in-chief. This advantage is sometimes referred to as "Brady" material, whereby constitutional due process allows greater defense access in order to prepare for the adjudication.[208] A request for production of evidence edifies this natural advantage (see Form 10.22 on the accompanying CD).

FIGURE 10.6 **Motions Relative to Criminal Practice**

I. Motions before trial.
  A. Motions challenging the jurisdiction of the court or the pleadings.
    1. Motion to dismiss the criminal complaint.
    2. Motion to dismiss based on the unconstitutionality of the statute.
    3. Motion to dismiss on the grounds the statute as applied denies the defendant's right to privacy.
    4. Motion to dismiss based on an unlawful arrest.
    5. Motion to dismiss based on an illegal stop.
    6. Motion to dismiss based on prearrest delay.
    7. Motion to dismiss on grounds of double jeopardy or res judicata.
    8. Motion to dismiss based on misconduct by the state.
    9. Motion to dismiss based on statute of limitations.
    10. Motion to strike surplusage or prejudicial material from complaint.
    11. Motion to dismiss or challenging the form or content of the information.
    12. Motion to strike codefendant's statement from the complaint.
    13. Motion to strike from complaint or information the name(s) of codefendant(s).
    14. Motion to dismiss based on insufficient evidence at preliminary examination.
  B. Bail.
    1. Motion for bail.
    2. Motion for reduction of bail.
    3. Motion for the release of posted bail.
  C. Representation of counsel.
    1. Motion to allow defendant to participate at trial as cocounsel.
    2. Motion to withdraw as counsel for the defendant.
    3. Motion and stipulation to substitution of counsel.
  D. Payment of expenses.
    1. Motion for appointment of expert(s).
    2. Motion for appointment of investigator.
    3. Motion for expenses to conduct survey or public opinion poll.
  E. Motions to suppress evidence.
    1. Motion to suppress evidence seized illegally from the person.
    2. Motion to suppress evidence seized illegally from an automobile.
    3. Motion to suppress evidence seized illegally from premises.
    4. Motion to suppress identification.
    5. Motion to suppress statements of the accused.
    6. Motion to suppress fruits of an illegal stop, arrest, search, seizure, or statement.
    7. Motion to suppress codefendant's statement.
  F. Insanity or incompetency.
    1. Motion for psychiatric and/or psychological examination.
    2. Motion for private examination and testing.
  G. Motions in limine.
    1. Motion in limine with respect to defendant's prior record.
    2. Motion in limine with respect to prior crimes or incidents of a same or similar nature.*
  H. Form, time, and place of trial.
    1. Motion for speedy trial.
    2. Motion for severance of counts.
    3. Motion for severance of defendants.
    4. Motion for change of place of trial.
    5. Motion for change of venue.
    6. Motion for continuance of trial.

*Whitty v. State, 34 Wis. 2d 278, 149 N.W. 2d 557 (1967).

FIGURE 10.6 (*continued*)

I. Discovery and inspection.
    1. Motion for discovery and inspection.
    2. Motion for discovery of defendant's confession and statement(s).
    3. Motion to inspect, examine, and test physical evidence.
    4. Motion to compel disclosure.
    5. Motion for disclosure of electronic and other surveillance.
    6. Motion for information necessary to receive a fair trial.
    7. Motion for disclosure of impeaching information.
    8. Motion to compel the state to reveal the name and address of a material witness.
    9. Motion to interview adverse witness.
    10. Motion for order allowing defendant's counsel to interview witnesses.
    11. Motion for in camera examination of informant.
    12. Motion for specific exculpatory evidence.
J. Publicity.
    1. Motion for restriction of publicity and/ or media coverage in court.
    2. Motion for temporary restraining order and preliminary injunction against the prosecutor, assistants, employees, and state and local law enforcement officers.
    3. Motion for order restraining prosecutorial misconduct.
    4. Motion to exclude television cameras from courtrooms.
K. Witnesses.
    1. Motion for summons of out-of-state witness.
    2. Motion for funds for expert witnesses.
    3. Motion for order allowing deposition of witness(es).
    4. Motion for in camera examination of informant.
    5. Motion for in camera examination of witness statements and masking of irrelevant material.
    6. Motion for disclosure of criminal record of witness.
    7. Motion for extradition of out-of-state witness.
    8. Motion and affidavit for bail for witness.
L. Miscellaneous motions.
    1. Motion for bill of particulars.
    2. Notice of alibi.
    3. Motion to return property to the accused.
II. Trial motions.
  A. Jury trial.
    1. Motion challenging jury array.
    2. Motion for inspection of court records re jury selection.
    3. Motion for individual voir dire and sequestration of jurors during voir dire.
    4. Motion to prevent state from investigating prospective jurors.
    5. Motion to disclose past and present relationships, associations, and ties between district attorney and prospective jurors.
    6. Motion to increase number of peremptory challenges.
  B. Preserving the record.
    1. Motion for complete recordation of all proceedings (voir dire, open and closing statements, conferences and proceedings out of presence of jury, instruction conferences and instructions, etc.).
    2. Motion for daily transcripts.
    3. Motion for permission to record court proceedings.
    4. Motion to include transcript of prior hearings.
    5. Motion to inspect and copy the entire file of the district attorney.
  C. Disqualifications of court personnel.
    1. Motion for substitution of judge.
    2. Motion to recuse.
    3. Motion for special prosecutor.
    4. Motion for disqualification of special prosecutor.
  D. Miscellaneous trial motions.
    1. Motion for an order sequestering witness.
    2. Motion to adjourn or for continuance.
III. Postconviction motions.
  A. Posttrial motions.
    1. Motion to withdraw plea.
    2. Motion for a new trial.
    3. Motion to modify sentence.
    4. Motion for postconviction relief.
    5. Notice of appeal.
    6. Motion for bail pending appeal.
    7. Motion for a weekend pass.
    8. Motion for a presentence report.
    9. Motion for a hearing on the content of a presentence report.
  B. Writs.
    1. Writ of habeas corpus.
    2. Petition for writ of habeas corpus.
    3. Affidavit in support of writ of habeas corpus.
    4. Affidavit of indigence.
    5. Writ of mandamus.
    6. Writ of prohibition.
  C. Stays of execution and sentence.
    1. Application for stay of sentence.
    2. Application to state supreme court or court of appeals for stay of sentence pending appeal.
    3. Order staying sentence pending appeal.

Generally defendants are entitled to the discovery of any information possessed by the government relative to defendant's statements, defendant's prior records, documents and tangible objects, reports of examinations, and tests.[209] The defendant must also give notice to the U.S. attorney of his or her intention to discover and request all favorable evidence . A general request for discovery and inspection may be made by a defendant according to the Federal Rules of Criminal Procedure at 16(a). (See Form 10.23 on the accompanying CD.) A motion regarding the disclosure of evidence that impeaches the prosecution or is exculpatory to defendant may be submitted. (See Form 10.24.)

Motions to Suppress or Exclude Evidence

The integrity of any prosecutor's case rests on the quality and constitutionality of the evidence submitted at trial. Criminal defense litigators look to suppress or exclude specific evidence acquired during the investigative phase or other police process. Suppression theories generally rest on the following arguments:

1. The warrant application or affidavit was faulty.
2. The warrant failed to describe the person, place, or things to be searched or seized with sufficient particularity or specificity.[210]
3. The warrant is not supported by sufficient facts or other corroborative evidence.[211]
4. The suspect was stopped and frisked and then questioned without reasonable suspicion of criminal activity.[212]
5. Incriminating evidence was produced by an illegal random stop of an automobile.[213]
6. A search of a vehicle or a stop and frisk occurred without any real concern for public safety or exigency.[214]
7. The incident to arrest search went beyond arm's length by including briefcases, duffel bags, and suitcases.[215]
8. A police search of the trunk of a vehicle was without any probable cause.[216]
9. The police claimed that they seized evidence in plain view—that is, seeing contraband in plain sight—yet still had no legal right to be on the premises.[217]
10. A search of the entire vehicle went beyond the personal portable effects of a defendant.
11. A vehicle was searched when there was no chance that evidence could be destroyed or lost or the defendant could alight.[218]
12. The police conducted an inventory or automobile search without any underlying grounds for impounding or towing a vehicle.[219]
13. The police performed strip searches for offenses that could not possibly lead to an inference of hidden contraband or weaponry.[220]
14. Consent for a search was nonexistent.[221]

15. Evidence from the body or person was extracted in a shocking and dehumanizing way.[222]

An affidavit and motion to suppress incriminating statements and illegal evidence may be acquired in the search of an automobile (see Form 10.25 on the accompanying CD).

Motion to Suppress Confession

Counsel and paralegals in criminal defense litigation continually analyze the legality of police conduct. If an argument can be presented or made regarding constitutional violation of rights based on the Fourth, Fifth, Sixth, or Fourteenth Amendment of the U.S. Constitution, then a suppression request can be made. Although public furor and clamor over these technical rights are growing, defense lawyers have an obligation to proceed with such argumentation.

Motion to Suppress or Exclude Results of Identification

If an identification process, such as a police lineup or a photographic display, is conducted irregularly, a court may conclude that these tactics are impermissibly suggestive. For example, if obvious racial or ethnic imbalances appear by either photography or display of only one or two pictures rather than multiple representations, a motion to suppress evidence of such identification can be made. (See Form 10.26 on the accompanying CD.)

Motion to Dismiss

Assuming a successful defense request for the suppression and exclusion of evidence, a motion to dismiss based on this previous proceeding is justified. (See Form 10.27 on the accompanying CD.)

Motions on Informants

The weight of evidence accorded informants generally is weak in comparison to other forms of evidence. Anonymous informants get the least respect; those with substantial track histories are rightfully given deference. Under fundamental theories of due process, a defendant has the obvious right to confront accusers. However, under certain circumstances, informants' rights to remain anonymous have been held superior to the right of confrontation. (See Form 10.28, which shows a motion to reveal the identity of an informant, on the accompanying CD.)

Technical Motions

Technical motions deal with highly procedural issues such as challenges to standing, jurisdiction, statutes of limitations, and the like. Although the subject matter of technical motions is less glamorous than that of substantive ones, successful advocacy of this form of motion can still cause dramatic results. See Figure 10.6 for a complete listing of technical motions.

Motion to Dismiss for Lack of Jurisdiction   This motion urges the court to dismiss the action because the jurisdiction selected by defendant or plaintiff is improper. (See Form 10.29 on the accompanying CD.)

Motion for Continuance   Although at odds with the judicial calendar, continuances are regularly granted in both state and federal courts. Although there are bona fide reasons for continuances, there is an abuse side to their usage. (See Form 10.30 on the accompanying CD.)

Motion for Severance   Codefendants or coconspirators often desire a separate action or a separate trial. This may occur when one may be turning state's evidence against the other, and a predictable conflict of interest would arise if they were tried together. A motion for severance is the appropriate pleading. (See Form 10.31 on the accompanying CD.)

Motion for a Lineup   When identification is an issue, or a case of misidentification is argued, a motion for a lineup may be in order. (See Form 10.32 on the accompanying CD.)

Posttrial Motions

Even after a criminal conviction, legal representation does not end. A plethora of posttrial motions and postconviction remedies are available to defense counsel. Paralegals will play an active role in this latter phase of criminal representation. Illustrative examples of posttrial motions and remedies are considered next.

Motion for Mistrial   A mistrial may be declared if the defense can prove any of the following: unfair and prejudicial publicity, civil rights violations, derogatory statements by jurors and court personnel, or arbitrary and capricious conduct by the prosecutor or the judge. The burden is to show adverse effect on the jury and the outcome. (See Form 10.33 on the accompanying CD.) Mistrials may be also declared in cases of deadlocked juries.

Motion for Judgment of Acquittal   Although this is rare, a judge may issue a judgment of acquittal if the basis for the conviction is plainly insufficient and the jury has clearly disregarded the obvious facts. A motion for judgment of acquittal is a pleadings option. (See Form 10.34 on the accompanying CD.)

Motion for a New Trial   If the verdict was contrary to the evidence and against the logical and consistent weight of evidentiary analysis, a motion for a new trial is the appropriate pleading. (See Form 10.35 on the accompanying CD.)

Sentencing Motions   Attacks on sentencing decision are rarely successful—though if constitutionally rooted and based on equal protection, the argument may win the day. Defense attorneys in today's federal criminal justice system are the underdogs in the sentencing process. The Federal Sentencing Guidelines, established November 1, 1987, sought to foster uniform justice sentencing patterns. Individualized circumstances are being replaced by rigid sentencing ranges. Many attorneys view these guidelines as being so restrictive as to leave them effectively powerless.[223]

The more able arguments involving sentencing are generally constitutional. Defendants who can argue that a sentence is excessive, cruel, and unusual based on either constitutional or statutory theories should file a motion to correct the sentence. (See Form 10.36 on the accompanying CD.)

When sentences are inconsistent with express guidelines, a motion for reduction is appropriate. (See Form 10.37 on the accompanying CD.) Sentencing disparity—that is, widespread differences in meting out punishments for identical offenses—is frequently the basis for challenge. Too much judicial discretion has caused inequities. Attempts to unify, through the Federal Sentencing Guidelines, which "restructured judicial discretion by delineating mandatory sentencing guidelines for defendants convicted of federal crimes, have made significant progress but still fail to check judicial capriciousness. Concurrently, the sentencing guidelines marked a fundamental shift in sentencing goals."[224]

Postconviction Remedies

Representation of criminal defendants continues even after incarceration. Most defendants, once incarcerated, believe that a state or federal judge will intervene in their particular situation. Prisoners hope for a reexamination of the evidence at trial, an order for a new trial, or the discovery of some circumstance or condition that proves a due process violation. At the U.S. Supreme Court, defendants hope for the retroactive application of some principle to their existing situations. To pursue most postconviction remedies, the advocate must secure the trial transcript. For indigent clients, a motion in pauperis, which if granted pays for the reproduction of the transcript, should be filed. (See Form 10.38 on the accompanying CD.)

Writs and petitions of habeas corpus request immediate release from confinement due to procedural or substantive error resulting in an invalid conviction. (See Form 10.39 on the accompanying CD.) In drafting the writ of habeas corpus, the defendant must give an objective analysis of the previous case, the status of the current appellate rulings, the reasons a plea was or was not taken or given, and the grounds for asking for a release.

TRIAL AIDS

Advocacy of a criminal case depends on a strong litigation team, with the paralegal being an essential player. As in all other aspects of law, the paralegal's organizational skills are simply indispensable. Keeping good records, compiling checklists, and creating exhibits and other litigation aids are all part of the regimen. (For a witness tracking form, see Form 10.40 on the accompanying CD. Other forms relating to exhibits, motions, and appealable issues are in Forms 10.41 through 10.45).

Summary

The law of crimes and its corresponding practice have been the chief aims of this chapter. Classifications of offenses, types of crimes, and the elements of offenses, whether against a person, property, or the public order, were fully covered. Defenses discussed included those involved with rights to self-help and defense of property, as well as the nature of self-defense.

An overview of criminal procedure was delivered, emphasizing stages where paralegals are most involved. From the initial summons to the filing of a complaint, from the preparation of affidavits to the petition for bail, the chapter delved into all aspects of criminal process. Other topics dealt with motion practice, arrest and search warrants, the nature of plea bargaining, and discovery and disclosure tactics.

Various trial aids were provided that help litigators keep accurate administrative and evidentiary records. Postconviction remedies, including writs of habeas corpus and other appellate processes, were also discussed.

Discussion Questions

1. Define crime.
2. How does your state criminal code define crime?
3. Identify and describe the classification of crime.
4. In what way does the law of insanity undermine the proof of mens rea?
5. Can you think of any other means or methods of classifying, categorizing, or typifying criminal conduct?
6. What types of new criminal behavior have come about in the last 10 years?
7. Can you name or identify any new criminal conduct definitions, legislation, or laws passed recently?
8. There has been significant reform of rape legislation in the last 20 years. Discuss generally some specific areas of reform and make suggestions regarding other areas of concern.
9. Should a person have the right to defend his or her domicile with any degree of force?
10. Discuss the influence of mitigation on criminal charges.
11. How do constitutional challenges impact criminal adjudications?
12. What are the similarities between the requirements for a search warrant and an arrest warrant?
13. Why are defendants granted preferred status in the discovery and disclosure process of a criminal case compared to a plaintiff's right?
14. If you were part of a criminal defense team, what motions would be most likely to lead to the suppression of evidence?

Research Assignment

1. Research the prejudicial effect of joinder of parties in the federal statutes. Where is the statute located? Is joinder automatically prejudicial to defendants? If a codefendant has confessed, and the confession incriminates other codefendants, is the confession admissible? If the joinder causes undue prejudice for a codefendant, what remedies exist? What rationale is used to support joinder?

Practical Exercises

1. Using the following fact pattern, complete an arrest form. If information is not included, use information of your own choosing:

Place of birth:	*Ewing, California*
Age:	*41*
Height:	*6'9"*
Weight:	*210 lbs.*
Hair:	*Blond*
Eyes:	*Blue*
Complexion:	*Fair*
Marital status:	*Single*
Marks:	*Scar from a slash across face*
Employment:	*No employer, no occupation*
Social Security number:	*000-00-0000*
Details of arrest:	*10/20/07; 5:18 p.m.; 13 Ambler Drive, Springfield, Delaware County, Pennsylvania*
Bail hearing:	*Upcoming*
Final disposition:	*Upcoming*
Juvenile information:	*N/A*

2. Using the following fact pattern, complete a criminal complaint:

Issuing authority:	*Judge Robert Stevens*
Complainant:	*Trooper Warren Michaels*
Political subdivision:	*Jamestown County, New York*
Date of complaint:	*August 1, 2007*

Defendant's name:	*Sally R. Jones*
Incident number:	*1612-2007*
UCR number:	*1190*
OTN:	*39-59-95*
Complaint number:	*CA-81-2007*
Year:	*2007*
Affiant:	*Trooper Warren Michaels, Midway Police Department, Jamestown County, New York*
Defendant's address:	*1814 Unitary Drive, Ellicottsville County, New York 14468*
Nicknames:	*None*

3. Locate your state's firearms legislation regarding illegal carrying and discharge of weapons, unlawful sales to minors, machine guns, firearm registration, and permissible ammunition. Answer the following questions:

   a. People convicted of certain crimes, such as manslaughter, aggravated battery, murder, aggravated and simple rape, and kidnapping, do not have the right to possess a firearm or carry any weapons. True or false? Why or why not?

   b. Guards and messengers employed by common carriers, banks, or trust companies may possess and carry machine guns while employed in and about the shipment, transportation, delivery, or guarding of any money, treasure, bullion, bonds, or other thing of value. True or false? Why or why not?

   c. Armor-piercing bullets can be permissibly sold to Department of Corrections officials and employees authorized to carry firearms while engaged in the performance of their official duties. True or false? Why or why not?

   d. What information is required to be kept by a manufacturer or merchant selling machine guns?

Internet Resources

Findlaw subjects: criminal law—www.findlaw.com/01topics/09criminal/index.html

Criminal law expert witnesses & consultants—marketcenter.findlaw.com/scripts/browse/4/152

The Federalist Society for Law & Policy Studies—www.fed-soc.org/Publications/practicegroupnewsletters/criminallaw/criminallaw.htm

Hieros Gamos: criminal law—hg.org/crime.html

International criminal court resources—www.lib.uchicago.edu/~llou/icc.html

LexisNexis criminal law practice area—www.lexisnexis.com/practiceareas/criminal

U.S. court rules—www.uscourts.gov/rules/newrules4.html

American Bar Association, Criminal Justice Section—www.abanet.org/crimjust

Courts.Net—www.courts.net

Criminal Defense Online—www.sado.org

Criminal law resources on the Internet—wings.buffalo.edu/law/bclc/

Endnotes

1. Illinois Bar Association, The Findings of the Competency Committee Relating to the Quality of Paralegal Services 17–22 (1989).

2. Model Penal Code §2.01 (Proposed Official Draft 1962).

3. *See* Restatement on Torts §2.05 (1934); WILLIAM L. CLARK & WILLIAM L. MARSHALL, A TREATISE ON THE LAW OF CRIMES 200 (1967).

4. *See* Summ. Pa. Jur. §1:6 at 7.

5. Model Penal Code §2.01(3).

6. *See* generally Frank J. Remington and Orrin L. Helstad, *The Mental Element in Crime—A Legislative Problem*, WIS. L. REV. 644 (1952); Rollin M. Perkins, *A Rationale of Mens Rea*, 52 HARV. L. REV. 905 (1935); Thomas A. Cowan, *A Critique of the Moralistic Conception of Criminal Law*, 97 U. PA. L. REV. 502 (1949); Dennis v. U.S., 341 U.S. 494, 71 S. Ct. 857, 96 L. Ed. 1137 (1951).

7. Model Penal Code §2.02 at 13 (1962).

8. CLARK & MARSHALL, *supra* note 3, §270 (1967).

9. Summ. Pa. Jur. §5:9 at 84.

10. Del. Code Ann. Tit. 11, §231 (2001).

11. Mo. Rev. Stat. §562.016 (2001).

12. *See generally* 2 EDWARD POLLOCK & FREDERIA W. MAITLAND, HISTORY OF ENGLISH LAW (1903); 4 SIR WILLIAM BLACKSTONE, COMMENTARIES; CLARK & MARSHALL, *supra* note 3, §108–115 (1967); CENTER FOR CRIMINAL JUSTICE, PRIVATE POLICE TRAINING MANUAL 34 (1985).

13. There are exceptions to this, including Pennsylvania. *See* 18 Pa. Stat. Ann. §1105.

14. *See* BLACKSTONE, *supra* note 12, at 205.

15. Bannon v. U.S., 156 U.S. 464, 467, 15 S.Ct. 467, 39 L.Ed. 494 (1894).

16. TASK FORCE ON ADMINISTRATION OF JUSTICE, THE PRESIDENT'S COMMISSION ON LAW ENFORCEMENT AND ADMINISTRATION OF JUSTICE, TASK FORCE REPORT: THE COURTS (1967).

17. *Id.* at 15.

18. As an example, *see* New York's misdemeanor classification of sexual misconduct, at Penal Law §130.20. Critics claim it is nothing more than an actual aggravated sexual assault.

19. U.S. Const. Amend. III, §3.

20. 18 U.S.C. § 2381 (2001).

21. 18 U.S.C. §§792 et seq., 2383, 2384 (2001).

22. *See* N.Y. Penal Law §§70.00, 220.00 (2001).

23. *See* for example, 16 Iowa §§902.9(5), 903.1(2), relating to punishments for Class D felonies and aggravated misdemeanors.

24. BLACKSTONE, *supra* note 12, at 5.

25. CLARK & MARSHALL, *supra* note 3, §2.02, at 113.

26. 18 Pa. Cons. Stat. §3731(E) (2001).

27. Code of the Town of West Hartford, Connecticut, §168-13(B) (2001).

28. *See generally* Rollin M. Perkins, *The Law of Homicide,* 36 J. CRIM. L. CRIMINOLOGY & POLICE SCI. 25 (1946); Herbert Wechsler and Jerome Michael, *A Rationale of the Law of Homicide,* 37 COLUM. L. REV. 701 (1937).

29. Model Penal Code §2.10.1 (1962).

30. Tenn. Code Ann. §39-13-202a (1999).

31. *See* Tennessee v. Brumit, No. M1999-00154-CCS-R3-CD (Tenn. Crim. App., decided April 28, 2000).

32. 2 FRANCIS WHARTON, WHARTON'S CRIMINAL LAW 247–248 (Charles E. Torcia ed., 15th ed. 1993).

33. Model Penal Code §2.10.2 (1962).

34. People v. Moran, 31 MICH. APP. 301, 310–318, 187 N.W. 2d 434, 438–443 (1971).

35. *Id.*

36. N.C. Gen. Stat. §14-17 (2000).

37. Neb. Rev. Stat. §28-304(1) (2001).

38. John Rockwell Snowden, *Second-Degree Murder, Malice, and Manslaughter in Nebraska: New Juice for an Old Cup,* 76 NEB. L. REV. 399, 410 (1997).

39. PHILLIP E. JOHNSON, CRIMINAL LAW 160 (5th ed. 1995); *see* RICHARD J. BONNIE ET AL., CRIMINAL LAW 658 (1997); GEORGE E. DIX & M. MICHAEL SHARLOT, CRIMINAL LAW 400 (4th ed. 1996).

40. State v. Elder, 982 S.W.2d 871, 876 (Tenn. Crim. App. 1998).

41. State v. Mitchell, No. W1999006610-CCA-R3-CD, 4 (Tenn. Crim. App., *decided* May 12, 1998), *citing* State v. Elder, 982 S.W.2d 871, 876 (Tenn. Crim. App. 1998).

42. Kara M. Houck, *People v. Dekens: The Expansion of the Felony-Murder Doctrine in Illinois,* 30 LOY. U. CHI. L.J. 557, 584 (1999).

43. *Id. See also* Md. Ann. Code Art. 27, §410 (Supp. 1998).

44. 720 Ill. Comp. Stat. Ann. 5/2-8 (West 1996).

45. *See* Case Note, *Criminal Law—Application of Felony Murder Rule Sustained Where Robbery Victim Killed Defendant's Accomplice,* 5 DEPAUL L. REV. 298, 302 (1956).

46. *See* People v. Payne, 194 N.E. 539, 543 (Ill. 1935).

47. For rare but contrasting results *see* Weick v. State, 420 A.2d 159, 163–164 (Del. 1980) (concluding that the felons were not responsible for the death of a cofelon because the felons did not commit the homicide); State v. Murrell, 585 P.2d 1017, 1019 (Kan. 1978) (noting that the jury acquitted a felon charged with felony murder because during the armed robbery either the police or the robbery victim killed the cofelon).

48. 18 Pa. Stat. Ann. §2503.

49. 18 Pa. Stat. Ann. §2504.

50. Monroe v. Smith, 197 F. SUPP. 2d 753 (E.D. Mich. 2001), *aff'd* 41 DEF. APPX. 730 (6th Cir. 2002).

51. *Id.*

52. People v. Roldan, 666 N.E.2d 553 (1996).

53. An incorrect application of manslaughter charges is quite evident in the prosecution of a Brooklyn High School student who raised his hand against a teacher. The teacher died the following day of a heart attack. *See* Ann Snider, *Pupil Cleared in Death of School Aide; Judge Finds Manslaughter Charge to Be Unsupported,* 218 N.Y.L.J., May 22, 1998, at 1.

54. Model Penal Code §§211.1-211.2 (1962).

55. Model Penal Code §211.1 (1962).

56. 18 Pa. Stat. Ann. §2705 (1986).

57. *See* 18 Pa. Stat. Ann. §§2705, 2706, 2708, 2709–2710.

58. Model Penal Code §212.1 (1962).

59. *See* State v. Williams, 111 ARIZ. 222, 526 P. 2d 1244 (1974); People v. Caudillo, 21 CAL. 3d 56, 146 CAL. RPTR. 859, 580 P. 2d 274 (1978).

60. N.C. Gen. Stat. §14-39 (2001).

61. Neb. Rev. Stat. §38-314 (2001).

62. Model Penal Code §212.3 (Proposed Official Draft 1962).

63. Model Penal Code §212.3 (1962).

64. R.I. Gen. Laws §11-37-1 (2001).

65. Ala. Code §13A-6-70 (2001).

66. Va. Code Ann. §18.2-61 (2001).

67. Charles P. Nemeth, *Character Evidence in Rape Trials in 19th Century New York: Chastity and the Admissibility of Specific Acts*, 6 WOMEN'S RIGHTS L. REP. (1980). *See also* CATHARINE A. MACKINNON, TOWARD A FEMINIST THEORY OF THE STATE 174 (1989).

68. Ark. Code Ann. §5-14-122 (2001).

69. Va. Code Ann. §18.2-76.1 (2001).

70. Hardwick v. Bowers, 478 U.S. 186 (1986); Lawrence v. Texas, 539 U.S. 558 (2003).

71. Mo. Rev. Stat. §566.067 (1999).

72. Michael W. Sheetz, *Cyberpredators: Police Internet Investigations under Florida Statute 847.0135,* 54 U. MIAMI L. REV. 405, 408 (2000).

73. Ariz. Rev. Stat. §13-3553 (2001).

74. Utah Code Ann. §76-7-102(1) (1999).

75. Model Penal Code §220.1 (1962).

76. 18 Pa. Stat. Ann. §3127.

77. CLARK & MARSHALL, *supra* note 3, §13.12, at 1014; *see also* BLACKSTONE, *supra* note 13, at 222; People v. Haggerty, 46 CAL. 354; Woolsey v. State, 30 TEX. APP. 346, 17 S. 546.

78. *See* 18 Pa. Stat. Ann. §§3301-07.

79. CLARK & MARSHALL, *supra* note 3, at 200.

80. CLARK & MARSHALL, *supra* note 3, at 984.

81. CLARK & MARSHALL, *supra* note 3, at 986–987.

82. *See* MCKINNEY'S CONSOL. LAWS OF NEW YORK, Ann. 39 §140 (1980).

83. *See* Albert Coates, *Criminal Intent in Burglary,* 2 N.C.L. REV. 110 (1924); Champlin v. State, 84 WIS. 2d 621, 267 N.W. 2d 295, (1978); State v. Ortiz, 92 N.M. 166, 584 P. 2d 1306 (1978).

84. CLARK & MARSHALL, *supra* note 3, at 1007.

85. Tenn. Code Ann. §39-14-402(a)–(d) (2001).

86. N.H. Rev. Stat. Ann. §635:1(1) (2001).

87. Summ. Pa. Jur. §24.8.

88. Model Penal Code §221.2 (1962).

89. 18 Pa. Cons. Stat. §3503 (2001).

90. Ariz. Rev. Stat. §629:1 (1996).

91. Model Penal Code §206.53 at 2 (Proposed Official Draft 1962).

92. Model Penal Code §221.1 (1962).

93. *See* People v. Beebe, 70 MICH. APP. 154, 245 N.W. 2d 547 (1976).

94. People v. Woods, 41 N.Y. 2d 279, 392 N.Y.S. 2d 400, 360 N.E. 2d 1082 (1977); Commonwealth v. Mays, 248 PA. SUPER. 318, 375 A. 2d 116 (1977).

95. People v. Woods, 41 N.Y. 2d 279, 392 N.Y.S. 2d 400, 360 N.E. 2d 1082 (1977); Commonwealth v. Mays, 248 PA. SUPER. 318, 375 A. 2d 116 (1977).

96. 18 U.C.S.A. §2113 (2001).

97. Cal. Penal Code §211215 (2001).

98. 678 A.2d 556 (DC App. 1996).

99. D.C. Code § 22-2901 (2001).

100. Zanders v. U.S., 678 A.2d 556, 564 (D.C. App. 1996).

101. JAMES CLEARY, PROSECUTING THE SHOPLIFTER, A LOSS PREVENTION STRATEGY (1986).

102. CLARK & MARSHALL, *supra* note 3, at 804-07.

103. Md. Stat. Ann., Art. 27 §340 (H) (1–12).

104. Model Penal Code §223.2 (1962).

105. THE AMERICAN LAW INSTITUTE, MODEL PENAL CODE, Reprint—Tentative Drafts, Nos. 1, 2, 3, 4, 56 (1953).

106. 18 Pa. Cons. Stat. Ann. §3903 (2001).

107. Mich. Stat. Ann. §28-588 (2000).

108. Model Penal Code §223.3 (1962).

109. *See* Ark. Code Ann. § 5-55-111(1) (Repl. 1997), Blackwell v. State, 338 ARK. 671, 1 S.W.3d 399 (1999).

110. Model Penal Code §206.2 (Proposed Official Draft 1962).

111. D.C. Code Ann. §22-3821 (2001).

112. Model Penal Code §223.4 (1962).

113. *See* U.S. v. Murphy, 193 F.3d 1 (1999); U.S. v. Smith, 198 F.3d 377 (1999).

114. 18 U.S.C. §1951 (2001).

115. Ohio Rev. Code Ann. §2905.11 (Anderson 1999).

116. 18 Pa. Stat. Ann. §3929 (a).

117. CLEARY, *supra* note 101.

118. Me. Rev. Stat. Ann. Tit. 17-A §703 (2002).

119. Me. Rev. Stat. Ann. Tit. 17-A §702 (2002).

120. Me. Rev. Stat. Ann. Tit. 17-A §702(1) (2002).

121. Or. Rev. Stat. §165.013 (2001).

122. CLARK & MARSHALL, *supra* note 3, at 954.

123. *See* 18 Pa. Stat. Ann. §4102.

124. *See* 18 Pa. Stat. Ann. §§4103, 4104.

125. *See* 18 Pa. Stat. Ann. §§4105, 4106; *see also* Md. Stat. Ann. Art. 27 §§141, 343(A)(1).

126. For the federal response to bank fraud, *see* 18 U.S.C. §1344 (2001).

127. 184 F.3d 180 (1999).

128. 184 F.3d 180, 188 (1999), *see also* 18 U.S.C. §1341 (2001).

129. Md. Stat. Ann. Art. 27, §141 (A) (1).

130. Model Penal Code §206.7 (Proposed Official Draft 1962).

131. N.Y. Penal Law §165.15 (2001). *See also* Abraham Abramovsky, *Theft of Services: Current State of the Law*, 216 N.Y.L.J., Oct. 31, 1996, at 3.

132. In 2000 there were 937,000 reported motor vehicle thefts, down 14 percent from the 1999 figure of 1,068,000. For more information, *see* CALLIE M. RENNISON, CRIMINAL VICTIMIZATION 2000, NCJ 187007, 2 (2001).

133. 18 Pa. Cons. Stat. Ann. §3928 (2001).

134. Model Penal Code §206.8 (Proposed Official Draft 1962).

135. Model Penal Code §206.8, at comment (Proposed Official Draft 1962).

136. Model Penal Code §206.4 (Proposed Official Draft 1962).

137. 18 Pa. Stat. Ann. §5501.

138. 18 Pa. Stat. Ann. §5104.

139. 18 Pa. Stat. Ann. §5507.

140. 18 Pa. Stat. Ann. §5506.

141. 18 Pa. Stat. Ann. §5502.

142. 18 Pa. Stat. Ann. §5503.

143. 18 Pa. Stat. Ann. §5505.

144. Ohio R.C. §2917.11 (B) (1).

145. 18 Pa. Cons. Stat. §5902 (2001).

146. 21 U.S.C.S. §801 (2001).

147. 21 U.S.C.S. §801 (2001).

148. 18 Pa. Cons. Stat. §780-113 (2001).

149. 18 Pa. Cons. Stat. §4301 (2001).

150. *See* 18 U.S.C. §2251 (1988); 47 U.S.C.S. §223(d)(1) & 223 (d)(2) (Law Co-Op. Supp. 1996); Communications Decency Act of 1996, Pub. L. No. 104–104, 502, 110 Stat. 133 (1996).

151. 18 Pa. Cons. Stat. §5903 (2001).

152. Tenn. Code Ann. §55-10-401 (2001).

153. 18 Pa. Stat. Ann. §5506.

154. 18 Pa. Stat. Ann. §5507.

155. 18 Pa. Stat. Ann. §5508; *see also* Ohio R.C. §2917.12.

156. 18 Pa. Stat. Ann. §5509.

157. Md. Stat. Ann., Art. 28 §581.

158. Md. Stat. Ann., Art. 28 §581.

159. NATIONAL INSTITUTE OF JUSTICE, CRIME AND PROTECTION IN AMERICA, A STUDY OF PRIVATE SECURITY AND LAW ENFORCEMENT RESOURCES AND RELATIONSHIPS (1985).

160. JOHN W. TURNER, VIOLENCE IN THE MEDICAL CARE SETTING, A SURVIVAL GUIDE 12 (1984).

161. CHRIS E. MCGOEY, "SECURITY GUARDS & OFFICERS: USE OF FORCE CONTINUUM." Available at http://www.crimedoctor.com/security_guards_2.htm (retrieved January 25, 2007).

162. *Id.*

163. Model Penal Code §3.04 (1962).

164. Model Penal Code §3.04 (1962).

165. Model Penal Code § 3.04(B) (Proposed Official Draft 1962).

166. 2 PAUL H. ROBINSON, CRIMINAL LAW DEFENSES §3-3, Model Codifications, app. A (1984).

167. Model Penal Code §3.05 (1962).

168. U.S. v. Peterson, 483 F. 2d 1222, 1223 (1973); *see also* State v. Goodseal, 186 NEB. 359, 183 N.W. 2d 258 (1971); Commonwealth v. Martin, 369 MASS. 640, 341 N.E. 885 (1976); Commonwealth v. Monico, 373 MASS. 298, 366 N.E. 2d 1241 (1977).

169. CENTER FOR CRIMINAL JUSTICE, PRIVATE POLICE TRAINING MANUAL 200 (1985).

170. *Id.*

171. Model Penal Code §3.06 (1962).

172. Model Penal Code §3.06 (1962).

173. The State of New Jersey recently expanded the right of the homeowner to protect his or her interests with deadly force.

174. State v. Miller, 267 N.C. 409, 411, 148 S.E. 2d 279, 281 (1966); *see also* Law v. State, 21 MD. APP. 13, 318 A. 2d 859 (1974); People v. Givens, 26 ILL. 2d 371, 186 N.E. 2d 255 (1962).

175. *See* Hampton v. Miller, 425 U.S. 484 (1976); United States v. Russell, 411 U.S. 423 (1973).

176. Model Penal Code §2.13 (Proposed Official Draft 1962).

177. CHARLES P. NEMETH & DAVID A. DAVIS, FLORIDA CRIMINAL PRACTICE (1996).

178. State v. Noble, 142 MONT. 284, 384 P. 2d 504, 508 (1963).

179. Herbert Weschler, *The Criteria of Criminal Responsibility*, U. CHI. L. REV. 367, 374–375 (1955).

180. Model Penal Code, Art. 4 (1962).

181. Daniel McNaghten's Case, 10 CL & F 200, 8 ENG. REP. 718 (1843).

182. Carter v. United States, 252 F2d 608, 102 U.S. APP. D.C. 227 at 234–235. (1954).

183. ROBERT L. GOLDSTEIN, THE INSANITY DEFENSE (1967); *see also* Morisette v. U.S., 342 U.S. 246 (1952); Durham v. U.S., 94 U.S. APP. D.C. 228, 214 F. 2d 862 (1954).

184. Delaware also has the plea.

185. *See* Mich. Stat. §768.36.

186. State v. Noble, 142 MONT. 284, 384 P2d 504, 508 (1963).

187. Model Penal Code §2.09 (1962).

188. 18 Pa. Cons. Stat. Ann. §309 (2001).

189. Criminal Resource Manual, 1816 Defenses—Duress (Oct. 1997), available at http://www.usdoj.gov/usao/eousa/foia_reading _room/usam/title9/crm01816.htm. *See* United States v. Bryan, 591 F.2d 1161, 1163 (5th Cir. 1979), *cert. denied*, 444 U.S. 1071 (1980); United States v. Boomer, 571 F.2d 543 (10th Cir.), *cert. denied*, 436 U.S. 911 (1978); United States v. Michelson, 559 F.2d 567, 569 (9th Cir. 1977); and United States v. Chapman, 455 F.2d 746, 749 (5th Cir. 1972).

190. Clark & Marshall, *supra* note 3, at 360–361.

191. Model Penal Code §3.02 (1962).

192. Charles P. Nemeth, *Character Evidence in Rape Trials in 19th Century New York: Chastity and the Admissibility of Specific Acts*, 6 Women's Rights L. Rev. (1980).

193. 18 Pa. Cons. Stat. Ann. §311 (2001).

194. James H. Rubin, *Legal Definition of Offenses by Children and Youths,* Ill. L. F. (1960).

195. The petitioner filed his direct appeal with this court using only his first and last names, so that appeal is styled "D.Y. v. State."

196. Section 15-20-21(11), Ala. Code 1975, defines *risk assessment* as "a written report on the assessment of risk for sexually reoffending conducted by a sexual treatment program approved by the Department of Youth Services. The report shall include, but not be limited to, the following regarding the criminal sexual offender: criminal history, mental status, attitude, previous sexual offender treatment and response to treatment, social factors, conditions of release expected to minimize risk of sexual reoffending, and characteristics of the criminal sex offense."

197. This mandamus petition was timely. The district attorney filed this petition seven days after the circuit court's ruling. See Rule 21(a), Ala.R.App.P., and State v. Gaines, [Ms. CR-03-1201, July 16, 2004] 932 So. 2nd 118, 2004 Ala. Crim. App. Lexis 131 (Ala.Crim.App. 2004).

198. We are aware that this court has strictly enforced the maximum three-year period of probation or commitment for youthful offenders contained in §15-19-6(a), Ala. Code 1975. *See* Warwick v. State, 843 So. 2d 832 (Ala.Crim.App. 2002) (defendant's five-year split sentence exceeded the maximum term of imprisonment under the youthful offender act); D.Y., *supra* (defendant's sentence of six consecutive three-year terms of imprisonment exceeded the maximum term of imprisonment under the youthful offender act); J.N.J. v. State, 690 So. 2d 519 (Ala.Crim.App. 1996) (defendant's sentence of five years' probation exceeded the maximum probationary period provided for under the youthful offender act). However, in this case D.B.Y.'s term of probation was tolled when the state filed its motion for a sexual offender risk assessment.

199. Though the language in §15-20-28, Ala. Code 1975, strongly suggests that as a matter of law a youthful offender's probation may be extended past the maximum three-year probation period in order to comply with this statute, because the state's motion was filed before D.B.Y.'s probation expired, we do not reach the question of whether a similar motion filed after a term of probation has expired would likewise be entitled to enforcement.

200. Model Penal Code §2.08 (1962).

201. Andre Moennsens, James Starr, & Fred Inbau, Scientific Discovery in Criminal Cases (1987).

202. 18 U.S.C. §3141G.

203. *See* Charles Whitebread, Criminal Procedure: Analysis of Constitutional Cases and Concepts (1980).

204. Comment, *Grand Jury Proceedings: The Prosecutor, The Trial Judge, and Undue Influence*, 39 U. Chi. L. Rev. 761 (1972).

205. Note, *Withdrawal of a Guilty Plea under Rule 32d*, 63 Yale L. J. 590 (1955).

206. Whitebread, supra note 203, at 283.

207. Fed. R. Crim. P. 17.1; *see generally* Fred Brewster, *Criminal Pre-Trials—Useful Techniques*, 29 F.R.D. 442 (1962).

208. Brady v. Maryland, 373 U.S. 83 (1963).

209. Fed. R. Crim. P. 16.

210. Steele v. U.S., 267 U.S. 498 (1925).

211. *See* Spinelli v. U.S., 393 U.S. 410 (1969); Draper v. U.S., 358 U.S. 307 (1959).

212. *See* Terry v. Ohio, 407 U.S 143 (1968); Adam v. Williams, 407 U.S. 143 (1972).

213. Delaware v. Prouse, 440 U.S. 648 (1979).

214. Pennsylvania v. Mimms, 434 U.S. 106 (1977).

215. Arkansas v. Sanders, 442 U.S 753 (1979).

216. Cady v. Dombrowski, 413 U.S. 433 (1973).

217. *See* Coolidge v. New Hampshire, 403 U.S. 443 (1971); Harris v. U.S., 390 U.S. 324 (1968).

218. New York v. Belton, 453 U.S 454 (1981).

219. South Dakota v. Opperman, 428 U.S. 364 (1976).

220. State v. Sheperd, 196 N. J. Super. 448 (1984).

221. Schneckloth v. Bustamonte, 412 U.S. 218 (1973).

222. *See* Schmerber v. California, 384 U.S. 757 (1966).

223. Shelia Balkan, *Pre-Sentence Strategy: Seeking Flexibility in Federal Guidelines,* 29 Trial 53 (March 1993).

224. Sentencing Reform Act of 1984, Pub. L. No. 98-473, 98 Stat. 1987 (codified as amended at 18 U.S.C. §§ 3551–3742 & 28 U.S.C. §§991–998 (1988). *See* Ilene H. Nagel, *Structuring Sentencing Discretion: The New Federal Guidelines*, 80 J. Crim. L. & Criminology 883, 886-887 (1990) (movement to redress "uses and abuses of unfettered judicial discretion" in federal sentencing practices resulted in passage of Sentencing Reform Act of 1984).

Chapter 11

The Law of Torts and Personal Injury

VI. **The Paralegal in Personal Injury Practice**
    A. **The Initial Interview**
    B. **Setting the Fee**
    C. **Obtaining Authorizations**
    D. **Tactical Considerations**
        1. **Statute of Limitations**
        2. **Conflicts of Interest**
        3. **Multiple Representation**
        4. **Meritorious Claims**
    E. **Auto Accident Cases**
        1. **Advocacy Approaches in the Auto Accident Case**
            a. **First Party Benefits**
            b. **Intentional Torts**
            c. **Underinsured or Uninsured Benefits**
    F. **Settlement Tactics**

VII. **The Paralegal and Medical Malpractice Cases**
    A. **The Legal Landscape**
    B. **The Role of Experts in Malpractice Litigation**
    C. **Legal Theories in a Malpractice Case**
        1. **Negligence**
        2. **Negligence in Contract**
    D. **ADR and Medical Malpractice**
    E. **Paralegal Responsibilities in a Medical Malpractice Case**
        1. **Authorizations/Releases**
        2. **Discovery Requirements**
        3. **Proof of Pain and Suffering**
        4. **Psychological/Psychiatric Reports**
        5. **Photographic Evidence**
        6. **Expert Reports**
        7. **Consent Forms**
    F. **Medical Malpractice Pleadings**

VIII. **The Paralegal and the Product Liability Case**
    A. **Theories of Litigation**
    B. **Processing the Product Liability Case**
    C. **Warranty in Product Liability Cases**

IX. **Defense Considerations**
    A. **Affirmative Defenses**
    B. **General Defenses**
        1. **Accord or Satisfaction**
        2. **Arbitration and Award**
        3. **Assumption of Risk**
        4. **Contributory Negligence**
        5. **Comparative Negligence**
        6. **Discharge**
        7. **Duress**
        8. **Estoppel**
        9. **Fraud**
        10. **Illegality**
        11. **Laches**
        12. **License/Privilege**
        13. **Res Judicata**
        14. **Statute of Limitations**
        15. **Statute of Frauds**
        16. **Waiver**

X. **Summary**

Discussion Questions

PERSONAL INJURY AND TORT LAW PARALEGAL JOB DESCRIPTION

Personal injury and tort law paralegals need to be proficient in the following competencies:

- Understand the various forms of tortious conduct.
- Distinguish between tortious and criminal conduct and the possibility of simultaneous occurrence.
- Distinguish between intentional and negligent tortious conduct and the possibility of simultaneous occurrence.
- Understand the nature of strict liability.
- Classify a claimant as trespasser, licensee, or invitee.
- Draft forms, checklists, and logs for use in assessing tort claims.
- Participate in the initial interview of clients to assess the merits of their claims.
- Apply the concepts of foreseeability, duty owed, and the reasonable person to the facts of the case.
- Determine the existence of multiple defendants in a claim.
- Determine the existence or nonexistence of a client's contributory or comparative negligence in a claim.
- Collect and assemble evidence of damages—physical and economic.
- Calculate damages based on injuries sustained.
- Locate and interview witnesses.
- Locate technical experts to assist in case evaluation and reconstruction.
- Perform legal research.
- Research and review insurance policy limits, as well as underinsured and uninsured benefits.
- Draft correspondence to product manufacturers, designers, and retailers.
- Create and maintain a tickler/calendaring system to ensure the integrity of a claim.
- Draft demand letters in personal injury, medical malpractice, and product liability cases.
- Draft follow-up correspondence regarding demand letter status.
- Draft pleadings appropriate to the tortious conduct claimed.
- Draft interrogatories, answers, defenses, and counterclaims or cross-claims.
- Know the various forms of affirmative defenses.
- Obtain medical authorizations.
- Determine what medical records are needed and request them.
- Arrange for independent medical exams.
- Draft submissions to a medical review panel board.
- Schedule appointments with clients, attorneys, adjusters, experts.
- Attend meetings of attorneys and doctors; prepare memoranda.
- Handle routine correspondence such as updating clients.
- Review all case files periodically and follow up on their status.
- Review medical and forensic publications.
- Conduct client interviews.
- Review medical records and reports (index and summarize).
- Extract data from medical reports and annotate them.
- Ascertain amounts and categories of damages for settlement.
- Obtain medical expert opinions.
- Prepare submissions to various funds or departments of insurance.
- Prepare pleadings required to open estates in wrongful death cases.
- Research and review general areas of the law in a case.
- Research and review medical topics.
- Design and prepare graphs, transparencies, charts, and trial aids.[1]

INTRODUCTION

The law of torts is concerned with personal harms, abridgement of rights to enjoyment of property, and affronts and insults to people and their economic or proprietary interests. Torts can be distinguished from criminal offenses in that they are individualistic, personalized harms rather than acts against society as a whole. Understanding the differences and distinctions between torts and crimes helps to illuminate the nature of civil wrongs. Look at the chart in Figure 11.1.

A tort is a civil wrong, a civil harm an individual suffers. A tort encompasses some type of breach of an obligation owed another or a failure in duty to another that causes calculable injury and corresponding damages. Professor Cook, in his work "A Proposed New Definition of Tort," sums this up well by labeling a tort:

> *An act or omission, not a mere breach of contract, and producing injury to another, without any existing lawful relation of which such act or omission is a natural outgrowth or incident.*[2]

From its Latin source *tortus,* meaning "twisted," a tort detours from the usual expectation in human conduct. A tort causes a wide array of problems—from inconvenience and ruin to reputation to significant bodily injury. Thomas E. Eimermann in *Fundamentals of Paralegalism* portrays this view:

> *The term* torts *covers a variety of noncriminal, noncontractual wrongs. A tort exists where a person (or a person's property) is harmed as a direct result of another person's failure to carry out a legal duty.*[3]

Review the following fact patterns, each of which illustrates the idea of tortious conduct:

Example 1

A newspaper prints a story about a political figure outlining his proclivities for womanizing, drinking, and drugs when it knows such statements are absolutely false.

FIGURE 11.1
Difference between Torts and Crimes

Source: Street Law: A Course in Practical Law, 6th ed., McGraw-Hill/Glencoe (2005). Used with permission.

Key Questions	Criminal Justice System	Civil Justice System
What interests are protected?	Wrongs against society (crimes)	Wrongs to an individual (breach of contract, torts, etc.)
Who are the parties to the case?	Prosecutor (state) and defendant	Plaintiff and defendant
What standard of proof is required?	Beyond a reasonable doubt	Preponderance of the evidence
What are the penalties?	Jail/prison, fines, probation (with requirements such as community service)	Money damages, injunctions
How does the Bill of Rights help ensure fair trials?	Right to a grand jury proceeding; protections against double jeopardy and self-incrimination (Fifth Amendment) Right to a speedy and public trial, right to confront and cross-examine witnesses, right to compulsory process for obtaining witnesses to testify, right to assistance of counsel (Sixth Amendment)	Right to a jury trial (Seventh Amendment)

Example 2

An individual business in serious competition with another business entity attempts to undermine the competitor's contracts with vendors and drivers.

Example 3

A world-renowned surgeon leaves a medical instrument within a patient's abdominal cavity after performing a liver transplant.

Example 4

An automobile driver passes through a stop sign, seriously injuring a completely innocent and nonnegligent victim.

In each of these scenarios, harm is identified, whether economic, reputational, or physical. This is the world of torts: finding an identifiable harm while simultaneously searching for obligation, duty, standards of care, and a measure of what the citizen usually does in daily life. Torts are concerned with obligations and failures to perform, to act, or to conduct oneself in a reasonable fashion. Tort law constitutes the study of obligation and responsibility—a field dedicated to human accountability and restoration of equilibrium. "Tort law is predicated on social policy that protects a plaintiff, as a member of a class of people to whom a duty is owed, in his or her interest to be free from unreasonable risks of injury."[4]

Goals and Purposes of Tort Law

The law of torts seeks to remedy injustice, imbalance, loss, or inadequacy caused by the tortious, wrongful conduct. Ernest J. Weinreb relates that tort law is a "mode of ordering"[5] that sets out parameters of human activity and generates consequence and liability in human action.

In a medical malpractice situation, the victim of negligent or intentional conduct of a physician or other medical specialist pleads for compensation to cover the cost of the civil harm. Although tort law generally expects every person to act with due care in daily life, it also promulgates various levels of professional expectation and imposes special standards of conduct relevant to reasonable professional behavior. Hence a neighbor has obligations relating to noise and fence encroachments, whereas just as compellingly a brain surgeon can be expected to operate competently. "Accordingly, society imposes special ethical and legal requirements on persons who are regularly employed by clients, not to bring about a specific, definable result, but to exercise specialized knowledge and skills on their behalf."[6]

To illustrate, a party who has been defamed, libeled, or slandered uses tort law to restore his or her reputation. The law of torts, and more specifically rules regarding slander, libel, and defamation, requires that people speak or write cautiously, without reckless disregard for known truth and without actual malice. In media circles, *reckless disregard* can be a slippery slope regarding definition. How much truth is required? Is nonmalicious mistake a sign of reckless disregard? Is careless reporting the same? These are cumbersome questions for the legal advocate, and judicial findings are not always consistent. Even so, "it is clear that reckless conduct is not measured by whether a reasonably prudent man would have published, or would have investigated before publishing; that there must be sufficient evidence to permit the conclusion that the defendant in fact entertained serious doubts as to the truth of his publication; and that publishing with such doubts shows reckless disregard for the truth and falsity and demonstrates actual malice."[7]

Although damage to reputation is instructive, diverse classes of conduct and behavior are governed by the law of torts. Consider the owner and keeper of a domestic animal. By every reasonable standard, that owner is responsible for the animal's conduct.[8]

Searching for standards of conduct that are acceptable, tort law delves into most facets of human interaction. Gauging, assessing, and evaluating the conduct of neighbors, adjoining landowners, friends scuffling and fighting, accident victims, patients assaulted and accosted by negligent and errant physicians, dangerous products and services, defective designs, and landowners', shopkeepers', and business invitees' rights, liabilities, and responsibilities, the law of torts delivers measures and rules for human interaction.

CLASSIFICATION OF TORTS

In simplest terms, torts can be divided into the following categories:

- Intentional torts.
- Negligence.
- Strict liability torts.

A comprehensive examination of each of these classifications will follow. Additionally, attention will be given to the most common areas of practice for the paralegal and attorney in the law of torts—namely, personal injury litigation involving automobiles and medical malpractice analysis. Pleadings and other practice skills–oriented documentation will be interspersed throughout the chapter.

Intentional Torts

An intentional tort is an act done with purpose, with knowledge, with reckless disregard of the result, or with gross disregard for the safety of others.[9] Not to be confused with the criminal mens rea as to intent, the proof of which must be beyond a reasonable doubt, intent in the civil realm, while still intentional, can be proven much more readily. Civil intent has been described often as a finding or inference that a person's conduct will result in natural and probable consequences. As former U.S. Supreme Court Justice Holmes noted in his work "Privilege, Malice and Intent,"

> *If the manifest probability of harm is very great, and the harm follows, we say that it is done maliciously or intentionally; if not so great but still considerable, we say the harm is done negligently; if there is no apparent danger, we call it mischance.*[10]

An intentional, tortious act is either one intended by the person or an act that has a predictable consequence. The defendant, the tortfeasor, knows that certain conduct predictably causes harm. In the civil realm, intent is not concerned with malevolence, evil, depraved heart, and criminal premeditation. In civil law, intent is fully personalized: It invades the interests of another, causing personal harm.

Therefore, intentional torts are acts, commissions, or omissions of responsibility or legal duty that are intentional in design. That is, they are consciously chosen, with full realization of the probability of harm. Although this may be a direct definition, intent can also be proven by implication or inference. In *Derosier v. New England Telephone and Telegraph,* the court relevantly digressed:

> *For an intended injury, the law is astute to discover even very remote causation. For one which the defendant merely ought to have anticipated, it has often stopped at an earlier stage of the investigation of causal connection and as to those where there was neither knowledge nor duty to foresee, it has usually limited accountability to direct immediate results. This is not because the defendant's act was a more immediate cause of one case than another's but because it had been felt to be just and reasonable that the liability should extend to results further removed when certain elements of fault are present.*[11]

Put another way, courts look to the nature of the act to infer intent. To summarize the position or argument, intent can be best described as

- A state of mind.
- About consequences of an act (or omission) and not about the act itself.
- Leading to a consequence or result.[12]

An examination of intentional torts follows.

Battery

Parties who enter slugfests with others—who attack, offensively touch, or harm individuals without provocation, justification, self-defense, or privilege—will find themselves potential subjects of battery lawsuits. Battery's key elements include

- Harmful or offensive contact.
- With intent.
- Causing injury.

An action in battery represents more than mere inconvenience or insult. Neither is it the result of a harmless practical joke, a gesture of affection, or some other nonoffensive form of conduct. The gist of the tort's proof rests in physical contact that is intentionally offensive and harmful to another person. As a result, the paralegal and attorney must vigorously evaluate the allegations of a client. Battery constitutes a serious action in damages. Evaluate the following questions to discern its suitability:

- Did the tortfeasor intend, under the standard definition, to harm another?
- Did the tortfeasor touch the client in an offensive, harmful way as reasonably understood?
- Did the offensive and harmful touching produce an actual injury, or is there only an imminent apprehension of potential bodily damage?

Simply put, "battery comprehends the first element of assault, the intentional act, and also required actual contact, rather than the mere fear of such contact."[13] Reasonable people can easily deduce its offensive nature. Lewd and lascivious touching; bludgeoning injury to the head; pushing, shoving, and punching; spitting on a victim or hurling human waste and urine at a party all signify a tortious battery. In these contexts, battery personally affronts the normal sensibilities of an ordinary individual. Despite this general proposition, there appears to be select support for a finding that smoke blown in the face of another may constitute battery. In one recent case, *Leichtman v. WLW Jacor Communications,*[14] the court held that allegations that the defendant intentionally blew cigar smoke in the plaintiff's face "for the purpose of causing physical discomfort, humiliation, and distress" were sufficient to state a cause of action for battery.[15] Form 11.1 on the accompanying CD is a complaint commencing a battery case.

Assault

By contrast, assault is an incomplete, unfulfilled battery. In most American jurisdictions, assault is also a criminal offense, just as battery has historically been.[16] The elements of assault are

- An overt act.
- Intent to cause harm to another.
- Imminent expectation of harm.

Compared to battery, an assault is a threat, an overt act, and an intentional deed that put a reasonable person in apprehension or fear of imminent bodily harm or injury. Although no actual, physical harm takes place, the mental apprehension of a serious expectant harm is enough to prove assault. In an early North Carolina case, *State v. Morgan,* the court aptly defined and described the law of assault:

> The law regards these acts as breaches of the peace because they directly invade that personal security which the law guarantees to every citizen. They do not excite an apprehension that his person may be attacked on a future occasion, and thus authorize a resort to cautionary remedies against it; but there are the beginnings of an attack, that excite terror of immediate personal harm or disgrace, and justify a resort to actual violence to repel the impending injury and insult.[17]

Any of these fact patterns would qualify for an assault action:

Example 1
A defendant attacks, though does not strike or hit, a victim with a club or other blunt instrument.

Example 2
A defendant threatens and shakes a gun at an innocent party.

Example 3
A defendant follows, tracks, and stalks someone for a while in a dark and deserted place.

The intentional nature of the conduct is integral to the examination of an assault and to a finding that the defendant does not carelessly or negligently make such gestures, threats, or affirmations.

To meet the standard of proof for an assault case, the plaintiff must demonstrate that the defendant intended, without jest or joke or nonvolitional conduct, to place the plaintiff in reasonable apprehension of bodily injury. Apprehension is not synonymous with fear, but is closer to understanding and awareness. Here the injured may or may not see fear but clearly recognizes that harm is a real possibility. The conduct of both parties must be measured against a standard of the reasonable person, not the fainthearted or overly paranoid.

It has been held that words may give rise to an action for assault. A party who states intensely "I will kill you" or "I intend to break every bone in your body" and who possesses the physical capacities to perform such a deed will be construed as performing the necessary overt act for a finding of assault.[18] Paralegals must review the client's story to determine the reasonable nature of a claim. If the paralegal is satisfied that the plaintiff's peace of mind has been severely injured, and if the facts warrant a conclusion that a normal, ordinary person would be in apprehension of bodily harm, a case may be legitimate. Form 11.2 on the accompanying CD contains complaint language for an assault action.

False Imprisonment

The elemental requirements in the proof of a false imprisonment case are these:

- Unlawful, unjustified, and illegal restraint or confinement.
- No reasonable chance of escape or alternative avenue to freedom.[19]

This tort action is a recurring problem for the retail industry, particularly as security guards protect retail assets by detaining suspected shoplifters. Although in many jurisdictions a merchant's privilege statute exists,[20] some jurisdictions still provide no privilege or immunity to such an action. Of course, there are many other circumstances in which wrongful detention that is unjustified or illegal may take place. In the public security area it can occur, such as in cases of mistaken identity or any other governmental action that would place a person in a restricted boundary without justification.

The restraint employed by the tortfeasor may be through personal physical pressure, by physical barriers, or by any technique that makes movement difficult.[21] To confine another person does not require a solid mass of walls, doors, locks, or other physical barrier. Confinement can rise by verbal threat or other coercion, including the assertion of legal authority, shop owners' rights, or threats to third parties. Equally required in the parameters of confinement is the nonexistence of, or unawareness of, any safe or reasonable means of escape.[22]

False imprisonment can result from official and nonofficial conduct. False imprisonment can also be asserted when conduct that was originally rightful, privileged, or authorized turns into abusive, unrestrained, and unreasonable restriction of the rights of the individual. "Where one is lawfully detained as a prisoner, but subsequently determined not to be guilty of any offense, the law requires only reasonable dispatch in executing a lawful order for release, the tort of false imprisonment arising in such circumstances only upon an unreasonable delay in release."[23]

The burden of proof on the proponent of a false imprisonment case must be that the defendant intended to cause the confinement. Again, malice may or may not exist in the case at hand, with the fact finder looking more intensely at whether the party intended to restrain or restrict the movement of the harmed party.[24] Pleadings related to a complaint action for false imprisonment are drafted in Form 11.3 on the accompanying CD.

Intentional Infliction of Mental Distress

In proving a case of mental distress, the plaintiff must establish these elements:

- Conduct that is extreme and outrageous.
- Conduct that is intentional.
- Actual damages.

Historically the damages for mental distress have been parasitic in nature—that is, they been tied to or accompanied by some actual physical, personal, or bodily injury.[25] Although early jurists accepted and recognized that psychic injuries were a natural part of a damage case, the quantification of such injuries was considered at best imprecise and incalculable.[26] Characterized as intangible, peculiar, and esoteric, claims for mental distress were slow in gaining full legal recognition.

ROSALIND NIMS V. JOEY HARRISON & JOHN GEORGE PAPAGIANNIS
768 SO.2D 1198 (FLA. 2000)

High school teacher brought actions against students for intentional infliction of emotional distress, alleging that students participated in production and distribution of newsletter in which author threatened to kill teacher and to rape her and all of her children. The Circuit Court, Leon County, Terry P. Lewis, J., dismissed complaints. Teacher appealed. The District Court of Appeal, Lawrence, J., held that teacher stated cause of action against students for intentional infliction of emotional distress.

Reversed and remanded with instructions.

In the 21st century it seems almost implausible that reservations once existed. Psychic damages are doled out generously. Modern respect for psychiatry and psychology has largely changed this perception. Despite the ease with which emotional damages are calculated, there are some that still call for better quantification of damage claims. A recent judicial finding held,

> *The court correctly avoided giving its opinion as an answer to the question but instead it reread the instructions: (1) that definite nervous disturbances caused by mental shock are classified as physical injuries and will warrant an award of damages for negligence if they are the proximate result of defendant's negligence and (2) that "if as the proximate result of physical consequences or physical injuries the plaintiff suffered loss of sleep, you may consider that in the matter of awarding damages."*[27]

Here the court holds to the older vision that emotional damages must be fixed to the physical cause. Hence loss of sleep alone will not suffice, but loss of sleep with a baseball bat to the head may work better. The historic reticence in the recognition of this tort is well founded if not prophetic. Today our legal system is awash in jury findings that compute emotional damages without much rigor. Millions are thrown about as if hard cash is play money. People show neither reticence nor hesitance in marching to the local courthouse over every insult and trifle. Is this a system that can sustain itself?

Should actions for mental distress arise from profanity, verbal abuse, and crude and indecent behavior that regularly engulfs our culture? Should petty insults and simple indignities qualify?

Under usual readings, this tort calls for conduct that is deemed "extreme and outrageous." These are not hollow words but a call for severity in the assessment. The following cases illuminate the principle of severity:

- Informing parents that their son had killed himself.[28]
- Delivering a bound, dead rat instead of a loaf of bread.[29]
- The mishandling, mutilation, disinterment, or improper burial of a body.[30]
- Harassing calls, threats of personal ruination, or continuous arrest threats.[31]

Each of these cases meets the extreme and outrageous threshold, though it may be fair to still argue a lack of real harm.[32] How does one calculate damages for rats versus pieces of bread? Undoubtedly the party intends to upset another, and the party engages in extreme conduct. However, while these components may be true, can damages be calculated? Individuals who are merely inconvenienced and insulted may not meet this rigorous burden. "The extreme and outrageous character of the conduct complained of may arise from the actor's knowledge that the person against whom the conduct is directed is peculiarly susceptible to emotional distress, by reason of some physical or mental condition or other peculiarity."[33] Carping, rumors, emotional taunting, and insults may seem appealing, although none of these things, in and of themselves, can necessarily prompt the type of damages a tort calls for.

A successful claim of intentional infliction of mental distress requires proof of conduct that is outrageous and extreme, but this element alone is insufficient to prove the tort. Damages fix the deal. A pleading outlining a complaint for intentional infliction of mental distress is provided in Form 11.4 on the accompanying CD.

Many American jurisdictions permit an action called *negligent* infliction of mental distress. However, most would argue this is not an intentional action because it measures conduct in negligent terms. Negligence looks not to intention but to result. As a result, the level of proof for the negligent version is much less demanding.[34] The same requisite standards involving extreme and outrageous conduct and result are still required, though proof of intention is not necessary. The view of those supportive of this tort rests in the fact that some careless, uncaring actors whose mistake is extreme should not avoid liability because of a lack of intent. The victim of said error, whether intentional or not, suffers significant and computable damages.[35]

Trespass

The hallmark of a trespass case is the proof of an intrusion. The elemental analysis under a trespass case includes these factors:

- An intrusion onto real property or chattel with intent.
- Interference with right to possess.
- Necessity of damages.

Trespass may take the form of an infringement on either land or chattels, the latter being specific personal property. Trespass concerns any intentional interference with one's right of enjoyment and exclusive possession of land and its privileges, powers, and immunities. It is an intrusion on one's right to use and enjoy. A trespass to land or chattels is not characterized as accidental or negligent conduct. Other tort remedies, such as private nuisance and other legal infringement actions, exist. A trespass is a conscious, deliberate, intentional deed whereby the trespasser invades the property of another. The numerous types of trespass include these:

- A trespasser walks over a surveyed boundary line without permission or right.
- A trespasser parks a car or other vehicle on adjoining property without privilege, right, easement, or grant.
- A trespasser dumps junk, trash, or refuse from his or her property onto an adjoining owner's property without privilege or right.
- A trespasser intentionally diverts chemicals, sludge, waste, or other materials onto an adjoining property without privilege or right.
- A trespasser diverts overflow water onto adjoining property without privilege or right.

In these fact patterns, a trespass is committed by an actual entry upon land, an intrusion of objects, substances, or other matter, or an intrusion by third parties or other entities that deprive a landowner of the appropriate enjoyment and use of his or her land. The trespasser's intent is to cause an intrusion. Remember that malevolence is not required—only an intent to trespass.

Cases involving trespass to land or chattels must ultimately deal with possessory interest and which party can make a superior claim. One can trespass even against a renter, lessee, or a person entitled by easement or other temporary right of possession. One can trespass as to certain mineral rights in coal or oil, even if taken mistakenly or in good faith.[36]

Therefore, a trespass is an attack on a possessory right. This right may not be simple ownership but part of a full array of property interests. The plaintiff must prove specific damages to maintain the action.[37] Trespass complaint pleadings are shown in Form 11.5 on the accompanying CD.

Trespassers who not only enter land but also destroy or damage goods, make use of goods without privilege or permission, or convert, move, or benefit from their usage to the detriment of the owner can be subject to a trespass action in chattel.[38]

Nuisance Actions

A nuisance is a legal action, applicable in both private and public settings, and defined as interference with the use and enjoyment of another person's land. It can be either an intentional or an unintentional act. The ownership or rightful possession of land necessarily involves the right not only to the unimpaired usage of the property itself but also to some reasonable comfort and convenience in its occupation. The unpleasant experience of having disorderly neighbors indicates the nature of nuisance. Examples of common nuisances are unrestrained animals, junk, trash, unsightly garbage disposal practices, pollution, environmental and toxic spills, dust, fire hazards, vibrations, blasting, and odors.

As with intentional infliction of mental distress, proof of the nuisance leaps beyond the trifle and petty annoyance. In a crowded society we all suffer certain physical and spatial inconvenience.

In the law of nuisance, the interference, the confrontation, whether it be aesthetic or environmental, needs to be substantial. Although there is no perfect measure of nuisance, a good rule relates to the impact the nuisance has on the market value of property being adversely affected. Loss of value from depreciation, an inability to rent or lease, or a general decline in the quality of life will all be relevant factors in a finding on nuisance. Whether the nuisance is significant and unreasonable is a reflection of a particular locality. Zoning regulations, rules regarding habitation and land, and local ordinances setting out restrictive behaviors all provide a measure of acceptable conduct. "A nuisance is the non-trespassory invasion of another's interest in the use and in the enjoyment of land. The term signifies such use of property or such a course of conduct that transgresses the restrictions which must be imposed due to the proximity of other persons or property in the community."[39] Proof of substantial and unreasonable interference, however, does not require complete ruination of the property impacted—only proof that the intrusion violates an individual's right to quietly enjoy the property.

Paralegals will draft multiple pleadings in cases of land intrusion. Often, if an action for intentional trespass exists, an auxiliary action for nuisance may also. In differentiating the nature of nuisance from trespass, consider this:

> The complaint in a trespass action for nuisance need not expressly allege that the matter complained of is a nuisance, or even use the word "nuisance"; it is sufficient to state the facts showing that the matter complained of is actually a nuisance. A complaint averring that as a result of the defendant's removal of landfill on his land, large quantities of water were diverted onto the plaintiff's land, thereby causing specified damages, states a cause of action for nuisance.[40]

An example of a complaint for nuisance is shown in Form 11.6 on the accompanying CD.

Other remedies in a nuisance case include injunctive relief or an order of abatement that results in the removal of the nuisance.[41] States are aggressively pursuing property owners who use their realty interest for illegal purposes. Unlike ordinary criminal prosecutions, nuisance abatement actions focus on cleaning up properties that are magnets for illegal activity in addition to punishing wrongdoers. Statutory authority generally looks to the following conduct before initiating the abatement action:

- Drug trafficking.
- Illegal gambling.
- Prostitution.
- Obscenity involving minors.
- Illegal liquor sales.

- Motor vehicle "chop shops."
- Inciting injury to persons or property.
- Murder.
- Sexual assault.
- Felonious assault.

Abatement cases have taken on increased prominence as public entities attempt to collect damages for cleaning up pollution.[42] The remedy of public nuisance is completely distinguishable from a private nuisance. It is a cause of action granted to governmental entities or bodies in their efforts to protect the public good and public health. Under this form of civil power, public agencies or bodies may declare certain activities nuisances for the purposes of their destruction, abatement, or termination. Common public nuisances are animal housing and care, unhealthful housing conditions, explosives, pit bull or other dangerous breeds of dogs, houses of prostitution, gambling houses, industrial concerns that cause health hazards to the public, and obstructions of highways or navigable streams.[43]

Conversion

When property is stolen or unlawfully taken, most think the only remedy is criminal in scope. Civil law provides another remedy: that of conversion. The elements of conversion are these:

- Wrongful taking or converting of chattel or personal property.
- Intent to do so.

- Withholding possession upon request or demand.
- Destruction, alteration, or permanent deprivation of that property.

Conversion, civil law's counterpart to the crime of theft, is an action that may be brought by a property owner who has been deprived of his or her property interest. Often compared to trespass to chattels, conversion is a substantial interference with the right to possession, enjoyment, usage, and ownership of specific property. The crux of a conversion case is the extent and seriousness of the interference with a property right. "Hence, conversion may be committed by intentionally dispossessing the owner or rightful possessor of the chattel, destroying or substantially altering it, without authority or beyond the terms of the authorized use, misdelivering it contrary to instructions, or refusing to surrender it following demand by the rightful owner or possessor."[44]

In a trespass to chattel, the interference is not permanent. But in conversion, the taking is long-term. For this reason, conversion was originally characterized as civil law's answer to theft. Conversion's taking, when compared to theft, opens up some new territory. Indeed, even cyberspace has witnessed the application of conversion principles to the conversion of domain names in sexual Web locations.[45] The permanency of conversion can also be demonstrated by its ultimate destruction, alteration, or long-term use of property, making it worthless to the original owner. Form 11.7 on the accompanying CD shows a complaint for conversion.[46]

Quasi-Intentional Torts

Some of the following tort actions are partially intentional in nature.

Deceit/Fraud

Consumers, unaware and innocent individuals, and even enlightened businesspeople can be and are regularly victimized by fraudulent misrepresentations. In the tort of deceit, the victim alleges that the tortfeasor's representations, which the victim justifiably relied on, caused substantial economic damages. The basic elements of the tort of deceit include these:

- False or misleading representations that deal with material, important facts.
- Knowledge, belief, or understanding on the part of the individual making the representation that his or her assertion is a falsehood. This is often referred to as the requirement of *scienter*.
- An intention to induce the plaintiff to rely on such falsehood or misrepresentation.
- Justifiable reliance on such a misrepresentation.
- Actual damages due to reliance.[47]

Modern culture is quite used to fraud and trickery in representation. In a world of bait and switch, unconscionable scams and schemes, and shady commercial activity, it is not surprising that deceit is a frequent cause of action. "Fraud consists in anything calculated to deceive, whether by single act or combination, or by suppression of truth, or a suggestion of what is false, either by direct falsehood or by innuendo, by speech or sentence, word of mouth, or look or gesture, and may be made up by any artifice by which a person is deceived to his disadvantage."[48]

For deceit to be meaningful, the misrepresentation must concern a material issue relative to the product and service in question. Deceit can be equated with good and sometimes aggressive salesmanship. Consumers have come to expect exaggeration and smooth talking in those selling their wares. Misrepresentation can also occur through silence or nondisclosure. Although there is no precise formula for deceit, courts will look at the facts on a case-by-case basis, evaluating those circumstances that would lead a reasonable person to be deceived. Generally these factors will play a role in a judicial determination:

- Degrees of intelligence of the parties.
- Ages of the parties.
- Levels of education and understanding of language.
- Relationship the parties have with each other.
- How the information is presented and disseminated.
- Types of facts that are not disclosed.
- Types of questions that have been asked and not answered.

- Nature of the documentation and contract itself.
- Actual proof of any active concealment or nondisclosure.

In the case of misrepresention, knowledge or *scienter* of the misrepresentation is crucial to the necessary proof of intentionality. Fraud and deceit demand more than careless error: they rely on affirmative knowledge of the falsehood.[48] Under the scienter principle, knowledge need not be absolute, but true enough for a person not to avoid its finding. Misrepresentation goes to the heart of the transaction, and at its center is the falsehood that triggers the consummation of the deal. Drawing the line between intent to mislead and being negligent or simply incompetent is challenging. Deceit consists of much more than ignorance or ineptitude; it is better described as a statement utterly contrived and intent on deception.

The misrepresentation must be about something central to the transaction, meaning that misrepresentation of a material fact rather than a peripheral question is required. "Courts also consider whether the defendant knew or should have known of facts making the plaintiff peculiarly susceptible to emotional distress and characterize a defendant's conduct as outrageous if it proceeds in the face of such knowledge."[49] Thus the misrepresentation's reliance often varies depending on individual victims. Standards for business merchants and ordinary consumers vary considerably. And for some classes of victims, deceit can only be termed unconscionable—say in the case of the elderly or the mentally retarded. Here principles in law are replaced by the equitable notion that victimization occurs even more readily in these groups.[50] A sample complaint for deceit and misrepresentation is shown in Form 11.8 on the accompanying CD.

Defamation

Defamation is an oral or written statement, communicated to a second party or published to the world at large, that is untrue and unjustified in content and that causes damage to another. Defamation is broken into two subcategories:

Libel: written defamation of a person's character.

Slander: oral defamation or derogatory remark about a person.[51]

The following elements are mandatory in analysis of a defamation case:

- A statement, either written or oral, tends to defame another.
- A statement is false and is neither privileged nor defensible.
- The statement causes its subject to be held in lower esteem.
- The statement has been communicated and published.
- Proof of special damages—or no proof of damages if involving the following conducts:
  - Propensities for crime.
  - Loathsome diseases.
  - Business, trade, or professional misconduct.

An act of defamation is gravely serious when compared to mockery or caricature. A defamatory communication is an utterance causing great embarrassment, contempt, ridicule, public or private derogation, a ruination of reputation, and a diminution of one's goodwill and the self-respect of its target. In short, the utterance leaves its target in personal disgrace. Defamation is a communication that harms the reputation of another within the community or place of employment and triggers economic or emotional harm to that individual.[52]

Whether a comment, remark, or communication is defamatory depends on numerous facts and conditions: the person's standing in the community; whether the person is a public or private figure; whether the comment involves a professional career or orientation; whether the comment involves a sexual proclivity or promiscuity; or whether the comment can be characterized as satirical, political, or privileged information.

For example, in the case of prosecutors, it is difficult to lodge a defamation action because in their function as prosecutor, they are, for the most part, granted absolute immunity. Critics have argued that this immunity grant fosters not only defamatory conduct on the part of prosecutors, but even worse. The human consequences of wrongful convictions are tragic. Imagine spending even one night on death row as an innocent person. Imagine spending a decade in prison. Even after the wrongly convicted are exonerated, the damage continues. The stigma of a prosecution and conviction is lasting. Employment prospects are greatly diminished. As former Labor Secretary Ray Donovan asked his prosecutor after his acquittal on criminal charges, "What office do I go to to get my reputation back?"[53]

Aside from this anomaly, the proponent of defamation must argue with substance. Ridicule and defamation are two different things, as are satire and defamation. By whom and how one can be defamed are the subjects of significant scholarly analysis.[54]

Are these statements defamatory or not?

- Calling an individual a "bastard."
- Charging that another individual has venereal disease.
- Asserting that a public politician has frequently been bribed.
- Claiming that a movie star has a drinking problem.
- Alleging that a public broadcaster was a coward during the Korean War.
- Alleging that parents neglected a child.
- Calling an individual a drunk.
- Characterizing a person as a womanizer.

Defamation exhibits far greater tolerance in cases involving public figures: politicians, celebrities, and high-profile people in the public spotlight. In the absence of actual malice, it is difficult to win a defamation case in the public realm. Media, historians, and others covering public figures have a sort of immunity unless the public figure can show sinister motivation on the part of the defaming party. The U.S. Supreme Court in *New York Times v. Sullivan*[55] demanded proof of actual malice and the utter disregard of the truth when evaluating public figure defamation cases. Willful and malicious disregard of the truth serves as the underpinning in an actionable defamation case regarding public figures. Balancing the rights to free speech with the privacy rights of public figures, the courts have overwhelmingly given preferred protection to the media. This was quite evident in the case of *Hustler Magazine v. Jerry Falwell*, where allegations of familial incest and drunkenness were characterized as political satire or simple ridicule.[56] Courts tend to require some subjective awareness of falseness or disregard of the truth before finding any right to bring forth an action in a public case.

In *Bose Corp. v. Consumer Union of the United States Inc.*, the U.S. Supreme Court reiterated the general standard that in defamatory falsehoods, an action for defamation about a public figure will not be upheld unless libelous or slanderous representations were made in complete and total reckless disregard of the truth.[57] Here are subsidiary questions to keep in mind when analyzing a case of defamation or slander:

- Is the person actually a public figure or public official?
- Do sports athletes, movie stars, and other people in the public eye constitute public figures?
- Is the defamatory remark, whether libel or slander, protected under some governmental privilege or immunity, such as in the case of a judge or public official making comment?
- Can actual damages be proven from the net effect of the statement?
- When do the rights of free press and free speech take a back seat to the personal rights of individuals?
- Do matters of personal privacy have a different protection for public figures when they do not relate to legitimate public interests?
- Does political opinion receive more favorable treatment than other forms of speech?
- Does truth always provide a defense?
- Is truth always definable?
- By whose standard is truth measured?
- How does one gauge the difference between political satire, intellectual jousting, ridicule, and a direct affront to a person's reputation?

Adding to the confusion of defamation are the tabloid materials available in any supermarket. These entertainment pieces report or allege every imaginable scenario between movie stars, professional athletes, politicians, and other individuals. Exactly what is the measure of truth in these publications? Does the public perceive these statements and affirmations to be the result of rigorous journalism, or does the public perceive such stories as delusion, fantasy, and Hollywood gossip? In cases involving public figures the advocate must objectively demonstrate that a defamatory meaning was conveyed. Paralegals delegated the task of preparing libel or slander pleadings can review Forms 11.9 and 11.10 on the accompanying CD.

Invasion of Privacy

The privacy right has both quasi-constitutional and civil foundations. In popular parlance, everyone expects some level of privacy in their daily existence. Some see privacy being whittled away at every corner. Supreme Court Justices Samuel Warren and Louis Brandeis addressed the question of how modern society has impinged upon fundamental privacy rights. In recounting the decimation of personal integrity and privacy, they stated,

> *The press is overstepping in every direction the obvious bounds of proprietary and of decency. Gossip is no longer the source of the idle and of the vicious but has become a trade, which is pursued with industry as well as effrontery. To satisfy the prurient taste, the details of sexual relations are spread broadcast in the columns of daily papers. To occupy the indolent, column upon column is filled with idle gossip which can only be procured by intrusion upon the domestic circle. The intensity and complexity of life, attendant upon advancing civilization, have rendered necessary some retreat from the world, and man, under the refining influence of culture has become more sensitive to publicity, so that solitude and privacy have become more essential to the individual; but modern enterprise and invention have, through invasions upon his privacy, subjected him to mental pain and distress, far greater than could be inflicted by mere bodily injury.*[58]

To say that modern society is intrusive is an understatement. With technological equipment, Internet blogs, chat rooms, electronic commerce and record keeping, governmental demands for Social Security numbers before the age of 2, terrorism, and a private enterprise system that collects much information about consumers and other clientele, we should be extremely concerned about how safe we are.[59] The tort of invasion of privacy approaches the encroachment from four differing directions: appropriation, false light, unreasonable intrusion, and disclosure of private facts.[60] The *Second Restatement of Torts* states,

> *(1) One who invades the right of privacy of another is subject to liability for the resulting harm to the interests of the other.*
>
> *(2) The right of privacy is invaded by*
>   *(a) unreasonable intrusion upon the seclusion of another, as stated in §652B;*
>   *(b) appropriation of the other's name or likeness, as stated in §652C; or*
>   *(c) unreasonable publicity given to the other's private life, as stated in §652D; or*
>   *(d) publicity that unreasonably places the other in a false light before the public, as stated in Restatement (Second) of Torts §652A (1977).*[61]

Each of these bases is considered highly invasive, and "a matter concerning the private life of another is subject to liability to the other for invasion of his privacy, if the matter publicized is of a kind that would be highly offensive to a reasonable person, and is not of legitimate concern to the public."[62]

Invasion of Privacy: Appropriation

Public and private figures often labor with great notoriety and fame; as a result, their presences, in the form of likeness, picture, name, trademark, signature, or any other personal trait or characteristic, are frequently appropriated without permission, grant, or right.[63] This intrusion is termed *invasion of privacy by appropriation*. The tort of invasion of privacy by appropriation consists of the following elements:

- Appropriation of the plaintiff's identity.
- An attempt to obtain advantage, whether economic, social, or through other means.
- Intrusion without permission, privilege, or legal right.

An example of a complaint highlighting the unauthorized use of a photograph for an advertisement is outlined in Form 11.11 on the accompanying CD.

Invasion of Privacy: Unreasonable Intrusion   An invasion of privacy can also take another approach—that of intrusion. By *intrusion* we mean not the garden variety but the special class of intrusion that shocks the ordinary citizen and is repulsive to people or common sensibility. The intrusion must pry deeply and be so distasteful that it offends the general standards of decency. Such intrusion is intentional rather than the result of carelessness and negligence. The elements are these:

- A highly offensive intrusion into the seclusion of another.
- A lack of permission, privilege, or right.
- An intention to intrude unreasonably.

Intrusion can be achieved by physical means or by eavesdropping or other technological invasion.

It is difficult to argue such invasion in a public setting. In other words, when a person visits the world, he or she can expect to pictured within it. "Courts are loathe to find violations of privacy when the alleged invasion takes place in public" because the court could not possibly anticipate all the possible infringements.[64]

Invasion of Privacy: Disclosure of Private Facts   Revelation of personal affairs and practices that are highly offensive and very personal in design may give rise to the disclosure principle in invasion of privacy. Although the facts may be true, they are not appropriate for the public domain. For example, pictures of a politician in a shower or looking unkempt, or a police chief shown drinking vodka at home, may or may not be examples of this tort. Here are required elements in this cause of action:

- Public disclosure of private facts.
- An intentional act.
- The facts disclosed must be private in nature.
- The private facts disclosed are highly offensive and objectionable to the reasonable person.

The trier of fact must be satisfied that the matter made public is so offensive and so objectionable that its public disclosure is unwarranted. An example of this tort's pleading is shown in Form 11.12 on the accompanying CD.

Invasion of Privacy: False Light in the Public Eye   Intending to depict private figures falsely, whether through visual or print media, knowing that the portrayal, the depiction, or the story itself is a complete falsity, can result in an action for a false light invasion of privacy. The *Restatement of Torts* holds,

> *One who gives publicity to a matter concerning another that places the other before the public in a false light is subject to liability to the other for invasion of his privacy, if*
> *(a) the false light in which the other was placed would be highly offensive to a reasonable person, and*
> *(b) the actor had knowledge of or acted in reckless disregard as to the falsity of the publicized matter and the false light in which the other would be placed.[65]*

As in the public disclosure of private facts, the invasion action is not available to those who are easily offended or hypersensitive in personality. Protection is granted to the reasonable man or woman whose personal and private life are grotesquely and inordinately portrayed.[66] In terms of publicity, such representation is highly offensive to the reasonable person.[67]

Malicious Prosecution

Parties who institute legal proceedings for the sole purpose of vengeance or vexatious harassment, without any justifiable claim, and who employ the legal system as a tool for a personal vendetta can be subject to an action for malicious prosecution. By most scholarly accounts, malicious prosecution is intentional. The elements required to establish this cause of action include the following:

- A criminal proceeding is instituted by a defendant against a specific plaintiff.
- The plaintiff is victorious in the criminal matter.

BROWNIE MILLER ET AL. V. NATIONAL BROADCASTING COMPANY ET AL.
187 CAL.APP.3D 1463, 232 CAL. RPTR. 668, 69 A.L.R.4TH 1027 (1987)

Wife and daughter sued television network, television news producer, and city alleging trespass, invasion of privacy, and infliction of emotional distress. After city was dismissed by stipulation, summary judgment was entered in favor of network and producer by the Superior Court, Los Angeles County, Charles E. Jones, J., and wife and daughter appealed. The Court of Appeal, L. Thaxton Hanson, J., held that (1) wife had stated cause of action for trespass, invasion of privacy, and infliction of emotional distress; (2) daughter had not stated cause of action; and (3) First Amendment protections for news gathering activities were outweighed by wife's right to privacy.

Affirmed in part and reversed in part.

- There is a finding of no probable cause for proceeding with the action.
- A finding occurs of malice, and that malice is the motive for bringing forth the action rather than a desire for justice.

A case of malicious prosecution will be upheld only if, in the underlying criminal action, the accused is acquitted or the case is dismissed or overturned at the appellate level. If the former defendant in the criminal case can demonstrate that the action brought against him or her was motivated with malicious intention—that is, without justice in mind or a desire for an equitable settlement—malice will be inferred. It is incorrect to assume that the term *malice* has the same meaning as in the criminal context.

Paralegals must always be attuned to the underlying action—searching for whether the person maliciously prosecuted was eventually victorious in the litigation. An underlying case that results in a negative judgment, regardless of the motivation of the initiator of the original action, will negate any action for malicious prosecution.[68] For an example of a malicious prosecution complaint, see Form 11.13 on the accompanying CD.

Abuse of Process

Quite similar to the malicious prosecution case is an abuse of process action. Instead of requiring that an underlying action be terminated or resolved favorably on behalf of the defendant, as in a case of malicious prosecution, abuse of process evaluates how the parties use the "system." By using the system, the litigant employs the justice system, in particular a civil lawsuit, for illegal reasons. In other words, judicial process is utilized as a procedural weapon: An aggressive orchestration of legal processes such as pleadings and counterclaims, cross-claims, affirmative defenses, and the like is used entirely for unjust ends. "Abuse of process is a tort that consists of the malicious or inappropriate use of legal process to accomplish some end not intended by the specific writ or other issued by the court. Essentially, the tort can be defined as the malicious perversion of a regularly issued process in an effort to obtain a result not lawfully warranted by the particular process."[69] The elements of the tort require these finding:

- Misuse of the legal process.
- Intent and malice.
- A definite act or threat not authorized by the process.

Stated another way, the legal system is used as a threat—a systematic domination imposed on innocent parties.[70]

Wrongful Death

Although wrongful death can be the result of a clear negligence case, it also can be the result of an intentional act. Wrongful death partially mirrors the criminal law of homicide. An action may be brought against any party who is responsible for the death of an individual and lacks any significant justification or defense. Civil remedies, such as wrongful death, are concurrent causes of action for any litigation team. A person killed by a drunk driver or mugged, robbed, and beaten to death in a robbery case has the alternative to sue the party responsible for the tragic death under a theory of wrongful death. In common law the action was legally implausible; the remedy presently arises from statutory authority. "Wrongful death statutes usually provide that the action can be maintained for any wrongful act, neglect, or default which causes death."[71]

Here are the required elements of a wrongful death action:

- Intentional or negligent act causing death of another.

- Proof of damages.

Wrongful death is most appropriate in multicount litigation plans when death arises under workers' compensation coverage, breach of contract or warranty, and theories of negligence and product liability. Paralegals should pay close attention to the wrongful death information sheet in Form 11.14 on the accompanying CD. Also available for the paralegal's review is a complaint for wrongful death in Form 11.15.

Economic Torts

Economic torts are primarily a modern legal invention; but despite their novelty, they play a critical role in the protection and maintenance of economic interests in the free market system. Commercial relationships can be just as significantly harmed as an individual, and in many cases it is difficult to distinguish the person from the business entity that has suffered. The most common economic torts are these:

- Disparagement.

- Slander of title.

- Trade libel.

- Injurious falsehood.

- Interference with contractual right.

- Interference with prospective advantage.[72]

The range of commercial interests is immeasurable in the modern economy but generally includes assets, leases, land, mineral rights, trademarks, and patents.[73] Under federal statutes, copyright, as well as other intellectual property actions, and unfair competition lawsuits are authorized. See Form 11.16 on the accompanying CD for an example of such a complaint. A cursory examination follows of the major torts in the business realm.

Injurious Falsehood/Disparagement

The elements consist of

- Publication of defamatory or derogatory statements.

- Affect on title or interest in business.

- Intent to interfere with relations.

- Proof of special damages.

In this cause of action, the injured business party must show that statements and conduct irreparably injure the business interest.

Interference with Contractual Relations

In the competitive marketplace, the stress and strain of winning clients and accounts can push businesspeople to the ethical edge. One way to gain accounts is to undercut and undermine the competition. Although all is fair in love and war, the right to compete has ethical and legal limitations. The crux of interference with contractual relations sits right in the midst of this ethical obligation because the party desires and intends to injure, destroy, or negatively impact another person's business. Negligent interference will not be enough for this tort; the burden of proof insists on clear intention.[74] The elements are these:

- Intention to interfere with a contractual right.
- Actual damages.
- Causation.

Proof of this tort is not easy, especially in light of the competitive American marketplace. Interference with contractual relationships and competitiveness in economic contracts and commercial interests are strange bedfellows. As businesspeople compete in differing territories and districts, one might argue that any comparison critique of a competitor's product is a sort of interference. Moreover, the tort's purpose is not to stifle the free market but to ensure a free and honorable system of competition. Intentional interference could be characterized in this way:

> It seems to us that where a party has entered into a contract with another to do or not to do a particular act or acts, he has as clear a right to its performance as he has to his property, either real or personal; and that knowingly to induce the other party to violate it is as distinct a wrong as it is to injure or destroy his property.[75]

Similarly, is it necessary to prove whether the conduct in question is the actual cause of damages? To induce another to breach a contract or to cause an actual repudiation or other defect in a relationship of a competing business interest requires assertions or acts that are tied to the acts of the intentional tortfeasor. Sour grapes for poor performance on the part of a competitor alleging interference may be a better explanation. To prove a case of intentional interference, the plaintiff must show that the defendant induced a breach of contractual interests by using threats, economic duress, coercion, unreasonable persuasion, unfair assertions, and subterfuge, which in turn caused an eventual repudiation.

NEGLIGENCE

Negligence is a failed human action, whether the neighbor or the brain surgeon, the police captain or the engineer—all of whom owe a duty to others in the performance of their tasks. Negligence is a cause of action that seeks a safe environment, identifies unsafe products and services, warns of incompetent and unpredictable professional behavior, and sets out expectations of action in the community. A negligent act is one that does not meet society's general expectations of reasonable conduct or due care. A negligent act is an error, a mistake, an accident that injures or harms another. In negligence we find the frail condition of the human species: a person who fails even though he or she knows what to do and how to do it and that his or her role or occupation has special obligations to others. The negligent individual knows better, or at least should have known that harm would arise. In some respects, negligence manifests misfeasance, nonfeasance, or, in a sense, even malfeasance. It can be acts affirmatively performed or negligently omitted. Negligence might be any of the following:

- A doctor who by carelessness and general disregard of medical standards fails to suture a patient.
- An automobile driver who carelessly neglects speed limits, stop signs, and stoplights and causes a serious injury to another.
- A product manufacturer who knows or under all reasonable standards should have known that a toy manufactured for a child's use can cause serious injury.
- A pet owner who is well aware of the pet's propensity to bite and injure others but lets it run without a leash.
- A landowner who owns property and knows that there are dangerous conditions yet takes no steps to repair them.
- A retail merchant who invites the public in for business yet provides an unsafe environment in which to do so.

On its face, negligence is basically the law of human mistake, the law of less than reasonable conduct, the law of error. The elements in any cause of negligence include the following:

- Duty or standard of care.
- Breach of that duty or standard of care.
- Causation, either legal or proximate in nature.
- Actual proof of damages.[76]

If negligence is concerned with human conduct that breaches or fails to adhere to a standard of care, the focus is less on pure mental state and more on human action. In this way, negligence is not an intentional tort. "Negligence is the absence or want of care which a reasonable person would exercise under the circumstances. It may consist of either the doing of that which a reasonably prudent person would not do under the circumstances, or failing to do that which a reasonably prudent person would do under the circumstances. The cause of action is based on the negligent conduct which occasioned the injury. The essence of the negligence complaint is that the defendant's conduct fell below the standard established by law for the protection of others against unreasonable risk of harm."[77] Like intentional torts, negligence is concerned with damages and relational causation between the act and injuries suffered on the part of the victim. However, negligence's mental state is not intentional.

Negligence also must gauge and calculate responsibility based not only on the fact that injury has taken place, but also on whether a person could have known, should have known, must have known, or was expected to have known that the failure to meet or exceed a basic standard of care would result in harm to another. Negligence needs foreseeability analysis in every case.

In applying the doctrine of foreseeability to a particular case, liability may be imposed even though no reported case deals with the same factual situation as is presented in the present litigation. Circumstances surrounding different accidents are varied, but the principle that determines the imposition of liability is constant, being based on the proposition that one who, by substandard conduct, causes injury to another is legally responsible if the harmful consequences of such conduct could reasonably have been foreseen.[78]

Foreseeability

Part of the negligence proof falls into the world of foreseeability. An actor cannot be responsible for that which is utterly unknown or unpredictable. If the negligent party did not know, should he or she have known? Is it reasonable to expect that human agents understand and know the consequences of their acts? Or are some circumstances simply not predictable? Although human beings cannot predict the weather well, there are some things that every agent needs to know, such as every reasonably foreseeable risk of threat and danger of injury. If one could not reasonably foresee an injury as a result of one's act, or if one's conduct was reasonable in light of what could be anticipated, there would be no negligence. Thus there is undoubtedly a great deal of flexibility, not to say downright inconsistency, in the application of "foreseeability" to "proximate cause." Undoubtedly this elasticity has served a useful purpose by providing a formula, not unlike that of the "reasonable person," to handle varied circumstances.

For example, a party who is exceeding the speed limit and weaving in and out of traffic can foresee potential or actual injury to others. At the same time, a party who rigorously adheres to the speed limit and drives in the proper manner and whose steering wheel breaks off, causing a collision and injuring others, could not foresee these events (unless of course it could be shown that he or she was aware of a faulty steering wheel and failed to repair it). Foreseeability also determines how far, extensive, and broad the scope of responsibility is. In the famous *Palsgraf v. The Long Island Railroad Company* case,[79] these questions are posed: To whom is the duty owed and how far does it extend? Who are the foreseeable and unforeseeable parties? How far does one's responsibility extend? What is the specific zone of danger as far as the chain of causation can be demonstrated? Determining how foreseeable events and consequences are is often like playing a game of legal dominoes. Justice Mitchell in the 1896 *Christensen v. Chicago, St. Paul Railway* case attempted to clarify foreseeability in the following way:

> *If a person had no reasonable ground to anticipate that a particular act would or might result in any injury to anybody, then, of course, the act would not be negligent at all; but if the act is negligent,*

HEATHER GEARY V. OE PLUS, LTD.
20 MASS.L.RPTR. 241, 2005 WL 3670415 (MASS.SUPER. 2005)
ROBERT RUFO, JUSTICE.

Plaintiffs Heather Geary and Steven Kelly, the administrators of the estates of Jarrod Drew and Timothy Kelly, respectively, have filed these wrongful death actions against OE Plus, Ltd. ("OE Plus"), and Lappen Auto Supply Co., Inc. ("Lappen"). Their complaints against OE Plus allege negligence, gross negligence, breach of implied warranty of merchantability, and breach of the implied warranty of fitness for a particular purpose. Geary's complaint also asserts a claim for negligence causing conscious pain and suffering. The plaintiffs' complaints against Lappen allege breach of the implied warranty of merchantability and breach of the implied warranty of fitness for a particular purpose. Defendants OE Plus and Lappen have each moved for summary judgment,

and both assert that the plaintiffs' claims are barred due to a lack of reasonable foreseeability and proximate cause. Moreover, they argue that the intoxicated driver's negligence which resulted in the decedents' deaths was an intervening, superseding cause which relieves them of any liability for the plaintiffs' injuries. Because the plaintiffs have joined their opposition to the defendants' motions for summary judgment, and the defendants' arguments in support of their summary judgment motions are identical, this court will consider all of the parties' arguments in this memorandum and order. For the following reasons, OE Plus and Lappen's motions for summary judgment are allowed.

BACKGROUND

The summary judgment record reveals the following undisputed facts. An alternator, manufactured by OE Plus and distributed by Lappen, was installed in a tow truck operated by A-1 Affordable Towing and Recovery (A-1 Towing). The alternator was defective. Approximately five months later, in the early morning hours of February 20, 2004, Timothy Kelly, an employee of A-1 Towing, was driving the tow truck southbound on Route 495, when he noticed the alternator light in the tow truck came on, indicating a problem with the alternator. Kelly radioed to the dispatcher at A-1 Towing that he was experiencing problems with the tow truck, and asked that another tow truck driver be sent to assist

him. Kelly eventually stopped the disabled tow truck in a break-down lane on Route 495. Jarrod Drew, another A-1 Towing employee, arrived with a flatbed tow truck to assist Kelly. As Kelly and Drew prepared the disabled tow truck to be lifted onto the flatbed truck, a vehicle driven by Daniel Cummings entered the breakdown lane and collided with the tow trucks. Cummings's vehicle also struck Kelly and Drew, and both were killed. It was later determined that Cummings was intoxicated, and he was criminally charged with, *inter alia,* operating a motor vehicle under the influence of alcohol and reckless operation causing motor vehicle homicide.

DISCUSSION

The court should allow summary judgment where there are no genuine issues of material fact and where the record entitles the moving party to judgment as a matter of law. See Mass.R.Civ.P. 56(c); *Cassesso v. Commissioner of Correction,* 390 Mass. 419, 422 (1983); *Community Nat'l Bank v. Dawes,* 369 Mass. 550, 553 (1976). A party moving for summary judgment who or which does not bear the burden of proof at trial may demonstrate the absence of a genuine dispute of material fact for trial either by submitting affirmative evidence negating an essential element of the non-moving party's case, or by showing that the nonmoving party has no reasonable expectation of proving an essential element of its case at trial. See *Flesner v. Technical Communications Corp.,* 410 Mass. 805, 809 (1991); *Kourouvacilis v. General Motors Corp.,* 410 Mass. 706, 716 (1991). It is necessary, however, for the summary judgment movant "to show by credible evidence from . . . affidavits and other supporting materials that there is no genuine issue of material fact and that [the party is] entitled, as matter of law, to a judgment." *Smith v. Massimiano,* 414 Mass. 81, 85 (1993).

While summary judgment is seldom granted in negligence actions, it is "appropriate, however, if a plaintiff has no reasonable expectation of proving that 'the injury to the plaintiff was a foreseeable result of the defendant's negligent conduct.'" *Hebert v. Enos,* 60 Mass.App.Ct. 817, 820–821 (2004), quoting *Kent v. Commonwealth,* 437 Mass. 312, 320 (2002). See also *Bergendahl v. Massachusetts Elec. Co.,* 45 Mass. App.Ct. 715, 725 (1998), cert. denied, 528 U.S. 929 (1999) ("While the issue of foreseeability is ordinarily a question of fact for the jury, the court may decide the issue as a matter of law . . . in the absence of evidence that the risk which resulted in the plaintiff's injury should reasonably have been anticipated by the defendant . . ."

The plaintiffs argue that the facts of this product liability case, viewed in their favor, establish that the decedents' deaths were a foreseeable consequence of Lappen's distribution and OE Plus's manufacture of the defective alternator. The plaintiffs argue that OE Plus and Lappen's motions for summary judgment should be denied because notwithstanding Cummings's intervening negligent conduct, a reasonable jury could conclude that the decedents' deaths were a foreseeable consequence of the failure of the defective alternator. In order to determine whether summary judgment should be allowed in this case, this court must examine whether the plaintiffs have a reasonable expectation of proving all of the elements of their claims at trial.

I. PLAINTIFFS' NEGLIGENCE CLAIMS

In negligence actions, "the plaintiff has the burden of proving each and every element of that claim: duty, breach of duty (or, the element of negligence), causation (actual and proximate), and damages." *Ulwick v. DeChristopher,* 411 Mass. 401, 408 (1991). It is well established that "'[o]ne cannot be held liable for negligent conduct unless it is causally related to injury of the plaintiff.' In addition to being the cause in fact of the injury, the plaintiff must show that the negligent conduct was a proximate or legal cause of the injury as well." *Kent,* 437 Mass. at 320, quoting *Wainwright v. Jackson,* 291 Mass. 100, 102 (1935) (other citations omitted). Because the defendants do not dispute that the alternator was defective, the sole issue presented by this summary judgment motion is whether the plaintiffs have established a reasonable expectation of proving the causation element of their negligence claim at trial.

"Whether negligent conduct is the proximate cause of an injury depends not on factual causation, but rather on whether the injury to the plaintiff was a foreseeable result of the defendant's negligent conduct." *Kent,* 437 Mass. at 320, citing *Jesionek v. Massachusetts Port Auth.,* 376 Mass. 101, 105 (1978). It has been stated that the cause of the injury must be "reasonably foreseeable," meaning that "one is bound to anticipate and provide against what usually happens and what is likely to happen, but is not bound in like manner to guard against what is . . . only remotely and slightly probable." *Hebert,* 60 Mass.App.Ct. at 821, citing *Falk v. Finkelman,* 268 Mass. 524, 527 (1929). The determination of "[t]he definition or scope of proximate cause (or foreseeable result) is in turn based on considerations of policy and pragmatic judgment." *Poskus v. Lombardo's of Randolph, Inc.,* 423 Mass. 637, 640 (1996). See also *Griffiths v. Campbell,* 425 Mass. 31, 35–36 (1997).

The plaintiffs argue that the defendants, as a manufacturer and supplier of tow truck parts, created the condition necessary for the decedents' deaths to occur. They argue that the type of harm which occurred in this case was highly foreseeable, due to the unfortunate frequency of drunk driving accidents in the Commonwealth, and cite to National Highway Traffic Safety Administration statistics which demonstrate the similar regularity of accidents which occur in highway breakdown lanes. They argue that it is foreseeable that a product defect which causes a tow truck to become disabled would put the tow truck driver in danger due to the emergency nature of that vehicle and its tendency to be in the highway breakdown lane. The defendants argue that the accident which resulted in the deaths of both decedents was not reasonably foreseeable, and to hold them responsible for what occurred in this case would defeat the pragmatic concerns which comprise the foundation of the foreseeability doctrine. They also contend that they are entitled to summary judgment because the actions of the intoxicated driver in this case were an intervening, superseding cause which relieves them of liability for the plaintiffs' resulting harm.

Although a jury could find that the defendants were negligent for manufacturing and distributing a defective alternator, their negligence was not the proximate cause of the decedents' deaths. "Proximate cause may be determined as a question of law when there is no dispute as to the effect of the facts established." *Kent,* 437 Mass. at 320, citing *Stamas v. Fanning,* 345 Mass. 73, 76 (1962). "If a series of events occur between the negligent conduct and the ultimate harm, the court must determine whether those intervening events have broken the chain of factual causation or, if not, have otherwise extinguished the element of proximate cause and become a superseding cause of the harm." *Kent,* 437 Mass. at 321, citing *Jesionek v. Massachusetts Port Auth.,* 376 Mass. 101, 105 (1978). "A superseding cause is an act of a third person or other force which by its intervention prevents the actor from being liable for harm to another which his antecedent negligence is a substantial factor in bringing about." *Jones v. Cincinnati, Inc.,* 32 Mass.App.Ct. 365, 366 n. 1 (1992), quoting *Restatement (Second) of Torts* §440 (1965). Here the intervening criminal act of Cummings, the intoxicated driver who struck and killed the decedents, was the proximate and superseding cause of the plaintiffs' injuries. This criminal act was "an intervening cause which the defendant was not bound to anticipate and guard against." *Poskus,* 423 Mass. at 637, citing *Galbraith v. Levin,* 323 Mass. 255, 261 (1948).

The facts would not warrant a jury's conclusion that the plaintiffs' injuries were within the reasonably foreseeable risk of harm created by the defendants' negligence. See *Poskus,* 423 Mass. at 640–641. As such, no rational jury could find the defendants liable for the plaintiffs' injuries, and summary judgment is allowed as to Counts I–III of Geary's complaint and Counts I and II of Kelly's complaint is allowed.

then the person guilty of it is equally liable for all of its natural and proximate consequences, whether he could have foreseen them or not. Otherwise expressed, the law is that if the act is one which the party ought, in the exercise of ordinary care, to have anticipated was liable to result in injury to others, then he is liable for any injury proximately resulting from it, although he could not have anticipated the particular injury which did happen. Consequences which follow in unbroken sequence, without an intervening efficient cause, from the original negligent act, are natural and proximate, and for such consequences the original wrongdoer is responsible, even though he could not have foreseen the particular results which did follow.[80]

Paralegals, in conjunction with attorneys must determine how far the chain of responsibility goes—what events and conditions can be tied legally or proximately to the original act of the negligent actor. In this way paralegals can determine how many plaintiffs and defendants might be involved in a negligence action. If foreseeability is liberally construed, more parties may be swept into the action. If foreseeability is restricted, victim counsel may bypass multiple sources of potential compensation for an injured party.

Causation

In the law of negligence, causation can be either *legal* or *proximate*. Paralegals will mostly hear attorneys and legal specialists using the term *proximate*—a legal attempt to determine whether an act, as in the case of negligence, or whether a breach of the standard of conduct and duty owed another, is causally connected to an identifiable injury. There must be a nexus, a damage connection, between the negligence alleged and the injury calculated or found. "Proximate or legal causation is traditionally defined as that which, in a natural and continuous sequence, broken by any sufficient intervening cause, produces injury, and without which the result would not have occurred."[81] The paralegal uses causation analysis in any fact pattern. In evaluating the client's story the paralegal must find whether the injuries alleged would not have occurred *but for* the action of the defendant in the case. Proximate causation is often referred to as the *but for* test. Evaluate these short examples:

But for the defendant driving through a stop sign, the injured party would not have cracked his vertebrae in an accident.

But for a doctor's medical malpractice, the injured party would not have lost her eyesight.

But for a railroad company's failure to maintain its tracks, an accident injuring 100 passengers would not have occurred.

But for an airline failing to maintain engine supports, an engine would not have fallen off the airplane.[82]

Another way of approaching proof of causation is to look at whether the defendant in a negligence case is the *substantial cause,* the substantial factor in the production of injury. This test is particularly helpful when multiple defendants exist. Which individual is substantially responsible or the most responsible party? Which defendant, in a case of manufacture and design of a product, is primarily responsible for injuries caused by faulty engineering? Is it the manufacturer, the distributor, the retailer, or the inspector who failed to review the product correctly? The fact finder calculates responsibility to the extent of a defendant's involvement.

When evaluating a negligence case, paralegals should watch for case scenarios that may have intervening causes. Assume an individual is in a parking lot of a retail establishment. If he is assaulted in the parking lot, does a case of negligence exist? If so, who bears responsibility? Is it the security company, the individual who inflicted injuries on the victim, or the company that owns and is responsible for the parking lot facility? At first glance there appear multiple parties whom the plaintiff can sue. In this case of negligence, the defendants will urge that certain intervening and supervening causes mitigate their responsibility. Criminal activity is frequently cited as an intervening cause because it is usually unforeseeable.[83] Intervening and supervening causes break the chain of causation, destroying the nexus between your theory of action and a party to whom damages may be responsibly claimed. The *Second Restatement of Torts* defines these forms of intervention:

> An intervening force is one which actively operates in producing harm to another after the actor's negligent conduct or omission has been committed.[84]
>
> A superseding cause is an act of a third person or other force which by its intervention prevents the actor from being liable for harm to another and which its antecedent negligence is a substantial factor in bringing about.[85]

Causation is a factor considered during the initial investigation. It behooves the paralegal when collecting information and assimilating data to prepare a memorandum of facts and ideas that formulates a chain of causation. Look at this causal sequence in Figure 11.2. In a suit for medical malpractice against the doctor, has there been a superseding or intervening cause of negligence?

Weigh the causation in Figure 11.3. Does the juvenile's act break the chain of causation in the liability of the railroad? Should the railroad foresee such activities?

FIGURE 11.2
Causal Sequence in
Medical Malpractice

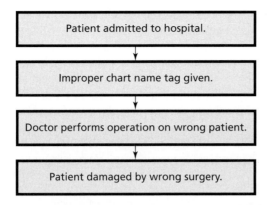

FIGURE 11.3
Causal Sequence with
Intervening Factor

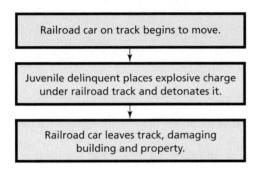

Defendants have been held liable for the consequences of any foreseeable intervening cause. However, acts of God, unpredictable in nature, relieve the originally responsible party from liability. Invariably courts and fact finders must assess who created the original situation that led to damage or injury. The question is one of negligence and the extent of obligation—whether the defendant's responsibility extends to interventions that are foreign to the risk the defendant created.

The Reasonable Person

Whether the accusation of negligence is reasonable largely depends on the standard of conduct or duty of care demanded. In finding a breach of due care, the fact finder discovers how the normal, reasonable person acts in similar circumstances. Negligence rests on finding liability when a person acts unreasonably and fails to foresee or predict conduct that most individuals would foresee as injurious to others. Who is the reasonable, ordinary, and prudent person? The *Second Restatement of Torts* at §283 suggests that a finding of negligence must be determined in a comparative sense with a "reasonable man under like circumstances."[86] Who is this ordinary man or woman? Professor A.P. Habert in his classic work, *Misleading Cases in the Common Law*, gives the following definition and standard:

> *He is an ideal, a standard, the embodiment of all those qualities which we demand of a good citizen . . . He is one who invariably looks where he is going, and is careful to examine the immediate foreground before he executes a leap or a bound; who neither star gazes nor is lost in meditation when approaching trap doors or at the margin of a dock; . . . who never mounts a moving omnibus and does not alight from any car while a train is in motion; . . . and will inform himself of the history and habits of a dog before administering a caress; . . . who never drives his ball until those in front of him have definitely vacated the putting green which is his own objective; who never from one year's end to another makes excessive demand upon his wife, his neighbors, his servants, his ox, or his ass; . . . who never swears, gambles, or loses his temper; who uses nothing except in moderation and even while he flogs his child is meditating only on the golden rule.*[87]

Looking for the reasonable person in most circumstances is a search for the average, not the superhuman or the divine.[88]

Conduct based on the average reasonable person serves as the evaluative standard. Moreover, conduct is further assessed in light of particular conditions and events. Determining how a car is reasonably driven is a far different exercise than finding what is reasonable conduct for an osteopath or a neurosurgeon. In the same light, what standard a lawyer will be held to in the representation of a client when charged with malpractice is governed by the reasonable standards of legal representation rather than the composite mental and intellectual attributes of a "super lawyer."

Similarly, differing expectations must exist regarding juveniles, the elderly, and those who represent that they possess a superior knowledge or professional standing. Who the reasonable person is—that is, determining what level of knowledge, skill, and mental capacity and what influence age and the severity and urgency of circumstances have upon this determination—must be assessed. In sum, the paralegal asks whether an ordinary, reasonable person would have acted the same way under similar sets of circumstances and conditions; the determination of a reasonable person depends on what the average person does or does not do. Ponder the reasonable person stereotype that exists for these occupations and roles:

- Heart transplant surgeon.
- Person of low intelligence.
- Police officer.
- Professor.
- Teacher.
- Paralegal practitioner.
- Negligence lawyer.
- Psychiatrist.
- Automobile driver.
- Psychologist.
- Public official.
- Manufacturer.
- Accountant.
- Engineer.
- Person of high intelligence.
- Architect.[89]

In short, the reasonable person is the average person, not the head of the class or the exceptional or best person. Reasonable means in the middle, according to what most can and do accomplish, not in the sense of intellectual and personal mediocrity but better stated as a character who does the best possible under the circumstances. In this regard, reasonable means the norm of living.[90]

Duty Owed: The Concept of Due Care

Before a finding of negligence, the questions of duty and obligation or due care must be fully analyzed. *Duty* or *due care* is defined as a legal obligation owed to another. "The general standard of negligence is the failure to exercise due care. Due care is the care a reasonably prudent person would exercise under the circumstances."[91] Generally, every person has a duty to each person and situation encountered, and this duty tells us to watch out for others, to not injure other people or their property or economic rights. Avoid unreasonable risks, mitigate accidents, and carry out one's business with the rights of others in mind. Due care can be gleaned from diverse situations and relationships:

- Doctor to patient.
- Teacher to student.
- Accountant to client.
- Attorney to client.
- Psychiatrist to client.
- Auto driver to pedestrian.
- Retailer to consumer.
- Manufacturer to retailer.
- Manufacturer to distributor.
- Distributor to consumer.
- Engineer to bridge builder.
- Architect to construction company.
- Police officer to private citizen.
- Public utility to environmental concerns.
- Department of transportation to highway rivers.
- Public transportation to riders.
- Builder to home buyer.
- Construction company to workers.
- Factory to employees.
- Grocery store to customers.
- Parent to child.
- Emergency medical personnel to accident victim.

Modern efforts to extend the obligation of due care are particularly evident in the *dram shop acts*—legislative enactments that make bars or taverns liable for the subsequent harm caused by their customers.

When formulating a case of negligence, the paralegal must identify relationships to discover the type of due care owed. A breach of due care lays the foundation for the negligence case. When duties and corresponding standards of conduct owed others have been breached, negligence is born. At the heart of the analysis are a duty and an obligation.

Breach can be discerned in the due care. Where and in what manner has the party failed? Where is the failure, the omission, the error, or other deed that results in specific injury to the plaintiff? A doctor who leaves a scalpel within the stomach wall of a patient cannot expect to avoid a finding of breach. How else could it be?

1. A physician–patient relationship exists, creating a duty.

2. An act was performed (surgery and leaving scalpel in stomach wall) that was negligent in light of what reasonable people do in a similar situation.

3. But for the act of the physician or because the physician was a substantial factor therein, an injury took place.

4. Damages ensued; the costs of correction are likely if not certain.

In this scenario, the practitioner discovers the path of negligence analysis. For every case before the paralegal, the a priori proof will be the existence of a duty, with that duty having a specific standard of care, whether for the average citizen or the heart surgeon. From this standard, one will evaluate conduct that harms another—the negligent act that we label a breach. With the breach established, there is one final step—causation—to show that the standard breached, by the party with a duty of due care, actually or proximately caused the injury in question, which in turn caused the resultant damages. Angela Holder's work *Medical Malpractice—Negligence in Post-Operative Care of a Patient* keenly lays out the diverse steps in negligence analysis.[92] More specifically, the elements of proof regarding physician malpractice edify this methodology:

> *The following facts and circumstances, among others, tend to establish the plaintiff's right to recover damages for negligent postoperative care:*
>
> - *Establishment of physician–patient relationship.*
> - *Condition leading to surgery.*
> - *Performance of surgery.*
> - *Onset of symptoms indicating complications.*
> - *Diagnosis of complication.*
> - *Treatment of complication.*
> - *Effects of complication.*
> - *Applicable standard of care and diagnosis and treatment of complication.*
> - *Defendant's failure to comply with applicable standard of care.*
> - *Proximate cause.*[93]

Again, remember the following legal sequence:

1. Existence of duty.

2. Standard of conduct.

3. Breach of conduct (as to the reasonable person's standard).

4. But for or substantial factor.

5. Damages.

The Pennsylvania Bar Institute offers some salient suggestions on the negligence action:

> *1. Who are the responsible parties?*
>
> *2. Duty, breach of duty, causation, damages?*
>
> *3. Is there more than one responsible party?*
>
> *4. Must an expert be contacted and retained to determine the identity of defendants?*
>
> *5. Is formal discovery likely to lead to additional defendants?*
>
> *6. Are there any contractual or statutory impediments to suit against one or more responsible parties?*
>
> *7. Is the statute of limitations a concern? Six months notice? Discovery rule?*
>
> *8. Do you have a potential conflict with any potential defendants?*

9. *Has a statute or regulation been violated?*

10. *If the case was referred to you, have any potential defendants been given a release?*

11. *Insurance coverage?*[94]

Special Problems: Owners and Occupiers of Land

Premises liability cases are a staple in tort litigation. Though not always comprising a negligence case, because injuries in the use of land can be based on warranty, contract, intentional tort, and even strict liability, premises liability cases graphically portray the differing standards of conduct and obligation within the negligence domain. Although all possessors and owners of land are required to exercise reasonable care in the maintenance of land, the extent of that duty or obligation depends on the occupier's status. Duty and the standard of due care owed will depend on how the individual occupier is classified.[95] Plaintiffs in a premises liability case can be characterized as follows: trespasser, licensee, or invitee.

Trespasser   A trespasser is a person who lacks both legal and equitable permission to enter property. If the trespasser is injured on the property, what legal obligation or standard of care is owed to the trespasser, if any? The *Second Restatement of Torts* defines a trespasser as "a person who enters or remains upon land in possession of another without a privilege to do so created by the possessor's consent or otherwise."[96] As a general principle, a trespasser has few rights in asserting damages for injuries caused by his or her intrusion on another's land. Nevertheless, the courts have been somewhat liberal in construing and creating unique designations of trespassers, such as *discovered* or *frequent.* When an owner or occupier of land knows that an individual continually trespasses on the land, the duty owed increases. If the landowner knows of a dangerous condition or peril and does not advise the discovered or frequent trespasser, liability may attach. There is ample precedential authority for a trespasser to have a right to collect damages under these circumstances.[97] Many courts now hold that a landowner has a duty of care to the discovered trespasser, including potential injuries from the operation of machinery. The landowner may also have a duty to warn of hidden dangers known to the landowner but not to the trespasser.[98]

Through a theory of *attractive nuisance,* children, while legally found to be trespassers, are granted preferential protection. Cases involving swimming pools and recreational facilities, which are inherently attractive to any child, and who lacks an understanding of peril or danger, prompt some jurisdictions to grant a higher protection than usually reserved for trespassers.[99] An example of a pleading regarding a child's injury when falling through a platform is shown in Form 11.17 on the accompanying CD.

Licensee   A licensee is any individual who has been given a privilege or a right to enter land. There are various categories of licensees. Visitors of employees are generally licensees when the purpose of their visit is not connected with the employment, even though the visitor gratuitously performs services beneficial to the employer. However, such visitors may obtain invitee status if they are requested to do work by the employer or by an employee with authority to make such a request. Such visitors may also be considered invitees when the employer permits or encourages them to enter to render services to the employees, as in the case of a caterer of food and drink or an insurance sales agent.

Employment seekers are usually held to be licensees, even if their quest is subsequently successful. However, if a visitor has responded to a general solicitation or has an appointment, she will be considered an invitee.[100]

What duty of care and standard of conduct is owed to licensees? Do social guests or neighbors visiting have a right to expect a higher standard than that afforded a trespasser? This sliding or ascending scale of legal responsibility illuminates negligence analysis. In the case of licensees, a higher protection, a more demanding standard of care, is expected from the landowner. Form 11.18 on the accompanying CD illustrates a complaint, petition, or declaration filed by a social guest injured by a sliding glass door.

Invitee   Invitees are afforded the highest level of personal protection in a premises liability case and simultaneously impose the highest standard of care on the landowner. An owner or occupier of property owes invitees protection from willful or wanton acts and has the obligation to keep the premises in reasonably safe condition. "Owners or occupiers owe invitees the additional duty of inspecting for and warning of dangerous conditions that the owner or occupier knew or should have known of."[101] Business establishments, as doors open, invite in the public. Because of this economic interchange, the standard of conduct, the standard of care, and the duty owed to the public are much higher than those owed a trespasser. Most of us have seen the doctrine in action. The sign on the floor that states "slippery when wet" or warning signs regarding dangerous conditions from a construction site or remodeling project evidence the responsibility that landowners have to invitees: to warn of potential harms.

Negligence Pleadings

The legal theory of negligence encompasses many actions, facts, and circumstances. A paralegal must evaluate fact patterns to determine whether multiple remedies and causes of action can be claimed. In cases of multiple defendants, one party may be acting intentionally while another may be acting in a negligent way.

 Negligence pleadings must reflect the plethora of potential causes and parties. Form 11.19 on the accompanying CD is a negligence pleading involving contractors and employees. The complaint outlines a breach of the standard of due care owed by an automobile driver. Note the particular pleading language:

> Driver was negligent in failing to keep a proper lookout and in failing to take, or attempt to take, reasonable avoidance action, or any avoidance action whatsoever . . . and otherwise failed to act prudently under the circumstances, all of which negligence and carelessness constituted the proximate cause of the collision.

Further discussion of negligence will be found in our examination of product liability and personal injury litigation.

STRICT LIABILITY

The intentional and negligent aspects of tortious conduct have been examined. The intentional tort requires an intentional deed—a wish for a specific end or result—whereas the negligent tort witnesses harm resulting from accident, carelessness, or disregard for the reasonable rights of another's person or property.

In cases of strict liability, a party who is injured will win the case, despite the issue of fault. It is the inherent dangerousness of the activity that imputes liability regardless of intention. Certain types of conduct and activities are deemed so inherently dangerous to the community that any resulting damages will result in strict liability. In the case of intentional tort, the party alleged to have committed an intentional act is found at fault for the intentional act—primarily because the end result was intended. In the case of negligence, fault is grounded in a factual and legal determination that a person did not meet or exceed a minimum standard of conduct under a duty owed to another party. By contrast, in a case of strict liability, the question of fault takes a back seat to the "the natural risk that occurs in certain economic behaviors that will result in liability no matter what."[102] From another vantage point, it is the product that contains defects; it is the product design that causes the harm. By contrast, in negligence cases the plaintiff must prove that the owner of the product misuses it or causes the injury. In strict liability, it does not matter what the owner or player does—the product itself will cause the injury. "Modern complexities, however, frequently make it very difficult for plaintiff to establish this. This is particularly so because he is usually at a relative disadvantage because the manufacturer has greater access to expertise, information, and resources. Imposing strict liability relieves plaintiff of the burden of proving fault."[103]

The basis of liability in any event "applies to anyone who sees any product in a defective condition unreasonably dangerous to the user or consumer."[104] But strict liability situations are rare when compared to intentional torts and negligence. Strict liability principles are usually relevant in these circumstances:

- Trespassing animals and livestock.
- Dangerous domestic animals.

WILMA PEGGY CARLIN V. SUTTER COUNTY
13 CAL.4TH 1104, 920 P.2D 1347, 56 CAL.RPTR.2D 162 (1996)

Prescription drug user brought products liability action against drug manufacturer for failure to warn about known or reasonably scientifically knowable dangerous propensities of drug. The Superior Court, Sutter County, Perry Parker, J., sustained manufacturer's demurrer without leave to amend. User petitioned for writ of mandate. The Court of Appeal, 46 Cal.App.4th 154, 38 Cal.Rptr.2d 576, issued writ. Manufacturer sought review. The Supreme Court, Mosk, Acting C.J., held that (1) user stated cause of action for strict liability premised on failure to warn, and (2) user stated cause of action for breach of warranty premised on failure to warn.
Affirmed.

- Activities that can be characterized as abnormally dangerous.
- Explosive and blasting activities.
- Defective products.

Liability is imposed even if not intended, if the tortfeasor did not act carelessly or negligently, and if there are no indications of fault or culpability. American jurisprudence has generally accepted the principle that in these cases "and if he or she fails to do so, he or she is absolutely liable for damages which are the natural consequence of its escape."[105] Form 11.20 on the accompanying CD includes a case of a captive wild animal that inflicts injury. In this complaint, if the plaintiff is able to show that the defendant was aware of these dangerous propensities, a strict liability action might be upheld.

Yet these traditional strict liability examples, while still less than generous, are evolving rather liberally. Most American jurisdictions have liberalized the strict liability concept, holding that any product that is defective and unreasonably dangerous provides a basis for strict liability argument. The *Second Restatement of Torts* holds,

> *(1) One who sells any product in a defective condition unreasonably dangerous to the user or consumer or to his property is subject to liability for physical harm thereby caused to the ultimate user or consumer, or to his property, if (a) the seller is engaged in the business of selling such a product, and (b) it is expected to and does reach the user or consumer without substantial change in the condition in which it is sold.*
>
> *(2) the rule stated in Subsection (1) applies although (a) the seller has exercised all possible care in the preparation and sale of his product, and (b) the user or consumer has not bought the product from or entered into any contractual relation with the seller.[106]*

The expansion of the strict liability doctrine has witnessed interesting results. A Pennsylvania Supreme Court decision illustrates how product strict liability theory could not be extended to *services.* In *Podrat v. Codman-Shurtleff, Inc.,*[107] a patient suffered injury when the tip of a pair of forceps broke off during back surgery. The court, citing the *Restatement,* denied a strict liability basis because the hospital delivered a service, not a product. Cases involving tires, lawn equipment, toasters, and other consumer goods are clearly defined as products.

WORKERS' COMPENSATION: A FORM OF STRICT LIABILITY

Workers' compensation is a legislative attempt to supplant traditional tort litigation with an employer–employee plan of compensation. Regardless of who is at fault, the compensation will be paid if an employee is injured on the job. Employees injured as a result of activities performed during the scope of employment need only demonstrate that their injuries were work-related, were caused during the scope of employment, and occurred while they performed the normal scope of employment. A worksheet collecting information for a compensation claim zeroes in on these issues in Form 11.21 on the accompanying CD.

FIGURE 11.4
Example of Workers'
Compensation

Source: Bureau of Workers' Disability Compensation, *An Overview of Workers' Compensation in Michigan,* Table 1 (2000), available at http://www.michigan. gov/documents/cis_bwuc_ over698_30939_7.pdf.

Specific Loss Schedule	Weeks	Specific Loss Schedule	Weeks
Thumb	65	Other toes	11
1st finger	38	Hand	215
2nd finger	33	Arm	269
3rd finger	22	Foot	162
4th finger	16	Leg	215
Great toe	33	Eye	162

Workers' compensation is clearly at odds with the common law because historically work-related injuries were subject to traditional tort litigation. The litigants assessed the negligent conduct of the employer, such as providing unsafe tools and equipment, a dangerous work environment, and a general failure to give warnings of dangers to which employees were entitled, and then deduced whether a meaningful case was possible. Today these historic means have been fully replaced by a strict liability program known as workers' compensation; the strict liability basis means that an injury will be compensable in the workplace regardless of who is at fault. Statutory language that evidences this strict liability might be as follows:

1. *An employee who receives a personal injury arising out of and in the course of employment by an employer who is subject to this act at the time of the injury, shall be paid compensation as provided in the act. In a case of death resulting from personal injury to the employee, compensation shall be paid to the employee's dependents as provided in this act. Time of injury or date of injury as used in this act in the case of a disease or in the case of an injury not attributable to a single event shall be the last day of work in the employment of which the employee was last subjected to the conditions that resulted in the employee's disability or death.*

2. *Mental disabilities and conditions of the aging process, including but not limited to the heart and cardiovascular conditions, shall be compensable if contributed to or aggravated or accelerated by the employment in a significant manner.*

3. *An employee going to and from his work, while on the premises where the employee's work is to be performed and within a reasonable time before and after his working hours, is presumed to be in the course of his or her employment.*[108]

Because of this legislative language, injuries on the job, from broken bones to lung disease, are statutorily computed in the compensation formula.

In some narrow circumstances, the employer operates with a dual persona—being both employer and employee. When this occurs the claimant has the option of either the workers' compensation action or a civil remedy by lawsuit. A schedule of benefits is provided under all American jurisdictions, an example of which is shown in Figure 11.4.

A paralegal's primary concern in the claimant interview for workers' compensation must be whether an injury exists and whether the injury is related to the work environment. Many workers' compensation cases can be negotiated to settlement in advance of the hearing if the parties act reasonably. If settlement is not possible, jurisdictions provide a hearing system with judicial referees to hear cases. A case that cannot be settled usually requires a petition or another documentation to request that hearing. An example of a petition for a hearing is outlined in Form 11.22 on the accompanying CD.

Doctors and other health specialists may submit their findings in writing and are made part of the hearing record. Check local rules. Negative decisions of the hearing board from either a defense or plaintiff perspective are not final and can be the subject of judicial review. Defense counsel may wish to evaluate a claimant's entire file. In this case, an authorization for release should be completed. (See Form 11.23 on the accompanying CD.)

THE PARALEGAL IN PERSONAL INJURY PRACTICE

The law of torts provides fertile ground for paralegal involvement in personal injury litigation. Personal injury cases develop in a host of situations: from traffic to hospitals, from stores to parking lots. Remember that a tort is harm against any person. Remember also the harm that is caused can be done in an intentional way, in a negligent way, or even without fault under strict liability analysis. Closely aligned to these multiple approaches are actions based on contract or warranty that plead specific damages. In personal injury practice, the following legal actions are likely:

- Automobile accidents: intentional or negligent conduct, strict liability.
- Defective products: intentional or negligent conduct, strict liability.
- Defective design of a building or structure: intentional or negligent conduct, strict liability.
- Public carrier negligence in the maintenance of planes, trains, and buses: intentional or negligent conduct, strict liability.
- Medical malpractice cases: intentional or negligent conduct, strict liability.
- Professional malpractice cases: intentional or negligent conduct, strict liability.

All of these scenarios are common in the world of the personal injury paralegal; remember that it is imperative that the processes of client interview, fact gathering, and case analysis be both timely and comprehensive. The initial obligations of a paralegal in a personal injury case are to calculate the damages, to allocate liability and responsibility, and to collect the necessary information to proceed with settlement or litigation. The personal injury paralegal's principal duty "is to screen clients for the attorney without necessitating the attorney's interaction. Depending on individual firm policy, the paralegal may make the 'first cut' when a person first contacts the office seeking legal redress."[109]

Personal injury litigation foretells an extremely bright future, with little reason to believe the opportunities will wane. Given the complexities of our medical system, the complexity of product design, the compression of drivers and road space, and the pace and intensity of modern living, it is unlikely that personal injury practices will dissipate.[110] Critics have labeled this activity as the "litigation explosion." Attorneys asserting such claims portray these actions as the simple affirmation of plaintiffs' rights. Whether a crisis exists is open to argument.[111] Most medical professionals reach the crisis conclusion. Negative caricatures of lawyers being ambulance chasers add to the crisis mentality. Dr. Robert J. Flemma, in his article *Medical Malpractice: A Dilemma in the Search for Justice,* delivers a unique perception:

> The rise in the number of malpractice claims is not solely a creation of the lawyers' ingenious advertising. Medicine itself has contributed to the problem: As the scientific aspects of medicine exploded, the physician became identified as a medical scientist. Mastery of scientific knowledge and technology led to many physicians apothesizing themselves and their profession. This unfortunately is a double-edged sword. Lost was the humility of imprecise knowledge and acquired was a hubris of technology. Physicians had been seduced into thinking that mastery of science and technology made them masters of the patient.[112]

While some sympathy should be reserved for the medical profession, these professionals often create their own state in life. For example, medical hospitals frequently display arrogance in malpractice cases and engage in a continuous cover-up or aggressive delay tactics. The fact of the matter is that medical institutions and medical professionals are "responsible for the negligence that causes serious personal injury and death within their walls. Some hospitals create an environment in which medical negligence thrives."[113]

That tension exists between lawyers and doctors is undeniable. Paralegals must be prepared for a certain level of antagonism between these professional groups. Carry out the role with extreme professionalism.

Because personal injury litigation calls for extraordinary organizational skill, forms, documents, checklists, and pleadings remain central components. Review Chapter 9, which outlines the investigative aspects of a civil case and includes much of the material referred to in this commentary.

The Initial Interview

At the initial interview the advocate determines the merit of the case at hand.[114] Using forms and documents, such as the checklist shown in Form 11.24 on the accompanying CD, is important in this early quality control. Gather as much information as possible, and be detailed and accurate in your presentation to the attorney. Master the parties, remedies, and potential defenses in an action. With your client, be confident, but always cautious, in his or her integrity and persuasiveness. The Michigan Institute of Continuing Legal Education gives realistic advice:

> *Perhaps more so than any other area of law, the client in a personal injury case can make the difference between winning and losing or between winning and winning big. Is your client one a jury will like and relate to? This is a very important factor in assessing your case. You want your client to create a favorable impression at trial. Evaluate him at the outset with an eye toward how much work will be required to emphasize his good traits and minimize his bad ones.*[115]

Setting the Fee

Attorneys set fees, but paralegals assist with the particulars. In most cases of personal injury, a contingent fee is the appropriate method of determining charges. Written contingent fee representation agreements are required for any contingent fee under the Code of Professional Responsibility as well as state ethical rules.[116] Two examples of attorney representation agreements are on the accompanying CD. First, a sliding scale percentage based on the amount and extent of litigation is shown in Form 11.25; and second, Form 11.26 mirrors a standardized representation agreement for a percentage of the recovery with a caveat that no fee is payable if unsuccessful. If after the initial consultation, counsel has decided not to represent the client, a courteous response outlining the refusal ensures goodwill and a possibility of future work (see Form 11.27).

Obtaining Authorizations

All personal injury cases require proof of medical, economic, or other compensatory damages. This requires signed authorizations that permit release of medical records, a subject covered in some detail in Chapter 9. Another example of an authorization for release of medical records is outlined in Form 11.28 on the accompanying CD. Releases for wages, IRS records, government benefits, and financial affairs may also be necessary. Another version that more narrowly highlights medical files and history is reproduced in Form 11.29. For employment history and documentation, use Form 11.30. Finally, to verify income, assets, and liabilities, copies of tax returns should be solicited (see Form 11.31).

Tactical Considerations

Paralegals keep track of multiple issues, and attorneys have come to expect that these professionals will adhere to the calendar. In any type of litigation, the paralegal must be attentive to both substantive and procedural issues. The following are a few examples.

Statute of Limitations

Is the right to file a cause of action ready to expire or has it expired? Most American jurisdictions have a two-year period for personal injury litigation.

Conflicts of Interest

A lawyer who takes a case with either an actual or a potential conflict of interest has opened the possibility of ethical discipline. Imputed conflicts resulting from employment changes are a common dilemma for personal injury litigators.

Multiple Representation

To the dismay of most attorneys, clients are not always satisfied with the initial representation of a given attorney. Therefore, clients shop for new attorneys to represent them. Paralegals must be aware that it is an ethical violation to snatch up disgruntled clients' cases without the consent and release of the former attorney. Communicate with previous counsel to prevent conflicts. See Form 11.32 on the accompanying CD.

Meritorious Claims

At times lawyers bring suit for frivolous claims—cases that are utterly disingenuous and without merit. Paralegals must resist becoming participants in a known frivolous action. The rules of civil procedure at both the state and federal levels have substantial penalties for filing actions that are totally lacking in merit, though critics of the litigation explosion rail against a system that does not apply these proscriptions. The decision as to whether a case is frivolous is left to the attorney, but a paralegal may not be a knowing party to a suit that is filed for vexatious purposes or pure harassment. (See the discussion under the ethical analysis in Chapter 2.)

Whether a case has merit is a factual and legal thicket. Even cases having remote potentiality for victory may still have merit. Merit should not be equated with the majoritarian view because minority positions in law sometimes evolve into fixed law. And merit also relates to viability as to collection. What value is a case without the slightest chance of collection? Merit ties itself to economic viability. Merit must also consider human motivations and questions of personal integrity. Stephen Sugarman argues that the culture of litigation has changed dramatically over the last century, and suing is no longer second-guessed by the masses:

> *In some quarters, accident victims today are viewed as too aggressive, too selfish, too greedy, and so on. But this point of view may well fail to constrain litigation, even if the victim perceives it. Perhaps the greater "individualism" of our society is relevant here. Perhaps the concentration of our population in larger, more anonymous urban areas is as well. The media may also have played a role: In recent years, newspapers, popular magazines, and TV have appeared to give much greater attention to personal injury cases and the large awards made in some of them.*[117]

Auto Accident Cases

Auto accident work is a staple of the personal injury lawyer. Given the data about frequency, this legal practice will not run dry. Auto accident cases demand organizational and documentary skills. Paralegals should use multiple forms of documents, memoranda, and data sheets that outline accident fact patterns. Clients should be active players in the composition and content of these forms. These documents memorialize the facts in the auto accident. By requiring the client to actively participate, such as filling out specific documentation, the client begins to develop a stake in the outcome and learns about the process. The client "must now search for and verify details of the accident that have been vague and uncertain in his mind up to this point—names of specific individuals and places, correct addresses and times. By the time the client has pored over the data sheets and finally completed them, he will be impressed with the Herculean task he has undertaken for himself and in which he has involved his attorney."[118] Two forms regularly used as data sheets are provided in Forms 11.33 and 11.34 on the accompanying CD.

Ask the client to diagram the accident as remembered. Again, active participation will corroborate the client's facts and allow the paralegal to gauge the veracity and credibility of the client's story. This drawing can be compared with the official police accident report, which is part of the official case record. Police reports and diagrams are discussed fully in Chapter 9.

Many other reports arise during the accident investigation. Photographs of the accident scene play a critical role in case evaluation. Paralegals should develop strong relationships with both police photographers and private photographers who work as independent contractors. There is no better tool of historical reproduction than the photographic technique. A photography log may be useful to a paralegal. (See Form 11.35 on the accompanying CD.)

Other damages that can be proven in an accident case are loss of economic value, wages, or property. Documentation regarding these matters is fully discussed in Chapter 9.

Advocacy Approaches in the Auto Accident Case

In an automobile accident case, multiple remedies and causes of action may exist. The negligence action is not mutually exclusive but is traditionally the cause of action first selected. Traditional negligence law asserts that certain careless acts, a breach of due care, resulted in actual injury and damage. The person who runs a stop sign or a red light, falls asleep at the wheel, or is distracted away from the roadway, thereby causing injury, will be deemed to have breached the standard of care and conduct owed to others in the operation of an automobile. However, negligence is only one remedy available. Others include the following.

First Party Benefits   Under contemporary no-fault provisions, an insured in a contractual capacity with an insurance company may collect benefits for injuries arising out of the ownership, operation, or utilization of a motor vehicle.[119] Insurers subsequently will subrogate one another based on fault questions.

Intentional Torts   Individuals who display conduct in excess of carelessness may do so intentionally. Although this situation is rare, cases of the intentional use of a vehicle to cause harm to another, inflicting bodily injury, destruction to property, or other intentional harm have occurred. Intentional tort theories such as assault, battery, wrongful death, and intentional infliction of mental duress may serve as alternative actions.

Underinsured or Uninsured Benefits A case involving substantial damages frequently looks to the injured party's own policy, which has provisions for underinsured and uninsured motorists' coverage. When the tortfeasor's policy limits do not adequately compensate the injury, the injured policy holder may seek damages under his or her own policy. Collection of underinsurance or uninsured motorists' proceeds is generally a cumbersome affair. Often the plaintiff's carrier will insist on a right to consent to any settlement, under the tortfeasor's own policy, before agreeing to any payment of underinsured or uninsured benefits. If consent is withheld without a justifiable reason, an action for bad faith, which most policies describe, may be available to the victim. The plaintiff's attorney is stuck in a sort of legal limbo because the attorney needs the consent of his client's insurer before entering any agreement with the defendant's company. Oddly, insurance companies use each other to avoid payment or at least hope to minimize the amount of payment. The equitable remedy of an injunction may prod the companies to pay the claim. See Form 11.36 on the accompanying CD. Paralegals who work in the auto negligence area will spend significant time with insurance companies.[120]

In general, the best policy is one marked by professionalism and courtesy. Because most auto litigation eventually is settled, the paralegal must possess and refine correspondence skills. A letter to an insurance company advising it of representation under an auto claim is outlined in Form 11.37 on the accompanying CD.

If the insurance company cannot be determined, the attorney also has a right to correspond directly with the tortfeasor. Form 11.38 on the accompanying CD requests the defendant/tortfeasor to have his or her insurance company contact the attorney and paralegal directly. In the case of first party benefits, a letter to the insured's carrier is appropriate. Form 11.39 includes a request for all benefits to which the attorney's client may be entitled. To determine the scope and amount of coverage available to the tortfeasor under his or her policy, use Form 11.40. Paralegals should be aware that information about policy coverage is often hard to get before formal discovery and is privileged in some jurisdictions.

Unfortunately some insurance companies stonewall requests. Follow-up letters that substantiate the record, especially in cases of future bad faith litigation, are essential. A short example is provided in Form 11.41 on the accompanying CD.

Before filing any lawsuit, the injured party and the tortfeasor, represented by the insurance company, should enter settlement discussions. A letter opening up such a dialogue is drafted in Form 11.42 on the accompanying CD.

Settlement Tactics

Paralegals will regularly help attorneys compile and draft settlement demand letters. A settlement demand letter, if done properly, can be a comprehensive document outlining damages, medical reports, expert opinions, legal theories, and mathematical calculation of an award desired. A typical demand letter usually includes these sections:

- Factual summation.
- Statement of medical conditions.
- Statement of economic damages.
- Case decisions and respective awards.
- Damages.

The settlement demand letter should be submitted with a cover letter soliciting negotiation in advance of formal litigation. (See Form 11.43 on the accompanying CD.)

Paralegals will find that responses from insurance companies are often evasive, delayed, and even insulting after submission of the demand letter. On the other hand, insurance companies are exposed to every imaginable demand—some beyond measure and significantly fraudulent. There is a culture of general resistance built by years of mistrust.

In all aspects of insurance practice, there is prodding, cajoling, and repetitive, insistent inquiry on the facts and merits. Insurance practice can be very frustrating work. An example of a follow-up letter is shown in Form 11.44 on the accompanying CD.

Sometimes a response or counteroffer may be offered, and it will likely be less than the client would authorize. Pursue the matter vigorously. Send another letter that appreciates the offer or takes issue with the quality of the offer. Put the insurance company on notice about good faith and its failure to act reasonably in the resolution of a claim. These negative facts often later bear positive fruit for a victim of an auto accident case. Regardless, the paralegal must continue to maintain a professional demeanor and relationship with the insurance company.

If the claims adjuster is unresponsive, send a certified or registered letter to the claims adjuster's supervisor or manager. Eventually some response to the demand letter will be forthcoming. Predictably the amount requested will never be the amount agreed to. Form 11.45 on the accompanying CD has been designed to reflect the natural give and take in the negotiation process. Proponents of reasonable demand letters argue that if a demand is close to a reasonable projection, the insurance company will provide a less than absurd counteroffer. However, most auto negligence attorneys have come to the conclusion that no matter what one requests or demands, counteroffers are usually paltry.

If your client and the tortfeasor reach an amicable settlement of the case, the insurance company will ask for a signed release that is either partial or general in nature. Be very cautious in accepting the language of insurance company releases. Releases that are too general should be avoided. Releases that are specific to the claim at hand and to the property in question are acceptable but narrow in design. See Form 11.46 on the accompanying CD.

General releases are effective for all parties to an action. A joint tortfeasor release works for only the parties listed. An example is shown in Form 11.47 on the accompanying CD. If the client is satisfied with the resolution of the case and the releases will not cause a loss of any other rights or interests with other parties, the paralegal should correspond with the insurance company.

Upon receipt of the settlement check for damages, certain fees and expenses must be paid in the disbursement process for doctors, attorneys, and other incidental charges. A draft letter like that in Form 11.48 on the accompanying CD explains the disbursement from the law office regarding a medical examination fee.

The client must also fully understand the disbursement process. A settlement disbursement sheet with an enclosed letter is provided for the paralegal's review in Form 11.49 on the accompanying CD. A signature on the settlement disbursement sheet is necessary to ensure that the client has a full and knowledgeable understanding of the disbursements. This also protects the lawyer from any later assertions of unethical conduct.

If the auto accident goes to litigation, pleadings preparation will be necessary. See the examples sprinkled throughout this chapter

THE PARALEGAL AND MEDICAL MALPRACTICE CASES

The Legal Landscape

As in auto accidents, medical malpractice cases may be based on multiple remedies and causes of action from negligence to intentional tortious conduct, from theory of contract to product liability principles. A dramatic explosion for medical malpractice claims has occurred in the last century.[121]

The cause of this increased litigiousness is the subject of considerable debate. Is the rise tied to a lowering standard of medical skill and proficiency? Is it increased sophistication in the practice of medicine or greater sophistication in medical science? Is it increased professional expectations on the part of the profession and the public alike? Or is it that medicine and the doctor–patient relationship have adopted a business approach that leads to a cold and calculated contractual relationship? Can the doctor–patient relationship be portrayed as follows?

> ... [A] commercial for a car or a detergent in selling both a product and the lure of success and happiness, or just as a hairdresser in selling both a service and an aura of beauty. So the modern doctor selling both medical treatment and the expectation of the amorphous quality we call health ... health becomes a thing rather than a way of living, and the doctor becomes a purveyor (and the patient a consumer) of things—pills and procedures, rather than a participant in a way of relating.[122]

No one would disagree that there has been a substantial escalation in medical malpractice premiums for medical specialists. See the chart in Figure 11.5.

The Rand Corporation, through a study by Professor Patricia Danzon titled "The Frequency and Severity of Medical Malpractice Claims: New Evidence," attempts to provide empirical evidence on the staggering growth of malpractice actions. The Rand report generally finds that

FIGURE 11.5
**Malpractice
Premium Growth
Rates, 2001–2002**

Source: U.S. General
Accounting Office.

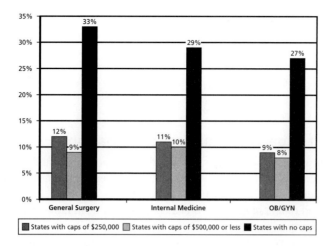

efforts to halt the escalation of malpractice claims have been ineffectual and that insurance premiums for medical professionals are not closely aligned to the economic reality of medical practice. Various factors were studied leading to the perception that malpractice is out of control:

- Growth rate in the last two decades.
- Number of claims filed.
- Availability of nonlegal/nontort sanctions for medical incompetency.
- Urbanization.
- Patient conditions.
- The nature of the doctor–patient relationship.
- The number of elderly people.
- The number of lawyers.

The summary conclusion about the data includes this finding:

> *However, it is worth noting that on average, severity has increased at almost twice the rate of inflation of consumer prices over the last decade. Thus, without further statutory controls, the income of successful malpractice claimants—or at least some subset of them—will continue to rise relative to the income of the population as a whole and relative to the income of other accident victims who are not compensated through the tort system. The optimal structure of tort awards therefore warrants further attention.*[123]

Clearly a crisis mentality exists in the medical profession. The medical establishment labels this legal onslaught as unjustified and spurred on by leeching lawyers and their feigned clients. Contrary to public opinion, this antagonism between the two camps is a relatively recent phenomenon. New York Court of Appeals Judge Judith Kaye puts the crisis in historical perspective:

> *That certainly was true during the decades that health care—though always of critical importance in the lives of human beings—did not so consistently raise broad public policy issues affecting the course and direction of society as a whole. I've searched through many early volumes of our case reports, even into the present century, and find very few cases dealing with physicians at all. The idea of lawyers and health care providers as adversaries is a relatively modern phenomenon.*[124]

Paralegals can expect that medical malpractice will be costly and the most intricate type of litigation in personal injury practice. Hospitals, doctors, emergency room personnel, nurses, and other medical personnel treasure their reputations for competency. Legal judgments against these personnel reflect badly not only on the individuals but also on their employers and the profession at large.

Another aspect generating an even greater malpractice problem is the absence of uniform and national standards for medical practices. Part of the reason relates to medicine often being more gray than black and white, with alternative medical approaches often achieving similar ends. Some call for the establishment of practice guidelines—measuring sticks that allow uniform judgments.

Indeed, if standard-of-care guidelines were to develop, one might find them playing a central role in malpractice litigation. Courts might take independent judicial notice of guidelines, or at least expect the opposing experts to brief the importance of the guideline to the case. Clear guidelines would thus help rationalize litigation by providing standards for courts, which now have to rely on less than objective battles of experts.[125]

What is clear is that the medical profession still lacks a cohesive and uniform view on competent medical practice, and that legislative attempts to infuse reason into the process are just as inadequate. Caps, damage limitations, and inclusions and exclusions appear to be temporary bandages in a system under siege.[126]

The Role of Experts in Malpractice Litigation

Malpractice litigation slavishly depends on the testimony and findings of the expert witness class. "Malpractice cases are difficult and expensive pieces of litigation. You will almost always have to get expert testimony to establish negligence."[127]

Attorneys and others in the legal arena consult with legal nurse consultants because of their expertise in nursing and healthcare. The primary role of the legal nurse consultant is to evaluate, analyze, and render informed opinions on the delivery of health care and the resulting outcomes. See Figure 11.6 for a description of the role of legal nurse consultants in litigation.

Because of this reliance on experts, attorneys and legal professionals often use private, for-profit referral services to help them locate experts in specific fields. These expert referral services find and refer experts who match the attorneys' criteria for expert credentials, location, and experience. One company that has been referring experts since 1956 is The TASA Group (TASA standing for Technical Advisory Service for Attorneys). Their web site is shown in Figure 11.7, and you can visit them online at www.tasanet.com.

Experts are allowed easy access into courts of law. Historically this was not the case. The seminal question was whether the expert's field of testimony had "crossed the barrier of judicial acceptability" and whether the expert was qualified to give testimony in this field of expertise. The case of *Frye v. United States,*[128] a landmark ruling still adhered to in many states, laid out a clear standard:

> *Just when a scientific principle of discovery crosses the line between the experimental and demonstrable stages is difficult to define. Somewhere in this twilight zone, the evidential force of the principle must be recognized, and while the courts will go a long way in admitting expert testimony deducted from a well-recognized scientific principle or discovery, the thing from which the deduction is made must be sufficiently established to have gained general acceptance in the particular field in which it belongs.*[129]

FIGURE 11.6
Role of the Legal Nurse Consultant in Litigation

Source: American Association of Legal Nurse Consultants, AALNC Position Statement on the Role of the Legal Nurse Consultant as Distinct from the Role of the Paralegal and Legal Assistant. Available at: http://www.aalnc.org/hire/roll.cfm (retrieved January 30, 2007).

The following list of activities helps to distinguish the practice of legal nurse consulting:

- Facilitating communications and thus strategizing with the legal professional for successful resolutions between parties involved in healthcare-related litigation or other medical-legal or healthcare-legal matters.

- Educating attorneys and/or others involved in the legal process regarding the healthcare facts and issues of a case or a claim.

- Researching and integrating healthcare and nursing literature, guidelines, standards, and regulations as related to the healthcare facts and issues of a case or claim.

- Reviewing, summarizing, and analyzing medical records and other pertinent healthcare and legal documents and comparing and correlating them to the allegations.

- Assessing issues of damages and causation relative to liability with the legal process.

- Identifying, locating, evaluating, and conferring with expert witnesses.

- Interviewing witnesses and parties pertinent to the healthcare issues in collaboration with legal professionals.

- Drafting legal documents in medically-related cases under the supervision of an attorney.

- Developing collaborative case strategies with those practicing within the legal system.

- Providing support during discovery, depositions, trial, and other legal proceedings.

- Testifying at depositions, hearings, arbitrations, or trials as expert health care witnesses.

- Contacting and conferring with vendors to develop demonstrative evidence or to collect costs of healthcare services, supplies, or equipment.

FIGURE 11.7
**Homepage of
The TASA Group, Inc.**

Source: Used courtesy of
The TASA Group, Inc.
Available at: http://www.
tasanet.com.

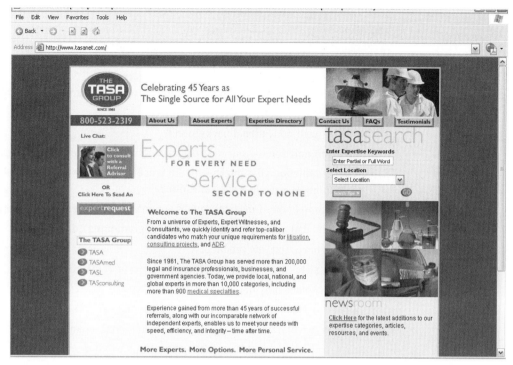

Frye once provided a series of benchmarks at the federal level, and as noted, most state jurisdictions followed these criteria. Determining whether evidence is reliable and has successfully engaged *Frye's* barrier of judicial acceptability depends on various factors. In general, experts and the field of their testimony are acceptable if these criteria are met:

1. The validity of the underlying scientific principle.
2. The validity of the technique or process that applies the principle.
3. The condition of any instrumentation used in the process.
4. Adherence to proper procedures.
5. The qualifications of the person who performs the test.
6. The qualifications of the person who interprets the results.[130]

The expanding array of scientific specialties, as well as those not so scientific, that are available as a source for testimony raises hard questions. Will courts require that the witnesses' opinions be reasonably based on trustworthy data? How far must judges inquire into the practice of other experts in the same field before allowing the trial witness to proffer an expert opinion? How much of the expert's supporting data will be received in evidence?[131]

In the late 1980s and into 2000, the U.S. Supreme Court altered the *Frye* legacy with a tumultuous series of decisions. Not all were happy with *Frye's* restrictiveness. The federal courts, by and through a pivotal ruling, *Daubert v. Merrell Dow Pharaceuticals, Inc.,*[132] have effectively made the *Frye* rule moot in their jurisdictions. *Daubert* has been the primary support of those hoping to achieve the admissibility of "sciences" once scorned. Strict reliance on the general consensus test of *Frye* is being replaced with a "more searching and flexible inquiry about the reliability and relevance of the offered evidence."[133] Under *Daubert*, judges are "gatekeepers" performing dual functions, screening "expert scientific testimony not merely to assure that the expert is qualified, but also to assure that the expert methodology is 'reliable.'"[134] Judges are to determine whether "the scientific evidence had sufficient testing, peer review, and publication."[135] *Daubert's* suggestions were toothless, and as a result, unpredictability at the lower courts became normal. It is questionable whether judges are even capable of performing the latter function.[136] Like it or not, until *Daubert* is modified, judges can take on an increasing screening role with respect to scientific evidence.[137]

Daubert's lenient and inconsistent results have generated enormous criticism. The U.S. Supreme Court's 1999 ruling in *Kumho Tire Co. v. Carmichael*[138] increased the gatekeeping role of the judge when it comes to the quality and content of expert evidence. Not only are the questions of qualification and field pertinent, but also the methodology behind the results testified to must be considered.[139] *Kumho* is a valiant attempt to banish a burgeoning "junk science" industry from the courtroom. Expert evidence should be primarily rooted in "real science"[140] that arises only from "careful and controlled experimentation."[141]

Whatever test applies, paralegals should scrutinize closely the expert's qualifications. Consider these factors:

1. What is your educational background?

2. At the completion of your medical studies, where did you serve your medical internship?

3. After completing your internship, did you engage in any postdoctoral studies or postgraduate training leading to a specialization?

4. Upon completion of medical studies and internship, where did you serve out your residency?

5. Have you had any postgraduate studies or continuing education?

6. Do you have a private practice?

7. In what states are you currently licensed and/or certified?

8. What hospitals do you have an affiliation with?

9. What professional organizations do you belong to?

10. Have you ever held an office in these professional organizations?

11. Have you ever received any honors as a result of your practice and profession?

12. Have you ever written any periodical articles or textbooks in your field of endeavor?

13. Have you ever held an academic appointment or done any college or university teaching?

14. Have you been found qualified to testify as an expert in court prior to this case?

15. Have you ever served as an expert in your field before a state, federal, local, or private agency?

16. Have you ever been appointed as expert by any one of the judges in this jurisdiction?[142]

For further information about experts, see Chapter 9.

Legal Theories in a Malpractice Case

Negligence

Often a cause of action for medical malpractice is grounded in negligence. Under negligence analysis, the requirement of a duty of care between a physician and patient is well established. A breach of that duty will depend on whether the doctor, physician, or other medical staff member has exercised a reasonable standard of care. Under usual circumstances, the standard of care will be that of an ordinary, diligent, and competent medical professional. The professional will be held not to the standard of a genius but to the average standard as most medical professionals would carry out their obligations. Here are some examples of malpractice:

- A physician may be considered negligent if she fails to hospitalize a patient when the standard of care indicates hospitalization is necessary.

- A physician may be considered to be in violation of his duty of care by his lack of diligence in attending to a patient.

- A physician may be considered in violation of her duty of care if she unjustifiably abandons or neglects her patient after sufficient notice, excuse, or mutual agreement.

- A physician may be considered to be in violation of his duty of care if he promises results that are not forthcoming, such as the side effects of the treatment prescribed or surgery performed.

- A physician may be considered in violation of her duty of care if she fails to explain or inform the patient of the nature of the proposed surgery and if she fails to obtain an intelligent consent to such surgery.[143]

Evaluate the awards in Figure 11.8.

Under a reasonable interpretation of facts and law, have these medical personnel failed? Have they acted reasonably? Have they neglected the types of performance reasonably expected of

FIGURE 11.8   **Large Malpractice Awards in California under MICRA**

Source: Californians Allied for Patient Protection, 1215 K Street, Suite 2015, Sacramento, CA 95814; http://www.micra.org/LargeAwardsUnderMICRA.pdf.

September 2003, San Francisco County
$70,000,000
Newborn with permanent mental retardation because of failure to diagnose a metabolic disease. The $500,000 award for past and future pain and suffering was reduced to $250,000 under MICRA.

December 2002, Alameda County
$84,250,000 total award
5 year-old boy with cerebral palsy and quadriplegia because of delayed treatment of jaundice after birth. The $750,000 award for noneconomic damages was reduced to $250,000 under MICRA.

October 2002, Contra Costa County
$59,317,500 total award
3 year-old girl with cerebral palsy as a result of birth injury.
The award included $100,000 in noneconomic damages for the child, $200,000 in noneconomic damages for the mother and $200,000 in noneconomic damages for the father.

January 1999, Los Angeles County
$21,789,549 total award
Newborn girl with cerebral palsy and mental retardation because of birth related injury.

October 1997, San Diego County
$25,000,000 total award
Boy with severe brain damage, spastic quadriplegia and mental retardation because too much anesthesia was administered during a procedure.

November 2000, San Bernardino County
$27,573,922 total award
25 year-old woman with quadriplegia because of a failure to diagnose a spinal injury.

July 2002, Los Angeles County
$12,558,852 total award
30 year-old homemaker with brain damage because of a lack of oxygen during recovery from surgery. The award included $250,000 in noneconomic damages for the plaintiff's husband and $676,921 for past and future household services.

July 1999, Los Angeles County
$30,800,000 total award
Newborn girl with cerebral palsy because of birth injuries.

April 1999, Orange County
$6,885,000 total award
Premature newborn girl with permanent blindness because of delay in treatment.

February 2000, Riverside County
$1,384,685 total award
39 year-old pregnant homemaker and mother who died because of misdiagnosis.
The $300,000 award for noneconomic damages was reduced to $250,000 under MICRA.

December 1999, San Francisco County
$50,239,557 total award
10 year-old boy with brain damage because of undiagnosed infection at birth.
The $324,000 noneconomic damage verdict was reduced to $250,000 under MICRA.

others in similar positions? In all medical malpractice negligence actions, a three-part analytical framework is needed:

1. What was the appropriate standard of care regarding the procedure in question?
2. Did the defendant meet this standard of care?
3. Was the defendant's failure to meet this standard a proximate cause of the plaintiff's injury?[144]

When is an incorrect diagnosis a negligent act? Is it negligent because another medical authority does not concur? What if the same symptoms can lead to multiple diagnoses?[145]

When evaluating a negligence action, reasonableness of action and general acceptability of the medical decision are the rules of measure. Tort law holds that a standard of conduct of the general practitioner of medicine is not that of the medical expert or the specialist, such as an orthopedic or neurosurgeon, but that of the general practitioner. General practitioners will be governed by standard medical practice "which the general medical community would follow based upon general information available. It is the practice of the majority of physicians, based upon their level of training and the standard textbook of medicine. These standards are incorporated into the rules and regulations of hospitals and in the explicit written instructions from drug manufacturers."[146] For expert witnesses in medical specialties, one must look to the average specialist—not the phenomenal exception to the rule of practice.

Professor Clark Havighurst of Duke University calls for contractual recognition of the expert standard of care. In a contract provision for the employment of a doctor, the following clause would be applicable:

> *The physician warrants that he or she possesses at least the skill and knowledge of a reasonably competent medical practitioner in the physician's specialty and undertakes to you that he or she will exercise that skill and knowledge in a reasonable and prudent manner in your case. In so doing, the physician may sometimes depart from practices customary among other physicians. Such departures shall not be deemed to breach the foregoing undertaking, however, unless they are expressly found to have been unreasonable and imprudent; evidence to support such a finding shall consist solely of the testimony of experts knowledgeable about scientific studies bearing on the appropriateness of the actions taken and about what, in light of all the circumstances including the cost of alternative measures, constitutes appropriate medical care.*[147]

Negligence in Contract

Recently an argument that malpractice cases should shift from tort actions to theories of contract has attracted considerable interest. Naturally any patient who seeks the medical assistance of a professional physician enters an express or implied contractual undertaking. Given the consent and other documents signed upon visitation, there is every reason to believe that an express contract exists. The characterization of the relationship is economic, and the appropriateness of the contractual remedy appears to have some strong intellectual and practitioner support.[148]

The emphasis in contract is clearer—an analysis of offers and promises: Did the physician deliver what was promised under the terms and conditions of the contract for services? A bit less emotional in design, this may be just what the system needs. Whether a contract remedy or a negligence analysis is more appropriate is a matter of academic dispute.[149]

Remedies in medical malpractice can be both in tort and in contract. Identify all potential defendants in this litigation and do not neglect ancillary medical personnel who may be involved in the malpractice. Allied medical personnel may include:

- Chiropractors.
- Anesthesiologists.
- Dentists.
- Paramedics.
- Nurses.
- Nurses' aides.
- Licensed practical nurses.
- Orderlies.
- Technicians.
- Lab personnel.
- Secretaries.
- Receptionists.
- Counselors.
- Medical consultants.
- Medical suppliers.
- Insurance personnel.
- Manufacturers of medical equipment and products.

ADR and Medical Malpractice

Never neglect alternative means of malpractice resolution. Indeed, various jurisdictions have mandated some informal review of any alleged malpractice before proceeding to the formal stage. In states like Pennsylvania, where medical specialists leave the state in droves, the traditional method of litigating medical malpractice may have seen its day. David Ruben urges his colleagues to consider arbitration before litigation:

> *It can be argued that traditional litigation has been ineffective in adjudicating medical malpractice claims because of disproportionate jury awards, inadequate or suspect expert testimony, and protracted court battles. Though physicians prevail in most jury verdicts, and thus vindicate their professional reputations, studies have estimated that approximately 40 percent of malpractice claims are without merit. The present system is incredibly expensive and inefficient and is largely based on subjective determinations of the jury.*[150]

The American Medical Association urges boards of arbitration that deliver nonbinding evaluations and recommendations or even binding judgments on the specific practices. Judicial review of the board's decisions will be based on administrative law principles rather than traditional civil and criminal reasoning.[151] Efforts to reform medical malpractice have included some of the following practices:

- Damage award caps.[152]
- Mediation panels and procedures.[153]
- Elimination of punitive damages.[154]
- Enforcement of collateral source rules, restricting double benefit.[155]

Paralegal Responsibilities in a Medical Malpractice Case

Pretrial activity in a medical malpractice case is quite demanding. Discovery and the acquisition of medical reports, records, and documents are essential paralegal functions. Sample letters requesting hospital records and other information are reproduced on the accompanying CD.

Authorizations/Releases

The following forms are on the accompanying CD:

    Form 11.50:   Hospital records.

    Form 11.51:   Hospital bills.

    Form 11.52:   Physician reports.

Discovery Requirements

Medical malpractice actions necessitate the discovery of hospital, staff, and institutional policies, procedures, and rules of conduct at the institution. The attorney and paralegal must gain access to "all the rules and regulations, bylaws, policies, procedures, and protocols of the defendant hospital and of its medical staff . . . also those policies about patient care, . . . including all instructions or standards related to their administration and performance."[156] Additionally, consultant reports of outside physicians must be obtained. Operation reports, anesthesia and recovery charts, if applicable, order sheets, laboratory reports, and other special examinations are components in the pretrial phase of a medical malpractice case. Paralegals who work in the malpractice area "must have a high degree of familiarity with the organization of the hospital record and the various parts that make up such a record. The observations of various medical personnel approaching the patient form a vital tool in attempting to reconstruct the patient's condition at any given time in the treatment (and therefore the correctness of the treatment) administered to the patient throughout the course of the hospital stay. For instance, the side-by-side comparison of a physician's notes and a progress record and the nurse's notes for the same given period of time can be of vital importance in the medical malpractice action, especially if there is a significant difference in the facts observed and reported in both sections of the record."[157]

As information is gathered, the calculation of medical costs and charges becomes more important. Medical expenses should be charted in a regular and uniform format. Some firms use a medical worksheet, an example of which is shown in Figure 11.9.

Proof of Pain and Suffering

A client's recollections and representations of his or her level of pain and suffering, discomfort, and permanent disability are useful both at the settlement phase and at trial. Tell the client to keep regular reports about any pain and anguish suffered. Also urge the client to keep a diary, highlighting states of depression, feelings of helplessness, and the results of any shock or trauma that affect his or her emotional outlook.

Proving damage claims relating to one's occupation, one's quality and enjoyment of life in the home, pain and suffering, and general trauma has historically been done by direct testimony. Of recent interest has been the use of video diaries, which chronicle extended periods in the normal living routine of a injured party. If a picture is worth a thousand words, what are 48 hours of video worth that intimately depict the many effects of injury?

In extreme cases of injury, defense attorneys claim such presentations are inflammatory or highly prejudicial. Excessive anguish may cause the court to construe prejudicial impact over

FIGURE 11.9
Example of a Medical
Worksheet

Client:			
Date of injury/incident:			
Outstanding medical expenses			
Facility/doctor	Date bill requested	Still in treatment?	Total due
Miscellaneous expenses			
Paid to:	For:	Date:	Total
Total of all medical expenses			

probative value. "Thus, films which show matters like the plaintiff repeatedly grimacing or yelling in pain or growling menacingly or uncommunicatively have not been admitted. If the court finds some portion of a videotape inadmissible, you should request permission to edit out the offensive portion and show the remainder."[158] Such videotapes are vigorously challenged because the opposition is not a party to their production, is suspicious of their content, and is aware of their obvious slant in presentation. This is particularly true in personal injury cases.[159] Day-in-the-life videos, such as those produced by B. and B. Enterprises (2 Half Mile Common, Westport, CT 06880), have been on the receiving end of serious legal challenges. In a case of medical malpractice, a videotape produced by B. and B. Enterprises was admitted into court. The hospital objected on the theory of prejudicial impact and, upon appeal, urged the court to overturn the damage finding. However, the court, in *Pisel v. Stamford Hospital*,[160] rejected the objection and, in its opinion, stated, "[A]fter examining the videotape with the above principles in mind, we agree with the trial court that the 'tape,' while not pleasant viewing, fairly presented to the jury Miss Pisel's condition and type of care she was required to receive."[161]

Companies that focus on the continuous agony of the plaintiff and adopt an overdone, tear-jerking approach in the guise of an objective appraisal of the plaintiff's injuries are to be shunned. Evaluate day-in-the-life videotapes with these criteria in mind:

- The film fairly depicts the daily activities of the plaintiff.
- The film demonstrates the plaintiff's adaptation to his or her injury.
- The film does not unduly distract the jury.
- The plaintiff who is the subject matter of the film can be cross-examined as to his or her self-serving portrayal on film—his or her conduct in the film.[162]

Other recommendations for the enlightened practitioner hoping to benefit from this demonstrative tool follow:

- Deal with a reputable filmmaker.
- Purge subjectivity in the videotape's production.

- Examine the videotape far in advance of litigation for editorial purposes.
- Disclose the content of the videotape during pretrial discovery.
- Summarize the technique or chronology used in the production of the videotape.
- Ensure honesty and accuracy; do not belabor and repeat the negative reality.
- Do not be cumulative in your approach.
- Afford opposing counsel the right to review the videotapes.
- Eliminate stipulations, if possible.
- Request cautionary or limiting instructions of the court.
- Prepare the videotape exhibits.
- Check jurisdictional rules.

The videotape as a form of demonstrative evidence has made substantial inroads into the litigation process.[163]

Psychological/Psychiatric Reports

Medical injuries often cause psychological and psychiatric damage. Collect any psychiatric or psychological reports that will help corroborate and verify the record.

Photographic Evidence

In cases involving specific physical injuries, photographs are an essential tool of proof. "A personal injury claim may last for more than a year, depending upon the applicable statute of limitations. Unless the client is permanently disabled or disfigured, many of his injuries will have disappeared by the time the case is brought to trial. Evidence of those injuries must somehow be preserved. There are two ways of doing this: maintaining tangible evidence such as casts, etc., and preserving injuries at the outset of the claim through photography."[164] Use the photo data tracking record at Figure 11.10.

Expert Reports

The credibility of any medical malpractice case will depend on whether expert physicians or other medical personnel will testify that the defendant in question did not adhere to the accepted skills and practice levels common in the professional community. Before proceeding with formal litigation, some outside assessment and review is necessary. An example of a medical report is shown in Figure 11.11.

Consent Forms

Informed consent plays a major role in a medical malpractice case. Its underlying theory is that the patient should have understood the dimensions and dynamics of the medical procedure to be performed and willingly consented. If the results were not acceptable or did not turn out as expected, the physician always relies on standardized forms confirming the patient's consent to the activity. The following standard must be proven by the physician for consent to be effective:

1. A fair explanation of the procedures to be followed, and their purposes, including identification of any procedures that are experimental.
2. A description of any attendant discomforts and risks reasonably to be expected.
3. A description of any benefits reasonably to be expected.
4. A disclosure of any appropriate alternative procedures that might be advantageous for the subject.
5. An offer to answer any inquiries concerning the procedure.
6. An instruction that the person is free to withdraw his consent and to discontinue participation in the project or activity at any time without prejudice to the subject.[165]

In cases of medical innovation and avant garde practice or medical therapy, standardized, preprinted documents can be subject to challenge. If the physician is unable to produce such

FIGURE 11.10
Example of a Photo Data Tracking Record

Case name: _____ Case number: _____

Exhibit number: _____ Photo number: _____

Firm: _____

Address: _____

Phone: _____

E-mail: _____

Attorney: _____

Client: _____

Incident location: _____

Time: _____

Date: _____

Individuals involved: _____

_____

Photographer: _____

Address: _____

E-mail: _____

Phone: _____

Years experience: _____

Used prior? _____

Available for testimony? _____

Photograph information: _____

Camera used: _____ Film/digital: _____

ISO number: _____ Number exposures: _____

Subject description: _____

_____

_____

Location: _____

Date taken: _____ Time taken: _____

Distance from subject: _____ Direction of camera: _____

If film: _____

Developing laboratory: _____

Time/date developed: _____

Film brand: _____ Speed: _____

Number of rolls:

acceptable consent documents, a medical malpractice case will be a more likely cause of action. Failure to provide evidence of informed consent can result in damages that include:

- Actual loss of income.
- Decrease in prospective earning capacity.
- Past and future medical expenses.
- Disfigurement or other damage to the plaintiff's body.
- Shortening of the plaintiff's life expectancy.
- Damage to family life and enjoyment of life.
- Past and future pain and suffering.
- Past and future fright, anxiety, and mental anguish.
- Appropriate wrongful death damages.
- Punitive damages when action is grounded in assault and battery.[166]

FIGURE 11.11

Example of a Medical Report

Dear Attorney _____:

I have carefully reviewed the material sent me concerning _____ and have discussed the contents with a colleague who is expert in both orthopedic surgery and rehabilitation medicine. As you have requested, I am now providing our perspective on the strengths and weaknesses of the case.

(1) Injuries to the acromioclavicular joints are divided into grades depending on the degree of rupture of the ligaments holding the joint together. _____ appears to have suffered a Grade III injury, involving complete rupture of all of the ligaments with physical separation of the clavicle and acromion process. As indicated by Dr. _____, the injury may be treated either conservatively or surgically, with the results being similar for each type of treatment in some studies (Dias et al., J. Bone Joint Surg. 69B: 719, 1987; Warren Smith and Ward, J. Bone Joint Surg. 69B: 715, 1987).

(2) In the series of patients described by Dias et al., all 53 patients with Grade III dislocation were treated by "broad arm slings for three to five weeks followed by mobilization of the shoulder. The purpose of the broad arm sling is to provide support and a minimal degree of immobilization for the affected shoulder. Although the type described by Dias et al. would include the type condemned by Dr. _____ as inadequate, only one of the patients with a painful subluxation was required to change her occupation, and the majority of the patients had a good outcome.

(3) Failure of management, defined as a poor cosmetic appearance of a persistently painful shoulder, did occur in about half of the patients managed conservatively. _____ experience was, therefore, not unique and cannot a priori be attributed to improper medical care. The surgical success of Warren Smith and Ward may have been somewhat better, but still left about 40% of the patients with a less-than-excellent result.

(4) One can question whether or not the outcome might have been somewhat better had rehabilitation therapy been begun sooner than seven weeks after _____'s accident. Given the fact that he appears to have made such good progress even after a somewhat long delay, however, this remains only a question.

(5) I and my consultant tend to agree with Dr. _____ that, as of _____, 20__, continued rehabilitation therapy was indicated. Assuming this was done, _____ may have made even more functional gains. Incidentally, Dr. _____'s opinion that "excision of a small portion of the distal clavicle" might help, appears to be supported in part by the work of Warren Smith and Ward.

(6) The exact extent of the functional deficit claimed by _____ is unclear from the material provided to me (assessments of Drs. _____ and _____). Should you elect to develop this case, a more detailed description of both subjective and objective findings present would be very helpful—that is, manual muscle and range of motion testing, dynamometer recordings of shoulder strength and range of motion, and electromyography if possible. However, even if the functional deficits are pronounced, each side may be able to mobilize both literature and expert opinion to support its contentions.

Sincerely yours,

Medical Malpractice Pleadings

Medical malpractice complaints may allege causes of action grounded in tort or contract or, for that matter, product liability principles. Assault and battery, classic intentional torts, may be alleged depending on the circumstances. Products and services that are defective in design, especially evident in cases of implantation, transplantation, blood filtering, and other technological advances, may be pertinent to the complaint's allegations. A full complaint that represents a standard medical malpractice action is shown in Form 11.53 on the accompanying CD.

In conclusion, medical malpractice is an expensive and highly contentious form of litigation. Consumers are regularly victimized by medical professionals. Paralegals and attorneys play a crucial role in the world of malpractice. Whether the remedy can be found in contract or in tort, or whether it is sought through a suggested avenue of tort reform or other reform-oriented compensatory scheme, restoration of the victim of malpractice is the chief aim of both the paralegal and attorney.[167]

THE PARALEGAL AND THE PRODUCT LIABILITY CASE

Theories of Litigation

It is undeniable that defective products cause personal injury. Product liability law provides a means to secure damages for injuries. Product liability litigation delivers various theories of action, including:

- Warranty litigation.
- Lemon law litigation.
- Consumer safety litigation.
- Product defect and design that causes economic losses and damages.
- Breach of implied warranties.
- Breach of warranty for a particular purpose.

Many of the avenues listed here also find root in the law of contracts and the Uniform Commercial Code. (See Chapters 5 and 6.)

Product liability is a multidimensional practice for lawyers and paralegals. The advocate might argue any of the following theories:

1. The product is negligent.
2. The product as designed and supplied is a breach of contract.
3. The product is inherently dangerous resulting in strict tort liability.
4. The product is in breach of express warranty.
5. The product is in breach of implied warranty.
6. The product is in breach of a warranty for a particular purpose.
7. The product is so defectively designed that the injury it caused could be classified as an intentional act.
8. The product is a breach of contractual agreement.
9. The product is a "lemon."

With product liability cases, courts balance the rights of consumers and business enterprises; they view clauses and provisions in express contracts; they deal with equitable principles of unconscionability and implied warranty and an abundance of other legal positions.

At the heart of every product liability case is proof of defectiveness. The *Second Restatement of Torts* at §402(a) holds that liability arises when a product is "in a defective condition that is unreasonably dangerous to persons or property."[168] In addition, statutory efforts to enunciate product defects have been drafted. A product action is

> *[B]ased on any legal or equitable theory of accountability brought for or on account of death or injury to person or property caused by or resulting from the manufacture, construction, design, formula, development of standards, preparation, processing, assembly, inspection, testing, listing, certifying, warning, instructing, marketing, advertising, packaging, or labeling of a product or a component of a product.*[169]

Statutory language allows consumers to use "any legal or equitable theory" to be made whole.[170]

Interpretation and judicial application of product liability principles have been mixed. Some jurisdictions tend to be consumer friendly, whereas others adhere to traditional principles of privity and contract. In any event there is great variety on how jurisdictions deal with product litigation. Patrick Lee, in his humorous analysis of product liability claims titled *Product Liability: The Great Question and Answer Search,* queries,

> *Think of these three categories: (1) the occurrence of an act and the behavior of the plaintiff; (2) the technology of the product and the behavior of the manufacturer; (3) the legal principles. This analysis applies whether you represent the plaintiff or the defendant. What you present in support of liability and support of defenses against liability will flow from an analysis of these three categories. By sorting the facts, you will understand which category will be most important.*[171]

Processing the Product Liability Case

Interview checklists that seek to confirm the product liability are beneficial. (See Form 11.54 on the accompanying CD.) Assume the client has been injured in the operation of a machine on an assembly line. The injuries are substantial and have led to complete and total disability. The client comes to the law firm seeking a remedy for such injury. Human factors must be considered in terms of the design interaction between human and machine. If the plaintiff can show that the engineering design and structure of the machine were not conducive to safe operation, there is an excellent chance of winning a product defect or design case. Attorneys must use experts who will give testimony, evaluate, and make reports about the safety of the machine for humans. When analyzing the accident, an expert in this area will do a partial task analysis to determine the contribution of the machine's design to the cause of the accident. The expert will not generally rely on published design standards but will reconstruct the sequence of events leading up to the accident in terms of

- What the human–machine system was doing.
- Within that context, what the operator (or victim) was trying to accomplish.
- What he did that led directly to the accident.
- How the machine design may have contributed to the accident by assisting him, encouraging him, or cooperating with him in engaging in behavior leading to the accident.[172]

In this factual scenario, the obligation of the paralegal is to reconstruct events and conditions showing that the machine or the product was inherently defective or unreasonably dangerous. Dr. William Bliss of the University of Florida, a specialist in experimental psychology and human factors analysis, claims that a machine can be viewed as inherently and unreasonably dangerous if the victim's legal team can accomplish the following ends:

1. It can qualify a specialized witness who can attest as such.
2. It can establish the design expertise of that witness.
3. It can establish accepted criteria for operation of a safe machine.
4. It can establish techniques and standards of accident investigations.
5. It can point out specific failures of the machinery to guard against injury.
6. It can point out specific failures to warn of operating deficiencies.
7. It can point out that the machine did not account for eventual human reaction over time.
8. It can state that the machine design is unreasonably dangerous and defective.
9. The expert can demonstrate causation.[173]

Challenging the manufacturing design of a product or other artifact is merely one aspect of product liability analysis.

Consider a vaccine that was administered to a patient. The patient suffered severe neurological injuries as the result of an adverse reaction to the vaccine. Traditional negligence analysis is necessary to bring suit against the manufacturer of the vaccine. Allegations that the vaccine was completely defective or negligently designed and was not accompanied by adequate warnings and notice are required:

- 1. Is there a relationship, a duty of care owed between a drug manufacturer and the person to whom it is administered? The answer generally is unequivocally yes.
- 2. Is there a standard of conduct that is expected in the drug industry?

HILL V. MERCEDES BENZ USA
— S.E.2D —, 2005 WL 1460007 (GA.APP.), 5 FCDR 1933 (GA. APP. 2005)

Background: Automobile purchasers brought breach of warranty action against automobile manufacturer. The trial court awarded summary judgment to manufacturer. Purchasers appealed.

Holdings: The Court of Appeals, Bernes, J., held that:

(1) triable issue existed as to whether dealership failed to successfully repair automobile;

(2) triable issue existed as to drivability of automobile at the time it was delivered; and

(3) purchaser provided adequate foundation for her opinion concerning diminished value of automobile.

Affirmed in part and reversed in part.

Genuine issue of material fact as to whether automobile dealership failed to successfully repair defective automobile precluded summary judgment on automobile buyer's breach of express warranty claim against automobile manufacturer.

- 3. Is it reasonable to expect that warnings are provided on labels?
- 4. Is it reasonable to expect that warnings are provided before the administration of a drug?
- 5. Is it reasonable to expect that the firm that produces and designs a drug will have some understanding that there may be adverse reactions?

Under most reasonable interpretations, the preceding answers must be affirmative. Causation may not be as easy to prove because the injury may be caused by another medical condition. But on these facts, we will assume that the injury was causally connected to the vaccine. If all of these standards are met, should such an action for product liability be based on a negligence theory? The answer is a very strong yes.[174] Language of a complaint relating to a product liability case based on negligence might be as follows:

> *That the said defendant, acting by and through its agents and employees, negligently designed, manufactured, assembled, marketed, distributed, and sold the said (product) in a defective condition (set out some particulars of the defect), and the said defendant was otherwise negligent in the design, manufacture, assembly, marketing, distribution, and sale of the said (product).*[175]

Warranty in Product Liability Cases

The topic of warranty was discussed in some detail in Chapter 5. The paralegal must recognize that a product sold to a consumer, business, or other entity carries with it an express, limited, or implied warranty. It is not unreasonable for consumers and businesses to expect that a product as advertised is inherently merchantable. This theory could be based on U.C.C. provisions, common law, or other statutory guideline. "In an action based on implied warranty, the plaintiff must establish that the product, when it left the defendant's control, was defective and not reasonably fit for the use intended, anticipated, or reasonably foreseeable (including foreseeable misuse) and that the defect was the proximate cause of the plaintiff's injury."[176] Here is an example of pleadings language in the case of an implied warranty:

> *That the said defendant, acting by and through its agents and employees, implicitly warranted that the said (product) was merchantable and was fit for the ordinary purposes for which said goods are used; that the said (product) was not merchantable, and was not fit for the said purposes, and the defendant breached its implied warranties as aforesaid.*[177]

Express warranties can be explicit written documents or an indisputable oral assertion describing and representing that a product will act according to specific standards. In personal injury litigation many express warranties exist; but limited warranties, whereby the manufacturer makes every effort to limit its potential liabilities, also are found. Chainsaws, power tools, and lawnmowers inflict serious harm, and manufacturers know it. Manufacturers prefer limited warranties; and by express language, these are usually included in the warranty papers and documentation received upon purchase. Successful challenge to limited warranties rests in theories of unconscionability and statutory protections that disapprove of these limitations. An example of a complaint for breach of an express warranty complaint is shown in Form 11.55 on the accompanying CD.

DEFENSE CONSIDERATIONS

To understand tort liability in the fullest sense, the litigant must anticipate the defense posture. Exactly what can a plaintiff expect from a sued defendant? What types of defense are applicable? Which defenses work best and in what particular fact patterns? Career tracks in paralegalism sometimes emphasize the defense over the prosecution. Government agencies often must contend with litigation, and its legal teams pick and choose the applicable defense strategy. Insurance work alone proves this point.

A plaintiff's claim should not be drafted without assessing potential or actual defense. At a minimum, the paralegal will have to become adept in the preparation of defense pleadings, whether in actual defense response or in subsequent responses of a plaintiff involved in a counterclaim.[178] Defenses, like most other legal principles, come in various shapes and colors.

Affirmative Defenses

A defendant must plead an affirmative defense. Failure to do so will result in a loss of said defense. Some common examples are statute of limitations, laches, necessity, alibi, insanity, and self-defense. Figure 11.12 contains standard language for this responsive pleading.

Other defenses are not mandatorily pled in the initial response to a complaint and may arise in later findings or in the evolution of an investigation. These types of defenses are sometimes called *general*.

General Defenses

Accord or Satisfaction

If a case has already been settled or satisfied in previous litigation, a plaintiff's action would be vigorously defended under a theory of accord and satisfaction. A legal document, such as a finding of the court, a jury verdict, or other legal document showing a previous legal resolution, would be pled and attached in the response. For example, proof of settlement by general release, an example of which is shown in Form 11.56 on the accompanying CD, would be proof of satisfaction.

FIGURE 11.12

Affirmative Defenses

> ### FIRST AFFIRMATIVE DEFENSE
> Plaintiff's complaint fails to state a claim upon which relief may be granted.
>
> ### SECOND AFFIRMATIVE DEFENSE
> Plaintiff was aware of the hazards and dangers attendant with said product in the way in which it being used. Plaintiff, therefore, assumed the risk of potential injury resulting.
>
> ### THIRD AFFIRMATIVE DEFENSE
> Any defect in the condition of the hairdryer was caused, created, or modified subsequent to manufacture and sale of the product to plaintiff.
>
> ### FOURTH AFFIRMATIVE DEFENSE
> Plaintiff failed to follow manufactuer's directions, which were set forth clearly and plainly in the instruction booklet included with the product. Plaintiff's own misuse of the product was the proximate cause of her alleged injuries. This misuse bars recovery by the plaintiff.
>
> WHEREFORE, defendant requests this court to dismiss plaintiff's complaint with costs, and to grant defendant such other relief as this court deems just.

Arbitration and Award

When plaintiff commences formal litigation, neglecting an agreed arbitration process, the proper defense is a stay based on the agreed arbitration. If an award has already been granted a previous arbitration, the defense of award is appropriate.

Assumption of Risk

Parties who assume the risk of certain conditions and events may bar recovery when making a claim for personal or property damages. For example, professional athletes in the NHL and NBA often get into physical scrapes. It is safe to say that injuries resulting from this ordinary and regular participation are not actionable, whereas the employment of excessive force by fellow athletes may negate the defense of assumption of risk. Employees may also be subject to the assumption of risk defense in high-risk occupations. See Form 11.57 on the accompanying CD for the recommended language.

Contributory Negligence

When an injured party plays a role in the injuries sustained, the argument of contributory negligence will likely be pled. By asserting contributory negligence, the defense shifts some part of the responsibility to the plaintiff—stressing the portion of the plaintiff's action that contributed to the injury. In an auto accident, the plaintiff may have been slightly in excess of the posted speed limit, and as a result assumed some portion of responsibility for the facts that caused the injury. Contributory negligence can be described as follows:

> *According to a small minority view, the contributory negligence of one beneficiary precludes all right of recovery, although there are innocent beneficiaries. This view is predicated in most instances upon the doctrine of imputation of the negligence of one beneficiary to the other beneficiaries who were not in fact contributorily negligent, under particular facts making the application of the imputed negligence doctrine appropriate, rather than on any independent rule which bars the risk of the innocent beneficiary because of the contributory negligence of another beneficiary.[179]*

Proof of contributory negligence is a complete defense in personal injury litigation and has been a harsh rule in many jurisdictions.[180]

Some argue that "contributory negligence is an antiquated doctrine abolished by almost all of the states."[181] As a result, more jurisdictions have adopted a comparative negligence formula, whereby liability computes and in some cases subtracts that portion of the plaintiff's negligence. A sample contributory negligence defense is drafted in Form 11.58 on the accompanying CD.

The hardship caused by the rule of contributory negligence has been labeled draconian[182] because the defense serves, in some jurisdictions, as a complete bar to a plaintiff's claim and a complete exoneration of a defendant. Justice Holt, in a 1938 Minnesota case, *Heg v. Sprague Werner & Co.,* cited this dilemma:

> *No one can appreciate more than we the hardship of depriving plaintiff of his verdict and of all right to collect damages from defendant; but the rule of contributory negligence, through no fault of ours, remains in our law and gives us no alternative other than to hold that the defendant is entitled to judgment notwithstanding the verdict. It would be hard to imagine a case more illustrative of the truth than in operation the rule of comparative negligence would serve justice more faithfully than that of contributory negligence.[183]*

Aside from the comparative negligence counter, some jurisdictions adhere to the doctrine of *last clear chance*. The harsh reality of contributory negligence will be softened if a "defendant in a personal injury or wrongful death action, usually one involving a motor vehicle accident, had the last clear chance to avoid the injury or death. This fact question arises most frequently in negligence actions in which the defendant asserts that the plaintiff's contributory negligence bars any recovery from the defendant, and the plaintiff alleges that, despite the plaintiff's contributory negligence, the defendant had the final opportunity to avoid the accident in question and failed to do so, so that the plaintiff is entitled to recover damages."[184]

Michael Cote, in his commentary on last clear chance, a doctrine that holds a defendant liable because that defendant did not exercise the last escape or last chance to avoid a collision or harm to another, lays out the critical factors in the doctrine:

- Presence of plaintiff (or his property) in position of peril.
- Plaintiff's inability to escape peril through use of ordinary care.
- Defendant's discovery of plaintiff's peril.
- Defendant's ability to prevent accident or injury.
- Defendant's failure to exercise ordinary care to prevent accident or injury.
- Proximate causal connection between defendant's failure and plaintiff's injury.[185]

Comparative Negligence

As a result of the injustice suffered due to the application of the contributory negligence doctrine, many jurisdictions have adopted the principle of comparative negligence: a test of comparison, calculating, differentiating, and distinguishing the respective behaviors of the plaintiff and defendant. Comparative analysis scrutinizes the level and fault and then assigns a value based on respective damages. Basically the court apportions damages by distinguishing levels of liability. Under modified systems of comparative negligence, a party who is at fault more than 51 percent will be barred from bringing the action. There are many statutory vagaries to this form of analysis.[186]

Accordingly, if a plaintiff is deemed 35 percent negligent and a defendant is computed at 65 percent, the eventual award will be reduced by the comparatively negligent finding of 35 percent. Therefore, if an award of $1 million is granted, $350,000 will be subtracted following comparative principles. The process becomes more complicated in cases involving multiple defendants:

> In a jurisdiction applying the rule of apportionment it would seem to be in the plaintiff's interest to hold down the number of defendants and not search too assiduously for joint tortfeasors. A large number of defendants can spread responsibility so thin that the plaintiff's negligence is likely to exceed that of each of the defendants. . . . The search for additional tortfeasors would seem to be in the interest of defendants as they seek to dilute their own individual responsibility to a point below that of the plaintiff.[187]

Whatever formula is employed, the paralegal must be capable in damage calculation and apportionment of fault and damages.

Discharge

Discharge from a debt, bankruptcy, legal obligation, or liability constitutes a pure defense. An example of a discharge pleading is outlined in Form 11.59 on the accompanying CD.

Duress

A party forced to perform certain conduct that results in harm to another, or who was emotionally coerced to act in a nonvolitional capacity, may plead the defense of duress. The doctrine of duress is evaluated in light of reasonable circumstances and conditions. A person whose personal interests or economic rights are threatened in an unreasonable fashion may argue the defense of duress.

Estoppel

Estoppel is an equitable remedy that acts like a defense—an assertion, affirmation, or agreement on a contractual obligation or subsequent modification that is relied on by others. Indeed so convincing is the lack of objection or appearance of consensus that one party acts to its own detriment under the belief that all is moving forward relative to any agreement.

Fraud

Fraud in the representation concerning material facts may provide a defense in contract or in tort. The defense of fraud has also been used in cases of personal injury and medical malpractice when an explanation of the terms and conditions of an experimental procedure was not provided to the patient. Justifiable reliance on the misrepresentation of material fact is required. (See Form 11.60 on the accompanying CD.)

Illegality

The defense of illegality is always available in both tort and contract. (See the relevant pleadings in Form 11.61 on the accompanying CD.)

Laches

Laches is an equitable defense barring an individual from asserting a right or a claim if a substantial period of time has passed since the injury occurred. Similar to the statute of limitations principle, the equitable defense of laches will exist if the plaintiff cannot explain or justify an unreasonable period or extended delay in commencing litigation.

License/Privilege

Governmental entities are legislatively granted rights, license, and privilege to carry out their function and purpose. In some cases these agencies have either whole or partial immunity when harm is caused. Cases of corporal punishment in schools, the historic principle of *in loco parentis* doctrine as applied to colleges and universities, and the scope and breadth of services performed by public law enforcement, correctional officers, and other public officials are illustrative examples of this defense. License and privilege can either be absolute or qualified.

Res Judicata

Actions in law or equity, previously resolved in another judicial forum, can be barred under a theory of *res judicata*. *Res judicata* literally means the matter has already been adjudicated. Whether the claim is identical to previous litigation or arises from the same or similar claim or controversy or under the same transactional basis is a central argument in *res judicata*. By checking and searching judgment records, paralegals can assure their supervising attorneys that a claim or controversy has yet to be adjudicated.

Statute of Limitations

The greatest cause of legal malpractice in America is the failure of attorneys to adhere to the statute of limitations. Because paralegals are given the job of establishing tickler files, calendars, and docket records of cases, the watchdog review of the statute of limitations rightfully rests on the paralegal, though the ultimate responsibility and liability always remains with the attorney.

Periods for the statute of limitations will vary from 90 days to a lifetime, depending on the nature of the offense, the legal action involved, and the discovery date of the legal injury or harm. In a busy litigation firm, the importance of date tracking cannot be overemphasized.[188]

Statute of Frauds

As discussed in the real estate chapter, the statute of frauds applies to any transaction involving real estate unless exempt under theories of estoppel and waiver. Aside from real estate contracts, certain contracts, such as personal service and commercial contracts in excess of $500.00, must be evidenced by writing to be enforceable.

Waiver

Similar to the doctrine of laches and estoppel, a party may waive rights under an existing contract or stated legal relationship. If a party waives, the party cannot later litigate a right waived. A party may waive a specific right not only by affirmative conduct but also by silence or failure to act.

Summary

Much has been said in this chapter about the nature of torts, negligence, strict liability, and the common practice areas of personal injury, malpractice, and product liability. More particularly, the chapter covered the following information:

The Law of Intentional Torts

An examination of the following intentional torts was made:

- Battery.
- Assault.

- False imprisonment.
- Intentional infliction of mental distress.
- Trespass.
- Theories of nuisance.
- Conversion.

Under the quasi-intentional classification, these areas were discussed:

- Deceit.
- Defamation.
- Invasion of privacy:
  - Appropriation.
  - Unreasonable intrusion.
  - Disclosure of private facts.
  - False light in the public eye.
- Malicious prosecution.
- Abuse of process.
- Wrongful death.

The following economic torts were also covered:

- Injurious falsehood.
- Interference with contractual relations.

The Law of Negligence

Contrasted with intentional acts, negligent acts cover the human foibles so common in social interaction and the predictable mistakes, errors, omissions, and commissions that the average person hopes to avoid. In detailed examination, doctrines involving foreseeability, the definitional aspects of a "reasonable" person, and corresponding standards of conduct expected were all addressed. The role of negligence in medical malpractice, premises, and product liability was also assessed.

Strict Liability

Strict liability involving inherently dangerous activities, such as the manufacture of explosives and chemical contaminants, nondomesticated animals, and other high-risk environments was fully covered. The emerging application of strict liability principles to product liability litigation was stressed. Strict liability principles find a home in workers' compensation programs, where fault is held irrelevant to the award of compensation.

Personal Injury Practice

Personal injury practice consumes increasing amounts of time for the professional paralegal. Whether in auto accident litigation, product liability, or medical malpractice, paralegals need to acquire specialized knowledge concerning this demanding field.

The image problems so rampantly negative for personal injury practice were fully and honestly examined. The question of crisis denotes a dual perspective: that of the practitioner who sees value in the work, and that of public policy, where a litigation explosion cannot be denied. A poll of any group of doctors would generally find the medical profession outraged by what it considers a litigious attack by a group of ambulance-chasing, greedy lawyers. Although there may be some truth or merit to this emotional position, this defensive stance is an exaggerated overreach. Half of the problem rests in the medical profession's extreme difficulty in regulating itself; the other half rests in the legal profession's expectation that the law provides a suitable remedy for all harms. States are jumping into the fray with caps and other reform ideas.

From every vantage point, personal injury litigation challenges both novice and seasoned practitioner. To be effective, the paralegal must be attentive to these recurring steps:

- Documentation is extremely important.
- Medical records and other expert opinion are essential.

- Pain and suffering must be quantified and proven.
- Property damages must be accounted for.
- Economic losses must be calculated.
- Damages of all types, including loss of consortium, loss of goodwill, interference with business relationships due to injury, and loss of future earnings are all essential parts of a claimant's case.

Whether the injury results from a product defect, a doctor's malpractice, or the negligent conduct of an automobile driver, a paralegal must display unceasing professionalism. Theodore Horn, in a 1957 article titled "The Handling of Plaintiff's Personal Injury Cases before Trial," republished in 1987 by *The Practical Lawyer* because of its timeless recommendations, sets out the methodology of personal injury practice:

- Do all the work of the case with the attitude that the case eventually will come to trial.
- Test every aspect of the client's claim by the yardstick of fairness and honesty.
- Do not allow the client's claim to be barred while it is being investigated.
- Move the case along vigorously at all stages. A speedy and thorough investigation of the facts, especially those about liability, is critical in court.
- Do not make a final evaluation of the client's injuries too quickly.
- Keep in mind the opponent's possible defenses.[189]

Some additional information was provided on practice in the auto accident injury case. Special emphasis was given to auto insurance practice and the tactics necessary to succeed.

Defenses

Litigation on behalf of any plaintiff requires a comprehensive understanding of defense strategy and tactics. Predicting the opposing counsel's approach comes about only with age and experience. Knowledge of the more typical defenses in civil actions will make the plaintiff's team better prepared and more assured of success. The typical defenses witnessed in civil practice, from accord and satisfaction to the statute of frauds and limitations, were presented.

In sum, the law of torts can forever stimulate the practicing paralegal. This area of legal practice provides challenges at every level of the legal system. Providing compensatory damages, restoring equilibrium, and making a person whole again serve the interests of justice.

Discussion Questions

1. If a client comes to a law office suffering injuries from a serious auto accident, what types of remedies and civil causes of action might be applicable?

2. What public figures are regularly the targets of actions causing an invasion of privacy?

3. Distinguish abuse of process from malicious prosecution.

4. Point out the differences and similarities between civil wrongs and criminal acts.

5. Civil liability extends as far as a zone of danger can be defined. Describe the zone. When are you in and when are you out?

6. Create a graphic illustration of the zone of danger with accompanying narrative.

7. Generally speaking, activities resulting in strict liability must be of an extremely serious nature. How is this principle evolving?

8. Think about your local hospital. If an act of malpractice occurs, what individuals might be responsible in an emergency room case?

9. What evidence will corroborate speed or vehicular direction in an auto accident case?

10. How can paralegals be certain that an insurance company is cooperating during negotiations? Can you think of any practical suggestions that will speed up an eventual settlement?

11. What products in the consumer marketplace regularly cause injuries as a result of defects and dangerous design?

12. Visit the following Web location for information about the Rodney King trial: http://www.law.umkc.edu/faculty/projects/ftrials/lapd/lapd.html. Which intentional torts would be applicable in this case?

13. Visit the following Web location for information about the OJ Simpson trial: http://www.law.umkc.edu/faculty/projects/ftrials/Simpson/simpson.htm. Although he was successful in his criminal prosecution, why did he lose on the civil side? Which torts seem to fit the facts?

Research Exercise

1. Parents of a teenager who committed suicide are seeking legal advice. The teenage boy consulted with a minister about his severe depression. His church claimed it could counsel those wishing its pastoral view. During his counseling sessions with the minister, he confided his desire to kill himself. The pastoral counselor took no steps to warn his parents or other authorities of the teenager's intentions. Later the teenager killed himself. Your assignment is to research the question of malpractice by clergy and answer the following questions. Where is the question of clergy negligence or malpractice considered? Is there any precedent for malpractice theory relating to clergy? What standard of care does a nontherapist clergy member owe someone counseled? During the discovery phase of a clergy malpractice case, what types of documents should be solicited?

Practical Exercises

1. Using the following information, prepare a complaint in an automobile accident case:

Plaintiff:	*Janet Wyrick*
Address:	*908 Salty Road, Fort Pierce, Beach County, Florida, 33213*
Attorney for plaintiff:	*Christopher Gardiner, Lawyers for the People, Inc.*
	725 Darlington Rd., Fort Pierce, FL 33214
Plaintiff's auto:	*2003 Chevy Cavalier, Florida license plate number COOL GAL*
Defendant:	*Ed Tournay*
Address:	*435 Blue Waters Way, Vero Beach, Beach County, Florida 33244*
Defendant's auto:	*2002 Ford Bronco, Florida license plate number 543-5644*
Date of accident:	*August 1, 2006*
Time of accident:	*10:45 p.m.*
Location of accident:	*Corner of A Boulevard and B Street, Fort Pierce, Beach County, Florida*
General damages:	*At least $400,000*
Specific damages:	*At least $1,000,000*

2. Using hypothetical information, complete a product liability complaint.

3. Complete a complaint for medical negligence using the following facts:

During a three-month period, a client experienced a dramatic escalation of low back pain. The client also experienced fever, chills, and lower extremity radiculopathy. The client sought treatment through his HMO on numerous occasions and was diagnosed with a degenerative lumbar condition. Anti-inflammatories were prescribed.

The client's low back pain continued, and the client then began experiencing significant breathing problems. He was ultimately hospitalized for what was suspected to be pneumonia and lumbar degeneration.

During the client's hospitalization, the client's HMO primary care physician arranged for a rheumatologist consultation to assess the client's low back pain. After taking a history, performing a physical examination, and reviewing the client's lab data and radiology films, the rheumatologist assessed the client as likely suffering from either rheumatologic disease or a lumbar spine infection.

Infection in the spine is well known to be an urgent care condition. If a spinal infection is not promptly diagnosed and treated, the patient is at risk of paralysis and even death. Magnetic resonance imaging (MRI) is the test of choice to confirm a spinal infection.

Despite the rheumatologist's suspicion of a possible spinal infection, no follow-up confirmation (by MRI) was ordered, and the client was released from the hospital without any further investigation or treatment devoted to the infection in his spine. The client's spinal infection was then left untreated for more than 30 days despite the client's numerous telephone calls and doctor visits relating to his back pain. Eventually the client became paralyzed from the neck down when the infection spread throughout his spine and a spinal epidural abscess invaded and damaged the client's spinal cord at C6–7.

The client was hospitalized again after the onset of paralysis. An MRI confirmed a massive spinal infection. The client then underwent spinal surgery and antibiotic therapy to clear the infection. Thereafter the client underwent a lengthy course of physical therapy to regain function in his arms and legs. The client eventually reacquired partial use of his arms and legs.

Internet Resources

Consumer Law Resource Page—consumerlawpage.com/resource/defect.shtml

Product Liability Lawyer—www.productliabilitylawyer.com

Crashworthiness: auto defect and recall information—www.crash-worthiness.com

'Lectric Law Library, Identify a Product Defect Page—www.lectlaw.com/files/bur17.htm

American Medical Forensic Specialists, Inc.—www.amfs.com

'Lectric Law Library, Medicine and Law—www.lectlaw.com/tmed.html

Hieros Gamos, guide to tort law—www.hg.org/torts.html

Cornell Law School, tort law overview—www.law.cornell.edu/wex/index.php/Tort

Findlaw legal subjects: injury and tort law—www.findlaw.com/01topics/22tort/index.html

Theories of tort law—http://plato.stanford.edu/entries/tort-theories/

American Guild of Court Videographers—www.agcv.com/

National Court Reporters Association—www.ncraonline.org/

NCRA, Certified Legal Video Specialist Section—http://clvs.ncraonline.org/index.shtml

Endnotes

1. ILLINOIS PARALEGAL ASSOCIATION, THE FINDINGS OF THE COMPETENCY COMMITTEE RELATING TO THE QUALITY OF PARALEGAL SERVICES 50–51 (1989).

2. Walter W. Cook, *A Proposed New Definition of Tort,* 12 HARV. L. REV. 335, 336 (1899).

3. THOMAS E. EIMERMANN, FUNDAMENTALS OF PARALEGALISM 13 (1980).

4. SUMMARY OF PA. JUR. 2D *Torts* 3 (199).

5. Ernest J. Weinreb, *Understanding Tort Law,* 23 VAL. U. L. REV. 485, 493 (1989).

6. Clark C. Havighurst, *Altering the Applicable Standard of Care,* 49 LAW & CONTEM. PROB. 265 (1986); *see also Malpractice Testimony: Competency of Physician or Surgeon from One Locality to Testify, in Malpractice Case, as to Standard of Care Required of Defendant Practicing in Another Locality,* 37 A.L.R.3d 420.

7. Stephen R. Pitcher, *Defamation with Actual Malice,* 14 AM. JUR. PROOF OF FACTS 2d 61 (1988).

8. Stephen R. Pitcher, *Knowledge of Animal's Vicious Propensities,* 13 AM. JUR. PROOF OF FACTS 473, 479 (1988).

9. For an excellent example of intentionality in tort law, *see* Anderson v. Piedmont Aviation, Inc., 68 F. Supp. 2d 682 (M.D.N.C. 1999).

10. Oliver W. Holmes, *Privilege, Malice, and Intent,* 8 HARV. L. REV. 1 (1894); *see also* RESTATEMENT (SECOND) OF TORTS §13.

11. Derosier v. New England Telephone and Telegraph, 81 N.H. 451, 130 A. 145 (1925).

12. *See generally Application of Comparative Negligence in Action Based on Gross Negligence, Recklessness, or the Like,* 10 A.L.R.4th 946.

13. SUMMARY OF PA JUR. 2d *Torts* §11.3 at 440 (1991).

14. 634 NE2d 697, 46 A.L.R.5th 939 (1994, Ohio Hamilton Co).

15. *Id. See also* Renee Vintzel Loridas, J.D., *Secondary Smoke as Battery,* 46 A.L.R.5th 813.

16. RESTATEMENT (SECOND) OF TORTS §24 (1977).

17. State v. Morgan, 25 N.C. 186 (1842).

18. Mitchell v. Daily, 133 Mich. App. 414, 350 N.W. 2d 772 (1984); Trot v. Merit Department Store, 106 A. D. 158, 484 N.Y.S. 2d 827 (1985).

19. RESTATEMENT (SECOND) OF TORTS §42 (1977).

20. *See* Fla. Stat. Ann. §812.015 (1989); Mo. Ann. Stat. §537.125 (1989); N.J. Stat. Ann. §2C: 20–11E (1989).

21. *See* Zohn v. Menard, Inc., 598 N.W.2d 323 (Iowa App. 1999).

22. CHARLES P. NEMETH, CRIMINAL LAW 178–179 (2004).

23. SUMMARY OF PA JUR 2D *Torts* §15.10 at 622 (1991).

24. Baggett v. National Bank and Trust Co., 174 Ga. App. 346, 33 S.E. 2d 108 (1985); Morales v. Lee, 668 S.W. 2d 867 (1984).

25. *See* Charles P. Nemeth, *Psychological Injuries: A Police Remedy in Intentional Infliction of Mental Distress,* 15 POLICE J. 244 (1982).

26. Calvert MacGruder, *Mental and Emotional Disturbance in the Law of Torts,* 49 HARV. L. REV. 1033 (1936); Fowler Harper & Mary C. McNeilly, *A Reexamination of the Basis for Liability for Emotional Distress,* WISC. L. REV. 426 (1938).

27. Espinosa v. Beverly Hospital, 114 CAL. APP. 2d 232, 249 P.2d 843 (1953).

28. Bielitski v. Obadiak, 61 Dom. L. Rep. 494 (1921).

29. Great Atlantic and Pacific Tea Company v. Roch, 160 Md. 189, 153 A. 22 (1930).

30. Boyle v. Chandler, 33 Del. 323, 138 A. 273 (1927).

31. *See* J.L. Borda, *One's Right to Enjoy Mental Peace and Tranquility,* 28 GEO. L J. 55 (1939).

32. For an interesting case on the threat of hanging and mental distress, *see* Vance v. Southern Bell Tel. & Tel. Co. 983 F.2d 1573, C.A. 11 (Fla., 1993).

33. Russell L. Ward, *Intentional Infliction of Emotional Distress,* 43 AM. JUR. PROOF OF FACTS 2d, 32 (1985).

34. *See* J.L. Borda, *One's Right to Enjoy Mental Peace and Tranquility,* 28 GEO. L J. 55 (1939).

35. Edmund C. Baird III, *No Pain, No Gain: The Third Circuit's "Sufficient Indicia of Genuineness" Approach to Claims of Negligent Infliction of Emotional Distress under the Federal Employers' Liability Act,* 71 WASH. U. L.Q. 1255 (1993).

36. Daniel F. Sullivan, *Good Faith of Mineral Trespasser,* 19 AM. JUR. PROOF OF FACTS 535 (1979).

37. RESTATEMENT (SECOND) OF TORTS §163 (1977).

38. 1 THOMAS A. STREET, FOUNDATIONS OF LEGAL LIABILITY 15 (1898). *See also* The New World of Internet Trespass in John D. Saba Jr., *Internet Property Rights: E-Trespass,* 33 ST. MARY'S L.J. 367 (2002).

39. SUMMARY OF PA JUR. 2d *Torts* §21:1 at 224–225 (1991).

40. 4 STANDARD PA PRACTICE 2d §23:88 at 606–607 (1982).

41. *See* 191 N.C. 419, 132 S.E. 5 (1926).

42. State of New York v. Shore Realty Corp., 759 F. 2d 1032 (2d Cir. 1985).

43. Philadelphia Electric Co. v. Hercules Inc., 762 F. 2d 303 (3d Cir. 1985); *see also* The Role of Nuisance and Tort in Albert C. Lin., *Beyond Tort: Compensating Victims of Environmental Toxic Injury,* 78 S. CAL. L. REV. 1439 (2005).

44. CHARLES P. NEMETH, PARALEGAL HANDBOOK 169 (1986).

45. Eric Kohm, *When "Sex" Sells: Expanding the Tort of Conversion to Encompass Domain Names,* 23 LOY. L.A. ENT. L. REV. 443 (2003).

46. *See also* O. HOLMES, THE COMMON LAW 227–228 (1881).

47. RESTATEMENT (SECOND) OF TORTS §525 (1977).

48. Carpenter, *Responsibility for Intentional, Negligent, or Innocent Misrepresentation,* 24 U. ILL. L. REV. 749 (1940).

49. David Polin, *Workers' Compensation: Special Mission Exception to Going-and-Coming Rule,* 32 AM. JUR. PROOF OF FACTS 2d 112 (1982).

50. Robyn L. Meadows, *Unconscionability as a Contract Policing Device for the Elder Client: How Useful Is It?* 38 AKRON L. REV. 741 (2005).

51. FREDRICK POLLOCK, LAW OF TORTS 243–249 (1929); Van Vechtner Veeder, *History and Theory of the Law of Defamation,* 3 COLUM. L. REV. 546 (1903).

52. RESTATEMENT (SECOND) OF TORTS §559 (1977).

53. Margaret Z. Johns, *Reconsidering Absolute Prosecutorial Immunity,* 2005 B.Y.U.L. REV. 53, 63 (2005).

54. *See* Note, *Actionable Defamation,* 9 CORNELL L. Q. 245 (1924); BURGRESS ELDRIDGE, THE LAW OF DEFAMATION 31 (1978); James M. Naughton & Eric R. Gilbertson, *Libelous Ridicule by Journalists,* 18 CLEV. MAR. L. REV. 450 (1969).

55. 376 U.S. 254 (1964).

56. Hustler Magazine v. Falwell, U.S. , 99 L. Ed. 2d 41, 108 S. Ct. 876 (1988).

57. Bose Corp. v. Consumer Union of the U.S., Inc., 466 U.S. 485 (1984).

58. Samuel D. Warren & Louis D. Brandeis, *The Right to Privacy,* 4 HARV. L. REV. 193, 196 (1980).

59. *See* Note, *Tort Recovery for Invasion of Privacy,* 59 NEB. L. REV. 808 (1980).

60. For an excellent analysis of the four types of invasion, *see* Beard v. Akzona, Inc., 517 F. SUPP. 128, 131 (E.D. Tenn. 1981).

61. RESTATEMENT (SECOND) OF TORTS 2d §§652A & 652E.

62. RESTATEMENT (SECOND) OF TORTS 2d §652(d) (1977).

63. Bradley H. Smith, *Torts—West v. Media General Convergence, Inc.: Tennessee's Recognition of the Tort of False Light Invasion of Privacy*, 32 U. Mem. L. Rev. 1053 (2002).

64. Jim Barr Coleman, *Digital Photography and the Internet: Rethinking Privacy Law*, 13 J.I.P.L. 205 (2005).

65. Restatement (Second) of Torts 2d §652E.

66. *See* Bryan R. Lasswell, *In Defense of False Light: Why False Light Must Remain a Viable Cause of Action*, 34 S. Tex. L. Rev. 149, 152 (1993); Robin Baker Perkins, *Comment: The Truth behind False Light—A Recommendation for Texas's Readoption of False Light Invasion of Privacy*, 34 Tex. Tech L. Rev. 1199 (2003).

67. Restatement (Second) of Torts §652(d) (1977).

68. *See* Dan B. Dobbs, *Belief and Doubt in Malicious Prosecution and Libel,* 21 Ariz. L. Rev. 607 (1979).

69. Larry Ball, *Abuse of Process—Debt Collection*, 7 Am. Jur. Proof of Facts 2d 417 (1975).

70. *See Malicious Prosecution: Defense of Acting on Advice of Justice of the Peace, Magistrate, or Lay Person,* 48 A.L.R.4th 250.

71. Stuart M. Speiser, Recovery for Wrongful Death (1975); Malone, *The Genesis of Wrongful Death,* 17 Stan. L. Rev. 1043 (1965). *See also* a curious application of the wrongful death in the case of fetuses at Jason Cuomo, *Symposium: Farley v. Sartin and Fetal Personhood Life Begins at the Moment of Conception for the Purposes of W. Va. Code §55-7-5: The Supreme Court of Appeals of West Virginia "Rewrites" Our Wrongful Death Statute,* 99 W. Va. L. Rev. 237 (1996).

72. Don A. Lynn, *Injurious Falsehood,* 52 Fl. B. J. 360 (1978); Note, *The Law of Commercial Disparagement: Business Defamations and Injuries,* 63 Yale L. J. 65 (1953); William L. Prosser, *Injurious Falsehood: The Basis of Liability,* 59 Colum. L. Rev. 425 (1959).

73. See *Liability for Tortious Interference with Prospective Contractual Relations Involving Sale of Business, Stock, or Real Estate,* 71 A.L.R.5th 491.

74. Dan B. Dobbs, *Tortious Interference with Contractual Relations,* 34 Ark. L. Rev. 335 (1980).

75. Raymond v. Ewington, 96 Texas 443, 72 S.W. 580 (1903).

76. Restatement (Second) of Torts §282 (1977).

77. Summary of Pa. Jur., 2d *Torts* §20:1 at 10 (1991).

78. Summary of Pa. Jur., 2d *Torts* §20:1 at 10 (1991). *See also* William H. Danne Jr., *Liability of Motorist Who Left Key in Ignition for Damage or Injury Caused by Stranger Operating the Vehicle,* J.D.45 A.L.R.3d 787.

79. Palsgraf v. Long Island R.R., 248 N.Y. 339, 162 N.E. 99 (1928); *see also* Leon Green, *The Palsgraf Case,* 30 Colum. L. Rev. 789 (1930).

80. Christensen v. Chicago, St. Paul, Minneapolis and Omaha Railway Co., 67 Minn. 94, 69 N.W. 640 (1896).

81. Summary of Pa Jur. 2d *Torts* §20:84 at 118 (1991).

82. Leon Green, *The Causal Relation in Negligence Law,* 60 Mich. L. Rev. 543 (1962); Wex S. Malone, *Ruminations on the Cause in Fact,* 9 Stan. L. Rev. 60 (1956).

83. Restatement (Second) of Torts §440–441 (1977).

84. *Id.*

85. *Id.*

86. *Id.,* §283 (1977).

87. Alan P. Herbert, Misleading Cases in the Common Law 12–16 (1930).

88. Warren Seavey, *Negligence—Subjective or Objective* 41 Harv. L. Rev. 1, 27 (1927); *see also* Osborne M. Reynolds, *The Reasonable Man of Negligence Law: A Health Report on the "Odious Creature,"* 23 Okla. L. Rev. 410 (1970).

89. Leon Green, *The Reasonable Man: Legal Fiction* or *Psycho-Social Reality,* 2 Law & Soc'y Rev. 241 (1968).

90. Ronald K.L. Collins, *Language, History, and the Legal Process: A Profile of the Reasonable Man,* 8 Rut.–Cam. L. J. 311 (1977).

91. Jennifer J. Aldrich, *General Standard of Negligence Applies in Determining a Vehicle Owner's Duty to Inspect a Mechanic's Repairs,* 42 S. C. L. Rev. 234, 236 (Autumn 1990); *see e.g.* Thomas v. Atlantic Greyhound Corp., 204 S.C. 247, 253, 29 S.E.2d 196, 198 (1944).

92. Angela R. Holder, *Medical Malpractice, Negligence in Postoperative Care of a Patient,* 26 Am. Jur. Proof of Facts 2d 183 (1988).

93. *Id.* at 213.

94. Pennsylvania Bar Institute, The Continuing Legal Education Arm of the Pennsylvania Bar Association, How to Handle the Personal Injury Case: Initial Client Interview to Jury Selection 28 (1990).

95. *See* Micah Echols, *Changing the Face of Premises Liability in Nevada: Davenport v. Comstock Hills-Reno [Fn1] Requiring an Affirmative Duty for Premises Owners to "Maintain" and Upgrade,* 37 UWLA L. Rev. 76 (2004); Thompson v. Katzer 86 Wash. App. 280, 936 P.2d 421, Wash. App. Div. 2, 1997.

96. Restatement (Second) of Torts §329 (1977).

97. Restatement (Second) of Torts §337 (1977); *see also* Anderson v. Greenbay and Western Railway Co., 99 Wis. 2d 514, 299 N.W. 2d 615 (1980); Bethay v. Philadelphia Housing Authority, 271 Pa. Super. 366, 413 A. 2d 710 (1979).

98. Bovino v. Metropolitan Dade County, 378 So. 2d 51 (Fla. App. 1980); *see also* Joyce v. Nash, 630 S.W. 2d 219 (Mo.App. 1982).

99. *See Liability of Owner of Vacant Building for Injury to Child Trespassing on Premises*, 99 A.L.R.2d 461.

100. Joseph A. Page, The Law of Premises Liability 40–41 (1976).

101. Institute of Continuing Legal Education, 1 Michigan Basic Practice Handbook, 209 (1986).

102. Fowler V. Harper, Law of Torts §155 (1933); Harry H. Ognal, *Some Facets of Strict Tortious Liability in the United States and Their Implications,* 33 Notre Dame L. Rev. 239 (1958).

103. John F. Vargo, *The Emperor's New Clothes: The American Law Institute Adorns a "New Cloth" for Section 402a Products Liability Design Defects—A Survey of the States Reveals a Different Weave,* 26 U. Mem. L. Rev. 493, 509 (1996).

104. Leon L. Wolfstone, *Glass Door Accidents,* 14 Am. Jur. Trials 112 (1968).

105. Summary of Pa Jur. 2d *Torts* §3:1 at 36 (1991).

106. Restatement (Second) of Torts §402(a) (1977).

107. Podrat v. Codman-Shurtleff, Inc., 384 Pa. Super 404, 558 A2d 895 (1989); and Grubb v. Albert Einstein Medical Center, 255 Pa. Super 381, 387 A2d 480 (1978).

108. *See* Mich. Stat. Ann. §17.237–301.

109. Burgess C. Eldridge, Personal Injury Paralegal 1.1 (1988).

110. Lawrence S. Charfoos & David W. Christensen, Personal Injury Practice: Technique and Technology 47 (1988).

111. David G. Warren & Richard Marritt, ed., Wisconsin's Medical Malpractice Crisis, A legislator's Guide to the Medical Malpractice Issue 55 (1976).

112. Robert J. Flemma, *Medical Malpractice: A Dilemma in the Search for Justice,* 68 Marq. L. Rev. 237, 256 (1985).

113. Mark S. Mandell, *Hospital Liability: Four Theories,* Trial, May 1992, at 16.

114. *Good Counsel,* Trial, Dec. 2001, at 66.

115. Institute of Continuing Legal Education, 1 Michigan Basic Practice Handbook 198 (1986).

116. *See* Model Rules of Professional Responsibility, 1.5.

117. Stephen D. Sugarman, *Symposium of the Law in the Twentieth Century: A Century of Change in Personal Injury Law,* 88 Cal. L. Rev. 2403, 2410 (2000).

118. Richard D. Grand, *Processing the Case,* 1 Am. Jur. Trials 208 (1988).

119. *See* Gary T. Schwartz, *Auto No-Fault and First-Party Insurance: Advantages and Problems,* 73 S. Cal. L. Rev. 611 (2000).

120. Some have argued that accident prevention and accident education should be a service of the insurance and legal industries. *See* Kenneth S. Abraham, *Liability Insurance and Accident Prevention: The Evolution of an Idea,* 64 Md. L. Rev. 573 (2005).

121. Glen O. Robinson, *The Medical Malpractice Crisis of the 1970s: A Retrospective,* 49 Law & Contemp. Probs. 1, 10 (1986).

122. L. Lander, Defective Medicine: Risk, Anger, and the Malpractice Crisis 92–95 (1978).

123. Patricia M. Danzon, *The Frequency and Severity of Medical Malpractice Claims: New Evidence,* 49 Law & Contemp. Probs. 57, 79 (1986).

124. Judith S. Kaye, *Medical Malpractice: A Judicial Outlook,* 21 Trial Law. Q. 62, 63 (1991).

125. Throne A. Brennan, *Practice Guidelines and Malpractice Litigation: Collision or Cohersion?* 16 J. Health Pol., Pol'y & L. 67, 73 (1991).

126. *See* Christopher J. Trombetta, *The Unconstitutionality of Medical Malpractice Statutes of Repose: Judicial Conscience versus Legislative Will,* 34 Vill. L. Rev. 397 (1989).

127. Institute of Continuing Legal Education, 1 Michigan Basic Practice Handbook 213 (1986).

128. Frye v. United States, 293 F. 1013 (D.C. Cir. 1923).

129. Frye v. United States, 293 F. 1013, 1014 (D.C. Cir. 1923).

130. Michael Graham, Evidence Text, Rules, Illustrations, and Problems 305–306 (1983).

131. Ronald Carlson, *Policing the Bases of Modern Expert Testimony,* 39 Vand. L. Rev. 577, 578 (1986).

132. 509 U.S. 579 (1993).

133. Ellen Moskovitz, *Junk Science,* 47 Hastings L.J. 48 (1996).

134. Michael H. Gottesman, *Should State Courts Impose a "Reliability" Threshold?"* Trial, Sept. 1997, at 20, 23.

135. Edward R. Cavanagh, *Decision Extends Daubert Approach to All Expert Testimony,* N.Y. St. B.J., July–Aug. 1999, at 9.

136. Paul Reidinger, *They Blinded Me with Science,* ABA B. J., Sept. 1996, at 58, 62.

137. In fact, the Federal Judicial Center has formally recognized the need for judicial involvement by increasing science training for district court judges and by publishing a handbook on scientific evidence, which includes detailed "reference guides" on scientific and technical specialties frequently encountered in the courtroom. Paul S. Miller & Bert W. Rein, *Whither Daubert? Reliable Resolution of Scientifically Based Causality Issues in Toxic Tort Cases,* 50 Rutgers L. Rev. 563 (1998).

138. 119 S.Ct. 1167 (1999).

139. Robert W. Littleton, *Supreme Court Dramatically Changes the Rules on Experts,* N.Y. St. B.J., July–Aug. 1999, at 8, 12.

140. *Id.*

141. *Id.*

142. Charles P. Nemeth, Evidence Handbook for Paralegals 169–170 (1993).

143. Deborah Larbalestrier, Paralegal Training Manual 144–445 (1981).

144. Lowry, *A Medical Malpractice Trial: Successful Techniques Presented and Analyzed,* 11 Am. J. Trial Advoc. 1 (1987).

145. David Schrager, *Strategy for Negligent Diagnosis Cases*, 22 TRIAL LAW. Q. 7, 14 (Fall 1991).

146. Lowry, *A Medical Malpractice Trial: Successful Techniques Presented and Analyzed,* 11 AM. J. TRIAL ADVOC. 1, 4 (1987).

147. Clark C. Havighurst, *Altering the Applicable Standard of Care*, 49 LAW & CONTEM. PROB. 265, 271 (1986).

148. M.S. FREED, CONTRACT AS PROMISE: A THEORY OF CONTRACTUAL OBLIGATION (1981); Richard Epstein, *Medical Malpractice: A Case for Contract*, AM. B. FOUND. RESEARCH J. 87 (1976).

149. Patrick S. Atiyah, *Medical Malpractice and the Contract/Tort Boundary*, 49 LAW & CONTEMP. PROBS. 287, 291 (1986).

150. Comment, *Medical Malpractice Arbitration: The Cure for What Ails the Pennsylvania Health Care System?* 4 J. AM. ARB. 95, 101 (2005).

151. Daniel A. Rottier, *American Medical Association Proposes Replacing Tort System for All Medical Malpractice Claims*, WIS. A. TRIAL LAW. 29 (1988).

152. *Construction and Application of State Statutory Cap on Punitive Damages in Tort Cases Exclusive of Medical Malpractice Actions*, 8 A.L.R.6th 439; Johnson v. St. Vincent Hospital, Inc., 404 N.E. 2d 585 (Ind. 1980).

153. Eastin v. Broomfield, 116 Ariz. 576, 570 P. 2d 744 (1977).

154. Robert M. Ackerman, *Medical Malpractice: A Time for More Talk and Less Rhetoric,* 37 MERCER L. REV. 725, 745 (1986).

155. Geoffrey N. Fieger, *Medical Malpractice Tort Reform: An Analysis and Comparison of Existing Acts*, MICH. B. J., March 1987, at 262.

156. Lowry, *A Medical Malpractice Trial: Successful Techniques Presented and Analyzed,* 11 AM. J. TRIAL ADVOC. 1, 5 (1987).

157. Julius W. Cohn & David C.C. Stark, *Medical Malpractice—Use of Hospital Records,* 22 AM. JUR. PROOF OF FACTS 2d 1, 7 (1988).

158. Philip H. Corboy & Robert A. Clifford, *Demonstrative Evidence*, in MASTER ADVOCATE HANDBOOK 183 (D. Lake Rumsey ed., 1986).

159. Greg Joseph, in his discussion of demonstrative videotape evidence, calls vigorously for the admission of day-in-the-life videotapes: "Day-in-the-life tapes document the effects of severe injury. They attempt to communicate the extent of injury by focusing on routine daily activities in the life of severely injured plaintiffs. The tapes are usually unpleasant and often emotionally draining to watch." Greg Joseph, *Demonstrative Videotape Evidence*, 22 TRIAL 60, 61 (1986).

160. 430 A.2d 1 (Conn. 1980).

161. *Id.* at 8.

162. JOHN TARANTINO, TRIAL EVIDENCE FOUNDATIONS 5–27 (1987).

163. *See* Robert D. Peltz, *Admissibility of "Day in the Life" Films*, 63 FLA. B.J. 55 (1989); Martha A. Churchill, *Day in the Life Films Subject to Court Challenge,* 32 FOR THE DEF. 24 (1990). The cases most often cited at the federal bench are Grimes v. Employer Mutual Liability Insurance Co., 73 F.R.D. 607 (D.Ala. 1977) (upheld the admissibility of videotapes) and Bolstridge v. Central Maine Power Co., 621 F.SUPP. 1202 (D.Me. 1985) (denied entry).

164. BURGRESS C. ELDRIDGE, PERSONAL INJURY PARALEGAL 6–7 (1988).

165. Angela R. Holder, *Physician's Failure to Obtain Informed Consent to Innovative Practice or Medical Research,* 15 AM. JUR. PROOF OF FACTS 2d. 711, 735 (1988).

166. Angela R. Holder, *Physician's Failure to Obtain Informed Consent to Innovative Practice or Medical Research,* 15 AM. JUR. PROOF OF FACTS 2d. 711, 745 (1988).

167. Peter C. Williams, *Abandoning Medical Malpractice*, 5 J. LEGAL MED. 549 (1984); *see also* Note, *Medical Malpractice: A Sojourn through the Jurisprudence Addressing Limitation of Liability,* 30 LOYOLA L. REV. 119 (1984).

168. RESTATEMENT (SECOND) OF TORTS §402(a) (1977).

169. Mich. Stat. Ann. §27A. 2945–2949.

170. Stephen J. Werber, *Product Liability in the Sixth Circuit, 1984–1985*, 17 U. TOL. L. REV. 527 (1986).

171. Patrick A. Lee, *Product Liability: The Great Question and Answer Search*, 13 LITIG. 17 (1987).

172. William D. Bliss, *Defective Product Design—Role of Human Factors*, 18 AM. JUR. PROOF OF FACTS 2d 117, 130–131 (1988).

173. *Id.* at117, 133.

174. *See* Abbot v. American Cyanamid Co. 844 F. 2d. 1108 (4th Cir. 1988).

175. JOINT COMMITTEE ON CONTINUING LEGAL EDUCATION OF THE VIRGINIA STATE BAR AND THE VIRGINIA STATE BAR ASSOCIATION, THE VIRGINIA LAWYER: A BASIC PRACTICE HANDBOOK 20–21 (1988).

176. INSTITUTE OF CONTINUING LEGAL EDUCATION, 1 MICHIGAN BASIC PRACTICE HANDBOOK 211 (1986).

177. JOINT COMMITTEE ON CONTINUING LEGAL EDUCATION OF THE VIRGINIA STATE BAR AND THE VIRGINIA STATE BAR ASSOCIATION, THE VIRGINIA LAWYER: A BASIC PRACTICE HANDBOOK 20–21 (1988).

178. Burgress C. Eldridge, Personal Injury Paralegal 11–20 (1988); Cynthia B. Monteiro, Paralegal Preparation of Pleadings (1988).

179. CRITICAL ISSUES: WRONGFUL DEATH: ANNOTATIONS FROM THE A.L.R. SYSTEM 438 (1990).

180. Jennifer J. Karangelen, *The Road to Judicial Abolishment of Contributory Negligence Has Been Paved by Bozman v. Bozman,* 34 U. BALT. L. REV. (2004).

181. *Id.* at 265.

182. Victor E. Schwartz, Comparative Negligence, §21.1 at 336 (1974); *see also* Robert E. Keeton, *Legal Process and Comparative Negligence Cases,* 17 Harv. J. On Legis. 1 (1980).

183. Heg v. Sprague, Werner & Co., 202 Minn. 425, 281 N.W. 261 (1938).

184. Michael Cote, *Last Clear Chance,* 32 Am. Jur. Proof of Facts 2d 625 (1988).

185. *Id.*

186. Frank Ray, *Uniform Comparative Fault Act—What Should It Provide?* 10 U. Mich. J. L. Ref. 220 (1977); Claude R. Sowle & Daniel O. Conkle, *Comparative Negligence vs. Constitutional Guarantee of Equal Protection: A Hypothetical Judicial Decision,* Duke L. J. 1083 (1979); Aaron D. Twerski, *The Use and Abuse of Comparative Negligence in Products Liability,* 10 Ind. L. Rev. 797 (1977).

187. Henry Wood, *Trial of a Personal Injury Case in Comparative Negligence Jurisdictions,* 21 Am. Jur. Trials 753–754 (1974).

188. Shepard's/McGraw-Hill, Shepard's Lawyer's Reference Manual 524–538 (1987).

189. Theodore A. Horn, *The Handling of Plaintiffs' Personal Injury Cases before Trial*, 30 Prac. Law. 29 (1987).Wilma Peggy Carlin v. Sutter County 13 Cal.4th 1104, 920 P.2d 1347, 56 Cal.Rptr.2d 162 (1996).

Chapter 12

Family Law

FAMILY LAW PARALEGAL JOB DESCRIPTION

Family law paralegals need to be proficient in the following competencies:

- Attend initial interviews with attorneys and clients.
- Collect background information about clients.
- Complete domestic relations questionnaire forms.
- Perform legal research.
- Draft notices to produce.
- Serve notice on opposing counsel.
- Arrange for service of documents.
- Conduct follow-up filing petitions and check service.
- Conduct timely briefings of clients concerning status of cases.
- Set trial dates and prepare necessary notification to all parties.
- Help clients prepare monthly income and expense sheets.
- Arrange for appraisal of real property and personal property.
- Schedule expert witness interviews and availability for trial.
- Close cases and clean up files.
- Research tax aspects of child support and maintenance.
- Determine protection available in domestic violence incidents.
- Draft petitions for name changes.
- Prepare forms necessary to transfer property.
- Inform or notify insurance companies that may be affected by family legal actions.
- Determine if property has been delivered to the rightful owner.
- Keep track of monetary property settlement payment dates.
- File legal documents to enforce judgments.
- Identify nonlegal problems that can be referred to other entities.
- Draft petitions for dissolution or response.
- Draft temporary motions, affidavits, and orders.
- Draft property settlement agreements.
- Determine child and spousal support needs.
- Draft decrees of dissolution and accompanying motions and affidavits.
- Draft motions and affidavits for modification.
- Communicate with opposing counsel or clients.
- Maintain contact; handle calls when legal advice is not needed.
- Obtain and organize information for discovery.
- Draft proposed stipulations.
- Confer with clients before court about issues relevant to hearings.
- Draft petitions for, consent for, and decrees of adoption.
- Draft postdecree pleadings as necessary.
- Prepare court documents, unusual petitions, and accountings.
- Develop and maintain manual or computerized accounting procedures.
- Develop and maintain a manual or computerized client database.
- Develop and maintain tax, probate, and other manuals.[1]

INTRODUCTION

Over the typical paralegal career, it will be rare not to come into contact with some facet of the law of domestic relations. Family law, in a somewhat tragic way, has become a booming legal practice area due to the obvious stresses on families in the American experience. As divorce rates rise and custody battles escalate, it is no wonder that opportunities for work and the related profits are so generous. Paralegals are rightfully considered central players in the delivery of this legal service. As Steve Berensen points out, the trend is toward the nonlawyer in the difficult world of domestic relations:

> *Responses that seek to increase provision of services by nonlawyers include efforts to increase the activity of legally trained, nonlawyer assistants such as paralegals, and mandatory court-ordered mediation of family law disputes. Efforts to increase the availability of representation by lawyers include cost reducing efforts such as unbundling or limited task representation and reduced-fee panels.*[2]

To be blunt, family law is a tough business, and those choosing to move in this direction cannot be fainthearted or overly sentimental. One hardened, battle-weary domestic relations attorney with over 40 years' experience profiles the necessary disposition. She handled squabbling spouses, battered wives and children, and uncaring fathers under severe emotional conditions. As a scarred survivor, she comments that any domestic relations lawyer should "get your fee first and don't worry about all that emotional stuff." At first glance such a statement appears coldhearted and irrational, though it makes perfect sense. Family law practitioners must maintain the delicate balance between being sympathetic and caring over their clients' situation while remaining objective and professional. It is impossible to represent a client well if the attorney has become too emotionally invested in the client's problems.[3] In this negative world, paralegals and lawyers provide essential services to families and marriages in distress and deal with a host of other issues:

- Separating married couples.
- Finding a marriage void or voidable.
- Stopping and halting physical and emotional abuse between spouses.
- Ensuring support payments.
- Ensuring a legal separation.
- Acquiring a divorce.
- Dividing children and custodial rights.
- Ensuring visitation rights.
- Creating, enforcing, and modifying specific support rights.
- Ensuring support or alimony for a nonindependent spouse.
- Protecting individuals from recurring physical abuse.
- Adopting children.

Most work performed by the domestic law practitioner and paralegal centers on emotional crisis. Understanding this is crucial to success.

Besides being emotionally taxing, family law is also sometimes subject to vacillating trends and fads more than other areas of law.[4] During the height of the family law reform era in the 1970s and early 1980s, alimony was viewed by many as an admission of weakness on the part of the receiving spouse. Feminist critiques of alimony were common. Alimony or spousal maintenance was often considered counterproductive to the developing independence or the already existing inherent independence of women suffering divisive marriages.[5] Now in many jurisdictions, alimony awards have been substantially decreased. However, the question of alimony is once again being reconsidered, and the pendulum may swing back to a more favorable view of this type of support.[6]

Faddishness manifests itself in other family law corners, such as the push for joint custody, the award of custody to the mentally retarded, and the heated debate over same sex relationships and adoption.[7] Family law often gets caught up in the times—and the times are not always wise or sensible. The proponents and reformers of family law often latch onto trendy ideas that sometimes do more harm than good.[8] In the context of change, family law has no rival. Consider the new theories of the past 20 years that are being tested and tried:

- No-fault divorce.
- Joint custody.
- Grandparents' visitation rights.
- Alimony: its rise, fall, and resurrection.
- Custody awards based on the best interests of the child.
- Attachment and garnishment mechanisms to ensure support.
- Inclusion and exclusion of homosexuals in the adoption of children.[9]
- Same sex marriage.
- Marriage and the problem of incest.

In Professor Sam Davis's *Rethinking American Family Law,* domestic relations law's conceptual volatility is tied to the people it serves and, as a result, is more likely to change its intellectual boundaries. Family law, he notes with insight, reflects the change in people as they live out their lives, and "values change; priorities change; institutions change. Ideas, definitions, theories, concepts, processes—all change."[10]

Those involved in family law often must grapple with trends and practices that may be inconsistent with their own value systems. In other words, family law may be an area not suitable for all paralegals because the statutory structure governing it may promote remedies and actions at odds with the practitioner.[11] If there is any truthful proposition, it is that the American family is changing—and in ways that not all can agree on. The statistics are powerful enough.

The traditional nuclear family consisting of a father and mother, as well as extended relatives, seems to be disappearing. "Census statistics show that fewer than one out of every eighteen American families approximate this model. Divorce, single parenting, and working women have contributed to this drastic change in lifestyle."[12] Demographic, cultural, and sociological studies of the American family all point to a dramatic change in its traditional structure. For example, Benjamin Schlesinger conducted an extensive study of the nature of remarriage or second marriages and emphasizes that even in the category of second marriages there are many combinations:

- A divorced man married to a single woman.
- A divorced man married to a widowed woman.
- A divorced man married to a divorced woman.
- A single man married to a divorced woman.
- A single man married to a widowed woman.
- A widowed man married to a single woman.
- A widowed man married to a widowed woman.
- A widowed man married to a divorced woman.[13]

Consider all the other players in the process such as stepparents, single parents deciding never to get married but still having children, grandparents taking over a split or broken family and adopting children, two-divorce families combining or blending their interests, and other variations. Sharyn Duffin attempts to describe and categorize families in her work *Yours, Mine, and Ours: Tips for Stepparents,* in which she describes the traditional nuclear family as classified into any of the following terminologies:

- Multiparent.
- Binuclear.
- Combined.
- Remarried.
- Second families.
- Serial monogamy.
- Instant.
- Split families.
- Joint.
- Stepfamilies.
- Merged.
- Mixed.
- Synergistic families.[14]

In law and legal rights, these varied definitions of family units create predictable confusion. Generally the traditional methods for evaluating parents' and children's rights in a domestic relations case are not always helpful. Besides value judgments made, it is apparent that traditional domestic relations law cannot serve these competing interests. Certainly demographic, cultural, and social forces are changing the American family.

New York State courts have radically altered the concept of biological families with a *functional* test of how people interact. If a relationship exists, despite biology, family rights exist. This form of analysis has led to a grant of visitation rights and adoption rights to homosexuals.[15]

Moral arguments aside, is *functionality* an objective legal criterion? Is it right for courts to "focus on the essential characteristics of a marital union, such as long-term commitment and economic interdependence, not merely in whether the two individuals were married in a licensed ceremony? The functional approach thus considers a broader class of individuals, such as homosexual and heterosexual couples who live together, to be a family unit."[16] Will this form of subjective analysis lead to an even more confusing approach in the determination of family rights?

And if one ponders a bit more, is the legal system the only mechanism appropriate in family law questions? Does the legal system truly provide a complementary service in matters of divorce, custody, and support? Are there alternatives, or are parallel systems under development that would deal with these questions? Historically the church, the synagogue, and the mosque played a crucial role in these affairs. Should they reemerge as models for the resolution of family law disputes? Rabbinical courts and tribunals are increasingly being utilized in various family law matters.[17] For some, the shoe of the American legal system and the foot of family law simply do not match.[18]

Although one surely cannot call for the elimination or radical reconstruction of how the legal system works in the family sector, it is worth some self-examination to make sure that the system does not whip up more litigiousness than alternative means. If anything, the paralegal must be in the business of resolution in this tumultuous area of law: It is the place where the counselor at law makes better sense than the aggressive advocate. This is an important preliminary concept for the paralegal to grasp—the inadequacy of the legal system and its inability to adapt to the emotionality of domestic relations law. A battleground mentality does the parties a clear injustice and delivers a "distorted view of their situation," with the usual result being further acrimony.[19]

Judicial intervention of this sort provides a convenient wall of protection, an emotional veneer that sometimes becomes impenetrable, according and affording parties the right not to deal directly with their problems. Some even argue that family law has two levels of victimization: that of the split or the dispute and that of a system that fails to efficiently resolve the dilemma:[20]

> *Remembering that an attorney is a counselor first, some mechanisms, some techniques of mediation, counseling, negotiating, and a resolution of problems through a conciliatory framework may be a much more sensible exercise. Some jurisdictions now mandate that divorcing parties take part in some form of mediation prior to the granting of a final decree of divorce.*[21]

ADMINISTRATIVE ASPECTS OF THE DOMESTIC RELATIONS CASE

Initial Client Contact

The importance of fact gathering in domestic relations cases cannot be emphasized enough. Because much of the activity is emotional, a client's commentary may be subject to exaggeration or vindictiveness, or it may result from deep psychological and emotional pain. Facts are often suspect in family law cases. Impress on the client a need for candor but just as compellingly accuracy. Make sure the client knows that the attorney and the paralegal are part of the *team*. The State Bar of Georgia's Family Law Section emphasizes the importance of the paralegal during initial client contact:

> A. Initial interview. *It is imperative during the initial interview with a client that the paralegal immediately is introduced as part of the divorce representation team. If this is done at the outset, the client then feels the paralegal is on equal footing in certain respects with the lawyer and immediately gains confidence and familiarity with the paralegal. The atmosphere and future progress of the case are often dependent on first impressions and reactions that clients gain.*

At this meeting, the paralegal should be introduced as a professional trained in family law procedure. The client should be aware that the lawyer may have times when availability is difficult, but the paralegal is always there as an ear for the client. When attorney and paralegal rates are explained to the client, he/she will realize how economically sensible it is to have contact with the paralegal rather than the attorney.[22]

See Form 12.1 on the accompanying CD for a family law intake form. The document elicits information regarding personal identification and address, names and number of children, known information about a spouse, and the general economic assets available in this marital relationship.

The family law information worksheet should be placed into the permanent file of a client once an agreement between the client and attorney has been reached. (See Form 12.2 on the accompanying CD.) Its contents indicate the jurisdiction of the action, a chronological listing of actions that may take place, the name of opposing counsel, and other relevant information.

In this area of law like no other, clients often tend to vacillate in their decisions. At first clients can be cooperative and then suddenly become noncooperative in providing essential information that will help in investigation. A request for a divorce may suddenly turn into reconciliation, and various other changes often occur during the separation phase of a domestic relations case. Standardized instructions are provided in the client instruction sheet (see Form 12.3 on the accompanying CD). Specific directions are given to the client about the law office's policies on telephones and the use of paralegals. Clients are urged to read all documentation, specifically about court dates. This handy document will be especially useful if a client claims you did not keep him or her informed of events or the importance of hearings and other matters.

Finally, evaluate facts skeptically because the facts being presented are obviously from a prejudiced viewpoint. The old maxim that it takes two to tango is generally true in the law of domestic relations. Although there is often a party who is abused and mistreated more than the other, more often both parties have some fault or responsibility. Conduct an extensive investigation before raising the expectations of any party. Also, seek at any cost to resolve the dispute in less adjudicated ways than those discussed in the next section.

Attorney's Fees

Attorney's fees in domestic relations cases are often difficult to collect. Clients, already victimized by personal trauma, resent the economic expense, and at best will grudgingly pay fees. Parties to domestic relations litigation sometimes regard attorneys' fees as wasted money. In a sense, they are exactly right. From an economic perspective, attorneys' fees in domestic relations cases are nonproductive investments—an expenditure necessitated by an inability to handle some facet of a relationship. In short, human failure is followed by economic loss. Attorney Jennifer Rose, experienced in the troublesome marriage of legal fees and domestic relations practice, states,

> *One of the worst secrets in legal practice is the toll that domestic relation work take can take on the lawyer's staff, resources, and psyche. Even the stiffest of iron constitutions sometimes bend under the strain of such emotionally overcharged work, and more than a few lawyers have found that their initial enthusiasm quickly turns to head-in-the-hands regret.*[23]

There is also a truism that no fee slides faster down the curve of gratitude than a domestic relations fee. Once a divorce has been granted, custody has been awarded, or support has been secured, client's memories become extremely vague and short, and they tend to disregard the efforts and energies expended in acquisition of the results. They often assert, "I could have done that myself." Within this financial framework, fee letters and fee agreements are absolutely mandatory; and generally such documentation should be used in every area of the practice of law. Jennifer Rose suggests ten commandments when handling fees:

1. *Decide what kind of profit you want to make from each client.*
2. *Tell your client what it's going to cost.*
3. *Always use a written retainer agreement.*
4. *Discuss cost-effectiveness with each client.*
5. *Bill regularly and descriptively.*
6. *Discuss payment options.*
7. *Assess the level of client satisfaction.*

8. *Cross-market your services.*
9. *Thank your referral source.*
10. *Reevaluate your profit margin at the end of each case.*[24]

The unpredictability and volatility of domestic relations fees cause continuous stress for the practitioner. Forms will take much of the worry out of fees. Review the sample fee letter that outlines the initial office visitation relative to a separation. (See Form 12.4 on the accompanying CD.) More than in any other area of law, fee discussions in domestic relations cases must be open, free, and frequent.[25] Another example of a retainer agreement in a divorce case is shown in Form 12.5.

CONTRACTUAL ISSUES IN THE LAW OF DOMESTIC RELATIONS

As can be expected, divorce, custody, and support litigation will take up the greatest amount of time of a family law practitioner. Clients should also be advised that alternatives to judicial involvement and formal litigation are available by select preliminary strategies. Most of the contentiousness in divorce, for example, could be mitigated by prenuptial and postnuptial agreements. Clients should be informed that the following techniques of contractual dispute resolution are also possible.

Prenuptial Agreements

In an age of staggering divorce rates, the protection of economic interests by prenuptial agreements is an intelligent approach. A prenuptial agreement is an agreement entered by the parties to a marriage before the marriage. Although critics call it an invitation to divorce, creating or at least promoting a self-fulfilling prophecy of marital breakdown, realists view a prenuptial agreement as the best form of preventive protection. Prenuptial agreements, to be enforceable, must be in writing under the Statute of Frauds and must have all the requisite clauses, provisions, and formalities of any valid contract. Consideration is supported by the marriage itself. A sample prenuptial agreement outlining the specific rights of the parties in the event of marital discord is shown in Form 12.6 on the accompanying CD.

Some highlighted clauses in the prenuptial agreement are these:

- Parties' retention of separate property and income.
- Understanding of each other's financial assets and income before entry into the marriage.
- Affirmation that the marriage is being entered volitionally and with full knowledge of the effect of the prenuptial agreement.
- Division of expenses and costs of maintaining a household.
- Estate planning provisions.
- Effect of a deceased spouse.
- Influence of a remarriage upon death of a spouse.
- Allocation formula of the value in an equitable division upon a divorce.
- Distribution of property to children upon death or divorce.
- Listing and valuation of each other's property interests if so desired.

Legalistic explanations of spousal rights have been criticized as unromantic; but given the odds of divorce, it may make sense to author such a document.

Family law practitioner Fred Morganroth sets out some timely advice on drafting enforceable prenuptial agreements:

- The agreement must be in writing and signed by the parties.
- The agreement must be voluntarily entered without fraud, mistake, or duress.
- The parties must be represented by independent legal counsel, who must explain to each client his or her obligations, rights, and alternatives and ensure that each party fully understands the terms of the agreement, as well as the nature of his or her waiver and/or relinquishment of rights. This includes an understanding of what differences would exist without the intended agreement.

- There must be a full, fair, and complete disclosure of each party's assets, liabilities, and income. This cannot be handled by a provision that merely recites that a disclosure was made. Attached to each agreement should be a detailed financial statement giving full disclosure. It is not sufficient to lump categories together or make generalizations such as these:

  - Stocks   30,000
  - Real estate   100,000
  - Business interests   50,000

- Each stock holding, each parcel of real estate, each limited partnership, and so forth should be separately itemized, valued, and broken down to ensure a complete, full, and fair disclosure. Similarly, liabilities should be separately itemized and listed. Having each party's financial statement prepared by a separate certified public accountant or an actuary would also be wise.

- The agreement must be fair and not unconscionable when the agreement is executed.

- Have the facts and circumstances changed since the agreement was executed to make its enforcement unfair and unreasonable?[26]

See Form 12.7 on the accompanying CD for a letter giving advice to clients in search of a prenuptial agreement.

Postnuptial Agreements

Postnuptial agreements define the rights of the parties in the event of marital dissolution. The same terms and conditions of the prenuptial agreement are posed:

- Emphasizing rights upon eventual divorce or separation.
- Equitably dividing property interests owned before the marriage and during its period of legitimacy.
- Property interests that will remain for all time separate and divided.

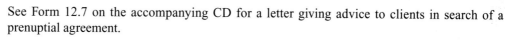

- Influence of the action for divorce on children of the parties.
- Other standardized miscellaneous matters.

A sample postnuptial agreement is outlined in Form 12.8 on the accompanying CD.

Separation Agreements

Parties currently living in an undesirable domestic situation should resist immediate divorce unless the circumstances are painfully futile. The nature of human beings and their relationships are complex and likely to change. Paralegals should dissuade clients from rash decisions. Allow time for emotion or rage to dissipate. Allow time for the parties to mediate and conciliate, and suggest a separation agreement. Separation agreements often provide that venting capacity. Lawyers should promote mediation rather than an adversarial interaction, and the separation agreement allows the parties to cool off and think rationally about their circumstances.

Depending on your jurisdiction, the utility of the separation agreement will largely depend on its enforceability. The validity and enforceability of separation agreements have come into question when not made a formal part of the final divorce decree.[27] See the separation agreement checklist in Form 12.9 on the accompanying CD for some helpful drafting advice.

Consider the separation agreement outlined in Form 12.10 on the accompanying CD. Most such agreements state that they are being entered for the purpose of defining the respective rights and obligations and property interests of each in the event of a granting of the dissolution of their marriage or the granting of a final decree of divorce to either party. By this language, separation agreements leave a door open, permit a line of communication, and foster one last clear chance for a resurrected relationship. Matters of custody, support, and temporary division of property are all fully discussed.

Cohabitation Agreements

Even without a declaration of formal marriage, contract principles, whether express or implied, may be pertinent to the enforcement of particular rights of parties who live together. In

Connecticut, by way of illustration, the courts are not hesitant to find enforceability in cohabitation agreements. In *Herring v. Daniels*[28] the court applied traditional contract principles:

> [W]here the parties have established an unmarried, cohabiting relationship, it is the specific conduct of the parties within that relationship that determines their respective rights and obligations, including the treatment of their individual property. . . . Any such finding must be determined by reference to the unique circumstances and arrangements between the parties present in each case. Those matters are questions of fact that are within the singular province of the trial court, and can only be determined by evaluating the credibility of the witnesses and weighing conflicting evidence.[29]

For sample language necessary in a cohabitation agreement, see Form 12.11 on the accompanying CD.

Breach of Engagement

From a common-law perspective, marriage is essentially a contract. The promise to marry is the offer. The acceptance of that offer constitutes an engagement. The parties' understanding that they intend to marry grows, matures, and becomes clearly defined as a result of the frequent meetings, the expressions of affection, possible physical intimacy, and mutual wishes and hopes. This interaction and oral promise create a binding contract. Although litigation involving engagement is rare, most American jurisdictions characterize the breach of promise to marry as a "heart-balm" action. The balm reminds us of a medicinal cure or salve in the event of a wounded heart. In modern times, such an action has been described as an anomaly. Most American jurisdictions have made some statutory modification to this right. For paralegals who come across an engagement dispute, a complaint for breach of a promise to marry is included in Form 12.12 on the accompanying CD.

THE ANNULMENT PROCESS

Instead of immediately embarking on a divorce action, a significant portion of the population, particularly individuals who have religious or spiritual restrictions on divorce, might consider the annulment process. Since the 12th century the right to annul marriages has been a remedy in both canon and civil law. Originally, within the ecclesiastical courts of England,[30] marriage could be declared annulled—that is, held to be nonexistent and without legal effect. The right to annul is still a civil remedy available in most jurisdictions.

If this question arises, inform the client that most religious denominations, such as Catholic, Lutheran, or Jewish faiths, have substantive and procedural steps in the matter of annulment. Steer the client to the local offices of the appropriate religious denomination, where information on this process will be available. For an example of the Roman Catholic annulment process, visit the Diocese of St. Cloud's Web site at www.stcdio.org/annul_proced.htm.

In sum, the religious aspects of divorce must be part of the paralegal plan in family law. As an example, a Catholic's whole perspective on divorce is changed if an annulment can be granted. A grant of annulment opens the potential for a new marriage without suffering sanctions from the church. Other religions have similar rules.[31]

An annulment declares a marriage either initially void or voidable. Potential grounds for annulment include these:

- Bigamy: A spouse is married to two or more partners.
- Incest: Marriage was entered with a party who has too close a consanguinity or affinity to the partner.
- Non-age: Marriage was entered by a minor.
- Duress: Marriage was entered under undue influence, threat, coercion, or other unreasonable force.
- Fraud: Marriage was entered under conditions or terms not known to one of the parties, such as a serious misrepresentation of identity, intentions, or capacity to marry.
- Mental disability: Marriage was entered with an individual who did not have the mental capacity to contract marriage.
- Physical disability: This generally relates to impotency or the inability to have children.

Review the complaint for an annulment shown in Form 12.13 on the accompanying CD.

PRELIMINARY LITIGATION

Most often the breakup of a family is a turbulent and traumatic event. The parties must contend with a wide array of complicated human problems; and while doing so, they often struggle with anger and rage, depression and alienation. The stakes are complex for family law clients. Consider these types of complications:

- Assuming the parties wish to live separately, who will stay in the primary residence?

- Who will have custody of the children?

- Who is to ensure that spouses and children are not physically abused?

- How can it be assured that mental and emotional abuse will not continue to take place?

- Is there a need for a protective order or other equitable remedy that will ensure the safety of spouses and children?

Because of these and other questions, steps need to be taken ensuring the health, safety, and economic support of the parties in a domestic relations case. Equitable remedies, such as temporary restraining orders, protective orders, injunctions, and criminal contempt remedies are used on a regular basis.[32]

Certain jurisdictions like Indiana formalize the preliminary issues by a pleading called a *motion for provisional order*. A document dealing with protection of self, right to domicile, and initial custody of children is filed.

Needless to say, these affairs are complicated, and some people debate whether the state and its courts are properly equipped to handle these complexities. Essentially two schools of thought on family intervention exist: first, those who advocate a laissez faire approach to familial problems; second, those who call for unbridled governmental intrusion.[33] "The experience of state intervention in a family can involve either affirmative, coercive behavior by state officials . . . or refusal by state officials to come to the aid of . . . a family."[34]

Courts cannot be expected to solve every problem in a domestic setting. Undeniably there has been an unrealistic expectation that in all matters courts have magical powers to resolve human differences. The state is simply incapable of mediating every dispute that comes before it. Yet the problems of families are acute under any measure. Rising rates of child abuse and molestation, as just one example, trigger a more aggressive form of intervention. Within this environment the paralegal or attorney in domestic relations must operate by carefully calculating the role of the state in the internal affairs of the family. Some remedial action is often needed in family disputes, especially involving economic and physical issues. First, such issues can be handled through a motion for a temporary restraining order. A sample of such a motion is shown in Form 12.14 on the accompanying CD.

Second, a temporary protection order, based on the motion and testimony of the parties, can be issued by the court. Under a temporary protection order, a spouse is "restrained and enjoined from annoying, harassing, threatening, or committing acts of domestic violence against plaintiff and is [further] enjoined from selling or moving or disposing of marital assets." (See Form 12.15 on the accompanying CD.) Many jurisdictions safeguard an abused spouse under protection from abuse laws and proceedings. (See Form 12.16.) Divorce attorney Patricia Grove and paralegal Mary Binter share their experienced advice on this temporary remedy:

> *Although many forms have the temporary terms motion papers and "canned" affidavits on the processor, I am a proponent of individualized pleadings. The use of form pleadings, designed of general language to fit a general case, is confusing not only to the client but to the opposing party. I have found that with the use of form pleadings, the opposing party frequently questioned my client about a particular relief claimed, and my client responded "that's what the lawyer asked for." It only takes a little additional time to fully individualize the temporary terms pleadings and affidavits, and this pays dividends in helping both parties understand what is being requested and why. The client should always feel comfortable with what he or she has signed.[35]*

A judicial order or decision may decide who is going to live in the marital home. An affiant or a petitioner who claims that he or she fears for the lives and safety of himself or herself and the minor children[36] can file a motion asking the court for an order removing the abusive spouse from the residence.[37]

Likewise, children must be accounted for in an abusive domestic situation. Motions requesting temporary custody and temporary support payments can be made. The affiant or petitioner may say that the opposing party is simply not suited to provide for the proper care of the minor children in question. Form 12.17 on the accompanying CD, from Colorado, illustrates a motion combining all of these requests into one document.

Other preliminary orders before the grant of a divorce decree are also possible. Paralegals should consider a request by the court for the temporary granting of

- Alimony.
- Attorney's fees.
- Injunctions halting a defendant from leaving the state.
- Protective orders or injunctions prohibiting the transfer of any property.

DIVORCE ACTIONS

Family law practitioners quickly discern that their relationships with paralegals are a good match. "More so than in many other areas of law, the family lawyer and legal assistant work together closely in providing supportive and cost-efficient legal services to the client."[38] From the outset of the divorce action, whether fault or no-fault in design, paralegals are essential players.

Initially paralegals should be aware that there is a growing trend toward mediation of divorce claims in lieu of the traditional adversarial context. The legal process gives only minimal recognition to the emotional trauma that underlies the severance of the marital relationship, and as a result promulgates rules and procedures that are less than attentive to the human cost.[39]

Mediation and dispute resolution, through the bar, private agencies, private or public masters, or other techniques, rests comfortably in the practice of family law. Mediation has many advantages over the traditional adversarial process:

- Mediation facilitates communication between the divorcing parties.
- Parties make their own agreements instead of having settlements imposed on them by a third party.
- The peaceful solution of conflicts helps to prevent problems from escalating.
- The mediation process takes problems out of the adversarial win–lose setting of the court into a setting that is nonadversarial and neutral.
- Solutions reached through mediation last longer because these solutions represent both parties' views and tend to be perceived as fair and acceptable.
- Mediation is less expensive and quicker than court processing, especially for minor disputes.
- Mediation helps spouses identify issues, reduce misunderstandings, vent emotions, clarify positions, find points of agreement, explore new areas of compromise, and ultimately negotiate an agreement.
- Mediation is conducted in private.
- Mediation permits the airing of all grievances, not only those that are legally operative.
- Mediation is procedurally simple and more likely to lead to truth finding.
- Mediation is capable of handling the causes of problems, not just the problems.
- Mediation reduces the alienation of the litigants and opens communication between them.
- Mediation aids disputing parties in resuming workable relationships with each other.
- Mediation enhances the adjustment of children following separation or divorce by promoting parental cooperation, reinforcing parent–child bonds, and encouraging visitation.
- Mediation reduces the anger, feelings of loss, sense of injustice, and separation from their children that many noncustodial parents experience.
- Mediation promotes child support payment performance of fathers following divorce.
- Mediation reduces governmental interference in the ordering of marital and family affairs.
- Mediation diminishes the emphasis on fault finding and blameworthiness.[40]

Mediation's proponents believe the process is a positive one. Mediation responds to a growing recognition that people, not systems, whether social or judicial, should solve their own problems and should not look strictly to lawyers and judicial officers for domestic relations tranquility.

Whether mediated or litigated, a divorce case needs an information base. A checklist that gathers such information is shown in Form 12.18 on the accompanying CD.

No-Fault Grounds for Divorce

In recognition of the dramatic increase in the number of divorces and in an effort to make the process of separation less painful, no-fault statutes have multiplied in the last 30 years. Arguing that the fault system is too restrictive, too arbitrary, and not realistic in light of today's family relationships, proponents of no-fault divorce say the emotional expenditure justifies the passage.[41] Although this is well intentioned, a host of states, including Pennsylvania and Kentucky, are revisiting the convenience side of the argument.[42] In fact, it is obvious that the ease of divorce precipitates higher rates of divorce.

A no-fault jurisdiction gives little credence or regard to a finding of fault in a marital breakup. In granting a decree of divorce, a no-fault advocate, and the court considering the complaint of petition, care little about the basis for the request, whether adultery, abuse, desertion, or abandonment of marital responsibilities. Instead no-fault statutes generally are characterized as follows.

Irreconcilable Differences Leading to Breakdown

A claim of irreconcilable differences purports that the marriage lacks any real hope of salvage, that the parties are fundamentally incapable of resolving their differences. The language of irreconcilable differences generally consists of subjective characterizations of failure and impossibility:

> *Irreconcilable differences exist between petitioner and respondent causing the irretrievable breakdown of the marriage bond.*[43]

How anyone could objectively measure the breakdown appears difficult enough for the parties, let alone the court.

Living Separate and Apart

The standard proof necessary to meet the no-fault grounds of living separate and apart can be as simple as the calendar calculation of a period in which spouses have lived physically and mentally separate and apart. See Form 12.19 on the accompanying CD for the language of such a pleading. Again, with little or no regard for fault, the court computes and calculates the period of living apart, whether it be six months or three years. A sample statute listing both fault and no-fault grounds is shown in Figure 12.1.

A petition for dissolution of the marriage shown in Form 12.20 on the accompanying CD contains the requisite language of this no-fault grounds, as well as averments regarding custody, alimony, property, and the rights of children. The parties, by amicable agreement, may wish to waive service requirements. (See Form 12.21.)

Incompatibility

Incompatibility is a catch-all basis in no-fault divorce—a state in which the parties indicate the complete impossibility of further cohabitation and the impossibility of marital maintenance. Although it is an elusive term, *incompatibility* includes "circumstances that indicate that the parties are no longer getting along and wish to end the marriage."[44] Here is some typical pleading language:

> *The tastes, mental dispositions, views, and likes and dislikes of plaintiff and defendant have become so widely separated and divergent that the parties are incompatible to such an extent that it is impossible for them to live together as husband and wife. The incompatibility between plaintiff and defendant is so great that there is no possibility of reconciliation between them.*[45]

Proving incompatibility, given its vague delineations, is, like other fault grounds, a formality with substance.

FIGURE 12.1 Grounds for Divorce from Bond of Matrimony

Source: Pa. Cons. Stat. Annot. §3301 (2005).

(a) FAULT.—The court may grant a divorce to the innocent and injured spouse whenever it is judged that the other spouse has:

(1) Committed willful and malicious desertion, and absence from the habitation of the injured and innocent spouse, without a reasonable cause, for the period of one or more years.

(2) Committed adultery.

(3) By cruel and barbarous treatment, endangered the life or health of the injured and innocent spouse.

(4) Knowingly entered into a bigamous marriage while a former marriage is still existing.

(5) Been sentenced to imprisonment for a term of two or more years upon conviction of having committed a crime.

(6) Offered such indignities to the innocent and injured spouse as to render that spouse's condition intolerable and life burdensome.

(b) INSTITUTIONALIZATION.—The court may grant a divorce from a spouse upon the ground that insanity or serious mental disorder has resulted in confinement in a mental institution for at least 18 months immediately before the commencement of an action under this part and where there is no reasonable prospect that the spouse will be discharged from inpatient care during the 18 months subsequent to the commencement of the action. A presumption that no prospect of discharge exists shall be established by a certificate of the superintendent of the institution to that effect and which includes a supporting statement of a treating physician.

(c) MUTUAL CONSENT.—The court may grant a divorce where it is alleged that the marriage is irretrievably broken and 90 days have elapsed from the date of commencement of an action under this part and an affidavit has been filed by each of the parties evidencing that each of the parties consents to the divorce.

(d) IRRETRIEVABLE BREAKDOWN.—

(1) The court may grant a divorce where a complaint has been filed alleging that the marriage is irretrievably broken and an affidavit has been filed alleging that the parties have lived separate and apart for a period of at least two years and that the marriage is irretrievably broken and the defendant either:

(i) Does not deny the allegations set forth in the affidavit.

(ii) Denies one or more of the allegations set forth in the affidavit but, after notice and hearing, the court determines that the parties have lived separate and apart for a period of at least two years and that the marriage is irretrievably broken.

(2) If a hearing has been held pursuant to paragraph (1)(ii) and the court determines that there is a reasonable prospect of reconciliation, then the court shall continue the matter for a period not less than 90 days nor more than 120 days unless the parties agree to a period in excess of 120 days. During this period, the court shall require counseling as provided in Section 3302 (relating to counseling). If the parties have not reconciled at the expiration of the time period and one party states under oath that the marriage is irretrievably broken, the court shall determine whether the marriage is irretrievably broken. If the court determines that the marriage is irretrievably broken, the court shall grant the divorce. Otherwise, the court shall deny the divorce.

(e) NO HEARING REQUIRED IN CERTAIN CASES.— If grounds for divorce alleged in the complaint or counterclaim are established under subsection (c) or (d), the court shall grant a divorce without requiring a hearing on any other grounds.

Fault Grounds for Divorce

Historically a divorce could only be granted to a party who was not at fault—that is, not responsible for the breakdown. Under equitable doctrines, such as clean hands and laches, if both parties were at fault, no divorce could be granted—a curious construction that befuddled jurists.[46] Traditional fault grounds are still important to litigators; and with the current reform push in various jurisdictions, the fault basis may take on elevated importance.

Adultery

Most American jurisdictions consider adultery a fault ground. Adultery is voluntary sexual intercourse of a married person with a person other than the offender's spouse. A case of adultery requires demonstration of an adulterous action and disposition or inclination by the offending spouse.

Desertion

Desertion is a willful, continuous, and intentional action to withdraw from the marital obligation and duty. The desertion is voluntary, without justification, and not a short-term event. To assert the grounds of desertion, four basic elements must be considered:

1. Voluntary separation by one spouse from another.
2. Intent not to resume marital cohabitation.
3. Lack of consent.
4. Simply leaving, leaving with intent not to return, and leaving without the consent of the other party.[47]

If spousal interaction recurs, despite its brevity, this ground is not provable.

Cruelty

The ground of cruelty exists in the majority of jurisdictions.[48] Quantifying cruelty is troublesome, though case law and statutory designs do pronounce that acts are cruel if they result in

- Willful infliction of pain.
- Excessive argumentation.
- Personal indignities.
- Barbarous treatment.
- Conduct that utterly destroys the marriage.
- Conduct that makes living together impossible.
- Physical and emotional abuse.
- Conduct that destroys one's personal well-being.
- False charges of prostitution.
- Impairment of the health of the victimized party.

By definition, almost any conduct can meet the standard of cruelty. Terms commonly used in divorce statutes relating to cruelty are *cruelty, extreme cruelty, cruel and inhuman treatment,* and the like. Several states permit divorce on the ground of "indignities." Most statutes that authorize a divorce on the ground of indignities also authorize a divorce on the ground of cruelty.[49]

Paralegals should search for conduct that causes indignity to another. Form 12.22 on the accompanying CD may be used to allege cruelty.

Miscellaneous Fault Grounds for Divorce

Depending on jurisdiction, an array of fault grounds exists. Here is a partial listing of these grounds:

- Grounds relating to capacity and competency to marry:
  - Bigamy.
  - Non-age.
  - Fraud.
  - Duress.
  - Physical disability or impotence.
  - Insanity.
  - Incest.
- Grounds relating to neglect of marital duties:
  - Nonsupport.
  - Neglect of duty.
- Grounds relating to the character of the offending spouse:
  - Drunkenness and drug addiction.
  - Conviction of specific crimes.
  - Habitual drunkenness.
  - Venereal disease.
  - Deviant sexual conduct.

A synopsis of divorce grounds, whether fault or no-fault, is outlined in Figure 12.2.

FIGURE 12.2 Grounds for Divorce by State

Source: Data from http://www.divorcesource.com/info/divorcelawsgr/states.shtml (retrieved January 22, 2007).

State	Fault Grounds	No-Fault Grounds	Separation Required?	Length of Separation
Alabama	☐	☐	☐	
Alaska	☐	☐		
Arizona	☐ ᵃ	☐		
Arkansas	☐	☐	☐	18 months
California		☐		
Colorado		☐		
Connecticut	☐	☐	☐	18 months
Delaware	☐	☐		
District of Columbia		☐	☐	6 months
Florida		☐		
Georgia	☐	☐		
Hawaii		☐	☐	2 years
Idaho	☐	☐	☐	5 years
Illinois	☐	☐	☐ ᵇ	2 years
Indiana	☐	☐		
Iowa		☐		
Kansas	☐	☐		
Kentucky		☐		
Louisiana	☐	☐	☐	180 days
Maine	☐	☐		
Maryland	☐		☐	1 year
Massachusetts	☐	☐		
Michigan		☐		
Minnesota		☐	☐	180 days
Mississippi	☐	☐		
Missouri		☐		
Montana		☐		
Nebraska	☐	☐		
Nevada	☐	☐	☐	1 year
New Hampshire	☐	☐		
New Jersey	☐		☐	18 months
New Mexico	☐	☐		

State				
New York	☐		☐	1 year
North Carolina	☐	☐	☐	1 year
North Dakota	☐	☐		
Ohio	☐	☐	☐	1 year
Oklahoma	☐	☐		
Oregon	☐	☐		
Pennsylvania	☐	☐	☐	2 years
Rhode Island	☐	☐	☐	3 years
South Carolina	☐	☐	☐	1 year
South Dakota	☐	☐		
Tennessee	☐	☐	☐ [c]	2 years
Texas	☐		☐	3 years
Utah	☐	☐	☐	3 years
Vermont	☐	☐	☐	6 months
Virginia	☐	☐	☐ [d]	1 year
Washington		☐		
West Virginia	☐	☐	☐	1 year
Wisconsin		☐		
Wyoming	☐	☐		1 year

[a]Arizona recognizes what is considered a "higher" form of marriage called a "covenant marriage." If the marriage is a covenant marriage, grounds must be alleged, including one-year separation.
[b]Length of separation may be waived upon written consent of both parties.
[c]Separation-based divorce allowed only if there are no minor children.
[d]May be reduced to six months if there are no children.

Litigating the Divorce Case Based on Fault

Complaint

A sample fault divorce complaint is shown in Form 12.23 on the accompanying CD. Note that paragraph 5 states, "During the term of the marriage, the Defendant treated the Plaintiff with such indignities as to render Plaintiff's condition in life intolerable and to entitle him/her to an absolute divorce." Setting out denials of a contested complaint is shown in Form 12.24.

Discovery

During the discovery process, paralegals must collect sizable amounts of information, ensuring an honest appraisal of the assets and economic interests of the parties. Some examples on the economic end can include the following list of information: tax returns, bank statements, certificates of deposit, brokerage accounts, financial statements, insurance records and policies, benefit statements regarding pensions, stock certificates, accounts receivable, credit information, loans and outstanding debts, and evidence of any personal or business litigation among the parties' interests.

In the process of litigating a domestic relations case, the normal activities of discovery and disclosure follow state civil procedure rules, though some states like Arizona have relaxed the traditional rules of discovery to allow easier access.[50] A sample inventory form from Arizona that will help in the economic determination of equitable distribution is provided in Form 12.25 on the accompanying CD.

A series of interrogatory requests are also made in the standard divorce process, again highlighting economic interests, property rights, wages and salaries, and other pertinent information for the determination. (See Form 12.26 on the accompanying CD.)

Naturally paralegals play an integral role in the discovery process. Written interrogatories and oral and/or written depositions will be a continuous responsibility of the paralegal. A notice of deposition form is shown in Form 12.27 on the accompanying CD. Other documentation about the discovery process is included in Form 12.28.

Defense Strategies

A complaint filed alleging a fault or no-fault ground may be defended like any other cause of action.[51] Singular or plural defenses may be presented by defense counsel in a divorce action and include, but are not limited to, the following strategies.

Connivance   The defense may assert that the grounds for divorce are nothing more than a sham. A party who originally consented to the grounds of fault cannot later be permitted to change his or her mind and say that he or she no longer consents. *Connivance* is the setting up of a situation so that the other person commits a wrongdoing. For example, a wife who invites her husband's lover to the house and then leaves for the weekend may be said to have connived his adultery. If the wife sues her husband for divorce, claiming he has committed adultery, the husband may argue as a defense that she connived—that is, set up—his actions. Simply put, if a married party agrees to connive, trick, and scheme to develop a ground for divorce, an equitable doctrine such as *clean hands* will negate the defense position. An advocate using the defense of connivance must show that a spouse "actively created an opportunity for the other to commit a specific offense, such as adultery or other matter, acquiesced and consented to the activity and then changed his or her position once it was committed."[52]

Collusion   Collusion is an agreement between a husband and a wife that one of them will commit an act to provide a ground for the obtainment of a fault divorce. Collusion is a deceitful agreement between two or more people, or between one of them and a third party, to bring an action against the other to obtain a judicial decision or some remedy that would not have been obtained unless the parties had combined for the purpose or suppressed material facts or otherwise. Of course, in this era of no-fault divorce activity, collusion is much less of an issue in divorce practice. It is essentially an act of fabrication in which both parties act in concert.[53]

Condonation   Condoning unethical, immoral, and fault-oriented activities in a marriage relationship can sometimes provide a defense. Essentially one spouse forgives the other for the transgression. Condonation is not a superficial statement of forgiveness. Using the defense of condonation, the advocate shows that the conduct was condoned not only voluntarily but with a desire for resumption of the marital relationship. When the parties resume living together as before, the defendant action is forgotten and condoned.

Recrimination   Recrimination is the absurd legal principle that holds that when both parties are equally at fault, no decree can be granted. The theory, a legal corollary to the clean hands doctrine, is that if both spouses are equally at fault, they will be left to stew in their own juices, married to each other, though they want a contrary result. Modern jurisdictions have limited the application of recrimination to specific grounds or to adultery only. Other jurisdictions have employed a "balancing process allowing only grounds of equal magnitude"[54] or have used the term *comparative rectitude* to serve as an offset in a recrimination case.

Miscellaneous Defenses to Divorce

- Technical defenses.
- Statute of limitations (in certain fault cases).
- Doctrine of laches (believe it or not, parties who have waited too long to get a divorce and did not complain of faulting conduct within the appropriate time will not be granted a divorce).
- *Res judicata* (if a divorce has already been granted in another jurisdiction, a divorce decree cannot be subsequently granted in another jurisdiction because the action has already been resolved).

Entry of Decree

Once a determination has been made that a fault or no-fault ground has been satisfactorily proven, the court will enter a divorce judgment or decree granting divorce to the parties who originally petitioned it. Other matters involving custody, property distribution, and visitation rights may be defined within the decree unless the parties have resolved those issues through a separation agreement or through another forum. Two sample divorce decrees are shown in Forms 12.29 and 12.30 on the accompanying CD.

EQUITABLE DIVISION OF PROPERTY

The legal aspects of property division in marital dissolution are many:

- The equitable distribution of all marital property.
- The payment of alimony if jurisdictionally permitted.
- The payment of support for children and/or a spouse.
- The payment for any extraordinary expenses of support, such as college educations or items of necessity.

Property division by state jurisdiction falls into the general categories shown in Figure 12.3.

Ideally the husband and wife who have decided that the marital relation is no longer functional or salvageable will divide property either through the mechanism of a separation agreement or through an informal understanding. Otherwise the courts take over. Supposedly courts want property divisions to be equitable, fair, and just. Many jurisdictions label the process of distributing the marital property as "equitable distribution."[55]

Judicial resolution may not be preferable in this area. Some practitioners and scholars think it best for the parties to negotiate these matters. Others hold that self-interest pervades the negotiation, and that necessitates judicial oversight. Professor Robert Mnookin refers to a bargaining mentality that fosters self-preservation:

> *Negotiated settlements will certainly reflect parental preferences with regard to these money and custody issues. Generally, self-interested judgments will not solely determine these preferences. One hopes that parental preferences reflect a desire for their children's happiness and well-being quite apart from any parental advantage. Nevertheless, some parents engage in divorce bargaining from preferences that reflect their selfish interests and ignore their children's needs.*[56]

A spirit of cooperation and familial understanding during a marital dissolution is often unrealistic. Economic interests are disproportionately valued or heightened in importance when judged in the climate of heated marital dispute. To decide sensibly the rationing of property, courts will view these issues:

- Ages of the parties.
- Earning capacity.
- Conduct during the marriage.
- Duration of the marriage.

FIGURE 12.3   **Property Division**

Source: NORMAN PERLBERGER, DIVORCE CODE, Appendix B, 2–3 (1998). © George T. Bisel Company, Inc.

A. *Community property* (9 states and Puerto Rico): Arizona, California, Idaho, Louisiana, Nevada, New Mexico, Texas, Washington, Wisconsin, and Puerto Rico.

B. Equitable distribution: 41 states divide property "equitably"; some consider "all" property, others "marital" property only. The District of Columbia, Puerto Rico, and the Virgin Islands also divide "marital" property equitably. Only 10 of those states consider fault in that determination:

1. Marital misconduct considered (19 states plus District of Columbia): Alabama, Connecticut, District of Columbia, Florida, Georgia, Hawaii, Idaho, Kansas, Louisiana, Michigan, Mississippi, Missouri, New Hampshire, New York, Rhode Island, South Carolina, Texas, Vermont, Virginia, and Wyoming.

2. The remaining 22 states (including Pennsylvania) have excluded "fault" from the determination of how property should be distributed between the parties.

- Station in life.
- Health and physical condition.
- Financial necessaries and financial circumstances.
- Economic valance of interest.

- Income-producing capacity.
- Skills and vocational talents.
- Property acquired and accumulated before the marriage.
- Any other fact of relevant interest.[57]

Minnesota Domestic Relations Judge Lindsay G. Arthur discusses the difficulty in uniform decision making when individualized and familial factors are considered:

> Factors—*Each particular case may have factors that the court should regard in doing equity as to the wife, the husband, and the children. It may or may not be appropriate to consider such matters as maintaining the parties' standard of living and station in life, the noneconomic services rendered to the marriage, the age of the parties and their physical conditions and special needs, their relative earning capacities, the duration of the marriage, the respective amounts of nonmarital property owned by each party, and the needs of the children, which may require appointing a guardian ad litem or attorney for the children if the parents' interests appear to conflict with those of the children; it may also require placing property in trust for the children, or rejecting a stipulation of the parents. Sometimes the tax consequences are a major factor, through the court need not compute these with precision.*[58]

The North Carolina General Statutes provide a list that weighs various factors in equitable distribution (see Figure 12.4).

 Before an evaluation can be made, the paralegal needs to assimilate data and information to assist in making judgments about property division. Certain property, like complex pension plans, trusts, and jointly owned property will need a professional appraisal and valuation. Using an equitable distribution property checklist is helpful. (See Form 12.31 on the accompanying CD.)

 A more expansive property settlement agreement checklist is provided in Form 12.32 on the accompanying CD. Information elicited will provide critical input in the determination of a property settlement agreement that preserves previous levels of support. This may include medical and dental costs, custody determinations, extraordinary expenses for children entering college or having extensive medical bills, visitation rights, retention of specific personal or real property, and responsibility for debt and attorneys' fees.

 Equitable division of property often heats up into open disputes. The parties need to be concerned about unlawful access to disputed property during the negotiation because a revengeful party may seek to destroy the property in question. If this is likely, a restraining order may be a wise action. (See Form 12.33 on the accompanying CD.)

FIGURE 12.4 **Factors in Equitable Distribution**

Source: North Carolina General Statutes, §50-20.

---

§50-20. Distribution by court of marital and divisible property.

(c) There shall be an equal division by using net value of marital property and net value of divisible property unless the court determines that an equal division is not equitable. If the court determines that an equal division is not equitable, the court shall divide the marital property and divisible property equitably. The court shall consider all of the following factors under this subsection:

(1) The income, property, and liabilities of each party at the time the division of property is to become effective.

(2) Any obligation for support arising out of a prior marriage.

(3) The duration of the marriage and the age and physical and mental health of both parties.

(4) The need of a parent with custody of a child or children of the marriage to occupy or own the marital residence and to use or own its household effects.

(5) The expectation of pension, retirement, or other deferred compensation rights that are not marital property.

(6) Any equitable claim to, interest in, or direct or indirect contribution made to the acquisition of such marital property by the party not having title, including joint efforts or expenditures and contributions and services, or lack thereof, as a spouse, parent, wage earner or homemaker.

(7) Any direct or indirect contribution made by one spouse to help educate or develop the career potential of the other spouse.

(8) Any direct contribution to an increase in value of separate property which occurs during the course of the marriage.

(9) The liquid or nonliquid character of all marital property and divisible property.

(10) The difficulty of evaluating any component asset or any interest in a business, corporation or profession, and the economic desirability of retaining such asset or interest, intact and free from any claim or interference by the other party.

(11) The tax consequences to each party, including those federal and State tax consequences that would have been incurred if the marital and divisible property had been sold or liquidated on the date of valuation. The trial court may, however, in its discretion, consider whether or when such tax consequences are reasonably likely to occur in determining the equitable value deemed appropriate for this factor.

. . .

(12) Any other factor which the court finds to be just and proper.

ALIMONY

Traditionally alimony was granted to a spouse who either lacked sufficient capacity to earn a living or who did not have the economic resources or vocational skills necessary for self-support. With changing gender roles and the growing economic independence of women, alimony manifests a curious inconsistency. On one hand, most people advocate economic and gender-based equality. Yet on the other hand, families witness, particularly in the case of mothers, well-educated former careerists who leave the workforce for the sake of children. Between these realities alimony, or support as it might be called, has a home.

Although the ideal of economic independence is well intentioned, it poorly serves those in need. "Indeed, the experience of the past twenty years has shown that older women often suffer a severe drop in their standard of living after a divorce. Such women often lack job skills and even knowledge of the contemporary workplace. Moreover, they often face age and sex discrimination."[59] In many cases, it may be an unreasonable expectation that women whose long-term marriages have ended are not entitled to economic assistance. True, the law provides support as a replacement mechanism, but in a less aggressive spirit. Alimony was an added support because of either an actual loss or deferred neglect of a career track or opportunity, failure to amass sufficient assets, and an unswerving dedication to a particular spouse.

Reimbursement alimony is already seen with great regularity concerning professional degrees. People who supported their spouses while in medical or law school have a valued interest in the eventual licensure. The South Carolina Supreme Court held reimbursement alimony appropriate in *Donohue v. Donohue.*[60] The contribution to education was one of the factors in the overall determination. The court held,

> *Generally, the contribution of one spouse to the education of the other spouse may be considered by giving the supporting spouse a larger distributive share of the marital property to be divided. This remedy is not, however, sufficient when little or no marital property has been accumulated during the marriage.*[61]

The merits of alimony rest on these fundamental functions: (1) to provide support for wives living apart from their husbands; (2) to serve as an economic buffer upon a divorce for an individual not trained in any particular occupational skill or away from its demands for an extended period; and (3) to provide reasonable and just compensation for the obvious sacrifices that homemakers and wives have made in the performance of their honorable duties. A sample complaint for alimony is provided in Form 12.34 on the accompanying CD.

Interrogatories, as shown previously in Form 12.26, that are part of the discovery process can also be used to discover particular information about the spouse to determine a reasonable demand for alimony. A spouse's wages, Social Security benefits, real property interests, stock holdings, insurance, and other circumstances may also merit a petition for an increase or reduction in alimony. See the complaint in Form 12.35 on the accompanying CD.

Determining the amount of alimony depends on many variables. As in all property divisions, courts look to lifestyles, conduct of the parties, occupational directions, and other factors that either maintain or undermine the lifestyle. The following factors are considered when granting alimony:

- The husband's ability to pay.
- The fault of the parties.
- The wife's needs.
- The previous standard of living.
- Accumulation of property before or contemporaneously with the marriage.
- The parties' financial responsibilities.
- The ages of the parties.
- The occupational skills of the parties.
- The health of the parties.

Alimony serves many interests for children and spouses. Primarily the grant permits spouses to make the transition from home to the workplace—and finally serves as a reminder to a former spouse that moral obligation does not end at divorce.

SUPPORT

An action for support, upon dissolution of the marriage, gauges the needs and demands of children and the spouse who cares for them. By judicial intervention and order, a grant of child support depends on factors similar to those discussed for equitable distribution and alimony. Most states have blended the notion of alimony into support actions. Review the support complaint and the resultant order of support in Forms 12.36 and 12.37 on the accompanying CD.

An order of support directs a spouse, usually a husband, to provide the economic needs of his spouse and children generally by a monthly, biweekly, or weekly payment. Support calculations are generally based on these factors:

- Ages of the child/children.
- Necessities of the child/children.
- Level of education or desire to become educated.
- Condition of the wife.
- Remarriage of the wife.
- Fault of the parties (though this is viewed unfavorably).
- Health expenses of the child/children.
- Parents' net income.
- Other dependents.
- Costs of residence.
- Any other factors necessary to prove either the raising of children or the daily living expenses of the spouse.

Support should refer to the actual and anticipated expenses for both the remaining spouse and children. A statement of expenses shown in Figure 12.5 presents an objective view of what these expenses may be. How a party is accustomed to living bears on the calculation of support.[62] (See Form 12.38 on the accompanying CD.)

The procedure and process relative to support are often guided by local court rules and, if applicable to the states, the Uniform Reciprocal Enforcement of Support Act (U.R.E.S.A.).[63] Various federal laws on support seek some uniformity in calculating support and its enforcement. These laws promote settlement between the parties; ensure fair and equal treatment to all people similarly situated by income and expenses; and define what constitutes income in the determination of support. Title 42 of the U.S. Code has requirements on disclosure both of information and parent location and collection processes.[64] Title 45 of the Code of Federal Regulations lays out standards for a Child Support Enforcement Program[65] and calls upon individual states to create a plan of support enforcement that encompass these criteria. (See Figure 12.6.)

In general, courts respond to a complaint or petition such as that shown previously in Form 12.36. The court, through hearings or the appointment of masters or mediator, will review relevant information about the economic resources of the parties.

Once an order of support has been issued, it is subject to modification. Modification or change can arise for a host of reasons including loss of job, children reaching adulthood, increase or decrease in salary, and other factors. Two examples of modification options in the support process are shown in Forms 12.39 and 12.40 on the accompanying CD.

The federal government has taken a vigorous role in the enforcement of interstate child support decrees since the mid-1970s. Under federal law, the Secretary of Health and Human Services is to monitor and enhance "child support management information systems" in all the states.[66] Under the Child Support Enforcement Act, 42 USCS §§651–669, states must do more than simply collect overdue support payments; they must also establish comprehensive systems to establish paternity, locate absent parents, and help families obtain support orders.

Some jurisdictions require notice of this action to the party whose refunds will be attached (see Figure 12.7).

FIGURE 12.5 A Statement of Expenses

Source: NEIL HUROWITZ, PENNSYLVANIA SUPPORT PRACTICE, THE COMPLETE LAWYER'S HANDBOOK OF SUCCESSFUL TECHNIQUES 272–273 (1980). © George T. Bisel Company, Inc.

SAMPLE WORKSHEET

Court docket #: ___07D0109___   Date worksheet completed: ___May 3, 2007___

Noncustodial parent gross annual income	$40,000 ($769/week)
Weekly support paid—child of prior marriage	$40
Custodial parent gross annual income	$28,000
2 children covered by order, ages 6 and 8	
Annualized day care cost	$4,160
Noncustodial weekly cost family group health insur.	$24

1. BASIC ORDER
   a. Noncustodial gross weekly income (less prior
      support orders actually paid for child/family
      other than the family seeking this order)   ___729___
   b. Basic child support order from chart
      (Attachment A)   (A) ___193___

2. ADJUSTMENT FOR AGE OF CHILDREN
   a. If age of oldest child is 13 – 18,
      calculate 10% times (A)   ___0___
   b. Adjusted order (A) + (2 a)   (B) ___193___

3. CUSTODIAL PARENT INCOME ADJUSTMENT
   a. Custodial parent gross income (annual)   ___28,000___

   b. Less $20,000 $20,000

   c. Less annual child care cost   ___4,160___

   d. Custodial adjusted gross   ___3,840___

   e. Noncustodial gross (annual)   ___40,000___

   f. Total available gross (d) + (e)   ___43,840___

   g. Line 3 (d) _3,840_ Line 3 (f) _43,840_

   h. 3 (d) divided by 3 (f)   ___.09___ %

   I. Adjustment for custodial income
      (Line 3 (h) %)   (B)   (C) ___17___

4. CALCULATION OF FINAL ORDER
   a. Adjusted order, (B) above   (B) ___193___

   b. Less adjustment for (C) above   (C) ___17___

   c. Less 50% weekly cost to obligor of family
      group health insurance [Section G. 1]   ___12___
                        or
      Plus 50% weekly cost of obligee's family
      group health insurance [Section G. 1]   +_____

5. **WEEKLY SUPPORT ORDER (B)** **(c) ±4 (c)** $___164___

FIGURE 12.6
State Plan Requirements for Child Support Enforcement Program

Source: Code of Federal Regulations, Title 45, Volume 2 (45CFR302.10). Revised as of October 1, 2006. From the U.S. Government Printing Office via GPO Access.

Sec. 302.10   Statewide operations.

The State plan shall provide that:

(a) It will be in operation on a statewide basis in accordance with equitable standards for administration that are mandatory throughout the State;

(b) If administered by a political subdivision of the State, the plan will be mandatory on such political subdivision;

(c) The IV-D [IV-D refers to Title IV-D of the Social Security Act] agency will assure that the plan is continuously in operation in all appropriate offices or agencies through:

(1) Methods for informing staff of State policies, standards, procedures and instructions; and

(2) Regular planned examination and evaluation of operations in local offices by regularly assigned State staff, including regular visits by such staff; and through reports, controls, or other necessary methods.

FIGURE 12.7
Notice of State's Intent to Intercept Funds for Payment of Past-Due Child Support

Source: Neil Hurowitz & Arthur S. Zanan, Pennsylvania Support Practice, The Complete Lawyer's Handbook of Successful Techniques 175–176 (1992 Supplement). © George T. Bisel Company, Inc.

COURT OF COMMON PLEAS
FAMILY COURT DIVISION
DOMESTIC RELATIONS BRANCH

Dear _____:

Federal law allows the court to intercept the 20___ Federal Income Tax Return of the defendant in your case, and to apply the intercepted funds to past due support owed to you under certain conditions:

1. The past due support must be owed for minor children.

2. The defendant must owe at least $500 in past due support at the time the court submits the case to the I.R.S.

3. You must provide the defendant's Social Security number or indicate if unknown.

4. You must apply for this service and be willing to have a fee of $25 deducted.

Note: If you have ever received welfare in _____ and an arrearage that accrued under your support order is due the _____ Department of Public Welfare, any monies intercepted will be applied to the welfare arrearage first. Any monies collected more than the welfare arrearage will be applied to your account.

To have your case included in this program, you must fill out the attached form, sign it, and return it by mail within ten (10) days to:

IRS Intercept Unit
Room 520
1600 Walnut Street
Philadelphia, Pennsylvania 19103

You must return this form even if you do not want to be included in the process.

CHILD CUSTODY

Traditionally common law determined that fathers were entitled to the custody and control of their children if the parents separated.[67] Modern custody analysis heavily depends on a test called "The Best Interests of the Child" as the chief criterion on which child custody decisions are made. There has been a contemporary recognition that the role of the mother in the rearing of a child, especially in the development of love, devotion, and affection, is essential.

Custody determinations, due to the physical and emotional well-being of the child, sometimes require immediate, urgent attention. In addition, modern custody practice is guided by statutory rules, particularly at the state and local level. Some more poignant examples of statutory authority are these:

- Uniform Child Custody Jurisdiction Act (UCCJA), 9(1A) U.L.A. 271 (1999).
- Uniform Child Custody Jurisdiction and Enforcement Act (UCCJEA), 9(1A) U.L.A. 657 (1999).
- Parental Kidnapping Prevention Act of 1980 (PKPA), 28 U.S.C. 1738A.[68]

A pleading that delineates the immediate need and complaint for temporary custody is shown in Form 12.41 on the accompanying CD.

Custody is more than just a geographic location; it also includes a spiritual sense of belonging. Courts rely heavily on the behavioral insight of family doctors, psychiatrists, psychologists, and family therapists. In more difficult cases, a motion for a psychological evaluation of the child and for the parents may be in order. Conduct this type of examination during the discovery phase.[69]

When custody is an issue, the client usually needs much handholding. A parent's fear of losing custody of a child is overwhelming, and the client is apt to call repeatedly needing constant reassurance. The legal assistant should endeavor to defuse the client's anxiety and advise the lawyer about the severity of the client's anxiety.[70]

At the center of the deliberations will be the court's focus on the "welfare of the child and not on which of the spouses was responsible for the failure of the marriage. The judicial concern is entirely with the child's physical, intellectual, moral, and spiritual well-being."[71]

Courts must look to complementary and competing factors in awarding custody:

- The child's wishes.
- The parents' wishes.
- The child's ability to interact with the parents.
- Siblings' desires and interactions with the child.
- The child's school record.
- The child's record in the community.
- The mental health of the child.
- The mental health of the parents.
- The physical health of the child.

- The physical health of the parents.
- The age of the child.
- The parents' moral fitness.
- The parents' sexual behavior.
- The child's temperament.
- The conditions of the home.
- The location of the home.
- Religious affiliation.
- Racial setting.[72]

An attorney acting as a custody advocate must show why his or her client is the preferred parent. The attorney can show what the best interests of the child are and provide a positive and moving portrayal of the client. A parent who is "capable of and motivated to care for and interact with the child sufficiently to meet the child's physical, emotional, and other needs"[73] while working amicably with the other parent and permitting access to the child when warranted is a much healthier situation than restrictive closure. "If the parties' major concern is the best interests of the children, they will, at some point during the litigation, make an effort to settle the custody issue with the court's approval, keeping in mind that if subsequent developments prove that their agreement was ill-advised, the matter can always be brought again to the attention of the court."[74]

Custody litigation has become a complex area of matrimonial law. Lawyers who practice in this area must have not only civil litigation skills, but also a personal ability to endure emotional stress not often found in other types of litigation. Custody cases require sophisticated use of expert witnesses as well as documentary and demonstrative evidence. Counsel must prepare for trial carefully and be skilled in the use of courtroom techniques.[75] Pleadings used for custody awards are illustrated in Form 12.42 on the accompanying CD. Partial custody can also be acquired through a petition shown in Form 12.43.

Some jurisdictions require the filing of an affidavit of child custody as shown in Form 12.44 on the accompanying CD. Within this document, the court requests information regarding past addresses of people in charge of the custody of the child or children, other litigation involving this child or children, and whether any other custody actions are pending. A petition to modify a custody decree is shown in Form 12.45.

Custody petitions are natural pleading corollaries in the divorce action. A complaint in divorce can ask the court to make an order or decision on custody. The decision of custody award is also directly and indirectly influenced by other litigation and documents of legal effect:

- Petitions in equity.
- Petitions for guardianship.
- Proceedings in aid of dependent or neglected children.

- Prenuptial agreements.
- Separation agreements.
- Postnuptial agreements.

Child custody can also be modified if circumstances and desires change. This is a likely event, particularly as children pass through various stages, such as from tender ages to puberty or the latter part of teenage years. (See Form 12.46 on the accompanying CD.)

Visitation Rights

A person who is awarded complete, total custody exerts both emotional and personal control over the child. Visitation rights are granted by the court depending on certain circumstances to the party not granted custody. Although there has been a movement toward joint or partial custody, physical and emotional protection from an offending parent rightfully restricts access. Of course, an offending parent may feel that any restriction on the right to see the child regularly is an affront to his or her integrity.[76]

A withdrawal of visitation rights can happen under many circumstances:

- Upon divorce and award of total and complete custody, a spouse refuses to allow the other spouse visitation rights.
- Upon award of joint custody, one spouse refuses the other visitation rights.
- Upon failure to pay support orders, alimony, or other economic interests, the aggrieved party uses visitation rights as a weapon.
- Upon divorce, separation, or annulment, grandparents are not permitted to visit grandchildren.
- Conduct of an offending spouse continues to violate a temporary restraining order or other protective remedy, causing the victimized spouse to refuse visitation.
- A spouse who has a right to visit refuses to do so, thereby waiving regular and consistent visitation rights.[77]

Sample documents regarding visitation rights are shown in Forms 12.47 through 12.49 on the accompanying CD.

To thwart needless litigation, if the parties are generally reasonable and lacking in serious flaws, courts encourage free and open visitation and discourage the use of visitation as a weapon in the dispute. Courts will deal with visitation in the primary litigation. "The right to reasonable visitation to the noncustodial parent is included in most divorce decrees, property settlement agreements, and decrees of legal separation. Even without an official grant of visitation rights, a parent is thought to have such right absent some showing of unfitness."[78] No matter how argumentative parents become, children should not become pawns in their battles.

Client Wrap-Up

Considering the diverse issues commonly seen in domestic practice, a letter confirming, outlining, and summarizing the case's history may be necessary. The Georgia Domestic Relations Forum provides an excellent example. (See Form 12.50 on the accompanying CD.)

ADOPTION

In adoption practice paralegals usually enjoy the brighter side of domestic relations. Despite this positive view, paralegals will quickly learn how obsessively bureaucratic the adoption process can be. Clients need to be prepared for the proliferation of requirements.

In most American jurisdictions, adoption can occur through either private or public means. Many clients who come into the law office have no idea about how and where they can initiate the adoption process. Consequently paralegals should maintain extensive form files and resource guides about adoption opportunities in their jurisdictions. Examples of adoption agencies and appropriate contacts include these:

- Catholic Social Services.
- Lutheran Family Services.
- Pearl S. Buck Foundation.
- World Child Incorporated.
- The State Division of Family and Youth Services.
- The County Division of Family and Youth Services.

- Crittendon Foster Homes.
- Other religious bodies and groups.
- Nonprofit enterprises dedicated to placement of adoptable children such as Golden Cradle.
- Law offices specializing in placement of children.

The paralegal also must be wary of illegal baby-making and transfer markets. Joan Hollinger, in her work *From Coitus to Commerce,*[79] outlines in depth the baby-making market and surrogacy schemes popularized in the case of *Sterns v. Marybeth Whitehead.*[80]

The process of adoption, once beyond the agency stage—that is, once the parties have filled out all applications and documents and have been reviewed by home visitation, psychological analysis, or other legislative requirements—turns to formal processing. The procedural aspects of adoption are not all that complex.

First, as shown in Form 12.51 on the accompanying CD, a petition of adoption is submitted to the court of proper jurisdiction outlining why the parties feel they are capable and competent in adopting a child. They may also be required to state that they have the consent of the natural parents or the appropriate licenses and other rights dictated under agency determinations. Commonly witnessed are adoptions by stepparents and less frequently, though increasingly, by grandparents.[81] Just as compellingly, the data demonstrate single parents' petitions for adoption in growing numbers.[82] An alternative prayer for the adoption of a child is illustrated in Form 12.52.

Before a petition can be confirmed or ordered, a notice must be sent to the natural parents to give them one last opportunity to revoke their informal or formal intentions to permit adoption. A consent to adoption by parent is shown in Form 12.53 on the accompanying CD.

After a satisfactory hearing, a requisite waiting period, and, if required under statute, the attainment of an interlocutory decree, a final decree of adoption or grant will be provided. Time periods usually run between 3 and 12 months. A decree of adoption is shown in Form 12.54 on the accompanying CD.

Cases of adoption in which one or both of the natural parents refuse consent are designated *involuntary.* The proponent of adoption in an involuntary case "must show by clear and convincing evidence; repeated and continued incapacity, abuse, neglect, or refusal; that such conduct caused the child to be without essential parental care, control, or subsistence and that causes of parental failure cannot or will not be remedied. Also, the court must consider the needs and welfare of the child as a separate element."[83]

Summary

At the commencement of this chapter, the unique emotional demands of family law practice were discussed. With the changing demographics of the American family, the increased and extraordinary pressures being placed on single parents, the miserable scourge of child abuse, and other social problems, the paralegal's role in family practice is a volatile yet essential one.

This chapter also examined contractual issues related to the law of domestic relations, including the role of agreements, both prenuptial and postnuptial, as well as simple separation agreements. Annulment and its effect on an underlying marriage were also thoroughly covered. Divorce, whether fault or no-fault, was comprehensively addressed with suggestions for forms, checklists, and other pleading documents used for daily practice.

Other important topics included the equitable division of property, the role of alimony, child and spousal support, and the award of custody and visitation rights. The procedural aspects of adoption with necessary pleadings, forms, and other documents were highlighted in the last section of the chapter.

Finally, the chapter challenged traditional judicial intervention in domestic matters, questioning both the efficacy and morality of legal solutions and urging alternative means of resolution. Even the courts have come to recognize part of their institutional inadequacy. Mediation, counseling, arbitration, and other informal means of problem solving are firmly suggested.

Discussion Questions

1. Without question, the traditional family has seen some revolutionary changes. Outline a few prominent ones.

2. What preventive steps can be taken to ensure an equitable division of property upon dissolution of a marriage?

3. Are there any shortcomings to the law's effort to eliminate fault in the determination of grounds for divorce?

4. Why is an annulment an important religious concern for many couples?

5. When preparing domestic relations pleadings, what issues must be considered in the drafting?

6. What factors are most important in the award of custody?

7. Support, custody, alimony, and other aspects of property division are often subject to modification. Give five examples of a change in circumstances that might result in a modification of an initial decree.

8. Is adoption now disfavored in any sectors of society?

9. What reforms or changes in family law would you like to see take place?

10. What types of family law disputes will exist in the future concerning the technological advances of procreation?

11. Most local courts publish forms for family law actions. Visit your local family court and create a form file.

12. Analyze the statute in your jurisdiction that governs the grounds or bases for divorce. List these grounds.

13. What are the requirements and qualifications for a marriage license in your jurisdiction?

14. What procedural steps must be taken to secure an annulment in your jurisdiction?

Research Exercise

1. Abe Lanko left his wife and children and over a period of five years has provided no support at all. He has moved 10 times, each time avoiding a contempt order or other enforcement technique. Every effort to enforce the support order for his three children has been unsuccessful. He simply moves from state to state, thumbing his nose at out-of-state court orders. Eileen Khought, a domestic relations paralegal, has been asked what remedies and options the Uniform Reciprocal Enforcement of Support Act (U.R.E.S.A.) recommends in light of these circumstances:

   A. Asserting jurisdiction under U.R.E.S.A. is a flexible argument when compared to other jurisdictional findings. Eileen Khought writes a draft memorandum to her supervisor indicating that because Abe had sexual relations in a hotel in a foreign state, whereby a child was conceived, personal jurisdiction exists despite present nonresidence. Is this true or false?

   B. Eileen is also asked whether attorneys' fees are awardable in a contested support case. She writes in the memorandum that the answer is yes, but only reasonable fees are awarded. Is this true or false?

C. Eileen Khought researches the content and style of interstate pleadings to establish or modify a support order. She advises her supervisory attorney that pleading style is a matter of personal choice and there should be no verification or relief clauses. Is this true or false?

D. Eileen researches another question: What if the statute of limitations has passed on the order's enforceability? What effect would this have?

Practical Exercises

1. Prepare a petition for divorce using the following facts, based on the no-fault ground of living separate and apart:

Wife's attorney:	*Deborah Sampson, Sampson, Simms & Simon, Suite 450, Three Attorney Central, Aurora, New Hampshire, 03333, 298-555-6800*
Husband:	*Benjamin Thomas Golden*
Date of marriage:	*January 21, 1990*
Court of jurisdiction:	*Dalton County, New Hampshire, General Court of Justice*
Civil action number:	*07-5564*
Names/ages of children:	*Thomas, age 13*
Wife's residence:	*Dalton County, New Hampshire, for more than six months*
Date of separation:	*July 17, 2003*
Wife:	*Susan Danson Golden*
Husband's residence:	*12 Bloom Avenue, Dalton County, New Hampshire, 03333*

2. Draft a petition for support using the following facts:

Place of marriage:	*Marsville, New Hampshire*
Additional income:	*Child: Trust fund from deceased maternal grandfather in the amount of $2,000 per month*
Child's residence:	*Same as plaintiff's*
Defendant's residence:	*56 Morton Avenue, Weston, New Hampshire, 03334*
Child's birth date:	*March 4, 1994*
Last support received:	*Voluntary $500.00 payment by defendant on June 29, 2004*
Plaintiff's residence:	*357 Applebaum Lane, Seneca, New Hampshire, 03335*

3. Assume that the petition for support in Exercise 2 was granted and that the defendant has not honored the order. Use the following additional facts to complete a motion for garnishment:

Date of court order:	*July 10, 2006*
Amount of arrearage:	*$3,000 effective April 10, 2006*
Requested amount to be withheld:	*$1,000 per month*
Name of employer:	*Do-Rite Manufacturing, P.O. Box 956, 12 Factory Drive, Weston, New Hampshire, 03334*
Disposable income:	*$3,000 monthly*
Amount of support order:	*$750.00 monthly*

Internet Resources

Cornell Law School, Legal Information Institute, Uniform Matrimonial and Family Laws Locator—www.law.cornell.edu/uniform/vol9.html

Divorcenet—www.divorcenet.com/

Cornell Law School, topic pages—www.law.cornell.edu/topics/divorce.html

Family law and divorce law information; child support calculators—www.alllaw.com/topics/family

National Center for Adoption Law and Policy, Capital University Law School—www.law.capital.edu/adoption

Adoption laws: information about international and domestic adoption law—laws.adoption.com

FindLaw.com, family law practice area—www.findlaw.com/01topics/15family/index.html

Endnotes

1. Illinois Paralegal Association, The Findings of the Competency Committee Relating to The Quality of Paralegal Services 30–32, 36 (1989).

2. Steven K. Berenson, *A Family Law Residency Program? A Modest Proposal in Response to the Burdens Created by Self-Represented Litigants in Family Court*, 33 Rutgers L.J. 105, 122 (2001).

3. *See* Pauline H. Tesler, *Collaborative Family Law*, 4 Pepp. Disp. Resol. L.J. 317 (2004).

4. For an excellent family law bibliography *see* Donald A. Hughes, *Family Law Bibliography,* 61 N. D. L. Rev. 335 (1985).

5. *See* Gilbert Y. Steiner, The Futility of Family Policy 14 (1981); Michael S. Wald, *The Family, State, and the Law*, 18 U. Mich. J. L. Ref. 799 (1985).

6. John C. Sheldon & Nancy Diesel Mills, *In Search of a Theory of Alimony*, 45 Me. L. Rev. 283 (1993).

7. See Robin Cheryl Miller, *Annotation: "Marriage between Persons of Same Sex,"* 81 A.L.R. 5th 1–40 (2000). This annotation, updated by an annual pocket supplement, provides citations and lengthy summaries of case law from the United States concerning the validity of same-sex marriages; *see also* Robin Cheryl Miller and Jason Binimow, *Annotation: "Marriage between Persons of the Same Sex—United States and Canadian Cases,"* 1 A.L.R. Fed 2d 1 (2005).

8. Martha Brannigan, *Permanent Alimony Makes a Comeback in Some Courts*, Wall St. J., Oct. 31, 1988.

9. Catherine A. West, *Gay and Lesbian Partners Are Family Too: Why Wisconsin Should Adopt a Family Consent Law*, 19 Wis. Women's L.J. 119 (2004).

10. Samuel M. Davis, *Rethinking American Law,* 61 N. D. L. Rev. 192 (1985).

11. *See* Jennifer Wriggins, *Marriage Law and Family Law: Autonomy, Interdependence, and Couples of the Same Gender*, 41 B.C.L. Rev. 265 (2000).

12. *Paternalism in the Law of Marriage*, 74 Ind. L.J. 801 (1999); Jeffrey Evans Stake, Steven Mintz, & Susan Kellogg, *Recent Trends in American Family History: A Commentary Describing Dimensions of Demographic and Cultural Change,* 21 Hous. L. Rev. 789 (1984).

13. Benjamin Schlesinger, Remarriage in Canada (1978); *see also* Benjamin Schlesinger, Remarriage: A Review and Annotated Bibliography (1983).

14. Sharyn Duffin, Yours, Mine, and Ours: Tips for Stepparents (1978).

15. *See* Braschi v. Stahl Assocs., 543 N.E.2d 49, 55 (N.Y. 1989). In *Braschi*, the court never referred to the couple as homosexuals, but it noted it could "reasonably conclude that these men were much more than mere roommates."

16. Note, *Family Law—Visitation Rights—New York Court of Appeals Refuses to Adopt a Functional Analysis in Defining Family Relationships*, 105 Harv. L. Rev. 941 (Feb. 1992).

17. For example, *see* the Rabbinical Council of America, *Prenuptial Agreement*, at http://www.rabbis.org/ Prenuptial_Agreement.cfm.

18. Thomas E. Carbonneau, *A Consideration of Alternatives to Divorce Litigation*, 4 U. Ill. L. Rev. 1125 (1986).

19. *Id*. at 1132.

20. Cozette Vergari, *A New Approach to Marital Dissolutions: Collaborative Family Law Seeks to Smooth the Transition into the Postdivorce Period,* L.A. Law., Dec. 2003, at 52.

21. Mary Kay Kisthardt, *Dispute Resolution Processes for Family Law Matters: An Annotated Bibliography 1987–97,* 14 J. Am. Acad. Matrim. Law. 469 (1997).

22. State Bar of Georgia, Family Law Section Newsletter 18 (Nov. 1987).

23. Jennifer J. Rose, *The Ten Commandments of Family Law Economics*, 39 Prac. Law. 85–86 (Jan. 1993).

24. *Id*. at 85, *et seq*.

25. Theodore P. Orenstein, *How to Use Your Billing Methods as a Public Relations Tool*, 5 Am. J. Fam. L 39 (1991).

26. Fred Morganroth, *Considerations in Preparing Enforceable Antenuptial Agreement*, 71 Mich. B.J. 264, 265–267 (1992); *see also Enforceability of Premarital Agreements Governing Support or Property Rights upon Divorce or Separation as Affected by Circumstances Surrounding Execution—Modern Status,* 53 A.L.R. 4th 85.

27. Given the agreement's contractual nature, does a divorce decree provisions make voidable? "In *Riffenburg v. Riffenburg,* the Supreme Court of Rhode Island considered the propriety of court modifications to a marital separation agreement incorporated by reference, but not merged into a final divorce decree. Reasoning that the unmerged separation agreements are contractual in nature, the court held that the judiciary lacked authority to modify the agreement's terms." Riffenberg v. Riffenberg, 585 A.2d 627 (R.I. 1991).

28. 70 Conn. App. 649 (2002).

29. *Id*. at 656.

30. 1 William S. Holdsworth, History of English Law 621 (1922).

31. *See* John M. Speca, *The Development of Jurisdiction in Annulment of Marriage Cases,* 22 U. Kan. L. Rev. 109 (1954).

32. June A. Eichbaum, *Toward an Autonomy-Based Theory of Constitutional Privacy: Beyond the Ideology of Familial Privacy,* 14 Harv. C. R.—C. L. L. Rev. 361 (1979).

33. Robert A. Burt, *Course of Freedom: A Response to Professor Chambers,* 18 U. Mich. J. L. Ref. 829 (1985).

34. *Id. See also* Frances E. Olson, *The Myth of State Intervention in the Family,* 18 U. Mich. J. L. Ref. 835 (1985).

35. For an analysis of intervention in sexual abuse and other critical situations *see* In re C.B., 611 N.W.2d 489 (Iowa 2000); Patricia L. Grove & Mary K. Binter, *The Use of Paralegal Assistants in Divorce Practice,* 4 Am. J. Fam. L. 41, 49 (1990).

36. Samuel M. Davis, *Child Abuse, A Pervasive Problem of the Eighties,* 61 N.D.L. Rev. 191 (1985).

37. *See* Leigh Goodmark, *Telling Stories, Saving Lives: The Battered Mothers' Testimony Project, Women's Narratives, and Court Reform,* 37 Ariz. St. L.J. 709 (2005).

38. Patricia L. Grove & Mary K. Binter, *The Use of Paralegal Assistants in Divorce Practice,* 4 Am. J. Fam. L. 41 (Spring 1990).

39. Thomas E. Carbonneau, *A Consideration of Alternatives to Divorce Litigation,* 4 U. Ill. L. Rev. 1125, 1130 (1986).

40. Gary A. Weissman & Christine M. Leick, *Mediation and Other Creative Alternatives to Litigating Family Law Issues,* 61 N. D. L. Rev. 263, 279–280 (1985).

41. Harry K. Crouse, Family Law 295 (1977).

42. Allen M. Parkman, *Reforming Divorce Reform,* 41 Santa Clara L. Rev. 379 (2001).

43. *See generally* 8A Am. Jur. Pleadings & Practice Forms 257 (1982).

44. *See* Hunter v. Hunter, 706 So.2d 753 (Ala. App. 1997); James V. Calvi & Susan Coleman, American Law & Legal System 260 (1990).

45. 8A Am. Jur. Pleadings & Practice Forms 257 (1982).

46. For an excellent discussion of fault grounds, *see* H. Clark, The Law of Domestic Relations 327 (1968).

47. *See* Lynn D. Wardle and Laurence C. Nolan, Fundamental Principles of Family Law 673–675 (2002); Howard L. Bass & M. L. Rein, Divorce Law: The Complete Practical Guide 27 (1976).

48. Note, *A Survey of Mental Cruelty as a Ground for Divorce,* 15 De Paul L. Rev. 159 (1965).

49. Wardle and Nolan, *supra* note 47, at 673.

50. *Summary of the New Rules,* Ariz. Att'y, Feb. 2006, at 34.

51. *See* Wardle and Nolan, *supra* note 47, at 674 *et seq.*

52. Harry K. Crouse, Family Law 283 (1977).

53. Note, *Collusive and Consensual Divorce in the New York Anomaly,* 39 Colum. L. Rev. 1121 (1936).

54. Harry K. Crouse, Family Law 281 (1977).

55. *Divorce: Equitable Distribution Doctrine,* 41 A.L.R.4th 481

56. Robert Mnookin, *Divorce Bargaining: The Limits on Private Ordering,* 18 U. Mich. J. L. Ref. 1015 (1984–1985).

57. Marcia O'Kelley, *Entitlements to Spousal Support after Divorce,* 61 N. D. L. Rev. 226–227 (1985).

58. Lindsay G. Arthur, *Property Distribution* 42 Juv. & Fam. Ct. J. 27, 28 (1991).

59. Martha Brannigan, *Permanent Alimony Makes a Comeback in Some Courts,* Wall St. J., Oct. 31, 1988, at B-1. For a fascinating look at the historical impact of fault on alimony, *see Adulterous Wife's Right to Permanent Alimony,* 86 A.L.R.3d 97.

60. Donohue v. Donohue, 299 S.C. 353, 384 S.E.2d 741 (1989).

61. *Id.* at 747.

62. For a look at how the lifestyles of the rich and famous impact support determinations, *see* Dennis M. Wasser & Bruce E. Cooperman, *Million-Dollar Babies: The Family Code Anticipates That in Extraordinarily High-Income Cases Guideline Child Support May Exceed the Needs of the Children,* L.A. Law., Feb. 2005, at 36.

63. *For example,* Pennsylvania has adopted the U.R.E.S.A. at 23 Pa. Cons. Stat. Ann. §6777.

64. 42 C.F.R. §232.12.

65. 42 C.F.R. §232.11.

66. 42 U.S.C. §652.

67. *See* Manuel E. Nestle, *Child Custody Determination on Termination of Marriage,* 39 Am. Jur. P.O.F. 2d 415 (1988).

68. James A. Cosby, *How Parents and Children "Disappear" in Our Courts—And Why It Need Not Ever Happen Again,* 53 Clev. St. L. Rev. 285 (2005–2006).

69. Brian P. Herth & Edward J. Winter Jr., *Child Custody Litigation,* 22 Am. Jur. Trial 94 (Supp. 1992).

70. Patricia L. Grove & Mary K. Binter, *The Use of Paralegal Assistants in Divorce Practice,* 4 Am. J. Fam. L. 41, 60–61 (Spring 1990). Custody determinations, like all other areas of family law. have seen radical change in the last three decades. See Liwen Mah, *The Legal Profession Faces New Faces: How Lawyers' Professional Norms Should Change to Serve a Changing American Population,* 93 Calif. L. Rev. 1721 (2005).

71. 25 Standard Pa Practice 2d §126:546 at 143 (1984).

72. *See* Beasley v. Davis, 92 Nev. 81, 545 P. 2d 206 (1976).

73. Manuel E. Nessle, *Child Custody Determination on Termination of Marriage,* 34 Am. Jur. P.O.F. 2d 417 (1988); *see also* R.D. Hursh, Annotation, *Simultaneous Injury to Person and Property as Giving Rise to Single Cause of Action,* 62 A.L.R. 2d 1008; Fredrick B. Stanton v. Helen B. Stanton, 66 A.L.R. 2d 1410; Eleanor Bower v. William C. Bower, 74 A.L.R. 2d 1073; Guardianship of Baby Girl Rutherford v. Adelle Rutherford, 98 A.L.R. 2d 417; Sheldon R. Sharpino, Annotation, *Validity, Construction, and Application of Uniform Child Custody Jurisdiction Act,* 96 A.L.R. 3d 968; Ramsey L. Klaff, *The Tender Years Doctrine: A Defense,* 70 Cal. L. Rev. 335 (March 1982).

74. Edward J. Winter Jr. & Brian R. Hersh, *Child Custody Litigation*, 22 Am. Jur. Trial 469 (1992).

75. Phyllis G. Bossin. *How to Handle Custody Cases*, 28 Trial 24 (June 1992).

76. For an analysis of how visitation is affected by behavior, *see* Leigh Goodmark, *Achieving Batterer Accountability in the Child Protection System,* 93 Ky. L.J. 613 (2004–2005); *see also* Carol S. Bruch, *Making Visitation Work: Dual Parenting Orders,* 1 Fam. Advoc. 22 (1978); Brigitte M. Bodenheimer, *Equal Rights, Visitation, and the Right to Move,* 1 Fam. Advoc. 18 (1978); *Comment, Postdivorce Visitation: A Study in the Deprivation of Rights,* 27 De Paul L. Rev. 113 (Fall 1977); Debra E. Wax, Annotation, *Interference by Custodian of Child with Noncustodian Parent's Visitation Rights as a Ground for a Change in Custody,* 28 A.L.R. 4th 9 (1984).

77. *See* Kyra Anderson Kerchum, *Denial of Child Visitation Rights*, 2 Am. Jur. Proof of Facts 2d 791 (1988).

78. *Id.* at 795.

79. Joan H. Hollinger, *From Coitus to Commerce: Legal and Social Consequences of Noncoital Reproduction,* 18 U. Mich. J. L. Ref. 870 *et seq.* (1985).

80. Nadine Brosnan, *Surrogate Mothers: Problems and Goals*, N.Y. Times, Feb. 27, 1984, at A-17.

81. Michelle Ognibene, *A Constitutional Analysis of Grandparents' Custody Rights*, 72 U. Chi. L. Rev. 1473 (2005).

82. *See* National Adoption Information Clearinghouse (DHHS), *Single Parent Adoption: What You Need to Know* (1994), available at http://naic.acf.hhs.gov/ pubs/f_single/f_singleb.cfm.

83. In re E.M., a.k.a. E.W.C. and L.M., a.k.a. L.C., Minors, 401 Pa. Super. 129, 584 A.2d 1014 (1991).

Real Estate

B. **Purchase Agreement/Contract of Sale Agreement**
1. **Common Provisions**
    a. **Outline of the Parties**
    b. **Legal Description of the Property**
    c. **Personal Property Exclusions/Inclusions**
    d. **Consideration**
    e. **Condition of Title**
    f. **Time and Place of Settlement**
    g. **Inspection Right**
    h. **Time of Possession Clause**
    i. **Prorations and Adjustments**
    j. **Loss Provisions**
    k. **Assessments**
    l. **Conditions and Contingencies**
    m. **Title Insurance Clause**
    n. **Integration Clause**
    o. **Brokerage Clause**
    p. **Signatures/Witnesses/Date of Execution**
    q. **Special Caution: Time Is of the Essence**
C. **Mortgages/Financing Techniques**
1. **Fixed Rate Mortgage**
2. **Adjustable Rate Mortgage**
3. **Roll-Over Mortgage**
4. **Assumed Mortgage**
5. **Graduated Payment Mortgage (GPM)**
6. **Purchase Money Mortgage (PMM)**
7. **Shared Appreciation Mortgage (SAM)**
8. **Blanket Mortgage**
9. **Balloon Mortgage**
10. **First Annuity Mortgage**
11. **Governmental Guarantees of Mortgage Loans**
12. **Reverse Mortgage**
13. **Installment Purchase Agreement**
D. **Financing Documentation**
E. **Abstraction of Title**
F. **Acquisition of Title Insurance**
G. **The Closing Process**
1. **Preparation of Documents**
    a. **Deeds**
    b. **Financing Documentation**
2. **Collection and Coordination of Closing Documentation**
3. **The Human Perspective on the Closing Process**
4. **Preparation of the Settlement Sheet**
    a. **Lines 701–704: Broker's Commission**
    b. **Lines 801–811: Financing Charges**
    c. **Lines 900–905: Prepaid Items**
    d. **Lines 1001–1008: Reserves**
    e. **Lines 1101–1113: Charges Related to Legal Settlement**
    f. **Lines 1201–1205: Recordation and Tax Expenses**
    g. **Lines 1301–1305: Additional Settlement Charges**
5. **Explanation of the Closing Process**

6. **Postclosing Activities**
   a. **Recordation of Mortgage and Other Related Documents**
   b. **Title Policy Issuance**
   c. **Escrow or Repair Issues**

V. **Summary**

Discussion Questions

 REAL ESTATE PARALEGAL JOB DESCRIPTION

Real estate paralegals need to be proficient in the following competencies:

- Draft closing documents, including deeds of conveyance, bills of sale, affidavits of title, American Land Title Association (ALTA) statements, releases, collateral assignment documents, leases, transfer declarations, assignments, closing/settlement statements, lien waivers, and rent and lease schedules.

- Set up and draft land trusts land trust documents, including trust agreements, directions to convey, letters of direction, assignments of beneficial interest, deeds in trust, trustee's deeds, and certified resolutions.

- Order title commitments and abstract searches, review exceptions to title, prepare or obtain necessary documents to correct or clear title, and obtain certain endorsements.

- Order and review plats of survey.

- Review leases, prepare tenant estoppel letters, and coordinate their execution.

- Contact holders of existing loans to arrange for payoff or to obtain lenders' estoppel letters.

- Order and review utility letters, soil tests, environmental surveys, zoning compliance letters, building permits, and building code violation printouts.

- Coordinate the details of closings with local counsel, real estate brokers, clients, title companies, and opposing counsel.

- Review management agreements and service contracts and prepare compilations.

- Attend property inspections.

- Prepare checklists of documents and items to be obtained or accomplished at closing.

- Attend and assist attorneys at closing.

- Coordinate postclosing matters, including recording documents, wiring funds, obtaining cancellation documents, issuance of owner's and loan policies, organizing and indexing files, plus overseeing preparation of closing document binders.

- Order and review estimates of redemption for real estate taxes.

- Have mortgages, deeds, assignment releases, and other documents recorded.

- Order and assemble duplicate tax receipts .

- Prepare Forms 1099A, 1099S, and 1096 for qualifying transactions.

- Draft and review permits.

- Draft, review, and plot legal descriptions.

- Redline changes in documents upon revision.

- Draft and arrange for filing of Uniform Commercial Code (U.C.C.) financing statements, amendments, extensions, or terminations.

- Analyze and digest leases, assignments, extensions, and amendments not of record.

- Arrange for payoff of notes and release of mortgages and trust deeds.

- Obtain closing figures from closing parties and determine necessary closing amounts.

- Notarize documents at closing, if qualified.

- Assist clients in obtaining liability insurance.

- Order U.C.C., Torrens , judgment, and tax lien searches.

- Monitor and obtain releases of bulk sales stop orders.

- Order certified copies of certain real estate and partnership documents.

- Prepare and file assumed name applications.
- Know and use certain county, city, and municipal offices regarding recordings, conveyances, land use planning, zoning, annexation, real estate tax matters, and building code violations.
- Maintain firm form files.
- Attend negotiations and discussions relating to the terms of sale contracts.
- Draft sale contracts, assignments thereof, and amendments thereto.
- Draft exchange agreements and attend relevant negotiations.
- Draft loan commitments and attend relevant negotiations.
- Draft installment sale contracts and attend relevant negotiations.
- Draft deeds and money, money lenders, joint order, and construction escrows.
- Draft partnership agreements, amendments, and certificates of partnership.
- Draft additional closing documents, including loan agreements, notes, security agreements, mortgages, estoppel certificates, buy–sell agreements, indemnification agreements, participation agreements, subordination agreements, nondisturbance agreements, guaranty and warranty, opinions of counsel, option agreements, trade name registrations, easement agreements, restrictive covenants, and all other closing documents necessary for a transaction to close.
- Prepare preliminary abstracts of title; draft opinions on the title and issue policy.
- Check for compliance with truth-in-lending requirements.
- Assist in resolving real estate tax problems such as reassessment/valuation complaints and tax parcel divisions or consolidations.[1]

INTRODUCTION: PARALEGAL FUNCTIONS

No better alliance exists in real estate practice than that of the attorney and paralegal. In real estate, attorneys, laden with documentation, mathematical calculations and prorations, coordination of parties and finance entities, real estate offices and agents, critically rely on the services of the paralegal.

From the initial contract formation to the day of closure, real estate paralegals tackle a multiplicity of tasks and functions, including document preparation, title research, settlement sheet calculation and tabulation, and coordination of closings. Paralegals are central players in American real estate practice and can be minimally expected to

- Communicate with real estate agents.
- Correspond and deal with real estate brokers.
- Interact with purchasers and sellers.
- Correspond and deal with title insurance companies.
- Communicate with mortgage companies or banks.
- Work with surveyors.
- Correspond and deal with government officials regarding taxes, septic certifications, and other matters.
- Interface with individuals at the deed recording office.
- Correspond with individuals who are lien holders or have competing or adverse interests in a property.
- Prepare legal descriptions.
- File papers and documents with appropriate government agencies.
- Prepare deeds.
- Abstract titles.
- Author residential mortgages.
- Prepare construction mortgages.
- Prepare loan closing documents.

- Draft and interpret contracts of sale.
- Analyze land or real estate tax records.
- Interpret appraisals.
- Draft attorney's certificates of title under the supervision of an attorney.
- Author promissory notes.
- Conduct title searches on the chain of title.
- Compute and calculate settlement sheets and other settlement documents.
- Record documents after real estate closing.
- Draft leases.
- Prepare papers and documentation related to a condominium structure.

As expansive as these duties appear, practice limitations relative to unauthorized practice of law are still relevant. As attorneys continually delegate tasks of real estate practice to paralegals and legal assistants, some state and local bar associations have raised the red flag. The Illinois State Bar Association's Real Estate Section and Unauthorized Practice of Law Committee issued these timely recommendations on legal assistants in real estate practice:

1. *All work of attorney assistants must be under the direct supervision of their employing attorney, and the employing attorney must be directly responsible for all of the work product of his or her attorney assistant.*

2. *Attorney assistants may prepare items which are standardized in form and which for the most part entail merely filling in the blanks from data available, such items to include, but are not limited to, deeds, mortgages, bills of sale, revenue declarations, provided however that the attorney employer assumes full responsibility for the preparation of the documents and each document is reviewed by the attorney employer.*

3. *In connection with these tasks, an attorney assistant may correspond or otherwise communicate with any party concerned with the transaction, but only for the purpose of obtaining factual information. Attorney assistants may not issue opinions relating to title or undertake or be assigned to perform any task which involves the giving of legal advice.*

4. *Attorney assistants may attend real estate closings of all types, but only in the company of the employing attorney and at such closings prepare computations, revisions of agreement, and perform similar tasks but only at the direction of, and under the supervision of, the employing attorney.*[2]

Clearly the tasks of legal interpretation and legal advocacy remain the province of the attorney; but few would argue that paralegals have not made substantial inroads into real estate practice. Legal assistant Ellen Mahoney sees the natural interplay between paralegalism and real estate:

Real estate law is primarily transactional and thus is particularly suited to the role of a legal assistant. Rather than delegating tasks as they evolve, attorneys can delegate many of the tasks to a legal assistant early on in a transaction who can then carry them through to closing. To the extent a legal assistant understands and is able to perform the variety of tasks, this will allow the attorney to focus on more substantive matters. The attorney may derive many benefits from the appropriate utilization of a legal assistant in his or her practice.[3]

To this extent paralegals are part of revolution in the delivery of legal services, "revaluing lawyering" in ways once never dreamt of.[4]

A successful career in real estate practice depends on mastery of not only the processes of real estate practice but also a full conceptual mastery of real estate law.

REAL PROPERTY: DEFINITIONS AND CHARACTERISTICS

Real property can be best understood when compared to other property forms. Property may be personal, intangible, or even intellectual in design. In the case of real property, one deals with something concrete and grounded. Some property forms or types, like privileges, licenses, or easements, are incorporeal—that is, they deal with a right to do something rather than the right to possess something. In real property we deduce a very reachable and delineable interest: the ground,

Land itself can constitute real property.

Source: Pixtal/age Fotostock.

the house, the barn, or whatever. *Real* is real, so to speak. *Real* means something actual—that you can touch, hold, or physically identify and possess. Even so, rights in real property can be termed *incorporeal*. Some property rights are "any intellectual or artificial conception(s), consisting of rights or groups of rights only, which inhere in and are supported by corporeal things, but are themselves of an invisible and intangible character, are known as incorporeal things."[5] Most people visualize real property as a house or building attached to a piece of land. But land in and of itself can be pure real property. Herbert Tiffany, in his treatise on real property, states that real property "includes whatever is parcel of the terrestrial globe, or is permanently affixed to such parcel."[6]

In addition to this view of land being real, any improvements or appurtenances can be considered real property. "Appurtenances are those incidental interests which attach to and pass with the land, such as trees, easements, and right of way. Manmade improvements also belong to real property if they are permanently attached to the land; examples are buildings, bridges, swimming pools, and the like."[7] Things permanently attached to land, often referred to as *fixtures,* are initially items of personal property such as a built-in sauna, swimming pool, or kitchen appliances. The integration of this personal property into the essential structure of the home causes personal property to evolve into a permanently affixed property form because its removal would be so cumbersome and so destructive the form becomes reclassified. See the accompanying photos for examples of specific fixtures. Can you identify them?

Kitchens frequently have a variety of permanently attached fixtures.

Source: Colin Paterson/Getty Images.

A typical example of real property includes both the land and the house.

Source: Royalty-Free/ CORBIS.

Real estate disputes are common in the matter of fixtures because the lines of personal and real sometime blur. A seller or buyer may disagree about whether an item is personal and may call for its exemption or inclusion in the transfer of property. Bruce Harwood lays out five key tests for the determination of whether an item is a fixture:

1. *The means and method of attachment.*
2. *The adaptation of the object outside the real property.*
3. *The intent of the party who originally affixed the object.*
4. *The relationship of the parties involved.*
5. *The existence of an agreement outlining the nature of the property.*[8]

In simplest terms, a property interest in realty is largely determined by the following questions and issues:

- Who is the owner of the property, whether actual or equitable in nature?
- Who has the right to possess, hold, or have occupancy of the property?
- Does anyone have a limited right of usage to property such as in the form of an easement?
- Does anyone have a right to control the property, whether by law or private agreement evidencing a privilege?

Determining the level of participation or interest in real property is a pressing concern for the real estate practitioner. Assessing the client's "bundle of rights" in a real estate transaction is accomplished by outlining the differing forms of possessory interest and estates in land—a subject reviewed in the next section.

Two major traditional classifications of real estate interests are these:

Freehold estate: An estate for life or in fee . . . an estate in land or other real property of uncertain duration; that is, either of inheritance or which may possibly last for the life of the tenant at the least (as distinguished from a leasehold); and held by a free tenure (as distinguished from copyhold or villeinage).

Leasehold estate: An estate in realty held under a lease; an estate for a fixed term of years.

The major distinction between the two classifications is duration. A freehold interest or estate is one whose duration is perpetual, of specific duration, or indefinite in design, whereas a leasehold estate or a less than freehold estate is simply a lease—a temporary period in which one party can use another party's property. A chart of interest in real property is outlined in Figure 13.1.

If the estate is freehold in nature, the language of a deed will include express language representing the free and unrestricted alienation. Review the general warranty deed in Form 13.1 on the accompanying CD. The deed represents a freehold interest by the draft language:

. . . Grantor, for valuable consideration paid by the Grantee, the receipt of which is hereby acknowledged, has and by these presents does grant, bargain, sell, and convey unto the Grantee in fee simple, all that certain lot or parcel of land . . .[9]

FIGURE 13.1
Interests in Real Property

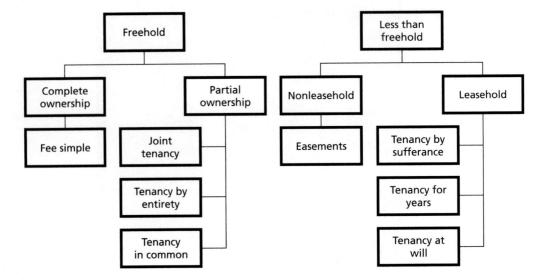

In contrast, the leasehold estate sets out a series of restrictions on the rights of ownership. Review a lease's time limitation on usage. Within these parameters—from unlimited, perpetual fee simple ownership to leasehold time limitations on property usage—lie an endless variety of real property rights.

Freehold Estates

The term *freehold* is derived from the feudal "free tenement." "Generally in common law one who held physical dominion or control over the land owned a freehold estate in the land."[10] Therefore, by connotation, *freehold* means to hold free, unassailably, for some period of time. Freehold estates are further subdivided into *estates of inheritance* and *estates that are not of inheritance*. Estates are also distinguished according to whether they provide future or present rights, thereby causing the often heard term *future estates*. A brief examination of these various freehold estates follows.

Fee Simple Estate

Known also as a *fee simple absolute estate*, a *fee simple property* consists of an entire estate of property and land held by the owner and his or her heirs and assigns forever. A fee simple estate carries with it the largest array and assortment of ownership rights possible. "It is the highest degree of ownership recognized by law and is an estate of inheritance for indefinite duration."[11] Freely and totally alienable, transferable, and without any inherent restrictions on marketable title, the fee simple estate is the preferred method of real property ownership (see Figure 13.2).

Fee Tail Estate

Although disfavored in the law because of its restrictions on alienability and transferability, the fee tail estate is given to a designated heir of the present owner of the property. The language associated with this estate is usually referred to as *words of limitation*—that is, specific instructions that the

FIGURE 13.2
Fee Simple Ownership Scheme

Source: HERBERT T. TIFFANY, THE LAW OF REAL PROPERTY AND OTHER INTERESTS IN LAND 41 (1970).

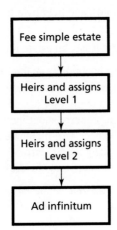

property can be alienated or transferred within a delineated range of individuals. The words employed in a grant usually are "This estate is hereby transferred to Sam Jones and the heirs of his body." By contrast, the words necessary to establish the fee simple absolute are "heirs and assigns forever."

The problem with the fee tail is the indeterminacy of length. There is simply no sensible way to measure the distance of this form of property right. Consider this:

> *Bob conveys to Sam and the heirs of his body. Sam and his wife have a son Eric. Sam is granted a fee tail. Bob retains a reversion. While Sam is alive, Eric doesn't have anything. But when Sam dies, if Eric is still alive, then Eric will inherit the fee tail.*

For public policy reasons and to promote commercial development, the fee tail estate is a modern-day anomaly that is statutorily prohibited in most American jurisdictions.

Life Estates

A *life estate* is nothing more than an estate "the duration of which is measured by a human life."[12] With this in mind, consider the following grant:

> *To John Stephens, I hereby grant and convey Blackacre for the period of his life.*

This life estate allows the tenant, John Stephens, possession of the property so long as he remains alive. Possession can be measured by either the tenant's or a third party's lifespan, the latter estate being referred to as an *estate pur autre vie* (estate for the life of another). Until the death of the other party, or if the estate is measured by the life tenant, no alienation or transfer to the life estate's heirs or assigns is permissible, unless the deed or other document permits. When the life tenant's estate is extinguished, the underlying real property interest reverts to another party—the most common being the initial grantor.[13]

One assuredly cannot predict the period of life of the occupant or the other party. A substantial body of common law and case law exists regarding life estates. Property is often conveyed using this technique to take care of widowed individuals or sons or daughters who have never married, are disabled, or who have economic or other personal failure. Alienation is usually not permissible, unless explicitly permitted in the deed, during the life of the tenant and during a rightful and proper period of possession, while use and profits and any other advantage of the land inures to the benefit of the life tenant. The party who has a right to the estate upon the termination of the life interest is known as the *remainderman* (see Figure 13.3).

Less Than Freehold Estates

Leases

Leases that are less than freehold estates are possessory interests in real estate for a calculated period of time. The requirements of any lease are

- Lessor.
- Lessee.
- Premises.
- A writing.
- A specific term.
- Terms, conditions, and place accurately described.[14]

FIGURE 13.3
Fee Simple Remainderman Scheme

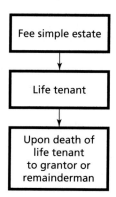

Under the definition of the Statute of Frauds, leases generally must be in writing if they are for a period of more than three years. Variations in the writing requirements do jurisdictionally exist. Leases have some typical conditions and requirements within them. The clauses and provisions in a lease are usually boilerplate addressing

- The parties to the lease.
- The premises that will be the subject of the lease.
- The right of usage and corresponding restrictions.
- The rent amount.
- The term and possession of the lease.[15]
- The rights to renewal.
- The rights to possession.
- The covenants to the lease.

Some jurisdictions supply lessees with an increased right of protection under the doctrine of "implied warranty of habitability." Both rental and ownership markets must contend with this doctrine's influence. Applied to apartment complexes, this warranty may have some application, particularly for lessees. Here the lessor is expected to lease a property that is habitable, with all the fundamental services and utilities, and in the absence thereof may be held to have breached the warranty. The warranty closely aligns with product warranty theories:

> With the advent of mass production and consumption of goods, caveat emptor for sales of goods largely disappeared, consumers became accustomed to buying goods with implied warranties of merchantability and when applicable for fitness for a particular purpose. Following World War II, the demand for and construction of houses exploded. Instances of poor construction quality in homes almost always resulted because of hurried construction and materials skimping. Unsophisticated purchasers streamed into court seeking relief. Accustomed to implied warranty for consumer goods, consumers logically expected the law to protect them when they purchased new homes.[16]

In the leasehold environment,

> a tenant may vacate the premises if the breach is material.[17] In such instances, the tenant may surrender possession of the property and terminate his obligation to pay rent under the lease. Second, if the tenant remains in possession and is sued by the landlord for possession and unpaid rent, the implied warranty of habitability may be presented as a total defense by the tenant. Where the landlord can be shown to not have delivered a premises that fails to meet the elementary standards of the warranty of habitability, the tenant's obligation to pay rent would be abated in full—the action for possession would fail because there would be no unpaid rent.[18]

Research local law to determine this doctrine's applicability in your area.

Standard leases discuss both landlord obligation and lessee rights as to express and implied covenants, rights of quiet enjoyment, warranties, services, and repairs. In the same document, clauses covering maintenance and repair and indemnification for destruction are drafted. Both lessor and lessee have a series of rights and obligations, all of which are fully discernible in a well-drafted lease. (See Form 13.2 on the accompanying CD.)

Varied jurisdictional requirements govern the application of a security deposit. As a general principle, security deposits are refundable after a finding by the landlord that no destruction or costs have been caused by the lessee because of destruction beyond "ordinary wear and tear." Tenants must contend with landlords who, without right or just cause, retain the security deposit. In landlord–tenant practice, paralegals are responsible for two fundamental aspects:

1. Preparing leases according to specific detail.

2. Preparing litigation documents for eviction or back payment of rent.

A short form lease is reproduced in Form 13.3 on the accompanying CD. Amendments to a existing lease are possible by the abridged form (see Form 13.4).

Estate for Years   An estate with a fixed period of time, whether it be a half year, a quarter, a day, a week, or other words that limit and provide fixed parameters for the right to possess and occupy, is known as an *estate for years.* In modern society, the most common technique of an estate for years is the use of a commercial or residential lease, covered in more detail in this chapter. An estate for years is generally created by the use of certain language, including the following terms: *lease, grant, let, devise.* An estate for years terminates according to an expiration clause upon the happening or nonoccurrence of a condition or contingency.[19]

Tenancy at Will   Another form of less than freehold interest, normally created by an oral or written lease, is a tenancy at will. The tenancy occurs when the premises are in the possession of an individual with the consent of the owner. Because no specific time period or other terms of duration are explicitly accounted for, the lease is considered to be at the will of both of the parties. This is another informal grant and interest in property, and the conduct of both lessee and lessor guides the creation of this estate. Under equitable principles, lessors, when choosing to terminate the tenancy, must give notice of that decision.

Tenancy by Other Durational Period   A typical lease satisfies this less than freehold interest. Forms 13.2 and 13.3, as already highlighted, outline the rights of the parties under this possessory interest.

Tenancy by Sufferance   When a tenant initially had a lawful possessory right, and upon expiration of that right holds over wrongfully, a tenancy by sufferance occurs. At the center of this tenancy is the illegitimacy of the holding over, where the lessor has neither granted nor extended an existing right of possession. Under this possessory right, "the tenancy at sufferance exists only as long as the landlord fails to indicate whether he will treat the occupier as a tenant or a trespasser. The landlord has his option, and if he indicates an intention that the tenancy will continue, the tenant is no longer a tenant by sufferance, but becomes, in most states, even against his will, a tenant from year to year on the terms of the previous tenancy so far as such terms are applicable thereto."[20]

Future Estates/Estates in Expectancy   A future interest is nothing more than "an interest which is not a present interest but which may become interest."[21] There are various types of future interests, and paralegals will usually encounter the conditional estate, estate on condition, and estate in expectancy. The concept of future interests becomes clearer when we consider specific grants. For example, in the case of a future interest known as a *condition precedent,* the right to claim an actual possessory interest in the estate and ownership does not occur until the happening of some condition.

Estates in or interests in real estate that have not come to fruition, whether for failure to meet a condition or contingency or other matter, are referred to as *conditional estates, estates on condition, estates in expectancy,* or *future interests.* Actual legal possession of the estate—that is, the right to claim an actual possessory interest in the estate and ownership—does not occur until the happening of some condition or contingency usually known as either

> condition precedent: *one which must happen or be performed before the estate to which it is annexed can vest or be enlarged. . . which calls for the happening of some event or the performance of some act after the terms of the contract have been agreed on, before the contract shall be binding on the parties.*

or

> condition subsequent: *one annexed to an estate already vested, by the performance of which such estate is kept and continued, and by the failure or nonperformance of which it is defeated, or . . . a future event, upon the happening of which the obligation becomes no longer binding upon the other party.*

The law does not favor conditions in the alienation and vesting of property. Whether precedent or subsequent in nature, conditions that violate public policy, that are impossible to fulfill, or that are vague and nondescript or impossible to interpret will be overturned.[22]

Words of common construction employed in the drafting of conditions either subsequent or precedent in real estate could include any of the following terms in the transfer:

> *"I hereby grant 200 acres of land on condition . . ."*
> *"I hereby grant 200 acres of land provided that . . . so that . . ."*

In an estate that is possessory only in a future context, a condition precedent means that a certain event, act, or condition must take place before the estate will vest. Assume that an estate is granted to John upon his marriage to Mary. If the marriage never takes place, the estate will never vest. A condition precedent exists to the vesting of the specific possession of the real property: that of actual marriage.

By contrast, a condition subsequent will permit the vesting of real estate upon the occurrence of a condition or a contingency that will ensure that the grantee has an estate as long as that specific condition does not take place. For illustration, assume that a piece of land is granted to Mary as long as she does not remarry. She will maintain an interest in the land as long as she chooses not to remarry. If she does remarry, the land will revert to its previous owner. In this case, Mary has an estate that may end on the breach of any given condition; but until that time, she has the same rights and powers as if the condition did not exist. A real interest or other possibility of reverter right remains in the party who granted it in the first place.

Be careful to distinguish an *estate by or on special limitation* that is created by grant or devise using other language similar to a condition but that is better labeled as words of limitation rather than construction. Here is some regularly employed language for an estate:

> *"I convey and grant 200 acres until I convey and grant . . ."*
>
> *"I convey and grant 200 acres while I convey and grant . . ."*
>
> *"I convey and grant 200 acres so long as . . ."*

The distinction between estates on condition and special limitation has some practical and pragmatic consequence. "Since in the latter case, the contingency is the proper termination of the estate, no estate can possibly remain in the grantee or lessee and hence the property ipso facto immediately reverts to the grantor or the lessor."[23]

Estates with conditions either precedent or subsequent generally can be further classified as either reversions or remainders. A reversion or remainder interest comes about if a condition subsequent occurs. That these distinctions are often obtuse and cumbersome in application is really no surprise. Herbert Tiffany explains the natural complexity:

> *The efforts of thousands of lawyers to draw a clear, definite, and always recognizable distinction have not resulted in a well-beaten path which the wayfaring court may safely follow, but in a labyrinth compared with which a plat of interlacing lines connecting all the stars of the firmament would be a model of simplicity. Attempts by the courts to blaze their way through the jungle of precedents and mark each turn and twist in the route by guideposts adorned with Latin quotations which everybody admires but nobody reads have not resulted in a clear highway which others can follow with any assurance of finding their way home again.[24]*

In a sense, the estate type largely depends on the language of conveyance. See the examples that follow.

Sample Conveyancing Language Creating Real Property Estates

Fee simple absolute estate:

> *I hereby grant and convey 200 acres of land to Bob and his heirs and assigns forever.*

Fee tail estate:

> *I hereby grant and convey 200 acres of land to Eleanor and the heirs of her body.*

Life estate:

> *I hereby grant and convey to Joseph, for as long as he lives, 200 acres of land.*

or

> *I hereby grant and convey to John, for as long as Joseph, his brother, lives, 200 acres of land.*

Estate for years:

> *I hereby grant and convey to Mary Claire my 200 acres for a period of 15 years.*

Estate from period to period:

> *I hereby grant and convey the right to remain on my 200 acres of property for a period of five weeks.*

Conditional estate—condition precedent:

> *I hereby grant and convey my 200 acres of land to Michael provided that he marries Sally.*

Estate of special limitation:

> *I hereby grant and convey to Jean Marie my 200 acres as long as the land is used for agricultural purposes.*

Conditional estate—condition subsequent:

> *I hereby grant and convey my 200 acres of land to Anne Marie and her heirs, provided that an amusement park is built.*

or

> *I hereby grant and convey my 200 acres of land to Anne Marie for life, provided that the land is not wasted or destroyed by environmental violation.*

Reversion:

> *I hereby grant and convey to my son, Stephen, 4,000 acres of land in western Pennsylvania for his life.*

In this last example the grantor has a right of reversion—that is, a right to the estate upon the death of his son Stephen. Reversionary rights also exist for failure of a condition or special limitation. "A reversion is always an interest left in the grantor. If such an interest is created in someone else, it will have a different name."[25]

Possibility of reverter:

> *I hereby grant and convey to my daughter Eleanor 4,000 acres of land in western California, but if the land is ever used for a museum, I may enter and repossess.*

With this type of language, the possibility of reverter "gives the grantor or his heirs the estate automatically once the limitation ends or occurs, but the power of termination merely gives him the option to terminate the previous estate."[26]

Remainder:

> *I hereby grant and convey my 300 acres of land in Hatteras, North Carolina, to Joseph Nemeth, for his life, then to John and his heirs.*

A person who has a future interest in land with the potentiality for a reversionary interest in land or a grant back of the land due to a failure of condition or other condition is referred to as a *remainderman*. From the facts shown here, John has a remainder interest upon the termination of the life estate in Joseph. The remainder would be in fee simple, of course.

Contingent remainder:

> *I hereby grant and convey my 5,000 acres of land in Buxton, North Carolina, to my daughter Mary Claire, the remainder of which to be given to her children who survive her.*

Because it cannot be determined which children will survive and who the remainderman will be, the remainder is classified as contingent. A contingent remainder exists when

- The remainderman (the person holding the remainder) is either unborn or unascertained.
- Some condition precedent or other termination of the prior estate must occur before the remainderman is entitled to take
- Both of the previous conditions occur.

Vested remainder:

> *I hereby grant and convey my two plots of land on Pamlico Sound to Anne Marie for her life and then to Stephen and his heirs.*

Stephen's interest is what is deemed a *vested remainder* because he exists and can make claim as a living being.

FIGURE 13.4
Sample Survey

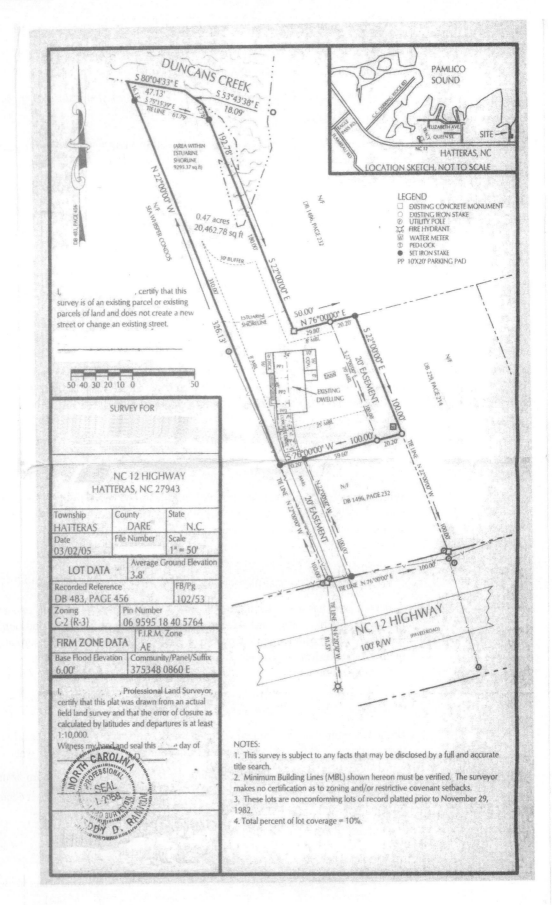

Can you identify the property most likely to be an easement?

Source: © Brand X Pictures/PunchStock.

Special Rights in Real Estate

Real property interests can be further categorized into incorporeal or nonpossessory interests. The more common examples are treated next.

Easements

Easements are nonpossessory interests in land that grant a privilege or limited right to use land in a certain way. Adjoining property owners, people without direct access, and people needing access for the public good, as in the case of utilities, desire limited, narrowly defined access to property. Consider the survey in Figure 13.4. Note that there are points of ingress and egress that cross over another person's property interest so that property owners may reach their destinations.

This easement, right of way, and privilege to use another's land is an interest in real property. These limited property interests are necessary in a complex and crowded society. Ponder the massive suburban expansion in modern America. How could society function without easements? "An easement granted for a particular purpose, or arising by prescription by an exercise of the right for such a purpose, necessarily comes to an end when the purpose ceases. A way of necessity ceases with the necessity on which it is based as when the dominant owner acquires land over which he has an outlet to the highway. The right to maintain, on adjoining land, a staircase leading to one's building terminates by the destruction of the building."[27]

Easements have also been employed to advance and preserve the cause of conservation of natural resources. Conservation easements—the limited right to use and enjoy the natural beauty of a particular parcel or piece of land—are in full bloom. Tax incentives have stimulated these programs.[28]

An easement is not a corporeal right but instead is an incorporeal, intangible right to use property. Easements can cover the subject matter of natural waterways, water courses, drains, trails and paths, roadways, tunnels, party walls, supportive buildings, fences, utility lines, rights of way, burial rights, preservation of views, and access to light and air.

Easements may also be created by direct, express reservation or exception, by implied usage or grant, or from necessity, prescription, and statutory permission or as accorded on a theory of estoppel.[29] An easement agreement setting out a right of way is shown in Form 13.5 on the accompanying CD.

Other Interests in Realty

License: A mere permission or authorization to use land, not a contract or a clear, legal property interest.

Profit a prendre: An economic and commercial right such as the taking of wood, sand, coal, minerals, and other materials for the sake of a business profit.[30]

Franchise or privilege: Granted by some governmental entity to specific parties such as the right to use public land for specified rights.

Dower: A kind of estate that entitles a widow to one-third of the lands of which her husband has possessed of a legal and inheritable estate during their marriage.[31]

Tenant/tenancy: A person who holds or has possession of real property.[32]

Forms of Ownership

Property can be held by any legal entity, including individuals, corporations, partnerships, non-profit entities, joint ventures, governmental agencies, religious organizations and groups, and any other entity, individual, or organization that has the capacity to contract.

Adverse Possession

Property also can be conveyed and acquired by happenstance. Under the doctrine of adverse possession, property passes by operation of law when over a sufficient period of time, a party not initially in rightful possession maintains an active and continuous presence without the real owner's claim, objection, or reclamation. Although this situation is not common, rural areas, where large tracts of land are not easily inspected or surveyed, sometimes witness litigation on theories of adverse possession. Title by adverse possession is acquired if these conditions are met:

1. Possession has been actual, known, and hostile to the original, rightful owner.
2. Possession has been open and notorious—that is, known by the owner as well as the community at large.
3. Possession has been exclusive in the adverse possessors.
4. Possession has been continuous and uninterrupted.
5. Possession has taken place under a claim of right.
6. Possession has been for the required statutory period, generally ranging between 7 and 30 years.[33]

Consider the example at Figure 13.5.

Singular Ownership

Any real property can be owned by a single individual or single legal entity. The individual title holder or owner is entitled to all rights, privileges, and benefits that come from ownership and need not worry about issues of partition, sharing of profits or losses, or other matters common in joint ownership. The individual is solely responsible for taxes and other obligations during his or her ownership.

Corporate or Other Business Entity Ownership

A corporation or other business entity can own property, not individually, but as the entity itself. Of course, under a joint venture or partnership, tax responsibility and civil and criminal responsibility may be directed toward the joint venturers or partners. In rare circumstances, civil and criminal liability may attach to corporate officers and directors. Customarily corporate ownership of real property is accomplished by board approval with a seal affixed to a corporate deed. The secretary of the corporation must always sign for this type of transaction.

Concurrent Ownership

Real property owned by more than one individual or entity is *concurrent*. To be classified as concurrent ownership, certain preconditions and unities of interest must be achieved:

- *Unity of time:* Co-owners or tenants in land must receive their interests at the same time.
- *Unity of title:* Co-owners or tenants in land must acquire title from the same source.
- *Unity of interest:* Tenants or co-owners must have equal interest in the land except in the case of tenants in common.

FIGURE 13.5
Example of Adverse Possession

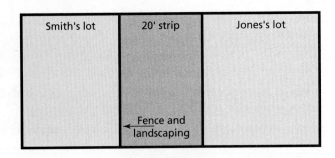

Smith's lot | 20' strip | Jones's lot

Fence and landscaping

- *Unity of possession:* This type of unity requires that each tenant have an equal right to possess the whole property for possessory purposes only.

- *Unity of person:* Applicable in tenancy by the entireties where husband and wife are viewed as the same.

Concurrent ownership has certain advantages as well as disadvantages. Judicial interpretation of concurrent ownership tends to emphasize alienability, transferability, and the duration of these estates rather than their limitation. As a result, the element of survivorship plays a crucial role in concurrent ownership. A leading characteristic of any joint tenancy is that "on the death of one joint tenant, the surviving joint tenant or tenants take the whole estate. If there are three joint tenants, on the death of one, the two survivors take the whole, and, on the death of one of these survivors, the last survivor does the same, and, on the death of this last survivor, the whole passes to his heirs, or to his personal representatives, if it is a leasehold estate. This doctrine is based on the fact that all the tenants together, as regards the feudal lord, constituted but one tenant, and this fictitious personality was considered as existent so long as any one of the tenants was alive."[34]

The Massachusetts Association of Realtors keenly covers joint ownership (see Figure 13.6). Common forms of joint tenancy are examined next.

FIGURE 13.6   Joint Tenancy

Joint Tenancy

What is joint tenancy?

Joint tenancy is a form of ownership by two or more individuals together. It differs from other types of co-ownership in that the surviving joint tenant immediately becomes the owner of the whole property upon the death of the other joint tenant. This is called a Right of Survivorship.

What is tenancy in common?

A tenancy in common is another form of co-ownership. It is the ownership of an asset by two or more individuals together, but without the rights of survivorship that are found in a joint tenancy. Thus, upon the death of one co-owner, his or her interest will not pass to the surviving owner or owners but will pass according to his or will. If there is no will, his or her share will pass according to the law determining heirs.

What are the advantages of joint tenancy?

The primary advantage of joint tenancy is the automatic transfer of ownership upon the death of one of the joint tenants. An asset that is passed from a deceased joint tenant to the surviving joint tenant(s) would not have to pass through the probate estate of the decedent. Therefore, joint tenancy is an efficient method to evade certain probate expenses and tasks. (It should be noted that joint tenancy will not avoid the incurrence of certain federal and state taxes.)

What are the disadvantages of joint tenancy?

Joint tenancy involves the co-ownership of a certain piece of property. There may be a difference of opinion among the co-owners as to the management of the property. Therefore, it may become difficult to perform such tasks as repairs, division of income, and so forth.

Titling property in joint tenancy may also lead to unintended consequences as to who inherits the property upon death. Even though your will leaves your property to certain named individuals, joint tenancy property will go to the surviving co-owner and will not pass based upon the will. A clause in a will which attempts to terminate certain joint tenancy is of no legal effect. Therefore, it is important for titling of assets to be considered as well as will drafting when doing your estate planning.

FIGURE 13.6 (*concluded*)

Is joint tenancy a substitute for a will?

Joint tenancy does not take the place of a will. It applies to a particular piece of property only. A properly drawn will disposes of all property not held in joint tenancy. A will can be changed as often as you choose. A joint tenancy agreement is difficult to change because one co-owner may simple refuse to do so.

How is joint tenancy created?

Joint tenancy is not established until something is affirmatively done by a party that owns property. State law controls the creation of a joint tenancy in both real and personal property. (Real property is land and attachments to land; personal property is all other kinds of property.)

For transfers of real property to two or more persons, the deed or conveyance must expressly state an intention to create a joint tenancy by noting that the property will be held not as tenants in common but as joint tenants with rights of survivorship. An example may be: To A & B, as joint tenants and not as tenants in common.

For transfers of personal property, such as stock certificates or bank accounts, the intention of the parties is controlling. Where there is a writing, such as a bank signature card, which is clear and unambiguous, the language on this written document will usually control on the issue of intent.

Can one joint tenant sell his or her interest in joint tenancy property?

This depends on the agreement between the joint tenants concerning co-ownership. Usually, each joint tenant owns an equal share in the whole property. Thus, if one joint tenant has a buyer for this share and there is no limitation between the joint tenants, then the sale may occur. It is important to note that a severance of the joint tenancy occurs upon a transfer by one of the joint tenants and, upon severance, the co-ownership then changes to tenancy in common (see above).

How does joint tenancy affect taxes on the death of a joint tenant?

Upon the death of any person, there are several different types of taxes that may be imposed that may affect joint property. These taxes include federal income tax, federal estate tax, federal gift tax, and Iowa inheritance tax. It should be noted that joint tenancy ownership may result in taxes which might not otherwise be required. Tax laws frequently change. The implications of tax laws should be considered when making the decision concerning the use of joint tenancy. It is therefore important to consult with an attorney concerning these issues.

What happens to joint tenancy property in the case of divorce?

Joint tenancy ownership of property between husband and wife may be divided by the Court in any divorce proceeding the same as other marital property.

FIGURE 13.7
Illustration of
Tenants in Common

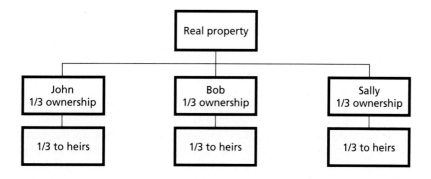

Tenants in Common   Labeled co-owner or cotenant, a *tenant in common* owns an undivided share and has a distinct piece of an entire estate except that he or she has no right to exclusive possession.

Consider Figure 13.7, in which John, Sally, and Bob each own a one-third interest in the real property that is separate and distinct from each other. Each has the same rights in respect to this realty as the others. This interest in land is generally created by a deed or other instrument that fosters a share-and-share-alike distribution or uses the term *equally*. A cotenant may not alienate, convey, mortgage, or devise his undivided interest without the consent of the cotenants unless there is agreement to the contrary. The cotenant's interest, upon death, passes to his or her heirs.

Joint Tenants   Most of the attributes of tenants in common reside within the *joint tenancy*. "The primary distinction between the tenancy in common and a joint tenancy is that joint tenancy involves a right of survivorship."[35] Survivorship under a joint tenancy plan has enormous implications. Contemplate the following fact pattern:

> *Chuck and Bart own a parcel of land in Pittsburgh, Pennsylvania, as joint tenants. Chuck dies, and his will states that his interest in the property will pass to his spouse. Under the law of joint tenancy, such a transfer will have no validity because survivorship rights are vested in the remaining joint tenant.*

Because of this harsh result, common law and current case law and statutory direction do not favor joint tenancy because it "made no provision for posterity."[36] Paralegals must be certain to label deeds, mortgages, and other evidence of ownership clearly by defining forms of current ownership as "tenants in common," "joint owners," or "tenancy by the entireties."

For litigation purposes, paralegals must prepare for disputes between tenants in common and joint tenants. In resolving these quandaries, courts confront issues such as the bankruptcy of one of the parties; failure of one of the parties to pay for debts, taxes, or improvements; failure to account properly or contribute between the cotenants; breach of contract between the cotenants; or other actions between the parties based on any theory in law. Consequently joint tenants and tenants in common should, for all practical purposes, have a partition plan upon entering this form of property ownership. Without a written plan or strategy for partition, a petition for property partition could be filed in the court of appropriate jurisdiction. An example of that complaint or petition is outlined in Form 13.6 on the accompanying CD.

Tenancy by the Entireties   As a general rule of law, and in the absence of explicit language to the contrary, a husband and wife take realty as *tenants by the entireties*. "At common law, the husband, having the right to control and dispose of his wife's land during their joint lives, was entitled to all the rents and profits of land held by entireties and could convey the land for the term of his life."[37]

The treatment of tenancy by the entireties differs by jurisdiction,[38] but for the most part has similar inclinations. Arguably, transfers of property that do not specifically mention or highlight the tenancy by the entireties nature of ownership could be viewed as other forms of joint tenancy. However, seeing the troubling results, American jurisdictions by law make any transfer to a husband and wife a tenancy by the entireties. This is a form of public policy response; an advantage to this form of concurrent ownership is that either spouse will have the benefit of full ownership under survivorship principles. Without the consent of spouses, division, severance, sale, or alienation of property cannot occur. A remedy in partition cannot be drafted until the spouses divorce. Also, creditors "cannot claim such property while both spouses are alive. Furthermore, in many states, state inheritance taxes are not imposed upon property held by entirety when the first spouse dies. However, property held by entirety may be subject to federal estate tax on the estate of the first spouse to die."[39]

Other Forms of Concurrent Ownership: Condominiums   Cooperative or concurrent ownership, especially in the condominium market, constitutes a significant market for the paralegal. Ads in newspapers and other popular publications grandiosely describe the positive values of time sharing, joint ownership, vacation sharing, and other parceled interests in real property. The reasons for the attraction to condominiums are many, but none are more compelling than the allowance for fee simple absolute ownership without fee simple obligation. The burdens of repair, maintenance of common areas, and other drudgeries of home ownership are replaced by or delegated to an association—a collective of owners who wish to avoid these recurring responsibilities. Some individuals dub a condominium as a freehold with lease characteristics.

Foundationally, the owner of a condominium unit has a fee simple interest but does not have an exclusive interest in the common areas of the property.[40] Literally defined, a *condominium* is an interest in real property consisting of an undivided interest in common in a portion of a parcel of real property, together with a separate interest in space.[41] Most individuals think of condominiums as large properties—apartment-type complexes that are being converted. "Under the condominium arrangement, the individual owner buys the exclusive right to occupy space where his unit is located. If his unit is located in a multistory building with other units above or below him, his exclusive right is to airspace his unit occupies. The apartment owner also receives an undivided interest in the land and common areas, such as the lobby, hallways, elevators, structure of the building, and the recreation facilities."[42] The maintenance and day-to-day oversight of the property are entrusted to an "association, which is all of the unit owners acting as a group to manage and maintain the condominium property. Through its bylaws and rules, the association's board of directors governs condominium administration. The board's powers include handling condominium revenues and expenditures as well as levying and collecting assessments for expenses."[43] Problems with fraud and corruption have been common within this association framework, and states are increasingly regulating their conduct.[44]

In essence, the condominium owner is like a tenant in common owning one piece of an entire tract yet having the same interests that other individuals have on a fractionalized basis. Condominiums ownership shares these characteristics:

- A master deed that identifies the property.
- Common areas of usage.
- A fractionalized or prorated formula of undivided interest in the entire property.
- An association or group of unit owners with corresponding bylaws.
- A maintenance agreement regarding all common areas, which usually include exterior walls, girders, roof, public halls, and major systems.
- A group of directors or other body of individuals who perform a governing function.
- Participation dues and other fees.
- Certain restrictions and guidelines on occupancy.[45]
- Some restrictions on alienability or preemptive transfer regulation.[46]

Condominiums are also not limited to residential purposes and have included medical and legal offices and even industrial buildings and complexes. Document preparation for either the establishment or subsequent ownership of a condominium is often handled by a paralegal. Skills of drafting and document organization are necessary for preparing the following:

- Master deed.
- Bylaws.
- Collection of blueprints and subdivision plans.
- Disclosure statements.
- Articles of incorporation.

- Recordation of the master deed.
- Proposed purchase agreement.
- Association documentation.
- Documentation of association's right of first refusal.

A sample document for condominium practice and procedure is outlined in Form 13.7 on the accompanying CD.

Other forms of concurrent ownership include cooperatives, which are nonprofit entities that purchase realty and then issue shares of stock to individuals who decide to invest and own. Additionally, a real estate investment trust, abbreviated as REIT (a money pool of numerous real estate investors operating like a mutual fund), is becoming familiar territory for the real estate paralegal. Another form of ownership is the *syndication:* a combination of two or more people who make a specific investment in real property. A summary of types of ownership is outlined in Figure 13.8.

FIGURE 13.8   Types of Ownership

Source: Frank W. Kovats, Principles and Practices of New Jersey Real Estate 67 (2005). Maywood, NJ: Kovco Publishing, Inc.

	Singular Ownership	Tenancy in Common	Joint Tenancy	Tenancy by Entireties*
Definition	Property held by one person, severed from all others.	Property held by two or more people with no right of survivorship.	Property held by two or more individuals (not corporations) with right of survivorship.	Property held by husband and wife with right of survivorship.
Creation	Any transfer to one person.	By express act; also by failure to express the tenancy.	Express intention plus four unities of time, title, interest, and possession.	Divorce automatically results in tenancy in common.
Possession	Total	Equal right of possession.	Equal right of possession.	Equal right of possession.
Title	One title in one person.	Each co-owner has a separate legal title to his or her undivided interest; will be equal interests unless expressly made unequal.	One title to the whole property because each tenant is theoretically deemed an owner of the whole; must be equal, undivided interests.	One title in the marital unit.
Conveyance	No restrictions (check release of marital rights if any).	Each co-owner's interest may be conveyed separately by its owners; purchaser becomes tenant in common.	Conveyance of one co-owner breaks his or her tenancy; purchaser becomes tenant in common.	Cannot convey without consent of spouse.
Effect of Death	Entire property subject to probate and included in gross estate for federal and state death taxes.	Decedent's fractional interest subject to probate and included in gross estate for federal and state death taxes. The property passes by will to devisees or heirs who take as tenants in common. No survivorship rights.	No probate and can't be disposed of by will; property automatically belongs to surviving cotenants (last one holds singularly). Entire property included in decedents' gross estate for federal estate tax purposes minus percentage attributable to survivor's contribution.	Right of survivorship, so no probate. Same death taxes as joint tenancy.
Creditor's Rights	Subject to creditor claims.	Co-owner's fractional interest may be sold to satisfy his or her creditor, who then becomes a tenant in common.	Joint tenant's interest also subject to execution sale; joint tenancy is broken and creditor becomes a tenant in common. Creditor gets nothing if debtor tenant dies before sale.	Only a creditor of both spouses can execute on the property.
Presumption	None.	Favored in doubtful cases; presumed to be equal interests.	Not favored so must be expressly stated.	Automatically created when names of both spouses appear on the deed.

* Husband and wife only.

LEGAL DESCRIPTIONS OF REAL PROPERTY

Understanding rights in land, the range and extent of real property interests, calls for an examination of the property's geographic and topographic parameters. A valid conveyance in land cannot occur unless the land is properly identified. Although the description does not have to be made with scientific certitude, the description must be drafted with enough particularity to make a binding conveyance. An acceptable description identifies the land. Survey carelessness or negligence in preparation of the deed and faulty visual inspection of the boundaries lays an improper foundation for the real estate transaction. The intention of the parties, as inferred from the terms of the legal description, controls the nature of the real estate conveyance.

For example, if a party proclaims an easement right, either by implication or necessity, won't a clear and unequivocal boundary line description of where the easement directs itself have to be known? In a dispute over riparian rights or damage done because of diversion of water, is it not important to know where the land tract extends to determine who has an interest in or claim over riparian rights? If permits are to be acquired for building on wetlands or other protected natural habitats, shouldn't a legal description precisely define the boundaries of a property? In sum, know where the property sits; understand its lines, its boundaries, its content, and quality before conveying it, defending it, or prosecuting an alleged violation. Practitioners must be cautious and exhibit professional care to ensure a legitimate land description.

> *It is one of the few ironies of real estate practice that few attorneys understand property descriptions or take care to review or draft them properly. The most common practice seems to be to regurgitate a description from a prior transaction by photocopying it and attaching it the current document as "Exhibit A." The property description delineates what is transferred. It is the focal point of the transaction and should be treated accordingly. Give the description the attention it deserves.*[47]

The blame for this neglect, on the part of some attorneys, is the sheer volume of land and homestead transactions—a reflection of increased mobility and wealth. It is not uncommon for a property to have been in the fee simple possession of more than 10 or 12 owners during a 30- or 40-year period. As a result of these multiple transfers, a robotic reliance on previous surveys, deeds, and other legal descriptions generates and perpetuates false descriptions. The paralegal must make certain that the legal description is accurate. Traditional measures of property lines rely on

- Informal historical references.
- Metes and bounds.
- Rectangular surveys.
- Recorded plats.
- Legal documents/legal descriptions.
- Mortgages, promissory notes, deeds of trust, title policies, indenture deeds, and written surveys.

Some Informal Suggestions

Common sense has much to do with defining and delineating property rights and corresponding boundaries. Historically some parts of the country accomplish real estate transactions without surveys—places like Smith Island or Tangier Island in Maryland and the Outer Banks of North Carolina. Even more startling is that land transactions are settled without the issuance of a deed—the deed is replaced by a handshake system of transfer. People simply know where the property line is; neighbors understand where it is; and this common understanding of boundary runs with the transference. Although such conduct does not meet the requirements of the Statute of Frauds and may certainly serve as a basis for legal malpractice, the informal technique of defining property by common understanding is a useful tool to verify and corroborate property boundaries and distances.

Second, the use of landmarks and other monuments corroborates a legal description. Within the legal description or survey are placed significant objects, such as a marker, a large tree, a fence, a wall, or another immovable object in the ground. These markers serve as beginning or ending points in the measurement of land and realty.

Third, visually inspect the property "to ensure that the property comports with the descriptions and the survey. The visit is also important to ensure no claims under a claim of adverse possession. Further, a visit to the property may turn up encumbrances such as utility easements that went unnoticed in the title insurer's or abstracter's review of record title."[48]

Visitation assists buyers concerned about the condition of the property, such as waste refuse and other destruction of the property, erosion, alluvial or riparian rights claims, continuing trespass problems, or an obvious zoning or permit difficulty.

Metes and Bounds Technique

Measuring land by metes and bounds has been a historically favorite method of land description. The metes and bounds technique relies on defined distances (metes) and general directions (bounds) from the point of a permanent monument. A description of a metes and bounds reference marker is outlined with a corresponding graphic in Figure 13.9.

Using natural geometric and concentric configurations, directions are shown in degrees. To draft and calculate a metes and bounds determination based on a written description, one must have the following rudimentary understanding:

- There are 360 degrees in a circle.
- There are 60 minutes in each degree.
- There are 60 seconds in each minute.

FIGURE 13.9
Example of Metes and Bounds

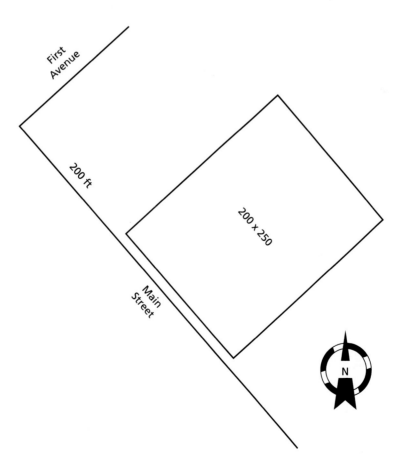

The reader or drafter of the legal description essentially acts as a compass traveling along each side of the parcel until the boundary has been marked off. A metes and bounds description in a deed might use this narrative:

> *Beginning at a point on the southerly side of Johnson Street, distant 40 feet southwesterly from the corner formed at the intersection of the easterly side of Johnson with the westerly side of Stacey Street, running then in a northerly direction and parallel with Stacey Street 400 feet and running thence southwesterly and parallel with Johnson for 70 feet, running thence southerly and again parallel with Stacey Street 200 feet to the southwesterly side of Johnson Street, running thence easterly along the southwesterly side of Johnson Street for 70 feet to the point or place of the beginning.*

Rectangular Survey System

The rectangular survey system has long been used by governmental entities, including townships, municipalities, and government agencies plotting or tracking public lands for survey purposes. An example of a township divided into grids is simply based on a compass reading utilizing north, south, east, and west designations. Also using north and south lines called *meridians* and east and west lines called *parallels,* governmental entities divided land into the following designations.

Check

A check is a system of 16 townships that are six square miles each. (See Figure 13.10.)

Township

A township within a check is further broken down into a 36-square-mile area and labeled as a section. (See Figure 13.11.)

Section and Quarters

A section contains 640 acres or one square mile. Sections are further divided into quarters and again divided as is necessary, depending on the development, plot, or planned strategy at the municipal level. (See Figure 13.12.)

A chart of land measurement equivalencies is outlined in Figure 13.13. Most of these terms are rarely used outside of real estate descriptions.

Recorded Plat or Survey

In many instances, particularly in burgeoning suburban areas, a recorded plat, survey, map, or lot–block tracking system is already available in the public recorder's office of the county where the land is located. Lots are already subdivided for purposes of development. Surveys also perform an invaluable contribution in bringing to the attention of landowners illegal intrusions, trespasses, or other encroachments to properties. A survey was previously shown in Figure 13.4.

FIGURE 13.10
Check System

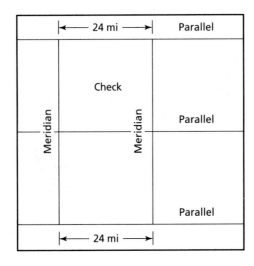

FIGURE 13.11
Township System

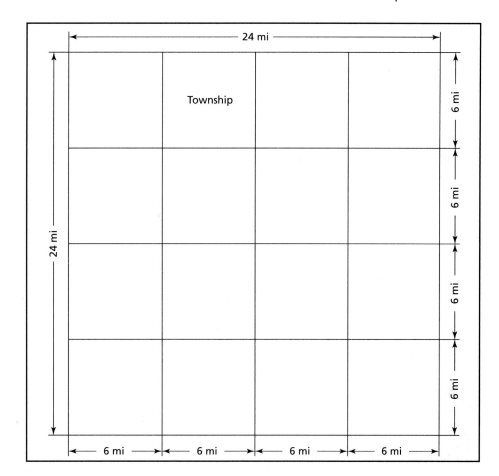

FIGURE 13.12
Sections and
Quarters System

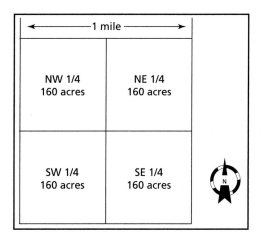

FIGURE 13.13
Land Measurement
Equivalencies

Linear:	1 link	= 7.92 inches
	1 rod	= 25 links, 16½ feet, 5½ yards
	1 chain	= 100 links, 66 feet, 4 rods
	1 mile	= 5,280 feet, 320 rods, 80 chains
Square:	1 acre	= 160 square rods, 10 square chains,
		= 4,840 square yards, 43,560 square feet
	1 section	= 640 acres, 1 square mile
	1 square mile	= 640 acres
	1 township	= 36 square miles

FIGURE 13.14
Legal Description of a Parcel of Land

That certain parcel of land situated in Hatteras Township, Dare County, NC, described as follows:

Lot No. 11 of the subdivision known as "Sutton Place Hatteras," as shown on map or plat made by Robert D. Kramer, Jr., Registered Surveyor, dated May 30, 1974, which map is recorded in Map Book 7 at Page 30 in the Dare County registry.

Legal Descriptions in Legal Documents

In any real estate closing or transaction, documents require a legal description. In the issuance of a title policy, a legal description is posted in the policy declarations. (See Figure 13.14 for an example.)

Mortgages also contain legal descriptions for enforceability, which are usually attached to the mortgage itself and are referred to in the document.

Graphic, precise legal descriptions reduce the litigation potential in real estate transactions. Review the instructions in Figure 13.15.

The best evidence of a transfer or conveyance between the parties is a deed document. Upon delivery of the deed, the party gets the property as described in the deed. Paralegals must make sure the legal description is accurate, agrees with the survey, and correlates with secondary documentation. At a minimum, the buyer wants the fullness of the property transaction. Incorrect legal descriptions may be litigated under theories of fraudulent conveyance or mistake of fact.

If a paralegal discovers inconsistencies or irregularities in the deed description versus the graphic survey, points of reference or monument/markers cited in the deed are given significant weight in the analysis of boundary lines. If a discrepancy occurs, a priority order of quality and clarification is given as follows:

1. Permanent monuments.
2. Formal and legal map references.

FIGURE 13.15
Instructions for Land Title Surveys

All surveys must be based on sufficient title abstracts and searches to prove ownership of premises and to determine effect of adverse conveyances, agreements, and miscellaneous recorded instruments.

Field surveys, whether city, town, or farm properties, must be made by an accurate, transit, balanced traverse of the property. Compass surveys are not acceptable. References to true meridian are preferred, but bearings may refer to magnetic meridian.

The map drawn from the survey must show all details graphically that bear witness to boundary lines and corners. Buildings and improvements must be located and shown on the plan. Boundary line distances and intersecting angles, as well as bearings, must be shown. Encroachments of all kinds and descriptions or evidences of adverse users must be located, shown, and reported. The surveyor reports and certifies as to the following:

1. Rights of way, old highways, or abandoned roads, lanes, or driveways, drains, sewer, water, gas, or oil pipelines across said premises.
2. Springs, streams, rivers, ponds, or lakes located, bordering on, or running through said premises.
3. Cemeteries or family burying grounds located on said premises.
4. Telephone, telegraph, or electric power poles, wires, or lines overhanging or crossing said premises and serving other properties.
5. Joint driveways or walkways; party walls or rights of support; porches, steps, or roofs used in common or joint garages.
6. Encroachments or overhanging projections. (If the buildings, projections, or cornices thereof, or signs affixed thereto, fences, or other indications of occupancy encroach upon or overhang adjoining properties, or the like encroach upon or overhang surveyed premises, specify all such.)
7. Fences, walls, shrubbery, or other evidences of physical boundary lines.
8. Evidences of recent building construction, repairs, or alterations.
9. Changes in grade or street alignment completed or proposed.
10. Are there indications of recent street or sidewalk construction or repairs?

3. Metes and bounds descriptions.

4. Specific land quantity statements.

5. Parcel numbers.

6. Plots or subdivisions.[49]

THE REAL ESTATE TRANSACTION

The typical real estate transaction encompasses a host of details. The parties alone require extraordinary control and oversight. Keeping track of individuals, personalities, financial institutions, title companies, real estate agents and brokers, vendors, vendees, and attorneys involves various human relations skills. Lawyers are no longer merely closers of the transaction, but active and decisive players from the initial date of contract negotiation until recordation of the deed.

Brokers and Agents

Most significantly, attorneys and paralegals generally deal with brokers and agents more than any other parties. Real estate agents have a vested interest in the form of commissions, which continually prods their interest level in the transaction.

Of course, the realty transaction need not have professional agents and brokers: Buyer–seller relationships can exist without them. Additionally, one real estate agent may dually represent both buyer and seller, though this arrangement has increasingly been critiqued as a conflict. For the most part, buyer and seller will have exclusive agents to represent them in the transaction. There may be only one broker of record, however. Because real estate work is commission based, how that commission will be paid depends on the fee agreement.

The relationship that exists between the broker, salesperson, and client constitutes one of agent and principal.[50] The broker is an agent for the purchaser or seller of the residence and consequently has a fiduciary obligation to act in the seller's or buyer's best interests. This obligation is "in addition to the contractual obligation between the parties established by the above-described listing agreements."[51] These words should be not hollow exhortations but ones rooted in professionalism and a sturdy ethical framework:

> *Operating under this philosophy, the brokers and agents have a series of duties to a seller, including*
>
> - *Good faith and undivided loyalty.*
> - *Full disclosure.*
> - *Reasonable care, skill, diligence, and judgment.*
> - *Obedience.*
> - *Confidentiality.*
> - *Accounting.*[52]

Understandably, a certain tension naturally exists between real estate brokers, sales agents, and the attorneys representing buyers and sellers. Lawyers are frequently labeled "deal killers" in the real estate market. On the other hand, lawyers perceive real estate agents as nothing but commission-collecting pariahs who will go to any extreme to collect their entitlement.

Of course these are exaggerated perceptions, but the disdain between lawyers and real estate agents represents a clear challenge for paralegals orchestrating the transaction. Granted, disputes over matters like the pace of closing are usual events. Misunderstandings about billing, lawyer meddling, threats of litigation, and disregard of contract language manifest the stress of the real estate transaction. However, the legendary professional bickering is counterproductive and should be replaced by cooperation and a mutual desire for the client's good. Despite these complexities, commissions are paid according to contractual terms. These agreements are commonly referred to as *listing agreements*.

Types of Listing Agreements

To *list* means to engage a property for sale. "Listings are generally generated or held by real estate brokers or agents. The broker, a licensed, state-approved professional, is directly responsible for a real estate office operation. Real estate agents work under the supervision of the broker.

A broker can be an agent and an agent can be a broker. But a real estate agent cannot operate on his or her own, because his or her agency depends on finding a real estate office to generate sales activity. Both brokers and agents have a contractual understanding that specifies how commissions are generated and split, and how expenses are allotted. Brokers and agents author listing agreements, whereby a seller engages them to sell the realty in question. In some states, buyer agency relationships are possible. The listing gives a right, under agreed terms and conditions, to the broker/agent to sell a property. The style, extent of agency, and other interpretive qualities of listing agreements vary enormously."

Exclusive Listing Agreement   The real estate agent may wish to be the exclusive agent of the seller. In an *exclusive listing* the owner agrees to appoint the broker as the sole, exclusive agent and grants the broker the exclusive right to sell or exchange the property in question. On the other hand, an open listing allows more brokers to market simultaneously.[53]

First, the exclusive right to sell agreement, which most real estate brokers/agents prefer, provides a commission to the broker/agent regardless of who sells the home. See Figure 13.16. Another example of a contract governing the behavior of real estate brokers and salespeople is the exclusive listing arrangement. An exclusive listing agreement requires the owner to sell the property only through that broker but does not require payment of a commission if the owner finds a buyer without the broker's assistance. In these facts, the real estate agent will get paid only if he or she provides the buyer. An example of an exclusive listing is shown in Figure 13.17.

Next, an *open listing* agreement permits a broker to receive a commission only if the broker finds the purchaser. No commission is paid whatsoever if the owner finds a purchaser, and the owner may use as many brokers as he or she wishes. Naturally, real estate agencies frown on this arrangement. For an example, see Form 13.8 on the accompanying CD.

Flat Fee Listing   Another type of listing agreement is the *flat fee listing* agreement, where broker and agent agree to a predetermined commission, despite the amount of the sale price. Because real estate commissions are usually tied to the sales price, the seller's effort to reduce the amount owed is not a warmly received gesture. Most brokers and agents do not like fixed commissions. See the example of this type of agreement in Form 13.9 on the accompanying CD.

Net Listing Agreement   In the *net listing* a broker or agent earns a commission only on the portion of the sales price that is in excess of a stated price. Here the broker/agent is rewarded for an aggressive sales price. Be wary of exaggerated appraisals in this listing format. An example of a net listing agreement is shown in Form 13.10 on the accompanying CD.

Purchase Agreement/Contract of Sale Agreement

An *agreement of sale* or *contract of sale agreement* is the documentary foundation for a real property transaction. This instrument should delineate the rights and obligations of each party, both purchaser and seller, regarding the transfer and grant of real property. In some jurisdictions, signing the document provides for an equitable transfer of ownership with settlement merely being the consummation of that agreement.

The Statute of Frauds requires that any transaction involving real property, to be enforceable, must be in writing and the form of that writing, while subject to jurisdictional variation, is of considerable consequence. Preprinted forms have taken the guesswork out of form content. The inherent design of such printed forms limits the scope of negotiation. However, despite this boilerplate tendency, parties may add or subtract by addendum, other clauses, or features of the transaction not evident in the printed forms.[54]

The real estate industry's historic reliance on the published form, often authored by local associations and groups of real estate specialists, tends to simplify too readily. Real estate practice can be complicated, and the standard forms do not always account for the array of complexities. These forms are not geared to specialized facts and circumstances. The Institute of Continuing Legal Education makes this clear: "A form is nothing more than someone else's effort at drafting. There may be legal constraints on what a form may contain or how it can be drafted, but there is nothing that makes any one form comprehensive or required."[55] A sound contract balances the interests of both sellers and buyers.

An example of a purchase agreement or agreement of sale is outlined in Form 13.11 on the accompanying CD. Sample checklists for buyers and sellers are provided in Figures 13.18 and 13.19.

FIGURE 13.16   Exclusive Brokerage Listing Contract

1	The printed portions of this form, except differentiated additions, have been approved by the Colorado
2	Real Estate Commission. (LC53-4-05)

3

4

5   **THIS IS A BINDING CONTRACT.   THIS FORM HAS IMPORTANT LEGAL**
6   **CONSEQUENCES AND THE PARTIES SHOULD CONSULT LEGAL AND TAX OR OTHER**
7   **COUNSEL BEFORE SIGNING.**
8   Compensation charged by real estate brokerage firms is not set by law. Such charges are established by
9   each real estate brokerage firm.

10

11   **DIFFERENT BROKERAGE RELATIONSHIPS ARE AVAILABLE WHICH INCLUDE**
12   **BUYER AGENCY, SELLER AGENCY, OR TRANSACTION-BROKERAGE.**

13

14   **EXCLUSIVE BROKERAGE LISTING CONTRACT**
15   **(ALL TYPES OF PROPERTIES)**

16

17

18   ☐ **SELLER AGENCY**   ☐ **TRANSACTION-BROKERAGE**

19

20

21   Date: _____

22

23   **1.   AGREEMENT.** Seller and Brokerage Firm enter into this exclusive, irrevocable contract as of
24   the date set forth above. However, this Listing Contract does not apply to a Sale of the Property to a
25   buyer procured solely by Seller without the assistance of Broker or any other person (Seller Sale).

26

27   **2.   BROKER AND BROKERAGE FIRM.**

28

29   ☐ **a.   Multiple-Person Firm.** If this box is checked, the individual designated by Brokerage
30   Firm to serve as the broker of Seller and to perform the services for Seller required by this contract is
31   called Broker. If more than one individual is so designated, then references in this contract to Broker
32   shall include all persons so designated, including substitute or additional brokers. The brokerage
33   relationship exists only with Broker and does not extend to the employing broker, Brokerage Firm, or to
34   any other brokers employed or engaged by Brokerage Firm who are not so designated.

35

36   ☐ **b.   One-Person Firm.** If this box is checked, Broker is a real estate brokerage firm with
37   only one licensed natural person. References in this contract to Broker or Brokerage Firm mean both the
38   licensed natural person and brokerage firm who shall serve as the broker of Seller and perform the
39   services for Seller required by this contract.

40

41   **3.   DEFINED TERMS.**

42

43   a.   **Seller:** _____

44

45   b.   **Brokerage Firm:**_____

46

47   c.   **Broker:** _____

48

No. LC53-4-05 EXCLUSIVE BROKERAGE LISTING CONTRACT (All Types of Properties) Page 1 of 11

FIGURE 13.16 (*continued*)

49
50   **d.**   **Property.** The Property is the following legally described real estate:
51
52
53 in the County of _____, Colorado,
54 commonly known as No. _____
55   Street Address   City   State   Zip
56 together with the interests, easements, rights, benefits, improvements, and attached fixtures appurtenant
57 thereto, all interest of Seller in vacated streets and alleys adjacent thereto, except as herein excluded.
58
59   **e.**   **Sale.** A Sale is the voluntary transfer or exchange of any interest in the Property or the
60 voluntary creation of the obligation to convey any interest in the Property, including a contract or lease.
61 It also includes an agreement to transfer any ownership interest in an entity which owns the Property.
62
63   **f.**   **Listing Period.** The Listing Period of this contract shall begin on _____,   and
64 shall continue through the earlier of (1) completion of the Sale of the Property or (2) _____
65 _____. Broker shall continue to assist in the completion of any transaction for
66 which compensation is payable to Brokerage Firm under § 16 of this contract.
67
68   **g.**   **Applicability of Terms.** A check or similar mark in a box means that such provision is
69 applicable. The abbreviation "N/A" means not applicable. The abbreviation "MEC" (mutual execution
70 of this contract) means the latest date upon which the parties have signed this contract.
71
72 **4.**   **BROKERAGE SERVICES AND DUTIES.** Brokerage Firm, acting through Broker, shall
73 provide brokerage services to Seller. The Broker, acting as either a Transaction-Broker or a Seller's
74 Agent, shall perform the following **Uniform Duties** when working with Seller:
75
76   **a.**   Broker shall exercise reasonable skill and care for Seller, including, but not limited to the
77 following:
78   **(1)**   Performing the terms of any written or oral agreement with Seller;
79   **(2)**   Presenting all offers to and from Seller in a timely manner regardless of whether
80   the Property is subject to a contract for Sale;
81   **(3)**   Disclosing to Seller adverse material facts actually known by Broker;
82   **(4)**   Advising Seller regarding the transaction and to obtain expert advice as to
83   material matters about which Broker knows but the specifics of which are beyond
84   the expertise of Broker;
85   **(5)**   Accounting in a timely manner for all money and property received; and
86   **(6)**   Keeping Seller fully informed regarding the transaction.
87
88   **b.**   Broker shall not disclose the following information without the informed consent of
89 Seller:
90   **(1)**   That Seller is willing to accept less than the asking price for the Property;
91   **(2)**   What the motivating factors are for Seller to sell the Property;
92   **(3)**   That Seller will agree to financing terms other than those offered;
93   **(4)**   Any material information about Seller unless disclosure is required by law or
94   failure to disclose such information would constitute fraud or dishonest dealing;
95   or

No. LC53-4-05 EXCLUSIVE BROKERAGE LISTING CONTRACT (All Types of Properties) Page 2 of 11

FIGURE 13.16   (*continued*)

96   (5)   Any facts or suspicions regarding circumstances that could psychologically
97   impact or stigmatize the Property.
98

99   **c.**   Seller consents to Broker's disclosure of Seller's confidential information to the
100   supervising broker or designee for the purpose of proper supervision, provided such supervising broker
101   or designee shall not further disclose such information without consent of Seller, or use such information
102   to the detriment of Seller.
103

104   **d.**   Brokerage Firm may have agreements with other sellers to market and sell their property.
105   Broker may show alternative properties not owned by Seller to other prospective buyers and list
106   competing properties for sale.
107

108   **e.**   Broker shall not be obligated to seek additional offers to purchase the Property while the
109   Property is subject to a contract for Sale.
110

111   **f.**   Broker has no duty to conduct an independent inspection of the Property for the benefit
112   of a buyer and has no duty to independently verify the accuracy or completeness of statements made by
113   Seller or independent inspectors.   Broker has no duty to conduct an independent investigation of a
114   buyer's financial condition or to verify the accuracy or completeness of any statement made by a buyer.
115

116   **g.**   Seller shall not be liable for the acts of Broker unless such acts are approved, directed, or
117   ratified by Seller.
118

119   **5.**   **ADDITIONAL DUTIES OF SELLER'S AGENT.**   If the Seller Agency box at the top of Page
120   1 is checked, Broker is a limited agent of Seller (Seller's Agent), with the following additional duties:
121

122   **a.**   Promoting the interests of Seller with the utmost good faith, loyalty, and fidelity.
123

124   **b.**   Seeking a price and terms that are acceptable to Seller.
125

126   **c.**   Counseling Seller as to any material benefits or risks of a transaction that are actually
127   known by Broker.
128

129   **6.**   **BROKERAGE RELATIONSHIP.**
130

131   **a.**   If the Seller Agency box at the top of page 1 is checked, Broker shall represent Seller as
132   a Seller's Agent. If the Transaction-Brokerage box at the top of page 1 is checked, Broker shall act as a
133   Transaction-Broker.
134

135   **b.**   **In-Company Transaction—Different Brokers.** When Seller and buyer in a transaction
136   are working with different brokers, those brokers continue to conduct themselves consistent with the
137   brokerage relationships they have established. Seller acknowledges that Brokerage Firm is allowed to
138   offer and pay compensation to brokers within Brokerage Firm working with a buyer.
139

140   **c.**   **In-Company Transaction—One Broker.** If Seller and buyer are both working with the
141   same broker, Broker shall function as:

No. LC53-4-05 EXCLUSIVE BROKERAGE LISTING CONTRACT (All Types of Properties) Page 3 of 11

FIGURE 13.16 (*continued*)

142

143   **(1)**   **SELLER'S AGENT.** If the Seller Agency box at the top of page 1 is checked,
144 the parties agree the following applies:

145

146 **Check One Box Only**

147

148 ☐   **(a) Seller Agency.** If this box is checked, Broker shall represent Seller as
149 Seller's Agent and shall treat the buyer as a customer. A customer is a party to a transaction with whom
150 Broker has no brokerage relationship. Broker shall disclose to such customer Broker's relationship with
151 Seller.

152

153 ☐   **(b) Seller Agency Unless Brokerage Relationship with Both.** If this box is
154 checked, Broker shall represent Seller as Seller's Agent and shall treat the buyer as a customer, unless
155 Broker currently has or enters into an agency or Transaction-Brokerage relationship with the buyer, in
156 which case Broker shall act as a Transaction-Broker, performing the duties described in § 4 and
157 facilitating sales transactions without being an advocate or agent for either party.

158

159   **(2)**   **TRANSACTION-BROKER.** If the Transaction-Brokerage box at the top of
160 page 1 is checked, or in the event neither box is checked, Broker shall work with Seller as a Transaction-
161 Broker. If Seller and buyer are working with the same broker, Broker shall continue to function as a
162 Transaction-Broker.

163

164 **7.**   **SELLER'S OBLIGATIONS TO BROKER.** Other than a Seller Sale, Seller agrees to conduct
165 all negotiations for the Sale of the Property only through Broker, and to refer to Broker all
166 communications received in any form from real estate brokers, during the Listing Period of this contract.
167 Seller represents that Seller ☐ **Is** ☐ **Is Not** currently a party to any listing agreement with any other
168 broker to sell the Property.

169

170 **8.**   **PRICE AND TERMS.**

171

172   **a.**   **Price.** U.S. $ _____

173

174   **b.**   **Terms.** ☐ **Cash** ☐ **Conventional** ☐ **FHA** ☐ **VA**
175   ☐ **Other:** _____
176 _____

177

178   **c.**   **Loan Discount Points.** _____
179 _____
180 _____

181

182   **d.**   **Buyer's Closing Costs (FHA/VA).** Seller shall pay closing costs and fees that Buyer is
183 not allowed to pay, in an amount not to exceed $_____ for only the following items: third party
184 document preparation, tax service, tax certificate, and_____
185 _____.

186

187   **e.**   **Earnest Money.** Minimum amount of earnest money deposit U.S. $_____ in the
188 form of _____.

189

No. LC53-4-05 EXCLUSIVE BROKERAGE LISTING CONTRACT (All Types of Properties) Page 4 of 11

FIGURE 13.16 (*continued*)

190 **f.** **Seller Proceeds.** Seller will receive net proceeds of closing as indicated:
191 ☐ **Cashier's Check** at Seller's expense; ☐ **Funds Electronically Transferred (Wire Transfer)** to an
192 account specified by Seller, at Seller's expense; or ☐ **Closing Company's Trust Account Check**.
193

194 **g.** **Advisory—Tax Withholding.** The Internal Revenue Service and the Colorado
195 Department of Revenue may require closing company to withhold a substantial portion of the proceeds
196 of this Sale when Seller either (1) is a foreign person or (2) will not be a Colorado resident after closing.
197 Seller should inquire of Seller's tax advisor to determine if withholding applies or if an exemption exists.
198

199 **9.** **DEPOSITS.** Brokerage Firm is authorized to accept earnest money deposits received by Broker
200 pursuant to a proposed Sale contract. Brokerage Firm is authorized to deliver the earnest money deposit
201 to the closing agent, if any, at or before the closing of the Sale contract.
202

203 **10.** **INCLUSIONS AND EXCLUSIONS.**
204

205 **a.** **Inclusions.** The Purchase Price includes the following items (Inclusions):
206

207 **(1)** **Fixtures.** If attached to the Property on the date of this contract, lighting, heating,
208 plumbing, ventilating, and air conditioning fixtures, TV antennas, inside telephone wiring and
209 connecting blocks/jacks, plants, mirrors, floor coverings, intercom systems, built-in kitchen appliances,
210 sprinkler systems and controls, built-in vacuum systems (including accessories), garage door openers
211 including ____ remote controls;
212
213
214

215 **(2)** **Personal Property.** If on the Property whether attached or not on the date of this
216 contract: storm windows, storm doors, window and porch shades, awnings, blinds, screens, window
217 coverings, curtain rods, drapery rods, fireplace inserts, fireplace screens, fireplace grates, heating stoves,
218 storage sheds, and all keys. If checked, the following are included: ☐ **Water Softeners**
219 ☐ **Smoke/Fire Detectors** ☐ **Security Systems** ☐ **Satellite Systems** (including satellite dishes); and
220 _____.
221 The Personal Property to be conveyed at closing shall be conveyed, by Seller, free and clear of
222 all taxes (except personal property taxes for the year of closing), liens and encumbrances, except _____
223 _____
224 _____.
225 Conveyance shall be by bill of sale or other applicable legal instrument.
226

227 **(3)** **Trade Fixtures.** The following trade fixtures: _____
228 _____
229 The Trade Fixtures to be conveyed at closing shall be conveyed, by Seller, free and clear of all
230 taxes (except personal property taxes for the year of closing), liens and encumbrances, except _____
231 _____
232 _____.
233 Conveyance shall be by bill of sale or other applicable legal instrument.
234

235 **(4)** **Parking and Storage Facilities.** ☐ **Use Only** ☐ **Ownership** of the
236 following parking facilities: _____; and the following storage facilities: _____
237 _____.

No. LC53-4-05 EXCLUSIVE BROKERAGE LISTING CONTRACT (All Types of Properties) Page 5 of 11

FIGURE 13.16 (*continued*)

238
239   **(5)   Water Rights.** The following legally described water rights:
240
241   Any water rights shall be conveyed by _____ deed or other applicable legal
242   instrument. The Well Permit # is _____.
243
244   **(6)   Growing Crops.** The following growing crops:
245
246
247   **b.   Exclusions.** The following are excluded: _____
248   _____
249
250   **11.   TITLE AND ENCUMBRANCES.** Seller represents to Broker that title to the Property is
251   solely in Seller's name. Seller shall deliver to Broker true copies of all relevant title materials, leases,
252   improvement location certificates, and surveys in Seller's possession and shall disclose to Broker all
253   easements, liens, and other encumbrances, if any, on the Property, of which Seller has knowledge. Seller
254   authorizes the holder of any obligation secured by an encumbrance on the Property to disclose to Broker
255   the amount owing on said encumbrance and the terms thereof. In case of Sale, Seller agrees to convey,
256   by a _____ deed, only that title Seller has in the Property. Property shall be conveyed
257   free and clear of all taxes, except the general taxes for the year of closing.
258   All monetary encumbrances (such as mortgages, deeds of trust, liens, financing statements) shall
259   be paid by Seller and released except as Seller and buyer may otherwise agree. Existing monetary
260   encumbrances are as follows: _____
261   _____.
262   The Property is subject to the following leases and tenancies: _____
263   _____.
264   If the Property has been or will be subject to any governmental liens for special improvements
265   installed at the time of signing a Sale contract, Seller shall be responsible for payment of same, unless
266   otherwise agreed. Brokerage Firm may terminate this contract upon written notice to Seller that title is
267   not satisfactory to Brokerage Firm.
268
269   **12.   EVIDENCE OF TITLE.** Seller agrees to furnish buyer, at Seller's expense, a current
270   commitment and an owner's title insurance policy in an amount equal to the Purchase Price in the form
271   specified in the Sale contract, or if this box is checked, ☐ **An Abstract of Title** certified to a current
272   date.
273
274   **13.   ASSOCIATION ASSESSMENTS.** Seller represents that the amount of the regular owners'
275   association assessment is currently payable at $_____ per _____ and that there
276   are no unpaid regular or special assessments against the Property except the current regular assessments
277   and except _____.
278   Seller agrees to promptly request the owners' association to deliver to buyer before date of closing a
279   current statement of assessments against the Property.
280
281   **14.   POSSESSION.** Possession of the Property shall be delivered to buyer as follows:
282   _____,
283   subject to leases and tenancies as described in §11.
284
285   **15.   MATERIAL DEFECTS, DISCLOSURES, AND INSPECTION.**

No. LC53-4-05 EXCLUSIVE BROKERAGE LISTING CONTRACT (All Types of Properties) Page 6 of 11

FIGURE 13.16 *(continued)*

286
287   **a.**   **Broker's Obligations.** Colorado law requires a broker to disclose to any prospective
288 buyer all adverse material facts actually known by such broker including but not limited to adverse
289 material facts pertaining to the title to the Property and the physical condition of the Property, any
290 material defects in the Property, and any environmental hazards affecting the Property which are
291 required by law to be disclosed. These types of disclosures may include such matters as structural
292 defects, soil conditions, violations of health, zoning, or building laws, and nonconforming uses and
293 zoning variances. Seller agrees that any buyer may have the Property and Inclusions inspected and
294 authorizes Broker to disclose any facts actually known by Broker about the Property.
295
296   **b.**   **Seller's Obligations.**
297
298   **(1)**   **Seller's Property Disclosure Form.** A seller is not required by law to provide a
299 written disclosure of adverse matters regarding the Property. However, disclosure of known material
300 latent (not obvious) defects is required by law. Seller ☐ **Agrees** ☐ **Does Not Agree** to provide a
301 Seller's Property Disclosure form completed to the best of Seller's current, actual knowledge.
302
303   **(2)**   **Lead-Based Paint.** Unless exempt, if the improvements on the Property include
304 one or more residential dwellings for which a building permit was issued prior to January 1, 1978, a
305 completed Lead-Based Paint Disclosure (Sales) form must be signed by Seller and the real estate
306 licensees, and given to any potential buyer in a timely manner.
307
308 **16.**   **COMPENSATION TO BROKERAGE FIRM.** Other than a Seller Sale, Seller agrees that any
309 Brokerage Firm compensation that is conditioned upon the Sale of the Property shall be earned by
310 Brokerage Firm as set forth herein without any discount or allowance for any efforts made by Seller or
311 by any other person in connection with the Sale of the Property.
312
313   **a.**   **Amount.** In consideration of the services to be performed by Broker, Seller agrees to
314 pay Brokerage Firm as follows:
315
316   **(1)**   **Sale Commission.** (a) _____% of the gross sales price in U.S. dollars, or
317 (b) _____.
318
319   **(2)**   **Lease Commission.** (a)____ % of the gross rent under the lease in U.S. dollars,
320 or (b) _____.
321
322   **b.**   **When Earned.** Such commission shall be earned upon the occurrence of any of the
323 following:
324
325   **(1)**   Any Sale of the Property, except a Seller Sale, within the Listing Period, by
326 Broker or by any other person;
327
328   **(2)**   Broker finding a buyer who is ready, willing, and able to complete the transaction
329 as specified herein by Seller; or
330
331   **(3)**   Any Sale of the Property, except a Seller Sale, within _____ calendar days
332 subsequent to the expiration of the Listing Period (Holdover Period) to anyone with whom Broker
333 negotiated and whose name was submitted, in writing, to Seller by Broker during the Listing Period

---

No. LC53-4-05 EXCLUSIVE BROKERAGE LISTING CONTRACT (All Types of Properties) Page 7 of 11

FIGURE 13.16 (*continued*)

334 (including any extensions thereof). However, Seller shall owe no commission to Brokerage Firm under
335 this subsection (3) if a commission is earned by another licensed real estate brokerage firm acting
336 pursuant to an exclusive agreement entered into during the Holdover Period.
337
338   **c.**   **When Applicable and Payable.** The commission obligation shall apply to a Sale, other
339 than a Seller Sale, made during the Listing Period or any extension of such original or extended term.
340 The commission described in subsection 16a(1) shall be payable at the time of the closing of the Sale as
341 contemplated by subsection 16b(1) or 16b(3), or upon fulfillment of subsection 16b(2) where either the
342 offer made by such buyer is defeated by Seller or by the refusal or neglect of Seller to consummate the
343 Sale as agreed upon.
344
345   **d.**   **Lease and Lease Option Commissions.** If the transaction consists of a lease or a lease
346 and right to purchase the Property, the commission relating to the lease shall be as provided in
347 subsection 16a(2), payable as follows: _____
348
349   **e.**   **Other Compensation.** _____
350
351 **17.**   **LIMITATION ON THIRD-PARTY COMPENSATION.** Neither Broker nor the Brokerage
352 Firm, except as set forth in § 16, shall accept compensation from any other person or entity in
353 connection with the Property without the written consent of Seller. Additionally, neither Broker nor
354 Brokerage Firm shall assess or receive markups or other compensation for services performed by any
355 third party or affiliated business entity unless Seller signs a separate written consent.
356
357 **18.**   **OTHER BROKERS' ASSISTANCE, MULTIPLE LISTING SERVICE, AND**
358 **MARKETING.** Seller has been advised by Broker of the advantages and disadvantages of various
359 marketing methods, the use of multiple listing services, and various methods of making the Property
360 accessible by other brokerage firms (e.g., using lock boxes, by-appointment-only showings, etc.), and
361 whether some methods may limit the ability of another broker to show the Property. After having been
362 so advised, Seller has chosen the following (check all that apply):
363
364   **a.**   The Property:
365   ☐ **Shall** ☐ **Shall Not** be submitted to one or more multiple listing services.
366   ☐ **Shall** ☐ **Shall Not** be submitted to one or more property information exchanges.
367   Seller authorizes the use of electronic and all other marketing methods except: _____
368 _____
369   Seller further authorizes use of the data by multiple listing services and property
370 information exchanges, if any.
371   Access to the Property by other brokerage firms may be by:
372   ☐ **Lock Box**
373   ☐ _____
374   Other instructions: _____
375
376   **b.**   Broker shall seek assistance from, and Brokerage Firm offers compensation to, the
377 following brokers outside of Brokerage Firm:
378   ☐ **Buyer Agents:** _____ % of the gross sales price in U.S. dollars.
379   ☐ **Transaction-Brokers:** ___ % of the gross sales price in U.S. dollars.
380

FIGURE 13.16   (*continued*)

381 **19.   FORFEITURE OF PAYMENTS.** In the event of a forfeiture of payments made by a buyer,
382 the sums received shall be divided between Brokerage Firm and Seller, one-half thereof to Brokerage
383 Firm but not to exceed the Brokerage Firm compensation agreed upon herein, and the balance to Seller.
384 Any forfeiture of payment under this section shall not reduce any Brokerage Firm compensation under
385 § 16.
386

387 **20.   COST OF SERVICES AND REIMBURSEMENT.** Unless otherwise agreed upon in writing,
388 Brokerage Firm shall bear all expenses incurred by Brokerage Firm, if any, to market the Property and
389 to compensate cooperating brokerage firms, if any. Neither Broker nor Brokerage Firm shall obtain or
390 order any other products or services unless Seller agrees in writing to pay for them promptly when due
391 (examples: surveys, radon tests, soil tests, title reports, engineering studies). Unless otherwise agreed,
392 neither Broker nor Brokerage Firm shall be obligated to advance funds for the benefit of Seller in order
393 to complete a closing. Seller shall reimburse Brokerage Firm for payments made by Brokerage Firm for
394 such products or services authorized by Seller.
395

396 **21.   MAINTENANCE OF THE PROPERTY.** Neither Broker nor Brokerage Firm shall be
397 responsible for maintenance of the Property, nor shall they be liable for damage of any kind occurring to
398 the Property, unless such damage shall be caused by their negligence or intentional misconduct.
399

400 **22.   NONDISCRIMINATION.** The parties agree not to discriminate unlawfully against any
401 prospective buyer because of the race, creed, color, sex, marital status, national origin, familial status,
402 physical or mental handicap, religion, or ancestry of such person.
403

404 **23.   RECOMMENDATION OF LEGAL AND TAX COUNSEL.** By signing this document,
405 Seller acknowledges that Broker has advised that this document has important legal consequences and
406 has recommended consultation with legal and tax or other counsel before signing this contract.
407

408 **24.   MEDIATION.** If a dispute arises relating to this contract, prior to or after closing, and is not
409 resolved, the parties shall first proceed in good faith to submit the matter to mediation. Mediation is a
410 process in which the parties meet with an impartial person who helps to resolve the dispute informally
411 and confidentially. Mediators cannot impose binding decisions. The parties to the dispute must agree
412 before any settlement is binding. The parties will jointly appoint an acceptable mediator and will share
413 equally in the cost of such mediation. The mediation, unless otherwise agreed, shall terminate in the
414 event the entire dispute is not resolved within 30 calendar days of the date written notice requesting
415 mediation is sent by one party to the other at the party's last known address.
416

417 **25.   ATTORNEY FEES.** In the event of any arbitration or litigation relating to this contract, the
418 arbitrator or court shall award to the prevailing party all reasonable costs and expenses, including
419 attorney and legal fees.
420

421 **26.   ADDITIONAL PROVISIONS.** (The following additional provisions have not been approved
422 by the Colorado Real Estate Commission.)
423
424
425
426 **27.   ATTACHMENTS.** The following are a part of this contract:
427
428

No. LC53-4-05 EXCLUSIVE BROKERAGE LISTING CONTRACT (All Types of Properties) Page 9 of 11

FIGURE 13.16 (*continued*)

429

430   **28.**   **NOTICE, DELIVERY, AND CHOICE OF LAW.**

431

432   **a.**   **Physical Delivery.** Except for the notice requesting mediation described in § 24 and

433 except as provided in § 28b below, any notice to the other party to this contract must be in writing, and

434 is effective upon receipt.

435

436   **b.**   **Electronic Delivery.** As an alternative to physical delivery, any signed document and

437 written notice may be delivered in electronic form by the following indicated methods only:

438 ☐ **Facsimile** ☐ **E-mail** ☐ **None**. Documents with original signatures shall be provided upon request

439 of any party.

440

441   **c.**   **Choice of Law.** This contract and all disputes arising hereunder shall be governed by

442 and construed in accordance with the laws of the State of Colorado that would be applicable to Colorado

443 residents who sign a contract in this state for property located in Colorado.

444

445 **29.**   **MODIFICATION OF THIS LISTING CONTRACT.** No subsequent modification of any of

446 the terms of this contract shall be valid, binding upon the parties, or enforceable unless made in writing

447 and signed by the parties.

448

449 **30.**   **COUNTERPARTS.** If more than one person is named as a Seller herein, this contract may be

450 executed by each Seller, separately, and when so executed, such copies taken together with one executed

451 by Broker on behalf of Brokerage Firm shall be deemed to be a full and complete contract between the

452 parties.

453

454 **31.**   **ENTIRE AGREEMENT.** This agreement constitutes the entire contract between the parties,

455 and any prior agreements, whether oral or written, have been merged and integrated into this contract.

456

457 **32.**   **COPY OF CONTRACT.** Seller acknowledges receipt of a copy of this contract signed by

458 Broker, including all attachments.

459

460

461 Brokerage Firm authorizes Broker to execute this contract on behalf of Brokerage Firm.

462

463

464 Date: _____   Date: _____

465

466 _____   _____

467 Seller   Seller

468 Address: _____

469 Phone No.: _____   Fax No.: _____

470 E-mail Address:_____

471

472

473 Date: _____   _____

474   Broker

475 Broker's Name: _____

476 Address: _____

No. LC53-4-05 EXCLUSIVE BROKERAGE LISTING CONTRACT (All Types of Properties) Page 10 of 11

FIGURE 13.16   (*continued*)

477	Phone No.: _____ Fax No.: _____
478	E-mail Address:_____
479	
480	Brokerage Firm's Name: _____
481	Address: _____
482	Phone No.: _____ Fax No.: _____
483	E-mail Address:_____
484	

No. LC53-4-05 EXCLUSIVE BROKERAGE LISTING CONTRACT (All Types of Properties) Page 11 of 11

FIGURE 13.17
Exclusive Listing
Agreement

EXCLUSIVE LISTING AGREEMENT

DATE

, BROKER

Agreement between

and   , Seller, in consideration of BROKER listing and endeavoring to procure a purchaser or tenant for the property known as

SELLER grants BROKER the sole exclusive right to sell or exchange the property for $ or to lease the property for $. The term of this listing shall be from   until midnight   .

Authorization to affix a lockbox to the property for use by all Multiple Listing Service Members is ____ is not ____ granted.

Authorization to post "For Sale" sign on property is ____ is not ____ granted.

SELLER agrees to pay BROKER a commission if this property, or any portion, is sold, leased, or exchanged by BROKER, other cooperating agent, SELLER, or any other person during the term of this Agreement. Commission shall be due and payable at the closing of title or upon execution of lease by landlord and tenant and payment of 1st month's rent.

Sale Commission:

_____

Rental Commission

_____

AS SELLER, YOU HAVE THE RIGHT TO INDIVIDUALLY REACH AN AGREEMENT ON ANY FEE, COMMISSION, OR OTHER VALUABLE CONSIDERATION WITH ANY BROKER. NO FEE, COMMISSION, OR OTHER CONSIDERATION HAS BEEN FIXED BY ANY GOVERNMENTAL AUTHORITY OR BY ANY TRADE ASSOCIATION OR MULTIPLE LISTING SERVICE. Nothing herein is intended to prohibit an individual broker from independently establishing a policy regarding the amount of fee, commission, or other valuable consideration to be charged in transaction by the broker.

BROKER offers the following commission to Sub-Agents
Buyer-Agents: SELLER and BROKER understand that if a purchaser has been obtained by a Buyer-Agent who has an Exclusive Buyer Agency Agreement with that purchaser, in that case the Buyer-Agent is representing the purchaser and has no relationship, fiduciary or otherwise, with the SELLER or BROKER, regardless of participation in brokerage fees.

BROKER offers the following commission to Transaction Brokers:

SELLER guarantees that if property is sold and closed he will have sufficient funds to satisfy all liens and encumbrances and pay brokerage commission as set forth in Agreement.

BROKER shall be entitled to a commission if the property is sold, leased, or exchanged within_____months after the end of the term of the listing or any extension thereof to a buyer who was introduced to the property during the term of the listing. However, SELLER shall not be obligated to pay such commission if a valid listing agreement is entered into during the term of said protection period with another licensed real estate broker and the sale, lease, or exchange of property is made during the term of said protection period.

BROKER shall be entitled to the following commission: if the property is sold no later than_____to a tenant obtained by BROKER. If a valid listing agreement is entered into with another licensed real estate broker, SELLER agrees to advise broker of aforementioned arrangement.

SELLER agrees to refer to BROKER every prospective buyer who directly contacts SELLER during the term of this Agreement.

SELLER represents that he/they is the sole owner of the property and has the legal right to sell, lease, or exchange the property and has no binding listing agreement with any other broker at the start of the period of this listing. SELLER states that the property information which has been filled in on the profile sheet for this listing is correct to the best of his knowledge, and SELLER will indemnify BROKER against loss resulting from reliance upon such information.

FIGURE 13.17
(*continued*)

SELLER acknowledges that he has received the Consumer Information Statement on New Jersey Real Estate Relationships. "I_____as an
Name of Licensee
authorized representative of _____intend, as of this time,
            Name of Brokerage Firm
to work with you, the SELLER, as a_____* (Indicate one of the following: sellers (landlord) agent only, seller's (landlord's) agent and disclosed dual agent if the opportunity arises, transaction broker).

SELLER acknowledges that he has read and received a copy of this Listing Agreement and that he has also read and understands the SELLER's responsibilities under New Jersey's Law Against Discrimination {N.J.S.A. 10:5-1 et.seq, as amended and supplemented) set forth on the reverse side of this Agreement

BROKER will list property in the following Multiple Listing Services (MLS):
whose member participants will act as cooperating agents of BROKER in the sale of the premises.

_____	_____	_____ L.S.
Listing Office	Date Signed	SELLER/Authorized Representative
By: _____	_____	_____ L.S.
Broker/Authorized Representative	Date Signed	SELLER/Authorized Representative

_____
_____
_____
Mailing Address

_____
Telephone Number

FIGURE 13.18
Checklist for Preparation and/or Review of the Agreement of Sale When Representing Buyer

Source: Andrene N. Plummer, *A Few New Solutions to a Very Old Problem: How the Fair Housing Act Can Be Improved to Deter Discriminatory Conduct by Real Estate Brokers*, 47 HOW. L.F. 163 (2003).

I. **Seller**
- List seller's name, address, and telephone numbers.
- Ascertain legal status of seller(s).
- If corporation, ascertain the state of incorporation.
- If partnership, is it general, limited, or limited liability? List names of the individuals.
- If husband and wife, do they both approve of the sale?
- If single person: Was the single person married when title was acquired? Was the single person married at any time thereafter the title was acquired? How was the marriage terminated?
- If executor or administrator, obtain proof of authority to sell.

II. **Buyer**
- List buyer(s) name, address, and telephone numbers.
- Ascertain manner in which buyer(s) will take and hold title:
  - As a partnership in the partnership name.
  - As a partnership in the individual names of the partners and their spouses, as joint tenants with rights of survivorship, tenants in common, or otherwise.
  - As husband and wife as tenants by the entireties.
  - As a single person(s).
- Ascertain purpose for property purchase:
  - Buyer's residence.
  - Speculation.

FIGURE 13.18
(*continued*)

- Subdivision.
- Commercial development.
- Other: _____.

III. The property

- List location: street, lot number, township, city, county, state.
- Describe any deed reference or boundaries necessary.
- If a metes and bounds description is available, insert it in the agreement of sale.
- If any personal property is to be sold with the land, add an addendum to the agreement, title it "Inventory," and list each item.

IV. The purchase price and financing

- List the total purchase price.
- Determine the amount of the down payment and due date(s).
- Ascertain manner in which payment of purchase price is to be made at time of final settlement:
  - Assumption of existing mortgage.
  - Purchase money mortgage.
  - Cash if no financial arrangements are made with a lending institution.
- Mortgage contingency clause: If buyer must obtain a loan commitment for financing the property, indicate the specifics in the mortgage contingency clause.
- Determine who is to retain down payment until final closing: the broker, buyer, seller, or attorney.

V. General considerations

- Determine settlement date (on or before X date).
- Determine from seller (or seller's attorney) exactly what personal property owned by seller is included in the sale, then list each item and the purchase price.
- Determine the amount of insurance seller is presently carrying on the property and insert this in the agreement of sale.
- Make sure there is only one remedy in agreement of sale in case of default by the buyer.
- Obtain statement as to what use property is zoned for.
- Make sure seller will convey to buyer good and marketable title.
- Make sure there is no pending or threatened condemnation.
- Make sure no deed restrictions affect any portion of the property or any special conditions, exceptions, covenants, or reservations.
- Make sure seller has complied with all laws, ordinances, and the like relating to the property.
- The question of discrimination in housing practice forever needs to concern agents.
- Make sure water, sewer, and electricity service are available.
- Make sure there are no notices of any violation by any governmental unit or agency and that if there are, seller will correct said violations at seller's cost and expense prior to settlement.
- Is any requisite approval of subdivision planning required? If so, note the dates for the necessary approval.
- Obtain approval of leases, if any. Are they assignable?
- Obtain approval or appraisal of property by lending institution, F.H.A, or V.A.
- Add a termite clause that benefits the buyer.
- Investigate rezoning or issuance of permits consonant with use of land.
- Fuel oil should be included in sale and purchase price.
- Is contract assignable by buyer(s)?
- Notice provisions: Does notice have to be received or is mailing adequate?

FIGURE 13.18
(*continued*)

- Is the successors and assigns clause in the contract?
- Entire agreement clause: If contained, no spoken evidence is allowed.
- A severability clause should prevent failure of entire agreement if one provision is invalid.
- Time of essence clause should state that time is of the essence in the contract. If silent, performance within a reasonable time will suffice.
- Has buyer placed any time limit within which seller must accept the contract?
- Is the signature page acceptable for proper execution?
- Is the agreement of sale dated?
- Were any amendments or modifications to the agreement of sale made? If so, are they legally sufficient?
- Real estate commissions: Are the commissions conditioned on the closing of the transaction if not already determined by the listing contract?
- Does the contract specify the party responsible to pay any real estate commissions?
- Is there representation and warranty by both parties that no other brokers are involved in the transaction?
- Are the breaches of the contract and what constitutes the breaches clearly stated and the remedies to the seller clearly stated?
- Are any surveys to be obtained? If so, by whom? Who is responsible for the costs and expenses of the surveys?
- Is the "not to be recorded clause" in the agreement?
- Special considerations and clauses:_____

FIGURE 13.19
Checklist for Preparation and/or Review of the Agreement of Sale When Representing Seller

I. **Seller**
- List seller(s)' name, address, and telephone numbers.
- Ascertain legal status of seller(s): if corporation, the state of incorporation.
- Sign a conveyance of the property: general or limited.
- If a partnership is holding title in the individual names of one or more partners, list names of the partners and whether they approve of the sale.
- If husband and wife, do both approve of the sale?
- If single person: Was the single person married when title was acquired or at any time thereafter? How was the marriage terminated?
- If a surviving joint tenant, how and when was the joint tenancy terminated?
- If an executor or administrator, is there proof of authority to sell?

II. **Buyer**
- List buyer's name, address, and telephone numbers.
- Ascertain the manner in which the buyer(s) will take and hold title:
  - As a partnership in the partnership name.
  - As a partnership in the individual names of the partners or the individual names of the partners and their spouses as joint tenants with right of survivorship, tenants in common, or otherwise.
  - As husband and wife as tenants by the entireties.
  - As a single person(s).

III. **The property**
- Location: street, lot number, ward, township, city, county, state.
- Attach as an addendum to the agreement of sale an inventory or description of any personal property to be sold with the land.

IV. **The purchase price and financing**
- List the total purchase price.
- List the manner in which the purchase price is to be paid:
  - The down payment or other deposit at signing of the agreement of sale and due date.

FIGURE 13.19
(*continued*)

- Assumption of existing mortgage.
- Purchase money mortgage.
- Cash (no financial arrangements with a lending institution).
- Assumption of existing encumbrances on property.
- The manner in which payment of the purchase price, if payable in installments, is to be secured.

V. General considerations

- Delivery of vacant property to buyer at time of final settlement.
- Approval of leases, if existing, and assignment of lease.
- Buyer's obtaining a loan or commitment for loans on the property (the mortgage contingency).
- Termite inspection: Insert pro-seller clause.
- Certification of zoning classification.
- Settlement date.
- Name and location of broker handling settlement, if any.
- Broker's commission specified.
- Other: _____

Common Provisions

Outline of the Parties Parties legally responsible for the purchase and sale of the property must be signatories unless a power of attorney designates otherwise. Without signatures, the agreement of sale is unenforceable. Pay close attention to whether any of the parties involved are tenants in common, joint tenants, joint venturers, or other concurrent owners of property rights. Where a corporation is involved, it is important to ensure that the signers of the deed (the corporate officers) can bind or obligate the corporation to the transaction. As such, it may be necessary to produce or prepare a corporate resolution authorizing and directing certain officers to act on behalf of the corporation.

Legal Description of the Property In most areas of the country a short legal description of the property is all that is necessary, as shown in the following example:

> *All that certain lot or piece of ground with the buildings and improvements thereon erected, situated in the township of _____, county of _____, state of _____, and known as _____ Street, as more particularly described in the deed to be delivered at settlement as hereafter provided.*

Personal Property Exclusions/Inclusions The agreement of sale should also outline exclusions or inclusions of specific personal property. Obviously fixtures pass with the realty unless a contrary agreement appears, but doubtful personal properties frequently become questions of contention and dispute. Examples include draperies, rods, washers and dryers, electrical appliances, tool sheds, industrial benches and tables, wall air conditioners, and other forms of property with qualities of both realty and personalty. Any items of personal property that may be subject to misinterpretation should be listed as exclusions or inclusions in the agreement, and if either party desires to sell or buy them, a specific price should be mentioned within the contract of sale or incorporated by reference. Other items of personalty that should receive some attention in the sales contract include rugs, carpeting, fireplace equipment, electric garage door openers, canvas patio canopies, tractors, television antennae, and chandeliers and other ornamental items.

Consideration The consideration aspect of any contract ensures a bargained-for exchange. The purchaser makes the offer in the agreement of sale for a specific price. The graphic formula shown here is how settlement will eventually occur:

	Purchase price	
−	Earnest money deposit	
=	Subtotal	_____
−	Cash at settlement	
=	Subtotal	_____
−	Mortgage	_____
=	Real estate transfer	

If the earnest money deposit is large enough, the funds should be placed in an interest-bearing account. In some jurisdictions, failure to state that interest is payable on earnest money deposits will result in no later claim, or if interest is paid, it will be credited to the seller's account. In cases of large real property acquisitions, interest amounts add up nicely. The agreement should account for this payment as so:

> *Earnest money deposit will be placed into an interest-bearing account, proceeds of principal and interest of which to be credited to purchaser at settlement.*

An alternative approach is to insist that the deposit be placed into the escrow account of a neutral party. If sellers and buyers eventually get into a severe dispute, the money will be in the third party's hands pending settlement. As Webster, Hetrick, and Outlaw point out in their work *North Carolina Real Estate for Brokers and Salesmen,*

> *The real estate broker is required to maintain a properly designated trust or escrow account for all "trust funds" (earnest money deposits, down payments, tenant security deposits, rents on money received from final settlement) that comes into his possession. [The broker is the temporary custodian of these trust funds and holds them as a fiduciary for the parties to the transaction. Trust funds must be maintained in a separate designated account in an insured bank or savings and loan association in North Carolina, and such funds may not be "commingled" with the broker's personal or business funds. The broker must also maintain detailed financial records relating to the trust account.]*[56]

In the event a dispute cannot be resolved, most jurisdictions permit *a motion for interpleader* to be filed in the court of appropriate jurisdiction. The interpleader document asks the court to exercise jurisdiction in a dispute between the vendor and purchaser in a real estate transaction, and to determine the legal and rightful owner of the property and the earnest money deposit.

As a final note under the consideration clause, the buyer will frequently assume and agree to pay for the seller's underlying mortgage. To assume a mortgage, a series of papers and documents that relieve the seller and oblige the buyer, under assumption of an existing mortgage, need crafting. Be aware that banks and financial institutions do not automatically permit assumptions unless consented to.[57]

Condition of Title   In any real estate contract, the purchaser bargains for a clear and marketable title. A marketable title is ensured through the issuance of a "general warranty deed subject to only unremovable liens."[58] Marketable title means that

> *The premises are to be conveyed free and clear of all liens, encumbrances, and easements excepting, however, mortgage encumbrances as herein before set forth [only if buyer is to take subject to an existing mortgage], ordinances, easements of roads and following items, none of which prevent the use of the premises as presently improved, as a single-family dwelling, none of which have been violated and none of which impose a financial burden on the buyer; existing building restrictions; privileges or rights of public service companies within the right of way of public roads or within ten feet of the perimeter of the real property subject to this agreement; agreements or like matters of record; otherwise the title to the above-described real estate shall be good and marketable and as such will be insured by the title company at regular rates.*[59]

A clear picture of title is mandatory because it ensures that

> *[F]irst, a clear assumption can take place and all debt, lien, and financial obligation will be removed before transfer; second, purchasers are made aware of any restrictions that the agreement may violate; third, easements and other restrictions are published; fourth, the buyer knows the extent of judgments and pending litigation; and fifth, a title policy of insurance will give both personal and legal assurance to the buyer.*[60]

A good and marketable title is one that can be fully insured. Determining the quality of title results from title abstraction, a research process engaged in by attorneys and now, more frequently, by paralegals. The abstraction of title satisfies the title insurance company as to property's alienability and the underlying marketability in this real estate transaction. As Professor Henry Hoagland and colleagues point out in their work *Real Estate Finance,*

> *From the date of earliest land records, abstracts attempt to include all actions of importance that may affect the quality of a title to the land in question. In addition to identifying maps, abstracts deal with deeds, mortgages, releases, taxes, leases, judgments and other liens, wills, pending suits, and a variety of other items that may cover forty or more categories.*[61]

A useful maxim is that title that is not insurable is not good and marketable title.

Time and Place of Settlement   The agreement of sale should outline an explicit period of time for settlement. The time of settlement should allow adequate time for the resolution of issues surrounding the transaction, such as curing of title defects, payment of past debts and creditor arrangements, and the inability of the seller to buy or find alternative temporary lodging. Timing should mirror the meeting of any conditions and contingencies in contract, especially those like finance and zoning. As a rule of thumb, settlement should and can occur within 90 to 120 days from the signing of the agreement. If it appears that some condition or contingency is not being met or satisfied, counsel for buyers and sellers should draft an endorsement to the agreement of sale that extends the time of settlement. An example of such an endorsement is illustrated in Form 13.12 on the accompanying CD.

Endorsements may serve other purposes too, such as changing mortgage amounts, changing from a fixed rate to a variable rate of interest, changing the amount of cash due upon settlement, changing time of possession, and altering responsibility for certain obligations and duties under the contract. Endorsements are addenda to the main contract and are fully integrated by implication and/or express language.

Unless there is an express agreement to the contrary, settlement will take place during a reasonable period of time.[62] Contracts governed by the *time of the essence* requirement are guided by the nuances of local practice, custom, and usage within the real estate industry.

For clarity, the location of settlement is often stated in the agreement of sale. Choices are many and include the offices of attorneys for sellers or purchasers, the real estate broker's office, the title insurance company's office, or any other agreed location.

Inspection Right   In most American jurisdictions, an inspection right exists for the benefit of the purchaser. Usually, one week to 24 hours before closing, purchasers have a right to inspect the premises and its major systems to determine operability, to verify habitability, and to ensure that all terms and conditions of the contract are being met. Under traditional custom and usage in the industry, the house should be in substantially the same condition as on the date of sale and turned over in broom-swept condition.

When defects in the home are known by the seller, the question of disclosure varies according to jurisdiction. Increasingly courts find that sellers have an obligation to disclose latent defects in the premises conveyed. To fail to disclose may give rise to action in fraud and misrepresentation. At the same time, buyers have an obligation to investigate. The doctrine of *caveat emptor* (let the buyer beware) still exists, though in a much softer form than its common-law counterpart

> *Therefore, negligent misrepresentation claims will be barred in whole (contributory negligence) or in part (comparative negligence) if the purchaser failed to investigate the premises. The purchaser's duty to investigate is especially strong in three situations: (1) when the defect is obvious; (2) when the realtor is not the purchaser's agent; and (3) when the realtor's representation is vague.*[63]

Time of Possession Clause   Even if settlement and closing occur on a specific date, possession can either take place concurrently or take place at an earlier or later date. Leasehold arrangements are often entered into by prospective buyers and sellers. In the case of a seller who wishes to remain after closing, a lease with pertinent insurance and risk of loss provisions is important. At the opposite end of the spectrum, a buyer who wishes to enter a residence before closing should have similar protections.

Prorations and Adjustments   Standard language in real estate contracts regarding proration of expenses, rents, taxes, and other assessments is usually this:

> *Taxes, rents, water rents, interest on mortgage encumbrances, sewer rental, and other assessments, if any, shall be apportioned pro rata as of the date of settlement. The apportionments for taxes shall be based upon actual fiscal years of the taxing authorities for which the subject taxes are levied. Interest on the mortgage encumbrance shall be deemed to be payable in arrears and shall be apportioned for the period between the date of payment immediately preceding closing and the date for payment immediately following closing. Rents on the lease shall be apportioned per diem on the basis of the installment for the month in which the closing occurred.*[64]

Loss Provisions   Depending on the jurisdiction, upon the signing of an agreement of sale, the risk of loss on real property may shift or transfer to the prospective purchaser. Watch this matter closely and give the client appropriate suggestions on insurance coverage pending closing.

Assessments   Policies on taxes, sewer assessments, local and county fees, and transfer tax vary considerably depending on jurisdiction and local practice.

Conditions and Contingencies   Real estate transfers are frequently conditioned or contingent on some event or circumstance. Conditions, as previously noted, may either be precedent or subsequent. In short, the condition, until fulfilled or met, creates an estate in expectancy. A contingency awaits a certain fulfillment such as the award of mortgage financing or grant of a zoning permit.

The typical conditional or contingent situations in real estate practice are

- Whether the agreement has effect if mortgage financing is not obtainable.
- Whether the agreement has effect if alternative mortgage financing is available other than that stated in the contract.
- Whether failure to acquire certification for septic systems will void a contract.
- Whether failure to be granted zoning will serve as an excusable condition or failure to meet a contingent requirement under a contract.
- Whether a political subdivision permits development of land in a certain way or right as envisioned under the original contract.
- Whether the condition of water and soil meets regulatory guidelines.
- Whether there is evidence of termite and insect infestation.
- Whether there is evidence of environmental contamination or toxic pollution.

A contract with a contingency or a condition is little more than a conditional contract that lacks enforceability until the condition is met. Conditions and contingencies in real estate law have triggered a formidable body of case law.

In *Hodorowicz v. Szulc,* the buyers' and sellers' contract provided that the buyers had to sell a house by a specific date, March 5. The Sellers did not meet the condition of sale by March 5. Finding a void contract for failure to meet a condition, the court noted,

> *It is also equally plain that before that contingency happened under the very terms of the contract, by lapse of time, the sellers had acquired an additional right to terminate it at their will and it therefore ceased to be binding upon the sellers and the purchasers could not have enforced it against the sellers anytime thereafter. When in May of 1955 the contingency happened and the property previously owned by the purchasers had been sold, the contract had already lost its binding power upon the sellers and there was therefore never a mutually binding and enforceable contract and agreement in effect between the parties.*[65]

In another case, the purchasers were to have a mortgage commitment within 60 days of the signing of the contract. When no commitment occurred within the 60-day period, the court held that these purchasers were under no obligation to perform under a contract that was void and nonexistent.

An Illinois case, *Dodson v. Nink,*[66] declared a contract of sale null and void because the purchasers would accept a VA loan but not agree to be responsible for any repair costs. In upholding the condition, the court strictly interpreted the contract:

> *Our holding merely gives effect to the agreement of the parties at the time the contract was entered into. When plaintiff contracted to purchase . . ., she did not agree . . . to repair the house to complete a sale. . . . We therefore conclude that the contingencies in both contracts did not occur, and that both contracts became void and unenforceable pursuant to their own terms. Plaintiff was thus entitled to the return of her earnest money.*[67]

The Delaware Supreme Court's respected Honorable Andrew D. Christie skillfully decided a similar case, *E. I. Dupont, et. al, v. Crompton-Townsend, Inc.*[68] In a dispute over a conditional clause on a survey in a standard real estate contract, Judge Christie used the following language:

> *Boundary lines for said subdivision to be subject to written approval of both the sellers and purchasers. Should written approval not be obtained from either party on or before July 30, 1976, then this contract shall be declared null and void and all monies on deposit refunded to purchasers.*[69]

When the purchasers decided not to approve the survey, the sellers balked and said the problems could have been corrected. In fact, the purchasers' objections to the survey were trivial. Judge Christie characterized the contract as "not a sale as to the purchase of a survey and to the terms on which a sale would take place if all the parties at a future date decided to agree to convert the conditional sales agreement into a binding contract by approving the survey."[70] Judge Christie, in strictly construing the contract, choosing not to infer or surmise the purchasers' motivations, held that the conditional language of the contract was unambiguous.

Both case law and scholarly legal analysis support the fundamental contention that a condition precedent, neither met nor waived, cannot lead to an obligation of contractual performance. Professor Milton Friedman of the Practicing Law Institute, in his treatise *Contract and Conveyance of Real Property,* notes,

> *The contract may also be conditional upon the buyers' obtaining a mortgage to finance the purchase, or a license or other permit to use the premises for some designed purpose. In these situations the condition precedent is not to the existence of a contract... but performance of the conditions is a condition precedent to further obligations under the contract. If there is no such performance, the buyer is entitled to refund his down payment.*[71]

In *Pena v. Security Title Company,*[72] the parties entered a binding contract for real estate with the conditional language "subject to buyer securing a loan of approximately $12,000.00." When the purchasers' loan application was rejected by the bank, the court construed the language as creating a conditional duty under the contract and,

> *... (that) the provision constituted a condition and unless such a loan was obtained, neither the bargain and sale terms nor the forfeiture provisions would become effective.*[73]

Pena referred extensively to *Hodorowicz v. Szulc,*[74] a case in which there were no written extensions, modifications, or waivers. The *Hodorowicz* court reviewed the issues by discussing first whether there was a contract at all because the condition was not met:

> *...[I]t becomes necessary for us to determine whether there was ever a binding and enforceable contract between the parties. If there was not, obviously there could be no breach and the statement of claim never stated a cause of action. It is clear that this contract was not enforceable at the time it was executed because of the condition contained in the clause stated in the contract... and that it only could become effective and enforceable, by either party, upon the happening of that contingency.*[75]

A review of case law unanimously supports the principle that a mortgage contingency is a condition precedent. In *Fischer v. Kennedy,*[76] the failure to acquire mortgage financing resulted in a contract being declared null and void. In *Roberts v. Maxwell,*[77] a purchaser's failure to procure a GI loan was held to be a condition precedent releasing the purchaser from further obligation on the contract.

Finally, paralegals must be aware of waiver and estoppel principles that might apply in a real estate dispute. On its face, the situation is simple enough: A condition not met nullifies a contract. However, some courts read into the contract the mind of a contract party who fails to give notice of the failure of condition. It is inferred, under theories of waiver and estoppel, that the party waives the condition because the party made no continuing objection to the enforcement of the condition. In addition, some cases see parties led on by nonconsenting parties to waiver and incur costs and even losses to keep a contract alive that the other party has no intention of honoring based on a failure of condition. Here the party would be estopped from avoiding the contract based on a failed condition.

The scope and coverage of conditional and contingent language will mirror the issue in the agreement. Conditions are generally memorialized in an addendum or additional clause. Examples are provided on the accompanying CD:

Home inspection: Form 13–13

Swimming pools: Form 13–14

Water and septic: Form 13–15

Radon: Form 13–16

UFFI: Form 13–17

Wood infestation: Form 13–18

Zoning: Form 13–19

Paralegals specializing in commercial practice must be alert to EPA regulations regarding toxic waste and underground storage tanks. The Comprehensive Environmental Response, Compensation, and Liability Act (CERCLA), commonly known as Superfund, was enacted by Congress on December 11, 1980. This law created a tax on the chemical and petroleum industries and provided broad federal authority to respond directly to releases or threatened releases of hazardous substances that may endanger public health or the environment. Over five years $1.6 billion was collected, and the tax went to a trust fund for cleaning up abandoned or uncontrolled hazardous waste sites. CERCLA

- Established prohibitions and requirements concerning closed and abandoned hazardous waste sites.
- Provided for liability of people responsible for releases of hazardous waste at these sites.
- Established a trust fund to provide for cleanup when no responsible party could be identified.

The law authorizes two kinds of response actions:

- Short-term removals, where actions may be taken to address releases or threatened releases requiring prompt response.
- Long-term remedial response actions that permanently and significantly reduce the dangers associated with releases or threatened releases of hazardous substances that are serious but not immediately life-threatening.[78]

Title Insurance Clause Title insurance protects the buyer from a possible cloud on the title. The agreement lays out not only the type of title necessary for alienation but also the type of title needed for acquisition of insurance.[79]

Integration Clause An integration clause is an essential proviso in any standardized contract. It ensures that the four corners of the document are the only haven for interpretation. An integration clause states emphatically that no other evidence outside the four corners of the document is considered germane, relevant, or legally admissible.

Brokerage Clause No real estate sales agreement can be complete without a recitation of real estate brokerage commissions. Usually this provision outlines a standard commission between single or dual brokers. At times the clause outlines the extent of damages for which a broker or real estate agent is obligated during a potential or actual dispute between buyers and sellers under a real estate contract.

Signatures/Witnesses/Date of Execution The contract is not binding if it is not fully executed. Although witnesses are a debatable legal requirement, they add credibility to the parties' intentions. The date of the contract is relevant because the time requirements for applying for mortgages, zoning certificates, and other issues come under a ticking clock from this date forward.

Special Caution: Time Is of the Essence In all standardized real estate contracts, time should be of the essence. "The proper meaning of the phrase 'time is of the essence' is that performance by one party at the time specified in the contract or within the period specified in the contract is essential in order to enable him to require performance from the other party."[80] Failure to adhere to time guidelines is the bane of many a disgruntled defendant in a real estate case. The time periods expressly laid out govern the conduct of the parties, and if they cannot be maintained, an addendum, endorsement, or written modification of the underlying contract is necessary. Here are some circumstances in which the time of the essence requirement comes up frequently:

- Bank application: Has the purchaser applied to a bank for financing?
- Mortgage commitment: Has the purchaser received a commitment from a bank for financing within the specific time periods?
- Earnest money deposit: Has the purchaser made the necessary earnest money deposit payments on schedule or as otherwise noted?
- Zoning: Has the purchaser or seller performed zoning requirements as outlined under the contract?
- Certificates: Have the buyer and seller acquired and provided evidence of certificates for water, soil, and percolation?
- Purchaser's failure to sell residence: If the contract is conditional on the purchaser selling his or her residence within a certain time frame, has that condition been met?

Contracts are drafted and written to protect both sides to a real estate transaction. The very existence of a condition or contingency related to mortgages ensures that a buyer of real estate will not be overwhelmed economically if he cannot get bank financing. If he or she does not have bank financing within the period accorded in the contract, does that buyer have a right to withdraw from the contract? Under technical interpretations, it would appear that the answer is affirmative.[81]

However, some jurisdictions have held that if a buyer does not continue to try—does not seek out alternative mortgage sources and does not show general good faith—the time requirement loses its punch.[82] Unfortunately for buyers and sellers in real estate, there has been much judicial intervention in the interpretation of a standardized contract. The crux of the matter in determining time of the essence is as follows:

- What are the reasonable expectations in the industry's definition of *time?*
- What are the circumstances behind the transaction?
- What are the parties' purposes in making the contract?
- What is the significance of timely performance?
- How reasonable is the date set for performance?
- Does the contract possess a "time is of the essence" designation?
- Is the bank or other agency whose subject matter deals with a condition or other contingency cooperating with the buyer?
- Does the lender or bank or other agency refuse to provide information necessary to effect the contract?
- Does the person who has a benefit of a condition promptly repudiate the contract after a failure of condition?
- Does the doctrine of waiver and estoppel play a role in the interpretation of time is of the essence?

Paralegals handling real estate contracts that include a time is of the essence clause should adhere to time frames religiously. As David Gee points out in his work *Time Is of the Essence of Real Estate Contracts,*

> *Where it clearly and unequivocally appears from the contract, by means of some expressed stipulation that time shall be essential, this expressed intention of the parties will be recognized in equity as well as at law, and that the time of completion or of performance or of complying with the terms will be regarded as of the essence of the contract. In such case notice to perform need not ordinarily be given nor reasonable time elapse following default before forfeiture or rescission may be declared.*[83]

The North Carolina Bar Association's Real Property section has written numerous checklists for contract agreements. See the example for income-producing property shown in Form 13.20 on the accompanying CD.

Mortgages/Financing Techniques

Gilmer's *Law Dictionary* has defined *mortgage* as "a conveyance of real or personal property to a person called the 'mortgagee,' to secure the payment of money by the 'mortgagor' and to become void upon the performance of such act."[84]

Mortgage requirements under a contract of sale should be specific. Diverse issues must be kept track of, including these:

- Application to the bank for a mortgage on time.

- Commitment within the prescribed time frame.

- Endorsements for any change in amount or rate.

- Sufficient cash and other assets to meet bank review for award of mortgage.

- Additions, addenda, or modifications to contract if time to secure mortgage has not been met.

- Assumption paperwork and documentation.

- Subordination documents if so necessary.

Aside from traditional bank financing, buyers may borrow from sellers or use pension proceeds, other savings, or governmental programs as the basis for purchase consideration.

The differences in bank rates, terms, and charges are mind-boggling. Paralegals spend significant time working with financial and banking professionals but should avoid becoming too chummy with a select few. When a paralegal steers a party continually to a bank that shows favoritism, the situation may give rise to an appearance of impropriety. Instead, evaluate your client, evaluate the types of loans available, and evaluate the up-front expenses, closing costs, settlement costs, and other cash outlays that will best fit the needs of your client. Select a bank based on its reputation as well as the services it can provide.

Once the financial source is chosen, the buyer needs to complete a loan application that outlines income levels, current debt and expenses, and assets. See Form 13.21 on the accompanying CD.

As financing becomes more complicated, paralegals spend time helping people with mandatory documentation. Other documents required by banks usually include verification of employment forms, verifications of deposits, verifications of credit checks, and verifications of histories on other mortgage accounts. For some examples, see Forms 13.22 and 13.23 on the accompanying CD.

Fixed Rate Mortgage

A fixed rate mortgage generally ranges from 3 to 21 percent, depending on economic conditions and Federal Reserve policy. The loan is generally amortized over a period of 10 to 40 years. An amortization schedule charts the present and future applications of payments to principal and interest over the life of the loan (see Figure 13.20).

Adjustable Rate Mortgage

This type of mortgage is subject to an initial rate that is usually anywhere between 2¼ and 8 percent based on economic conditions and Federal Reserve policy. The loan is amortized over a 10- to 40-year period but can change depending on refinancing options or conversion rights exercisable over three- to seven-year periods. An example of an adjustable mortgage and a rider is shown in Form 13.24 on the accompanying CD.

Roll-Over Mortgage

A roll-over mortgage is a short-term mortgage to which a lender will commit by rolling it over one or more times for additional periods at then-existing rates of interest.

Assumed Mortgage

An assumed mortgage is a mortgage that is assumed by a new buyer, providing the bank does not have a "due on sale" clause—a provision forcing complete satisfaction of the mortgage when taken over by another mortgagor.

FIGURE 13.20 Amortization Table

Amortization Table for $500,000.00 borrowed on May 10, 2006

Month	6	7	8	9	10	11	12	1	2	3	4	5
Year	2006	2006	2006	2006	2006	2006	2006	2007	2007	2007	2007	2007
Payment ($)	3,582.16	3,582.16	35,82.16	3,582.16	3,582.16	3,582.16	3,582.16	3,582.16	3,582.16	3,582.16	3,582.16	3,582.16
Principal Paid ($)	1,082.16	1,087.57	1,093.00	1,098.47	1,103.96	1,109.48	1,115.03	1,120.60	1,126.21	1,131.84	1,137.50	1,143.18
Interest Paid ($)	2,500.00	2,494.59	2,489.15	2,483.69	2,478.19	2,472.67	2,467.13	2,461.55	2,455.95	2,450.32	2,444.66	2,438.97
Total Interest ($)	2,500.00	4,994.59	7,483.74	9,967.43	12,445.62	14,918.30	17,385.42	19,846.97	22,302.92	24,753.24	27,197.90	29,636.87
Balance ($)	498,917.84	497,830.28	496,737.27	495,638.81	494,534.84	493,425.36	492,310.34	491,189.73	490,063.52	488,931.69	487,794.19	486,651.01

Month	6	7	8	9	10	11	12	1	2	3	4	5
Year	2007	2007	2007	2007	2007	2007	2007	2008	2008	2008	2008	2008
Payment ($)	3,582.16	3,582.16	3,582.16	3,582.16	3,582.16	3,582.16	3,582.16	3,582.16	3,582.16	3,582.16	3,582.16	3,582.16
Principal Paid ($)	1,148.90	1,154.64	1,160.42	1,166.22	1,172.05	1,177.91	1,183.80	1,189.72	1,195.67	1,201.65	1,207.66	1,213.69
Interest Paid ($)	2,433.26	2,427.51	2,421.74	2,415.94	2,410.10	2,404.24	2,398.35	2,392.44	2,386.49	2,380.51	2,374.50	2,368.46
Total Interest ($)	32,070.12	34,497.63	36,919.37	39,335.31	41,745.41	44,149.66	46,548.01	48,940.45	51,326.93	53,707.44	56,081.94	58,450.40
Balance ($)	485,502.11	484,347.46	483,187.04	482,020.82	480,848.77	479,670.86	478,487.06	477,297.34	476,101.67	474,900.02	473,692.37	472,478.68

Month	6	7	8	9	10	11	12	1	2	3	4	5
Year	2008	2008	2008	2008	2008	2008	2008	2009	2009	2009	2009	2009
Payment ($)	3,582.16	3,582.16	3,582.16	3,582.16	3,582.16	3,582.16	3,582.16	3,582.16	3,582.16	3,582.16	3,582.16	3,582.16
Principal Paid ($)	1,219.76	1,225.86	1,231.99	1,238.15	1,244.34	1,250.56	1,256.82	1,263.10	1,269.41	1,275.76	1,282.14	1,288.55
Interest Paid ($)	2,362.39	2,356.29	2,350.17	2,344.01	2,337.81	2,331.59	2,325.34	2,319.06	2,312.74	2,306.39	2,300.01	2,293.60
Total Interest ($)	60,812.80	63,169.09	65,519.26	67,863.26	70,201.08	72,532.67	74,858.01	77,177.06	79,489.80	81,796.20	84,096.21	86,389.82
Balance ($)	471,258.91	470,033.05	468,801.06	467,562.91	466,318.57	465,068.01	463,811.19	462,548.09	461,278.68	460,002.92	458,720.78	457,432.23

Month	6	7	8	9	10	11	12	1	2	3	4	5
Year	2009	2009	2009	2009	2009	2009	2009	2010	2010	2010	2010	2010
Payment ($)	3,582.16	3,582.16	3,582.16	3,582.16	3,582.16	3,582.16	3,582.16	3,582.16	3,582.16	3,582.16	3,582.16	3,582.16
Principal Paid ($)	1,294.99	1,301.47	1,307.98	1,314.52	1,321.09	1,327.69	1,334.33	1,341.00	1,347.71	1,354.45	1,361.22	1,368.03
Interest Paid ($)	2,287.16	2,280.69	2,274.18	2,267.64	2,261.07	2,254.46	2,247.82	2,241.15	2,234.45	2,227.71	2,220.93	2,214.13
Total Interest ($)	88,676.98	90,957.66	93,231.84	95,499.48	97,760.55	100,015.01	102,262.83	104,503.98	106,738.43	108,966.13	111,187.07	113,401.20
Balance ($)	456,137.23	454,835.76	453,527.79	452,213.27	450,892.18	449,564.49	448,230.15	446,889.15	445,541.44	444,186.99	442,825.77	441,457.74

| Month | 6 | 7 | 8 | 9 | 10 | 11 | 12 | 1 | 2 | 3 | 4 | 5 |
Year	2010	2010	2010	2010	2010	2010	2010	2011	2011	2011	2011	2011
Payment ($)	3,582.16	3,582.16	3,582.16	3,582.16	3,582.16	3,582.16	3,582.16	3,582.16	3,582.16	3,582.16	3,582.16	3,582.16
Principal Paid ($)	1,374.87	1,381.74	1,388.65	1,395.59	1,402.57	1,409.58	1,416.63	1,423.71	1,430.83	1,437.99	1,445.18	1,452.40
Interest Paid ($)	2,207.29	2,200.41	2,193.51	2,186.56	2,179.58	2,172.57	2,165.52	2,158.44	2,151.32	2,144.17	2,136.98	2,129.75
Total Interest ($)	115,608.49	117,808.90	120,002.41	122,188.97	124,368.55	126,541.13	128,706.65	130,865.09	133,016.41	135,160.58	137,297.56	139,427.31
Balance ($)	440,082.88	438,701.14	437,312.49	435,916.89	434,514.32	433,104.74	431,688.11	430,264.39	428,833.56	427,395.57	425,950.40	424,497.99

| Month | 6 | 7 | 8 | 9 | 10 | 11 | 12 | 1 | 2 | 3 | 4 | 5 |
Year	2011	2011	2011	2011	2011	2011	2011	2012	2012	2012	2012	2012
Payment ($)	3,582.16	3,582.16	3,582.16	3,582.16	3,582.16	3,582.16	3,582.16	3,582.16	3,582.16	3,582.16	3,582.16	3,582.16
Principal Paid ($)	1,459.67	1,466.96	1,474.30	1,481.67	1,489.08	1,496.52	1,504.01	1,511.53	1,519.08	1,526.68	1,534.31	1,541.98
Interest Paid ($)	2,122.49	2,115.19	2,107.86	2,100.49	2,093.08	2,085.63	2,078.15	2,070.63	2,063.07	2,055.48	2,047.84	2,040.17
Total Interest ($)	141,549.80	143,664.99	145,772.85	147,873.33	149,966.41	152,052.04	154,130.19	156,200.82	158,263.89	160,319.37	162,367.21	164,407.38
Balance ($)	423,038.33	421,571.36	420,097.06	418,615.39	417,126.32	415,629.79	414,125.79	412,614.26	411,095.18	409,568.50	408,034.18	406,492.20

| Month | 6 | 7 | 8 | 9 | 10 | 11 | 12 | 1 | 2 | 3 | 4 | 5 |
Year	2012	2012	2012	2012	2012	2012	2012	2013	2013	2013	2013	2013
Payment ($)	3,582.16	3,582.16	3,582.16	3,582.16	3,582.16	3,582.16	3,582.16	3,582.16	3,582.16	3,582.16	3,582.16	3,582.16
Principal Paid ($)	1,549.69	1,557.44	1,565.23	1,573.06	1,580.92	1,588.83	1,596.77	1,604.75	1,612.78	1,620.84	1,628.95	1,637.09
Interest Paid ($)	2,032.46	2,024.71	2,016.93	2,009.10	2,001.23	1,993.33	1,985.39	1,977.40	1,969.38	1,961.31	1,953.21	1,945.06
Total Interest ($)	166,439.84	168,464.55	170,481.48	172,490.58	174,491.81	176,485.14	178,470.53	180,447.93	182,417.31	184,378.62	186,331.83	188,276.89
Balance ($)	404,942.51	403,385.06	401,819.83	400,246.78	398,665.85	397,077.03	395,480.26	393,875.50	392,262.73	390,641.89	389,012.94	387,375.85

| Month | 6 | 7 | 8 | 9 | 10 | 11 | 12 | 1 | 2 | 3 | 4 | 5 |
Year	2013	2013	2013	2013	2013	2013	2013	2014	2014	2014	2014	2014
Payment ($)	3,582.16	3,582.16	3,582.16	3,582.16	3,582.16	3,582.16	3,582.16	3,582.16	3,582.16	3,582.16	3,582.16	3,582.16
Principal Paid ($)	1,645.28	1,653.50	1,661.77	1,670.08	1,678.43	1,686.82	1,695.26	1,703.73	1,712.25	1,720.81	1,729.42	1,738.06
Interest Paid ($)	1,936.88	1,928.65	1,920.39	1,912.08	1,903.73	1,895.33	1,886.90	1,878.42	1,869.90	1,861.34	1,852.74	1,844.09
Total Interest ($)	190,213.77	192,142.43	194,062.81	195,974.89	197,878.61	199,773.95	201,660.85	203,539.27	205,409.18	207,270.52	209,123.26	210,967.35
Balance ($)	385,730.57	384,077.07	382,415.30	380,745.22	379,066.79	377,379.97	375,684.72	373,980.98	372,268.73	370,547.92	368,818.51	367,080.44

Graduated Payment Mortgage (GPM)

A GPM has an initial lower rate, affording first-time home buyers a lower payment option and gradually increasing payments. The Federal Housing Administration has an extensive program for this. Graduated payment mortgages can have both adjustable and fixed characteristics.

Purchase Money Mortgage (PMM)

Any mortgage given by the vendor to secure the payment of all or part of the purchase price is called a *purchase money mortgage*. As noted previously, sellers frequently provide the best sources of financing available for a real estate transaction.[85]

Shared Appreciation Mortgage (SAM)

In a time of escalating housing prices, vendors frequently want a stake in the acceleration of housing values, and as a result they will provide a competitive rate and other terms for a piece of the profits later. This is frequently referred to as a *SAM loan*.

Blanket Mortgage

A *blanket mortgage* is one that covers more than one piece of property and is generally used in the commercial end of the real estate business. "Subdividers sometimes give a blanket mortgage as part payment for acreage. As each lot is sold, it is released from the mortgage by a grant with the mortgagee according to a schedule of release credits."[86]

Balloon Mortgage

A *balloon mortgage* is a mortgage payable and due, in total, within a very short span of time, ordinarily between one and five years. However, the nature of the mortgage permits a favorable amortization schedule—usually between 20 and 30 years serving best the commercial investment market. It provides a window of opportunity for someone who wants to take advantage of a solid investment. Although the entire amount may be due in a short time, the amortization schedule makes the monthly payments reasonable in amount.

First Annuity Mortgage

Frequently individuals have built up substantial equity in their properties. As a result, a certain amount of money is taken out of the property and turned into an annuity with payments being made to service the debt while providing financial security to select individuals.

Governmental Guarantees of Mortgage Loans

Government-backed mortgage programs insure or guarantee the loans made on certain types of property under specified conditions. These loans are commonly known as *government mortgages*. Of course this is a misnomer because the banks are lending the money. The federal government is simply insuring the risk in case of default. Government-backed programs include FHA (Federal Housing Administration); VA (Veteran's Administration); and FMHA (Farmer's Home Administration).

Reverse Mortgage

A *reverse mortgage* is a popular vehicle with senior citizens when home equity is substantial and the parties wish to draw on some portion of its value. Thus once illiquid wealth becomes available.[87]

Installment Purchase Agreement

In installment contracts, the purchaser gets possession of the property while paying installments. Here are some advantages to the vendee:

- Getting possession of the property before full payment of the cost of the property.
- Fixing the price at the beginning of the period rather than later.
- Getting more time to assemble more cash to apply against the purchase price.
- Obtaining tax advantages during the whole term of the contract, though this has been substantially affected by the Tax Reform Act of 1986.[88]

Financing Documentation

Financial documentation is a major paralegal responsibility in the real estate transaction. In essence there are two closings in the real estate deal: one between buyers and sellers, and the other involving the bank. Typical documentation includes these elements:

Figure 13.21: Mortgage

Figure 13.22: Mortgage note

Figure 13.23: Truth-in-lending disclosure statement

Figure 13.24: Estimate of closing costs

(Also see Chapter 6 for a discussion of promissory notes on real property.)

FIGURE 13.21 Mortgage

Prepared by: <TOP.PREPARER>
Return original to: <FIRM.NAME>
              <FIRM.ADDRESS>
              <FIRM.CITY>, <FIRM.ST> <FIRM.ZIP>

[Space above This Line for Recording Data]

....

MORTGAGE

   THIS MORTGAGE ("Security Instrument") is given on <TOP.CLOSING_DATE>. The mortgagor is <BUYER.NAME> ("Borrower"). This Security Instrument is given to <LENDER.NAME>, which is organized and existing under the laws of the State of <FIRM.STATE>, and whose principal office and mailing address is <LENDER.ADDRESS>, <LENDER.CITY>, <LENDER.ST> <LENDER.ZIP> ("Lender").

   Borrower owes Lender the principal sum of <LENDER.LOAN_AMT> Dollars (U.S. <LENDER.LOAN_AMT>). This debt is evidenced by Borrower's note dated the same date as this Security Instrument ("Note"), which provides for monthly payments, with the full debt, if not paid earlier, due and payable on <USER_FIELD>. This Security Instrument secures to Lender: (a) the repayment of the debt evidenced by the Note, with interest, and all renewals, extensions, and modifications of the Note; (b) the payment of all other sums, with interest, advanced under paragraph 7 to protect the security of this Security Instrument; and (c) the performance of Borrower's covenants and agreements under this Security Instrument and the Note. This Security Instrument and the Note secured hereby are subject to modification (including changes in the interest rate, the due date, and other terms and conditions), as defined in New Jersey Laws 1985, ch. 353, 1 *et seq.*, and upon such modification, shall have the benefit of the lien priority provisions of that law. The maximum principal amount secured by this Security Instrument is <LENDER.LOAN_AMT>. For these purposes, Borrower does hereby mortgage, grant, and convey to Lender the following described property located in <PROPERTY.MUNI_TYPE> of <PROPERTY.CITY>, <PROPERTY.COUNTY>, <PROPERTY.ST>.

<NOTES.BOX1>
<USER_FIELD>

which has the address of <PROPERTY.LOCATION>   <PROPERTY.CITY>
                          [Street]   [City]
<PROPERTY.ST> <PROPERTY.ZIP>
            [State and Zip Code]   ("Property Address");

   TOGETHER WITH all the improvements now or hereafter erected on the property, and all easements, appurtenances, and fixtures now or hereafter a part of the property. All replacements and additions shall also be covered by this Security Instrument. All of the foregoing is referred to in this Security Instrument as the "Property."

   BORROWER COVENANTS that Borrower is lawfully seized of the estate hereby conveyed and has the right to mortgage, grant, and convey the Property and that the Property is unencumbered, except for encumbrances of record. Borrower warrants and will defend generally the title to the Property against all claims and demands, subject to any encumbrances of record.

   THIS SECURITY INSTRUMENT combines uniform covenants for national use and nonuniform covenants with limited variations by jurisdiction to constitute a uniform security instrument covering real property.

FIGURE 13.21 (*continued*)

UNIFORM COVENANTS. Borrower and Lender covenant and agree as follows:

1. **Payment of Principal and Interest; Prepayment and Late Charges.** Borrower shall promptly pay when due the principal of and interest on the debt evidenced by the Note and any prepayment and late charges due under the Note.

2. **Funds for Taxes and Insurance.** Subject to applicable law or to a written waiver by Lender, Borrower shall pay to Lender on the day monthly payments are due under the Note, until the Note is paid in full, a sum ("Funds") for (a) yearly taxes and assessments which may attain priority over this Security Instrument as a lien on the Property; (b) yearly leasehold payments or ground rents on the Property, if any; (c) yearly hazard or property insurance premiums; (d) yearly flood insurance premiums, if any; (e) yearly mortgage insurance premiums, if any; and (f) any sums payable by Borrower to Lender, in accordance with the provisions of paragraph 8, in lieu of the payment of mortgage insurance premiums. These items are called "Escrow Items." Lender may, at any time, collect and hold Funds in an amount not to exceed the maximum amount a lender for a federally related mortgage loan may require for Borrower's escrow account under the federal Real Estate Settlement Procedures Act of 1974 as amended from time to time, 12 U.S.C. 2601 *et seq.* ("RESPA"), unless another law that applies to the Funds sets a lesser amount. If so, Lender may, at any time, collect and hold Funds in an amount not to exceed the lesser amount. Lender may estimate the amount of Funds due on the basis of current data and reasonable estimates of expenditures of future Escrow Items or otherwise in accordance with applicable law.

   The Funds shall be held in an institution whose deposits are insured or by a federal agency, instrumentality, or entity (including Lender if Lender is such an institution) or in any Federal Home Loan Bank. Lender shall apply the Funds to pay the Escrow Items. Lender may not charge Borrower for holding and applying the Funds, annually analyzing the escrow account, or verifying the Escrow Items, unless Lender pays Borrower interest on the Funds and applicable law permits Lender to make such a charge. However, Lender may require Borrower to pay a one-time charge for an independent real estate tax reporting service used by Lender in connection with this loan, unless applicable law provides otherwise. Unless an agreement is made or applicable law requires interest to be paid, Lender shall not be required to pay Borrower any interest or earnings on the Funds. Borrower and Lender may agree in writing, however, that interest shall be paid on the Funds. Lender shall give to Borrower, without charge, an annual accounting of the Funds, showing credits and debits to the Funds and the purpose for which each debit to the Funds was made. The Funds are pledged as additional security for all sums secured by this Security Instrument.

   If the Funds held by Lender exceed the amounts permitted to be held by applicable law, Lender shall account to Borrower for the excess Funds in accordance with the requirements of applicable law. If the amount of the Funds held by Lender at any time is not sufficient to pay the Escrow Items when due, Lender may so notify Borrower in writing, and, in such case Borrower shall pay to Lender the amount necessary to make up the deficiency. Borrower shall make up the deficiency in no more than twelve monthly payments, at Lender's sole discretion.

   Upon payment in full of all sums secured by this Security Instrument, Lender shall promptly refund to Borrower any Funds held by Lender. If, under paragraph 21, Lender shall acquire or sell the Property, Lender, prior to the acquisition or sale of the Property, shall apply any Funds held by Lender at the time of acquisition or sale as a credit against the sums secured by this Security Instrument.

3. **Application of Payments.** Unless applicable law provides otherwise, all payments received by Lender under paragraphs 1 and 2 shall be applied first, to any prepayment charges due under the Note; second, to amounts payable under paragraph 2; third, to interest due; fourth, to principal due; and last, to any late charges due under the Note.

4. **Charges; Liens.** Borrower shall pay all taxes, assessments, charges, fines, and impositions attributable to the Property which may attain priority over this Security Instrument, and leasehold payments or ground rents, if any. Borrower shall pay these obligations in the manner provided in paragraph 2, or if not paid in that manner, Borrower shall pay them on time directly to the person owed payment. Borrower shall promptly furnish to Lender all notices of amounts to be paid under this paragraph. If Borrower makes these payments directly, Borrower shall promptly furnish to Lender receipts evidencing the payments.

   Borrower shall promptly discharge any lien which has priority over this Security Instrument unless Borrower (a) agrees in writing to the payment of the obligation secured by the lien in a manner acceptable to Lender; (b) contests in good faith the lien by, or defends against enforcement of the lien in, legal proceedings which in the Lender's opinion operate to prevent the enforcement of the lien; or (c) secures from the holder of the lien an agreement satisfactory to Lender subordinating the lien to this Security Instrument. If Lender determines that any part of the Property is subject to a lien which may attain priority over this Security Instrument, Lender may give Borrower a notice identifying the lien. Borrower shall satisfy the lien or take one or more of the actions set forth above within 10 days of the giving of notice.

5. **Hazard or Property Insurance.** Borrower shall keep the improvements now existing or hereafter erected on the Property insured against loss by fire, hazards included within the term "extended coverage," and

any other hazards, including floods or flooding, for which Lender requires insurance. This insurance shall be maintained in the amounts and for the periods that Lender requires. The insurance carrier providing the insurance shall be chosen by Borrower subject to Lender's approval which shall not be unreasonably withheld. If Borrower fails to maintain coverage described above, Lender may, at Lender's option, obtain coverage to protect Lender's rights in the Property in accordance with paragraph 7.

All insurance policies and renewals shall be acceptable to Lender and shall include a standard mortgage clause. Lender shall have the right to hold the policies and renewals. If Lender requires, Borrower shall promptly give to Lender all receipts of paid premiums and renewal notices. In the event of loss, Borrower shall give prompt notice to the insurance carrier and Lender. Lender may make proof of loss if not made promptly by Borrower.

Unless Lender and Borrower otherwise agree in writing, insurance proceeds shall be applied to restoration or repair of the Property damaged, if the restoration or repair is economically feasible and Lender's security is not lessened. If the restoration or repair is not economically feasible or Lender's security would be lessened, the Insurance proceeds shall be applied to the sums secured by this Security Instrument, whether or not then due, with any excess paid to Borrower. If Borrower abandons the Property, or does not answer within 30 days a notice from Lender that the insurance carrier has offered to settle a claim, then Lender may collect the insurance proceeds. Lender may use the proceeds to repair or restore the Property or to pay the sums secured by this Security Instrument, whether or not then due. The 30-day period will begin when the notice is given.

Unless Lender and Borrower otherwise agree in writing, any application of proceeds to principal shall not extend or postpone the due date of the monthly payments referred to in paragraphs 1 and 2 or change the amount of the payments. If under paragraph 21 the Property is acquired by Lender, Borrower's right to any insurance policies and proceeds resulting from damage to the Property prior to the acquisition shall pass to Lender to the extent of the sums secured by this Security Instrument immediately prior to the acquisition.

6. **Occupancy, Preservation, Maintenance, and Protection of the Property; Borrower's Loan Application; Leaseholds.** Borrower shall occupy, establish, and use the Property as Borrower's principal residence within sixty days after the execution of this Security Instrument and shall continue to occupy the Property as Borrower's principal residence for at least one year after the date of occupancy, unless the Lender otherwise agrees in writing, which consent shall not be unreasonably withheld, or unless extenuating circumstances exist which are beyond Borrower's control. Borrower shall not destroy, damage, or impair the Property, allow the Property to deteriorate, or commit waste on the Property. Borrower shall be in default if any forfeiture action or proceeding, whether civil or criminal, is begun that in Lender's good faith judgment could result in forfeiture of the Property or otherwise materially impair the lien created by this Security Instrument or Lender's security interest. Borrower may cure such a default and reinstate, as provided in paragraph 18, by causing the action or proceeding to be dismissed with a ruling that, in Lender's good faith determination, precludes forfeiture of the Borrower's interest in the Property or other material impairment of the lien created by this Security Instrument or Lender's security interest. Borrower shall also be in default if Borrower, during the loan application process, gave materially false or inaccurate information or statements to Lender (or failed to provide Lender with any material information) in connection with the loan evidenced by the Note, including, but not limited to, representations concerning Borrower's occupancy of the Property as a principal residence. If this Security Instrument is on a leasehold, Borrower shall comply with all the provisions of the lease. If Borrower acquires fee title to the Property, the leasehold and the fee title shall not merge unless Lender agrees to the merger in writing.

7. **Protection of Lender's Rights in the Property.** If Borrower fails to perform the covenants and agreements contained in this Security Instrument, or there is a legal proceeding that may significantly affect Lender's rights in the Property (such as a proceeding in bankruptcy, probate, for condemnation or forfeiture, or to enforce laws or regulations), then Lender may do and pay for whatever is necessary to protect the value of the Property and the Lender's rights in the Property. Lender's actions may include paying any sums secured by a lien which has priority over this Security Instrument, appearing in court, paying reasonable attorneys' fees, and entering on the Property to make repairs. Although Lender may take action under paragraph 7, Lender does not have to do so.

Any amounts disbursed by Lender under this paragraph 7 shall become additional debt of Borrower secured by this Security Instrument. Unless Borrower and Lender agree to other terms of payment, these amounts shall bear interest from the date of disbursement at the Note rate and shall be payable, with interest, upon notice from Lender to Borrower requesting payment.

8. **Mortgage Insurance.** If Lender required mortgage insurance as a condition of making the loan secured by this Security Instrument, Borrower shall pay the premiums required to maintain the mortgage insurance in effect. If, for any reason, the mortgage insurance coverage required by Lender lapses or ceases to be in effect, Borrower shall pay the premiums required to obtain coverage substantially equivalent to the mortgage insurance previously in effect, at a cost substantially equivalent to the cost to Borrower of the mortgage insurance previously in effect, from an alternate mortgage insurer approved by Lender. If substantially equivalent

FIGURE 13.21 (*continued*)

mortgage insurance is not available, Borrower shall pay to Lender each month a sum equal to one-twelfth of the yearly mortgage insurance premium being paid by Borrower when the insurance coverage lapsed or ceased to be in effect. Lender will accept, use, and retain these payments as a loss reserve in lieu of mortgage insurance. Loss reserve payments may no longer be required, at the option of the Lender, if mortgage insurance coverage (in the amount and for the period that Lender requires) provided by an insurer approved by Lender again becomes available and is obtained. Borrower shall pay the premiums required to maintain mortgage insurance in effect, or to provide a loss reserve, until the requirement for mortgage insurance ends in accordance with any written agreement between Borrower and Lender or applicable law.

9. **Inspection.** Lender or its agent may make reasonable entries upon and inspections of the Property. Lender shall give Borrower notice at the time of or prior to an inspection specifying reasonable cause for the inspection.

10. **Condemnation.** The proceeds of any award or claim for damages, direct or consequential, in connection with any condemnation or other taking of any part of the Property, or for conveyance in lieu of condemnation, are hereby assigned and shall be paid to Lender.

In the event of a total taking of the Property, the proceeds shall be applied to the sums secured by this Security Instrument, whether or not then due, with the excess paid to Borrower. In the event of a partial taking of the Property in which the fair market value of the Property immediately before the taking is equal to or greater than the amount of the sums secured by this Security Instrument immediately before the taking, unless Borrower and Lender otherwise agree in writing, the sums secured by this Security Instrument shall be reduced by the amount of the proceeds multiplied by the following fraction: (a) the total amount of the sums secured immediately before the taking, divided by (b) the fair market value of the Property immediately before the taking. Any balance shall be paid to Borrower. In the event of a partial taking of the Property in which the fair market value of the Property immediately before the taking is less than the amount of the sums secured immediately before the taking, unless Borrower and Lender otherwise agree in writing or unless applicable law otherwise provides, the proceeds shall be applied to the sums secured by this Security Instrument whether or not the sums are then due.

If the Property is abandoned by Borrower, or if, after notice by Lender to Borrower that the condemnor offers to make an award or settle a claim for damages, Borrower fails to respond to Lender within 30 days after the date the notice is given, Lender is authorized to collect and apply the proceeds, at its option, either to restoration or repair of the Property or to the sums secured by this Security Instrument, whether or not then due.

Unless Lender and Borrower otherwise agree in writing, any application of proceeds to principal shall not extend or postpone the due date of the monthly payments referred to in paragraphs 1 and 2 or change the amount of such payments.

11. **Borrower Not Released; Forbearance by Lender Not a Waiver.** Extension of the time for payment or modification of amortization of the sums secured by this Security Instrument granted by Lender to any successor in interest of Borrower shall not operate to release the liability of the original Borrower or Borrower's successors in interest. Lender shall not be required to commence proceedings against successor in interest or refuse to extend time for payment or otherwise modify amortization of the sums secured by this Security Instrument by reason of any demand made by the original Borrower or Borrower's successors in interest. Any forbearance by Lender in exercising any right or remedy shall not be a waiver of or preclude the exercise of any right or remedy.

12. **Successors and Assigns Bound; Joint and Several Liability; Co-signers.** The covenants and agreements of this Security Instrument shall bind and benefit the successors and assigns of Lender and Borrower, subject to the provisions of paragraph 17. Borrower's covenants and agreements shall be joint and several. Any Borrower who cosigns this Security Instrument but does not execute the Note (a) is cosigning this Security Instrument only to mortgage, grant. and convey that Borrower's interest in the Property under the terms of this Security Instrument; (b) is not personally obligated to pay the sums secured by this Security Instrument; and (c) agrees that Lender and any other Borrower may agree to extend, modify, forbear, or make any accommodations with regard to the terms of this Security Instrument or the Note without that Borrower's consent.

13. **Loan Charges.** If the loan secured by this Security Instrument is subject to a law which sets maximum loan charges, and that law is finally interpreted so that the interest or other loan charges collected in connection with the loan exceed the permitted limits, then (a) any such loan charge shall be reduced by the amount necessary to reduce the charge to the permitted limit; and (b) any sums already collected from Borrower which exceed permitted limits will be refunded to Borrower. Lender may choose to make this refund by reducing the principal owed under the Note or by making a direct payment to Borrower. If a refund reduces principal, the reduction will be treated as a partial prepayment without any prepayment charge under the Note.

14. **Notices.** Any notice to Borrower provided for in this Security Instrument shall be given by delivering it or by mailing it by first class mail unless applicable law requires use of another method. The notice shall be directed to the Property Address or any other address Borrower designates by notice to Lender. Any notice

to Lender shall be given by first class mail to Lender's address stated herein or any other address as Lender designates by notice to Borrower. Any notice provided for in this Security Instrument shall be deemed to have been given to Borrower or Lender when given as provided in this paragraph.

15. **Governing Law; Severability.**   This Security Instrument shall be governed by federal law and the law of the jurisdiction in which the Property is located. In the event that any provision or clause of this Security Instrument or the Note conflicts with applicable law, such conflict shall not affect other provisions of this Security Instrument or the Note which can be given effect without the conflicting provision. To this end the provisions of the Security Instrument and the Note are declared to be severable.

16. **Borrower's Copy.**   Borrower shall be given one conformed copy of the Note and of this Security Instrument.

17. **Transfer of the Property or a Beneficial Interest in Borrower.**   If all or any part of the Property or any interest in it is sold or transferred (or if a beneficial interest in Borrower is sold or transferred and Borrower is not a natural person) without Lender's prior written consent, Lender may, at its option, require immediate payment in full of all sums secured by this Security Instrument. However, this option shall not be exercised by Lender if exercise is prohibited by federal law as of the date of this Security Instrument.

   If Lender exercises this option, Lender shall give Borrower notice of acceleration. The notice shall provide a period of not less than 30 days from the date the notice is delivered or mailed within which Borrower must pay all sums secured by this Security Instrument. If Borrower fails to pay these sums prior to the expiration of this period, Lender may invoke any remedies permitted by this Security Instrument without further notice or demand on Borrower.

18. **Borrowers Right to Reinstate.**   If Borrower meets certain conditions, Borrower shall have the right to have enforcement of this Security Instrument discontinued at any time prior to the earlier of (a) 5 days (or such other period as applicable law may specify for reinstatement) before the sale of the Property pursuant to any power of sale contained in this Security Instrument; or (b) entry of a judgment enforcing this Security Instrument. Those conditions are that Borrower (a) pays Lender all sums which then would be due under this Security Instrument and the Note as if no acceleration had occurred; (b) cures any default of any other covenants or agreements; (c) pays all expenses incurred in enforcing this Security Instrument, including, but not limited to, reasonable attorney's fees; and (d) takes such action as Lender may reasonably require to assure that the lien of this Security Instrument, Lender's rights in the Property, and Borrower's obligation to pay the sums secured by this Security Instrument shall continue unchanged. Upon reinstatement by Borrower, this Security Instrument and the obligations secured hereby shall remain fully effective as if no acceleration had occurred. However, this right to reinstate shall not apply in the case of acceleration under paragraph 17.

19. **Sale of Note; Change of Loan Servicer.**   The Note or a partial interest in the Note (together with this Security Instrument) may be sold one or more times without prior notice to Borrower. A sale may result in a change in the entity (known as the "Loan Servicer") that collects the monthly payments due under the Note and this Security Instrument. There also may be one or more changes of the Loan Servicer unrelated to the sale of the Note. If there is a change of the Loan Servicer, Borrower will be given written notice of the change in accordance with paragraph 14 above and applicable law. The notice will state the name and address of the new Loan Servicer and the address to which payments should be made. The notice will also contain any other information required by applicable law.

20. **Hazardous Substances.**   Borrower shall not permit the presence, use, disposal, storage, or release of any Hazardous Substances on or in the Property. Borrower shall not do, nor allow anyone else to do, anything affecting the Property that is in violation of any Environmental Law. The preceding two sentences shall not apply to the presence, use, or storage on the Property of small quantities of Hazardous Substances that are generally recognized to be appropriate to normal residential uses and to maintenance of the Property.

   Borrower shall promptly give Lender written notice of any investigation, claim, demand, lawsuit, or other action by any governmental or regulatory agency or private party involving the Property and any Hazardous Substance or Environmental Law of which Borrower has actual knowledge. If Borrower learns, or is notified by any governmental or regulatory authority, that any removal or other remediation of any Hazardous Substance affecting the Property is necessary, Borrower shall promptly take all necessary remedial actions in accordance with Environmental Law.

   As used in paragraph 20, "Hazardous Substances" are those substances defined as toxic or hazardous substances by Environmental Law and the following substances: gasoline, kerosene, other flammable or toxic petroleum products, toxic pesticides and herbicides, volatile solvents, materials containing asbestos or formaldehyde, and radioactive materials. As used in this paragraph 20, "Environmental Law" means federal laws and the laws of the jurisdiction where the Property is located that relate to health, safety. or environmental protection.

   NON-UNIFORM COVENANTS. Borrower and Lender further covenant and agree as follows:

FIGURE 13.21 *(continued)*

21. **Acceleration; Remedies.** Lender shall give notice to Borrower prior to acceleration following Borrower's breach of any covenant or agreement in this Security Instrument (but not prior to acceleration under paragraph 17 unless applicable law provides otherwise). The notice shall specify (a) the default; (b) the action required to cure the default; (c) a date, not less than 30 days from the date the notice is given to Borrower, by which the default must be cured; and (d) that failure to cure the default on or before the date specified in the notice may result in acceleration of the sums secured by this Security Instrument, foreclosure by judicial proceeding, and sale of the Property. The notice shall further inform Borrower of the right to reinstate after acceleration and the right to assert in the foreclosure proceeding the nonexistence of a default or any other defense of Borrower to acceleration and foreclosure. If the default is not cured on or before the date specified in the notice, Lender at its option may require immediate payment in full of all the sums secured by this Security Instrument without further demand and may foreclose this Security Instrument by judicial proceeding. Lender shall be entitled to collect all expenses incurred in pursuing the remedies provided in this paragraph 21, including, but not limited to, attorney's fees and costs of title evidence permitted by Rules of Court.

22. **Release.** Upon payment of all sums secured by this Security Instrument, Lender shall cancel this Security Instrument without charge to Borrower. Borrower shall pay any recordation costs.

23. **No Claim of Credit for Taxes.** Borrower will not make deduction from or claim credit on the principal or interest secured by this Security Instrument by reason of any governmental taxes, assessments, or charges. Borrower will not claim any deduction from the taxable value of the Property by reason of this Security Instrument.

24. **Riders to this Security Instrument.** If one or more riders are executed by Borrower and recorded together with this Security Instrument, the covenants and agreements of each such rider shall be incorporated into and shall amend and supplement the covenants and agreements of this Security Instrument as if the rider(s) were a part of this Security Instrument. [Check applicable box(es)]

[<X>] Adjustable Rate Rider   [<X>] Condominium Rider   [<X>] 1–4 Family Rider
[<X>] Graduated Payment Rider   [<X>] Planned Unit Development Rider   [<X>] Biweekly Payment Rider
[<X>] Balloon Rider   [<X>] Rate Improvement Rider   [<X>] Second Home Rider
[<X>] Other(s) *[specify]* <USER_FIELD>

    BY SIGNING BELOW, Borrower accepts and agrees to the terms and covenants contained in this Security Instrument and in any rider(s) executed by Borrower and recorded with it.

Signed, sealed, and delivered in the presence of:

_____ (SEAL)
<BUYER.NAME> —Borrower

_____ (SEAL)
<BUYER.NAME> —Borrower

_____ (SEAL)
<BUYER.NAME> —Borrower

_____ (SEAL)
<BUYER.NAME> —Borrower
.... [Space below This Line for Acknowledgment] ....
....

STATE OF _____
COUNTY OF _____
I, _____, a Notary Public in and for said county and
state do hereby certify that _____, personally
known to me to be the same person(s) whose names is/are subscribed to the foregoing instrument, appeared
before me this day in person, and acknowledged that he/she/they signed and delivered the said instrument as
his/her/their free and voluntary act, for the uses and purposes therein set forth.
    Given under my hand and official seal, this_____ day of _____

_____
Notary Public

My Commission expires:

FIGURE 13.22   Mortgage Note

MORTGAGE NOTE

<TOP.CLOSING_DATE>	<PROPERTY.CITY>	<PROPERTY.ST>
	[City]	[State]
	<PROPERTY.LOCATION>	

[Property Address]

1. BORROWER'S PROMISE TO PAY

In return for a loan that I have received, I promise to pay U.S. <LENDER.LOAN_AMT> (this amount is called "principal"), plus interest, to the order of the Lender. The Lender is <LENDER.NAME>. I understand that the Lender may transfer this Note. The Lender or anyone who takes this Note by transfer and who is entitled to receive payments under this Note is called the "Note Holder."

2. INTEREST

Interest will be charged on unpaid principal until the full amount of principal has been paid. I will pay interest at a yearly rate of <NOTES.AMT1>.

The interest rate required by this Section 2 is the rate I will pay both before and after any default described in Section 6(B) of this Note.

3. PAYMENTS

(A) Time and Place of Payments

I will pay principal and interest by making payments every month.

I will make my monthly payments on the <USER_FIELD> day of each month beginning on <USER_FIELD>. I will make these payment every month until I have paid all of the principal and interest and any other charges described below that I may owe under this Note. My monthly payments will be applied to interest before principal. If, on <USER_FIELD>, I still owe amounts under this Note, I will pay those amounts in full on that date, which is called the "maturity date."

I will make my monthly payments at <LENDER.ADDRESS> or at a different place if required by the Note Holder.

(B) Amount of Monthly Payments

My monthly payment will be in the amount of U.S. <NOTES.AMT2>

4. BORROWER'S RIGHT TO PREPAY

I have the right to make payments of principal at any time before they are due. A payment of principal only is known as a "prepayment." When I make a prepayment, I will tell the Note Holder in writing that I am doing so.

I may make a full prepayment or partial prepayments paying any prepayment charge. The Note Holder will use all of my prepayments to reduce the amount of principal that I owe under this Note. If I make a partial prepayment, there will be no changes in the due date or in the amount of my monthly payment unless the Note Holder agrees in writing to those changes.

5. LOAN CHARGES

If a law, which applies to this loan and which sets maximum loan charges, is finally interpreted so that the interest or other loan charges collected or to be collected in connection with this loan exceed the permitted limits, then (i) any such loan charge shall be reduced by the amount necessary to reduce the charge to the permitted limit; and (ii) any sums already collected from me which exceeded permitted limits will be refunded to me. The Note Holder may choose to make this refund by reducing the principal I owe under this Note or by making a direct payment to me. If a refund reduces principal, the reduction will be treated as a partial prepayment.

6. BORROWER'S FAILURE TO PAY AS REQUIRED

(A) Late Charge for Overdue Payments

If the Note Holder has not received the full amount of any monthly payment by the end of <USER_FIELD> calendar days after the date it is due, I will pay a late charge to the Note Holder. The amount of the charge will be <NOTES.AMT3> of my overdue payment of principal and interest. I will pay this late charge promptly but only once on each late payment.

(B) Default

If I do not pay the full amount of each monthly payment on the date it is due, I will be in default.

(C) Notice of Default

If I am in default, the Note Holder may send me a written notice telling me that if I do not pay the overdue amount by a certain date, the Note Holder may require me to pay immediately the full amount of principal which has not been paid and all the interest that I owe on that amount. That date must be at least 30 days after the date on which the notice is delivered or mailed to me.

(D) No Waiver by Note Holder

Even if, at a time when I am in default, the Note Holder does not require me to pay immediately in full as described above, the Note Holder will still have the right to do so if I am in default at a later time.

(E) Payment of Note Holder's Costs and Expenses

If the Note Holder has required me to pay immediately in full as described above, the Note Holder will have the right to be paid back by me for all of its costs and expenses in enforcing this Note to the extent not prohibited by applicable law. Those expenses include, for example, reasonable attorneys' fees.

7. GIVING OF NOTICES

Unless applicable law requires a different method, any notice that must be given to me under this Note will be given by delivering it or by mailing it by first class mail to me at the Property Address above or at a different address if I give the Note Holder a notice of my different address.

Any notice that must be given to the Note Holder under this Note will be given by mailing it by first class mail to the Note Holder at the address stated in Section 3(A) above or at a different address if I am given a notice of that different address.

8. OBLIGATIONS OF PERSONS UNDER THIS NOTE

If more than one person signs this Note, each person is fully and personally obligated to keep all of the promises made in this Note, including the promise to pay the full amount owed. Any person who is a guarantor, surety, or endorser of this Note is also obligated to do these things. Any person who takes over these obligations, including the obligations of a guarantor, surety, or endorser of this Note, is also obligated to keep all of the promises made in this Note. The Note Holder may enforce its rights under this Note against each person individually or against all of us together. This means that any one of us may be required to pay all of the amounts owed under this Note.

9. WAIVERS

I and any other person who has obligations under this Note waive the rights of presentment and notice of dishonor. "Presentment" means the right to require the Note Holder to demand payment of amounts due. "Notice of dishonor" means the right to require the Note Holder to give notice to other persons that amounts due have not been paid.

10. UNIFORM SECURED NOTE

This Note is a uniform instrument with limited variations in some jurisdictions. In addition to the protections given to the Note Holder under this Note, a Mortgage, Deed of Trust, or Security Deed (the "Security Instrument"), dated the same date as this Note, protects the Note Holder from possible losses which might result if I do not keep the promises which I make in this Note. That Security Instrument describes how and under what conditions I may be required to make immediate payment in full of all amounts I owe under this Note. Some of those conditions are described as follows:

Transfer of the Property or a Beneficial Interest in Borrower. If all or any part of the Property or any interest in it is sold or transferred (or if a beneficial interest in Borrower is sold or transferred and Borrower is not a natural person) without Lender's prior written consent, Lender may, at its option, require immediate payment in full of all sums secured by this Security Instrument. However, this option shall not be exercised by Lender if exercise is prohibited by federal law as of the date of this Security instrument.

If Lender exercises this option, Lender shall give Borrower notice of acceleration. The notice shall provide a period of not less than 30 days from the date the notice is delivered or mailed within which Borrower must pay all sums secured by this Security Instrument. If Borrower fails to pay these sums prior to the expiration of this period, Lender may invoke any remedies permitted by this Security Instrument without further notice or demand on Borrower.

WITNESS THE HAND(S) AND SEAL(S) OF THE UNDERSIGNED.

_____(Seal)
<BUYER.NAME>—Borrower

_____(Seal)
<BUYER.NAME>—Borrower

_____(Seal)
<BUYER.NAME>—Borrower
[Sign Original Only]

FIGURE 13.23
Truth in Lending Disclosure Statement

TRUTH-IN-LENDING DISCLOSURE STATEMENT
(THIS IS NEITHER A CONTRACT NOR A COMMITMENT TO LEND)

Applicants: Prepared By:

Property Address:

Application No: Date Prepared:

ANNUAL PERCENTAGE RATE	FINANCE CHARGE	AMOUNT FINANCED	TOTAL OF PAYMENTS
The cost of your credit as a yearly rate	The dollar amount the credit will cost you	The amount of credit provided to you or on your behalf	The amount you will have paid after making all payments as scheduled
%	$	$	$

☐ REQUIRED DEPOSIT: The annual percentage rate does not take into account your required deposit
PAYMENTS: Your payment schedule will be:

Number of Payments	Amount of Payments **	When Payments Are Due	Number of Payments	Amount of Payments **	When Payments Are Due	Number of Payments	Amount of Payments **	When Payments Are Due
		Monthly Beginning:			Monthly Beginning:			Monthly Beginning:

☐ DEMAND FEATURE: This obligation has a demand feature.
☐ VARIABLE RATE FEATURE: This loan contains a variable rate feature. A variable rate disclosure has been provided earlier.

CREDIT LIFE/CREDIT DISABILITY: Credit life insurance and credit disability insurance are not required to obtain credit, and will not be provided unless you sign and agree to pay the additional cost.

Type	Premium	Signature
Credit Life		I want credit life insurance. Signature:
Credit Disability		I want credit disability insurance. Signature:
Credit Life and Disability		I want credit life and disability insurance. Signature:

INSURANCE: The following insurance is required to obtain credit:
☐ Credit life insurance ☐ Credit disability ☐ Property insurance   ☐ Flood insurance
You may obtain the insurance from anyone you want that is acceptable to creditor.
☐ If you purchase   ☐ property   ☐ flood insurance from creditor you will pay $ for a one-year term.
SECURITY: You are giving a security interest in:
☐ The goods or property being purchased   ☐ Real property you already own.
FILING FEES: $
LATE CHARGE: If a payment is more than   days late, you will be charged   % of the payment
PREPAYMENT: If you pay off early, you
☐ may   ☐ will not   have to pay a penalty.
☐ may   ☐ will not   be entitled to a refund of part of the finance charge.
ASSUMPTION: Someone buying your property
☐ may   ☐ may, subject to conditions   ☐ may not   assume the remainder of your loan on the original terms.
See your contract documents for any additional information about nonpayment, default, any required repayment in full before the scheduled date, and prepayment refunds and penalties.
☐ * means an estimate   ☐ all dates and numerical disclosures except the late payment disclosures are estimates.

* * NOTE: The Payments shown above include reserve deposits for Mortgage Insurance (if applicable), but exclude Property Taxes and Insurance.

THE UNDERSIGNED ACKNOWLEDGES RECEIVING A COMPLETED COPY OF THIS DISCLOSURE.

_____   (Applicant) (Date)   _____   (Applicant) (Date)

_____   (Applicant) (Date)   _____   (Applicant) (Date)

_____   (Lender) (Date)

Calyx Form - til.hp (02/95)

FIGURE 13.24 Estimate of Closing Costs

GOOD FAITH ESTIMATE

Lender:		Sales Price:
Address:		Base Loan Amount:
		Total Loan Amount:
Applicant(s):		Interest Rate:
		Type of Loan:
Property Address:		Preparation Date:
		Loan Number:

The information provided below reflects estimates of the charges which you are likely to incur at the settlement of your loan. The fees listed are estimates — actual charges may be more or less. Your transaction may not involve a fee for every item listed.
The numbers listed beside the estimates generally correspond to the numbered lines contained in the HUD-1 or HUD-1A settlement statement which you will be receiving at settlement. The HUD-1 or HUD-1A settlement statement will show you the actual cost for items paid at settlement.

800	ITEMS PAYABLE IN CONNECTION WITH LOAN:		1100	TITLE CHARGES:	
801	Origination Fee @ % + $	$	1101	Closing or Escrow Fee	$
802	Discount Fee @ % + $	$	1102	Abstract or Title Search	$
803	Appraisal Fee	$	1103	Title Examination	$
804	Credit Report	$	1105	Document Preparation Fee	$
805	Lender's Inspection Fee	$	1106	Notary Fee	$
806	Mortgage Insurance Application Fee	$	1107	Attorney's Fee	$
807	Assumption Fee	$	1108	Title Insurance	$
808	Mortgage Broker Fee	$			$
810	Tax Related Service Fee	$			$
811	Application Fee	$			$
812	Commitment Fee	$			$
813	Lender's Rate Lock-In Fee	$			$
814	Processing Fee	$			$
815	Underwriting Fee	$	1200	GOVERNMENT RECORDING AND TRANSFER CHARGES:	
816	Wire Transfer Fee	$	1201	Recording Fee	$
		$	1202	City/County Tax/Stamps	$
900	ITEMS REQUIRED BY LENDER TO BE PAID IN ADVANCE:		1203	State Tax/Stamps	$
901	Interest for days @ $ /day	$	1204	Intangible Tax	$
902	Mortgage Insurance Premium	$			$
903	Hazard Insurance Premium	$			$
904	County Property Taxes	$			$
905	Flood Insurance	$			$
		$	1300	ADDITIONAL SETTLEMENT CHARGES:	
			1301	Survey	$
1000	RESERVES DEPOSITED WITH LENDER:		1302	Pest Inspection	$
1001	Hazard Ins. Mo. @$ Per Mo.	$			$
1002	Mortgage Ins. Mo. @$ Per Mo.	$			$
1004	Tax & Assmt. Mo. @$ Per Mo.	$			$
1006	Flood Insurance	$			$
		$		TOTAL ESTIMATED SETTLEMENT CHARGES:	$
	"S"/"B" designates those costs to be paid by Seller/Broker.			"A" designates those costs affecting APR.	

TOTAL ESTIMATED MONTHLY PAYMENT:		TOTAL ESTIMATED FUNDS NEEDED TO CLOSE:	
Principal & Interest	$		
Real Estate Taxes	$	Payoff Payment	$
Hazard Insurance	$	Estimated Closing Costs	$
Flood Insurance	$	Estimated Prepaid Items / Reserves	$
Mortgage Insurance	$	Total Paid Items (Subtract)	$
Other	$	Other	$
TOTAL MONTHLY PAYMENT	$	CASH FROM BORROWER	$

THIS SECTION IS COMPLETED ONLY IF A PARTICULAR PROVIDER OF SERVICE IS REQUIRED. Listed below are providers of service which we required you to use. The charges indicated in the Good Faith Estimate above are based upon the corresponding charge of the below designated providers.

ITEM NO.	NAME & ADDRESS OF PROVIDER	TELEPHONE NO.	NATURE OF RELATIONSHIP

These estimates are provided pursuant to the Real Estate Settlement Procedures Act of 1974, as amended (RESPA). Additional information can be found in the HUD Special Information Booklet, which is to be provided to you by your mortgage broker or lender, if your application is to purchase residential property and the Lender will take a first lien on the property.

Applicant	Date	Applicant	Date
Applicant	Date	Applicant	Date

☐ This Good Faith Estimate is being provided by
  a mortgage broker, and no lender has yet been obtained.

Most financial documents are standardized boilerplate. Maintain close and continuous contact with the mortgage or banking officer in this matter and ask about any preference regarding forms. Mortgages usually contain some legal subtleties as to the legal description of the property and an outline of specific rights and obligations of both mortgagor and mortgagee. Additionally, express language regarding the consequences of default and the assessment of costs is within the body of the document. Policies on recordation and the implications of notice in case of default are blended into the document as well.

Other documentation includes the "truth-in-lending" disclosure, as well as an estimate of closing costs. Both documents inform the buyer about interest rates and payoff.

The Department of Housing and Urban Development's Web site holds a wealth of information for prospective buyers regarding charges and other costs to expect in a real estate settlement. Visit the department's Web site at http://www.hud.gov/offices/hsg.

Abstraction of Title

Although paralegals are not permitted to give legal opinions, the task of tracking a chain of title to ensure that it is clear and marketable, good and freely alienable, is often delegated to them. The paralegal must be technically proficient and mechanically inclined and have an eye for detail and attention.

Searching a title involves extracting a sometimes simple, sometimes complicated history of the ownership of a specific piece of land or realty, often extending back as far as the original owners of the land during America's colonial period. At best the abstract produces a chain of owners fully accounted for, at least in the public records. Abstraction is not a perfect science because "a purchaser's quiet possession of the property could be upset if the person who examined the title . . . negligently overlooked some flaw in the title that appears on the public records, or if the flaw in the title existed because of something that would not become apparent from even the closest examination of the public records."[89]

Such impediments, difficulties, and issues that cloud or confuse title are often called *encumbrances*. Even if not on the public record, they still might exist. Carol and James Irvin in their work, *Ohio Real Estate Law*, explain some troubling examples of items that are not on the public record:

- Valid but unrecorded documents.
- Forged documents.
- Signatures made under duress.
- Signatures made by incompetents.
- Legally ineffective documents due to some legal error.
- Improperly executed documents.[90]

In the abstraction or historical review of any property, recurring items will appear on the public record and should be cleared, resolved, or dealt with before the conveyance of any real property can take place. These encumbrances include the following:

- Unsatisfied mortgages. (Satisfied mortgages need documentation. See Form 13.25 on the accompanying CD.)
- Unsatisfied liens.
- Judgments of courts of local or federal jurisdiction.
- Federal tax claims.
- Estate tax claims.
- Corporate taxes.
- Welfare liens.
- Sales and use taxes.
- Unemployment compensation contributions.
- Personal income tax claims.

- Use tax claims.
- Inheritance and estate tax claims.
- Real estate tax claims.
- Municipal claims for services.
- Municipal assessments.
- Rights of way.
- Building and use restrictions.
- Easements.
- Ground rents.
- Leases.
- Water rents.
- Lis pendens (notice of pending legal action).[91]

Some of these defects are serious, and some are not. The ultimate determination is not whether title is free of all defects and doubt, but whether the apparent defects affect marketability. The trend in modern real estate transactions seems to be that a marketable title is one which is unencumbered, is not subject to liens, and will enable a purchaser to hold it during his period of ownership peacefully—that is, without any legitimate adverse claims.[92]

Of course, defects may be curable. Factoring in the economic costs of perfecting a defective title is a recurring seller consideration. Then too, the purchaser may not be driven away from the transaction if he or she finds the defect less onerous than it first appears.

Not all defects are discovered in registries of deeds or mortgage books. Some defects to title can be gleaned from a physical inspection of the property itself. Consider these conditions:

- Fences and party walls near or on the boundary lines.
- People occupying the premises who are not the owners.
- Recent municipal improvements or alterations for which municipal claims or mechanic's liens may be filed.
- Streams or bodies of water on the property that may be subject to riparian rights of others.[93]

And defects can clearly be derived from gaps or breaks in the chain of ownership. In a sort of genealogy of deeds, the abstractor visits the governmental offices that track and compile a registry of deeds. The abstractor wants to connect the line or lineage of ownership from the initial date of land purchase. In establishing the chain of title, the abstractor must compile certain information in chronological order from the first deed to the most current. This is often designated as the *bring-down* process. In synoptic and abbreviated form, deeds in the chain of title can be characterized on standardized sheets:

- Names of grantors and marital status.
- Names of grantees and marital status.
- Date of deed.
- Verification of the description of property on the deed.
- Tax stamps as required.
- Transfer stamps as required.
- Form and type of acknowledgement.

- Deed book volume and page references.
- Dates of recordation.
- Easements and restrictions.
- Any unusual features.
- Comparison of preceding deed.
- List of any defects or encumbrances throughout history.

All research into the chain of title will involve the following issues:

- Who is the grantor? Who is the grantee? (Look to grantee/grantor indexes.)
- What was the date of the transfer? (If you are in a jurisdiction that has a chronological listing of transfer dates, you are in luck.)
- What is the street address? (If there is a city directory or street name, you may be in luck as well. Certain jurisdictions will record deeds by city directories or other recorded plats.)
- Lien, judgment, or lis pendens rolls. (If you have evidence of a specific lien, you can track a deed by cross-referencing judgment rolls with the deed book location noted.)

Two forms illustrating a conveyance chain of title are provided in Forms 13.26 and 13.27 on the accompanying CD.

A typical search can be summarized as follows:

A. Search against prospective genitor, mortgagor or ground rent assignor.

    I. Conveyance search:

        1. Make a conveyance search by searching at the office of the Recorder of Deeds for flaws in the title.

        2. Verify the conveyance search at the Registry Bureau.

    II. Encumbrance search:

        1. For mortgages, look in the mortgage index at the office of the Recorder of Deeds.

        2. For judgments of the supreme, superior, or commonwealth court, look in the office of the clerk of the court of common pleas of the county (or embracing such county) where the property is situated.

3. For federal court judgments and federal liens, look in the office of the clerk of the United States District Court. While there, search also for possible marshal's sales and bankruptcies to complete the conveyance search, and for notices or suits filed against estates involved.

4. For judgments of the criminal courts and road damage awards, look in the office of the clerk of the courts.

5. In the office of the prothonotary of the court of common pleas, search:
   (a) Judgment index for judgments, mechanic's liens, state taxes, and possible revival of liens of debts of decedents who died before January 1, 1950.
   (b) Locality index for municipal liens and taxes.
   (c) Ejectment and miscellaneous indexes for pending actions affecting the title. Local court rules may specify searching the judgment index.
   (d) Federal tax lien index for federal tax liens filed on or before August 6, 1963, or after December 7, 1965.
   (e) For possible sheriff's sales prior to April 22, 1905.

6. For possible liens of debts of or claims against decedents who died on or after January 1, 1950, in the office of the clerk of the orphans' court.

7. For unpaid municipal taxes, water, and sewer charges.

8. If any corporation has been in the title, a search should be ordered from the Department of Revenue for taxes due the commonwealth by the corporation, assessed for the period during which it held title, that are still unpaid.

9. Obtain affidavits, receipts, and so on to protect against possible unfiled tax, municipal, and mechanic's liens and liens for inheritance and federal estate taxes.

III. Personally examine the property:

1. For possible easements not appearing in the record chain of title.

2. For rights of occupant.

3. For indications of recent improvements, alterations, and so forth, inside and out, for which a municipal or mechanic's lien might be filed.

4. For walls and fences, especially on or near the boundary liens.

B. Search against prospective assignor or mortgagee.

I. Search against the original mortgagor:

1. As fully as if he or she were a prospective grantor or mortgagor, in order to establish the validity, extent, priority, and nature of the mortgage to be assigned.

II. Search against all holders of the mortgage:

1. During the periods when they held the mortgage, respectively, for any adverse assignments.

2. During the periods when they held title to the mortgage, respectively, for any releases of mortgage, and during such periods and for four months after the expiration of each, respectively, for possible bankruptcy of the holder.

III. Supplemental to search:

1. See that the assignment to be given is in proper form.

2. See that bonds, warrants, and mortgages to be assigned are produced and delivered.

3. Insist upon execution by the mortgagor and owner and delivery of a declaration of no set-off.[94]

Despite best professional efforts, no title report can guarantee a perfect historical representation of the property subject to conveyance.[95] As a result, the industry has long sought to insure the guarantee by the adoption of a form of insurance called *title insurance*. "Efforts to insure titles date back to the last century and were primarily organized by and for the benefit of attorneys who wanted protection from errors that they might make in the interpretation of abstracts. As time passed, title insurance or title guarantee became available to anyone wishing to purchase it."[96]

The practice of title insurance is a specialization of the law itself.[97] The title insurance industry was created to provide assurance to attorneys and their employees—namely paralegals—in this process. Insurance by no means provides an escape route for conduct that is grossly negligent. It is merely a safeguard against predictable human error.

Acquisition of Title Insurance

As already noted, title insurance is a policy like any other: a pool or a group of funds of other people who secure each other's interests from error. Attorneys usually become either authorized representatives and agents or participating attorneys in specific title insurance groups.[98] Although attorneys can purchase the title insurance without an alliance or allegiance to any particular company, when not aligned the rates are less competitive. Title insurance, given its cost and relative benefit, is an absolute must in a real estate transaction. Paralegals acquire title insurance policies usually after the abstraction has been completed. Once the attorney or paralegal has advised the title company of defects or difficulties, a title policy will not be issued until defects are cured, or until they are exempted or conditioned from coverage under a specific policy.

In the typical real estate transaction, an attorney applies for title insurance when a client seeks representation in a real estate transaction. An application completed by the paralegal, under the supervision of an attorney, providing preliminary information about the title intended for abstraction. (See Form 13.28 on the accompanying CD.) In the process of representation, the attorney sets out to compile a title report. There is no standardized or uniform format regarding the title report, but all title reports have information that must be reported for the purposes of issuing a policy. Some examples include the status of tax assessments, the nature of easements, the nature of any unpaid charges, the nature of any rights of way, and reverters or other unsatisfied debts or obligations.

The title company will also ask the present owner of the property subject to conveyance and the current purchaser to file affidavits positively affirming there are no violations of zoning, outstanding purchase money obligations, unrecorded leases or agreements, or other matter not discoverable in the public record. (These documents are reproduced in Forms 13.29 and 13.30 on the accompanying CD.)

Once the title report is filed, a final certificate of title is issued by the attorney. It states,

> *I hereby certify that I have searched all the records that affect title to the premises described in the above-numbered report of title, commitment, or interim binder from the date thereof as to the date of this final certificate, and I find that the following instruments affecting title thereto have been recorded subsequent to the date of said report (if so applicable).*

After the title abstraction process is complete and the title has become marketable or cured, with defects remedied, the title company will issue a title policy. The title policy provides a guarantee that the title is free and alienable subject to specific conditions. Any special conditions are listed under separate schedules of the report. (See Figure 13.25 for a sample title insurance policy.)

In many jurisdictions, title companies perform title abstraction. Jurisdictional differences in real estate practice vary considerably. The title insurance company also expects that all objections, defects, encumbrances, and difficulties uncovered during the abstraction process will be cured, waived, or exempted, or a policy will not be issued. Consider these suggestions as examples of how defects or problems can be cured:

Mechanic's liens: Pay off any outstanding obligations.

Unpaid taxes: Pay off any unpaid taxes.

Sewer and water rents: Pay appropriate municipal authority.

Judgments: Get a record of satisfaction of judgment.

Mortgages: Get a satisfaction piece.

If the seller refuses to correct a defect or provide what is known as *quiet title,* an action to remove title clouds can be brought against a recalcitrant seller. (An example of a suit to quiet title is provided in Form 13.31 on the accompanying CD.)

FIGURE 13.25   Sample Title Insurance Policy

*Appraisal * Title * Settlement * Default*   1616 Mockingbird Lane, NY 08833-2568

Phone:908.555.7400 * Toll Free:800.555.2349 * Fax:908.555.3421 * Toll Free:555.555.3422 * www.titlecommitmentco.com

```
Created File: 16:34:09  01/19/2006

                         TITLE COMMITMENT
AGENT IN BEHALF OF:TITLE INSURANCE COMPANY

                           SCHEDULE A

1.                                   2.
Commitment No.: R-232561             Policy to be Issued: Owner's
   Date Issued: 07/18/2005           Amount of Policy: $250,000
Date Effective: 07/12/2005           Account No: US0086
                                     Proposed Insured:
                                     COMPANY CORP, INC.
3.
The estate or interest in the land described or referred to in this
Commitment and covered herein is a fee simple and title to the estate or
interest in said land is at the effective date hereof VESTED IN:


GRANTEE:
 GEORGE LEWIS KING AND MICHELLE KING
 Tenancy: HUSBAND AND WIFE
GRANTOR:
 JANICE J. KING AND SOPHIA KING
DEED DATED: 09/11/1924  RECORDED: 09/15/1924  VOLUME: 175,
PAGE: 454, CONSIDERATION: $NOT STATED.


4.
          LEGAL DESCRIPTION:

          ALL THAT TRACT OR PARCEL OF LAND, SITUATE IN THE TOWN OF
          VINYARD, COUNTY OF VINCENT AND STATE OF NEW YORK, IN DISTRICT
          NUMBER ONE: KNOWN AND DISTINGUISHED AS LOT NUMBER EIGHTY-ONE
          (81) IN TOWNSHIP NUMBER TWELVE(12) OF VINCENT'S PATENT,
          CONTAINING NINETY-EIGHT (98) ACRES OF LAND, AND BEING THE
          SAME PREMISES CONVEYED TO BILL F. MOONEY BY GEORGE
          JEFFERSON BY DEED RECORDED IN THE VINCENT COUNTY CLERK'S OFFICE
          IN LIBER V OF DEEDS AT PAGE 981.

          ALSO ALL THAT TRACT OR PARCEL OF LAND, SITUATE IN THE TOWN
          OF VINYARD, COUNTY OF VINCENT AND STATE OF NEW YORK, UPON LOT
          NUMBER FORTY-TWO (42) IN TOWNSHIP NUMBER SIXTEEN 916) OF
          SCRIBA'S PATENT BOUNDED AS FOLLOWS: ON THE SOUTH, BY THE
          PARCEL ABOVE DESCRIBED; ON THE EAST BY LANDS FORMERLY OF
          CHRISTIAN JOHNSON AND ON THE NORTH AND WEST BY LANDS
          FORMERLY OWNED BY REUBEN CHAPMAN, CONTAINING FIVE (5) ACRES
          OF LAND, BE THE SAME MORE OR LESS, AND BEING THE SAME
```

FIGURE 13.25 (*continued*)

PREMISES CONVEYED TO WILLIAM F. CHESBRO BY HARVEY W. SMITH
AND WIFE BY DEED RECORDED IN THE OSWEGO COUNTY CLERK'S
OFFICE IN LIBER 195 OF DEES AT PAGE 194.

EXCEPTING THEREFROM, HOWEVER, THE FOLLOWING DESCRIBED LANDS
AND BUILDING ERECTED THEREON, TO WIT:

BEGINNING AT A POINT IN THE CENTER OF THE ROAD KNOWN AS
OWENS ROAD, NORTH 77 DEGREES 02' 30" WEST FROM THE
SOUTHWEST CORNER OF THE FARM NOW OR FORMERLY OF VINCENT
SPATARO; THENCE RUNNING ALONG THE CENTER OF SAID ROAD,
NORTH 76 DEGREES 55' 00" WEST, 217.88' TO A POINT; THENCE
RUNNING OVER TO A SET STAKE NORTH 16 DEGREES 00' 00" WEST,
234.00' TO A STAKE; THENCE RUNNING SOUTH 65 DEGREES 17' 52"
EAST 166.93' TO A STAKE; THENCE RUNNING SOUTH 34 DEGREES
02' 00" EAST, 58.35' TO A STAKE; THENCE RUNNING SOUTH 13
DEGREES 11' 30" WEST, PASSING OVER A SET STAKE 160.37' TO
THE PLACE OF BEGINNING.

SCHEDULE B — SECTION 1

The following are the requirements to be complied with:

1. INSTRUMENT(S) CREATING THE ESTATE OR INTEREST TO BE INSURED MUST BE
    APPROVED, EXECUTED, DELIVERED, AND FILED FOR RECORD.

2. a.) THE OPTION TO LEASE MUST BE EXERCISED AND ASSIGNED TO THE
    PROPOSED INSURED (NAMED HEREIN) OR A NEW LEASE MUST BE EXECUTED AND
    THE LEASE OR MEMORANDUM THEREOF MUST BE RECORDED.
    b.) A FINAL SURVEY AND CERTIFIED DESCRIPTIONS OF THE LEASED PARCEL,
    ACCESS AND UTILITY EASEMENTS MUST BE FURNISHED.
    c.) EASEMENTS (ACCESS AND UTILITY) MUST BE RECORDED.
    d.) AN ESTOPPEL LETTER MUST BE FURNISHED, FROM THE LANDLORD,
    INDICATING THAT THE LEASE IS IN FULL FORCE AND EFFECT AND THERE ARE
    NO DEFAULTS THEREUNDER.

SCHEDULE B — SECTION 2

The premises endorsed hereon are subject to the following items, which
together with items not removed in Schedule B-1, will be excepted in the
policy.

1. DEFECTS, LIENS, ENCUMBRANCES, ADVERSE CLAIMS OR OTHER MATTERS,
    IF ANY, CREATED, FIRST APPEARING IN THE PUBLIC RECORDS OR ATTACHING
    SUBSEQUENT TO THE EFFECTIVE DATE HEREOF BUT PRIOR TO THE DATE THE PROPOSED
    INSURED ACQUIRES FOR VALUE OF RECORD THE ESTATE OR INTEREST OR MORTGAGE
    THEREON COVERED BY THIS COMMITMENT.

2. RIGHTS OR CLAIMS OF PARTIES IN POSSESSION NOT SHOWN BY THE PUBLIC RECORDS.

3. ENCROACHMENTS, OVERLAPS, BOUNDARY LINE DISPUTES, OR OTHER MATTERS
    WHICH WOULD BE DISCLOSED BY AN ACCURATE SURVEY OR INSPECTION OF THE
    PREMISES.

4. EASEMENTS OR CLAIMS OF EASEMENTS NOT SHOWN IN THE PUBLIC RECORDS.

5. ANY LIEN OR RIGHT TO A LIEN, FOR SERVICES, LABOR, OR MATERIAL HERETOFORE OR HEREAFTER FURNISHED, IMPOSED BY LAW AND NOT SHOWN BY THE PUBLIC RECORDS.

6. TAXES OR SPECIAL ASSESSMENTS WHICH ARE NOT SHOWN AS EXISTING LIENS BY THE PUBLIC RECORDS.

SCHEDULE B OF THE POLICY OR POLICIES TO BE ISSUED WILL CONTAIN EXCEPTIONS TO THE FOLLOWING MATTERS UNLESS THE SAME ARE DISPOSED OF TO THE SATISFACTION OF THE COMPANY:

************************************ TAXES ***********************************

FOR CURRENT TAX INFORMATION, INCLUDING PENALTIES, INTEREST, AND AMOUNT GOOD UNTIL DATES, PLEASE CONTACT THE VINCENT COUNTY TREASURER'S OFFICE.

1. THE FOLLOWING TAX INFORMATION REFERS TO TAX MAP NUMBER 2232.00-04-10.01:

   REAL ESTATE TAX FOR THE YEAR 2005 ARE PAID.

   ALL TAXES, LIENED OR UNLIENED, ARE SUBJECT TO PENALTY AND INTEREST AND SHOULD BE VERIFIED WITH LOCAL AUTHORITIES TO INSURE PROPER PAYOFF.

   PLEASE CONTACT THE OR YOUR CUSTOMER FOR ALL PAID TAX RECEIPTS.

********************************** MORTGAGES **********************************

NONE.

********************************** LIENS ************************************

NONE.

****************************** MISCELLANEOUS *********************************

NONE.

********************* STANDARD OR SPECIAL EXCEPTIONS *********************

1. SUBJECT TO AN EASEMENT TO CENTRAL NEW YORK CORPORATION, RECORDED APRIL 16, 1940, IN LIBER 239, FOLIO 20.

2. SUBJECT TO UTILITY EASEMENT TO POWER CORPORATION, RECORDED OCTOBER 5, 1976, IN LIBER 221, FOLIO 726.

3. SUBJECT TO AN AGREEMENT BETWEEN ROBERT LEWIS KING, ET UX, AND OIL COMPANY, RECORDED APRIL 4, 1977, IN BOOK 12, PAGE 4019.

4. SUBJECT TO AN OIL AND GAS LEASE BETWEEN ROBERT LEWIS MCDONALD, ET UX, AND

FIGURE 13.25 (*continued*)

MASON DIXON ENERGY, INC., RECORDED FEBRUARY 6, 2002, IN INSTRUMENT 2002-001939.

5. THE LEGAL DESCRIPTION CONTAINED IN THIS COMMITMENT REPRESENTS THE PROPERTY AS SET FORTH IN THE MOST RECENT (RECORDED) VESTING DEED. THIS LEGAL DESCRIPTION DOES NOT PURPORT TO DESCRIBE THE PROPOSED TOWER SITE. THE FINAL POLICY OF TITLE INSURANCE WILL CONTAIN A MODIFIED LEGAL DESCRIPTION BASED UPON a.) A CURRENT SURVEY OF THE PROPERTY AND b.) EVIDENCE OF RECORDING OF THE LEASE PURCHASE AGREEMENT AND ANY ANCILLARY ACCESS AGREEMENTS, EASEMENTS, RIGHTS OF WAY, ETC.

6. A PROPOSED ACCESS ROAD AND/OR EASEMENT FOR INGRESS, EGRESS, AND UTILITIES APPEARS ON THE SITE SKETCH OR HAS BEEN MADE PART OF THE LEASE PURCHASE AGREEMENT. THE COMPANY DOES NOT INSURE THE ACCESS OR THE EASEMENT UNTIL SUCH TIME AS a.) THE WIDTH AND LOCALITY OF EACH HAS MET WITH THE APPROVAL OF APPLICABLE GOVERNMENTAL AUTHORITIES AND UTILITY PROVIDERS AND b.) THE INSTRUMENTS GRANTING ACCESS, INGRESS, AND EGRESS HAVE BEEN FILED AMONG THE PUBLIC RECORDS.

* *

YOUR PREMIUM FOR THIS NEW TITLE INS. POLICY IN THE AMT OF $250,000 IS $1,319.00.

IF THIS IS A REFINANCE WITHIN TEN YEARS YOU MAY BE ENTITLED TO A REDUCED PREMIUM. CONTACT US IMMEDIATELY FOR DETAILS.

PLEASE CALL NATIONAL REAL ESTATE INFORMATION SERVICES
FOR AN UPDATED TITLE QUOTATION IF THE AMOUNT BEING FINANCED CHANGES OR ANY ENDORSEMENTS NEED TO BE INCLUDED.

------------------------------END OF COMMITMENT----------------------------

        THIS PDF COMMITMENT SERVES AS THE TRUE AND ACTUAL ORIGINAL.

MORTGAGE TAX AND RECORDING INFORMATION IS SUBJECT TO CHANGE. FOR INFORMATION, PLEASE CONTACT OSWEGO COUNTY CLERK'S OFFICE.
IF YOU REQUIRE FURTHER ASSISTANCE, PLEASE CONTACT OUR CUSTOMER SERVICE DEPARTMENT.

  PLEASE MAIL YOUR MORTGAGE INFORMATION FOR FILING TO:

            REGULAR MAIL OR OVERNIGHT EXPRESS:

            ARNOLD DRUMMOND
            23 WASHINGTON ST.
            SUITE 777
            BALDWIN, NY 16452

  FED EXP # : 1-800-238-5355 (On Federal Express Air Bills, please be sure
                      to check FEDEX LETTER box in Standard Overnight
                      column.)

TITLE INSURANCE COMMITMENT

We agree to issue policy to you according to the terms of the Commitment. When we show the policy amount and your name as the proposed insured in Schedule A, this Commitment becomes effective as of the Commitment Date shown in Schedule A.

If the Requirements shown in this Commitment have not been met within six months after the Commitment Date, our obligation under this Commitment will end. Also, our obligation under this Commitment will end when the Policy is issued and then our obligation to you will be under the Policy.

Our obligation under this Commitment is limited by the following:
The Provisions in Schedule A.
The Requirements in Schedule B-1.
The Exceptions in Schedule B-II.

This Commitment is not valid without SCHEDULE A and Sections I and II of SCHEDULE B.

THIS COMMITMENT (substitute preliminary report or binder where appropriate) IS NOT AN ABSTRACT, EXAMINATION, REPORT, OR REPRESENTATION OF FACT OR TITLE AND DOES NOT CREATE AND SHALL NOT BE THE BASIS OF ANY CLAIM FOR NEGLIGENCE, NEGLIGENT MISREPRESENTATION, OR OTHER TORT CLAIM OR ACTION. THE SOLE LIABILITY OF COMPANY AND ITS TITLE INSURANCE AGENT SHALL ARISE UNDER AND BE GOVERNED BY THE CONDITIONS OF THE COMMITMENT.

IN WITNESS WHEREOF, the underwriter named herein has caused its corporate name and seal to be hereunto affixed by its duly authorized officers on the date shown in Schedule A.

CONDITIONS

1. DEFINITIONS

 (a) "Mortgage" means mortgage, deed of trust, or other security instrument.
 (b) "Public Records" means title records that give constructive notice
 of matters affecting your title — according to the state statutes where
 your land is located.

2. LATER DEFECTS
 The Exceptions in Schedule B — Section II may be amended to show any defects, liens, or encumbrances that appear for the first time in the public records or are created or attach between the Commitment Date and the date on which all of the Requirements (a) and (c) of Schedule B — Section I are met. We shall have no liability to you because of this amendment.

3. EXISTING DEFECTS
 If any defects, liens, or encumbrances existing at Commitment Date are not shown in Schedule B, we may amend Schedule B to show them. If we do amend Schedule B to show these defects, liens, or encumbrances, we shall be liable to you according to Paragraph 4 below unless you

FIGURE 13.25 (*continued*)

```
knew of this information and did not tell us about it in writing.
```

```
4. LIMITATION OF OUR LIABILITY
   Our only obligation is to issue to you the Policy referred to in this
   Commitment when you have met its Requirements. If we have any liability
   to you for any loss you incur because of an error in this Commitment,
   our liability will be limited to your actual loss caused by your relying
   on this Commitment when you acted in good faith to comply with the
   Requirements shown in Schedule B — Section I or eliminate with our
   written consent any Exceptions shown in Schedule B — Section II. We
   shall not be liable for more than the Policy Amount shown in Schedule A
   of this Commitment, and our liability is subject to the terms of the Policy
   form to be issued to you.
```

```
5. CLAIMS MUST BE BASED ON THIS COMMITMENT
   Any claim, whether or not based on negligence, which you may have against
   us concerning the title to the land must be based on this Commitment and
   is subject to its terms.
```

In today's busy real estate practice, title insurance is an absolute necessity:

> *The role of the title insurer, and measures that the company takes to minimize its risks, shape the format and function of the title report itself. Thus the report states what a search of the public records has disclosed about the status of title as it relates to the contemplated transaction and further describes what gaps must be filled in, and what documents and proofs must be produced, in order for the title insurer to be able to issue a policy after settlement insuring that the title on that day is as stated therein.*[99]

A bank will insist on a title insurance policy before it will disburse any mortgage funds. Title insurance policies are generally mandatory for financial institutions but optional on the part of the purchaser of real estate. Attorneys routinely advise the purchase of title insurance by the client to protect the entire investment of the purchaser, considering the economic implications.

The Closing Process

Closing refers to that set of "procedures that must be followed in order to conclude a transaction involving the purchase and transfer of real property."[100]

Preparation of Documents

Governmental regulatory requirements, as well as internal policies of financial institutions, cause a blizzard of paperwork in the closing process. The paralegal and attorney prepare the documents for eventual settlement.

Deeds The primary evidence of transferred title in real property is accomplished by the execution and delivery of a deed. A deed defines the limits of the conveyance and ownership interest. A deed information worksheet is provided in Form 13.32 on the accompanying CD and is a useful preliminary tool in the initial draft stage.

A deed is a formal legal document that should be recorded. Although not a mandatory practice, recording gives notice to others as to the priority of ownership and serves as a mechanism to identify the rights and priorities of competing parties to realty. See Form 13.33 on the accompanying CD.

All deeds minimally contain the following provisions:

- Names of the parties.
- Consideration, whether nominal or actual.
- Specific words of conveyance, such as grant or convey, grant, bargain or sell, or the like.
- Description of the property—another place where the legal description will be provided.

- Habendum clause—that is, that the property is taken freely and clearly or with certain reservations or restrictions. Habendum is often known as the "to have and to hold" clause.
- Execution and acknowledgement clause.

The grantor must be competent to convey, and the grantee must be capable of receiving the grant of the property. Any person who is competent to make a valid contract is competent to be a grantor. Minors and mentally incompetent (*non compos mentis*) individuals do nothing more than negotiate voidable or void contracts.[101]

Deeds alienate property under various tactics—some more restrictive, others expansive. Deeds set out exactly what is the subject of transfer. Under the "*general warranty deed*" a grantor warrants that the property is being alienated, transferred, and conveyed without any reservation and is free and clear of any encumbrances or defects. (See Form 13.34 on the accompanying CD.) By contrast, the *limited warranty deed* is not as unequivocal. By its very language, the purchaser realizes that "no representation or guarantee of good title is made, but the grantor's title is conveyed absolutely."[102] This deed is also known as a *bargain and sale deed*. (See Form 13.35.)

A quit claim deed, shown in Form 13.36 on the accompanying CD, conveys whatever title the grantor has; it contains no covenants, no warranties, nor implication of the grantor's ownership. It is essentially an "as-is" deed that people should become a party to cautiously.

A *deed of trust* is used in some jurisdictions. (See Form 13.37 on the accompanying CD.) A deed of trust signifies an underlying mortgage. Under a deed of trust, the borrower conveys the land to a third party trustee to hold for the mortgage lender to secure a debt, subject to the condition that the conveyance shall be void and terminated on payment of the debt at maturity. Most deeds of trust contain a power of sale giving the trustee the power to sell the land in case of default and to apply the proceeds from the sale toward payment of the debt. It is also called a *trust deed*.[103]

Here are some miscellaneous deed forms covering other territory:

- Executor's deed (see Form 13.38 on the accompanying CD).
- Referee's deed.
- Guardian's deed.
- Sheriff's deed.

- Deed of surrender.
- Deed of release.
- Corporate deed (see Form 13.39).

In cases of guardianship, infancy, or incompetency, the guardian signs in place of the ward, the incompetent, or the mentally disabled party. Each of these deeds shares basic language and provisional components.

Under the deed's habendum clause—that is, the provision that indicates the extent and nature of title held—the grantor states that certain covenants will run with the land, *covenants* being certain rights and duties that are passed to grantees. Covenants like the covenant of quiet enjoyment pass with the land except in the case of a quit claim or sheriff's deed. Other specific covenants or rights with the land require explicit express language within the deed. (Review Form 13.40 on the accompanying CD.) Some deeds seeks specific limitations in the usage of property. For an example of a deed limiting the use of land to single-family residences, see Form 13.41.

For mineral rights accepted and reserved to the grantor not permitting their running with the land, see Form 13.42 on the accompanying CD. Riparian rights will also be noted in the deed. Typical language might be this:

> *Together with all and singular buildings, improvements, waters, woods, ways, rights, liberties, privileges, hereditaments, and appurtenances to the same belonging, or in any ways appertaining, and the reversions and remainders, rents, issues, and profits thereof and of every part and parcel thereof.*

Financing Documentation As previously discussed, paralegals frequently prepare banking documentation. For purposes of review, those documents include any of the following:

- Mortgage.
- Mortgage note.
- Deed of trust.

- Promissory note.
- Installment note.
- Rider for adjustable rate purposes.

Throughout this chapter are various examples of these financial documents:

- Regulation Z: Buyer's estimate of closing costs.
- Valuation forms necessary for closing.
- Title documents: As noted in the section on acquisition of title insurance, any of these are necessary for a complete and total settlement package: owner's affidavit, purchaser's affidavit, attorney's title opinion, attorney's final certificate of title, title binder (sometimes issued at closing previous to a formal issuance of a title policy), or title policy.

Collection and Coordination of Closing Documentation

Many tasks must be attended to before a closing can take place. The paralegal must be certain that the following items are completed to be submitted in the closing package to the bank or other financing authority:

- Survey.
- Loan pay-off statements.
- Judgment certificates.
- Assumption statements and other documentation.
- Notice requirements under government loan programs.
- Leases if applicable.
- Receipts for payment of all taxes, whether state, local, or special assessments.
- Certificates for septic, soil, percolation, and zoning rights.
- Insurance policies that cover hazard and occupational activities.

- Rough draft of a settlement sheet to be submitted to all the parties for their inspection before a settlement. A general form is provided by most title insurance companies that assist in the settlement process. Review Form 13.43 on the accompanying CD as a good example.
- Certificate of attorney as required.
- Termite inspection report: Contracts are usually conditional upon satisfactory termite reports.
- Satisfaction pieces for mortgages.
- Evidence of satisfied judgments.
- Evidence of satisfied liens.
- Releases as needed.
- Septic tank inspection reports.
- Premise inspection documents.
- Certificates of occupancy.
- Final accounting.
- Checks from escrow account, whether real estate or attorney's office.
- Zoning certificates and waivers.
- Utility bills.
- Calculation of earnest money deposit interest.

Robert Schreiner, in his work *Real Estate Closings,* also provides sensible advice on the process of starting early and compiling useful worksheets. He emphasizes that the attorney must read the sales contract carefully, "including the counterproposals and extension agreements, with a view toward comprehending the contents of these documents as related to the settlement sheets and other closing-related activities."[104] (See Form 13.44 on the accompanying CD for a complete outline of closing activities.)

The Human Perspective on the Closing Process

Paralegals soon learn that nervousness and anxiety are part of the closing culture and atmosphere. Competent paralegals can relieve the pressure by exhibiting a professional demeanor and by being well prepared. Although closings and settlements are not earth-shattering experiences, you can presume a problem or two will crop up during the process. Sellers and buyers have familiar interests, yet competing ones. Thus all are interested in effecting the closing without any detriment to their positions. "Expediency is the prevailing attitude at the closing. The parties always seem to be in a hurry to get in and get out and do not want anything to interfere with the actual completion of the transaction."[105]

Sometimes the purchaser never even appears for a closing. Under general principles of law and equity, a purchaser must be ready, willing, and able to effect settlement. According to Frances Crable in his work *Purchaser Not Ready, Willing, and Able to Make a Closing,*

> *The phrase "ready, willing, and able" as applied to the purchaser under a land sale contract is of long standing in equity. According to the language sometimes employed by the authorities, a party to a contract seeking specific performance against the other must show himself "ready, willing, desirous, prompt, and eager" to perform.*[106]

The reasons why purchasers fail to arrive at closing are varied. Some lack the funds to close; others change their minds or their hearts. Others simply forget the day and time. Whatever the motivation, the seller has the right, all things being equal, to a buyer ready willing and able to close. One potential remedy for a seller is an action for specific performance.

Other civil actions may make sense. The aggrieved party (the seller) can argue diverse damage issues, including how long the house was off the market, what losses were incurred in subsequent resale efforts, legal expenses to sell again, and other consequential damages.[107]

Aside from all the documentary responsibilities, the paralegal must orchestrate personalities at every level. Closings produce some ugly human behavior and acute irrationality. The action gets quite heated in some circles. "In some instances, some real estate brokers choose to have parties attend at separate times, evidently because of fear of conflict and controversy."[108] This portrayal, of course, may be overblown and, as Schreiner indicates, is probably "a groundless fear when the sales contract was well written and when the closing has been properly prepared and is skillfully handled."[109] Clearly being well prepared, confident in demeanor, and insistent on time lines and other courtesies goes a long way to tempering any situation.

The location of a closing or settlement should be a place that is mutually convenient to all the parties, such as a title insurance office, a real estate office, a bank, or either party's attorney's office. "Make sure you have sufficient support staff available at the closing to witness, notarize, and copy documents. You may also need someone to type additions or corrections to the documents or to prepare new documents. If you arrange for the closing at a location where typing or photocopying assistance is not available, you may face some awkward moments."[110] Advise all necessary parties who should be at the closing well in advance of the date. Generally the buyer and seller, along with their attorneys, the closing officer, and at times a real estate representative are expected to be at closing. During the closing process, paralegals must communicate with many parties:

- Seller.
- Attorney for seller.
- Buyer.
- Attorney for buyer.
- Banker.
- Title insurance company.
- Hazard policy insurance company.
- Paralegals from other offices.
- Government agencies.
- Mortgage authorities.
- Tax officials.
- Zoning authorities.
- Parties who must be advised to attend the closing.
- Real estate agents.
- Brokers.

Preparation of the Settlement Sheet

As required under federal law, particularly when bank financing is involved, the parties to a closing must receive a settlement statement. This statement advises both sellers and buyers of the amounts due from and to them, as well as the corresponding charges.[111] From lines 700 through 1400 of the back sheet of the closing statement, proceeds payable from either buyer's or seller's funds are includable. (See Form 13.45, which shows a HUD-1 settlement sheet, on the accompanying CD.)

On the front of the settlement sheet, a reconciliation of expense and incoming deposits and mortgage funds is calculated for final distribution at settlement. The preparer must complete page 2 before finalizing the computations on the front of the closing statement. A more particular analysis of the settlement statement follows.

Lines 701–704: Broker's Commission   Typically a broker's commission is either paid in one sum to one broker who is the sole broker in the matter or divided evenly or under another agreed formula. Within these lines, a calculation is made—usually 6 or 7 percent of the total purchase price.

Lines 801–811: Financing Charges   In this section, charges relating to the acquisition of financing are listed:

801–802: Loan origination and loan discount fees, also known as points and up-front charges, are calculated. Unless there is an agreement to the contrary, the borrower or purchaser is always responsible for points under a real estate contract. Certain FHA programs and other governmental programs, however, charge that expense to the seller.

803: An appraisal fee, generally running from $150 to $350 for a typical residential appraisal, is usually the borrower's expense.

804: A credit report, required under all mortgage application analyses, is the borrower's expense and ranges anywhere from $25 to $75.

805: The lender's inspection fee is generally an optional expense borne by the borrower if he or she desires an engineer's report, a home warranty report, or another type of analysis.

806–807: A mortgage insurance application fee will be required when the loan is less than 80 percent loan to value ratio; this assumption fee is determinable by the contractual relationship between the current seller and his or her bank. These amounts are payable, as a rule, by the borrower.

Lines 900–905: Prepaid Items   All lending institutions require certain prepayments to ensure proper payments of interest, taxes, and insurance. Interest, because it is paid in arrears, is required to be paid in advance. Each day before the end or termination of a month is calculated as a day's interest. If a closing takes place on May 2, there will be 29 days of interest payable at the amortized rate of interest at so many dollars per day. That, of course, is the borrower's expense. Another result would be reached if settlement occurred on the last day of the month, in which case only one day's interest would be payable. Cash buyers on tight budgets generally choose to have a closing on the last day of the month.

Lines 1001–1008: Reserves   In this section, a lender may require certain reserves to be deposited. Those reserves include hazard insurance, mortgage insurance, city and county taxes, as well as other assessments. Customarily lenders require between three and nine months' reserves deposited with them to ensure the economic viability of a loan.

Lines 1101–1113: Charges Related to Legal Settlement   Settlement closing fees, abstract searches, title searches, title binders, document preparation, notary fees, and title insurance acquisition are all calculated in this section. Again, these are basically buyer's expenses to ensure a free, good, and marketable title.

Lines 1201–1205: Recordation and Tax Expenses   This section includes recordation expenses for deeds, mortgages, and releases, as well as the payment of transfer and city and county taxes, which are borne equally by the seller and the buyer.

Lines 1301–1305: Additional Settlement Charges   Any additional settlement charges, including survey, pest inspection, water and sewer assessments, and other extraordinary charges are listed at this point depending on who is responsible. Termite inspection may be the expense of the purchaser, but repairs may be the expense of the seller depending on jurisdiction.

Once these charges are calculated throughout, the total settlement charges for both borrower and seller are written on lines 101 and 401, respectively, on the front of the settlement sheet. Then simple mathematical calculation determines who owes what amount and who is due what amount.

At lines 102 and 103, personal property and settlement charges are added to the contract sales price. Therefore, if a house costs $1 million, and there are $200,000 worth of personal property and a settlement charge of $5,000, the gross amount due is $1,205,000. Additionally, city and town taxes, county taxes, and other assessments are always prorated, resulting in a gross amount due from the borrower. From those amounts, lines 201–209 (deposit or earnest money, new loans or existing loans taken subject to, and items that are unpaid by the seller) are subtracted. At line 220 the total paid by the borrower is subtracted from the total gross amount due from the borrower, resulting in a net figure at line 303 of the cash amount to or from the borrower.

On the opposite side of the settlement statement, the contract sales price, plus personal property charges due a seller, minus any adjustments for items paid in advance, result at line 420 in a gross amount due to a seller. At lines 501–509, the seller has to meet any existing obligations, including excess deposits, settlement charges to the seller, existing loans, payoffs of mortgage loans, or adjustments for any items that are unpaid up to the settlement. At line 520, there is a total reduction of the amount due to the seller; line 600 shows cash at settlement to or from the seller; line 601 shows the gross amount due to the seller; line 602 shows reductions in the amount due to the seller, resulting in the net cash to or from the seller as a final calculation.

Various sample problems are provided at the end of this chapter on how to calculate a settlement sheet. For mathematical purposes, a buyer and seller must calculate the amounts they have placed in earnest money, the amounts they owe above and beyond the contract price, and all the expenses of a closing.

Explanation of the Closing Process

Once a settlement sheet has been calculated, all interested parties must be informed of the rights and obligations of each individual before a formal transfer can take place. Across the American landscape, paralegals no longer sit as bystanders to the closing process. Instead the role and function of paralegals at closing are now fairly well entrenched, though a few states retain the attorney requirement.[112] Many things need to be explained and accomplished at the closing:

- Explain the settlement sheet to each interested party.
- Explain all documents on financing and other related matters to all of the parties.
- Acquire signatures on all necessary documents.
- Collect all monies due the necessary parties, including seller and real estate broker.
- Collect all checks, ensuring that they are certified and accountable.
- Pay all debts and obligations at the closing.
- Pay off any liens, judgments, or other matters for which there are sufficient funds to do so.
- Get seller's new and future address.
- Put return addresses on documents being recorded.
- Surrender of keys held by broker.
- Make a memo of those present at the closing.
- Make sure that the following utilities are transferred and correctly accounted for: gas and electric meter readings, telephone, water service.
- Make sure that all tax bills are properly paid and accounted for.
- Complete all mortgage satisfaction pieces.
- Make sure that the hazard insurance policy is submitted to the financial institution.
- Give copies of the settlement sheet and other documentation necessary to all interested parties.
- Submit a title binder policy to the purchaser.
- Complete any other closing-related activities.

After attending to these multiple tasks, the paralegal will bind all the necessary documents, package them in good order, and send the appropriate portions to the relevant parties. Copies of everything eventually go to the mortgage company with a file for the buyer and the buyer's counsel. Most banks give explicit instructions on what to do with this settlement package. See the sample instructions here:

> *a. The entire settlement package normally must be returned to the mortgage company within an extremely short period of time after settlement. ADHERE TO THEIR TIMETABLE. If there is a lack of the required adherence, they will contact your office immediately.*
>
> *b. In all fairness to the mortgage companies, their livelihood depends upon packaging and selling the mortgages that they grant to mortgagors. It is incumbent upon their system of operation that the mortgages be turned around and sold in as short a period as possible. Your office's cooperation will be most appreciated by them.[113]*

Additionally, all checklists written at settlement should be recorded in a disbursement schedule such as that shown in Form 13.46 on the accompanying CD.

Postclosing Activities

The paralegal's tasks usually do not end with the final calculation of the settlement sheet and successful closing. Postclosing requirements include the following.

Recordation of Mortgage and Other Related Documents   Mortgages, notes, liens, promissory notes, or any other financing statements must be recorded as soon as possible after closing. This, again, is to ensure a perfection of title regarding race or notice statutes.

Title Policy Issuance   As discussed previously, title insurance companies are usually willing to issue only an initial or preliminary binder covering the real estate transaction. Once all documents and other requirements are fulfilled, a title insurance policy of full legal effect will be issued. Make sure that a full premium is paid for both the bank and the purchaser.

Escrow or Repair Issues   Frequently, upon final inspection by the purchaser, corrective repairs are necessary. If the plumbing and electrical systems are inoperable, the attorney should escrow a designated amount—say $500 or $1,000—to cover the cost of future repairs. The parties should execute an escrow agreement to protect their relative interests. (See Form 13.47 on the accompanying CD.) The paralegal must monitor this situation to see that those repairs have taken place, and refund the balance if necessary.[114] Use the suggested flowchart at Form 13.48[115] to track the history of escrow.

Finally, "review the closing statement and any closing memoranda to insure that no matters are left unresolved. For example, certain documents or letters may need to be forwarded to different parties."[116]

Summary

The law of real estate requires paralegals to master many skills. The paralegal frees the attorney from the many technical and administrative aspects of real estate practice, allowing counsel to tackle other matters.

Real estate coverage within this chapter was comprehensive. The chapter began with a full examination of types, kinds, and definitions of real property. From the freehold estate to the easement, no form of real property interest was avoided. The subtleties of joint ownership were fully gauged, as well as newer means of joint ownership such as the condominium and joint venture. Methods of property description were presented and included metes and bounds, rectangular surveys, recorded plats, and the importance of legal descriptions in deeds.

The chapter's chief thrust was the real estate transaction, from an analysis of the agreement of sale to final closing. The role of conditions and contingencies was comprehensively addressed, as well as the various clauses in standard real estate contracts. Other coverage included deeds, mortgages and related financing documentation, and other relevant documentation that encompasses the typical real estate sale. Abstraction of title, the role of title insurance, and practical hints and suggestions about what to search for in insuring the integrity of title were fully developed within the chapter's content. The final emphasis in the chapter related to the settlement and closing process, with special emphasis on the closing statements. Sample closing exercises are available at the end of this chapter to ensure mastery of this important aspect of real estate practice. Postclosing activities were also highlighted.

Discussion Questions

1. Contact a local realtor in your area. Collect forms for real estate practice and learn about the Multiple Listing Service process in your jurisdiction.

2. Have you ever considered becoming a real estate agent? Do you think the professions of paralegal and real estate agent are complementary or antagonistic?

3. How would you classify the property you currently live in? Is it fee simple? Is it a life estate? Is it a leasehold?

4. What type of lease assures the least protection?

5. Married people own real property by what designation?

6. What would be defined as a fixture within your residence?

7. Why are condominiums slightly different from traditional fee simple estates?

8. What techniques of legal description exist?

9. Why is title insurance important when lawyers have underlying malpractice insurance?

10. What are the most common disagreements that might arise relative to any agreement of sale?

11. What conditions or contingencies can be expected in a typical real estate transaction?

Practical Exercises

1. A broker receives a 6 percent commission on the sale of a house for $42,000. What is the amount of the commission? (The commission equals the sale price times the commission rate.)

2. If a broker received a commission of $8,000 on the sale of a property and his commission rate was 7 percent, what was the price of the house? (Selling price equals commission divided by commission rate.)

3. As a rule of calculation the following applies: Interest equals principal times rate times time. Find the interest on $2,000 at 6 percent per annum for three months.

4. Calculate the interest on $1,000 at 7 percent per annum for two months and five days.

5. Points or other origination charges are based on the value of the money borrowed. The term *two points* equals 2 percent. Four and one-half points equals 4½ percent. A loan amount is $110,000. If there is a two and one-half point origination fee, what will be its amount?

6. Most jurisdictions have a transfer tax of 1 or 2 percent. Solve the following problem: The sale price of a house is $300,000. The transfer tax rate is 2 percent. Calculate the transfer tax. If the transfer tax is to be split between seller and buyer, what will each have to pay?

7. Prorations are made on taxes, assessments, water bills, utilities, and possibly insurance. Prorations will be made on an annualized to daily basis. Calculate the following problem: With the fiscal year commencing July 1, 2007, the taxes are $312 and have not been paid. The home is sold, and the transaction closing took place on February 15, 2008. What amount would be credited to the buyer at closing?

8. Sale of a property is to take place on April 5, 2007. The 2006 tax bill was paid in full and equaled $462. The tax for 2007 is not known. Compute the prorated taxes that will be credited to a purchaser.[117]

9. Complete a blank settlement sheet based on the following facts:

    Settlement date: October 1, 2007
    Contract price: $47,000.00
    Two brokers—commission: 5% each
    Earnest money deposit: $3,000.00
    Amount to be mortgaged: None
    Yearly city/town taxes: $110.40 (paid in advance by seller)
    Yearly county taxes: $128.17 (not yet paid by seller)
    Yearly school tax: $647.28 (tax year July 1–June 30; not yet paid by seller)
    Closing fee: $100.00

Title examination fee: $50.00

Title insurance binder fee: $25.00

Title insurance fee: $141.00

Deed recording fee: $15.50

Transfer tax: 1% for seller; 1% for buyer

Pest inspection fee: $200.00 for seller, $50.00 for buyer

Internet Resources

National Association of Realtors—www.realtor.org

NAR Ebooks—ebooks.realtor.org

ABA Real Estate, Probate and Trust Section—www.abanet.org/rppt/home.html

American Land Title Association—www.alta.org/index.cfm

National Association of Insurance Commissioners—www.naic.org/

U.S. Department of Housing and Urban Development—www.hud.gov/

National Association of Mortgage Brokers—www.namb.org

National Association of Mortgage Field Services—www.namfs.org

Mortgage Bankers Association of America—www.mbaa.org

Home Inspectors Nationwide Directory—www.homeinspections-usa.com

National Association of Certified Home Inspectors—www.nachi.org

---

Endnotes

1. ILLINOIS PARALEGAL ASSOCIATION, THE FINDINGS OF THE COMPETENCY COMMITTEE RELATING TO THE QUALITY OF PARALEGAL SERVICES 58–61 (1989).

2. Illinois State Bar Association, *Use of Attorney Assistants in Real Estate Transactions*, ILL. B.J. 616 (August 1984).

3. Ellen S. Mahoney, *The Role of a Legal Assistant in Real Estate Practice*, MICH. B.J. 1159, 1160 (Nov. 1991).

4. Susan D. Carle, *Revaluing Lawyering for Middle-Income Clients*, 70 FORDHAM L. REV. 719 (2001).

5. HERBERT T. TIFFANY, THE LAW OF REAL PROPERTY AND OTHER INTERESTS IN LAND 4 (1970).

6. *Id.*

7. EDWARD WEICH, REAL ESTATE 1 (1975).

8. BRUCE T. HARWOOD, REAL ESTATE: AN INTRODUCTION TO THE PROFESSION 28 (1978).

9. NORTH CAROLINA BAR FOUNDATION AND THE REAL PROPERTY SECTION OF THE NORTH CAROLINA BAR ASSOCIATION, 1 NORTH CAROLINA REAL PROPERTY FORMS BOOKS, 9-1–9-2 (1987).

10. *See* THOMAS F. BERGIN & PAUL L. HASKELL, PREFACE IN LAND AND FURTHER INTERESTS 42 (1966).

11. FRANK W. KOVATS, PRINCIPLES AND PRACTICES OF NEW JERSEY REAL ESTATE 55 (1984).

12. *See* THOMAS F. BERGIN & PAUL L. HASKELL, PREFACE IN LAND AND FURTHER INTERESTS 37 (1966).

13. *Quantum or Character of Estate or Interest Created by Language Providing Premises as a Home, or Giving or Granting Same for Such Use*, 45 A.L.R.2d 699.

14. PENNSYLVANIA BAR INSTITUTE, REAL ESTATE PRACTICE 92 (1982).

15. *Lease Provisions Allowing Termination or Forfeiture for Violation of Law*, 92 A.L.R.3d 967.

16. Note, *Implied Warranty of Habitability, Doctrine in Residential Property Conveyances: Policy-Backed Change,* 62 WASH. L. REV. 742–743 (1947).

17. Christopher S. Brennan, *The Next Step in the Evolution of the Implied Warranty of Habitability: Applying the Warranty to Condominiums,* 67 FORDHAM L. REV. 3041 (1999).

18. PENNSYLVANIA BAR INSTITUTE, REAL ESTATE PRACTICE 98–99 (1982).

19. HERBERT T. TIFFANY, THE LAW OF REAL PROPERTY AND OTHER INTERESTS IN LAND 58–62 (1970).

20. *Id.* at 67–68.

21. THOMAS F. BERGIN & PAUL L. HASKELL, PREFACE IN LAND AND FUTURE INTERESTS 61 (1966).

22. HERBERT T. TIFFANY, THE LAW OF REAL PROPERTY AND OTHER INTERESTS IN LAND 79–83 (1970).

23. *Id.* at 89.

24. *Id.* at 102.

25. ROBERT BERNHARDT, REAL PROPERTY 44 (1975).

26. *Id.* at 45.

27. HERBERT T. TIFFANY, THE LAW OF REAL PROPERTY AND OTHER INTERESTS IN LAND 350 (1970).

28. Nancy A. McLaughlin, *Increasing the Tax Incentives for Conservation Easement Donations—A Responsible Approach,* 31 ECOLOGY L.Q. 1 (2004).

29. BRUCE T. HARWOOD, REAL ESTATE: AN INTRODUCTION TO THE PROFESSION 55–57 (1978).

30. *Oil and Gas Royalty as Real or Personal Property,* 56 A.L.R.4th 539.

31. THOMAS F. BERGIN & PAUL L. HASKELL, PREFACE IN LAND AND FUTURE INTERESTS 40 (1966).

32. WESLEY GILMER, THE LAW DICTIONARY 317 (1986).

33. Martin J. Foncello, *Adverse Possession and Takings Seldom Compensation for Chance Happenings,* 35 SETON HALL L. REV. 667 (2005).

34. HERBERT T. TIFFANY, THE LAW OF REAL PROPERTY AND OTHER INTERESTS IN LAND 160 (1970).

35. INSTITUTE FOR PARALEGAL TRAINING, INTRODUCTION TO REAL ESTATE LAW 137 (1978).

36. HERBERT T. TIFFANY, THE LAW OF REAL PROPERTY AND OTHER INTERESTS IN LAND 162 (1970).

37. *Id.* at 167.

38. Substitute Senate Bill No. 201, 1985.

39. INSTITUTE FOR PARALEGAL TRAINING, INTRODUCTION TO REAL ESTATE LAW 138 (1978).

40. INSTITUTE OF CONTINUING LEGAL EDUCATION, 1 MICHIGAN BASIC PRACTICE HANDBOOK 93 (1986).

41. HERBERT T. TIFFANY, THE LAW OF REAL PROPERTY AND OTHER INTERESTS IN LAND 184 (1970).

42. BRUCE T. HARWOOD, REAL ESTATE: AN INTRODUCTION TO THE PROFESSION 172 (1978).

43. Mark R. Hinkston, *Wisconsin's Revised Condominium Ownership Act,* WIS. LAW., Sept. 2004, at 10.

44. For example, *see* Wis. Stat. §703.15.

45. Preston Tower Condominium Association v. S. B. Realty, Inc., 685 S.W. 2d 98 (Tex. App. 1985).

46. Cambridge Co. v. East Slope Investment Corp., 700 P. 2d 537 (Colo. 1985).

47. INSTITUTE OF CONTINUING LEGAL EDUCATION, 1 MICHIGAN BASIC PRACTICE HANDBOOK 86 (1986).

48. *Id.* at 87.

49. INSTITUTE FOR PARALEGAL TRAINING, INTRODUCTION TO REAL ESTATE LAW 133 (1978).

50. Implied in the agency relationship is the fiduciary duty to each other. *See Failure of Real Estate Broker to Disclose to Principal Fee-Splitting Agreement with Adverse Party, or Adverse Party's Broker, as Breach of Fiduciary Duty Barring Claim for Commission,* 63 A.L.R.3d 1211.

51. INSTITUTE OF CONTINUING LEGAL EDUCATION, 1 MICHIGAN BASIC PRACTICE HANDBOOK 53 (1986).

52. CHARLES P. NEMETH, PA REAL ESTATE AGREEMENTS OF SALE 51 (1996).

53. CHARLES P. NEMETH, THE REALITY OF REAL ESTATE 18 (2000).

54. PENNSYLVANIA BAR INSTITUTE, REAL ESTATE PRACTICE 1 (1982).

55. INSTITUTE OF CONTINUING LEGAL EDUCATION, 1 MICHIGAN BASIC PRACTICE HANDBOOK 56 (1986).

56. JAMES A. WEBSTER JR., PATRICK K. HETRICK, & LARRY A. OUTLAW, NORTH CAROLINA REAL ESTATE FOR BROKERS AND SALESMEN 220 (3rd ed. 1986).

57. PENNSYLVANIA BAR INSTITUTE, REAL ESTATE PRACTICE 6 (1982).

58. CAROL K. IRVIN & JAMES D. IRVIN, OHIO REAL ESTATE LAW 74 (1982).

59. ROBERT BERNHARDT, REAL PROPERTY 256 (1975).

60. CAROL K. IRVIN & JAMES D. IRVIN, OHIO REAL ESTATE LAW 252 (1982).

61. H.E. HOAGLAND, LEO D. STONE, & WILLIAM BRUEGGEMAN, REAL ESTATE FINANCE 132 (1977).

62. Clover v. Grubbs, 367 Pa. 257 (1951).

63. Clearance E. Hagglund, *Caveat Emptor: Realty Purchaser's Duty to Investigate,* 20 REAL EST. L.J. 373 (1992).

64. PENNSYLVANIA BAR INSTITUTE, REAL ESTATE PRACTICE 9–10 (1982).

65. Hodorowicz v. Szulc, 16 Ill. App. 2d 317, 147 N.E. 2d 887, 889 (1958). *See also* Goldberg v. Abastasi, 272 Md. 61, 321 A. 2d 155 (1974).

66. Dodson v. Nink, 72 Ill. App. 3d 51, 390 N.E. 2d 546.

67. Dodson v. Nink, 72 Ill. App. 3d 51, 390 N.E. 2d 546, 550.

68. E.I. Du Pont, et al., v. Crompton-Townsend, Inc., No. C.A. 1284 (Superior Court of Del., New Castle County, 1976); *see also* Forrest Creek v. McLean Savings, 831 F. 2d 1238 (4th Cir. 1987). For a precise, rigid application of conditional principles, see Ditman v. Huyer, No. 990 (Ct. of Common Pleas of Greene County, Pa., November 3, 1988).

69. E.I. Du Pont, et al. v. Crompton-Townsend, Inc., No. C.A. 1284 at 26 (Superior Court of Del., New Castle County, 1976).

70. *Id.*

71. MILTON R. FRIEDMAN, CONTRACT AND CONVEYANCE OF REAL PROPERTY 123 (1979).

72. Pena v. Security Title Company, 267 S.W.2d 847 (Tex. Civ. App. 1954).

73. Pena v. Security Title Company, 267 S.W.2d 847, 848 (Tex. Civ. App. 1954).

74. Hodorowicz v. Szulc, 16 Ill. App. 2d 317, 147 N.E. 2d 887 (1958).

75. Hodorowicz v. Szulc, 16 Ill. App. 2d 317, 147 N.E. 2d 887, 888–889 (1958).

76. Fischer v. Kennedy, 106 Conn. 484, 138 A. 503 (1927).

77. Roberts v. Maxwell, 94 Ga. App. 406, 94 S.E. 2d 764 (1959).

78. *See* Title 42—The Public Health and Welfare, United States Code, available at http://www.access.gpo.gov/uscode/title42/title42.html.

79. PENNSYLVANIA BAR INSTITUTE, REAL ESTATE PRACTICE 14 (1982).

80. David Gee, *Time Is of the Essence of Real Estate Contracts,* 13 AM. JUR. PROOF OF FACTS 2d 585 (1987).

81. *See* Loper v. O'Rourke, 382 N.Y.S. 2d 663 (1976).

82. *See Sufficiency of Real Estate Buyer's Efforts to Secure Financing upon Which Sale Is Contingent,* 78 A.L.R.3d 880

83. David Gee, *Time Is of the Essence of Real Estate Contracts,* 13 AM. JUR. PROOF OF FACTS 2d 585, 589 (1987).

84. WESLEY GILMER, THE LAW DICTIONARY 219 (1986).

85. H.E. HOAGLAND, LEO D. STONE, & WILLIAM BRUEGGEMAN, REAL ESTATE FINANCE 39 (1977).

86. *Id.* at 42.

87. Jean Reilly, *Reverse Mortgages: Backing into the Future* 5 ELDER L.J. 17 (1997).

88. CAROL K. IRVIN & JAMES D. IRVIN, OHIO REAL ESTATE LAW 204 (1982).

89. *Id.* at 250.

90. *Id.*

91. CHARLES P. NEMETH, THE REALITY OF REAL ESTATE 95–96 (2000).

92. INSTITUTE FOR PARALEGAL TRAINING, INTRODUCTION TO REAL ESTATE LAW 101 (1978).

93. PENNSYLVANIA BAR INSTITUTE, REAL ESTATE PRACTICE 42 (1982).

94. TIMOTHY G. O'NEILL, 2 LADNER ON CONVEYANCING IN PENNSYLVANIA §19.20 (1988).

95. For a fascinating look at the impossibility of the perfect title, *see* Matthew Baker, Thomas J. Miceli, C.F. Sirmans, & Geoffrey K. Turnbull, *Optimal Title Search,* 31 J. LEGAL STUD. 139 (2002).

96. BRUCE T. HARWOOD, REAL ESTATE: AN INTRODUCTION TO THE PROFESSION 304–305 (1978).

97. *Handling Title Insurance Claims,* 15 AM. JUR. TRIALS 467–454 (1987).

98. Lawrence J. Nagy, *Evidence of Title in Residential Closings: Do Lenders Demand Too Much of Lawyers?* N.J. LAW. May–June 1993, at 29.

99. INSTITUTE FOR PARALEGAL TRAINING, INTRODUCTION TO REAL ESTATE LAW 110 (1978).

100. OHIO TRANSACTION GUIDE, CLOSING AND PROCEDURES RELATED TO CLOSING, §200.00.

101. JAMES A. WEBSTER JR., PATRICK K. HETRICK, & LARRY A. OUTLAW, NORTH CAROLINA REAL ESTATE FOR BROKERS AND SALESMEN 83 (1986).

102. EDWARD WEICH, REAL ESTATE 89 (1975).

103. JAMES A. WEBSTER JR., PATRICK K. HETRICK, & LARRY A. OUTLAW, NORTH CAROLINA REAL ESTATE FOR BROKERS AND SALESMEN 788 (1986).

104. ROBERT E. SCHREINER, REAL ESTATE CLOSINGS 197 (1983).

105. INSTITUTE OF CONTINUING LEGAL EDUCATION, MICHIGAN BASIC PRACTICE HANDBOOK 96 (1986).

106. Frances Crable, *Purchaser Not Ready, Willing, and Able to Make a Closing Payment,* 9 AM. JUR. PROOF OF FACTS 2d 123 (1987); *see also* 4 JOHN N. POMEROY, A TREATISE ON EQUITY JURISPRUDENCE, §1407 (5th ed. 1941).

107. *See* George A. Locke, *Vendor's Waiver of Strict Compliance with Terms of Land Sales Contracts,* 2 AM. JUR. PROOF OF FACTS 2d 137 (1987); Larry Ball, *Purchaser's Abandonment of a Land Sales Contract,* 5 AM. JUR. PROOF OF FACTS 2d 165 (1987); Larry Ball, *Inability to Clear Objectionable Title,* 5 AM. JUR. PROOF OF FACTS 2d 507 (1987).

108. ROBERT E. SCHREINER, REAL ESTATE CLOSINGS 223 (1983).

109. *Id.*

110. INSTITUTE OF CONTINUING LEGAL EDUCATION, 1 MICHIGAN BASIC PRACTICE HANDBOOK 98 (1986).

111. Helen W. Gunnarsson, *Watch Out for (Un)Real Estate Deals: Don't Let Your Clients Lead You Down the Road to a RESPA Violation by Misstating the Price of Real Estate,* 92 ILL. B.J. 337 (2004); *Unauthorized Practice of Law—Real Estate Closings,* 119 A.L.R.5th 191.

112. Janet Kennedy Dawson, *The Role of Laypersons in the Closing of Residential Real Estate Transactions: North Carolina's New Approach,* 7 N.C. BANKING INST. 277 (2003); Melissa K. Walker, *Sharing Their Piece of the Real Estate Pie: An Analysis of the Necessity of Lawyers at Residential Real Estate Closings in the Context of the Adoption of Recent Opinions of the North Carolina State Bar,* 26 CAMPBELL L. REV. 59 (2004); Joyce Palomar, *The War between Attorneys and Lay Conveyancers— Empirical Evidence Says "Cease Fire!"* 31 CONN. L. REV. 423 (1999).

113. WILLIAM F. HOFFMEYER, THE PENNSYLVANIA REAL ESTATE SETTLEMENT PROCEDURES MANUAL 68 (Mar. 1990).

114. Robert L. Flores, *A Comparison of the Rules and Rationales for Allocating Risks Arising in Realty Sales Using Executory Sale Contracts and Escrows,* 59 MO. L. REV. 307 (1994).

115. *See* Flow Chart, Tehama County Association of Realtors, 956 Walnut Street, Red Bluff, CA 96080; 530-529-0430; http://tcaor.com/PDF_Forms/Flow%20Chart.pdf.

116. INSTITUTE OF CONTINUING LEGAL EDUCATION, 1 MICHIGAN BASIC PRACTICE HANDBOOK 104 (1986).

117. For excellent problems in real estate mathematics, *refer to* M. FLOGERG, PRACTICE IN REAL ESTATE MATHEMATICS (1975).

Chapter 14

Civil Process, Litigation, and Pleadings

C. Interrogatories
D. Alternate Discovery Applications
1. Production of Documents
2. Rule 35: Request for Physical and Mental Examination
3. Rule 36: Request for Admissions
4. Stipulations

V. Motion Practice
A. Motions on Pleadings
B. Motions on the Parties
C. Other Technical Motions
1. Statute of Limitations
2. Motion to Consolidate
3. Motions for Discovery
4. Motion *Nunc Pro Tunc*
D. Miscellaneous Motions
1. Motion for a Continuance
2. Motion in Limine
3. Motion for a Summary Judgment
4. Motion for a Default Judgment
5. Motion for Directed Verdict
E. Postjudgment Motions—Motion to Reconsider or Reargue

VI. Trial
A. The Paralegal's Role in Trial Preparation
1. Assistance with Witnesses
2. Jury Verdict Analysis and Voir Dire
3. Trial Notebook
4. Document Production
5. Trial Equipment
6. Jury Instructions
B. Posttrial Activities
1. Judgments
2. Appeals

VII. Summary

Discussion Questions

 CIVIL LITIGATION PARALEGAL JOB DESCRIPTION

Civil litigation paralegals need to be proficient in the following competencies:

- Arrange for outside investigators.
- Handle computerized research for source materials.
- Conduct factual research.
- Conduct initial client interviews.
- Draft demand letters.
- Photograph accident scenes, evidence, and parties.
- Locate, interview, and obtain statements of witnesses.
- Trace documents and physical evidence.
- Search records from private and public sources.
- Draft documents, including complaints, answers, interrogatories, requests for production of documents, requests for examination, requests for admissions, affidavits, motions for extension of time, trial briefs, voir dire questions, jury instructions, and so on.

- Review client files and gather and organize factual data.
- Prepare and serve subpoenas and subpoena *duces tecum*.
- Index and abstract documents.
- Review documents for response to production requests.
- Prepare statistical and economic information.
- Review and summarize medical and other records.
- Index and summarize depositions and deposition exhibits.
- Stay current with procedures of local, state, and federal courts.
- Organize witness files.
- Arrange for publication of legal notices.
- Maintain court calendar (docket) on tickler system.
- Arrange for extensions of time by telephone, letter, or motion.
- Meet with clients to prepare answers to interrogatories; obtain clients' documents to be produced: medical records, wage and wage loss information, tax statements, photographs, bills or expenses that were incurred because of the lawsuits, and the like.
- Attend and organize document productions.
- Attend on-site and expert inspections.
- Prepare, organize, and supervise document control systems.
- Create databases and procedures for computerized systems.
- Input information into computer systems.
- Research facts for depositions.
- Draft outlines and questions for depositions.
- Prepare witnesses for depositions.
- Schedule, attend, and take notes at depositions.
- Organize exhibits and request copies of transcripts.
- Follow up after depositions for additional information.
- Segregate and record documents not to be produced as well as privileged materials for attorney review.
- Locate expert witnesses, interview them, and prepare written reports.
- Prepare statistical and factual memoranda.
- Prepare case status reports to be submitted to clients.
- Compile product history and obtain information about similar products, market surveys, and industrial statistics in product liability cases.
- Draft legal memoranda or briefs.
- Perform legal research, check citations, and Shepardize.
- Review and analyze cases continually for further discovery.
- Prepare and exchange lists of names of witnesses and exhibits.
- Prepare trial notebooks and witness files.
- Prepare graphs, charts, and the like.
- Arrange for court reporters and computerized transcripts.
- Prepare, mark, and index exhibits.
- Prepare outlines of anticipated testimony.
- Meet with witnesses, help prepare witness and client testimony, and coordinate attendance at trial.
- Analyze video and audio evidence at trial.
- Draft pretrial statements, settlement calculations (including comparative analyses of potential settlement terms), and settlement conference memoranda.
- Obtain jury lists and perform biographical research on jurors.
- Draft bills of costs.
- Draft settlement documents, including releases, dismissals, and satisfaction.
- Maintain list of exhibits offered, admitted, or objected to.
- Prepare digests, abstracts, indexes, and summaries of transcripts.
- Help in jury selection: Prepare voir dire questions, observe jurors' reactions and responses, and review and analyze jurors' questionnaires.

- Attend trial: Take notes of testimony and reactions of jurors, witnesses, and counsel; organize exhibits and documents; coordinate witnesses and experts.
- Prepare drafts of document lists and testimony used to impeach opposition witnesses.
- Help prepare witnesses.
- Gather documents and pertinent information with which to familiarize witnesses with case issues and facts.
- Draft notices of appeal.
- Order hearing transcripts; prepare recaps or outlines of transcripts.
- Set up timetables for filings.
- Check citations in and Shepardize. briefs.
- Prepare records for appeals.

THE PARALEGAL'S ROLE IN CIVIL PROCESS, LITIGATION, AND PLEADINGS

The American justice system is adversarial in nature: It is a place of verbal and analytical combat. A victim, claimant, or other legal entity, called a *plaintiff,* makes another party, called a *defendant,* the target of a lawsuit, criminal action, or equitable remedy. Attorneys are known as *counsel* and may represent either side. Between these competing interests is a judge who acts, not strictly as a mediator, but as a boundary between the two. The judge is an instructor on the law and acts like a legal ringmaster attempting to provide balance in the courtroom. The decision makers, members of a jury, are known as *jurors.* Their verdicts are the hallmark of Western jurisprudence. In the American courtroom the right side of the courtroom is where the plaintiff is settled with counsel; the left is where the defendant sits. The judge sits in between, within the neutral zone; the jury sits in a box to the side, usually on a platform.

Whether working for defendant or plaintiff, the paralegal influences the flow of litigation. In a civil action, where a person alleges a personal harm or wrong (such as in a product liability case), a burden of proof of "preponderance of evidence" or "clear and convincing proof" must be met by the plaintiff. In a criminal case, the burden of proof means proof "beyond a reasonable doubt." The adversarial process requires one party to prove a legal or factual assertion while the other party attempts to rebut the assertion. The adversarial system is also affected by burdens of persuasion—a key evidentiary issue in collateral legal issues. For example, in affirmative defenses in criminal and civil cases, the burden of persuasion may rest upon a defendant who alleges that he or she is insane or who claims that jurisdictional defenses or other procedural or substantive matters have a bearing on innocence. Presumptions also exist within the adversarial system, such as the presumption of innocence in criminal litigation, as well as the presumption of sanity and the presumption of competence.

In American litigation dual representation and advocacy are both permissible and fostered. Two sides of a story are allowed to be told, permitting challenge, direct questioning, cross-examination, and a testing of human and evidentiary credibility. Litigation is a study of conduct between defense and prosecution, as well as the role and responsibilities of the judiciary. Litigation's thrust is procedural. How a case can commence, how it can be argued, and how it can be advocated are procedural questions in the civil and criminal systems. How defendants and plaintiffs adjudicate their claims is largely determined by established rules of trial advocacy and conduct. Litigation is governed by rules, standards, and guidelines at both the state and federal levels. On the federal level, such rules are found in the Federal Rules of Evidence (Fed. R. Evid.), Federal Rules of Civil Procedure (Fed. R. Civ. P.), Federal Rules of Criminal Procedure (Fed. R. Crim. P.), and Federal Rules of Appellate Procedure (Fed. R. App. P.).

How litigation is conducted depends not only on these formal guidelines but also on an understanding of what an adversarial action is. Milford Meyer discusses litigation as follows:

> *The trial of a lawsuit is an adversary business. It is not a disinterested investigation.*
> *The object of war is to defeat the enemy.*
> *The aim of the legal system is to achieve justice, but the advocate's role in that system is to achieve the best possible result for his client without departing from established principles and the standards of ethics of his profession.*[1]

If litigation is a war, what are the rules of war? If litigation is an antagonistic, adversarial process, what boundaries of conduct do lawyers and paralegals heed? A "winning at all costs" mentality may produce the results a plaintiff desires but could tarnish the reputation of the justice system. Though to be adversarial is not to be unethical, this mentality is eventually self-destructive. James W. McElheney calls for zealous adherence to ethical and human principles:

> *Finally having a reputation with the judges and lawyers in the community for being scrupulously fair and honest, also being thought of as a man who truly "knows the law," is more valuable than rubies. A judge is sometimes called the thirteenth juror. No matter if the local rules forbid the judge from commenting on the weight of the evidence, if the judge thinks you are fair and honest. it will show in subtle little ways that will influence the jury throughout its deliberations.*[2]

The entire field of litigation and advocacy is guided not only by technical rules of application, but also by ethical dimensions, competency, integrity, and professional demeanor.[3] Paralegals must be careful and cautious about their respective scope. Advocacy is the province of the attorney. Litigation support implies supervision from an attorney. Indeed it is unfortunate that so many of today's litigators cannot connect notions of truth with fervent representation. Daniel Walfish notes eloquently that lawyers and judges fail to "seriously address the issue of a lawyer's responsibility for truth in an adversarial system."[4] Criticism of the adversary system may have resulted more from the personal failures of lawyers rather than from the system itself. Arthur R. Miller of Harvard University states in "The Adversary System: Dinosaur or Phoenix,"

> *The inability of the American judicial system to adjudicate civil disputes economically and efficiently is one of the most pressing issues facing the court today. It is axiomatic that justice delayed is justice denied. From the perspective of most people ensnared in the litigation process, a half-decade wait for the resolution of a serious dispute is intolerable.*[5]

Miller characterizes judicial gridlock as being prompted chiefly by lawyers and judges. The burden of guilt for the failures of the American justice system must be spread among all the parties. Public perceptions about the American justice system are not high. Lawyers and judges alike, in terms of their reputation and status, rank very low in both quantitative and qualitative studies. Others tie the decline of professionalism to an abdication of what it means to be in or of a profession.

> *Another important factor leading to the observed declines in civility and professionalism is the increasingly national character of law practice. The expansion of the market for legal services from being local to being national in scope contributes to the decline in civility and professionalism in at least three ways. First, by reducing the amount of "repeat dealing" that occurs among opposing counsel, national practice reduces the costs to attorneys of bad behavior because few, if any, social sanctions, such as stigma or ostracism, emerge to constrain behavior.*[6]

The historical controls of the professional class have been thrown overboard, and as a result, there is a marked decrease in "empathy and camaraderie among lawyers."[7]

J. Michael McWilliams, past president of the American Bar Association, labels the current situation a "justice deficit." "The central message emerging from the survey is unmistakable: The justice system in many parts of the United States is on the verge of collapse due to both inadequate funding and unbalanced funding."[8] The recurring criticism that the system is suffering from a litigation explosion lacks uniform support. Undeniably caseloads have increased, but whether this growth is out of control is debatable. Former American Trial Lawyers Association (ATLA) president Roxanne Barton Conlin states,

> *Recent empirical studies continue to explode popular myths about the civil justice system.*
>
> *These new studies reconfirm that there is no "explosion" of tort cases threatening the viability of America's courts and businesses. In fact, there never has been.*
>
> *The new studies address state court caseloads, punitive damages, verdicts and actual payments, levels of injury compensation, and the amount of business litigation claiming judicial resources. Conclusions from these studies contrast sharply with folklore perpetuated by tort system critics. It is time for detractors of the U.S. civil justice system to focus on the facts that independent researchers have uncovered.*[9]

The shortcomings of the adversarial system are a subject of dramatic concern to all members of the legal community, including paralegals. The American College of Trial Lawyers and the America Law Institute comment,

> *Even a brief survey makes it clear that the American legal profession and the legal system confront a period of major turmoil and change. For the system to retain its vitality, a change within the framework of the high ethical principles that have guided it in the past must occur through the informed efforts of the profession itself. Perhaps the greatest problem facing us is to insure that principles do not fall to the demand for efficiency. Only by sponsoring needed reforms can the legal profession itself control the process of change and insure the continuity of the present system. If we fail to make the changes from within, they will come about from without, with danger to the continuity of the guiding ethical principles that set our profession apart from all other professions.*[10]

Whatever merits this argument and discussion may have, its chief purpose edifies the dilemma: that the critique is now generally systematic.[11] The paralegal must contribute to the betterment of the process. Paralegals, like other nonlawyers, will play a critical role in the reformation of an overburdened system. Herbert Kritzer lumps paralegals into the new track known as a "law worker."[12] It is agreed that the process moves too slowly and that the existing technical and procedural rules need refinement and improvement. Continuous efforts are made to improve the efficacy and direction of the legal system. The paralegal profession and the direction in which it is going are clearly integral contributors to that process.

This chapter will examine civil procedure guidelines—a series of technical and procedural precepts that outline the processes of litigation and pleadings preparation. Discovery techniques and other pretrial activities, as well as trial and posttrial sequences, will be assessed and analyzed. Because paralegals must prepare pleadings, litigation paperwork, and other documentation, the chapter's approach is practical. The Federal Rules of Civil Procedure are used as a model because most states have either adopted or imitated the content of these rules.

LITIGATION: SOME PRELIMINARY CONSIDERATIONS

Selecting a Forum

Choosing a suitable court for resolution of a legal matter is known as *choice of forum* or the *establishment of jurisdiction*. The place or locality in which a case belongs can be either exclusive or multiple. In other words, lawyers often have a choice of where a case can be litigated. Definitionally, the forum is the place where plaintiffs and defendants can adjudicate and litigate their claims. Choosing the correct forum depends on some of the following tactical factors.

Jurisdiction

Jurisdiction is the power or authority of a court to hear or decide a given case or question of fact or law. In exercising jurisdiction, a court proclaims by legislative right some legal entitlement or control over a particular subject matter or territory, or over specific parties or actions. The Supreme Court of the United States has what is known as *original jurisdiction* in the following cases:

> (a) *The Supreme Court shall have original and exclusive jurisdiction of all controversies between two or more states.*
> (b) *The Supreme Court shall have original but not exclusive jurisdiction of*
>   (1) *All actions or proceedings to which ambassadors, other public ministers, consuls, or vice consuls of foreign states are parties;*
>   (2) *All controversies between the United States and a state;*
>   (3) *All actions or proceedings by a state against the citizens of another state or against aliens.*[13]

Another option for the Supreme Court is to exercise jurisdiction under the doctrine of certiorari (discussed in detail in Chapter 3).

Jurisdiction may also exist exclusively in a particular tribunal or court and to the detriment of any other legal power or authority. Exclusive jurisdiction is usually achieved by legislative grant:

Federal tax questions: U.S. Tax Court

Federal questions: U.S. District Court

Patents and trademarks: U.S. Patent and Trademark Court

Tort actions against the United States: U.S. Court of Claims

Military justice: U.S. Court of Military Appeals

Subject matter jurisdiction is another example of forum or locale election. This type of jurisdiction has also been referred to as *in rem* (over the subject matter) jurisdiction. Tax courts, for example, have subject matter control over tax litigation, as do patent courts over patents. Jurisdiction also can be based *in personam*—that is, "over the person" where an act has occurred, where the party resides, or where the person is within the territorial limits of a particular court. Selected courts have specific subject matter jurisdiction, such as family or juvenile law courts. Other examples of subject matter courts are wills and trusts; probate or surrogates courts; crimes; courts of common pleas; criminal divisions; youth crime; juvenile courts of appeals; and superior, supreme, or other appellate division courts. Courts also can be forums of general jurisdiction, handling any form of case in law and equity.

Most trial courts at the state level are considered courts of general jurisdiction because they have criminal, civil, and equitable divisions. Jurisdiction also depends on locality or geography—the most obvious distinction being our dual federal/state system. The jurisdiction of a state court rests in its locality or territorial area. Citizens of the state must opt for this forum in first order (initially) unless the legal issues are not state-oriented and are typified as federal questions, or the parties exercise diversity jurisdiction (in which the parties to a suit are citizens of different states).

On many occasions, a plaintiff or defendant may have a multiplicity of claims or causes of action that are both federal and nonfederal in nature. Because of this dual status, claimants sometimes forum-shop and elect the forum that offers the most favorable legal precedent. The proliferation of cases at the federal level in which other jurisdictional bases can be founded is testimony to this practice.

Federal Jurisdiction Federal jurisdiction can be based on any of the following theories:

- Cases presenting questions arising under the Constitution, laws, or treaties of the United States (a federal question).
- Cases involving sums of more than $75,000.
- Cases involving differing geographic jurisdictions involving diversity of citizenship.
- Cases of original jurisdiction.

It is not difficult to get into a federal court.[14] For example, if you are from the state of Hawaii and are driving your car and are hit by someone from the state of Nebraska and the damages exceed the sum of $75,000, you can get into a federal court based on a diversity principle.[15] At 28 U.S.C. Section 1332, the diversity requirement is outlined:

> (a) *The district courts shall have original jurisdiction of all civil actions where the matter in controversy exceeds the sum or value of $75,000, exclusive of interest and costs, and is between—*
> (1) *Citizens of different states;*
> (2) *Citizens of a state and citizens or subjects of a foreign state;*
> (3) *Citizens of different states and in which citizens or subjects of a foreign state are additional parties; and*
> (4) *A foreign state, defined in Section 1603(a) of this title [28 U.S.C.S. §1603(a)], as plaintiff and citizens of a state or of different states.*[16]

The ease in which federal jurisdiction can be asserted has resulted in staggering workloads for most American federal judges. According to Judge Thomas R. MacMillan, almost 12,000 cases were filed in the federal court in Chicago in 1985. The typical federal judge rendered three or four substantive decisions every week while disposing of more than 40 new cases every month.[17]

A comparison data chart compiled by the director of the administrative offices of the United States courts is reproduced in Figure 14.1.[18] The monumental increase in cases from 1990 through 2000 is illustrated.

Figure 14.1 also reveals the nature of jurisdiction based on a finding of federal question or dispute. Federal courts have original jurisdiction over federal questions. By most accounts, the

FIGURE 14.1
U.S. District Court, Civil Filings, September 1990–2000

Source: What Has Contributed to a Decade of Increasing Civil Case Filings? THE THIRD BRANCH (Admin. Office of the U.S. Courts, Washington, D.C.) Dec. 2001, available at http://www.uscourts.gov/ttb/dec01ttb/filings.html, last visited 1/17/05.

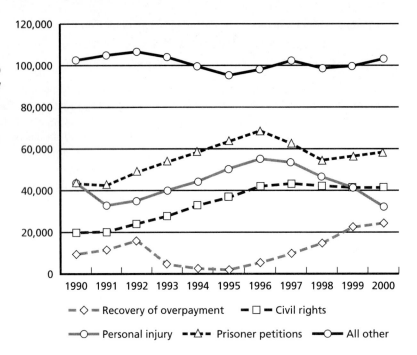

reach of the legislative tentacles of federal law is incalculable. Issues of constitutional dimension involving privacy, free speech, civil rights, and procedural challenge tend to have a federal nexus, as do tax matters, environmental concerns, work and safety standards, and a whole array of other legislative, administrative, and governmental activities. An assertion that a federal claim, question, or issue exists is not a secondary challenge or extraneous matter. Instead "the federal claim must be a substantial one rather than a superficial claim that is being used merely as an excuse for finding federal jurisdiction over a state claim."[19] Often there is crossover between cases that are primarily federal yet still have a state flavor.

Another permissible form of jurisdiction based on overlapping jurisdictional rights between state and federal courts is pendent jurisdiction. The exercise of pendent jurisdiction is complex for advocates. In *United Mine Workers v. Gibbs*[20] the Supreme Court set out certain guidelines to help resolve competing claims at the federal and state level:

(a) *If the state law claim is such that there is a strong need for the expertise of the state courts to correctly adjudicate it, then the federal court should not entertain that claim.*

(b) *If the state issues dominate the case… in terms of proof of the scope of the issues raised or of the comprehensiveness of the remedies sought, the state claims may be dismissed without prejudice and left for resolution for the state tribunals.*

(c) *If the case involves the question of whether federal law has preempted the field to the exclusion of state law, it is very appropriate for the district court to exercise its pendent jurisdiction and examine both the state and federal elements so that a federal forum can resolve the preemption problems.*

(d) *If the exercise of jurisdiction over both the state and federal elements would lead to confusion of the jury, the state element should not be entertained. Confusion exists when the jury is unable to tell which standards of liability and damages apply to which aspects of the case.*[21]

Form 14.1 on the accompanying CD includes an allegation of jurisdiction based on diversity and amount. If jurisdiction is challenged, a motion may be made to dismiss a complaint based on a lack of jurisdiction over the subject or the person.[22] Cases improperly filed within the state court may, upon a petition to transfer, be moved to a federal court.[23] A writ of mandamus is an alternative procedure for the change of jurisdiction.[24]

State Jurisdiction State jurisdiction basically entails state matters, granting jurisdiction on geographic subject matter and other bases. A federal court will remand a case to the state court if at any time before final judgment it finds that the cause has been removed improvidently and without jurisdiction.[25]

Venue

In addition to a jurisdictional change, an argument based on venue can be made. Venue is closely aligned to jurisdiction. It determines the proper location for litigation based on efficiency and justice. The American Law Institute points out several factors pertinent to a motion for a change of venue, including "whether physical evidence is more accessible in the transferee district than in the transferor district, whether more witnesses are residents of the transferee district than the transferor district, and whether testimony could be presented live in the new district rather than by deposition as it would have been in the old district."[26] A sample motion to dismiss based on improper venue is provided in Form 14.2 on the accompanying CD. The most common justification for a venue change is based on unreasonable, prejudicial trial publicity.

Identification of the Parties

All litigation requires the attorney and paralegal to identify the eligible plaintiffs and defendants to the action. It should never be assumed that only one plaintiff or defendant is involved. Consider the following fact pattern to discern the potential plaintiffs and defendants:

Harry Simms was driving his car on Route 94, a poorly maintained state highway in the Commonwealth of Virginia. Harry was driving his car in a safe, reasonable fashion and is not contributorily or comparatively negligent. Coming around the bend traveling at 10 miles over the speed limit was one John Simons, whose car went out of control and smashed into Harry's car, causing many injuries and damages to both property and person. Because of the collision, Harry's car's gas tank exploded, and Harry lost complete control of the vehicle. He was able, however, to alight from the vehicle, even though he suffered substantial burns and other injuries. Harry's sudden stop on this state highway caused three other individuals to collide into a guardrail, all of whom suffered extensive injuries.

Who would the potential plaintiffs be under this factual scenario? Would they include Harry? Would they be the three individuals who suffered injuries because of the negligence of John Simons?

Are there any other potential plaintiff actions brought because of the conduct of John Simons? What about the state highway authority for the destruction of its guardrail and other property? What about the costs of repairs? Should the negligent party be responsible? Who are the potential defendants? Is it John? Is it the state highway authority? Is it the manufacturer of Harry's car? Is it John Simons's automobile manufacturer?

Link all the factors in this case. Why did Harry's gas tank explode? Although John was negligent for exceeding the speed limit and not exercising the due care and standard of conduct necessary to respect the rights of other people and property, was his speed so excessive as to make him totally liable for the incident? If the highway was poorly maintained, poorly designed, engineered with defects in turn angle, or constructed without proper safeguards, is it possible to sue a governmental entity that is responsible for the road? Is there any likelihood that this event could have been prevented by a proper braking and rollover automotive design? What if John's accelerator locked?

Clearly such analysis is extensive, but the potentiality of prospective parties can turn into actual ones. The lesson here is to think about the case on an extended basis, developing a causation chart of all parties to whom responsibility could be attributed. In the selection of defendants, "the plaintiff attorney must be sure that the defendants named are both viable and liable. Viable defendants are those whom it will not prove fruitless to sue. If some absolute defense exists barring the imposition of liability on a potential defendant, that defendant absent a change in law will neither be viable nor liable."[27] The identification of defendants in a typical automobile negligence case could include other drivers, a person who has placed a hazard in a road as a practical joke, employers who have hired individuals to drive their automobiles during their employment, or a tavern owner or other party who has sufficiently contributed to the defendant's state of intoxication.[28]

Medical malpractice defendants might include physicians, nurses, hospital medical assistants, emergency personnel, health maintenance organizations (HMOs), manufacturers of medical equipment, medical service providers, medical suppliers, independent contracting medical consultants, professional corporations, or any other medical personnel.

A search for potential defendants must also occur in a product liability analysis. If a product or design is claimed to be defective, who is the party to be sued? Parties might include retailers, manufacturers, designers, distributors, component part manufacturers, wholesalers, material suppliers, deliverers, and so on.[29] Every action should be prosecuted in the name of the real party in interest. An executor, administrator, guardian, bailee, trustee of an express trust, a party with whom or in whose name a contract has been made for the benefit of another, or a party authorized by statute may sue in that person's own name without joining the party for whose benefit the action is brought; and when a statute of the United States so provides, an action for the use or benefit of another should be brought in the name of the United States. No action will be dismissed on the ground that it is not prosecuted in the name of the real party in interest until a reasonable time has been allowed after objection for ratification of commencement of the action by, or joinder or substitution of, the real party in interest; and such ratification, joinder, or substitution will have the same effect as if the action had been commenced in the name of the real party in interest.[30]

Third Party Practice

A complete acknowledgment of all potential defendants or plaintiffs depends on third party analysis. Third parties may be brought willingly and unwillingly into litigation. Under the Federal Rules, this is often referred to as the *process of joinder*. Under the philosophical foundation of the Federal Rules, parties who have a stake in the outcome of any case can be permissibly joined. At Rule 19, the language provides,

> *Persons to Be Joined if Feasible. A person who is subject to service of process and whose joinder will not deprive the court of jurisdiction over the subject matter of the action shall be joined as a party in the action if (1) in the person's absence complete relief cannot be accorded among those already parties, or (2) the person claims an interest relating to the subject of the action and is so situated that the disposition of the action in the person's absence may (i) as a practical matter impair or impede the person's ability to protect that interest or (ii) leave any of the persons already parties subject to a substantial risk of incurring double, multiple, or otherwise inconsistent obligations by reason of the claimed interest. If the person has not been so joined, the court shall order that the person be made a party. If the person should join as a plaintiff but refuses to do so, the person may be made a defendant, or, in a proper case, an involuntary plaintiff. If the joined party objects to venue and joinder of that party would render the venue of the action improper, that party shall be dismissed from the action.[31]*

Under Rule 21 of the Federal Rules of Civil Procedure, improper joinder is discussed:

> *Misjoinder of parties is not ground for dismissal of an action. Parties may be dropped or added by order of the court on motion of any party or of its own initiative at any stage of the action and on such terms as are just. Any claim against a party may be severed and proceeded with separately.[32]*

Joinder may be requested for fraudulent purposes. If multiple parties are involved, a given defendant or plaintiff may duplicitously agree to a claim of diversity[33]—all the while agreeing not to pursue on another but target only the remaining parties. The intent here is to find a more agreeable court.[34]

A complaint, interpleader, or other declaratory relief may draw in third parties in a search for a justiciable resolution. Rule 22 states specifically,

> (1) *Persons having claims against the plaintiff may be joined as defendants and required to interplead when their claims are such that the plaintiff is or may be exposed to double or multiple liability. It is not ground for objection to the joinder that the claims of the several claimants or the titles on which their claims depend do not have a common origin or are not identical but are adverse to and independent of one another, or that the plaintiff avers that the plaintiff is not liable in whole or in part to any or all of the claimants. A defendant exposed to similar liability may obtain such interpleader by way of cross-claim or counterclaim. The provisions of this rule supplement and do not in any way limit the joinder of parties permitted in Rule 20.*
>
> (2) *The remedy herein provided is in addition to and in no way supersedes or limits the remedy provided by Title 28, U.S.C.§§ 1335, 1397, and 2361. Actions under those provisions shall be conducted in accordance with these rules.[35]*

Litigants are expected to use a summons to put third parties on notice of an impending action. A third party summons and illustrative examples of interpleader complaints are shown in Forms 14.3, 14.4, and 14.5 on the accompanying CD.

Class Action

Another special situation emerging in the identification of parties to a civil action involves the finding of a class of plaintiffs or defendants. Under Rule 23 of the Federal Rules, a *class action* is maintainable if the following elements are satisfied:

> *Class Actions Maintainable. An action may be maintained as a class action if the prerequisites of subdivision (a) are satisfied, and in addition*
>
> (1) *the prosecution of separate actions by or against individual members of the class would create a risk of*
>> (A) *inconsistent or varying adjudications with respect to individual members of the class which would establish incompatible standards of conduct for the party opposing the class, or*
>> (B) *adjudications with respect to individual members of the class which would as a practical matter be dispositive of the interests of the other members not parties to the adjudications or substantially impair or impede their ability to protect their interests; or*
>
> (2) *the party opposing the class has acted or refused to act on grounds generally applicable to the class, thereby making appropriate final injunctive relief or corresponding declaratory relief with respect to the class as a whole; or*
>
> (3) *the court finds that the questions of law or fact common to the members of the class predominate over any questions affecting only individual members, and that a class action is superior to other available methods for the fair and efficient adjudication of the controversy. The matters pertinent to the findings include (A) the interest of members of the class in individually controlling the prosecution or defense of separate actions; (B) the extent and nature of any litigation concerning the controversy already commenced by or against members of the class; (C) the desirability or undesirability of concentrating the litigation of the claims in the particular forum; (D) the difficulties likely to be encountered in the management of a class action.*[36]

Class actions can be found in cases of consumer litigation, civil rights violations, serious public nuisance, and other cases with similarly situated persons.[37] The finding of a class recognizes that singular adjudication of claims would be so impractical, inefficient, and duplicitous that it would place an extraordinary strain on the entire legal system.[38] One party becomes the "represented" plaintiff for all other plaintiffs who are similarly situated. Certain specific legal requirements must be met to qualify as class action. Paralegals can help with the research and preparing pleadings in the determination of classes (see Forms 14.6 and 14.7 on the accompanying CD). Those recommending that a class be found have to clarify that the finding will result in a fair resolution of claims for multiple parties.

Alternatives to Legal Remedies

Equitable Remedies

It is well known that most American jurisdictions have merged legal and equitable principles. Equitable remedies are "a type of justice that developed separately from the common law, and which tends to complement it. The current meaning is to classify disputes and remedies according to their historical relationship and development. Under modern rules of civil procedure, law and equity have been unified."[39] Certain remedies are permissible under an equity jurisdiction, including injunctions, restraining orders, and orders of specific performance. Because *equity* can take on several meanings, it is advisable to narrow the particular meaning one attributes to this term in a given context. One commentator has identified the following different senses for *equity* (excluding the meaning relating to mortgaged property): what is fair and just; natural law; a system of law that corrects failures of justice in a main body of the law; and a body of legal precepts that introduces into law.[40] In cases of extreme hardship, danger, damage, and loss, the law's slow pace does not provide a remedy, but equity may. In cases in which the damage is ongoing and continuous (such as personal service contracts, nuisances, or trespass), the law does not always remedy the situation. Paralegals are more likely to be involved with equitable principles if they specialize in real estate, domestic relations, and labor law. When a continuing trespass encroaches upon a neighbor's property, a remedy of a temporary restraining order or an injunction may be proper. When picketers are blocking the entrance to an industrial complex, hospital, or other subject of protest, an equitable remedy will often be the strategy of choice.

A list of regularly drafted equitable actions follows:

- Motion for preliminary injunction (see Form 14.8 on the accompanying CD).
- Motion for temporary restraining order (see Form 14.9).
- Temporary restraining order (see Form 14.10).
- Complaint for temporary restraining order and preliminary and permanent injunction (see Form 14.11).
- Petition or application for writ of mandamus.
- Writ of quo warranto.

Equitable remedies and principles are subject to extraordinary judicial discretion. As Robert Cover, Owen M. Fiss, and Judith Resnik comment,

> Note . . . the variety of remedies possible and the substantial discretion of judges when selecting remedies. Further, consider the function of a remedy. Are the goals to respond to the damage inflicted? To prevent future harm? To deter others? To punish the wrongdoer?
>
> Difficulty in accomplishing these goals will vary with the nature of the defendant; a single individual may be more easily deterred or punished than an enterprise, whose behavior comprises actions of a myriad of individuals.[41]

Alternative Dispute Resolution (ADR)

Legal and equitable remedies are not the exclusive means of dispute resolution. An enhanced emphasis on alternative dispute resolution (ADR) now exists. "The growth has been attributed to a number of circumstances—first, problematic and sometimes staggering court backlog has been the impetus for designing alternative dispute resolution mechanisms and for diverting cases to them; secondly, the costs of prolonged litigation have prompted the consideration of alternatives to traditional judicial proceedings; and finally, there is a growing recognition that not all complaints require adversarial setting for their resolution and that, in some circumstances, such a setting may actually be detrimental to reaching a satisfactory resolution as receptivity to innovative mechanics increases."[42] Federal courts have instituted court-annexed arbitration, which provides for the involuntary assignment of an eligible case. Procedural rules are relaxed, and the Federal Rules of Evidence are generally used as guides rather than strict rules of admissibility. The power of subpoena is enforceable. A panel of three arbitrators hears the testimony of the parties and their witnesses. If a party is dissatisfied with the award, it may reject it by demanding a formal trial de novo within a set period (usually 30 days). If such a demand is not filed, the arbitration award will be entered as a judgment of the court after the expiration of the 30 days. The judgment has the same force and effect as any civil judgment, except that it is not appealable. If a trial de novo is granted, the court may not admit evidence regarding the arbitration proceeding.[43] The U.S. Department of Justice has been promoting alternative dispute resolution through its Federal Mediation and Conciliation Service. The Civil Justice Reform Act of 1990[44] requires "each federal district court to develop a civil justice delay-and-expense-reduction including consideration of the use of ADR."[45] Private sector involvement in dispute resolution has been substantial, including these groups: the American Bar Association Special Committee on Alternative Dispute Resolution; the American Arbitration Association; the National Institute for Dispute Resolution; the Better Business Bureau Arbitration Panel; JUDICATE: The National Court System; United States Arbitration and Mediation; JAMS/Endispute; and U.S. Mediation.

There are a variety of programs available. Figure 14.2 shows explanatory literature disseminated by one of the providers.

Alternative dispute mechanisms are relatively recent phenomena:

- Why is there such a drive toward the privatization of dispute resolution?
- Does arbitration really play a significant role in the reduction of court overload at both the federal and state levels?
- Is alternative dispute resolution merely a panacea or an anathema to our historical method of dispute resolution?
- Is it more costly or more efficient?
- Has there been an objective, quantifiable assessment of the arbitration process?[46]

FIGURE 14.2   **How Predispute Arbitration Works**

Source: © National Arbitration Forum. National Arbitration Forum, P.O. Box 50191, Minneapolis, MN 55405-0191.

> People agree to use arbitration in a contract, such as the contract signed when purchasing a car or found on a sales invoice or notice from a bank.
>
> Arbitration is used only when people have a legal dispute they cannot settle on their own.
>
> Typically, to begin an arbitration, one party completes an arbitration claim form, files it with the arbitration administrator, and pays a filing fee, if any. The other party responds.
>
> In some systems the parties can have a document hearing, where an arbitrator studies the paperwork or electronic documents submitted by each party, makes a decision, and issues an arbitration award.
>
> Or the parties could opt for a participatory hearing, where each party submits evidence and appears before an arbitrator who studies the evidence, makes a decision, and issues an arbitration award.
>
> The arbitration decision or award is legally enforceable and often reviewable by the courts.

According to the U.S. Department of Justice's *Dispute Resolution: Techniques and Applications*, "Given the very nature of conflicts and conflicting parties, coupled with the need to resolve disputes more quickly and, in some cases, more personally than the traditional judicial system allows, the dispute resolution field promises to continue expanding into new areas."[47] Guided by relaxed rules of evidence and less rigorous standards of advocacy and generally operating in a commonsense, common-language approach, companies that provide dispute resolution services are experiencing a wave of popularity.[48]

PREPARATION OF AN ACTION IN LAW

The Complaint

Once jurisdiction has been set, the parties have been identified, and a determination has been made, the litigation turns to the preparation of a formal complaint—that is, asserting a theory of action of law or equity. Effective pleadings should be clear and concise.[49] The complaint, a document seeking relief on a specific set of facts and conditions, is statutorily guided, as by Rule 8 of the Federal Rules of Civil Procedure, which states specifically,

> *(a) Claims for Relief. A pleading which sets forth a claim for relief, whether an original claim, counterclaim, cross-claim, or third party claim, shall contain (1) a short and plain statement of the grounds upon which the court's jurisdiction depends, unless the court already has jurisdiction and the claim needs no new grounds of jurisdiction to support it, (2) a short and plain statement of the claim showing that the pleader is entitled to relief, and (3) a demand for judgment for the relief the pleader seeks. Relief in the alternative or of several different types may be demanded.*[50]

 The full text of a standardized complaint is shown in Form 14.12 on the accompanying CD. Portions of the complaint will be analyzed in the following sections. Structurally, a complaint formulates the plaintiff's claim and notifies the defendant of that claim.

Whether considered under modern code pleading requisites or those of common law, the objectives remain the same. A claim of equitable or legal rights gives rise to a controversy of which the judicial process serves as a forum for resolution. At a minimum, a complaint must consist of the following components.

Caption

Every complaint must have a caption identifying the court of jurisdiction and the parties. Figure 14.3 includes a caption for the U.S. Supreme Court.[51]

Introduction

The plaintiff, defendant, third party, or other interested individual legally empowered to bring an action will state an introductory paragraph such as the one shown in Figure 14.4.[52]

FIGURE 14.3
Caption for the
U.S. Supreme Court

IN THE SUPREME COURT OF THE UNITED STATES
_____ TERM 20____
No. _____

_____ ,
_____ [Plaintiff or Petitioner or Appellant],

vs.

_____ ,
_____ [Defendant or Respondent or Appellee]

_____ [*Designate type of process, pleading, order, etc.*]

FIGURE 14.4
Introductory
Paragraph

The plaintiff complains of the defendant and for cause of action alleges:
    [*Set forth allegations.*]

Residency

For jurisdictional purposes, the party filing the complaint must state his or her residency (see Figure 14.5).[53] If federal court jurisdiction is based on diversity, a diversity description is mandatory (see Figure 14.6).[54] Figure 14.7 outlines the language of a federal question.

Body of the Complaint

To support the underlying cause of action, the plaintiff's complaint must substantially and accurately state the facts supporting the allegations. Each set of facts should be stated briefly in separately numbered paragraphs, beginning with a statement identifying the parties. Pleading language is usually called an *averment* or a *statement of a claim*. At Rule 8(e), multiple averments must be accounted for in this fashion:

> (2)   *A party may set forth two or more statements of a claim or defense alternately or hypothetically, either in one count or defense or in separate counts or defenses. When two or more statements are made in the alternative and one of them if made independently would be sufficient, the pleading is not made insufficient by the insufficiency of one or more of the alternative statements. A party may also state as many separate claims or defenses as the party has regardless of consistency and whether based on legal, equitable, or maritime grounds. All statements shall be made subject to the obligations set forth in Rule 11.*[55]

FIGURE 14.5   Statement of Residency

Plaintiff, _____, is a resident of _____ [city] _____, _____ [county] _____, state of _____.
Defendant, _____, is a resident of _____[city]_____, _____[county]_____, state of _____.

FIGURE 14.6   Allegation of Jurisdiction Founded on Diversity of Citizenship and Amount

Plaintiff is a [citizen of the state of _____] [corporation incorporated under the law of the state of _____ having its principal place of business in the state of _____].
Defendant is a corporation incorporated under the laws of the state of _____ having its principal place of business in a state other than the state of _____[state of plaintiff's residency]_____. The matter in controversy exceeds, exclusive of interest and costs, the sum of _____ dollars.

FIGURE 14.7 Allegation of Jurisdiction Founded on the Existence of a Federal Question

The action arises under [the Constitution of the United States, Article ___, Section ___; [the _____ Amendment to the Constitution of the United States, Section _____]; [the Act of _____, _____ Stat. _____; U.S.C., Title _____ § _____]; [the Treaty of the United States dealing with _____] as hereinafter more fully appears.

 See Figure 14.8 for an example of a pleading format highlighting the averments or statements of claim in the body of the complaint. Alternatively, the Federal Rules permit averments of claims or defenses to be in numbered paragraphs. An example of this format is shown in Form 14.12 on the accompanying CD. Specific counts (whether claims or defenses) can also be drafted with that express designation (see Figure 14.9).

Rule 10 of the Federal Rules of Civil Procedure highlights this separation of claim or defense and discusses the adoption by reference and exhibit requirements:

> (b) *Paragraphs; Separate Statements. All averments of claim or defense shall be made in numbered paragraphs, the contents of each of which shall be limited as far as practicable to a statement of a single set of circumstances; and a paragraph may be referred to by number in all succeeding pleadings. Each claim founded upon a separate transaction or occurrence and each defense other than denials shall be stated in a separate count or defense whenever a separation facilitates the clear presentation of the matters set forth.*

> (c) *Adoption by Reference; Exhibits. Statements in a pleading may be adopted by reference in a different part of the same pleading or in another pleading or in any motion. A copy of any written instrument which is an exhibit to a pleading is a part thereof for all purposes.*[56]

An example of adoption by reference can be seen in paragraphs 5 and 15 of Figure 14.9.

The importance of clarity in pleadings cannot be overemphasized. Rule 8(e) of the Federal Rules of Civil Procedure calls for all pleadings to be concise and direct:

> (e) *Pleading to be Concise and Direct; Consistency.*
> (1) *Each averment of a pleading shall be simple, concise, and direct. No technical forms of pleading or motions are required.*[57]

Prayer for Relief

After jurisdiction has been established and a cause of action based on meritorious facts and law has been found and alleged through specific and general means, the proponent of any cause of action is required to pray or ask for specific forms of relief. It is not enough simply to complain and allege injury and harm. One must specify what one is asking the court to do under these facts—what types of remedy and relief are being sought.

FIGURE 14.8 Averments (Statement of Claim)

Source: Reprinted/Adapted with the permission of Wolters Kluwer Law & Business, from Marcy Fawcett Delesandri, *Paralegal Litigation: Forms and Procedures*, 3rd edition Form 2–28 at p. 89 (2003).

IV.

Defendant maintained a dangerous and unsafe condition which exposed patrons of their establishment to undue harm.

V.

The defendant operated the hotel in such a negligent manner that as a proximate result plaintiff was injured in her health, strength, and activity, sustaining severe shock and injuries to her nervous system and person, causing plaintiff mental and physical pain and suffering and resulting in her disability.

VI.

As a direct and proximate result of said carelessness and negligence of the defendant, plaintiff was compelled to and did incur expenses for medical care, hospitalization, and other incidentals, and will have to incur additional like expenses in the amounts presently unknown to her. Plaintiff, therefore, asks leave either to amend the complaint so as to show the amount of her medical expenses when ascertained or prove said amount at the time of trial.

FIGURE 14.9 Expressly Designated Counts

COUNT ONE	COUNT TWO
5. Paragraphs 1 through 4 are incorporated by reference as if fully set out herein.	15. Paragraphs 1 through 14 are incorporated as if fully set out herein.
6. On or about September 3, 2006, Defendant, Albert Mole, on behalf of himself and/or on behalf of Defendant, of which he was/is Director, entered into a written Retainer Agreement with Plaintiff, Johnny Right.	16. Plaintiff Johnny Right performed services for Defendants from September 5, 2006, to March 5, 2007, or a total of six months.
A copy of the Retainer Agreement is annexed hereto as Exhibit A.	17. During this time period, Defendants made no complaint about Plaintiff's work and, in fact, regularly requested additional work.

FIGURE 14.10 General Prayer for Relief

Wherefore, plaintiff prays the decree of the court forever enjoining defendant from the performance of said acts complained of, and for judgment for damages in the sum of $25,000, legal costs, and such other relief as the court may find to be proper.

Rule 8(a) of the Federal Rules of Civil Procedure outlines the general rules of pleading. It states that any pleading must contain "a demand for judgment for the relief the pleader seeks. Relief in the alternative or of several different types may be demanded."[58] As an example, in a case of wrongful termination of an employee, the following forms of relief are possible: reinstatement, damages for lost income, damages to reputation, damages for emotional distress, damages for loss of consortium, damages for intentional interference to contract, economic disparagement, injurious falsehood, and defamation. The prayer must state what the plaintiff expects.

Determination of the relief sought is obviously interconnected with the nature of injury. A prayer for relief may be a fairly generic request (see Figure 14.10) looking for a specific dollar sum or "any such other relief as the court may find to be proper."[59] In the case of contract law, a determination of rights under the written instrument involving a construction activity is asked to be interpreted and found as binding and enforceable (see Figure 14.11).[60] Plaintiffs in personal injury actions tend to be looking for medical expenses, damages and other injuries not yet ascertainable (see Figure 14.12).[61] A more specific enumeration of damages in a personal injury action can be reviewed in Figure 14.13.[62]

Types of Damages Determining the dollar value of a claim is complex. Many questions need to be answered before calculating the amount of an award. What kinds of losses should be included? Out-of-pocket expenses? Lost goodwill? The consequential losses resulting from the absence of an operating business? Should the plaintiff be restored to the position he or she would have

FIGURE 14.11 Prayer for Finding a Written Instrument Binding and Enforceable

Wherefore, plaintiff demands judgment against defendant as follows:
1. That the court declare the rights and other legal relations of the plaintiff and the defendant created by reason of the written instrument dated March 23, 2006, and annexed to the complaint herein and marked Exhibit D.
2. That the court declare that the defendant has no rights whatever in and to the 1968 Ford Fairlane in question by reason of said written instrument.
3. That, in the event that this court declare that the written instrument constitutes a binding and enforceable agreement between plaintiff and the defendant, this court order and direct defendant to account to plaintiff and to pay plaintiff for towing expenses associated with removing vehicle from the property of defendant.
4. For the costs and disbursements of this action.
5. That plaintiff have such other and further relief as to this court may seem just and proper.

FIGURE 14.12 Prayer for Medical Expenses

Wherefore, plaintiff prays the court to grant all reasonable medical, including physician, hospital and nursing, expenses, the exact amount of which is unknown to plaintiff at this time; and leave of court will be asked to insert the true amount when determined; and plaintiff further prays that the court will grant such other and further relief as it may deem proper.

FIGURE 14.13 Prayer for Specific Damages

Wherefore, plaintiff prays for judgment against defendants in the sum of $150,000, plus the reasonable medical expenses, the costs herein incurred, and for such other and further relief as this court may deem proper.

occupied had the breach not occurred? Should emotional distress over the breach of contract be included in the damage calculation? Are only *compensatory* damages to be paid? Or may *punitive* damages, designed as a kind of fine to punish the wrongdoer, also be awarded?[63]

The calculation of damages by private sector experts and consulting services influences the nature of not only the lawyer's decision to prosecute but also the evaluation of the total claim. Many private companies handle product liability cases, wage loss evaluations, and medical malpractice evaluations. Among the services these companies provide are

- Preliminary case screenings.
- Case analysis and evaluation.
- Assistance in discovery and trial preparation.
- Trial strategy tips.
- Literature searches.
- Educational seminars on technical subject matter.
- Document and application filing.
- Selection and recommendation of expert witnesses.
- Practice trials.
- Preparation for settlement conferences.

Damages are especially important in cases of medical malpractice and personal injury litigation. The damage elements may include

- Wage loss.
- Automobile repair.
- Car rental cost.
- Towing cost.
- Car storage cost.
- Property damage.
- Loss of personal property.
- Alternative transportation expenses.
- Physician expenses.
- Laboratory expenses.
- Hospital expenses.
- Ambulance expenses.
- Medication expenses.
- Physical therapy.
- Nurses.
- Home health care.
- Housekeeping expense.
- Miscellaneous expenses including wheelchairs, fracture devices, heating pads, and so on.[64]

Issues that must be evaluated to determine the severity of such losses are added to these basic damage calculations. Consider these questions:

- How old is the client?
- What is his or her life expectancy?
- Does the client have any dependents?
- What is the education level of the client?
- What was the client's occupational role?
- What was his or her annual income?
- What benefits has he or she lost?
- What is the best estimate of future medical care costs?
- What type of insurance coverage exists?[65]

FIGURE 14.14
Signature Clause

_____ [Signature]

_____ [Name]

Attorney for _____

[Plaintiff/Defendant]

_____ [Address]

The Georgia Institute of Continuing Legal Education suggests,

> *It is very important that your client's total injuries and damages are understood fully before settlement negotiations are started, or at least before a final settlement is reached. Physical as well as psychic damages may be applicable.*[66]

Make sure, through the client's treating physician, that all injuries are known and that all foreseeable results of existing injuries have appeared. The best way to ensure that all foreseeable results are known is to wait until the physician determines that the patient has fully recovered—at least to the extent he or she ever will recover.[67] Damage calculation and summarization should be included in the trial notebook.

The paralegal needs to be aware of the types of damages that can be claimed in a civil action. As a general principle, damages are the payment of compensation to a person who has suffered a detriment or an injury, whether to person or property rights or through the unlawful act of omission or negligence of another party. A party who files a complaint asserts, alleges, and avers specific damages. The law affords various damage remedies. Whether it is a case of auto accident, trespass, medical malpractice action, or product liability, the injured party seeks at a minimum to be made whole. A list appears in Chapter 9 showing the applicability of damage options in cases that paralegals may handle. In preparing a prayer for relief, boilerplate language is usually adapted to cover these varied types of damage claims.

Signature

Rule 11 of the Federal Rules of Civil Procedure holds that any pleading, motion, or other paper presented by an attorney shall be signed by at least one attorney of record with the attorney's individual name and address. Under this requirement, the attorney, by his or her signature, certifies that "to the best of the person's knowledge, information, and belief, formed after an inquiry reasonable under the circumstances,"[68] the pleading is not improper, unwarranted, or lacking in evidentiary support or factual foundation. A signature clause used in complaint drafting is shown in Figure 14.14.[69]

Verification

A verification clause in a complaint is the plaintiff's affirmation that the facts and allegations outlined in the body of the complaint are true and correct to the best of his or her information and knowledge. It must be signed, subscribed, and sworn before witnesses (and sometimes a notary public). In many jurisdictions, an intentional, malicious, or malevolent disregard of the truth and fact in a formal pleading will give rise to both criminal and civil actions (see the verification clause in Figure 14.15).[70]

Other Matters

In most jurisdictions, the Office of the Prothonotary or court administrator is the central filing location for case initiation. Depending on the jurisdiction or locality, appendixes, attachments, and other matter may be required in the pleading of a case involving a contract dispute. A party who files a breach

FIGURE 14.15
Verification Clause

The plaintiff above-named, being duly sworn, says:
I have read the foregoing complaint, the contents of which are true to the best of my own knowledge.

_____ [Signature]

FIGURE 14.16

PACER Home Page

Source: Administrative Office of the U.S. Courts, PACER Service Center. Available at: http://pacer.psc.uscourts.gov/.

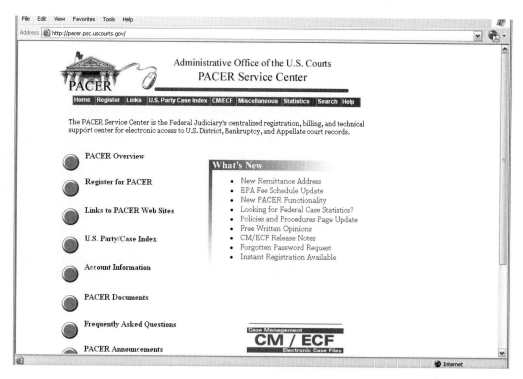

of contract suit should attach and label all employment contracts and other matters that are evidenced by documentation. In the Federal Courts, electronic filing is now required. The PACER program is the Federal Judiciary's centralized system for filing, billing, and technical support (see Figure 14.16).

Service of Process

Summons

For a cause of action to have procedural validity, it must be served on or delivered to the named opposing party (or parties) and completed within the statute of limitations. Paralegals must be familiar with the statutes of limitations that determine when a cause of action will no longer be permitted. If a filing is appropriate, civil actions generally can be commenced either by issuance of a Praecipe or with a summons and complaint. A *Praecipe* simply puts the court and the other party on notice that you intend to file an action. Under Rule 4 of the Federal Rules of Civil Procedure, an action can be commenced upon the filing of a complaint with a court clerk, who will then issue a summons and deliver the summons to the plaintiff or the plaintiff's attorney. The attorney is responsible for a prompt service of that complaint on the opposing party. The form of the summons is standardized. (One example is shown in Form 14.13 on the accompanying CD.) A summons may be required to include a civil cover sheet such as is required in the federal system (see Form 14.14). Instructions for attorneys are shown on the second page of Form 14.14. This task is frequently delegated to a paralegal.

Service Methods

Service of process can be accomplished personally, by mail, or by publication. The 1993 amendments to the Federal Rules of Civil Procedure liberalized the service methods:

> (c) (1) *A summons shall be served together with a copy of the complaint. The plaintiff is responsible for service of a summons and complaint within the time allowed...and shall furnish the person effecting service with the necessary copies of the summons and complaint.*
>
> (2) *Service may be effected by any person who is not a party and who is at least 18 years of age. At the request of the plaintiff, however, the court may direct that service be effected by a United States marshal, deputy United States marshal, or other person or officer specially appointed by the court for the purpose. Such an appointment must be made when the plaintiff is authorized to proceed in forma pauperis pursuant to 28 U.S.C. U §1915 or is authorized to proceed as a seaman under 28 U.S.C. §1916.*[71]

The growing philosophy in service is to allow any party to do so by the easiest means available—usually mail. Although the federal rules still note the use of the marshal, or at the state level a sheriff, the rules allow waiver of personal service to save costs. Rule 4(d) lays out the new waiver of service mechanism:

> (d) *Waiver of Service; Duty to Save Costs of Service; Request to Waive.*
>
> (1) *A defendant who waives service of a summons does not thereby waive any objection to the venue or to the jurisdiction of the court over the person of the defendant.*
>
> (2) *An individual, corporation, or association that is subject to service under subdivision (e), (f), or (h) and that receives notice of an action in the manner provided in this paragraph has a duty to avoid unnecessary costs of serving the summons. To avoid costs, the plaintiff may notify such a defendant of the commencement of the action and request that the defendant waive service of a summons.*
>
> *The notice and request*
>
> (A) *shall be in writing and shall be addressed directly to the defendant, if an individual, or else to an officer or managing or general agent (or other agent authorized by appointment or law to receive service of process) of a defendant subject to service under subdivision (h);*
>
> (B) *shall be dispatched through first-class mail or other reliable means;*
>
> (C) *shall be accompanied by a copy of the complaint and shall identify the court in which it has been filed;*
>
> (D) *shall inform the defendant, by means of a text prescribed in an official form promulgated pursuant to Rule 84, of the consequences of compliance and of a failure to comply with the request;*
>
> (E) *shall set forth the date on which the request is sent;*
>
> (F) *shall allow the defendant a reasonable time to return the waiver, which shall be at least 30 days from the date on which the request is sent, or 60 days from that date if the defendant is addressed outside any judicial district of the United States; and*
>
> (G) *shall provide the defendant with an extra copy of the notice and request, as well as a prepaid means of compliance in writing.*
>
> *If a defendant located within the United States fails to comply with a request for waiver made by a plaintiff located within the United States, the court shall impose the costs subsequently incurred in effecting service on the defendant unless good cause for the failure be shown.*
>
> (3) *A defendant that, before being served with process, timely returns a waiver so requested is not required to serve an answer to the complaint until 60 days after the date on which the request for waiver of service was sent, or 90 days after that date if the defendant was addressed outside any judicial district of the United States.*
>
> (4) *When the plaintiff files a waiver of service with the court, the action shall proceed, except as provided in paragraph (3), as if a summons and complaint had been served at the time of filing the waiver, and no proofs of service shall be required.*
>
> (5) *The costs to be imposed on a defendant under paragraph (2) for failure to comply with a request to waive service of a summons shall include the costs subsequently incurred in effecting service under subdivision (e), (f), or (h), together with the costs, including a reasonable attorney's fee, of any motion required to collect the costs of service.*[72]

A federal notice and request for waiver are shown in Form 14.15 on the accompanying CD.

Not all jurisdictions promote the waiver concept. A first attempt at the personal service method is still mandatory in some places. If this fails, it is possible to perform service by publication in a newspaper, legal magazine, or publication with regular readership. Form 14.16 on the accompanying CD outlines the affidavit of publication that would be attached to the court's record.[73] Paralegals should know the process service companies in their area.

Defendants who are difficult to find make service of process difficult. Carole A. Bruno provides 20 dependable ways to locate defendants:

1. Write the defendant at his or her last known address; request a corrected address from the postmaster by writing that an address correction is requested.

2. Send a certified or registered letter marked return receipt requested.

3. Check with the local postmaster.

4. Send a telegram via Western Union's report delivery and address service.

5. Check with a local credit bureau.

6. Contact the defendant's landlord and past landlord.

7. Contact the mortgagee if the property is still owned by the defendant.

8. Contact neighbors, local stores, gas stations, and previous addresses.

9. Contact gas, electric, water, and telephone companies for recorded changes of address.

10. Check the civil and criminal divisions of local and county courts and state police for relevant information.

11. Check the county and local court records within the defendant's jurisdiction for real estate ownership and other official records.

12. Check all known lodges, clubs, unions, churches, and veterans' organizations.

13. Contact all known relatives and friends of both the defendant and his or her spouse.

14. Contact the local Army, Navy, Air Force, or Marine recruiting boards.

15. Contact the defendant's banks—both checking and savings accounts.

16. Contact the defendant's present and past employers.

17. Contact trade references, finance companies, and banks.

18. Check your state and neighboring states for motor vehicle information.

19. Check with the defendant's automobile dealer or auto mechanic.

20. Offer a reward for information about the defendant.[74]

In addition, an Internet search for information about the defendant may prove fruitful.

Computation of Time

Once service has been perfected, computation of time has an added meaning. An answer to a complaint or other affirmative pleading is mandated within a specific period of time. Rule 6 of the Federal Rules describes the computation process:

> *Rule 6. Time.*
>
> (a) *Computation. In computing any period of time prescribed or allowed by these rules, by the local rules of any district court, by order of court, or by any applicable statute, the day of the act, event, or default from which the designated period of time begins to run shall not be included. The last day of the period so computed shall be included, unless it is a Saturday, a Sunday, or a legal holiday, or, when the act to be done is the filing of a paper in court, a day on which weather or other conditions have made the office of the clerk of the district court inaccessible, in which event the period runs until the end of the next day which is not one of the aforementioned days. When the period of time prescribed or allowed is less than 11 days, intermediate Saturdays, Sundays, and legal holidays shall be excluded in the computation. As used in this rule and in Rule 77(c), "legal holiday" includes New Year's Day, Birthday of Martin Luther King, Jr., Washington's Birthday, Memorial Day, Independence Day, Labor Day, Columbus Day, Veterans Day, Thanksgiving Day, Christmas Day, and any other day appointed as a holiday by the President or the Congress of the United States, or by the state in which the district court is held.*
>
> (b) *Enlargement. When by these rules or by a notice given thereunder or by order of court an act is required or allowed to be done at or within a specified time, the court for cause shown may at any time in its discretion (1) with or without motion or notice order the period enlarged if request therefor is made before the expiration of the period originally prescribed or as extended by a previous order, or (2) upon motion made after the expiration of the specified period permit the act to be done where the failure to act was the result of excusable neglect; but it may not extend the time for taking any action under Rules 50(b) and (c)(2), 52(b), 59(b), (d), and (e), and 60(b), except to the extent and under the conditions stated in them.*
>
> (c) *Unaffected by Expiration of Term. [Rescinded Feb. 28, 1966, eff. July 1, 1966.]*
>
> (d) *For Motions—Affidavits. A written motion, other than one which may be heard ex parte, and notice of the hearing thereof shall be served not later than 5 days before the time specified for the hearing, unless a different period is fixed by these rules or by order of the court. Such an order may for cause shown be made on ex parte application. When a motion is supported by affidavit, the affidavit shall be served with the motion; and, except as otherwise provided in Rule 59(c), opposing affidavits may be served not later than 1 day before the hearing, unless the court permits them to be served at some other time.*

(e) *Additional Time after Certain Kinds of Service. Whenever a party must or may act within a prescribed period after service and service is made under Rule 5(b)(2)(B), (C), or (D), 3 days are added after the prescribed period would otherwise expire under subdivision (a).*[75]

Answer

Under Rule 12 of the Federal Rules of Civil Procedure, an answer to a complaint, a cross-claim, or a reply to a counterclaim must be made within 20 days after it has been served. Rule 12(a) states specifically,

Rule 12.   Defenses and Objections—When and How Presented—By Pleading or Motion—Motion for Judgment on the Pleadings.

(a) *When Presented.*
   (1) *Unless a different time is prescribed in a statute of the United States, a defendant shall serve an answer*
      (A) *within 20 days after being served with the summons and complaint, or*
      (B) *if service of the summons has been timely waived on request under Rule 4(d), within 60 days after the date when the request for waiver was sent, or within 90 days after that date if the defendant was addressed outside any judicial district of the United States.*
   (2) *A party served with a pleading stating a cross-claim against that party shall serve an answer thereto within 20 days after being served. The plaintiff shall serve a reply to a counterclaim in the answer within 20 days after service of the answer, or, if a reply is ordered by the court, within 20 days after service of the order, unless the order otherwise directs.*
   (3) (A) *The United States, an agency of the United States, or an officer or employee of the United States sued in an official capacity shall serve an answer to the complaint or cross-claim—or a reply to a counterclaim—within 60 days after the United States attorney is served with the pleading asserting the claim.*
      (B) *An officer or employee of the United States sued in an individual capacity for acts or omissions occurring in connection with the performance of duties on behalf of the United States shall serve an answer to the complaint or cross-claim—or a reply to a counterclaim—within 60 days after service on the officer or employee, or service on the United States attorney, whichever is later.*
   (4) *Unless a different time is fixed by court order, the service of a motion permitted under this rule alters the periods of time as follows:*
      (A) *if the court denies the motion or postpones its disposition until the trial on the merits, the responsive pleading shall be served within 10 days after notice of the court's action; or*
      (B) *if the court grants a motion for a more definite statement, the responsive pleading shall be served within 10 days after the service of the more definite statement.*
(b) *How Presented. Every defense, in law or fact, to a claim for relief in any pleading, whether a claim, counterclaim, cross-claim, or third-party claim, shall be asserted in the responsive pleading thereto if one is required, except that the following defenses may at the option of the pleader be made by motion: (1) lack of jurisdiction over the subject matter, (2) lack of jurisdiction over the person, (3) improper venue, (4) insufficiency of process, (5) insufficiency of service of process, (6) failure to state a claim upon which relief can be granted, (7) failure to join a party under Rule 19. A motion making any of these defenses shall be made before pleading if a further pleading is permitted. No defense or objection is waived by being joined with one or more other defenses or objections in a responsive pleading or motion. If a pleading sets forth a claim for relief to which the adverse party is not required to serve a responsive pleading, the adverse party may assert at the trial any defense in law or fact to that claim for relief. If, on a motion asserting the defense numbered (6) to dismiss for failure of the pleading to state a claim upon which relief can be granted, matters outside the pleading are presented to and not excluded by the court, the motion shall be treated as one for summary judgment and disposed of as provided in Rule 56, and all parties shall be given reasonable opportunity to present all material made pertinent to such a motion by Rule 56.*
(c) *Motion for Judgment on the Pleadings. After the pleadings are closed but within such time as not to delay the trial, any party may move for judgment on the pleadings. If, on a motion for judgment on the pleadings, matters outside the pleadings are presented to and not excluded by the court, the motion shall be treated as one for summary judgment and disposed of as provided in Rule 56, and all parties shall be given reasonable opportunity to present all material made pertinent to such a motion by Rule 56.*

(d) *Preliminary Hearings. The defenses specifically enumerated (1) –(7) in subdivision (b) of this rule, whether made in a pleading or by motion, and the motion for judgment mentioned in subdivision (c) of this rule shall be heard and determined before trial on application of any party, unless the court orders that the hearing and determination thereof be deferred until the trial.*

(e) *Motion for More Definite Statement. If a pleading to which a responsive pleading is permitted is so vague or ambiguous that a party cannot reasonably be required to frame a responsive pleading, the party may move for a more definite statement before interposing a responsive pleading. The motion shall point out the defects complained of and the details desired. If the motion is granted and the order of the court is not obeyed within 10 days after notice of the order or within such other time as the court may fix, the court may strike the pleading to which the motion was directed or make such order as it deems just.*

(f) *Motion to Strike. Upon motion made by a party before responding to a pleading or, if no responsive pleading is permitted by these rules, upon motion made by a party within 20 days after the service of the pleading upon the party or upon the court's own initiative at any time, the court may order stricken from any pleading any insufficient defense or any redundant, immaterial, impertinent, or scandalous matter.*

(g) *Consolidation of Defenses in Motion. A party who makes a motion under this rule may join with it any other motions herein provided for and then available to the party. If a party makes a motion under this rule but omits therefrom any defense or objection then available to the party which this rule permits to be raised by motion, the party shall not thereafter make a motion based on the defense or objection so omitted, except a motion as provided in subdivision (h)(2) hereof on any of the grounds there stated.*

(h) *Waiver or Preservation of Certain Defenses.*

    (1) *A defense of lack of jurisdiction over the person, improper venue, insufficiency of process, or insufficiency of service of process is waived (A) if omitted from a motion in the circumstances described in subdivision (g), or (B) if it is neither made by motion under this rule nor included in a responsive pleading or an amendment thereof permitted by Rule 15(a) to be made as a matter of course.*

    (2) *A defense of failure to state a claim upon which relief can be granted, a defense of failure to join a party indispensable under Rule 19, and an objection of failure to state a legal defense to a claim may be made in any pleading permitted or ordered under Rule 7(a), or by motion for judgment on the pleadings, or at the trial on the merits.*

    (3) *Whenever it appears by suggestion of the parties or otherwise that the court lacks jurisdiction of the subject matter, the court shall dismiss the action.*[76]

Standard practice requires that an answer address both the technical and substantive issues of a complaint. Technical challenges to a complaint's content can be included in an answer to a complaint. Additionally, the answer to any complaint can raise challenges permissible under the Federal Rules of Civil Procedure, such as these:

- *lack of jurisdiction over the subject matter or person*
- *improper venue*
- *insufficiency of process or service of process*
- *failure to state a claim upon which relief can be granted or join a party under Rule 19..*[77]
  Motions can be filed before a formal answer is made. Until a motion has been argued before a tribunal, an answer is not required. The forthcoming section on motion practice will illustrate some of the more traditional challenges to complaints.

An answer with denials can be either general or specific. Allegations may be admitted or denied based on the defendant's information or belief that he or she is without sufficient information upon which to formulate either an admission or denial. A responsive pleading may proclaim that an allegation states a conclusion of law or fact that cannot be answered. The paralegal must mirror the allegations made in the complaint, clause by clause, and directly answer those assertions and affirmations cited in the cause of action:

1. General denial[78] (see Forms 14.17 and 14.18 on the accompanying CD).
2. Incorporation of previous answer[79] (see Form 14.19).
3. Basis of information and belief[80] (see Forms 14.20 and 14.21).

Just as the plaintiff has a duty and obligation to draft a meritorious complaint, the defendant must not be a party to falsity, fraud, and substantial misrepresentation. In other words, to aver a lack of knowledge or information, one should not be blind to truth and reality.

The answer with denials is either general or specific in design. Allegations may be admitted or denied based on the defendant's information or belief. "If he or she is without sufficient information on which to formulate either an admission or denial, then such a position should be stated. A responsive pleading may proclaim that an allegation states a conclusion of law or fact that cannot be answered."[81]

Counterclaim

When the answer is filed, the defendant can initiate a counterclaim against the plaintiff. This is usually done after the complaint has been answered and affirmative defenses have been raised within the body of the answer. An example of a counterclaim is shown in Form 14.22 on the accompanying CD.

Rules for drafting counterclaims are the same as for the original complaint. A counterclaim is merely a complaint filed by a defendant against the original party plaintiff. Counterclaims can be either compulsory or permissive in nature and are guided by Rule 13 of the Federal Rules of Civil Procedure:

(a) *Compulsory Counterclaims. A pleading shall state as a counterclaim any claim which at the time of serving the pleading the pleader has against any opposing party, if it arises out of the transaction or occurrence that is the subject matter of the opposing party's claim and does not require for its adjudication the presence of third parties of whom the court cannot acquire jurisdiction. But the pleader need not state the claim if (1) at the time the action was commenced the claim was the subject of another pending action, or (2) the opposing party brought suit upon the claim by attachment or other process by which the court did not acquire jurisdiction to render a personal judgment on that claim, and the pleader is not stating any counterclaim under this Rule 13.*

(b) *Permissive Counterclaims. A pleading may state as a counterclaim any claim against an opposing party not arising out of the transaction or occurrence that is the subject matter of the opposing party's claim.*[82]

Part of the rationale behind Rule 13's compulsory dimension is the policy that problems arising out of the same events and by the same parties should be resolved at the same time.

Cross-Claim

Paralegals must be alert for potential cross-claims against co-parties. Rule 13 states that "a pleading may state as a cross-claim any claim by one party against a co-party arising out of the transaction or occurrence that is the subject matter either of the original action or of a counterclaim therein or relating to any property that is the subject matter of the original action."[83] See Form 14.23 on the accompanying CD for an example of a cross-claim. Cross-claims are most likely in cases with multiple defendants.

Defenses

An answer must contain specific defenses to the content of a complaint. Operating under the pressure of waiver or dismissal of defense rights, a paralegal must state absolutely any affirmative defense that may have merit under a cause of action. Failure to plead an affirmative defense may result in waiver. However, adopting an extremely defensive posture caused by fear of dismissal or waiver has led to some unmeritorious assertions of affirmative defenses. Mark Bower has commented on the implications:

We have frequently seen all kinds of affirmative defenses raised at the joinder of issue, only to be withdrawn or stricken later as being completely without merit. The defense of "lack of jurisdiction" for failure to make proper service of process is commonplace. Some malpractice defense firms are notorious for pleading jurisdictional defenses in every answer as a matter of course. The statute of limitations defense has been seen in cases commenced within a few weeks after the cause of action arose, or where the plaintiff is an infant who has a statute of limitation tolled for years into the future. The defense of "failure to state a cause of action" has been asserted despite the service of a detailed complaint which alleges every element and ingredient of a complete claim. Culpable conduct is frequently alleged against brain-damaged babies, presumably for their own negligence in passing through the birth canal with difficulty. When pressed, the defense firms simply insist that these defenses had to be raised or else could not have been raised later.[84]

A review of potential affirmative defenses is provided in the defense analysis in Chapter 11.[85] An example of an answer posing affirmative defenses is shown in Form 14.24 on the accompanying CD. The relevant defenses are these:

Accord and satisfaction: an agreement between two (or more) people, one of whom has a right of action against the other, that the latter should do or give, and the former accept, something in satisfaction of the rights of action.[86]

Arbitration and award: the voluntary settlement of a controversy by mutually agreeing to submit the controversy to arbitration so that the decision in the arbitration is binding on the parties.[87]

Assumption of risk: a defense to a claim for negligent injury to a person or property—that is, a person who voluntarily exposes himself or herself or his or her property to a known danger may not recover for injuries thereby sustained.[88]

Contributory negligence: the failure by a plaintiff to exercise care, which contributed to the plaintiff's injury.[89]

Discharge in bankruptcy: the order by which a bankrupt party is released from liability for his or her debts, which were incurred before the adjudication in bankruptcy.[90]

Duress: imprisonment; compulsion; coercion or the threat thereof.[91]

Estoppel: an admission or declaration by which a person is concluded (that is, prevented) from bringing evidence to controvert or to prove the contract.[92]

Failure of consideration: the neglect, refusal, or inability of a contracting party to do, perform, or furnish, after making and entering a contract, the consideration agreed upon.[93]

Fraud: a broad term for all kinds of acts that have as their objective the gain of an advantage to another's detriment by deceitful or unfair means.[94]

Illegality: the condition of being contrary to law.

Laches: negligence or unreasonable delay in pursuing a legal remedy, concurrent with a resultant prejudice to the opposing party, whereby a person forfeits his or her rights.[95]

License: permission or authority to do something that would be wrong or illegal to do if the permission or authority were not granted.[96]

Payment: the satisfaction of a debt or an obligation to pay money.[97]

Release: the giving up or surrender of a claim or right of action.[98]

Res judicata: a controversy already judicially decided.[99]

Statute of frauds: various state legislative acts that have as their main object the desire to take away the facilities for fraud, and the temptation to perjury, which arose in verbal obligations, the proof of which depended on oral evidence. Its most common provisions are these:

> *(a) all leases, excepting those for less than three years, shall have the force of leases at will only, unless they are in writing and signed by the parties or their agents; (b) assignments and surrenders of leases and interests in land must be in writing; (c) all declarations and assignments of trusts must be in writing, signed by the party (trust arising by implication of law are, however, excepted); (d) no action shall be brought upon a guarantee, or upon any contract for sale of land, or any interest in or concerning them, or upon any agreement which is not to be performed within a year, unless agreement is in writing and signed by the party to be charged or his agent; (e) no contract for the sale of goods for a certain proceed or more, e.g., $500.00 (U.C.S. §2-201) shall be good, unless the buyer accepts part, or gives something in part payment, or some memorandum thereof be signed by the parties to be charged or their agents.*[100]

Statute of limitations: a procedural bar to a plaintiff's action that does not begin to run until after the cause of action has accrued and the plaintiff has a right to maintain a lawsuit.[101]

Waiver: a positive act by which a legal right is relinquished.[102]

Replies

Remember that any cause of action commencing with a complaint is responded to by an answer. In some states, material allegations of fact set forth in an answer are deemed to be agreed to by the plaintiff unless a formal reply follows. In most jurisdictions replies are not required unless the allegations or averments are material. Replies also are opportunities for new matters to be introduced.

A demur (not inconsistent with the complaint) could be argued. A reply, general in nature and construction, is reproduced in Form 14.25 on the accompanying CD.[103]

Amendments of the Pleadings

The Federal Rules of Civil Procedure provide a liberal avenue for amendment and supplemental pleadings activities. Rule 15 states in part,

> (a) *Amendments. A party may amend the party's pleading once as a matter of course at any time before a responsive pleading is served or, if the pleading is one to which no responsive pleading is permitted and the action has not been placed upon the trial calendar, the party may so amend it at any time within 20 days after it is served. Otherwise a party may amend the party's pleading only by leave of court or by written consent of the adverse party; and leave shall be freely given when justice so requires. A party shall plead in response to an amended pleading within the time remaining for response to the original pleading or within 10 days after service of the amended pleading, whichever period may be the longer, unless the court otherwise orders.*
>
> (b) *Amendments to Conform to the Evidence. When issues not raised by the pleadings are tried by express or implied consent of the parties, they shall be treated in all respects as if they had been raised in the pleadings. Such amendment of the pleadings as may be necessary to cause them to conform to the evidence and to raise these issues may be made upon motion of any party at any time, even after judgment; but failure so to amend does not affect the result of the trial of these issues.*[104]

Amendments to pleadings use the same captions, parties, and identification clauses that are used in pleadings and simply state for the parties' understanding and the court's record what specific changes will be in the original pleading. Amendments can take place with or without court leave, depending on jurisdiction rules. Courts are authorized by their discretionary powers, before or after judgment and in furtherance of justice, to allow any pleadings to be amended, corrected, or modified by

- Striking or adding the name of a party.
- Correcting a mistake.
- Inserting other allegations material to the case.
- Conforming the pleading or proceedings to the facts proved when the amendment does not change the claim or defense.[105]

The tone of Rule 15(a) is to permit amendment and to ensure that the grant to amend "shall be freely given when justice so requires."[106]

Default

At this stage of the litigation process, a complaint has been filed; an answer has been returned; replies, cross-claims, and counterclaims have been completed; and amendments and supplemental pleadings have been completed. The paralegal must develop a tracking or tickler system to keep track of the pleadings. It is imperative to be aware of the failure of any party to answer within the exact period of time. If a defendant does not provide an answer to a legal and properly served complaint, default remedies are available. The proper strategy is a petition or motion for a default judgment, requesting the court to make a decision based on the defendant's failure to answer in conjunction with the substantive merit of the case alleged. A default judgment motion is shown in Form 14.26 on the accompanying CD.[107]

THE DISCOVERY PROCESS

Some Initial Considerations

As the plaintiff, attorney, and paralegal move toward the trial stage of a cause of action, many preliminary steps are necessary. Much of the paralegal's time is spent in the discovery stage of litigation. Under both federal rules and state principles, the courts are not allowed to be forums of tactical surprise. Instead the rules of discovery and disclosure emphasize free exchange of information long before a trial date. Hidden witnesses or surprise papers and documents used for theatrical effect are disfavored practices. The rules of discovery and disclosure outline reasonable steps for the interchange of information between plaintiff and defendant. The techniques of disclosure and discovery are straightforward and consist of several techniques:

Interrogatories: Interrogatories are a series of written questions passed from either side asking about specific information.

Deposition: Depositions can be oral or written. They usually result from a conference between opposing counsel, witnesses, and opposing parties in which testimony is taken by a court reporter (or sometimes by video).

Production of documents: By using the subpoena *duces tecum,* documents of the opposition may be requested and copied for review and inspection. The work product of an attorney or any other material that qualifies as privileged is excluded from this inspection.

Medical reports: By informal or formal means, past or present medical reports, tests, or examinations can be ordered and acquired.

Discovery conference:[108] The parties may voluntarily arrange meetings to exchange information or may be obligated under local practice rules to conduct conferences about the extent of discovery. An example of a pretrial conference order is shown in Form 14.27 on the accompanying CD.

Pretrial conference: Although judges are not specifically empowered to be mediators or facilitators to discovery, in the federal courts they have taken increased steps to help resolve cases before the formal trial date.

Under Rule 16 of the Federal Rules of Civil Procedure, the pretrial conference serves various purposes:

- Expediting the disposition of the action.
- Establishing early and continuing control so that the case will not be protracted because of lack of management.
- Discouraging wasteful pretrial activities.
- Improving the quality of the trial through more thorough preparation.
- Facilitating the settlement of the case.[109]

Tactically, the discovery process does much more. "It provides for the revelation of the essential strengths and weaknesses of each party's case, thereby permitting the realistic appraisal of settlement possibilities that make trial unnecessary. It makes possible the conduct of the case by attorneys so well informed on the merits and demerits of each side that, if a trial is necessary, they can effectively present their clients' cases."[110] Under the Federal Rules of Civil Procedure, the scope of discovery is liberally construed as long as the request is relevant to the subject matter of the pending litigation. Parties may obtain discovery about any matter not privileged, as long as it relates to the claim or defense of any party.

This includes the existence, description, nature, custody, condition, and location of any books, documents, or other tangible things, and the identity and location of people having knowledge of any discoverable matter.[111] The American Trial Lawyers Association examines the scope and parameters of discovery, stating,

> *The broad reach of the relevancy standard embraces not only the discovery of information relating to the merits or the substance of problems involved in a case but also to information related to disputes peripheral to the merits. Material relevant to disputes over jurisdiction and venue is discoverable. Information of importance to the question of damages rather than to the assessment of liability may be discovered.*[112]

Determining what is nondiscoverable as attorney's "work product" is a process not yet totally resolved. *Work product* normally means the ardor, endurance, and sacrifice a lawyer is making to prepare a case, including his or her research, theories, and thoughts of defense and strategy, notes, and internal memoranda. Whether information of this type should be considered discoverable by the opposition is addressed by Rule 26:

> *(1) Requiring that before a party can obtain trial preparation material from another side, he must show (a) that he has a substantial need for the material in the preparation of his case; and (b) he is unable to obtain the substantial equivalent of the material by other means without undue hardship; and*
>
> *(2) Affording special protection against discovery of the creative aspects of trial preparations, mental impressions, conclusions, and legal theories.[113]*

Rule 26 goes on to state without qualification, "in ordering discovery of such materials when the required showing has been made, the court shall protect against disclosure of the mental impressions, conclusions, opinions, or legal theories of an attorney."[114] However, the paralegal will often correspond and talk with opposing counsel to obtain this information informally. The paralegal should not hand over an entire file; he or she should remove any items that are personal and unique to legal representation and deliver those that are normally expected to be part of the discovery process, such as medical reports, expert reports, witness lists, papers and documents that are part of the public record, and other documents.

Some general discovery principles and guidelines might include these:

1. Discovery must be reasonable and relevant.

2. Discovery must not be a "fishing expedition."

3. Discovery must respect privileged information.

4. Discovery should not be too expensive, irrationally based, or duplicitous.

5. Discovery should not be a request for the opposition to perform the paralegal's work.

6. Discovery should not be vexatious or for the sole purpose of harassment.[115]

Rule 26(b)(2) addresses these practice issues:

> *The frequency or extent of use of the discovery methods set forth in subdivision (a) shall be limited by the court if it determines that:*
>
> *(i) the discovery sought is unreasonably cumulative or duplicative, or is obtainable from some other source that is more convenient, less burdensome, or less expensive; (ii) the party seeking discovery has had ample opportunity by discovery in the action to obtain the information sought; or (iii) the burden or expense of the proposed discovery outweighs its likely benefit, taking into account the needs of the case, the amount in controversy, the parties' resources, the importance of the issues at stake in the litigation, and the importance of the proposed discovery in resolving the issues. The court may act upon its own initiative after reasonable notice or pursuant to a motion under Rule 26(c).[116]*

The discovery process should be well planned and focused. Discovery that induces responses will adhere to these suggestions:

- Make certain that a reasonable person could say, "I know what they want." Use as few imprecise words as possible.

- Make certain that a judge will be able to decide if the responses to your requests are adequate.

- Draft definitions with enough breadth to make certain requests do not escape your attention.

- After drafting requests, consider whether each can be redrafted in a less complex fashion.

- Ask yourself how the answer to each request will provide you with information helpful to the case. Decide whether some requests can be eliminated or consolidated.

- Consider ways the response to your request could be acceptable yet vague, and then try to redraft the questions to eliminate the vagueness.[117]

Use software programs to track the avalanche of paper and documentary requirements. See Figure 14.17 for an example.

Depositions

Depositions are oral exchanges by which testimony is taken under oath through the examination of opposing counsel. The proceedings, questions, and answers are recorded either by videotape or by transcription by an official court reporter. Depositions are usually taken in the offices of

FIGURE 14.17

Example of Software Program Used to Track Documents

Source: Legal Files. Available at: http://www.legalfiles.com/LawFirms.htm.

attorneys or judges, in conference rooms, or in other mutually agreed locations. Under typical rules of federal and state procedure, a subpoena is used to advise a party of an upcoming deposition[118] (see Form 14.28 on the accompanying CD). Both common courtesy and legal rules dictate that sufficient notice be given to a party to be deposed (see Form 14.29).

As a form of discovery, a deposition is tactically reliable because it places the client in the "hot seat," thereby assessing his or her credibility. Paralegals must prepare witnesses for depositions, arrange the locations of the events, give notice to all individuals who must attend, and arrange for court reporters or videotape equipment.

It is always a good idea to give the witness written instructions before any deposition proceedings to allay any fears the witness might have. Offering this information helps give the witness confidence to handle the deposition. Use of these or other documents and learning tools make repetitive explanations less likely.

Deposition practice should not be automatic. Depending on the client's character, the opposition may use the deposition as an opportunity for impeachment. The strength of the proponent's case may be undermined. Other reasons for bypassing the deposition process are these:

- Depositions are expensive.
- Depositions force an opponent to prepare.
- Depositions preserve adverse testimony.
- Depositions dilute unfavorable statements that may already have been obtained.
- Depositions reveal what a lawyer believes is important.[119]

The proper way to prepare a witness to testify depends on the type of case involved. Witnesses should be advised that the plan of the deposition will include these typical concerns:

1. Name.
2. Home address.
3. Home telephone number.
4. Work address.
5. Work telephone number (needed to help locate the deponent for trial).
6. Name of a close local relative (in case the deponent cannot later be located).

7. Address and telephone number of a close local relative.

8. Whether the deponent has been a party or witness in a civil or criminal lawsuit before.

9. Whether the deponent has ever testified at a trial before.

10. With whom the deponent has discussed the case: when, how long, and who was present?

11. Whether the deponent has made any notes, diagrams, or drawings regarding the incident. If so, where are they?

12. Whether the deponent is aware of any diagrams, drawings, reports, photographs, models or exhibits regarding the incident.

13. Whether the deponent is aware of any witnesses to the incident. If so, who are they? What do they know? What did they observe? (Obtain their addresses and phone numbers.)

14. Whether the deponent has talked with attorneys or parties involved in the case.

15. How long the deponent has known any witnesses or parties to the lawsuit.[120]

In addition, a witness in an accident case should know something about the vehicles, the occupants, a description of the accident scene, details of the occurrence, police report, medical history, and extent of damages. It is of great benefit to the practicing paralegal to summarize the strengths and weaknesses of the deponent.

Paralegals are often asked to prepare deposition questions. Dianne D. Zalewski calls for paralegals to be exacting, chronological, and objective when preparing deposition questions:

> *Develop a logical sequence in your line of questioning. Use your chronology of events as a guide. For example, your attorney will want to establish the sequence of events before the accident, then discover in detail exactly what occurred during the accident, and finally, solicit responses about subsequent actions by various persons involved. After the accident has been fully covered, your attorney will want to know if a witness has given any statements, if the opposing party has learned of any new witness, or if other information has been discovered since the accident.*[121]

The deposition process plays a key role in the examination of expert testimony. Expert witnesses can be engaged by either the plaintiff or the defendant. Their testimony, testing results, knowledge, and opinions are traditionally discoverable if the other party expects to call that expert witness to trial. Deposing questions should solicit the expert's background and testimonial range and a summary of the grounds for each finding or opinion.[122] The opinion of experts plays a critical part in the evaluation of a case's strengths and weaknesses. Questions for expert deponents depend on their area of expertise. Some sample sets of inquiries regarding expert testimony in the deposition are shown in Chapter 9, which covers investigation.

Paralegals also will be involved in extensive postdeposition activity. When the finished transcripts have been received from the court reporter, they are often voluminous. As a result, indexes and other quick techniques for keeping track of deposition content are essential. A deposition log is one technique of summarization (see Form 14.30 on the accompanying CD).

Deposition summary letters that outline the major facts and issues surfacing from the testimony transcribed in a deposition are also beneficial. Deposition documents can be overwhelming. Extracting essential information in an abridged format can be accomplished by a deposition digest. Brenda Piatz offers the following step-by-step process:

> 1. *Review notes, memos, and letters from the client regarding the facts and issues.*
>
> 2. *Read the entire deposition cursorily, attempting to spot testimony regarding important points.*
>
> 3. *Reread the deposition slowly and carefully to get the overall context of the subject clearly in mind, making notations.*
>
> 4. *Read two to five pages ahead of yourself to allow the testimony to fall into place and make sense. As you read, keep asking yourself, "How can the substance of what the deponent said be summarized succinctly and accurately? Has the witness been consistent? Are there inconsistencies or gaps in what the witness said or failed to say with what the client previously told the attorney or what was uncovered in investigation? Has the witness been incomplete in his or her answers? What questions should be followed up in later discovery?"*
>
> 5. *Draw a schematic map, diagram, or chart to help explain, if applicable, or as an aid to the attorney.*

6. *Write or dictate a brief narrative of the witness's testimony. Sometimes it may be necessary to quote the testimony word for word.*

7. *Make a list of lines and page numbers where particular answers are important to a point or issue.*

8. *Have the summary typed and place the original in the front of the deposition. You may want to bind it into the deposition transcript so it will not fall out and be lost.*[123]

Paralegals must give significant attention to the integrity and accuracy of the deposition transcript. Given the liberal admissibility of a deposition, any inconsistencies or evidence that impeaches the deponent may provide insight into the merits of the case, especially when considering issues of credibility.

Interrogatories

Interrogatories, the submission of written questions to the opposing party, are an acceptable method of discovery. Interrogatories are a series of questions, usually lengthy and all-encompassing. As in other forms of discovery, the questioning must be relevant and sensible and must not be a "fishing expedition" for information. David Young alleges that despite the generic proscription against such sport, the courts manifest amazing tolerance for even the most irrelevant expeditions.[124]

Moreover, the interrogatories must not be so burdensome as to create an economic hardship for the answering party. According to Rule 33(b), interrogatories may relate to any matters that can be asked about under Rule 26(b) on depositions, and the answers may be used to the extent permitted by the rules of evidence.[125] Interrogatories can be used in any cause of action, ranging from accident cases to product liability cases. In an accident case, for example, a defendant or a plaintiff may be asked whether he or she was driving at a certain rate of speed or whether a part in the car appeared to be defective. Unlike in a deposition, there is no opportunity to cross-examine an answer that is given in written form.

However, their ease of preparation and economic efficacy make them of indispensable value in the evaluation of a civil action. Moreover, for some purposes, interrogatories are more effective than depositions. Often the deposition of an opposing party cannot be taken profitably unless certain fundamental facts can be learned about the party and his or her case in order to be used in preparation of the deposition.[126] Information sought and found in the interrogatory process can include, but is not limited to, the following types:

- Business statistics.
- Lists of documents.
- Information about corporations and other business structures.
- Detailed technical information.
- Identification of documents.
- Witness statements.
- Clarification of witness statements.

- Available physical evidence.
- Explanations to technical questions.
- Information about finances and tax records.
- Information about licenses.
- Identities of experts.
- Scope of insurance coverage.
- Data about products and services.
- Data about automobiles.[127]

Paralegals must prepare interrogatories precisely. Queries should be narrow in scope and design rather than broad-based. With standardized interrogatories, opposing counsel can object to a question's content if the question has no relevance. Some standardized interrogatories are shown in Forms 14.31 and 14.32 on the accompanying CD.

Objections to interrogatories may be properly grounded in these theories:

1. The information sought is not relevant to the case.

2. The information sought is privileged.

3. The information sought is for trial preparation, and the necessary demonstration of substantial need and inability to obtain the equivalent has not been made.

4. The information sought refers to specially retained nonwitness experts, and the necessary showing of need and inability to obtain the substantial equivalent has not been made.

5. The inquiry places an unreasonably great burden on the respondent.[128]

Interrogatories are increasingly being submitted and responded to by electronic means.[129]

A motion objecting to the scope or range of discovery questions is a justifiable pleading (see Form 14.33 on the accompanying CD).[130] The key to drafting interrogatories is to understand the nature of the cause of action, distinguishing the issues between the litigants and focusing on specific problems between competing interests. The complaint, answer, and other documentation in the record should be evaluated before questions are posed. The body of any set of interrogatories always will consist of these components:

- Background interrogatories.
- Interrogatories dealing with the pleadings.
- Interrogatories that cover specific facts of the case at hand.
- Interrogatories that deal with legal and factual issues.
- Interrogatories that attempt to summarize the facts.

A timetable for interrogatories (Form 14.34 on the accompanying CD) and an interrogatory log (Form 14.35) are tools that should be part of the regular interrogatory process. Because interrogatories become part of the court's formal record, a caption is necessary (see Form 14.36 for the federal caption heading).[131] Once interrogatories have been filed, a response is required within a specific period, usually ranging between 30 and 45 days. Responses should be directed to the questions posed. They should not be evasive, deliberately misleading, or false. Vague references to the responding party's pleadings are insufficient, particularly when the purpose of the interrogatory is to clarify vague pleadings.[132] Accuracy is essential. (See the sample pleading response technique shown in Form 14.37).[133] Paralegals need to carefully draft, compile, and analyze interrogatories. If a paralegal goes on a fishing expedition during the interrogatories, the responses received will be useless and indeterminable. If the paralegal's concept of the case is unfocused, the lines of questioning, issues of the case, matters to be resolved, and problems to be settled will never be clarified. "Interrogatories should be drafted to survive any objections by the parties served. Courts are increasingly sensitive to charges that overuse of interrogatories constitutes abusive discovery. Entire sets of interrogatories have been struck down because they are too long or too many or because they are too vague or unintelligible."[134]

Alternate Discovery Applications

Production of Documents

Under traditional civil process, the Federal Rules permit other techniques of discovering the opposing party's information. Under Rule 34 on production of documents, document requests can be attached to a list of interrogatories or to the pleadings themselves. The scope of Rule 34 is concerned with providing litigants the opportunity to inspect "and copy, any designated documents (including writings, drawings, graphs, charts, photographs, phonorecords, and other data compilations from which information can be obtained, translated if necessary) . . . or to inspect and copy, test, or sample any tangible things which constitute or contain matters within the scope of Rule 26(b)."[135] Several means may be used to accomplish this end, but the record must reflect that a formal request was made. Attorneys who work with each other regularly provide easy access for inspecting and copying documents. A plaintiff's request for the production of documents under Rule 34 is shown in Form 14.38 on the accompanying CD.

Under any reasonable standard, a party who wishes to inspect or produce cannot demand reproduction at the expense of the opposition; nor should it insist that reproduction costs or any other incidental expenses be incurred by anyone but the person making the request. Requests for documents should be screened for legitimacy. Here are some common objections to requests:

- The documents are not in the possession, custody, or control of the responding party.
- The documents no longer exist.
- The documents are not yet prepared.
- The documents are irrelevant.
- The documents impose undue burden or expense to produce.
- The documents are mental impressions or opinions of a lawyer.
- The documents are sought through an excessively broad request.
- The documents are sought through a vague and ambiguous request.[136]

If a counsel balks at a production request, a motion to compel will allow a judicial resolution (see Form 14.39 on the accompanying CD).[137]

Rule 35: Request for Physical and Mental Examination

According to Rule 35, a request for a mental or a physical examination of an opposing party may be a proper method of gaining discovery:

> *Rule 35. Physical and Mental Examination of Persons.*
>
> (a) *Order for Examination. When the mental or physical condition (including the blood group) of a party or other person in the custody or under the legal control of a party, is in controversy, the court in which the action is pending may order the party to submit to a physical or mental examination by a suitably licensed or certified examiner or to produce for examination the person in the party's custody or legal control. The order may be made only on motion for good cause shown and upon notice to the person to be examined and to all parties and shall specify the time, place, manner, conditions, and scope of the examination and the person or persons by whom it is to be made.*
>
> (b) *Report of Examiner.*
>
> (1) *If requested by the party against whom an order is made under Rule 35(a) or the person examined, the party causing the examination to be made shall deliver to the requesting party a copy of the detailed written report of the examiner setting out the examiner's findings, including results of all tests made, diagnoses, and conclusions, together with like reports of all earlier examinations of the same condition. After delivery the party causing the examination shall be entitled upon request to receive from the party against whom the order is made a like report of any examination, previously or thereafter made, of the same condition, unless, in the case of a report of examination of a person not a party, the party shows that the party is unable to obtain it. The court on motion may make an order against a party requiring delivery of a report on such terms as are just, and if an examiner fails or refuses to make a report the court may exclude the examiner's testimony if offered at trial.*
>
> (2) *By requesting and obtaining a report of the examination so ordered or by taking the deposition of the examiner, the party examined waives any privilege the party may have in that action or any other involving the same controversy, regarding the testimony of every other person who has examined or may thereafter examine the party in respect of the same mental or physical condition.*
>
> (3) *This subdivision applies to examinations made by agreement of the parties, unless the agreement expressly provides otherwise. This subdivision does not preclude discovery of a report of an examiner or the taking of a deposition of the examiner in accordance with the provisions of any other rule.*[138]

A request alone will not suffice for a subsequent court order. Relevance will play a crucial role in the court's judgment about the issuance of the order. Merely alleging mental difficulties does not meet a threshold for decision making, as is evident in recent sexual harassment cases. Rule 35 motions may "distinguish between plaintiffs who allege current mental injury from those who claim past pain and suffering. If emotional distress is claimed to have been experienced in the past, courts tend to deny motions to compel mental evaluations. In contrast, courts have ordered examinations of plaintiffs who allege that they are currently suffering from mental illness due to their harassment, especially when they plan to proffer expert testimony in support of their claims."[139]

   If an informal request does not produce the examination results, a motion for an order directing the plaintiff or defendant to submit to a mental or physical examination is in order. Form 14.40 on the accompanying CD contains the required language.[140] A court that concurs in a judgment that a mental or physical exam should be taken by a plaintiff or defendant will order the party to submit (see Form 14.41).[141]

Rule 36: Request for Admissions

   Rule 36 permits either side to request admissions of specific facts regarding genuineness of legal documents or truth of any tactical matter or legal conclusion. Admitting to a specific fact, document, or legal issue assists in the clarification of issues during the litigation process. Once an admission is made, it is extremely difficult for the party who has done so to withdraw it. Admissions practice narrows the issues by eliminating noncontentious matters and automatically authenticating documents and other matters that have foundational or other admissibility requirements. A request for admissions is shown in Form 14.42 on the accompanying CD.[142] An answer to a request for admissions is shown in Form 14.43.[143]

Stipulations

Defendants and plaintiffs may stipulate as to certain facts and events to make them a formal part of the court's record. This technique is known as *stipulation*. In Form 14.44 on the accompanying CD, the stipulation shown is "as if made in open court and entered on the minutes of the proceedings."[144]

Much information that could be formally acquired through techniques of court order, petition, or the like can also be obtained through cordial and professional relationships. Attorneys have an obligation to treat opposing counsel with professional deference and regard. If a request is made that can be informally followed, why not follow through? The goodwill that one generates with other lawyers and members of the legal community goes a long way. In many cases, a court order forcing discovery on a given issue could have been prevented by lawyers simply acting maturely. Moreover, the federal courts can impose sanctions for failure to cooperate in a discovery process. Any attorney who exhibits abusive discovery conduct is bound to receive judicial discipline. Most attorneys, if approached judiciously, will be courteous and accessible.

MOTION PRACTICE

In contrast to complaints, petitions, answers, and replies, a motion is a request for a judicial authority to review a given aspect of a case or controversy. Motion practice exists at all stages of the legal process, including the pretrial stage, the trial, and many postconviction and postjudgment processes. The sheer volume of motions has triggered novel approaches to calendaring, docket control, and even the assignment of judges and special masters to handle the extraordinary load.[145]

A motion seeks a specific resolution of a singular aspect of a claim, controversy, or cause of action. A paralegal's skills in drafting, researching, and filing motions will be in demand regularly. Although most cases never reach trial, many cases involve motion practice. One should be wary of misuse, misapplication, and/or technical procedural errors in the use of motions. A paralegal should ask himself or herself these questions:

- Is the timing of the motion correct?
- Have I allowed sufficient time for a response to the motion filed?
- Have I chosen the correct court?
- Have I moved to include third parties?
- Did I amend my motion in a timely fashion?
- Have I restricted the content of my motion to matters in the pleadings?
- Have I filed appeals to motion results?
- Have I attempted to settle the basis of the motion?
- Am I prepared to advocate my motion?
- Have I filed and served my motion in a timely manner?[146]

A paralegal must know how to prepare motion documentation. Accordingly, a summary review of standardized motions follows.

Motions may be technical or substantive. All motion pleadings require notice to the opposing party. (A notice of motion is shown in Form 14.45 on the accompanying CD.)[147]

Motions on Pleadings

Pleadings themselves (that is, the complaint, answer, cross-claim, or counterclaim) can be technically and legally deficient. Parties who wish to challenge, clarify, or verify the nature of a pleading may file the following motions:

Motion to make a pleading more definite and specific: See Form 14.46 on the accompanying CD for an example.

Motion to strike pleading: See Form 14.47 for an example.

Motion for judgment on the pleadings: See Form 14.48 for an example.

Motion to dismiss—no justiciable controversy: See Form 14.49 for an example.[148]

Motions on the Parties

Motions also can be based on a technical deficiency in the pleading regarding the subject matter or the jurisdiction of the person. Such motions include these:

Motion to dismiss based on no jurisdiction: See Form 14.50 on the accompanying CD for an example.[149]

Motion to dismiss as a class action: See Form 14.51 for an example.

Third-party practice motions.

Third-party defendants or plaintiffs can be joined under theories of intervention, interpleader, or additional defendant practice. Form 14.52 includes a motion to intervene. Form 14.53 includes a motion to join a third party.

Other Technical Motions

Statute of Limitations

Other technical motions can be presented through standard motion practice. Form 14.54 on the accompanying CD is a motion to dismiss based on the statute of limitations.[150]

Motion to Consolidate

See Form 14.55 on the accompanying CD for an example.

Motions for Discovery

As reviewed in the discovery section, a party who is not cooperating in the discovery process can be ordered to produce documents and tangible items under Rule 34 of the Federal Rules of Civil Procedure.

Motion Nunc Pro Tunc

On its face, the content of the Federal Rules of Civil Procedure outlines some stringent rules regarding computational times for answers in litigation practice, such as the 20-day response time for an answer to a complaint. For example, a party who has failed to follow a time limit and becomes victimized by a default judgment may be able to request, under a motion *nunc pro tunc,* to open the answer period.

Because the rules are liberally construed, the courts may waive or reopen time frames if they find a reasonable explanation. One should never assume, however, that a motion *nunc pro tunc* will ever be granted. Use Form 14.56 on the accompanying CD to correct a clerical omission in an agreement between the parties.

Miscellaneous Motions

Motion for a Continuance

Parties who are not ready for a trial, legal hearing, or other matters should file a motion for continuance (see Form 14.57 on the accompanying CD).[151]

Motion in Limine

A motion in limine can be made to restrict the testimony of a party in a cause of action (see Form 14.58 on the accompanying CD).

Motion for a Summary Judgment

A summary judgment (which takes place when a court summarily finds in favor of either plaintiff or defendant) can be requested before a trial or jury judgment is rendered. This motion is made when a party proclaims that there is no genuine issue of material fact in dispute. A motion for summary judgment can be either total or partial (see Forms 14.59 and 14.60 on the accompanying CD).[152]

Motion for a Default Judgment

A party who has not responded to pleadings, who has not defended himself or herself in an action, and who has failed to appear in an action will lose by default judgment (see Form 14.61 on the accompanying CD).[153] A motion to set aside a default judgment, based on a meritorious defense that the defendant did not have an opportunity to produce, can be presented through the pleading shown in Form 14.62.[154]

Motion for Directed Verdict

At the end of a plaintiff's case, a motion for a directed verdict is a permissible litigation strategy (see Form 14.63 on the accompanying CD).[155] A directed verdict may take place in a case in which the party with the burden of proof has failed to present sufficient evidence.

Postjudgment Motions—Motion to Reconsider or Reargue

A defendant or plaintiff who is not satisfied with the results of a judicial finding may file a motion to reconsider (see Form 14.64 on the accompanying CD) or for leave to reargue (see Form 14.65).[156] In some jurisdictions, the appropriate motion is a judgment notwithstanding the verdict. See the following Massachusetts statutory authority:

> *Rule 50. Motion for a Directed Verdict and for Judgment Notwithstanding the Verdict*
>
> (b) *Motion for Judgment Notwithstanding the Verdict. Whenever a motion for a directed verdict made at the close of all the evidence is denied or for any reason is not granted, the court is deemed to have submitted the action to the jury subject to a later determination of the legal questions raised by the motion. Not later than 10 days after entry of judgment, a party who has moved for a directed verdict may serve a motion to have the verdict and any judgment entered thereon set aside and to have judgment entered in accordance with the motion for a directed verdict; or if a verdict was not returned such party, within 10 days after the jury has been discharged, may serve a motion for judgment in accordance with the motion for a directed verdict. A motion for a new trial may be joined with this motion, or a new trial may be prayed for in the alternative. If a verdict was returned the court may allow the judgment to stand or may reopen the judgment and either order a new trial or direct the entry of judgment as if the requested verdict had been directed. If no verdict was returned the court may direct the entry of judgment as if the requested verdict had been directed or may order a new trial.*[157]

Paralegals should be familiar with different software and data files in motion practice. Many software companies offer comprehensive packages in litigation.

TRIAL

Although paralegals are not litigators and are not responsible for the direct examination and cross-examination of witnesses and parties, they are essential players in the actual advocacy process. They perform many tasks in preparation for trial, including some of the following administrative tasks:

- Carrying and maintaining visual aids.
- Doing research.
- Taking notes about a trial and witness testimony that may be the basis of a motion for new trial.
- Maintaining exhibits and documents.
- Monitoring witnesses and the client.
- Informing the witness what to wear to trial, how to act, and so on.
- Helping witnesses or clients in small ways, such as directing them to restaurants for the lunch break.[158]
- Ensuring that all papers and documents have been filed properly.
- Creating charts, diagrams, and other evidence tools or arranging for outside graphic companies to create them.
- Maintaining responsibility for all demonstrative evidence.

Some nonadministrative tasks may include these:

- Assessing witness depositions/testimony for impeachment purposes.
- Assessing completeness of direct examinations and cross-examinations.
- Assisting in the assessment of evidence.
- Assessing juror reactions.

In addition to these duties, Peggy N. Kerley, Paul A. Sukys, and Joanne Banker Hames point out that the litigation paralegal's job varies from firm to firm and from case to case. In a complex litigation case, one may be part of a litigation team along with attorneys, other paralegals, and legal secretaries, in which case the responsibilities are limited to one aspect of the case.[159] As expected, this coordination of people, tangible items, documents, trial notebooks, binders, evidence logs, and the payment of fees, costs, and expenses is the job of a skilled administrator. The consequences of negligence in management can be catastrophic. Lawyers are always accountable—even for the gross errors of paralegals to whom they delegate.[160]

Schum and Tillers call upon the advocate at trial to "marshal evidence" to prove one's point.[161] Collecting and organizing evidence is a key paralegal function.

It has been suggested that every paralegal should be responsible for compiling a pleadings folder containing copies of original and amended complaints, answers, and other pleadings documents.[162] In addition to assembling these documents, the paralegal should prepare a cover sheet that summarizes the complaint and the responses and should cross-reference these summaries with the original documents. Bruno advises all paralegals to create a comprehensive trial notebook for each case, dividing the topical considerations within the notebook into the following categories:

- Preparation.
- Laptop and demonstrative equipment.
- Agenda/game plan/trial strategy.
- Analysis of the issues.
- Guidelines of proof.
- Evaluation of prospective jurors.
- Voir dire notes.
- Case summaries.
- List of witnesses.
- Witness files.
- Witness sheets for direct examination.
- Notes for opening statement.
- Notes for cross-examination.
- Index of discovery material to be used at trial.
- Notes and briefs about law and evidence and trial motions.
- Requests for charge.
- PowerPoint presentations.
- Notes for final arguments.
- Lists of exhibits and exhibit file.
- Trial agenda.
- To-do lists.
- Medical briefs.
- Equipment for repair.
- Technical notes.[163]

The Paralegal's Role in Trial Preparation

The role of the paralegal in the typical trial process can include

- Case evaluation.
- Pretrial conference.
- Pretrial motions.
- Commencement of trial.
- Jury selection.
- Opening statements.
- Plaintiff's case direct examination.
- Cross-examination.
- Rebuttal.
- Defendant's case.
- Plaintiff's cross-examination.
- Defense rebuttal.
- Motions (if applicable).
- Closing arguments.
- Submission of jury instructions.
- Court's instruction to jury.
- Jury deliberations.
- Appeal.
- Posttrial motion and other activity.[164]

Assistance with Witnesses

The examination of both lay and expert witnesses is a serious responsibility. A paralegal must account for witnesses, as well as make certain that witnesses are prepared for testimony. Witnesses may be friendly or hostile. Those who are friendly need adequate coaching and explanation of the litigation process. Those who are hostile must be properly subpoenaed.

Rule 45(b) of the Federal Rules of Civil Procedure states,

> *A subpoena may be served by any person who is not a party and is not less than 18 years of age. Service of a subpoena upon a person named therein shall be made by delivering a copy thereof to such person and, if the person's attendance is commanded, by tendering to that person the fees for one day's attendance and the mileage allowed by law. When the subpoena is issued on behalf of the United States or an officer or agency thereof, fees and mileage need not be tendered. Prior notice of any commanded production of documents and things or inspection of premises before trial shall be served on each party in the manner prescribed by Rule 5(b).[165]*

In most law firms and agencies the paralegal has the responsibility to ensure that witnesses have been put on notice of their obligation to attend. (An example of a witness subpoena is reproduced in Form 14.66 on the accompanying CD.) Keeping track of witnesses to subpoena can be accomplished by using Form 14.67.

The following forms relating to witnesses should also be included in the trial notebook:

• Witness list (see Form 14.68 on the accompanying CD).

• Information sheets about witnesses: This document is an informational cover sheet about each witness verifying subpoena dates, deposition participation, and relevant forms of testimony (see Form 14.69).

• Witness checklists: This form focuses on an observance of physical injury of continuing benefit to a case of personal injury or medical malpractice. It includes questions regarding the injury itself, restrictions of movement, and third parties who witness the ongoing malady.

• Deposition index (see Form 14.70).

Another paralegal function is to follow the testimony of both plaintiff and defendant. A paralegal's review of the content of direct examinations and cross-examinations should help the attorney in the trial process, especially when challenges to evidence or the substance and merit of a case, or motions for summary judgment or directed verdicts are necessary. Suggested guidelines for witness testimony at trial are reproduced in Forms 14.71 and 14.72 on the accompanying CD.

Jury Verdict Analysis and Voir Dire

Jury verdict inclination is surmised during the voir dire process. Paralegals should become familiar with verdict review and analysis materials that are commercially available. Jury verdicts are

FIGURE 14.18
National Jury Verdict Review and Analysis

Source: Jury Verdict Review & Analysis. Available at www.jvra.com.

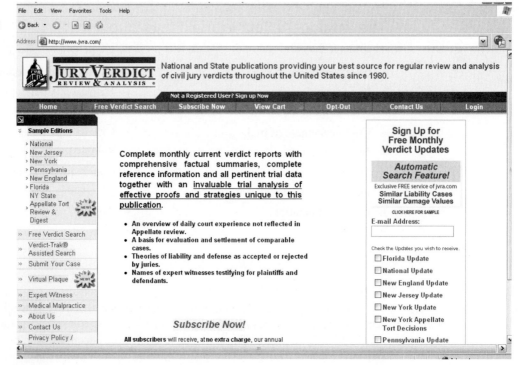

tabulated in terms of dollar sums in the National Jury Verdict Review and Analysis.[166] Paralegals can review services such as this to determine the range of damages awarded in similarly situated cases.

The paralegal's observation skills are essential in *voir dire*—the selection of jurors. For example, how does a juror feel about individuals who do not pay their bills? What does a juror think of doctors who make mistakes? McAllaster comments,

> *The trial lawyer must get enough information to identify those jurors with strong feelings about perceived, excessive verdicts, while at the same time educating the rest of the panel about the significant damages in your case and your intent to ask them to award only those damages which you have proved to them. . . . It is the trial lawyer's challenge to stay in touch with commonly held opinions and to use that knowledge to his or her advantage when selecting a jury in a given case.*[167]

Useful practice tools regarding selection and attributes of actual or potential jury members include question sheets such as that shown in Form 14.73 on the accompanying CD. Another document used to compile potential juror background information, experience, employment, personality traits, and familial data is shown in Form 14.74.

The Georgia Lawyer's Basic Practice Handbook suggests recording pertinent information concerning each juror. "[T]ype on a clean jury chart the name and pertinent information regarding each juror so that during the course of the trial, you may think in terms of the experiences that those jurors have had and appeal to those experiences in the closing argument."[168]

Trial Notebook

The paralegal's function in trial litigation is multifaceted. There is a continuous responsibility to account for witnesses, evidence, exhibits, and even a case's theories of argument and research. Many documents and forms are designed to help the paralegal do this.

Janice E. Hall, a litigation paralegal, focuses on the importance of the trial notebook:

> *All in all, consider your trial notebook the most important part of your trial preparation. Put in the extra touches which can make it useful and efficient, and begin it early. If you do all these things, then you will not only impress your attorney but you will know that you did everything possible to obtain a positive outcome for your client.*[169]

A typical trial notebook may include the following tabs:

- Pretrial notes.
- Proof analysis.
- Checklists.
- Research.
- Procedures.
- Stipulations.
- Pretrial orders.
- Discovery digest.
- Pretrial motions.
- Jury selection.

- Opening statement.
- Research/evidence.
- Research/substantive.
- Plaintiff's witnesses.
- Defendant's witnesses.
- Exhibits list.
- Rebuttal charges.
- Final argument.
- Trial motions.
- Notes during trial.[170]

A checklist for the trial notebook is included in Form 14.75 on the accompanying CD. Forms included in a typical trial notebook include these:

Form 14.76: Things to do

Form 14.77: Plaintiff's exhibits

Form 14.78: Proof outline

Form 14.79: Law of the case

Form 14.80: Expense report

Form 14.81: Argument notes

Document Production

The paralegal is expected to handle record keeping, administrative tracking, personality coordination, and investigative tasks. Document indexes can be helpful in the organization of documents at trial. (See Form 14.82 on the accompanying CD for a useful index.)

Document production does not have to be unpleasant. Once you become comfortable with the procedures of document production, you will begin to enjoy them. This is the stage of the game where you can actually roll up your sleeves and discover the pieces of information that can lead you to wonderful clues and aids to preparing your case. It is an opportunity to show how valuable a paralegal can be, and it can give you a sense of accomplishment.[171]

Some forms of evidence do not lend themselves to storage in the law firm during a lengthy litigation because of their size or daily use on a job site. Photographs of these exhibits may be taken and retained in the client's file for use in preparing the case for trial, at which time the original piece of evidence may be introduced. Ensuring that evidence is preserved in its original form may be one of the paralegal's responsibilities.[172] Keeping meticulous notes of arguments, both opening and closing, is also a duty of the paralegal involved in trial litigation. The Georgia Institute of Continuing Legal Education notes,

> *What are the major arguments and points? For instance, in a criminal case, one may want to emphasize the burden of proof or the identity issue. In a misrepresentation case, one may want to emphasize the lack of knowledge of the defendant or the falsity of the statement. One should record these thoughts in a trial notebook concerning possible types of arguments or analogies. One should not wait until the night before trial to prepare the opening and closing.*[173]

Trial Equipment

Trial kits or equipment packages are necessary for each trial. The contents will vary depending on the cause of action advocated. See Figure 14.19 for the suggested contents of a personal injury kit relating to an automobile accident.

Jury Instructions

Once the closing arguments have been completed, paralegals may help the attorney prepare jury instructions that are to be submitted to the judge. A set of jury instructions, delivered by the judge, outlines the law in the case before the court. Ideally jury instructions are a scholarly, unemotional, and neutral exposition of the law as applied to the facts at hand. Attorneys have a right to submit the specific instructions they wish to have included in the judge's presentation to the

FIGURE 14.19
Personal Injury Kit

Trial Kit Contents: Personal Injury	
Litigation bag	Lined paper pad (2)
Blue pens	Blue car labeled "Johnson"
Black pens	Red car labeled "Wood"
Red pens	Yellow car labeled "Cline"
Green pens	Four-way traffic light
Highlighters	Magnetic board
Pencils	White board (scene predrawn)
Erasers	Whiteboard markers:
Stapler and staples	Red
Paper clips (small and large)	Yellow
Colored paper clips	Blue
Rubber bands	Easel
Scissors	Day-in-the-life video—Johnson
Ruler	Accident reconstruction video
Correction fluid	Trial exhibit folders
Band-Aids	Johnson's cast
Tylenol	Trial notebook

jury after both sides have rested. A sample request for input on instructions to the jury is shown in Form 14.83 on the accompanying CD. An objection to instructions is shown in Form 14.84.[174] The attorney's input in the drafting of jury instructions can be either mandatory or discretionary. Input is permitted by most local rules of civil and criminal procedure and is solicited by many members of the judiciary. Instructions play a key role in the jury's deliberations and therefore are subject to challenge or exception. Those challenges and exceptions must be formalized in the record to preserve them for appellate purposes. In addition, standardized jury instructions are published by major law publishers. (See Figure 14.20[175] for a list of standardized jury instructions from Connecticut.) Form 14.85 shows a selected portion of jury instructions in a murder trial.

FIGURE 14.20 Standardized Jury Instructions

Before Start of Evidence
1.1 Obligation of juror's oath
1.2 Description of the order of the trial
1.3 No deliberations until completion of evidence and charge
1.4 Note taking
1.5 Questions by jurors
1.6 Limitation on contact with jurors
1.7 Schedule of the trial
1.8 Communications with the court
1.9 Deaf or hearing-impaired jurors: interpreter
1.10 Replacement of regular juror with alternate juror

During Evidence
1.11 Instructions before recesses
1.12 Instructions before adjournment for the day
1.13 Effect of side bars/argument without jury
1.14 Exhibits marked for identification only
1.15 Stricken evidence [time of striking]
1.16 Evidence admitted for limited purpose
1.17 Ruling on objections
1.18 Prerecorded testimony
1.19 Jury view

After Evidence
1.20 Role of judge/role of jury
1.21 Duty to follow the law
1.22 Duty to decide on the evidence
1.23 Direct and circumstantial evidence
1.23 (a) Use of medical records
1.24 Stipulations/undisputed facts
1.25 Admissions from pleadings
1.26 Admissions from requests to admit
1.27 Admissions from superseded pleadings
1.28 Judicial notice
1.29 Learned treatises
1.30 Use of deposition
1.31 Limiting instructions on evidence
1.32 Stricken evidence [final charge]
1.33 Ruling on objections
1.34 Burden of proof—claims
1.35 Burden of proof—affirmative defenses
1.36 Standard of proof
1.37 Separation of liability and damages
1.38 Bifurcation of liability and damages
1.39 Credibility of witnesses
1.40 False testimony
1.41 Expert witnesses
1.42 Hypothetical question

1.43 Corporation [other entity] as a party
1.44 Directed verdict
1.45 Use of notes during deliberations
1.46 Mention of insurance
1.47 Sympathy/prejudice
1.48 Suggested amount of damages
1.49 Process for jury's deliberations
1.49 (a) Duty to deliberate
1.50 Restrictions on deliberations
1.51 Procedures for reporting verdict
1.52 Discharge of alternate juror(s)
1.53 Deadlocked jury
1.54 Reconsider verdict
1.55 Discharge jury

General Negligence
2.1 Negligence—definition
2.2 Distinction between statutory and common-law negligence
2.3 Common-law negligence defined
2.4 Reasonable care
2.5 Standard of care applicable to children
2.6 Standard of care of others in relation to children
2.7 Duty—foreseeability
2.8 Standard of care of volunteer (common law)
2.9 Standard of care of person suffering from an infirmity
2.10 Specifications of negligence—complaint
2.11 Specifications of negligence—special defense

Automobile
2.12 Statutory negligence—reckless driving
2.13 Statutory negligence—speeding
2.14 Statutory negligence—traveling unreasonably fast
2.15 Statutory negligence—slow speed
2.16 Statutory negligence—passing
2.17 Statutory negligence—left turn
2.18 Statutory negligence—right of way at intersections
2.19 Statutory negligence—lights
2.20 Statutory negligence—unsafe tires
2.21 Statutory negligence—brakes
2.22 Statutory negligence—failing to drive a reasonable distance apart
2.23 Statutory negligence—driving in right-hand lane
2.25 Right to assume that others will obey the law
2.26 Lookout
2.27 Failure to sound horn
2.28 Sudden emergency

Posttrial Activities

Judgments

After the delivery of jury instructions, if applicable, a judgment is made by applying the law to the acts at hand. When a judgment comes down, a decree is issued. Various examples of such decrees are shown in Forms 14.86 and 14.87 on the accompanying CD.

Appeals

Parties who are not satisfied with the judgment of a court generally can appeal. If a decision to appeal is affirmative, notice of the appeal must be given to the opposing party (see Form 14.88 on the accompanying CD). A civil docketing statement outlining the nature of the appeal usually is required (see Form 14.89).

Examples of notice or petition to appeal from a tax court and administrative agency are shown in Forms 14.90 and 14.91 on the accompanying CD.

Summary

The chapter's main purpose was twofold: to review the rules of civil procedure governing the conduct of civil litigation and to give the paralegal a step-by-step analysis of a typical civil action, from commencement of the action to appeal of a judgment or other decree.

The chapter contained a wide array of topics, including the nature of jurisdiction, the identification of parties, third party practice and class action analysis, and alternatives to typical legal remedies.

The paralegal was walked through a typical civil action, with substantial discussion of the summons and complaint and their drafting requirements. Service of process to give the complaint legal effect was covered in detail. Responsive pleadings were thoroughly reviewed, such as answers, replies, counterclaims, cross-claims, affirmative defenses, and the processes of amendment and supplementation.

The discovery process, which is crucial to successful case evaluation and trial preparation, was addressed thoroughly. Sample interrogatories were provided. The role of motions in civil practice was emphasized, including motions on the pleadings and parties, technical motions, and motions that address the merits of a case or a decision.

Finally, the paralegal's role in trial advocacy and process was examined. A growing trend holds paralegals responsible for recordkeeping; administrative and personal oversight; preparation of exhibits; tracking of real and physical evidence; preparation of witness testimony; involvement in jury selection and analysis; and preparation of jury instructions.

Discussion Questions

1. Can you envision a judicial system that is not adversarial in nature? Describe some options.

2. Are there alternatives to formal litigation? What other methods are popular?

3. How would you define a *meritorious claim?*

4. In a case of product liability, who could be the potential plaintiffs and defendants?

5. In an auto accident case, what types of jurisdiction could be claimed?

6. When is it appropriate to award punitive damages in addition to compensatory damages?

7. If service of process cannot be made in person, what are the alternatives?

8. Give an example of a pleading that avers or claims something with the necessary conciseness, specificity, and precision as outlined in the Federal Rules.

9. Although there are many formal techniques of discovery, can you explain some informal techniques of finding out information?

10. Why do admissions and stipulations save time, cost, and energy?

11. If a case has no merit, no substantive dispute, and no factual disagreement, what types of motions should an attorney file?

Research Assignment

1. Answer the following questions regarding federal civil negligence complaints using the federal code and rules. Which rule governs the adjustment or change of any pleadings in the federal system? Does service of a complaint on a defendant make any changes to the complaint impossible? If additional facts or damages come to light after the complaint has been served, how should they be made part of the case's formal record? Will any change to the original complaint need court approval?

Practical Exercises

1. Assume that a liability claim is directed toward the manufacturer and distributor of an elevator. Prepare the body of a complaint employing these factual allegations:

   - The elevator car had various operating devices and controls that were broken.
   - There was no protective barrier between the floor level and the elevator shaft when the plaintiff/victim fell into it.
   - The elevator electrical components were defective, were constructed of substandard wiring, and had rusted and corroded joints and bolts.
   - The ropes of the elevator that guide the shaft up a vertical path were crushed, worn, broken, and excessively in disrepair.
   - All safety devices were improperly adjusted, corroded, and not appropriately lubricated.
   - The elevator mechanism did not include a safety device when a jam or other intrusion took place.

2. Prepare a defendant's answer to a complaint using the following information:
   - Defendant warned plaintiff about the currently defective and inoperable state of the elevator.
   - Defendant warned plaintiff that only authorized personnel were permitted to operate the elevator.
   - Defendant posted signs and warnings in well-illuminated locations.
   - Defendant alleges that plaintiff did not exercise reasonable care in entering a business location that was declared off limits.
   - Defendant alleges that all statutory ordinances, laws, and regulations were adhered to in the maintenance of the elevator.
   - Defendant states that plaintiff should have or could have known that the elevator shaft was lower than the adjoining floor at the time he fell into it.
   - Defendant responds that it was foreseeable that a human being could be caught between a moving elevator and an elevator shaft wall.
   - Defendant responds that it is not responsible for defects, if there were any, because it did not engineer, design, or construct the elevator.

3. Complete a request for production of documents, using the information from Exercises 1 and 2. Be sure the discovery addresses documents relevant to an elevator shaft incident.

Internet Resources

Legal Information Institute: civil procedure—www.law.cornell.edu/wex/index.php/Civil_procedure

Hieros Gamos: guide to litigation law—www.hg.org/litg.html

CataLaw: litigation and procedure—www.catalaw.com/topics/Litigation.shtml

Federal Judicial Center: materials on electronic discovery and civil litigation—www.fjc.gov/public/home.nsf/autoframe?openform&url_r=pages/196

The 'Lectric Law Library Lawcopedia's general litigation matters—www.lectlaw.com/tlit.htm

U.S. Attorney's Manual—www.usdoj.gov/usao/eousa/foia_reading_room/usam/index.html

National Center for State Courts: civil procedure—www.ncsconline.org/WC/Events/PreCivView.htm

Endnotes

1. Milford Meyer, Pennsylvania Trial Advocacy Handbook 24 (1976).

2. James W. McElheney, Trial Handbook: A Practical Primer on Trial Advocacy 19 (1981).

3. Daniel Walfish, *Making Lawyers Responsible for the Truth: The Influence of Marvin Frankel's Proposal for Reforming the Adversary System,* 35 Seton Hall L. Rev. 613 (2005).

4. *Id.* at 618.

5. Arthur R. Miller, *The Adversary System: Dinosaur or Phoenix,* 69 Minn. L. Rev. 1 (1984).

6. Jonathan Macey, *Ethics in Corporate Representation: Occupation Code 541110: Lawyers, Self-Regulation, and the Idea of a Profession,* 74 Fordham L. Rev. 1079, 1079 (2005).

7. *Id.*

8. J. Michael McWilliams, *Our Justice Deficit,* 29 Trial 19 (April 1993).

9. Roxanne Barton Conlin, *"Litigation Explosion": Tempest in a Teapot?* 27 Trial 114 (Nov. 1991).

10. American College of Trial Lawyers, ALI–ABA Committee on Continuing Professional Responsibility, Civil Trial Manual 38 (1974).

11. *See generally* Deborah L. Rhode, *Frivolous Litigation and Civil Justice Reform: Miscasting the Problem, Recasting the Solution,* 54 Duke L.J. 447 (2004); Mitchell J. Nathanson, *It's the Economy (and Combined Ratio), Stupid: Examining the Medical Malpractice Litigation Crisis Myth and the Factors Critical to Reform,* 108 Penn St. L. Rev. 1077 (2004); Michael P. Murphy, *Note: Tort Reform: Would a Noneconomic Damages Cap Be Constitutional, and Is One Necessary in Iowa?* 53 Drake L. Rev. 813 (2005).

12. Herbert M. Kritzer, *The Future Role of "Law Workers": Rethinking the Forms of Legal Practice and the Scope of Legal Education,* 44 Ariz. L. Rev. 917 (2002).

13. 28 U.S.C.S. §1251 (2005).

14. *See generally* Christiana Ochoa Summer, *Symposium: Part III: Courts: Access to U.S. Federal Courts as a Forum for Human Rights Disputes: Pluralism and the Alien Tort Claims Act,* 12 Ind. J. Global Leg. Stud. 631 (2005).

15. *See* Joseph M. Creed, *Choice of Law under the Multiparty, Multiforum Trial Jurisdiction Act of 2002,* 17 Regent U.L. Rev. 157, (2004–2005).

16. 28 U.S.C.S. §1332 (2005).

17. Thomas R. Macmillan, *The Changing Patterns of Litigation in One Federal Court,* 34 Fed. B. News & J. 179 (1987).

18. *What Has Contributed to a Decade of Increasing Civil Case Filings?* The Third Branch (Admin. Office of the U.S. Courts, Washington, D.C.) Dec. 2001, available at http://www.uscourts.gov/ttb/dec01ttb/filings.html, last visited 1/17/05.

19. American College of Trial Lawyers, *supra* note 10, at 75.

20. United Mine Workers v. Gibbs, 383 U.S. 715 (1966).

21. American College of Trial Lawyers, *supra* note 10, at 75–76; *see also* E.H. Schopler, *Annotation, Federal Civil Procedure Rule 17(C) Relating to Representation of Infant or Incompetent Person,* 68 A.L.R. 2d 752 (1959); P.H. Vartanian, Annotation, *Duty of Federal Court to Exercise Jurisdiction Dependent on Diversity of Citizenship to Follow State Statutes and State Court Decisions, in the Application or Enforcement of Equitable Principles or Rights,* 115 A.L.R. 1007 (1938) and 160 A.L.R. 1243 (1946).

22. *See for example* 19A Am. Jur. Pleadings & Practice Forms 614 (1985).

23. That litigants shop for the most sympathetic forum is now well established. *See generally* Richard Maloy, *Forum Shopping? What's Wrong with That?* 24 Quinnipiac L. Rev. 25 (2005).

24. James A. Dooley, *Selecting the Forum—Plaintiff's Position,* 3 Am. Jur. Trials 605 (1987).

25. *Id.* at 609; *see also* 28 U.S.C. §1447 (2005).

26. American College of Trial Lawyers, *supra* note 10, at 80.

27. Lawrence S. Charfoos & David W. Christensen, Personal Injury Litigation: Technique and Technology 570 (1988); *see also* Thomas A. Dickerson, *Selecting Viable and Liable Travel Law Defendants,* 87 Case & Com. 28 (1982).

28. Jonathan M. Purver, *Tavern Keeper's Liability under the Dram Shop Act,* 32 Am. Jur. Proof of Facts 357 (1982).

29. *Id.*

30. Fed. R. Civ. Pro. 17 (2005).

31. Fed. R. Civ. Pro. 19 (2005).

32. Fed. R. Civ. Pro. 21 (2005).

33. *See generally* Richard Maloy, *Forum Shopping? What's Wrong with That?* 24 Quinnipiac L. Rev. 25 (2004).

34. Laura I. Asbury, *Comment: A Practical Guide to Fraudulent Joinder in the Eighth Circuit,* 57 Ark. L. Rev. 913 (2005): "Fraudulent joinder occurs when a plaintiff joins both a diverse and a nondiverse defendant in a state action, but has no intention of prosecuting the case against the nondiverse defendant, or has no reasonable basis to support his claim against the nondiverse defendant. In such a case, the joinder of a nondiverse and diverse defendant 'may be shown by a petition for removal to be only a fraudulent device to prevent a removal.'"

35. Fed. R. Civ. Pro. 22 (2005).

36. Fed. R. Civ. Pro. 23 (2005).

37. For a fascinating finding on class actions relative to firearms, see D.C. v. Beretta, USA, et al., 872 A.2d 633 (2005).

38. *See generally* John Bronsteen, *Class Action Settlements: An Opt-In Proposal*, 2005 U. ILL. L. REV. 903 (2005).

39. WESLEY GILMER JR., THE LAW DICTIONARY 125 (6th ed. 1986).

40. BRYAN A. GARNER, A DICTIONARY OF MODERN LEGAL USAGE 220 (1987).

41. ROBERT COVER, OWEN M. FISS, & JUDITH RESNIK, PROCEDURE 190–191 (1988).

42. U.S. DEPARTMENT OF JUSTICE, DISPUTE RESOLUTION: TECHNIQUES AND APPLICATIONS, A SELECTED BIBLIOGRAPHY v (1985).

43. Irving R. Kaufman, *Reform for a System in Crisis: Alternative Dispute Resolution in the Federal Courts*, 59 FORDHAM L. REV., 17–18 (Oct. 1990).

44. Pub. L. No. 101-650, Tit. I §103(A), 104 Stat 5091 (codified at 28 U.S.C. §473(A) (Supp. II 1990).

45. Eric D. Green, *Voluntary ADR: Part of the Solution*, 29 TRIAL 35 (April 1993).

46. CHARLES P. NEMETH, LITIGATION, PLEADINGS, AND ARBITRATION 591 (1990).

47. U.S. Department of Justice, *supra* note 42, at vi.

48. For an assessment of a publicly annexed ADR program, *see generally* Honorable Howard H. Dana Jr., *Court-Connected Alternative Dispute Resolution in Maine*, 57 ME. L. REV. 349 (2005); *see also* Joshua Isaacs, *Current Development 2004–2005: A New Way to Avoid the Courtroom: The Ethical Implications Surrounding Collaborative Law*, 18 GEO. J. LEGAL ETHICS 833 (2005).

49. *See generally* Joseph Kimble, *Plain Language: Guiding Principles for Restyling the Federal Rules of Civil Procedure (Part 2)*, MI BAR JNL., Oct. 2005, at 52.

50. Fed. R. Civ. Pro. 8 (2005)

51. For related pleadings, *see* 5 AM. JUR PLEADINGS & PRACTICE FORMS 427 (1968).

52. For related pleadings, *see* 5 AM. JUR. PLEADINGS & PRACTICE FORMS 430 (1968).

53. For related pleadings, *see* 5 AM. JUR. PLEADINGS & PRACTICE FORMS 448 (1968).

54. For related pleadings, *see* 5 AM. JUR. PLEADINGS & PRACTICE FORMS 449 (1968) and 14 FED. PROC. FORMS, Form 367 (1978).

55. Fed. R. Civ. Pro. 8 (2005).

56. Fed. R. Civ. Pro. 10 (2005).

57. Fed. R. Civ. Pro. 8 (2005).

58. Fed. R. Civ. Pro. 8 (2005).

59. For related pleadings, *see* 5 AM. JUR. PLEADINGS & PRACTICE FORMS 503 (1968).

60. For related pleadings, *see* 5 AM. JUR. PLEADINGS & PRACTICE FORMS 422 (1968).

61. *See generally* 5 AM. JUR. PLEADINGS & PRACTICE FORMS 462 (1968).

62. *See generally* 5 AM. JUR. PLEADINGS & PRACTICE FORMS 462 (1968).

63. R. COVER et al., *supra* note 41, at 191–192.

64. JOHN TARANTINO & DAVID OLIVEIRA, LITIGATING NECK AND BACK INJURIES 1-35–1-36 (1988).

65. CYNTHIA MONTEIRO, PARALEGAL PREPARATION AND PLEADINGS 3-719 (1988).

66. For an analysis of recent reform efforts in the area of medical malpractice and damages, *see* Ronen Avraham, *Should Pain-and-Suffering Damages Be Abolished from Tort Law? More Experimental Evidence,* 55 UNIV. OF TORONTO L.J. 941 (2005).

67. THE INSTITUTE OF CONTINUING LEGAL EDUCATION IN GEORGIA, GEORGIA LAWYER'S BASIC PRACTICE HANDBOOK 12.3 (1988).

68. Fed. R. Civ. Pro. 11 (2005).

69. *See generally* 5 AM. JUR. PLEADINGS & PRACTICE FORMS 559 (1968).

70. *See generally* 5 AM. JUR. PLEADINGS & PRACTICE FORMS 561 (1968).

71. Fed. R. Civ. Pro. 4 (C) (1) and (2) (2005).

72. Fed. R. Civ. Pro. 4 (2005)

73. For related pleadings, *see* 25 AM. JUR. PLEADINGS & PRACTICE FORMS 180 (1973).

74. CAROLE A. BRUNO, PARALEGAL'S LITIGATION HANDBOOK 179–184 (1980).

75. Fed. R. Civ. Pro. 6 (2005).

76. Fed. R. Civ. Pro. 12 (2005).

77. Fed. R. Civ. Pro. 12 (2005).

78. *See also* 19a AM. JUR. PLEADINGS & PRACTICE FORMS 508, 509 (1985).

79. *See also* 19a AM. JUR. PLEADINGS & PRACTICE FORMS 509 (1985).

80. *See also* 19a AM. JUR. PLEADINGS & PRACTICE FORMS 514 (1985).

81. Nemeth, *supra* note 46, at 229.

82. Fed. R. Civ. Pro. 13 (A) and (B) (2005).

83. Fed. R. Civ. Pro. 13 (A) and (B) (2005).

84. Mark R. Bower, *Baseless Affirmative Defenses*, 17 TRIAL LAW. Q. 54, 60 (1986).

85. For a fascinating look at the seatbelt defense, see the Wyoming law highlighted in Tori R. A. Kricken, *The Viability of "The Seatbelt Defense" in Wyoming Implications of and Issues Surrounding Wyoming Statute §31-5-1402(F),* 5 WYO. L. REV. 133 (2005).

86. Gilmer, *supra* note 39, at 6.

87. *Id*. at 29.

88. *Id*. at 33.

89. *Id*. at 86.

90. *Id*. at 109–110.

91. *Id*. at 118.

92. *Id.* at 127–128.

93. *Id.* at 136

94. *Id.* at 149.

95. *Id.* at 193.

96. *Id.* at 201.

97. *Id.* at 248.

98. *Id.* at 284.

99. *Id.* at 288.

100. *Id.* at 149.

101. *Id.* at 202.

102. *Id.* at 339.

103. For related pleadings, *see* 19a Am. Jur. Pleadings & Practice Forms 530 (1985).

104. Fed R. Civ. Pro. 15 (2005).

105. Fed R. Civ. Pro. 15(A) and (B) (2005).

106. Fed R. Civ. Pro. 15(A) and (B) (2005).

107. *See generally* Arvo Van Alstyne, *Tactics and Strategy of Pleading*, 3 Am. Jur. Trials 681 (1987).

108. Fed. R. Civ. P. 26(F) (2005).

109. Fed. R. Civ. P. 16(a) (2005).

110. American College of Trial Lawyers, *supra* note 10, at 179.

111. Fed. R. Civ. P. 26 (2002).

112. American College of Trial Lawyers, *supra* note 10, at 181.

113. American College of Trial Lawyers, *supra* note 10, at 182.

114. Fed. R. Civ. P. 26 (B) (3) (2005).

115. *See* Fed. R. Civ. P. 26 (2005).

116. Fed. R. Civ. P. 26 (2005).

117. Cynthia Vaughn Tupis, *Tips for Compelling and Limiting Discovery*, 9 Legal Assistant Today 164, 168–169 (May–June 1992).

118. Fed. R. Civ. P. 45(B) (2005). For related pleadings, *see* Anderson Ohio Civil Practice, Form 6.19 (1988).

119. Robert E. Oliphant, Deposition Tactics and Considerations 15–17 (1988).

120. *Id.* at 72–73.

121. Dianne D. Zalewski, Paralegal Discovery 2-6–2-6.1(1988).

122. Fed. R. Civ. P. 26(B)(4).

123. Brenda Piatz, *Organizing and Digesting Depositions*, 6 Legal Assistant Today 45, 47 (July–Aug. 1990). Copyright 1993 James Publishing, Inc. Reprinted with permission from Legal Assistant Today. For subscription information call 714-755-5450.

124. "No matter how liberally the standard of 'relevant to the subject matter' or leading 'to the discovery of admissible evidence' is applied in favor of permitting discovery, the concept of relevance is still the primary focus at depositions in determining the permissible scope of discovery.... Thus the concept of relevance would not prohibit 'fishing expeditions,' but it did assure that there be at least some bait on the hook before the fish was obligated to bite." David Young, Esq., *A New Theory of Relativity: The Triumph of the Irrelevant at Depositions*, 36 U.W.L.A. L. Rev. 56, 59 (2005).

125. Fed. R. Civ. P. 33(b) & 26(b) (2005).

126. American College of Trial Lawyers, *supra* note 10, at 211.

127. Noel H. Thompson, *How to Use Written Interrogatories Effectively*, 16 Prac. Law. 81 (1970).

128. American College of Trial Lawyers, *supra* note 10, at 217.

129. Lloyd S. van Oostenrijk, *Paper or Plastic? Electronic Discovery and Spoliation in the Digital Age*, 42 Hous. L. Rev. 1163 (2005); *see also* Ophir D. Finkelthal, *Scope of Electronic Discovery and Methods of Production*, 38 Loy. L.A. L. Rev. 1591 (2005); Sonia Salinas, *Electronic Discovery and Cost Shifting: Who Foots the Bill?* 38 Loy. L.A. L. Rev. 1639 (2005).

130. For related pleadings, *see* Anderson Ohio Civil Practice, Form 6.79 (1988).

131. *See also* 5 Am. Jur. Pleadings & Practice Forms 109 (1968).

132. American College of Trial Lawyers, *supra* note 10, at 216–217.

133. For some general yet expert discussion of discovery technique and practice, *see* Matthew Bender, Bender's Form of Discovery (1973); D. Danner, Patterned Discovery of Medical Malpractice (1985); D. Harney, Medical Malpractice (1973). For related pleadings, *see* Anderson Ohio Civil Practice, Form 6.127 (1988).

134. Charfoos & Christensen, *supra* note 27, at 638.

135. Fed. R. Civ. P. 34(A) (2005).

136. Cynthia Vaughn Tupis, *Tips for Compelling and Limiting Discovery*, 9 Legal Assistant Today 164, 168 (May–June 1992).

137. For related pleadings, *see* 18 Am. Jur. Pleadings & Practice Forms 323 (1986).

138. Fed. R. Civ. P. 35 (2005).

139. Margaret Bull Kovera & Stacie A. Cass, *Compelled Mental Health Examinations, Liability Decisions, and Damage Awards in Sexual Harassment Cases: Issues for Jury Research*, 8 Psych. Pub. Pol. and L. 96, 98 (2005).

140. For related pleadings, *see* Anderson Ohio Civil Practice, Form 6.111 (1988).

141. For related pleadings, *see* Anderson Ohio Civil Practice, Form 6.115 (1988).

142. For related pleadings, *see* Anderson Ohio Civil Practice, Form 6.155 (1988).

143. For related pleadings, *see* Anderson Ohio Civil Practice, Form 6.157 (1988).

144. *See generally* 20 Am. Jur. Pleadings & Practice Forms 162 (1972).

145. Mark A. Fellows & Roger S. Haydock, *The Role of Special Masters in the Judicial System: Federal Court Special Masters: A Vital Resource in the Era of Complex Litigation,* 31 Wm. Mitchell L. Rev. 1269 (2005).

146. Scott Cagan, *Twelve Motion Practice, Blunders in U.S. District Court,* N.Y. St. B. J. 46 (April 1990).

147. *See generally* 18 Am. Jur. Pleadings & Practice Forms 312 (1986).

148. For related pleadings, *see* 8 Fed. Proc. Forms 23 (1976).

149. For related pleadings, *see* 19a Am. Jur. Pleadings & Practice Forms 633 (1985).

150. For related pleadings, *see* 15 Fed. Proc. Forms 368 (1985).

151. *See also* 18 Am. Jur. Pleadings & Practice Forms 321 (1986).

152. *See generally* 23 Am. Jur. Pleadings & Practice Forms 94 (1973) and 23 Am. Jur. Pleadings & Practice Forms 101 (1983).

153. *See generally* 18 Am. Jur. Pleadings & Practice Forms 325 (1986).

154. *Id.*

155. *See generally* 18 Am. Jur. Pleadings & Practice Forms 326 (1986).

156. *See generally* 18 Am. Jur. Pleadings & Practice Forms 313, 314 (1986).

157. Mass. R. Civ. P. Rule 50.

158. Bruno, *supra* note 74, at 364.

159. Peggy N. Kerley, Paul A. Sukys, & Joanne Banker Hames, Civil Litigation for The Paralegal (1992).

160. Some courts have been kinder. "In 2004, the United States Court of Appeals for the Ninth Circuit, sitting *en banc,* decided Pincay v. Andrews, referred to here as Pincay II. In Pincay II, the court affirmed a district court's finding of excusable neglect—and thus its decision to extend a party's time to appeal—when a lawyer left to a paralegal serving as his law firm's calendaring clerk responsibility for calendaring appellate deadlines and the paralegal calendared the wrong date." Douglas R. Richmond, *Neglect, Excusable and Otherwise,* 2 Seton Hall Cir. Rev. 119, 120 (2005); Pincay v. Andrews, 351 F.3d 947, 951 (9th Cir. 2003), *reh'g granted,* 367 F.3d 1087 (9th Cir. 2004), vacated, 389 F.3d 853 (9th Cir. 2004) (en banc).

161. David Schum & Peter Tillers, *Marshalling Evidence for Adversary Litigation,* 13 Cardozo L. Rev. 657 (1991).

162. Thomas Eimermann, Fundamentals of Paralegalism 551 (3d ed. 1992).

163. Bruno, *supra* note 74, at 91.

164. See local statutes and rules for trial procedure. *See also* Heather Holland, *Paperless? Hah! Less Paper—Absolutely Basic Records Management Concepts,* 18 Utah Bar J. 45 (2005).

165. Fed. R. Civ. P. 45 (B)(1) (2005).

166. Jury Verdict Review Publications, Inc., *National Jury Verdict Review & Analysis,* at http://www.jvra.com (follow "National" hyperlink under "Sample Editions").

167. Carolyn McAllaster, *Voir Dire Tips,* Trial Briefs 16, 17 (Fall 1987).

168. ICLE Georgia, *supra* note 67, at 16.88.

169. Janice E. Hall, *Building Trial Notebooks,* 8 Legal Assistant Today 60, 64 (Jan.–Feb. 1991).

170. ICLE Georgia, *supra* note 67, at 16.85.

171. Marcy Davis Fawcett, Paralegal Litigation Forms 6-13 (1988).

172. Kerley et al., *supra* note 159, at 85.

173. ICLE Georgia, *supra* note 67, at 16.88–16.89.

174. For related pleadings, *see* 1 Fed. Proc. Forms 911 (1975).

175. State of Connecticut, Judicial Branch, *Civil Jury Instructions,* available at http://www.jud.state.ct.us/civiljury/default.htm.

Appendix A

Paralegal Associations

National/International

The American Alliance of Paralegals, Inc.
16815 East Shea Blvd.
Suite 110, Box 101
Fountain Hills, AZ 85268
www.aapipara.org

American Association for Paralegal Education
19 Mantua Road
Mt. Royal, NJ 08061
www.aafpe.org

Canadian Association of Paralegals
P.O. Box 967, Station "B"
Montreal, Quebec
Canada, H3B 3K5
www.caplegal.ca

International Paralegal Management Association
Headquarters
P.O. Box 659
Avondale Estates, GA 30002-0659
www.paralegalmanagement.org/ipma

National Association of Legal Assistants
1516 S. Boston, #200
Tulsa, OK 74119
www.nala.org

National Association of Legal Secretaries
314 East Third Street, Suite 210
Tulsa, OK 74120
www.nals.org

National Federation of Paralegal Associations, Inc.
P.O. Box 2016
Edmonds, WA 98020
www.paralegals.org

National Paralegal Association
Box 406
Solebury, PA 18963
www.nationalparalegal.org

Alabama

Alabama Association of Paralegals, Inc.
P.O. Box 55921
Birmingham, AL 35255-5921
www.aaopi.com

NE Alabama Litigation Support Association
P.O. Box 1218
Gadsden, AL 35901
www.freewebs.com/nealsa

Alaska

Alaska Association of Paralegals
P.O. Box 101956
Anchorage, AK 99510-1956
www.alaskaparalegals.org

Arizona

Arizona Paralegal Association
P.O. Box 392
Phoenix, AZ 85001
www.azparalegal.org

Arkansas

Arkansas Paralegal Association
400 West Capitol, Suite 1900
Little Rock, AR 72201
www.arparalegal.org

California

California Alliance of Paralegal Associations
P.O. Box 1089
San Leandro, Ca 94577-0126
www.caparalegal.org

California Lawyers' Assistants, Secretaries, & Students
442½ Pacific Avenue
Alameda, CA 94501
www.lawguru.com/users/law/class/class.html

Cuyamaca Association of Paralegal Students
Cuyamaca College
900 Rancho San Diego Parkway
El Cajon, CA 92019
www.cuyamaca.edu/CAPS

Los Angeles Paralegal Association
P.O. Box 71708
Los Angeles, CA 90071
www.lapa.org

Orange County Paralegal Association
P.O. Box 8512
Newport Beach, CA 92658
www.ocparalegal.org

Sacramento Valley Paralegal Association
P.O. Box 453
Sacramento, CA 95812-0453
www.svpa.org

San Francisco Paralegal Association
985 Darien Way
San Francisco, CA 94125
www.sfpa.com

Santa Barbara Paralegal Association
Santa Barbara Superior Court Dept. 1
1100 Anacapa Street
Santa Barbara, CA 93101
www.sbparalegals.org

Sequoia Paralegal Association
P.O. Box 3884
Visalia, CA 93278-3884
www.sequoiaparalegals.com

Colorado

Colorado Association of Professional Paralegals
& Legal Assistants
P.O. Box 8944
Denver, CO 80201
www.capplaweb.org

Rocky Mountain Paralegal Association
P.O. Box 481864
Denver, CO 80248-1864
www.rockymtnparalegal.org

Connecticut

Central Connecticut Paralegal Association, Inc.
P.O. Box 230594
Hartford, CT 06123-0594
http://paralegals.org/displaypersonalwebpage
.cfm?id=883983

Connecticut Association of Paralegals
P.O. Box 134
Bridgeport, CT 06601-0134
backup.paralegals.org/Connecticut

Delaware

Delaware Paralegal Association
P.O. Box 1362
Wilmington, DE 19899-1362
www.deparalegals.org

District of Columbia

National Capital Area Paralegal Association
P.O. Box 27607
Washington, DC 20038-7607
www.ncapa.com

Florida

Central Florida Paralegal Association, Inc.
P.O. Box 1107
Orlando, FL 32802
www.cfpainc.com

Gainesville Association of Paralegals, Inc.
P.O. Box 2519
Gainesville, FL 32602
www.afn.org/~gala

Northeast Florida Paralegal Association, Inc.
221 North Hogan St., Box 164
Jacksonville, FL 32202
www.nefpa.org

Paralegal Association of Florida
P.O. Box 7073
West Palm Beach, FL 33405
www.pafinc.org

South Florida Paralegal Association
P.O. Box 31-0745
Miami, FL 33231-0745
www.sfpa.info

Georgia

Georgia Association of Paralegals
1199 Euclid Avenue
Atlanta, GA 30307
www.gaparalegal.org

Hawaii

Hawaii Paralegal Association
P.O. Box 674
Honolulu, HI 96809
www.hawaiiparalegal.org

Illinois

Illinois Paralegal Association
P.O. Box 452
New Lenox, IL 60451-0452
www.ipaonline.org

Indiana

Indiana Paralegal Association, Inc.
P.O. Box 44518
Indianapolis, IN 46204
www.indianaparalegals.org

The Michiana Paralegal Association, Inc.
P.O. Box 11458
South Bend, IN 46634
backup.paralegals.org/Michiana/home.html

Iowa

Iowa Association of Legal Assistants
P.O. Box 93153
Des Moines, IA 50393
www.ialanet.org

Kansas

Kansas Association of Legal Assistants
P.O. Box 47031
Wichita, KS 67201
www.accesskansas.org/kala

Kansas Paralegal Association
P.O. Box 1675
Topeka, KS 66601
www.accesskansas.org/ksparalegals

Kentucky

Kentucky Paralegal Association
P.O. Box 2675
Louisville, KY 40201-2675
www.kypa.org

Louisville Association of Paralegals
P.O. Box 70265
Louisville, KY 40270-0265
www.loupara.com

Louisiana

New Orleans Paralegal Association
P.O. Box 30604
New Orleans, LA 70190
backup.paralegals.org/NewOrleans

Tulane University Paralegal Association
1400 Poydras Street, Suite 841
New Orleans, LA 70118
http://www.uc.tulane.edu/

Maryland

Maryland Association of Paralegals, Inc.
550 M Ritchie Highway PMB# 203
Severna Park, MD 21146
backup.paralegals.org/Maryland/home.html

Massachusetts

Massachusetts Paralegal Association, Inc.
P.O. Box 1381
Marblehead, MA 01945
www.massparalegal.org

Michigan

Legal Assistants Association of Michigan
P.O. Box 6826
Traverse City, MI 49696
www.laamnet.org

Minnesota

Minnesota Paralegal Association
1711 W. County Road B #300N
Roseville, MN 55113
www.mnparalegals.org

Missouri

Kansas City Paralegals Association
1912 Clay Street
North Kansas City, MO 64116
www.kcparalegals.org

St. Louis Association of Legal Assistants
P.O. Box 69218
St. Louis, MO 63169-0218
www.slala.org

Nebraska

Nebraska Association of Legal Assistants
P.O. Box 24943
Omaha, NE 68124
www.neala.org

New Jersey

Legal Assistants Association of New Jersey
P.O. Box 142
Caldwell, NJ 07006
www.laanj.org

New York

Adirondack Paralegal Association
338 Reynolds Road
Ft. Edward, NY 12828

Capital District Paralegal Association, Inc.
P.O. Box 12562
Albany, New York 12212-2562
www.timesunion.com/communities/cdpa/

Empire State Alliance of Paralegal Associations
http://www.geocities.com/empirestateparalegals/
empirestateparalegals@yahoo.com

Long Island Paralegal Association
1877 Bly Road
East Meadow, NY 11554
http://www.liparalegals.org/main_web/homepage_main.htm

Onondaga County Bar Association
Legal Assistants' Committee
1000 State Tower Building
Syracuse, NY 13202
http://www.onbar.org/

Oswego County Paralegal Association
Hancock & Estabrook, LLP
1500 Tower 1
P.O. Box 4976
Syracuse, NY 13221

Paralegal Association of Rochester
P.O. Box 40567
Rochester, NY 14604
http://www.par.itgo.com/

Western New York Paralegal Association
P.O. Box 207
Buffalo, NY 14201
www.wnyparalegals.org

North Carolina

North Carolina Paralegal Association
P.O. Box 36264
Charlotte, NC 28236-6264
www.ncparalegal.org

Ohio

Cincinnati Paralegal Association
P.O. Box 1515
Cincinnati, OH 45201
www.cincinnatiparalegals.org

Cleveland Association of Paralegals
P.O. Box 14517
Cleveland, OH 44114-0517
www.capohio.org/~newcap/

Northeastern Ohio Paralegal Association
P.O. Box 80068
Akron, OH 44308-0068
backup.paralegals.org/NortheasternOhio

Paralegal Association of Central Ohio
P.O. Box 15182
Columbus, Ohio 43215-0182
www.pacoparalegals.org

Oklahoma

Oklahoma Paralegal Association
714 Maple Drive
Weatherford, OK 73096
www.okparalegal.org

Oregon

Oregon Paralegal Association
P.O. Box 8523
Portland, OR 97207
www.oregonparalegals.org

Pennsylvania

Central Pennsylvania Paralegal Association (CPPA)
P.O. Box 11814
Harrisburg, PA 17108
home.comcast.net/~cppageneral

Chester County Paralegal Association
P.O. Box 295
15 West Gay Street
West Chester, PA 19381
www.chescoparalegal.org

Philadelphia Association of Paralegals
P.O. Box 59179
Philadelphia, PA 19102-9179
www.philaparalegals.com

Pittsburgh Paralegal Association
P.O. Box 2845
Pittsburgh, PA 15230
www.pghparalegals.org

Rhode Island

Rhode Island Paralegals Association
P.O. Box 1003 Providence, RI 02901
backup.paralegals.org/RhodeIsland

Tennessee

Tennessee Paralegal Association
P.O. Box 21723
Chattanooga, TN 37424
www.tnparalegal.org

Texas

Alamo Area Professional Legal Assistants, Inc.
P.O. Box 524
San Antonio, TX 78292
www.aapla.org

Capital Area Paralegal Assn.
P.O. Box 773
Austin, TX 78767
www.capatx.org

Dallas Area Paralegal Association
P.O. Box 12533
Dallas, TX 75225-0533
www.dallasparalegals.org

Fort Worth Paralegals Association
P.O. Box 17021
Fort Worth, TX 76102
www.fwpa.org

Houston Legal Assistants Association
Lyric Centre, Suite 900 (400 Louisiana)
Houston, TX 77002
hmpa-hlaa.com/MAMBO

Houston Paralegal Association
P.O. Box 61863
Houston, Texas 77208-1863
www.houstonparalegalassociation.org

SE Texas Association of Legal Assistants
P.O. Box 813
Beaumont, TX 77704
www.setala.org

South Texas Organization of Paralegals, Inc.
P.O. Box 2486
San Antonio, TX 78299-2486
www.southtexasparalegals.org

Washington

Washington State Paralegal Association
P.O. Box 58530
Seattle, WA 98138-1530
www.wspaonline.com

West Virginia

Legal Assistants of West Virginia
P.O. Box 3422
Charleston, WV 25334-3422
www.lawv.org

Wisconsin

Madison Area Paralegal Association
P.O. Box 2242
Madison, Wisconsin 53701-2242
www.madisonparalegal.org

Paralegal Association of Wisconsin
P.O. Box 510892
Milwaukee WI 53203-0151
www.wisconsinparalegal.org

Appendix B

THE CONSTITUTION OF THE UNITED STATES

We the People of the United States, in Order to form a more perfect Union, establish Justice, insure domestic Tranquility, provide for the common defence, promote the general Welfare, and secure the Blessings of Liberty to ourselves and our Posterity, do ordain and establish this Constitution for the United States of America.

ARTICLE I

Section 1. All legislative Powers herein granted shall be vested in a Congress of the United States, which shall consist of a Senate and House of Representatives.

Section 2. The House of Representatives shall be composed of Members chosen every second Year by the People of the several States, and the Electors in each State shall have the Qualifications requisite for Electors of the most numerous Branch of the State Legislature.

No Person shall be a Representative who shall not have attained to the Age of twenty five Years, and been seven Years a Citizen of the United States, and who shall not, when elected, be an Inhabitant of that State in which he shall be chosen.

Representatives and direct Taxes shall be apportioned among the several States which may be included within this Union, according to their respective Numbers, which shall be determined by adding to the whole Number of free Persons, including those bound to Service for a Term of Years, and excluding Indians not taxed, three fifths of all other Persons. The actual Enumeration shall be made within three Years after the first Meeting of the Congress of the United States, and within every subsequent Term of ten Years, in such Manner as they shall by Law direct. The Number of Representatives shall not exceed one for every thirty Thousand, but each State shall have at Least one Representative; and until such enumeration shall be made, the State of NewHampshire shall be entitled to chuse three, Massachusetts eight, Rhode-Island and Providence Plantations one, Connecticut five, New-York six, New Jersey four, Pennsylvania eight, Delaware one, Maryland six, Virginia ten, North Carolina five, South Carolina five, and Georgia three.

When vacancies happen in the Representation from any State, the Executive Authority thereof shall issue Writs of Election to fill such Vacancies.

The House of Representatives shall chuse their Speaker and other Officers; and shall have the sole Power of Impeachment.

Section 3. The Senate of the United States shall be composed of two Senators from each State, chosen by the Legislature thereof for six Years; and each Senator shall have one Vote.

Immediately after they shall be assembled in Consequence of the first Election, they shall be divided as equally as may be into three Classes. The Seats of the Senators of the first Class shall be vacated at the Expiration of the second Year, of the second Class at the Expiration of the fourth Year, and of the third Class at the Expiration of the sixth Year, so that one third may be chosen every second Year; and if Vacancies happen by Resignation, or otherwise, during the Recess of the Legislature of any State, the Executive thereof may make temporary Appointments until the next Meeting of the Legislature, which shall then fill such Vacancies.

No Person shall be a Senator who shall not have attained to the Age of thirty Years, and been nine Years a Citizen of the United States, and who shall not, when elected, be an Inhabitant of that State for which he shall be chosen.

The Vice President of the United States shall be President of the Senate, but shall have no Vote, unless they be equally divided.

The Senate shall chuse their other Officers, and also a President pro tempore, in the Absence of the Vice President, or when he shall exercise the Office of President of the United States.

The Senate shall have the sole Power to try all Impeachments. When sitting for that Purpose, they shall be on Oath or Affirmation. When the President of the United States is tried, the Chief Justice shall preside: And no Person shall be convicted without the Concurrence of two thirds of the Members present.

Judgment in Cases of Impeachment shall not extend further than to removal from Office, and disqualification to hold and enjoy any Office of honor, Trust or Profit under the United States: but the Party convicted shall nevertheless be liable and subject to Indictment, Trial, Judgment and Punishment, according to Law.

Section 4. The Times, Places and Manner of holding Elections for Senators and Representatives, shall be prescribed in each State by the Legislature thereof; but the Congress may at any time by Law make or alter such Regulations, except as to the Places of chusing Senators.

The Congress shall assemble at least once in every Year, and such Meeting shall be on the first Monday in December, unless they shall by Law appoint a different Day.

Section 5. Each House shall be the Judge of the Elections, Returns and Qualifications of its own Members, and a Majority of each shall constitute a Quorum to do Business; but a smaller Number may adjourn from day to day, and may be authorized to compel the Attendance of absent Members, in such Manner, and under such Penalties as each House may provide.

Each House may determine the Rules of its Proceedings, punish its Members for disorderly Behaviour, and, with the Concurrence of two thirds, expel a Member.

Each House shall keep a Journal of its Proceedings, and from time to time publish the same, excepting such Parts as may in their Judgment require Secrecy; and the Yeas and Nays of the Members of either House on any question shall, at the Desire of one fifth of those Present, be entered on the Journal.

Neither House, during the Session of Congress, shall, without the Consent of the other, adjourn for more than three days, nor to any other Place than that in which the two Houses shall be sitting.

Section 6. The Senators and Representatives shall receive a Compensation for their Services, to be ascertained by Law, and paid out of the Treasury of the United States. They shall in all Cases, except Treason, Felony and Breach of the Peace, be privileged from Arrest during their Attendance at the Session of their respective Houses, and in going to and returning from the same; and for any Speech or Debate in either House, they shall not be questioned in any other Place.

No Senator or Representative shall, during the Time for which he was elected, be appointed to any civil Office under the Authority of the United States, which shall have been created, or the Emoluments whereof shall have been encreased during such time; and no Person holding any Office under the United States, shall be a Member of either House during his Continuance in Office.

Section 7. All Bills for raising Revenue shall originate in the House of Representatives; but the Senate may propose or concur with Amendments as on other Bills.

Every Bill which shall have passed the House of Representatives and the Senate, shall, before it become a Law, be presented to the President of the United States: If he approve he shall sign it, but if not he shall return it, with his Objections to that House in which it shall have originated, who shall enter the Objections at large on their Journal, and proceed to reconsider it. If after such Reconsideration two thirds of that House shall agree to pass the Bill, it shall be sent, together with the Objections, to the other House, by which it shall likewise be reconsidered, and if approved by two thirds of that House, it shall become a Law. But in all such Cases the Votes of both Houses shall be determined by yeas and Nays, and the Names of the Persons voting for and against the Bill shall be entered on the Journal of each House respectively. If any Bill shall not be returned by the President within ten Days (Sundays excepted) after it shall have been presented to him, the Same shall be a Law, in like Manner as if he had signed it, unless the Congress by their Adjournment prevent its Return, in which Case it shall not be a Law.

Every Order, Resolution, or Vote to which the Concurrence of the Senate and House of Representatives may be necessary (except on a question of Adjournment) shall be presented to the President of the United States; and before the Same shall take Effect, shall be approved by him, or being disapproved by him, shall be repassed by two thirds of the Senate and House of Representatives, according to the Rules and Limitations prescribed in the Case of a Bill.

Section 8. The Congress shall have Power to lay and collect Taxes, Duties, Imposts and Excises, to pay the Debts and provide for the common Defence and general Welfare of the United States; but all Duties, Imposts and Excises shall be uniform throughout the United States;

> To borrow Money on the credit of the United States;
>
> To regulate Commerce with foreign Nations, and among the several States, and with the Indian Tribes;
>
> To establish an uniform Rule of Naturalization, and uniform Laws on the subject of Bankruptcies throughout the United States;
>
> To coin Money, regulate the Value thereof, and of foreign Coin, and fix the Standard of Weights and Measures;
>
> To provide for the Punishment of counterfeiting the Securities and current Coin of the United States;
>
> To establish Post Offices and post Roads;
>
> To promote the Progress of Science and useful Arts, by securing for limited Times to Authors and Inventors the exclusive Right to their respective Writings and Discoveries;
>
> To constitute Tribunals inferior to the supreme Court;
>
> To define and punish Piracies and Felonies committed on the high Seas, and Offences against the Law of Nations;
>
> To declare War, grant Letters of Marque and Reprisal, and make Rules concerning Captures on Land and Water;
>
> To raise and support Armies, but no Appropriation of Money to that Use shall be for a longer Term than two Years;
>
> To provide and maintain a Navy;
>
> To make Rules for the Government and Regulation of the land and naval Forces;
>
> To provide for calling forth the Militia to execute the Laws of the Union, suppress Insurrections and repel Invasions;
>
> To provide for organizing, arming, and disciplining, the Militia, and for governing such Part of them as may be employed in the Service of the United States, reserving to the States respectively, the Appointment of the Officers, and the Authority of training the Militia according to the discipline prescribed by Congress;
>
> To exercise exclusive Legislation in all Cases whatsoever, over such District (not exceeding ten Miles square) as may, by Cession of particular States, and the Acceptance of Congress, become the Seat of the Government of the United States, and to exercise like Authority over all Places purchased by the Consent of the Legislature of the State in which the Same shall be, for the Erection of Forts, Magazines, Arsenals, dock-Yards, and other needful Buildings;—And
>
> To make all Laws which shall be necessary and proper for carrying into Execution the foregoing Powers, and all other Powers vested by this Constitution in the Government of the United States, or in any Department or Officer thereof.

Section 9. The Migration or Importation of such Persons as any of the States now existing shall think proper to admit, shall not be prohibited by the Congress prior to the Year one thousand eight hundred and eight, but a Tax or duty may be imposed on such Importation, not exceeding ten dollars for each Person.

The Privilege of the Writ of Habeas Corpus shall not be suspended, unless when in Cases of Rebellion or Invasion the public Safety may require it.

No Bill of Attainder or ex post facto Law shall be passed.

No Capitation, or other direct, Tax shall be laid, unless in Proportion to the Census or enumeration herein before directed to be taken.

No Tax or Duty shall be laid on Articles exported from any State.

No Preference shall be given by any Regulation of Commerce or Revenue to the Ports of one State over those of another; nor shall Vessels bound to, or from, one State, be obliged to enter, clear, or pay Duties in another.

No Money shall be drawn from the Treasury, but in Consequence of Appropriations made by Law; and a regular Statement and Account of the Receipts and Expenditures of all public Money shall be published from time to time.

No Title of Nobility shall be granted by the United States: And no Person holding any Office of Profit or Trust under them, shall, without the Consent of the Congress, accept of any present, Emolument, Office, or Title, of any kind whatever, from any King, Prince, or foreign State.

Section 10. No State shall enter into any Treaty, Alliance, or Confederation; grant Letters of Marque and Reprisal; coin Money; emit Bills of Credit; make any Thing but gold and silver Coin a Tender in Payment of Debts; pass any Bill of Attainder, ex post facto Law, or Law impairing the Obligation of Contracts, or grant any Title of Nobility.

No State shall, without the Consent of the Congress, lay any Imposts or Duties on Imports or Exports, except what may be absolutely necessary for executing it's inspection Laws: and the net Produce of all Duties and Imposts, laid by any State on Imports or Exports, shall be for the Use of the Treasury of the United States; and all such Laws shall be subject to the Revision and Controul of the Congress.

No State shall, without the Consent of Congress, lay any Duty of Tonnage, keep Troops, or Ships of War in time of Peace, enter into any Agreement or Compact with another State, or with a foreign Power, or engage in War, unless actually invaded, or in such imminent Danger as will not admit of delay.

ARTICLE II

Section 1. The executive Power shall be vested in a President of the United States of America. He shall hold his Office during the Term of four Years, and, together with the Vice President, chosen for the same Term, be elected, as follows:

Each State shall appoint, in such Manner as the Legislature thereof may direct, a Number of Electors, equal to the whole Number of Senators and Representatives to which the State may be entitled in the Congress: but no Senator or Representative, or Person holding an Office of Trust or Profit under the United States, shall be appointed an Elector.

The Electors shall meet in their respective States, and vote by Ballot for two Persons, of whom one at least shall not be an Inhabitant of the same State with themselves. And they shall make a List of all the Persons voted for, and of the Number of Votes for each; which List they shall sign and certify, and transmit sealed to the Seat of the Government of the United States, directed to the President of the Senate. The President of the Senate shall, in the Presence of the Senate and House of Representatives, open all the Certificates, and the Votes shall then be counted. The Person having the greatest Number of Votes shall be the President, if such Number be a Majority of the whole Number of Electors appointed; and if there be more than one who have such Majority, and have an equal Number of Votes, then the House of Representatives shall immediately chuse by Ballot one of them for President; and if no Person have a Majority, then from the five highest on the List the said House shall in like Manner chuse the President. But in chusing the President, the Votes shall be taken by States, the Representation from each State having one Vote; A quorum for this purpose shall consist of a Member or Members from two thirds of the States, and a Majority of all the States shall be necessary to a Choice. In every Case, after the Choice of the President, the Person having the greatest Number of Votes of the Electors shall be the Vice President. But if there should remain two or more who have equal Votes, the Senate shall chuse from them by Ballot the Vice President.

The Congress may determine the Time of chusing the Electors, and the Day on which they shall give their Votes; which Day shall be the same throughout the United States.

No Person except a natural born Citizen, or a Citizen of the United States, at the time of the Adoption of this Constitution, shall be eligible to the Office of President; neither shall any Person be eligible to that Office who shall not have attained to the Age of thirty five Years, and been fourteen Years a Resident within the United States.

In Case of the Removal of the President from Office, or of his Death, Resignation, or Inability to discharge the Powers and Duties of the said Office, the Same shall devolve on the Vice President, and the Congress may by Law provide for the Case of Removal, Death, Resignation or Inability, both of the President and Vice President, declaring what Officer shall then act as

President, and such Officer shall act accordingly, until the Disability be removed, or a President shall be elected.

The President shall, at stated Times, receive for his Services, a Compensation, which shall neither be increased nor diminished during the Period for which he shall have been elected, and he shall not receive within that Period any other Emolument from the United States, or any of them.

Before he enter on the Execution of his Office, he shall take the following Oath or Affirmation:—"I do solemnly swear (or affirm) that I will faithfully execute the Office of President of the United States, and will to the best of my Ability, preserve, protect and defend the Constitution of the United States."

Section 2. The President shall be Commander in Chief of the Army and Navy of the United States, and of the Militia of the several States, when called into the actual Service of the United States; he may require the Opinion, in writing, of the principal Officer in each of the executive Departments, upon any Subject relating to the Duties of their respective Offices, and he shall have Power to grant Reprieves and Pardons for Offences against the United States, except in Cases of Impeachment.

He shall have Power, by and with the Advice and Consent of the Senate, to make Treaties, provided two thirds of the Senators present concur; and he shall nominate, and by and with the Advice and Consent of the Senate, shall appoint Ambassadors, other public Ministers and Consuls, Judges of the supreme Court, and all other Officers of the United States, whose Appointments are not herein otherwise provided for, and which shall be established by Law: but the Congress may by Law vest the Appointment of such inferior Officers, as they think proper, in the President alone, in the Courts of Law, or in the Heads of Departments.

The President shall have Power to fill up all Vacancies that may happen during the Recess of the Senate, by granting Commissions which shall expire at the End of their next Session.

Section 3. He shall from time to time give to the Congress Information of the State of the Union, and recommend to their Consideration such Measures as he shall judge necessary and expedient; he may, on extraordinary Occasions, convene both Houses, or either of them, and in Case of Disagreement between them, with Respect to the Time of Adjournment, he may adjourn them to such Time as he shall think proper; he shall receive Ambassadors and other public Ministers; he shall take Care that the Laws be faithfully executed, and shall Commission all the Officers of the United States.

Section 4. The President, Vice President and all civil Officers of the United States, shall be removed from Office on Impeachment for, and Conviction of, Treason, Bribery, or other high Crimes and Misdemeanors.

ARTICLE III

Section 1. The judicial Power of the United States shall be vested in one supreme Court, and in such inferior Courts as the Congress may from time to time ordain and establish. The Judges, both of the supreme and inferior Courts, shall hold their Offices during good Behaviour, and shall, at stated Times, receive for their Services a Compensation, which shall not be diminished during their Continuance in Office.

Section 2. The judicial Power shall extend to all Cases, in Law and Equity, arising under this Constitution, the Laws of the United States, and Treaties made, or which shall be made, under their Authority;—to all Cases affecting Ambassadors, other public Ministers and Consuls;—to all Cases of admiralty and maritime Jurisdiction;—to Controversies to which the United States shall be a Party;—to Controversies between two or more States;—between a State and Citizens of another State;—between Citizens of different States;—between Citizens of the same State claiming Lands under Grants of different States, and between a State, or the Citizens thereof, and foreign States, Citizens or Subjects.

In all Cases affecting Ambassadors, other public Ministers and Consuls, and those in which a State shall be Party, the supreme Court shall have original Jurisdiction. In all the other Cases before mentioned, the supreme Court shall have appellate Jurisdiction, both as to Law and Fact, with such Exceptions, and under such Regulations as the Congress shall make.

The Trial of all Crimes, except in Cases of Impeachment, shall be by Jury; and such Trial shall be held in the State where the said Crimes shall have been committed; but when not committed within any State, the Trial shall be at such Place or Places as the Congress may by Law have directed.

Section 3. Treason against the United States, shall consist only in levying War against them, or in adhering to their Enemies, giving them Aid and Comfort. No Person shall be convicted of Treason unless on the Testimony of two Witnesses to the same overt Act, or on Confession in open Court.

The Congress shall have Power to declare the Punishment of Treason, but no Attainder of Treason shall work Corruption of Blood, or Forfeiture except during the Life of the Person attainted.

ARTICLE IV

Section 1. Full Faith and Credit shall be given in each State to the public Acts, Records, and judicial Proceedings of every other State. And the Congress may by general Laws prescribe the Manner in which such Acts, Records and Proceedings shall be proved, and the Effect thereof.

Section 2. The Citizens of each State shall be entitled to all Privileges and Immunities of Citizens in the several States.

A Person charged in any State with Treason, Felony, or other Crime, who shall flee from Justice, and be found in another State, shall on Demand of the executive Authority of the State from which he fled, be delivered up, to be removed to the State having Jurisdiction of the Crime.

No Person held to Service or Labour in one State, under the Laws thereof, escaping into another, shall, in Consequence of any Law or Regulation therein, be discharged from such Service or Labour, but shall be delivered up on Claim of the Party to whom such Service or Labour may be due.

Section 3. New States may be admitted by the Congress into this Union; but no new State shall be formed or erected within the Jurisdiction of any other State; nor any State be formed by the Junction of two or more States, or Parts of States, without the Consent of the Legislatures of the States concerned as well as of the Congress.

The Congress shall have Power to dispose of and make all needful Rules and Regulations respecting the Territory or other Property belonging to the United States; and nothing in this Constitution shall be so construed as to Prejudice any Claims of the United States, or of any particular State.

Section 4. The United States shall guarantee to every State in this Union a Republican Form of Government, and shall protect each of them against Invasion; and on Application of the Legislature, or of the Executive (when the Legislature cannot be convened), against domestic Violence.

ARTICLE V

The Congress, whenever two thirds of both Houses shall deem it necessary, shall propose Amendments to this Constitution, or, on the Application of the Legislatures of two thirds of the several States, shall call a Convention for proposing Amendments, which, in either Case, shall be valid to all Intents and Purposes, as Part of this Constitution, when ratified by the Legislatures of three fourths of the several States, or by Conventions in three fourths thereof, as the one or the other Mode of Ratification may be proposed by the Congress; Provided that no Amendment which may be made prior to the Year One thousand eight hundred and eight shall in any Manner affect the first and fourth Clauses in the Ninth Section of the first Article; and that no State, without its Consent, shall be deprived of its equal Suffrage in the Senate.

ARTICLE VI

All Debts contracted and Engagements entered into, before the Adoption of this Constitution, shall be as valid against the United States under this Constitution, as under the Confederation.

This Constitution, and the Laws of the United States which shall be made in Pursuance thereof; and all Treaties made, or which shall be made, under the Authority of the United States, shall be the supreme Law of the Land; and the Judges in every State shall be bound thereby, any Thing in the Constitution or Laws of any State to the Contrary notwithstanding.

The Senators and Representatives before mentioned, and the Members of the several State Legislatures, and all executive and judicial Officers, both of the United States and of the several States, shall be bound by Oath or Affirmation, to support this Constitution; but no religious Test shall ever be required as a Qualification to any Office or public Trust under the United States.

ARTICLE VII

The Ratification of the Conventions of nine States, shall be sufficient for the Establishment of this Constitution between the States so ratifying the Same.

The Word, "the," being interlined between the seventh and eighth Lines of the first Page, the Word "Thirty" being partly written on an Erazure in the fifteenth Line of the first Page, The Words "is tried" being interlined between the thirty second and thirty third Lines of the first Page and the Word "the" being interlined between the forty third and forty fourth Lines of the second Page.

Attest William Jackson Secretary

Done in Convention by the Unanimous Consent of the States present the Seventeenth Day of September in the Year of our Lord one thousand seven hundred and Eighty seven and of the Independence of the United States of America the Twelfth In witness whereof We have hereunto subscribed our Names.

THE BILL OF RIGHTS: A TRANSCRIPTION

Note: The following text is a transcription of the first 10 amendments to the Constitution in their original form. These amendments were ratified December 15, 1791, and form what is known as the *Bill of Rights*.

Amendment I [1791]

Congress shall make no law respecting an establishment of religion, or prohibiting the free exercise thereof; or abridging the freedom of speech, or of the press; or the right of the people peaceably to assemble, and to petition the Government for a redress of grievances.

Amendment II [1791]

A well regulated Militia, being necessary to the security of a free State, the right of the people to keep and bear Arms, shall not be infringed.

Amendment III [1791]

No Soldier shall, in time of peace be quartered in any house, without the consent of the Owner, nor in time of war, but in a manner to be prescribed by law.

Amendment IV [1791]

The right of the people to be secure in their persons, houses, papers, and effects, against unreasonable searches and seizures, shall not be violated, and no Warrants shall issue, but upon probable cause, supported by Oath or affirmation, and particularly describing the place to be searched, and the persons or things to be seized.

Amendment V [1791]

No person shall be held to answer for a capital, or otherwise infamous crime, unless on a presentment or indictment of a Grand Jury, except in cases arising in the land or naval forces, or in the Militia, when in actual service in time of War or public danger; nor shall any person be subject for the same offence to be twice put in jeopardy of life or limb; nor shall be compelled in any criminal case to be a witness against himself, nor be deprived of life, liberty, or property, without due process of law; nor shall private property be taken for public use, without just compensation.

Amendment VI [1791]

In all criminal prosecutions, the accused shall enjoy the right to a speedy and public trial, by an impartial jury of the State and district wherein the crime shall have been committed, which district shall have been previously ascertained by law, and to be informed of the nature and cause of the accusation; to be confronted with the witnesses against him; to have compulsory process for obtaining witnesses in his favor, and to have the Assistance of Counsel for his defence.

Amendment VII [1791]

In Suits at common law, where the value in controversy shall exceed twenty dollars, the right of trial by jury shall be preserved, and no fact tried by a jury, shall be otherwise re-examined in any Court of the United States, than according to the rules of the common law.

Amendment VIII [1791]

Excessive bail shall not be required, nor excessive fines imposed, nor cruel and unusual punishments inflicted.

Amendment IX [1791]

The enumeration in the Constitution, of certain rights, shall not be construed to deny or disparage others retained by the people.

Amendment X [1791]

The powers not delegated to the United States by the Constitution, nor prohibited by it to the States, are reserved to the States respectively, or to the people.

Note: The capitalization and punctuation in this version are from the enrolled original of the Joint Resolution of Congress proposing the Bill of Rights, which is on permanent display in the Rotunda of the National Archives Building, Washington, DC.

THE CONSTITUTION: AMENDMENTS 11–27

Constitutional Amendments 1–10 make up what is known as The Bill of Rights. Amendments 11–27 are listed next.

AMENDMENT XI [1795]

Note: Article III, section 2, of the Constitution was modified by Amendment XI.

The Judicial power of the United States shall not be construed to extend to any suit in law or equity, commenced or prosecuted against one of the United States by Citizens of another State, or by Citizens or Subjects of any Foreign State.

AMENDMENT XII [1804]

The Electors shall meet in their respective states and vote by ballot for President and Vice-President, one of whom, at least, shall not be an inhabitant of the same state with themselves; they shall name in their ballots the person voted for as President, and in distinct ballots the person voted for as Vice-President, and they shall make distinct lists of all persons voted for as President, and of all persons voted for as Vice-President, and of the number of votes for each, which lists they shall sign and certify, and transmit sealed to the seat of the government of the United States, directed to the President of the Senate;—the President of the Senate shall, in the presence of the Senate and House of Representatives, open all the certificates and the votes shall then be counted;—The person having the greatest number of votes for President, shall be the President, if such number be a majority of the whole number of Electors appointed; and if no person have such majority, then from the persons having the highest numbers not exceeding three on the list of those voted for as President, the House of Representatives shall choose immediately, by ballot, the President. But in choosing the President, the votes shall be taken by states, the representation from each state having one vote; a quorum for this purpose shall consist of a member or members from two-thirds of the states, and a majority of all the states shall be necessary to a choice. [And if the House of Representatives shall not choose a President whenever the right of choice shall devolve upon them, before the fourth day of March next following, then the Vice-President shall act as President, as in case of the death or other constitutional disability of the President.—]* The person having the greatest number of votes as Vice-President, shall be the Vice-President, if such number be a majority of the whole number of Electors appointed, and if no person have a majority, then from the two highest numbers on the list, the Senate shall choose the Vice-President; a quorum for the purpose shall consist of two-thirds of the whole number of Senators, and a majority of the whole number shall be necessary to a choice. But no person constitutionally ineligible to the office of President shall be eligible to that of Vice-President of the United States.

AMENDMENT XIII [1865]

Section 1. Neither slavery nor involuntary servitude, except as a punishment for crime whereof the party shall have been duly convicted, shall exist within the United States, or any place subject to their jurisdiction.

Section 2. Congress shall have power to enforce this article by appropriate legislation.

AMENDMENT XIV [1868]

Section 1. All persons born or naturalized in the United States, and subject to the jurisdiction thereof, are citizens of the United States and of the State wherein they reside. No State shall make or enforce any law which shall abridge the privileges or immunities of citizens of the United States; nor shall any State deprive any person of life, liberty, or property, without due process of law; nor deny to any person within its jurisdiction the equal protection of the laws.

Section 2. Representatives shall be apportioned among the several States according to their respective numbers, counting the whole number of persons in each State, excluding Indians not taxed. But when the right to vote at any election for the choice of electors for President and Vice-President of the United States, Representatives in Congress, the Executive and Judicial officers of a State, or the members of the Legislature thereof, is denied to any of the male inhabitants of such State, being twenty-one years of age,* and citizens of the United States, or in any way abridged, except for participation in rebellion, or other crime, the basis of representation therein shall be reduced in the proportion which the number of such male citizens shall bear to the whole number of male citizens twenty-one years of age in such State.

Section 3. No person shall be a Senator or Representative in Congress, or elector of President and Vice-President, or hold any office, civil or military, under the United States, or under any State, who, having previously taken an oath, as a member of Congress, or as an officer of the United States, or as a member of any State legislature, or as an executive or judicial officer of any State, to support the Constitution of the United States, shall have engaged in insurrection or rebellion against the same, or given aid or comfort to the enemies thereof. But Congress may by a vote of two-thirds of each House, remove such disability.

Section 4. The validity of the public debt of the United States, authorized by law, including debts incurred for payment of pensions and bounties for services in suppressing insurrection or rebellion, shall not be questioned. But neither the United States nor any State shall assume or pay any debt or obligation incurred in aid of insurrection or rebellion against the United States, or any claim for the loss or emancipation of any slave; but all such debts, obligations and claims shall be held illegal and void.

Section 5. The Congress shall have the power to enforce, by appropriate legislation, the provisions of this article.

AMENDMENT XV [1870]

Section 1. The right of citizens of the United States to vote shall not be denied or abridged by the United States or by any State on account of race, color, or previous condition of servitude.

Section 2. The Congress shall have the power to enforce this article by appropriate legislation.

AMENDMENT XVI [1913]

The Congress shall have power to lay and collect taxes on incomes, from whatever source derived, without apportionment among the several States, and without regard to any census or enumeration.

AMENDMENT XVII [1913]

The Senate of the United States shall be composed of two Senators from each State, elected by the people thereof, for six years; and each Senator shall have one vote. The electors in each State shall have the qualifications requisite for electors of the most numerous branch of the State legislatures.

When vacancies happen in the representation of any State in the Senate, the executive authority of such State shall issue writs of election to fill such vacancies: *Provided,* That the legislature of any State may empower the executive thereof to make temporary appointments until the people fill the vacancies by election as the legislature may direct.

This amendment shall not be so construed as to affect the election or term of any Senator chosen before it becomes valid as part of the Constitution.

AMENDMENT XVIII [1919]

[Repealed by Amendment XXI]

Section 1. After one year from the ratification of this article the manufacture, sale, or transportation of intoxicating liquors within, the importation thereof into, or the exportation thereof from the United States and all territory subject to the jurisdiction thereof for beverage purposes is hereby prohibited.

Section 2. The Congress and the several States shall have concurrent power to enforce this article by appropriate legislation.

Section 3. This article shall be inoperative unless it shall have been ratified as an amendment to the Constitution by the legislatures of the several States, as provided in the Constitution, within seven years from the date of the submission hereof to the States by the Congress.

AMENDMENT XIX [1920]

The right of citizens of the United States to vote shall not be denied or abridged by the United States or by any State on account of sex.

Congress shall have power to enforce this article by appropriate legislation.

AMENDMENT XX [1933]

Section 1. The terms of the President and the Vice President shall end at noon on the 20th day of January, and the terms of Senators and Representatives at noon on the 3d day of January, of the years in which such terms would have ended if this article had not been ratified; and the terms of their successors shall then begin.

Section 2. The Congress shall assemble at least once in every year, and such meeting shall begin at noon on the 3d day of January, unless they shall by law appoint a different day.

Section 3. If, at the time fixed for the beginning of the term of the President, the President elect shall have died, the Vice President elect shall become President. If a President shall not have been chosen before the time fixed for the beginning of his term, or if the President elect shall have failed to qualify, then the Vice President elect shall act as President until a President shall have qualified; and the Congress may by law provide for the case wherein neither a President elect nor a Vice President shall have qualified, declaring who shall then act as President, or the manner in which one who is to act shall be selected, and such person shall act accordingly until a President or Vice President shall have qualified.

Section 4. The Congress may by law provide for the case of the death of any of the persons from whom the House of Representatives may choose a President whenever the right of choice shall have devolved upon them, and for the case of the death of any of the persons from whom the Senate may choose a Vice President whenever the right of choice shall have devolved upon them.

Section 5. Sections 1 and 2 shall take effect on the 15th day of October following the ratification of this article.

Section 6. This article shall be inoperative unless it shall have been ratified as an amendment to the Constitution by the legislatures of three-fourths of the several States within seven years from the date of its submission.

AMENDMENT XXI [1933]

Section 1. The eighteenth article of amendment to the Constitution of the United States is hereby repealed.

Section 2. The transportation or importation into any State, Territory, or Possession of the United States for delivery or use therein of intoxicating liquors, in violation of the laws thereof, is hereby prohibited.

Section 3. This article shall be inoperative unless it shall have been ratified as an amendment to the Constitution by conventions in the several States, as provided in the Constitution, within seven years from the date of the submission hereof to the States by the Congress.

AMENDMENT XXII [1951]

Section 1. No person shall be elected to the office of the President more than twice, and no person who has held the office of President, or acted as President, for more than two years of a term to which some other person was elected President shall be elected to the office of President more than once. But this Article shall not apply to any person holding the office of President when this Article was proposed by Congress, and shall not prevent any person who may be holding the office of President, or acting as President, during the term within which this Article becomes operative from holding the office of President or acting as President during the remainder of such term.

Section 2. This article shall be inoperative unless it shall have been ratified as an amendment to the Constitution by the legislatures of three-fourths of the several States within seven years from the date of its submission to the States by the Congress.

AMENDMENT XXIII [1961]

Section 1. The District constituting the seat of Government of the United States shall appoint in such manner as Congress may direct:

A number of electors of President and Vice President equal to the whole number of Senators and Representatives in Congress to which the District would be entitled if it were a State, but in no event more than the least populous State; they shall be in addition to those appointed by the States, but they shall be considered, for the purposes of the election of President and Vice President, to be electors appointed by a State; and they shall meet in the District and perform such duties as provided by the twelfth article of amendment.

Section 2. The Congress shall have power to enforce this article by appropriate legislation.

AMENDMENT XXIV [1964]

Section 1. The right of citizens of the United States to vote in any primary or other election for President or Vice President, for electors for President or Vice President, or for Senator or Representative in Congress, shall not be denied or abridged by the United States or any State by reason of failure to pay poll tax or other tax.

Section 2. The Congress shall have power to enforce this article by appropriate legislation.

AMENDMENT XXV [1967]

Section 1. In case of the removal of the President from office or of his death or resignation, the Vice President shall become President.

Section 2. Whenever there is a vacancy in the office of the Vice President, the President shall nominate a Vice President who shall take office upon confirmation by a majority vote of both Houses of Congress.

Section 3. Whenever the President transmits to the President pro tempore of the Senate and the Speaker of the House of Representatives his written declaration that he is unable to discharge the powers and duties of his office, and until he transmits to them a written declaration to the contrary, such powers and duties shall be discharged by the Vice President as Acting President.

Section 4. Whenever the Vice President and a majority of either the principal officers of the executive departments or of such other body as Congress may by law provide, transmit to the

President pro tempore of the Senate and the Speaker of the House of Representatives their written declaration that the President is unable to discharge the powers and duties of his office, the Vice President shall immediately assume the powers and duties of the office as Acting President.

Thereafter, when the President transmits to the President pro tempore of the Senate and the Speaker of the House of Representatives his written declaration that no inability exists, he shall resume the powers and duties of his office unless the Vice President and a majority of either the principal officers of the executive department or of such other body as Congress may by law provide, transmit within four days to the President pro tempore of the Senate and the Speaker of the House of Representatives their written declaration that the President is unable to discharge the powers and duties of his office. Thereupon Congress shall decide the issue, assembling within forty-eight hours for that purpose if not in session. If the Congress, within twenty-one days after receipt of the latter written declaration, or, if Congress is not in session, within twenty-one days after Congress is required to assemble, determines by two-thirds vote of both Houses that the President is unable to discharge the powers and duties of his office, the Vice President shall continue to discharge the same as Acting President; otherwise, the President shall resume the powers and duties of his office.

AMENDMENT XXVI [1971]

Section 1. The right of citizens of the United States, who are eighteen years of age or older, to vote shall not be denied or abridged by the United States or by any State on account of age.

Section 2. The Congress shall have power to enforce this article by appropriate legislation.

AMENDMENT XXVII [1992]

No law, varying the compensation for the services of the Senators and Representatives, shall take effect, until an election of representatives shall have intervened.

Appendix C

Model Executor's Account
First and Final Account

First and Final Account of
William C. Doe, Executor
for
ESTATE of John Doe, Deceased

Date of death: November 14, 2006   Date of executor's appointment: November 23, 2006
Accounting for the period: November 30, 2007

Purpose of account: William C. Doe, executor, offers this account to acquaint interested parties with the transactions that have occurred during his administration.

The account also indicates the proposed distribution of the estate. It is important that the account be carefully examined.

Requests for additional information or questions or objections can be discussed with:

[Name of executor, counsel, or other appropriate person]
[Address and telephone number]

SUMMARY OF ACCOUNT			
	Page	Current Value	Fiduciary Acquisition Value
Proposed distribution to beneficiaries	645	$102,974.56	$ 90,813.96
Principal			
Receipts	636		$160,488.76
Net gain (or loss) on sales or other disposition	638		$ 2,662.00
Less disbursements:			
Debts of decedent	639	$ 485.82	
Funeral expenses	638	1,375.00	
Administration expenses	639	194.25	
Federal and state taxes	639	5,962.09	
Fees and commissions	639	11,689.64	19,706.80
Balance before distributions			$143,443.96
Distributions to beneficiaries	641		52,630.00
Principal balance on hand	641		$ 90,813.96

	Page	Current Value	Fiduciary Acquisition Value
For information:			
Investments made	642		
Changes in investment holdings	642		
Income			
Receipts	643		$ 2,513.40
Less disbursements	643		178.67
Balance before distributions			$ 2,334.73
Distributions to beneficiaries	644		2,334.73
Income balance on hand			-0-
Combined balance on hand			$ 90,813.96

RECEIPTS OF PRINCIPAL		
Assets Listed in Inventory (Valued as of Date of Death)		*Fiduciary Acquisition Value*
Cash		
First National Bank: checking account	$ 516.93	
Prudent Saving Fund Society: savings account	2,518.16	
Cash in possession of decedent	42.54	$ 3,077.63
Tangible Personal Property		
Jewelry:		
1 pearl necklace		515.00
Furniture		
1 antique highboy	$ 2,000.00	
1 antique side table	60.00	
1 antique chair	55.00	2,115.00
Stocks		
200 shares Home Telephone & Telegraph Co., common	$ 25,000.00	
50 shares Best Oil Co., common	5,000.00	
1,000 shares Central Trust Co., capital	50,850.00	
151 shares Electric Data Corp., common	1,887.50	
50 shares Fabulous Mutual Fund	1,833.33	
200 shares XYZ Corporation, common	6,000.00	90,570.83
Realty		
Residence: 86 Norwood Road West Hartford, CT		$ 50,000.00
	Total inventory	$146,278.46

Receipts Subsequent to Inventory
(Valued When Received)

2/22/07	Proceeds of sale: Best Oil Co., rights to subscribe received 2/15/07	$ 50.00	
3/12/07	Fabulous Mutual Fund, capital gains dividend received in cash	32.50	
5/11/07	Refund of overpayment of 2006 U.S. individual income tax	127.80	
9/25/07	From Richard Roe, ancillary administrator, net proceeds on sale of oil and gas leases in Jefferson Parish, Louisiana	10,000.00	$ 10,210.30

Adjustment to Carrying Value

Increased value of 200 shares XYZ Corporation. Common stock upon audit of federal estate tax return:	$ 10,000.00	
Adjusted value upon audit	[6,000.00]	$ 4,000.00
Value per inventory		
Total receipts of principal		$160,488.76

GAINS AND LOSSES ON SALES OR OTHER DISTRIBUTIONS

			Gain	Loss
2/7/07	100 shares Home Telephone & Telegraph Co., common			
	Net proceeds	$ 14,025.00		
	Fiduciary acquisition value	$ 12,500.00	$1,525.00	
3/15/07	1,000 shares Central Trust Co., capital			
	Net proceeds	27,467.00		
	Fiduciary acquisition value	$ 25,425.00	2,042.00	
3/15/07	200 shares XYZ Corporation, common			
	Fiduciary acquisition value	10,000.00		1,000.00
	Net proceeds	9,000.00		
5/21/07	35 shares Electric Data Corp., common			
	Net Proceeds	530.00		
	Fiduciary acquisition value	437.50	92.50	
7/20/07	35 shares Electric Data Corp., common Net proceeds	10,000.00		
	Fiduciary acquisition value	9,997.50	2.50	
	Total gains and losses		$ 3,662.00	$ 1,000.00
	Less loss		1,000.00	
	Net gain		$ 2,662.00	

DISBURSEMENTS OF PRINCIPAL

Debts of Decedent

1/25/07	John T. Hill, M.D., professional services	$ 250.00	
4/12/07	State tax commissioner, 2006 state capital gains tax	156.00	
1/25/07	Thomas Pharmacy, prescriptions	23.82	
2/1/07	Sanders Hardware, purchases per bill dated 12/15/06	<u>56.00</u>	$ 485.82

Funeral Expenses

1/10/07	Smith Funeral Home, services	1,200.00	
2/15/07	Jones Memorials, grave marker	<u>175.00</u>	1,375.00

Administration Expenses

11/14/06	Clerk of court, probate costs	72.00	
2/22/07	Henry Smith, appraisal of jewelry and antiques	50.00	
11/16/08	Arden, Miles & Solomon, disbursements	56.00	
	Various miscellaneous affidavits, registered mail, toll telephone charges, and other costs	16.25	194.25

Federal and State Taxes

8/13/07	State tax commissioner, state death tax		2,501.33	
8/13/07	Internal Revenue Service, federal estate tax		2,663.29	
11/15/07	Internal Revenue Service, U.S. fiduciary income tax for fiscal year ending 7/31/07 (attributable to capital gains)		283.84	
11/23/07	Internal Revenue Service, Deficiency in federal estate tax Interest 8/14/07 to 11/24/07	<u>$505.248.39</u> <u>8.39</u>	<u>513.63</u>	5,962.09

Fees and Commissions

11/16/07	Albert Schryver, Esq., fee as guardain ad litem	375.00	
11/16/07	William C. Doe, executor's principal commission 5% on $50,000 4% on $50,000 3% on $60,488	6,314.64	
11/26/07	Arden, Miles & Soloman, attorney's fees	<u>5,000.00</u>	<u>11,689.64</u>
			$19,706.80

DISTRIBUTION OF PRINCIPAL TO BENEFICIARIES

To Janet Doe, in satisfaction of gift under Article FIRST of Will

12/1/06	1 pearl necklace	$ 515.00	
	1 antique highboy	2,000.00	
	1 antique side table	60.00	
	1 antique side chair	55.00	$ 2,630.00

To Janet Doe, in satisfaction of gift under Article SECOND of Will

12/1/06	Residence: 86 Norwood Road West Hartford, CT	50,000.00
	Total distributions of principal to beneficiaries	$ 52,630.00

PRINCIPAL BALANCE ON HAND

		Current Value 12/10/07 or as noted	Fiduciary Acquisition Value
Cash		$ 5,305.63	$ 5,305.63
Stocks:			
50 shares	Best Oil Co., common	4,500.00	5,000.00
1,000 shares	Central Trust Co., capital: value at most recent sale, 9/18/07	32,168.76	25,425.00
116 shares	Electric Data Corp., common: not traded, value per company books, 12/29/06	1,684.00	1,450.00
50 shares	Fabulous Mutual Fund	4,016.17	1,833.33
200 shares	Home Telephone & Telegraph Co., common	16,000.00	12,500.00
$40,000	U.S. Treasury Bills due 12/14/07	39,300.00	39.300.00
		$102,974.56	$90,813.96

INFORMATION SCHEDULE—PRINCIPAL

			Cost
	Investments Made		
2/1/07	$10,000 U.S. Treasury Bonds, 3% Less accrued interest collected 6/29/07	$10,022.50 25.00	$ 9,997.50
9/14/07	$40,000 U.S. Treasury Bills, due 12/14/07		39,300.00
	Changes in Investment Holdings Central Trust Co.		
11/14/06	1,000 shares capital stock, par $5 inventoried		$50,850.00
1/15/06	1,000 shares additional received in 2:1 split, _____ par reduced to $2.50 2,000 shares par $2.50 carried at		50,850.00
3/15/06	1,000 shares sold, carried at _____ 1,000 shares remaining, carried at		25,425.00 $25,425.00
	Home Telephone & Telegraph Co.		
11/14/07	200 shares common par $10, inventoried		$25,000.00

2/7/07	<u>100</u> shares sold, carried at		12,500.00
	100 shares remaining, carried at		12,500.00
3/30/07	100 shares additional received in 2:1 split,		
	____ par reduced to $5		
	<u>200</u> shares par $5 carried at		$ 12,500

RECEIPTS OF INCOME

Dividends

Best Oil Co., common			
1/2/07 to 10/2/07: 50 shares		$ 20.00	
Central Trust Co., common			
1/15/07: 2,000 shares	$600.00		
4/13/07 to 10/15/07:			
1,000 shares	<u>900.00</u>	1,500.00	
Electric Data Corp., common			
12/29/07 to 3/30/07: 151 shares	30.20		
6/29/07 to 9/28/07: 116 shares	<u>23.20</u>	53.40	
Fabulous Mutual Fund			
3/12/07 to 9/12/07: 50 shares		140.00	
Home Telephone & Telegraph Co., common			
2/1/07: 200 shares	225.00		
5/1/07 to 11/1/07: 200 shares (after stock split)	<u>450.00</u>	<u>675.00</u>	$ 2,388.40
Interest			
U.S. Treasury Bonds, 3% due 7/1/10			
6/29/07: $10,000	150.00		
Less accrued interest paid			
on purchase 2/1/07	(25.00)	125.00	125.00
Total			$ 2,513.40

DISBURSEMENTS OF INCOME

11/15/07	U.S. fiduciary income tax for fiscal year ended 7/31/07 (allocable to income)	53.00
	To be paid:	
	William C. Doe—executor's income commission 5% on $2,513.40	125.67
		$ 178.67

DISTRIBUTIONS OF INCOME TO BENEFICIARIES

	To William C. Doe, trustee under Article FOURTH (A) for Walter Doe	
11/16/07	Cash	$1,167.37
	to Sharon Doe	
11/16/07	Cash	1,167.36
	Total	$ 2,334.73

PROPOSED DISTRIBUTION TO BENEFICIARIES		Current Value 12/10/07 or as Noted	Fiduciary Acquisition Value
Per Article FOURTH (A) of Will: to William C. Doe, Trustee for Walter Doe			
25 shares	Best Oil Co., common	$ 2,250.00	$ 2,500.00
500 shares	Central Trust Co., capital	16,084.38[1]	12,712.50
58 shares	Electric Data Corp., common	842.00[2]	725.00
25 shares	Fabulous Mutual Fund	2,008.09	916.67
100 shares	Home Telephone & Telegraph Co., common	8,000.00	6,250.00
$20,000 U.S. Treasury Bills, due 12/14/06		19,650.00	19,650.00
Cash		2,652.81	2,652.81
		$ 51,487.28	$45,406.98
Per Article FOURTH (A) of Will: to Sharon C. Doe			
25 shares	Best Oil Co., common	$ 2,250.00	$2,500.00
500 shares	Central Trust Co., capital	16,084.38[1]	12,712.50
58 shares	Electric Data Corp., common	842.00[2]	725.00
25 shares	Fabulous Mutual Fund	2,008.09	916.67
100 shares	Home Telephone & Telegraph Co., common	8,000.00	6,250.00
$20,000 U.S. Treasury Bills, due 12/14/07		19,650.00	19,650.00
Cash		2,652.81	2,652.81
		$ 51,487.28	$45,406.98
	Total	$102,974.56	$90,813.96

[1] Central Trust Co.: valued at most recent sale, 9/18/07.
[2] Electric Data Corp.: not traded, valued per company books, 12/29/06.

WILLIAM C. DOE, executor under the last will and testament of JOHN DOE, deceased, hereby declares under oath [penalties of perjury] that he has fully and faithfully discharged the duties of his office; that the foregoing first and final account is true and correct and fully discloses all significant transactions occurring during the accounting period; that all known claims against the estate have been paid in full; that, to his knowledge, there are no claims now outstanding against the estate; and that all taxes presently due from the estate have been paid.

/s/ WILLIAM C. DOE
Executor

Subscribed and sworn to
by WILLIAM C. DOE before me this
_____ day of _____, 20_____.

_____
Notary Public
[Execution under oath before a notary or under penalty of perjury is optional, depending on rules of the local jurisdiction.]

Appendix D

PARTIAL LIST OF INTERNET PROVIDERS THAT HELP FIND MISSING WITNESSES

- 007-People-Finder.com—www.007-people-finder.com: Helps find people anywhere in the United States with searches by name, age, date of birth, and Social Security number.
- Aaron's Private Investigations—www.aaronspi.com: Specializes in skip tracing and locating adoptees, missing relatives, and more.
- Absolute Research Solutions, LLC—www.ars-pi.com: Specializes in locating people, conducting employee background checks, and other personal and corporate research.
- Accurate Information Services—www.accurate-people-finder.com: Provides background checks, SSN verification, public records screening services, and more.
- Accurate People Search—www.accuratepeoplesearch.com: Provides access to databases to search for old friends, classmates, family members, and more.
- Adolescent Guidance Services (AGS)—www.escort-transport.com: Special emphasis is placed on locating and returning runaways through nonviolent crisis intervention techniques. Also offers youth transport services to schools, mental health facilities, wilderness programs, social engagements, and judicial facilities.
- BestPeopleSearch.com—www.bestpeoplesearch.com: Investigators who help find missing people, perform background checks, and locate address and phone information.
- BigHugs.com—www.bighugs.com: Locates lost family, friends, and loved ones. Free adoption registry. Several links to investigative sites.
- Brownstone Investigation Services—www.brownstoneinvestigator.com: Locates missing people with multiple search techniques.
- Champion & Champion—www.champion-champion.com: Worldwide genealogical research firm specializing in missing and unknown heirs.
- Computrace People Search—www.amerifind.com: Missing person service experienced in locating people.
- Deadbeat Dad/Mom Finders—www.deadbeatdadfinders.com: Locates missing parents for child support collection. Services also include background checks for criminal history, bankruptcies, judgments, liens, and lawsuits.
- Find People Fast—www.fpf.com: Performs computer searches to help locate lost or missing relatives, friends, or other people in the united States.
- Finders Genealogists Ltd.—www.findersuk.com: U.K.-based firm of probate genealogists providing international tracing services for missing and unknown beneficiaries.
- FindMissingPeople.com—www.findmissingpeople.com: Source for online search tools.
- Findersusa.com—www.findersusa.com: Location of missing people, family, heirs, and descendants as well as asset searches and background reports.
- Fraser & Fraser International Probate Research—www.fraserandfraser.com: Specializes in locating missing heirs and beneficiaries, with offices throughout Europe and a worldwide network of agents.
- GIsearch.com—www.gisearch.com: Helps locate lost friends, reunite fellow military service members, and honor armed forces veterans.

- Global Tracing Services, Inc.—www.heirsearchusa.com: Locates missing heirs, beneficiaries, insured parties, plaintiffs, defendants, witnesses, and more.
- Harpernet Investigative Services—www.harpernet.com: Private detective agency specializing in video surveillance and helping find people.
- Harvey E. Morse, P.A.—www.probate.com: Specializes in locating people who are entitled to money or assets of which they are unaware; site includes a list of "most wanted" individuals.
- Infoquest, Inc.—www.infoquestinc.com: Extensive people search services.
- International Genealogical Search Inc.—www.heirsearch.com: Prove heirship and locate missing heirs.
- OmniTrace—www.omnitrace.com: Specializes in missing person and adoption searches worldwide.
- PeopleFind.com—www.peoplefind.com: Offering a directory of services to find old friends, family members, public records, and more.
- People-Finder.tv—www.people-finder.tv: Offers an online people search as well as investigative services.
- PeopleSearch.com—www.peoplesearch.com: Searches for missing people and does due diligence and background checks.
- Pro People Search—www.propeoplesearch.com: Helps locate missing people.
- Quicktrace—www.quick-trace.com: Service locating missing people, tracing family, reuniting lost relatives, and searching for service pals.
- Search America—www.searchamerica.com: Finds people in order to collect money and reduce bad debts.
- Search International Inc.—www.searchint.com: Specializes in locating missing heirs and beneficiaries.
- Seekers of the Lost—www.seeklost.com: Helps find missing friends, family, and military people through database searches.
- Trackstar—www.missingperson.net: Services include background checks and locating missing people.
- USA People Search—www.usa-people-search.com: Provides instant search results that include a possible 20-year address history, phone numbers, and birth dates. Background checks with nationwide criminal records available.
- U.S. Locator's People Search Services—www.uslocate.com: Helps find people anywhere in the United States. Search by name and age or Social Security number.
- U.S. Search.com—www.ussearch.com: Provider of location, verification, and screening services for consumer and enterprise clients.
- YourReputation.com—www.yourreputation.com: Lets users find out the reputation of a person by seeing what other people are saying about their past contacts and experiences with them.

Appendix E

Web Directory of Expert Service Providers

- **A Medical Expert Witness Resource**
  http://amedicalexpertwitness.com/
  Expert witnesses for case review, deposition, and trial testimony in all specialties for plaintiff and defense cases.

- **ABC Psychology Divorce Education Project**
  http://www.geocities.com/Paris/Cafe/6612/
  Custody and parenting divorce issues; forensic psychologists and psychiatrists. Also hosts of When Marriage Ends e-newsletter.

- **Accessibility Development Associates, Inc.**
  http://www.adaconsults.com/
  Consulting firm specializing in compliance with the Americans with Disabilities Act.

- **Accreditation Commission for Traffic Accident Reconstruction (ACTAR)**
  http://www.actar.org/
  Founded in 1990 to establish the minimum requirements needed to practice as a certified traffic accident reconstructionist. Certification exams offered.

- **Acme Research Services**
  http://www.acmeinfosys.com/
  Expert legal, medical, and scientific research.

- **Accountability Services, Inc.**
  http://www.legalbills.com/
  Legal cost control and auditing financials.

- **ADV Trial Monitoring**
  http://www.advtrialmonitoring.com/
  Trial attendance and observation services.

- **A.I.M.**
  http://www.cutcomp.com/expert.htm
  Expert testimony on commercial insurance, particularly workers' compensation insurance.

- **Aggressive Process Servers**
  http://www.lawguru.com/users/law/npsnps/
  Nationwide process servers and skip tracers.

- **Reginald F. Allard, Jr.**
  http://www.expertcop.com/
  Police practices expert witness in cases involving the use of force and arrest protocols.

Source: The Washburn School of Law

- **All Pets Veterinary Group**
  http://firms.findlaw.com/ALLPETS/
  Expert witness testimony in dog bite injury, veterinary malpractice, and animal abuse, as well as veterinary consultation, case review, and research.

- **American Academy of Forensic Science**
  http://www.aafs.org/

- **American Association of Legal Nurse Consultants**
  http://www.aalnc.org/

- **Americana Safety Associateshttp://www.aalnc.org/, Inc.**
  http://www.oshaexpert.com/
  Forensic safety consulting and expert witness services nationwide, including personal injury, negligence, and wrongful death cases.

- **Applied Technical Services, Inc.**
  http://www.atslab.com/
  Multidiscipline private testing lab providing expert services in accident reconstruction and simulation, forensic engineering, product liability, failure analysis, workplace accidents, fires, explosions, metallurgy, chemistry, and related areas.

- **Aptech Engineering Services, Inc.**
  http://www.aptecheng.com/
  Metallurgy and failure analysis expert consultants.

- **Animators at Law**
  http://www.animators.com/
  Courtroom computer animation and graphics.

- **Ardea Consulting**
  http://www.ardeacon.com/
  Wildlife and ecotoxicology expertise.

- **Associated Legal Research Services of Texas**
  http://www.webspawner.com/users/medlegalconsult/
  Expert testimony and legal research nationwide.

- **Astleford, Inc.**
  http://www.mindspring.com/%7Eastinc/expert.html
  Product liability and personal injury cases. Electrical and mechanical engineering experts.

- **Athena Research & Consulting**
  http://firms.findlaw.com/jrnixon/
  Consulting and expert witness services in the area of firearms and ballistics. Service available for criminal and civil litigation assignments. World-class, court-qualified expert with excellent credentials. Nationwide service. Firearms, ballistics, and wound ballistics. Case strategy, range and caliber determination, performance testing, ballistics matching, failure analysis (firearms and ammunition), wound analysis, crime and accident scene reconstruction (including video).

- **Atlanta Trial Lawyers**
  http://www.atlantatriallawyers.com/
  Individual representation in serious personal injury and wrongful death claims resulting from car or truck accidents, defective products, medical malpractice, nursing home neglect, premises accidents, and toxic substances.

- **Attorney Locate**
  http://www.attorneylocate.com/

- **Axsen—Legal Web Design**
  http://www.legalwebdesigner.com/
  Web design and hosting for legal professionals.

- **Background Information Searches**
  http://www.biscx.com/

- **Ken Barnes**
  http://krbarnes.8k.com/
  Expert witness—law enforcement, jails, prisons. Professor of the administration of justice providing expert reports and testimony, plaintiff/defense, civil or criminal.

- **BCL Immigration Services**
  http://www.workpermit.com/
  Immigration experts to English-speaking countries.

- **Beauregard Investigations**
  http://members.aol.com/beauinvest/prof2/index.htm
  A full-service investigative agency located in Southern California.

- **Martin L. Bell, MD, JD**
  http://www.bellmdjd.com/
  Experienced expert witness in general medicine, plastic and reconstructive surgery, cosmetic surgery, hair restoration surgery, and burns.

- **Richard Brown Investigations**
  http://planetdeland.com/rbi.htm

- **Business Risks International, Inc.**
  http://www.businessrisks.com/
  Full-service investigative firm specializing in liability and risk reduction services.

- **Biomedia**
  http://www.medart.com/
  Courtroom exhibits and animations.

- **Bradley-Huggins Consulting Group**
  http://bhcgi.com/
  Law practice management consulting.

- **Michael A. Brook**
  http://www.chemistry.mcmaster.ca/faculty/brook/brook.html
  PhD consulting organic and polymer chemist offering expert witness services in organic and polymer synthesis, silanes (coupling agents), and silicones.

- **Bureau of Private Investigation**
  http://pibureau.com/
  Experienced in criminal law, constitutional law, civil rights, administrative law, and civil law. Serving the islands of Hawaii.

- **Cardomon Group Litigation Support Home Page**
  http://www.cardomon.com/
  Litigation support services.

- **Robert D. Carrow**
  http://www.carrow.com/
  Expertise in the law of England and Wales.

- **Center for Forensic Economic Studies**
  http://www.cfes.com/

- **C.E.S. Consulting Inc.**
  http://www.duianddreexpert.com/
  Case review and expert testimony. Expert on maintenance and operation of the Intoxilyzer 5000 Series. Drug recognition, retrograde extrapolation, and police procedures.

- **Richard A. Clarke**
  http://firms.findlaw.com/Dickie/
  Nationally recognized expert in many aspects of commercial lending and problem loan resolution.

- **Climet Systems**
  http://www.climetsystems.com/
  Reconstruction of weather conditions for civil and criminal litigation. Expert testimony. Site investigations.

- **CN Expert Nurse Consultants**
  http://commerce.prodigybiz.com/customer/c/cnlegalnurseconsultants/

- **Collision Research Associates**
  http://www.collision-research.com/
  Traffic accident investigation and reconstruction.

- **Corbett Toxicology**
  http://www.tconl.com/%7Ecorbett
  Consultant and expert witness in chemical toxicology and carcinogenesis based in Omaha.

- **Credit and Collection Tools on the Internet**
  http://www.i-collections.com/
  San Diego–based credit and collection site that features the best Internet tools for credit professionals. Sponsored by the law office of Mark P. Krones.

- **College Hill Internet Consultants**
  http://www.collegehill.com/
  Internet consulting and Web design.

- **Linda L. Collins**
  http://handwritinganalysis.net/
  Forensic document and handwriting examiner.

- **Computer Forensics Network**
  http://computerforensics.net/

- **Consolidated Consultants Co.**
  http://www.freereferral.com/
  Referral service.

- **The Consus Group**
  http://www.consusgroup.com/
  Analysis of contracts, industries, and companies, providing critical intelligence for the business and legal communities.

- **Continental Hoisting Consultants**
  http://www.chcelevator.com/
  Specializing in elevators and escalators.

- **Coonis Private Investigations**
  http://www.ccon.com/locate/
  Hidden bank accounts and people field services.

- **CRS and Associates**
  http://www.adata.com/%7Ecrspi/
  Corporate fraud, background investigations, surveillance, media research, and other services.

- **Data Recovery Services**
  http://www.legalforensics.com/
  Computer forensics services.

- **Dean P. Cary, CRNA**
  http://home.earthlink.net/%7Edustycary
  Legal consulting, expert witness testimony, chart review.

- **Dental Expert**
  http://www.mindsource.org/neer/
  Dental malpractice expert.

- **Discovery Handwriting Services**
  http://www.documentexam.com/
  Forensic document examiner using the latest technical equipment, including stereoscopic microscope, ultraviolet light, scanner, and digital camera to analyze documents and signatures.

- **Divorced from Justice**
  http://www.divorcedfromjustice.com/
  Provides a statement of rights for litigants in divorce and other information on consumer-related issues for litigants in divorce. Karen Winner, company president, is a qualified expert witness in legal malpractice cases involving the mistreatment of women by attorneys.

- **Domestic Violence Consultant & Expert Witness**
  http://www.lawinfo.com/biz/lemon.htm
  Nancy K.D. Lemon domestic violence legal consulting, assisting other attorneys with their cases and testifying as an expert. Works only in the greater Bay Area, California; has worked in the domestic violence field for 20 years and has been an attorney for 19 years.

- **Duncan Investigations**
  http://www.janieduncan.com/
  Serving individuals, insurance companies, law firms, national organizations, and all levels of government.

- **Ecology and Environment, Inc.**
  http://www.ecolen.com/
  Multidisciplinary scientific, engineering, and technical support for environmental and occupational forensic matters. Services available throughout the United States and abroad.

- **Electrical and Mechanical Engineer and Expert Witness**
  http://www.ljkamm.com/
  Lawrence Kamm.

- **EnviroCop1**
  http://members.aol.com/envirocop1/
  Environmental investigator.

- **ERGO/GERO Expert Witness Services**
  http://www.ergogero.com/
  Human factors errors in road, medical, and other accidents. Specialists in intellectual property and trademark infringement litigation.

- **Environmental Insurance Claims Alliance (EICA)**
  http://members.aol.com/eiclaims/
  Evaluation of hazardous waste cleanup claims.

- **Environmental Networking Facilities**
  http://www.networking-facilities.net/index.asp
  Add your curriculum vitae to the ENF database for keyword access by anyone.

- **Essential Edge**
  http://www.essentialedge.com/

- **Expert Law**
  http://www.expertlaw.com/

- **Expert Witness Services**
  http://firms.findlaw.com/jhguth
  Works in a variety of tort cases.

- **Exponent**
  http://www.exponent.com/
  Expert witnesses in over 50 scientific disciplines.

- **Expert Forensic Psychiatry and Medicine**
  http://www.forensic-psych.com/
  Harvard Medical School's graduate and senior faculty, expert medicine and psychiatry/law and ethics Web site. A free educational resource for health and legal professionals and the general public.

- **Express Search Inc.**
  http://www.expresssearch.com/
  Patent and trademark services.

- **Flanagan and Associates, Inc.**
  http://www.webcom.com/flanagan/EXPERT.html
  Water and wastewater control experts.

- **Forensic Construction Management**
  http://www.tectonicsystems.com/
  Construction-related delay damages, analysis of damages, preparation of delay and damage documentation, expert witnesses, and construction management training.

- **Forensic Neuropsychology**
  http://www.forensicneuropsychology.com/
  Licensed psychologist.

- **Forensic Panel Letter**
  http://www.forensicpanel.com/
  Updated throughout the week with commentaries from doctors, professors, and experts who provide an insider feel on recent higher court decisions and scientific research. This database also features hundreds of articles and other original content on forensic behavioral sciences, DNA, toxicology, and pathology.

- **Forensic Psychology Associates**
  http://www.psylaw.com/
  Specializing in trial consultation.

- **Forensic Strategy Services**
  http://www.forensicstrategy.com/
  Forensics related to computers and data. Newsletter and services in trial consultation.

- **Forensic Training Consultants**
  http://www.magma.ca/%7Ekew/
  Physical evidence comparisons such as fingerprints, footwear and vehicle tire impressions, torn or broken edges such as paper, wood, metal, and bare foot impressions.

- **Forensic Meteorology Associates, Inc.**
  http://www.forensic-weather.com/
  Nationwide, full-service litigation support, and expert testimony.

- **Forensic Science Consultants**
  http://firms.findlaw.com/rockyabq
  Expert consultant and witness services in the fields of firearm and tool mark examination and identification, shooting scene reconstruction, trajectory analysis, proximity determination, and shoe and tire print comparisons.

- **ForensisGroup, Inc.**
  http://www.forensisgroup.com/
  Forensic engineering and construction.

- **Frankenfeld's Interactive Economics Page**
  http://frankenfeld.com/
  Economic consulting and litigation support.

- **Dr. Jed Friend**
  http://www.jedfriend.com/
  Expert witness testimony in the areas of family and marital law, labor and management, personal injury (vocational rehabilitation testing), and medical malpractice.

- **Futuretech Design**
  http://www.cgernon.com/ftd/
  Forensic mechanical engineering consultants providing studies, depositions, reports, and testimony for mechanical failures and agriculture.

- **Fyler Associates**
  http://www.fyler.com/
  Legal nurse consultants.

- **Gemini Executive Search, Inc.**
  http://www.geminies.com/
  International recruiting; executive long-term health care and assisted living placement.

- **CW Girard**
  http://www.cwgirard.com/
  Expert court reporter.

- **Golden Gate Weather Services**
  http://www.ggweather.com/
  Weather and climate research and expert testimony.

- **Haard Translating Services**
  http://www.haardtranslating.com/haardtranslating.html
  Company located in Miami specializing in judicial interpreters and translators for trials, depositions, hearings, and workers' compensation cases.

- **Handwriting & Document Examiner**
  http://www.reedwrite.com/
  Reed C. Hayes, CDE.

- **John H. Hanst**
  http://www.hanst.com/hanst.html
  Recreational hazards experts.

- **Penny Harrington**
  http://www.pennyharrington.com/
  Expert witness.

- **Harris Technical Services**
  http://www.harristechnical.com/
  Accident reconstruction experts.

- **Health Capital Consultants**
  http://www.healthcapital.com/
  Technical litigation support services and assistance to legal counsel focused on health care transactions, such as valuation, antitrust issues, fraud and abuse, compensation disputes, and other types of cases containing complex legal, financial, and health care industry issues.

- **Healthcare Negligence Control, Inc.**
  http://www.healthadministration.com/
  Expert witness for all health entities.

- **Henz Meteorological Services**
  http://www.hmsweather.com/
  Forensic meteorology for law firms and the insurance industry.

- **Hernandez Investigations and Research**
  http://www.hernandezpi.com/
  Investigative research to business and the legal profession in California and Oregon.

- **HGC Contract Consultants**
  http://firms.findlaw.com/chart
  Complex construction scheduling; change order and claims analysis.

- **Gregory Hidley**
  http://www-soe.ucsd.edu/%7Eghidley
  Director of engineering computing at UCSD. Expertise in computing, networking, systems security, software engineering, Y2K, and all other computing questions.

- **Hoffmann and Feige, Inc.**
  http://www.hoffmann-feige.com/
  Failure analysis and quality assurance.

- **Hermele and Kozin LLP**
  http://www.livg.com/members.cfm?Temp=585014Koz0319B99
  A CPA firm dedicated to assisting attorneys and law firms in the business aspects of lawyering.

- **Legal Video Sync**
  http://www.legalvideosync.com/

- **IMS Expert Services**
  http://www.ims-expertservices.com/
  Expert witnesses and case consultants; a search service for experts in narrow, conflict-rife specialties.

- **Intercept Investigations**
  http://www.intercept-spytech.com/
  Private investigators, consultants, and sales of investigation, surveillance, security, counterfeit detection, and countermeasures equipment worldwide.

- **International Medical Litigation Consultants**
  http://www.medlit.info/
  Consulting services to personal injury and plaintiff medical malpractice lawyers and their clients.

- **Inter-Pro Investigations**
  http://firms.findlaw.com/Gus/
  Private investigator, New York.

- **Investigative Consultants International**
  http://www.investcon.com/
  Corporate investigations.

- **IPSIS**
  http://www.ipsis-usa.com/
  Economic consultants specializing in the proof and measurement of economic damages, and toxicologists specializing in the adverse effects of drugs.

- **Ivey Engineering & Construction Services, Inc.**
  http://www.iveycon.com/
  Litigation support (expert witness work, etc.) in the field of construction law.

- **Jersey Weather Service**
  http://www.monmouth.com/%7Ejws/forensic.htm
  Meteorological and climatological data and analytical weather reports for investigative or forensic purposes.

- **JL & Associates, Ltd.**
  http://www.jlassoc.com/
  Private investigation.

- **John W. Kennish, CPP, CFE**
  http://www.kennish.com/
  Security consultant and expert witness.

- **JurisPro Expert Witness Directory**
  http://www.jurispro.com/

- **Kemic Bioresearch**
  http://www.kemic.com/
  Consulting services and extensive expert experience in pharmacology and toxicology (occupational, clinical, and forensic aspects).

- **Law Firm Pro**
  http://www.lawfirmpro.com/
  Matches attorneys to professional legal consultants.

- **Law Technology**
  http://www.well.com/user/lawtech
  Law-related computer/security/software services.

- **LawDepot.com**
  http://www.lawdepot.com/?pid=link-washlaw-dir
  Legal automation specialists.

- **LawInfo.com**
  http://www.lawinfo.com/index.cfm/fuseaction/Client.about
  Providing public access to prequalified, prescreened attorneys and to free legal resources.

- **LawSearch**
  http://www.lawsearch.gov.au/

- **Lawyer's Guide to Cross-Cultural Depositions**
  http://www.languagealliance.com/white-paper/
  From All Language Alliance.com.

- **Legal Arts Multimedia, LLC**
  http://www.legalarts.com/
  Demonstrative evidence for litigation graphics, animation, digital video, and interactive programming.

- **Legal Language Service**
  http://www.alsintl.com/legal.htm
  Service of process, translation, and interpreting.

- **Legal Research Texas Style**
  http://www.geocities.com/texashoods/research.htm
  Links to legal research and government sites, with Texas emphasis.

- **Legal Translations**
  http://www.legaltranslator.com/
  Translation of commercial, corporate, and corporate documents.

- **Legal Translations and Interpretation Tips**
  http://www.languagealliance.com/legal-translation-tips/
  Tips from Language Alliance that can affect your law firm's reputation.

- **Legal Video**
  http://www.legalvideoinc.com/

- **Lifesaving Resources, Inc.**
  http://www.lifesaving.com/
  Expert witness services in the areas of aquatics safety and water rescue in matters pertaining to drowning, aquatic injury, lifesaving, lifeguards, surveillance, rescue procedures, incident prevention, victim recognition, and lifeguard training.

- **Litigation Strategies Group**
  http://www.litigationstrat.com/
  Strategic case and records reviews. Educates attorneys about the scientific, medical, and technological aspects of their cases.

- **London Associates International**
  http://www.londonmedarb.com/
  Objective assessments, consultations, reports, and expert witness services.

- **Guy Magny**
  http://www.hawk.igs.net/%7Eguymagny/
  Forensic handwriting and document examiner.

- **Mallar Law Consulting**
  http://mallarlaw.com/
  Management and law consultants.

- **Marcus Business Services**
  http://www.marcosbusiness.com/
  Arabic/English translation services for law professionals.

- **Mark R. McDermott**
  http://www-fhs.mcmaster.ca/vdgp/mcdermott/
  PhD consulting immunologist. Consultant and expert witness in immunology, vaccines, mucosal immunity, and immunodiagnostic tests.

- **Medical-Legal Art**
  http://www.medical-legal.com/

- **Medical Litigation Consultants**
  http://www.medmal-inc.com/
  Expert professional litigation support services.

- **Medicine & Psychiatry Expert**
  http://www.forensic-psych.com/

- **Med-Mal Experts, Inc.**
  http://www.medmalexperts.com/
  Greg Kane, MD. is a board-certified internal medicine doctor who practices malpractice consulting full-time. He also refers attorneys to medical school clinical faculty experts.

- **Barrett Miller**
  http://www.safety-engineer.com/
  Safety expert, slip and fall, OSHA.

- **Mining Engineer-Consultant**
  http://home.att.net/%7Eehollop/ehollop.html
  Mine health and safety, mining regulations, training, fatal and accident investigations, research, mine and tunnel design, ground control, rock mechanics, surface and underground mining.

- **Nacomex USA, Inc.**
  http://www.nacomex.com/
  Computer valuation analysis and consulting.

- **National Association of Forensic Economics**
  http://www.nafe.net/

- **National Audio Video Forensic Laboratory**
  http://www.pimall.com/nais/n.perl.html
  Norman Perle, forensic audio expert, American Board of Recorded Evidence nationally certified expert.

- **James Allan Natte, PhD**
  http://www.mattepolygraph.com/
  Forensic psychophysiology using the polygraph.

- **Network Consulting**
  http://www.istal.com/smoke/
  ADA and handicap accessibility expert.

- **Neville's Forensic Art Service**
  http://www.forensicartist.com/
  A Web site dedicated to the services provided by the forensic artist.

- **NLJ Experts**
  http://www.nljexperts.com/
  15,000 experts, expert witnesses, investigators, court reporters, consultants, and litigation support professionals. Search by category or keyword.

- **North American Medical Jurisprudence**
  http://www.namj.com/
  Professionals in both the medical and legal fields.

- **NorthShore Process Service/ELMO**
  http://firms.findlaw.com/srsr/
  Legal process service with local coverage and nationwide forwarding. Discounts available.

- **Jim O'Boyle**
  http://www.elevatorsafety.com/
  Certified safety professional with over 30 years of progressively more responsible safety experience. Over 19 years with a major elevator company as director of safety and codes.

- **O'Donnell Consulting Engineering, Inc.**
  http://www.odonnellconsulting.com/
  Mechanical engineering and metallurgy expert witnesses.

- **Offshore Management International**
  http://www.pananet.com/offshore/main.html
  Offshore corporate and trust services.

- **Oklahoma Private Investigators Association**
  http://www.opia.com/home/default.asp
  A database of private investigators in Oklahoma.

- **Oman Consulting**
  http://www.rdoman.com/
  Expert analysis and testimony in automobile and industrial accidents.

- **Onecle Sample Contracts**
  http://contracts.onecle.com/
  Provides various sample contracts.

- **OSHAware, Inc.**
  http://www.oshaware.net/
  Work-related injuries, falls, OSHA, and general industry and construction accidents.

- **Orma & Associates**
  http://www.orma.com/
  Insurance claims consulting firm.

- **PaperStreet Web Design**
  http://www.paperst.com/
  Web design for law firms and legal professionals.

- **Valeria V. Parisi, RN, LNC**
  http://www.valpar.com/
  Legal nurse consultant.

- **Alan M. Perlman, PhD**
  http://www.alanperlman.com/
  Forensic linguistics: Linguistics PhD provides analysis of language of questioned documents, wills, contracts, and the like, and offers expert opinion on authorship and on the meaning of particular words, phrases, and clauses.

- **Personal Injury Attorneys**
  http://www.lawinfo.com/index.cfm/fuseaction/Client.lawarea/categoryid/32
  Use this site to find personal injury attorneys in all 50 states. From LawInfo.

- **Personnel Management Consultants, LLC**
  http://www.vocex.com/
  Vocational expert, vocational evaluation, earning capacity analysis, medical/legal file reviews, legal nurse consultant, life care planning.

- **PI Resources and Locator**
  http://www.piresourcesandlocator.com/

- **J.L. Pierson & Co.**
  http://www.jlpierson.com/
  Expert in business valuations.

- **Pilko & Associates Inc.**
  http://www.pilko.com/
  A management consulting firm specializing in environmental, health, and safety issues.

- **Placement Associates, Ltd./PA Experts**
  http://www.expertwitness.com/mooney/
  Physician assistant expert witness.

- **Point Alpha Associates**
  http://www.angelfire.com/biz/ptalpha/
  Registered California process servers. Located in Poway, California, and serving all of San Diego County.

- **Preston Mills Inc.**
  http://firms.findlaw.com/jhofius/
  Specializing in helping private and public entities comply with state and federal disability discrimination laws.

- **Priori**
  http://www.tsri.com/
  Stuart Soffer, forensic computer science expert witness.

- **Private Security and Intelligence Agency**
  http://www.mobrien.com/ui.html
  Global security intelligence agency, personal protection, bodyguards, detectives, communication security, and network security.

- **PRN Legal Nurse Corporation**
  http://www.prnlnc.com/
  Assists attorneys with medical-related cases and locating expert witnesses.

- **Pro-Ag Consultants**
  http://www.firms.findlaw.com/tracey/
  Expert witness and consultation for agricultural-related issues: crop loss, pesticide misuse, beneficial impact from pesticides, entomological issues.

- **Process Service Network**
  http://www.processnet1.com/
  Process servers anywhere in the world, specializing in "hard-to-serve" and international cases.

- **Procounsel Consultancy & Training**
  http://www.procounsel.co.uk/
  Human relations consultancy and training in the commercial and public sectors.

- **PsyBar**
  http://www.psybar.com/
  Psychiatric and psychological experts.

- **Psychiatry & Law Updates**
  http://www.reidpsychiatry.com/
  Psychiatry and psychiatry forensic expert.

- **Public Utility Home Page**
  http://www.publicutilityhome.com/

- **Questioned Document Examination Page**
  http://qdewill.com/
  Learn about the theories, applications, equipment, cases, and other aspects of forensic document and handwriting examination.

- **Rachlin Cohen & Holtz**
  http://www.rchcpa.com/
  Certified public accountants and consultants providing litigation support: accounting, auditing, business damages, white-collar crime.

- **Regional Investigative Services**
  http://inaccs.com.bb/pi/
  Investigations throughout the Caribbean.

- **Registered Nurse Expert**
  http://www.rnexperts.com/

- **Rehman Technology Services, Inc.**
  http://www.surveil.com/
  Expert testimony in the areas of child exploitation, computers, computer forensics, online services, the Internet, and electronic surveillance.

- **Research Associates**
  http://www.researchassociates.net/
  General legal research for the legal profession.

- **Risk Management Consulting**
  http://www.riskmanco.com/
  Expert medical record review, litigation support in medical malpractice cases, insight into physician credentialing and privileging, and information about JCAHO standards.

- **Rocky Mountain Instrumental Laboratories, Inc.**
  http://www.rockylab.com/
  Forensic toxicology, serology, gunshot residue, and fire debris analysis.

- **Dan Rohling and Associates**
  http://firms.findlaw.com/rohling/
  Consulting and expert witness for the funeral industry, including embalming procedures and regulations, crematory procedures and regulation, cemetery procedures and regulations—nationwide.

- **The Safe Child Program**
  http://www.safechild.org/
  Expert witness services: Assess cases; provide opinions and testimony in the area of child abuse (sexual, physical, emotional) and neglect. Broad experience in institutional abuse including day care, schools, youth organization, churches, and foster care.

- **Safety Engineer Page**
  http://www.safety-engineer.com/
  Useful information about expert witnesses.

- **Sewell Investigations**
  http://www.sewellinvest.prodigybiz.com/
  Expert testimony on traffic reconstruction and law enforcement management, including computer simulation, animations, and computerized photogrammetry.

- **Dr. Michael Sidman**
  http://www.sidman.com/legal/index.htm
  Engineering.

- **Sigma Animation, Inc.**
  http://www.sigma-animation.com/
  Forensic animation and 3D analysis.

- **Orrin Skretvedt**
  http://pages.prodigy.net/oskretvedt/skretvedts/Expert.htm
  OSHA regulation expert witness for asbestos, respirators, PPE, confined space, lead, silica, IAQ, and industrial hygiene or safety.

- **Solender Group Inc.**
  http://solendergroupinc.com/
  Forensic construction defect experts.

- **Sensimetrics Corporation**
  http://www.sens.com/
  Expert witness in forensic analysis of sound recordings and speech, voice identification, testing of integrity of sound recordings, enhancement of sound recordings, and preparation and authentication of transcripts.

- **Summit Engineering**
  http://www.summitengr.com/
  Engineers consulting in accident analysis.

- **Vic Sunshine**
  http://www.omnisafety.com/
  Expert testimony in construction, forensics, and OSHA training.

- **Ta-Dah!**
  http://www.legalist.com/
  Litigation graphics for the construction and environmental industries.

- **Tampa Accidental Injury, Criminal Defense, & Business Law Attorneys**
  http://www.kfblaw.com/
  Florida accidental injury, criminal defense, dog bites, nursing home abuse, slip and fall, wrongful death, and product liability cases, with over 50 years of combined experience.

- **TBA Forensic Engineering and Sciences**
  http://firms.findlaw.com/ThomasBoehly/index.htm
  Expert witness engineers: electrical, mechanical, fires, industrial accidents, OSHA, metallurgy, and more. Twenty years of experience providing technical investigations in the insurance and legal professions.

- **Technical Experts Corporation**
  http://technicalexperts.net/
  Chemical consulting services ranging from expert witness testimony to the design of pharmaceutical, biotechnology, metallurgical, polymer, petrochemical, and environmental plants.

- **Telecom Visions, Inc.**
  http://telecomexpertwitness.com/
  Telecommunications expert with 30 years of experience, including testimony before the FCC.

- **Telecommunications Consulting Group, Inc.**
  http://www.teleconsultingroup.com/expert.htm
  Expert witness testimony and litigation support for telecommunications network engineering and related business planning matters.

- **Thinktwice, Inc.**
  http://www.thinktwicelegal.com
  Visual communications for litigation. Provides a full range of graphics services for all stages

of litigation, including pleadings, pretrial hearings, ADR, and trials. Services include strategic planning, story development, display boards, fully rendered animations, and video and multimedia presentations.

- **TossicologiaNet**
  http://www.toxpert.com/
  Expert in biochemical toxicology and pharmacology.

- **Toxicology Labs, Inc.**
  http://www.toxlabsomaha.com/
  Forensic toxicology for attorneys.

- **Roundtable of Toxicology Consultants**
  http://rtctox.com/
  Independent consultants.

- **Trial Behavior Consulting Firm**
  http://www.trialbehavior.com/
  Nationwide legal consulting services.

- **Trialexhibits.com**
  http://www.trialexhibits.com/
  Custom color graphics and enlargements.

- **Brent E. Turvey**
  http://www.corpus-delicti.com/brent/brent_cv.html
  Forensic science expert in criminal profiling, crime scene analysis, crime reconstruction, offender signature analysis, and victimology.

- **Gerald H. Vandenburg, PhD, ABPP**
  http://firms.findlaw.com/geraldv/
  Board-certified forensic psychologist, expert witness, and consultant.

- **Venable**
  http://www.venable.com/
  Serves clients in all areas of corporate law and litigation, including intellectual property, technology, labor and employment, and government contracts.

- **National Court Reporters Association**
  http://www.verbatimreporters.com/

- **V/G Associates**
  http://www.vgassociates.com/
  Legal nurse consultants.

- **The Virtual Chase**
  http://www.hslc.org/%7Etyburski/home.html
  A research site for legal professionals.

- **The Virtual Law**
  http://members.tripod.com/Jomato/
  Thousands of links about juridical questions in Internet areas.

- **Visual Expert**
  http://www.visualexpert.com/
  Expert witness for accidents involving human error in vision, perception, and attention: highway signs and displays, legibility, lighting, recognition, warnings, computer interfaces, and the like. Intellectual property disputes where visual similarity is at issue.

- **VisionQuest**
  http://www.vq.com/overview_home.htm
  Innovative and effective intervention services for at-risk youth and families.

- **Vocational Economics Inc.**
  http://www.vocecon.com/
  Expert testimony on lost earnings.

- **Pogos Voskanian, MD**
  http://www.forensic-psychiatrist.com/
  Forensic psychiatric evaluations; also fluent in Russian and Armenian.

- **Wade Industries**
  http://www.wadeindustries.com/
  Attorney fee audits and legal cost containment.

- **Robert Wadman**
  http://rwadman.freeyellow.com/
  Former DEA agent, former police chief in several jurisdictions. Professor of criminal justice at Weber State University.

- **Walsh Pfeffer Co.**
  http://firms.findlaw.com/Pfeffer/
  Securities dispute case evaluators and expert witnesses.

- **Welch Consulting**
  http://www.welchcon.com/
  Leading consulting firm in economics and statistics.

- **Workers' Compensation Forum**
  http://www.ggmmlaw.com/

- **The Wilmington Institute Network**
  http://www.winthecase.com/
  A leading trial consulting firm.

- **Ralph Witherspoon, CCP**
  http://www.security-expert.org/
  Premises liability and negligent security cases.

- **Wreck Check Assessments of Boston**
  http://www.wreckcheckboston.com/
  Diminished value assessments of collision-damaged vehicles.

- **Perry J. Zucker, Ltd.**
  http://www.trafficdoc.com/
  Engineers providing technical reports, pretrial preparation, and expert witness testimony concerning vehicle accidents (reconstruction), traffic violations, product liability, and general accident cases.

Index